A Child's World

Infancy through Adolescence

THIRTEENTH EDITION

A Child's World
Infancy through Adolescence

Gabriela Martorell

Diane E. Papalia

Ruth Duskin Feldman

McGraw
Hill
Education

A CHILD'S WORLD: INFANCY THROUGH ADOLESCENCE, THIRTEENTH EDITION

Published by McGraw-Hill Education, 2 Penn Plaza, New York, NY 10121. Copyright © 2014 by McGraw-Hill Education. All rights reserved. Printed in the United States of America. Previous editions © 2011, 2008, and 2006. No part of this publication may be reproduced or distributed in any form or by any means, or stored in a database or retrieval system, without the prior written consent of McGraw-Hill Education, including, but not limited to, in any network or other electronic storage or transmission, or broadcast for distance learning.

Some ancillaries, including electronic and print components, may not be available to customers outside the United States.

This book is printed on acid-free paper.

4 5 6 7 8 9 0 DOW/DOW 1 0 9 8 7 6 5

ISBN 978-0-07-803543-2
MHID 0-07-803543-0

Senior Vice President, Products & Markets: *Kurt L. Strand*
Vice President, General Manager, Products & Markets: *Michael Ryan*
Vice President, Content Production & Technology Services: *Kimberly Meriwether David*
Managing Director: *William R. Glass*
Brand Manager: *Allison McNamara*
Senior Director of Development: *Dawn Groundwater*
Digital Product Analyst: *Neil Kahn*
Digital Development Editor: *Sarah Colwell*
Marketing Manager: *Ann Helgerson*
Director, Content Production: *Terri Schiesl*
Lead Content Project Manager: *Mary E. Powers*
Buyer: *Susan K. Culbertson*
Design: *Margarite Reynolds*
Cover Image: *Multi-bits*
Content Licensing Specialist: *Shawntel Schmitt*
Compositor: *Aptara®, Inc.*
Typeface: *10.5/12 Adobe Garamond Pro*
Printer: *R. R. Donnelley*

All credits appearing on page or at the end of the book are considered to be an extension of the copyright page.

Library of Congress Cataloging-in-Publication Data

Papalia, Diane E.
    A child's world : infancy through adolescence / Diane E. Papalia, Gabriela Martorell, Virginia Wesleyan College,
Ruth Duskin Feldman. – Thirteenth Edition.
        pages cm
    Includes index.
    ISBN 978–0–07–803543–2 — ISBN 0–07–803543–0 (hard copy : alk. paper) 1. Child development.
2. Child psychology. 3. Adolescence. I. Martorell, Gabriela. II. Feldman, Ruth Duskin. III. Title.
    HQ767.9.P36 2014
    305.231–dc23   2013029115

The Internet addresses listed in the text were accurate at the time of publication. The inclusion of a website does not indicate an endorsement by the authors or McGraw-Hill Education, and McGraw-Hill Education does not guarantee the accuracy of the information presented at these sites.

www.mhhe.com

Diane E. Papalia As a professor, Diane E. Papalia taught thousands of undergraduates at the University of Wisconsin–Madison. She received her bachelor's degree, majoring in psychology, from Vassar College and both her master's degree in child development and family relations and her PhD in life-span developmental psychology from West Virginia University. She has published numerous articles in such professional journals as *Human Development, International Journal of Aging and Human Development, Sex Roles, Journal of Experimental Child Psychology,* and *Journal of Gerontology.* Most of these papers have dealt with her major research focus, cognitive development from childhood through old age. She is especially interested in intelligence in old age and factors that contribute to the maintenance of intellectual functioning in late adulthood. She is a Fellow in the Gerontological Society of America. She is the coauthor of *Human Development,* now in its eleventh edition, with Sally Wendkos Olds and Ruth Duskin Feldman; of *Adult Development and Aging,* now in its third edition, with Harvey L. Sterns, Ruth Duskin Feldman, and Cameron J. Camp; and of *Child Development: A Topical Approach* with Dana Gross and Ruth Duskin Feldman.

Gabriela Alicia Martorell was born in Seattle, Washington, but moved as a toddler to Guatemala. At eight, she moved back to the United States and lived in Northern California until leaving for her undergraduate training at University of California, Davis. After obtaining her BS in Psychology, she earned her PhD in Developmental and Evolutionary Psychology at University of California, Santa Barbara. Since that time, she has served a number of learning institutions including Portland State University, Norfolk State University, and her current full-time position at Virginia Wesleyan College. Gabi has taught graduate and undergraduate courses in introductory psychology, research methods, lifespan human development, infant development, child development, adolescent development, adulthood and aging, cultural issues in psychology, evolutionary psychology, developmental psychopathology, and community-based learning courses in Early Childhood Education and Adult Development and Aging. She is committed to teaching, mentoring and advising. She is currently conducting research on attachment processes in immigrant Latino/a adolescents that was funded by the Virginia Foundation for Independent Colleges, and is Co-Investigator for a National Science Foundation grant focused on student retention and success in science, technology, engineering, and math. She lives in Virginia with her husband Michael, daughters Amalia and Clara, and two dogs.

Ruth Duskin Feldman is an award-winning writer and educator. With Diane E. Papalia and Sally Wendkos Olds, she coauthored the fourth, seventh, eighth, ninth, tenth, eleventh and **twelfth** editions of Human Development and the eighth, ninth, tenth, eleventh, and **twelfth** editions of A Child's World. She also is coauthor of *Adult Development and Aging* and of *Child Development: A Topical Approach.* A former teacher, she has developed educational materials for all levels from elementary school through college and has prepared ancillaries to accompany the Papalia-Olds books. She is author or coauthor of four books addressed to general readers, including *Whatever Happened to the Quiz Kids? Perils and Profits of Growing Up Gifted,* republished in 2000 as an Authors Guild Back-in-Print edition of iUniverse. She has written for numerous newspapers and magazines and has lectured extensively and made national and local media appearances throughout the United States on education and gifted children. She received her bachelor's degree from Northwestern University, where she was graduated with highest distinction and was elected to Phi Beta Kappa.

To my husband
who picked up the slack for me
on all the long working evenings
and weekends, mostly without complaint.

To my daughters,
for joyfully and furiously bringing to life
the magic of development right in
front of me, every day.

And last to my dogs, for parking themselves
under the table to be my footrests while I worked
and for providing me with a reason to get outside
at least once a day to stretch my legs.

To our parents,
Madeline and Edward Papalia,
Leah and Samuel Wendkos,
and Boris and Rita Duskin,
for their unfailing love, nurturance, and
confidence in us, and for their abiding conviction
that childhood is a wondrous time of life.

And to our children,
Anna Victoria,
Nancy, Jennifer, and Dorri,
Steven, Laurie, and Heidi,

And our grandchildren,
Stefan, Maika, Anna, Lisa, and Nina,
Daniel, Emmett, Rita, Carol, Eve, Isaac, Delilah, and Raphael,
who have helped us revisit childhood
and see its wonders and challenges.

brief contents

contents

part 1

③ part

Infancy and Toddlerhood

4 part Early Childhood

⑥ Adolescence

A Child's World: fostering your students' success. Informed by real student data and supported by real infants and children, *A Child's World* takes a practical approach to research and recognizes that just as every child develops in their own way, your students also learn in their own ways. With our adaptive, personalized learning program, LearnSmart, students are guided toward success on their terms. With integrated resources like Milestones of Child Development and short author tutorials on some of the most challenging learning objectives, *A Child's World* makes a difference for your students.

A Powerful Revision Based on Real Data from Real Students

Here's how it used to be: The revision process for a new edition typically began with asking several dozen instructors what they would change and what they would keep. Also, experts in the field were asked to provide comments that point out new material to add and dated material to remove. Using all these reviews, authors would revise the material. But now, a new tool has revolutionized that paradigm.

• Student Data

McGraw-Hill authors now have access to real data from real students to create their revisions. This data is anonymously collected from the many students who use *LearnSmart*, the adaptive learning system that provides students with an individualized assessment of their own progress. Because virtually every text paragraph is tied to several questions that students answer while using *LearnSmart*, empirical data showing the specific concepts with which students have the most difficulty is easily pinpointed.

This student data from *LearnSmart* is in the form of a *heat map*, which graphically illustrates "hot spots" in the text that cause students the most difficulty. Using these hot spots, McGraw-Hill authors can refine the wording and content in the new edition to make these areas clearer than before.

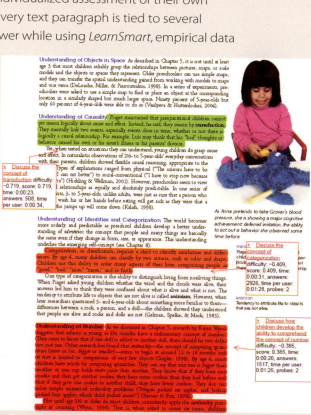

- **StudySmart**

In addition to those areas that have been reworked for clarity in *A Child's World*, Thirteenth Edition, "StudySmart" icons are placed in the most important hot spots in the chapter based on student data. These icons lead students to digital assets that enhance their understanding of challenging concepts. The assets may be a video of a child that demonstrates a milestone, an animated figure to explain a concept visually, or a video of one of the book's authors to further explain the topic.

Students will see "StudySmart" QR codes throughout the chapters related to challenging concepts. One example in Chapter 1 is "Domains of Development." When students scan the QR code with their smartphones, they can access that digital asset for an enhanced explanation or alternate view of that material.

In addition, in each chapter students will find "Connect StudySmart" icons in the margin focusing on a specific challenging concepts such as "Operant Conditioning." These guide students to assignable and assessable digital activities that are part of Connect Child Development. This means instructors and students can determine how well they understand that concept prior to taking the high-stakes test.

study smart

Domains of Development

connect

study smart

Operant Conditioning

Engage with Real Life as It Unfolds

Many of the Connect StudySmart icons guide students to McGraw-Hill's Milestones, another opportunity to enhance learning.

McGraw Hill's Milestones is a powerful tool that allows students to experience life as it unfolds, from infancy to through emerging adulthood. This tool consists of two essential components that work together to capture key changes throughout child development—**Milestones of Child Development** and **Milestones: Transitions**.

In **Milestones of Child Development**, students track the early stages of physical, social, and emotional development. By watching one child over time or comparing various children, Milestones provides a unique, experiential learning environment that can only be achieved by watching real human development as it happens—all in pre-, transitional, and post-milestone segments.

In **Milestones: Transitions**, students meet a series of people—from teenagers to individuals in late adulthood—to hear individual perspectives on changes that occur throughout the life span. Through a series of interviews, students are given the opportunity to think critically while exploring the differences in attitudes on everything from body image to changes in emotion, sexuality, cognitive processes, and death and dying.

Real Research, Applications, Culture

We continue to emphasize *A Child's World* hallmarks of research, practical applications, and culture. In addition to updating the research base of each chapter, "The Research World" features provide an in-depth examination of research topics such as Chapter Two's adaptive value of immaturity. "The Everyday World" features deal with a variety of practical applications such as Chapter Five's comforting a crying baby. Stressing the cultural and historical influences on development, the "Around the World" features explore cultural and socioeconomic issues. In this edition, Gabriela Martorell's research with immigrant populations and her current involvement on an NSF grant designed to increase the retention of underrepresented students in the STEM areas (science, technology, engineering, and math) further contribute to this emphasis.

McGraw-Hill Connect Child Development

McGraw-Hill Connect engages students in the course content so they are better prepared, are more active in discussion, and achieve better results.

• LearnSmart

Powered by McGraw-Hill Connect® Child Development, LearnSmart is our response to today's student. LearnSmart is designed to maximize productivity and efficiency in learning, helping students "know what they know" while helping them learn what they don't know. In fact, instructors using LearnSmart are reporting that their students' performance is improving by a letter grade or more. Through this unique tool, instructors have the ability to identify struggling students quickly and easily, *before* the first exam.

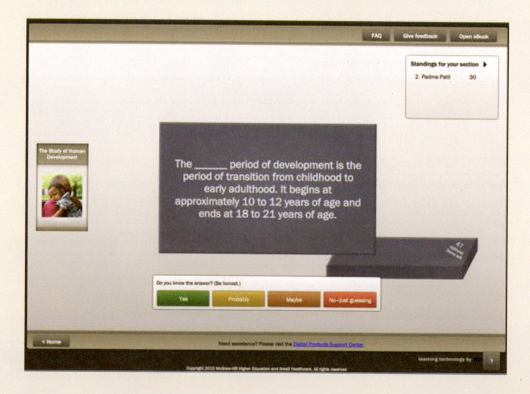

Regardless of individual study habits, preparation, and approaches to the course, students will find that *A Child's World* connects with them on a personal, individual basis and provides a road map for real success in the course.

• Streamlined Course Management and Powerful Reporting

Whether a class is face-to-face, hybrid, or entirely online, *A Child's World* provides the tools needed to reduce the amount of time and energy that instructors must expend to administer their course. Easy-to-use course management allows instructors to spend less time administering and more time teaching.

- **At-Risk Student Reports:** The At-Risk Report provides instructors with one-click access to a dashboard that identifies students who are at risk of dropping out of a course due to low engagement levels.

- **Category Analysis Reports:** The Category Analysis report is the place to find out how your students are performing relative to specific learning objectives and goals.

- **Item Analysis Reports:** The Item Analysis report is the best way to get a bird's-eye view of a single assignment. You'll be able to tell if students are improving or if the concepts are something you want to spend additional time on in class.

- **Student Performance Reports:** The student performance report helps you search for a specific student in your class and focus on that student's progress across your assignments.

- **Assignment Results and Statistics Reports:** The Assignment Results report shows your entire class's performance across all of your assignments. Assignment Statistics reports will give you quick data on each assignment including the mean score, high score, and low scores, as well as the number of times it was submitted.

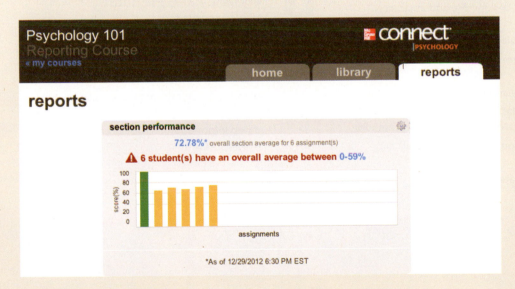

In addition to updating references, adding interesting margin notes, updating statistics, and the change in the design, this is a chapter-by-chapter list of topics that are new or have been revised based on the heat map data from students using Connect.

1 Studying a Child's World

- Revised the section on studying the life span
- Added material on developmental trajectories
- Revised information about minority children in the United States
- Updated statistics on poverty and ethnicity

2 A Child's World: How We Discover It

- Expanded "Issue 1: Is Development Active or Reactive" section
- Revised sections on mechanistic and organismic views of development
- Expanded material about Freud's ideas
- Revised the relationship between qualitative change and stage theories throughout the chapter
- Added an example of how Erikson's stages feed in to each other
- Added examples of concrete and abstract schemes
- Expanded disequilibrium material
- Revised exosystem influences and added an example
- Revised ethology and evolutionary psychology
- Expanded material about qualitative and quantitative research and the scientific method
- Revised the section on developmental research designs.
- Revised ethics material

3 Forming a New Life: Conception, Heredity, and Environment

- Updated material on multiple births
- Expanded information on the human genome
- Revised information on dominant and recessive genes
- Revised information on polygenic inheritance
- Expanded the description of epigenesis
- Revised the section on phenotype and genotype
- Expanded the description of incomplete dominance
- Expanded the description of sex-linked inheritance
- Expanded the section on heritability
- Added a simile for canalization
- Added an example of nonshared environmental influences

4 Pregnancy and Prenatal Development

- Revised the description of implantation
- Added information on organogenesis in text and figure
- Updated research on what fetuses can hear in utero
- Updated information on rubella cases in developing countries

5 Birth and the Newborn Baby

- Updated maternal and infant mortality rates
- Revised definition of *parturition*
- Expanded stages of labor, electronic fetal monitoring, and fontanels
- Added information on the functioning of body systems in neonates
- Added information on the Brazelton Neonatal Behavioral Assessment Scale
- Added an example of internal clocks
- Added information on cultural differences in infant sleep schedules
- Updated information on birth complications
- Revised the distinction between low birth weight and small-for-date infants
- Added additional information to the section on childbirth and bonding

6 Physical Development and Health during the First Three Years

- Added examples of cephalocaudal and proximodistal principles
- Added information on the cerebral hemispheres and their functions
- Revised information on cell death
- Added an example of a reflex
- Added information on plasticity
- Expanded sections on ecological systems and dynamic systems theories on motor development
- Updated worldwide neonatal mortality rate information

7 Cognitive Development during the First Three Years

- Revised the description of operant conditioning
- Expanded the use of conditioning techniques in the study of infant memory
- Revised the description of intelligent behavior
- Expanded the description of developmental tests
- Revised the section on early intervention
- Updated the section on imitative abilities
- Added an example of pictorial competence
- Expanded the description of scale error and the dual representation hypothesis
- Expanded the description of habituation and dishabituation
- Added an example of how visual preference is used in infant research
- Revised the use of habituation as a method to investigate visual recognition
- Added examples for categorization and causality
- Revised the description of the violation of expectations paradigm and its use for the investigation of object permanence
- Revised the section on number
- Revised the section on conceptual understanding and perceptual awareness
- Added examples of implicit and working memory
- Expanded the description of phonemes
- Added material about early sensitization of infants to their native language
- Added an example of syntax
- Revised the section on overregularization
- Revised and added an example to learning theoretical approach to language learning
- Revised the section on child-directed speech

8 Psychosocial Development during the First Three Years

- Added an example of an emotional response
- Updated the figure on differentiation of emotions
- Revised the introduction to temperament
- Expanded the example of a slow-to-warm up child
- Revised stability of temperament material
- Expanded the description of behavioral inhibition
- Revised the link to goodness of fit in the behavioral inhibition section
- Revised trust versus mistrust
- Expanded the description of attachment categories
- Revised the explanation of internal working models
- Revised the description of mutual regulation
- Added an example of social referencing
- Revised the description of socialization and internalization
- Added an example of how attentional processes impact socialization
- Revised the descriptions of conscience and compliance
- Revised the description of gender typing
- Updated data on maternal employment

9 Physical Development and Health in Early Childhood

- Expanded the brain development section
- Revised information on handedness
- Updated mortality information on children 5 years and younger
- Updated food security statistics
- Updated information on homelessness and health insurance

10 Cognitive Development in Early Childhood

- Revised the introduction to the Piagetian approach
- Expanded the section on symbolic function
- Revised the section on understanding causality
- Added an example to understanding identities and categorization
- Revised the research example of egocentrism
- Expanded conservation material
- Revised and added examples for basic processes and capacities in memory
- Added examples of episodic and generic memories
- Revised and added examples for influences on memory retention
- Expanded the definition of *intelligence*
- Revised information on scaffolding and the zone of proximal development
- Added an example of fast mapping
- Revised descriptions of grammar and syntax
- Added an example for pragmatics
- Revised the definition of *emergent literacy*
- Expanded the introduction to the child in kindergarten

11 Psychosocial Development in Early Childhood

- Revised the example of self-definition
- Revised developmental changes in self-esteem
- Added an example of helpless response pattern
- Revised the section on emotional understanding
- Added an example of initiative
- Revised the introduction to gender differences
- Revised the biological approach to gender differences
- Revised the discussion of evolutionary approach to gender
- Added supporting research on family influences
- Revised information to emphasize the developmental importance of play
- Revised information about levels of play
- Expanded dramatic play material
- Revised some information about reinforcement and punishment
- Expanded an example of inductive reasoning
- Added a table on parenting styles
- Added an example of instrumental aggression
- Revised the section on gender differences in aggression
- Revised the section on only children

12 Physical Development and Health in Middle Childhood

- Expanded brain development material
- Updated accidental death data in children
- Added an example of social anxiety

13 Cognitive Development in Middle Childhood

- Expanded spatial relationships and causality material
- Revised categorization material
- Expanded inductive and deductive reasoning
- Revised conservation material
- Revised the link between culture and mathematical reasoning
- Revised moral reasoning material
- Added an example to illustrate links between attention, memory, and planning
- Revised the description of executive functioning
- Added an example of selective attention
- Revised working memory material
- Expanded the description of metamemory
- Revised the section on mnemonics
- Added an example of the link between information processing and Piagetian tasks
- Added a definition of *psychometrics*
- Revised the section on cultural influences on IQ
- Added information on Gardner's theories of intelligence
- Revised the section on Sternberg's Triarchic Theory
- Added information to the section on dynamic tests of intelligence
- Expanded the definition of *syntax*
- Added examples to the section on reading
- Expanded the description of metacognition
- Added an example of self-efficacy
- Revised the definition of *special needs*
- Updated data on learning disabilities
- Revised the description of convergent and divergent thinking

14 Psychosocial Development in Middle Childhood

- Revised information about self-concept
- Revised self-esteem material
- Revised the description of emotional self-regulation
- Revised information on family atmosphere
- Expanded the description of coregulation
- Updated data on children living in poverty
- Updated data on living arrangements in children under 18
- Updated data on father-absent homes
- Revised the section on custody, visitation, and co-parenting
- Expanded the section on sociometric popularity
- Revised the section on levels of friendship in school-age children
- Added an example of a hostile attributional bias
- Expanded the description of resilience

15 Physical Development and Health in Adolescence

- Expanded the description of adolescence as a social construct
- Revised the section on adolescence as a time of opportunity and risk
- Revised the description of puberty
- Revised the section on family influences on pubertal timing
- Expanded the section on the adolescent brain
- Updated data on sleep needs and problems
- Added *binge drinking* as a key term
- Updated data on alcohol, marijuana, tobacco use, and depression rates in adolescents

16 Cognitive Development in Adolescence

- Revised the definition of *hypothetical-deductive reasoning*
- Revised information about evaluation of Piaget's approach
- Revised and added an example to language development in adolescence
- Expanded Kohlberg's theory of moral reasoning
- Revised examples of reasoning
- Revised and added an example to evaluation of Kohlberg's approach
- Revised the description of Gilligan's theory
- Added an example of prosocial moral reasoning
- Added the description of inductive disciplinary techniques
- Revised information about student motivation and self-efficacy
- Revised the description of brain differences by gender
- Updated data on high school drop out rates and on master's degrees obtained by women

17 Psychosocial Development in Adolescence

- Expanded the section on identity versus identity confusion and added *fidelity* as a key term
- Revised definitions of *crisis* and *commitment*
- Expanded examples of foreclosure and moratorium
- Revised gender differences in identity formation
- Revised some material in the section on ethnic factors in identity formation
- Added an example of cultural socialization
- Updated data on sexual activity in grades 9–12, contraceptive usage, sexually transmitted infections, and teenage pregnancies
- Revised relationships with family and peers
- Added examples of individuation
- Added an example of behavioral control techniques
- Added information on parental monitoring
- Revised trends in sibling relationships in adolescence
- Expanded the description of antisocial behavior
- Revised information on authoritative parenting
- Revised the description of collective efficacy

integrated instructor resources

The password-protected Online Learning Center for *A Child's World,* Thirteenth Edition, contains valuable tools for instructors to use in the classroom. This site includes chapter-by-chapter Instructor' Manual, Test Bank files, and PowerPoint presentations. Contact your local McGraw-Hill representative for log-in information: **www.mhhe.com/martorellacw13**

- **Instructors Manual**—The instructor's manual includes classroom activities available to both new and experienced instructors. Among the featured resources are teaching outlines, suggested lecture topics, and classroom discussions and activities. The manual is available in electronic format, for convenient access, editing, and printing.

- **Test Bank**—Each chapter's test bank holds approximately 100 questions that are designed to test factual, conceptual, and practice-based understanding. The test bank is compatible with **EZTest,** McGraw-Hill's **Computerized Test Bank** program.

  With the introduction of LearnSmart—an adaptive student study tool—to this edition of *A Child's World,* test bank questions have been modified to reflect a seamless integration between student study tools and instructor assessment tools. With updates to incorporate LearnSmart and Connect Learning Objective tags into EZTest, it will not only be easier for instructors to create assessments, but assessments that reflect student study habits. This alignment will benefit both students and instructors by creating cohesion between the key concepts that are read, understood, practiced, and ultimately, assessed.

- **PowerPoint Presentations**—These slides cover the key points of each chapter and include charts and graphs from the text. The PowerPoint presentations serve as an organization and navigation tool integrated with examples and activities from an expert instructor. The slides can be used as is or modified to meet your needs.

acknowledgments

We would like to express out gratitude to the many friends and colleagues who, through their work and their interest, helped us clarify our thinking about child development. The following reviewers, who are affiliated with both two-year and four-year institutions, provided a number of excellent recommendations:

Akins, Ericka *East Mississippi Community College*
Atkins, LaDonna *University of Central Oklahoma*
Brewer, Laura *Hudson Valley Community College*
Calhoun, Tamara *Hudson Valley Community College*
Conrad, Ruth *Broward University*
Crosetti, Laura *Monroe Community College*
Edwards-Rowell, Tyra *Holmes Community College*
Fordham, Kim *North Idaho College*
Goth-Owens, Judy *Lansing Community College*
Green, Kathleen *North Idaho College*
Hall, Cheryl *Lansing Community College*
Harmelink, Virginia *Pima Community College*
Lao, Joseph *Hunter College*
Miller, Kendra *Anoka Ramsey Community College*
Shelton, Jaimie *Stanly Community College*
Willard, Wanda *Monroe Community College*
Wise, Patrick *Monroe Community College*

As always, we welcome your comments!

Gabriela Martorell
Diane Papalia
Ruth Duskin Feldman

A Child's World

Infancy through Adolescence

did you know outline

did you know?

▷ In some societies there is no concept of adolescence?

▷ Many scholars today agree that the construction of race is not a concept that can be defended on a biological basis?

▷ More than 16 million U.S. children live in poverty and are at risk for health, cognitive, emotional, and behavioral problems?

In this chapter, we describe how the field of child development has itself developed. We identify aspects of development and show how they interrelate. We summarize major developments during each period of a child's life. We look at influences on development and the contexts in which each occurs.

Studying a Child's World

There is nothing permanent except change.

—Heraclitus, fragment (6th century BC)

1. What is child development, and how has its study evolved?

2. What do developmental scientists study?

3. What influences make one child different from another?

4. What are six fundamental points about child development on which consensus has emerged?

guidepost

1 What is child development, and how has its study evolved?

child development
Scientific study of processes of change and stability in children from conception through adolescence.

Developmental psychologists have helped identify key achievements in development across childhood. Many parenting web sites include lists of these milestones to help track.

The Study of Child Development: Then and Now

From the moment of conception, children begin a process of change that will continue throughout their lives. A single cell becomes a tiny group of cells that eventually becomes a living, breathing baby. And though this single cell develops into a unique individual, the changes human beings experience have common patterns. Babies grow and become children, who grow and become adolescents and then adults. Individuals grow in patterned ways, and they show consistency over time with respect to their unique characteristics. For example, about 10 to 15 percent of children are consistently shy, and another 10 to 15 percent are very bold. Although various influences can modify these traits, they tend to persist to a moderate degree, especially in children at one extreme or the other. This is discussed further in Chapter 8.

The field of **child development** focuses on the scientific study of systematic processes of change and stability in human children. Developmental scientists—people engaged in the professional study of child development—look at ways in which children change from conception through adolescence as well as at characteristics that remain fairly stable. Which of a child's characteristics are most likely to endure? Which are likely to change, and why? These are among the questions developmental scientists seek to answer.

The work of developmental scientists can have a dramatic impact on children's lives. Research findings often have direct applications to child rearing, education, health, and social policy. For example, researchers found that Boston public school students who went to school hungry or lacked essential nutrients in their diet had poorer grades and more emotional and behavior problems than their classmates. After the schools started a free breakfast program, participating students improved their math grades, were absent and tardy less often, and had fewer emotional and behavioral problems (Kleinman et al., 2002).

Research findings influence child rearing, education, heath, and social policy. When researchers determined that students performed better when they had a good breakfast, a number of schools instituted breakfast programs.

EARLY APPROACHES

The formal *scientific* study of child development is relatively new. Looking back, we can see dramatic changes in the ways of investigating the world of childhood.

Forerunners of the scientific study of child development were *baby biographies,* journals kept to record the early development of a single child. One journal, published in 1787, contained the German philosopher Dietrich Tiedemann's observations of his infant son's sensory, motor, language, and cognitive development (1787/1897). Typical of the speculative nature of such observations was Tiedemann's erroneous conclusion, after watching the infant suck more continuously on a cloth tied around something sweet than on a nurse's finger, that sucking appeared to be "not instinctive, but acquired" (Murchison & Langer, 1927, p. 206).

It was Charles Darwin, originator of the theory of evolution, who first emphasized the *developmental* nature of infant behavior. In the belief that human beings could better understand themselves by studying their origins—both as a species and as individuals—Darwin in 1877 published notes on his son Doddy's sensory, cognitive, and emotional development during his first 12 months (Keegan & Gruber, 1985). Darwin's journal gave baby biographies scientific respectability; about 30 more were published during the next three decades (Dennis, 1936).

DEVELOPMENTAL PSYCHOLOGY BECOMES A SCIENCE

By the end of the nineteenth century, several advances in the Western world had paved the way for the scientific study of child development. Scientists had unlocked the mystery of conception and were arguing with renewed vigor about the relative importance of nature and nurture (inborn characteristics and external influences). Advances in medicine, including the discovery of germs and the development of vaccines, made it possible for many more children to survive infancy. Child welfare laws designed to protect children from long workdays let them spend more time in school, and parents and teachers became more concerned with identifying and meeting children's developmental needs. The new science of psychology suggested that people could better understand themselves by learning what had influenced them as children.

Still, this new discipline had far to go. Adolescence was not considered a separate period of development until the early twentieth century, when G. Stanley Hall, a pioneer in child study, published a popular (though somewhat unscientific) book called *Adolescence.* The establishment of research institutes in the 1930s and 1940s at universities such as Iowa, Minnesota, Columbia, Berkeley, and Yale marked the emergence of child psychology as a true science with professionally trained practitioners. Longitudinal studies, such as Arnold Gesell's (1929) studies of stages in motor development, provided research-based information about developments that normally occur at various ages. Other major studies that began around 1930—the Fels Research Institute Study, the Berkeley Growth and Guidance Studies, and the Oakland (Adolescent) Growth Study—produced much information on long-term development.

STUDYING THE LIFE SPAN

When the field of developmental psychology first emerged as a scientific discipline, most researchers focused their energies on infant and child development. Growth and development are more obvious during these times given the rapid pace of change. As the field matured, however, it became clear that development did not just include infancy and childhood. On the day of birth, a child has already had nine months of development, and environmental influences experienced during that time can have lifelong consequences. And, once childhood has passed, development continues; adults develop and change, just as children do, and development continues until death.

Today, researchers consider development to be from "womb to tomb," comprising the entire human life span from conception to death. Moreover, they acknowledge that development can be either positive (e.g., becoming toilet trained or enrolling in a college course after retirement) or negative (e.g., once again wetting the bed after a traumatic

what's your view

How will studying child development influence your understanding of the phases and stages of childhood?

G. Stanley Hall was the originator of the common stereotype of adolescence as a time of storm and strife, although later research showed his conclusions to be overstated.

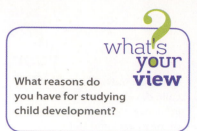

what's your view

What reasons do you have for studying child development?

event or isolating yourself after retirement). For these reasons, events such as the timing of parenthood, maternal employment, and marital satisfaction are now also studied under the umbrella of developmental psychology. This book focuses on development from conception to adolescence; however, some factors about adult development are included because they have an influence on how children develop.

Development is messy. It's complex and multifaceted and shaped by interacting arcs of influence. Therefore, development is best understood with input from a variety of theoretical and research orientations and is most appropriately studied using multiple disciplines. Thus, the study of development has been interdisciplinary almost from the start (Parke, 2004b). Students of child development draw collaboratively from a wide range of disciplines, including psychology, psychiatry, sociology, anthropology, biology, genetics, family science, education, history, and medicine. This book includes findings from research in all these fields.

NEW FRONTIERS

Although children have been the focus of scientific study for more than 100 years, this exploration is ever evolving. The questions developmental scientists seek to answer, the methods they use, and the explanations they propose are more sophisticated and more varied than they were even 10 years ago. These shifts reflect progress in understanding as new investigations build on or challenge those that went before. They also reflect advances in technology. Sensitive instruments that measure eye movements, heart rate, blood pressure, muscle tension, and the like are illuminating biological influences and correlates of development that were previously hidden. Digital technology and computers enable investigators to scan infants' facial expressions for early signs of emotions and to analyze how mothers and babies communicate. Advances in brain imaging make it possible to probe the mysteries of temperament, to investigate the neural basis of language, and to pinpoint the sources of logical thought.

checkpoint can you . . .

▷ Trace highlights in the evolution of the study of child development?

▷ Give examples of practical applications of research on child development?

guidepost 2 What do developmental scientists study?

The Study of Child Development: Basic Concepts

The processes of change and stability that developmental scientists study occur in all domains, or aspects, of the self and throughout all of childhood and adolescence.

DOMAINS OF DEVELOPMENT

Developmental scientists study three *domains,* or aspects, of the self: physical, cognitive, and psychosocial. Growth of the body and brain, sensory capacities, motor skills, and health are parts of biological or **physical development**. Learning, attention, memory, language, thinking, reasoning, and creativity make up **cognitive development**. Emotions, personality, and social relationships are aspects of **psychosocial development**.

Although we talk separately about physical, cognitive, and psychosocial development, these domains are interrelated: each affects the others. As one researcher pointed out, "Our brains work better, our thinking is sharper, our mood brighter, and our vulnerability to disease diminished if we are physically fit" (Diamond, 2007, p. 153). For example, a child with frequent ear infections may develop language more slowly than a child without this physical problem. During puberty, dramatic physical and hormonal changes affect the developing sense of self.

Cognitive advances are closely related to physical, emotional, and social factors. For example, the ability to control your body's movements opens up a world of exploration to the infant, a world that grows more accessible with each advance in motor development. Understanding and using language depends on certain physical structures in the brain. A child who is precocious in language development may gain in self-esteem and social acceptance.

physical development
Growth of body and brain, including biological and physiological patterns of change in sensory capacities, motor skills, and health.

cognitive development
Pattern of change in mental abilities, such as learning, attention, memory, language, thinking, reasoning, and creativity.

psychosocial development
Pattern of change in emotions, personality, and social relationships.

Psychosocial development can affect cognitive and physical functioning. Indeed, without meaningful social connections, physical and mental health can suffer. Motivation and self-confidence are important contributors to school success, whereas negative emotions such as fear and anxiety can impair school performance.

Thus, although for simplicity's sake we look separately at physical, cognitive, and psychosocial development, development is a unified process. Throughout the text, we highlight links among the three major domains of development.

> The interactions between domains of development can be conceptualized as a giant spiderweb where one thread of development is affected by what is going on in the rest of the web. A vibration experienced in one area is experienced by the whole web.

study smart

Domains of Development

PERIODS OF DEVELOPMENT

Division of the life span into periods of development is a **social construction:** a concept or practice that may appear natural and obvious to those who accept it, but in reality is an invention of a particular culture or society. There is no objectively definable moment when a child becomes an adult or a young person becomes old. In fact, our understanding of childhood itself can be viewed as a social construction. In contrast to the relative freedom children have in the United States today, young children in colonial times were treated much like small adults and were expected to do adultlike tasks such as knitting socks and spinning wool (Ehrenreich & English, 2005). Inuit parents in the Canadian Arctic believe that young children are not yet capable of thought and reason and therefore are lenient when their children cry or become angry. On the other hand, parents on the Pacific Island of Tonga regularly beat 3- to 5-year-olds, whose crying is attributed to willfulness (Briggs, 1970; Morton, 1996).

The concept of adolescence as a period of development in industrial societies is quite recent. Until the early twentieth century, young people in the United States were considered children until they left school, married or got a job, and entered the adult world. By the 1920s, with the establishment of comprehensive high schools to meet the needs of a growing economy and with more families able to support extended formal education for their children, the teenage years had become a distinct period of development (Keller, 1999). In many preindustrial societies, the concept of adolescence does not exist. The Chippewa Indians, for example, have only two periods of childhood: from birth until the child walks, and from walking to puberty. What we call *adolescence* is viewed as part of adulthood (Broude, 1995).

In this book, we follow a sequence of five periods generally accepted in Western industrial societies. After examining the crucial changes that occur in the first period, before birth, we trace physical, cognitive, and psychosocial development through infancy and toddlerhood, early childhood, middle childhood, and adolescence (Table 1.1). Again, these age divisions are approximate and arbitrary.

social construction
Concept about the nature of reality based on societally shared perceptions or assumptions.

> **what's your view ?**
>
> Why do you think various societies divide the periods of development differently?

Peer groups become increasingly important in middle childhood and adolescence and strongly influence behavior.

	Typical Major Developments in Five Periods of Child Development		
TABLE 1.1			
Age Period	**Physical Developments**	**Cognitive Developments**	**Psychosocial Developments**
Prenatal Period (conception to birth)	Conception occurs by normal fertilization or other means. The genetic endowment interacts with environmental influences from the start. Basic body structures and organs form; brain growth spurt begins. Physical growth is the most rapid in the life span. Vulnerability to environmental influences is great.	Abilities to learn and remember and to respond to sensory stimuli are developing.	Fetus responds to mother's voice and develops a preference for it.
Infancy and Toddlerhood (birth to age 3)	All senses and body systems operate at birth to varying degrees. The brain grows in complexity and is highly sensitive to environmental influence. Physical growth and development of motor skills are rapid.	Abilities to learn and remember are present, even in early weeks. Use of symbols and ability to solve problems develop by end of 2nd year. Comprehension and use of language develop rapidly.	Attachments to parents and others form. Self-awareness develops. Shift from dependence to autonomy occurs. Interest in other children increases.
Early Childhood (ages 3 to 6)	Growth is steady; appearance becomes more slender and proportions more adultlike. Appetite diminishes, and sleep problems are common. Handedness appears; fine and gross motor skills and strength improve.	Thinking is somewhat egocentric, but understanding of other people's perspectives grows. Cognitive immaturity results in some illogical ideas about the world. Memory and language improve. Intelligence becomes more predictable. Preschool experience is common, and kindergarten experience is more so.	Self-concept and understanding of emotions become more complex; self-esteem is global. Independence, initiative, and self-control increase. Gender identity develops. Play becomes more imaginative, more elaborate, and usually more social. Altruism, aggression, and fearfulness are common. Family is still the focus of social life, but other children become more important.
Middle Childhood (ages 6 to 11)	Growth slows. Strength and athletic skills improve. Respiratory illnesses are common, but health is generally better than at any other time in life span.	Egocentrism diminishes. Children begin to think logically but concretely. Memory and language skills increase. Cognitive gains permit children to benefit from formal schooling. Some children show special educational needs and strengths.	Self-concept becomes more complex, affecting self-esteem. Coregulation reflects gradual shift in control from parents to child. Peers assume central importance.
Adolescence (ages 11 to about 20)	Physical growth and other changes are rapid and profound. Reproductive maturity occurs. Major health risks arise from behavioral issues, such as eating disorders and drug abuse.	Ability to think abstractly and use scientific reasoning develops. Immature thinking persists in some attitudes and behaviors. Education focuses on preparation for college or vocation.	Search for identity, including sexual identity, becomes central. Relationships with parents are generally good. Peer group may exert a positive or negative influence.

Although individual differences exist in the way children deal with the characteristic events and issues of each period, developmental scientists suggest that certain basic needs must be met and certain tasks mastered for normal development to occur. Infants, for example, are dependent on adults for food, clothing, and shelter as well as for human contact and affection. They form attachments to parents and caregivers, who also become attached to them. With the development of speech and self-locomotion, toddlers become more self-reliant; they need to assert their autonomy but also need parents to set limits on their behavior. During early childhood, children develop more self-control and more interest in other children. During middle childhood, control over behavior gradually shifts from parent to child, and the peer group becomes increasingly important. A central task of adolescence is the search for identity—personal, sexual, and occupational. As adolescents become physically mature, they deal with conflicting needs and emotions as they prepare to leave the parental nest.

▷ **checkpoint**
can you . . .

▷ Identify three domains of development and give examples of how they are interrelated?

▷ Name five periods of child development (as defined in this book) and list several key issues or tasks of each period?

Influences on Development

What makes each child unique? Although students of development are interested in the universal developmental processes experienced by all children, they also must consider **individual differences** in characteristics, influences, and developmental outcomes. Children differ in gender, height, weight, and body build; in health and energy level; in intelligence; and in temperament, personality, and emotional reactions. The contexts of their lives differ too: the homes, communities, and societies they live in, the relationships they have, the kinds of schools they go to (or whether they go to school at all), and how they spend their free time. Because of this, every child has a different developmental trajectory—a unique and individual path to follow. One of the primary challenges in developmental psychology is to identify the universal influences on development, and then apply those to the understanding of individual differences in developmental trajectories.

guidepost 3

What influences make one child different from another?

Hypnotizability is one individual difference between people. Only about 10 percent of the population is highly hypnotizable.

Spiegel, 1985

individual differences
Differences among children in characteristics, influences, or developmental outcomes.

HEREDITY, ENVIRONMENT, AND MATURATION

Some influences on development originate primarily with **heredity**, inborn traits or characteristics inherited from a child's biological parents. Other influences come largely from the inner and outer **environment**, the world outside the self beginning in the womb, and the learning that comes from experience—including *socialization*, a child's induction into the value system of the culture. Which of these factors—heredity or environment—has more impact on development? This issue inspires intense debate. Theorists differ in the relative importance they give to *nature* (heredity) and *nurture* (environmental influences both before and after birth).

Today, scientists have found ways to measure more precisely the roles of heredity and environment in the development of specific traits within a population. When we look at a particular child, however, research with regard to almost all characteristics points to a blend of inheritance and experience. Thus, even though intelligence is strongly affected by heredity, environmental factors such as parental stimulation, education, and peer influences also affect it. Although there still is some dispute about the relative importance of nature and nurture, contemporary theorists and researchers are more interested in finding ways to explain how they work together rather than arguing about which factor is more important. In other words, they are more concerned with the processes governing development than the outcome of any one particular characteristic.

Many typical changes of infancy and early childhood, such as the emergence of the abilities to walk and talk, are tied to **maturation** of the body and brain—the unfolding

heredity
Inborn characteristics inherited from the biological parents.

environment
Totality of nonhereditary, or experiential, influences on development.

maturation
Unfolding of a universal natural sequence of physical and behavioral changes.

study smart

Nature/Nurture

of a universal, natural sequence of physical changes and behavior patterns. These maturational processes, which are seen most clearly in the early years, act in concert with the influences of heredity and environment. As children grow into adolescents and then into adults, individual differences in innate characteristics (heredity) and life experience (environment) play an increasing role as children adapt to the internal and external conditions in which they find themselves.

Even in processes that all children undergo, rates and timing of development vary. Throughout this book, we talk about average ages for the occurrence of certain events, such as the first word, the first step, the first menstruation or wet dream, and the development of logical thought. But these ages are merely averages, and there is wide variation among children with respect to these norms. Only when deviation from the average is extreme should we consider development exceptionally advanced or delayed.

To understand child development, then, we need to look at the *inherited* characteristics that give each child a special start in life. We also need to consider the many *environmental*, or experiential, factors that affect children, especially such major contexts as family, neighborhood, socioeconomic status, race/ethnicity, and culture. We need to consider how heredity and environment interact. We need to understand which developments are primarily maturational and which are not. We need to look at influences that affect many or most children at a certain age or a certain time in history and also at those that affect only certain individuals. Finally, we need to look at how timing can accentuate the impact of certain influences.

CONTEXTS OF DEVELOPMENT

Human beings are social beings. Right from the start they develop within a social and historical context. For an infant, the immediate context normally is the family; and the family in turn is subject to the wider and ever-changing influences of neighborhood, community, and society.

nuclear family
Two-generational household unit consisting of one or two parents and their biological children, adopted children, or stepchildren.

Family The **nuclear family** is a household unit generally consisting of one or two parents and their children, whether biological, adopted, or stepchildren. Historically, the two-parent nuclear family has been the dominant family unit in the United States and other Western societies. However, the nuclear family today is different from what it used to be. Instead of the large, rural family in which parents and children worked side by side on the family farm, we now see smaller, urban families in which both parents work outside the home and children spend much of their time in school or child care. The increased incidence of divorce also has affected the nuclear family. Children of divorced parents may live with one or the other parent or may move back and forth between them. The household may include a stepparent and stepsiblings or a parent's live-in partner, and there are increasing numbers of unmarried parents and gay and lesbian households (Dye, 2010; Hernandez, 1997, 2004; Teachman, Tedrow, & Crowder, 2000).

extended family
Multigenerational kinship network of parents, children, and other relatives, sometimes living together in an extended-family household.

In many societies in Asia, Africa, and Latin America and among some U.S. families that trace their lineage to those countries, the **extended family**—a multigenerational kinship network of grandparents, aunts, uncles, cousins, and more distant relatives—is the traditional family form. Many or most people live in *extended-family households*, where they have daily contact with kin. Adults often share breadwinning and child-raising responsibilities, and children are responsible for younger brothers and sisters. Often these households are headed by women (Aaron, Parker, Ortega, & Calhoun, 1999; Johnson et al., 2003).

Today the extended-family household is becoming slightly less typical in some developing countries due to industrialization and migration to urban centers (Brown & Gilligan, 1990; Gorman, 1993; Kinsella & Phillips, 2005). Meanwhile, in the United States, economic pressures, housing shortages, and out-of-wedlock childbearing have helped to fuel a trend toward three- and even four-generational family households. There were nearly 4 million such households—almost 4 percent of all households—in 2000, many of them in places with large numbers of recent immigrants living with relatives, such as Hawaii and California (U.S. Census Bureau, 2001, revised 2008).

Culture and Race/Ethnicity **Culture** refers to a society's or group's total way of life, including customs, traditions, laws, knowledge, beliefs, values, language, and physical products, from tools to artworks—all of the behavior and attitudes that are learned, shared, and transmitted among members of a social group. Culture is constantly changing, often through contact with other cultures. Today cultural contact among adults and children alike is enhanced by computers and telecommunications; e-mail, text messaging, and instant messaging offer almost immediate communication across the globe, and digital services such as iTunes give people around the world easy access to American music and movies.

An **ethnic group** consists of people united by a distinctive culture, ancestry, religion, language, or national origin, all of which contribute to a sense of shared identity and shared attitudes, beliefs, and values. By 2050, due to rising immigration and high birthrates among immigrant families, ethnic minorities in the United States are expected to become the majority. In fact, in 2008, roughly a third of all children and nearly half of children under the age of 5 (U.S. Census Bureau, 2008a, 2009d) were from a minority group. The proportion of minority children is increasing, and it is predicted that minority children will make up more than half of the child population by 2023. By 2050, 62 percent of the nation's children are projected to be members of what are now minority groups, and the proportion of Hispanic or Latino/a children—39 percent—will surpass the 38 percent who will be non-Hispanic white (U.S. Census Bureau, 2008a; Figure 1.1a and 1.1b). Already, nearly one-fourth of U.S. kindergarteners and one-fifth of all kindergarten through twelfth grade are Hispanic (U.S. Census Bureau, 2009b, 2009c).

Ethnic and cultural patterns affect child development by their influence on the composition of a household, its economic and social resources, the way its members act toward one another, the foods they eat, the games children play, the way they learn, how well they do in school, the occupations adults engage in, and the way family members think about and perceive the world. For example, as we mentioned, children of immigrant or minority families are more likely than other U.S. children to live in extended-family households. In time, however,

> When we are immersed in a culture, it is difficult to see how much of what we do is affected by it. For example, there are regional differences in the United States regarding what soft drinks are called. The term *pop* is most common in the Midwest, Great Plains, and Northwest, *coke* is commonly used in the South and New Mexico, and *soda* is primarily used in California and bordering states.

culture
A society's or group's total way of life, including customs, traditions, beliefs, values, language, and physical products—all learned behavior passed on from adults to children.

ethnic group
A group united by ancestry, race, religion, language, or national origin that contributes to a sense of shared identity.

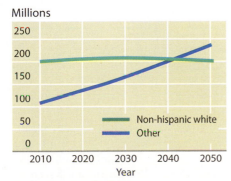

(a) Population projections

Source: U.S. Census Bureau, 2008a.

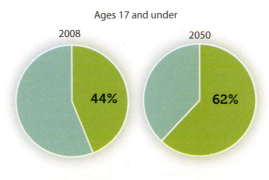

(b) Percent minority children

FIGURE 1.1

Population Projections for Non-Hispanic White and Minority Groups, 2008–2050

(a) *According to Census Bureau projections, racial/ethnic minorities will reach 54 percent of the U.S. population, exceeding the proportion of non-Hispanic white people, by 2050. (b) Also by 2050, "minority" children under age 18 are expected to make up 62 percent of the child population.*

CHILDREN OF IMMIGRANT FAMILIES

1.1

The United States has always been a nation of immigrants and ethnic groups, but the primary ethnic origins of the immigrant population have shifted from Europe and Canada—the homelands of 97 percent of immigrants in 1910—to Latin America, the Caribbean, Asia, and Africa, which now account for 88 percent of all immigrants.

Nearly one-fourth (24 percent) of U.S. children lived in immigrant families in 2007. Faster-growing than any other group of children in the country, they are the leading edge of the coming shift of racial and ethnic minorities to majority status. Whereas earlier waves of immigrants were almost entirely white and Christian, more than one-third (37 percent) of children in immigrant families have nonwhite parents. Many of these families are Confucian, Buddhist, Hindu, Jewish, Muslim, Shinto, Sikh, Taoist, or Zoroastrian, and, although predominantly Spanish-speaking, they speak a wide variety of languages.

Immigrant families are widely dispersed. Children in immigrant families account for at least 10 percent of all children in 27 states and the District of Columbia, but they are most highly concentrated in California, Texas, New York, Florida, and Illinois, which together are home to 64 percent of children of immigrants.

More immigrants come from Mexico (40 percent) than from any other country (Hernandez, Denton, & Macartney, 2008). An estimated 5 million Mexican-born children or children of Mexican-born parents live in the United States. Many of these parents work at low-paying jobs in the food service, maintenance, construction, farming, and manufacturing industries, earning less than $20,000 a year full time. With anti-immigrant sentiment rising, undocumented parents live in constant fear of losing their jobs (if they can find one) and of being deported (Children in North America Project, 2008). Nearly half of all children in immigrant families (47.9 percent) live in poverty (Hernandez, Denton, & Macartney, 2007), and many do not have health insurance despite being eligible, even though most of the parents work hard to support their families.

Most children of immigrants live with two parents (married or cohabiting), but these children are nearly twice as likely as other children to live in extended-family households with grandparents, other relatives, and even nonrelatives, often in overcrowded housing. Children in immigrant families are more than three times as likely as those in native families to have fathers who have not finished high school (40 percent as compared to 12 percent). Immigrant parents often have high educational aspirations for their children but lack the knowledge and experience to help their children succeed in school. (Issues concerning the education of immigrant children are discussed in later chapters.)

A little-known fact is that almost one in four children in immigrant families (24 percent) has one parent born in the United States, and nearly half (48 percent) have a parent who is a naturalized citizen. More than two out of three (68 percent) have parents who have lived in the United States for 10 years or more, and nearly four out of five (79 percent) of the children were born in the United States. In fact, nearly two out of three (63 percent) children living with undocumented parents are themselves natural-born citizens.

As immigration fuels dramatic changes in the United States population, developmental issues affecting children in immigrant families will become increasingly important subjects for research.

Source: Unless otherwise cited, the source for this box is Hernandez, Denton, and Macartney (2008).

what's your view

Are you or any members of your family immigrants or children of immigrants? If so, what factors helped or hindered your (or their) adjustment to life in the United States? How do you imagine life may be different for children of immigrants 40 years from now?

what's your view

How might you be different if you had grown up in a culture other than your own?

immigrants tend to *acculturate*, or adapt, by learning the language, customs, and attitudes needed to get along in the dominant culture while trying to preserve some of their cultural practices and values (Johnson et al., 2003). Box 1.1 looks at immigrant families in the United States.

Within broad ethnic boundaries, much diversity exists. The European-descended "white majority" consists of many distinct ethnicities—German, Belgian, Irish, French, Italian, and so on. Cuban Americans, Puerto Ricans, and Mexican Americans—all

Hispanic Americans—have different histories and cultures and may be of African, European, Native American, or mixed descent (Johnson et al., 2003; Sternberg, Grigorenko, & Kidd, 2005). African Americans from the rural South differ from those of Caribbean ancestry. Asian Americans hail from several countries with distinct cultures, from modern, industrial Japan to communist China to the remote mountains of Nepal, where many people still practice their ancient way of life. American Indians consist of hundreds of recognized nations, tribes, bands, and villages (Lin & Kelsey, 2000).

Many scholars now agree that the term *race*, historically and popularly viewed as an identifiable biological category, is a social construct. There is no clear scientific consensus on its definition, and it is impossible to measure reliably (American Academy of Pediatrics Committee on Pediatric Research, 2000; Bonham, Warshauer-Baker, & Collins, 2005; Helms, Jernigan, & Macher, 2005; Lin & Kelsey, 2000; Smedley & Smedley, 2005; Sternberg et al., 2005). Human genetic variation occurs along a broad continuum, and 90 percent of such variation occurs *within* rather than among socially defined races (Bonham et al., 2005; Ossorio & Duster, 2005). Nevertheless, race as a social category clearly remains a factor in research because it makes a difference in "how individuals are treated, where they live, their employment opportunities, the quality of their health care, and whether [they] can fully participate" in their society (Smedley & Smedley, 2005, p. 23).

Categories of culture, race, and ethnicity are fluid (Bonham et al., 2005; Sternberg et al., 2005), "continuously shaped and redefined by social and political forces" (Fisher et al., 2002, p. 1026). Geographic dispersion and adaptation to local conditions together with a steady rise in interracial marriages—more than 5 percent of U.S. marriages in 2000 (Lee & Edmonston, 2005)—have produced a wide variety of physical and cultural characteristics within populations (Smedley & Smedley, 2005; Sternberg et al., 2005). A person such as President Barack Obama, with a black father from Kenya and a white mother from Kansas, may fall into more than one racial or ethnic category and may identify more strongly with one or another at different times. Indeed, according to a 2007 estimate, 1.6 percent of the U.S. population is of two or more races (Central Intelligence Agency, 2008). A term such as *black*, *Hispanic*, *Asian*, or *white* can be an **ethnic gloss:** an overgeneralization that obscures or blurs such variations (Parke, 2004b; Trimble & Dickson, 2005).

Socioeconomic Status and Neighborhood A family's **socioeconomic status (SES)** is based on family income and the educational and occupational levels of the adults in the household. Throughout this book, we examine many studies that relate SES to developmental processes (such as mothers' verbal interactions with their children) and to developmental outcomes (such as health and cognitive performance). SES affects these processes and outcomes indirectly, through such associated factors as the kinds of homes and neighborhoods people live in and the quality of nutrition, medical care, and schooling available to them.

> People in the United States are more likely to self-disclose personal information than are people in Japan. Why might this be? The freer social structure in the United States might be one reason. When you can make and break friendships easily, you need to cement social bonds as much as possible.
>
> Schug, Yuki, & Maddux, 2010

ethnic gloss
Overgeneralization about an ethnic or cultural group that blurs or obscures variations within the group or overlaps with other such groups.

socioeconomic status (SES)
Combination of economic and social factors, including income, education, and occupation, that describe an individual or family.

The existence of Kian and Remee Hodgson, who as fraternal twins share approximately 50 percent of their genes, calls into question the concept of race as a biological construct.

FIGURE 1.2

Development Indicators by Country

The general socioeconomic level of a country (as measured by its per capita gross national income, or GNI) is related to its people's survival, health, and living conditions, which vary greatly throughout the world. Children's chances in life are far better in industrialized countries, such as the United States, Japan, and the nations of western Europe, than in the least developed countries, such as those of sub-Saharan Africa.

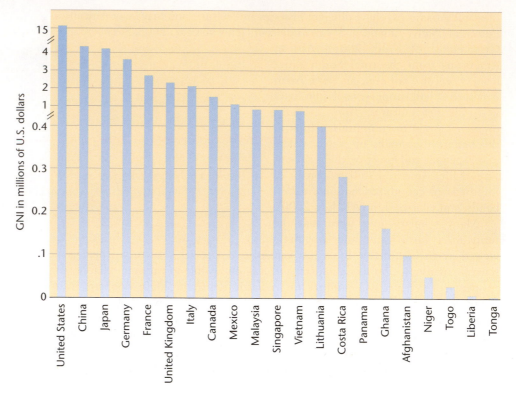

Source: World Development Indicators database, World Bank, accessed January 13, 2013.

More than half of the world's population (53 percent) live on less than the international poverty standard of $2 a day (Population Reference Bureau, 2006), and 19 percent—but twice as many in the least economically developed countries—live on less than $1 a day (United Nations Children's Fund, 2007; Figure 1.2). Even in the United States, where poverty thresholds depend on family size and composition, more than 16 million children—21.9 percent of all children under age 18—live in poverty, and 7.4 million children—almost 7 percent—are in extreme poverty (Children's Defense Fund, 2012; DeNavas-Walk, Proctor & Smith, 2012).*

Furthermore, child poverty in the United States has increased since the 1990s (Figure 1.3), and poor children throughout North America have become poorer in comparison with the rest of the child population. Poverty rates vary by geographic region and are highest among racial and ethnic minorities. In the United States, about 39 percent of black children and more than 35 percent of Latino children are poor as compared to 10 percent of white children. Children living with single parents or stepparents or with nonparental caregivers, such as grandparents, and those with less educated parents are especially likely to be poor (Children's Defense Fund, 2012; Children in North America Project, 2008).

Poverty is stressful and can damage the physical, cognitive, and psychosocial well-being of children and families. Poor children are more likely than other children to go hungry; to have frequent illnesses; to lack access to health care; to experience accidents, violence, and family conflict; and to show emotional or behavioral problems. Their cognitive potential and school performance suffer as well (Children in North America Project, 2008; Children's Defense Fund, 2012; Evans, 2004; Wadsworth & Santiago, 2008). The harm done by poverty is often indirect, through its impact on parents' emotional state and parenting practices and on the home environment they create (see Chapter 10). Threats to well-being multiply if, as often happens, several **risk factors**—conditions that increase the likelihood of a negative outcome—are present.

risk factors
Conditions that increase the likelihood of a negative developmental outcome.

*A family of four was considered extremely poor in 2012 if their household income was below $10,600, half of the official poverty line (Children's Defense Fund, 2012).

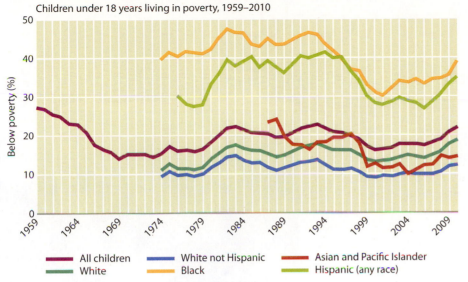

Children under 18 years living in poverty, 1959–2010

Legend:
— All children
— White
— White not Hispanic
— Black
— Asian and Pacific Islander
— Hispanic (any race)

Source of Data: U.S. Bureau of the Census, Historical Poverty Tables, People. Table 3.

FIGURE 1.3

Child Poverty Rates, United States, 1959–2010

The child poverty rate dropped substantially in the 1960s, then rose significantly in the early 1980s. Great strides were made in decreasing child poverty in the late 1990s, owing in part to the strong economy. However, the child poverty rate was higher in 2007 than at the beginning of the decade. Child poverty is closely tied to the overall health of the economy, rising in periods of recession.

Affluence doesn't necessarily protect children from risk. Some children in affluent families face pressure to achieve and are often left on their own by busy parents. These children have high rates of substance abuse, anxiety, and depression (Luthar & Latendresse, 2005).

The composition of a neighborhood affects the way children develop. Living in a neighborhood with large numbers of people who are poor and unemployed makes it less likely that effective social support will be available (Black & Krishnakumar, 1998). Positive development can occur despite serious risk factors, however (Kim-Cohen, Moffitt, Caspi, & Taylor, 2004). Consider the television star Oprah Winfrey, the singer and songwriter Shania Twain, the actor and director Ashton Kutcher, and former U.S. president Bill Clinton, all of whom grew up in poverty.

The Historical Context At one time developmental scientists paid little attention to the historical context—the time in which people live. Then, as the early longitudinal studies of childhood extended into the adult years, investigators began to focus on how certain experiences, tied to time and place, affect the course of people's lives (Box 1.2). Today, as we discuss in the next section, the historical context is an important part of the study of development.

NORMATIVE AND NONNORMATIVE INFLUENCES

To understand similarities and differences in development, we need to look at **normative** influences—biological or environmental events that affect many or most people in a society in similar ways— and also at events that touch only certain individuals (Baltes & Smith, 2004).*

Normative age-graded influences are highly similar for people in a particular age group. The timing of biological events is fairly predictable within a normal range. For example, children don't experience puberty at age 3 or menopause at 12.

Media exposure is a normative influence on children today, and toddlers are now skillful at using iPhone apps developed specifically for them. How might this shape their development?

Stout, 2010

checkpoint
can you . . .

▷ Discuss the concepts of maturation and individual differences?

▷ Give examples of the influences of family and neighborhood composition, socioeconomic status, culture, race/ethnicity, and historical context?

normative
Characteristic of an event that occurs in a similar way for most people in a group.

*Unless otherwise noted, this section is based largely on Baltes and Smith (2004).

STUDYING THE LIFE COURSE: GROWING UP IN HARD TIMES

1.2

Our awareness of the need to look at the life course in its social and historical context is indebted in part to Glen H. Elder Jr. In 1962, Elder arrived on the campus of the University of California, Berkeley, to work on the Oakland Growth Study, a longitudinal study of social and emotional development in 167 urban young people born around 1920. The study had begun at the outset of the Great Depression of the 1930s, when the participants, about half of whom came from middle-class homes and had spent their childhoods in the boom years of the Roaring Twenties, were entering adolescence. Elder (1974) observed how societal disruption can alter family processes and, through them, children's development.

As economic stress changed parents' lives, it changed children's lives too. Deprived families reassigned economic roles. Fathers, preoccupied with job losses and irritable about loss of status within the family, sometimes drank heavily. Mothers got outside jobs and took on more parental authority. Parents argued more. Adolescents tended to show developmental difficulties.

Still, for boys, particularly, the long-term effects of the ordeal were not entirely negative. Boys who got jobs to help out became more independent and were better able to escape the stressful family atmosphere than were girls, who helped at home. As adults, these men were strongly work oriented but also valued family activities and cultivated dependability in their children.

Effects of a major economic crisis depend on a child's stage of development, Elder noted. The children in the Oakland sample were already teenagers during the 1930s. They could draw on their own emotional, cognitive, and economic resources. A child born in 1929 would have been entirely dependent on the family. On the other hand, the parents of the Oakland children, being older, may have been less resilient in dealing with the loss of a job, and their emotional vulnerability may well have affected the tone of family life and their treatment of their children.

Fifty years after the Great Depression, in the early 1980s, a precipitous drop in the value of midwestern agricultural land pushed many farm families into debt or off the land. This farm crisis gave Elder the opportunity to replicate his earlier research on families suffering from an economic depression, this time in a rural setting. In 1989, he and his colleagues (Conger, Ge, Elder, Lorenz, & Simons 1994; Conger & Conger, 2002) interviewed 451 Iowa farm and small-town two-parent families with a seventh grader and a sibling no more than 4 years younger. The researchers

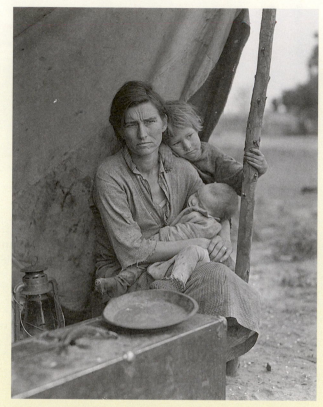

Glen Elder's studies of children growing up during the Great Depression showed how a major sociohistorical event can affect children's current and future development.

also videotaped family interactions. Because virtually no minorities lived in Iowa at the time, all the participating families were white.

As in the Depression-era study, many of these rural parents, under pressure of economic hardship, developed emotional problems. Depressed parents were more likely to fight with each other and to mistreat or withdraw from their children. The children, in turn, tended to lose self-confidence, to be unpopular, and to do poorly in school. But whereas in the 1980s this pattern of parental behavior fit both mothers and fathers, in the 1930s it was less true of mothers, whose economic role before the collapse had been more marginal (Conger & Elder, 1994; Conger et al., 1993; Elder, 1998).

The Iowa study, now called the Family Transitions Project, continues. Family members have been reinterviewed yearly, with a focus on how a family crisis experienced in early adolescence affects the transition to adulthood. The adolescents who were in seventh grade when the study

Continued

began were followed through high school. Each year they completed a list of stressful events they had experienced and were tested on measures of anxiety and depression and self-reported delinquent activities. For both boys and girls, a self-reinforcing cycle appeared. Such negative family events as economic crisis, illness, and getting in trouble at school tended to intensify sadness, fear, and antisocial conduct, which, in turn, led to future adversities, such as the divorce of parents (Kim, Conger, Elder, & Lorenz, 2003).

Elder's work, like other studies of the life course, gives researchers a window into processes of development and their links with socioecoconomic change. Eventually it may enable us to see long-term effects of early hardship on the lives of people who experienced it at different ages and in varying family situations.

Source: Unless otherwise referenced, this discussion is based on Elder (1998).

what's your view Can you think of a major cultural event within your lifetime that shaped the lives of families and children? How would you go about studying such effects?

Normative history-graded influences are significant events (such as the Great Depression or World War II) that shape the behavior and attitudes of a **historical generation:** a group of people who experience the event at a formative time in their lives. For example, the generations that came of age during the Depression and World War II tend to show a strong sense of social interdependence and trust that has declined among more recent generations (Rogler, 2002). Depending on when and where they live, entire generations may feel the impact of famines, nuclear explosions, or terrorist attacks. In Western countries, medical advances as well as improvements in nutrition and sanitation have dramatically reduced infant and child mortality. As children grow up today, they are influenced by computers, digital television, the Internet, and other technological developments. Social changes such as the increase in employed mothers and the increase in single-parent households have greatly altered family life.

A historical generation is not the same as an age **cohort:** a group of people born at about the same time. A historical generation may contain more than one cohort, but not all cohorts are part of historical generations unless they experience major, shaping historical events at a formative point in their lives (Rogler, 2002).

Nonnormative influences are unusual events that have a major impact on *individual* lives because they disturb the expected sequence of the life cycle. They are either typical events that happen at an atypical time of life (such as the death of a parent when a child is young) or atypical events (such as surviving a plane crash). Some of these influences are largely beyond a person's control and may present rare opportunities or severe challenges that the person perceives as a turning point. On the other hand, young people sometimes help create their own nonnormative life events—say, by driving after drinking or by applying for a scholarship—and thus participate actively in their own development. Taken together, the three types of influences—normative age-graded, normative history-graded, and nonnormative—contribute to the complexity of human development as well as to the challenges people experience in trying to build their lives.

historical generation
A group of people strongly influenced by a major historical event during their formative period.

cohort
A group of people born at about the same time.

nonnormative
Characteristic of an unusual event that happens to a particular person or a typical event that happens at an unusual time of life.

TIMING OF INFLUENCES: CRITICAL OR SENSITIVE PERIODS

In a well-known study, Konrad Lorenz (1957), an Austrian zoologist, got newborn ducklings to follow him as they would a mother duck. Lorenz showed that newly hatched ducklings will instinctively follow the first moving object they see, whether or not it is a member of their species. This phenomenon is called **imprinting**, and Lorenz believed that it is automatic and irreversible. Usually, this instinctive bond is with the mother; but if the natural course of events is disturbed, other attachments, like the one

imprinting
Instinctive form of learning in which, during a critical period in early development, a young animal forms an attachment to the first moving object it sees, usually the mother.

to Lorenz—or none at all—can form. Imprinting, said Lorenz, is the result of a *predisposition toward learning:* the readiness of an organism's nervous system to acquire certain information during a brief critical period in early life.

A **critical period** is a specific time when a given event, or its absence, has a specific impact on development. If a necessary event does not occur during a critical period of maturation, normal development will not occur; and the resulting abnormal patterns may be irreversible (Knudsen, 1999; Kuhl, Conboy, Padden, Nelson, & Pruitt, 2005). However, the length of a critical period is not absolutely fixed; if ducklings' rearing conditions are varied to slow their growth, the usual critical period for imprinting can be extended, and imprinting itself may even be reversed (Bruer, 2001).

Do human children experience critical periods, as ducklings do? One example occurs during gestation. If a woman receives X-rays, takes certain drugs, or contracts certain diseases at certain times during pregnancy, the fetus may show specific ill effects, depending on the nature of the insult and on its timing. Many environmental influences may affect development irreversibly after pregnancy as well. If a muscle problem interfering with the ability to focus both eyes on the same object is not corrected within a critical period early in childhood, depth perception probably will not develop (Bushnell & Boudreau, 1993).

plasticity
Modifiability of performance.

sensitive periods
Times in development when a given event or its absence usually has a strong effect on development.

However, the concept of critical periods in humans is controversial. Because many aspects of development, even in the biological/neurological domain, have been found to show **plasticity**, or modifiability of performance, it may be more useful to think about **sensitive periods**, when a developing person is especially responsive to certain kinds of experiences (Bruer, 2001). Further research is needed to discover "which aspects of behavior are likely to be altered by environmental events at specific points in development and which aspects remain more plastic and open to influence across wide spans of development" (Parke, 2004b, p. 8). Box 1.3 discusses how the concepts of critical and sensitive periods apply to language development.

checkpoint can **you** . . .

▷ Give examples of normative age-graded, normative history-graded, and nonnormative influences?

▷ Explain the concept of "critical" periods and give examples?

An Emerging Consensus

As the study of children has matured, a broad consensus has emerged on several fundamental points concerning child development, which sum up our introduction to this book:

1. *All domains of development are interrelated.* Although developmental scientists often look separately at the three domains of development—physical, cognitive, and psychosocial—each affects the others.

2. *Normal development includes a wide range of individual differences.* Each child, from the start, is unlike anyone else in the world. One child is outgoing, another shy. One is agile, another awkward. Some of the influences on individual development are inborn; others come from experience. Most often, these influences work together. Family characteristics, gender, social class, race/ethnicity, and the presence or absence of physical, mental, or emotional disability all affect the way a child develops within the universal processes of human maturation.

3. *Children help shape their development and influence others' responses to them.* Right from the start, through the ways in which they respond to the world around them and via the responses they evoke in others, infants mold their environment and then respond to the environment they have helped create. Influence is *bidirectional:* When babies babble and coo, adults tend to talk to them, which then makes babies "talk" more.

4. *Historical and cultural contexts strongly influence development.* Each child develops within a specific environment, bounded by time and place. A child born in the

the research world

IS THERE A CRITICAL PERIOD FOR LANGUAGE ACQUISITION?

In 1967 Eric Lenneberg (1967, 1969) proposed a critical period for language acquisition beginning in early infancy and ending around puberty. Lenneberg argued that it would be difficult, if not impossible, for a child who had not yet acquired language by the onset of puberty to do so after that age.

In 1970, a 13-year-old girl named Genie (not her real name) offered the opportunity for a test of Lenneberg's hypothesis. Genie was discovered in a suburb of Los Angeles (Curtiss, 1977; Fromkin, Krashen, Curtiss, Rigler, & Rigler, 1974; Pines, 1981; Rymer, 1993). The victim of an abusive father, she had been confined for nearly 12 years to a small room in her parents' home, tied to a potty chair, and cut off from normal human contact. When found, she recognized only her own name and the word *sorry*. Could Genie be taught to speak, or was it too late? The National Institutes of Mental Health (NIMH) funded a study to provide intensive testing and language training for Genie.

Genie's progress during the study both challenged and supported the idea of a critical period for language acquisition. Genie learned some simple words and could string them together into primitive sentences. She also learned the fundamentals of sign language. But "her speech remained, for the most part, like a somewhat garbled telegram" (Pines, 1981, p. 29). Her mother regained custody, cut her off from the NIMH researchers, and then eventually sent her into the foster care system. A series of abusive foster homes rendered Genie silent once more.

What explains Genie's initial progress and her inability to sustain it? Her understanding of her name and the single word *sorry* may mean that her language-learning mechanisms had been triggered early in the critical period, allowing later learning to occur. The timing of the NIMH language training and her ability to learn some simple words at age 13 may indicate that she was still in the critical period, though near its end. On the other hand, her extreme abuse and neglect may have impacted her so much that she could not be considered a true test of the critical period (Curtiss, 1977).

Genie's case dramatizes the difficulty of acquiring language after the early years of life, but, because of the complicating factors, it does not permit conclusive judgments about whether such acquisition is possible. Some researchers consider the prepubertal years a sensitive rather than critical period for learning language (Newport, Bavelier, & Neville, 2001; Schumann, 1997). Brain imaging research has found that even if the parts of the brain best suited to language processing are damaged early in childhood, nearly normal language development can continue as other parts of the brain take over (Boatman et al., 1999; Hertz-Pannier et al., 2002; M. H. Johnson, 1998). In fact, shifts in brain organization and utilization occur throughout the course of normal language learning (M. H. Johnson, 1998; Neville & Bavelier, 1998).

If either a critical or a sensitive period for language learning exists, what explains it? Do the brain's mechanisms for acquiring language decay as the brain matures? That would seem strange because other cognitive abilities improve. An alternative hypothesis is that this very increase in cognitive sophistication interferes with an adolescent's or adult's ability to learn a language. Young children acquire language in small chunks that can be digested readily. Older learners, when they first begin learning a language, tend to absorb a great deal at once and then may have trouble analyzing and interpreting it (Newport, 1991).

what's your view

Have you had difficulty learning a new language as an adult? If so, does this box help you understand why?

United States today is likely to have very different experiences from a child born in colonial America or from a child born in Greenland or Afghanistan.

5. *Early experience is important, but children can be remarkably resilient.* A traumatic incident or a severely deprived childhood may well have grave emotional consequences, but the life histories of countless people show that the effects of painful experience, such as growing up in poverty or the death of a parent, often can be overcome.

6. *Development in childhood affects development throughout the life span.* At one time it was believed that growth and development end, as this book does, with adolescence. Today developmental psychologists agree that development is lifelong—from womb to tomb. As long as people live, they have the potential to change.

Now that you have had a brief introduction to the field of child development and its basic concepts, we can look more closely at the issues developmental scientists think about and how they do their work. In Chapter 2, we discuss some influential theories of how development takes place and the methods investigators commonly use to study it.

▷ **checkpoint can you . . .**

▷ Summarize six fundamental points of agreement that have emerged from the study of child development?

summary and key terms

guidepost ❶

The Study of Child Development: Then and Now

What is child development, and how has its study evolved?

- Child development as a field of scientific study focuses on processes of change and stability from conception through adolescence.

- The scientific study of child development began toward the end of the nineteenth century. Adolescence was not considered a separate phase of development until the early twentieth century. The field of child development is now part of the study of the entire life span, or human development.

- Ways of studying child development are still evolving, making use of advanced technologies.

  child development (4)

guidepost ❷

The Study of Child Development: Basic Concepts

What do developmental scientists study?

- The three major domains, or aspects, of development that developmental scientists study are physical, cognitive, and psychosocial. Each affects the others.

- The concept of periods of development is a social construction. In this book, child development is divided into five periods: the prenatal period, infancy and toddlerhood, early

childhood, middle childhood, and adolescence. In each period, children have characteristic developmental needs and tasks.

  physical development (6)
  cognitive development (6)
  psychosocial development (6)
  social construction (7)

guidepost ❸

Influences on Development

What influences make one child different from another?

- Influences on development come from both heredity and environment. Many typical changes during childhood are related to maturation. Individual differences increase with age.

- In some societies, the nuclear family predominates; in others, the extended family.

- Socioeconomic status (SES) affects developmental processes and outcomes through the quality of home and neighborhood environments and of nutrition, medical care, supervision, and schooling. The most powerful neighborhood influence seems to be neighborhood income. Multiple risk factors increase the likelihood of poor outcomes.

- Other important environmental influences stem from culture, ethnicity, and historical context. In large, multiethnic societies, immigrant groups often acculturate to the majority culture while preserving aspects of their own.

- Influences may be normative (age graded or history graded) or nonnormative.

- There is evidence of critical or sensitive periods for certain types of early development, but the existence of critical periods is controversial.

individual differences (*9*)

heredity (*9*)

environment (*9*)

maturation (*9*)

nuclear family (*10*)

extended family (*10*)

culture (*11*)

ethnic group (*11*)

ethnic gloss (*13*)

socioeconomic status (SES) (*13*)

risk factors (*14*)

normative (*15*)

historical generation (*17*)

cohort (*17*)

nonnormative (*17*)

imprinting (*17*)

critical period (*18*)

plasticity (*18*)

sensitive periods (*18*)

guidepost ❹ An Emerging Consensus

What are six fundamental points about child development on which consensus has emerged?

- Consensus has emerged on several important points. These include (1) the interrelationship of domains of development, (2) the existence of a wide range of individual differences, (3) the bidirectionality of influence, (4) the importance of history and culture, (5) children's potential for resilience, and (6) continuity of development throughout life.

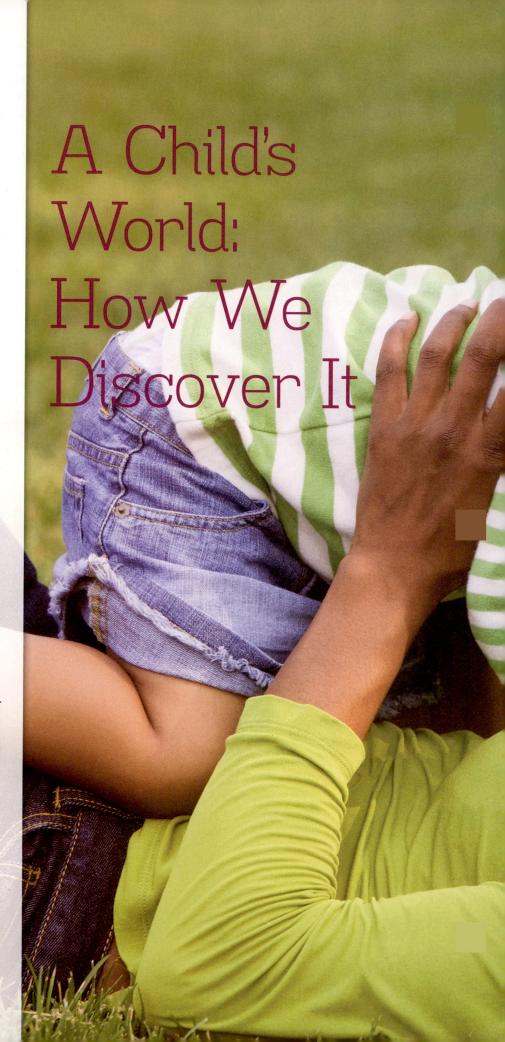

A Child's World: How We Discover It

did you know?

▷ Theories are never "set in stone"; they are always open to change as a result of new findings?

▷ Children shape their world as it shapes them?

▷ Cross-cultural research enables us to determine which aspects of development are universal and which are culturally influenced?

Here, we present an overview both of major theories of human development and of research methods used to study it. In the first part of the chapter, we explore major issues and theoretical perspectives that underlie much research in child development. In the remainder of the chapter, we look at how researchers gather and assess information so that, as you read further in this book, you will be better able to judge whether research findings and conclusions rest on solid ground.

did you know outline

The most exciting phrase to hear in science, the one that heralds new discoveries, is not "Eureka" but "That's funny . . ."

—Isaac Asimov

1. What purposes do theories serve, and what are two basic issues on which developmental theorists differ?

2. What are five theoretical perspectives on child development, and what are some theories that are representative of each?

3. How do developmental scientists study children, and what are the advantages and disadvantages of each research method?

4. What ethical problems may arise in research on children?

guidepost 1

What purposes do theories serve, and what are two basic issues on which developmental theorists differ?

theory
Coherent set of logically related concepts that seeks to organize, explain, and predict data.

hypotheses
Possible explanations for phenomena, used to predict the outcome of research.

People generally think theories are less well supported than laws, but in scientific terms the opposite is true. Laws are observations without explanations. Theories, by contrast, are observations with explanations. So theories have more support, not less.

Basic Theoretical Issues

When Ahmed graduated from high school with honors in math and science, his father, an award-winning engineer, beamed. "The apple doesn't fall far from the tree," he said.

Statements like that one, which abound in everyday life, are informal, or intuitive, theories about why children develop as they do. Scientists have formal theories about human development. Like laypeople's informal theories, scientific theories are not dry, abstract, or esoteric. They deal with the substance of real life.

A scientific **theory** is a set of logically related concepts or statements that seeks to describe and explain development and to predict what kinds of behavior might occur under certain conditions. Theories organize and explain *data*, the information gathered by research. As painstaking research adds, bit by bit, to the body of knowledge, theoretical concepts help us make sense of, and see connections between, isolated pieces of data.

Theory and research are interwoven strands in the intricate fabric of scientific study. Theories inspire further research and predict its results. They do this by generating **hypotheses**, tentative explanations or predictions that can be tested by further research. Research can indicate whether a theory is accurate in its predictions but cannot conclusively show a theory to be true. Theories can be disproved, but never proved. Theories change to incorporate new findings. Sometimes research supports a hypothesis and the theory on which it was based. At other times, scientists must modify their theories to account for unexpected data. Research findings often suggest additional hypotheses to be examined and provide direction for dealing with practical issues.

A theory is based on certain assumptions, which may or may not turn out to be true. For example, Charles Darwin's theory of evolution, which preceded modern cell biology, assumed that all life forms evolved from a single ancestor—an assumption that has been challenged by newer evolutionary research (Liu, 2006; Woese, 1998). Alternatively, despite the fact that Gregor Mendel's seminal work on particulate genetics had not yet been discovered by the scientific community, Darwin's theory required an explanation of how traits in their entirety could be passed on to offspring. At the time he developed his theory, no such explanation existed. Darwin logically surmised that such a process must exist, and this aspect of his work was later supported.

Developmental science cannot be completely objective. Theories and research about human behavior are products of very human individuals, whose inquiries and interpretations are inevitably influenced by their own values and experience. In striving for greater objectivity, researchers must scrutinize how they and their colleagues conduct their work, the assumptions on which it is based, and how they arrive at their conclusions.

Throughout this book, we examine many, often conflicting, theories. In assessing them, it is important to keep in mind that they reflect the outlooks of the human beings who originated them. The way theorists explain development depends in part on their assumptions about two basic issues: (1) whether children are active or reactive in their own development, and (2) whether development is continuous or occurs in stages. A third issue, whether development is more influenced by heredity or by environment, was introduced in Chapter 1 and is discussed more fully in Chapter 3.

ISSUE 1: IS DEVELOPMENT ACTIVE OR REACTIVE?

Psychology is an outgrowth of philosophy in many ways, and indeed philosophers have frequently grappled with questions of psychology and development. Exactly how does the child learn? What happens during that process?

There have been various perspectives on these issues. For example, the eighteenth-century English philosopher John Locke held that a young child is a *tabula rasa*—a "blank slate"—upon which society "writes." How the child developed, in either positive or negative ways, depended entirely upon experiences. In contrast, the French philosopher Jean Jacques Rousseau believed that children are born "noble savages" who develop according to their own positive natural tendencies if not corrupted by society. This debate remains important today, although it is informed by what we currently understand. In modern terms, we speak of heredity and environmental influences. We introduced this issue in Chapter 1, and we will address it more fully in Chapter 3.

There are additional philosophical debates about development, and the same basic issues that philosophers argued about support the classic and continuing theories that psychologists use to make sense of development. In this section, we address the debate about active and reactive development. Psychologists who believe in reactive development conceptualize the developing child as a hungry sponge that soaks up experiences and is shaped by this input over time. Psychologists who believe in active development argue that people seek to create experiences for themselves and are motivated to learn about the world around them. Things aren't just happening to them, they are involved in making their world what it is.

> Remember *Calvin and Hobbes* comic strips? The names of the two primary characters were drawn from other philosophers who speculated on our essential nature.

> These issues are also applicable in the real world. For instance, if you believe in the worth of programs like Head Start, that implies you believe in the power of environmental influences. If you think such programs are not worth the financial investment, that implies you feel heredity is more important. Which do you believe?

Mechanistic Model The debate over Locke's and Rousseau's philosophies led to two contrasting models, or images, of development: mechanistic and organismic. Locke's view was the forerunner of the **mechanistic model**. In this model, people are like machines that react to environmental input (Pepper, 1942, 1961). A machine is the sum of its parts. To understand it, we can break it down into its smallest components and then reassemble it.

Machines do not operate of their own volition; they react automatically and passively to physical forces or inputs. Fill a car with gas, turn the ignition key, press the accelerator, and the vehicle will move. In the mechanistic view, human behavior is much the same: It results from the operation of biological parts in response to external or internal stimuli. If we know enough about how the human "machine" is put together and about the forces acting on it, we can predict what the person will do.

Mechanistic research seeks to identify the factors that make people behave as they do. For example, in seeking to explain why some high school students drink too much

mechanistic model
Model that views human development as a series of predictable responses to stimuli.

connect

study smart

Mechanistic and Organismic Models of Development

alcohol, a mechanistic theorist might look for environmental influences, such as advertising and whether the student's friends are heavy drinkers.

Organismic Model Rousseau was the precursor of the **organismic model**. This model sees children as active, growing organisms that set their own development in motion (Pepper, 1942, 1961). They initiate events; they do not just react. Thus, the driving force for change is internal. Environmental influences do not *cause* development, though they can speed or slow it. Because human behavior is viewed as an organic whole, it cannot be predicted by breaking it down into simple responses to environmental stimulation. The meaning of a family relationship, for example, goes beyond what can be learned from studying its individual members and their day-to-day interactions. An organismic theorist, in studying why some high school students drink too much, would be likely to look at what kinds of situations they choose to participate in, and with whom. Do they choose friends who prefer to party or to study?

For organicists, development has an underlying, orderly structure, though it may not be obvious from moment to moment. As a fertilized egg cell develops into an embryo and then into a fetus, it goes through a series of qualitative changes not overtly predictable from what came before. Swellings on the head become eyes, ears, mouth, and nose. The brain begins to coordinate breathing, digestion, and elimination. Sex organs form. Similarly, organicists describe development after birth as a progressive sequence of stages, moving toward full maturation.

ISSUE 2: IS DEVELOPMENT CONTINUOUS OR DISCONTINUOUS?

The mechanistic and organismic models also differ on the second issue: Is development *continuous*, that is, gradual and incremental, or *discontinuous*, that is, abrupt or uneven? Mechanist theorists see development as continuous: as occurring in small incremental stages (Figure 2.1a). Development is always governed by the same processes and involves the gradual refinement and extension of early skills into later abilities, allowing one to make predictions about future characteristics on the basis of past performance. This type of change is known as **quantitative change**—a change in number or amount, such as height, weight, or vocabulary size. A primary characteristic of quantitative change is that you are measuring fundamentally the same thing over time, even if there might be more or less of it.

Organismic theorists see development as discontinuous; as marked by the emergence of new phenomena that could not be easily predicted on the basis of past functioning. Development at different points in the lifespan is, in this view, fundamentally different in nature—not just more or less of the same thing. It is a change in kind, structure, or organization, not just in number. This type of change is known as **qualitative change**.

Organismic theorists are proponents of what are called *stage theories*. In these approaches, development is seen as occurring in a series of distinct stages, like stair steps (Figure 2.1b). At each stage, what is going on is fundamentally different from what was happening at the previous stage. Each stage builds on the previous one and prepares the way for the next. Thus, stages cannot be skipped and development only proceeds in a positive direction. Moreover, it is believed that these processes are universal and account for the development of all humans everywhere, although the particular timing may vary a bit.

organismic model
Model that views human development as internally initiated by an active organism, and as occurring in a sequence of qualitatively different stages.

connect

studysmart

Quantitative and Qualitative Changes

quantitative change
Change in number or amount, such as in height, weight, or size of vocabulary.

qualitative change
Change in kind, structure, or organization, such as the change from nonverbal to verbal communication.

Quantitative change is like counting apples; there are fewer or more apples, but they are all apples. Qualitative change is like comparing apples and oranges.

Be careful here. If you google "quantitative" and "qualitative," you are likely to find web pages that focus on quantitative and qualitative statistics, not change. Although these are somewhat related concepts, they are not the same thing.

checkpoint
can you . . .

▷ Explain the relationships among theories, hypotheses, and research?

▷ Discuss two issues regarding child development?

▷ Contrast the mechanistic and organismic models?

▷ Compare quantitative and qualitative change and give an example of each?

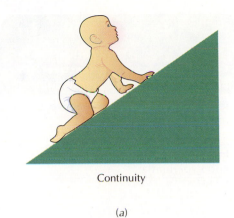
Continuity

(a)

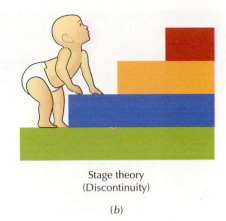
Stage theory
(Discontinuity)

(b)

FIGURE 2.1

Quantitative and Qualitative Change

A major difference among developmental theories is (a) whether it proceeds continuously, as learning theorists and information-processing theorists propose, or (b) whether development occurs in distinct stages, as Freud, Erikson, and Piaget maintained.

Theoretical Perspectives

Theories can generally be characterized as either mechanistic or organismic, and as describing change as either continuous or discontinuous, even if those beliefs are not directly stated. But all developmental theories have implicit assumptions that underlie their approach. These assumptions influence the questions researchers ask, the methods they use, and the ways they interpret data. Therefore, to evaluate and interpret research, it is important to recognize the theoretical perspective on which it is based.

Five major perspectives underlie much influential theory and research on child development: (1) psychoanalytic, which focuses on unconscious emotions and drives; (2) learning, which studies observable behavior; (3) cognitive, which analyzes thought processes; (4) contextual, which emphasizes the impact of the historical, social, and cultural context; and (5) evolutionary/sociobiological, which considers evolutionary and biological underpinnings of behavior. Following is a general overview of the basic propositions, methods, and causal emphasis of each of these perspectives and some leading theorists within each perspective. These are summarized in Table 2.1 on page 28 and will be referred to throughout this book.

PERSPECTIVE 1: PSYCHOANALYTIC

Sigmund Freud (1856–1939) was a Viennese physician who had a profound effect upon the field of psychology. He was the originator of the **psychoanalytic perspective**, and believed in reactive development, as well as qualitative changes over time. Freud proposed that humans were born with a series of innate, biologically based drives such as hunger, sex, and aggression. He thought that people were highly motivated to satisfy their urges, and that much of development involved learning how to do so in socially acceptable ways. In addition to these biologically based influences, Freud also believed that early experiences shaped later functioning, and thus drew attention to childhood as an important precursor to adult behavior. While this seems obvious to us now, at the time he developed his theories most psychologists did not acknowledge childhood as a formative period on the lifespan. Freud also believed in and promoted the idea that there was a vast, hidden reserve to our psyche, and what we consciously know about and experience is only the small tip of the iceberg of who we are. Following is a summary of Freud's theory of psychosexual development. Other theorists, including Erik H. Erikson, whom we discuss next, have expanded and modified Freud's theory.

Sigmund Freud: Psychosexual Development Freud (1953, 1964a, 1964b) believed that people are born with biological drives that must be redirected to make it possible to live in society. He proposed three hypothetical parts of the personality: the id, the ego, and the superego. Newborns are governed by the *id*, which operates under the pleasure

What are five theoretical perspectives on child development, and what are some theories that are representative of each?

connect
study smart

Theoretical Perspectives

connect
study smart

Application of Theories

psychoanalytic perspective
View of human development as being shaped by unconscious forces.

guidepost 2

Although this is not originally what it stood for, an easy way to remember what the id wants is by remembering "instinctual desires."

TABLE 2.1 Five Perspectives on Human Development

Perspective	Important Theories	Basic Propositions	Stage-Oriented	Causal Emphasis	Active/Reactive Individual
Psycho-analytic	Freud's psychosexual theory	Behavior is controlled by powerful unconscious urges.	Yes	Innate factors modified by experience	Reactive
	Erikson's psychosocial theory	Personality is influenced by society and develops through a series of crises.		Interaction of innate and experiential factors	Active
Learning	Behaviorism, or traditional learning theory (Pavlov, Skinner, Watson)	People are responders; the environment controls behavior.	No	Experience	Reactive
	Social learning (social cognitive) theory (Bandura)	Children learn in a social context by observing and imitating models; they are active contributors to learning.		Experience modified by innate factors	Active and reactive
Cognitive	Piaget's cognitive-stage theory	Qualitative changes in thought occur between infancy and adolescence. Children are active initiators of development.	Yes	Interaction of innate and experiential factors	Active
	Vygotsky's sociocultural theory	Social interaction is central to cognitive development.	No	Experience	
	Information-processing theory	Human beings are processors of symbols.	No	Interaction of innate and experiential factors	
Contextual	Bronfenbrenner's bioecological theory	Development occurs through interaction between a developing person and five surrounding, interlocking contextual systems of influences, from microsystem to chronosystem.	No	Interaction of innate and experiential factors	Active
Evolutionary/ sociobiological	Evolutionary Psychology Bowlby's attachment theory	Human beings are the product of adaptive processes; evolutionary and biological bases for behavior and predisposition toward learning are important.	No	Interaction of innate and experiential factors	Active and reactive (theorists vary)

principle—the drive to seek immediate satisfaction of needs and desires. When gratification is delayed, as it is when infants have to wait to be fed, they begin to see themselves as separate from the outside world. The *ego*, which represents reason, develops gradually during the first year or so of life and operates under the reality principle. The ego's aim is to find realistic ways to gratify the id that are acceptable to the superego, which develops at about age 5 or 6. The *superego* includes the conscience and incorporates socially approved "shoulds" and "should nots" into the child's own value system. The superego is highly demanding; if its standards are not met, a child may feel guilty and anxious. The ego mediates between the impulses of the id and the demands of the superego.

Freud proposed that personality forms through unconscious childhood conflicts between the inborn urges of the id and the requirements of civilized life. These conflicts occur in an unvarying sequence of five maturation-based stages of **psychosexual development** (Table 2.2), in which sensual pleasure shifts from one body zone to another—from the mouth to the anus and then to the genitals. At each stage, the behavior that is the chief source of gratification (or frustration) changes—from feeding to elimination and eventually to sexual activity.

Freud considered the first three stages—those of the first few years of life—to be crucial for personality development. According to Freud, if children receive too little or too much gratification in any of these stages, they are at risk of *fixation*—an arrest in development that can show up in adult personality. For example, babies whose needs are not met during the *oral stage*, when feeding is the main source of sensual pleasure, may grow up to become nail-biters or smokers or to develop "bitingly" critical personalities. A person who, as a toddler, had too-strict toilet training may be fixated at the *anal stage*, when the chief source of pleasure was moving the bowels. Such a person may be obsessively clean, rigidly tied to schedules and routines, or defiantly messy.

According to Freud, a key event in psychosexual development occurs in the *phallic stage* of early childhood. Boys develop sexual attachment to their mothers, and girls to their fathers, and they have aggressive urges toward the same-sex parent, whom they regard as a rival. Freud called these developments the *Oedipus* and *Electra complexes*. Girls, according to Freud, experience *penis envy*, the repressed wish to possess a penis and the power it stands for.

Children eventually resolve their anxiety over these feelings by identifying with the same-sex parent and move into the *latency stage* of middle childhood, a period of relative emotional calm and intellectual and social exploration. They redirect their sexual energies into other pursuits, such as schoolwork, relationships, and hobbies.

The *genital stage*, the final one, lasts throughout adulthood. The sexual urges repressed during latency now resurface to flow in socially approved channels, which Freud defined as heterosexual relations with persons outside the family of origin.

Freud's theory made historic contributions and inspired a whole generation of followers, some of whom took psychoanalytic theory in new directions. Some of Freud's ideas, such as his notions of the Oedipus crisis and penis envy, now are widely considered obsolete. Others, such as the concepts of the id and superego, cannot be scientifically tested. While Freud opened our eyes to the importance of early sexual urges, many psychoanalysts today reject his narrow emphasis on sexual and aggressive drives to the exclusion of other motives. Although the specific components of his theory generally have not been supported in research, several of his central themes have nonetheless "stood the test of time" (Westen, 1998, p. 334). Freud made us aware of the importance of unconscious thoughts, feelings, and motivations; the role of childhood experiences in forming personality; the ambivalence of emotional responses, especially responses to parents; the role of mental representations of the self and others in the establishment of intimate relationships; and the path of normal development from an immature, dependent state to a mature, interdependent one. In all these ways, Freud left an indelible mark on psychoanalysis and developmental psychology (Gedo, 2001; Westen, 1998).

We need to remember that Freud's theory grew out of his place in history and in society. Freud based his theories about normal development not on a population of average children but on a clientele of upper-middle-class adults, mostly women, in therapy. His concentration on the influences of sexual urges and early experience did not take into account other, and later, influences on personality—including the influences of society and culture, which many heirs to the Freudian tradition, such as Erik Erikson, stress.

The Viennese physician Sigmund Freud developed an influential but controversial theory of childhood emotional development.

psychosexual development
In Freudian theory, an unvarying sequence of stages of personality development during infancy, childhood, and adolescence, in which gratification shifts from the mouth to the anus and then to the genitals.

connect

study smart

Psychoanalytic Perspective

TABLE 2.2 Development Stages according to Various Theories

Psychosexual Stages (Freud)	Psychosocial Stages (Erikson)	Cognitive Stages (Piaget)
Oral *(birth to 12–18 months)*. Baby's chief source of pleasure involves mouth-oriented activities (sucking and feeding).	**Basic trust versus mistrust** *(birth to 12–18 months)*. Baby develops sense of whether world is a good and safe place. Virtue: hope.	**Sensorimotor** *(birth to 2 years)*. Infant gradually becomes able to organize activities in relation to the environment through sensory and motor activity.
Anal *(12–18 months to 3 years)*. Child derives sensual gratification from withholding and expelling feces. Zone of gratification is anal region, and toilet training is important activity.	**Autonomy versus shame and doubt** *(12–18 months to 3 years)*. Child develops a balance of independence and self-sufficiency over shame and doubt. Virtue: will.	**Preoperational** *(2 to 7 years)*. Child develops a representational system and uses symbols to represent people, places, and events. Language and imaginative play are important manifestations of this stage. Thinking is still not logical.
Phallic *(3 to 6 years)*. Child becomes attached to parent of the other sex and later identifies with same-sex parent. Supergo develops. Zone of gratification shifts to genital region.	**Initiative versus guilt** *(3 to 6 years)*. Child develops initiative when trying out new activities and is not overwhelmed by guilt. Virtue: purpose.	
Latency *(6 years to puberty)*. Time of relative calm between more turbulent states.	**Industry versus inferiority** *(6 years to puberty)*. Child must learn skills of the culture or face feelings of incompetence. Virtue: skill.	**Concrete operations** *(7 to 11 years)*. Child can solve problems logically if they are focused on the here and now but cannot think abstractly.
Genital *(puberty through adulthood)*. Reemergence of sexual impulses of phallic stage, channeled into mature adult sexuality.	**Identity versus identity confusion** *(puberty to young adulthood)*. Adolescent must determine sense of self ("Who am I?") or experience confusion about roles. Virtue: fidelity. **Intimacy versus isolation** *(young adulthood)*. Person seeks to make commitments to others; if unsuccessful, may suffer from isolation and self-absorption. Virtue: love. **Generativity versus stagnation** *(middle adulthood)*. Mature adult is concerned with establishing and guiding the next generation or else feels personal impoverishment. Virtue: care. **Integrity versus despair** *(late adulthood)*. Elderly person achieves acceptance of own life, allowing acceptance of death, or else despairs over inability to relive life. Virtue: wisdom.	**Formal operations** *(11 years through adulthood)*. Person can think abstractly, deal with hypothetical situations, and think about possibilities.

Note: All ages are approximate.

Erik Erikson: Psychosocial Development Erik Erikson (1902–1994), a German-born psychoanalyst who originally was part of Freud's circle in Vienna, modified and extended Freudian theory by emphasizing the influence of society on the developing personality. Erikson was a pioneer in the life-span perspective. Whereas Freud maintained that early childhood experiences permanently shape personality, Erikson contended that ego development is lifelong. Note that both theorists, as they proposed stage theories, believed in qualitative change.

Erikson's (1950, 1982; Erikson, Erikson, & Kivnick, 1986) theory of **psychosocial development** covers eight stages across the life span (see Table 2.2); we discuss the first five of these stages in the appropriate chapters. Each stage involves what Erikson originally called a "crisis" in personality—a major psychosocial challenge that is particularly important at that time but will remain an issue to some degree throughout the rest of life.* These issues, which emerge according to a maturational timetable, must be satisfactorily resolved for healthy ego development.

Each stage requires the balancing of a positive trait and a corresponding negative one. Although the positive quality should predominate, some degree of the negative is needed as well for optimal development. The critical theme of infancy, for example, is *basic trust versus basic mistrust*. People need to trust the world and the people in it, but they also need to learn some mistrust to protect themselves from danger. The successful outcome of each stage is the development of a particular "virtue" or strength—in this first stage, the virtue of *hope*. The resolution of later crises or conflicts depends upon the resolution reached in previous stages. In other words, successful resolution of one crisis put the child in a particularly good position to address the next crisis, a process that occurs iteratively across the life span. So, for example, a child who successfully developed a sense of trust in infancy would be well prepared for the development of a sense of autonomy—the second psychosocial challenge—in toddlerhood. After all, if you feel that others have your back, you are more likely to try to develop your skills knowing that they will be there to comfort you if you fail.

Erikson's theory is important because of its emphasis on social and cultural influences and on development beyond adolescence. He is perhaps most widely known for his concept of the *identity crisis* (see Chapter 17), which has generated considerable research and public discussion.

PERSPECTIVE 2: LEARNING

The **learning perspective** maintains that development results from *learning*, a long-lasting change in behavior based on experience or adaptation to the environment. Learning theorists are concerned with discovering the objective laws that govern changes in observable behavior. They see development as continuous (not in stages) and emphasize quantitative change.

Learning theorists have helped to make the study of human development more scientific by focusing on observable, quantifiable behaviors. Their terms are defined precisely, and their theories can be tested in the laboratory. Two important learning theories are *behaviorism* and *social learning (social cognitive) theory*.

Learning Theory 1: Behaviorism **Behaviorism** is a mechanistic theory, which describes observed behavior as a predictable response to experience. Thus, behaviorists consider development as reactive and continuous. Although biology sets limits on what people do, behaviorists view the environment as much more influential. They hold that human beings at all ages learn about the world the same way other organisms do: by reacting to conditions, or aspects of their environment, that they find pleasing, painful, or threatening. Moreover, they argue that learning occurs throughout the life span. The processes governing the way you learn to walk are very similar to those governing the emergence of language. Behavioral research focuses on *associative learning*, in which a mental link is formed between two events. Two kinds of associative learning are *classical conditioning* and *operant conditioning*.

*Erikson later dropped the term "crisis" and referred instead to conflicting or competing tendencies.

The psychoanalyst Erik H. Erikson departed from Freudian theory in emphasizing societal, rather than chiefly biological, influences on personality.

psychosocial development
In Erikson's eight-stage theory, the socially and culturally influenced process of development of the ego, or self.

checkpoint
can you . . .

▷ Identify the chief focus of the psychoanalytic perspective?

▷ Name Freud's five stages of development and three parts of the personality?

▷ Tell how Erikson's theory differs from Freud's and list its eight stages?

learning perspective
View of human development that holds that changes in behavior result from experience.

behaviorism
Learning theory that emphasizes the predictable role of environment in causing observable behavior.

Classical Conditioning While studying the role of saliva in dogs' digestive processes, Russian physiologist Ivan Pavlov (1849–1936) stumbled upon a phenomenon he labeled "psychic reflexes." Pavlov's dogs were presented with meat powder and then had their saliva collected. He noticed that his dogs began to salivate when they saw their handlers or when they heard clicking noises produced by the device that distributed the meat powder, before the meat powder was even presented. Pavlov tried pairing the meat powder with various stimuli such as the ringing of a bell and the dogs learned to salivate at the sound of a bell. These experiments were the foundation for **classical conditioning**, in which a response (salivation) to a stimulus (the bell) is elicited after repeated association with a stimulus that normally elicits the response (food).

> Pavlov was originally studying salivary enzymes in dogs. He put a plate of meat in front of them so he could collect their saliva. He made his breakthrough discovery when he realized the dogs were salivating before the meat was presented to them.

The American behaviorist John B. Watson (1878–1958) applied stimulus-response theories to children, claiming that he could mold any infant in any way he chose. His writings influenced a generation of parents to apply principles of learning theory to child raising. In one of the earliest and most famous demonstrations of classical conditioning in human beings, he taught an 11-month-old baby known as "Little Albert" to fear a furry white rat (Watson & Rayner, 1920).

In this study, Albert was exposed to a loud noise when he started to stroke the rat. The noise frightened him, and he began to cry. After repeated pairings of the rat with the loud noise, Albert whimpered with fear when he saw the rat. Moreover, Albert also started showing fear responses to white rabbits and cats, and the beards of elderly men. Although the study had methodological flaws and was extremely unethical, it did demonstrate that a baby could be conditioned to fear something he or she had not been afraid of before.

> You can think of classical conditioning as the before—what happens to provoke a response. And, operant conditioning can be thought of as the after—what happens after a response occurs that shapes the likelihood of it happening again.

Classical conditioning occurs throughout life. Food preferences may be a result of conditioned learning. Fear responses to objects like a car or a dog may be the result of an accident or a bad experience.

Operant Conditioning Angel lies in his crib. When he starts to babble ("ma-ma-ma"), his mother smiles and repeats the syllables. Angel learns that his behavior (babbling) can produce a desirable consequence (loving attention from a parent), and so he learns to keep babbling to attract his mother's attention. An originally accidental behavior (babbling) has become a conditioned response.

This type of learning is called **operant conditioning** because the individual learns from the consequences of "operating" on the environment. Unlike classical conditioning, operant conditioning involves voluntary behavior, such as Angel's babbling and involves the consequences rather than the predictors of behavior.

The American psychologist B. F. Skinner (1904–1990), who formulated the principles of operant conditioning, worked primarily with rats and pigeons, but Skinner (1938) maintained that these principles apply to human beings as well. He found that an organism will tend to repeat a response that has been reinforced by desirable consequences and will suppress a response that has been punished. Thus, **reinforcement** is the process by which a behavior is strengthened, increasing the likelihood that the behavior will be repeated. In Angel's case, his mother's attention reinforces his babbling. **Punishment** is the process by which a behavior is weakened, *decreasing* the likelihood of repetition. If Angel's mother frowned when he babbled, he would be less likely to babble again. Whether a consequence is reinforcing or punishing depends on the person.

What is reinforcing for one person may be punishing for another. For a child who likes being alone, being sent to his or her room could be reinforcing rather than punishing.

Reinforcement is most effective when it immediately follows a behavior. If a response is no longer reinforced, it will eventually be *extinguished*, that is, return to its original (baseline) level. If, after a while, no one repeats Angel's babbling, he may babble less often than if his babbles still brought reinforcement.

Behavior modification, or behavior therapy, is a form of operant conditioning used to eliminate undesirable behavior, such as temper tantrums, or to instill desirable behavior, such as putting away toys after play. For example, every time a child puts toys away, she or he gets a reward, such as praise or a treat or new toy. Behavior modification is particularly effective among children with special needs, such as those with mental or emotional disabilities. However, Skinnerian psychology is limited in application because it does not adequately address individual differences, cultural and social influences, or other aspects of human development that can be attributed to a combination of factors—not solely learned associations.

Learning Theory 2: Social Learning (Social Cognitive) Theory The American psychologist Albert Bandura (b. 1925) developed many of the principles of **social learning theory**. Whereas behaviorists see the environment, acting on the child, as the chief impetus for development, Bandura (1977, 1989; Bandura & Walters, 1963) suggests that the impetus for development is bidirectional. Bandura called this concept **reciprocal determinism**—the child acts on the world as the world acts on the child.

Classic social learning theory maintains that people learn appropriate social behavior chiefly by observing and imitating models—that is, by watching other people, such as parents, teachers, or sports heroes and learning both about what potential behaviors might be, as well as learning about the likely consequences of such behaviors. This process is called **observational learning**, or *modeling*. People tend to choose models who are prestigious, who control resources, or who are rewarded for what they do—in other words, whose behavior is perceived as valued in their culture. Note that this is an active process. Imitation of models is the most important element in how children learn a language, deal with aggression, develop a moral sense, and learn gender-appropriate behaviors. Observational learning can occur even if a person does not imitate the observed behavior.

Bandura's (1989) updated version of social learning theory is *social cognitive theory*. The change of name reflects a greater emphasis on cognitive processes as central to development. Cognitive processes are at work as people observe models, learn "chunks" of behavior, and mentally put the chunks together into complex new behavior patterns. Rita, for example, imitates the toes-out walk of her dance teacher but models her dance steps after those of Carmen, a slightly more advanced student. Even so, she develops her own style of dancing by putting her observations together into a new pattern.

Through feedback on their behavior, children gradually form standards for judging their own actions and become more selective in choosing models who exemplify those standards. They also begin to develop a sense of **self-efficacy**, the confidence that they have what it takes to succeed.

PERSPECTIVE 3: COGNITIVE

The **cognitive perspective** focuses on thought processes and the behavior that reflects those processes. This perspective encompasses both organismic and mechanistically influenced theories. It includes Piaget's cognitive-stage theory and Vygotsky's sociocultural theory of cognitive development. It also includes the information-processing approach and neo-Piagetian theories, which combine elements of information-processing and Piagetian theory.

Jean Piaget's Cognitive-Stage Theory Our understanding of how children think owes a great deal to the work of the Swiss theoretician Jean Piaget (1896–1980). Piaget's **cognitive-stage theory** was the forerunner of today's "cognitive

The American psychologist B. F. Skinner formulated the principles of operant conditioning.

social learning theory
Theory that behaviors also are learned by observing and imitating models. Also called *social cognitive theory*.

reciprocal determinism
Bandura's term for bidirectional forces that affect development.

observational learning
Learning through watching the behavior of others.

self-efficacy
Sense of one's capability to master challenges and achieve goals.

cognitive perspective
Perspective that looks at the development of mental processes such as thinking.

cognitive-stage theory
Piaget's theory that children's cognitive development advances in a series of four stages involving qualitatively distinct types of mental operations.

According to social learning theory, children learn by imitating the behavior of adult models.

checkpoint
can you . . .

▷ Identify the chief concerns, strengths, and weaknesses of the learning perspective?

▷ Tell how classical conditioning and operant conditioning differ?

▷ Contrast reinforcement and punishment?

▷ Compare behaviorism and social learning (or social cognitive) theory?

connect

study smart

Organization/Schemes/ Piaget

organization
Piaget's term for the creation of categories or systems of knowledge.

schemes
Piaget's term for organized patterns of thought and behavior used in particular situations.

adaptation
Piaget's term for adjustment to new information about the environment.

assimilation
Piaget's term for incorporation of new information into an existing cognitive structure.

accommodation
Piaget's term for changes in a cognitive structure to include new information.

equilibration
Piaget's term for the tendency to seek a stable balance among cognitive elements; achieved through a balance between assimilation and accommodation.

The Swiss psychologist Jean Piaget studied children's cognitive development by observing and talking with his own youngsters and others.

revolution" with its emphasis on mental processes. Piaget, a biologist and philosopher by training, viewed development organismically, as the product of children's efforts to understand and act on their world. He also believed that development was discontinuous; thus, his theory describes development as occurring in stages.

As a young man studying in Paris, Piaget set out to standardize the tests Alfred Binet had developed to assess the intelligence of French schoolchildren. Although his original role was to develop norms for the age at which children could pass particular tasks, Piaget instead became intrigued by the children's wrong answers, finding in them clues to their thought processes. He realized that children showed specific types of logical errors depending on their age.

Piaget's *clinical method* combined observation with flexible questioning. To find out how children think, Piaget followed up their wrong answers with more questions, and then designed tasks to test his tentative conclusions. In this way he discovered that a typical 4-year-old believes that pennies or flowers are more numerous when arranged in a line than when heaped or piled up. From his observations of his own and other children, Piaget created a comprehensive theory of cognitive development.

Piaget suggested that cognitive development begins with an inborn ability to adapt to the environment and is initially based on motor activities such as reflexes. By rooting for a nipple, feeling a pebble, or exploring the boundaries of a room, young children develop a more accurate understanding of their surroundings and greater competence in dealing with them. This cognitive growth occurs through three interrelated processes: organization, adaptation, and equilibration.

Organization is the tendency to create categories, such as birds, by observing the characteristics that individual members of a category, such as sparrows and cardinals, have in common. According to Piaget, people create increasingly complex cognitive structures called **schemes**, ways of organizing information about the world that govern the way the child thinks and behaves in a particular situation. As children acquire more information, their schemes become more complex. Take sucking, for example. A newborn infant has a simple scheme for sucking but soon develops varied schemes for how to suck at the breast, a bottle, or a thumb. The infant may have to open her mouth wider, or turn her head to the side, or suck with varying strength. Schemes are originally concrete in nature (e.g., how to suck on objects) and become increasingly abstract over time (e.g., what a dog is).

Adaptation is Piaget's term for how children handle new information in light of what they already know. Adaptation occurs through two complementary processes: (1) **assimilation**, taking in new information and incorporating it into existing cognitive structures; and (2) **accommodation**, adjusting one's cognitive structures to fit the new information.

How does the shift from assimilation to accommodation occur? Piaget argued that children strive for a stable balance—or **equilibration**—between their cognitive structures and new experiences. In other words, children want what they understand of the world to match what they observe around them. When children's understanding of the world does not match what they are experiencing, children find themselves in a state of disequilibrium. Disequilibrium can be thought of as an uncomfortable motivational state, and it pushes children into accommodation. For example, a child knows what birds are and sees a plane for the first time. The child labels the plane a "bird" (assimilation). Over time the child notes differences between planes and birds, which makes her somewhat uneasy (disequilibrium) and motivates her to change her understanding (accommodation) and provide a new label for the plane. She then is at equilibrium. By organizing new mental and behavioral patterns that integrate the new experience, the child restores equilibrium. Thus, assimilation and accommodation work together to produce equilibrium. Throughout life, the quest for equilibrium is the driving force behind cognitive growth.

Piaget described cognitive development as occurring in four qualitatively different stages (listed in Table 2.2 and discussed in detail in later chapters), which represent universal patterns of development. At each stage a child's mind develops a new way of operating. From infancy through adolescence, mental operations evolve from learning based on simple sensory and motor activity to logical, abstract thought.

Piaget's observations have yielded much information and some surprising insights. Piaget has shown us that children's minds are not miniature adult minds. Knowing how children think makes it easier for parents and teachers to understand and teach them. Piaget's theory has provided rough benchmarks for what to expect of children at various ages and has helped educators design curricula appropriate to varying levels of development.

Piaget wrote his first scientific paper at the age of 10—on the sighting of an albino sparrow.

Yet Piaget may have seriously underestimated the abilities of infants and young children. Some contemporary psychologists question his distinct stages, pointing instead to evidence that cognitive development is more gradual and continuous (Courage & Howe, 2002). Research beginning in the late 1960s has challenged Piaget's idea that thinking develops in a single, universal progression of stages leading to formal thought. Instead, children's cognitive processes seem closely tied to specific content (what they are thinking *about*) as well as to the context of a problem and the kinds of information and thought a culture considers important (Case & Okamoto, 1996; Hong, Morris, Chiu, & Benet-Martinez, 2000). We explore further critiques of Piaget's work in the chapters that follow.

Lev Vygotsky's Sociocultural Theory The Russian psychologist Lev Semenovich Vygotsky (1896–1934) focused on the social and cultural processes that guide children's cognitive development. Vygotsky's (1978) **sociocultural theory**, like Piaget's theory, stresses children's active engagement with their environment; but, whereas Piaget described the solo mind taking in and interpreting information about the world, Vygotsky saw cognitive growth as a *collaborative* process. Children, said Vygotsky, learn through social interaction. There is no such thing as development without context, and there are as many ways to develop as there are different cultures and different experiences. Children acquire cognitive skills as part of their induction into a way of life. Shared activities help children internalize their society's modes of thinking and behaving and make those folkways their own. Vygotsky placed special emphasis on *language*—not merely as an expression of knowledge and thought but as an essential tool for learning and thinking about the world.

According to Vygotsky, adults or more advanced peers must help direct and organize a child's learning before the child can master and internalize it. This guidance is most effective in helping children cross the **zone of proximal development (ZPD)**, the gap between what they are already able to do and what they could achieve with assistance from another person (*proximal* means "nearby"). Children in the ZPD for a particular task can almost, but not quite, perform the task on their own, and it is within this psychological space that most learning occurs. Responsibility for directing and monitoring learning gradually shifts from the adult to the child—much as, when an adult teaches a child to float, the adult first supports the child in the water and then lets go gradually as the child's body relaxes into a horizontal position.

Some followers of Vygotsky (Wood, 1980; Wood, Bruner, & Ross, 1976) have applied the metaphor of scaffolds—the temporary platforms on which construction workers stand—to this way of teaching. **Scaffolding** is the temporary support that parents, teachers, or others give a child in doing a task until the child can do it alone. For example, when a child is learning to float, a parent or teacher supports a child's back, first with a hand, then with only a finger, until the child can float without support.

Vygotsky's theory has important implications for education and for cognitive testing. Tests that focus on a child's potential for learning provide a valuable alternative to standard intelligence tests that assess what the child has already learned, and many children may benefit from the sort of expert guidance Vygotsky prescribes.

The Information-Processing Approach The **information-processing approach** seeks to explain cognitive development by analyzing the processes involved in making sense of incoming information and performing tasks effectively: such processes as attention,

sociocultural theory
Vygotsky's theory of how contextual factors affect children's development.

zone of proximal development (ZPD)
Vygotsky's term for the difference between what a child can do alone and what the child can do with help.

scaffolding
Temporary support to help a child master a task.

information-processing approach
Approach to the study of cognitive development by observing and analyzing the mental processes involved in perceiving and handling information.

According to the Russian psychologist Lev Semenovich Vygotsky, children learn through social interaction.

checkpoint
can you...

▷ Contrast Piaget's assumptions
and methods with those of
classical learning theory?

▷ List three interrelated principles
that bring about cognitive
growth, according to Piaget, and
give an example of each?

▷ Explain how Vygotsky's theory
differs from Piaget's and define
the concepts of ZPD and
scaffolding?

memory, planning strategies, decision making, and goal setting. The information-processing approach is not a single theory but a framework that undergirds a wide range of theories and research.

Some information-processing theorists compare the brain to a computer: There are certain inputs (such as sensory impressions) and certain outputs (such as behaviors). Information-processing theorists are interested in what happens in the middle. How does the brain use sensations and perceptions, say, of an unfamiliar word, to recognize that word again? Why does the same input sometimes result in different outputs? In large part, information-processing researchers use observational data to *infer* what goes on between a stimulus and a response. For example, they may ask a person to recall a list of words and then observe any difference in performance if the person repeats the list over and over before being asked to recall the words. Through such studies, some information-processing researchers have developed *computational models* or flowcharts that analyze the specific steps people go through in gathering, storing, retrieving, and using information.

Information-processing theorists, like Piaget, see people as active thinkers about their world. Unlike Piaget, they generally do *not* propose stages of development. Instead, they view development as continuous. They note age-related increases in the speed, complexity, and efficiency of mental processing and in the amount and variety of material that can be stored in memory. Brain imaging research, discussed later in this chapter, supports important aspects of information-processing models, such as the existence of separate physical structures to handle conscious and unconscious memory (Schacter, 1999; Yingling, 2001).

The information-processing approach has practical applications. It enables researchers to estimate an infant's later intelligence from the efficiency of sensory perception and processing. It enables parents and teachers to help children learn by making them more aware of their own mental processes and of strategies to enhance them. Psychologists often use information-processing models to test, diagnose, and treat learning problems.

Neo-Piagetian Theories Since the 1980s, in response to criticisms of Piaget's theory, some developmental psychologists have sought to integrate elements of his theory with the information-processing approach. Instead of describing a single, general system of increasingly logical mental operations, these neo-Piagetians focus on *specific* concepts, strategies, and skills, such as number concepts and comparisons of "more" and "less." They suggest that children develop cognitively by becoming more efficient at processing information. Because of this emphasis on efficiency of processing, the neo-Piagetian approach helps account for individual differences in cognitive ability and for uneven development in various domains.

checkpoint
can you...

▷ Describe what information-
processing researchers do?

▷ Explain how neo-Piagetian
theory differs from the Piagetian
approach?

PERSPECTIVE 4: CONTEXTUAL

contextual perspective
View of child development that sees the individual as inseparable from the social context.

bioecological theory
Bronfenbrenner's approach to understanding processes and contexts of child development that identifies five levels of environmental influence.

microsystem
Bronfenbrenner's term for a setting in which a child interacts with others on an everyday, face-to-face basis.

According to the **contextual perspective**, development can be understood only in its social context. Contextualists see the individual, not as a separate entity interacting with the environment but as an inseparable part of it. (Vygotsky's sociocultural theory, which we discussed as part of the cognitive perspective, also can be classified as contextual.)

The American psychologist Urie Bronfenbrenner's (1917–2005) **bioecological theory** (1979, 1986, 1994; Bronfenbrenner & Morris, 1998) identifies five levels of environmental influence, ranging from very intimate to very broad: microsystem, mesosystem, exosystem, macrosystem, and chronosystem (Figure 2.2). To understand the complexity of influences on development, we must see a child within the context of these multiple environments.

A **microsystem** is the everyday environment of home, school, or neighborhood, including face-to-face relationships with parents, friends, classmates, teachers, or neighbors. How, for example, does a new baby affect the parents' lives? How do their feelings and attitudes affect the baby?

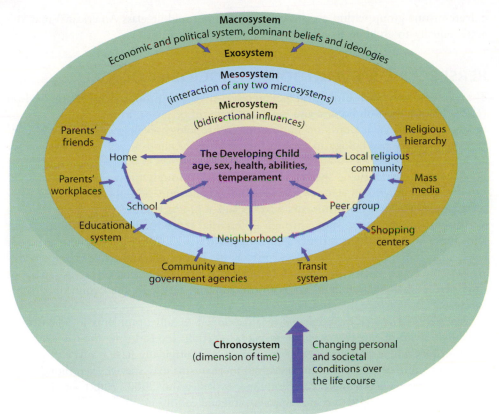

FIGURE 2.2

Bronfenbrenner's Bioecological Theory

Concentric circles show five levels of environmental influence on the individual, from the most intimate environment (the microsystem) to the broadest (the chronosytem)—all within the perpendicular dimension of time.

The **mesosystem** is the interlocking of various microsystems. It may include linkages between home and school (such as parent-teacher conferences) or between the family and the peer group (such as relationships that develop among families of children in a neighborhood play group). For example, a parent's bad day at work might affect interactions with a child later that evening in a negative way. Despite never having actually gone to the workplace, the child is still affected by it.

The mesosystem focuses on interactions between microsystems, but the **exosystem** consists of interactions between a microsystem and an outside system or institution. Though the effects are indirect, they can still have a profound impact on a child. For example, different countries have policies on what type, if any, of maternal or paternal leave accommodations are available for new parents. And, whether or not a parent has the option to stay home with a newborn is a substantial influence on development. Thus governmental policies trickle down and can affect a child's day-to-day experiences.

The **macrosystem** consists of overarching cultural patterns, such as dominant beliefs, ideologies, and economic and political systems. How is a child's development affected by living in a capitalist or socialist society?

Finally, the **chronosystem** adds the dimension of time: change or constancy in the child and the environment. Time marches on, and as it does, changes occur. These can include changes in family composition, place of residence, or parents' employment, as well as larger events such as wars, ideology, political system, and economic cycles.

According to Bronfenbrenner, a person is not merely an outcome of development but a shaper of it. People affect their own development through their biological and psychological characteristics, talents and skills, disabilities, and temperament.

By looking at systems that affect individuals in and beyond the family, this bioecological approach helps us to see the variety of influences on development. The contextual perspective also reminds us that findings about the development of children in one

mesosystem
Bronfenbrenner's term for linkages between two or more microsystems.

exosystem
Bronfenbrenner's term for linkages between two or more settings, one of which does not contain the child.

macrosystem
Bronfenbrenner's term for a society's overall cultural patterns, including values, customs, and social systems.

chronosystem
Bronfenbrenner's term for effects of time on other developmental systems.

checkpoint can **you** . . .

▷ State the chief assumptions of the contextual perspective?

▷ Name and differentiate Bronfenbrenner's five systems of contextual influence?

culture or one group within a culture (such as white, middle-class Americans) may not apply equally to children in other societies or cultural groups.

PERSPECTIVE 5: EVOLUTIONARY/SOCIOBIOLOGICAL

The **evolutionary/sociobiological perspective** originally proposed by E. O. Wilson (1975) focuses on evolutionary and biological bases of behavior. Influenced by Darwin's theory of evolution, it draws on findings of anthropology, ecology, genetics, ethology, and evolutionary psychology to explain the adaptive, or survival, value of behavior for an individual or species.

According to Darwin, species have developed through the related processes of *survival of the fittest* and *natural selection.* Individuals with heritable traits *fitted* (better adapted) to their environments survive and reproduce more than those that are less fitted (less adapted). Thus, through differential reproduction success, individuals with more adaptive characteristics pass on their traits to future generations at higher levels than individuals that are less adaptively fit. In this way, adaptive characteristics are selected to be passed on, and the less adaptive ones die out. Over vast spans of time, these small, incremental changes add up, and result in the evolution of new species.

Evolved mechanisms are behaviors that developed to solve problems in adapting to an earlier environment. For example, aversion to certain foods during the first trimester of pregnancy, when the fetus is most vulnerable, may originally have evolved to protect the fetus from toxic substances. Such evolved mechanisms may survive even though they no longer serve a useful purpose (Bjorklund & Pellegrini, 2000, 2002), or they may evolve further in response to changing environmental conditions. Although most evolved mechanisms are tailored to a specific problem, others, such as human intelligence, are viewed as having evolved to help people face a wide range of problems (MacDonald, 1998; MacDonald & Hershberger, 2005).

Ethology is the study of the adaptive behaviors of animal species in natural contexts. For example, ethologists might study squirrels' burying of nuts in the fall or how spiders spin webs. The assumption is that such behaviors evolved through natural selection. Ethologists are most interested in investigating distinctive behaviors expressed by animals of different species. By comparing animals of different species, they seek to identify which behaviors are universal and which are specific to a particular species or modifiable by experience.

For example, one widespread characteristic throughout the animal kingdom is called *proximity-seeking*, or, more casually, "staying close to mommy." This was first studied by Konrad Lorenz (refer to Chapter 1) in newborn ducklings, who imprint on the first moving object they see and then follow it unceasingly until they are old enough to survive on their own. Other animals also engage in this behavior, and following Lorenz's work, an explosion of research focused on proximity-seeking in the young of different animals. It became clear that this innate tendency was an important adaptive behavior. Those baby animals that did not stay close to their mothers tended not to survive, and hence, reproduce later in life.

But why discuss animal research in a human development text? The answer is that the human species has also been subject to the forces of evolution and is thus likely to also have innate adaptive behaviors. In fact, one of the most influential theories in developmental psychology was strongly influenced by the ethological approach. The British psychologist John Bowlby (1969) drew upon his knowledge of proximity-seeking behavior in animals of different species as he formed his ideas about attachment in humans. He viewed infants' attachment to a caregiver as a mechanism that evolved to protect them from predators (attachment is discussed more fully in Chapter 8).

A related extension of the ethological approach can be found in **evolutionary psychology**. While ethologists focus most closely on cross-species comparisons, evolutionary

evolutionary/sociobiological perspective
View of human development that focuses on evolutionary and biological bases of social behavior.

The peak of morning sickness is in the first trimester, which corresponds to the formation of nearly all the major body structures. So the mother is least likely to consume potentially damaging foods during the most sensitive time period.

ethology
Study of distinctive adaptive behaviors of species of animals that have evolved to increase survival of the species.

evolutionary psychology
Application of Darwinian principles of natural selection and survival of the fittest to human psychology.

psychologists focus on humans and apply Darwinian principles to human behavior. Evolutionary psychologists believe that, just as we have a heart specialized as a pump, lungs specialized for air exchange, and thumbs specialized for grasping, we also have aspects of our human psychology specialized for solving specific adaptive problems. According to this theory, people unconsciously strive, not only for personal survival, but also to perpetuate their genetic legacy. They do so by seeking to maximize their chances of having offspring who will survive to reproduce, hence passing down their characteristics.

It is important to note that an evolutionary perspective does not reduce human behavior to the effects of genes seeking to reproduce themselves, despite arguing that ultimately, the transmission of genes is what drives many evolved behaviors. Evolutionary psychologists place great weight on the environment to which humans must adapt and the flexibility of the human mind. For example, we are a relatively aggressive species—that is part of our species architecture. But, we are also sensitive to those situations in which aggression is a viable strategy, and how aggressively we behave is shaped strongly by the culture in which we develop.

Evolutionary developmental psychologists apply evolutionary principles to child development. They study such topics as parenting strategies, attachment, gender differences in play, and peer relations, and they identify characteristics that help children of various ages adapt, or adjust, to the circumstances in which they find themselves. Box 2.1 discusses an apparent irony: the adaptive value of immature behavior.

A SHIFTING BALANCE

No one theory of development is universally accepted, and no one theoretical perspective explains all facets of development. As the study of child development has evolved, the mechanistic and organismic models have shifted in influence. Most of the early pioneers in the field, including Freud, Erikson, and Piaget, favored organismic, or stage, approaches. The mechanistic view gained support during the 1960s with the popularity of learning theories.

Today much attention is focused on the biological and evolutionary bases of behavior. Instead of looking for broad stages, developmental scientists seek to discover what specific kinds of behavior show continuity and what processes are involved in each. Rather than abrupt changes, a close examination of Piaget's stages of cognitive development, for example, reveals gradual, sometimes imperceptible advances that add up to a qualitative shift. Similarly, most infants do not learn to walk overnight, but rather by a series of tentative movements that gradually become more self-assured. Even when observable behavior seems to change suddenly, the biological or neurological processes that underlie that behavioral change may be continuous (Courage & Howe, 2002). To some extent, the interpretation of advances as quantitative or qualitative depends on the size of the lens being used to investigate them.

Instead of debating active versus reactive development, investigators often find that influences are *bidirectional:* people change their world even as it changes them. A baby girl born with a cheerful disposition is likely to get positive responses from adults, which strengthens her trust that her smiles will be rewarded and motivates her to smile more. A teacher who offers constructive criticism and emotional support to his students is likely to elicit greater efforts to achieve. Improved student performance, in turn, is likely to encourage him to keep using this teaching style.

Developmental theories grow out of, and are tested by, research. Although most researchers draw from a variety of theoretical perspectives, research questions and methods often reflect a researcher's particular theoretical orientation. For example, in trying to understand how a child develops a sense of right and wrong, a behaviorist would examine the way the parents respond to the child's behavior: what kinds of behavior they punish or praise. A social learning theorist would focus on imitation of moral

checkpoint
can **you** . . .

▷ Identify the chief focus of the evolutionary/sociobiological perspective, and explain how Darwin's theory of evolution underlies this perspective?

▷ Tell what kinds of topics ethologists and evolutionary psychologists study?

what's
your
view

Which theoretical perspective would be most useful for (a) a mother trying to teach her child to say "please," (b) a teacher interested in stimulating critical thinking, and (c) a researcher studying siblings' imitation of one another?

THE ADAPTIVE VALUE OF IMMATURITY

2.1

In comparison with other animals and even with other primates, human beings take a long time to grow up. Chimpanzees reach reproductive maturity in about 8 years, rhesus monkeys in about 4 years, and lemurs in only 2 years or so. Human beings, in contrast, do not reach full growth and physical maturity until the early teenage years and, at least in modern industrialized societies, typically reach cognitive and psychosocial maturity even later. During much of that time, they remain largely dependent on their parents or other caregivers.

From the point of view of evolutionary theory, this prolonged period of immaturity may be essential to survival and well-being. Human beings are social animals, and a long, protective childhood may serve as essential preparation for the social problem-solving skills needed in adulthood. Human communities and cultures are highly complex, and there is much to learn in order to know the ropes. Thus childhood may be an evolved mechanism that allows for the development of social competency.

Human intelligence, too, may be an evolved characteristic. The fossil record indicates that during the past 4 million years the human brain has tripled in volume. At the same time, its period of development has nearly doubled. The human brain, despite its rapid prenatal growth, is much less fully developed at birth than the brains of other primates; if the human fetus's brain attained full size before birth, its head would be too big to go through the birth canal and women's hips are as wide as they can be to still support upright walking. Instead, the human brain continues to grow in size and complexity throughout childhood, eventually far surpassing the brains of our simian cousins in the capacities for language and thought. The human brain's slower development gives it greater *plasticity*, or flexibility, as not all connections are hardwired at an early age. One theorist has called this plasticity "the human species's greatest adaptive advantage" (Bjorklund, 1997, p. 157).

The extended period of immaturity and dependency during infancy and childhood allows children to spend much of their time in play; and, as Piaget and Vygotsky both maintained, it is largely through play that cognitive development occurs. Play also enables children to develop motor skills and experiment with social roles. It is a vehicle for creative imagination and intellectual curiosity, the hallmarks of the human spirit. Rather than being a distraction used to burn off energy before getting to the real business of learning, it is within play that many of our most important fundamental skills and abilities are developed.

Some aspects of immaturity serve immediate adaptive purposes. For example, some primitive reflexes, such as rooting for the nipple, which are protective for newborns, disappear when no longer needed. Research on animals suggests that the immaturity of early sensory and motor functioning may protect infants from overstimulation. By limiting the amount of information they have to deal with, it may help them focus on experiences essential to survival, such as feeding and attachment to the mother. Later, infants' limited memory capacity may simplify the processing of linguistic sounds and facilitate early language learning.

Limitations on the way young children think also may have adaptive value. For example, young children are unrealistic in assessing their abilities, believing they can do more than they actually can. This immature self-judgment, by reducing fear of failure, may encourage children to try new things.

All in all, evolutionary theory and research suggest that immaturity is not necessarily equivalent to deficiency and that some attributes of infancy and childhood have persisted because they are appropriate to the tasks of a particular time of life.

Source: Bjorklund, 1997; Bjorklund & Pellegrini, 2000, 2002; Flinn & Ward, 2005.

what's your view

Can you think of additional examples of the adaptive value of immaturity? Can you think of ways in which immaturity may *not* be adaptive?

examples, possibly in stories or in movies. An information-processing researcher might do a task analysis to identify the steps a child goes through in determining the range of moral options available and then in deciding which option to pursue.

With the vital connection between theory and research in mind, let's look at the methods developmental researchers use.

Research Methods

Researchers in child development work within two methodological traditions: quantitative and qualitative. Each of these traditions has different goals and different ways of seeing and interpreting reality and uses different means of collecting and analyzing data.

How do developmental scientists study children, and what are the advantages and disadvantages of each research method?

QUANTITATIVE AND QUALITATIVE RESEARCH

Generally, when most people think of scientific research, they are thinking of what is called quantitative research. **Quantitative research** deals with objectively measurable, numerical data that can answer questions such as "how much?" or "how many?" and that is amenable to statistical analysis. For example, quantitative researchers might study the fear and anxiety that children feel before surgery by asking them to answer questions, using a numerical scale, about how fearful or anxious they are. This data could then be compared to data for children not facing surgery to determine if a statistically significant difference exists between the two groups. Alternatively, quantitative researchers might collect physiological data such as heart rate or stress hormone levels of children facing surgery, and then compare that data to data for children not facing surgery. The important component is not the particular way in which the data is collected, but rather that the data consists of numbers and quantifiable amounts that can be manipulated mathematically. Quantitative research on child development is based on the **scientific method**, which has traditionally characterized most scientific inquiry. Its usual steps are:

1. *Identification of a problem* to be studied, often on the basis of a theory or of previous research;
2. *Formulation of hypotheses* to be tested by research;
3. *Collection of data;*
4. *Statistical analysis of the data* to determine whether they support the hypothesis;
5. *Formation of tentative conclusions;* and
6. *Dissemination of findings* so other observers can check, learn from, analyze, repeat, and build on the results.

Qualitative research, in contrast, focuses on the how and why of behavior. It more commonly involves nonnumerical (verbal or pictorial) descriptions of participants' subjective understanding, feelings, or beliefs about their experiences. Qualitative researchers might study the same subject areas as quantitative researchers, but their perspective informs both how they collect data as well as its interpretation. For example, if qualitative researchers were to study children's emotional state prior to surgery, they might do so with unstructured interviews given to presurgical children, or by asking children to draw their perceptions of the upcoming event. Whereas the goal in quantitative research is to generate hypotheses from previous research and empirically test them, the goal in qualitative research is to understand the "story" of the event. Thus, qualitative research is more flexible and informal, and such researchers might be more interested in gathering and exploring large amounts of data to see what hypotheses might emerge than in running statistical analyses on numerical data.

The selection of quantitative or qualitative methods may depend on the purpose of the study, how much is already known about the topic, and the researcher's theoretical orientation. Quantitative research often is done in controlled laboratory settings; qualitative research typically is conducted in everyday settings, such as the home or school. Quantitative investigators seek to remain detached from study participants so as not to influence the results; qualitative investigators may get to know participants to better understand why they think, feel, and act as they do, and it is assumed they are to some extent interpreting the results through the lens of their own experiences and characteristics.

quantitative research
Research that deals with objectively measurable data.

scientific method
System of established principles and processes of scientific inquiry, which includes identifying a problem to be studied, formulating a hypothesis to be tested by research, collecting data, analyzing the data, forming tentative conclusions, and disseminating findings.

The Scientific Method

qualitative research
Research that involves the interpretation of nonnumerical data, such as subjective experiences, feelings, or beliefs.

TABLE 2.3 Comparing Qualitative and Quantitative Research

	Qualitative Research	Quantitative Research
Purpose and focus	Discovering and interpreting meaning and perceptions.	Testing a hypothesis developed before the research begins.
Standardization and replicability	The study is particular to the participant group. Replication is rare.	The study is standardized so that replication is possible.
Sampling	Subjects are selected to fit the purpose of the study.	Subjects are selected randomly.
Data	The primary data produced are words. Raw qualitative data may be researcher's notes, audiotapes, or transcripts of informal interviews. Secondary data such as existing written material and observations are often used.	The primary data are numbers or fixed responses that can be quantified.
Methods	Data are gathered using less structured methods, such as observation and interviews, to generate rich description. Questions are typically open-ended, allowing for flexibility in response. The researcher is the main instrument of inquiry, aided by semistructured interview guides, observation strategies, and a thorough review of secondary data. Research generally takes place in the field and often involves face-to-face encounters with the participants.	Methods and instruments are structured beforehand to gather standardized data that can be coded or numerated. Questions are asked in such a way that the answers are a fixed set of choices. Instruments such as surveys are carefully designed to measure specific variables and are administered systematically, in a standardized fashion, to avoid researcher bias. Research can take place without direct contact with the subject, for example, by telephone or mailed surveys.
Analysis	Data are analyzed by systematically organizing and interpreting information using categories, themes, and motifs that identify patterns and relationships.	Data are analyzed using standardized statistics and procedures.
Results	Results are in-depth explanations for patterns of behavior.	Results tend to summarize patterns of similarities, variability, size, direction, and/or significance of any differences between specific groups.

Source: Adapted from Mathie & Carnozzi (2005).

Each of these methodologies uses different types of sampling and data collection. Table 2.3 summarizes the differences between the two types of research.

SAMPLING

sample
Group of participants chosen to represent the entire population under study.

Because studying an entire *population* (a group to whom the findings may apply) is usually too costly and time-consuming, investigators select a **sample**, a smaller group within the population. To be sure that the results of quantitative research are true generally, the sample should adequately represent the population under study—that is, it should show relevant characteristics in the same proportions as in the entire population. Otherwise the results cannot properly be *generalized*, or applied to the population as a whole. To judge how generalizable the findings are likely to be, the researchers must control who is in the study. For example, if the proportion of African Americans in a given population is estimated to be about 15 percent, then any sample drawn from that population should have approximately 15 percent African American research participants.

Often quantitative researchers seek to achieve representativeness through **random selection**, in which each person in a population has an equal and independent chance of being chosen. If we wanted to study the effects of an educational program, one way to select a random sample would be to put all the names of participating children into a large bowl, stir it, and then draw out a certain number of names. A random sample, especially a large one, is likely to represent the population well. Unfortunately, a random sample of a large population is often difficult to obtain. Instead, many studies use samples selected for convenience or accessibility (for example, children born in a particular hospital or attending a particular day care center). The findings of such studies may not apply to the whole population.

In qualitative research, sampling is usually *focused* rather than random; participants are chosen for their ability to communicate the nature of a certain experience, such as how it feels to go through puberty or to undergo a particular type of surgery. The size and nature of the sample depend on the purpose of the study. In some studies samples are relatively small; in others, a broader sample may better represent variations within a population. A carefully selected qualitative sample may have a fair degree of generalizability.

One problem with the results of Cosmo magazine polls is that they are not a random sample. The data come from "people who answer Cosmo magazine polls," a select group of individuals.

FORMS OF DATA COLLECTION

Common ways of gathering data (Table 2.4) include *self-reports* (verbal or visual reports by study participants), *observation* of participants in laboratory or natural settings, and *behavioral* or *performance measures*. Depending in part on time and financial constraints,

random selection
Selection of a sample in such a way that each person in a population has an equal and independent chance of being chosen.

checkpoint
can you . . .

▷ Contrast quantitative and qualitative research and give an example of each?

▷ Summarize the six steps in the scientific method and tell why each is important?

▷ Explain the purpose of random selection and tell how it can be achieved?

There is no one "best way" of collecting data; rather, each technique has costs and benefits associated with it.

TABLE 2.4	Major Methods of Data Collection		
Type	**Main Characteristics**	**Advantages**	**Disadvantages**
Self-report: diary, visual reports, interview, or questionnaire	Participants are asked about some aspect of their lives; questioning may be highly structured or more flexible; self-report may be verbal or visual.	Can provide firsthand information about a person's life, attitudes, or opinions. Visual techniques (i.e., drawing, mapping, graphing) avoid need for verbal skills.	Participant may not remember information accurately or may distort responses in a socially desirable way; how question is asked or by whom may affect answer.
Naturalistic observation	People are observed in their normal setting, with no attempt to manipulate behavior.	Provides good description of behavior; does not subject people to unnatural settings that may distort behavior.	Lack of control; observer bias.
Laboratory observation	Participants are observed in the laboratory, with no attempt to manipulate behavior.	Provides good descriptions; offers greater control than naturalistic observation because all participants are observed under same controlled conditions.	Observer bias; controlled situation can be artificial.
Behavioral and performance measures	Participants are tested on abilities, skills, knowledge, competencies, or physical responses.	Provides objectively measurable information; avoids subjective distortions.	Cannot measure attitudes or other nonbehavioral phenomena; results may be affected by extraneous factors.

researchers may use one or more of these data collection techniques in any research design. Qualitative research tends to rely on self-reports, often in the form of in-depth, open-ended interviews or visual techniques (such as asking participants to draw or paint their impressions of an experience), and on observation in natural settings. Quantitative research typically uses standardized, structured methods involving numerical measurements of behavior or performance.

Let's look more closely at several common methods of data collection.

Self-Reports: Diaries, Visual Techniques, Interviews, and Questionnaires The simplest form of self-report is a *diary* or log. Adolescents may be asked, for example, to record what they eat each day or the times when they feel depressed. In studying young children, *parental self-reports*—diaries, journals, interviews, or questionnaires—are commonly used, often together with other methods, such as videotaping or recording. Parents may be videotaped playing with their babies and then may be shown the tapes and asked to explain why they acted or reacted as they did. Visual representation techniques—asking participants to draw or paint or to provide maps or graphs that illuminate their experience—can avoid reliance on verbal skills.

In a face-to-face or telephone *interview*, researchers ask questions about attitudes, opinions, or behavior. In a *structured* interview, each participant is asked the same set of questions. An *open-ended* interview is more flexible; the interviewer can vary the topics and order of questions and can ask follow-up questions based on the responses. To reach more people and to protect their privacy, researchers sometimes distribute a printed or online *questionnaire*, which participants fill out and return.

By questioning a large number of people, investigators can get a broad picture—at least of what the respondents *say* they believe or do or did. However, people willing to participate in interviews or fill out questionnaires may not accurately represent the population as a whole. Furthermore, heavy reliance on self-reports may be unwise because people may not have thought about what they feel and think or honestly may not know. They may forget when and how events took place or may consciously or unconsciously distort their replies to fit what is considered socially desirable.

How a question is asked, and by whom, can affect the answer. When questioned about risky or socially disapproved behavior, such as sexual habits and drug use, respondents may be more candid in responding to a computerized survey than to a face-to-face interview.

Naturalistic and Laboratory Observation Observation can take two forms: *naturalistic observation* and *laboratory observation*. In **naturalistic observation**, researchers look at children in real-life settings. The researchers do not try to alter behavior or the environment; they simply record what they see. In **laboratory observation**, researchers observe and record behavior in a controlled situation, such as a laboratory. By observing all participants under the same conditions, investigators can more clearly identify any differences in behavior not attributable to the environment.

Both kinds of observation can provide valuable descriptions of behavior, but they have limitations. For one, they do not explain *why* children behave as they do, though the observers may suggest interpretations. Then, too, an observer's presence can alter behavior. When children know they are being watched, they may act differently. Further, there is a risk of *observer bias:* the researcher's tendency to interpret data to fit expectations or to emphasize some aspects and minimize others. The issue of observer bias is most relevant to quantitative research, which must be *replicable* (repeatable) by other researchers to see whether they obtain similar results.

At one time, laboratory observation was favored as a means to more rigorous control. Now such technological devices as portable digital recorders and computers increase objectivity and enable researchers to analyze moment-by-moment changes in facial expressions or other behavior (Gottman & Notarius, 2000). Such methods can make naturalistic observation more accurate and objective than it otherwise would be.

what's your view?

Which interview technique do you think would yield more reliable results—structured or open-ended?

naturalistic observation
Research method in which behavior is studied in natural settings without intervention or manipulation.

laboratory observation
Research method in which all participants are observed under the same controlled conditions.

Observation doesn't work terribly well for very rare events either. Suppose you wanted to do research on heroic rescues and decided to wait by a bridge to observe whether anyone helps when people try to commit suicide by jumping off. How long would you be waiting?

Behavioral and Performance Measures For quantitative research, investigators typically use objective measures of behavior or performance instead of, or in addition to, self-reports or observation. Tests and other behavioral and neuropsychological measures, including mechanical and electronic devices, may be used to assess abilities, skills, knowledge, competencies, or physiological responses, such as heart rate and brain activity. Although these measures are less subjective than self-reports or personal observation, such factors as fatigue and self-confidence can affect results.

Some written tests, such as intelligence tests, compare performance with that of other test-takers. Such tests can be meaningful and useful only if they are both *valid* (that is, the tests measure the abilities they claim to measure) and *reliable* (that is, the results are reasonably consistent from one time to another). To avoid bias, tests must be *standardized*, that is, given and scored by the same methods and criteria for all test-takers.

When measuring any characteristic, intelligence for example, it is important to define exactly what is to be measured in a way that other researchers will understand so they can comment on the results. For this purpose, researchers use an **operational definition**—a definition stated solely in terms of the operations or procedures used to produce or measure a phenomenon. Intelligence can be defined as the ability to achieve a certain score on a test covering logical relationships, memory, and vocabulary recognition. Some people may disagree with this definition, but no one can reasonably claim that it is not clear.

For most of the history of psychology, theorists and researchers studied cognitive processes apart from the physical structures of the brain in which these processes occur. Now sophisticated imaging instruments, such as functional magnetic resonance imaging (fMRI) and positron emission tomography (PET), make it possible to see the brain in action, and the field of **cognitive neuroscience** is linking our understanding of cognitive functioning with what happens in the brain (Gazzaniga, 2000; Humphreys, 2002; Posner & DiGirolamo, 2000).

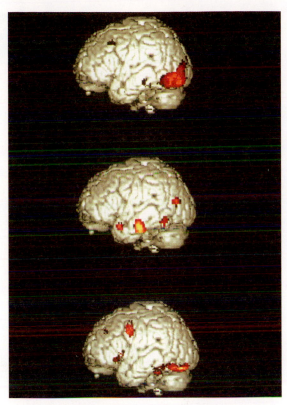

Researchers can analyze a PET (position emission tomography) scan to observe the link between cognitive activity and what happens in the brain. The regions shown in color are activated when objects are seen (top), recognized (middle), and named (bottom).

operational definition
Definition stated solely in terms of the operations or procedures used to produce or measure a phenomenon.

cognitive neuroscience
Study of links between neural processes and cognitive abilities.

EVALUATING QUANTITATIVE AND QUALITATIVE RESEARCH

In comparison with quantitative research based on the scientific method, qualitative research has both strengths and limitations. On the positive side, qualitative research can examine a question in great depth and detail, and the research framework can readily be revised in the light of new data. Findings of qualitative research can be a rich source of insights into attitudes and behavior. The interactive relationship between investigators and participants can humanize the research process and reveal information that would not emerge under the more impersonal conditions of quantitative research. On the other hand, qualitative research tends to be less rigorous and more subject to bias than quantitative research. Because samples are often small and usually not random, results are less generalizable and replicable than the results of quantitative research. The large volume of data makes analysis and interpretation time-consuming, and the quality of the findings and conclusions depends greatly on the skills of the researcher (Mathie & Carnozzi, 2005).

Yet the line between these methodologies is not necessarily clear-cut. Qualitative data may be analyzed quantitatively—for example, by statistical analysis of interview transcripts or videotaped observations to see how many times certain themes or behaviors occur. Conversely, quantitative data may be illuminated by qualitative research—for example, by interviews designed to examine the motivations and attitudes of children who make high scores on achievement tests (Yoshikawa, Weisner, Kalil, & Way, 2008).

A current trend is to combine qualitative and quantitative methods. For example, quantitative research might reveal what proportion of teenagers in a particular country smoke tobacco and the average age at which they began to do so. Qualitative research, using in-depth interviews or focus groups, might discover why certain participants

connect
studysmart

Validity/Reliability

checkpoint
can **you** . . .

▷ Compare the advantages and disadvantages of various forms of data collection and give examples of how qualitative and quantitative methods can be combined?

▷ Explain how brain research contributes to the understanding of cognitive processes and social behaviors and attitudes?

TABLE 2.5 Basic Research Designs

Type	Main Characteristics	Advantages	Disadvantages
Case study	In-depth study of single individual.	Flexibility; provides detailed picture of one person's behavior and development; can generate hypotheses.	May not generalize to others; conclusions not directly testable; cannot establish cause and effect.
Ethnographic study	In-depth study of a culture or subculture.	Can help overcome culturally based biases in theory and research; can test universality of developmental phenomena.	Subject to observer bias.
Correlational study	Attempt to find positive or negative relationship between variables.	Enables prediction of one variable on basis of another; can suggest hyptheses about causal relationships.	Cannot establish cause and effect.
Experiment	Controlled procedure in which an experimenter controls the independent variable to determine its effect on the dependent variable; may be conducted in the laboratory or field.	Establishes cause-and-effect relationships; is highly controlled and can be repeated by another investigator; degree of control greatest in the laboratory experiment.	Findings, especially when derived from laboratory experiments, may not generalize to situations outside the laboratory.

started smoking, and these findings might then be tested by quantitative research on a larger, more representative sample. In combination, quantitative and qualitative research often can provide more complex and more complete information about child development than can either method alone.

BASIC RESEARCH DESIGNS

A research design is a plan for conducting a scientific investigation: what questions are to be answered, how participants are to be selected, how data are to be collected and interpreted, and how valid conclusions can be drawn. Four basic designs used in developmental research are case studies, ethnographic studies, correlational studies, and experiments. The first two designs are qualitative; the last two are quantitative. Each design has advantages and drawbacks, and each is appropriate for certain kinds of research problems (Table 2.5).

Just as there is no one "best way" to collect data, there is no one best way to conduct research. Each design has costs and benefits associated with it.

case study
Study of a single subject, such as an individual or family.

Case Studies A **case study** is a study of a single case or individual, such as Genie, the 13-year-old girl who never learned to talk (refer to Box 1.3 in Chapter 1). Some theories, most notably Freud's, grew primarily out of clinical case studies, which included careful observation and interpretation of what patients said and did. Case studies also may use behavioral or physiological measures and biographical, autobiographical, or documentary materials.

Case studies offer useful in-depth information. They can explore sources of behavior and test treatments. They also can suggest potentially fruitful areas for other research. A related advantage is flexibility; the researcher is free to explore avenues of inquiry that arise during the course of the study. However, case studies, being qualitative in design, have shortcomings. From studying Genie, for instance, we learn much about the development of a single child, and although it is oftentimes assumed that some findings are relevant to all children, we cannot be sure the information applies to children in general. Furthermore, case studies cannot explain behavior with certainty or make strong causal statements because there is no way to test their conclusions. Even though it seems reasonable that Genie's severely deprived environment contributed to or even caused her language deficiency, it is impossible to know how she would have developed with a normal upbringing.

Ethnographic Studies An **ethnographic study** seeks to describe the pattern of relationships, customs, beliefs, technology, arts, and traditions that make up a society's way of life. In a way, it is like a case study of a culture. Ethnographic research can be qualitative, quantitative, or both. It uses a combination of methods, including informal, unstructured interviewing and **participant observation**. Participant observation is a form of naturalistic observation in which researchers live or participate in the societies or smaller groups they observe, as anthropologists often do for long periods of time.

Because of ethnographers' involvement in the events or societies they are observing, their findings are especially open to observer bias. On the positive side, ethnographic research can help overcome cultural biases in theory and research, as discussed in Box 2.2. Ethnography demonstrates the error of assuming that principles developed from research in Western cultures are universally applicable.

Correlational Studies A **correlational study** is an attempt to find a *correlation*, or statistical relationship, between *variables*, phenomena that change or vary among people or can be varied for purposes of research. Correlations are expressed in terms of direction (positive or negative) and magnitude (degree). Two variables that are related *positively* increase or decrease together. As we report in Chapter 14, studies show a positive, or direct, correlation between televised violence and aggressiveness; that is, children who watch more violent television tend to fight more than children who watch less violent television. Two variables have a *negative*, or inverse, correlation if, as one increases, the other decreases. Studies show a negative correlation between amount of schooling and the risk of developing dementia (mental deterioration) due to Alzheimer's disease in old age. In other words, the less education, the more dementia (Katzman, 1993).

Correlations are reported as numbers ranging from +1.0 (a perfect positive relationship) to −1.0 (a perfect negative relationship). So, for example correlations of +0.6 and −0.6 are equal in strength, but in the opposite direction. Perfect correlations are rare. The closer a correlation comes to +1.0 or −1.0, the stronger the relationship, either positive or negative. A correlation of 0 means the variables have no relationship (Figure 2.3).

Correlations enable us to predict one variable on the basis of another. On the basis of the positive correlation between viewing televised violence and aggressiveness, we can predict that children who watch violent shows are more likely to get into fights than children who do not watch such shows. The greater the magnitude of the correlation between two variables, the greater the ability to predict one from the other.

> *A correlation of +/− 1.0 essentially means you are measuring the same thing in different ways. For example, inches and centimeters are perfectly correlated.*

ethnographic study
In-depth study of a culture, which uses a combination of methods including participant observation.

participant observation
Research method in which the observer lives with the people or participates in the activity being observed.

correlational study
Research design intended to discover whether a statistical relationship between variables exists.

connect

study smart

Correlations

FIGURE 2.3

Scatter Plots of Positive, Negative, and No Correlations

Correlational studies may find positive or negative correlations or no correlation. In a positive, or direct, correlation (a), data plotted on a graph cluster around a line showing that one variable (X) increases as the other variable (Y) increases. In a negative, or inverse, correlation (b), one variable (X) increases as the other variable (Y) decreases. No correlation, or a zero correlation (c), exists when increases and decreases in two variables show no consistent relationship (that is, data plotted on a graph show no pattern).

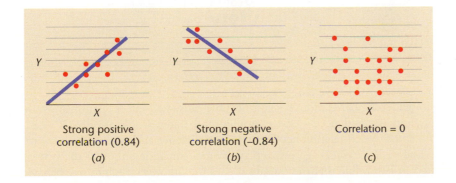

Strong positive correlation (0.84)
(a)

Strong negative correlation (−0.84)
(b)

Correlation = 0
(c)

around the world

PURPOSES OF CROSS-CULTURAL RESEARCH

2.2

When David, a European American child, was asked to identify the missing detail in a picture of a face with no mouth, he said, "The mouth." But Ari, an Asian immigrant child in Israel, said that the *body* was missing. Because art in his culture does not present a head as a complete picture, he thought the absence of a body was more important than the omission of "a mere detail like the mouth" (Anastasi, 1988, p. 360).

By looking at children from different cultural groups, researchers can learn in what ways development is universal (and thus intrinsic to the human condition) and in what ways it is culturally determined. For example, children everywhere learn to speak in the same sequence, advancing from cooing and babbling to single words and then to simple combinations of words. The words vary from culture to culture, but around the world toddlers put them together to form sentences similar in structure. Such findings suggest that the capacity for learning language is universal and inborn.

On the other hand, culture can influence early motor development. African babies, whose parents often prop them in a sitting position and bounce them on their feet, tend to sit and walk earlier than U.S. babies (Rogoff & Morelli, 1989). The society in which children grow up also influences the skills they learn. In the United States, children learn to read, write, and use computers. In rural Nepal, they learn how to drive water buffalo and find their way along mountain paths.

One important reason to conduct research among different cultural groups is to recognize biases in traditional Western theories and research that often go unquestioned until they are shown to be a product of cultural influences. Because much research in child development has focused on Western industrialized societies, typical development in these societies may be seen as the *norm*, or standard of behavior. Measuring against this norm leads to narrow—and often wrong—ideas about development. Pushed to its extreme, this belief can cause the development of children in other ethnic and cultural groups to be seen as deviant.

Barriers exist to our understanding of cultural differences, particularly those involving minority subcultures.

As with David and Ari in our opening example, a question or task may have different conceptual meanings for different cultural groups. Sometimes the barriers are linguistic. In a study of children's understanding of kinship relations among the Zinacanta people of Chiapas, Mexico (Greenfield & Childs, 1978), instead of asking "How many brothers do you have?" the researchers—knowing that the Zinacantas have separate terms for older and younger siblings—asked, "What is the name of your older brother?" Using the same question across cultures might have obscured, rather than revealed, cultural differences and similarities (Parke, 2004b).

Results of observational studies of ethnic or cultural groups may be affected by the ethnicity of the researchers. For example, in one study European American observers noted more conflict and restrictiveness in African American mother-daughter relationships than African American observers did (Gonzales, Cauce, & Mason, 1996).

In this book we discuss several influential theories developed from research in Western societies that do not hold up when tested on people from other cultures—theories about gender roles, abstract thinking, moral reasoning, and other aspects of human development. Throughout this book, we consistently look at children in cultures and subcultures other than the dominant one in the United States to show how closely development is tied to society and culture and to add to our understanding of normal development in many settings. In so doing, however, we need to keep in mind the pitfalls involved in cross-cultural comparisons.

what's your view

? Can you think of a situation in which you made an incorrect assumption about a person because you were unfamiliar with her or his cultural background?

Although strong correlations suggest possible cause-and-effect relationships, these are merely hypotheses and need to be examined and tested very critically. We cannot be sure from a positive correlation between televised violence and aggressiveness that watching televised violence *causes* aggressive play; we can conclude only that the two variables are related. It is possible that the causation goes the other way: Aggressive behavior may lead children to watch more violent programs. Or a third variable—perhaps an inborn predisposition toward aggressiveness or a violent living environment—may cause a child *both* to watch violent programs and to act aggressively. Similarly, we cannot be sure that schooling protects against dementia; it may be that another variable, such as socioeconomic status, might explain both lower levels of schooling and higher levels of dementia. The only way to show with certainty that one variable causes another is through experimentation—a method that, when studying human beings, is not always possible for practical or ethical reasons.

Experiments An **experiment** is a controlled procedure in which the experimenter manipulates variables to learn how one affects another. Scientific experiments must be conducted and reported in such a way that another experimenter can *replicate* them, that is, repeat them in exactly the same way with different participants to verify the results and conclusions.

Groups and Variables A common way to conduct an experiment is to divide the participants into two kinds of groups. An **experimental group** consists of people who are to be exposed to the experimental manipulation or *treatment*—the phenomenon the researcher wants to study. Afterward, the effect of the treatment will be measured one or more times to find out what changes, if any, it caused. A **control group** consists of people who are similar to the experimental group but do not receive the treatment or may receive a different treatment. An experiment may include one or more of each type of group. If the experimenter wants to compare the effects of different treatments (say, of two methods of teaching), the overall sample may be divided into *treatment groups*, each of which receives one of the treatments under study. To ensure objectivity, some experiments, particularly in medical research, use *double-blind* procedures, in which neither participants nor experimenters know who is receiving the treatment and who is instead receiving an inert *placebo*.

One team of researchers (Whitehurst et al., 1988) wanted to find out what effect *dialogic reading*, a special method of reading picture books to very young children, might have on their language and vocabulary skills. The researchers compared two groups of middle-class children ages 21 to 35 months. In the *experimental group*, the parents adopted the new read-aloud method (the *treatment*), which consisted of encouraging children's active participation and giving frequent, age-based feedback. In the *control group*, parents simply read aloud as they usually did. After 1 month, the children in the experimental group were 8½ months ahead of the control group in level of speech and 6 months ahead in vocabulary; after 10 months, the experimental group was still 6 months ahead of the controls. It is fair to conclude, then, that this read-aloud method improves language and vocabulary skills.

In this experiment, the type of reading approach was the *independent variable*, and the children's language skills were the *dependent variable*. An **independent variable** is something over which the experimenter has direct control. A **dependent variable** is something that may or may not change as a result of changes in the independent variable; in other words, it *depends* on the independent variable. In an experiment, a researcher manipulates the independent variable to see how changes in it will affect the dependent variable.

> Dependent variables are also known as "end measures" because their values are used to check whether you were right at the end of the study.

Random Assignment If an experiment finds a significant difference in the performance of the experimental and control groups, how do we know that the cause was the independent variable—in other words, that the conclusion is valid? For example, in the read-aloud study, how can we be sure that the reading method and not some other factor (such as intelligence) caused the difference in language development of the two

> The number of churches in a town is highly correlated with the number of liquor bottles found in the garbage cans of the town. But it would be inappropriate to conclude that religion drives people to drink. Rather a third variable—population size—explains this relationship. We always need to include critical thinking in our observations.

experiment
Rigorously controlled, replicable procedure in which the researcher manipulates variables to assess the effect of one on the other.

experimental group
In an experiment, the group receiving the treatment under study.

control group
In an experiment, a group of people, similar to those in the experimental group, who do not receive the treatment under study.

independent variable
In an experiment, the condition over which the experimenter has direct control.

dependent variable
In an experiment, the condition that may or may not change as a result of changes in the independent variable.

study the same person or group of people over time, sometimes years apart. They may measure a single characteristic, such as vocabulary size, intelligence, height, or aggressiveness, or they may look at a number of variables in concert to find relationships among them.

The Oakland Growth Study was a groundbreaking longitudinal study of the physical, intellectual, and social development of 167 fifth and sixth graders in Oakland, California. The study, discussed in Box 1.2 in Chapter 1, began at the outset of the Great Depression of the 1930s. The children were followed intensively until the age of 18 to 19 years, and then on 5 occasions during their adult years. The data collected included interviews, health assessments, personality inventories, and fact-sheet questionnaires. The researchers found that the societal disruption of the Great Depression seemed to negatively affect family processes and child development. Just as with cross-sectional designs, there is a caveat. Because individual people are studied over time, researchers have access to each person's specific individual trajectory. This is rich and valuable data because it can show each person's development over time. However, it might be the case that the results from one cohort might not apply to a study on a different cohort. For example, the results of a study on children born in the 1920s, such as the Oakland Growth Study, might not apply to children born in the 1990s. Therefore, care must be taken in the interpretation of longitudinal research too.

In attempting to determine the best research design, neither cross-sectional nor longitudinal design is superior. Rather, both designs have strengths and weaknesses (Table 2.6). For example, cross-sectional design is fast—we don't have to wait 30 years for results. This also makes it a more economical choice. Moreover, because participants are assessed only once, we don't have to consider *attrition* (people dropping out of the study) or repeated testing (which can produce practice effects). But, as cross-sectional design uses group averages, this can obscure individual differences and trajectories. More important, the results can be affected by the differing experiences of people born at different times as previously explained.

Longitudinal research shows a different and complementary set of strengths and weaknesses. Because the same people are studied repeatedly over time, researchers can track individual patterns of continuity and change. This does make longitudinal studies more time-consuming and expensive than cross-sectional studies. In addition, repeated testing of participants can result in practice effects. For example, your performance on an intelligence test might get better over time from practice rather than from any

TABLE 2.6 Cross-Sectional, Longitudinal, and Sequential Research			
Type of Study	**Procedure**	**Advantages**	**Disadvantages**
Cross-sectional	Data are collected on people of different ages at the same time.	Can show similarities and differences among age groups; speedy, economical; presents no problem of attrition or repeated testing.	Cannot establish age effects; masks individual differences; can be confounded by cohort effects.
Longitudinal	Data are collected on same person or persons over a period of time.	Can show age-related change or continuity; avoids confounding age with cohort effects.	Is time-consuming, expensive; presents problems of attrition, bias in sample, and effects of repeated testing; results may be valid only for cohort tested or sample studied.
Sequential	Data are collected on successive cross-sectional or longitudinal samples.	Can avoid drawbacks of both cross-sectional and longitudinal designs.	Requires large amount of time and effort and analysis of very complex data.

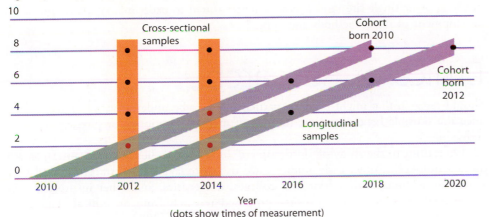

Age of participants (years)

FIGURE 2.5

A Sequential Design

Two successive cross-sectional groups of 2-, 4-, 6-, and 8-year-olds are tested in 2012 and 2014. Also, a longitudinal study of a group of children first measured in 2012, when they were 2 years old, is followed by a similar longitudinal study of another group of children who were 2 years old in 2014.

increase in intelligence. Attrition can also be problematic in longitudinal research as it tends to be nonrandom, which can introduce a positive bias to the study: Those who stay with the study tend to be above average in intelligence and socioeconomic status and those who drop out tend to have more chaotic lives and worse overall outcomes. Moreover, practical issues, such as turnover in research personnel, loss of funding, or the development of new measures or methodologies, can introduce potential problems with data collection.

With the design of sequential studies researchers are attempting to overcome the drawbacks of longitudinal and cross-sectional design. Sequential designs track people of different ages (like cross-sectional designs) over time (like longitudinal designs). Another variation of this involves a sequence of longitudinal studies running concurrently but starting in waves one after the other.

The combination of cross-sectional and longitudinal designs (as shown in Figure 2.5) allows researchers to separate age-related changes from cohort effects, and provides a more complete picture of development than would be possible with either design alone. The major drawbacks of sequential studies relate to time, effort, and complexity. Sequential designs require large numbers of participants and the collection and analysis of huge amounts of data over a period of years. Interpreting their findings and conclusions can demand a high degree of sophistication.

COLLABORATIVE RESEARCH

Researchers use various means to share and pool data. One is the archiving of data sets for use by other researchers. Another is *meta-analysis*, which provides a systematic overview of the research on a topic through statistical analysis of the combined findings of multiple studies. Generally, meta-analyses are used for controversial findings and are an attempt to reconcile disparities across a large number of studies. A problem with meta-analysis is that the designs and methodologies of the studies may be inconsistent, making interpretation of the results less than precise.

Still another increasingly common approach is collaborative research by multiple researchers at multiple sites, sometimes with government or foundation funding. This collaborative model can trace development within a population on a very broad scale. It makes possible larger, more representative samples; makes it easier to carry out longitudinal studies that might otherwise be hampered by researcher attrition and burnout; and permits a blending of theoretical perspectives (Parke, 2004b). An example of collaborative research is the National Institute of Child Health and Human Development (NICHD) Study of Early Child Care, discussed in Chapter 8.

A difficulty with the collaborative model is the need for group consensus on all aspects of the research, from the initial design to writing the report. Achieving consensus

Attrition is not random; it is almost always biased in some fashion. For example, the people most likely to drop out of a study are those with the most chaotic lifestyles. The people still in the study at its conclusion might look really good, but it could be because the people who were not doing well are gone.

checkpoint
can you . . .

▷ List advantages and disadvantages of longitudinal, cross-sectional, and sequential research?

▷ Discuss advantages and disadvantages of collaborative research?

can be cumbersome and may require difficult compromises. The more flexible single-investigator or single-site model may be better suited to experimental work and to the development of novel methods and approaches.

guidepost

4 What ethical problems may arise in research on children?

Ethics of Research

Should research that might harm its participants ever be undertaken? How can we balance the possible benefits against the risk of mental, emotional, or physical injury to individuals?

Objections to the study of "Little Albert" (described earlier in this chapter), as well as to a number of other early studies, gave rise to today's more stringent ethical standards. Institutional review boards at colleges, universities, and other institutions that receive federal funding must review proposed research from an ethical standpoint. Guidelines of the American Psychological Association (2002) cover such issues as *informed consent* (consent freely given with full knowledge of what the research entails), *avoidance of deception*, *protection of participants* from *harm and loss of dignity*, guarantees of *privacy and confidentiality*, the *right to decline or withdraw* from an experiment at any time, and the responsibility of investigators to *correct any undesirable effects*, such as anxiety or shame.

In resolving ethical dilemmas, researchers should be guided by three principles. The first is beneficence, which is the obligation to maximize potential benefits to participants and to minimize potential harm. For example, suppose you are a researcher studying the effect of failure on self-esteem. If you are going to deceive some of your participants by telling them they failed on a laboratory task, what steps will you take to mitigate any potential harm you might cause to them? The second principle is respect for participants' autonomy and protection of those who are unable to exercise their own judgment. For example, if you are conducting research with toddlers, and a 2-year-old refuses to participate, should you force the child to participate? What is the appropriate action in this case? The third principle is justice, which, in this case, is the inclusion of diverse groups together with sensitivity to any special impact the research may have on them. For example, it may be important that your study includes an appropriate and representative selection of diverse people. If this is the case, have you developed culturally appropriate materials and methods to use?

Developmental psychologists must be particularly careful as their research frequently involves vulnerable individuals, such as infants or children. In response, the Society for Research in Child Development (2007) has developed standards for age-appropriate treatment of children in research, covering such principles as avoidance of physical or psychological harm, obtaining the child's assent as well as a parent's or guardian's informed consent, and responsibility to follow up on any information that could jeopardize the child's well-being. For example, infants' and very young children's ability to cope with the stress of the research situation may hinge on the presence of a parent or trusted caregiver, a familiar setting and procedure, and familiar objects.

Let's look more closely at a few specific ethical considerations that can present problems.

RIGHT TO INFORMED CONSENT

Informed consent exists when participants voluntarily agree to be in a study, are competent to give consent, are aware of the risks as well as the potential benefits, and are not being exploited. The National Commission for the Protection of Human Subjects of Biomedical and Behavioral Research (1978) recommends that children age 7 or over be asked to give their consent to take part in research and that any children's objections should be overruled only if the research promises direct benefit to the child.

However, some ethicists argue that young children cannot give meaningful, voluntary *consent* because they cannot fully understand what is involved. They can merely

TABLE 2.7	Developmental Considerations in Children's Participation in Research	
Younger Children Are Especially Vulnerable to	**Older Children Are Especially Vulnerable to**
Stressful or unfamiliar situations	Apparent approval or disapproval by the researcher
Absence of parent or caregiver	Sense of failure, threats to self-esteem
Situations arousing inappropriate shame, guilt, or embarrassment	Expressed or implied comparisons with others
Coercion, deception, and unreasonable demands	Implied racial, ethnic, or socioeconomic biases
	Threats to privacy

Source: Based on Thompson, 1990.

assent, that is, agree to participate. Young children are less capable than adults of understanding what they are getting into and of making an informed decision on whether to participate. The usual procedure, therefore, when children under age 18 are involved, is to ask the parents or legal guardians and sometimes school personnel to give consent. For other issues about consent to consider, see Table 2.7 (Thompson, 1990).

AVOIDANCE OF DECEPTION

Can informed consent exist if participants are deceived about the nature or purpose of a study or about the procedures to which they will be subjected? Suppose that children are told they are trying out a new game when they are actually being tested on their reactions to success or failure? Experiments like this have added to our knowledge but at the cost of the participants' right to know what they were getting involved in.

Ethical guidelines call for withholding information *only* when it is essential to the study; and then investigators should avoid methods that could cause pain, anxiety, or harm. Participants should be debriefed afterward to let them know the true nature of the study and why deception was necessary and to make sure they have not suffered as a result.

RIGHT TO SELF-ESTEEM

Some studies have a built-in *failure factor*. Researchers give harder and harder tasks until the participant is unable to do them. Might this inevitable failure affect a participant's self-worth? Similarly, when researchers publish findings that middle-class children are academically superior to poor children, unintentional harm may be done to some participants' self-esteem. Even if such studies may lead to beneficial interventions for poor children, they also may affect teachers' expectations and students' performance.

RIGHT TO PRIVACY AND CONFIDENTIALITY

Not all ethical issues have clear answers; some hinge on researchers' judgment and scruples. In this gray area are issues having to do with privacy and with protecting the confidentiality of personal information that participants may reveal in interviews or questionnaires.

What if, during the course of research, an investigator suspects that a child may have a learning disability or some other treatable condition? Is the researcher obliged to share such information with the parents or guardians or to recommend services that may help, when sharing the information might contaminate the research findings? Such

what's your view

Should informed consent involve telling participants about what your hypotheses for your research are? Why or why not?

checkpoint
can you . . .

▷ Identify three principles that should govern inclusion of participants in research?

▷ Discuss four rights of research participants?

▷ Give examples of how children's developmental needs can be considered in research?

a decision should not be made lightly; sharing information of uncertain validity might create damaging misconceptions about a child. However, researchers need to know, and inform participants of, their legal responsibility to report abuse or neglect or any other illegal activity of which they become aware.

The final word in these introductory chapters is that this entire book is far from the final word. Although we have tried to incorporate the most important and up-to-date information about how children develop, developmental scientists are constantly learning more. As you read this book, you are certain to come up with questions. By thinking about them and perhaps eventually conducting research to find answers, it is possible that you, now embarking on the study of child development, will someday add to our knowledge about the interesting species to which we all belong.

summary and key terms

guidepost 1
Basic Theoretical Issues

What purposes do theories serve, and what are two basic issues on which developmental theorists differ?

- A theory is used to organize and explain data and generate hypotheses that can be tested by research.
- Developmental theories differ on two basic issues: the active or reactive character of development and the existence of stages of development.
- Two contrasting models of development are the mechanistic model and the organismic model. Mechanistic theories deal with quantitative change; organismic theories, with qualitative change.

theory (24)
hypotheses (24)
mechanistic model (25)
organismic model (26)
quantitative change (26)
qualitative change (26)

guidepost 2
Theoretical Perspectives

What are five theoretical perspectives on child development, and what are some theories that are representative of each?

- The psychoanalytic perspective sees development as motivated by unconscious emotional drives and conflicts. Leading examples are Freud's and Erikson's theories.

psychoanalytic perspective (27)
psychosexual development (29)
psychosocial development (31)

- The learning perspective views development as a result of learning based on experience. Leading examples are Watson's and Skinner's behaviorism and Bandura's social learning (social cognitive) theory.

learning perspective (31)
behaviorism (31)
classical conditioning (32)
operant conditioning (32)
reinforcement (32)
punishment (32)
social learning theory (33)
reciprocal determinism (33)
observational learning (33)
self-efficacy (33)

- The cognitive perspective is concerned with thought processes. Leading examples are Piaget's cognitive-stage theory, Vygotsky's sociocultural theory, the information-processing approach, and neo-Piagetian theories.

cognitive perspective (33)
cognitive-stage theory (33)
organization (34)
schemes (34)
adaptation (34)
assimilation (34)
accommodation (34)
equilibration (34)
sociocultural theory (35)
zone of proximal development (ZPD) (35)
scaffolding (35)
information-processing approach (35)

- The contextual perspective focuses on interaction between the individual and the social context. A leading example is Bronfenbrenner's bioecological theory, although Vygotsky's sociocultural theory also can be considered a contextual approach.

  contextual perspective (36)

  bioecological theory (36)

  microsystem (36)

  mesosystem (37)

  exosystem (37)

  macrosystem (37)

  chronosystem (37)

- The evolutionary/sociobiological perspective is based in part on Darwin's theory of evolution and describes adaptive behaviors that promote survival. A leading example is Bowlby's attachment theory.

  evolutionary/sociobiological perspective (38)

  ethology (38)

  evolutionary psychology (38)

guidepost ❸ Research Methods

How do developmental scientists study children, and what are the advantages and disadvantages of each research method?

- Research can be quantitative, qualitative, or both.
- To arrive at sound conclusions, researchers use the scientific method.
- Random selection of a research sample can provide generalizability.

  quantitative research (41)

  scientific method (41)

  qualitative research (41)

  sample (42)

  random selection (43)

- Three forms of data collection are self-reports, observation, and behavioral or performance measures.

  naturalistic observation (44)

  laboratory observation (44)

  operational definition (45)

  cognitive neuroscience (45)

- Two qualitative designs used in developmental research are the case study and ethnographic study. Cross-cultural research can indicate whether certain aspects of development are universal or culturally influenced.

- Two quantitative designs are the correlational study and experiment. Only experiments can firmly establish causal relationships.

  case study (46)

  ethnographic study (47)

  participant observation (47)

  correlational study (47)

  experiment (49)

- Experiments must be rigorously controlled so as to be valid and replicable. Random assignment of participants can ensure validity.

- Laboratory experiments are easiest to control and replicate, but findings of field experiments may be more generalizable. Natural experiments may be useful in situations in which true experiments would be impractical or unethical.

  experimental group (49)

  control group (49)

  independent variable (49)

  dependent variable (49)

  random assignment (50)

- The two most common designs used to study age-related development are longitudinal and cross-sectional. Cross-sectional studies compare age groups; longitudinal studies describe continuity or change in the same participants. The sequential study is intended to overcome the weaknesses of the other two designs but can be expensive and time-consuming.

  cross-sectional study (51)

  longitudinal study (51)

  sequential study (51)

guidepost ❹ Ethics of Research

What ethical problems may arise in research on children?

- Researchers seek to resolve ethical issues on the basis of principles of beneficence, respect, and justice.

- Ethical issues in research on child development involve the rights of participants to informed consent, avoidance of deception, protection from harm and loss of dignity or self-esteem, and guarantees of privacy and confidentiality.

- Standards for protecting children used in research cover such points as parental informed consent and avoidance of harm or jeopardy to the child's well-being.

chapter **3**

did you know?

▷ "Identical" twins may not be exactly identical?

▷ More than 1,000 genetic tests are available to help physicians clarify diagnoses, select appropriate treatments, and identify people at high risk for certain preventable conditions?

▷ Even on characteristics with a strong hereditary basis, environment can have a substantial impact?

We begin this chapter by examining how a life is conceived. We consider the mechanisms and patterns of heredity—the inherited factors that affect development—and how genetic counseling can help couples make the decision whether to become parents. We look at how heredity and environment work together and how their effects on development can be understood.

outline

did you know

Forming a New Life: Conception, Heredity, and Environment

Genes and family may determine the foundation of the house, but time and place determine its form.

—Jerome Kagan, as quoted in *Childhood*, Robert H. Wozniak (1991)

1. How does conception normally occur, and how have beliefs about conception changed?

2. What causes infertility, and what are alternative ways of becoming parents?

3. What genetic mechanisms determine sex, physical appearance, and other characteristics?

4. How are birth defects and disorders transmitted?

5. How do scientists study the relative influences of heredity and environment, and how do heredity and environment work together?

6. What roles do heredity and environment play in physical health, intelligence, and personality?

guidepost 1 How does conception normally occur, and how have beliefs about conception changed?

Conceiving a New Life

The timing and circumstances of parenthood can have vast consequences for a child. Whether a pregnancy is welcomed or unwanted, whether it comes about through normal or extraordinary means, whether the parents are married or unmarried or of the same sex or different sexes, and how old the parents are when a child is born or adopted all are *microsystem* issues identified in Bronfenbrenner's bioecological approach, discussed in Chapter 2. Whether the culture encourages large or small families, whether it values one sex over the other, and how much it supports families with children are *macrosystem* issues likely to influence the child's development. We'll explore such contextual issues throughout this book. For now, let's look at conception and then at options for couples unable to conceive normally.

CHANGING THEORIES OF CONCEPTION*

Most adults, and even most children in industrialized countries, have a reasonably accurate idea of where babies come from. However, it is also the case that folk beliefs regarding the origin of new life have been common throughout history. For example, the belief that children came from wells, springs, or rocks was common in north and central Europe as late as the beginning of the twentieth century. Conception was believed to be influenced by cosmic forces. A baby conceived under a new moon would be a boy; during the moon's last quarter, a girl (Gélis, 1991). Even today, beliefs about spiritual influences on conception persist in many traditional societies. Among the Warlpiri people of Australia, for example, a baby conceived in a place associated with a particular spirit is believed to have been given life by that spirit (DeLoache & Gottlieb, 2000). And even in modern Western countries such as the United States, beliefs about how personality might be shaped by the time of year in which children are born are relatively common.

Theories about conception date back to ancient times. The Greek physician Hippocrates, known as the father of medicine, held that a fetus results from the joining of male and female seeds. The philosopher Aristotle had a contrary view that "the woman functions only as a receptacle, the child being formed exclusively by means of the sperm" (Fontanel & d'Harcourt, 1997, p. 10). According to Aristotle, the production

*Unless otherwise referenced, this discussion is based on Eccles (1982) and Fontanel and d'Harcourt (1997).

of male babies was in the natural order of things; a female came about only if development was disturbed.

Between the seventeenth and nineteenth centuries, a debate raged between two schools of biological thought. Harking back to Aristotle, the *animalculists* (so named because the male sperm were then called *animalcules*) claimed that fully formed "little people" were contained in the heads of sperm, ready to grow when deposited in the nurturing environment of the womb. The *ovists*, inspired by the work of the English physician William Harvey, held an opposite but equally incorrect view: that a female's ovaries contained tiny, already formed humans whose growth was activated by the male's sperm. Finally, in the late eighteenth century, the German-born anatomist Kaspar Friedrich Wolff supported the theory of a gradual building up of structures. His research focused on the idea that groups of cells that were initially unspecialized differentiated into various tissues, organs, and systems. This view was later supported by the French pathologist Xavier Bichat.

HOW FERTILIZATION TAKES PLACE

Tania wanted to have a baby. She carefully watched the calendar, counting the days after each menstrual period to take advantage of her "fertile window," the time during which conception is possible. When after 2 months Tania had not yet achieved her pregnancy, she wondered what possibly might have gone wrong. What Tania didn't realize is that although a woman is usually fertile between the 6th and 21st days of the menstrual cycle, the timing of the fertile window can be highly unpredictable (Wilcox, Dunson, & Baird, 2000). This means that although conception is far more likely at certain times, she may be able to conceive at any time during the month. Concurrently, while conception is more likely during certain parts of the month, it may not always occur during that time.

Fertilization, or conception, is the process by which sperm and ovum—the male and female gametes, or sex cells—combine to create a single cell called a **zygote**, which then duplicates itself again and again by cell division to produce all the cells that make up a baby. However, conception is not as simple as it sounds. Several independent events need to coincide to conceive a child. And, as we discuss in the next chapter, not all conceptions end in birth.

At birth, a girl is believed to have about 2 million immature ova in her two ovaries, each ovum in its own small sac, or follicle. In a sexually mature woman, ovulation—rupture of a mature follicle in either ovary and expulsion of its ovum—occurs about once every 28 days until menopause. The ovum is swept along through one of the fallopian tubes by tiny hair cells, called cilia, toward the uterus, or womb.

Sperm are produced in the testicles (testes), or reproductive glands, of a mature male at a rate of several hundred million a day and are ejaculated in the semen at sexual climax. Deposited in the vagina, they try to swim through the cervix (the opening of the uterus) and into the fallopian tubes, but only a tiny fraction make it that far. As we will see, which sperm meets which ovum has tremendous implications for the new person.

Fertilization normally occurs while the ovum is passing through the fallopian tube. If fertilization does not occur, the ovum and any sperm cells in the woman's body die. The sperm are absorbed by the woman's white blood cells, and the ovum passes through the uterus and exits through the vagina.

Infertility

An estimated 7 percent of U.S. couples experience **infertility**, which is defined as an inability to conceive a baby after 12 months of trying (Centers for Disease Control and Prevention [CDC], 2005a; Wright, Chang, Jeng, & Macaluso, 2006). Women's fertility begins to decline in the late 20s, with substantial decreases during the 30s. Men's fertility is less affected by age but declines significantly by the late 30s (Dunson, Colombo, & Baird, 2002).

fertilization
Union of sperm and ovum to produce a zygote; also called *conception*.

zygote
One-celled organism resulting from fertilization.

infertility
Inability to conceive after 12 months of trying.

checkpoint
can **you** . . .

▷ Compare folk, historic, and scientific views of conception?

▷ Explain how and when fertilization normally takes place?

What causes infertility, and what are alternative ways of becoming parents?

Infertility can burden a marriage emotionally. Partners may become frustrated and angry with themselves and each other and may feel empty, worthless, and depressed (Abbey, Andrews, & Halman, 1992; Jones & Toner, 1993). However, only when infertility leads to permanent, involuntary childlessness is it likely to be associated with long-term psychological distress (McQuillan, Greil, White, & Jacob, 2003).

Infertility is far from a new concern. To enhance fertility, ancient doctors advised men to eat fennel, and women to drink the saliva of lambs and wear necklaces of earthworms. It was recommended that, after intercourse, a woman lie flat with her legs crossed and "avoid becoming angry" (Fontanel & d'Harcourt, 1997, p. 10). By the Renaissance, the list of foods recommended to spur conception ranged from squabs and sparrows to cocks' combs and bull's genitals. In the early seventeenth century, Louise Bourgeois, midwife to Marie de Médicis, the queen of France, advocated bathing the vagina with chamomile, mallow, marjoram, and catmint boiled in white wine.

CAUSES OF INFERTILITY

Today we know that the most common cause of infertility in men is production of too few or insufficiently motile sperm. Although only one sperm is needed to fertilize an ovum, a sperm count lower than 60 to 200 million per ejaculation makes conception unlikely. In some instances an ejaculatory duct may be blocked, preventing the exit of sperm, or sperm may be unable to swim well enough to reach the cervix. Some cases of male infertility seem to have a genetic basis. For example, some men appear to have gene mutations or chromosome deletions affecting the quality and quantity of sperm they produce (Krausz, 2010; Phillips, 1998).

In a woman, common causes of infertility include the failure to produce ova or to produce normal ova; mucus in the cervix, which might prevent sperm from penetrating it; or a disease of the uterine lining, which might prevent implantation of the fertilized ovum. A major cause of declining fertility in women after age 30 is deterioration in the quality of ova (Broekmans, Soules, & Fauser, 2009). However, the most common cause is blockage of the fallopian tubes, preventing ova from reaching the uterus. In about half of these cases, the tubes are blocked by scar tissue from sexually transmitted diseases (Rhoton-Vlasak, 2000). Table 3.1 lists major causes and treatments of male and female infertility.

TREATMENTS FOR INFERTILITY

Sometimes hormone treatment, drug therapy, or surgery may correct the problem. However, these solutions come at a cost. Fertility drugs given to women having difficulty getting pregnant increase the likelihood of multiple, high-risk births (Box 3.1). Men with low-quality sperm may take daily supplements of coenzyme Q10 to increase their sperm motility (Balercia et al., 2004). However, men increase their risk of producing sperm with chromosomal abnormalities (Levron et al., 1998) when using supplements such as these.

Unless there is a known cause for failure to conceive, the chances of success after 18 months to 2 years are high (Dunson, 2002). For couples struggling with infertility, science today offers several alternative ways to parenthood.

ALTERNATIVE WAYS TO PARENTHOOD: ASSISTED REPRODUCTIVE TECHNOLOGY

Louise Brown, the world's first documented "test-tube baby," was born July 25, 1978, in Oldham, England. She had been conceived by the then-experimental method of *in vitro fertilization* (IVF), when Patrick Steptoe, a gynecologist, and Robert Edwards, a physiologist at Cambridge University, placed a ripe ovum from her mother, Lesley Brown, in a shallow glass dish with fluid containing sperm from her father, John Brown. After 2 days, during which the resulting single-celled organism multiplied to eight cells, the embryo was implanted in Lesley's womb. While the outcome of this experiment was a single baby,

TABLE 3.1 Common Causes of Infertility in Men and Women

Condition	Explanations	Treatments
MALE CAUSES		
Abnormal sperm production or function	Abnormal shape or motility of sperm. Low or no sperm production. Undescended testicles. Varicose veins in the scrotum. Testosterone deficiency. Klinefelter's syndrome. Sexually transmitted diseases.	Fertility drugs. Surgery to repair varicose veins or other obstructions. Artificial insemination with donor sperm. Injecting sperm directly into ovum.
Impaired delivery of sperm into vagina	*Sexual problems*, including erectile dysfunction, premature ejaculation, and painful intercourse. *Physical problems*, including failure to produce semen, blockage of ejaculatory ducts, other structural defects, and antibodies that weaken or disable sperm.	*Sexual problems* can be treated with medication or behavioral therapy. *Physical problems* may require surgery. Assisted reproduction techniques may include in vitro fertilization, electrical stimulation of ejaculation, or surgical retrieval of sperm (if blockage is present).
Age	Gradual decline in fertility, commonly in men older than 35.	
General health and lifestyle issues	Emotional stress, malnutrition, obesity, alcohol and drugs, tobacco smoking, cancer treatments, severe injury, surgery, and other medical conditions may impair sperm production.	Correct health and lifestyle problems if possible.
Environmental exposure	Overexposure to heat (in saunas or hot tubs), toxins, and certain chemicals, such as pesticides, lead, and chemical solvents.	Avoid unhealthy exposures.
FEMALE CAUSES		
Fallopian tube damage or blockage	*Most frequent cause:* inflammation of the fallopian tube due to chlamydia, a sexually transmitted disease; tubal damage with scarring may result in an ectopic pregnancy, in which the fertilized egg is unable to pass through the fallopian tube and implant in the uterus. *Other causes:* benign uterine fibroid tumors and pelvic adhesions (bands of scar tissue) formed after pelvic infections, appendicitis, or pelvic or abdominal surgery.	Laparoscopic surgery to repair or open fallopian tubes; in vitro fertilization.
Endometriosis	Uterine tissue implanted outside the uterus can lead to scarring and inflammation, which may prevent transfer of ovum to fallopian tube and cause pelvic pain. Ovarian cysts.	Ovulation therapy (medication to stimulate ovulation) or in vitro fertilization.
Ovulation disorders	Any condition that prevents the release of a mature ovum from the ovary. Specific causes include hormonal deficiencies, injury to hypothalamus or pituitary gland, pituitary tumors, excessive exercise, and eating disorders.	Fertility drugs.
Polycystic ovary syndrome	Increase in production of the hormone androgen can prevent production of mature ovum. Common symptoms are absent or infrequent menstruation; dark or thick hair on chin, upper lip, or abdomen; acne; and oily skin.	Fertility drugs, particularly clomiphene.
Early menopause	Ovarian failure before age 35 may be associated with autoimmune disease, hypothyroidism (too little thyroid hormone), radiation or chemotherapy for cancer treatment, or tobacco smoking.	In vitro fertilization with donated ova.

Source: Based on Mayo Clinic, 2013. Retrieved March 15, 2013, from www.mayoclinic.com/health/infertility/DS00310/DSECTION=causes

the everyday world

MULTIPLE BIRTHS

3.1

In early 2009 Nadya Suleman gave birth to octuplets. They are only the second full set of octuplets to be born alive in the United States and, one week after their birth, surpassed the worldwide survival rate set by the Chukwu octuplets in 1998. The six boys and two girls were born 9 weeks prematurely and include two sets of identical twins (Mohajer, 2009a).

Both the Suleman and the Chukwu octuplets were the result of in virto fertilization in which multiple embryos were implanted in the mother's uterus. However, multiple births occur naturally as well. While twins are the most common variation, triplets, quadruplets, and other multiple births are possible.

Dizygotic, or *fraternal*, twins are the result of two separate eggs being fertilized by two different sperm to form two unique individuals. Genetically, they are like siblings who inhabit the same womb at the same time, and they can be the same or different sex. Dizygotic twins tend to run in families and are the result of multiple eggs being released at one time. This tendency may have a genetic basis and seems to be passed down from a woman's mother (Martin & Montgomery, 2002; National Center for Health Statistics [NCHS], 1999). Thus, when dizygotic twins skip generations, it is normally because a mother of dizygotic twins has only sons to whom she cannot pass on the tendency (NCHS, 1999).

Monozygotic twins are the result of a far different process. They result from the cleaving of one fertilized egg and, thus, are generally genetically identical. They can still differ outwardly, however, given that people are the result of the interaction between genes and environmental influences and not just a product of genetics. And, even if twins are in the same womb or are raised in the same family, there are different environmental experiences that affect each of them. For example, in one condition that affects only monozygotic twins (twin-to-twin transfusion syndrome), the blood vessels of the placenta form abnormally, and the placenta is shared unequally between the twins. Thus, one twin receives a smaller share of nutrients than does the other. While mortality is high, if the twins both survive, they appear very different at birth despite being genetically identical. Generally, one twin is significantly larger than the other.

Moreover, environmental differences add up over time. The differences between identical twins generally magnify as twins grow older, especially if they live apart. So, for example, 3-year-old monozygotic twins appear more similar than 30-year-old monozygotic twins. These differences may result from chemical modifications in a person's genome shortly after conception or may be due to later experiences or environmental factors, such as exposure to smoke or other pollutants (Fraga et al., 2005). This process, known as *epigenesis*, is discussed later in this chapter.

Doctors recently identified a rare third type of twins, called *semi-identical*—the result of two sperm cells fusing with a single ovum which then splits into two separate zygotes. Only one case of this has been identified thus far, and doctors believe that while possible, the chances of it occurring again are slim. The identified twins are more genetically similar than dizygotic twins (because they share all their maternal genetic material) but less similar than monozygotic twins (because they don't share all the same paternal genetic material) (Souter et al., 2007).

The rate of monozygotic twins (about 4 per 1,000 live births) is constant at all times and places, but the rate of dizygotic twins, the more common type, varies (Martin & Montgomery, 2002; NCHS, 1999). For example, West African and African American women are more likely to have dizygotic twins than Caucasian women, who, in turn, are more likely to have them than Chinese or Japanese women (Martin & Montgomery, 2002).

The incidence of multiple births in the United States has grown rapidly since 1980. By 2006 the twin birthrate had risen by 70 percent, from 18.9 to 32.1 twins per 1,000 live births. However, the birthrate for triplets and higher multiples, which had quadrupled during the 1980s and 1990s, has since taken a 21 percent downturn (Martin et al., 2009). Two related factors in the rise in multiple births are (1) the trend toward delayed childbearing and (2) the increased use of fertility drugs, which spur ovulation, and of assisted reproductive techniques such as in vitro fertilization, which tend to be used by older women (Martin et al., 2009).

The upsurge in multiple births is troubling because such births are associated with increased risks: complications of pregnancy, premature delivery, low-birth-weight infants, and disability or death of an infant (Hoyert, Mathews, Menacker, Strobino, & Guyer, 2006; Jain, Missmer, & Hornstein, 2004; Martin et al., 2009; Wright, Schieve, Reynolds, & Jeng, 2003). The families often suffer as well. Among 249 mothers who had given birth with the help of assisted reproductive technology and were surveyed when their children were between 1 and 4 years old, each additional multiple birth child increased the risk of maternal depression, more than doubled the chances of a lower

Continued

quality of life and a sense of social stigma, and quadrupled the likelihood of difficulty meeting basic material needs (Ellison et al., 2005). In response to such concerns, the American Society of Reproductive Medicine recommends limitations on artificial procedures involving three or more embryos, and these guidelines may account for the recent decrease in triplets and higher multiple births (Practice Committee, 2006).

▷ **Would you want to have twins or higher multiples?**

▷ **If you are a twin or higher multiple, how does that experience affect you?**

▷ **If you learned that you were bearing octuplets, what would you do?**

3.1

the consequences of this groundbreaking work extended far outside the confines of this one family. Steptoe and Edwards's work gave birth to a new branch of medicine: **assisted reproductive technology (ART)**, or conception through artificial means (International Committee for Monitoring Assisted Reproductive Technologies [ICMART], 2006; "Louise Brown," 1984; "Test-Tube Baby," 1978; "The First Test-Tube Baby," 1978).

Since Louise Brown's birth, more than 3 million children worldwide have been conceived through ART (ICMART, 2006; Reaney, 2006). In 2005, U.S. women delivered more than 52,000 babies with technological help, representing about 1 percent of all babies born in the United States in that year (Wright, Chang, Jeng, & Macaluso, 2008).

With the in vitro method, the most common assisted reproductive procedure and the one Lesley Brown used, a woman first receives fertility drugs to stimulate the production of multiple ova. Then the ova are surgically removed, fertilized in a laboratory dish, and implanted in the woman's uterus. These implanted ova are less likely to become established in the womb and more likely to result in miscarriage. In an attempt to increase the odds of a successful pregnancy, it is common to transplant multiple ova, but this procedure also increases the likelihood of multiple, usually premature births. Because women generally release multiple ova after receiving fertility drugs, women are cautioned against engaging in sexual activity before removal of the eggs. If women do have sex, they risk the fertilization and implantation of multiple eggs. In 2006, nearly half (48 percent) of infants born through ART were twins or higher multiples (Saswati et al., 2009). As we discuss in Box 3.1, births of multiples come concurrent with increased risk.

A newer technique, *in vitro maturation* (IVM) is performed earlier in the monthly cycle, when egg follicles are developing. Harvesting a large number of follicles before ovulation is complete and then allowing them to mature in the laboratory can make hormone injections unnecessary and thus diminish the likelihood of multiple births (Duenwald, 2003). However, if multiple fertilized ova are transplanted, then multiple births remain probable.

IVF also addresses severe male infertility. A single sperm can be injected into the ovum—a technique called *intracytoplasmic sperm injection* (ICSI). This procedure is now used in the majority of IVF cycles (Van Voorhis, 2007). Singleton infants conceived through IVF or ICSI are 2 to 4 times more likely than naturally conceived infants to have certain types of heart defects, cleft lip, and gastrointestinal defects although the incidence of such defects is still quite small (Reefhuis et al., 2008).

Artificial insemination—injection of sperm into a woman's vagina, cervix, or uterus— can be used to facilitate conception if a man has a low sperm count, allowing a couple to produce their own biological offspring. If the man is infertile, a couple may choose *artificial insemination by a donor* (AID). If the woman has no explainable cause of infertility, the chances of success can be greatly increased by stimulating her ovaries to produce excess ova and injecting semen directly in the uterus (Guzick et al., 1999). Although success rates have improved (Duenwald, 2003), only 35 percent of women who attempted assisted reproduction in 2005 had live births (Wright et al., 2008). This statistic speaks more to issues related to maternal age and ova quality, however, than it does for the

assisted reproductive technology (ART)
Methods used to achieve conception through artificial means.

ability of science to aid conception as the likelihood of success with IVF using a mother's own ova drops precipitously as a woman advances in age (Van Voorhis, 2007).

A woman who is producing poor-quality ova or who has had her ovaries removed may try *ovum transfer*. In this procedure, an ovum, or *donor egg*, provided by a fertile younger woman is fertilized in the laboratory and implanted in the prospective mother's uterus. IVF using donor eggs tends to be highly successful (Van Voorhis, 2007). Alternatively, the ovum can be fertilized in the donor's body by artificial insemination. The embryo is retrieved from the donor and inserted into the recipient's uterus. Two other techniques with relatively higher success rates are *gamete intrafallopian transfer* (GIFT) and *zygote intrafallopian transfer* (ZIFT), in which either the egg and sperm or the fertilized egg are inserted in the fallopian tube (Schieve et al., 2002; Society for Assisted Reproductive Technology, 1993, 2002).

Assisted reproduction can result in a tangled web of legal, ethical, and psychological dilemmas (ISLAT Working Group, 1998; Schwartz, 2003). Who should have access to these methods? Should the children know about their parentage? Should genetic tests be performed on prospective donors and surrogates? When IVF results in multiple fertilized ova, should some be discarded so as to improve the chances of health for the survivors? What should be done with any unused embryos?

Dr. Michael Kamrava, the fertility doctor who helped Nadya Suleman (see Box 3.1) become pregnant, came under investigation by the state medical board when it was learned that Suleman already had six children ages 2 to 7 from previous fertility treatments and that she had had Dr. Kamrava implant six leftover embryos in her uterus (two of which evidently split) and refused to abort any of them. There also were questions about the unemployed single mother's ability to support and care for 14 children (Adams, 2009; Dillon, 2009; Mohajer, 2009a, 2009b, 2009c). Although this is an extreme example of potential ethical concerns related to ART, it is nonetheless true that such events raise very serious questions about ethics and legal oversight that have not yet been addressed. At least two states, Missouri and Georgia, are considering legislation to limit the number of embryos fertility clinics can implant.

The issues multiply when a *surrogate mother* is involved (Schwartz, 2003). The surrogate, a fertile woman, is impregnated by the prospective father, usually by artificial insemination. She agrees to carry the baby to term and give it to the father and his partner. But who is the "real" parent—the surrogate or the woman whose baby she bears? What if a surrogate wants to keep the baby, as has happened in a few highly publicized cases? What if the intended parents refuse to go through with the contract? Courts in most states view surrogacy contracts as unenforceable, and some states have either banned the practice or placed strict conditions on it. The American Academy of Pediatrics (AAP) Committee on Bioethics (1992) recommends that surrogacy be considered a tentative, preconception adoption agreement. The committee also recommends a prebirth agreement on the period of time in which the surrogate may assert parental rights.

Another controversial aspect of surrogacy is the payment of money. The creation of a "breeder class" of poor and disadvantaged women who carry the babies of the well-to-do strikes many people as wrong. Similar concerns have been raised about payment for donor eggs (Gabriel, 1996). Some countries, such as France and Italy, have banned commercial surrogacy. In the United States, it is illegal in some states and legal in others, and regulations differ from state to state (Warner, 2008).

Mechanisms of Heredity

The science of genetics is the study of *heredity:* the genetic transmission of heritable characteristics from parents to offspring. When ovum and sperm unite—whether by normal fertilization or by assisted reproduction—they endow the baby-to-be with a genetic makeup that influences a wide range of characteristics from color of eyes and hair to health, intellect, and personality.

what's
your
view

If you or your partner were infertile, would you consider or undertake one of the methods of assisted reproduction described here? Why or why not?

checkpoint
can **you** . . .

▷ Identify several causes and treatments of male and female infertility?

▷ Describe four means of assisted reproduction, and mention issues they raise?

▷ Distinguish between monozygotic and dizygotic twins, and tell how each comes about?

guidepost
3

What genetic mechanisms determine sex, physical appearance, and other characteristics?

THE GENETIC CODE

The "stuff" of heredity is a chemical called **deoxyribonucleic acid (DNA)**. The double-helix structure of DNA resembles a long, spiraling ladder whose steps are made of pairs of chemical units called *bases* (Figure 3.1). The bases—adenine (A), thymine (T), cytosine (C), and guanine (G)—are the "letters" of the **genetic code**, which cellular machinery "reads."

Chromosomes are coils of DNA that consist of smaller segments called **genes**, the functional units of heredity. Each gene is located in a definite position on its chromosome and contains thousands of bases. The sequence of bases in a gene tells the cell how to make the proteins that enable it to carry out its specific functions. The complete sequence of genes in the human body constitutes the **human genome**. Of course, every unique human has a unique genome, and the more closely related two people are, the more similar their particular genomes will be. The human genome is not meant to be a recipe for making a particular human, and in fact was developed with the use of multiple study participants as well as nonhuman organisms. Rather, the human genome is a reference point or representative genome that shows the location of all human genes.

Every cell in the normal human body except the sex cells (sperm and ova) has 23 pairs of chromosomes—46 in all. Through a type of cell division called *meiosis*, which the sex cells undergo when they are developing, each sex cell ends up with only 23 chromosomes—one of each pair. Thus, when sperm and ovum fuse at conception, they produce a zygote with 46 chromosomes, 23 from the father and 23 from the mother (Figure 3.2).

At the moment of conception, the single-celled zygote receives all the biological information needed to guide its development into a unique individual. Through *mitosis*, a process by which the nonsex cells divide in half over and over again, the DNA replicates itself, so that each newly formed cell has the same DNA structure as all the others. Thus each cell division creates a genetic duplicate of the original cell, with the same hereditary information. When development is normal, each cell (except the sex cells) continues to have 46 chromosomes identical to those in the original zygote. As the cells divide, they differentiate, specializing in a variety of complex bodily functions that enable the child to grow and develop.

Genes spring into action when conditions call for the information they can provide. Genetic action that triggers the growth of body and brain is often regulated by hormonal levels—both in the mother and in the developing baby—that are affected by such environmental conditions as nutrition and stress. Thus, from the start, heredity and environment are interrelated.

DNA is the genetic material in all living cells. It consists of four chemical units, called bases. These bases are the letters of the DNA alphabet. A (adenine) pairs with T (thymine) and C (cytosine) pairs with G (guanine). There are 3 billion base pairs in human DNA.

Letters of the DNA alphabet

T = Thymine
A = Adenine
G = Guanine
C = Cytosine

FIGURE 3.1

DNA: The Genetic Code
Source: Ritter, 1999.

deoxyribonucleic acid (DNA)
Chemical that carries inherited instructions for the development of all cellular forms of life.

New research indicates that a single gene—Pax6—is responsible for regulating human brain development.

Zhang et al., 2010

genetic code
Sequence of bases within the DNA molecule; a set of rules that govern the formation of proteins that determine the structure and functions of living cells.

chromosomes
Coils of DNA that consist of genes.

genes
Small segments of DNA located in definite positions on particular chromosomes; functional units of heredity.

human genome
The complete sequence of genes in the human body.

connect

study smart

The Genetic Code

The human genome was first sequenced in 2006. More recently, the Neandertal genome was also sequenced, and analysis of the commonalities between Neandertal and human genes suggests that we engaged in limited interbreeding. In other words, some of their genes live on in us.

Green et al., 2010

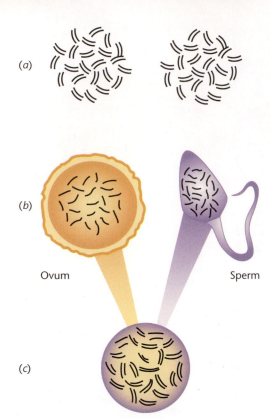

(a)

(b)

Ovum

Sperm

(c)

Zygote

FIGURE 3.2

Hereditary Composition of the Zygote

(a) Body cells of women and men contain 23 pairs of chromosomes, which carry the genes, the basic units of inheritance. (b) Each sex cell (ovum and sperm) has only 23 single chromosomes because of meiosis, a special kind of cell division in which the total number of chromosomes is halved. (c) At fertilization, the 23 chromosomes from the sperm join the 23 from the ovum so that the zygote receives 46 chromosomes, or 23 pairs.

autosomes
In humans, the 22 pairs of chromosomes not related to sexual expression.

sex chromosomes
Pair of chromosomes that determines sex: XX in the normal human female, XY in the normal human male.

Indeed, the human genome itself has changed—and continues to change—in response to environmental conditions. One research team has estimated that at least 7 percent of the genome has been evolving during the past 40,000 years at a faster rate than ever before as a result of changes in diet and new diseases, such as AIDS, malaria, and yellow fever (Hawks, Wang, Cochran, Harpending, & Moyzis, 2007). For example, after the agricultural revolution about 10,000 years ago, when early farmers switched from hunting animals to domesticating and milking them, a new gene that enabled digestion of lactose spread to more than 80 percent of the European population. Lactose intolerance remains common, however, in Asia and Africa, where dairy farming is less widespread (Krause, 2009).

WHAT DETERMINES SEX?

In many villages in Nepal, it is common for a man whose wife has borne no male babies to take a second wife. In some societies, a woman's failure to produce sons is justification for divorce. In Muslim villages in central Turkey, a traditional belief is that the foods a woman eats influence the sex of her baby—red meat and tomato sauce making it more likely she will have a boy, white foods such as chicken and rice, a girl (Delaney, 2000). The irony in these customs and beliefs is that it is the father's sperm that genetically determines a child's sex.

At the moment of conception, the 23 chromosomes from the sperm and the 23 from the ovum form 23 pairs. Twenty-two pairs are **autosomes**, chromosomes not related to sexual expression. The 23rd pair are **sex chromosomes**—one from the father and one from the mother—which govern the baby's sex.

Sex chromosomes are either *X chromosomes* or *Y chromosomes*. The sex chromosome of every ovum is an X chromosome, but the sperm may contain either an X or a Y chromosome. The Y chromosome contains a gene for maleness, the *SRY gene*. When an ovum (X) is fertilized by an X-carrying sperm, the zygote formed is XX, a female. When an ovum (X) is fertilized by a Y-carrying sperm, the resulting zygote is XY, a male (Figure 3.3).

Initially, the embryo's rudimentary reproductive system appears almost identical in males and in females. About 6 to 8 weeks after conception, male embryos normally start producing the male hormone testosterone. Exposure of a genetically male embryo to steady, high levels of testosterone ordinarily results in the development of a male body with male sexual organs. However, the process is not automatic. Research with mice has found that hormones must first signal the SRY gene, which then triggers cell differentiation and formation of the testes. Without this signaling, a genetically male mouse will develop female genitals instead of male ones (Hughes, 2004; Meeks, Weiss, & Jameson, 2003; Nef et al., 2003). It is likely that a similar mechanism occurs in human males. The development of the female reproductive system is equally complex and depends on a number of variants. One of these is the signaling molecule called *Wnt-4*, a variant form of which can masculinize a genetically female fetus (Biason-Lauber, Konrad, Navratil, & Schoenle, 2004; Hughes, 2004; Vainio, Heikkiia, Kispert, Chin, & McMahon, 1999). Thus sexual differentiation appears to be a more complex process than simple genetic determination.

Further complexity arises from the fact that women have two X chromosomes, whereas men have only one. For many years researchers believed that the duplicate genes on one of a woman's two X chromosomes are inactivated. Recently, however, researchers sequencing the X chromosome discovered that only 75 percent of the genes on the extra X chromosome are inactive. About 15 percent remain active, and 10 percent are active in some women but not in others (Carrel & Willard, 2005).

This variability in gene activity could help explain gender differences both in normal traits and in disorders linked to the X chromosome (discussed later in this chapter). The extra X chromosome also may help explain why women are generally healthier and live longer than men: Harmful changes in a gene on one X chromosome may be offset by a backup copy on the other X chromosome (Migeon, 2006).

PATTERNS OF GENETIC TRANSMISSION

During the 1860s, Gregor Mendel, an Austrian monk, laid the foundation for our understanding of patterns of inheritance. He crossbred pea plants that produced only yellow seeds with pea plants that produced only green seeds. The resulting hybrid plants produced only yellow seeds, meaning, he said, that yellow was *dominant* over green. Yet when he bred the yellow-seeded hybrids with each other, only 75 percent of their offspring had yellow seeds, and the other 25 percent had green seeds. This showed, Mendel said, that a hereditary characteristic (in this case, the color green) can be *recessive;* that is, be carried by an organism that does not express, or show, it.

Mendel also tried breeding for two traits at once. Crossing pea plants that produced round yellow seeds with plants that produced wrinkled green seeds, he found that color and shape were independent of each other. Mendel thus showed that hereditary traits are transmitted separately, a concept now known as particulate inheritance.

Today we know that the genetic picture in humans is far more complex than Mendel imagined. Although some human traits, such as the presence of facial dimples, are inherited via simple dominant transmission, most human traits fall along a continuous spectrum and result from the actions of many genes in concert. Nonetheless, Mendel's ground breaking work laid the foundations for our modern understanding of genetics.

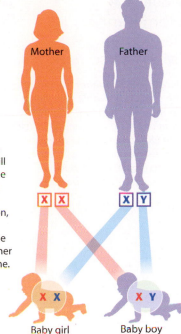

Fathers have an X and a Y chromosome, while mothers have two X chromosomes. In the case of a daughter, the baby will receive one X chromosome from the father and one X chromosome from the mother. In the case of a son, the father donates the Y chromosome—making the baby male—and the mother donates the X chromosome.

Mother Father

X X   X Y

X X   X Y

Baby girl   Baby boy

FIGURE 3.3

Determination of Sex

Dominant and Recessive Inheritance Do you have dimples? If so, you probably inherited them through *dominant inheritance*. If your parents have dimples but you do not, *recessive inheritance* occurred. How do these two types of inheritance work?

Genes that can produce alternative expressions of a characteristic (such as the presence or absence of dimples) are called **alleles**. Alleles are alternate versions of the same gene. Every person receives one maternal and one paternal allele for any given trait. When both alleles are the same, the person is **homozygous** for the characteristic; when they are different, the person is **heterozygous**. In **dominant inheritance**, the dominant allele is always expressed, or shows up as a trait in that person. The person will look the same whether or not he or she is heterozygous or homozygous because the recessive allele doesn't show. In **recessive inheritance**, for the trait to be expressed the person must have two recessive alleles, one from each parent. If a recessive trait is expressed, that person cannot have a dominant allele.

Let's take the presence of dimples as an example. Dimples are a dominant trait, so you will have dimples if you receive at least one copy (D) from either parent. If you

Hetero means different and homo means the same, just as when we speak of heterosexual and homosexual orientations. Thus, heterozygous individuals have two different alleles, homozygous individuals have two of the same allele.

alleles
Two or more alternative forms of a gene that can occupy the same position on paired chromosomes and affect the same trait.

homozygous
Possessing two identical alleles for a trait.

heterozygous
Possessing differing alleles for a trait.

dominant inheritance
Pattern of inheritance in which, when a child receives different alleles, only the dominant one is expressed.

recessive inheritance
Pattern of inheritance in which a child receives identical recessive alleles, resulting in expression of a nondominant trait.

FIGURE 3.4

Dominant and Recessive Inheritance

Because of dominant inheritance, the same observable phenotype (in this case, dimples) can result from two different genotypes (DD and Dd). A phenotype expressing a recessive characteristic (such as no dimples) must have a homozygous genotype (dd).

Mother

Father

Dd

Dd

DD

Dd

Dd

dd

Dimples are unusual in that they are inherited through simple dominant transmission. Most traits are influenced by multiple genes, often in combination with other factors.

polygenic inheritance
Pattern of inheritance in which multiple genes at different sites on chromosomes affect a complex trait.

mutations
Permanent alterations in genes or chromosomes that usually produce harmful characteristics but provide the raw material of evolution.

phenotype
Observable characteristics of a person.

genotype
Genetic makeup of a person, containing both expressed and unexpressed characteristics.

inherited one allele for dimples from each parent (Figure 3.4), you are homozygous for this trait and have one or more dimples. If you receive one copy of the dimpling allele (D) and one copy of an allele for lack of dimples (d), you are heterozygous. In both cases, your expressed characteristic is that you have dimples. The only situation in which you would not have dimples is if you received two recessive copies (d), one from each parent.

Relatively few traits are determined in this simple fashion. Most traits result from **polygenic inheritance**, the interaction of many genes. For example, there is not an "intelligence" gene that determines whether or not you are smart. Rather, a large number of genes work in concert to determine your intellectual potential. Like intelligence, most individual variations in complex behaviors or traits are governed by the additive influences of many genes with small but identifiable effects. In other words, they are polygenic. While single genes often determine abnormal traits, there is no single gene that by itself significantly accounts for individual differences in any complex normal behavior.

Traits may also be affected by **mutations:** permanent alterations in genetic material. A study comparing genomes of four racial/ethnic groups found that the lighter skin color of Caucasians and Asians resulted from slight mutations—a change of just 1 letter of DNA code out of the 3.1 billion letters in the human genome—tens of thousands of years ago (Lamason et al., 2005). Mutations generally result from copying errors and are usually harmful.

Genotypes and Phenotypes: Multifactorial Transmission If you have dimples, that trait is part of your **phenotype**, the observable characteristics through which your **genotype**, or underlying genetic makeup, is expressed. Except for monozygotic twins, no two people have the same genotype. The phenotype is the product of the genotype and any relevant environmental influences. The difference between genotype and phenotype helps explain why a clone (a genetic copy of an individual) or even an identical twin can never be an exact duplicate of another person.

As Figure 3.4 illustrates, people with different genotypes may exhibit the same phenotype. For example, a child who is homozygous for a dominant dimples allele will have dimples, but so will a child who is heterozygous for that same allele. Because it is dominant, the dimples are expressed, and the recessive nondimpling allele is hidden.

Furthermore, the hidden alleles can float around undetected for generations and then be expressed if both parents carry a hidden copy. For example, if you are heterozygous for dimples, and you find a mate who is also heterozygous for dimples, then by chance, approximately one-fourth of your children should not have dimples. This is because there is a 25 percent chance that any particular child will inherit *both* of the recessive alleles, and thus express the recessive trait (a lack of dimples). Note that there is a 75 percent chance the child will have dimples; however, this can occur in two different ways. The dimpled children might either be homozygous for the trait (25 percent chance) or heterozygous for it (50 percent chance). But, because the dominant trait is always expressed, all that you would know, upon seeing a dimpled child, is that the child had to have at least *one* dimpling allele.

Dimples have a strong genetic base, but for most traits experience modifies the expression of the genotype—a phenomenon called **multifactorial transmission**. Multifactorial transmission illustrates the action of nature and nurture influences and how they mutually and reciprocally affect outcomes. Imagine that Steven has inherited musical talent. If he takes music lessons and practices regularly, he may delight his family with his performances. If his family likes and encourages classical music, he may play Bach preludes; if the other children on his block influence him to prefer popular music, he may eventually form a rock group. However, if from early childhood he is not encouraged and not motivated to play music, and if he has no access to a musical instrument or to music lessons, his genotype for musical ability may not be expressed (or may be expressed to a lesser extent) in his phenotype. Some physical characteristics (including height and weight) and most psychological characteristics (such as intelligence and personality traits, as well as musical ability) are products of multifactorial transmission. Many disorders arise when an inherited predisposition interacts with an environmental factor, either before or after birth.

Later in this chapter we discuss in more detail how environmental influences work together with the genetic endowment to influence development.

Epigenesis: Environmental Influence on Gene Expression

Until recently, most scientists believed that the genes a child inherits were firmly established during fetal development, though their effects on behavior could be modified by experience. Now, mounting evidence suggests that gene expression itself is controlled by a third component, a mechanism that regulates the functioning of genes within a cell without affecting the structure of the cell's DNA. Genes are turned off or on as they are needed by the developing body or triggered by the environment. This phenomenon is called **epigenesis**, or *epigenetics*. Far from being fixed once and for all, epigenetic activity is affected by a continual bidirectional interplay with nongenetic influences (Gottlieb, 2007; Mayo Foundation for Medical Education and Research, 2009; Rutter, 2007).

Epigenesis (meaning "on, or above, the genome") refers to chemical molecules (or "tags") attached to a gene that alter the way a cell "reads" the gene's DNA. If we think of the human genome as a computer, we can visualize this epigenetic framework as the software that tells the DNA when to work. Because every cell in the body inherits the same DNA sequence, the function of the chemical tags is to differentiate various types of body cells, such as brain cells, skin cells, and liver cells. In this way, genes for the types of cells that are needed are turned on, and genes for unneeded cells are left off. Now that scientists have mapped the human genome, they are joining forces internationally to decode the epigenome (Mayo Foundation for Medical Education and Research, 2009).

Epigenetic changes can occur throughout life in response to environmental factors such as nutrition, sleep habits, stress, and physical affection. In one twin study, blood analysis

connect
study smart

Genotype and Phenotype

multifactorial transmission
Combination of genetic and environmental factors to produce certain complex traits.

epigenesis
Mechanism that turns genes on or off and determines functions of body cells.

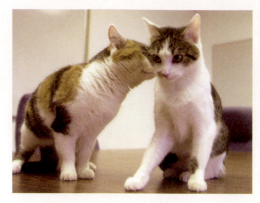

Rainbow, on the left, nuzzles her clone, Cc, on the right. They are genetically identical, but have different appearances and personalities.

checkpoint
can you . . .

▷ Explain why no two people, other than monozygotic twins, have the same genetic heritage?

▷ Explain why it is the sperm that determines a baby's sex?

▷ Tell how dominant inheritance and recessive inheritance work, and why most normal traits are not the product of simple dominant or recessive transmission?

▷ Explain how epigenesis and genome imprinting work and give examples?

guidepost

4 How are birth defects and disorders transmitted?

showed epigenetic differences in 35 percent of the sample, and these differences were associated with age and lifestyle factors such as diet, physical activity, and smoking (Fraga et al., 2005). Sometimes errors arise, which may lead to birth defects or disease (Gosden & Feinberg, 2007). Epigenetics may contribute to such common ailments as cancer, diabetes, and heart disease. It may explain why one monozygotic twin is susceptible to a disease such as schizophrenia whereas the other twin is not, and why some twins get the same disease but at different ages (Fraga et al., 2005; Wong, Gottesman, & Petronis, 2005).

Cells are particularly susceptible to epigenetic modification during critical periods such as puberty and pregnancy (Mayo Foundation for Medical Education and Research, 2009; Rakyan & Beck, 2006). Furthermore, epigenetic modifications, especially those that occur early in life, may be heritable. Studies of human sperm cells found age-related epigenetic variations capable of being passed on to future generations (Rakyan & Beck, 2006). Thus good health and nutritional practices throughout a woman's reproductive years may help ensure the health of her future children and grandchildren.

One example of epigenesis is *genome*, or *genetic*, *imprinting*. Imprinting is the differential expression of certain genetic traits, depending on whether the trait has been inherited from the mother or the father. In imprinted gene pairs, genetic information inherited from the parent of one sex is activated, but genetic information from the other parent is suppressed. Imprinted genes play an important role in regulating fetal growth and development. When a normal pattern of imprinting is disrupted, abnormal fetal growth or congenital growth disorders may result (Hitchins & Moore, 2002).

A parental "battle of the sexes" may explain the role of imprinting in certain growth disorders. According to evolutionary theory, the father benefits from having large offspring who are likely to survive and thrive at no personal cost to him, whereas the mother incurs the costs of bearing and suckling a large infant. Thus fathers normally imprint growth-enhancing genes, such as *IGF2*, for expression, whereas mothers tend to silence these genes, thus keeping a fetus's growth balanced against her need to preserve some bodily resources. If, however, both parents' copies of a growth-enhancing gene are expressed, a fetus will be overgrown; if both copies are silenced, the fetus's growth will be restricted. One controversial theory suggests a link between imprinting-related growth problems and personality disorders such as autism, depression, and schizophrenia (Badcock & Crespi, 2006, 2008; Crespi, 2008). While the specifics of such theories remain to be determined, it is indeed the case that the field of epigenetics holds the potential for answering many of our questions about mechanisms of inheritance.

Disturbances in genome imprinting may explain why the child of a diabetic father but not of a diabetic mother is likely to develop diabetes and why the opposite is true for asthma (Day, 1993). Imprinting problems also may explain why children who inherit Huntington's disease from their fathers are far more likely to be affected at an early age than children who inherit the Huntington's gene from their mothers (Sapienza, 1990), and why children who receive a certain allele from their mothers are more likely to have autism than those who receive that allele from their fathers (Ingram et al., 2000).

Genetic and Chromosomal Abnormalities

Most birth disorders are fairly rare, affecting only about 3 percent of live births (Waknine, 2006). Nevertheless, they are the leading cause of infant death in the United States, accounting for 19.5 percent of all deaths in the first year in 2005 (Kung, Hoyert, Xu, & Murphy, 2008). The most prevalent defects are cleft lip and cleft palate, followed by Down syndrome. Other serious malformations involve the eye, the face, the mouth, or the circulatory, gastronomical, or musculoskeletal systems (Centers for Disease Control and Prevention [CDC], 2006b; Table 3.2).

TABLE 3.2 Some Birth Defects

Problem	Characteristics of Condition	Who Is at Risk	What Can Be Done
Alpha$_1$ antitrypsin deficiency	Enzyme deficiency that can lead to cirrhosis of the liver in early infancy and emphysema and degenerative lung disease in middle age.	1 in 1,000 white births	No treatment.
Alpha thalassemia	Severe anemia that reduces ability of the blood to carry oxygen; nearly all affected infants are stillborn or die soon after birth.	Primarily families of Malaysian, African, and Southeast Asian descent	Frequent blood transfusions.
Beta thalassemia (Cooley's anemia)	Severe anemia resulting in weakness, fatigue, and frequent illness; usually fatal in adolescence or young adulthood.	Primarily families of Mediterranean descent	Frequent blood transfusions.
Cystic fibrosis	Overproduction of mucus, which collects in the lung and digestive tract; children do not grow normally and usually do not live beyond age 30; the most common inherited *lethal* defect among white people.	1 in 2,000 white births	Daily physical therapy to loosen mucus; antibiotics for lung infections; enzymes to improve digestion; gene therapy (in experimental stage).
Duchenne muscular dystrophy	Fatal disease usually found in males, marked by muscle weakness; minor mental retardation is common; respiratory failure and death usually occur in young adulthood.	1 in 3,000 to 5,000 male births	No treatment.
Hemophilia	Excessive bleeding, usually found in males; in its most severe form, can lead to crippling arthritis in adulthood.	1 in 10,000 families with a history of hemophilia	Frequent transfusions of blood with clotting factors.
NEURAL-TUBE DEFECTS			
Anencephaly	Absence of brain tissues; infants are stillborn or die soon after birth.	1 in 1,000	No treatment.
Spina bifida	Incompletely closed spinal canal, resulting in muscle weakness or paralysis and loss of bladder and bowel control; often accompanied by hydrocephalus, an accumulation of spinal fluid in the brain, which can lead to mental retardation.	1 in 1,000	Surgery to close spinal canal prevents further injury; shunt placed in brain drains excess fluid and prevents mental retardation.
Phenylketonuria (PKU)	Metabolic disorder resulting in mental retardation.	1 in 15,000	Special diet begun in first few weeks of life can prevent mental retardation.
Polycystic kidney disease	*Infantile form:* enlarged kidneys, leading to respiratory problems and congestive heart failure. *Adult form:* kidney pain, kidney stones, and hypertension resulting in chronic kidney failure.	1 in 1,000	Kidney transplants.

Continued

TABLE 3.2   Some Birth Defects   *Continued*

Problem	Characteristics of Condition	Who Is at Risk	What Can Be Done
Sickle-cell anemia	Deformed, fragile red blood cells that can clog the blood vessels, depriving the body of oxygen; symptoms include severe pain, stunted growth, frequent infections, leg ulcers, gallstones, susceptibility to pneumonia, and stroke.	1 in 500 African Americans	Painkillers, transfusions for anemia and to prevent stroke, antibiotics for infections.
Tay-Sachs disease	Degenerative disease of the brain and nerve cells, resulting in death before age 5.	Historically found mainly in eastern European Jews	No treatment.

Source: Adapted from AAP Committee on Genetics, 1996; NIH Consensus Development Panel, 2001; Tisdale, 1988, pp. 68–69.

Not all genetic or chromosomal abnormalities are apparent at birth. Tay-Sachs (a fatal degenerative disease of the central nervous system most common in Jews of eastern European ancestry), and sickle-cell anemia (a blood disorder more common among African Americans) do not generally appear until at least 6 months of age. Likewise, cystic fibrosis (a condition most common in people of northern European descent in which excess mucus accumulates in the lungs and digestive tract) may not appear until age 4. Some diseases show an even later onset, such as glaucoma (a disease in which fluid pressure builds up in the eyes) and Huntington's disease (a progressive degeneration of the nervous system), which do not typically appear before middle age.

Note that in addition to these variable time lines, some genetic diseases also are more common in people of certain races or ethnicities.

It is in genetic defects and diseases that we see most clearly the operation of dominant and recessive transmission, and also of a variation, *sex-linked inheritance*, discussed in a subsequent section.

DOMINANT OR RECESSIVE INHERITANCE OF DEFECTS

Most of the time, normal genes are dominant over those carrying abnormal traits, but sometimes the gene for an abnormal trait is dominant. When one parent has one dominant abnormal gene and one recessive normal gene and the other parent has two recessive normal genes, each of their children has a 50-50 chance of inheriting the abnormal gene. Among the 1,800 disorders known to be transmitted by dominant inheritance are achondroplasia (a type of dwarfism) and Huntington's disease. Although they can be quite serious, defects transmitted by dominant inheritance are less likely to be lethal at an early age than those transmitted by recessive inheritance. This is because if a dominant gene is lethal at an early age, then affected children would be likely to die before reproducing. Therefore, that gene would not be passed on to the next generation and would soon disappear from the population.

Recessive defects are expressed only if the child is homozygous for that gene; in other words, a child must inherit a copy of the recessive gene from each parent to be affected. Because recessive genes are not expressed if the parent is heterozygous for that trait, it may not always be apparent that a child is at risk for receiving two alleles of a recessive gene. However, we do know that certain ethnic groups are more likely to carry particular recessive genes, and this can be used to gauge the likelihood of the child being affected. Defects transmitted by recessive genes tend to be lethal at an earlier age, in contrast to those transmitted by dominant genes. This is because recessive genes can be transmitted by heterozygous carriers who do not themselves have the disorder. Thus they are able to reproduce and pass the genes down to the next generation.

Some traits are only party dominant or party recessive. In **incomplete dominance**, a trait is not fully expressed. Normally the presence of a dominant/recessive gene pair results in the full expression of the dominant gene and the masking of the recessive gene. In incomplete dominance, the resulting phenotype is a combination of both genes. For example, people with only one sickle-cell allele and one normal allele do not have sickle-cell anemia with its distinctive, abnormally shaped blood cells. Their blood cells are not the typical round shape either. They are an intermediate shape, which shows that the sickle-cell gene for these people is incompletely dominant.

incomplete dominance
Pattern of inheritance in which a child receives two different alleles, resulting in partial expression of a trait.

SEX-LINKED INHERITANCE OF DEFECTS

In **sex-linked inheritance** (Figure 3.5), certain recessive disorders affect male and female children differently. This is due to the fact that males are XY and females are XX. In humans, the Y chromosome is smaller and carries far fewer genes than the X chromosome. One outcome of this is that males receive only one copy of any gene that happens to be carried on the sex chromosomes, whereas females receive two copies. So, if a woman has a "bad" copy of a particular gene, she has a back-up copy. However, if a male has a "bad" copy of a particular gene, that gene will be expressed.

Heterozygote females who carry one "bad" copy of a recessive gene and one "good" one are called carriers. If such a woman has children with an unaffected male (in other words, a man who has a "good" copy of the gene), she has a 50 percent chance of passing the disorder on to any sons they might have. This is because if they have a son (who is XY by virtue of being male), the father *must* have contributed a Y chromosome. Thus, the X chromosome *had* to come from the mother, and because she has one "good" copy and one "bad" one, either outcome

sex-linked inheritance
Pattern of inheritance in which certain characteristics carried on the X chromosome inherited from the mother are transmitted differently to her male and female offspring.

Children with Turner syndrome are always girls. Because so little information is carried on the Y chromosome, an embryo with only a Y chromosome and no X chromosome is not viable. Alternatively, an embryo with an X chromosome, but no Y, often is.

FIGURE 3.5

Sex-Linked Inheritance

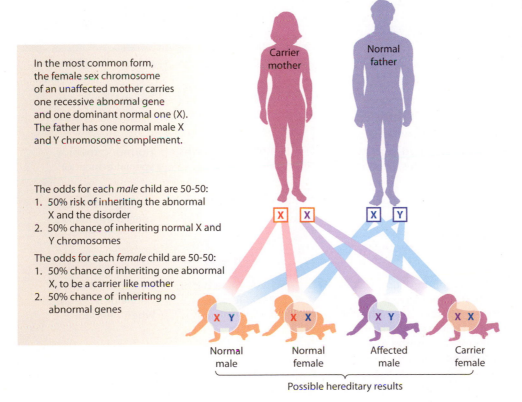

In the most common form, the female sex chromosome of an unaffected mother carries one recessive abnormal gene and one dominant normal one (X). The father has one normal male X and Y chromosome complement.

The odds for each *male* child are 50-50:
1. 50% risk of inheriting the abnormal X and the disorder
2. 50% chance of inheriting normal X and Y chromosomes

The odds for each *female* child are 50-50:
1. 50% chance of inheriting one abnormal X, to be a carrier like mother
2. 50% chance of inheriting no abnormal genes

Carrier mother

Normal father

X X   X Y

Normal male   Normal female   Affected male   Carrier female

Possible hereditary results

is equally likely. Daughters (who are XX by virtue of being female) might have been protected because the father will pass on his "good" copy to daughters. Thus, girls have a 50 percent chance either of being completely unaffected or of carrying a hidden recessive copy of the gene. Occasionally, a female does inherit a sex-linked condition. In this case, the father must have a "bad" copy, and the mother must also be a carrier or herself have the condition.

For this reason, sex-linked recessive disorders are more common in males than females. For example, red-green color blindness, hemophilia (a disorder in which blood does not clot when it should), and Duchenne muscular dystrophy (a disorder that results in muscle degeneration and eventually death) are all more common in males, and all result from genes located on the X chromosome.

CHROMOSOMAL ABNORMALITIES

Chromosomal abnormalities typically occur because of errors in cell division, which result in an extra or missing chromosome. Some of these errors happen in the sex cells during meiosis. For example, Klinefelter syndrome is caused by an extra female sex chromosome (shown by the pattern XXY). Turner syndrome results from a missing sex chromosome (XO). The likelihood of errors in meiosis may increase in offspring of women age 35 or older (University of Virginia Health System, 2004). (Table 3.3 shows characteristics of selected sex chromosome disorders.) Other chromosomal abnormalities, such as **Down syndrome**, occur in the autosomes during cell division.

The most common genetic disorder in children (Davis, 2008), Down syndrome, is responsible for about 40 percent of cases of moderate-to-severe mental retardation (Pennington, Moon, Edgin, Stedron, & Nadel, 2003). The condition is also called *trisomy-21* because it is characterized by an extra 21st chromosome in 90 percent of cases, or, in 3–4 percent of cases, by the translocation of part of the 21st chromosome onto another chromosome before or at conception. Translocation is the rearrangement

checkpoint can you . . .

▷ Compare the operation of dominant inheritance, recessive inheritance, sex-linked inheritance, and genome imprinting in transmission of birth defects?

Another common sign of Down syndrome involves the lines that palm readers use to tell your fortune. In children with Down syndrome, there is a single horizontal line across the palm.

Down syndrome
Chromosomal disorder characterized by moderate-to-severe mental retardation and by such physical signs as a downward-sloping skin fold at the inner corners of the eyes.

TABLE 3.3 Sex Chromosome Abnormalities			
Pattern/Name	**Characteristics***	**Incidence**	**Treatment**
XYY	Male; tall stature; tendency to low IQ, especially verbal.	1 in 1,000 male births	No special treatment.
XXX (triple X)	Female; normal appearance, menstrual irregularities, learning disorders, mental retardation.	1 in 1,000 female births	Special education.
XXY (Kleinfelter)	Male; sterility, underdeveloped secondary sex characteristics, small testes, learning disorders.	1 in 1,000 male births	Hormone therapy, special education.
XO (Turner)	Female; short stature, webbed neck, impaired spatial abilities, no menstruation, infertility, underdeveloped sex organs, incomplete development of secondary sex characteristics.	1 in 1,500 to 2,500 female births	Hormone therapy, special education.
Fragile X	Minor-to-severe mental retardation; symptoms, which are more severe in males, include delayed speech and motor development, speech impairments, and hyperactivity; the most common *inherited* form of mental retardation.	1 in 1,200 male births; 1 in 2,000 female births	Educational and behavioral therapies when needed.

*Not every affected person has every characteristic.

of genetic material within the same chromosome or the transfer of a segment of one chromosome to another nonhomologous one. The most obvious physical characteristic associated with the disorder is a downward-sloping skin fold at the inner corners of the eyes. Children with Down syndrome also tend to have slowed growth, poor muscle tone, congenital heart defects, thick hands, ear infections and early hearing loss, gastrointestinal defects or issues, and impaired communication, language, memory, and motor skills (Davis, 2008).

Approximately 1 in every 700 babies born alive has Down syndrome. Although the risk of having a child with Down syndrome rises with age (Society for Neuroscience, 2008), because of the higher birthrates of younger women, there are actually more young mothers with children with Down syndrome (National Institute of Child Health and Human Development, 2008). In 95 percent of cases the extra chromosome seems to come from the mother's ovum; in the other 5 percent, from the father's sperm (Antonarakis & Down Syndrome Collaborative Group, 1991).

The brains of children with Down syndrome appear nearly normal at birth but shrink in volume by young adulthood, particularly in the hippocampal area and prefrontal cortex, resulting in cognitive dysfunction, and in the cerebellum, leading to problems with motor coordination and balance (Davis, 2008; Pennington et al., 2003). With early intervention, however, the prognosis for these children is brighter than was once thought. Children with Down syndrome, like other children with disabilities, benefit cognitively, socially, and emotionally when placed in regular classrooms rather than in special schools (Davis, 2008; see discussion of mainstreaming in Chapter 13) and when provided with regular, intensive therapies designed to help them achieve important skills. As adults, many live in small group homes and support themselves; they tend to do well in structured job situations. More than 70 percent of people with Down syndrome live into their 60s, but they are at elevated risk of early death from various causes, including leukemia, cancer, Alzheimer's disease, and cardiovascular disease (Bittles, Bower, Hussain, & Glasson, 2006; Hayes & Batshaw, 1993; Hill et al., 2003).

genetic counseling
Clinical service that advises prospective parents of their probable risk of having children with hereditary defects.

GENETIC COUNSELING AND TESTING

When Alicia became pregnant after 5 years of marriage, she and her husband, Eduardo, were overjoyed. They turned their study into a nursery and eagerly looked forward to bringing the baby home. But the baby never entered that brightly decorated nursery. He was born dead, a victim of Edwards syndrome, a condition in which a child is born with an extra 18th chromosome and suffers from a variety of birth defects, including abnormalities in the heart, kidneys, gastrointestinal system, and brain. The couple, heartbroken, were afraid to try again. They still wanted a baby but feared that they might not be able to conceive a normal child.

Genetic counseling can help prospective parents like Alicia and Eduardo assess their risk of bearing children with genetic or chromosomal defects. People who have already had a child with a genetic defect, who have a family history of hereditary illness, who suffer from conditions known or suspected to be inherited, or who come from ethnic groups at higher-than-average risk of passing on genes for certain diseases can get information about their likelihood of producing affected children.

Geneticists have made great contributions to avoidance of birth defects. For example, since so many Jewish couples have been tested for Tay-Sachs genes, far fewer Jewish babies have been born with the disease (Kolata, 2003). Similarly, screening and

Although Down syndrome is a major cause of mental retardation, children with this chromosomal abnormality can live productive lives.

FIGURE 3.6

Karyotype of a
Femal with Down
Sydrome

A karyotype is a photograph that shows the chromosomes when they are separated and aligned for cell division. We know that this is a karyotype of a person with Down syndrome because there are three chromosomes instead of the usual two on pair 21. Because pair 23 consists of two Xs, we know that this is the karyotype of a female.

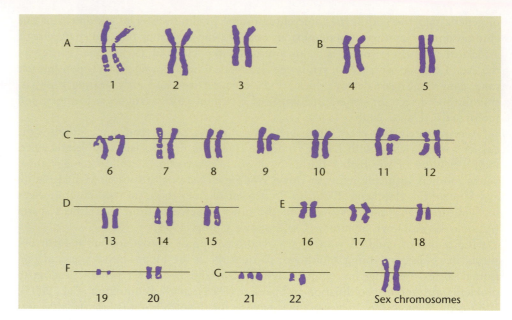

Source: Babu & Hirschhorn, 1992; March of Dimes, 1987.

what's your view ?

Should genetic counseling be compulsory before marriage?

checkpoint can you . . .

▷ Describe three ways in which chromosomal disorders occur?

▷ Explain the purposes of genetic counseling?

guidepost

5 How do scientists study the relative influences of heredity and environment, and how do heredity and environment work together?

counseling of women of childbearing age from Mediterranean countries, where beta thalassemia (refer to Table 3.2) is common, have resulted in a decline in births of affected babies and greater knowledge of the risks of being a carrier (Cao, Rosatelli, Monni, & Galanello, 2002).

A genetic counselor takes a family history and gives the prospective parents and any biological children physical examinations. Laboratory investigations of blood, skin, urine, or fingerprints may be performed. Chromosomes from body tissues may be analyzed and photographed, and the photographs enlarged and arranged according to size and structure on a chart called a *karyotype*. This chart can show chromosomal abnormalities and can indicate whether a person who appears normal might carry a genetic defect that could be transmitted to a child (Figure 3.6). The counselor tries to help clients understand the mathematical risk of a particular condition, explains its implications, and presents information about alternate courses of action.

Today researchers are rapidly identifying genes that contribute to many serious diseases and disorders as well as those that influence normal traits. Their work is likely to lead to widespread genetic testing to reveal genetic profiles—a prospect that involves dangers as well as benefits (Box 3.2).

Nature and Nurture: Influences of Heredity and Environment

Which is more important, nature or nurture? That question was a major issue among philosophers, early psychologists, and the general public. By now it has become clear that, although certain rare physical disorders are virtually 100 percent inherited, phenotypes for most complex normal traits, such as those having to do with health, intelligence, and personality, are subject to a complex array of hereditary and environmental forces. Let us explore how scientists study and explain the influences of heredity and environment and how these two forces work together.

GENETIC TESTING

The mapping of the human genome has advanced our ability to identify which genes affect specific traits or behaviors (Parke, 2004b). *Genomics*, the scientific study of the functions and interactions of the various genes, has untold implications for *medical genetics*, the application of genetic information to therapeutic purposes (McKusick, 2001; Patenaude, Guttmacher, & Collins, 2002). Scientists are able to identify genes that cause, trigger, or increase susceptibility to particular disorders and even to tailor specific drug treatments to specific individuals. Already, more than 1,000 genetic tests are available from clinical testing laboratories, helping physicians clarify diagnoses, select appropriate treatments, and identify people at high risk for certain preventable conditions (U.S. Department of Energy, Office of Science, 2008a). Genetic screening of newborns is saving lives and preventing mental retardation by permitting early identification and treatment of such disorders as sickle-cell anemia and phenylketonuria (PKU) (Holtzman, Murphy, Watson, & Barr, 1997; Khoury, McCabe, & McCabe, 2003).

On the other hand, genetic testing involves ethical and political issues related to privacy and fair use of genetic information. Although medical data are supposed to be confidential, some courts have ruled that blood relatives have a legitimate claim to information about a patient's genetic health risks that may affect them, even though such disclosures violate confidentiality (Clayton, 2003).

A major concern, particularly regarding commercial tests aimed at currently healthy people, is *genetic determinism:* the misconception that a person with a gene for a disease is bound to get the disease. All such testing can tell us is the *likelihood* that a person will contract a disease. Most diseases involve a complex combination of genes or depend in part on lifestyle or other environmental factors. Until recently, federal and state laws failed to provide adequate protection, and fear of discrimination and social stigmatization kept many people from having genetic tests recommended by their doctors (Clayton, 2003; Khoury et al., 2003; U.S. Department of Energy, Office of Science, 2008a). The federal Genetic Information Nondiscrimination Act, signed in 2008, prohibits discrimination based on genetic testing (Wexler, 2008).

The psychological impact of test results is also troubling. Predictions are imperfect; a false positive result may cause needless anxiety, and a false negative result may lull a person into complacency. A panel of experts has recommended against genetic testing for diseases for which there is no known cure (Institute of Medicine [IOM], 1993). Further concerns, especially with home testing kits being marketed directly to the public, are the possibilities of error and of misinterpretation of test results (U.S. Department of Energy, Office of Science, 2008a).

A particularly chilling prospect is that genetic testing could be misused to justify sterilization of people with "undesirable" genes or abortion of a normal fetus with the "wrong" genetic makeup (Plomin & Rutter, 1998). Gene therapy has the potential for similar abuse. Should it be used to make a short child taller or a chubby child thinner? To improve an unborn baby's appearance or intelligence? The path from therapeutic correction of defects to genetic engineering for cosmetic or functional purposes may well be a slippery slope, leading to a society in which some parents could afford to provide the "best" genes for their children and others could not (Rifkin, 1998).

Genetic testing opens the door to *gene therapy,* an experimental technique for repairing or replacing defective genes or regulating the extent to which a gene is turned on or off. Gene therapy has been used successfully to treat congenital blindness, advanced melanoma (skin cancer), and myeloid blood disorders (Bainbridge et al., 2008; Morgan et al., 2006; Ott et al., 2006; U.S. Department of Energy, Office of Science, 2008b).

Genetic testing has the potential to revolutionize medical practice. It is important to ensure that the benefits outweigh the risks.

what's your view

Angelina Jolie, an American actress and activist, opted to receive a double mastectomy after genetic testing indicated she had a gene variant putting her at high risk for breast cancer. Would you choose to undergo major surgery based on the results of genetic testing?

Keep in mind that a high heritability estimate does not mean that a trait cannot be influenced by the environment. If the environment changes, the heritability estimate may change as well.

STUDYING THE RELATIVE INFLUENCES OF HEREDITY AND ENVIRONMENT

One approach to the study of heredity and environment is quantitative: It seeks to measure how much a trait in a given population is influenced by heredity and how much by environment. This is the traditional goal of the science of **behavioral genetics**.

Measuring Heritability Behavioral geneticists have developed a means of estimating how much of a trait is due to genetics and how much is the result of environmental influences by using a concept known as **heritability**. Every trait is a consequence of genes and environment. By looking at groups of people with known genetic relationships, and assessing whether or not they are *concordant*, meaning *the same*, on a given trait, behavioral geneticists can estimate the relative influence of genes and environments.

For example, we may wish to know what the relative influences of genes and environment are for homosexuality. One way to estimate this is to look at large groups of monozygotic and dizygotic twins and calculate how concordant they are on the trait. In other words, if one twin is homosexual, what are the chances the other twin is as well? Remember that monozygotic twins generally share 100 percent of their genes, while dizygotic twins share approximately 50 percent. If genes are implicated in homosexuality, the concordance rates for monozygotic twins should be higher than that of those for dizygotic twins because they share more genes. If genes don't matter, the concordance rate should be the same for both types of twins. By the same token, if the environment exerts a large influence on a trait, people who live together should be more similar on traits than people who do not live together, and this variable can also be used to determine heritability.

There are multiple variations of this basic approach. For example, immediate family members might be compared to more distant relatives, adopted children might be compared to their biological and adopted parents, or twins adopted by two different families might be compared to twins raised in the same family—but the essential logic is the same. If we know, on average, how many genes people share by virtue of knowing their genetic relationship, and whether or not they are raised together or apart, we can measure how similar they are on traits and work backward to determine the relative environmental influence.

Heritability is expressed as a percentage ranging from 0.0 to 1.0: The higher the number, the greater the heritability of a trait. A heritability estimate of 1.0 indicates that genes are 100 percent responsible for variances in the trait within the population. A heritability estimate of 0 percent would indicate the environment shaped a trait exclusively. Note that heritability does not refer to the influences that shaped any one particular person because those influences are virtually impossible to separate. Nor does heritability tell us how traits develop. It merely indicates the statistical extent to which genes contribute to a trait at a certain time within a given population.

Types of Heritability Studies *Family studies* measure the *degree* to which biological relatives share certain traits and whether the closeness of the familial relationship is associated with the degree of similarity. In other words, the more closely two people are related, the more likely it is that they will be similar on a trait if that trait is indeed genetically influenced. Therefore, researchers use concordance rates on traits to infer genetic influences. However, family studies cannot rule out environmental influences. A family study alone cannot tell us whether obese children of obese parents inherited the tendency, whether they are overweight because their diet is like that of their parents, or whether or how those two factors interact. For that reason, researchers do adoption studies, which are an attempt to separate the effects of heredity from those of a shared environment.

Adoption studies look at similarities between adopted children and their adoptive families and also between adopted children and their biological families. When adopted children are more like their biological parents and siblings in a particular trait (say, obesity), we see the influence of heredity. When they resemble their adoptive families more, we see the influence of environment.

Monozygotic twins separated at birth are sought by researchers who want to study the impact of genes on personality. These twins, adopted by different families and not reunited until age 31, both became firefighters. Was this a coincidence, or did it reflect the influence of heredity?

Studies of twins compare pairs of monozygotic twins with same-sex dizygotic twins. Same-sex twins are used so as to avoid any confounding effects of gender. Monozygotic twins are twice as genetically similar, on average, as dizygotic twins, who are no more genetically similar than siblings. When monozygotic twins are more **concordant** on a trait than dizygotic twins, we see the likely effects of heredity.

When monozygotic twins show higher concordance for a trait than do dizygotic twins, the likelihood of a genetic factor can be studied further through adoption studies. Studies of monozygotic twins separated in infancy and reared apart have found strong resemblances between the twins. Twin and adoption studies support a moderate to high hereditary basis for many normal and abnormal characteristics (McGuffin, Riley, & Plomin, 2001).

Critics of behavioral genetics claim that its assumptions and methods tend to maximize the importance of hereditary effects and minimize environmental ones. They point out that a high heritability estimate, suggesting strong genetic influences, does not imply that the environment should not be able to make a difference in the expression of that trait. Furthermore, there are great variations in the findings depending on the source of the data. For example, twin studies generally estimate higher heritability than adoption studies do. This wide variability, critics say, "means that no firm conclusions can be drawn about the relative strength of these influences on development" (Collins, Maccoby, Steinberg, Hetherington, & Bornstein, 2000, p. 221).

But in actuality, behavioral geneticists recognize that the effects of genetic influences, especially on behavioral traits, are rarely inevitable. Even in a trait strongly influenced by heredity, the environment can have substantial impact (Rutter, 2002). In fact, environmental interventions sometimes can overcome genetically determined conditions. For example, a special diet begun soon after birth often can prevent mental retardation in children with the genetic disease phenylketonuria (PKU) (Widamann, 2009; refer to Table 3.2).

HOW HEREDITY AND ENVIRONMENT WORK TOGETHER

Today many developmental scientists have come to regard a solely quantitative approach to the study of heredity and environment as simplistic. They see these two forces as fundamentally intertwined. Instead of looking at genes and experience as operating independently on an organism, scientists influenced by contemporary evolutionary and

concordant
Term describing the tendency of twins to share the same trait or disorder.

checkpoint
can **you** . . .

▷ State the basic assumption underlying studies of behavioral genetics and explain how it applies to family studies, adoption studies, and twin studies?

▷ Cite criticisms of the behavioral genetics approach?

Pieter Gijselaar, 7 feet tall, poses next to an elevator in Amsterdam. In the past 150 years the Dutch have become the tallest people on earth, and experts say they are still growing. Gijselaar spends much of his life ducking doorways.

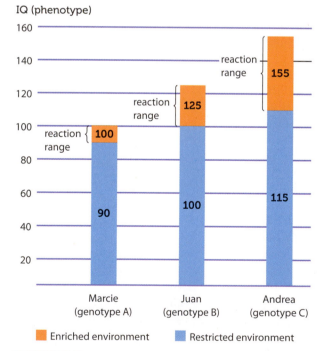

FIGURE 3.7

Intelligence and Reaction Range

Children with different genotypes for intelligence will show varying reaction ranges when exposed to a restricted (blue portion of bar) or enriched (entire bar) environment.

developmental theory see both as part of a complex *developmental system* (Gottlieb, 1991; Lickliter & Honeycutt, 2003). From conception on, a combination of constitutional (biological and psychological), social, economic, and cultural factors help shape development. The more advantageous these circumstances and the experiences to which they give rise, the greater is the likelihood of optimum development. Let us consider several ways in which inheritance and experience work together.

Reaction Range and Canalization Many characteristics vary, within limits, under differing hereditary or environmental conditions. The concepts of *reaction range* and *canalization* can help us visualize how this happens.

Reaction range is the conventional term for a range of potential expressions of a hereditary trait. Body size, for example, depends largely on biological processes, which are genetically regulated. Even so, a range of sizes is possible, depending on environmental opportunities and constraints and a person's own behavior. In societies in which nutrition has dramatically improved, such as the Netherlands, an entire generation has grown up to tower over the generation before. The better-fed children share their parents' genes but also have responded to a healthier world. Once a society's average diet becomes adequate for more than one generation, however, children tend to grow to heights similar to their parents'. Height has genetic limits; we do not see people who are only a foot tall or any who are 10 feet tall.

Heredity can influence whether a reaction range is wide or narrow. In other words, the genotype places limits on the range of possible phenotypes. For example, a child born with a defect producing mild cognitive limitations is more able to respond to a favorable environment than a child born with more severe limitations. The child with a mild impairment has a wider range of reaction. Likewise, a child with high native intelligence is likely to benefit more from an enriched home and school environment than a child with less ability (Figure 3.7).

Some traits have an extremely narrow range of reaction. The metaphor of **canalization** illustrates how heredity restricts the range of development for some traits. After a heavy storm, the rainwater that has fallen on a pavement has to go somewhere. If the street has potholes, the water will fill them. If deep canals have been dug along the edges of the street, the water will flow into the canals. Highly canalized traits, like eye color, are analogous to the deep canals. They are strongly programmed by genes and there is little opportunity for variance in their expression. In other words, because of the deep, genetically dug channel, it would take an extreme change in environment to alter their course.

In humans, walking and talking are essential to adult functioning. Not surprisingly, these are highly canalized.

Behaviors that depend largely on maturation seem to appear when a child is ready. Normal babies follow a predictable sequence of motor development: crawling, walking, and running, in that order, at certain approximate ages. This sequence is said to be canalized, in that children will follow this same blueprint irrespective of many variations in the environment. Many highly canalized traits tend to be those necessary for survival. In the case of very important traits such as these, natural selection has designed them to develop in a predictable and reliable way within a variety of environments and a multitude of influences. They are too important to be left to chance.

Cognition and personality are not highly canalized. They are more subject to variations in experience: the kinds of families children grow up in, the schools they attend, and the people they encounter. Consider reading. Before children can learn to read, they must reach a certain level of cognitive, language, and perceptual skills. No 2-year-old could read this sentence, no matter how enriched the infant's home life might be. Environment plays a large part in reading skills development, as we discuss in Chapter 7. Parents who play letter and word games and who read to their children are likely to have children who learn to read earlier than if these skills are not encouraged or reinforced.

Recently scientists have begun to recognize that a usual or typical *experience*, too, can dig canals, or channels for development (Gottlieb, 1991). For example, infants who hear only the sounds peculiar to their native language soon lose the ability to perceive sounds characteristic of other languages. Throughout this book you will find many examples of how socioeconomic status, neighborhood conditions, and educational opportunity can powerfully shape developmental outcomes, from the pace and complexity of language development to the likelihood of early sexual activity and antisocial behavior.

Genotype–Environment Interaction

Genotype–environment interaction usually refers to the effects of similar environmental conditions on genetically different individuals, and a discussion of these interactions is a way to conceptualize and talk about the different ways nature and nurture interact. To take a

> One of the environmental factors that has been identified as protective against severe allergies in children is early exposure to animals.
>
> Wegienka et al., 2011

familiar example, many children are exposed to pollen and dust, but those with a genetic predisposition are more likely to develop allergic reactions. Interactions can work the other way as well: Genetically similar children often develop differently depending on their home environments (Collins et al., 2000; Figure 3.8). As we discuss in Chapter 8, a child born with a difficult temperament may develop adjustment problems in one family and thrive in another, depending largely on parental handling. Thus it is the interaction of hereditary and environmental factors, not just one or the other, that produces certain outcomes.

Genotype–Environment Correlation

The environment often reflects or reinforces genetic differences. That is, certain genetic and environmental influences tend to act in the same direction. This is called **genotype–environment correlation**, or *genotype–environment covariance*, and it works in three ways to strengthen the phenotypic expression of a genotypic tendency (Bergeman & Plomin, 1989; Scarr, 1992; Scarr & McCartney, 1983): The first two ways are common among younger children, the third among older children and adolescents.

- *Passive correlations:* Parents, who provide the genes that predispose a child toward a trait, also tend to provide an environment that encourages the development of that trait. For example, a musical parent is likely to create a home environment in which music is heard regularly, to give a child music lessons, and to take the child to musical events. If the child inherited the parent's musical talent, the child's musicality will reflect a combination of genetic and environmental influences. This type of

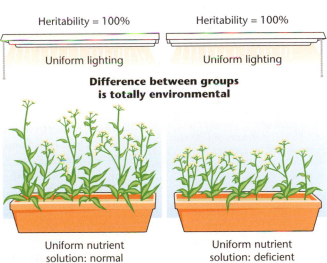

FIGURE 3.8

Example of Gene–Environment Interaction

The two plants have the same hereditary endowment, but the one grown in a deficient nutrient mix is dwarfed in height. This graphic illustrates why traits with high heritability can also be affected by environmental variables.

Source: Gray & Thompson, 2004.

correlation is called *passive* because the child does not control it. The child has inherited the environment, as well as genes that might make that child particularly well-suited to respond to those particular environmental influences. Passive correlations are most applicable to young children, whose parents have a great deal of control over their early experiences. In addition, passive correlations function only when a child is living with a biologically related parent.

The easiest way to remember this is to recall that, when you are living with your biological parents, you are inheriting both genes and environments from them. Sometimes those two complement each other precisely because they came from the same source.

- *Reactive, or evocative, correlations:* Children with differing genetic makeups evoke different responses from adults. If a child shows interest and ability in music, parents who are not musically inclined may react by making a special effort to provide that child with musical experiences. This response, in turn, strengthens the child's genetic inclination toward music.

Another way to think of this is that children evoke, or pull out, certain responses from others.

- *Active correlations:* As children get older and have more freedom to choose their own activities and environments, they actively select experiences consistent with their genetic tendencies. A shy child is more likely than an outgoing child to spend time in solitary pursuits. An adolescent with a talent for music probably will seek out musical friends, take music classes, and go to concerts if such opportunities are available. This tendency to seek out environments compatible with one's genotype is called *niche-picking;* it helps explain why identical twins reared apart tend to be quite similar. Children are to some extent creating the environment they inhabit.

What Makes Siblings So Different? The Nonshared Environment Although two children in the same family may bear a striking physical resemblance, siblings can differ greatly in intellect and especially in personality (Plomin & Daniels, 2011). One reason may be genetic differences, which lead children to need different kinds of stimulation or to respond differently to a similar home environment. For example, one child may be more affected by family discord than another (Horowitz et al., 2010). In addition, studies in behavioral genetics suggest that many of the experiences that strongly affect development do not function in the same way for different children in a family (McGuffin et al., 2001; Plomin & Daniels, 1987; Plomin & DeFries, 1999).

nonshared environmental effects The unique environment in which each child grows up, consisting of distinctive influences or influences that affect one child differently from another.

In addition, there are also what have been called **nonshared environmental effects**. These nonshared environmental effects result from the unique environment in which each child in a family grows up. Children in a family have a shared environment—the home they live in, the people in it, and the activities a family jointly engages in—but they also, even if they are twins, have experiences that are not shared by their brothers and sisters. Parents and siblings may treat each child differently. Certain events, such as illnesses and accidents, and experiences outside the home (for example, with teachers and peers) affect one child and not another. For example, if you are the oldest child in a family, one of your early influences was the ability to have your parents' undivided attention. A second-born or later child is not born into that same environment. Later siblings must share their parents' attention. Thus, despite being in the same family, the influences are not identical. Indeed, some behavioral geneticists have concluded that although heredity accounts for most of the similarity between siblings, the nonshared environment accounts for most of the difference (McClearn et al., 1997; Plomin, 1996; Plomin, 2004; Plomin & Daniels, 1987; Plomin & DeFries, 1999; Plomin, Owen, & McGuffin, 1994). However, methodological challenges and additional empirical evidence point to the more moderate conclusion that nonshared environmental effects do not greatly outweigh shared ones; rather, there seems to be a balance between the two (Rutter, 2002).

what's your view

In what ways are you like your mother and in what ways like your father? How are you similar and dissimilar to your siblings? Which differences would you guess come chiefly from heredity and which from environment? Can you see possible effects of both?

Genotype–environment correlations may play an important role in the nonshared environment. Children's genetic differences may lead parents and siblings to react to them differently and treat them differently, and genes may influence how children perceive and respond to that treatment and what its outcome will be. Children also mold their environments by the choices they make—what they do and with whom—and their genetic makeup influences these choices. A child who has inherited artistic talent may spend a great deal of time creating "masterpieces" in solitude, whereas a sibling who is athletically inclined may spend more time playing ball with friends. Thus, not only will the children's abilities (in, say, painting or soccer) develop differently, but their social lives will be different as well. These differences tend to be accentuated as children grow older and have more experiences outside the family (Bergeman & Plomin, 1989; Bouchard, 1994; Plomin, 1990, 1996; Plomin et al., 1994; Scarr, 1992; Scarr & McCartney, 1983).

The old nature-nurture debate is far from resolved; we know now that the problem is far more complex than previously thought. Future research will continue to augment and refine our understanding of the forces affecting child development.

Some Characteristics Influenced by Heredity and Environment

Keeping in mind the complexity of unraveling the influences of heredity and environment, let us look at what is known about their roles in producing certain characteristics.

PHYSICAL AND PHYSIOLOGICAL TRAITS

Not only do monozygotic twins generally look alike, but they also are more concordant than dizygotic twins in their risk for medical disorders such as high blood pressure, heart disease, stroke, rheumatoid arthritis, peptic ulcers, and epilepsy (Brass, Isaacsohn, Merikangas, & Robinette, 1992; Plomin et al., 1994). Life span, too, seems to be influenced by genes (Hjelmborg et al., 2006).

Obesity is measured by body mass index, or BMI (comparison of weight to height). A child who is at or above the 95th percentile of BMI for his or her age and sex is considered obese. Obesity is a multifactorial condition; twin studies, adoption studies, and other research suggest that 40 to 70 percent of the risk is genetic, but environmental influences contribute to it (Chen et al., 2004).

More than 430 genes or chromosome regions are associated with obesity (Nirmala, Reddy, & Reddy, 2008; Snyder et al., 2004). One key gene on chromosome 10 normally controls appetite, but an abnormal version of this gene can stimulate hunger and overeating (Boutin et al., 2003). Functional MRI studies point to an allele that restricts the activity of dopamine, a brain chemical that normally signals when a person is full (Stice, Spoor, Bohon, & Small, 2008).

The risk of obesity is 2 to 3 times higher for a child with a family history of obesity, especially severe obesity (Nirmala et al., 2008). However, this increased risk is not solely genetic. The kind and amount of food eaten in a particular home or in a particular social or ethnic group and the amount of exercise that is encouraged can increase or decrease the likelihood that a child will become overweight. The rise in the prevalence of obesity in Western countries seems to result from the interaction of a genetic predisposition with overeating, supersized portions, and inadequate exercise (Arner, 2000; see Chapters 9, 12, and 15). In addition, some research suggests that obesity spreads through social ties. If one sibling is obese, the other sibling is likely to become obese as well. The same is true of spouses and friends, but not of neighbors (Christakis & Fowler, 2007).

checkpoint can you...

▷ Explain and give at least one example of reaction range, canalization, and genotype–environment interaction?

▷ Differentiate the three types of genotype–environment correlation?

▷ List three types of influences that contribute to nonshared environmental effects?

guidepost 6

What roles do heredity and environment play in physical health, intelligence, and personality?

obesity
Extreme overweight in relation to age, sex, height, and body type.

INTELLIGENCE

Heredity exerts a strong influence on general intelligence (as measured by intelligence tests) and, to a lesser extent, on specific abilities such as memory, verbal ability, and spatial ability (McClearn et al., 1997; Petrill et al., 2004; Plomin et al., 1994; Plomin & DeFries, 1999; Plomin & Spinath, 2004). Several genes have been tentatively associated with intelligence, but only one of these associations has been replicated so far (Dick et al., 2007; Posthuma & de Gues, 2006). However, intelligence is a trait that is polygenic; it is influenced by the additive effects of large numbers of genes working together. Intelligence also depends in part on brain size and structure, which are under strong genetic control (Toga & Thompson, 2005). Experience counts too; as Figure 3.7 shows, an enriched or impoverished environment can substantially affect the development and expression of innate ability (Ceci & Gilstrap, 2000).

Indirect evidence of the role of heredity in intelligence comes from adoption and twin studies. Adopted children's IQs are consistently closer to the IQs of their biological mothers than to those of their adoptive parents and siblings, and monozygotic twins are more alike in intelligence than dizygotic twins (Petrill et al., 2004; Plomin & DeFries, 1999).

The genetic influence, which is primarily responsible for stability in cognitive performance, increases with age, probably as a result of niche-picking. The shared family environment seems to have a dominant influence on young children but almost no influence on adolescents, who are more apt to find their own niche by actively selecting environments compatible with their hereditary abilities and related interests. The non-shared environment, in contrast, is influential throughout life and is primarily responsible for changes in cognitive performance (Bouchard, 2004; Petrill et al., 2004; Toga & Thompson, 2005).

PERSONALITY

Scientists have identified genes directly linked with specific aspects of personality, such as a trait called *neuroticism*, which may contribute to depression and anxiety (Lesch et al., 1996). Heritability of personality traits appears to be between 40 and 50 percent, and there is little evidence of shared environmental influence (Bouchard, 2004).

Temperament, one's characteristic style of approaching and reacting to situations, appears to be largely inborn and is often consistent over the years, though it may respond to special experiences or parental handling (Thomas & Chess, 1984; Thomas, Chess, & Birch, 1968). Siblings—both twins and nontwins—tend to be similar in temperament (Saudino, Wertz, Gagne, & Chawla, 2004). An observational study of 294 twin pairs (about half of them monozygotic and half dizigotic) found significant genetic influences on behavior regulation (Gagne & Saudino, 2010).

PSYCHOPATHOLOGY

There is evidence for a strong hereditary influence on such mental disorders as schizophrenia, autism, alcoholism, and depression. All tend to run in families and to show greater concordance between monozygotic twins than between dizygotic twins. However, heredity alone does not produce such disorders; an inherited tendency can be triggered by environmental factors. (Autism is discussed in Box 6.1 in Chapter 6 and depression in Chapters 14 and 15.)

Schizophrenia is a neurological disorder that affects about 1 percent of the U.S. population each year and is usually diagnosed between ages 15 and 25 (Society for Neuroscience, 2008); it is characterized by loss of contact with reality;

temperament
Characteristic disposition, or style of approaching and reacting to situations.

schizophrenia
Neurological disorder marked by loss of contact with reality; hallucinations and delusions; loss of coherent, logical thought; and inappropriate emotionality.

hallucinations and delusions; loss of coherent, logical thought; and inappropriate emotionality. One might wonder why genes coding for such a debilitating disease might have evolved. However, schizophrenia tends to be associated with creativity and may have developed as a by-product of natural selection for positive cognitive abilities (Crespi, Summers, & Dorus, 2007). Estimates of heritability are as high as 80 to 85 percent (McGuffin, Owen, & Farmer, 1995; Picker, 2005). However, monozygotic twins are not always concordant for schizophrenia, perhaps due to epigenesis (Fraga et al., 2005; Wong et al., 2005).

A wide array of rare gene mutations, some of which involve missing or duplicated segments of DNA, may increase susceptibility to schizophrenia (Chen et al., 2009; Vrijenhoek et al., 2008; Walsh et al., 2008). Researchers also have looked at possible nongenetic influences, such as a series of neurological insults in fetal life (Picker, 2005; Rapoport, Addington, Frangou, & Psych, 2005); exposure to influenza or the mother's loss of a close relative in the first trimester of pregnancy (Brown, Begg, et al., 2004; Khashan et al., 2008); or maternal rubella or respiratory infections in the second and third trimesters. Infants born in urban areas or in late winter or early spring appear to be at increased risk, as are those whose mothers experienced obstetric complications or who were poor or severely deprived as a result of war or famine (Picker, 2005). Studies in the Netherlands, Finland, and China have found a link between fetal malnutrition and schizophrenia (St. Clair et al., 2005; Susser & Lin, 1992; Wahlbeck, Forsen, Osmond, Barker, & Eriksson, 2001).

Advanced paternal age is also a risk factor for schizophrenia. In large population-based studies, the risk of the disorder was heightened when the father was 30 years old or more (Byrne, Agerbo, Ewald, Eaton, & Mortensen, 2003; Malaspina et al., 2001; Sipos et al., 2004).

In this chapter we have looked at some ways in which heredity and environment act to make children what they are. A child's first environment is the world within the womb, which we discuss in Chapter 4.

checkpoint can you . . .

▷ Assess the evidence for genetic and environmental influences on obesity, intelligence, temperament, and schizophrenia?

summary and key terms

guidepost 1 Conceiving a New Life

How does conception normally occur, and how have beliefs about conception changed?

- Early beliefs about conception reflected unscientific approaches to the understanding of nature and of male and female anatomy.
- Fertilization, the union of an ovum and a sperm, results in the formation of a one-celled zygote, which then duplicates itself by cell division.

fertilization (61)

zygote (61)

guidepost 2 Infertility

What causes infertility, and what are alternative ways of becoming parents?

- The most common cause of infertility in men is a low sperm count; the most common cause in women is blockage of the fallopian tubes.
- Assisted reproductive technology may involve ethical and practical issues.
- Multiple births can occur either by the fertilization of more than one ovum by different sperm or by the splitting of a single fertilized ovum.

- Dizygotic (fraternal) twins have different genetic makeups and may be of different sexes. On average, they share 50 percent of their genes. Monozygotic (identical) twins have much the same genetic makeup but may differ in temperament or other respects.

infertility (61)

assisted reproductive technology (ART) (65)

guide**post** ❸

Mechanisms of Heredity

What genetic mechanisms determine sex, physical appearance, and other characteristics?

- The basic functional units of heredity are the genes, which are made of deoxyribonucleic acid (DNA). DNA carries the biochemical instructions that govern the formation and functions of various body cells. The genetic code, the chemical structure of DNA, determines all inherited characteristics. Each gene is located by function in a definite position on a particular chromosome. The complete sequence of genes in the human body is the human genome.

deoxyribonucleic acid (DNA) (67)

genetic code (67)

chromosomes (67)

genes (67)

human genome (67)

- At conception, each normal human being receives 23 chromosomes from the mother and 23 from the father. These form 23 pairs of chromosomes—22 pairs of autosomes and 1 pair of sex chromosomes. A child who receives an X chromosome from each parent is genetically female. A child who receives a Y chromosome from the father is genetically male.

- The simplest patterns of genetic transmission are dominant and recessive inheritance. When a pair of alleles are the same, a person is homozygous for the trait; when they are different, the person is heterozygous.

autosomes (68)

sex chromosomes (68)

alleles (69)

homozygous (69)

heterozygous (69)

dominant inheritance (69)

recessive inheritance (69)

- Most normal human characteristics are the result of polygenic inheritance or multifactorial transmission. Except in the case of monozygotic twins, each child inherits a unique genotype, which then interacts with the environment to determine the phenotype.

- The epigenetic framework controls the functions of particular genes; it can also be affected by environmental factors.

polygenic inheritance (70)

mutations (70)

phenotype (70)

genotype (70)

multifactorial transmission (71)

epigenesis (71)

guide**post** ❹

Genetic and Chromosomal Abnormalities

How are birth defects and disorders transmitted?

- Birth defects and diseases may result from simple dominant, recessive, or sex-linked inheritance; from mutations; from genome imprinting; from chromosomal abnormalities; or from errors in growth.

- Genetic counseling can provide information about the mathematical odds of bearing children with certain defects. Genetic testing involves risks as well as benefits.

incomplete dominance (75)

sex-linked inheritance (75)

Down syndrome (76)

genetic counseling (77)

guide**post** ❺

Nature and Nurture: Influences of Heredity and Environment

How do scientists study the relative influences of heredity and environment, and how do heredity and environment work together?

- Research in behavioral genetics is based on the assumption that the relative influences of heredity and environment within a population can be measured statistically. If heredity is an important influence on a trait, genetically closer persons will be more similar in that trait. Family studies, adoption studies, and studies of twins enable researchers to measure the heritability of traits.

- Critics claim that traditional behavioral genetics is too simplistic. Instead, they study complex developmental systems, reflecting a confluence of constitutional, economic, social, and biological influences.

- The concepts of reaction range, canalization, genotype–environment interaction, genotype–environment correlation (or covariance), and niche-picking describe ways in which heredity and environment work together.

- Siblings tend to be more different than alike in intelligence and personality. Many experiences that strongly affect development are different for each sibling.

   behavioral genetics (80)

   heritability (80)

   concordant (81)

   reaction range (83)

   canalization (83)

genotype–environment interaction (83)

genotype–environment correlation (83)

nonshared environmental effects (84)

Some Characteristics Influenced by Heredity and Environment

What roles do heredity and environment play in physical health, intelligence, and personality?

- Health, obesity, longevity, intelligence, and temperament are influenced by both heredity and environment, and their relative influences may vary across the life span.

- Schizophrenia is a highly heritable neurological disorder that also is environmentally influenced.

   obesity (85)

   temperament (86)

   schizophrenia (86)

guideposts for study

1. What are the three stages of prenatal development, and what happens during each stage?

2. What environmental influences can affect prenatal development?

3. What techniques can assess a fetus's health and well-being, and what is the importance of prenatal and preconception care?

guidepost 1 What are the three stages of prenatal development, and what happens during each stage?

connect

studysmart

Stages of Prenatal Development

gestation
Period of development between conception and birth.

gestational age
Age of an unborn baby, usually dated from the first day of an expectant mother's last menstrual cycle.

cephalocaudal principle
Principle that development proceeds in a head-to-tail direction; that is, that upper parts of the body develop before lower parts of the trunk.

studysmart

Cephalocaudal and Proximodistal Principles of Growth

Prenatal Development: Three Stages

For many women, the first clear (though not necessarily reliable) sign of pregnancy is a missed menstrual period. But even before that first missed period, a pregnant woman's body undergoes subtle but noticeable changes. Table 4.1 lists early signs and symptoms of pregnancy. Although these signs are not unique to pregnancy, a woman who experiences one or more of them may wish to take a home pregnancy test or to seek medical confirmation that she is pregnant.

> Pregnancy tests identify the presence of human chorionic gonadotropin, which is only produced by embroyos and fetuses. So there are no false positives. A pregnancy might not be viable, but a positive pregnancy test usually tells a women a conception has occurred.

During **gestation**, the period between conception and birth, an unborn child undergoes dramatic processes of development. The normal range of gestation is between 37 and 41 weeks (Martin et al., 2009). **Gestational age** is usually dated from the first day of an expectant mother's last menstrual cycle.

Prenatal (prebirth) development takes place in three stages: *germinal, embryonic,* and *fetal.* (Table 4.2 gives a month-by-month description.) During these three stages of gestation, the fertilized ovum, or *zygote,* grows into an *embryo* and then a *fetus.*

What turns a single-celled zygote into a creature with a specific shape and pattern? Research suggests that an identifiable group of genes is responsible for this transformation in vertebrates, including human beings. These genes produce molecules called *morphogens,* which are switched on after fertilization and begin sculpting arms, hands, fingers, vertebrae, ribs, a brain, and other body parts (Echeland et al., 1993; Krauss, Concordet, & Ingham, 1993; Riddle, Johnson, Laufer, & Tabin, 1993).

Both before and after birth, development proceeds according to two fundamental principles: Growth and motor development occur from the top down and from the center of the body outward.

The **cephalocaudal principle** (from Latin, meaning "head to tail") dictates that development proceeds from the head to the lower part of the trunk. An embryo's head, brain, and eyes develop earliest and are disproportionately large until the other parts catch up. At 2 months of gestation, the embryo's head is half the length of the body. By the time of birth, the head is only one-fourth the length of the body but is still disproportionately

TABLE 4.1 Early Signs and Symptoms of Pregnancy

Physical Change	Causes and Timing
Tender, swollen breasts or nipples	Increased production of the female hormones estrogen and progesterone stimulates breast growth to prepare for producing milk (most noticeable in a first pregnancy).
Fatigue; need to take extra naps	Woman's heart is pumping harder and faster to produce extra blood to carry nutrients to the unborn baby. Stepped-up production of hormones takes extra effort. Progesterone depresses central nervous system and may cause sleepiness. Concerns about pregnancy may sap energy.
Slight bleeding or cramping	*Implantation bleeding* may occur about 10 to 14 days after fertilization when fertilized ovum attaches to lining of uterus. Many women also have cramps (similar to menstrual cramps) as the uterus begins to enlarge.
Nausea with or without vomiting	Rising levels of estrogen produced by placenta and fetus cause stomach to empty more slowly. Also, heightened sense of smell may trigger nausea in response to certain odors, such as coffee, meat, dairy products, or spicy foods. *Morning sickness* may begin as early as 2 weeks after conception, but usually around 4 to 8 weeks, and may occur at any time of day.
Food cravings	Hormonal changes may alter food preferences, especially during first trimester, when hormones have greatest impact.
Frequent urination	Enlarging uterus during first trimester exerts pressure on the bladder.
Frequent, mild headaches	Increased blood circulation caused by hormonal changes may bring on headaches.
Constipation	Increase in progesterone may slow digestion, food passes more slowly through intestinal tract.
Mood swings	Flood of hormones early in pregnancy can produce emotional highs and lows.
Faintness and dizziness	Lightheaded feeling may be triggered by blood vessel dilation and low blood pressure; also may be triggered by low blood sugar.
Raised basal body temperature	Basal body temperature (taken first thing in the morning) normally rises soon after ovulation each month and then drops during menstruation. When menstruation ceases, temperature remains elevated.

Source: Mayo Clinic, 2005.

large. According to the **proximodistal principle** (from Latin, "near to far"), development proceeds from parts near the center of the body to outer ones. The embryo's head and trunk develop before the limbs, and the arms and legs before the fingers and toes.

THE GERMINAL STAGE (FERTILIZATION TO 2 WEEKS)

During the **germinal stage**, the first 2 weeks after fertilization, the zygote divides, becomes more complex, and is implanted in the wall of the uterus (Figure 4.1).

Within 36 hours after fertilization, the zygote enters a period of rapid cell division and duplication, or *mitosis*. Some 72 hours after fertilization, it has divided into 16 to 32 cells; 24 hours later it has 64 cells.

While the fertilized ovum is dividing, it is also making its way down the fallopian tube to the uterus, a journey of 3 or 4 days. Its form changes into a *blastocyst*, a fluid-filled sphere, which floats freely in the uterus until the 6th day after fertilization, when it begins to implant itself in the uterine wall. Only about 10 to 20 percent of fertilized ova complete the task of **implantation** and continue to develop. Where the egg implants will determine the placement of the placenta.

Before implantation, as cell differentiation begins, some cells around the edge of the blastocyst cluster on one side to form the *embryonic disk*, a thickened cell mass from which the embryo begins to develop. This mass is already differentiating into two layers. The upper layer, the *ectoderm*, will become the outer layer of skin, the nails, hair, teeth, sensory organs, and the nervous system, including the brain and spinal cord. The inner layer, the *endoderm*, will become the digestive system, liver, pancreas, salivary glands,

proximodistal principle
Principle that development proceeds from within to without; that is, that parts of the body near the center develop before the extremities.

germinal stage
First 2 weeks of prenatal development, characterized by rapid cell division, increasing complexity and differentiation, and implantation in the wall of the uterus.

implantation
The attachment of the blastocyst to the uterine wall, occurring at about day 6.

TABLE 4.2 Prenatal Development

Month	Description
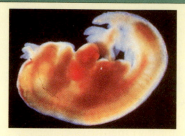 1 month	During the first month, growth is more rapid than at any other time during prenatal or postnatal life: The embryo reaches a size 10,000 times greater than the zygote. By the end of the first month, it measures about ½ inch in length. Blood flows through its veins and arteries, which are very small. It has a minuscule heart, beating 65 times a minute. It already has the beginnings of a brain, kidneys, liver, and digestive tract. The umbilical cord, its lifeline to the mother, is working. By looking very closely through a microscope, it is possible to see the swellings on the head that will eventually become eyes, ears, mouth, and nose. Its sex cannot yet be detected.
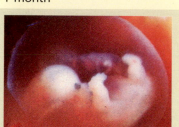 7 weeks	By the end of the second month, the fetus is less than 1 inch long and weighs only 1/13 ounce. Its head is half its total body length. Facial parts are clearly developed, with tongue and teeth buds. The arms have hands, fingers, and thumbs, and the legs have knees, ankles, and toes. The fetus has a thin covering of skin and can make handprints and footprints. Bone cells appear at about 8 weeks. Brain impulses coordinate the function of the organ system. Sex organs are developing; the heartbeat is steady. The stomach produces digestive juices; the liver, blood cells. The kidneys remove uric acid from the blood. The skin is now sensitive enough to react to tactile stimulation. If an aborted 8-week-old fetus is stroked, it reacts by flexing its trunk, extending its head, and moving back its arms.
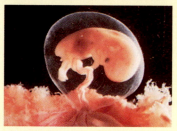 3 months	By the end of the third month, the fetus weighs about 1 ounce and measures about 3 inches in length. It has fingernails, toenails, eyelids (still closed), vocal cords, lips, and a prominent nose. Its head is still large—about one-third its total length—and its forehead is high. Sex can easily be detected. The organ systems are functioning, and so the fetus may now breathe, swallow amniotic fluid into the lungs and expel it, and occasionally urinate. Its ribs and vertebrae have turned into cartilage. The fetus can now make a variety of specialized responses: It can move its legs, feet, thumbs, and head; its mouth can open and close and swallow. If its eyelids are touched, it squints; if its palm is touched, it makes a partial fist; if its lip is touched, it will suck; and if the sole of the foot is stroked, the toes will fan out. These reflexes will be present at birth but will disappear during the first months of life.
 4 months	The body is catching up to the head, which is now only one-fourth the total body length, the same proportion it will be at birth. The fetus now measures 8 to 10 inches and weighs about 6 ounces. The umbilical cord is as long as the fetus and will continue to grow with it. The placenta is now fully developed. The mother may be able to feel the fetus kicking, a movement known as *quickening*, which some societies and religious groups consider the beginning of human life. The reflex activities that appeared in the third month are now brisker because of increased muscular development.
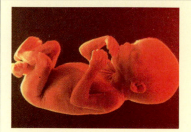 5 months	The fetus, now weighing about 12 ounces to 1 pound and measuring about 1 foot, begins to show signs of an individual personality. It has definite sleep-wake patterns, has a favorite position in the uterus (called its *lie*), and becomes more active—kicking, stretching, squirming, and even hiccuping. By putting an ear to the mother's abdomen, it is possible to hear the fetal heartbeat. The sweat and sebaceous glands are functioning. The respiratory system is not yet adequate to sustain life outside the womb; a baby born at this time does not usually survive. Coarse hair has begun to grow for eyebrows and eyelashes, fine hair is on the head, and a woolly hair called *lanugo* covers the body.

Continued

TABLE 4.2 Prenatal Development *Continued*

Month	Description
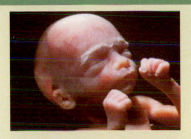 6 months	The rate of fetal growth has slowed down a little—by the end of the sixth month, the fetus is about 14 inches long and weighs 1¼ pounds. It has fat pads under the skin; the eyes are complete, opening, closing, and looking in all directions. It can hear, and it can make a fist with a strong grip. A fetus born during the sixth month still has only a slight chance of survival because the breathing apparatus has not matured. However, medical advances have made survival increasingly likely.
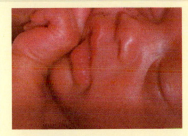 7 months	By the end of the seventh month, the fetus, about 16 inches long and weighing 3 to 5 pounds, has fully developed reflex patterns. It cries, breathes, and swallows, and it may suck its thumb. The lanugo may disappear at about this time, or it may remain until shortly after birth. Head hair may continue to grow. The chances that a fetus weighing at least 3½ pounds will survive are good, provided it receives intensive medical attention. It will probably need to be kept in an isolette until a weight of 5 pounds is attained.
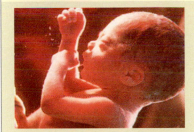 8 months	The 8-month-old fetus is 18 to 20 inches long and weighs between 5 and 7 pounds. Its living quarters are becoming cramped, and so its movements are curtailed. During this month and the next, a layer of fat develops over the fetus's entire body, which will enable it to adjust to varying temperatures outside the womb.
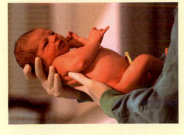 9 months—newborn	About a week before birth, the fetus stops growing, having reached an average weight of about 7½ pounds and a length of about 20 inches, with boys tending to be a little longer and heavier than girls. Fat pads continue to form, the organ systems are operating more efficiently, the heart rate increases, and more wastes are expelled through the umbilical cord. The reddish color of the skin is fading. At birth, the fetus will have been in the womb for about 266 days, although gestational age is usually estimated at 280 days because most doctors date the pregnancy from the mother's last menstrual period.

Note: Even in these early stages, individuals differ. The figures and descriptions given here represent averages.

and respiratory system. Later a middle layer, the *mesoderm*, will develop and differenti-ate into the inner layer of skin, muscles, skeleton, and excretory and circulatory systems.

Other parts of the blastocyst begin to develop into organs that will nurture and protect the embryo: the *amniotic cavity*, or *amniotic sac*, with its outer layers, the *amnion* and *chorion*, the *placenta*, and the *umbilical cord* (Figure 4.2). The *amniotic sac* is a fluid-filled membrane that encases the developing embryo, giving it room to move. The *placenta*, which contains both maternal and embryonic tissue, develops in the uterus to allow oxygen, nourishment, and wastes to pass between mother and embryo. It is con-nected to the embryo by the *umbilical cord*. Nutrients from the mother pass from her blood to the embryonic blood vessels and are then carried, via the umbilical cord, to the embryo. In turn, embryonic blood vessels in the umbilical cord carry embryonic

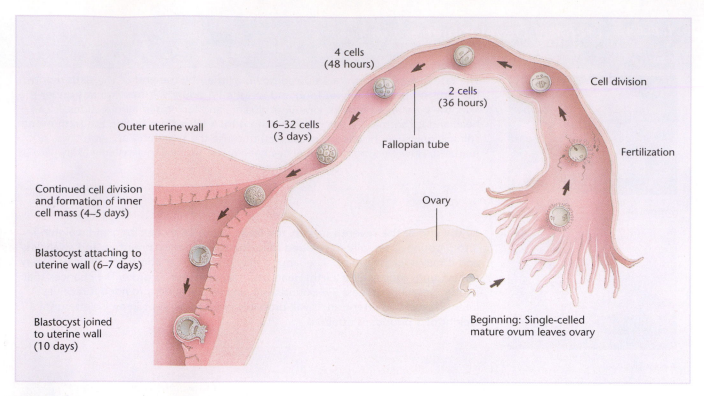

FIGURE 4.1

Early Development of a Human Embryo

This simplified diagram shows the progress of the ovum as it leaves the ovary, is fertilized in the fallopian tube, and then divides while traveling to the lining of the uterus. Now a blastocyst, it is implanted in the uterus, where it will grow larger and more complex until it is ready to be born.

wastes to the placenta, where they can be eliminated by maternal blood vessels. The mother's and embryo's circulatory systems are not directly linked; instead, this exchange occurs by diffusion across the blood vessel walls. The placenta also helps to combat internal infection and gives the unborn child immunity to various diseases. It produces the hormones that support pregnancy, prepare the mother's breasts for lactation, and eventually stimulate the uterine contractions that will expel the baby from the mother's body. In short, it is a complex life support system for the developing child.

FIGURE 4.2

The Developing Embryo (Approximately 6 Weeks Gestational Age)

Throughout its development, the embryo is enclosed and cushioned by the expandable, fluid-filled amniotic cavity. The umbilical cord develops to contain the embryonic blood vessels that carry blood to and from the placenta. Diffusion across the chorionic villi removes wastes from the embryonic blood and adds nutrients and oxygen without commingling of maternal of embryonic blood.

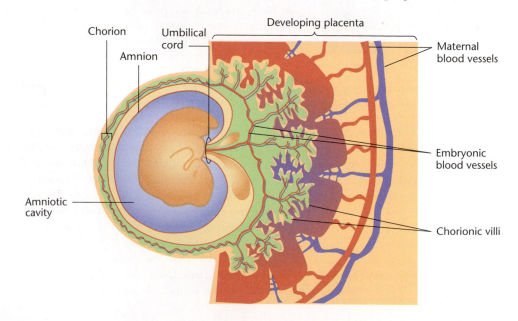

THE EMBRYONIC STAGE (2 TO 8 WEEKS)

During the **embryonic stage**, from about 2 to 8 weeks, the organs and major body systems—respiratory, digestive, and nervous—develop rapidly. This process is known as *organogenesis*. This is a critical period when the embryo is most vulnerable to destructive influences in the prenatal environment (Figure 4.3). Any organ system or structure that is developing at the time of exposure is most likely to be affected. Because of this, defects that occur later in pregnancy are likely to be less serious as the major organ systems and physical structures of the body are complete. (In Chapter 6, we discuss brain growth and development, which begins during the embryonic stage and continues after birth and beyond.)

The most severely defective embryos usually do not survive beyond the first *trimester*, or 3-month period, of pregnancy. A **spontaneous abortion**, commonly called a *miscarriage*, is the expulsion from the uterus of an embryo or fetus that is unable to survive outside the womb. As many as 1 in 4 recognized pregnancies end in miscarriage, and the actual figure may be as high as 1 in 2 because many spontaneous abortions take place before the woman realizes she is pregnant. About 3 out of 4 miscarriages occur during the first trimester (Neville, n.d.).

The Puritans in colonial New England believed that miscarriages could be brought on by violent passion, such as grief or anger, or by violent movements, as in dancing, running, or horseback riding (Reese, 2000). We now know that most miscarriages result from abnormal pregnancies; about 50 to 70 percent involve chromosomal abnormalities (Hogge, 2003) and result in miscarriages mainly in early stages of pregnancy. Smoking, drinking alcohol, and drug use increase the risks of miscarriage later in pregnancy (American College of Obstetricians and Gynecologists, 2002). Losing an unborn baby can be extremely painful, as we discuss in Box 4.1.

embryonic stage
Second stage of prenatal development (2 to 8 weeks), characterized by rapid growth and development of major body systems and organs.

spontaneous abortion
Natural expulsion from the uterus of a embryo that cannot survive outside the womb; also called *miscarriage*.

FIGURE 4.3
When Birth Defects Occur

Body parts and systems are most vulnerable during organogenesis, when they are developing most rapidly, generally within the first trimester of pregnancy.

Note: Intervals of time are not all equal.

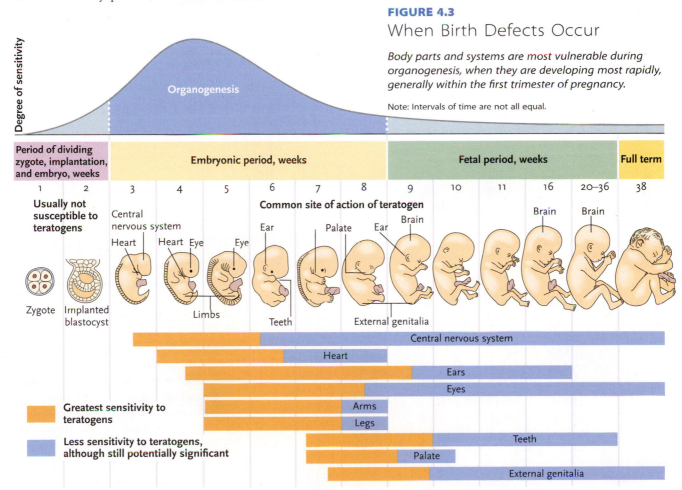

Source: J. E. Brody, 1995; data from March of Dimes.

around the world

MOURNING A MISCARRIAGE OR STILLBIRTH

At a Buddhist temple in Tokyo, small statues of infants accompanied by toys and gifts are left as offerings to Jizo, an enlightened being who is believed to watch over miscarried and aborted fetuses and eventually, through reincarnation, to guide them into a new life. The ritual of *mizuko kuyo*, a rite of apology and remembrance, is observed as a means of making amends to the lost life (Orenstein, 2002).

The Japanese word *mizuko* means "water child." Japanese Buddhists believe that life flows into an organism gradually, like water, and a mizuko is somewhere on the continuum between life and death (Orenstein, 2002). In English, in contrast, there is no word for a miscarried, aborted, or stillborn fetus, nor any ritual of mourning. Families, friends, and health professionals tend to avoid talking about such losses, which may seem insignificant compared with the loss of a living child (Van, 2001). Or people make unhelpful comments such as, "It was better this way" or "This happens all the time." (See table for advice on what to say to someone who has suffered a pregnancy loss.) Grief can be more wrenching without social support, and "the silence our society casts over the topic makes it hard for women and families to get the information and help they need" (Grady, 2002, p. 1).

How do prospective parents cope with the loss of a child they never knew? Each person's or couple's experience of loss is unique (Van, 2001). A woman may feel a sense of inadequacy or failure. She may feel anger (at herself or others for not being able to prevent the miscarriage or stillbirth, or at her partner for not being supportive enough), guilt (if the woman had mixed feelings about becoming a mother, or if she thinks the loss of the baby may have resulted from something she did), or anxiety ("Will I be able to have another child?"). Children in the family may blame themselves, especially if they had some negative feelings about the expected birth. The parents may mourn not only for what is now lost but for what the lost child might have become. Feelings of pain and grief may recur, often on the expected due date or on the anniversary of the loss (Neville, n.d.).

Differences in the ways men and women grieve may be a source of tension and divisiveness in a couple's relationship (Caelli, Downie, & Letendre, 2002). The man may have been less focused on the pregnancy, and his body does not give him physical reminders of the loss (Grady, 2002). In one small study, 11 men whose child had died in utero reported being overcome with frustration and helplessness during and after the delivery, but several found relief in supporting their partners (Samuelsson, Radestad, & Segesten, 2001). In another study, grieving parents perceived their spouses and extended families as most helpful and their doctors as least helpful. Some bereaved parents benefited from a support group, and some did not (DiMarco,

Talking to Someone Who Has Had a Miscarriage or Stillbirth

When Speaking to a Friend Who Has Experienced Pregnancy Loss

Do…	Bring up the subject; ignoring the loss can be painful.
	Listen with empathy and compassion.
	Express sadness and regret.
	Let your friend grieve, cry, and take the time necessary to heal.
Don't…	Minimize or trivialize the loss or pain.
	Ask why it happened—often there is no real answer.
	Expect your friend to move on before she is ready.

Source: Grady, 2002.

Menke, & McNamara, 2001). Couples who have gone through pregnancy loss may need extra-compassionate care during a later pregnancy (Caelli et al., 2002).

Grief counselors suggest that adjustment to a pregnancy loss may be eased if the parents are allowed to see and hold their deceased baby—something that is often not possible. Here are some other suggestions (Brin, 2004; Grady, 2002; Neville, n.d.):

- Set aside time to talk about the loss.
- Create and hold a memorial ceremony or ritual; online resources may help.
- Name the miscarried or stillborn baby.
- Plant a tree or flowering bush in the lost baby's name.
- Write poetry or keep a journal.
- Put items such as an ultrasound photo, a lock of hair, or a mold of the baby's hands or feet in a memory box.
- Create a special certificate.
- Seek private counseling or a support group. In one study of women who had experienced stillbirth, those who attended support groups had fewer symptoms of traumatic stress than those who did not attend support groups (Cacciatore, 2007).

what's your view

▷ Have you ever had a spontaneous abortion (miscarriage) or stillbirth, or do you know anyone who has? If so, how did you or your acquaintance cope with the loss? How did others react to it?

▷ Do you think recognition of such losses through ceremonies or rituals would be helpful?

Males are more likely than females to be spontaneously aborted or to be *stillborn* (dead at or after the 20th week of gestation; see Chapter 5). Thus, although about 125 males are conceived for every 100 females, only about 105 boys are born for every 100 girls. Males' greater vulnerability continues after birth: More of them die early in life, and at every age they are more susceptible to many disorders. As a result, there are only 96 males for every 100 females in the United States (Martin et al., 2009; U.S. Department of Health and Human Services [USDHHS] 1996a).

THE FETAL STAGE (8 WEEKS TO BIRTH)

The appearance of the first bone cells at about 8 weeks signals the **fetal stage**, the final stage of gestation. During this period, the fetus grows rapidly to about 20 times its previous length, organs and body systems become more complex, and the fetus puts on a layer of fat in preparation for birth. Right up to that moment, "finishing touches" such as fingernails, toenails, and eyelids continue to develop.

Fetuses are not passive passengers in their mothers' wombs. They breathe, kick, turn, flex their bodies, do somersaults, squint, swallow, make fists, hiccup, and suck their thumbs. The flexible membranes of the uterine walls and amniotic sac, which surround the protective buffer of amniotic fluid, permit and stimulate limited movement. Fetuses also can feel pain, but it is unlikely that they do so before the third trimester (Lee, Ralston, Drey, Partridge, & Rosen, 2005).

Scientists can observe fetal movement through **ultrasound**, the use of high-frequency sound waves to detect the outline of the fetus. Other instruments can monitor heart rate, changes in activity level, states of sleep and wakefulness, and cardiac reactivity.

Obesity can affect the quality of an ultrasound. Normally, the sound waves bounce off the fetus floating in the amnion, a process that is disrupted in the presence of high levels of abdominal body fat.

The movements and activity level of fetuses show marked individual differences, and their heart rates vary in regularity and speed. There also are differences between males and females. Male fetuses, regardless of size, are more active and tend to

fetal stage
Final stage of prenatal development (from 8 weeks to birth), characterized by increased differentiation of body parts and greatly enlarged body size.

ultrasound
Prenatal medical procedure using high-frequency sound waves to detect the outline of a fetus and its movements, used to determine whether a pregnancy is progressing normally.

connect

study**smart**

Prenatal

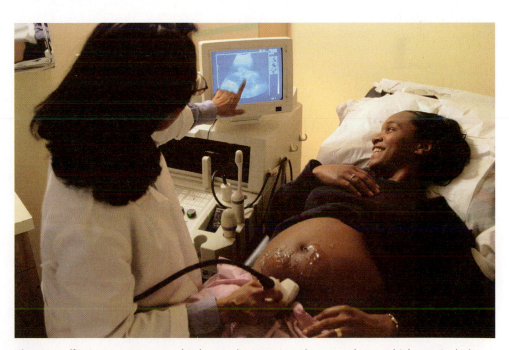

The most effective way to prevent birth complications is early prenatal care, which may include ultrasound checkups, such as this woman is having, to follow the fetus's development. Ultrasound is a diagnostic tool that presents an immediate image of the fetus in the womb.

move more vigorously than female fetuses throughout gestation (Almli, Ball, & Wheeler, 2001). Thus infant boys' tendency to be more active than girls may be at least partly inborn (DiPietro, Hodgson, Costigan, Hilton, & Johnson, 1996; DiPietro et al., 2002).

Beginning at about the 12th week of gestation, the fetus swallows and inhales some of the amniotic fluid in which it floats. The amniotic fluid contains substances that cross the placenta from the mother's bloodstream and enter the fetus's bloodstream. Partaking of these substances may stimulate the budding senses of taste and smell and may contribute to the development of organs needed for breathing and digestion (Mennella & Beauchamp, 1996; Ronca & Alberts, 1995; Smotherman & Robinson, 1995, 1996). There are also indications that early exposure to different flavors in the amniotic fluid may influence later taste preferences (Beauchamp & Mennella, 2009; Eliot, 1999). Mature taste cells appear at about 14 weeks of gestation. The olfactory system, which controls the sense of smell, also is well developed before birth (Bartoshuk & Beauchamp, 1994; Mennella & Beauchamp, 1996; Savage, Fisher, & Birch, 2007).

Fetuses respond to the mother's voice and heartbeat and the vibrations of her body, suggesting that they can hear and feel. Hungry infants, no matter on which side they are held, turn toward the breast in the direction from which they hear the mother's voice (Noirot & Algeria, 1983, cited in Rovee-Collier, 1996). Thus familiarity with the mother's voice may have an evolutionary survival function: to help newborns locate the source of food. Responses to sound and vibration seem to begin at 26 weeks of gestation, rise, and then reach a plateau at about 32 weeks (Kisilevsky & Haines, 2010; Kisilevsky, Muir, & Low, 1992). In addition, fetuses nearing full-term show the basic ability to recognize the voice of their mother and of their native language (Kisilevsky et al., 2009).

Fetuses seem to learn and remember. In one experiment, 3-day-old infants sucked more on a nipple that activated a recording of a story their mother had frequently read aloud during the last 6 weeks of pregnancy than they did on nipples that activated recordings of two other stories. Apparently, the infants recognized the pattern of sound they had heard in the womb. A control group, whose mothers had not recited a story before birth, responded equally to all three recordings (DeCasper & Spence, 1986). Similar experiments have found that newborns age 2 to 4 days prefer musical and speech sequences heard before birth. They also prefer their mother's voice to those of other women, female voices to male voices, and their mother's native language to another language (DeCasper & Fifer, 1980; DeCasper & Spence, 1986; Fifer & Moon, 1995; Kisilevsky et al., 2003; Lecanuet, Granier-Deferre, & Busnel, 1995; Moon, Cooper, & Fifer, 1993). They also seem to show recognition of smell (Varendi, Porter & Winberg, 1997).

Prenatal Development: Environmental Influences

MATERNAL FACTORS

In traditional societies, pregnancy is recognized as a dangerous time for both a woman and her unborn baby. Among the Beng people of West Africa's Ivory Coast, for example, a woman who has "taken a belly" is warned to stay away from corpses, lest her baby be born diseased; not to offend someone who might curse her pregnancy; and not to eat certain foods, such as pureed yams, lest her labor be difficult (Gottlieb, 2000). Such unscientific beliefs have a basis in fact: Because the prenatal environment is the mother's body, virtually everything that affects her well-being, from her diet to her moods, may alter her unborn child's environment and influence its growth and health.

A **teratogen** is an environmental agent, such as a virus, a drug, or radiation, that can interfere with normal prenatal development. However, not all environmental hazards are equally risky for all fetuses. An event, substance, or process may be teratogenic for some fetuses but have little or no effect on others. Sometimes vulnerability may depend on a gene either in the fetus or in the mother. For example, fetuses with a particular

---

In one study, babies recognized the Dr. Suess book read to them by their mother daily during the last trimester of pregnancy, even when the book was read by a different person.

DeCasper & Spence, 1986

checkpoint
can you . . .

▷ Identify two principles that govern physical development and give examples of their application during the prenatal period?

▷ Explain why defects and miscarriages are most likely to occur during the embryonic stage?

▷ Summarize findings about fetal activity, sensory development, and memory?

guidepost 2

What environmental influences can affect prenatal development?

teratogen
Environmental agent, such as a virus, a drug, or radiation, that can interfere with normal prenatal development and cause developmental abnormalities.

variant of a growth gene, called *transforming growth factor alpha*, have greater risk than other fetuses of developing a cleft palate if the mother smokes while pregnant (Zeiger, Beaty, & Liang, 2005). The timing of exposure (refer to Figure 4.3), the dose, duration, and interaction with other teratogenic factors also may make a difference.

Nutrition and Maternal Weight According to the evolutionary biologist David Haig (1993), pregnancy creates an unconscious conflict between a prospective mother and her fetus over the nutrients the mother provides. From an evolutionary perspective, it is adaptive for the fetus to obtain maximum amounts of nutrients from the mother, whereas it is adaptive for the mother to limit the transfer of nutrients to the fetus to maintain her own health and her ability to bear future children. Yet because the fetus has direct access to the maternal blood supply through the placenta, the mother does not have much control over the amount of nutrients she "loses" to her fetus. It is important, then, for an expectant mother to take in enough nutrients to adequately feed both herself and her fetus.

Pregnant women typically need 300 to 500 additional calories a day, including extra protein. Women of normal weight and body build who gain 16 to 40 pounds are less likely to have birth complications or to bear babies whose weight at birth is dangerously low or overly high. Yet about 1 in 3 mothers gain more or less than the recommended amounts (Martin et al., 2009). Either too much or too little weight gain can be risky. If a woman does not gain enough, her baby is likely to suffer growth retardation in the womb, to be born prematurely, to experience distress during labor and delivery, or to die at or near birth. Some research has shown that maternal calorie restriction during pregnancy might put children at risk for later obesity, perhaps by setting their metabolism to be thrifty (Caballero, 2006).

A woman who gains too much weight risks having a large baby that needs to be delivered by induced labor or cesarean section (Chu et al., 2008; Martin et al., 2009). Among 41,540 pregnant U.S. women, those who gained more than 40 pounds doubled their chances of bearing a baby weighing 9 pounds or more. A fetus that large poses serious risks to both mother and baby during delivery and is likely to become overweight or obese later in life (Hillier et al., 2008).

Desirable weight gain depends on body mass index (BMI) before pregnancy. Women who are overweight or obese before becoming pregnant or in the early months of pregnancy tend to have longer deliveries, to need more health care services (Chu et al., 2008), and to bear infants with birth defects (Stothard, Tennant, Bell, & Rankin, 2009; Watkins, Rasmussen, Honein, Botto, & Moore, 2003). A recent study conducted by the U.S. Centers for Disease Control and Prevention of more than 12,000 infants found that women who were overweight or obese before pregnancy were about 18 percent more likely than normal weight women to have a baby with certain kinds of heart defects (Gilboa et al., 2009). Obesity also increases the risk of other complications of pregnancy, including miscarriage, difficulty inducing labor, and a greater likelihood of cesarean delivery (Brousseau, 2006; Chu et al., 2008).

What an expectant mother eats is also important. For example, newborns whose mothers ate fish high in DHA, an omega-3 fatty acid found in certain fish, such as Atlantic salmon and tuna, showed more mature sleep patterns (a sign of advanced brain development) than infants whose mothers' blood had lower levels of DHA (Cheruku, Montgomery-Downs, Farkas, Thoman, & Lammi-Keefe, 2002; Colombo et al., 2004) and also were more attentive at 12 and 18 months of age (Colombo et al., 2004).

Only fairly recently have we learned of the critical importance of folic acid, or folate (a B vitamin), in a pregnant woman's diet. For some time, scientists have known that China has the highest incidence in the world of babies born with anencephaly and spina bifida, but it was not until the 1980s that researchers linked that fact with the timing of the babies' conception. Traditionally, Chinese couples marry in January or February and try to conceive as soon as possible. Thus their pregnancies often begin in the winter, when rural women have little access to fresh fruits and vegetables, important sources of folic acid.

Babies whose mothers drink large amounts of carrot juice in the last trimester are more likely to like carrots.
Mennella, Jagnow, & Beauchamp, 2001

Moderate, regular exercise is beneficial for pregnant women and does not seem to endanger the fetus.

After medical detective work established the lack of folic acid as a cause of anencephaly and spina bifida, China embarked on a massive program to give folic acid supplements to prospective mothers. The result was a large reduction in the prevalence of these defects (Berry et al., 1999). Addition of folic acid to enriched grain products has been mandatory since 1998 in the United States, where the incidence of these defects also has fallen (Honein, Paulozzi, Mathews, Erickson, & Wong, 2001). Women of childbearing age are urged to take folate supplements and to include this vitamin in their diets by eating plenty of fresh fruits and vegetables even before becoming pregnant, as damage from folic acid deficiency can occur during the early weeks of gestation (American Academy of Pediatrics [AAP] Committee on Genetics, 1999; Mills & England, 2001). If all women took 5 milligrams of folic acid each day before pregnancy and during the first trimester, an estimated 85 percent of neural-tube defects could be prevented (Wald, 2004).

Vitamin D deficiency during pregnancy in women with a gene variant called DRB1*1501 may increase the risk of a child's developing multiple sclerosis later in life. This gene–environment interaction is most common in northern European regions that get little sunshine, an important source of Vitamin D (Ramagopalan et al., 2009).

Malnutrition Prenatal malnutrition may have long-range effects. In rural Gambia, in western Africa, people born during the *hungry season*, when foods from the previous harvest are depleted, are 10 times more likely to die in early adulthood than people born during other parts of the year (Moore et al., 1997). In a study done in the United Kingdom, children whose mothers had had low vitamin D levels late in pregnancy showed low bone mineral content at age 9, potentially increasing their risk of osteoporosis in later life (Javaid et al., 2006). And, as we reported in Chapter 3, studies have revealed a link between fetal undernutrition and schizophrenia.

It is important to identify malnutrition early in pregnancy so that it can be treated. Malnourished women who take dietary supplements while pregnant tend to have bigger, healthier, more active, and more visually alert infants (J. L. Brown, 1987; Vuori et al., 1979); and women with low zinc levels who take daily zinc supplements are less likely to have babies with low birth weight and small head circumference (Hess & King, 2009). In a large-scale randomized study of low-income households in 347 Mexican communities, women who took nutrient-fortified dietary supplements while pregnant or lactating tended to have infants who grew more rapidly and were less likely to be anemic (Rivera, Sotres-Alvarez, Habicht, Shamah, & Villalpando, 2004).

Physical Activity and Strenuous Work Among the Ifaluk people of the Western Caroline Islands, women are advised to refrain from harvesting crops during the first 7 months of pregnancy, when the developing fetus is thought to be weak, but resume manual labor during the last 2 months to encourage a speedy delivery (Le, 2000). Actually, moderate exercise any time during pregnancy does not seem to endanger the fetuses of healthy women (Committee on Obstetric Practice, 2002; Riemann & Kanstrup Hansen, 2000). Regular exercise helps prevent constipation and improves respiration, circulation, muscle tone, and skin elasticity, all of which contribute to a more comfortable pregnancy and an easier, safer delivery (Committee on Obstetric Practice, 2002). Employment during pregnancy generally entails no special hazards. However, strenuous working conditions, occupational fatigue, and long working hours may be associated with a greater risk of premature birth (Bell, Zimmerman, & Diehr, 2008; Luke et al., 1995).

The American Congress of Obstetricians and Gynecologists (2002) recommends that women in low-risk pregnancies be guided by their own abilities and stamina. The safest course seems to be for pregnant women to exercise moderately, not pushing themselves and not raising their heart rate above 150, and, as with any exercise, to taper off at the end of each session rather than stop abruptly.

checkpoint
can you . . .

▷ Summarize recommendations concerning an expectant mother's diet and physical activity?

Drug Intake Practically everything an expectant mother takes in makes its way to the uterus. Drugs may cross the placenta, just as oxygen, carbon dioxide, and water do. Vulnerability is greatest in the first few months of gestation during the formation of the major systems and structures of the body. What are the effects of the use of specific drugs during pregnancy? Let's look first at medical drugs; then at alcohol, nicotine, and caffeine; and finally at some illegal drugs: marijuana, cocaine, and methamphetamine.

Medical Drugs It once was thought that the placenta protected the fetus against drugs the mother took during pregnancy—until the early 1960s, when a tranquilizer called *thalidomide* was banned after it was found to have caused stunted or missing limbs, severe facial deformities, and defective organs in some 12,000 babies. The thalidomide disaster sensitized medical professionals and the public to the potential dangers of taking drugs while pregnant.

Among the medicinal drugs that may be harmful are the antibiotic tetracycline; certain barbiturates, opiates, and other central nervous system depressants; several hormones, including diethylstilbestrol (DES) and androgens; certain anticancer drugs, such as methotrexate; Accutane, a drug often prescribed for severe acne; drugs used to treat epilepsy; and several antipsychotic drugs. (Einarson & Boskovic, 2009; Koren, Pastuszak, & Ito, 1998). Angiotensin-converting enzyme (ACE) inhibitors and nonsteroidal anti-inflammatory drugs (NSAIDs), such as naproxen and ibuprofen, have been linked to birth defects when taken anytime from the first trimester on (Cooper et al., 2006; Ofori, Oraichi, Blais, Rey, & Berard, 2006).

The AAP Committee on Drugs (2001) recommends that *no* medication be prescribed for a pregnant or breast-feeding woman unless it is essential for her health or her child's. When practical and consistent with the essentiality of controlling her symptoms, a woman should be withdrawn from psychotropic medication prior to conception. Infants whose mothers took antidepressants such as Prozac during pregnancy tend to show signs of disrupted neurobehavioral activity (Zeskind & Stephens, 2004) and are at increased risk of severe respiratory failure (Chambers et al., 2006). Certain antipsychotic drugs used to manage severe psychiatric disorders, like lithium, may have serious potential effects on the fetus, including withdrawal symptoms at birth (AAP Committee on Drugs, 2001). If medication is utilized, the most effective drug with the fewest side effects should be selected. Pregnant women should not take over-the-counter drugs without consulting a doctor (Koren et al., 1998).

Research has shown that most psychotropic drugs administered to a lactating woman can be found in her breast milk. The concentration tends to be low, and, therefore, there is little likelihood of an effect on the infant. Thus there appears to be no concrete evidence at the present time with which to recommend that a woman requiring psychotropic medication avoid breast-feeding. However, it must be emphasized that if a mother chooses to breast-feed while receiving medications, the infant should be observed for signs of drug effects (AAP Committee on Drugs, 1982).

Alcohol As many as 5 infants in 1,000 born in the United States suffer from **fetal alcohol syndrome (FAS)**, a combination of retarded growth, facial and bodily malformations, and disorders of the central nervous system. FAS and other, less severe, alcohol-related conditions are estimated to occur in nearly 1 in every 100 births (Sokol, Delaney-Black, & Nordstrom, 2003).

Prenatal alcohol exposure is the most common cause of mental retardation and the leading preventable cause of birth defects in the United States (Sokol et al., 2003) and is a risk factor for development of drinking problems and alcohol disorders in young adulthood (Alati et al., 2006; Baer, Sampson, Barr, Connor, & Streissguth, 2003).

The more the mother drinks, the greater are the effects. Moderate or heavy drinking during pregnancy seems to disturb an infant's neurological and behavioral functioning, and this may affect early social interaction with the mother, which is vital to emotional development (Hannigan & Armant, 2000; Nugent, Lester, Greene, Wieczorek-Deering, & Mahony, 1996). Heavy drinkers who continue to drink after

Thalidomide had been tested for safety in rats, and that research did not suggest there would be problems. Although animal research can be a useful tool, it must be interpreted carefully because results may not generalize across species.

what's your view

The drug Accutane is most commonly used for severe acne, although it has multiple other applications, including treatment of some cancers. However, Accutane is highly teratogenic and can cause of variety of severe birth defects, including mental retardation, facial abnormalities, and hearing and vision problems. Should the use of Accutane be permitted for women of child-bearing age? What safeguards should be required?

fetal alcohol syndrome (FAS)
Combination of mental, motor, and developmental abnormalities affecting the offspring of some women who drink heavily during pregnancy.

becoming pregnant are likely to have babies with reduced skull and brain growth as compared with babies of nondrinking women or expectant mothers who stop drinking (Handmaker et al., 2006).

FAS-related problems can include, in infancy, reduced responsiveness to stimuli, slow reaction time, and reduced visual acuity (sharpness of vision) (Carter et al., 2005; Sokol et al., 2003); and, throughout childhood, short attention span, distractibility, restlessness, hyperactivity, learning disabilities, memory deficits, and mood disorders (Sokol et al., 2003) as well as aggressiveness and problem behavior (Sood et al., 2001). Some FAS problems recede after birth; but others, such as retardation, behavioral and learning problems, and hyperactivity, tend to persist. Enriching these children's education or general environment does not always seem to enhance their cognitive development (Kerns, Don, Mateer, & Streissguth, 1997; Spohr, Willms, & Steinhausen, 1993; Streissguth et al., 1991; Strömland & Hellström, 1996), but recent interventions targeted at cognitive skills in children with FAS are showing promise (Paley & O'Connor, 2011). Children with FAS may be less likely to develop behavioral and mental health problems if they are diagnosed early and are reared in stable, nurturing environments (Streissguth et al., 2004).

Breast-feeding mothers should avoid alcoholic beverages because alcohol has been shown to become concentrated in breast milk, and its use can inhibit milk production. An occasional, small alcoholic drink is acceptable, but breast-feeding should be avoided for 2 hours after the drink (Anderson, 1995).

Nicotine Maternal smoking has been identified as the single most important factor in low birth weight in developed countries (DiFranza, Aligne, & Weitzman, 2004). Women who smoke during pregnancy are more than 1½ times as likely as nonsmokers to bear low-birth-weight babies (weighing less than 5½ pounds at birth). Even light smoking (fewer than five cigarettes a day) is associated with a greater risk of low birth weight (Hoyert, Mathews, Menacker, Strobino, & Guyer, 2006; Martin et al., 2007; Shankaran et al., 2004).

Tobacco use during pregnancy also brings increased risks of miscarriage, growth retardation, stillbirth, small head circumference, sudden infant death, colic (uncontrollable, extended crying for no apparent reason) in early infancy, hyperkinetic disorder (excessive movement), and long-term respiratory, neurological, cognitive, and behavioral problems (AAP Committee on Substance Abuse, 2001; DiFranza et al., 2004; Hoyert, Mathews, et al., 2006; Linnet et al., 2005; Martin et al., 2007; Pendlebury et al., 2008; Shah, Sullivan, & Carter, 2006; Shankaran et al., 2004; Smith et al., 2006; Sondergaard, Henriksen, Obel, & Wisborg, 2001). The effects of prenatal exposure to secondhand smoke on cognitive development tend to be worse when the child also experiences socioeconomic hardships, such as substandard housing, malnutrition, and inadequate clothing during the first 2 years of life (Rauh et al., 2004).

Caffeine Can the caffeine a pregnant woman consumes in coffee, tea, cola, or chocolate cause trouble for her fetus? For the most part, results have been mixed. It does seem clear that caffeine is *not* a teratogen for human babies (Christian & Brent, 2001). A controlled study of 1,205 new mothers and their babies showed no effect of reported caffeine use on low birth weight, premature birth, or retarded fetal growth (Santos, Victora, Huttly, & Carvalhal, 1998). On the other hand, in a controlled study of 1,063 pregnant women, those who consumed at least two cups of regular coffee or five cans of caffeinated soda daily had twice the risk of miscarriage as those who consumed no caffeine (Weng, Odouli, & Li, 2008). Four or more cups of coffee a day during pregnancy is related to increased risk of sudden death in infancy (Ford et al., 1998).

Marijuana, Cocaine, and Methamphetamine Studies of marijuana use by pregnant women are sparse and the results inconsistent. However, some limited evidence suggests that heavy marijuana use can lead to birth defects, low birth weight, withdrawal-like symptoms (excessive crying and tremors) at birth, and increased risk of attention disorders and learning problems later in life (March of Dimes Birth Defects Foundation, 2004b). In two longitudinal studies, prenatal use of marijuana was associated

Because it would be unethical to conduct the kind of randomized, experimental research that would answer the question, we cannot determine what "safe" levels of drinking are.

A woman who drinks and smokes while pregnant is taking grave risks with her future child's health.

with impaired attention, impulsivity, and difficulty in use of visual and perceptual skills after age 3, suggesting that the drug may affect functioning of the brain's frontal lobes (Fried & Smith, 2001).

Cocaine use during pregnancy has been associated with spontaneous abortion, delayed growth, premature labor, low birth weight, small head size, birth defects, impaired neurological development, and mild cognitive deficits into preadolescence (Bennett, Bendersky, & Lewis, 2008; Bunikowski et al., 1998; Chiriboga, Brust, Bateman, & Hauser, 1999; Macmillan et al., 2001; March of Dimes Birth Defects Foundation, 2004a; Scher, Richardson, & Day, 2000; Shankaran et al., 2004). In some studies, cocaine-exposed newborns show acute withdrawal symptoms and sleep disturbances (O'Brien & Jeffery, 2002). In a more recent study, high prenatal cocaine exposure was associated with childhood behavior problems, independent of the effects of alcohol and tobacco exposure (Bada et al., 2007). So great has been the concern about "crack babies" that some states have taken criminal action against expectant mothers suspected of using cocaine (Box 4.2).

Other studies, however, have found no specific connection between prenatal cocaine exposure and physical, motor, cognitive, emotional, or behavioral deficits that could not also be attributed to other risk factors, such as low birth weight; exposure to tobacco, alcohol, or marijuana; or a poor home environment (Frank, Augustyn, Knight, Pell, & Zuckerman, 2001; Messinger et al., 2004; Singer et al., 2004). Many of the effects associated with prenatal cocaine exposure may be due to indirect effects such as these rather than stemming directly from the drug itself.

Methamphetamine use among pregnant women is an increasing concern in the United States. In a study of 1,618 infants, 84 were found to have been exposed to methamphetamine. The methamphetamine-exposed infants were more likely to have low birth weight and to be small for their gestational age than the remainder of the sample. This finding suggests that prenatal methamphetamine exposure is associated with fetal growth restriction (Smith et al., 2006).

Early treatment for alcohol, nicotine, and other substance abuse can greatly improve health outcomes. Among 2,073 women enrolled in an early prenatal care program, risks of stillbirth, preterm delivery, low birth weight, and placental separation from the uterus were no higher than for a control group of 46,553 women with no evidence of substance abuse, whereas risks for 156 untreated substance abusers were dramatically higher (Goler, Armstrong, Taillac, & Osejo, 2008).

Maternal Illnesses Both prospective parents should try to prevent all infections—common colds, flu, urinary tract and vaginal infections, as well as sexually transmitted diseases. If the mother does contract an infection, she should have it treated promptly.

Acquired immune deficiency syndrome (AIDS) is a disease caused by the human immunodeficiency virus (HIV), which undermines functioning of the immune system. If an expectant mother has the virus in her blood, *perinatal transmission* may occur: The virus may cross over to the fetus's bloodstream through the placenta during pregnancy, labor, or delivery or, after birth, through breast milk.

The biggest risk factor for perinatal HIV transmission is a mother who is unaware she has HIV. In the United States, new pediatric AIDS cases have declined steadily since 1992 due to routine testing and treatment of pregnant women and newborn babies and to advances in the prevention, detection, and treatment of HIV infection in infants. The risk of transmission also can be reduced by choosing cesarean delivery, especially when an infected woman has not received antiretroviral therapy, and by promotion of alternatives to breast-feeding among high-risk women (CDC, 2006a).

Rubella (German measles), if contracted by a woman before her 11th week of pregnancy, is almost certain to cause deafness and heart defects in her baby. Chances of catching rubella during pregnancy have been greatly reduced in Europe and the United States since the late 1960s, when a vaccine was developed that is now routinely administered to infants and children. Recent efforts in less developed countries to provide rubella vaccinations have resulted in a decrease of reported rubella cases of over 80 percent from 2000 to 2009 (Reef, Strebel, Dabbagh, Gacic-Dobo, & Cochi, 2011).

Another way of saying this is that many of the effects of prenatal cocaine exposure are indirect rather than direct consequences. This is similar to the fact that maternal heroin addiction is related to greater risk of being HIV positive. It's not that the heroin directly causes HIV infection, it's that heroin is related to lifestyle issues that can cause infection.

Does society's interest in protecting unborn children justify coercive measure against pregnant women who ingest harmful substances?

acquired immune deficiency syndrome (AIDS)
Viral disease that undermines effective functioning of the immune system.

Because some parents are reluctant to vaccinate their children, rates of rubella in the United States are now on the rise.

the everyday world

FETAL WELFARE VERSUS MOTHERS' RIGHTS

A South Carolina hospital routinely tested the urine of pregnant women suspected to be using illegal drugs and reported the evidence to police. Ten women were arrested, some of them in their hospital rooms almost immediately after childbirth. They sued, arguing that the urine tests constituted an unconstitutional search of their persons without their consent (Greenhouse, 2000a). The U.S. Supreme Court invalidated the hospital's drug testing policy (Harris & Paltrow, 2003).

Another South Carolina woman was convicted of homicide after an autopsy revealed evidence of cocaine in her stillborn baby's body. The woman was sentenced to 12 years in prison. The South Carolina Supreme Court upheld the conviction, and the U.S. Supreme Court declined to hear an appeal (Drug Policy Alliance, 2004).

In both these cases the issue was the conflict between protection of a fetus and a woman's right to privacy or to make her own decisions about her body. It is tempting to require a pregnant woman to adopt practices that will ensure her baby's health or to stop or punish her if she does not. But what about her personal freedom? Can a woman's civil rights be abridged to protect the unborn?

The argument about the right to choose abortion, which rests on whether a fetus has the legal rights of a person, is far from settled. But what can or should be done about a woman who does *not* choose abortion but instead goes on carrying her unborn baby while engaging in behavior destructive to it, or who refuses tests or treatment that medical providers consider essential to the baby's welfare?

Ingesting Harmful Substances

Does a woman have the right to knowingly ingest a substance, such as alcohol or another drug, that can kill or damage her unborn child?

At least 36 states have enacted fetal homicide laws criminalizing acts that cause the death of an unborn child, and at least 19 of these laws apply to the earliest stages of pregnancy (National Conference of State Legislatures, 2008). In addition, congressional passage of the Unborn Victims of Violence Act of 2004, in response to the murder of a pregnant woman that also took the life of her unborn son, for the first time established a fetal right to life separate from the mother's in federal cases (Reuters, 2004b).

Some of the state statutes have been used to prosecute pregnant women who consume substances harmful to their fetuses. Since 1985, more than 240 women have been charged with such offenses as child endangerment or abuse, illegal drug delivery to a minor, murder, or manslaughter (Harris & Paltrow, 2003). Penalties can include forced confinement and termination of parental rights (Reutter, 2005).

Advocates for fetal rights argue that substance abuse should be against the law for an expectant mother even if it is legal for other adults. Opponents claim that jailing a pregnant woman is unworkable and self-defeating and cannot undo damage already done to the fetus. They say that expectant mothers who have a drinking or drug problem need education and treatment, not prosecution (Drug Policy Alliance, 2004; Marwick, 1997, 1998; Reutter, 2005).

Intrusive Medical Procedures

In January 2004, Melissa Ann Rowland of Salt Lake City was charged with the murder of one of her newborn twins, who was born dead. Until it was too late, Rowland had refused doctors' urgent recommendation that she have a cesarean section. The second child, a girl, was born alive with cocaine and alcohol in her system and was subsequently adopted. Rowland, who had a history of mental health problems, pleaded guilty to a reduced charge of child endangerment, agreed to enter a drug treatment program, and was sentenced to 18 months of probation (Associated Press, 2004b; Johnson, 2004).

Should a woman be forced to submit to intrusive procedures that pose a risk to her, such as a surgical delivery or intrauterine transfusions, when doctors say such procedures are essential to the delivery of a healthy baby? Should a woman in a fundamentalist sect that rejects modern medical care be taken into custody until she gives birth? Such measures have been defended as protecting the rights of the unborn, but women's rights advocates claim that they reflect a view of women as mere vehicles for carrying offspring and not as persons in their own right (Greenhouse, 2000b). Also, forcing intrusive measures on a pregnant woman may jeopardize the doctor-patient relationship. If failure to follow medical advice could bring forced surgery, confinement, or criminal charges, some women might avoid doctors altogether and thus deprive their fetuses of needed prenatal care (Nelson & Marshall, 1998). Courts have held that "neither fetal rights nor state interests on behalf of the fetus supersede[s] women's rights as ultimate medical decision maker" (Harris & Paltrow, 2003, p. 1698). However, this may not be the last word regarding situations in which fetal welfare conflicts with women's rights.

Continued

Continued

Does society's interest in protecting an unborn child justify coercive measures against pregnant women who ingest harmful substances or refuse medically indicated treatment?

a. Should pregnant women who refuse to stop drinking or to get treatment be incarcerated until they give birth?

b. Should mothers who repeatedly give birth to children with FAS be sterilized?

c. Should liquor companies be held liable if adequate warnings against use during pregnancy are not on their products?

d. Would your answers be the same regarding smoking or use of cocaine or other potentially harmful substances?

4.2

An infection called *toxoplasmosis*, caused by a parasite harbored in the bodies of cattle, sheep, and pigs and in the intestinal tracts of cats, typically produces either no symptoms or symptoms like those of the common cold. In an expectant woman, however, especially in the second and third trimesters of pregnancy, it can cause fetal brain damage, severely impaired eyesight or blindness, seizures, miscarriage, stillbirth, or death of the baby. If the baby survives, there may be later problems, including eye infections, hearing loss, and learning disabilities. Treatment with antiparasitic drugs during the first year of life can reduce brain and eye damage (McLeod et al., 2006). To avoid infection, expectant mothers should not eat raw or very rare meat, should wash hands and all work surfaces after touching raw meat, should peel or thoroughly wash raw fruits and vegetables, and should not dig in a garden where cat feces may be buried. Women who have a cat should have it checked for the disease, should not feed it raw meat, and, if possible, should have someone else empty the litter box (March of Dimes Foundation, 2002).

Offspring of mothers with diabetes are 3 to 4 times more likely than offspring of other women to develop a wide range of birth defects (Correa et al., 2008). Research on mice suggests why: High blood glucose levels, typical in diabetics, deprive an embryo of oxygen, with resultant cell damage, during the first 8 weeks of pregnancy when its organs are forming. Women with diabetes need to be sure their blood glucose levels are under control *before* becoming pregnant (Li, Chase, Jung, Smith, & Loeken, 2005). Use of multivitamin supplements during the 3 months before conception and the first 3 months of pregnancy can help reduce the risk of diabetes-associated birth defects (Correa, Botto, Liu, Mulinare, & Erickson, 2003).

Maternal Anxiety and Stress Some tension and worry during pregnancy are normal and do not necessarily increase risks of birth complications such as low birth weight (Littleton, Breitkopf, & Berenson, 2006). Moderate maternal anxiety may even spur organization of the developing brain. In a series of studies, 2-year-olds whose mothers had shown moderate anxiety midway through pregnancy scored higher on measures of motor and mental development than did age-mates whose mothers had not shown anxiety during pregnancy (DiPietro, 2004; DiPietro, Novak, Costigan, Atella, & Reusing, 2006).

On the other hand, a mother's self-reported anxiety during pregnancy has been associated with an 8-month-old's inattentiveness during a developmental assessment (Huizink, Robles de Medina, Mulder, Visser, & Buitelaar, 2002) and a preschooler's negative emotionality or behavioral disorders in early childhood (Martin, Noyes, Wisenbaker, & Huttunen, 2000; O'Connor, Heron, Golding, Beveridge, & Glover, 2002).

Unusual maternal stress during pregnancy may have harmful effects on the unborn child (Dingfelder, 2004; Huizink, Mulder, & Buitelaar, 2004). In one study, pregnant

Your veterinarian can run an easy blood test on your cat to scan for the presence of the parasite. Alternatively, your blood can be tested for antibodies to toxoplasmosis. If you were previously exposed, you are in the clear.

women whose partners or children died or were hospitalized for cancer or heart attacks were at elevated risk of giving birth to children with malformations, such as cleft lip, cleft palate, and heart malformations (Hansen, Lou, & Olsen, 2000). Even stress *before conception* may have injurious long-term effects. In one experiment, when female rats were subjected to ongoing, unpredictable stressors, such as 24-hour isolation, food and water deprivation, constant light, crowding, and electric shocks, for 7 days before being mated, their adult offspring engaged in less social interaction than the offspring of a control group, and the female offspring of the stressed mothers were more fearful. These findings suggest that a child born to a woman who has suffered from early physical, emotional, or sexual abuse may bear permanent scars (Shachar-Dadon, Schulkin, & Leshem, 2009).

Maternal Age On December 30, 2006, in Barcelona, Spain, Maria del Carmen Bousada became the oldest woman on record to give birth. She had become pregnant after in vitro fertilization (IVF) and delivered twins by cesarean section about a week before her 67th birthday. In August and November, 2008, two Indian women who claimed to be 70, Omkari Panwar and Rajo Devi, apparently topped that record, also giving birth after IVF. However, these women's ages could not be confirmed because they had no birth certificates.

Birthrates of U.S. women in their 30s and 40s are at their highest levels since the 1960s, in part due to multiple births associated with fertility treatments—an example of a history-graded influence. The number of births to women in their early 40s more than doubled between 1990 and 2008, and the number of births to women in their late 40s nearly quadrupled (Figure 4.4). Births to women ages 50 to 54 have increased an average of 15 percent each year since 1997 (Martin et al., 2009).

Although most risks to the baby's health are not much greater than for babies born to younger mothers, the chance of miscarriage or stillbirth rises with maternal age, reaching 90 percent for women age 45 or older (Heffner, 2004). Women over 30 to 35 are more likely to experience complications due to diabetes, high blood pressure, or severe bleeding and are at higher risk of premature delivery. Their babies are more likely to show retarded fetal growth, birth defects, and chromosomal abnormalities, such as Down syndrome. However, due to widespread screening among older expectant mothers, fewer malformed infants are born nowadays (Berkowitz,

FIGURE 4.4

Rate of First Births, by Age of Mother

From 1970 to 2008 the proportion of first births to women age 35 years and over increased nearly 8 times. In 2008, about 9.8 in 1,000 first births were to women age 40–44 years old and over compared with a rate of 3.8 in 1,000 first births in 1981.

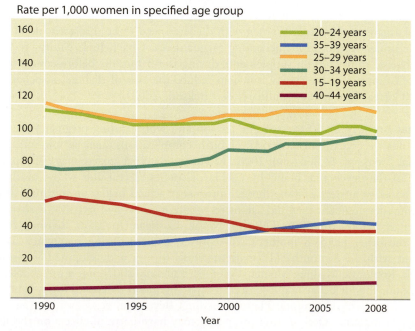

Rate per 1,000 women in specified age group

- 20–24 years
- 35–39 years
- 25–29 years
- 30–34 years
- 15–19 years
- 40–44 years

Year

Source: CDC/NCHS. National Vital Statistics System.

Skovron, Lapinski, & Berkowitz, 1990; P. Brown, 1993; Cunningham & Leveno, 1995; Heffner, 2004).

Adolescents also tend to have premature or underweight babies (Fraser, Brockert, & Ward, 1995; Martin et al., 2007). These newborns are at heightened risk of death in the 1st month, disabilities, or health problems. Teenage pregnancy is discussed further in Chapter 17.

Outside Environmental Hazards Air pollution, chemicals, radiation, extremes of heat and humidity, and other hazards of modern life can affect prenatal development. Pregnant women who regularly breathe air that contains high levels of fine combustion-related particles are more likely to bear infants who are premature or undersized (Parker, Woodruff, Basu, & Schoendorf, 2005) or have chromosomal abnormalities (Bocskay et al., 2005). Exposure to high concentrations of disinfection by-products is associated with low birth weight and slowed fetal growth (Hinckley, Bachand, & Reif, 2005). Women who work with chemicals used in manufacturing semiconductor chips have about twice the rate of miscarriage as other female workers (Markoff, 1992), and women exposed to DDT tend to have more preterm births (Longnecker, Klebanoff, Zhou, & Brock, 2001). Two common insecticides, chlorpyrifos and diazinon, apparently have caused stunting of prenatal growth (Whyatt et al., 2004). Research in the United Kingdom found a 33 percent increase in risk of nongenetic birth defects among families living within 2 miles of hazardous waste sites (Vrijheld et al., 2002).

Fetal exposure to low levels of environmental toxins, such as lead, mercury, and dioxin, as well as nicotine and ethanol, may help explain the sharp rise in asthma, allergies, and autoimmune disorders such as lupus (Dietert, 2005). In a longitudinal study of a birth cohort of children born in high-traffic areas of Manhattan and the Bronx, where asthma prevalence (more than 25 percent) is among the highest in the United States, children exposed prenatally to polycyclic aromatic hydrocarbons emitted by carbon-containing fuels were at heightened risk of developing asthma symptoms by age 5. Both maternal exposure to the hydrocarbons and the children's asthma symptoms were associated with epigenetic changes in the gene ACSL3, which affects the lungs (Perera et al., 2009). Childhood cancers, including leukemia, have been linked to pregnant mothers' drinking chemically contaminated groundwater (Boyles, 2002) and use of home pesticides (Menegaux et al., 2006). Infants exposed prenatally even to low levels of lead, especially during the third trimester, tend to show IQ deficits during childhood (Schnaas et al., 2006).

Women who have routine dental X-rays during pregnancy triple their risk of having full-term, low-birth-weight babies (Hujoel, Bollen, Noonan, & del Aguila, 2004). In utero exposure to radiation 8 through 15 weeks after fertilization has been linked to mental retardation, small head size, chromosomal malformations, Down syndrome, seizures, and poor performance on IQ tests and in school (Yamazaki & Schull, 1990).

In the 1920s to 1970s, a shoe-fitting machine that enabled customers to view their feet X-rayed within shoes was a common gimmick in shoe stores. Now that we know how damaging X-rays are for both adults and children, these machines are no longer in use.

checkpoint
can **you** . . .

▷ Discuss the short- and long-term effects on the developing fetus of a mother's use of medical and recreational drugs during pregnancy?

▷ Summarize the risks of maternal illnesses and stress, delayed childbearing, and exposure to chemicals and radiation?

PATERNAL FACTORS

A man's exposure to lead, marijuana or tobacco smoke, large amounts of alcohol or radiation, DES, pesticides, or high ozone levels may result in abnormal or poor quality sperm (Sokol et al., 2006; Swan et al., 2003). Offspring of male workers at a British nuclear processing plant were at elevated risk of being born dead (Parker, Pearce, Dickinson, Aitkin, & Craft, 1999). Babies whose fathers had diagnostic X-rays within the year prior to conception or had high lead exposure at work tended to have low birth weight and slowed fetal growth (Chen & Wang, 2006; Lin, Hwang, Marshall, & Marion, 1998; Shea, Little, & ALSPAC Study Team, 1997).

Men who smoke have an increased likelihood of transmitting genetic abnormalities (AAP Committee on Substance Abuse, 2001). A pregnant woman's exposure to the father's secondhand smoke has been linked with low birth weight, infant respiratory infections, sudden infant death, and cancer in childhood and adulthood (Ji et al., 1997; Rubin, Krasilnikoff, Leventhal, Weile, & Berget, 1986; Sandler, Everson, Wilcox, & Browder, 1985; Wakefield, Reid, Roberts, Mullins, & Gillies, 1998). In a study of 214 nonsmoking mothers in New York City, exposure to *both* paternal smoking and urban air pollution resulted in a 7 percent reduction in birth weight and a 3 percent reduction in head circumference (Perera et al., 2004).

Older fathers may be a significant source of birth defects due to damaged or deteriorated sperm. Birthrates for fathers ages 30 to 49 have risen substantially since 1980 (Martin et al., 2009). Advancing paternal age is associated with increases in the risk of several rare conditions, including dwarfism (Wyrobek et al., 2006). Advanced age of the father also may be a factor in a disproportionate number of cases of schizophrenia (Byrne, Agerbo, Ewald, Eaton, & Mortensen, 2003; Malaspina et al., 2001), bipolar disorder (Frans et al., 2008), and autism and related disorders (Reichenberg et al., 2006; Tsuchiya et al., 2008).

checkpoint can **you** . . .

▷ Identify several ways in which environmentally caused defects can be influenced by the father?

guidepost

3 What techniques can assess a fetus's health and well-being, and what is the importance of prenatal and preconception care?

study smart

Fetal Development

Monitoring and Promoting Prenatal Development

Not long ago, almost the only decision parents had to make about their babies before birth was the decision to conceive; most of what happened in the intervening months was beyond their control. Now scientists have developed an array of tools to assess an unborn baby's progress and well-being.

Progress is being made in the use of noninvasive procedures, such as ultrasound and blood tests, to detect chromosomal abnormalities. Screening is most effective when begun during the first trimester (Simpson, 2005). In one study, a combination of three noninvasive tests conducted at 11 weeks of gestation predicted the presence of Down syndrome with 87 percent accuracy. When the 11-week tests were followed by further noninvasive testing early in the second trimester, accuracy reached 96 percent (Malone et al., 2005). Amniocentesis and chorionic villus sampling, which provide definitive evidence of a genetic issue, can be used earlier in pregnancy and have been shown to carry only a slightly higher miscarriage risk (Caughey, Hopkins, & Norton, 2006; Eddleman et al., 2006). Embryoscopy can assist in diagnosis of nonchromosomal disorders, and umbilical cord sampling allows direct access to fetal DNA for diagnosis. See Table 4.3 for a summary of assessment techniques.

Screening for defects and diseases is only one reason for the importance of early prenatal care. Early, high-quality prenatal care, which includes educational, social, and nutritional services, can help prevent maternal or infant death and other birth complications. It can provide first-time mothers with information about pregnancy, childbirth, and infant care. Poor women who get prenatal care benefit by being put in touch with other needed services, and they are more likely to get medical care for their infants after birth (Shiono & Behrman, 1995).

DISPARITIES IN PRENATAL CARE

In developing countries, 1 in every 4 pregnant women gets no prenatal care, and more than 4 out of 10 give birth with no skilled attendant. These facts may help explain why almost 40 percent of deaths of children under age 5 occur during the first 4 weeks of life from complications of birth (UNICEF, 2007).

In the United States prenatal care is widespread, but not universal as in many European countries; and it lacks uniform national standards and guaranteed financial coverage. Use of early prenatal care (during the first 3 months of pregnancy) rose modestly

TABLE 4.3 Prenatal Assessment Techniques

Technique	Description	Uses and Advantages	Risks and Notes
Ultrasound (sonogram), sonoembryology	High-frequency sound waves directed at the mother's abdomen produce a picture of fetus in uterus. Sonoembryology uses high-frequency transvaginal probes and digital image processing to produce a picture of embryo in uterus.	Monitor fetal growth, movement, position, and form; assess amniotic fluid volume; judge gestational age; detect multiple pregancies. Detect major structural abnormalities or death of a fetus. Guide amniocentesis and chorionic villus sampling. Help diagnose sex-linked disorders. Sonoembryology can detect unusual defects during embryonic stage.	No known risks; done routinely in many places. Can be used for sex-screening of unborn babies.
Embryoscopy, fetoscopy	Tiny viewing scope is inserted in woman's abdomen to view embryo or fetus.	Can guide fetal blood transfusions and bone marrow transplants. Can assist in diagnosis of nonchromosomal genetic disorders.	Embryoscopy is still in research stage. Riskier than other prenatal diagnostic procedures.
Amniocentesis	Sample of amniotic fluid is withdrawn and analyzed under guidance of ultrasound. Most commonly used procedure to obtain fetal cells for testing.	Can detect chromosomal disorders and certain genetic or multifactorial defects; more than 99 percent accuracy rate. Usually performed in women age 35 and over; recommended if prospective parents are known carriers of Tay-Sachs disease or sickle-cell anemia or have family history of Down syndrome, spina bifida, or muscular dystrophy. Can help diagnose sex-linked disorders.	Normally not performed before 15 weeks' gestation. Results usually take 1 to 2 weeks. Small (0.5 percent to 1 percent) added risk of fetal loss or injury; early amniocentesis (at 11 to 13 weeks' gestation) is more risky and not recommended. Can be used for sex-screening of unborn babies.
Chorionic villus sampling (CVS)	Tissues from hairlike chorionic villi (projections of membrane surrounding fetus) are removed from placenta and analyzed.	Early diagnosis of birth defects and disorders. Can be performed between 10 and 12 weeks' gestation; yields highly accurate results within a week.	Should not be performed before 10 weeks' gestation. Some studies suggest 1 to 4 percent more risk of fetal loss than with amniocentesis.
Preimplantation genetic diagnosis	After in vitro fertilization, a sample cell is removed from the blastocyst and analyzed.	Can avoid transmission of genetic defects or predispositions known to run in the family; a defective blastocyst is not implanted in uterus. Can test for more than 100 disorders. Can screen for defective embryo that might be miscarried. Often used with in vitro fertilization.	No known risks.
Umbilical cord sampling (cordocentesis, or fetal blood sampling)	Needle guided by ultrasound is inserted into blood vessels of umbilical cord.	Allows direct access to fetal DNA for diagnostic measures, including assessment of blood disorders and infections, and therapeutic measures such as blood transfusions.	Fetal loss or miscarriage is reported in 1 to 2 percent of cases; increases risk of bleeding from umbilical cord and fetal distress.

Continued

TABLE 4.3 Prenatal Assessment Techniques *Continued*

Technique	Description	Uses and Advantages	Risks and Notes
Maternal blood tests	A sample of the prospective mother's blood is tested for levels of alpha fetoprotein (AFP), human chorionic gonadotropin (hCG), and cestriol.	May indicate defects in formation of brain or spinal cord (anencephaly or spina bifida); also can predict Down syndrome and other abnormalities. Permits monitoring of pregnancies at risk for low birth weight or stillbirth.	No known risks, but false negatives are possible. Ultrasound and/or amniocentesis needed to confirm suspected conditions.

Sources: Chodirker et al., 2001; Cicero, Curcio, Papageorghiou, Sonek, & Nicolaides, 2001; Cunniff & Committee on Genetics, 2004; Kurjak, Kupesic, Matijevic, Kos, & Marton, 1999; Tarkan, 2005; and Verlinsky et al., 2002.

between 1990 and 2003 but then plateaued and declined slightly in 2006, possibly due to changes in welfare and Medicaid policies. In 32 states using reporting standards in effect in 1988, 3.6 percent of prospective mothers received no prenatal care in 2006 or did not begin it until the third trimester of pregnancy. Utilization rates were poorer (7.9 percent with no or late prenatal care) in 18 states in which revised definitions of prenatal care have been adopted since 2003. However, most of the difference can be attributed to changes in reporting and not to actual changes in prenatal care utilization (Martin et al., 2009).

Meanwhile, rates of low birth weight and premature birth continue to rise (see Chapter 5). Why? One answer is the increasing number of multiple births, which often are early births, with heightened risk of death within the first year. However, rates of preterm birth and low birth weight also have increased for single births (Martin et al., 2009).

A second answer is that the benefits of prenatal care are not evenly distributed. Although usage of prenatal care has grown, especially among ethnic groups that have tended not to receive early care, the women most at risk of bearing low-birth-weight babies—teenage and unmarried women, those with little education, and some minority women—are still least likely to receive it (Martin et al., 2006; National Center for Health Statistics [NCHS], 2005; USDHHS, 1996a). In 2006, as in earlier years, non-Hispanic black and Hispanic women were more than twice as likely as non-Hispanic white women to receive late or no care (Martin et al., 2009).

A related concern is an ethnic disparity in fetal and postbirth mortality. After adjusting for such risk factors as SES, overweight, smoking, hypertension, and diabetes, the chances of perinatal death (death between 20 weeks gestation and 1 week after birth) remain 3.4 times higher for blacks, 1.5 times higher for Hispanics, and 1.9 times higher for other minorities than for whites (Healy et al., 2006).

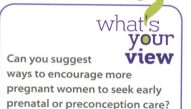

what's your view?

Can you suggest ways to encourage more pregnant women to seek early prenatal or preconception care?

THE NEED FOR PRECONCEPTION CARE

A more fundamental answer is that even early prenatal care is insufficient; care should begin *before* pregnancy to identify preventable risks. The Centers for Disease Control and Prevention ([CDC], 2006c) has issued comprehensive, research-based guidelines for *preconception care* for all women of childbearing age. Such care should include the following:

- *Physical examinations* and the taking of medical and family histories.
- *Vaccinations* for rubella and hepatitis B.
- *Risk screening* for genetic disorders and infectious diseases such as STDs.
- *Counseling* women to avoid smoking and alcohol, maintain a healthy body weight, and take folic acid supplements.

Interventions should be provided where risks are indicated and also between pregnancies for women who have had poor pregnancy outcomes in the past.

The CDC (2006c) urges all adults to create a reproductive life plan to focus attention on reproductive health, avoid unintended pregnancies, and improve pregnancy outcomes. The CDC also calls for increased health insurance for low-income women to make sure they have access to preventive care.

Good preconception and prenatal care can give every child the best possible chance for entering the world in good condition to meet the challenges of life outside the womb—challenges we discuss in the next three chapters.

checkpoint can you . . .

▷ Describe seven techniques for identifying defects or disorders prenatally?

▷ Discuss possible reasons for disparities in utilization of prenatal care?

▷ Tell why early, high-quality prenatal care is important and why preconception care is needed?

summary and key terms

guidepost 1

Prenatal Development: Three Stages

What are the three stages of prenatal development, and what happens during each stage?

- Prenatal development occurs in three stages of gestation: the germinal, embryonic, and fetal stages.
- Growth and development both before and after birth follow the cephalocaudal principle (head to tail) and the proximodistal principle (center outward).
- As many as 1 in 2 conceptions end in spontaneous abortion, usually in the first trimester of pregnancy.
- As fetuses grow, they move less, but more vigorously. Swallowing amniotic fluid, which contains substances from the mother's body, stimulates taste and smell. Fetuses seem able to hear, exercise sensory discrimination, learn, and remember.

gestation (92)

gestational age (92)

cephalocaudal principle (92)

proximodistal principle (93)

germinal stage (93)

implantation (93)

embryonic stage (97)

spontaneous abortion (97)

fetal stage (99)

ultrasound (99)

guidepost 2

Prenatal Development: Environmental Influences

What environmental influences can affect prenatal development?

- The developing organism can be greatly affected by its prenatal environment. The likelihood of a birth defect may depend on the timing and intensity of an environmental event and its interaction with genetic factors.
- Important environmental influences involving the mother include nutrition, physical activity, smoking, intake of alcohol or other drugs, maternal illnesses, maternal stress, maternal age, and external environmental hazards, such as chemicals and radiation. External influences and paternal age may affect the father's sperm.

teratogen (100)

fetal alcohol syndrome (FAS) (103)

acquired immune deficiency syndrome (AIDS) (105)

guidepost 3

Monitoring and Promoting Prenatal Development

What techniques can assess a fetus's health and well-being, and what is the importance of prenatal and preconception care?

- Ultrasound, amniocentesis, chorionic villus sampling, embryoscopy, preimplantation genetic diagnosis, umbilical cord sampling, and maternal blood tests can be used to determine whether an unborn baby is developing normally.
- High-quality prenatal care, begun early, is important for healthy development. It can lead to detection of defects and disorders and may help reduce low birth weight and other birth complications.
- Racial/ethnic disparities in prenatal care may be a factor in disparities in low birth weight and perinatal death.
- Preconception care for every woman of childbearing age would reduce unintended pregnancies and increase the chances of good pregnancy outcomes.

Birth and the Newborn Baby

did you know?

▷ At 32 percent of all births, the cesarean rate in the United States is among the highest in the world?

▷ In some cultures, babies have no regular sleep schedules but are allowed to fall asleep whenever they naturally do?

▷ Baby boys' deliveries are more likely to involve complications than baby girls'?

In this chapter, we describe how babies come into the world, what newborn babies look like, and how their body systems work. We discuss techniques used to assess newborn health and the different ways in which birth complications can affect development. We also consider how the birth of a baby affects the people most vital to the infant's well-being: the parents.

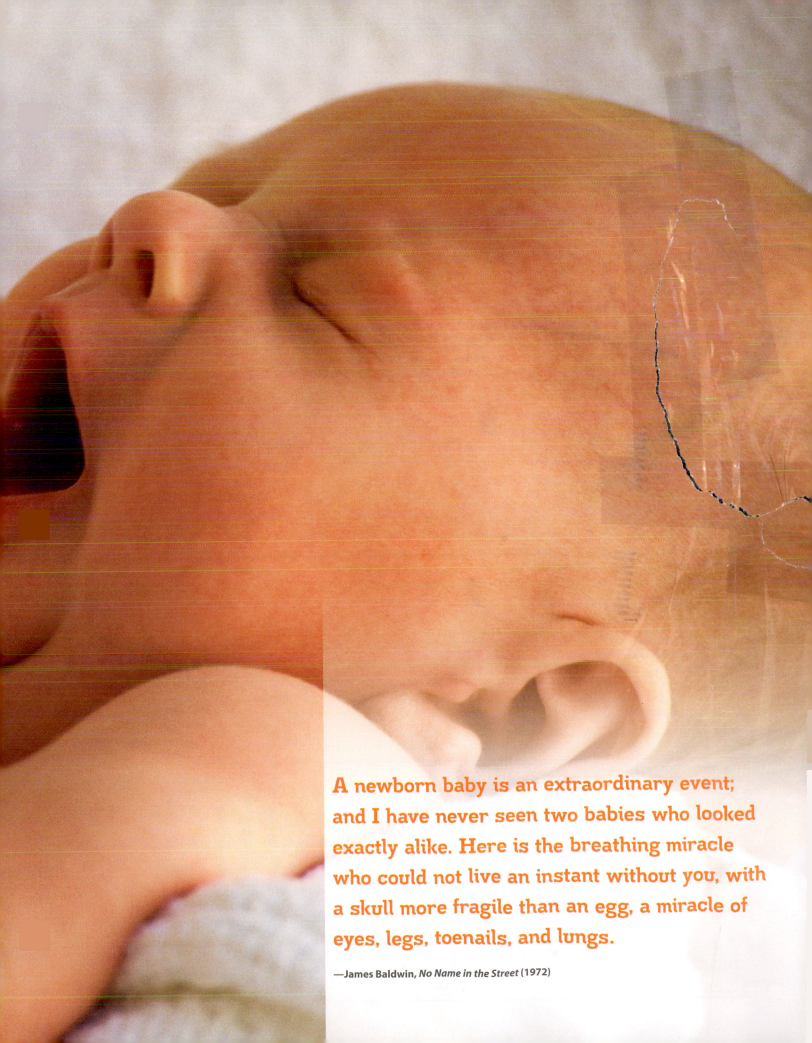

A newborn baby is an extraordinary event; and I have never seen two babies who looked exactly alike. Here is the breathing miracle who could not live an instant without you, with a skull more fragile than an egg, a miracle of eyes, legs, toenails, and lungs.

—James Baldwin, *No Name in the Street* (1972)

1. How do customs surrounding birth reflect culture, and how has childbirth changed in developed countries?

2. How does labor begin, what happens during each of the three stages of childbirth, and what alternative methods of delivery are available?

3. How do newborn infants adjust to life outside the womb, and how can we tell whether a new baby is healthy and is developing normally?

4. What complications of childbirth can endanger newborn babies, and what are the long-term prospects for infants with complicated births?

5. How do parents bond with and care for their baby?

guidepost 1

How do customs surrounding birth reflect culture, and how has childbirth changed in developed countries?

Childbirth and Culture: How Birthing Has Changed*

Customs surrounding childbirth reflect the beliefs, values, and resources of a culture. A Mayan woman in Yucatan gives birth in the hammock in which she sleeps every night; both the father-to-be and a midwife are expected to be present. To evade evil spirits, mother and child remain at home for a week (Jordan, 1993). By contrast, among the Ngoni in East Africa, men are excluded from the birth. In rural Thailand, a new mother generally resumes normal activity within a few hours of giving birth (Broude, 1995; Gardiner & Kosmitzki, 2005).

Prior to the twentieth century, childbirth in Europe and in the United States followed somewhat similar patterns. Birth was a female social ritual. The woman, surrounded by female relatives and neighbors, sat up in her bed or perhaps in the stable, modestly draped in a sheet; if she wished, she might stand, walk around, or squat over a birth stool. Chinks in the walls, doors, and windows were stuffed with cloth to keep out chills and evil spirits. The prospective father was nowhere to be seen. Not until the fifteenth century was a doctor present, and then only for wealthy women if complications arose.

The midwife who presided over the event had no formal training; she offered "advice, massages, potions, irrigations, and talismans." Salves made of fat of viper, gall of eel, powdered hoof of donkey, tongue of chameleon, or skin of snake or hare might be rubbed on the prospective mother's abdomen to ease her pain or hasten her labor; but "the cries of the mother during labor were considered to be as natural as those of the baby at birth" (Fontanel & d'Harcourt, 1997, p. 28).

Given the lack of accurate knowledge about female anatomy and the birth process, the midwives' ministrations sometimes did more harm than good. A sixteenth-century textbook instructed midwives to stretch and dilate the membranes of the genital parts and cut or break them with their fingernails, to urge the patient to go up and down stairs screaming at the top of her lungs, to help her bear down by pressing on her belly, and to pull out the placenta immediately after the birth (Fontanel & d'Harcourt, 1997).

*This discussion is based largely on Eccles, 1982; Fontanel and d'Harcourt, 1997; Gélis, 1991; and Scholten, 1985.

The *Guinness Book of World Records* reports that the highest number of births from one woman is held by a Russian woman who, from 1725 to 1765, gave birth to 16 sets of twins, 7 sets of triplets, and 4 sets of quadruplets over the course of 29 pregnancies.

After the baby emerged, the midwife cut and tied the umbilical cord and cleaned and examined the newborn, testing the reflexes and joints. The other women helped the new mother wash and dress, made her bed with clean sheets, and served her food to rebuild her strength. Within a few hours or days, a peasant mother would be back at work in the fields; a more affluent or noble woman could "lie in" and rest for several weeks.

REDUCING THE RISKS OF CHILDBIRTH

Childbirth in those times was "a struggle with death" (Fontanel & d'Harcourt, 1997, p. 34) for both mother and baby. In seventeenth- and eighteenth-century France, a woman had a 1 in 10 chance of dying while or shortly after giving birth. Thousands of babies were stillborn, and 1 out of 4 who were born alive died during their 1st year. At the end of the nineteenth century in England and Wales, an expectant mother was almost 50 times more likely to die in childbirth than is a woman giving birth today (Saunders, 1997).

Not much about childbirth has changed in some developing countries in sub-Saharan Africa and South Asia. There, 60 million women deliver at home each year without the benefit of skilled care, and more than 500,000 women and 4 million newborns die in or shortly after childbirth (Sines, Syed, Wall, & Worley, 2007).

After the turn of the twentieth century, childbirth began to be professionalized, at least in urban settings. The growing use of maternity hospitals led to somewhat safer, more antiseptic conditions for childbirth. This served to reduce mortality for women, and the new field of obstetrics grew. In 1900, only 5 percent of U.S. deliveries occurred in hospitals; by 1920, in some cities 65 percent did (Scholten, 1985). A similar trend took place in Europe. Most recently, in the United States, 99 percent of babies are born in hospitals, and 91.5 percent of births are attended by physicians. Nearly 8 percent are attended by midwives, usually certified nurse-midwives (Martin et al., 2009).

The dramatic reductions in risks surrounding pregnancy and childbirth in the industrialized world, particularly during the past 50 years, are largely due to the availability of antibiotics, blood transfusions, safe anesthesia, improved hygiene, and drugs for inducing labor when necessary. In addition, improvements in prenatal assessment and care make it far more likely that a baby will be born healthy. Mortality rates for both mothers and children have decreased dramatically as noted in Figures 5.1 and 5.2.

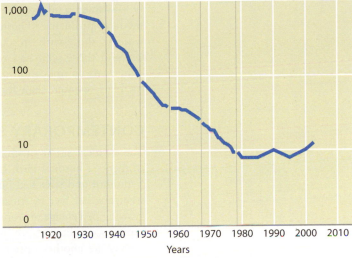

FIGURE 5.1

Maternal Mortality Rates, United States, 1915–2003

Since 1915 the maternal mortality rate in the United States has dropped from 607.9 deaths per 100,000 live births for the birth registration area to 12.1 deaths per 100,000 live births in 2003.

Note: Prior to 1933, data for birth-registration states only. Line breaks are shown between successive *International Classification of Diseases* revisions.

Source: National Center for Health Statistics, 2007; S. L. Clark, 2012

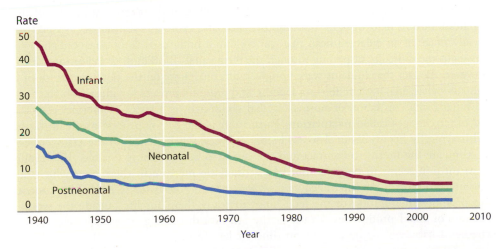

Source: Heron et al., 2009

FIGURE 5.2

Infant, Neonatal, and Postneonatal Mortality Rates, 1940–2006

The U.S. infant mortality rate has decreased from 47.0 infant deaths per 1,000 live births in 1940 to 6.7 in 2006. During the same period, the neonatal rate decreased 85 percent, from 28.8 to 4.5 deaths per 1,000 live births, and the postneonatal rate decreased 88 percent from 18.3 to 2.2 deaths per 1,000 live births.

Still, childbirth is not risk-free for women or babies. Among the nearly 4 million U.S. women who gave birth each year between 1993 and 1997, 31 percent experienced medical problems (Daniel, Berg, Johnson, & Atrash, 2003). Black women, obese women, those with difficult medical histories, those who had previous cesarean deliveries, and those who had several children are at elevated risk of hemorrhage and other dangerous complications; and the risk of dying in childbirth is at least 4 times higher for black women than for white women (Chazotte, quoted in Bernstein, 2003).

CONTEMPORARY SETTINGS FOR CHILDBIRTH

The medicalization of childbirth has had social and emotional costs. To many modern women, "a hospital birth has become a surgical act in which the woman is hooked up to a monitor and stretched out on a table under glaring lights and the stares of two or three strangers, her feet in stirrups" (Fontanel & d'Harcourt, 1997, p. 57). Today a small but growing percentage of women in economically developed countries are reviving the intimate experience of home birth, which can involve the whole family. Freestanding, homelike birth centers are another option. Some studies suggest that planned home births with speedy transfer to a hospital available in case of need can be as safe as hospital births for low-risk deliveries attended by skilled, certified midwives or nurse-midwives (American College of Nurse-Midwives, 2005). However, the American College of Obstetricians and Gynecologists (ACOG, 2008) and the American Medical Association (AMA, 2008) oppose home births, maintaining that complications can arise suddenly, even in low-risk pregnancies, and hospitals or accredited birthing centers are best equipped to respond to such emergencies.

However, in response to these social trends, hospitals are finding ways to "humanize" childbirth. Labor and delivery may take place in a quiet, homelike birthing room, under soft lights, with the father present as a coach and older siblings invited to visit after the birth. The woman is given local anesthesia if she wants and needs it, but she can see and consciously participate in the birth process and can hold her newborn on her belly immediately afterward. Rooming-in policies allow a baby to stay in the mother's room much or all of the time. By "demedicalizing the experience, some hospitals and birthing centers are seeking to establish—or reestablish—around childbirth an environment in which tenderness, security, and emotion carry as much weight as medical techniques" (Fontanel & d'Harcourt, 1997, p. 57).

The Birth Process

Emily woke up with some strange sensations in her belly. She had felt the baby, her first, moving all through her second and third trimesters, but this felt different. Her due date was still 2 weeks off. Could she be feeling the birth contractions she had heard and read so much about? Was she in labor?

Labor is an apt term for the process of giving birth. Chiefly because of the size of the fetal head, birth is hard work for both mother and baby. From an evolutionary perspective, the advantage of an enlarged head that can contain a brain capable of advanced thought outweighs the difficulty of passing through the birth canal (Bjorklund & Pellegrini, 2000). However, the fact that humans walk upright puts constraints on the potential width of a woman's pelvis, making childbirth a lengthy and arduous process for most women.

What brings on labor, or normal vaginal childbirth, is a series of uterine, cervical, and other changes called **parturition**. Parturition is the act or process of giving birth, and it typically begins about 2 weeks before delivery, when sharply rising estrogen levels stimulate the uterus to contract and the cervix to become more flexible. The timing of parturition seems to be determined by a dramatic increase in the rate at which the placenta produces a protein called *corticotropin-releasing hormone* (CRH). This protein also promotes maturation of the fetal lungs to ready them for life outside the womb. The rate of CRH production as early as the 5th month of pregnancy may help predict whether a baby will be born early, on time, or late (Smith, 1999, 2007).

checkpoint can you . . .

▷ Identify three ways in which childbirth has changed in developed countries?

▷ Give reasons for the reduction in risks of pregnancy and childbirth?

▷ Weigh the comparative advantages of various settings and attendants for childbirth?

guidepost 2 How does labor begin, what happens during each of the three stages of childbirth, and what alternative methods of delivery are available?

parturition
The act or process of giving birth.

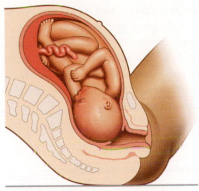

Stage one: Baby positions itself

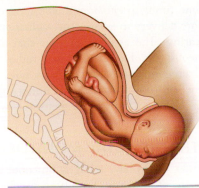

Stage two: Baby begins to emerge

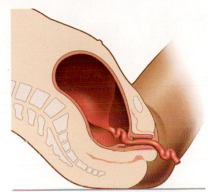

Stage three: Placenta is expelled

FIGURE 5.3

The Three Stages of Childbirth

(a) During the first stage of labor, a series of stronger and stronger contractions dilates the cervix, the opening to the mother's womb. (b) During the second stage, the baby's head moves down the birth canal and emerges from the vagina. (c) During the brief third stage, the placenta and umbilical cord are expelled from the womb. Then the cord is cut.

The uterine contractions that expel the fetus begin—typically, about 266 days after conception—as tightenings of the uterus. A woman may have felt false contractions (known as *Braxton-Hicks contractions*) at times during the final months of pregnancy, or even as early as the second trimester, when the muscles of the uterus tighten for up to 2 minutes. These contractions may help tone the uterine muscles and promote the flow of blood to the placenta but do not result in any of the cervical changes required for birth to take place. In comparison with Braxton-Hicks contractions, which are relatively mild and irregular and then subside, real labor contractions are more frequent, rhythmic, and painful, and they increase in frequency and intensity.

STAGES OF CHILDBIRTH

Labor takes place in three overlapping stages (Figure 5.3).

Stage 1: Dilation of the Cervix
The first stage, dilation of the cervix, is the longest, typically lasting 12 to 14 hours for a woman having her first child. In subsequent births the first stage tends to be shorter. During this stage, regular and increasingly frequent uterine contractions—15 to 20 minutes apart at first—cause the cervix to shorten and dilate, or widen, in preparation for delivery. Toward the end of the first stage, contractions occur every 2 to 5 minutes. This stage lasts until the cervix is fully open (10 centimeters, or about 4 inches) so the baby can descend into the birth canal.

Stage 2: Descent and Emergence of the Baby
The second stage, descent and emergence of the baby, typically lasts up to an hour or two. It begins when the baby's head begins to move through the cervix into the vaginal canal, and it ends when the baby emerges completely from the mother's body. If this stage lasts longer than 2 hours, signaling that the baby may need help, a doctor may grasp the baby's head with forceps or, more often, use vacuum extraction with a suction cup to pull it out of the mother's body. At the end of this stage, the baby is born but is still attached to the placenta in the mother's body by the umbilical cord, which must be cut and clamped.

Stage 3: Expulsion of the Placenta
The third stage, expulsion of the placenta, lasts between 10 minutes and 1 hour. During this stage the placenta and the remainder of the umbilical cord are expelled from the mother.

At one time, an *episiotomy*, a surgical cut between the vagina and anus, was made just before delivery to enlarge the vaginal opening, speed delivery, and prevent the vagina from tearing. The assumption was that a "clean" incision would heal better than a spontaneous tear. However, many studies have suggested this procedure led to more harm than good, and most experts now agree that episiotomy should not be done routinely. It is recommended only under special circumstances, such as a very large baby, a forceps birth, or indications of trouble with the baby's heart rate.

ELECTRONIC FETAL MONITORING

While most births have a happy outcome, labor and delivery are nonetheless risky. For that reason, technologies have been developed for the purpose of monitoring the fetus prior to delivery. **Electronic fetal monitoring** can be used to track the fetus's heartbeat during labor and delivery and to indicate how the fetal heart is responding to the stress of uterine contractions. Monitoring is most commonly done with the use of sensors attached to the woman's midsection and held in place with an electric belt. The sensors monitor heart rate and alert medical personnel of potentially problematic changes. The procedure was used in 85.4 percent of live births in the United States in 2003 (Martin et al., 2005).

Electronic fetal monitoring can provide valuable information in high-risk deliveries, including those in which the fetus is very small, is premature, is in a breech position (feet or buttocks down), or seems to be in distress, or in which labor is induced through administration of drugs. However, monitoring can have drawbacks if used routinely in low-risk pregnancies. It is costly; it restricts the mother's movements during labor; and, most important, it has an extremely high false-positive rate, suggesting that fetuses are in trouble when they are not. Such warnings may prompt doctors to deliver by the riskier cesarean method rather than the vaginal one (Banta & Thacker, 2001; Nelson, Dambrosia, Ting, & Grether, 1996).

VAGINAL VERSUS CESAREAN DELIVERY

The usual method of childbirth, previously described, is *vaginal delivery*. Alternatively, **cesarean delivery** can be used to surgically remove the baby from the uterus through an incision in the mother's abdomen. In 2007, a record-high 32 percent of U.S. births were by cesarean delivery, a 53 percent increase since 1996 (Menacker & Hamilton, 2010). Use of this procedure also increased in European countries during the 1990s, and despite a modest decrease in 2008 to 30 percent, cesarean birthrates in the United States are among the highest in the world (Gibbons et al., 2010).

The operation is commonly performed when labor progresses too slowly, when the fetus seems to be in trouble, or when the mother is bleeding vaginally. Often a cesarean is needed when the fetus is in the breech position (feet or buttocks first) or in the transverse position (lying crosswise in the uterus) or when the head is too big to pass through the mother's pelvis.

The increase in cesarean rates is attributed largely to rising proportions of older first-time mothers, who tend to have multiple births, and of very premature infants (Martin et al., 2009) for whom cesarean delivery significantly reduces the risk of dying during the 1st month of life (Malloy, 2008). Physicians' fear of malpractice suits and women's preferences also may play a part in the choice of cesarean deliveries (Ecker & Frigoletto, 2007; Martin et al., 2006, 2007, 2009), as may the increased revenue hospitals generate when a woman has a cesarean rather than a vaginal birth.

Cesarean deliveries carry risks of serious complications for the mother, such as bleeding, infection, damage to pelvic organs, postoperative pain, and heightened risks of problems in future pregnancies (Ecker & Frigoletto, 2007). They also deprive the baby of important benefits of normal birth such as the surge of hormones that clears the lungs of excess fluid, mobilizes stored fuel to nourish cells, and sends blood to the heart and brain. In making the baby more alert and ready to interact with another person, these hormones also may promote bonding with the mother (Lagercrantz & Slotkin, 1986). In addition, cesarean delivery can negatively impact breast-feeding, which can also affect bonding (Zanardo et al., 2010). Vaginal delivery also seems to influence a mother's attachment to her baby due to the action of oxytocin, a hormone involved in uterine contractions that stimulates maternal behavior in animals. There are indications that oxytocin may have similar effects in humans. In one study, fMRIs of the brains of mothers who had delivered vaginally showed more sensitivity to their newborns' cries than the brains of mothers who had had elective cesarean deliveries (Swain et al., 2008).

Oxytocin is involved in a variety of positive social interactions outside of the maternal relationship as well. For example, nasal sprays of oxytocin can help people who are low in social competence accurately read the emotions of others.

Bartz, 2010

Once a woman has had one cesarean delivery, many physicians warn that a vaginal birth after cesarean (VBAC) should be attempted only with caution. VBACs have been associated with greater (though still low) risks of uterine rupture and brain damage (Landon et al., 2004) as well as infant death (Smith, Pell, Cameron, & Dobbie, 2002). As the risks of such deliveries have become widely known, the rate of VBACs among U.S. women has fallen sharply. Today, if a woman has had a cesarean delivery, chances are about 92 percent that any subsequent deliveries will be by cesarean (Martin et al., 2009). However, an elective repeat cesarean before 39 weeks gestation, when the fetal lungs are fully mature, greatly increases the risk that the infant will have breathing problems, infections, or low blood sugar and will need intensive care (Tita et al., 2009). Thus, a recent NIH (2010) consensus development conference has concluded that a trial of labor is a reasonable option for women who have had a previous low transverse uterine incision.

MEDICATED VERSUS NONMEDICATED DELIVERY

For centuries, pain was considered an unavoidable part of giving birth. Then, in the mid-19th century, sedation with ether or chloroform became common practice as more births took place in hospitals (Fontanel & d'Harcourt, 1997).

Because of growing concerns that the use of drugs that might pose risks for babies, and a desire to enable both parents to participate fully in a natural, empowering experience, several alternative methods of **natural**, or **prepared**, **childbirth** were developed during the twentieth century. In 1914 Dr. Grantly Dick-Read, an English gynecologist, suggested that pain in childbirth was caused mostly by fear of the unknown and the resulting muscular tension. His "Childbirth without Fear" method educates expectant mothers about the physiology of reproduction and trains them in physical fitness and in breathing and relaxation during labor and delivery.

The Lamaze method, introduced by the French obstetrician Fernand Lamaze in the late 1950s, acknowledges that labor is painful and teaches expectant mothers to work actively with their bodies through controlled breathing. The woman is trained to pant or breathe rapidly in sync with the increasing intensity of her contractions and to concentrate on other sensations to ease the perception of pain. She learns to relax her muscles as a conditioned response to the voice of her coach (usually the prospective father or a friend), who attends classes with her, takes part in the delivery, and helps with the exercises. Other pain management methods use mental imagery, massage, gentle pushing, variations of upright posture, and deep breathing. One technique, introduced by the French physician Michael Odent, is submersion of the laboring mother in a soothing pool of water. Perhaps most extreme is the Bradley Method, which disavows all obstetrical procedures and other medical interventions.

study smart

Medicated versus Nonmedicated Delivery

natural, or **prepared, childbirth**
Method of childbirth that seeks to reduce or eliminate the use of drugs, enable both parents to participate fully, and control perceptions of pain.

TABLE 5.1 Neonatal Skin Conditions

Condition	Description	Cause	Duration
Blue coloring	Bluish color on hands and feet*	Immature blood circulation	Normal color should appear within several days
Milia	Tiny, white, hard, pimplelike spots on nose, chin, or forehead	Immature oil glands	Disappear on their own
Stork bites (or salmon patches)	Small pink or red patches on eyelids, between the eyes, on upper lip, or back of neck, most visible during crying	Concentration of immature blood vessels	Most soon fade and disappear
Mongolian spots	Blue or purple splotches on lower back and buttocks	Concentration of pigmented cells; tends to occur in dark-skinned babies	Usually disappears within first 4 years
Erythema toxicum	Red rash similar to flea bites, usually on chest and back	Cause unknown; appears in half of all babies, but most commonly in premature babies	Usually disappears in a few days
Acne neonatorum (baby acne)	Pimples on cheeks and forehead	Maternal hormones; about one-fifth of neonates develop this condition in 1st month	Disappears in a few months
Strawberry hemangioma (strawberry mark)	Bright or dark red, raised or swollen, bumpy area, usually on head	Concentration of tiny, immature blood vessels; often develop within first 2 months; most common in premature babies and in girls	Often grow in size for several months and then fade gradually, disappearing by age 9
Port wine stain	Flat pink, red, or purple birthmark, usually on head or neck but may cover large areas of body	Concentration of dilated capillaries (tiny, immature blood vessels)	Do not disappear; may become darker and bleed as child grows older; may be treated by laser surgery

*Bluish coloring on other parts of body is abnormal.

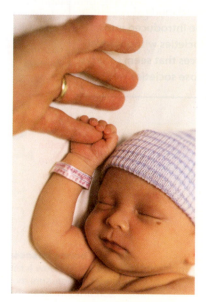

New babies weigh an average of 7½ pounds and have distinctive features, including a large head.

Table 5.1), birthmarks (which are permanent), and a receding chin (which makes it easier to nurse). Newborn infants also have areas on their heads known as *fontanels* where the bones of the skull do not meet. Many people refer to these holes as soft spots, and they are necessary because of the large size of a baby's head. Fontanels are covered by a tough membrane that allows for flexibility in shape, and thus, ease the passage of the neonate through the vaginal canal. In fact, many vaginally delivered newborns have a misshaped skull for a few weeks after birth. This has occurred as a result of squeezing through the vaginal canal. Over time, the skull rounds out again to a more typical form. And, in the first 18 months of life, the plates of the skull gradually fuse together.

Many newborns have a pinkish cast; their skin is so thin that it barely covers the capillaries through which blood flows. However, a baby's skin color can vary greatly, depending on the baby's age, racial or ethnic origin, health status, temperature, the environment, and whether the baby is crying. During the first few days, some neonates are very hairy because some of the *lanugo*, a fuzzy prenatal hair on the shoulders, back, forehead, and cheeks, has not yet fallen off. It appears most often in premature babies. Almost all new babies (except those born postterm, after 41 weeks of gestation), are covered with *vernix caseosa* ("cheesy varnish"), a white, oily, cheeselike substance that is formed in the womb by secretions from the fetal oil glands and protects against infection. This coating is absorbed into the skin after birth.

Gifted children tend to weigh more at birth.

TABLE 5.2 A Comparison of Prenatal and Postnatal Life

Characteristic	Prenatal Life	Postnatal Life
Environment	Amniotic fluid	Air
Temperature	Relatively constant	Fluctuates with atmosphere
Stimulation	Minimal	All senses stimulated by various stimuli
Nutrition	Dependent on mother's blood	Dependent on external food and functioning of digestive system
Oxygen supply	Passed from maternal bloodstream via placenta	Passed from neonate's lungs to pulmonary blood vessels
Metabolic elimination	Passed into maternal bloodstream via placenta	Discharged by skin, kidneys, lungs, and gastrointestinal tract

"Witch's milk," a secretion that sometimes leaks from the swollen breasts of newborn boys and girls around the 3rd day of life, was believed to have special healing powers during the Middle Ages. Like the whitish or blood-tinged vaginal discharge of some newborn girls, this fluid emission results from high levels of the hormone estrogen, which is secreted by the placenta just before birth, and goes away within a few days or weeks. A newborn, especially if premature, also may have swollen genitals.

BODY SYSTEMS

Before birth, blood circulation, respiration, nourishment, elimination of waste, and temperature regulation are accomplished through the mother's body. While all these systems, with the exception of the lungs, are functioning to some degree by the time a full-term birth occurs, the mother's own body systems are still involved and the fetus is not yet an independent entity. After birth, all of the baby's systems and functions must operate on their own (Table 5.2). Most of this transition occurs during the first 4 to 6 hours after delivery (Ferber & Makhoul, 2004).

During pregnancy, the fetus and mother have separate circulatory systems and separate heartbeats. The fetus's blood is cleansed through the umbilical cord, which carries "used" blood to the placenta and returns a fresh supply (refer to Figure 4.2 in Chapter 4). A neonate's blood circulates wholly within the baby's own body; the heartbeat at first is fast and irregular, and blood pressure does not stabilize until about the 10th day of life.

The fetus gets oxygen through the umbilical cord, which also carries away carbon dioxide. Once birth occurs, a newborn must start breathing and take over this function for itself. Most babies start to breathe as soon as they are exposed to air. If breathing has not begun within about 5 minutes, the baby may suffer permanent brain injury from **anoxia**, lack of oxygen, or *hypoxia*, a reduced oxygen supply. Anoxia or hypoxia may occur during delivery (though rarely so) as a result of repeated compression of the placenta and umbilical cord with each contraction. This form of *birth trauma* can leave permanent brain damage, causing mental retardation, behavior problems, or even death. Babies can have difficulty taking in enough oxygen after birth as well. Because infants' lungs have only one-tenth as many air sacs as adults' do, infants (especially those born prematurely) are susceptible to respiratory problems.

In the uterus, the fetus relies on the umbilical cord to bring food from the mother and to carry fetal body wastes away. After birth, babies must fully take over these functions for themselves. Many babies are born alert and ready to begin feeding. They have a strong sucking reflex to take in milk, and their own gastrointestinal secretions to digest it. Babies must also eliminate toxins from their bodies independently. During the first few days infants secrete *meconium*, a stringy, greenish-black waste matter formed in the

anoxia
Lack of oxygen, which may cause brain damage.

Although still experimental, early data suggest that "Cool Caps," designed to lower the temperature of the brain of babies suffering from anoxia, may slow or prevent brain damage by reducing the brain's energy needs.

Gluckman et al., 2005

neonatal jaundice
Condition in many newborn babies caused by immaturity of the liver and evidenced by a yellowish appearance; can cause brain damage if not treated promptly.

checkpoint
can **you** . . .

▷ Describe the normal size and appearance of a newborn, and name several temporary skin conditions and other changes that occur within the first few days?

▷ Compare four fetal and neonatal body systems?

▷ Identify two dangerous conditions that can appear soon after birth?

The APGAR is popular because it's easy to remember and requires no fancy medical equipment, making it useful to quickly asses the health of a newborn.

Apgar scale
Standard measurement of a newborn's condition; it assesses appearance, pulse, grimace, activity, and respiration.

fetal intestinal tract. In addition, babies begin to urinate on a regular basis, and the volume of urine is proportionate to food intake. When the bowels and bladder are full, the sphincter muscles open automatically; a baby will not be able to control these muscles for many months.

The layers of fat that develop during the last 2 months of fetal life enable healthy full-term infants to keep their body temperature constant after birth despite changes in air temperature. Newborn babies also maintain body temperature by increasing their activity when air temperature drops. These early fat deposits also provide babies with a reserve of energy until their mother's milk comes in.

Three or four days after birth, about half of all babies (and a larger proportion of babies born prematurely) develop **neonatal jaundice:** their skin and eyeballs look yellow. This kind of jaundice is caused by the immaturity of the liver and failure to filter out bilirubin, a by-product resulting from the breakdown of red blood cells. Usually it is not serious, does not need treatment, and has no long-term effects. However, because healthy U.S. newborns usually go home from the hospital within 48 hours or less, jaundice may go unnoticed and may lead to complications (AAP Committee on Quality Improvement, 2002). Severe jaundice that is not monitored and treated promptly may result in brain damage.

MEDICAL AND BEHAVIORAL ASSESSMENT

Although the great majority of births result in normal, healthy babies, some do not. The first few minutes, days, and weeks after birth are crucial for development. It is important to know as soon as possible whether a baby has any problem that needs special care.

The Apgar Scale One minute after delivery, and then again 5 minutes after birth, most babies are assessed using the **Apgar scale** (Table 5.3). Its name, after its developer, Dr. Virginia Apgar (1953), helps us remember its five subtests: *a*ppearance (color), *p*ulse (heart rate), *g*rimace (reflex irritability), *a*ctivity (muscle tone), and *r*espiration (breathing). The newborn is rated 0, 1, or 2 on each measure, for a maximum score of 10. A 5-minute score of 7 to 10—achieved by 98.4 percent of babies born in the United States in 2006—indicates that the baby is in good to excellent condition (Martin et al., 2009). A score of 5 to 7 at 1 minute may mean the baby needs help to establish breathing; nurses may dry him vigorously with a towel while oxygen is held under his nose, and the test should be repeated every 5 minutes up to 20 minutes (AAP Committee on Fetus and Newborn & American College of Obstetricians and Gynecologists [ACOG] Committee on Obstetric Practice, 2006).

TABLE 5.3 Apgar Scale			
Sign*	**0**	**1**	**2**
Appearance (color)	Blue, pale	Body pink, extremities blue	Entirely pink
Pulse (heart rate)	Absent	Slow (below 100 beats per minute)	Rapid (over 100 beats per minute)
Grimace (reflex irritability)	No response	Grimace	Coughing, sneezing, crying
Activity (muscle tone)	Limp	Weak, inactive; some flexing of arms and legs	Strong, active
Respiration (breathing)	Absent	Irregular, slow	Good, crying

*Each sign is rated in terms of absence or presence from 0 to 2; highest overall score is 10.

A score below 5 (unlikely except in a small percentage of premature newborns or those delivered by emergency cesarean) may reflect a variety of problems. For example, the heart or respiratory system may not be working at peak levels. In this event, a mask may be placed over the newborn's face to pump oxygen directly into the lungs; or, if breathing still does not start, a tube can be placed in the windpipe. In addition, medications and fluids may be administered through the blood vessels in the umbilical cord to strengthen the heartbeat. If resuscitation is successful, bringing the baby's score to 5 or more, long-term damage is unlikely. Scores of 0 to 3 at 10, 15, and 20 minutes after birth are increasingly associated with cerebral palsy (muscular impairment due to brain damage prenatally or during birth) or other neurological problems (AAP Committee on Fetus and Newborn & ACOG Committee on Obstetric Practice, 1996, 2006).

In general, Apgar scores at 5 minutes reliably predict survival during the 1st month of life (Martin et al., 2009). However, a low Apgar score alone does not necessarily indicate anoxia or predict neonatal death. Prematurity, low birth weight, trauma, infection, birth defects, medication given to the mother, and other conditions may affect the scores (AAP Committee on Fetus and Newborn & ACOG Committee on Obstetric Practice, 1996, 2006).

Assessing Neurological Status: The Brazelton Scale The **Brazelton Neonatal Behavioral Assessment Scale (NBAS)** is a neurological and behavioral test to measure a neonate's responses to the environment. It is used to help parents, health care providers, and researchers assess neonates' responsiveness to their physical and social environment, to identify strengths and possible vulnerabilities in neurological functioning, and to predict future development. The test, suitable for infants up to 2 months old, is named for its developer, Dr. T. Berry Brazelton (1973, 1984; Brazelton & Nugent, 1995, 2001). It assesses *motor organization* as shown by such behaviors as activity level and the ability to bring a hand to the mouth; *reflexes*; *state changes*, such as irritability, excitability, and ability to quiet down after being upset; *attention and interactive capacities*, as shown by general alertness and response to visual and auditory stimuli; and indications of *central nervous system instability*, such as tremors and changes in skin color. The NBAS takes about 30 minutes, and scores are based on a baby's best performance.

Brazelton Neonatal Behavioral Assessment Scale (NBAS) Neurological and behavioral test to measure a neonate's responses to the environment.

Neonatal Screening for Medical Conditions As we mentioned in Chapter 3, children who inherit the enzyme disorder phenylketonuria, or PKU, will become mentally retarded unless they are fed a special diet beginning in the first 3 to 6 weeks of life (National Institute of Child Health & Human Development, 2010). Screening tests administered soon after birth often can discover this and other correctable defects. Generally, blood is collected via a heelstick from newborn babies at the hospital and used to screen for this and other conditions.

Routine screening of all newborn babies for such rare conditions as PKU (1 case in 15,000 births), congenital hypothyroidism (1 in 3,600 to 5,000), galactosemia (1 in 60,000 to 80,000), and other, even rarer, disorders is expensive. Yet the cost of testing thousands of newborns to detect one case of a rare disease may be less than the cost of caring for one mentally retarded person for a lifetime. Now, with more sophisticated blood tests, a single blood specimen can be screened for 20 or more disorders, so about half of all states as well as many developed countries have expanded their mandatory screening programs (Howell, 2006). In a study of newborns in several New England states, infants identified by screening were less likely to become retarded or to need hospitalization than those identified by clinical diagnosis. However, the tests can generate false positive results, suggesting that a problem exists when it does not, and may trigger anxiety and costly, unnecessary treatment (Waisbren et al., 2003).

checkpoint can you . . .

▷ Discuss the uses of the Apgar test, the Brazelton Scale, and routine postbirth screening for rare disorders?

STATES OF AROUSAL AND ACTIVITY LEVELS

Are you an early bird or a night owl? Do you get particularly sleepy or alert at certain points of the day? When do you get hungry? These tendencies are likely related to your

TABLE 5.4 States of Arousal in Infancy

State	Eyes	Breathing	Movements	Responsiveness
Regular sleep	Closed; no eye movement	Regular and slow	None, except for sudden, generalized startles	Cannot be aroused by mild stimuli.
Irregular sleep	Closed; occasional rapid eye movements	Irregular	Muscles twitch, but no major movements	Sounds or light bring smiles or grimaces in sleep.
Drowsiness	Open or closed	Irregular	Somewhat active	May smile, startle, suck, or have erections in response to stimuli.
Alert inactivity	Open	Even	Quiet; may move head, limbs, and trunk while looking around	An interesting environment (with people or things to watch) may initiate or maintain this state.
Waking activity and crying	Open	Irregular	Much activity	External stimuli (such as hunger, cold, pain, being restrained, or being laid down) bring about more activity, perhaps starting with soft whimpering and gentle movements and turning into a rhythmic crescendo of crying or kicking, or perhaps beginning and enduring as uncoordinated thrashing and spasmodic screeching.

Source: Adapted from Prechtl & Beintema, 1964; Wolff, 1969.

state of arousal
Infant's physiological and behavioral status at a given moment in the periodic daily cycle of wakefulness, sleep, and activity.

connect

studysmart

Sleep

own internal clock. This clock regulates your states of arousal and activity over the course of a day. Babies also have an internal clock that regulates their daily cycles of eating, sleeping, and elimination and perhaps even their moods. These periodic cycles of wakefulness, sleep, and activity, which govern an infant's **state of arousal**, or degree of alertness (Table 5.4), seem to be inborn and highly individual. Changes in state are coordinated by multiple areas of the brain and are accompanied by changes in the functioning of virtually all body systems (Ingersoll & Thoman, 1999; Scher, Epstein, & Tirosh, 2004). The establishment of "stable and distinct" states of arousal is associated with newborn health and positive outcomes.

Most new babies sleep about 75 percent of their time—up to 18 hours a day—but wake up every 3 to 4 hours, day and night, for feeding (Ferber & Makhoul, 2004; Hoban, 2004). Newborns' sleep alternates between quiet (regular) and active (irregular) sleep. Active sleep appears to be the equivalent of rapid eye movement (REM) sleep, which in adults is associated with dreaming. Active sleep appears rhythmically in cycles of about 1 hour and accounts for up to 50 percent of a newborn's total sleep time. The amount of REM sleep declines to less than 30 percent of daily sleep time by age 3 and continues to decrease steadily throughout life (Hoban, 2004).

In addition to daily sleep cycles, our bodies experience other ones. For example, we experience regular nasal dominance cycles that we may only notice when we have increased congestion as the result of a cold. One nostril is dominant, and this switches on a regular basis over the course of the day.

Eccles, 1978

Beginning in the 1st month, nighttime sleep periods gradually lengthen and total sleep time diminishes as babies grow more wakeful in the daytime. Some infants begin to sleep through the night as early as age 3 months. By 6 months, an infant typically sleeps for 6 hours straight at night, but brief nighttime waking is normal even during late infancy and toddlerhood. A 2-year-old typically sleeps about 13 hours a day, including a single nap, usually in the afternoon (Hoban, 2004).

Babies' sleep rhythms and schedules vary across cultures. Among the Micronesian Truk and the Canadian Hare peoples, babies and children have no regular sleep schedules; they fall asleep whenever they feel tired. Some U.S. parents try to time the evening feeding to encourage nighttime sleep. Mothers in rural Kenya allow their babies to nurse as they please, and their 4-month-olds continue to sleep only 4 hours at a stretch (Broude, 1995). In many predominantly Asian countries, bedtimes are later and total sleep time is shorter than in predominantly Caucasian countries (Mindell, Sadeh, Wiegand, How, & Goh, 2010).

Some parents and caregivers spend a great deal of time and energy trying to change babies' states—mostly by soothing a fussy infant to sleep. This is particularly important for low-birth-weight babies because quiet babies maintain their weight better. Steady stimulation is the time-proven way to soothe crying babies: by rocking or walking them, wrapping them snugly, or letting them hear rhythmic sound. Box 5.2 offers suggestions for comforting a crying baby.

▶ **checkpoint**
can **you . . .**

▷ Discuss patterns of sleep, arousal, and activity and variations in newborns' states?

▷ Tell how sleep patterns change, and how cultural practices can affect these patterns?

connect

study smart

Swaddling

Complications of Childbirth— and Their Aftermath

What complications of childbirth can endanger newborn babies, and what are the long-term prospects for babies with complicated births?

"It must be a boy," say some mothers whose labor and delivery prove long and difficult. This old wives' tale is grounded in some truth: boys' deliveries are more likely to involve complications than girls', in part because boy babies tend to be larger (Bekedam, Engelsbel, Mol, Buitendijk, & van der Pal-de Bruin, 2002; Eogan, Geary, O'Connell, & Keane, 2003).

Although the great majority of births result in normal, healthy babies, some, sadly, do not. Some are born prematurely or very small, some remain in the womb too long, and some are born dead or die soon after birth. Let's look at these potential complications of birth and how they can be avoided or treated to maximize the chances of favorable outcomes.

LOW BIRTH WEIGHT

Low-birth-weight babies (LBW) are those neonates born weighing less than 2,500 grams (5 pounds) at birth. There are two types of LBW babies: those born early and those born small. Typical gestation is 40 weeks, and babies born before the 37th week of gestation are known as **preterm (premature) infants**. Being born early is closely associated, as might be expected, with being smaller than a full-term infant. More than

low-birth-weight babies
Infants who weigh less than 5½ pounds (2,500 grams) at birth because of prematurity or being small-for-date.

preterm (premature) infants
Infants born before completing the 37th week of gestation.

FIGURE 5.4

Birth Complications, United States, 2005

Percentages of live births that were: (a) preterm (less than 37 weeks gestation); or (b) low birth weight (less than 2,500 grams). Low-birth-weight babies can be preterm or small-for date, or both.

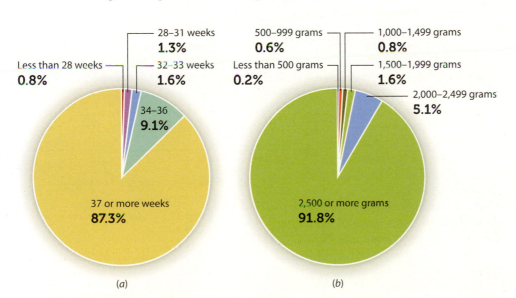

Source: Adapted from Mathews & MacDorman, 2008, figures 2 and 3.

the everyday world

5.2

COMFORTING A CRYING BABY

All babies cry. It is their first communicative signal and is their way of letting us know they are hungry, uncomfortable, lonely, or unhappy. And because few sounds are as distressing as a baby's cry, parents or other caregivers usually rush to feed or pick up a crying infant. Once an infant's problem has been solved, the baby generally quiets down and falls asleep or gazes about in alert contentment. At other times, the caregiver cannot figure out what the baby wants, and the baby may continue to cry and cry. It is worth trying to find ways to help. Parents who cannot figure out why their baby continues to cry for a persistent period of time may become stressed, irritable, and depressed. Moreover, babies are affected by frequent crying as well. Babies whose cries do not bring relief seem to become less self-confident, feeling that they cannot affect their own lives.

In Chapter 8 we discuss several kinds of crying and what the crying may mean. Unusual, persistent crying patterns may be early signs of trouble. For healthy babies who just seem unhappy, the following may help (Eiger & Olds, 1999):

- Hold the baby, perhaps laying the baby on his or her stomach on your chest, to feel your heartbeat and breathing. Or sit with the baby in a comfortable rocking chair.
- Put the baby in a carrier next to your chest and walk around.
- If you are upset, ask someone else to hold the baby; infants sometimes sense and respond to their caregivers' moods.
- Pat or rub the baby's back, or "bicycle" their legs in case a bubble of air is causing discomfort.
- Wrap the baby snugly in a small blanket; some infants feel more secure when firmly swaddled from neck to toes, with arms held close to the sides.
- Make the baby warmer or cooler; put on or take off clothing or change the room temperature.
- Give the baby a massage or a warm bath.
- Sing or talk to the baby. Or provide a continuous or rhythmic sound, such as music from the radio, a simulated heartbeat, or background noise from a whirring fan, vacuum cleaner, or other appliance.
- Take the baby out for a ride in a stroller or car seat—at any hour of the day or night. In bad weather, some parents walk around in an enclosed mall; the distraction helps them as well as the baby.

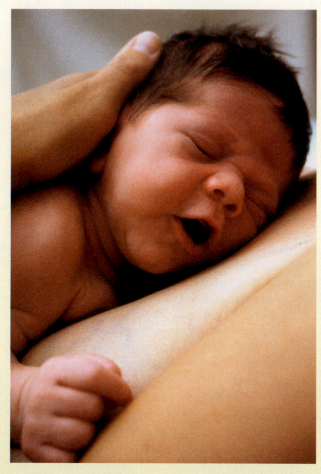

This crying baby may quiet when held stomach down on his mother's chest.

- If someone other than a parent is taking care of the baby, it sometimes helps if the caregiver puts on a robe or a sweater that the mother or father has recently worn so the baby can sense the familiar smell.

what's your view

▷ Have you ever tried to soothe a crying baby?

▷ What techniques seemed to work best?

TABLE 5.5	Percentage of Low-Birth-Weight Infants by Selected United Nations Regions, 1999–2006*	
		% Low-Birth-Weight Infants
WORLD		**15**
Industrialized countries		7
Developing countries		16
Least developed countries		17
AFRICA		
Eastern and Southern Africa		14
Sub-Saharan Africa		14
Western and Central Africa		14
Northern Africa and Middle East		16
ASIA		
Eastern Asia and Pacific		6
South Asia		29
EASTERN EUROPE (CEE/CTS)		**6**
LATIN AMERICA AND CARIBBEAN		**9**

*Data refer to the most recent year available during 1999–2006.

Source: UNICEF, 2008b.

43 percent of preterm infants are of low birth weight, as compared with only about 3 percent of full-term infants (Martin et al, 2009). Some babies, known as **small-for-date (small-for-gestational-age) infants**, are born at or around their due date, but are smaller than would be expected. These babies weigh less than 90 percent of babies of the same gestational age. They are small, not because they were born early and did not have a chance to finish putting on weight, but for other reasons, most commonly inadequate prenatal nutrition, which slows fetal growth.

An estimated 15 percent of all infants worldwide are born with low birth weight, and the percentages are far greater in less economically developed countries (UNICEF, 2008b; Table 5.5).

The true extent of low birth weight may be much higher because as many as 3 out of 4 newborns in the developing world are not weighed. Low birth weight in developing regions stems primarily from the mother's poor health and nutrition. In a double-blind study of 8,468 pregnant women in Tanzania, daily multivitamin supplements reduced the incidence of low birth weight (Fawzi et al., 2007). In the industrialized world, smoking during pregnancy is the leading factor in low birth weight (UNICEF & WHO, 2004).

In the United States, 8.3 percent of infants born in 2006 were low-birth-weight babies—the highest percentage in four decades. In the same year, 12.8 percent of U.S. infants were preterm, 36 percent more than in the early 1980s. Much of the rise in low-birth-weight and preterm births is likely due to delayed childbearing, multiple births, and use of fertility drugs and induced and cesarean deliveries; but low birth weight and prematurity also have increased among single births (Martin et al., 2009).

Birth weight and length of gestation are the two most important predictors of an infant's survival and health (Mathews & MacDorman, 2008). Together they constitute the second leading cause of death in infancy in the United States after birth defects and the leading cause during the neonatal period (Kung, Hoyert, Xu, & Murphy, 2008; Hoyert, Heron, Murphy, & Kung, 2006). Preterm birth is involved in nearly half of

small-for-date (small-for-gestational-age) infants
Infants whose birth weight is less than that of 90 percent of babies of the same gestational age as a result of slow fetal growth.

neurological birth defects, such as cerebral palsy, and more than one-third of infant deaths; altogether, low-birth-weight infants account for more than two-thirds of infant deaths. Late preterm infants, delivered between 34 and 36 weeks' gestation, tend to weigh more and to fare better than those born earlier in gestation; but in comparison with full-term babies, they too are at greater risk of early death or long-term adverse effects (Martin et al., 2006, 2007, 2009; Mathews & MacDorman, 2008). Internationally, low birth weight is an underlying factor in 60 to 80 percent of neonatal deaths worldwide (UNICEF, 2008b).

The United States has been more successful than any other country in saving low-birth-weight babies, but the rate of such births to U.S. women remains higher than in some European and Asian nations (UNICEF & WHO, 2004). Preventing preterm births would greatly increase the number of babies who survive the first year of life, but such measures as enhanced prenatal care, nutritional interventions, home monitoring of uterine activity, and administration of drugs, bed rest, and hydration for women who go into labor early have failed to stem the tide (Goldenberg & Rouse, 1998; Lockwood, 2002). One promising treatment is a form of the hormone progesterone called *hydroxy-progesterone caproate*, or *17P*. In a 2½-year trial at 13 major medical research centers, giving 17P to women who had borne premature babies reduced repeat preterm births by as much as one-third (Meis et al., 2003).

Who Is Likely to Have a Low-Birth-Weight Baby? Factors increasing the likelihood that a woman will have an underweight baby include (1) *demographic and socioeconomic factors*, such as being African American, under age 17 or over 40, poor, unmarried, or undereducated, and being born in certain regions, such as the southern and plains states (Thompson, Goodman, Chang, & Stukel, 2005); (2) *medical factors predating the pregnancy*, such as having no children or more than four, being short or thin, having had previous low-birth-weight infants or multiple miscarriages, having had low birth weight oneself, or having genital or urinary abnormalities or chronic hypertension; (3) *prenatal behavioral and environmental factors*, such as poor nutrition, inadequate prenatal care, smoking, use of alcohol or other drugs (especially heavy or binge drinking, which increases the risk of preterm delivery), or exposure to stress, high altitude, or toxic substances; and (4) *medical conditions associated with the pregnancy*, such as vaginal bleeding, infections, high or low blood pressure, anemia, too little weight gain (Arias, MacDorman, Strobino, & Guyer, 2003; S. S. Brown, 1985; Chomitz, Cheung, & Lieberman, 1995; Nathanielsz, 1995; O'Leary, Nassar, Kurinczuk, & Bower, 2009; Shiono & Behrman, 1995; Wegman, 1992; Zhu, Rolfs, Nangle, & Horan, 1999), and having last given birth less than 12 months or more than 5 years before (Conde-Agudelo, Rosas-Bermúdez, & Kafury-Goeta, 2006; DeFranco, Stamilio, Boslaugh, Gross, & Muglia, 2007). Depression during pregnancy is another risk factor; screening for depression is a critical part of prenatal care (Yonkers, quoted in Bernstein, 2003).

The high proportion (11.85 percent) of low-birth-weight babies in the non-Hispanic black population—more than twice as high as among white and Hispanic babies (Martin et al., 2009)—is a major factor in the high mortality rates of black babies (Hoyert, Mathews, et al., 2006; Martin et al., 2007; MacDorman & Mathews, 2008; see Chapter 6). Researchers have identified a genetic variant that may help explain the high rates of premature delivery among African American women (Wang et al., 2006). Other suggested reasons for the greater prevalence of low birth weight, preterm births, and infant mortality among African American babies include (1) health behaviors and SES; (2) higher levels of stress in African American women; (3) greater susceptibility to stress; (4) the impact of racism, which may contribute to or exacerbate stress; and (5) ethnic differences in stress-related body processes, such as blood pressure and immune reactions (Giscombé & Lobel, 2005).

Immediate Treatment and Outcomes The most pressing fear regarding very small babies is that they will die in infancy. Because their immune systems are not fully developed, they are especially vulnerable to infection, which has been linked to slowed growth and developmental delays (Stoll et al., 2004). Moreover, their status sometimes requires a variety of invasive interventions, increasing the chances of infection. Also, these infants' nervous systems may be too immature for them to perform functions basic to survival, such as sucking, so they may need to be fed intravenously (through the veins). Feeding them mothers' milk can help prevent infection (AAP Section on Breastfeeding, 2005; Furman, Taylor, Minich, & Hack, 2003). Because they do not have enough fat to insulate them and to generate heat, it is hard for them to stay warm. Low Apgar scores in a preterm newborn are a strong indication of the need for intensive care (Weinberger et al., 2000).

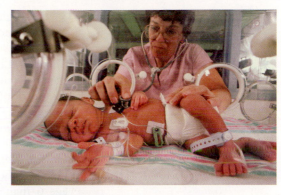

The antiseptic, temperature-controlled crib, or isolette, in which this premature baby lies has holes through which the infant can be examined, touched, and massaged. Frequent human contact helps low-birth-weight infants thrive.

A low-birth-weight or at-risk preterm baby is placed in an *isolette* (an antiseptic, temperature-controlled crib) and fed through tubes. To counteract the sensory impoverishment of life in an isolette, hospital workers and parents are encouraged to give these small babies special handling. Gentle massage seems to foster growth, weight gain, motor activity, alertness, and behavioral organization, as assessed by the Brazelton NBAS (T. Field, 1998b; T. Field, Diego, & Hernandez-Reif, 2007), and can shorten the hospital stay (T. Field, Hernandez-Reif, & Freedman, 2004; Standley, 1998). However, their appearance, as well as their tendency to be less engaged with parents during interactions, can lead to difficulties with respect to the bonding process.

Premature infants tend to show uneven state development. Compared with full-term infants the same age, they are more alert and wakeful and have longer stretches of quiet sleep and more REMs in active sleep. On the other hand, their sleep can be more fragmented, with more transitions between sleeping and waking (Holditch-Davis, Schwarts, & Hudson-Barr, 2004; Ingersoll & Thoman, 1999). **Kangaroo care**, a method of skin-to-skin contact in which a newborn is laid face down between the mother's breasts for an hour or so at a time after birth, can help preemies—and full-term infants—make the adjustment from fetal life to the jumble of sensory stimuli in the outside world. This soothing maternal contact seems to reduce stress on the central nervous system and help with self-regulation of sleep and activity (Ferber & Makhoul, 2004).

kangaroo care
Method of skin-to-skin contact in which a newborn is laid face down between the mother's breasts.

Respiratory distress syndrome, also called *hyaline membrane disease*, is common in preterm babies who lack an adequate amount of *surfactant*, an essential lung-coating substance that keeps air sacs from collapsing. These babies may breathe irregularly or stop breathing altogether. Since 1994, administering surfactant to high-risk preterm newborns has dramatically increased survival rates (Corbet et al., 1995; Goldenberg & Rouse, 1998; Horbar et al., 1993; Martin et al., 2005; Msall, 2004; Stoelhorst et al., 2005) as well as neurological and developmental status at 18 to 22 months (Vohr, Wright, Poole, & McDonald for the NICHD Neonatal Research Network Follow-up Study, 2005). Since 2000 the percentage of extremely low-birth-weight infants who survived unimpaired has increased further (Wilson-Costello et al., 2007).

Long-Term Outcomes Even if low-birth-weight babies survive the dangerous early days, their future is in question. For example, both preterm and small-for-gestational-age infants may be at increased risk of adult-onset diabetes, and small-for-gestational-age infants appear to be at increased risk of cardiovascular disease (Hofman et al., 2004; Sperling, 2004). Among a cohort born in Norway in 1967, and followed longitudinally, preterm birth led to heightened risk of death throughout childhood, diminished reproductive rates in adulthood, and, for women, increased risk of bearing preterm infants themselves (Swamy, Ostbye, & Skjaerven, 2008). In another Norwegian cohort, the shorter the period of gestation, the greater the likelihood of cerebral palsy, mental retardation, autistic disorders, and low educational and job-related income levels (Moster, Lie, & Markestad, 2008).

A brain lipid called Docosahexaenoic acid (DHA) is not adequately developed in infants born before 33 weeks' gestation and can lead to impaired mental development. In a longitudinal study of infants born before that gestational age, girls, but not boys, who received compensating high doses of fatty acids through breast milk or infant formula until what would have been full term showed better mental development at 18 months than premature girls who had been fed a low-DHA diet (Makrides et al., 2009).

In longitudinal studies of extremely low-birth-weight infants (about 1 to 2 pounds at birth) and infants born before 26 weeks of gestation, the survivors tend to be smaller than full-term children and more likely to have neurological, sensory, cognitive, educational, and behavioral problems (Anderson, Doyle & the Victorian Infant Collaborative Study Group, 2003; Marlow, Wolke, Bracewell, & Samara for the EPICure Study Group, 2005; Mikkola et al., 2005; Saigal, Stoskopf, Streiner, & Burrows, 2001; Samara, Marlow, & Wolke for the EPICure Study Group, 2008). Among a cohort of extremely low-birth-weight infants born in Finland in 1996–1997, only 26 percent showed normal development at age 5 (Mikkola et al., 2005). And in a study of children born in the United Kingdom and Ireland in 1995, those born at or before 25 weeks of gestation—especially boys—were about 5 times more likely to show serious behavior problems at age 6 than a control group who had not been born preterm, possibly because early separation from the mother affects the developing brain (Samara et al., 2008).

The less low-birth-weight children weigh at birth, the lower their IQs and achievement test scores tend to be and the more likely they are to require special education or to repeat a grade (Saigal, Hoult, Streiner, Stoskopf, & Rosenbaum, 2000). Cognitive deficits, especially in memory and processing speed, have been noted among very-low-birth-weight babies (those weighing less than 1,500 grams or 3½ pounds at birth) by age 5 or 6 months, continuing throughout childhood (Rose & Feldman, 2000; Rose, Feldman, & Jankowski, 2002), and persisting into adulthood (Fearon et al., 2004; Greene, 2002; Hack et al., 2002; Hardy, Kuh, Langenberg, & Wadsworth, 2003). Very-low-birth-weight children and adolescents also tend to have more behavioral and mental health problems than those born at normal weight (Hack et al., 2004).

On the other hand, in a longitudinal study of 296 infants who weighed, on average, just over 2 pounds at birth and were considered borderline retarded, most showed cognitive improvement in early childhood and intelligence in the normal range by age 8. Children in two-parent families, those whose mothers were highly educated, those who had not suffered significant brain damage, and those who did not need special help did best (Ment et al., 2003). And, in a prospective longitudinal study of 166 extremely low-birth-weight babies born from 1977 to 1982 in Ontario, Canada, where health care is universal, a significant majority overcame earlier difficulties to become functioning young adults, finishing high school, working, and living independently and many of them pursuing postsecondary education. The children were predominantly white and from two-parent families, about half of them of high SES. Children with disabilities had been integrated into regular schools and provided with classroom assistants (Saigal et al., 2006). Birth weight alone, then, does not necessarily determine the outcome. Environmental factors make a difference, as we discuss in a subsequent section. More specifically, babies are highly resilient, and a high-quality postnatal environment can do much to mitigate the potential effects of being born small.

POSTMATURITY

postmature
A fetus not yet born as of 42 weeks' gestation.

When people think about birth complications, they generally think about the issues related to being born too early or too small. However, babies can also be negatively affected by staying too long in the womb. In fact, nearly 6 percent of pregnant women in the United States have not gone into labor after 42 or more weeks' gestation (Martin et al., 2009). At that point, a baby is considered **postmature**. Postmature babies tend to be long and thin as they continue to grow in the womb but do not receive a sufficient blood supply toward the end of gestation. The placenta becomes less efficient as the pregnancy progresses, resulting in a decrease in the levels of nutrients and oxygen that are available to the baby. The baby's greater size also complicates labor; the mother has to deliver a baby the size of a normal 1-month-old.

Because postmature fetuses are at risk of brain damage or even death, doctors sometimes induce labor or perform cesarean deliveries. The increasing use of both of these techniques probably explains a decline in postterm births in recent years (Martin et al., 2006).

STILLBIRTH

Stillbirth, the sudden death of a fetus at or after the 20th week of gestation, is a tragic union of opposites—birth and death. Sometimes fetal death is diagnosed prenatally; in other cases, the baby's death is discovered during labor or delivery.

Worldwide, about 3.2 million fetuses are stillborn annually (Lawn et al., 2010). In the United States the incidence of stillbirth has fallen steadily since 1990, mainly due to a decline in third-trimester deaths. Still, the number of reported stillbirths—25,894, or 6.22 for every 1,000 live births plus fetal deaths in 2005—is nearly as great as the total of all infant deaths (Kung et al., 2008; MacDorman & Kirmeyer, 2009). Boys are more likely to be stillborn than girls, non-Hispanic black fetuses are more likely to be stillborn than fetuses of other racial/ethnic groups, and twins and higher multiples are more likely to be stillborn than singletons. Use of assisted reproductive technologies may increase the risk of stillbirth (MacDorman & Kirmeyer, 2009).

Although the cause of stillbirth is often not clear, many stillborn fetuses are small for gestational age, indicating malnourishment in the womb (Surkan, Stephansson, Dickman, & Cnattingius, 2004). In 2005 more than one-third (35 percent) of stillborn fetuses in the United States weighed less than 500 grams at delivery, and one-half weighed less than 750 grams (MacDorman & Kirmeyer, 2009). The reduction in stillbirths may be due to electronic fetal monitoring, ultrasound, and other measures to identify fetuses at risk for restricted growth. Fetuses believed to have problems can have prenatal surgery in the womb to correct congenital problems or be delivered prematurely (Goldenberg, Kirby, & Culhane, 2004; Goldenberg & Rouse, 1998).

Stillbirth has been called an "invisible death." Family members may struggle for years to come to terms with their loss in a social environment that denies the legitimacy of the loss (Cacciatore, DeFrain, & Jones, 2008, p. 1). A stillbirth is what family therapist Pauline Boss (2006, 2007) calls an *ambiguous loss*, one that leaves the bereaved parents with more questions than answers. The bereaved parents may ask themselves, "Why did our baby die? Did I contribute to the death? Should we have another baby? Will this happen again? Could I endure it?" Although the stillborn baby is physically absent, "the baby's psychological presence continues for the rest of the family members' lives" (Cacciatore et al., 2008, p. 4). A mother may express shame over her body's failure to produce a live, healthy baby and may wonder whether her husband blames her. Siblings may show such physical symptoms as insomnia, lack of appetite or overeating, regression in development, anxiety, irritability, anger, apathy, nervous tics, muscle tension, emotional outbursts, and tearfulness (Cacciatore et al., 2008). (Refer to Box 4.1 in Chapter 4 for ways to ease a loss due to stillbirth.)

CAN A SUPPORTIVE ENVIRONMENT OVERCOME EFFECTS OF BIRTH COMPLICATIONS?

From an evolutionary standpoint, people—like other organisms—thrive, reproduce, and survive in environments suitable to their needs and expectations. Thus appropriate environmental characteristics can help an infant develop optimally. Furthermore, human beings are adaptable and resilient, especially during the early years. A major longitudinal study suggests that, given a supportive environment, resilience can occur even in the face of a difficult start in life.

For nearly five decades, Emmy E. Werner (1987, 1995; Werner & Smith, 2001) and a team of pediatricians, psychologists, public health workers, and social workers have followed 698 children, born in 1955 on the Hawaiian island of Kauai, from gestation to middle adulthood. The researchers interviewed the mothers-to-be, monitored their pregnancies, and interviewed them again when the children were ages 1, 2, and 10. They observed the children at home, gave them aptitude, achievement, and personality tests in elementary and high school, and obtained progress reports from their teachers. The young people themselves were interviewed periodically after they reached adulthood.

stillbirth
Death of a fetus at or after the 20th week of gestation.

checkpoint can you . . .

▷ Discuss the risk factors, treatment, and outcomes for low-birth-weight babies?

▷ Explain the risks attending postmaturity?

▷ State risk factors for stillbirth, and explain why stillbirth rates have decreased?

Although they are fragile and must be handled carefully, low-birth-weight babies who are cuddled and held gain weight and are released from the hospital faster.

Thanks to positive environments and their own resilience, fully a third of the at-risk children studied by Emmy Werner and her colleagues developed into self-confident, successful adults.

protective factors
Factors that reduce the impact of potentially negative influences and tend to predict positive outcomes.

▷ Name three protective factors identified by the Kauai study?

The physical and psychological development of children who had suffered low birth weight or other birth complications were seriously impaired *only* when the children grew up in persistently poor environmental circumstances. Unless the early damage was so serious as to require institutionalization, those children who had a stable and enriching environment did well (E. E. Werner, 1985, 1987). In fact, they had fewer language, perceptual, emotional, and school problems than did children who had *not* experienced unusual stress at birth but who had received little intellectual stimulation or emotional support at home (E. E. Werner, 1989; E. E. Werner et al., 1968). The children who had been exposed to *both* birth-related problems and later stressful experiences had the worst health and the most delayed development (E. E. Werner, 1987).

Most remarkable is the resilience of children who escaped damage despite *multiple* sources of stress. Even when birth complications were combined with chronic poverty, family discord, divorce, or parents who were mentally ill, many children came through relatively unscathed. Of the 276 children who at age 2 had been identified as having four or more risk factors, two-thirds developed serious learning or behavior problems by age 10 or, by age 18, had become pregnant, gotten in trouble with the law, or become emotionally disturbed. Yet by age 30, one-third of these highly at-risk children had managed to become "competent, confident, and caring adults" (E. E. Werner, 1995, p. 82). Of the full sample, about half of those on whom the researchers were able to obtain follow-up data successfully weathered the age-30 and age-40 transitions. Women tended to be better adapted than men (E. Werner & Smith, 2001).

Protective factors, which tended to reduce the impact of early stress, fell into three categories: (1) individual attributes, such as energy, sociability, and intelligence; (2) affectionate ties with at least one supportive family member; and (3) rewards at school, work, or place of worship that provide a sense of meaning and control over one's life (E. E. Werner, 1987). Although the home environment seemed to have the most marked effect in childhood, in adulthood the individuals' own qualities made a greater difference (E. E. Werner, 1995).

This study underlines the need to look at development in context. It shows how biological and environmental influences interact, making resiliency possible even in babies born with serious complications. (Characteristics of resilient children are further discussed in Chapter 14.)

Newborns and Parents

Childbirth is a major transition, not only for the baby, but for the parents as well. Suddenly almost all their time and energy (it seems) is focused on this newcomer in their lives. Parents (and, perhaps, siblings) are getting acquainted with this newcomer and developing emotional bonds. Especially with a first birth, a newborn brings insistent demands that challenge the parents' ability to cope—and may affect their marital relationship.

INFANT CARE: A CROSS-CULTURAL VIEW

Infant care practices and patterns of interaction with infants vary greatly around the world, depending on environmental conditions and the culture's view of infants' nature and needs. In Bali, infants are believed to be ancestors or gods brought to life in human form and thus must be treated with utmost dignity and respect. The Beng of West Africa think that young babies can understand all languages, whereas people in the Micronesian atoll of Ifaluk believe that babies cannot understand language at all, and therefore adults do not speak to them (DeLoache & Gottlieb, 2000).

In some societies infants have multiple caregivers. Among the Efe people of central Africa, for example, infants typically receive care from five or more people in a given hour and are routinely breast-fed by other women besides the mother (Tronick, Morelli, & Ivey, 1992). Among the Gusii in western Kenya, where infant mortality is high, parents are more likely than those in industrial societies to keep their infants close to them, respond quickly when they cry, and feed them on demand (LeVine, 1974, 1989, 1994). The same is true of Aka foragers in central Africa, who move around frequently in small, tightly knit groups marked by extensive sharing, cooperation, and concern about danger. However, Ngandu farmers in the same region, who tend to live farther apart and to stay in one place for long periods of time, are more likely to leave their infants alone and to let them fuss or cry, smile, vocalize, or play (Hewlett, Lamb, Shannon, Leyendecker, & Schölmerich, 1998).

We need to remember, then, that patterns of parent-infant interaction we take for granted may be culture-based. Moreover, from the very first day, the ways in which babies' needs and desires are managed begins the lifelong process of socialization.

CHILDBIRTH AND BONDING

How and when does the **mother-infant bond**—the close, caring connection between mother and newborn—develop? Some researchers studying this topic have followed the ethological approach (introduced in Chapter 2), which considers behavior in human beings, as in animals, to be biologically influenced and emphasizes critical or sensitive periods for development of certain behaviors.

As we mentioned in Chapter 1, Konrad Lorenz (1957) demonstrated that newly hatched ducklings will follow the first moving object they see, usually the mother—a phenomenon called **imprinting**. However, research has concluded that, unlike the animals Lorenz studied, a critical period for bonding does *not* exist in human beings (Chess & Thomas, 1982; Klaus & Kennell, 1982; Lamb, 1983). Infants do indeed need to develop attachment figures; however, this process occurs over a span of time (rather than instantly as with birds) and can take a variety of forms. This finding can relieve the worry and guilt sometimes felt by adoptive parents and those who have to be separated from their infants after birth.

Fathers, like mothers, form close bonds with their babies. This may even be influenced at a biological level; there are indications that involved fathers show decreases in testosterone levels over the course of a pregnancy, suggesting their bodies' physiology is helping to prepare them for engagement in parenting behaviors (Berg & Wynne-Edwards, 2001; Gettle, McDade, Feranil, & Kuzawa, 2011; Gray, Yang, & Pope Jr., 2006). The babies contribute simply by doing the things typical babies do: opening their eyes, grasping their fathers' fingers, or moving in their fathers' arms. Fathers who are present at the birth of a child often see the event as a "peak emotional experience" (May & Perrin, 1985), or as the best thing that has happened to them (Longworth & Kingdon, 2010). A man, however, can become emotionally committed to his newborn whether or not he attended the birth (Palkovitz, 1985). This relationship is also often impacted by the quality of the relationship between the mother and father (Fagan, Palkovitz, Roy, & Farrie, 2009).

Charles Darwin (1872) suggested that we are prewired by natural selection to want to care for infants. We find them cute, not because there is anything objectively cute about them but because our minds see them that way. We find their cries an aversive sound, and rush to help them because those parents who took good care of their newborns were the parents who passed their genes on to us. In other words, we are biologically prepared by evolution to engage in the parenting relationship. From an evolutionary perspective, parental bonding may be a mechanism to ensure that the parents invest the tremendous energy and resources needed to enable a helpless infant to survive and reproduce. Evolutionary developmental psychologists point out that child rearing involves a balancing act between the needs of the parents and those of the offspring (Bjorklund & Pellegrini, 2000). Bonding helps ensure that the benefits to the parents are worth the cost.

A study using magnetic brain imaging suggests a neurological basis for parental bonding. Adults' brains showed an almost immediate surge of activity in response to

mother-infant bond
Mother's feeling of close, caring connection with her newborn.

imprinting
Instinctive form of learning in which, during a critical period in early development, a young animal forms an attachment to the first moving object it sees, usually the mother.

In a series of classic experiments, Harry Harlow and Margaret Harlow showed that food is not the most important way to a baby's heart. When infant rhesus monkeys could choose whether to go to a wire surrogate mother or a warm, soft terry-cloth mother, they spent more time clinging to the cloth mother, even if they were being fed by bottles connected to the wire mother.

the faces of unfamiliar infants, but not to the equally attractive faces of unfamiliar adults, in an area of the frontal cortex involved in processing feelings of reward and pleasure (Kringelbach et al., 2008).

WHAT DO NEWBORNS NEED FROM THEIR MOTHERS?

For many years in psychology, the parent-child bond was understood as being driven by an associationist model. In other words, theorists thought babies became attached to their parents because parents provided food, which babies naturally enjoyed. Over time, babies would start to associate their parents with the provision of food and would then become attached. For example, both the learning and psychoanalytic theorists viewed attachment in this manner. However, a series of pioneering experiments by Harry Harlow and his colleagues established that more than feeding is involved in the mother-infant bond. In these experiments, rhesus monkeys were separated from their mothers 6 to 12 hours after birth and raised in a laboratory. The infant monkeys were put into cages with one of two kinds of surrogate "mothers": a plain cylindrical wire-mesh form or a form covered with terry cloth. Although numerous variations of the study were conducted, the essential question across all the studies was "to which mother would the baby monkeys become attached?" If earlier theorists were right, then the babies should have become attached to the wire "mother" because she provided food. However, what actually happened was that the monkeys became attached to the soft terry cloth "mother." When the monkeys were allowed to spend time with either kind of "mother," they all spent more time clinging to the cloth surrogates, and in an unfamiliar room, the babies "raised" by cloth surrogates showed more natural interest in exploring than those "raised" by wire surrogates, even when the appropriate "mothers" were there.

Apparently, the monkeys also remembered the cloth surrogates better. After a year's separation, the "cloth-raised" monkeys eagerly ran to embrace the terry-cloth forms, whereas the "wire-raised" monkeys showed no interest in the wire forms (Harlow & Zimmerman, 1959). None of the monkeys in either group grew up normally, however (Harlow & Harlow, 1962), and none were able to nurture their own offspring (Suomi & Harlow, 1972).

In another study, baby rats whose mothers licked them frequently turned out to be less anxious and fearful and produced lower levels of stress hormones than rats who had been licked less. The researchers found that this maternal contact activated a gene that relieves stress (Caldji, Diorio, & Meaney, 2003).

It is hardly surprising that a dummy mother would not provide the same kinds of stimulation and opportunities for positive development as a live mother and that a mother's physical demonstrativeness would soothe her baby's stress. These studies show that feeding is not the most important thing babies get from their mothers. Mothering includes the comfort of close bodily contact and, at least in monkeys, the satisfaction of an innate need to cling.

Human infants also have needs that must be satisfied if they are to grow up normally. It is the task of parents to try to meet those needs.

THE FATHER'S ROLE

The fathering role has different meanings in different cultures. The role may be taken or shared by someone other than the biological father: the mother's brother, as in Botswana (where young mothers remain with their childhood family until their partners are in their 40s), or a grandfather, as in Vietnam (Engle & Breaux, 1998; Richardson, 1995; Townsend, 1997). In some societies, fathers are more involved in their young children's lives—economically, emotionally, and in time spent—than in other cultures. In many parts of the world, what it means to be a father has changed and indeed continues to change (Engle & Breaux, 1998).

Among the Huhot of Inner Mongolia, a province of China, fathers traditionally are responsible for economic support and discipline and mothers for nurturing (Jankowiak, 1992). Fathers are stern and aloof, and their children respect and fear them. Men almost never hold infants. Fathers interact more with toddlers but perform child care duties only if the mother is absent. However, urbanization and maternal employment are changing these attitudes. Fathers—especially college-educated fathers—now seek more intimate relationships with children, especially sons. China's official one-child policy has accentuated this change, leading both parents to be more deeply involved with their only child (Engle & Breaux, 1998).

Concepts of fathering have changed in recent decades. This father comforting his son will play an important part in the child's development.

Among the Aka of central Africa, in contrast with the Huhot, fathers are as nurturant and emotionally supportive as mothers. In fact, "Aka fathers provide more direct infant care than fathers in any other known society" (Hewlett, 1992, p. 169).

In the United States and some other countries, fathers' involvement in caregiving and play has greatly increased since 1970 as more mothers have begun to work outside the home and concepts of fathering have changed (Cabrera, Tamis-LeMonda, Bradley, Hoffreth, & Lamb, 2000; Casper, 1997; Pleck, 1997; Wood & Repetti, 2004). A father's frequent and positive involvement with his child, from infancy on, is directly related to the child's well-being and physical, cognitive, and social development (Cabrera et al., 2000; Kelley, Smith, Green, Berndt, & Rogers, 1998; Shannon, Tamis-LeMonda, London, & Cabrera, 2002).

HOW PARENTHOOD AFFECTS MARITAL SATISFACTION

Marital satisfaction typically declines during the child-raising years. An analysis of 146 studies including nearly 48,000 men and women found that parents report lower marital satisfaction than nonparents do, and the more children, the less satisfied parents are with their marriage. The difference is most striking among mothers of infants; 38 percent report high marital satisfaction compared with 62 percent of childless wives, probably due to restriction on mothers' freedom and the need to adjust to a new role (Twenge, Campbell, & Foster, 2003). Two prospective longitudinal studies had similar findings: young couples who had babies reported a small but steady decline in marital satisfaction, whereas couples who remained childless did not (Schulz, Cowan, & Cowan, 2006; Shapiro & Gottman, 2003).

What accounts for the typical decline in satisfaction? New parents are likely to experience multiple stressors, which may affect their health and state of mind. They may feel isolated and lose sight of the fact that other parents are going through similar problems. The division of household tasks between the man and the woman can become an issue: For example, if a woman who was previously working outside the home now stays home, the burden of housework and child care falls mostly on her (Cowan & Cowan, 2000; Schulz et al., 2006). Something as simple as a baby's crying, which keeps the parents up at night, can lessen marital satisfaction during the 1st year of parenthood (Meijer & van den Wittenboer, 2007).

A new baby's effect on the parents' marriage may depend on how the couple approaches parenthood. Researchers who interviewed 96 expectant couples and followed them for 6 years after their first babies were born found that those who had jointly decided when to begin trying to conceive tended to experience as much or more

what's your view

▷ "Despite the increasingly active role many of today's fathers play in child raising, a mother will always be more important to babies and young children than a father." Do you agree or disagree?

▷ How do you think your relationship with your father might have been different if you had grown up among the Huhot of Inner Mongolia? Among the Aka people?

what's your view

Marital satisfaction declines with the birth of a child. Typically, couples with children are compared to couples without children. But, are researchers using the right comparison group? Might there be a difference between couples who don't have children because they don't want them, and couples who don't have children because they can't?

checkpoint
can you . . .

▷ Give examples of cultural differences in care and treatment of newborns?

▷ Summarize findings on bonding between parents and newborns?

▷ Compare the roles of mothers and fathers in meeting newborns' needs?

▷ Discuss how parenthood affects marital satisfaction?

marital satisfaction after the birth as before. Couples whose pregnancy was unplanned, who had mixed feelings about it, or who disagreed about whether or not to have a baby accounted almost completely for the average decline in marital satisfaction (Cowan & Cowan, 2009).

Parents who participate in professionally led couples discussion groups about parenting issues and relationships, beginning in the last trimester of pregnancy, report significantly smaller declines in satisfaction. Such discussions can help new parents take stock of the way the changes in their lives are affecting their relationships with each other and with their babies and can encourage them to search for their own solutions (Schulz et al., 2006).

The birth of a baby, as momentous an achievement as it is, marks the launching of a challenging but rewarding journey—the journey through a child's world. In Part 3, we examine our rapidly growing understanding of the physical, cognitive, and psychosocial developments of infancy and toddlerhood.

summary and key terms

guidepost ❶ Childbirth and Culture: How Birthing Has Changed

How do customs surrounding birth reflect culture, and how has childbirth changed in developed countries?

- In Europe and the United States, childbirth before the twentieth century was similar to childbirth in some developing countries today. Birth was a female ritual that occurred at home and was attended by a midwife. Pain relief was minimal, and risks for mother and baby were high.

- The development of obstetrics as a science professionalized childbirth. Births took place in hospitals, attended by physicians. Medical advances dramatically improved safety.

- Today some women choose delivery at home attended by midwives. However, the safety of home births, even in normal, low-risk pregnancies, is in dispute.

guidepost ❷ The Birth Process

How does labor begin, what happens during each of the three stages of childbirth, and what alternative methods of delivery are available?

- Labor normally begins after a preparatory period of parturition.

- The vaginal birth process consists of three stages: (1) dilation of the cervix, (2) descent and emergence of the baby, and (3) expulsion of the umbilical cord and the placenta.

- Electronic fetal monitoring is widely used during labor and delivery. It is intended to detect signs of fetal distress, especially in high-risk births.

- The rate of cesarean births in the United States is at a record high.

- Natural or prepared childbirth can minimize the need for pain-killing drugs and maximize parents' active involvement. Modern epidurals can give effective pain relief with smaller doses of medication than in the past.

- The presence of a doula can provide physical benefits as well as emotional support.

parturition (*118*)
electronic fetal monitoring (*120*)
cesarean delivery (*120*)
natural, or prepared, childbirth (*121*)
doula (*122*)

guidepost ❸ The Newborn Baby

How do newborn infants adjust to life outside the womb, and how can we tell whether a new baby is healthy and is developing normally?

- The neonatal period is a time of transition from intrauterine to extrauterine life. During the first few days, the neonate loses weight and then regains it; the lanugo (prenatal hair) falls off, and the protective coating of vernix caseosa dries up. The fontanels (soft spots) in the skull close within the first 18 months.

- At birth, the circulatory, respiratory, gastrointestinal, and temperature regulation systems become independent of the mother's. If a newborn cannot start breathing within about 5 minutes, brain injury may occur.

- Newborns have a strong sucking reflex and within the first few days will secrete meconium from the intestinal tract. They are commonly subject to neonatal jaundice, due to immaturity of the liver.

- At 1 minute and 5 minutes after birth, a neonate's Apgar score can indicate how well he or she is adjusting to

A 2-year-old is kind of like having a blender, but without a top on it.

—Jerry Seinfeld

extrauterine life. The Brazelton Neonatal Behavioral Assessment Scale can assess an infant's responses to the environment and predict future development.

- Neonatal screening is done for certain rare but potentially dangerous conditions, such as PKU and congenital hypothyroidism. It is being expanded to include more conditions.
- A newborn's state of arousal is characterized by periodic cycles of wakefulness, sleep, and activity, which seem to be inborn.
- Neonates sleep the majority of the time, but are awake for longer and longer time periods with age.
- Individual differences in newborns' activity levels show stability and may be early indicators of temperament.
- Parents' responsiveness to babies' states and self-initiated activity levels is an important bidirectional influence on development.

neonatal period (*122*)

neonate (*122*)

anoxia (*125*)

neonatal jaundice (*126*)

Apgar scale (*126*)

Brazelton Neonatal Behavioral Assessment Scale (NBAS) (*127*)

state of arousal (*128*)

guidepost ❹ Complications of Childbirth— and Their Aftermath

What complications of childbirth can endanger newborn babies, and what are the long-term prospects for infants with complicated births?

- Complications of childbirth include low birth weight, prematurity, postmature birth, and stillbirth.
- Low-birth-weight babies may be either preterm (premature) or small-for-date (small-for-gestational-age). Low birth

weight is a major factor in infant mortality and can cause long-term physical and cognitive problems. Very-low-birth-weight babies have an even less promising prognosis.

- A supportive postnatal environment and other protective factors often can improve the outcome for babies who experience birth complications.
- Postmature births have decreased with the increase in induced and cesarean deliveries.
- Stillbirth has been substantially reduced in the United States but still accounts for half of perinatal deaths in the developing world.

low-birth-weight babies (*129*)

preterm (premature) infants (*129*)

small-for-date (small-for-gestational-age) infants (*131*)

kangaroo care (*133*)

postmature (*134*)

stillbirth (*135*)

protective factors (*136*)

guidepost ❺ Newborns and Parents

How do parents bond with and care for their baby?

- Researchers following the ethological approach have suggested that there is a sensitive period for the formation of the mother-infant bond, much like imprinting in some animals. However, research has not confirmed this hypothesis. Fathers can bond with their babies whether or not they are present at the birth.
- Infants have strong needs for maternal closeness and warmth as well as physical care.
- Fathering roles differ in various cultures.
- Child-raising practices and caregiving roles vary around the world.

mother-infant bond (*137*)

imprinting (*137*)

did you know?

▷ The American Academy of Pediatrics recommends that babies be exclusively breast-fed for the first 6 months?

▷ Although the brain's early development is genetically directed, its structure is continually modified both positively and negatively by environmental experience?

▷ Vision is the least developed sense at birth?

▷ Cultural practices, such as how much freedom babies have to move about, can affect the age at which they begin to reach motor milestones?

In this chapter, we explore how sensory perception goes hand in hand with an infant's growing motor skills and shapes the astoundingly rapid development of the brain. We examine typical growth patterns of body and brain, and we see how a nourishing environment can stimulate both. We study how young infants become busy, active toddlers and how parents and other caregivers can foster healthy growth and development. We discuss threats to infants' life and health, including abuse and neglect, and ways to ward them off.

Physical Development and Health during the First Three Years

---

guideposts for study

1. What principles govern early growth and physical development?

2. How and what should babies be fed?

3. How does the brain develop, and how do environmental factors affect its early growth?

4. How do the senses develop during infancy?

5. What are the early milestones in motor development, and what are some influences on it?

6. How can we enhance babies' chances of survival and health?

7. What are the causes and consequences of child abuse and neglect, and what can be done about them?

guidepost

1 What principles govern early growth and physical development?

connect

study smart

Patterns of Growth

Early Growth and Physical Development

PRINCIPLES OF EARLY GROWTH AND PHYSICAL DEVELOPMENT

Early growth and physical development follow the maturational principles introduced in Chapter 5: the cephalocaudal principle and the proximodistal principle. According to the *cephalocaudal principle*, growth occurs from top down. Because the brain grows so rapidly before birth, a newborn baby's head is disproportionately large. By 1 year, the brain is 70 percent of its adult weight, but the rest of the body is only 10 to 20 percent of adult weight. The head becomes proportionately smaller as the child grows in height and the lower parts of the body develop (Figure 6.1).

Sensory and motor development proceed according to the same principle; infants learn to use the upper parts of the body before the lower parts. So, for example, a baby learns to use her arms for grasping prior to learning to use her legs for walking, and holds her head up before she can sit unaided.

According to the *proximodistal principle* (inner to outer), growth and motor development proceed from the center of the body outward. In the womb, the head and trunk develop before the arms and legs, then the hands and feet, and then the fingers and toes. During infancy and early childhood, the limbs continue to grow faster than the hands and feet. In addition, babies learn to use the parts of their bodies closest to the center of their body before they learn to use the outermost parts. For example, babies first learn to control their arms when reaching, then use their hands in a scooping motion, then finally learn to use their thumb and pointer finger in a pincer grip.

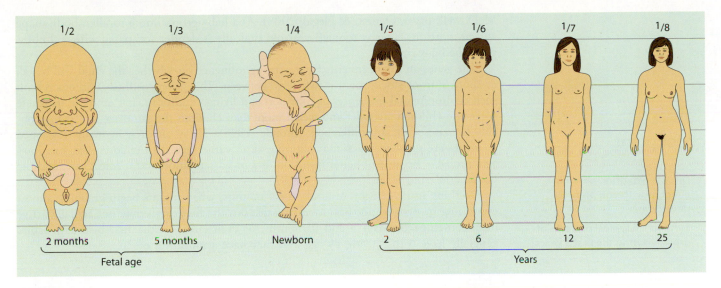

1/2	1/3	1/4	1/5	1/6	1/7	1/8
2 months	5 months	Newborn	2	6	12	25
Fetal age			Years			

FIGURE 6.1

Changes in Proportions of the Human Body during Growth

The most striking change is that the head becomes smaller relative to the rest of the body. The fractions indicate head size as a proportion of total body length at several ages. More subtle is the stability of the trunk proportion (from neck to crotch). The increasing leg proportion is almost exactly the reverse of the decreasing head proportion.

GROWTH PATTERNS

Children grow faster during the first 3 years, especially during the first few months, than they ever will again (Figure 6.2). By 5 months, the average U.S. baby boy's birth weight has doubled to nearly 16 pounds, and by 1 year, has more than tripled to exceed 25 pounds. This rapid growth rate tapers off during the 2nd and 3rd years. A boy typically gains about 5½ pounds by his second birthday and 3 more pounds by his third, when he tips the scales at almost 34 pounds. A boy's height typically increases by 10 inches during the 1st year (making the average 1-year-old boy nearly 30 inches tall), by 5 inches during the 2nd year (so that the average 2-year-old boy is about 3 feet tall), and by 2½ inches during the 3rd year (to approach 39 inches). Girls follow a similar pattern but are slightly smaller at most ages (Kuczmarski et al., 2000;

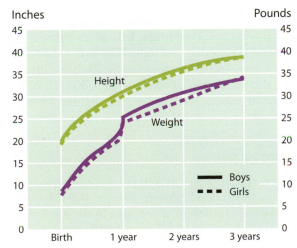

Note: Curves shown are for the 50th percentiles for each sex.

Source: McDowell et al., 2008.

FIGURE 6.2

Growth in Height and Weight during Infancy and Toddlerhood

Babies grow most rapidly in both height and weight during the first few months of life and then taper off somewhat by age 3. Baby boys are slightly larger, on average, than baby girls.

McDowell, Fryar, Ogden, & Flegal, 2008). As a baby grows into a toddler, body shape and proportions change, too; a 3-year-old typically is slender compared with a chubby, potbellied 1-year-old.

The genes an infant inherits have a strong influence on whether the child will be tall or short, thin or stocky, or somewhere in between. This genetic influence interacts with such environmental influences as nutrition and living conditions. For example, Japanese American children are taller and weigh more than children the same age in Japan, probably because of dietary differences (Broude, 1995). Today children in many developed countries are growing taller and maturing at an earlier age than children did a century ago, probably because of better nutrition, improved sanitation and medical care, and the decrease in child labor.

Teething usually begins around 3 or 4 months, when infants begin grabbing almost everything in sight to put into their mouths; but the first tooth may not actually arrive until sometime between 5 and 9 months, or even later. By the first birthday, babies generally have 6 to 8 teeth; by age 2½, they have a mouthful of 20.

Nutrition and Feeding Methods

Mammals breast-feed their newborns, so from the beginnings of human history, babies were breast-fed. In fact, babies fed nonhuman milk were likely to fall ill and die. Following the discovery of germs in 1878, mothers were warned to avoid the "poisonous bottle" at all costs (Fontanel & d'Harcourt, 1997, p. 121).

With the advent of dependable refrigeration, pasteurization, and sterilization in the first decade of the twentieth century, manufacturers began to develop formulas to modify and enrich cow's milk for infant consumption and to improve the design of bottles. Bottle-feeding became safe, nutritious, and popular. During the next half-century, formula feeding became the norm in the United States and some other industrialized countries. By 1971, only 25 percent of U.S. mothers even tried to nurse (Ryan, 1997).

Since then, recognition of the benefits of breast milk has brought about a striking reversal of this pattern. According to a large national random survey, 77 percent of infants born in 2005–2006 were breast-fed (McDowell, Wang, & Kennedy-Stephenson, 2008). However, only about 36 percent of U.S. infants are still breast-fed at 6 months, and only 16 percent are breast-fed exclusively for that long (Forste & Hoffman, 2008). Breast-feeding varies among ethnic groups; only 65 percent of non-Hispanic black infants are ever breast-fed, as compared with 80 percent of Mexican American and 79 percent of non-Hispanic white infants (McDowell, Wang, et al., 2008). Immigrant women are more likely to breast-feed, presumably reflecting customs in their countries of origin (Singh, Kogan, & Dee, 2007). Worldwide, only 38 percent of infants less than 6 months old are exclusively breast-fed (UNICEF, 2008b).

BREAST OR BOTTLE?

Feeding a baby is an emotional as well as a physical act. Warm contact with the mother's body fosters the emotional bond between mother and baby. An infant suckling at the breast triggers the release of oxytocin, a hormone in the mother's brain that promotes trust and causes the mammary gland to release milk (Rossoni et al., 2008). Still, bonding can take place through bottle-feeding and through many other caregiving activities, most of which can be performed by fathers as well as mothers. The quality of the relationship between parent and child and the provision of abundant affection and cuddling is as important, if not more so, as the feeding method.

▷ checkpoint
can you . . .

▷ Discuss two principles that affect growth and physical development?

▷ Summarize typical patterns of growth during the first 3 years?

guidepost
2
How and what should babies be fed?

TABLE 6.1 Benefits of Breast-Feeding over Formula-Feeding

Breast-fed babies . . .

- Are less likely to contract infectious illnesses such as diarrhea, respiratory infections, otitis media (an infection of the middle ear), and staphylococcal, bacterial, and urinary tract infections.
- Have a lower risk of sudden infant death syndrome and of postneonatal death.
- Have less risk of inflammatory bowel disease.
- Have better visual acuity, neurological development, and long-term cardiovascular health, including cholesterol levels.
- Are less likely to develop obesity, asthma, eczema, diabetes, lymphoma, childhood leukemia, and Hodgkin's disease.
- Are less likely to show language and motor delays.
- Score slightly higher on cognitive tests at school age and into young adulthood; but cognitive benefits have been questioned.
- Have fewer cavities and are less likely to need braces.

Breast-feeding mothers . . .

- Enjoy quicker recovery from childbirth with less risk of postpartum bleeding.
- Are more likely to return to their prepregnancy weight and less likely to develop long-term obesity.
- Have reduced risk of anemia and almost no risk of repeat pregnancy while breast-feeding.
- Report feeling more confident and less anxious.
- Are less likely to develop osteoporosis or ovarian and premenopausal breast cancer.

Sources: AAP Section on Breastfeeding, 2005; Black, Morris, & Bryce, 2003; Chen & Rogan, 2004, Dee, Li, Lee, & Grummer-Strawn, 2007; Kramer et al., 2008; Lanting, Fidler, Huisman, Touwen, & Boersma, 1994; Mortensen, Michaelson, Sanders, & Reinisch, 2002; Ogbuanu, Karmaus, Arshad, Kurukulaaratchy, & Ewart, 2009; Owen, Whincup, Odoki, Gilg, & Cook, 2002; Singhal, Cole, Fewtrell, & Lucas, 2004; Soliday, 2007; United States Breastfeeding Committee, 2002.

Nutritionally speaking, though, breast-feeding is almost always best for infants—and mothers (Table 6.1). The American Academy of Pediatrics [AAP] Section on Breastfeeding (2005) recommends that babies be *exclusively* breast-fed for 6 months. Breast-feeding should begin immediately after birth and should continue for at least 1 year, longer if mother and baby wish. A recent study on the benefits of breast-feeding has determined that if 90 percent of U.S. mothers complied with the AAP's recommendation to breast-feed for 6 months, it could potentially prevent 911 infant deaths and save the United States $13 billion annually (Bartick & Reinhold, 2010). The only acceptable alternative to breast milk is an iron-fortified formula that is based on either cow's milk or soy protein and contains supplemental vitamins and minerals. Infants weaned during the 1st year should receive iron-fortified formula. At 1 year, babies can switch to full-fat cow's milk (AAP Section on Breastfeeding, 2005).

On average, an ounce of breast milk has about 22 calories in it.

Kellymom Breast Feeding and Parenting, 2006

Since 1991, some 16,000 hospitals and birthing centers worldwide have been designated as "Baby-Friendly" under a United Nations initiative for encouraging institutional support of breast-feeding. These institutions offer new mothers rooming-in, tell them of the benefits of breast-feeding, help them start nursing within 1 hour of birth, show them how to maintain lactation, encourage on-demand feeding, give infants nothing but breast milk unless medically necessary, and establish ongoing breast-feeding support groups. Breast-feeding in U.S. hospitals and elsewhere greatly increased after the program went into effect, and mothers were more likely to continue nursing (Kramer et al., 2001; Labarere et al., 2005; Merewood, Mehta, Chamberlain, Philipp, & Bauchner, 2005).

Increases in breast-feeding in the United States are most notable in socioeconomic groups that historically have been less likely to breast-feed: black women, teenage women, poor women, working women, and those with no more than high school education, but many of these women do not continue breast-feeding. Postpartum maternity leave,

connect
study smart

Nutritional Benefits of Breast-feeding

Breast milk can be called the "ultimate health food" because it offers so many benefits to babies—physical, cognitive, and emotional.

what's your view

"Every mother who is physically able should breast-feed." Do you agree or disagree? Give reasons.

checkpoint can you . . .

▷ Summarize pediatric recommendations regarding early feeding and the introduction of cow's milk, solid foods, and fruit juices?

▷ Cite factors that contribute to overweight or obesity in later life?

flexible scheduling, the ability to take relatively frequent and extended breaks at work to pump milk, privacy for nursing mothers at work and at school, as well as education about the benefits of breast-feeding and availability of breast pumping facilities might increase its prevalence in these groups (Guendelman et al., 2009; Ryan, Wenjun, & Acosta, 2002; Taveras et al., 2003).

Breast-feeding is inadvisable if a mother is infected with the AIDS virus or any other infectious illness, if she has untreated active tuberculosis, if she has been exposed to radiation, or if she is taking any drug that would not be safe for the baby (AAP Section on Breastfeeding, 2005). The risk of transmitting HIV infection to an infant continues as long as an infected mother breast-feeds (Breastfeeding and HIV International Transmission Study Group, 2004). However, by receiving treatment with nevirapine or with both nevirapine and zidovudine during the first 14 weeks of life, HIV-infected breastfeeding mothers can significantly reduce this risk (Kumwenda et al., 2008).

STARTING SOLID FOODS

Contrary to recommendations for earlier generations, healthy babies should consume *nothing* but breast milk or iron-fortified formula for the first six months. Pediatric experts recommend that iron-enriched solid foods—usually beginning with cereal—be introduced gradually between ages 6 and 12 months. At this time, too, water may be introduced (AAP Section on Breastfeeding, 2005). Unfortunately, many parents do not follow these guidelines. According to random telephone interviews with parents and caregivers of more than 3,000 U.S. infants and toddlers, 29 percent of infants are given solid food before 4 months, 17 percent drink juice before 6 months, and 20 percent drink cow's milk before 12 months.

Furthermore, like older children and adults, many infants and toddlers eat too much and eat the wrong kinds of food. From 7 to 24 months, the median food intake is 20 to 30 percent above normal daily requirements (Fox, Pac, Devaney, & Jankowski, 2004). By 19 to 24 months, French fries become the most commonly consumed vegetable. About 30 percent of children this age eat no fruit, but 60 percent eat baked desserts, 20 percent candy, and 44 percent sweetened beverages each day (American Heart Association [AHA] et al., 2006).

While infants and toddlers in the U.S. may eat too much, in many low-income communities around the world, malnutrition in early life is widespread—and often fatal. Malnutrition is implicated in more than half of deaths of children globally, and many children are irreversibly damaged by age 2 (World Bank, 2006). Malnutrition and its impact on development is discussed in Chapter 9.

IS BEING OVERWEIGHT A PROBLEM IN INFANCY?

Overweight has increased in infancy as in all age groups in the United States. In 2000–2001, 5.9 percent of U.S. infants up to 6 months old were classified as overweight, meaning that their weight for height was in the 95th percentile for age and gender, up from 3.4 percent in 1980. An additional 11.1 percent were at risk for overweight (in the 85th percentile), up from 7 percent in 1980 (Kim, Peterson, et al., 2006). Rapid weight gain during the first 4 to 6 months is associated with future risk of overweight (AHA et al., 2006).

Two factors seem to influence most strongly the chances that an overweight child will become an obese adult: whether the child has an obese parent, and the age of the child. Before age 3, parental obesity is a stronger predictor of a child's obesity as an adult than is the child's own weight (AAP Committee on Nutrition, 2003). Among 70 children followed from age 3 months to 6 years, little difference in weight and body composition appeared by age 2 between children with overweight mothers and children with lean mothers. However, by age 4, those with overweight mothers tended to weigh more and, by age 6, also had more body fat than those with lean mothers (Berkowitz, Stallings, Maislin, & Stunkard, 2005). Thus, a 1- or 2-year-old who has an obese parent—or especially two obese parents—may be a candidate for preventive efforts. Children that age who are at risk of overweight or obesity may be given reduced fat (2 percent) milk; after age 2, they can drink skim (fat-free) milk (Daniels, Greer, & the Committee on Nutrition, 2008).

The Brain and Reflex Behavior

What makes newborns respond to a nipple? What tells them to start the sucking movements that allow them to control their intake of fluids? These are functions of the **central nervous system**—the brain and *spinal cord* (a bundle of nerves running through the backbone) and of a growing peripheral network of nerves extending to every part of the body (Figure 6.3). Through this network, sensory messages travel to the brain, and motor commands travel back.

How does the brain develop, and how do environmental factors affect its early growth?

central nervous system
Brain and spinal cord.

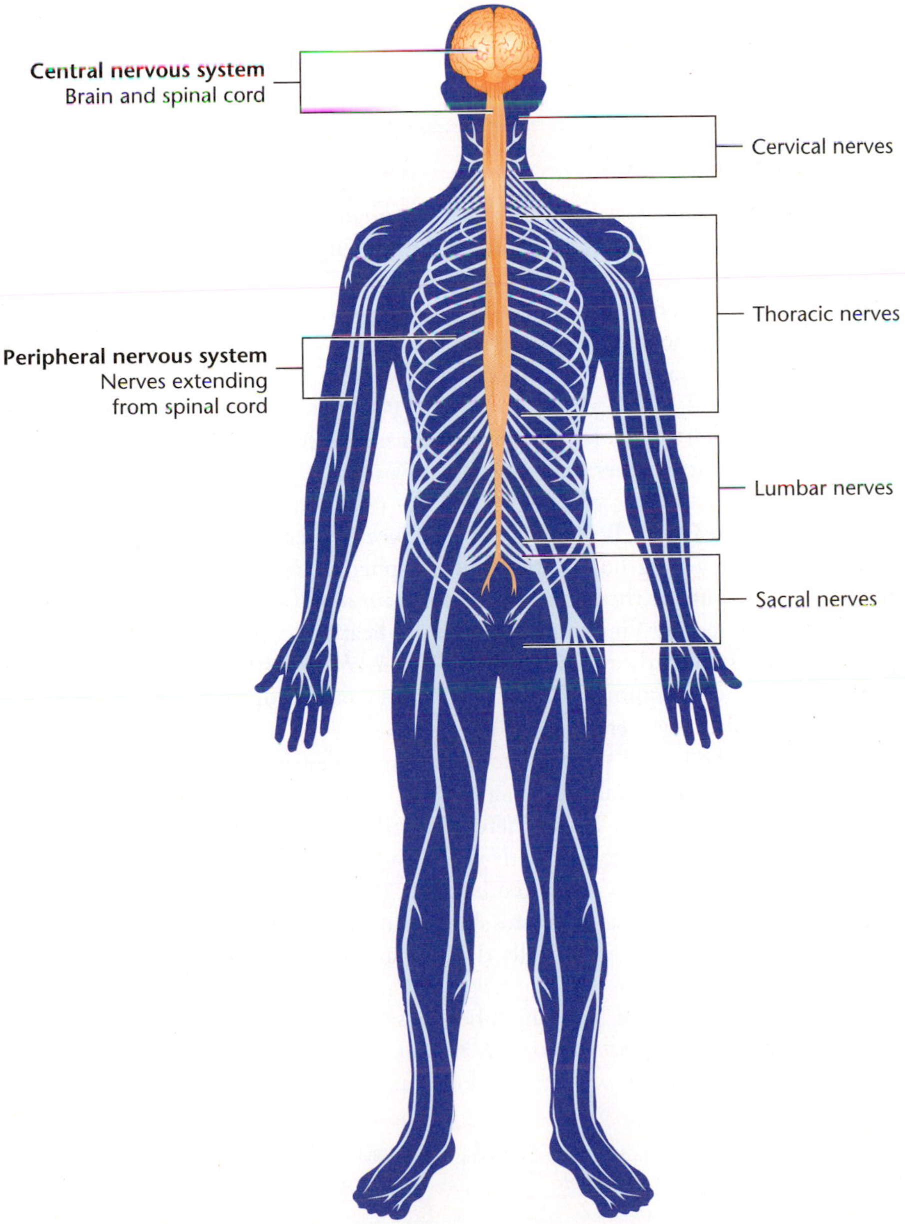

FIGURE 6.3

The Human Nervous System

The central nervous system consists of the brain and spinal cord. The brain sends nerve signals to specific parts of the body through peripheral nerves. Cervical nerves serve the neck and arms; thoracic nerves serve the main part of the body; lumbar nerves serve the legs; and sacral nerves serve the bowels and bladder.

Central nervous system
Brain and spinal cord

Cervical nerves

Thoracic nerves

Peripheral nervous system
Nerves extending from spinal cord

Lumbar nerves

Sacral nerves

Brain Development during Gestation

Fetal nervous system development begins at about 3 weeks. At 1 month, major regions of the brain appear: the forebrain, midbrain, and hindbrain. As the brain grows, the front part expands to form the cerebrum, the seat of conscious brain activity. The cerebellum grows most rapidly during the 1st year of life.

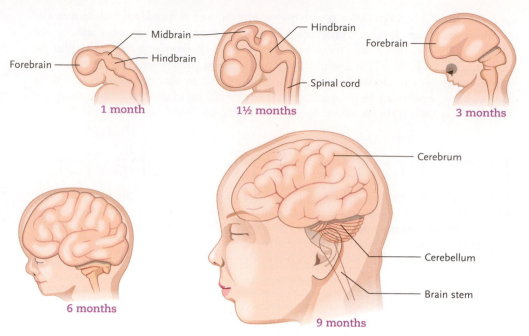

Source: Adapted from Cowan, W. M., 1979.

Mothers' brains have been shown to increase in size after childbirth in key areas regulating motivation, emotional processing, sensory integration, reasoning, and judgment. Researchers suspect the experience of holding and cuddling a newborn infant triggers this effect, and that it helps mothers be more effective in their interactions with infants.

Kinsley & Meyer, 2010

lateralization
Tendency of each of the brain's hemispheres to have specialized functions.

study smart

Four Lobes of the Brain

BUILDING THE BRAIN

The growth of the brain is a lifelong process fundamental to physical, cognitive, and emotional development. Through various brain-imaging tools, researchers are gaining a clearer picture of how brain growth occurs.

The brain at birth is only about one-fourth to one-third of its eventual adult volume (Toga, Thompson, & Sowell, 2006); it reaches nearly 90 percent of adult weight (3½ pounds) by age 3. By age 6, it is almost adult weight; but specific parts of the brain continue to grow and develop into adulthood (Gabbard, 1996*). The brain's growth occurs in fits and starts called *brain growth spurts*. Different parts of the brain grow more rapidly at different times.

Major Parts of the Brain Beginning about 3 weeks after conception, the brain gradually develops from a long hollow tube into a spherical mass of cells (Figure 6.4). By birth, the growth spurt of the spinal cord and *brain stem* (the part of the brain responsible for such basic bodily functions as breathing, heart rate, body temperature, and the sleep-wake cycle) has nearly run its course. The *cerebellum* (the part of the brain that maintains balance and motor coordination) grows fastest during the 1st year of life (Casaer, 1993; Knickmeyer et al., 2008).

The *cerebrum*, the largest part of the brain, is divided into right and left halves, or hemispheres, each with specialized functions. This specialization of the hemispheres is called **lateralization**. The left hemisphere is mainly concerned with language and logical thinking; the right hemisphere with visual and spatial functions such as map reading and drawing. Joining the two hemispheres is a tough band of tissue called the *corpus callosum*, which enables them to share information and coordinate commands. The corpus callosum grows dramatically during childhood, reaching adult size by about age 10.

Each cerebral hemisphere has four lobes or sections, which control different functions. They include the *occipital, parietal, temporal,* and *frontal lobes* (Figure 6.5). The occipital lobe is the smallest of the four lobes and is primarily concerned with visual

*Unless otherwise referenced, the discussion in this section is largely based on Gabbard (1996), Society for Neuroscience (2008), and Toga et al. (2006).

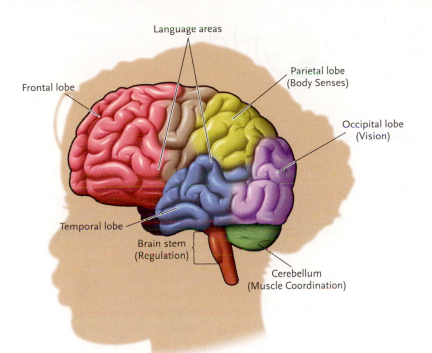

FIGURE 6.5

The Human Brain

Language areas

Frontal lobe

Parietal lobe
(Body Senses)

Occipital lobe
(Vision)

Temporal lobe

Brain stem
(Regulation)

Cerebellum
(Muscle Coordination)

processing. The parietal lobe is involved with integrating sensory information from the body. It helps us move our bodies through space and manipulate objects in our world. The temporal lobe helps us interpret smells and sounds and is involved in memory. Last, the frontal lobes, the newest region of the brain, are involved with a variety of higher-order processes, such as goal setting, inhibition, reasoning, planning and problem solving. The regions of the *cerebral cortex* (the outer surface of the cerebrum) that govern vision, hearing, and other sensory information grow rapidly in the first few months after birth and are mature by age 6 months, but the areas of the frontal cortex responsible for abstract thought, mental associations, remembering, and deliberate motor responses grow little during this period and remain immature through adolescence (Gilmore et al., 2007).

The brain growth spurt that begins at about the third trimester of gestation and continues until at least age 4 is important to the development of neurological functioning. Smiling, babbling, crawling, walking, and talking—all the major sensory, motor, and cognitive milestones of infancy and toddlerhood—reflect the rapid development of the brain, particularly the cerebral cortex. (Box 6.1 discusses autism, a disorder related to abnormal brain growth.)

Brain Cells The brain is composed of *neurons* and *glia*. **Neurons**, or nerve cells, send and receive information. *Glia*, or glial cells, nourish and protect the neurons. They are the support system for our neurons.

neurons
Nerve cells.

Beginning in the 2nd month of gestation, an estimated 250,000 immature neurons are produced every minute through mitosis (cell division). At birth, most of the more than 100 billion neurons in a mature brain are already formed but are not yet fully developed. The number of neurons increases most rapidly between the 25th week of gestation and the first few months after birth. This cell proliferation is accompanied by a dramatic growth in cell size.

Originally the neurons are simply cell bodies with a nucleus, or center, composed of deoxyribonucleic acid (DNA), which contains the cell's genetic programming. As the brain grows, these rudimentary cells migrate to various parts of it (Bystron, Rakic, Molnar, & Blakemore, 2006). Most of the neurons in the cortex are in place by 20 weeks of gestation, and its structure becomes fairly well defined during the next 12 weeks.

the research world

THE AUTISM "EPIDEMIC"

Autism Spectrum Disorders (ASD), also known as Pervasive Developmental Disorders (PDDs), can cause severe and pervasive impairment in thinking, feeling, language, and the ability to relate to others. *Autism* is a disorder of brain functioning characterized by lack of normal social interaction, impaired communication, repetitive movements, and a highly restricted range of activities and interests. Most children with autism are also mentally retarded. ASDs are usually first diagnosed in early childhood and range from severe forms of autism, through pervasive development disorder not otherwise specified (PDD-NOS), to much milder forms, and Asperger syndrome (National Institute of Mental Health [NIMH], 2009).

Autism seems to involve a lack of coordination between different regions of the brain needed for complex tasks (Just, Cherkassky, Keller, Kana, & Minshew, 2007; Williams, Goldstein, & Minshew, 2006). Postmortem studies have found fewer neurons in the amygdala in the brains of people who had autism (Schumann & Amaral, 2006). People with autism also show deficits in executive function and theory of mind, discussed in Chapter 10 (Zelazo & Müller, 2002).

Asperger syndrome is a related but less severe disorder. Children with Asperger syndrome usually function at a higher level than children with autism and have normal to high intelligence. However, they are profoundly deficient with respect to interpreting and understanding social interaction. They tend to have large vocabularies and stilted speech patterns and often are awkward and poorly coordinated. Their odd or eccentric behavior makes social contacts difficult (NINDS, 2007).

Perhaps due in part to increased awareness and more accurate diagnosis, the reported prevalence of these conditions has increased markedly since the mid-1970s. ASD prevalence was reported to be 110 per 10,000 children in the United States in 2007. Odds of having ASD were 4 times higher for boys than girls. Non-Hispanic black and multiracial children had lower odds of ASD than Non-Hispanic white children (Kogan et al., 2009). In California alone, for reasons that are not fully explained, the incidence of autism has increased more than 7-fold, from 6.2 in 10,000 children born in 1990 to 42.5 in 10,000 born in 2001 (Hertz-Picciotto & Delwiche, 2009).

The greater prevalence of autism in boys has been attributed to a number of factors, among them (1) boys'

larger brain size and the larger-than-average brains of autistic children (Gilmore et al., 2007); (2) boys' natural strength in systematizing and the propensity of autistic children to systematize (Baron-Cohen, 2005); and (3) high fetal testosterone levels in boys' amniotic fluid, which have been associated with impaired social relationships and restricted interests at age 4 (Knickmeyer, Baron-Cohen, Raggatt, & Taylor, 2005). These findings support the idea of autism as an extreme version of the normal male brain. A controversial hypothesis is that autism and related disorders result from imbalances in brain development due to the expression of imprinted genes from the father or lack of expression of genes from the mother, or both (Badcock & Crespi, 2006, 2008; Crespi, 2008).

Autism and related disorders run in families and have a strong genetic basis (Constantino, 2003; Ramoz et al., 2004; Rodier, 2000). An international team of researchers has identified at least one gene and pinpointed the location of another that may contribute to autism (Szatmari et al., 2007). Deletions and duplications of gene copies at chromosome 16 may account for a small number of cases (Eichler & Zimmerman, 2008; Weiss et al., 2008).

Environmental factors, such as exposure to certain viruses or chemicals, may trigger an inherited tendency toward autism (Rodier, 2000). Many parents have blamed thimerosal, a preservative used in vaccines, for the increased incidence of autism. The prevalence of the disorder did decline when the U.S. Public Health service recommended the use of thimerosal-free vaccines (Geier & Geier, 2006), but the Centers for Disease Control and Prevention (2004), on the basis of multiple studies on thimerosal and its effects, has found no conclusive link between the preservative and autism. Nonetheless, thimerosal has been removed from vaccines in an attempt to allay parents' fears about its effects. Later research also has failed to find a relationship between childhood vaccination and autism (Baird et al., 2008; Thompson et al., 2007), and in February 2009 a special claims court ruled against families seeking compensation for alleged vaccine-related injuries (Freking & Neergaard, 2009). Other factors, such as certain complications of pregnancy, advanced parental age, first births, threatened fetal loss, epidural anesthesia, induced labor, and cesarean delivery have been associated with higher incidence of autism (Juul-Dam,

Continued

Townsend, & Courchesne, 2001; Glasson et al., 2004; Reichenberg et al., 2006).

Studies of younger siblings of affected children found that those who did not respond to their names by age 12 months or who showed deficits in communicative and cognitive skills at 16 months were likely to develop an autism-related disorder or developmental delay (Nadig et al., 2007; Stone, McMahon, Yoder, & Walden, 2007). Studies like these offer promise for early detection and treatment at a time when the brain is most plastic and systems related to communication are beginning to develop (Dawson, 2007).

Very early signs of possible autism or related disorders include the following (Johnson, Myers, & The Council on Children with Disabilities, 2007):

- No joyful gazing at a parent or caregiver
- No back-and-forth babbling between infant and parent (beginning about age 5 months)
- Not recognizing a parent's voice
- Failure to make eye contact
- Delayed onset of babbling (past 9 months)
- No or few gestures, such as waving or pointing
- Repetitive movements with objects

Later, as speech develops, these are important signs:

- No single words by 16 months
- No babbling, pointing, or other communicative gestures by 1 year
- No two-word phrases by 2 years
- Loss of language skills at any age

Though no known cure is available, substantial improvement may occur with highly structured early educational interventions that help the child develop independence and personal responsibility; speech and language therapy; and instruction in social skills, along with medical management as necessary (Myers, Johnson, & Council on Children with Disabilities, 2007).

6.1

what's your view? Have you ever known anyone with autism? If so, in what ways did that person's behavior seem unusual?

Once in place, the neurons sprout *axons* and *dendrites*—narrow, branching, fiber-like extensions. Axons send signals to other neurons, and dendrites receive incoming messages from them, through *synapses*, the nervous system's communication links. The synapses are tiny gaps, which are bridged with the help of chemicals called *neurotransmitters*, which are released by the neurons. Eventually a particular neuron may have anywhere from 5,000 to 100,000 synaptic connections to and from the body's sensory receptors, its muscles, and other neurons within the central nervous system.

The multiplication of dendrites and synaptic connections, especially during the last 2½ months of gestation and the first 6 months to 2 years of life (Figure 6.6), accounts for much of the brain's growth and permits the emergence of new perceptual, cognitive, and motor abilities. As the neurons multiply, migrate to their assigned locations, and develop connections, they undergo the complementary processes of *integration* and *differentiation*. Through **integration**, the neurons that control various groups of muscles coordinate their activities. Through **differentiation**, each neuron takes on a specific, specialized structure and function.

At first the brain produces many more neurons and synapses than it needs. The large number of excess neurons provided by this early proliferation give the brain flexibility—there are many more connections than will ever be needed, thus many potential paths are available to the growing brain. As early experience shapes the brain, the paths are selected, and unused paths are pruned away. This process involves **cell death**, which, though sounding negative, is a way to calibrate the developing brain to the local environment and help it work

As an analogy, think of this as a sports team. *Integration* involves all members of the team learning to work together in an coordinated fashion. *Differentiation* involves each team member taking on a specific position that he or she plays.

integration
Process by which neurons coordinate the activities of muscle groups.

differentiation
Process by which cells acquire specialized structure and function.

cell death
In brain development, normal elimination of excess cells to achieve more efficient functioning.

EARLY REFLEXES

When your pupils contract as you turn toward a bright light, they are acting involuntarily. Such an automatic, innate response to stimulation is called a **reflex behavior**. Reflex behaviors are controlled by the lower brain centers that govern other involuntary processes, such as breathing and heart rate.

Human infants have an estimated 27 major reflexes, many of which are present at birth or soon after (Gabbard, 1996; see Table 6.2 for examples). *Primitive reflexes*, such as sucking, rooting for the nipple, and the Moro reflex (a response to being startled or beginning to fall), are related to instinctive needs for survival and protection. Some primitive reflexes may be part of humankind's evolutionary legacy. One example is the grasping reflex, by which infant monkeys hold on to their mothers' fur. Human infants show an analogous reflex wherein they grasp any object placed in their palm tightly, a holdover from our ancestral past.

As the higher brain centers become active during the first 2 to 4 months, infants begin to show *postural reflexes:* reactions to changes in position or balance. For example, infants who are tilted downward extend their arms in the parachute reflex, an instinctive attempt to break a fall. *Locomotor reflexes*, such as the walking reflexes, resemble voluntary movements that do not appear until months after these reflexes have disappeared.

Most of the early reflexes disappear during the first 6 months to 1 year. Reflexes that continue to serve protective functions, such as blinking, yawning, coughing, gagging, sneezing, shivering, and the pupillary reflex (dilation of the pupils in the dark), remain. Disappearance of unneeded reflexes on schedule is a sign that motor pathways in the cortex have been partially myelinated, enabling a shift to voluntary behavior. Thus we can evaluate a baby's neurological development by seeing whether certain reflexes are present or absent.

MOLDING THE BRAIN: THE ROLE OF EXPERIENCE

Although the brain's early development is genetically directed, its structure is continually modified both positively and negatively by environmental experience. The physical architecture of our brain is a reflection of the experiences we have had throughout our lives—our brains are not static. Rather, they are living, changeable organs that respond to environmental influences. The technical term for this malleability, or modifiability, of the brain is **plasticity**. Plasticity may be an evolutionary mechanism to enable adaptation to environmental change (Pascual-Leone, Amedi, Fregni, & Merabet, 2005; Toga et al., 2006).

Plasticity enables learning. Individual differences in intelligence may reflect differences in the brain's ability to develop neural connections in response to experience (Garlick, 2003). Early experience have lasting effects on the capacity of the central nervous system to learn and store information (Society for Neuroscience, 2008).

There are two sides to every coin: Just as plasticity allows learning in response to appropriate environmental input, it can also lead to damage in the case of harmful input. During the formative period of early life when the brain is most plastic, it is especially vulnerable. Exposure to hazardous drugs, environmental toxins, or maternal stress before or after birth can threaten the developing brain, and malnutrition can interfere with normal cognitive growth. Early abuse or sensory impoverishment can leave an imprint on the brain as it adapts to the environment in which the developing child must live, delaying neural development or affecting brain structure (AAP, Stirling, and the Committee on Child Abuse and Neglect and Section on Adoption and Foster Care; American Academy of Child and Adolescent Psychiatry, Amaya-Jackson; & National Center for Child Traumatic Stress, Amaya-Jackson, 2008). In one study, a monkey raised until age 6 months with one eyelid closed became permanently blind in that eye, apparently through loss of working connections between that eye and the visual cortex. Thus, if certain cortical connections are not made early in life, these circuits may shut down forever (Society for Neuroscience, 2008). Other research suggests that lack of environmental input may inhibit the normal process of cell death and the streamlining of neural connections, resulting in smaller head size and reduced brain activity (C. A. Nelson, 2008).

TABLE 6.2 Early Human Reflexes

Reflex	Stimulation	Baby's Behavior	Typical Age of Appearance	Typical Age of Disappearance
Moro	Baby is dropped or hears loud noise.	Extends legs, arms, and fingers; arches back, draws back head.	7th month of gestation	3 months
Darwinian (grasping)	Palm of baby's hand is stroked.	Makes strong fist, can be raised to standing position if both fists are closed around a stick.	7th month of gestation	4 months
Tonic neck	Baby is laid down on back.	Turns head to one side, assumes "fencer" position, extends arms and legs on preferred side, flexes opposite limbs.	7th month of gestation	5 months
Babkin	Both of baby's palms are stroked at once.	Mouth opens, eyes close, neck flexes, head tilts forward.	Birth	3 months
Babinski	Sole of baby's foot is stroked.	Toes fan out, foot twists in.	Birth	4 months
Rooting	Baby's cheek or lower lip is stroked with finger or nipple.	Head turns, mouth opens, sucking movements begin.	Birth	9 months
Walking	Baby is held under arms, with bare feet touching flat surface.	Makes steplike motions that look like well-coordinated walking.	1 month	4 months
Swimming	Baby is put into water face down.	Makes well-coordinated swimming movements, holds breath.	1 month	4 months

Moro reflex

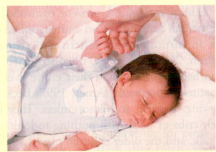

Darwinian reflex

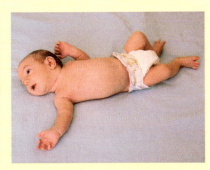

Tonic neck reflex

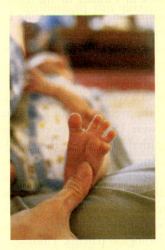

Babinski reflex

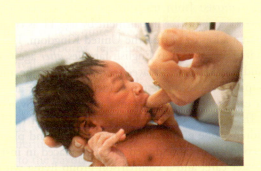

Rooting reflex

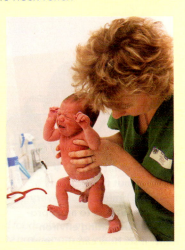

Walking reflex

HEARING

Hearing, too, is functional before birth; fetuses respond to sounds and seem to learn to recognize them. From an evolutionary perspective, early recognition of voices and language heard in the womb may in part lay the foundation for the relationship with the mother, which is critical to early survival (Rakison, 2005).

Auditory discrimination develops rapidly after birth. Even 3-day-old infants can tell new speech sounds from those they have heard before (L. R. Brody, Zelazo, & Chaika, 1984). In addition, infants as young as 2 days old were able to recognize a word they hear up to a day earlier (Swain, Zelano, & Clifton, 1993). At 1 month, babies can distinguish sounds as close as *ba* and *pa* (Eimas, Siqueland, Jusczyk, & Vigorito, 1971).

Because hearing is a key to language development and hearing impairments are the most common cause of speech delays, hearing impairments should be identified as early as possible. Hearing loss occurs in 1 to 3 of 1,000 infants (Gaffney, Gamble, Costa, Holstrum, & Boyle, 2003).

SIGHT

Vision is the least developed sense at birth, perhaps because there is so little to see in the womb. From an evolutionary developmental perspective, the other senses are more directly related to a newborn's survival. Visual perception and the ability to use visual information—identifying caregivers, finding food, and avoiding dangers—become more important as infants become more alert and active (Rakison, 2005).

The eyes of newborns are smaller than those of adults, the retinal structures are incomplete, and the optic nerve is underdeveloped. A neonate's eyes focus best from about 1 foot away—just about the typical distance from the face of a person holding a newborn. This focusing distance may have evolved to promote mother-infant bonding.

Newborns blink at bright lights. Their peripheral vision is very narrow; it more than doubles between 2 and 10 weeks of age (Tronick, 1972). The ability to follow a moving target also develops rapidly in the first months, as does color perception (Haith, 1986).

Visual acuity at birth is approximately 20/400 but improves rapidly, reaching the 20/20 level by about 8 months (Kellman & Arterberry, 1998; Kellman & Banks, 1998). *Binocular vision*—the use of both eyes to focus, enabling perception of depth and distance—usually does not develop until 4 or 5 months (Bushnell & Boudreau, 1993).

Early screening is essential to detect any problems that interfere with vision. Infants should be examined by 6 months for visual fixation preference, ocular alignment, and any signs of eye disease. Formal vision screening should begin by 3 years (AAP Committee on Practice and Ambulatory Medicine and Section on Ophthalmology, 2002).

checkpoint
can you . . .

▷ Describe the early development of the senses?

▷ Tell how breast-feeding plays a part in the development of smell and taste?

▷ Describe why early auditory and visual screening is important?

Motor Development

Babies do not have to be taught such basic motor skills as rolling over, crawling, and walking. They just need room to move and freedom to see what they can do. When the central nervous system, muscles, and bones are ready and the environment offers the right opportunities for exploration and practice, babies keep surprising the adults around them with their new abilities.

guidepost

5

What are the early milestones in motor development, and what are some influences on it?

systems of action
Increasingly complex combinations of motor skills that permit a wider or more precise range of movement and more control of the environment.

MILESTONES OF MOTOR DEVELOPMENT

Motor development is marked by a series of milestones: achievements that develop systematically, each newly mastered ability preparing a baby to tackle the next. Babies first learn simple skills and then combine them into increasingly complex **systems of action**, which permit a wider or more precise range of movement and more effective control of the environment. In developing the precision grip, for example, an infant first tries to pick things up with the whole hand, fingers closing against the palm like a rake. Later the baby masters the *pincer grasp*, in which thumb and index finger meet at the tips to form a circle, making it possible to pick up tiny objects. In learning to walk, an infant first gains control of separate movements of the arms, legs, and feet before putting these movements together to take that momentous first step.

The **Denver Developmental Screening Test** (Frankenburg, Dodds, Fandal, Kazuk, & Cohrs, 1975) is used to chart normal progress between ages 1 month and 6 years and to identify children who are not developing normally. The test measures **gross motor skills** (those using large muscles), such as rolling over and catching a ball, and **fine motor skills** (using small muscles), such as grasping a rattle and copying a circle. It also assesses language development (such as knowing the definitions of words) and personality and social development (such as smiling spontaneously and dressing without help). The newest edition, the Denver II Scale (Frankenburg et al., 1992), includes revised norms (Table 6.3 gives examples).

When we talk about what the "average" baby can do, we refer to the 50 percent Denver norms. Actually, normality covers a wide range; about half of all babies master these skills before the ages given, and about half do so afterward. The Denver norms were developed with reference to a Western population and are not necessarily valid in assessing children from other cultures.

As we trace typical progress in head control, hand control, and locomotion, notice how these developments follow the cephalocaudal (head to tail) and proximodistal (inner to outer) principles outlined earlier. Note, too, that although boy babies tend to be a little bigger and more active than girl babies, there are no gender differences in infants' motor development (Mondschein, Adolph, & Tamis-Lemonda, 2000).

Head Control At birth, most infants can turn their heads from side to side while lying on their backs. While lying chest down, many can lift their heads enough to turn them.

At 4 months, she can raise her head high from a prone position. She was a little later in doing so than some babies, but such variations in timing are normal.

Denver Developmental Screening Test
Screening test given to children age 1 month to 6 years to determine whether they are developing normally.

gross motor skills
Physical skills that involve the large muscles.

fine motor skills
Physical skills that involve the small muscles and eye-hand coordination.

TABLE 6.3 Milestones of Motor Development

Skill	50 percent	90 percent
Rolling over	3.2 months	5.4 months
Grasping rattle	3.3 months	3.9 months
Sitting without support	5.9 months	6.8 months
Standing while holding on	7.2 months	8.5 months
Grasping with thumb and finger	8.2 months	10.2 months
Standing alone well	11.5 months	13.7 months
Walking well	12.3 months	14.9 months
Building tower of two cubes	14.8 months	20.6 months
Walking up steps	16.6 months	21.6 months
Jumping in place	23.8 months	2.4 years
Copying circle	3.4 years	4.0 years

Note: This table shows the approximate ages when 50 percent and 90 percent of children can perform each skill, according to the Denver Training Manual II.

Source: Adapted from Frankenburg et al., 1992.

No matter how enticing a mother's arms are, this baby is staying away from them. As young as he is, he can perceive depth and wants to avoid falling off what looks like a cliff.

between their changing physical characteristics and new and varied characteristics of their environment. Babies' bodies continually change with age—their weight, center of gravity, and muscular strength, and abilities. And each new environment provides a new challenge for babies to master. For example, sometimes a baby might have to make her way down a slight incline, and other times might have to navigate stairs. With experience, then, instead of relying on solutions that previously worked, babies learn to continually gauge their abilities and adjust their movements to meet the demands of their current environment.

This process of "learning to learn" (Adolph, 2008, p. 214) is an outcome of both perception and action. It involves visual and manual exploration, testing of alternatives, and flexible problem solving. What worked at one time may not work now, and what worked in one environment may not work well in another. For example, when faced with steep downward slopes, infants who have just begun to crawl or walk seem unaware of the limits of their abilities, and are more likely to plunge recklessly down steep slopes. But, infants who have been crawling for some time are better at judging slopes and know how far they can push their limits without losing their balance. They also explore the slope before attempting it (Adolph, 2000, 2008; Adolph et al., 2003; Adolph & Eppler, 2002). For example, they may gauge the steepness with their hands first, or turn around to go down backward as if they are going down stairs. They have learned *how* to learn about the slope through their everyday experiences.

This is not a stage approach, and thus does not imply that locomotion develops in functionally related, universal stages. Rather, the baby is somewhat like a small scientist testing out new ideas in each situation. According to Gibson, "each problem space has its own set of information-generating behaviors and its own learning curve" (Adolph, 2008, p. 214). So, for example, babies who learn how far they can reach for a toy across a gap while in a sitting position without tumbling over must acquire this knowledge anew for situations involving crawling. Likewise, when crawling babies who have mastered slopes begin to walk, they have to learn to cope with slopes all over again (Adolph & Eppler, 2002).

HOW MOTOR DEVELOPMENT OCCURS: THELEN'S DYNAMIC SYSTEMS THEORY

Traditionally, motor development was thought to be genetically determined and largely automatic. Presumably, the maturing brain would produce a predetermined set of motor abilities at the appropriate point in development. Today, many developmental psychologists consider this view too simplistic. Instead, motor development is considered to be a continuous process of interaction between the baby and the environment (Thelen, 1995; Smith & Thelen, 2003).

Ester Thelen, in her influential **dynamic systems theory (DST)**, argued that "behavior emerges in the moment from the self-organization of multiple components" (Spencer et al., 2006, p. 1523). Infant and environment form an interconnected, dynamic system. Opportunities and constraints presented by the infant's physical characteristics, motivation, energy level, motor strength, and position in the environment at a particular moment in time affect whether and how an infant achieves a goal. Ultimately, a solution emerges as the baby explores various combinations of movements and assembles those

study smart

Ecological vs. Systems Views of Motor Development

dynamic systems theory (DST)
Thelen's theory that holds that motor development is a dynamic process of active coordination of multiple systems within the infant in relation to the environment.

that most efficiently contribute to that end. Furthermore, the solution must be flexible and subject to modification in changing circumstances. Rather than being solely in charge of it, the maturing brain is but one component of a dynamic process. Indeed, no one factor determines the pace of development, and there is not some predetermined timetable that specifies when a particular skill will emerge. Rather, normal babies tend to develop the same skills in the same order because they are built approximately the same way and have similar challenges and needs. However, because these factors can vary from baby to baby, this approach also allows for variability in the timeline of individual development.

Thelen used the walking reflex to illustrate her approach. When neonates are help upright with their feet touching a surface, they spontaneously make coordinated stepping movements. This behavior usually disappears by the 4th month. Not until the latter part of the 1st year, when a baby is getting ready to walk, do the movements appear again. The traditional explanation focused on cortical control, and the belief was that an older baby's deliberate walking was a new skill masterminded by the developing brain. However, this explanation did not make sense to Thelen. She wondered why the stepping reflex—which used the same series of movements that would become walking—should stop, particularly as other early behaviors, such as kicking, persisted. The answer, she suggested might lay in other relevant variables that could affect movement. For example, babies' legs become thicker and heavier during the early months of life, but the large leg muscles used to control movements are not yet strong enough to handle the increased weight (Thelen & Fisher, 1982; 1983). In support of this hypothesis, when infants who had stopped stepping were held in warm water, stepping reappeared. Presumably, the water helped support their legs and lessened the pull of gravity on their muscles, allowing them to once again demonstrate the skill. Their ability to produce the movement had not changed—only the physical and environmental conditions that inhibited or promoted it. Thus, maturation alone cannot explain such an observation, said Thelen. These same systems of dynamic influences affect all motor movements, from reaching for a rattle to sitting independently to learning to walk.

CULTURAL INFLUENCES ON MOTOR DEVELOPMENT

Although motor development follows a virtually universal sequence, its pace does respond to certain cultural factors. According to some research, African babies tend to be more advanced than U.S. and European infants in sitting, walking, and running. In Uganda, for example, babies typically walk at 10 months, as compared with 12 months in the United States and 15 months in France (Gardiner & Kozmitzki, 2005). Asian babies tend to develop these skills more slowly. Such differences may be related in part to ethnic differences in temperament (Kaplan & Dove, 1987; see Chapter 8) or may reflect a culture's child-rearing practices (Gardiner & Kozmitzki, 2005).

Some cultures actively encourage early development of motor skills. In many African and West Indian cultures with advanced infant motor development, adults use special *handling routines*, such as bouncing and stepping exercises, to strengthen babies' muscles (Hopkins & Westra, 1988). In one study, Jamaican infants, whose mothers used such handling routines daily, sat, crawled, and walked earlier than English infants, whose mothers gave them no such special handling (Hopkins & Westra, 1990).

On the other hand, some cultures discourage early motor development. Children of the Ache in eastern Paraguay do not begin to walk until age 18 to 20 months (Kaplan & Dove, 1987). Ache mothers pull their babies back to their laps when the infants begin to crawl away. The Ache mothers closely supervise their babies to protect them from the hazards of nomadic life. Yet, as 8- to 10-year-olds, Ache children climb tall trees, chop branches, and play in ways that enhance their motor skills (Kaplan & Dove, 1987). Normal development, then, need not follow the same timetable to reach the same destination, and there are many paths leading to proficiency in motor movements.

connect

study smart

Bipedal Posture and
Dynamic Systems Theory

checkpoint
can **you** . . .

▷ Trace a typical infant's progress in head control, hand control, and locomotion, according to the Denver norms?

▷ Discuss how maturation, perception, and culture influence early motor development?

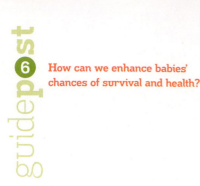

guidepost

6 How can we enhance babies' chances of survival and health?

Health

REDUCING INFANT MORTALITY

Great strides have been made in protecting the lives of new babies, but these advances are not evenly distributed. Worldwide, 47 infants die during their first year for every 1,000 live births—about 6 million infant deaths. Nearly 60 percent of these deaths, 3.7 million, occur during the first month—about three-quarters of them in the first week and between one-quarter and one-half in the first 24 hours. In fact, a baby is about 500 times more likely to die on the first day of life than at 1 month of age. The vast majority of these early deaths are in developing countries, especially in South Asia and West and Central Africa (UNICEF, 2007, 2008b; Figure 6.8).

The chief causes of neonatal death worldwide, accounting for 86 percent of all neonatal deaths, are severe infections, including sepsis or pneumonia, tetanus, and diarrhea (36 percent); preterm delivery (27 percent); and asphyxia (difficulty breathing) at birth (23 percent) (UNICEF, 2008b). Many of these deaths are preventable, resulting from a combination of poverty, poor maternal health and nutrition, infection, and inadequate medical care (Lawn et al., 2005; UNICEF, 2008b). About two-thirds of maternal deaths from complications of childbirth occur during the immediate postnatal period, and infants whose mothers have died are more likely to die than infants whose mothers remain alive (Sines, Syed, Wall, & Worley, 2007; UNICEF, 2008b). Community-based postnatal care for mothers and babies in the first few days after birth might save many of these lives.

infant mortality rate
Proportion of babies born alive who die within the 1st year.

In the United States, the **infant mortality rate**—the proportion of babies who die within the first year—has fallen almost continuously since the beginning of the 20th century, when 100 infants died for every 1,000 born alive. However, the rate plateaued from 2000 to 2006, when 6.69 infants died for every 1,000 live births, largely due to a 9 percent increase in preterm births during that 5-year period. More than half of U.S. infant deaths take place in the first week of life, and about two-thirds occur during the neonatal period (Heron et al., 2009).

sudden infant death syndrome (SIDS)
Sudden and unexplained death of an apparently healthy infant.

Birth defects are the leading cause of infant deaths in the United States, followed by disorders related to prematurity or low birth weight, **sudden infant death syndrome (SIDS)**, maternal complications of pregnancy, and complications of the placenta, umbilical cord, and membranes (Heron et al., 2009). The proportion of preterm and low-birth-weight births has increased steadily since the mid-1980s. In 2005, more than two-thirds of all deaths in infancy were of preterm babies, and more than half were of very preterm infants. In that same year, only 0.8 percent of U.S. infants were born weighing less than 1,000 grams (about 2 pounds), but they represented nearly half (48.2 percent) of all infant deaths (Mathews & MacDorman, 2008; Figure 6.9).

FIGURE 6.8

Neonatal Mortality Rate, 2011

Most neonatal deaths occur in sub-Saharan Africa and Asia.

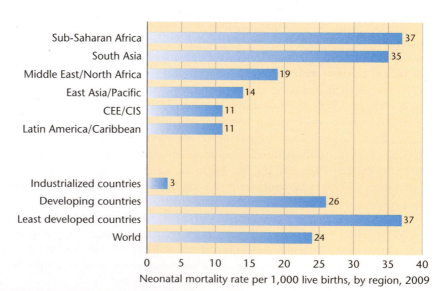

Neonatal mortality rate per 1,000 live births, by region, 2009

Source: UNICEF, 2012.

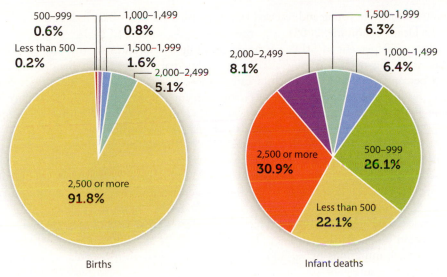

500–999
0.6%

1,000–1,499
0.8%

Less than 500
0.2%

1,500–1,999
1.6%

2,000–2,499
5.1%

2,500 or more
91.8%

Births

1,500–1,999
6.3%

2,000–2,499
8.1%

1,000–1,499
6.4%

2,500 or more
30.9%

500–999
26.1%

Less than 500
22.1%

Infant deaths

Source: Mathews & MacDorman, 2008, Figures 2 & 3.

FIGURE 6.9

Percentage of Live Births and Infant Deaths by Birth Weight in Grams: United States, 2005

Low-birth-weight babies constitute less than 10 percent of live births but nearly 70 percent of infant deaths.

The overall improvement in U.S. infant mortality rates since 1990, even at a time when more babies are born perilously small, is attributable largely to prevention of SIDS (discussed below) as well as to effective treatment for respiratory distress and medical advances in keeping very small babies alive (Arias, MacDorman, Strobino, & Guyer, 2003). Another factor is a striking reduction in air pollution in some cities due to losses of manufacturing (Greenstone & Chay, 2003). Still, mainly because of the prevalence of preterm births and low birth weight, U.S. babies have less chance of reaching their first birthday than do babies in many other developed countries. The U.S. infant mortality rate in 2008 was higher than in 44 countries worldwide (U.S. Census Bureau, 2009a).

Racial/Ethnic Disparities in Infant Mortality Although infant mortality has declined for all races and ethnic groups in the United States, large disparities remain. Black babies are nearly 2½ times as likely to die in their 1st year as white and Hispanic babies. This disparity largely reflects the greater prevalence of low birth weight and SIDS among African Americans. Infant mortality among American Indians and Alaska Natives is about 1½ times that among white babies, mainly due to SIDS and fetal alcohol syndrome (American Public Health Association, 2004; Mathews & MacDorman, 2008).

Intragroup variations are often overlooked. Within the Hispanic population, Puerto Rican infants are nearly twice as likely to die as Cuban infants (Hoyert, Heron, et al., 2006). Asian Americans, overall, are least likely to die in infancy, but Hawaiian infants are more than 3 times as likely to die as Chinese American infants (National Center for Health Statistics [NCHS], 2006).

Racial or ethnic disparities in access to and quality of health care for minority children (Federal Interagency Forum on Child and Family Statistics, 2005; Flores, Olson, & Tomany-Korman, 2005) clearly help account for differences in mortality, but behavioral factors also may play a part. Obesity, smoking, and alcohol consumption contribute to poor outcomes of pregnancy. African Americans have the highest obesity rates, and American Indians and Alaska Natives tend to be heavy smokers and drinkers. Rates of prenatal care vary from about 89 percent of non-Hispanic white expectant mothers down to about 76 percent of American Indians and Alaska Natives (NCHS, 2006). Because causes and risk factors for infant mortality vary among ethnic groups, efforts to further reduce infant deaths need to focus on factors specific to each ethnic group (Hesso & Fuentes, 2005).

Sudden Infant Death Syndrome Sudden infant death syndrome (SIDS), sometimes called *crib death*, is the sudden death of an infant under age 1 year in which the cause of death remains unexplained after a thorough investigation that includes an autopsy. SIDS is the leading cause of postneonatal infant death in the United States (Anderson & Smith, 2005). It peaks between 2 and 3 months and is most common among African American and American Indian/Alaska Native babies, boy babies, those born preterm, and those

The back-to-sleep campaign is a great example of a successful public health campaign. However, it comes with unexpected consequences. Because babies spend less time trying to push up on their arms to see the world, several motor milestones (such as rolling over) are now delayed relative to where they used to be.

Davis, Moon, Sachs, & Ottolini, 1998

whose mothers are young and received late or no prenatal care (AAP Task Force on Sudden Infant Death Syndrome, 2005).

About 20 percent of SIDS deaths occur while the infant is in the care of someone other than the parents (AAP Task Force on Sudden Infant Death Syndrome, 2005), 16.5 percent among infants in child care (Moon, Sprague, & Patel, 2005). SIDS most likely results from a combination of factors. An underlying biological defect may make some infants vulnerable during a critical period to certain contributing or triggering experiences, such as prenatal exposure to smoke—an identified risk factor (AAP Task Force on Sudden Infant Death Syndrome, 2005). The underlying defect may be a delay in maturation of the neural network that is responsible for arousal from sleep in the presence of life-threatening conditions (AAP Task Force on Sudden Infant Death Syndrome, 2005), a disturbance in the brain mechanism that regulates breathing (Tryba, Peña, & Ramirez, 2006), or a genetic factor (Opdal & Rognum, 2004).

At least six gene mutations affecting the heart have been linked to SIDS cases (Ackerman et al., 2001; Cronk et al., 2006; Tester et al., 2006). Nearly 10 percent of victims have mutations or variations in genes associated with irregular heart rhythms, according to a survey of 201 SIDS deaths in a single cohort in Norway (Arnestad et al., 2007; Wang et al., 2007). A gene variant that appears in 1 out of 9 African Americans may help explain the greater incidence of SIDS among black babies (Plant et al., 2006; Weese-Mayer et al., 2004).

An important clue has emerged from the discovery of defects in the brain stem, which regulates breathing, heartbeat, body temperature, and arousal. Autopsies of 31 SIDS babies and 10 babies who had died of other causes found that all 31 SIDS babies (but not the other babies) had defects in the brain's ability to use serotonin (Paterson et al., 2006). These defects may prevent SIDS babies who are sleeping face down or on their sides from waking or turning their heads when they breathe stale air containing carbon dioxide trapped under their blankets (AAP Task Force, 2000; Kinney et al., 1995; Panigrahy et al., 2000; Waters, Gonzalez, Jean, Morielli, & Brouillette, 1996). Sleeping with a fan, which circulates the air, has been associated with a 72 percent reduction in SIDS risk (Coleman-Phox, Odouli, & DeKun, 2008).

Research strongly supports a relationship between SIDS and sleeping on the stomach. SIDS rates declined in the United States by 53 percent between 1992 and 2001 (AAP Task Force on Sudden Infant Death Syndrome, 2005) and in some other countries by as much as 70 percent following recommendations that healthy babies be laid on their backs to sleep (Dwyer, Ponsonby, Blizzard, Newman, & Cochrane, 1995; Hunt, 1996; Skadberg, Morild, & Markestad, 1998; Willinger, Hoffman, & Hartford, 1994). On the other hand, U.S. infant mortality rates attributed to accidental suffocation or strangulation in bed quadrupled between 1984 and 2004, from 2.8 to 12.5 deaths per 1,000 live births, with the greatest increase after 1996 especially for black boys less than 4 months old, (Shapiro-Mendoza, Kimball, Tomashek, Anderson, & Blanding, 2009). This change may in part reflect a more precise distinction between SIDS and accidental suffocation. Sharing a bed with the mother is a common practice in some cultures; its possible role in SIDS and in suffocation has been controversial, as we discuss in Box 6.2.

Doctors recommend that infants not sleep on soft surfaces, such as pillows or quilts, or under loose covers, which, especially when the infant is face down, may increase the risk of overheating or rebreathing (breathing exhaled waste products) (AAP Task Force on Sudden Infant Death Syndrome, 2005; see Table 6.4 for a list of the Task Force's recommendations). The risk of SIDS is increased 20-fold when infants sleep in adult beds, sofas, or chairs, or on other surfaces not designed for infants (Scheers, Rutherford, & Kemp, 2003). Studies associate use of pacifiers with lower risk of SIDS (AAP Task Force on Sudden Infant Death Syndrome, 2005; Hauck, Omojokun, & Siadaty, 2003, 2005; Mitchell, Blair, & L'Hoir, 2006). Contrary to popular reports, studies show no connection between immunizations and SIDS (AAP Task Force on Sudden Infant Death Syndrome, 2005).

Injuries Unintentional injuries are the fifth leading cause of death in infancy in the United States (Heron et al., 2009) and the third leading cause of death after the first 4 weeks,

Recent research suggests that the use of a fan can significantly reduce the risk of SIDS, especially in warm rooms and for infants who sleep on their sides or stomach.

Coleman-Phox, Odouli, & Li, 2008.

SLEEP CUSTOMS

In many cultures, infants do not have special places to sleep. Gusii infants in Kenya fall asleep in someone's arms or on a caregiver's back. In many societies, infants sleep in the same room with their mothers for the first few years of life and frequently in the same bed, making it easier to nurse at night (Broude, 1995). In the United States, it is customary to have a separate bed or a separate room for the infant, but bed sharing is common among younger and poorer inner-city families, African and Asian Americans, and in the South. According to a national survey, the percentage of babies sleeping with a parent or other caregiver more than doubled between 1993 and 2000 (Brenner et al., 2003; Willinger, Ko, Hoffman, Kessler, & Corman, 2003). This practice has become controversial.

In interviews, middle-class U.S. parents and Mayan mothers in rural Guatemala revealed their societies' child-rearing values and goals in their explanations about sleeping arrangements (Morelli, Rogoff, Oppenheim, & Goldsmith, 1992). The U.S. parents, many of whom kept their infants in the same room but not in the same bed for the first 3 to 6 months, said they moved the babies to separate rooms because they wanted to make them self-reliant and independent. The Mayan mothers kept infants and toddlers in the maternal bed until the birth of a new baby, when the older child would sleep with another family member or in a bed in the mother's room. The Mayan mothers valued close parent-child relationships and expressed shock at the idea that anyone would let a baby sleep in a room all alone.

Some investigators find benefits in the shared sleeping pattern, sometimes called *bed sharing* or *cosleeping*.

Observational studies have found that the physical closeness of mother and baby tends to facilitate breast-feeding, touching, and maternal responsiveness (AAP Task Force on Sudden Infant Death Syndrome, 2005; Baddock, Galland, Bolton, Williams, & Taylor, 2006; McKenna & Mosko, 1993; McKenna, Mosko, & Richard, 1997). By snuggling up together, mother and baby stay oriented toward each other's subtle body signals, and mothers can respond more quickly and easily to an infant's first whimpers of hunger.

However, under certain conditions, bed sharing can increase the risk of sudden infant death syndrome or suffocation, as a parent may roll over onto the baby while asleep. The risk seems to be particularly high when the infant is under 8 to 11 weeks, when more than one person cosleeps with the baby, or when a bed sharer has been smoking, drinking alcohol, or is overtired (AAP Task Force on Sudden Infant Death Syndrome, 2005). Both the United Kingdom Department of Health and the American Academy of Pediatrics advise that the safest place for an infant to sleep is in a crib in the parents' room for the first 6 months (AAP Task Force on Sudden Infant Death Syndrome, 2005).

what's your view

In view of medical evidence that bed sharing between mother and infant may contribute to SIDS, should mothers from cultures in which sharing a bed is customary be discouraged from doing so?

---

following SIDS and birth defects (Anderson & Smith, 2005). Infants have the second highest death rate from unintentional injuries among children and adolescents, exceeded only by 15- to 19-year-olds. About two-thirds of injury deaths in the 1st year of life are by suffocation. Among children ages 1 to 4, traffic accidents are the leading cause of unintentional injury deaths, followed by drowning and burns. Falls are by far the major cause of nonfatal injuries in both infancy (52 percent) and toddlerhood (43 percent). Boys of all ages are more likely to be injured and to die from their injuries than girls (Borse et al., 2008). Black infants are 2½ times as likely to die of injuries as white infants and more than 3 times as likely to be victims of homicide (Tomashek, Hsia, & Iyasu, 2003).

In a study of 990 infants brought to emergency rooms in Kingston, Ontario, by far the most injuries were caused by falls (61.1 percent), by ingesting harmful substances (6.6 percent), and by burns (5.7 percent) (Pickett, Streight, Simpson, & Brison, 2003). These statistics speak to the importance of baby-proofing the home environment, as many accidents are avoidable.

or against a wall. Head trauma is the leading cause of death in child abuse cases in the United States (Dowshen, Crowley, & Palusci, 2004). About 20 percent of shaken babies die within a few days. Survivors may be left with a wide range of disabilities from learning and behavioral disorders to neurological injuries, paralysis or blindness, or a permanent vegetative state (King, McKay, Sirnick, & The Canadian Shaken Baby Study Group, 2003; National Center on Shaken Baby Syndrome, 2000; NINDS, 2006).

CONTRIBUTING FACTORS: AN ECOLOGICAL VIEW

As in Bronfenbrenner's bioecological theory, abuse and neglect reflect the interplay of multiple layers of contributing factors involving the family, the community, and the larger society.

Characteristics of Abusive and Neglectful Parents and Families In nearly 80 percent of cases of maltreatment, the perpetrator is the child's parent, usually the mother; and 90 percent of these perpetrators are the victim's biological parents (USDHHS, Administration on Children, Youth and Families, 2008). Maltreatment by parents is a symptom of extreme disturbance in child rearing, usually aggravated by other family problems, such as poverty, lack of education, alcoholism, depression, or antisocial behavior. Although most neglect occurs in very poor families, most low-income parents do not neglect their children.

Characteristics of the household environment are related to the likelihood a child will be physically abused (Jaffee et al., 2004). Abuse may begin when a parent who is already anxious, depressed, or hostile tries to control a child physically but loses self-control and ends up shaking or beating the child. Parents who abuse children tend to have marital problems and to fight physically. Their households are often disorganized, and they experience more stressful events than other families.

Abuse and neglect sometimes occur in the same families (USDHHS, Administration on Children, Youth and Families, 2006). Substance abuse is a factor in one- to two-thirds of cases of abuse and neglect (USDHHS, 2009). Sexual abuse often occurs along with other family disturbances such as physical abuse, emotional maltreatment, substance abuse, and family violence (Kellogg and the Committee on Child Abuse and Neglect, 2005).

Community Characteristics and Cultural Values What makes one low-income neighborhood a place where children are highly likely to be maltreated and another, matched for ethnic population and income levels, safer? Two cultural factors associated with child abuse are societal violence and physical punishment of children. In countries where violent crime is infrequent and children are rarely spanked, such as Japan, China, and Tahiti, child abuse is rare (Celis, 1990). In addition, more frequent use of corporal punishment is related to higher rates of violence in societies (Lansford & Dodge, 2008). In the United States, homicide, domestic violence, and rape are common, and many states still permit corporal punishment in schools. According to a representative sampling, more than 90 percent of parents of 3- and 4-year-olds and about 50 percent of parents of 12-year-olds report using physical punishment at home (Straus, 2010; Straus & Stewart, 1999; see Box 11.2 in Chapter 11 for a discussion of effects of corporal punishment).

HELPING FAMILIES IN TROUBLE

After making a determination of maltreatment, Child Protective Services agencies determine what steps, if any, need to be taken and marshal community resources to help. Agency staff may try to help the family resolve their problems or arrange for alternative care for children who cannot safely remain at home. Services for children who have been abused and for their parents include shelters, education in parenting skills, and therapy. Parents Anonymous and other organizations offer free, confidential support groups. However, availability of these services is often limited (Burns et al., 2004).

When authorities remove children from their homes, the usual alternative is foster care. Foster care removes a child from immediate danger, but it is often unstable, further alienates the child from the family, and may turn out to be another abusive situation. Often a child's basic health and educational needs are not met (David and Lucile Packard Foundation, 2004; National Research Council [NRC], 1993b). Although most foster children who leave the system are reunited with their families, about 28 percent reenter foster care within the next 10 years (Wulczyn, 2004). Children who have been in foster care are more likely than other children to become homeless, to become involved in criminal activity, and to become teenage mothers (David and Lucile Packard Foundation, 2004).

Better than dealing with the results of maltreatment is to prevent it from occurring. Some prevention activities, such as public service announcements, are aimed at raising awareness among the general population. Others, such as parenting classes for single teen mothers, are targeted to high-risk families or to families where abuse or neglect has already occurred (Child Welfare Information Gateway, 2008b).

LONG-TERM EFFECTS OF MALTREATMENT

Without help, maltreated children often grow up with serious problems and may continue the cycle of maltreatment when they have children of their own. An estimated one-third of adults who were abused and neglected in childhood victimize their own children (National Clearinghouse on Child Abuse and Neglect Information [NCCANI], 2004).

Long-term effects of maltreatment include poor physical, mental, and emotional health; impaired brain development; cognitive, language, and academic difficulties; memory problems; emotional instability; problems in attachment and social relationships; and attentional and behavioral problems (AAP, Stirling, Committee on Child Abuse and Neglect and Section on Adoption and Foster Care, American Academy of Child and Adolescent Psychiatry, Amaya-Jackson, & National Center for Child Traumatic Stress, 2008; Brunson et al., 2005; Glaser, 2000; NCCANI, 2004; Pollack, 2008). As adolescents, children who have been abused or neglected are at heightened risk of poor academic achievement, delinquency, pregnancy, alcohol and drug use, and suicide (Dube et al., 2001, 2003; Lansford et al., 2002; NCCANI, 2004). As adults, they tend to be in poor health and to develop fatal illnesses, such as stroke, cancer, and heart disease (AAP, American Academy of Child and Adolescent Psychiatry, & National Center for Child Traumatic Stress, 2008). Adults who were maltreated early in life tend to be anxious or depressed; those who were older when maltreated are more likely to show aggression and to engage in substance abuse (Kaplow & Widom, 2007). Long-term reactions to the chronic stress of maltreatment may be triggered by a sight, sound, or smell that evokes memories or dreams of childhood trauma (AAP, American Academy of Child and Adolescent Psychiatry, & National Center for Child Traumatic Stress, 2008).

How does maltreatment produce such effects? Childhood abuse or neglect can delay or alter brain development and undermine emotion regulation (AAP, American Academy of Child and Adolescent Psychiatry, & National Center for Child Traumatic Stress, 2008; Pollack, 2008). Physically abused children tend to judge ambiguous facial expressions as angry, and electrical activity in their brains increases when they search for angry faces (Pollak & Kistler, 2002; Shackman, Shackman, & Pollak, 2007; Tupler & DeBellis, 2006). These children may interpret a minor slight or stern rebuke as threatening and, mistakenly believing themselves to be in danger, respond inappropriately. Their exaggerated response may then elicit a negative reaction from the other person, which seems to confirm the child's original appraisal of the situation. Because the child's behavior is rooted in physiological adaptations to an abnormal environment, the behavior is highly resistant to change (AAP, American Academy of Child and Adolescent Psychiatry, & National Center for Child Traumatic Stress, 2008).

Severe neglect can alter hormonal responses to stress, impair immune response, and lower oxytocin levels, weakening social bonding (Wismer Fries, Ziegler, Kurian, Jacoris, & Pollak, 2005). Severely neglected infants tend to be demanding, anxious, and hard to console, and their already challenged parents may respond with anger or further distance themselves from the child (AAP, American Academy of Child and Adolescent Psychiatry, & National Center for Child Traumatic Stress, 2008).

Even preschool children can experience episodes of clinical depression, although it may look a bit different than it does in adults. For example, depressed preschool children may have episodes of normal functioning interspersed with periods of sadness or irritation throughout the day.

1. What are six approaches to the study of cognitive development?

2. How do infants learn, and how long can they remember?

3. Can infants' and toddlers' intelligence be measured, and how can it be improved?

4. How did Piaget describe infants' and toddlers' cognitive development, and how have his claims stood up?

5. How can we measure infants' ability to process information, and when do babies begin to think about characteristics of the physical world?

6. What can brain research reveal about the development of cognitive skills?

7. How does social interaction with adults advance cognitive competence?

8. How do babies develop language, and what influences linguistic progress?

guidepost 1

What are six approaches to the study of cognitive development?

behaviorist approach
Approach to the study of cognitive development that is concerned with the basic mechanics of learning.

psychometric approach
Approach to the study of cognitive development that seeks to measure the quantity of intelligence a person possesses.

Piagetian approach
Approach to the study of cognitive development that describes qualitative stages in cognitive functioning.

checkpoint can you . . .

▷ Compare six approaches to the study of cognitive development and identify their goals?

Studying Cognitive Development: Six Approaches

How do babies learn to solve problems? When does memory develop? What accounts for individual differences in cognitive abilities? Can we measure a baby's intelligence or predict how smart that baby will be in the future? These questions have long intrigued developmental scientists, many of whom have taken one of six approaches to their study:

- The **behaviorist approach** studies the basic *mechanics* of learning. Behaviorists are concerned with how behavior changes in response to experience.

- The **psychometric approach** measures *quantitative* differences in abilities that make up intelligence by using tests that indicate or predict these abilities.

- The **Piagetian approach** looks at changes, or stages, in the *quality* of cognitive functioning. It is concerned with how the mind structures its activities and adapts to the environment.

- The **information-processing approach** focuses on perception, learning, memory, and problem solving. It aims to discover how children process information from the time they encounter it until they use it.

- The **cognitive neuroscience approach** examines the hardware of the central nervous system. It seeks to identify what brain structures are involved in specific aspects of cognition.

- The **social-contextual approach** examines the effects of environmental aspects of the learning process, particularly the role of parents and other caregivers.

All six of these approaches help us understand how cognition develops.

Behaviorist Approach: Basic Mechanics of Learning

How do infants learn, and how long can they remember?

guidepost 2

Babies are born with the ability to learn from what they see, hear, smell, taste, and touch, and they have some ability to remember what they learn. Although learning theorists recognize maturation as a limiting factor, their main interest is in mechanisms of learning. Let's look first at two learning processes that behaviorists study: *classical conditioning* and *operant conditioning*. Later we will consider *habituation*, a form of learning that information-processing researchers use to study infants' abilities.

CLASSICAL AND OPERANT CONDITIONING

Eager to capture Anna's memorable moments on film, her father took pictures of the infant smiling, crawling, and showing off her other achievements. Whenever the flash went off, Anna blinked. One evening when Anna was 11 months old, she saw her father hold the camera up to his eye—and she blinked *before* the flash. She had learned to associate the camera with the bright light, so that the sight of the camera alone activated her blinking reflex.

Anna's blinking is an example of **classical conditioning**, in which a person learns to make a reflex or involuntary response (in this case, blinking) to a stimulus (the camera) that originally did not provoke the response. Classical conditioning enables infants to anticipate an event before it happens by forming associations between stimuli (such as the camera and the flash) that regularly occur together. Classically conditioned learning becomes *extinct*, or fades, if it is not reinforced by repeated association. Thus, if Anna frequently saw the camera without the flash, she would eventually stop blinking.

While classical conditioning focuses on the prediction of events (a flash) based on their associates (a camera), **operant conditioning** focuses on the consequences of behaviors and how they affect the likelihood of that behavior occurring again. Specifically, behaviors may be reinforced and become more likely to occur, or they may be punished and become less likely to occur. For example, a baby may learn that when she babbles, her parents respond with smiles and attention, and thus she may increase this behavior in order to receive even more smiles and attention. In other words, she has been reinforced for her babbling. By contrast, a baby may see that when she throws her food, her parents tend to frown and speak sharply to her; thus, she might learn not to throw her food in order to keep her parents happy. She has thus been punished for throwing her food.

INFANT MEMORY

Can you remember anything that happened to you before you were about 2 years old? Chances are you can't. Developmental scientists have proposed various explanations for this common phenomenon. Piaget (1969) argued that early events are not retained in memory because the brain is not yet developed enough to store them. Freud, by contrast, believed that early memories are stored but often repressed because they are emotionally distressing. Other researchers (Nelson, 2005) take an evolutionary developmental approach and argue that abilities develop as they become useful for adapting to the environment. Early procedural and perceptual knowledge is not the same as the later explicit, language-based memories of specific events used by adults. Infancy is a time of great change, and retention of those early experiences is not likely to be useful for very long. Thus, we do not remember events that occurred in infancy, and this explains the infantile amnesia experienced by most adults.

Luckily, we can use operant conditioning techniques to "ask" infants questions about what they remember. For example, Carolyn Rovee-Collier and her associates (1996, 1999) brought 2- to 6-month-old infants in to their laboratory and attached a

information-processing approach Approach to the study of cognitive development by observing and analyzing processes involved in perceiving and handling information.

cognitive neuroscience approach Approach to the study of cognitive development that links brain processes with cognitive ones.

social-contextual approach Approach to the study of cognitive development that focuses on environmental influences, particularly parents and other caregivers.

classical conditioning Learning based on associating a stimulus that does not ordinarily elicit a particular response with another stimulus that does elicit the response.

operant conditioning Learning based on reinforcement or punishment.

Operant conditioning techniques can help us "ask" babies what they remember. Babies 2 to 6 months old who are conditioned to kick in order to activate a mobile remember this skill even if the mobile is removed for up to 2 weeks. When the mobile is returned, the baby starts kicking as soon as he sees it.

string between one of their ankles and a mobile. The babies soon learned that when they kicked their leg, the mobile moved. As this was reinforcing to them, the number of kicks increased. When they were later brought in to the same laboratory, they repeated the kicking even though their ankle was no longer attached to the mobile. The fact that they kicked more than other infants who had not been conditioned in this fashion showed that the recognition of the mobiles triggered a memory of their initial experience with them. Similar research has been conducted with older infants and toddlers, and in this way researchers have been able to determine that the length of time a conditioned response lasts increases with age. At 2 months of age, the typical infant can remember a conditioned response for 2 days, while 18-month-olds can remember it for 13 weeks (Hartshorn et al., 1998; Rovee-Collier, 1996, 1999).

While young infants do have the capacity to remember events, this memory is less robust than for older children. Infant memory appears to be linked specifically to the original cues encoded during conditioning. For example, 2- to 6-month-olds trained to press a lever to make a train go around a track repeated the learned behavior only when they saw the original train. But by 9 to 12 months, infants and toddlers could generalize their memory and press the lever to make a different train move if no more than 2 weeks had gone by since the conditioning. By the same token, 3-, 9-, and 12-month-olds could recognize a mobile or train in a different setting than the one in which they were trained. However, after a long delay, they were no longer able to do so (Rovee-Collier, 1999).

Research using operant conditioning techniques has thus illustrated that infants' memory processes may not differ fundamentally from those of older children and adults except that their retention time is shorter and memory is more dependent on encoding cues. Moreover, studies have found that just as with adults, memory can be aided by reminders. Brief, nonverbal exposure to the original stimulus can sustain a memory from early infancy through age 1½ to 2 years (Rovee-Collier, 1999).

▷ **checkpoint**
can you . . .

▶ Give examples of classical and operant conditioning in infants?

▶ Summarize what studies of operant conditioning have shown about infant memory?

Psychometric Approach: Developmental and Intelligence Testing

Can infants' and toddlers' intelligence be measured, and how can it be improved?

Although there is no clear scientific consensus on a definition of intelligence, most professionals agree on some basic criteria. Intelligence enables people to acquire, remember, and use knowledge; to understand concepts and relationships; and to solve everyday problems. Moreover, **intelligent behavior** is presumed to be *goal-oriented*, meaning it exists for the purposes of attaining a goal. It is also presumed to be *adaptive* in that it helps an organism adjust to the varying circumstances of life.

The precise nature of intelligence has been debated for many years, and so has the best way to measure it. The modern intelligence testing movement began in the early twentieth century, when school administrators in Paris asked the psychologist Alfred Binet to devise a way to identify children who could not handle academic work and needed special instruction. The test that Binet and his colleague, Theodore Simon, developed was the forerunner of psychometric tests that score intelligence by numbers.

The goals of psychometric testing are to measure quantitatively the factors that are thought to make up intelligence (such as comprehension and reasoning) and, from the results of that measurement, to predict future performance (such as school achievement). **IQ (intelligence quotient) tests** consist of questions or tasks that are supposed to show how much of the measured abilities a person has, by comparing that person's performance with norms established by a large group of test-takers who were in the standardization sample.

For school-age children, intelligence test scores can predict academic performance fairly accurately and reliably, as we discuss in Chapter 13. Testing infants and toddlers is another matter. Because babies cannot tell us what they know and how they think, the most obvious way to gauge their intelligence is by assessing what they can do. But if they do not grasp a rattle, it is hard to tell whether they do not know how, do not feel like doing it, do not realize what is expected of them, or have simply lost interest.

intelligent behavior
Behavior that is goal oriented and adaptive to circumstances and conditions of life.

IQ (intelligence quotient) tests
Psychometric tests that seek to measure intelligence by comparing a test-taker's performance with standardized norms.

> *Piaget, whom you will read about in a few pages, first became interested in children's cognition while working on this project. Put to work standardizing reasoning tasks for the intelligence tests, he became more interested in the logical errors children made than in their correct answers to the questions.*

TESTING INFANTS AND TODDLERS

Although it is virtually impossible to measure infants' intelligence, it is possible to test their functioning with development tests. These tests assess infants on tasks and compare their performance with norms established on the basis of what large numbers of infants and toddlers can do at particular ages. So, for example, if a child is unable to perform a task that the "average baby" can do by a particular age, then that child may be delayed in that area. By contrast, a baby can also be ahead of the curve by performing better than her same-age peers.

The **Bayley Scales of Infant and Toddler Development** (Bayley, 1969, 1993, 2005) is a widely used developmental test designed to assess children from 1 month to 3½ years. Scores on the

connect

study smart

The Bayley Scales

Bayley Scales of Infant and Toddler Development
Standardized test of infants' and toddlers' mental and motor development.

> *Only two of the Bayley Scales items correlate to later IQ: speed of habituation (how quickly they get bored by items) and preference for novelty (whether or not they like new stimuli). More on this later.*

► checkpoint
can **you** . . .

▷ Tell why developmental tests are sometimes given to infants and toddlers, and describe one such widely used test?

Many parenting Web sites include lists of milestones to help parents track their baby's development. These milestones are similar to the items on the Bayley scales in that they describe what the average baby of that age should be able to do.

Bayley-III (Bayley, 2005) indicate a child's strengths and weaknesses in each of five developmental areas: *cognitive*, *language*, *motor*, *social-emotional*, and *adaptive behavior*. Separate scores, called *developmental quotients* (DQs), are calculated for each scale. DQs are most commonly used for early detection of emotional disturbances and sensory, neurological, and environmental deficits and in helping parents and professionals plan for a child's needs.

ASSESSING THE IMPACT OF THE HOME ENVIRONMENT

Intelligence was once thought to be fixed at birth, but we now know that it is influenced by both inheritance and experience. As discussed in Chapter 6, early brain stimulation is a key to future cognitive development. What characteristics of the early home environment may influence measured intelligence and other measures of cognitive development?

Using the **Home Observation for Measurement of the Environment (HOME)** (R. H. Bradley, 1989; Caldwell & Bradley, 1984), trained observers interview the primary caregiver and rate on a yes-or-no checklist the intellectual stimulation and support observed in a child's home. The version for infants and toddlers (Table 7.1) lasts about 1 hour. HOME scores are significantly correlated with measures of cognitive development (Totsika & Sylva, 2004).

Home Observation for Measurement of the Environment (HOME) Instrument designed to measure the influence of the home environment on children's cognitive growth.

TABLE 7.1 The Infant-Toddler HOME Inventory (age 0 to 3)

Name of Subscale	Description	Example Item
Emotional and verbal responsivity of the primary caregiver (*items* 1–11)	The communicative and affective interactions between the caregiver and the child	Mother spontaneously vocalizes to the child at least twice during visit Mother caresses or kisses child at least once during visit
Avoidance of restriction and punishment (*items* 12–19)	How the adult disciplines the child	Primary caregiver (PC) does not shout at child during visit PC does not express overt annoyance with or hostility toward the child
Organization of the physical and temporal environment (*items* 20–25)	How the child's time is organized outside the family house. What the child's personal space looks like	When PC is away, care is provided by one of three regular substitutes The child's play environment appears safe and free of hazards
Provision of appropriate play materials (*items* 26–34)	Presence of several types of toys available to the child and appropriate for his/her age	Child has one or more large muscle activity toys or pieces of equipment Provides equipment appropriate to age, such as infant seat, infant rocker, playpen
Parental involvement with the child (*items* 35–40)	How the adult interacts physically with the child	PC tends to keep child within visual range and look at him/her often PC talks to child while doing her work
Opportunities for variety in daily stimulation (*items* 40–45)	The way the child's daily routine is designed to incorporate social meetings with people other than the mother	Father provides some caregiving every day Family visits or receives visits from relatives approximately once a month

Source: Totsika & Sylva (2004).

One important factor that HOME assesses is parental responsiveness. HOME gives credit to the parent of an infant or toddler for caressing or kissing the child during an examiner's visit. Researchers pay particular attention to this because longitudinal research has illustrated the importance of parental responsiveness. Parental responsiveness at 6 months has been positively correlated to IQ, achievement test scores, and classroom behavior at 13 years of age (Bradley, Corwyn, Burchinal, McAdoo, & Coll, 2001).

Other important variables that have been identified with the HOME inventory include the number of books in the home, the presence of playthings that encourage the development of concepts, and parents' involvement in children's play. In an analysis of HOME assessments of 29,264 U.S. children, learning stimulation was consistently associated with kindergarten achievement scores, language competence, and motor and social development (Bradley, Corwyn, Burchinal, et al., 2001).

Of course, some HOME items may be less culturally relevant in non-Western than in Western families (Bradley, Corwyn, McAdoo, & Coll, 2001). Also, we cannot be sure on the basis of HOME and correlational findings that parental responsiveness or an enriched home environment actually increases a child's intelligence. All we can say is that these factors are associated with high intelligence and achievement. Intelligent, well-educated parents may be more likely to provide a positive, stimulating home environment; and, because they also pass their genes on to their children, there may be a genetic influence as well. This is an example of a *passive genotype–environment correlation*, described in Chapter 3.

Other research has identified seven aspects of the early home environment that support cognitive and psychosocial development and help prepare children for school. These aspects are (1) encouraging exploration of the environment; (2) mentoring in basic cognitive and social skills; (3) celebrating developmental advances; (4) guidance in practicing and extending skills; (5) protection from inappropriate disapproval, teasing, and punishment; (6) communicating richly and responsively; and (7) guiding and limiting behavior. The consistent presence of all seven aspects early in life is "causally linked to many areas of brain functioning and cognitive development" (Ramey & Ramey, 2003, p. 4). Table 7.2 lists specific suggestions for helping babies develop cognitive competence.

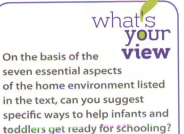

what's your view

On the basis of the seven essential aspects of the home environment listed in the text, can you suggest specific ways to help infants and toddlers get ready for schooling?

checkpoint can you . . .

▸ Identify aspects of the home environment that may influence intelligence, and tell why such influence is hard to show?

Prevention is when you intervene before a problem exists, often on the basis of known risk factors. Intervention is when you intervene to help with an existing problem.

TABLE 7.2 Fostering Competence

Findings from studies using the HOME scales, and from neurological studies and other research suggest the following guidelines for fostering infants' and toddlers' cognitive development:

- In the early months, *provide sensory stimulation* but avoid overstimulation and distracting noises.

- As babies grow older, *create an environment that fosters learning*—one that includes books, interesting objects (which do not have to be expensive toys), and a place to play.

- *Respond to babies' signals.* This establishes a sense of trust that the world is a friendly place and gives babies a sense of control over their lives.

- *Give babies the power to effect changes* through toys that can be shaken, molded, or moved. Help a baby discover that turning a doorknob opens a door, flicking a light switch turns on a light, and opening a faucet produces running water for a bath.

- *Give babies freedom to explore.* Do not confine them regularly during the day in a crib, jump seat, or small room and only for short periods in a playpen. Baby-proof the environment and let them go!

- *Talk to babies.* They will not pick up language from listening to the radio or television; they need interaction with adults.

- In talking to or playing with babies, *enter into whatever they are interested in* at the moment instead of trying to redirect their attention to something else.

- *Arrange opportunities to learn basic skills*, such as labeling, comparing, and sorting objects (say, by size or color), putting items in sequence, and observing the consequences of actions.

- *Applaud new skills and help babies practice and expand them.* Stay nearby but do not hover.

- *Read to babies in a warm, caring atmosphere from an early age.* Reading aloud and talking about the stories develop preliteracy skills.

- *Use punishment sparingly.* Do not punish or ridicule results of normal trial-and-error exploration.

Sources: R. R. Bradley & Caldwell, 1982; R. R. Bradley, Caldwell, & Rock, 1988; R. H. Bradley, 1989; C. T. Ramey & Ramey, 1998a, 1998b, 2003; S. L. Ramey & Ramey, 1992; Staso, quoted in Blakeslee, 1997; J. H. Stevens & Bakeman, 1985; B. L. White, 1971; B. L. White, Kaban, & Attanucci, 1979.

early intervention
Systematic process of providing services to help families meet young children's developmental needs.

EARLY INTERVENTION

Early intervention is a systematic process of planning and providing therapeutic and educational services for families that need help in meeting infants', toddlers' and preschool children's developmental needs. Such programs are expensive, and thus assessment research is needed to justify continued funding.

Thus, a large number of research programs have sought to determine the effectiveness of intervention programs. For example, both Project CARE (Wasik, Ramey, Bryant, & Sparling, 1990) and the Abcedarian (ABC) Project (Campbell, Ramey, Pungello, Sparling, & Miller-Johnson, 2002) have been investigated with randomly assigned, controlled experimental designs. These programs involved a total of 174 at-risk babies who participated in the research from age 6 weeks through 5 years. In each project, an experimental group was enrolled in Partners for Learning, a full-day, year-round early childhood education program at a university child development center. Control groups received pediatric and social work services, but they were not enrolled in Partners for Learning (Ramey & Ramey, 2003).

In both projects, the children who received the early intervention showed a widening advantage over the control groups in developmental test scores between 12 to 18 months, and performed equal to or better than the average for the general population. By age 3, the average IQ in the Abcedarian experimental group was 101 and of the CASE experimental group was 105. By contrast, the control groups had an IQ of 84 and 93, respectively (Ramey & Ramey, 1998b).

These findings, and others like them, show that early educational intervention can help offset environmental risks and provide significant benefits even if the striking early gains that are often seen do not persist. The most effective early interventions are those that (1) start early and continue throughout the preschool years; (2) are highly time-intensive (that is, occupy more hours in a day or more days in a week, month, or year); (3) are center-based, providing direct educational experiences, not just parental training; (4) take a comprehensive approach, including health, family counseling, and social services; and (5) are tailored to individual differences and needs. As occurred in the two North Carolina projects, initial gains tend to diminish without sufficient ongoing environmental support (Brooks-Gunn, 2003; Ramey & Ramey, 1996, 1998a).

Early Head Start, a federally funded intervention for low-income families, is discussed in Chapter 10.

checkpoint
can **you . . .**

▷ Summarize findings about the value of early intervention?

guidepost
4
How did Piaget describe infants' and toddlers' cognitive development, and how have his claims stood up?

Piagetian Approach: The Sensorimotor Stage

The first of Piaget's four stages of cognitive development is the **sensorimotor stage**. During this stage, from birth to approximately age 2, infants learn about themselves and their world through their developing sensory and motor activity as they change from creatures who respond primarily through reflexes and random behavior into goal-oriented toddlers.

sensorimotor stage
In Piaget's theory, first stage in cognitive development, during which infants learn through senses and motor activity.

schemes
Piaget's term for organized patterns of thought and behavior used in particular situations.

SUBSTAGES OF THE SENSORIMOTOR STAGE

The sensorimotor stage consists of six substages (Table 7.3) that flow from one to another as a baby's **schemes**, organized patterns of thought and behavior, become more elaborate. During the first five substages, babies learn to coordinate input from their senses and organize their activities in relation to their environment. During the sixth substage, they progress from trial-and-error learning to the use of symbols and concepts to solve simple problems.

TABLE 7.3 Six Substages of Piaget's Sensorimotor Stage of Cognitive Development*

Substages	Ages	Description	Behavior
1. Use of reflexes	Birth to 1 month	Infants exercise their inborn reflexes and gain some control over them. They do not coordinate information from their senses. They do not grasp an object they are looking at.	Dorri begins sucking when her mother's breast is in her mouth.
2. Primary circular reactions	1 to 4 months	Infants repeat pleasurable behaviors that first occur by chance (such as thumb sucking). Activities focus on the infant's body rather than the effects of the behavior on the environment. Infants make first acquired adaptations; that is, they suck different objects differently. They begin to coordinate sensory information and grasp objects.	When given a bottle, Dylan, who is usually breast-fed, is able to adjust his sucking to the rubber nipple.
3. Secondary circular reactions	4 to 8 months	Infants become more interested in the environment; they repeat actions that bring interesting results (such as shaking a rattle) and prolong interesting experiences. Actions are intentional but not initially goal directed.	Alejandro pushes pieces of dry cereal over the edge of his high chair tray one at a time and watches each piece as it falls to the floor.
4. Coordination of secondary schemes	8 to 12 months	Behavior is more deliberate and purposeful (intentional) as infants coordinate previously learned schemes (such as looking at and grasping a rattle) and use previously learned behaviors to attain their goals (such as crawling across the room to get a desired toy). They can anticipate events.	Anica pushes the button on her musical nursery rhyme book, and "Twinkle, Twinkle, Little Star" plays. She pushes this button over and over again, choosing it instead of the buttons for the other songs.
5. Tertiary circular reactions	12 to 18 months	Toddlers show curiosity and experimentation; they purposefully vary their actions to see results (for example, by shaking different rattles to hear their sounds). They actively explore their world to determine what is novel about an object, event, or situation. They try out new activities and use trial and error in solving problems.	When Bjorn's big sister holds his favorite board book up to his crib bars, he reaches for it. His first efforts to bring the book into his crib fail because the book is too wide. Soon, Bjorn turns the book sideways and hugs it, delighted with his success.
6. Mental combinations	18 to 24 months	Because toddlers can mentally represent events, they are no longer confined to trial and error to solve problems. Symbolic thought enables toddlers to begin to think about events and anticipate their consequences without always resorting to action. Toddlers begin to demonstrate insight. They can use symbols, such as gestures and words, and can pretend.	Jenny plays with her shape box, searching carefully for the right hole for each shape before trying—and succeeding.

*Infants show enormous cognitive growth during Piaget's sensorimotor stage, as they learn about the world through their senses and their motor activities. Note their progress in problem solving and the coordination of sensory information. All ages are approximate.

Much of this early cognitive growth comes about through **circular reactions**, in which an infant learns to reproduce pleasurable or interesting events originally discovered by chance. Initially, an activity produces a sensation so enjoyable that the baby wants to repeat it. The repetition then feeds on itself in a continuous cycle in which cause and effect keep reversing (Figure 7.1). The original chance behavior has been consolidated into a new scheme.

In the *first substage* (birth to about 1 month), neonates begin to exercise some control over their inborn reflexes, engaging in a behavior even when its normal stimulus is not present. For example, newborns suck reflexively when their lips are touched. But they soon learn to find the nipple even when they are not touched, and they suck at times when they are not hungry. These newer behaviors illustrate how infants modify and extend the scheme for sucking.

circular reactions
Piaget's term for processes by which an infant learns to reproduce desired occurrences originally discovered by chance.

connect

study smart

Piaget's 6 Substages of Sensorimotor Stage and Schemes/Organization

FIGURE 7.1

Primary, Secondary,
and Tertiary Circular
Reactions

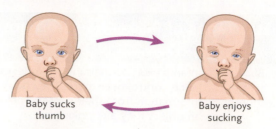

(a) **Primary circular reaction:** Action and
response both involve infant's own body
(1 to 4 months).

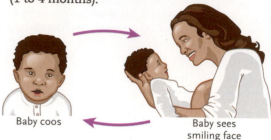

(b) **Secondary circular reaction:** Action gets
a response from another person or object,
leading to baby's repeating original action
(4 to 8 months).

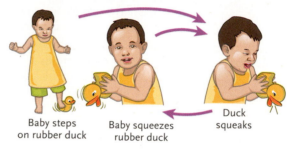

(c) **Tertiary circular reaction:** Action gets
one pleasing result, leading baby to perform
similar actions to get similar results
(12 to 18 months).

*This 8-month-old baby crawling after a ball is in the fourth
substage of Piaget's sensorimotor stage, coordination of
secondary schemes.*

In the *second substage* (about 1 to 4 months), babies learn to repeat a pleasant bodily
sensation first achieved by chance (say, sucking their thumbs, as shown in Figure 7.1a).
Piaget called this a *primary circular reaction*. Also, babies begin
to turn toward sounds, showing the ability to coordinate different kinds of sensory information (vision and hearing).

The *third substage* (about 4 to 8 months) coincides with a
new interest in manipulating objects and learning about their
properties. Babies engage in *secondary circular reactions:* intentional actions repeated not merely for their own sake, as in the
second substage, but to get results *beyond the infant's own body.*
For example, a baby this age will repeatedly shake a rattle to hear
its noise or (as shown in Figure 7.1b) coo when a friendly face
appears, so as to make the face stay longer.

By the time infants reach the *fourth substage, coordination of
secondary schemes* (about 8 to 12 months), they have built on the
few schemes they were born with. They have learned to generalize from past experience to solve new problems, and they can
distinguish means from ends. They will crawl to get something
they want, grab it, or push away a barrier to it (such as someone

else's hand). They try out, modify, and coordinate previous schemes to find one that works. This substage marks the development of complex, goal-directed behavior.

In the *fifth substage* (about 12 to 18 months), babies begin to experiment with new behavior to see what will happen. Once they begin to walk, they can more easily explore their environment. They now engage in *tertiary circular reactions*, varying an action to get a similar result, rather than merely repeating pleasing behavior they have accidentally discovered. For example, a toddler may squeeze a rubber duck that squeaked when stepped on, to see whether it will squeak again (as shown in Figure 7.1c). For the first time, children show originality in problem solving. By trial and error, they try out behaviors until they find the best way to attain a goal.

The *sixth substage, mental combinations* (about 18 months to 2 years), is a transition into the preoperational stage of early childhood. **Representational ability**—the ability to mentally represent objects and actions in memory, largely through symbols such as words, numbers, and mental pictures—frees toddlers from immediate experience. They can pretend, and their representational ability affects the sophistication of their pretending (Bornstein, Haynes, O'Reilly, & Painter, 1996). They can think about actions before taking them. They no longer have to go through laborious trial and error to solve problems.

During these six substages, infants develop the abilities to think and remember. They also develop knowledge about aspects of the physical world, such as objects and spatial relationships. Researchers inspired by Piaget have found that some of these developments conform fairly closely to his observations, but other developments, including representational ability, may occur earlier than Piaget claimed. (Table 7.4 compares Piaget's views on these and other topics with more current findings; refer to this table as you read on.)

DO IMITATIVE ABILITIES DEVELOP EARLIER THAN PIAGET THOUGHT?

One-year-old Clara watches carefully as her older sister brushes her hair. When her sister puts the brush down, Clara carefully picks it up and tries to brush her hair. Although she gets it wrong, brushing with the flat end rather than the bristles, Clara nonetheless has learned something about the function of the object she saw her older sister holding.

Imitation is an important means of learning, and it becomes increasingly valuable late in the first year of life as babies try out new skills (Nelson, 2005). Piaget noted this behavior in his own observations, and maintained that **visible imitation**—imitation that uses body parts such as hands or feet that babies can see—develops first and is then followed by **invisible imitation**—imitation that involves parts of the body that babies cannot see—at 9 months.

However, it appears as if imitative abilities may have earlier roots than Piaget thought. For instance, studies have shown that babies less than 72 hours old can imitate adults by opening their mouths and sticking out their tongues (Meltzoff & Moore, 1989), although this ability does seem to disappear by about 2 months of age (Bjorklund & Pellegrini, 2000).

Researchers have proposed a variety of explanations for this behavior. Some researchers argue that early imitative behavior is the basis for later *social cognition*—the ability to understand the goals, actions, and feelings of others (Meltzoff, 2007). In this view, babies are presumed to have an evolved "like me" mechanism that underlies their later ability to understand their social interaction. In other words, before a child can model others' thoughts and minds, they model their behaviors, and this early physical imitation eventually leads to an understanding of mental

representational ability
Piaget's term for capacity to store mental images or symbols of objects and events.

▷ **checkpoint**
can **you . . .**

▷ Summarize major developments during the six substages of the sensorimotor stage?

▷ Explain how primary, secondary, and tertiary circular reactions work?

▷ Tell why the development of representational ability is important?

visible imitation
Imitation with parts of one's body that one can see.

invisible imitation
Imitation with parts of one's body that one cannot see.

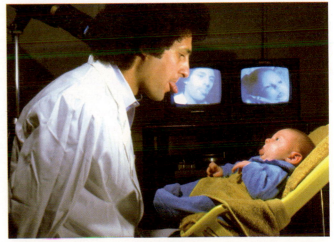

Is this infant imitating the researcher's stuck-out tongue? Studies by Andrew N. Meltzoff suggest that infants as young as 2 weeks are capable of invisible imitation. But other researchers found that only the youngest babies make this response, suggesting that the tongue movement may merely be exploratory behavior.

TABLE 7.4	Key Developments of the Sensorimotor Stage	
Concept or Skill	**Piaget's View**	**More Recent Findings**
Imitation	Invisible imitation develops around 9 months; deferred imitation begins after development of mental representations in the sixth substage (18–24 months).	Controversial studies have found invisible imitation of facial expressions in newborns and deferred imitation as early as 6 weeks. Deferred imitation of complex activities seems to exist as early as 6 months.
Object permanence	Develops gradually between the third and sixth substage. Infants in the fourth substage (8–12 months) make the A-not-B error.	Infants as young as 3½ months (second substage) seem to show object knowledge, though interpretation of findings is in dispute.
Symbolic development	Depends on representational thinking, which develops in the sixth substage (18–24 months).	Understanding that pictures stand for something else occurs at about 19 months. Children under 3 tend to have difficulty interpreting scale models.
Categorization	Depends on representational thinking, which develops during the sixth substage (18–24 months).	Infants as young as 3 months seem to recognize perceptual categories, and 7-month-olds categorize by function.
Causality	Develops slowly between 4–6 months and 1 year, based on an infant's discovery, first of effects of own actions and then of effects of outside forces.	Some evidence suggests early awareness of specific causal events in the physical world, but general understanding of causality may be slower to develop.
Number	Depends on use of symbols, which begins in the sixth substage (18–24 months).	Infants as young as 5 months may recognize and mentally manipulate small numbers, but interpretation of findings is in dispute.

states. Researchers have also argued that infants have an innate predisposition to imitate human faces that may serve the evolutionary purpose of communication with a caregiver (Rakinson, 2005). Last, some researchers have argued that the tongue thrust may simply be exploratory behavior aroused by the sight of an adult tongue—or of some other, narrow, pointed object approaching an infant's mouth (Kagan, 2008). If so, the use of the word *imitation* to describe young infants' behavior in this situation may be misleading.

Piaget also believed that children under 18 months could not engage in **deferred imitation**. Deferred imitation is the reproduction of an observed behavior after the passage of time. As the behavior is no longer happening, deferred imitation thus requires that a stored symbol of the action can be recalled. Piaget argued that young children could not engage in deferred imitation because they lacked the ability to retain mental representations.

However, Piaget relied heavily on asking children for explanations of their behavior in his research, and as toddlers have a limited ability to describe what they remember, he may have underestimated their abilities. Indeed, even babies as young as 6 weeks appear to be able to imitate an adult's facial movements after a 24-hour delay, as long as they are in the presence of the same adult. This finding suggests that even very young

deferred imitation
Piaget's term for reproduction of an observed behavior after the passage of time by calling up a stored symbol of it.

babies can retain a mental representation of simple events, at least for relatively short periods of time (Meltzoff & Moore, 1994). Deferred imitation abilities become more sophisticated with age. Deferred imitation of novel or complex events seems to begin by about 6 to 9 months (Bauer, 2002). Note that the findings on deferred imitation agree with those on operant conditioning (Rovee-Collier, 1999), and both sets of data suggest that infants are capable of remembering after a delay.

In another form of imitation, **elicited imitation**, infants and toddlers are induced to imitate a specific series of actions they have seen, but not done before. For example, more than 40 percent of 9-month-olds can reproduce a simple two-step procedure, such as dropping a toy car down a vertical chute and then pushing a car with a rod to make it roll to the end of a track and turn on a light. Moreover, they can do this after a delay of one-month on the basis of only the initial demonstration and explanation and without further training (Bauer, 2002; Bauer, Wiebe, Carver, Waters, & Nelson, 2003). It may be that how well they perform on this task is tied to how well they consolidate the memory into long-term storage. Brain scans of infants looking at photos of the procedure a week after the initial session indicate that the memory traces of infants who later performed well on the task were more robust than scans of those who did not do as well (Bauer et al., 2003).

Elicited imitation is much more reliable during the 2nd year; nearly 8 out of 10 toddlers 13 to 20 months old can repeat an unfamiliar, multistep sequence (such as putting together a metal gong and causing it to ring) a year after seeing it done (Bauer, 1996; Bauer, Wenner, Dropik, & Wewerka, 2000). Prior practice helps to reactivate children's memories, especially if some new items have been substituted for the original ones (Hayne, Barr, & Herbert, 2003). Four factors seem to determine young children's long-term recall: (1) the number of times a sequence of events has been experienced, (2) whether the child actively participated or merely observed, (3) whether the child is given verbal reminders of the experience, and (4) whether the sequence of events occurs in a logical, causal order (Bauer et al., 2000).

DEVELOPMENT OF KNOWLEDGE ABOUT OBJECTS AND SPACE

The ability to perceive the size and shape of objects and to discern their movements may be an early evolved mechanism for avoidance of predators (Rakison, 2005). The *object concept*—the idea that objects have independent existence, characteristics, and locations in space—is a later *cognitive* development fundamental to an orderly view of physical reality. The object concept is the basis for children's awareness that they themselves exist apart from objects and other people. It is essential to understanding a world full of objects and events.

When Does Object Permanence Develop? One aspect of the object concept is **object permanence**, the realization that an object or person continues to exist when out of sight. According to Piaget, object permanence develops gradually during the sensorimotor stage. At first, infants have no such concept. By the third substage, from about 4 to 8 months, they will look for something they have dropped, but if they cannot see it, they act as if it no longer exists. In the fourth substage, about 8 to 12 months, they will look for an object in a place where they first found it after seeing it hidden, even if they later saw it being moved to another place. Piaget called this the **A-not-B error**. In the fifth substage, 12 to 18 months, they no longer make this error; they will search for an object in the last place they saw it hidden. However, they will not search for it in a place where they did not see it hidden. By the sixth substage, 18 to 24 months, object permanence is fully achieved; toddlers will look for an object even if they did not see it hidden.

Esther Thelen's dynamic systems theory proposes that the decision of where to search for a hidden object is not about what babies *know*, but about what they *do*, and why. One factor is how much time has elapsed between the infant's seeing the object hidden in a new place and the infant's reaching for it. If the elapsed time is brief, the infant is more likely to reach for the object in the new location. When the time interval is longer,

elicited imitation
Research method in which infants or toddlers are induced to imitate a specific series of actions they have seen but not necessarily done before.

object permanence
Piaget's term for the understanding that a person or object still exists when out of sight.

A-not-B error
Tendency for 8- to 12-month-old infants to search for a hidden object in a place where they previously found it rather than in the place where they most recently saw it being hidden.

however, the memory of having previously found the object in the old place inclines the infant to search there again, and that inclination grows stronger the more times the infant has found it there (Smith & Thelen, 2003; Spencer, Smith, & Thelen, 2001; Spencer et al., 2006).

Other research suggests that babies may fail to search for hidden objects because they cannot yet carry out a two-step or two-handed sequence of actions, such as moving a cushion or lifting the cover of a box before grasping the object. When given repeated opportunities, during a period of 1 to 3 months, to explore, manipulate, and learn about such a task, infants at 6 to 12 months can succeed (Bojczyk & Corbetta, 2004).

When object permanence is tested by hiding the object only by darkness, making it retrievable in one motion, infants in the third substage (4 to 8 months) perform surprisingly well (Goubet & Clifton, 1998).

Methods based only on infants' looking behavior eliminate the need for any motor activity and thus can be used at very early ages. As we discuss next, some research using information-processing methodology suggests that infants as young as 3 or 4 months seem not only to have a sense of object permanence but also have some understanding of causality, categorization, number, and other principles governing the physical world.

Symbolic Development, Pictorial Competence, and Understanding of Scale Much of the knowledge people acquire about their world is gained, not through direct observation or experience but through *symbols,* intentional representations of reality. Learning to interpret symbols is, then, an essential task of childhood. One aspect of symbolic development is the growth of *pictorial competence,* the ability to understand the nature of pictures (DeLoache, Pierroutsakos, & Uttal, 2003). For example, think of how suns are represented in children's books. Generally they are drawn as a yellow circle with radiating spires. A child who understands that this simple graphic stands in for the ball of light in the sky has attained some degree of pictorial competence.

In studies carried out in both the United States and Africa's Ivory Coast, Judy DeLoache and her colleagues (DeLoache et al., 2003; DeLoache, Pierroutsakos, Uttal, Rosengren, & Gottlieb, 1998; Pierroutsakos & DeLoache, 2003) have observed infants using their hands to explore pictures as if they were objects—feeling, rubbing, patting, or grasping them or attempting to lift a depicted object off the page. This manual exploration of pictures diminishes by 15 months, but not until about 19 months do children point at a picture of a bear or telephone while saying its name ("beh" or "teltone"), showing an understanding that a picture is a symbol of something. By age 2, children understand that a picture is *both* an object and a symbol (Preissler & Bloom, 2007).

Although toddlers may spend a good deal of time watching television, they at first seem unaware that what they are seeing is a representation of reality (Troseth, Saylor, & Archer, 2006). In one series of experiments, 2- and 2½-year-olds watched on a video monitor as an adult hid an object in an adjoining room. When taken to the room, the 2½-year-olds found the hidden object easily, but 2-year-olds could not. Yet the younger children did find the object if they had watched through a window as it was being hidden (Troseth & DeLoache, 1998). Apparently, what the 2-year-olds lacked was representational understanding of screen images. In a follow-up experiment, 2-year-olds who were told face to face where to find a hidden toy were able to do so, whereas 2-year-olds who received the same information from a person on a video were not (Troseth et al., 2006).

Have you ever seen toddlers try to put on a hat that is too small for their head, or sit in a chair much too tiny to hold them? This is known as a *scale error*—a momentary misperception of the relative sizes of objects. In one study, 18- to 36-month-olds were first allowed to interact with play objects that fit their body size, such as a toy car

In one study, 18- to 36-month-olds were observed trying to slide down tiny slides, and squeeze into toy cars after similar, but larger child-sized objects were removed from their playrooms.

to ride in, a chair to sit in, or a plastic slide to slide down. Then, the life-size objects were replaced with miniature replicas. The children were then videotaped trying to slide down tiny slides, sit in dollhouse chairs, and squeeze their bodies into miniature cars. Why would they treat the objects as if they were full size?

The researchers suggested that these actions might in part be based on a lack of impulse control—the children wanted to play with the objects so badly that they ignored perceptual information about size. However, toddlers might also be exhibiting faulty communication between immature brain systems that ordinarily work together during interactions with familiar objects. One brain system enables the child to recognize and categorize an object ("That's a chair") and plan what to do with it ("I'm going to sit in it"). A separate system may be involved in perceiving the size of the object and using visual information to control actions pertaining to it ("It's big enough to sit on"). When communication between these areas breaks down, children momentarily, and amusingly, treat the objects as if they were full size (DeLoache, Uttal, & Rosengreen, 2004).

The **dual representation hypothesis** offers yet another proposed explanation for scale errors. An object such as a toy chair has two potential representations. The chair is both an object in its own right, as well as a symbol for a class of things ("chairs"). According to this hypothesis, it is difficult for toddlers to simultaneously mentally represent both the actual object and the symbolic nature of what it stands for at the same time. In other words, they can either focus on the particular chair they are faced with ("This is a miniature chair") or the symbol and what it represents ("Chairs are for sitting in"), and so they may confuse the two (DeLoache, 2006; DeLoache et al., 2003).

EVALUATING PIAGET'S SENSORIMOTOR STAGE

According to Piaget, the journey from reflex behavior to the beginnings of thought is a long, slow one. For a year and a half or so, babies learn only from their senses and movements; not until the last half of the 2nd year do they make the breakthrough to conceptual thought. Now, as we have seen, research using simplified tasks and modern tools suggests that certain limitations Piaget saw in infants' early cognitive abilities, such as object permanence, may instead have reflected immature linguistic and motor skills. The answers that Piaget received were as much a function of the ways in which he asked the questions as they were a reflection of the actual abilities of young children.

In terms of describing what children do under certain circumstances, and the basic progression of skills, Piaget was correct. He was an astute observer of child behavior. However, in some ways infants and toddlers are more cognitively competent than Piaget imagined. This does not mean that infants come into the world with minds fully formed. As Piaget observed, immature forms of cognition precede more mature forms. We can see this, for example, in the errors young infants make in searching for hidden objects. However, Piaget may have been mistaken in his emphasis on motor experience as the primary engine of cognitive growth. Infants' perceptions are far ahead of their motor abilities, and today's methods enable researchers to make observations and inferences about those perceptions. The relationship between perception and cognition is a major area of investigation, and we discuss it in the next section.

Information-Processing Approach: Perceptions and Representations

Information-processing researchers analyze the separate parts of a complex task, such as Piaget's object search tasks, to figure out what abilities are necessary for each part of the task and at what age these abilities develop. Information-processing researchers also measure and draw inferences from what infants pay attention to and for how long.

dual representation hypothesis
Proposal that children under age 3 have difficulty grasping spatial relationships because of the need to keep more than one mental representation in mind at the same time.

On the basis of observations by Piaget and the research they inspired, what factors would you consider in purchasing a toy for an infant or toddler?

checkpoint can you . . .

▷ Summarize Piaget's views on imitation, object permanence, pictorial competence, and understanding of scale?

▷ Explain why Piaget may have underestimated some of infants' cognitive abilities, and discuss the implications of more recent research?

How can we measure infants' ability to process information, and when do babies begin to think about characteristics of the physical world?

HABITUATION

At about 6 weeks, Stefan lies peacefully in his crib near a window, sucking a pacifier. It is a cloudy day, but suddenly the sun breaks through, and an angular shaft of light appears on the end of the crib. Stefan stops sucking for a few moments, staring at the pattern of light and shade. Then he looks away and starts sucking again.

We don't know what was going on in Stefan's mind when he saw the shaft of light, but we can tell by his sucking and looking behavior at what point he began paying attention and when he stopped.

In order to do research with babies, researchers need to figure out how to ask questions in ways that babies can answer. Natural behaviors such as those performed by Stefan give researchers a means by which to do this. **Habituation** is a type of learning in which repeated or continuous exposure to a stimulus (such as a shaft of light) reduces attention to that stimulus (such as looking away). It can be compared to boredom, and the rate of habituation (how quickly infants look away) can thus be used to ask infants how interesting they think various objects are.

Researchers study habituation in newborns by repeatedly presenting a stimulus such as a sound or visual pattern, and then monitoring responses such as heart rate, sucking, eye movements, and brain activity. A baby who has been sucking typically stops or sucks less vigorously when a stimulus is first presented in order to pay attention to the stimulus. After the stimulus loses its novelty, the infant generally resumes sucking vigorously. This indicates that habituation has occurred. If a new sight or sound is presented, however, the baby's attention is generally captured once again, and the baby will reorient toward the interesting stimuli and once again sucking slows. This response to a new stimulus is called **dishabituation**.

Researchers gauge the efficiency of infants' information processing by measuring how quickly babies habituate to familiar stimuli, how fast their attention recovers when they are exposed to new stimuli, and how much time they spend looking at the new and the old. Liking to look at new things and habituating to them quickly correlates with later signs of cognitive development, such as a preference for complexity, rapid exploration of the environment, sophisticated play, quick problem solving, and the ability to match pictures. In fact, as we will see, speed of habituation and other information-processing

habituation
Type of learning in which familiarity with a stimulus reduces, slows, or stops a response.

dishabituation
Increase in responsiveness after presentation of a new stimulus.

Habituation

Can this baby tell the difference between Raggedy Ann and Raggedy Andy? This researcher may find out by seeing whether the baby has habituated to—gotten used to—one face (as shown by sucking on a nipple) and then stops sucking on the nipple when a new face appears, showing recognition of the difference.

abilities show promise as predictors of intelligence (Bornstein & Sigman, 1986; Colombo, 1993; Fagan, Holland, & Wheeler, 2007; McCall & Carriger, 1993).

VISUAL AND AUDITORY PROCESSING ABILITIES

The tendency to spend more time looking at one sight rather than another is known as **visual preference**. Researchers can use this natural tendency to ask babies which of two objects they prefer. For example, if babies given a choice between looking at a curved or straight line spend more time focused on the curved line, the implication is that babies like curved lines more than straight lines. With this technique, researchers have determined that babies less than 2 days old prefer curved lines to straight lines, complex patterns to simple patterns, three-dimensional objects to two-dimensional objects, and moving objects to stationary objects. Newborns also prefer pictures of faces or facelike configurations to pictures of other things. Last, infants tend to prefer new sights to familiar ones (Fantz, 1963, 1964, 1965; Fantz, Fagen, & Miranda, 1975; Fantz & Nevis, 1967; Rakison, 2005; Turati, Simion, Milani, & Umilta, 2002), a tendency known as *novelty preference.*

The finding that babies like to look at new things afforded researchers with yet another tool with which to ask them questions. Babies can be shown a stimulus and be allowed to habituate to it. Then, they can be concurrently presented with the familiar stimulus, as well as an additional novel stimulus, and their visual preference can be measured. If the baby spends longer looking at the novel stimulus, then that suggests that the baby recognizes the familiar stimulus. In other words, because the novel stimulus is new and babies like new things, it is more interesting and thus warrants a better look that the previously seen, more boring, stimulus. This behavior demonstrates **visual recognition memory**, an ability that depends on the capacity to form and refer to mental representations (P. R. Zelazo, Kearsley, & Stack, 1995).

Contrary to Piaget's view, habituation and novelty preference studies suggest that at least a rudimentary representational ability exists at birth or soon after and quickly becomes more efficient. Individual differences in efficiency of information processing reflect the speed with which infants form and refer to such mental images. When shown two sights at the same time, infants who quickly shift attention from one to another tend to have better recognition memory and stronger novelty preference than infants who take longer looks at each sight (Jankowski, Rose, & Feldman, 2001; Rose, Feldman, & Jankowski, 2001; Stoecker, Colombo, Frick, & Allen, 1998).

Speed of processing increases rapidly during the first year of life. It continues to increase during the second and third years, as toddlers become better able to separate new information from information they have already processed (Rose, Jankowski, & Feldman, 2002; P. R. Zelazo et al., 1995).

Auditory discrimination studies also are based on attentional preference. Such studies have found that newborns can tell sounds they have already heard from those they have not. In one study, infants who heard a certain speech sound 1 day after birth appeared to remember that sound 24 hours later, as shown by a reduced tendency to turn their heads toward the familiar sound and even a tendency to turn away (Swain, Zelazo, & Clifton, 1993).

Piaget believed that the senses are unconnected at birth and are only gradually integrated through experience. If so, this integration begins almost immediately. The fact that neonates will look at a source of sound shows that they associate hearing and sight. A more sophisticated ability is **cross-modal transfer**, the ability to use information gained from one sense to guide another—as when a person negotiates a dark room by feeling for the location of familiar objects or identifies objects by sight after feeling them with eyes closed. In one study, 1-month-olds showed that they could transfer information gained from sucking (touch) to vision. When the infants saw a rigid object (a hard plastic cylinder) and a flexible one (a wet sponge) being manipulated by a pair of hands, the infants looked longer at the object they had just sucked (Gibson & Walker, 1984).

Failure to engage in joint attention is an early warning sign of autism.

Researchers also study how attention itself develops. From birth to about 2 months, the amount of time infants typically gaze at a new sight increases. Between about 2 and

Given the growing usage of electronic readers, tablet computers, and smartphones, researchers are now beginning to turn their attention to these media influences as well, theorizing they might also affect cognitive processes in young children.

9 months, looking time decreases as infants learn to scan objects more efficiently and shift attention. Later in the 1st year and into the 2nd, when sustaining attention becomes more voluntary and task-oriented, looking time plateaus or increases (Colombo, 2002; Colombo et al., 2004).

The capacity for *joint attention*—which is of fundamental importance to social interaction, language acquisition, and the understanding of others' intentions and mental states—develops between 10 and 12 months, when babies follow an adults' gaze by looking or pointing in the same direction (Brooks & Meltzoff, 2002, 2005). In one longitudinal study, 10- and 11-month-olds' ability to follow an adult's gaze and the length of time they spent looking at the object at which the adult was gazing predicted their spoken vocabulary at ages 18 months and 2 years. Infants who spontaneously pointed at the object as well as looking at it had the fastest vocabulary growth, perhaps because parents tend to supply a label when infants point (Brooks & Meltzoff, 2005, 2008).

Some research suggests that watching television (Box 7.1) may impede attentional development. In a nationally representative longitudinal study, the more hours children spent viewing television at ages 1 and 3, the more likely they were to have attentional problems by age 7 (Christakis, Zimmerman, DiGiuseppe, & McCarty, 2004). However, other research suggests that this link may occur at only the highest levels of television viewing, if at all (Foster & Watkins, 2010).

INFORMATION PROCESSING AS A PREDICTOR OF INTELLIGENCE

Because of a weak correlation between infants' scores on developmental tests such as the Bayley Scales and their later IQ, many psychologists believed that the cognitive functioning of infants had little in common with that of older children and adults—in other words, that there was a discontinuity in cognitive development. Piaget believed this too. However, when researchers assess how infants and toddlers process information, some aspects of mental development seem to be fairly continuous from birth (Bornstein et al., 2006; McCall & Carriger, 1993). Children who, from the start, are efficient at taking in and interpreting sensory information later score well on intelligence tests.

In many longitudinal studies, habituation and attention-recovery abilities during the first 6 months to 1 year of life were moderately useful in predicting childhood IQ. So was visual recognition memory (Bornstein & Sigman, 1986; Colombo, 1993; McCall & Carriger, 1993). In one study, a combination of visual recognition memory at 7 months and cross-modal transfer at 1 year predicted IQ at age 11 and also showed a modest relationship to processing speed and memory at that age (Rose & Feldman, 1995, 1997).

Visual reaction time and *visual anticipation* can be measured by the *visual expectation paradigm*. In this research design, a series of computer-generated pictures briefly appears, some on the right and some on the left side of an infant's peripheral visual field. The same sequence of pictures is repeated several times. The infant's eye movements are measured to see how quickly his or her gaze shifts to a picture that has just appeared (reaction time) or to the place where the infant expects the next picture to appear (anticipation). These measurements are thought to indicate attentiveness and processing speed, as well as the tendency to form expectations on the basis of experience. In a longitudinal study, visual reaction time and visual anticipation at 3½ months correlated with IQ at age 4 (Dougherty & Haith, 1997).

All in all, there is much evidence that the abilities infants use to process sensory information are related to the cognitive abilities intelligence tests measure. Still, we need to be cautious in interpreting these findings. Most of the studies used small samples. Also, the predictability of childhood IQ from measures of habituation and recognition memory is only modest. Furthermore, predictions based on information-processing measures alone do not take into account the influence of environmental factors (Colombo & Janowsky, 1998; Laucht, Esser, & Schmidt, 1994; McCall & Carriger, 1993). For example, maternal responsiveness in early infancy seems to play a part in the link between early attentional abilities and cognitive abilities later in childhood (Bornstein & Tamis-LeMonda, 1994) and even at age 18 (Sigman, Cohen, & Beckwith, 1997).

checkpoint
can you . . .

▷ Explain how habituation measures the efficiency of infants' information processing?

▷ Identify several early perceptual and processing abilities that serve as predictors of intelligence?

DO INFANTS AND TODDLERS WATCH TOO MUCH TELEVISION?

Six-month-old Caitlin bounces up and down, claps, and laughs out loud as the bright images of her Baby Einstein DVD flash across the screen. Caitlin has been watching Baby Einstein since she was 5 weeks old.

Caitlin is neither precocious nor unusual. According to a random survey of 1,000 parents of preschoolers (Zimmerman, Christakis, & Meltzoff, 2007), by 3 months of age, 40 percent of U.S. infants watch an hour of television, DVDs, or videos every day. By age 2, 90 percent of U.S. children watch television an average of 1½ hours a day. Another national survey (Vandewater et al., 2007) found that 68 percent of children age 2 and under watched television daily, and almost one-fifth of these children had television sets in their bedrooms. Many of these very young children watch alone despite evidence that parental involvement and participation increase the positive impact of educational shows.

During the past 10 years an avalanche of media geared to infants and toddlers has become commercially available. Television shows now aim at children as young as 12 months; computer games have been developed with special keyboards for infants as young as 9 months; and educational DVDs target 1-month-old infants.

This increased screen time flies in the face of recommendations by the American Academy of Pediatrics Committee on Public Education (2001) that children under age 2 be discouraged from watching television at all. Instead, the committee recommends they engage in activities that promote brain development, such as talking, playing, singing, and reading with parents. In one survey (Rideout, Vandewater, & Wartella, 2003), children under age 2 spent more than twice as much time watching TV as they spent being read to (see figure). "Heavy watchers" were less likely to learn to read by age 6.

In view of the potential developmental risks, why do parents expose their infants and toddlers to television and other visual media? One reason is the belief that media is educational (Zimmerman et al., 2007). Yet in a prospective longitudinal study, time spent watching television between birth and age 2 did not improve language or visual motor skills at age 3 (Schmidt, Rich, Rifas-Shiman, Oken & Taveras, 2009).

Other reasons parents give for exposing infants to media are the belief that viewing is enjoyable or relaxing for the child and the use of media as an electronic babysitter (Zimmerman et al., 2007). In one national survey almost one-fifth of the children age 2 and under who watched television daily had TV sets in their bedrooms. The two

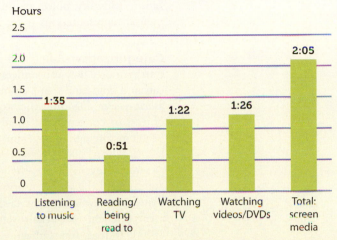

Average amount of time children under 2 spend on media and other activities in a typical day, according to mothers' reports.

Note: These data include only children who participate in these activities.

Source: Rideout et al., 2003.

most common reasons for this practice were to free the family television for other family members and to keep the child occupied (Vandewater et al., 2007).

What impact does constant media use have on neurological and cognitive development? Does it stimulate aggressive behavior? Does having a TV in the bedroom interfere with sleep? Do video and computer games help visual and spatial skills or risk eyestrain and ergonomic problems? There is already evidence that background media interfere with toddlers' concentration on play (Anderson & Pempek, 2005), but further study is needed to determine how heavy exposure to television affects infants' and toddlers' development. One thing is clear: Time spent on media takes away time from exploratory play and from interaction with family members, both of which are developmentally important activities.

Source: Unless otherwise referenced, this box is based on Rideout, Vandewater, and Wartella (2003); Vandewater et al. (2007); and Zimmerman et al. (2007).

what's your view
At what age would you let a baby watch television or play a computer game, and what restrictions, if any, would you place on such activities?

INFORMATION PROCESSING AND THE DEVELOPMENT OF PIAGETIAN ABILITIES

As we discussed earlier in this chapter, evidence suggests that several of the cognitive abilities Piaget identified as developing toward the end of the sensorimotor stage seem to arise much earlier. Research based on infants' visual processing has given developmental scientists a window into the timing of such cognitive developments as categorization, causality, object permanence, and number, all of which depend on formation of mental representations (refer to Table 7.4).

Categorization Adults can understand that plants and animals are both living things. Furthermore, they can understand that some animals are pets, that among those pets are cats and dogs, and that a chihuahua is a type of dog. These nested relationship are known as *categories*. Dividing the world into meaningful categories is vital to thinking about objects or concepts and their relationships. It is the foundation of language, reasoning, problem solving, and memory; without it, the world would seem chaotic and meaningless (Rakison, 2005).

According to Piaget, the ability to classify, or group things into categories, does not appear until the sixth sensorimotor substage, around 18 months. Yet by looking longer at items in a new category, even 3-month-olds seem to know, for example, that a dog is not a cat (French, Mareschal, Mermillod, & Quinn, 2004; Quinn, Eimas, & Rosenkrantz, 1993). Indeed, brain imaging has found that basic components of the neural structures needed to support categorization are functional within the first 6 months of life (Quinn, Westerlund, & Nelson, 2006).

Infants at first seem to categorize on the basis of *perceptual* features, such as shape, color, and pattern, but by 12 to 14 months their categories become *conceptual*, based on real-world knowledge, particularly of function (Mandler, 1998, 2007; Mandler & McDonough, 1993, 1996, 1998; Oakes, Coppage, & Dingel, 1997). In one series of experiments, 10- and 11-month-olds recognized that chairs with zebra-striped upholstery belong in the category of furniture, not animals (Pauen, 2002). When infants were allowed to handle tiny models, even 7-month-olds could tell that animals are different from vehicles or furniture. As time goes on, these broad concepts become more specific. For example, 2-year-olds recognize particular categories, such as "car" and "airplane," within the overall category of "vehicles" (Mandler, 2007).

Causality Eight-month-old Aviva accidentally squeezes her toy duck and it quacks. Startled, she drops it, and then, staring at it intently, she squeezes it again. She laughs when the duck once again quacks and looks up at her mother with a wide smile. Aviva is beginning to understand causality—the principle that one event (squeezing) causes another (quacking). Piaget maintained that this understanding develops slowly during the 1st year of life. At about 4 to 6 months, as infants become able to grasp objects, they begin to recognize that they can act on their environment. Thus, said Piaget, the concept of causality is rooted in a dawning awareness of the power of one's own intentions. However, according to Piaget, infants do not yet know that causes must come before effects; and not until close to 1 year do they realize that forces outside of themselves can make things happen.

Some information-processing researchers suggest that a mechanism for recognizing causality may exist earlier (Mandler, 1998), possibly even at birth. However, studies suggest that an understanding of causality does not emerge until at least the second half of the 1st year, when infants have gained experience in observing how and when objects move (Saxe & Carey, 2006). Infants 6½ months old have shown by habituation and dishabituation that they seem to see a difference between events that are the immediate cause of other events (such as a brick striking a second brick, which is then pushed out of position) and events that occur with no apparent cause (such as a brick moving away from another brick without having been struck by it) (Leslie, 1982, 1984, 1995).

Other researchers have replicated these findings with 6½-month-olds but not with younger infants (Cohen & Amsel, 1998). These investigators attribute the growth of causal understanding to a gradual improvement in information-processing skills. As infants accumulate more information about how objects behave, they are better able to see causality as a general principle operating in a variety of situations (Cohen & Amsel, 1998; Cohen, Chaput, & Cashon, 2002; Cohen & Oakes, 1993; Cohen, Rundell, Spellman, & Cashon, 1999; Oakes, 1994).

One research team set up a "blicket detector," rigged to light up and play music only when certain objects (called "blickets") were placed on it. Children as young as 2 years were able to decide, by watching the device operate, which objects were blickets (because they activated the blicket detector) and which were not (Gopnik, Sobel, Schulz, & Glymour, 2001). In a follow-up study, 2-year-olds correctly placed the blicket on the detector even when the decision depended on making inferences from ambiguous information, as when two different objects, one a blicket and one not, had been placed on the detector at the same time (Sobel, Tenenbaum, & Gopnik, 2004).

Research also has explored infants' expectations about hidden causes. In one experiment, 10- to 12-month-olds looked longer when a human hand emerged from the opposite side of a lighted stage onto which a beanbag had been thrown than when the hand emerged from the same side as the beanbag, suggesting that the infants understood that the hand probably had thrown the beanbag. The infants did *not* have the same reaction when a toy train rather than a hand appeared or when the thrown object was a self-propelled puppet (Saxe, Tenenbaum, & Carey, 2005). In another set of experiments, infants as young as 7 months used the motion of a beanbag to infer the position of a hand, but not of a toy block (Saxe, Tzelnic, & Carey, 2007). Thus 7-month-olds appear to know that (1) an object incapable of self-motion must have a causal agent to set it in motion, (2) a hand is a more likely causal agent than a toy train or block, and (3) the existence and position of an unseen causal agent can be inferred from the motion of an inanimate object. In still another experiment, 7-month-olds who had begun to crawl recognized self-propulsion of objects, but noncrawling 7-month-olds did not. This finding suggests that infants' ability to identify self-propelled motion is linked to the development of self-locomotion, which gives them new ways of perceiving objects in their world (Cicchino & Rakison, 2008).

Object Permanence When Piaget investigated object permanence, he used infants' motor responses to gauge whether or not infants understood that a hidden object still existed. Their failure to reach for the hidden object was interpreted to mean they did not. However, it was possible that infants understood object permanence but could not demonstrate this knowledge with motor activity. At that time, infant development research methodologies were more limited and a better means of investigation did not exist. However, once researchers developed the basic habituation and visual preference paradigms described earlier, this allowed them to ask babies the question in a different way, using what has since become known as the violation-of-expectations paradigm.

Violation-of-expectations begins with a familiarization phase in which infants see an event happen normally. After the infant becomes bored and has habituated to this procedure, the event is changed in a way that conflicts with—or violates—normal expectations. If then baby then looks longer at this changed event, researchers assume that the additional interest shown by the baby implies that the baby is surprised.

For example, in one experiment, infants as young as 3½ months were first shown an animation of a carrot moving back and forth behind a screen (Hespos & Baillargeon, 2008). The center of the screen was notched, so that a tall carrot should have shown momentarily as it moved in front of the notch. In the "possible" event, the carrot could be seen as it passed in front of the notch. In the "impossible" event, the carrot would appear at one side, never show in the middle, and then emerge out the opposite side.

violation-of-expectations
Research method in which dishabituation to a stimulus that conflicts with experience is taken as evidence that an infant recognizes the new stimulus as surprising.

FIGURE 7.2

How Early Do Infants Show Object Permanence?

In this violation-of-expectations experiment, 3½-month-olds watched a short carrot and then a tall carrot slide along a track, disappear behind a screen, and then reappear. After they became accustomed to seeing these events, the opaque screen was replaced by a screen with a large notch at the top. The short carrot did not appear in the notch when passing behind the screen; the tall carrot, which should have appeared in the notch, also did not. The babies looked longer at the tall, than at the short, carrot event, suggesting they were surprised that the tall carrot did not reappear in the notch.

Source: Baillargeon & DeVos, 1991.

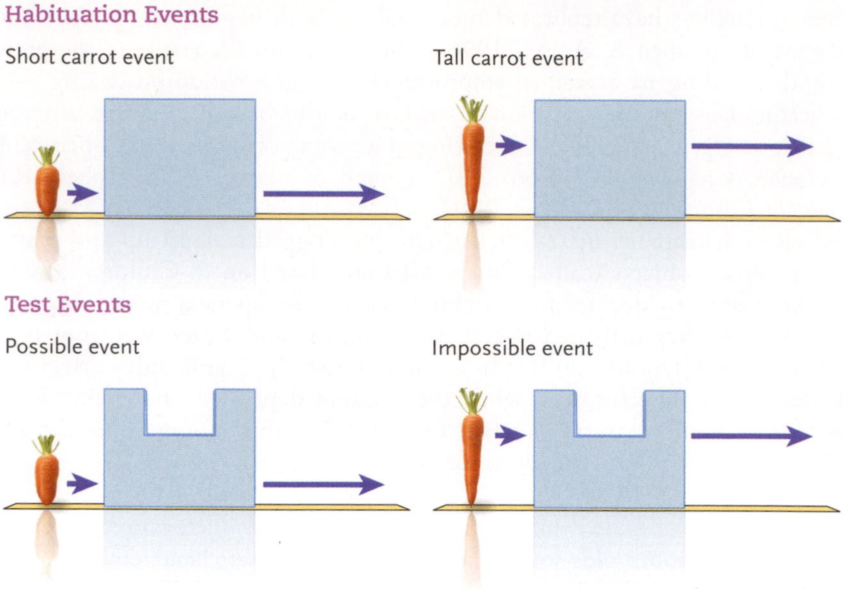

Habituation Events

Short carrot event

Tall carrot event

Test Events

Possible event

Impossible event

Babies may use a rudimentary understanding of probability in figuring out other people's preferences. For example, if they see a person pick a blue toy out of a box filled primarily with red toys, they will assume that person likes blue toys. If a person picks a blue toy out of a box filled with equal amounts of red and blue toys, they are less likely to assume there was a preference for blue toys. In a way, they are performing a statistical analysis of the likelihood of each act, and basing their assumptions on that.

Kushnir & Wellman, 2010

Infants showed surprise by looking longer at the "impossible" event, indicating that the "impossible" event violated their expectations.

The reason this procedure was important to the study of object permanence is that in order to be surprised by the carrot's failure to show, babies needed to be able to remember that it continued to exist. Thus, such studies suggest that at least a rudimentary form of object permanence may be present in the early months of life. On the other hand, critics point out an infant's perception that an object that disappears on one side of a visual barrier looks the same as the object that reappears on the other side does not necessarily imply cognitive knowledge that the object continues to exist behind the barrier (Meltzoff & Moore, 1998).

Number The violation-of-expectations paradigm can also be used to ask babies questions about their understanding of number. Karen Wynn (1992) tested whether 5-month-old babies can add and subtract small numbers of objects. The infants watched as Mickey Mouse dolls were placed behind a screen, and a doll was either added or taken away. The screen then was lifted to reveal either the number of dolls that should have been there or a different number of dolls. Babies looked longer at surprising "wrong" answers than at expected "right" ones, suggesting that they had mentally computed the right answers. This understanding of number seems to begin long before Piaget's sixth substage.

According to Wynn, this research suggests that numerical concepts are inborn. However, skeptics point out that the idea that these concepts are inborn is mere speculation, as the infants in these studies were already 5 and 6 months old. Furthermore, the infants might simply have been responding *perceptually* to the puzzling presence of a doll they saw removed from behind the screen or the absence of a doll they saw placed there (Cohen & Marks, 2002; Haith, 1998; Haith & Benson, 1998). Other researchers suggest that, although infants do seem to discriminate visually between sets of, say, two and three objects, they may merely notice differences in the overall contours, area, or collective mass of sets of objects rather than compare the number of objects in the sets (Clearfield & Mix, 1999; Mix, Huttenlocher, & Levine, 2002).

In response to such criticisms, McCrink and Wynn (2004) designed an experiment to find out whether 9-month-olds can add and subtract numbers too large for mere perceptual discrimination. The infants saw 5 abstract objects go behind an opaque square. Five more objects then appeared and went behind the square. The infants looked longer when the screen dropped to reveal 5 objects than when it revealed 10. Similarly, when 10 objects went behind the square and 5 emerged and went away, the infants looked longer when the screen dropped to reveal 10 objects than when it revealed 5. The authors concluded that "humans possess an early system that supports numerical combination and manipulation" (p. 780). Again, however, this finding does not establish whether numerical concepts are present at birth.

It is likely that qualitative differences exist between the numerical representations of infants and the number concepts of school age children—most likely because of the tremendous changes in brain structure, organization, and function during and after the 1st year of life. For example, even 3-year-olds do not seem to know that the number of items in an array remains the same if they are rearranged—an important aspect of the number concept. As one prominent developmental scientist wrote, "Attributing number concepts to infants simply because they can discriminate among arrays containing different numbers of elements is analogous to attributing a number competence to pigeons who can be taught to peck at a key exactly four times" (Kagan, 2008, p. 1613). Numerical concepts likely develop slowly over many years.

EVALUATING INFORMATION-PROCESSING RESEARCH ON INFANTS

Violation-of-expectations studies and other recent information processing research with infants raises the possibility that at least rudimentary forms of categorization, causal reasoning, object permanence, and number sense may be present in the early months of life. One proposal is that infants are born with reasoning abilities—*innate learning mechanisms* that help them make sense of the information they encounter—or that they acquire these abilities very early (Baillargeon, 1994). Some investigators go further, suggesting that infants at birth may already have intuitive *core knowledge* of basic physical principles in the form of specialized brain modules that help infants organize their perceptions and experience (Spelke, 1994, 1998).

However, these interpretations are controversial. Theorists argue whether an infant's visual interest in an impossible condition reveals a *perceptual* awareness that something unusual has happened or a *conceptual* understanding of the way things work. For instance, if an infant looks longer at one scene than another, it may be because the infant can perceptually discriminate between the two. In other words, the two scenes *look* different from each other and because infants like to look at new things, they gaze longer at the "impossible" condition. Alternatively, it's possible that an infant, in becoming accustomed to a habituation event, has developed an expectation about what should happen that is then violated by the surprising event. In other words, they look longer because their *concept* of what should have happened was challenged (Goubet & Clifton, 1998; Haith, 1998; Haith & Benson, 1998; Kagan, 2008; Mandler, 1998; Munakata, 2001; Munakata, McClelland, Johnson, & Siegler, 1997).

Defenders of violation-of-expectations research insist that a conceptual interpretation best accounts for the findings (Baillargeon, 1999; Spelke, 1998), but a variation on one of Baillargeon's experiments suggests caution. In her original research, Baillargeon (1994) showed infants of various ages a "drawbridge" rotating 180 degrees. When the infants became habituated to the rotation, a barrier was introduced in the form of a box. At 4½ months, infants seemed to show (by looking longer) they understood that the drawbridge could not move through the entire box, but not until 6½ months did infants recognize that the drawbridge cannot pass through 80 percent of the box. Later investigators replicated the experiment but eliminated the box. At 5 months, infants still looked longer at the 180-degree rotation than at a lesser degree of rotation, even though no barrier was present—suggesting that they simply were demonstrating a preference for greater movement (Rivera, Wakeley, & Langer, 1999). Still other researchers showed that the "drawbridge effect" could result simply from the mechanics of habituation and dishabituation (Schöner & Thelen, 2006). Thus, critics say, we must be careful

checkpoint can you . . .

▷ Describe the violation-of-expectations research method, tell how and why it is used, and list some criticisms of it?

▷ Discuss four areas in which information-processing research seems to contradict Piaget's account of development?

guidepost

6 What can brain research reveal about the development of cognitive skills?

implicit memory
Unconscious recall, generally of habits and skills; sometimes called *procedural memory*.

explicit memory
Intentional and conscious memory, generally of facts, names, and events; sometimes called *declarative memory*.

study smart

Implicit and Explicit Memory

working memory
Short-term storage of information being actively processed.

about overestimating infants' cognitive abilities from data that may have simpler explanations or may represent only partial achievement of mature abilities (Haith, 1998; Kagan, 2008).

Is it likely that mechanisms to acquire knowledge of physical principles would become functional long before babies can put that knowledge to practical use? According to some evolutionary theorists, the answer is no (Nelson, 2005; Rakison, 2005). Evolutionary principles suggest that people develop various capacities at times of life when they are adaptive, or useful. Thus infants are endowed at birth with basic attentional, perceptive, and learning abilities that adequately meet their needs for that period of life. It is possible that the ability to find meaning in what they perceive develops later, as do specialized learning abilities for specific domains such as language (Rakison, 2005).

Cognitive Neuroscience Approach: The Brain's Cognitive Structures

Current brain research bears out Piaget's assumption that neurological maturation is a major factor in cognitive development. Brain growth spurts (periods of rapid growth and development) coincide with changes in cognitive behavior similar to those Piaget described (Fischer, 2008; Fischer & Rose, 1994, 1995).

Some researchers have used brain scans to determine which brain structures are tied to cognitive functions and to chart developmental changes. These brain scans provide physical evidence of the location of two separate long-term memory systems—*implicit* and *explicit*—that acquire and store different kinds of information (Vargha-Khadem et al., 1997). **Implicit memory** refers to remembering that occurs without effort or even conscious awareness, for example, knowing how to tie your shoe or throw a ball, and it most commonly pertains to habits and skills. Implicit memory seems to develop early in development and is demonstrated by such actions as an infant's kicking on seeing a familiar mobile (Nelson, 2005). **Explicit memory**, also called *declarative memory*, is conscious or intentional recollection, usually of facts, names, events, or other things that can be stated or declared. Delayed imitation of complex behaviors is evidence that declarative memory is developing in late infancy and toddlerhood.

In early infancy, when the structures responsible for memory storage are not fully formed, memories are relatively fleeting. The maturing of the *hippocampus*, a structure deep in the temporal lobes, along with the development of cortical structures coordinated by the hippocampal formation make longer-lasting memories possible (Bauer, 2002; Bauer et al., 2003).

The *prefrontal cortex* (the large portion of the frontal lobe directly behind the forehead) is believed to control many aspects of cognition. This part of the brain develops more slowly than any other (Diamond, 2002; M. H. Johnson, 1998). During the second half of the 1st year, the prefrontal cortex and associated circuitry develop the capacity for **working memory**. Working memory is short-term storage of information the brain is actively processing, or working on. For example, when you try to figure out how much an item on sale will cost at the register, you are using working memory to make the calculations. Working memory can be overwhelmed, as in when someone speaking to you while you try to calculate the sale price interrupts this process.

Working memory appears relatively late in development and may be responsible for the slow development of object permanence, which seems to be seated in a rearward area of the prefrontal cortex (Nelson, 1995). By 12 months, this region may be developed enough to permit an infant to avoid the A-not-B error by controlling the impulse to search in a place where the object previously was found (Bell & Fox, 1992; Diamond, 1991).

Although memory systems continue to develop beyond infancy, the early emergence of the brain's memory structures underlines the importance of environmental stimulation from the first months of life. Social-contextual theorists and researchers pay particular attention to the impact of environmental influences.

Social-Contextual Approach: Learning from Interactions with Caregivers

How does social interaction with adults advance cognitive competence?

Researchers influenced by Vygotsky's sociocultural theory study how the cultural context affects early social interactions that may promote cognitive competence. **Guided participation** refers to mutual interactions with adults that help structure children's activities and bridge the gap between a child's understanding and an adult's. This concept was inspired by Vygotsky's view of learning as a collaborative process. Guided participation often occurs in shared play and in ordinary, everyday activities in which children learn informally the skills, knowledge, and values important in their culture.

In one cross-cultural study (Göncü, Mistry, & Mosier, 2000; Rogoff, Mistry, Göncü, & Mosier, 1993), researchers visited 14 homes with 1- to 2-year-olds in each of four places: a Mayan town in Guatemala, a tribal village in India, and middle-class urban neighborhoods in Salt Lake City and Turkey. The investigators interviewed caregivers about their child-rearing practices and watched them help the toddlers learn to dress themselves and to play with unfamiliar toys.

Cultural differences affected the types of guided participation the researchers observed. In the Guatemalan town and the Indian village where children saw mothers sewing and accompanied their mothers at work in the fields, the children customarily played alone or with older siblings while the mother worked nearby. After initial demonstration and instruction, mostly nonverbal, in, for example, how to tie shoes, the children took over, while the parent or other caregiver remained available to help. The U.S. toddlers, who had full-time caregivers, interacted with adults in the context of child's play rather than work or social worlds. Caregivers managed and motivated children's learning with praise and excitement. Turkish families, who were in transition from a rural to an urban way of life, showed a pattern somewhere between.

guided participation
Participation of an adult in a child's activity in a manner that helps to structure the activity and to bring the child's understanding of it closer to that of the adult.

> *Rogoff points out that despite the varied ways in which children learn, they all learn what they need to learn to be effective adults in that culture. She argues there is no "one best way"; rather, there are multiple, equally valid ways of learning.*

The cultural context, then, influences the way caregivers contribute to cognitive development. Direct adult involvement in children's play and learning may be better adapted to a middle-class urban community, in which parents or caregivers have more time, greater verbal skills, and possibly more interest in children's play and learning, than in a rural community in a developing country, in which children frequently observe and participate in adults' work activities (Rogoff et al., 1993). However, despite the different means by which caregivers teach their children valuable life skills, all children learn the things they need to learn to be effective members of society.

checkpoint can you . . .

▷ Identify the brain structures apparently involved in explicit, implicit, and working memory, and mention a task made possible by each?

▷ Tell how brain research helps explain Piagetian developments and memory operations?

▷ Explain how cultural patterns affect guided participation in toddlers' learning?

guidepost

8 How do babies develop
language, and what influences
linguistic progress?

language
Communication system based on
words and grammar.

Language Development

The day William Erasmus Darwin, affectionately known as Doddy, was born, his father, Charles, began keeping a diary of observations of his newborn son. These notes, published in 1877, called scientific attention to the developmental nature of infant behavior.

*Charles and
"Doddy" Darwin*

Darwin was particularly interested in documenting his son's progress in self-expression, first nonverbally and then through language. Through smiling, crying, laughing, facial expressions, and sounds of pleasure or pain, Doddy managed to communicate with his parents even before uttering his first word. One of his first meaningful verbal expressions was "Ah!"—uttered when he recognized an image in a mirror.

Doddy's exclamation is a striking example of the connection between **language**, a communication system based on words and grammar, and cognitive development. Once children know words, they can use them to represent objects and actions. They can reflect on people, places, and things; and they can communicate their needs, feelings, and ideas in order to exert control over their lives. How do infants "crack" this communicative "code"?

Let's look first at the typical sequence of language development (Table 7.5). Next we will note some special characteristics of early speech and then examine competing explanations of how infants acquire language.

SEQUENCE OF EARLY LANGUAGE DEVELOPMENT

Before babies can use words, they make their needs and feelings known through sounds that progress from crying to cooing and babbling, then to accidental imitation, and then to deliberate imitation. These sounds are known as **prelinguistic speech**. Infants also grow in the ability to recognize and understand speech sounds and to use meaningful gestures. Babies typically say their first word around the end of their 1st year, and toddlers begin speaking in sentences about 8 months to 1 year later.

prelinguistic speech
Forerunner of linguistic speech;
utterance of sounds that are not words.
Includes crying, cooing, babbling, and
accidental and deliberate imitation of
sounds without understanding their
meaning.

Early Vocalization *Crying* is a newborn's first means of communication. Different pitches, patterns, and intensities signal hunger, sleepiness, or anger (Lester & Boukydis, 1985). Adults find crying aversive for a reason—it motivates them to find the source of the problem and fix it. Crying has great adaptive value.

Between 6 weeks and 3 months, babies start *cooing* when they are happy—squealing, gurgling, and making vowel sounds like "ahhh." At about 3 to 6 months, babies begin to play with speech sounds, matching the sounds they hear from people around them.

Babbling—repeating consonant-vowel strings, such as "ma-ma-ma-ma"—occurs between ages 6 and 10 months and is often mistaken for a baby's first word. Babbling is not real language because it does not hold meaning for the baby, but it becomes more wordlike over time.

Imitation is key to early language development. First, babies *accidentally* imitate language sounds and then imitate themselves making these sounds. Generally, they are reinforced by their parents' positive responses and thus encouraged to produce such sounds more and more over time. At about 9 to 10 months, infants *deliberately* imitate sounds without understanding them. Once they have a repertoire of sounds, they string them together in prelinguistic speech patterns that sound like language but seem to have no meaning. Once infants become familiar with the sounds of words and phrases, they begin to attach meanings to them (Fernald, Perfors, & Marchman, 2006; Jusczyk & Hohne, 1997).

Sometimes making a particular sound results in a tongue position more or less suited toward making another sound. So, for example, "da" is easier to say for a baby than "bi." When you look at the most common kinship terms across cultures, they almost all use some variation of "ba," "pa," "da," and "ma." These are, not coincidentally, the easiest sounds for babies to make.

Perceiving Language Sounds and Structure Imitation of language sounds requires the ability to perceive subtle differences between sounds, and infants can do this from or even before birth. Their brains seem to be preset to discriminate basic linguistic units,

TABLE 7.5 Language Milestones from Birth to 3 Years

Age in Months	Development
Birth	Can perceive speech, cry, make some response to sound.
1½ to 3	Coos and laughs.
3	Plays with speech sounds.
5 to 6	Recognizes frequently heard sound patterns.
6 to 7	Recognizes all phonemes of native language.
6 to 10	Babbles in strings of consonants and vowels.
9	Uses gestures to communicate and plays gesture games.
9 to 10	Intentionally imitates sounds.
9 to 12	Uses a few social gestures.
10 to 12	No longer can discriminate sounds not in own language.
10 to 14	Says first word (usually a label for something).
10 to 18	Says single words.
12 to 13	Understands symbolic function of naming; passive vocabulary grows.
13	Uses more elaborate gestures.
14	Uses symbolic gesturing.
16 to 24	Learns many new words, expanding expressive vocabulary rapidly, going from about 50 words to as many as 400; uses verbs and adjectives.
18 to 24	Says first sentence (2 words).
20	Uses fewer gestures; names more things.
20 to 22	Has comprehension spurt.
24	Uses many two-word phrases; no longer babbles; wants to talk.
30	Learns new words almost every day; speaks in combinations of three or more words; understands very well; makes grammatical mistakes.
36	Says up to 1,000 words, 80 percent intelligible; makes some mistakes in syntax.

Source: Bates, O'Connell, & Shore, 1987; Capute, Shapiro, & Palmer, 1987; Kuhl, 2004; Lalonde & Werker, 1995; Lenneberg, 1969; Newman, 2005.

perceive linguistic patterns, and categorize them as similar or different (Kuhl, 2004). This process of sound discrimination apparently begins in the womb, as we described in Chapter 4 (DeCasper, Lecanuet, Busnel, Granier-Deferre, & Maugeais, 1994). This process continues in the first year of life as infants become rapidly sensitized to their native language.

Phonemes are the smallest units of sound in speech. For example, the word *dog* has 3 phonemes: the *d*, the *o*, and the *g* sound. Every language has its own unique phonology, or system of sounds, that are used in the production of speech. At first, infants can discriminate the phonemes of any language. In time, however, the ongoing process of pattern perception and categorization commits the brain's neural networks to further learning of the patterns of the infant's native language and constrains future learning of nonnative language patterns (Kuhl & Rivera-Gaxiola, 2008). By age 6 to 7 months, hearing babies have learned to recognize the approximately 40 phonemes of their native language and to adjust to slight differences in the way different speakers form those sounds (Kuhl, Williams, Lacerda, Stevens, & Lindblom, 1992). The ability to discriminate native-language sounds at this age predicts individual differences in language abilities during the second year (Tsao, Liu, & Kuhl, 2004), whereas nonnative sound discrimination does not (Kuhl, Conboy, Padden, Nelson, & Pruitt, 2005).

Starting as early as 6 months for vowels and by 10 months for consonants, recognition of native phonetic sounds significantly increases, while discrimination of nonnative sounds declines. By the end of the first year, babies lose their sensitivity to sounds that are not part of the language or languages they usually hear spoken (Kuhl & Rivera-Gaxiola, 2008). Although the ability to perceive nonnative sounds is not entirely lost, the brain no longer routinely discriminates them (Bates, O'Connell, & Shore, 1987; Lalonde & Werker, 1995; Werker, 1989). Deaf babies undergo a similar restrictive process with regard to recognition of signs (Kuhl & Rivera-Gaxiola, 2008). Presumably, this increased sensitivity to native sounds or gestures help the child more efficiently acquire language. Indeed, babies who lack early exposure to this patterning feature of language—whether spoken or signed—during a critical or sensitive period are unlikely to acquire language normally (Kuhl, 2004; Kuhl et al., 2005; refer to Box 1.3 in Chapter 1). How does this change occur? One hypothesis, for which there is evidence from behavioral studies and brain imaging, is that infants mentally compute the relative frequency of particular phonetic sequences in their language and learn to ignore sequences they infrequently hear (Kuhl, 2004). Another hypothesis, also supported by behavioral and brain imaging studies, is that early language experience modifies the neural structure of the brain, facilitating rapid progress toward detection of word patterns in the native language while suppressing attention to nonnative patterns that would slow native language learning. These early pattern-detection skills predict continuity of language development: In one study, toddlers who at 7½ months had shown better neural discrimination of native phonemes were more advanced in word production and sentence complexity at 24 months and at 30 months than toddlers who, at 7½ months, had been better able to discriminate phonetic contrasts in other nonnative languages (Kuhl & Rivera-Gaxiola, 2008).

In addition to learning what the phonemes in their language are, babies also learn the rules for how they fit together. For example, in English, the sound combination in "kib" is acceptable, although "kib" is not a word. However, the nonsense word "bnik" breaks the phonological rules in English as a "b" and an "n" are not typically found next to each other within the same word. Between 6 and 12 months, babies begin to become aware of the phonological rules of their language. In one series of experiments, 7-month-olds listened longer to "sentences" containing a different order of nonsense sounds from the order to which the infants had been habituated. The sounds used in the test were different from those used in the habituation phase, so the infants' discrimination must have been based on the patterns of repetition alone. This finding suggests that infants may have a mechanism for discerning abstract rules of sentence structure (Saffran, Pollak, Seibel, & Shkolnik, 2007).

Gestures Before babies can speak, they point (Liszkowski, Carpenter, & Tomasello, 2008). Pointing is important to language acquisition and serves several functions. At 11 months, Maika pointed to her cup to show that she wanted it. She also pointed to a dog chasing his tail, using the gesture to communicate with her mother about an interesting sight. At 12 months, she pointed at a pen her brother had dropped and was looking for. This use of pointing to provide information showed that she drew an inference about her brother's state of mind and wanted to help—an early indication of *social cognition*, discussed in Chapter 8 (Liszkowski, Carpenter, Striano, & Tomasello, 2006; Liszkowski et al., 2008; Tomasello, Carpenter, & Liszkowski, 2007). Pointing helps regulate joint interactions and does not need to be taught.

One way in which this structure is reflected is in babies' babbling. One-year-olds babble in their native language. In other words, their babbling follows the phonological rules of their language.

Babies generally start pointing with their entire hand, and then move to using their pointer finger.

Also by 12 months, Maika learned some *conventional social gestures:* waving bye-bye, nodding her head to mean *yes*, and shaking her head to signify *no*. By about 13 months, she used more elaborate *representational gestures*; for example, she would hold an empty cup to her mouth to show that she wanted a drink or hold up her arms to show that she wanted to be picked up.

Symbolic gestures, such as blowing to mean *hot* or sniffing to mean *flower*, often emerge around the same time as babies say their first words, and they function much like words. Both hearing and deaf babies use such gestures in much the same ways (Goldin-Meadow, 2007). By using them, babies show an understanding that symbols can refer to specific objects, events, desires, and conditions. Gestures usually appear before children have a vocabulary of 25 words and drop out when children learn the word for the idea they were gesturing and can say it instead (Lock, Young, Service, & Chandler, 1990).

Learning gestures seems to help babies learn to talk. Early gestures are a good predictor of later vocabulary size (Goldin-Meadow, 2007). In one study, researchers captured video interactions between toddlers and their parents at home for 90 minutes every 4 months. Parents' use of gestures predicted their child's use of gestures at 14 months, which in turn predicted the size of the child's vocabulary at 42 months (Rowe, Özçaliskan, & Goldin-Meadow, 2008).

Toddlers often combine gestures with words. Gesture-word combinations serve as a signal that a child is about to begin using multiword sentences (Goldin-Meadow, 2007).

First Words The average baby says a first word sometime between 10 and 14 months, initiating **linguistic speech**—verbal expression that conveys meaning. At first an infant's total verbal repertoire is likely to be "mama" or "dada." Or it may be a simple syllable that has more than one meaning depending on the context in which the child utters it. "Da" may mean "I want that," "I want to go out," or "Where's Daddy?" A word like this, in which an entire sentence is expressed in one word, is called a **holophrase**.

Long before infants can connect sounds to meanings, they learn to recognize sound patterns they hear frequently, such as their name. Infants 5 months old listen longer to their name than to other names (Newman, 2005). One method researchers use to measure infants' perception of word sounds is to record their eye movements while listening to names for pictures on a screen, such as *apple* or *dog*. Infants at 8 months or younger start learning the forms of words by discerning such perceptual cues as syllables that usually occur together (such as *ba* and *by*) and store these possible word forms in memory. They also notice pronunciation, stress placed on syllables, and changes in pitch. This early auditory learning lays the foundation for vocabulary growth (Swingley, 2008).

Babies understand many words before they can use them. Six-month-olds look longer at a video of their mothers when they hear the word "mommy" and of their fathers when they hear "daddy," suggesting that they are beginning to associate sound with meaning—at least with regard to special people (Tincoff & Jusczyk, 1999). By 13 months, most children understand that a word stands for a specific thing or event, and they can quickly learn the meaning of a new word (Woodward, Markman, & Fitzsimmons, 1994).

Between 10 months and 2 years, the process by which babies learn words gradually changes from simple association to following social cues. At 10 months, infants associate a name they hear with an object they find interesting whether or not the name is the correct one for that object. At 12 months, they begin to pay attention to cues from adults, such as looking or pointing at an object while saying its name. However, they still learn names only for interesting objects and ignore uninteresting ones. By 18 to 24 months, children follow social cues in learning names, regardless of the intrinsic interest of the objects (Golinkoff & Hirsh-Pasek, 2006; Pruden, Hirsh-Pasek, Golinkoff, & Hennon, 2006). Pointing is one of the primary scaffolds for learning word meaning.

This child is communicating by pointing at something that catches her eye. Gesturing comes naturally to young children and seems to be an important part of language learning.

linguistic speech
Verbal expression designed to convey meaning.

holophrase
Single word that conveys a complete thought.

Language Development: 10–18 months

At 24 months, children quickly recognize names of familiar objects in the absence of visual cues (Swingley & Fernald, 2002).

Receptive vocabulary—what infants understand—continues to grow as verbal comprehension gradually becomes faster and more accurate and efficient (Fernald et al., 2006). Generally, infants have a far greater receptive vocabulary than expressive—or spoken—vocabulary. By 18 months, 3 out of 4 children can understand 150 words and can say 50 of them (Kuhl, 2004). Children with larger vocabularies and quicker reaction times can recognize spoken words from just the first part of the word. For example, when they hear "daw" or "ki," they will point to a picture of a dog or kitten (Fernald, Swingley, & Pinto, 2001). This early language learning is closely related to later cognitive development. In a longitudinal study, children's speed of recognition of spoken words and vocabulary size at 25 months predicted linguistic and cognitive skills, including the efficiency of working memory, at 8 years (Marchman & Fernald, 2008).

Addition of new words to the *expressive* (spoken) *vocabulary* is slow at first. Then, sometime between 16 and 24 months, a "naming explosion" may occur, though this phenomenon does not appear to occur in all children (Ganger & Brent, 2004). Within a few months, a toddler may progress from saying about 50 words to saying several hundred (Courage & Howe, 2002). Rapid gains in spoken vocabulary reflect increases in speed and accuracy of word recognition during the second year (Fernald, Pinto, Swingley, Weinberg, & McRoberts, 1998; Fernald et al., 2006) as well as an understanding that things belong in categories (Courage & Howe, 2002).

Nouns seem to be the easiest type of word for most children to learn. In cross-cultural studies, it did not matter whether a family's native language was Spanish, Dutch, French, Hebrew, Italian, Korean, or American English; in all these languages, parents reported that their 20-month-old children knew more nouns than any other class of words (Bornstein & Cote, 2004). At 24 months, children quickly recognize names of familiar objects in the absence of visual cues (Swingley & Fernald, 2002).

First Sentences The next linguistic breakthrough comes when a toddler puts two words together to express one idea ("Dolly fall"). Generally, children do this between 18 and 24 months, but this age range varies greatly. Although prelinguistic speech (such as babbling) is fairly closely tied to chronological age, linguistic speech is not. Most children who begin talking fairly late catch up eventually—and many make up for lost time by talking nonstop to anyone who will listen. (True delayed language development is discussed in Chapter 10.)

A child's first sentences typically deal with everyday events, things, people, or activities (Braine, 1976; Rice, 1989; Slobin, 1973). Children typically use **telegraphic speech**, consisting of only a few essential words. When Rita says, "Damma deep," she seems to mean "Grandma is sweeping the floor." Children's use of telegraphic speech and the form it takes vary, depending on the language being learned (Braine, 1976; Slobin, 1983). Word order generally conforms to what a child hears; Rita does not say, "Deep Damma," when she sees her grandmother pushing a broom. In other words, children illustrate their implicit understanding of the structure of their language with the word order they use.

Does the omission of functional words such as *is* and *the* mean that a child does not know these words? Not necessarily; the child may merely find them hard to reproduce. Even during the 1st year, infants are sensitive to the presence of functional words; at 10½ months, they can tell a normal passage from one in which the functional words have been replaced by similar-sounding nonsense words (Jusczyk, 2003).

Sometime between 20 and 30 months, children show increasing competence in **syntax**, the fundamental rules for putting sentences together in their language. Syntax is why a sentence like "man bites dog" differs from "dog bites man," and it allows us to understand and produce an infinite number of utterances. They also become increasingly aware of the communicative purpose of speech and of whether their words are being understood (Dunham, Dunham, & O'Keefe, 2000; Shwe & Markman, 1997), a sign of growing sensitivity to the mental lives of others. By age 3, speech is fluent,

If you want to help a toddler learn color words, label the object you are referring to, then name the color.

Dye, 2010

telegraphic speech
Early form of sentence use consisting of only a few essential words.

The term *telegraphic speech* is derived from the fact that telegrams charged by the word. To save money, people would eliminate all but the essential components of speech, much in the same way that babies use only the words best able to communicate their intent.

syntax
Rules for forming sentences in a particular language.

longer, and more complex; although children often omit parts of speech, they usually get their meaning across well.

CHARACTERISTICS OF EARLY SPEECH

Early speech has a character all its own—no matter what language a child is speaking (Slobin, 1970, 1990). As we have seen, children *simplify*. They use telegraphic speech to say just enough to get their meaning across ("No drink milk!").

Children *understand grammatical relationships they cannot yet express*. At first, Nina may understand that a dog is chasing a cat, but she cannot string together enough words to express the complete action. Her sentence comes out as "Puppy chase" rather than "Puppy chase kitty."

Children also make mistakes with respect to what category a word describes by either underextending or overextending word meaning. When they *underextend word meanings*, they use words in too narrow of a category. Lisa's uncle gave her a toy car, which the 13-month-old called her "koo-ka." Then her father came home with a gift, saying, "Look, Lisa, here's a little car for you." Lisa shook her head. "Koo-ka," she said and ran and got the one from her uncle. To her, *that* car—and *only* that car—was a little car, and it took some time before she called any other toy cars by the same name. Lisa was underextending the word *car* by restricting it to a single object.

Alternatively, children also *overextend word meanings* by using words in too broad of a category. At 14 months, Ajay jumped in excitement at the sight of a gray-haired man on the television screen and shouted, "Gampa!" Ajay was *overextending*, or over-generalizing, a word; he thought that because his grandfather had gray hair, all gray-haired men could be called "Grandpa." As children develop a larger vocabulary and get feedback from adults on the appropriateness of what they say, they overextend less. ("No, honey, that man looks a little like Grandpa, but he's somebody else's grandpa, not yours.")

Children *overregularize rules*. Over regularization is a language error, but it nonetheless illustrates children's growing knowledge of syntax. It occurs when children inappropriately apply a syntactical rule. For instance, when children say sentences such as "Daddy goed to the store," "I drawed that," or "we eated dinner," they are applying the English language rule "add –ed to a verb to make it past tense." It takes a while for children to learn the rule as well as the exceptions to it and they demonstrate this process to us in the words they say. For example, children commonly use the exceptions to the rule first. They generally learn these by rote for phrases they commonly hear ("Daddy went to the store"). Then, they learn the rule, and use that to fill in the blanks on the fly when they can't recall the exception ("Daddy goed to the store"). By early school age as they become more proficient in language, they memorize the exceptions and begin to apply them, once again saying the phrase correctly ("Daddy went to the store").

> English is generally considered to be a challenging second language to learn. Part of the reason for this is that English has so many exceptions to the rules.

checkpoint
can you . . .

▷ Trace the typical sequence of milestones in early language development, pointing out the influence of the language babies hear around them?

▷ Describe five ways in which early speech differs from adult speech?

CLASSIC THEORIES OF LANGUAGE ACQUISITION: THE NATURE-NURTURE DEBATE

Is linguistic ability learned or inborn? In the 1950s, a debate raged between two schools of thought: one led by B. F. Skinner, the foremost proponent of learning theory, and the other by the linguist Noam Chomsky.

Skinner (1957) maintained that language learning, like other learning, is based on experience and learned associations. According to classic learning theory, children learn language through the processes of operant conditioning. At first, babies utter sounds at random. Caregivers reinforce the sounds that happen to resemble adult speech. Infants then repeat these reinforced sounds and language is gradually shaped. Social learning theorists extended this early model to account for imitation. According to social learning theory, babies imitate the sounds they hear adults make and, again, are reinforced for doing so.

For example, Lila, while babbling to herself, inadvertently says "da." Her parents hear her, and provide her with smiles, attention, and praise for this sound. Lila is thus reinforced, and thus continues to say "da." Eventually, her parents tire of this, and no longer provide as much reinforcement for the sound. But then, Lila happens to say "dada." Now her parents once again reward her lavishly. Again, their praise eventually tapers off, and now the word is only reinforced when her father is actually present. Over time, her parents' selective reinforcement of closer and closer approximations to speech in the right context results in the shaping of language. In addition, Lila's imitation of her parents' utterances gives them a variety of sounds and words to reinforce.

Observation, imitation, and reinforcement probably do contribute to language development, but, as Chomsky (1957) persuasively argued, they cannot fully explain it. For one thing, word combinations and nuances are so many and so complex that they cannot all be acquired by specific imitation and reinforcement. Then, caregivers often reinforce utterances that are not strictly grammatical, as long as they make sense ("Gampa go bye-bye"). Adult speech itself is an unreliable model to imitate, as it is often ungrammatical, containing false starts, unfinished sentences, and slips of the tongue. Also, learning theory does not account for children's imaginative ways of saying things they have never heard—as when 2-year-old Anna described a sprained ankle as a "sprangle" and said she didn't want to go to sleep yet because she wasn't "yawny."

Chomsky's view is called **nativism**. Unlike Skinner's learning theory, nativism emphasizes the active role of the learner. Chomsky (1957, 1972, 1995) proposed that the human brain has an innate capacity for acquiring language; babies learn to talk as naturally as they learn to walk. He suggested that an inborn **language acquisition device (LAD)** programs children's brains to analyze the language they hear and to figure out its rules.

Support for the nativist position comes from newborns' ability to differentiate similar sounds, suggesting that they are "born with perceptual mechanisms that are tuned to the properties of speech" (Eimas, 1985, p. 49). Nativists point out that almost all children master their native language in the same age-related sequence without formal teaching. Furthermore, the brains of human beings, the only animals with fully developed language, contain a structure that is larger on one side than on the other, suggesting that an inborn mechanism for sound and language processing may be localized in the larger hemisphere—the left for most people (Gannon, Holloway, Broadfield, & Braun, 1998). The existence of sensitivity periods for language also support the nativist position.

Still, the nativist approach does not explain precisely how such a mechanism operates. It does not tell us why some children acquire language more rapidly and efficiently than others, why children differ in linguistic skill and fluency, or why (as we'll see) speech development appears to depend on having someone to talk with, not merely on hearing spoken language. Nativism also doesn't address motivational aspects of language development—that babies are compelled to and rewarded for communicating.

Deaf babies seem to learn sign language in much the same fashion and in the same sequence as hearing infants learn speech. Just as hearing babies of hearing parents imitate vocal utterances, deaf babies of deaf parents seem to imitate the sign language they see their parents using, first stringing together meaningless motions and then repeating them over and over in what has been called *hand-babbling*. As parents reinforce these gestures, the babies attach meaning to

> Just as deaf babies hand-babble, deaf parents engage in baby-talk (aka motherese or parentese) with gestures.

nativism
Theory that human beings have an inborn capacity for language acquisition.

language acquisition device (LAD)
In Chomsky's terminology, an inborn mechanism that enables children to infer linguistic rules from the language they hear.

around the world

INVENTING SIGN LANGUAGE

All human communities have *language*, a system of symbols to communicate thoughts. Children normally learn, without special instruction, the language to which they are exposed from birth. But what if children cannot acquire the language that surrounds them? Will they invent one?

To answer that question, researchers have studied children born deaf to hearing parents who do not know a sign language and do not expose their children to one. These children communicate spontaneously through gestures that are organized differently from the casual gestures their parents use. The children's gestures are language-like; they correspond to parts of speech, such as nouns and verbs, which are combined into sentence-like strings. For example, one child, inviting an adult to share a snack, first pointed at the snack, then brought his hand to his mouth to gesture *eat*, and then pointed at the adult. Still, these *home signs*, as they have been called, do not constitute a full blown language system because the children lack nonhearing partners with whom to communicate.

In the 1980s, when deaf Nicaraguan schoolchildren who were being taught lip-reading in Spanish were brought together for the first time, they developed a true sign language, which, as adapted by successive cohorts of deaf children, has evolved from simple gestures into words and sentences that follow linguistic rules (Senghas & Coppola, 2001; Senghas, Kita, & Ozyürek, 2004). Likewise, Al-Sayyid Bedouin Sign Language, which

emerged spontaneously in an isolated village in Israel's Negev desert, has a distinct, systematic grammatical structure unlike that of Israeli Sign Language or of the Arabic dialect spoken by hearing members of the community (Sandler, Meir, Padden, & Aronoff, 2005). Unlike Nicaraguan Sign Language, Bedouin Sign Language is passed on from parents to children, as occurs in hearing families.

All sign languages, including American Sign Language, probably came into existence through a similar process. These languages are structured much like spoken language, and children exposed to them from birth acquire them as naturally as hearing children acquire spoken language. One difference, though, is that hand signs are easier than speech to invent and understand. Thus the development of new sign languages offers "a unique opportunity to glimpse language in its infant stages and watch it grow" (Goldin-Meadow, 2007, p. 4).

Source: Unless otherwise cited, this box is indebted to Goldin-Meadow (2007).

what's your view

Does the creation of Nicaraguan Sign Language seem to support nativist or learning theories of language acquisition?

---

them (Petitto & Marentette, 1991; Petitto, Holowka, Sergio, & Ostry, 2001). For more on the development of sign language, especially in children without linguistic models, see Box 7.2.

Learning theory does not explain the correspondence between the ages at which linguistic advances in both hearing and nonhearing babies typically occur (Padden, 1996; Petitto, Katerelos, et al., 2001; Petitto & Kovelman, 2003). Deaf babies begin hand-babbling between ages 7 and 10 months, about the age when hearing infants begin voice-babbling (Petitto, Holowka, et al., 2001; Petitto & Marentette, 1991). Deaf babies also begin to use sentences in sign language at about the same time that hearing babies begin to speak in sentences (Meier, 1991; Newport & Meier, 1985). This finding suggests that an inborn language capacity may underlie the acquisition of both spoken and signed language and that advances in both kinds of language are tied to brain maturation.

Most developmental scientists today believe that language acquisition, like most other aspects of development, depends on an intertwining of nature and nurture. Children, whether hearing or deaf, probably have an inborn capacity to acquire language, which may be activated or constrained by experience.

checkpoint can you . . .

▷ Summarize how learning theory and nativism seek to explain language acquisition, and point out strengths and weaknesses of each theory?

CHAPTER 7 Cognitive Development during the First Three Years | **209**

INFLUENCES ON LANGUAGE DEVELOPMENT

What determines how quickly and how well children learn to understand and use language? Research has focused on influences both within and outside the child.

Brain Development The tremendous brain growth during the early months and years is closely linked with language development. A newborn's cries are controlled by the *brain stem* and *pons*, the most primitive parts of the brain and the earliest to develop (refer to Chapter 6). Repetitive babbling may emerge with the maturation of parts of the *motor cortex*, which control movements of the face and larynx. A brain imaging study points to the emergence of a link between the brain's phonetic perception and motor systems as early as 6 months—a connection that strengthens by 6 to 12 months (Imada et al., 2006). The development of language actively affects brain networks, committing them to the recognition of native language sounds only (Kuhl, 2004; Kuhl et al., 2005). In other words, language exposure helps shape the developing brain, and then the developing brain helps the infant learn language.

Brain scans, which measure changes in electrical potential at particular brain sites during cognitive activity, confirm the sequence of vocabulary development outlined earlier in this chapter. In toddlers with large vocabularies, brain activation tends to focus on the left temporal and parietal lobes, whereas in toddlers with smaller vocabularies, brain activation is more scattered (Kuhl & Rivera-Gaxiola, 2008). Cortical regions associated with language continue to develop until at least the late preschool years or beyond—some, even until adulthood.

In about 98 percent of people, the left hemisphere is dominant for language, though the right hemisphere participates as well (Knecht et al., 2000; Nobre & Plunkett, 1997; Owens, 1996). Images of babbling babies show that, as in adult speech, the mouth opens more on the right side than on the left. Because the brain's left hemisphere controls activity on the right side of the body, lateralization of linguistic functions apparently takes place very early in life (Holowka & Petitto, 2002; refer to Chapter 6). Language lateralization increases into young adulthood, enabling continued growth in language skills (Szaflarski, Holland, Schmithorst, & Weber-Byars, 2004).

Social Interaction: The Role of Parents and Caregivers Language is a social act. It requires interaction. Language takes not only the necessary biological machinery and cognitive capacity but also interaction with a live communicative partner. Children who grow up without normal social contact—for example, those who are linguistically isolated, or who have autism—do not develop language normally. And, those who learn about language only through television and do not interact with a live partner will not learn to speak the language either. In a laboratory experiment, native Mandarin speakers read to and played with 9-month-old infants regularly for 4 to 6 weeks. Behavioral tests and brain scans up to 1 month after the final session showed that the infants had learned—and retained—Mandarin syllables not used in English. By contrast, a control group who had been exposed to the same Mandarin speech through televised or audio-only tutors did no better than another control group who had heard only English (Kuhl & Rivera-Gaxiola, 2008).

Parents or other caregivers play an important role at each stage of language development. They do so (1) by providing *opportunities for communicative experience*, which motivate babies to learn language, and (2) by providing *models of language use* (Hoff, 2006). The age of parents or caregivers, the way they interact with and talk with an infant, the child's birth order, child care experience, and, later, schooling, peers, and television exposure all affect the pace and course of language acquisition. So does the wider culture. The milestones of language development described in this chapter are typical of Western, middle-class children who are spoken to directly. They are not necessarily typical in all cultures, nor at all socioeconomic levels (Hoff, 2006).

checkpoint
can you . . .

▷ Name areas of the brain involved in early language development, and tell the function of each?

Playing peek-a-boo involves turn-taking, which is what also happens within conversations and most social interactions.

Prelinguistic Period At the babbling stage, adults help an infant advance toward true speech by repeating the sounds the baby makes and rewarding her efforts. The baby finds this imitation engaging, and soon joins in the game and repeats the sounds back. Parents' imitation of babies' sounds affects the amount of infant vocalization (Goldstein, King, & West, 2003) and the pace of language learning (Hardy-Brown & Plomin, 1985; Hardy-Brown, Plomin, & DeFries, 1981; Schmitt, Simpson, & Friend, 2011). It also helps babies experience the social aspect of speech, the sense that a conversation consists of alternating or taking turns (Kuhl, 2004), an idea most babies seem to grasp at about age 7½ to 8 months. Even as early as 4 months, babies in a game of peekaboo show sensitivity to the structure of social exchange with an adult (Rochat, Querido, & Striano, 1999).

> Research showed that mothers who took their babies to baby sign-language classes were more stressed than mothers who did not. Given that length of time spent in classes was not related to increased stress, the researchers concluded that the classes did not cause stress. What is an alternative explanation for the finding?
>
> Howlett, Kirk, & Pine, 2010

Pointing is also important in language acquisition. Caregivers may help babies understand spoken words by, for example, pointing to a doll and saying, "Please give me Kermit," encouraging the infant to follow the caregiver's gaze (Kuhl, 2004). If the baby doesn't respond, the adult may pick up the doll and say, "Kermit." In one longitudinal study, mothers' responsiveness to 9-month-olds' and, even more so, to 13-month-olds' vocalization and play predicted the timing of language milestones, such as first spoken words and sentences (Tamis-LeMonda, Bornstein, & Baumwell, 2001).

Vocabulary Development How can parents facilitate language development in their children? When babies begin to talk, parents or caregivers can boost vocabulary development by repeating their first words and pronouncing them correctly. Joint attention, discussed earlier in this chapter, leads to more rapid vocabulary development (Hoff, 2006). In one longitudinal study, mothers' responsiveness to 9-month-olds' and, even more so, to 13-month-olds' vocalization and play predicted the timing of language milestones, such as first spoken words and sentences (Tamis-LeMonda et al., 2001). This is not surprising—a shared understanding and focus on an event or object coupled with maternal labeling is an extremely supportive framework for language acquisition.

A strong relationship exists between the frequency of specific words in mothers' speech and the order in which children learn these words (Brent & Siskind, 2001; Huttenlocher, Haight, Bryk, Seltzer, & Lyons, 1991) as well as between mothers' talkativeness and the size of toddlers' vocabularies (Huttenlocher, 1998; Schmitt, Simpson, & Friend, 2011). Mothers with higher socioeconomic status tend to use richer vocabularies and longer utterances, and their 2-year-olds have larger spoken vocabularies—as much as 8 times as large as those of low-SES children the same age (Hoff, 2003; Ramey & Ramey, 2003). By age 3, vocabularies of low-income children vary greatly, depending in large part on the diversity of word types they have heard their mothers use (Pan, Rowe, Singer, & Snow, 2005).

However, parental sensitivity and responsiveness may count even more than the number of words a mother uses. In a yearlong study of 290 low-income families of 2-year-olds, both parents' sensitivity, positive regard for the child, and the cognitive stimulation they provided during play predicted the child's receptive vocabulary and cognitive development at ages 2 and 3 (Tamis-LeMonda et al., 2004).

In households where more than one language is spoken, babies achieve similar milestones in each language on the same schedule as children who hear only one language (Petitto, Katerelos, et al., 2001; Petitto & Kovelman, 2003). However, children learning two languages tend to have smaller vocabularies in each language than children

"Peekaboo!" This game, played the world over, helps babies develop cognitive concepts such as anticipation.

When babies hear CDS, their heart rate slows, a physiological state that is consistent with orienting toward and absorbing information.

learning only one language (Hoff, 2006). Bilingual children often use elements of both languages, sometimes in the same utterance—a phenomenon called **code mixing** (Petitto, Katerelos, et al., 2001; Petitto & Kovelman, 2003). In Montreal, children as young as 2 in dual-language households differentiate between the two languages, using French with a predominantly French-speaking father and English with a predominantly English-speaking mother (Genesee, Nicoladis, & Paradis, 1995). This ability to shift from one language to another is called **code switching**. (Chapter 13 discusses second-language learning.)

Child-Directed Speech You do not have to be a parent to speak "parentese." If, when you talk to an infant or toddler, you speak slowly in a sing-songy high-pitched voice with exaggerated ups and downs, simplify your speech, exaggerate vowel sounds, and use short words and sentences and much repetition, you are using **child-directed speech (CDS)**, sometimes called *parentese*, *motherese*, or *baby talk*. Most adults and even children do it naturally, and even other babyish stimuli such as puppies or kittens can elicit it.

Such "baby talk" has been documented in many languages and cultures (Kuhl et al., 1997), suggesting it is universal in nature. In one cross-cultural observational study, mothers in the United States, Russia, and Sweden were audiotaped speaking to their 2- to 5-month-old infants. Whether the mothers were speaking English, Russian, or Swedish, they produced more exaggerated vowel sounds when talking to the infants than when talking to other adults. At 20 weeks, the babies' babbling contained distinct vowels that reflected the phonetic differences to which their mothers' speech had alerted them (Kuhl et al., 1997).

Most researchers believe that CDS helps infants learn their native language or at least pick it up faster by exaggerating and directing attention to the distinguishing features of speech sounds (Kuhl et al., 2005). Moreover, infants are "captured" attentionally by the sound and find it highly engaging, resulting in more rapid learning (Fernauld, 1985.) A few theorists challenge the value of CDS. They contend that babies speak sooner and better if they hear and can respond to more complex adult speech

Despite controversy over the value of child-directed speech, or parentese, this simplified way of speaking does appeal to babies and is highly supportive of language acquisition.

(Gleitman, Newport, & Gleitman, 1984; Oshima-Takane, Goodz, & Derevensky, 1996). Nonetheless, infants themselves prefer to hear simplified speech. This preference is clear practically from birth, and it does not seem to depend on any specific experience (Cooper & Aslin, 1990; Kuhl et al., 1997; Kuhl & Rivera-Gaxiola, 2008; Werker, Pegg, & McLeod, 1994).

PREPARING FOR LITERACY: THE BENEFITS OF READING ALOUD

Most babies love to be read to. The frequency with which caregivers read to them can influence how well children speak and eventually how well and how soon they develop **literacy**—the ability to read and write. In a study of 2,581 low-income families, about half of the mothers reported reading daily to their preschool children between 14 months and 3 years. Children who had been read to daily had better cognitive and language skills at age 3 (Raikes et al., 2006) and better reading comprehension at age 7 than do their peers (Crain-Thoreson & Dale, 1992; Sénéchal & LeFevre, 2002; Wells, 1985).

The way parents or caregivers read to children makes a difference. Adults tend to have one of three styles of reading to children: the describer, comprehender, and performance-oriented style. A *describer* focuses on describing what is going on in the pictures and invites the child to do so as well ("What are the Mom and Dad having for breakfast?"). A *comprehender* encourages the child to look more deeply at the meaning of a story and to make inferences and predictions ("What do you think the lion will do now?"). A *performance-oriented* reader reads the story straight through, introducing the main themes beforehand and asking questions afterward. An adult's read-aloud style is best tailored to the needs and skills of the child. In an experimental study of 50 4-year-olds in Dunedin, New Zealand, the describer style resulted in the greatest overall benefits for vocabulary and print skills, but the performance-oriented style was more beneficial for children who started out with large vocabularies (Reese & Cox, 1999).

Social interaction in reading aloud, play, and other daily activities is a key to much of childhood development. Children call forth responses from the people around them and, in turn, react to those responses. In Chapter 8, we look more closely at these bidirectional influences as we explore early psychosocial development.

checkpoint
can you . . .

▷ Explain the importance of social interaction, and give at least three examples of how parents or caregivers help babies learn to talk?

▷ Assess the arguments for and against the value of child-directed speech (CDS)?

▷ Tell why reading aloud to children at an early age is beneficial, and describe an effective way of doing so?

literacy
Ability to read and write.

summary and key terms

❶ Studying Cognitive Development: Six Approaches

What are six approaches to the study of cognitive development?

- Six approaches to the study of cognitive development are the behaviorist, psychometric, Piagetian, information-processing, cognitive neuroscience, and social-contextual approaches.
- All of these approaches can shed light on how early cognition develops.

behaviorist approach (*178*)

psychometric approach (*178*)

Piagetian approach (*178*)

information-processing approach (*179*)

cognitive neuroscience approach (*179*)

social-contextual approach (*179*)

❷ Behaviorist Approach: Basic Mechanics of Learning

How do infants learn, and how long can they remember?

- Two types of learning that behaviorists study are classical conditioning and operant conditioning.

classical conditioning (*179*)

operant conditioning (*179*)

- Rovee-Collier's research suggests that infants' memory processes are much like those of adults, though this conclusion has been questioned. Infants' memories can be jogged by periodic reminders.

guidepost 3 Psychometric Approach: Developmental and Intelligence Testing

Can infants' and toddlers' intelligence be measured, and how can it be improved?

- Psychometric tests measure factors presumed to make up intelligence.
- Developmental tests, such as the Bayley Scales of Infant and Toddler Development, can indicate current functioning but are generally poor predictors of later intelligence.
- Socioeconomic status, parenting practices, and the home environment may affect measured intelligence.
- If the home environment does not provide the necessary conditions that pave the way for cognitive competence, early intervention may be needed.

guidepost 4 Piagetian Approach: The Sensorimotor Stage

How did Piaget describe infants' and toddlers' cognitive development, and how have his claims stood up?

- During Piaget's sensorimotor stage, infants' schemes become more elaborate. They progress from primary to secondary to tertiary circular reactions and finally to the development of representational ability, which makes possible deferred imitation, pretending, and problem solving.
- Object permanence develops gradually, according to Piaget.
- Research suggests that a number of abilities, including imitation and object permanence, develop earlier than Piaget described. He may have underestimated young infants' grasp of object permanence and their imitative abilities.

guidepost 5 Information-Processing Approach: Perceptions and Representations

How can we measure infants' ability to process information, and when do babies begin to think about characteristics of the physical world?

- Information-processing researchers measure mental processes through habituation and other signs of visual and perceptual abilities. Contrary to Piaget's view, such research suggests that representational ability is present virtually from birth.
- Indicators of the efficiency of infants' information processing, such as speed of habituation, tend to predict later intelligence.
- Such information-processing research techniques as habituation, novelty preference, and the violation-of-expectations method have yielded evidence that infants as young as 3½ to 5 months may have a rudimentary grasp of such Piagetian abilities as categorization, causality, object permanence, a sense of number, and an ability to reason about characteristics of the physical world. Some researchers suggest that infants may have innate learning mechanisms for acquiring such knowledge. However, the meaning of these findings is in dispute.

guidepost 6 Cognitive Neuroscience Approach: The Brain's Cognitive Structures

What can brain research reveal about the development of cognitive skills?

- Explicit memory and implicit memory are located in different brain structures.

- Working memory emerges between ages 6 and 12 months.
- Neurological developments help explain the emergence of Piagetian skills and memory abilities.

implicit memory (*200*)

explicit memory (*200*)

working memory (*200*)

⑦ Social-Contextual Approach: Learning from Interactions with Caregivers

How does social interaction with adults advance cognitive competence?

- Social interactions with adults contribute to cognitive competence through shared activities that help children learn skills, knowledge, and values important in their culture.

guided participation (*201*)

⑧ Language Development

How do babies develop language, and what influences linguistic progress?

- The acquisition of language is an important aspect of cognitive development.
- Prelinguistic speech includes crying, cooing, babbling, and imitating language sounds. By 6 months, babies have learned the basic sounds of their language and have begun to link sound with meaning. Perception of categories of sounds in the native language may commit the neural circuitry to further learning in that language only.
- Before they say their first word, babies use gestures.
- The first word typically comes sometime between 10 and 14 months, initiating linguistic speech. For many children a "naming explosion" occurs sometime between 16 and 24 months.

- The first brief sentences generally come between 18 and 24 months. By age 3, syntax and communicative abilities are fairly well developed.
- Early speech is characterized by simplification, underextending and overextending word meanings, and overregularizing rules.
- Two classic theoretical views about how children acquire language are learning theory and nativism. Today, most developmentalists hold that an inborn capacity to learn language may be activated or constrained by experience.
- Influences on language development include neural maturation and social interaction.
- Family characteristics, such as socioeconomic status, adult language use, and maternal responsiveness, affect a child's vocabulary development.
- Children who hear two languages at home generally learn both at the same rate as children who hear only one language, and they can use each language in appropriate circumstances.
- Child-directed speech (CDS) seems to have cognitive, emotional, and social benefits, and infants show a preference for it. However, some researchers dispute its value.
- Reading aloud to a child from an early age helps pave the way for literacy.

language (*202*)

prelinguistic speech (*202*)

linguistic speech (*205*)

holophrase (*205*)

telegraphic speech (*206*)

syntax (*206*)

nativism (*208*)

language acquisition device (LAD) (*208*)

code mixing (*212*)

code switching (*212*)

child-directed speech (CDS) (*212*)

literacy (*213*)

1. When and how do emotions develop, and how do babies show them?

2. How do infants show temperament differences, and how enduring are those differences?

3. How do infants gain trust in their world and form attachments, and how do infants and caregivers read each other's nonverbal signals?

4. When and how does the sense of self arise, and how do toddlers exercise autonomy and develop standards for socially acceptable behavior?

5. When and how do gender differences appear?

6. How do infants and toddlers interact with siblings and other children?

7. How do parental employment and early child care affect infants' and toddlers' development?

guidepost

1 When and how do emotions develop, and how do babies show them?

personality
The relatively consistent blend of emotions, temperament, thought, and behavior that makes each person unique.

emotions
Subjective reactions to experience that are associated with physiological and behavioral changes.

Foundations of Psychosocial Development

Although babies share common patterns of development, each, from the start, shows a distinct **personality:** the relatively consistent blend of emotions, temperament, thought, and behavior that makes each person unique. One baby may usually be cheerful; another easily upset. One toddler plays happily with other children; another prefers to play alone. Such characteristic ways of feeling, thinking, and acting, which reflect both inborn and environmental influences, affect the way children respond to others and adapt to their world. From infancy on, personality development is intertwined with social relationships (Table 8.1). This combination is called *psychosocial development.*

In our exploration of psychosocial development we first look at emotions, which shape responses to the world. Then we focus on temperament, an early building block of personality. Last, we discuss an infant's earliest social experiences in the family and how parents can influence behavioral differences between girls and boys.

EMOTIONS

Recall the last time you were were scared by a horror movie. Your heart was probably racing in your chest, and you may have breathed more heavily. It's likely your eyes were fixed on the screen and you were focused closely on the action unfolding in front of you. If someone were to grab you suddenly, you would probably have been easily startled. You were feeling the emotion of fear. **Emotions**, such as fear, are subjective reactions to experience that are associated with physiological and behavioral changes. A person's characteristic pattern of emotional reactions begins to develop during infancy and is a basic element of personality. People differ in how often and how strongly they feel a particular emotion, in the kinds of events that may produce it, in the physical manifestations they show, and in how they act as a result. Culture influences the way people feel about a situation and the way they show their emotions. For example, some Asian cultures, which stress social harmony,

TABLE 8.1 Highlights of Infants' and Toddlers' Psychosocial Development, Birth to 36 Months

Approximate Age, Months	Characteristics
0–3	Infants are open to stimulation. They begin to show interest and curiosity, and they smile readily at people.
3–6	Infants can anticipate what is about to happen and experience disappointment when it does not. They show this by becoming angry or acting warily. They smile, coo, and laugh often. This is a time of social awakening and early reciprocal exchanges between the baby and the caregiver.
6–9	Infants play "social games" and try to get responses from people. They "talk" to, touch, and cajole other babies to get them to respond. They express more differentiated emotions, showing joy, fear, anger, and surprise.
9–12	Infants are intensely preoccupied with their principal caregiver, may become afraid of strangers, and act subdued in new situations. By 1 year, they communicate emotions more clearly, showing moods, ambivalence, and gradations of feeling.
12–18	Toddlers explore their environment, using the people they are most attached to as a secure base. As they master the environment, they become more confident and more eager to assert themselves.
18–36	Toddlers sometimes become anxious because they now realize how much they are separating from their caregiver. They work out their awareness of their limitations in fantasy and in play and by identifying with adults.

Source: Adapted from Sroufe, 1979.

discourage expressions of anger but place much importance on shame. The opposite is often true in American culture, which stresses self-expression, self-assertion, and self-esteem (Cole, Bruschi, & Tamang, 2002).

First Signs of Emotion Newborns plainly show when they are unhappy. They let out piercing cries, flail their arms and legs, and stiffen their bodies. It is harder to tell when they are happy. During the 1st month, they become quiet at the sound of a human voice or when they are picked up, and they may smile when their hands are moved together to play pat-a-cake. As time goes by, infants respond more to people— smiling, cooing, reaching out, and eventually going to them.

These early signals or clues to babies' feelings are important indicators of development. When babies want or need something, they cry; when they feel sociable, they smile or laugh. When their messages bring a response, their sense of connection with other people grows. Their sense of control over their world grows too, as they see that their cries bring help and comfort and that their smiles and laughter elicit smiles and laughter in return. They become more able to participate actively in regulating their states of arousal and their emotional life.

Crying Crying is the most powerful way—and sometimes the only way—infants can communicate their needs. Some research has distinguished four patterns of crying (Wolff, 1969): the basic *hunger cry* (a rhythmic cry, which is not always associated with hunger); the *angry cry* (a variation of the rhythmic cry, in which excess air is forced through the vocal cords); the *pain cry* (a sudden onset of loud crying without preliminary moaning,

Emotional Expression

When a healthy baby cries for more than 3 hours a day, 3 days a week, for more than 3 weeks with no apparent cause for the distress, the reason is usually colic.

sometimes followed by holding the breath); and the *frustration cry* (two or three drawn-out cries, with no prolonged breath-holding) (Wood & Gustafson, 2001).

Some parents worry that picking up a crying baby will spoil the infant. However, if parents wait until cries of distress escalate to shrieks of rage, it may become more difficult to soothe the baby; and such a pattern, if experienced repeatedly, may interfere with an infant's developing ability to regulate, or manage, his or her emotional state (R. A. Thompson, 1991, 2011). Ideally, the most developmentally sound approach may be to *prevent* distress, making soothing unnecessary.

Smiling and Laughing The earliest faint smiles occur spontaneously soon after birth, apparently as a result of subcortical nervous system activity. These involuntary smiles frequently appear during periods of REM sleep (refer to Chapter 5). Through 1 month of age, smiles are often elicited by high-pitched tones when an infant is drowsy. During the 2nd month, as visual recognition develops, babies smile more at visual stimuli, such as faces they know (Sroufe, 1997; Wolff, 1963).

These early smiles are known as "windy grins" because they sometimes occur in response to gas.

An infant's earliest smiles are involuntary, but beginning at 1 month, smiles generally become more frequent and more social. This baby may be smiling at the sight of a parent or caregiver.

Crying enables this baby to communicate his needs. Parents generally learn to recognize whether their baby is crying because of hunger, anger, frustration, or pain.

Social smiling, when newborn infants gaze at their parents and smile at them, does not develop until the 2nd month of life. Social smiling signals the infant's active, positive participation in the relationship. The development of smiling involves both changes in the timing of smiles and in the form of the smiles themselves. Laughter is a smile-linked vocalization that becomes more common between 4 and 12 months when it may signify the most intense positive emotion (Salkind, 2005).

Through 6 months of age, infant smiles reflect an emotional exchange with a partner. As babies grow older, they become more actively engaged in mirthful exchanges. A 6-month-old may giggle in response to the mother making unusual sounds or appearing with a towel over her face; a 10-month-old may laughingly try to put the towel back on her face when it falls off. This change reflects cognitive development: By laughing at the unexpected, babies show that they know what to expect. By turning the tables, they show awareness that they can make things happen. Laughter also helps babies discharge tension, such as fear of a threatening object (Sroufe, 1997).

By 12 to 15 months, infants are intentionally communicating to the partner about objects. Anticipatory smiling—in which infants smile at an object and then gaze at an adult while continuing to smile—may be the first step. Anticipatory smiling rises sharply between 8 and 10 months and seems to be among the first types of communication in which the infant refers to an object or experience.

Early smiles may help predict later development. Four-month-olds who smile more in response to a mobile show a more exuberant temperament style at 4 years, being more likely to talk and engage. Six-month-old infants who smile at a still face are more likely to be securely attached at 12 months. So the form of infant smiles as well as their timing changes with development. Just as infants exercise more control over when they smile between 3 and 6 months, they also become more capable of using very intense smiles to participate in highly arousing social situations.

When Do Emotions Appear? Emotional development is an orderly process; complex emotions unfold from simpler ones. According to one model of emotional development (Lewis, 1997; Figure 8.1), babies soon after birth show signs of contentment, interest, and distress. These are diffuse, reflexive, mostly physiological responses to sensory stimulation or internal processes. During the next 6 months or so, these early emotional states differentiate into true emotions: joy, surprise, sadness, disgust, and, last, anger and fear—reactions to events that have meaning for the infant. As we discuss in a subsequent section, the emergence of these basic, or primary, emotions is related to the biological clock of neurological maturation.

Self-conscious emotions, such as embarrassment, envy, and empathy (discussed in more detail in a subsequent section) arise only after children have developed **self-awareness:** the cognitive understanding that they have a recognizable identity, separate and different from the rest of their world. This consciousness of self seems to emerge between 15 and 24 months. Self-awareness is necessary before children can be aware of being the focus of attention, identify with what other "selves" are feeling, or wish they had what someone else has. By about age 3, having acquired self-awareness plus a good deal of knowledge about their society's accepted standards, rules, and goals, children become better able to evaluate their thoughts, plans, desires, and behavior against what

self-conscious emotions
Emotions, such as embarrassment, empathy, and envy, that depend on self-awareness.

self-awareness
Realization that one's existence and functioning are separate from those of other people and things.

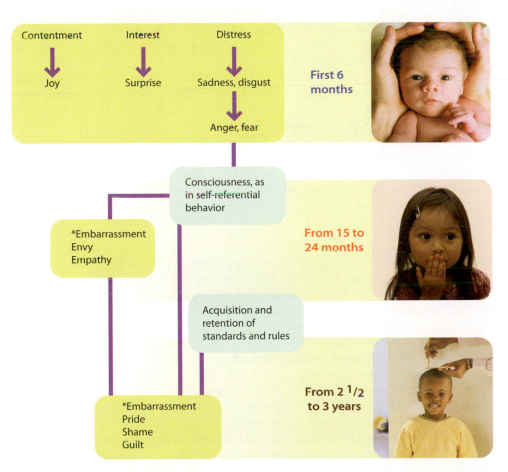

FIGURE 8.1

Differentiation of Emotions during the First 3 Years

The primary, or basic, emotions emerge during the first 6 months or so; the self-conscious emotions develop around 18 to 24 months, as a result of the emergence of self-awareness (consciousness of self) together with accumulation of knowledge about societal standards and rules.

*Note: There are two kinds of embarrassment. The earlier kind does not involve evaluation of behavior and may simply be a response to being singled out as the object of attention. The second kind, evaluative embarrassment, which emerges during the 3rd year, is a mild form of shame.

Source: Adapted from Lewis, 1997, Fig. 1, p. 120.

is considered socially appropriate. Only then can they demonstrate the **self-evaluative emotions** of pride, guilt, and shame (Lewis, 1995, 1997, 1998, 2007). In other words, children must understand that they are separate from someone else—and that others might have opinions about the wrongness or rightness of their behavior—before they can understand and feel these social emotions.

Guilt and shame are distinct emotions, even though both may be responses to wrongdoing. Children who fail to live up to behavioral standards may feel guilty (that is, regret their behavior), but they do not necessarily feel a lack of self-worth, as when they feel ashamed. Their focus is on a bad *act*, not a bad *self* (Eisenberg, 2000).

Brain Growth and Emotional Development The development of the brain after birth is closely connected with changes in emotional life. This is a bidirectional process: Emotional experiences not only are affected by brain development but also can have long-lasting effects on the structure of the brain (Mlot, 1998; Sroufe, 1997).

Four major shifts in brain organization correspond roughly to changes in emotional processing (Schore, 1994; Sroufe, 1997; refer to Figure 6.6). During the first 3 months, differentiation of basic emotions begins as the *cerebral cortex* becomes functional, bringing cognitive perceptions into play. REM sleep and reflexive behavior, including the spontaneous neonatal smile, diminish.

The second shift occurs around 9 or 10 months, when the *frontal lobes* begin to interact with the *limbic system*, a seat of emotional reactions. At the same time, limbic structures such as the *hippocampus* become larger and more adultlike. Connections between the frontal cortex and the *hypothalamus* and limbic system, which process sensory information, may facilitate the relationship between the cognitive and emotional spheres. As these connections become denser and more elaborate, an infant can experience and interpret emotions at the same time.

The third shift takes place during the 2nd year, when infants develop self-awareness, self-conscious emotions, and a greater capacity for regulating their emotions and activities. These changes, which may be related to myelination of the frontal lobes, are accompanied by greater physical mobility and exploratory behavior.

The fourth shift occurs around age 3, when hormonal changes in the autonomic (involuntary) nervous system coincide with the emergence of evaluative emotions. Underlying the development of such emotions as shame may be a shift away from dominance by the *sympathetic system*, the part of the autonomic system that prepares the body for action, and the maturation of the *parasympathetic system*, the part of the autonomic system that is involved in excretion and sexual excitation.

Altruistic Helping, Empathy, and Social Cognition A guest of 18-month-old Alex's father—a person Alex had never seen before—dropped his pen on the floor, and it rolled under a cabinet, where the guest couldn't quite reach it. Alex, being small enough, crawled under the cabinet, retrieved the pen, and gave it to the guest. By acting out of concern for a stranger with no expectation of reward, Alex showed **altruistic behavior** (Warneken & Tomasello, 2006).

Altruistic behavior seems to come naturally to toddlers. Well before the second birthday, children often help others, share belongings and food, and offer comfort (Zahn-Waxler, Radke-Yarrow, Wagner, & Chapman, 1992). However, rewarding such behavior may undermine it. In an experiment in Leipzig, Germany, 20-month-olds repeatedly helped an adult by picking up dropped objects, even when doing so required them to stop playing. Children who received a material reward for their help were less likely to help again than children who received only praise or no reward (Warneken & Tomasello, 2008).

In another experiment, when the researcher was having trouble reaching a goal, 18-month-olds helped in 6 out in 10 situations. They did not help in situations when the researcher did not appear to be having trouble—for example, when he deliberately dropped a pen. Such behavior may reflect **empathy**, the ability to imagine how another person might feel in a particular situation (Zahn-Waxler et al., 1992). As we have mentioned, this ability to "put oneself in another person's place" emerges during the 2nd year, and it increases with age (Eisenberg, 2000; Eisenberg & Fabes, 1998).

The roots of empathy, however, can be seen in early infancy. Two- to three-month-olds react to others' emotional expressions (Tomasello, 2007). Six-month-olds engage in *social evaluation*, valuing someone on the basis of that person's treatment of others. In one series of experiments (Hamlin, Wynn, & Bloom, 2007), 6- and 10-month-old infants saw a wooden character ("the climber") repeatedly attempt to climb a hill. On the third attempt, the infants saw the climber either assisted by a "helper," who pushed up from behind, or pushed down by a "hinderer." When the infants in both age groups were encouraged to reach for either the helper or the hinderer, they overwhelmingly chose the helper. In a follow-up study, the infants saw a neutral character that followed the same route as either the helper or hinderer but did not interact with the climber. When given a choice between the helper and the neutral character, the infants preferred the helper; and between the neutral character and the hinderer, they preferred the neutral character.

Research in neurobiology has recently identified special brain cells called *mirror neurons*, which may underlie empathy and altruism. **Mirror neurons**, located in several parts of the brain, fire when a person does something but also when he or she observes someone else doing the same thing. By "mirroring" the activities and motivations of others, they allow a person to see the world from someone else's point of view. Mirror neurons have been linked to imitative learning as well as to the emergence of self-awareness, of language, and of abstract reasoning. Autism spectrum disorders (refer to Box 6.1 in Chapter 6) may represent a breakdown or suppression of the mirroring system; children with autism and related disorders are less empathic, less emotionally connected to others, and less able to read their emotional states than are other children, and brain imaging shows less mirror neuron activity in their brains (Iacoboni, 2008; Iacoboni & Mazziotta, 2007; Oberman & Ramachandran, 2007).

Empathy depends on **social cognition**, the cognitive ability to understand that others have mental states and to gauge their feelings and intentions. Piaget maintained that **egocentrism** (inability to see another person's point of view) delays the development of this ability until the concrete operational stage of middle childhood, but more recent research suggests that social cognition begins much earlier. In one study, 9-month-olds (but not 6-month-olds) reacted differently to a person who was unwilling to give them a toy than to a person who tried to give them a toy but accidentally dropped it. This finding suggests that the older infants had gained some understanding of another person's intentions (Behne, Carpenter, Call, & Tomasello, 2005).

Young children often engage in what is known as overimitation, closely copying all actions they see an adult do, even if some of those actions are clearly irrelevant or impractical. Chimps, by contrast, will skip steps that don't accomplish anything. Researchers think our universal propensity to overimitate may be tied to the depth and complexity of our culture.

Nielsen & Tomaselli, 2010

Shared Intentionality and Collaborative Activity The motivation to help and share and the ability to understand the intentions of others together contribute to an important development between 9 and 12 months of age, collaboration with caregivers in joint activities, such as a child holding and handing over a pair of socks and a caregiver dressing the child. Such activities require **shared intentionality:** joint attention to a mutual goal (Tomasello, 2007).

Collaborative activities increase during the 2nd year of life as toddlers become more adept at communication—first with gestures, then with words. At 12 months, Jasmine points at a ball to show that she wants to play a game of rolling it back and

mirror neurons
Neurons that fire when a person does something or observes someone else doing the same thing.

social cognition
Ability to understand that other people have mental states and to gauge their feelings and intentions.

egocentrism
Piaget's term for inability to consider another person's point of view; a characteristic of young children's thought.

checkpoint
can you . . .

▷ Explain the significance of patterns of crying, smiling, and laughing?

▷ Trace a proposed sequence of emergence of the basic, self-conscious, and evaluative emotions and its connection with neurological development?

▷ Discuss the emergence of altruistic behavior, empathy, social cognition, and collaborative activity, and tell how these developments are related?

shared intentionality
Joint attention to a mutual goal.

temperament
Characteristic disposition or style of approaching and reacting to situations.

easy children
Children with a generally happy temperament, regular biological rhythms, and a readiness to accept new experiences.

difficult children
Children with irritable temperament, irregular biological rhythms, and intense emotional responses.

slow-to-warm-up children
Children whose temperament is generally mild but who are hesitant about accepting new experiences.

Easy babies, such as this little girl, respond to a wide variety of situations happily and with minimal fear.

forth with her father. When the ball rolls under a chair, she points to let her father know where it is. And when her father loses interest in the game, she points to remind him that it is his turn. The vocabulary explosion that frequently occurs during the 2nd year enables more complex and flexible collaborative communication (Tomasello, 2007).

TEMPERAMENT

From the very first day of life, all babies are unique. Some babies are fussy, while others are happy and placid. Some are active, kicking and squirming restlessly at the slightest provocation, some lay calmly taking in the world through wide eyes. Some babies like meeting new people, some shrink from contact.

Psychologists call these early individuals differences **temperament**. Temperament can be defined as an early-appearing, biologically-based tendency to respond to the environment in predictable ways. Temperament affects how children approach and react to the outside world, as well as how they regulate their mental, emotional, and behavioral functioning (Rothbart, Ahadi, & Evans, 2000; Rueda & Rothbart, 2009). Temperament is closely linked to emotional responses to the environment given that many responses, such as smiles or cries, are often emotional in nature. However, unlike emotions such as fear, excitement, and boredom, which come and go, temperament is relatively consistent and enduring. Individual differences in temperament, which are thought to derive from a person's basic biological makeup, form the core of the developing personality.

Studying Temperament Patterns: The New York Longitudinal Study To better appreciate how temperament affects behavior, let's look at three sisters. Amy, the eldest, was a cheerful, calm baby who ate, slept, and eliminated at regular times. She greeted each day and most people with a smile, and the only sign that she was awake during the night was the tinkle of the musical toy in her crib. When Brooke, the second sister, woke up, she would open her mouth to cry before she even opened her eyes. She slept and ate little and irregularly; she laughed and cried loudly, often bursting into tantrums; and she had to be convinced that new people and new experiences were not threatening before she would have anything to do with them. The younger sister, Christina, was midway in her responses. She was wary of new situations but would eventually warm up. For example, if she went on a playdate to a new friend's house, she would at first hide behind her mother's legs shyly peeking out. However, within a half hour, she would be happily chattering away and playing with her new friend.

Amy, Brooke, and Christina exemplify the three main types of temperament found by the New York Longitudinal Study (NYLS). In this pioneering study on temperament, researchers followed 133 infants into adulthood. The researchers collected data from parents on how active the children were; how regular they were in hunger, sleep, and bowel habits; how readily they accepted new people and situations; how they adapted to changes in routine; how sensitive they were to noise, bright lights, and other sensory stimuli; how intensely they responded; whether their mood tended to be pleasant, joyful, and friendly or unpleasant, unhappy, and unfriendly; and whether they persisted at tasks or were easily distracted (Thomas, Chess, & Birch, 1968).

The researchers were able to place most of the children in the study into one of three categories (Table 8.2).

- Forty percent were **easy children** like Amy: generally happy, rhythmic in biological functioning, and accepting of new experiences.

- Ten percent were what the researchers called **difficult children** like Brooke: more irritable and harder to please, irregular in biological rhythms, and more intense in expressing emotion.

- Fifteen percent were **slow-to-warm-up children** like Christina: mild but slow to adapt to new people and situations (Thomas & Chess, 1977, 1984).

TABLE 8.2 Three Temperamental Patterns (according to the New York Longitudinal Study)

Easy Child	Difficult Child	Slow-to-Warm-Up Child
Has moods of mild to moderate intensity, usually positive.	Displays intense and frequently negative moods; cries often and loudly; also laughs loudly.	Has mildly intense reactions, both positive and negative.
Responds well to novelty and change. Quickly develops regular sleep and feeding schedules.	Responds poorly to novelty and change. Sleeps and eats irregularly.	Responds slowly to novelty and change. Sleeps and eats more regularly than the difficult child, less regularly than the easy child.
Takes to new foods easily. Smiles at strangers.	Accepts new foods slowly. Is suspicious of strangers.	Shows mildly negative initial response to new stimuli (a first encounter with a new person, place, or situation).
Adapts easily to new situations. Accepts most frustrations with little fuss.	Adapts slowly to new situations. Reacts to frustration with tantrums.	
Adapts quickly to new routines and rules of new games.	Adjusts slowly to new routines.	Gradually develops liking for new stimuli after repeated, unpressured exposures.

Source: Adapted from A. Thomas & Chess, Genesis and evolution of behavioral disorders: From infancy to early adult life. *American Journal of Psychiatry, 141*(1) 1984, pp. 1–9. Copyright © 1984 by the American Psychiatric Association. Reproduced with permission.

Some children (including 35 percent of the NYLS sample) do not fit neatly into any of these three categories. A baby may eat and sleep regularly but be afraid of strangers. A child may be easy most of the time, but not always. Another child may warm up slowly to new foods but adapt quickly to new babysitters (Thomas & Chess, 1984). A child may laugh intensely but not show intense frustration, and a child with rhythmic toilet habits may show irregular sleeping patterns (Rothbart et al., 2000). All these variations are normal.

How Is Temperament Measured? Because the complex interviewing and scoring procedures used in the NYLS are cumbersome, many researchers use short-form questionnaires. A parental self-report instrument, the Rothbart Infant Behavior Questionnaire (IBQ) (Gartstein & Rothbart, 2003; Rothbart et al., 2000) focuses on several dimensions of infant temperament similar to those in the NYLS: activity level, positive emotion (smiling and laughing), fear, frustration, soothability, and duration of orienting (a combination of distractibility and attention span) as well as such additional factors as intensity of pleasure, perceptual sensitivity, and attentional shifting. Parents rate their infants with regard to recent concrete events and behaviors ("How often during the past week did the baby smile or laugh when given a toy?" rather than "Does the baby respond positively to new events?").

Although parental ratings are the most commonly used measures of children's temperament, their validity is in question. For example, studies of twins have found that parents tend to rate a child's temperament by comparison with other children in the family—for example, labeling one child inactive in contrast to a more active sibling (Saudino, 2003a). Still, observations by researchers may reflect biases as well (Seifer, 2003). Parents see their children in a variety of day-to-day situations, whereas a laboratory observer sees only how the child reacts to particular standardized situations. Thus a combination of methods may provide a more accurate picture of how temperament affects child development (Rothbart & Hwang, 2002; Saudino, 2003a, 2003b).

How Stable Is Temperament? Newborn babies show different patterns of sleeping, fussing, and activity, and these differences tend to persist to some degree (Korner, 1996;

The way you ask a question often influences the answers you find. The researchers in this study based their data on parental reports—what the parents said about their children—so it is not surprising that the most salient dimensions that emerged were the relative difficulty or easiness of the children.

Korner et al., 1985). Studies using the IBQ have found strong links between infant temperament and childhood personality at age 7 (Rothbart, Ahadi, Hershey, & Fisher, 2001; Rothbart et al., 2000). Other researchers, using temperament types similar to those of the NYLS, have found that temperament at age 3 closely predicts aspects of personality at ages 18 and 21 (Caspi, 2000; Caspi & Silva, 1995; Newman, Caspi, Moffitt, & Silva, 1997).

That temperament is relatively stable speaks to the underlying biological influences on temperament. Temperament appears to be largely inborn, probably hereditary (Braungart, Plomin, DeFries, & Fulker, 1992; Emde et al., 1992; Schmitz, Saudino, Plomin, Fulker, & DeFries, 1996; Thomas & Chess, 1984). Thus, it is not surprising that we find stability in temperament over time. That does not mean, however, that temperament is fully formed at birth. Temperament develops as various emotions and self-regulatory capacities appear (Rothbart et al., 2000) and can change in response to parental treatment and other life experiences (Belsky, Fish, & Isabella, 1991; Kagan & Snidman, 2004).

For example, temperament is affected by culturally influenced child-raising practices. Infants in Malaysia, an island group in Southeast Asia, tend to be less adaptable, more wary of new experiences, and more readily responsive to stimuli than U.S. babies. This may be because Malay parents do not often expose young children to situations that require adaptability, and they encourage infants to be acutely aware of sensations, such as the need for a diaper change (Banks, 1989).

goodness of fit
Appropriateness of environmental demands and constraints to a child's temperament.

There is a relationship between what a parent says a baby will be like before a child is born and what a parent later says about that child as an infant. In particular, the perceptions of a child as difficult precede the birth of that child. What might explain this finding?

Pauli-Pott, Mertesacker, Bade, Haverkock, & Beckman, 2003

Temperament and Adjustment: "Goodness of Fit" According to the NYLS, the key to healthy adjustment is **goodness of fit**—the match between a child's temperament and the environmental demands and constraints the child must deal with. We can think of goodness of fit as a descriptor of the child-caregiver relationship, or of the fit between the child and the wider social context. If a very active child is expected to sit still for long periods, if a slow-to-warm-up child is constantly pushed into new situations, or if a persistent child is constantly taken away from absorbing projects, tensions may occur. Infants with difficult temperaments may be more susceptible to the quality of parenting than infants with easy or slow-to-warm-up temperaments and may need more emotional support combined with respect for their autonomy (Belsky, 1997, 2005; Stright, Gallagher, & Kelley, 2008). Caregivers who recognize that a child acts in a certain way, not out of willfulness, laziness, stupidity, or spite but largely because of inborn temperament, may be less likely to feel guilty, anxious, or hostile, to feel a loss of control, or to be rigid or impatient. They can anticipate the child's reactions and help the child adapt—for example, by giving early warnings of the need to stop an activity or by gradually introducing a child to new situations.

Shyness and Boldness: Influences of Biology and Culture As we have explained, temperament has a biological basis. One biologically-based individual difference that has been identified as being important is *behavioral inhibition.* Behavioral inhibition is a trait, which has to do with how boldly or cautiously a child approaches unfamiliar objects and situations, and it is associated with certain biological characteristics (Kagan & Snidman, 2004).

Behavioral inhibition is most clearly seen when babies are presented with novel stimuli. When babies who were high in behavioral inhibition were presented with a new stimulus, they became overly aroused, pumping their arms and legs vigorously and sometimes arching their backs. This feeling of being over-aroused eventually became unpleasant for them, and most cried. Approximately 20 percent of babies respond in this way. Babies low in behavioral inhibition, however, respond quite differently. When presented with a new stimulus, these babies are relaxed. They show little distress or motor activity, and often calmly stare at new stimuli, sometimes smiling at it. About 40 percent of babies respond in this manner. These differences between babies are theorized to be the result of an underlying difference in physiology. The researchers suggested that inhibited children may be born with an unusually excitable amygdala. The amygdala detects and reacts to unfamiliar events, and, in the case of behaviorally inhibited children, responds vigorously and easily to most novel events (Kagan & Snidman, 2004).

Infants identified as inhibited or uninhibited seemed to maintain these patterns to some degree during childhood (Kagan, 1997; Kagan & Snidman, 2004), along with specific differences in physiological characteristics. Inhibited children were more likely to have a thin body build, narrow face, and blue eyes, whereas uninhibited children were taller, heavier, and more often brown-eyed. In addition, inhibited children showed higher and less variable heart rates than uninhibited children, and the pupils of their eyes dilated more (Arcus & Kagan, 1995). It may be that the genes that contribute to reactivity and inhibited or uninhibited behavior also influence these physiological traits (Kagan & Snidman, 2004).

These findings suggest, again, that experience can moderate or accentuate early tendencies. Male toddlers who were inclined to be fearful and shy were more likely to remain so at age 3 if their parents were highly accepting of the child's reactions. In contrast, if parents exposed their sons to new situations that were somewhat, but not overly frightening, the boys tended to become less inhibited over time as they developed strategies to handle their arousal. (Park, Belsky, Putnam, & Crnic, 1997). In other research, when mothers responded neutrally to infants who were behaviorally inhibited, the inhibition tended to remain stable or increase. These authors suggested that caregivers' sensitivity may affect the neural systems that underlie reactions to stress and novelty (Fox, Hane, & Pine, 2007). In other words, when parents were a good fit to their child's innate inhibited temperament, children were more likely to outgrow inhibition. Other environmental influences, such as birth order, race/ethnicity, culture, relationships with teachers and peers, and unpredictable events also can reinforce or soften a child's original temperament bias (Kagan & Snidman, 2004).

Developmental Issues in Infancy

How does a dependent newborn, with a limited emotional repertoire and pressing physical needs, become a child with complex feelings and the abilities to understand and control them? Much of this development revolves around issues regarding relationships with caregivers.

DEVELOPING TRUST

For a far longer period than the young of most mammals, human babies are dependent on others for food, protection, and nurturance. According to Erikson, this extended period results in the first stage of psychosocial development being centered upon forming a sense of trust.

Erikson (1950) argued that at each stage in the lifespan, we are faced with a challenge and a complementary risk (see Table 2.2 in Chapter 2). As babies, our first challenge involves forming a **basic sense of trust versus mistrust**. If we are successful, we develop a sense of the reliability of people and objects in our world. We feel safe and loved. The risk, however, is that, instead, we develop a sense of mistrust and feel that those around us cannot be counted on in times of need.

This stage depends heavily on early experiences. The stage begins in infancy and continues until about 18 months. Ideally, babies develop a balance between trust (which lets them form intimate relationships) and mistrust (which enables them to protect themselves). If trust predominates, as it should, children develop hope and the belief that they

what's your view

In the United States, many people consider shyness undesirable. How should a parent handle a shy child? Do you think it is best to accept the child's temperament or try to change it?

checkpoint
can you . . .

▷ Describe the three patterns of temperament identified by the New York Longitudinal Study?

▷ Assess evidence for the stability of temperament?

▷ Explain the importance of "goodness of fit"?

▷ Discuss evidence of biological influences on behavioral inhibition?

guidepost 3

How do infants gain trust in their world and form attachments, and how do infants and caregivers read each other's nonverbal signals?

connect

studysmart

Trust and Autonomy

basic sense of trust versus basic mistrust
Erikson's first stage in psychosocial development, in which infants develop a sense of the reliability of people and objects.

Diane's sensitivity to Anna's needs contributes to the development of Anna's sense of basic trust—her ability to rely on the people and things in her world. Trust is necessary, according to Erikson, for children to form intimate relationships.

can fulfill their needs and obtain their desires (Erikson, 1982). If mistrust predominates, children will view the world as unfriendly and unpredictable and will have trouble forming quality relationships.

The critical element in developing trust is sensitive, responsive, consistent caregiving. Erikson saw the feeding situation as the setting for establishing the right mix of trust and mistrust. Can the baby count on being fed when hungry, and can the baby therefore trust the mother as a representative of the world? Trust enables an infant to let the mother out of sight "because she has become an inner certainty as well as an outer predictability" (Erikson, 1950, p. 247).

DEVELOPING ATTACHMENTS

When Ahmed's mother is near, he looks at her, smiles at her, babbles to her, and crawls after her. When she leaves, he cries; when she comes back, he squeals with joy. When he is frightened or unhappy, he clings to her. Ahmed has formed his first attachment to another person.

Attachment is a reciprocal, enduring emotional tie between an infant and a caregiver, each of whom contributes to the quality of the relationship. From an evolutionary point of view, attachments have adaptive value for babies, ensuring that their psychosocial as well as physical needs will be met (MacDonald, 1998). According to ethological theory, infants and parents are biologically predisposed to become attached to each other, and attachment promotes a baby's survival.

Studies of functional MRIs of Japanese and U.S. mothers identified neural bases for attachment. In the Japanese study, certain areas of a mother's brain were activated at the sight of her own 16-month-old baby smiling at the mother or crying for her, but not at the sight of other infants showing those behaviors (Noriuchi, Kikuchi, & Senoo, 2008). A U.S. study highlighted the pleasure a new mother gets from seeing her infant's smiling face. In this longitudinal study, researchers videotaped the infants' faces during play at 5 to 10 months of age. At least 3 months later, the mothers saw these images for the first time. Happy-faced images of their own infant—but not of

checkpoint can **you** . . .

▷ Explain the importance of basic trust, and identify the critical element in its development?

connect

study**smart**

Emotions and Attachment

attachment
Reciprocal, enduring tie between two people—especially between infant and caregiver—each of whom contributes to the quality of the relationship.

another infant—activated maternal reward-processing brain regions associated with the brain chemical dopamine. For reasons that are not clear, sad facial expressions on their own and other infants did *not* elicit such differing maternal responses (Strathearn, Li, Fonagy, & Montague, 2008).

Studying Patterns of Attachment The study of attachment owes much to the ethologist John Bowlby (1951), a pioneer in the study of bonding. From his knowledge of Harlow's seminal work with rhesus monkeys demonstrating the importance of contact comfort rather than food (see Chapter 5) and from observations of disturbed children in a London psychoanalytic clinic, Bowlby became convinced of the importance of the mother-baby bond and warned against separating mother and baby without providing good substitute care. Mary Ainsworth (1967), a student of Bowlby's in the early 1950s, went on to study attachment in African babies in Uganda through naturalistic observation in their homes. Ainsworth later devised the **Strange Situation**, a now-classic laboratory-based technique designed to assess attachment patterns between an infant and an adult. Typically, the adult is the mother (though other adults have taken part as well), and the infant is 10 to 24 months old.

The Strange Situation consists of a sequence of eight episodes of gradually increasing stress, which takes less than half an hour. The episodes are designed to trigger the emergence of attachment-related behaviors. During that time, the mother twice leaves the baby in an unfamiliar room, the first time with a stranger. The second time she leaves the baby alone, and the stranger comes back before the mother does. The mother then encourages the baby to explore and play again and gives comfort if the baby seems to need it (Ainsworth, Blehar, Waters, & Wall, 1978). Of particular concern is the baby's response each time the mother returns.

When Ainsworth and her colleagues observed 1-year-olds in the Strange Situation and at home, they found three main patterns of attachment. These are *secure* (the most common category, into which about 60 to 75 percent of low-risk North American babies fall) and two forms of anxious, or insecure, attachment: *avoidant* (15 to 25 percent) and *ambivalent*, or *resistant* (10 to 15 percent) (Vondra & Barnett, 1999).

Babies with **secure attachment** sometimes cry or protest when a caregiver leaves, but they quickly and effectively obtain the comfort they need once the caregiver returns. Some babies with secure attachment are comfortable being left with a stranger for a short period of time; however, they clearly indicate they prefer the caregiver to the stranger, often smiling at, greeting, or approaching the caregiver during the reunion episode. Secure babies are flexible and resilient in the face of stress. Babies with **avoidant attachment**, by contrast, are outwardly unaffected by a caregiver leaving or returning. They generally continue to play in the room and frequently interact with the stranger. However, upon the caregiver's return they act as if they are ignoring or rejecting the caregiver, sometimes deliberately turning away. Avoidantly attached babies tend to show little emotion, either positive or negative. Last, babies who exhibit **ambivalent (resistant) attachment** are generally anxious even before the caregiver leaves, sometimes approaching the caregiver for comfort when the stranger looks at or approaches them for interaction. They are extremely reactive to the caregiver's departure from the room and generally become extremely upset. Upon the caregiver's return, these babies tend to remain upset for long periods of time, kicking, screaming, refusing to be distracted with toys, and sometimes arching back and away from contact. They show a mix of proximity-seeking and angry behaviors and are very difficult to settle. Note that in all of these cases what the baby does during the caregiver's absence is not diagnostic of attachment categorization. Some babies cry, some do not. What is diagnostic, however, is what the babies do when the caregiver returns. After all, the important component is the attachment relationship and how the babies use a caregiver to obtain comfort *while* in his or her presence.

These three attachment *patterns* are universal in all cultures in which they have been studied—cultures as different as those in Africa, China, and Israel—though the percentage of infants in each category varies (van IJzendoorn & Kroonenberg, 1988;

Strange Situation
Laboratory technique used to study infant attachment.

secure attachment
Pattern in which an infant is quickly and effectively able to find comfort from a caregiver when faced with a stressful situation.

avoidant attachment
Pattern in which an infant rarely cries when separated from the primary caregiver and avoids contact on his or her return.

ambivalent (resistant) attachment
Pattern in which an infant becomes anxious before the primary caregiver leaves, is extremely upset during his or her absence, and both seeks and resists contact on his or her return.

A baby's attachment style is best determined when a mother soothes an upset child rather than by how that child acts when she is not around.

van IJzendoorn & Sagi, 1999). Attachment *behaviors*, however, vary across cultures. Among the Gusii of East Africa, on the western edge of Kenya, infants are greeted with handshakes, and Gusii infants reach out for a parent's hand much as Western infants cuddle up for a hug (van IJzendoorn & Sagi, 1999).

Other research (Main & Solomon, 1986) identified a fourth pattern, **disorganized-disoriented attachment**. Babies with the disorganized pattern seem to lack a cohesive strategy to deal with the stress of the Strange Situation. Instead, they show contradictory, repetitive, or misdirected behaviors (such as seeking closeness to the stranger instead of the mother or showing a fear response upon the caregiver's entry). They may greet the mother brightly when she returns but then turn away or approach without looking at her. They seem confused and afraid (Carlson, 1998; van IJzendoorn, Schuengel, & Baermans-Kranenburg, 1999).

Disorganized attachment is thought to occur in at least 10 percent of low-risk infants but in much higher proportions in certain at-risk populations, such as premature children and those whose mothers abuse alcohol or drugs (Vondra & Barnett, 1999). It is most prevalent in babies with mothers who are insensitive, intrusive, or abusive; who are fearful or frightening and thus leave the infant with no one to alleviate the fear the mother arouses; or who have suffered unresolved loss or have unresolved feelings about their childhood attachment to their own parents. The natural tendency of infants is to approach the mother when they are frightened. When they are frightened *by* the mother, this puts into place an incompatible motivational system and results in the collapse of strategies. The likelihood of disorganized attachment increases in the presence of multiple risk factors, such as maternal insensitivity plus marital discord plus parenting stress. Disorganized attachment is a reliable predictor of later behavioral and adjustment problems (Bernier & Meins, 2008; Carlson, 1998; van IJzendoorn et al., 1999).

Some infants seem to be more susceptible to disorganized attachment than others. Some manage to form organized attachments despite atypical parenting, while others who are *not* exposed to atypical parenting form disorganized attachments (Bernier & Meins, 2008). One explanation might be a *gene-environment interaction* (discussed in Chapter 3). Studies have identified a variant of the DRD4 gene as a possible risk factor for disorganized attachment, and the risk increases nearly 19-fold when the mother has an unresolved loss (Gervai et al., 2005; Lakatos et al., 2000, 2002; van IJzendoorn & Bakermans-Kranenburg, 2006). Another explanation might be a *gene-environment correlation* (also discussed in Chapter 3). The infant's inborn characteristics may place unusually stressful demands on a parent and thus elicit parenting behaviors that promote disorganized attachment (Bernier & Meins, 2008).

Contrary to Ainsworth's original findings, babies seem to develop attachments to both parents at about the same time, and security of attachment to father and mother is usually quite similar (Brown, Schoppe-Sullivan, Mangelsdorf, & Neff, 2010; Fox, Kimmerly, & Schafer, 1991).

How Attachment Is Established By the time babies are a year of age, they have established a characteristic style of attachment. According to Bowlby, attachment styles are the result of expectations formed because of repeated interactions with a caregiver. For example, if every time a baby cries the mother responds quickly and sensitively to that bid for comfort, then over time, the baby comes to expect that response. By contrast, if a mother responds inconsistently to crying, then babies form a very different set of expectations regarding the likely responses of the mother to their cries.

disorganized-disoriented attachment Pattern in which an infant, after separation from the primary caregiver, shows contradictory behaviors on his or her return.

Babies with disorganized-disoriented attachment may seem confused or afraid when faced with the Strange Situation.

> Sensitive mothering is related to another important developmental achievement, at least in the eyes of parents. Mothers who respond sensitively to their infants end up with babies who fall asleep faster, sleep longer, and wake less often.
>
> Teti, Bo-Ram, Mayer, & Countermine, 2010

Bowlby called these sets of expectations working models, and theorized that these early working models then became the blueprint for the dynamics of that relationship. As long as the mother continues to act the same way, the model holds up. If her behavior changes—not just once or twice but repeatedly—the baby may revise the model, and security of attachment may change. Note that because the working model emerges as a result of interactions between both partners in the relationship, babies can have different working models (and attachment styles) with different people.

A baby's working model of attachment is related to Erikson's concept of basic trust. Secure attachment reflects trust; insecure attachment, mistrust. Securely attached babies have learned to trust not only their caregivers but also their own ability to get what they need. Not surprisingly, mothers of securely attached infants and toddlers tend to be sensitive and responsive (Ainsworth et al., 1978; Braungart-Rieker, Garwood, Powers, & Wang, 2001; De Wolff & van IJzendoorn, 1997; Isabella, 1993; NICHD Early Child Care Research Network, 1997). Equally important are mutual interaction, stimulation, a positive attitude, warmth and acceptance, and emotional support (De Wolff & van IJzendoorn, 1997; Lundy, 2003).

Alternative Methods to Study Attachment Although much research on attachment has been based on the Strange Situation, some investigators have questioned its validity. The Strange Situation *is* strange; it is also artificial. It asks mothers not to initiate interaction, exposes babies to repeated comings and goings of adults, and expects the infants to pay attention to them. Also, the Strange Situation may be less valid in some non-Western cultures. Research on Japanese infants, who are less commonly separated from their mothers than U.S. babies, showed high rates of resistant attachment, which may reflect the extreme stressfulness of the Strange Situation for these babies (Miyake, Chen, & Campos, 1985).

Because attachment influences a wider range of behaviors than are seen in the Strange Situation, some researchers have begun to supplement it with methods that enable them to study children in natural settings. The Waters and Deane (1985) Attachment Q-set (AQS) has mothers or other home observers sort a set of descriptive words or phrases ("cries a lot"; "tends to cling") into categories ranging from most to least characteristic of the child and then compare these descriptions with expert descriptions of the prototypical secure child. An analysis of 139 studies found the observer version (but not the maternal report version) a valid measure of attachment security, correlating well with results from the Strange Situation and with measures of maternal sensitivity. The AQS also seems to have cross-cultural validity (van IJzendoorn, Vereijken, Bakermans-Kranenburg, & Riksen-Walraven, 2004). In a study using the AQS, mothers in China, Colombia, Germany, Israel, Japan, Norway, and the United States described their children as behaving more like than unlike the "most secure child." Furthermore, the mothers' descriptions of "secure-base" behavior were about as similar across cultures as within a culture. These findings suggest that the tendency to use the mother as a secure base is universal, though it may take somewhat varied forms (Posada et al., 1995).

The Role of Temperament How much influence does temperament exert on attachment and in what ways? Findings vary (Susman-Stillman, Kalkoske, Egeland, & Waldman, 1996; Vaughn et al., 1992). In a study of 6- to 12-month-olds and their families, both a mother's sensitivity and her baby's temperament influenced attachment patterns (Seifer, Schiller, Sameroff, Resnick, & Riordan, 1996). Neurological or physiological conditions may underlie temperament differences in attachment. For example, variability in heart rate is associated with irritability, and heart rate seems to vary more in insecurely attached infants (Izard, Porges, Simons, Haynes, & Cohen, 1991).

A baby's temperament may have not only a direct impact on attachment but also an indirect impact through its effect on the parents. In a series of studies in the Netherlands (Van den Boom, 1989, 1994), 15-day-old infants classified as irritable were much more likely than nonirritable infants to be insecurely (usually avoidantly) attached at 1 year. However, irritable infants whose mothers received home visits, with instruction on how to soothe their babies, were as likely to be rated as securely attached as the nonirritable infants. Thus irritability on an infant's part may prevent the development of secure attachment but not if the mother has the skills to cope with the baby's temperament (Rothbart et al., 2000). Goodness of fit between parent and child may well be a key to understanding security of attachment.

Stranger Anxiety and Separation Anxiety Chloe used to be a friendly baby, smiling at strangers and going to them, continuing to coo happily as long as someone—anyone—was around. Now, at 8 months, she turns away when a new person approaches and howls when her parents try to leave her with a babysitter. Chloe is experiencing both **stranger anxiety**, wariness of a person she does not know, and **separation anxiety**, distress when a familiar caregiver leaves her.

Stranger anxiety and separation anxiety used to be considered emotional and cognitive milestones of the second half of infancy, reflecting attachment to the mother. However, newer research suggests that although stranger anxiety and separation anxiety are fairly typical, they are not universal. Whether a baby cries when a parent leaves or when someone new approaches may say as much about the baby's temperament or life circumstances than about security of attachment (R. J. Davidson & Fox, 1989).

Babies rarely react negatively to strangers before age 6 months, commonly do so by 8 or 9 months, and do so more and more throughout the rest of the 1st year (Sroufe, 1997). This change may reflect cognitive development. Chloe's stranger anxiety involves memory for faces, the ability to compare the stranger's appearance with her mother's, and perhaps the recollection of situations in which she has been left with a stranger. If Chloe were allowed to get used to the stranger gradually in a familiar setting, she might react more positively (Lewis, 1997; Sroufe, 1997).

Separation anxiety may be due not so much to the separation itself as to the quality of substitute care. When substitute caregivers are warm and responsive and play with 9-month-olds *before* they cry, the babies cry less than when they are with less responsive caregivers (Gunnar, Larson, Hertsgaard, Harris, & Brodersen, 1992).

Stability of care is also important. Pioneering work by René Spitz (1945, 1946) on institutionalized children emphasizes the need for substitute care to be as close as possible to good mothering. Research has underlined the value of continuity and consistency in caregiving, so children can form early emotional bonds with their caregivers.

Today, neither intense fear of strangers nor intense protest when the mother leaves is considered to be a sign of secure attachment. Researchers measure attachment more by what happens when the mother returns than by how many tears the baby sheds when she leaves.

Long-Term Effects of Attachment As attachment theory proposes, security of attachment seems to affect emotional, social, and cognitive competence (Sroufe, Coffino, & Carlson, 2010; van IJzendoorn & Sagi, 1997) presumably through the action of internal working models. The more secure a child's attachment to a nurturing adult, the easier it seems to be for the child to develop good relationships with others. If children, as infants, had a secure base and could count on parents' or caregivers' responsiveness, they are likely to feel confident enough to be actively engaged in their world (Jacobsen & Hofmann, 1997). In a study of 70 15-month-olds, those who were securely attached to their mothers, as measured by the Strange Situation, showed less stress in adapting to child care than did insecurely attached toddlers (Ahnert, Gunnar, Lamb, & Barthel, 2004).

Securely attached toddlers tend to have larger, more varied vocabularies than those who are insecurely attached (Meins, 1998). They have more positive interactions with peers, and their friendly overtures are more likely to be accepted (Fagot, 1997). Insecurely attached toddlers tend to show more fear, distress, and anger, whereas securely attached children are more joyful (Kochanska, 2001).

Between ages 3 and 5, securely attached children are likely to be more curious, competent, empathic, resilient, and self-confident; to get along better with other children; and to form closer friendships than children who were insecurely attached as

---

stranger anxiety
Wariness of strange people and places, shown by some infants from age 6 to 12 months.

separation anxiety
Distress shown by someone, typically an infant, when a familiar caregiver leaves.

Babies, at least when they are themselves down on the ground, respond more negatively to tall strangers than to short strangers.

Weinraub, 1978

infants (Arend, Gove, & Sroufe, 1979; Elicker, Englund, & Sroufe, 1992; J. L. Jacobson & Wille, 1986; Waters, Wippman, & Sroufe, 1979; Youngblade & Belsky, 1992). They interact more positively with parents, preschool teachers, and peers and are better able to resolve conflicts (Elicker et al., 1992; Sroufe, Egeland, Carlson, & Collins, 2005). They tend to have a more positive self-image (Elicker et al., 1992; Verschueren, Marcoen, & Schoefs, 1996).

Secure attachment seems to prepare children for the intimacy of friendship (Carlson, Sroufe, & Egeland, 2004). In middle childhood and adolescence, securely attached children (at least in Western cultures, where most studies have been done) tend to have the closest, most stable friendships (Schneider, Atkinson, & Tardif, 2001; Sroufe, Carlson, & Shulman, 1993).

Insecurely attached children, in contrast, are more likely to have inhibitions and negative emotions in toddlerhood, hostility toward other children at age 5, and dependency during the school years (Calkins & Fox, 1992; Fearon, Bakersmans-Kranenburg, van Ijzendoorn, Lapsley, & Roisman, 2010; Kochanska, 2001; Lyons-Ruth, Alpern, & Repacholi, 1993; Sroufe et al., 1993). Those with disorganized attachment tend to have behavior problems at all levels of schooling and psychiatric disorders at age 17 (Carlson, 1998).

In a longitudinal study of 1,364 families with 1-month-old infants, children who were avoidantly attached at 15 months tended to be rated by their mothers as less socially competent than secure children and by their teachers as more aggressive or anxious during the preschool and school-age years. However, effects of parenting on the children's behavior during these years were more important than early attachment. Insecure or disorganized children whose parenting had improved were less aggressive in school than those whose parenting did not improve or got worse. Secure children, on the other hand, were relatively immune to parenting that became less sensitive, perhaps because their early working models buoyed them up even under changed conditions. This study suggests that the continuity generally found between attachment and later behavior can be explained by continuity in the home environment (NICHD Early Child Care Research Network, 2006).

Intergenerational Transmission of Attachment Patterns The *Adult Attachment Interview* (AAI) (George, Kaplan, & Main, 1985; Main, 1995; Main, Kaplan, & Cassidy, 1985) asks adults to recall and interpret feelings and experiences related to their childhood attachments. Studies using the AAI have found that the way adults recall early experiences with parents or caregivers is related to their emotional well-being and may influence the way they respond to their own children (Adam, Gunnar, & Tanaka, 2004; Dozier, Stovall, Albus, & Bates, 2001; Pesonen, Raïkkönen, Keltikangas-Järvinen, Strandberg, & Järvenpää, 2003; Slade, Belsky, Aber, & Phelps, 1999). A mother who was securely attached to *her* mother or who understands why she was insecurely attached can accurately recognize her baby's attachment behaviors, respond encouragingly, and help the baby form a secure attachment to her (Bretherton, 1990). Mothers who are preoccupied with their past attachment relationships tend to show anger and intrusiveness in interactions with their children. Their recollections of these relationships may or may not be accurate in terms of the reality of the relationships, but their memories of experiences with caregivers will affect their relationships with children. Depressed mothers who dismiss memories of their past attachments tend to be cold and unresponsive to their children (Adam et al., 2004). Parents' attachment history also influences their perceptions of their baby's temperament, and those perceptions may affect the parent-child relationship (Pesonen et al., 2003).

Fortunately, the cycle of insecure attachment can be broken. In one study, 54 first-time Dutch mothers who were classified by the AAI as insecurely attached received home visits in which they were either given video feedback to enhance sensitive parenting or participated in discussions of their childhood experiences in relation to their current caregiving. After the interventions, these mothers were more sensitive than a control group who had not received the visits. Maternal gains in sensitivity were most effective in affecting the security of infants who had negative emotional temperaments (Klein-Velderman, Bakermans-Kranenburg, Juffer, & van IJzendoorn, 2006).

checkpoint
can **you** . . .

▷ Identify four patterns of attachment?

▷ Discuss how attachment is established, including the role of temperament?

▷ Identify factors affecting stranger anxiety and separation anxiety?

▷ Tell how long-term behavioral differences are influenced by attachment patterns?

EMOTIONAL COMMUNICATION WITH CAREGIVERS: MUTUAL REGULATION

At 1 month, Max gazes attentively at his mother's face. At 2 months, when his mother smiles at him and rubs his tummy, he smiles back. By the 3rd month, Max smiles first, inviting his mother to play (Lavelli & Fogel, 2005).

Infants are communicating beings; they have a strong drive to interact with others. The ability of both infant and caregiver to respond appropriately and sensitively to each other's mental and emotional states is known as **mutual regulation**. Infants take an active part in mutual regulation by sending behavioral signals, like Max's smile, that influence the way caregivers behave toward them (Lundy, 2003). Mutual regulation can be thought of as an emotional dance between infant and caregiver, and when it is happening correctly, both caregiver and infant accurately read and then respond to each other's cues. When a baby's goals are met, the baby is joyful or at least interested (Tronick, 1989). If a caregiver ignores an invitation to play or insists on playing when the baby has signaled "I don't feel like it," the baby may feel frustrated or sad. When babies do not achieve desired results, they keep on sending signals to repair the interaction. Normally, interaction moves back and forth between well-regulated and poorly regulated states, and babies learn from these shifts how to send signals and what to do when their initial signals are not effective. Mutual regulation helps babies learn to read others' behavior and to develop expectations about it. Even very young infants can perceive emotions expressed by others and can adjust their own behavior accordingly (Legerstee & Varghese, 2001; Montague & Walker-Andrews, 2001; Termine & Izard, 1988), but they are disturbed when someone—whether the mother or a stranger, and regardless of the reason—breaks off interpersonal contact (Striano, 2004). (Box 8.1 discusses how a mother's depression may contribute to developmental problems in her baby.)

Measuring Mutual Regulation: The "Still-Face" Paradigm

The **still-face paradigm** (Tronick, Als, Adamson, Wise, & Brazelton, 1978) is a research procedure usually used to measure mutual regulation in 2- to 9-month-old infants, though even newborns have shown the still-face response (Nagy, 2008). In the *still-face* episode, which follows a normal face-to-face interaction, the mother suddenly becomes stony-faced, silent, and unresponsive. Then, a few minutes later, she resumes normal interaction, the *reunion* episode. During the still-face episode, infants tend to stop smiling and looking at the mother. They may make faces, sounds, or gestures or may touch themselves, their clothing, or a chair, apparently to comfort themselves or to relieve the emotional stress created by the mother's unexpected behavior (Cohn & Tronick, 1983; E. Z. Tronick, 1989; Weinberg & Tronick, 1996). In essence, they become dysregulated.

How do infants react during the reunion episode? In one study, 6-month-olds showed even more positive behavior during that episode—joyous expressions and utterances and gazes and gestures directed toward the mother—than before the still-face episode. Nonetheless, the persistence of sad or angry facial expressions, "pick-me-up" gestures, distancing, and indications of stress, as well as an increased tendency to fuss and cry, suggested that the negative feelings stirred by a breakdown in mutual regulation were not readily eased (Weinberg & Tronick, 1996).

Social Referencing

Ann toddles warily toward the new playground and stops at the entrance, staring at the laughing, screaming children scaling the bright structure. Unsure of herself, she turns toward her mother and makes eye contact. Her mother smiles at her and Ann, emboldened by her mother's response, walks in and starts to climb the structure. When babies look at their caregivers upon encountering an ambiguous event, they are engaging in **social referencing**, seeking out emotional information to guide behavior (Hertenstein & Campos, 2004). In social referencing, one person forms an understanding of how to act in an ambiguous, confusing, or unfamiliar situation by seeking out and interpreting another person's perception of it.

Research provides experimental evidence of social referencing at 1 year (Moses, Baldwin, Rosicky, & Tidball, 2001). When exposed to jiggling or vibrating toys fastened to the

mutual regulation
Process by which infant and caregiver communicate emotional states to each other and respond appropriately.

still-face paradigm
Research procedure used to measure mutual regulation in infants 2 to 9 months old.

connect
study smart

Interactional Synchrony

what's your view

Do you see any ethical problems with the still-face paradigm or the Strange Situation? If so, do you think the benefits of these kinds of research are worth any potential risks?

social referencing
Understanding an ambiguous situation by seeking out another person's perception of it.

HOW POSTPARTUM DEPRESSION AFFECTS EARLY DEVELOPMENT

Reading emotional signals lets mothers assess and meet their babies' needs and helps babies respond to the mother's behavior toward them. What happens when that communication system seriously breaks down, and can anything be done about it?

Much media attention has focused on postpartum depression. Celebrities such as Brooke Shields and Marie Osmond have shared stories of their personal battles with this distressing condition.

Postpartum depression (PPD)—major or minor depression occurring within 4 weeks of giving birth—affects about 12 to 20 percent of new mothers, according to a survey taken in 17 states. Younger mothers, unmarried mothers, those with lower educational attainment, and those who received Medicaid benefits for their delivery are more likely to report postpartum depressive symptoms (Centers for Disease Control and Prevention, 2008b).

Depression may also be brought on by the significant emotional and lifestyle changes new mothers face. First-time mothers are at especially high risk (Munk-Olsen, Laursen, Pedersen, Mors, & Mortensen, 2006). High levels of corticotrophin-releasing hormone, which may help prepare expectant mothers' bodies for the stress of childbirth, may trigger postpartum depression (Yim et al., 2009). Low-income women with diabetes have a more than 50 percent increased risk of PPD (Kozhimannil, Pereira, & Harlow, 2009).

Unless treated promptly, postpartum depression may affect the way a mother interacts with her baby, with detrimental effects on the child's cognitive and emotional development (Gjerdingen, 2003). Depressed mothers are less sensitive to their infants than nondepressed mothers, and their interactions with their babies are generally less positive (NICHD Early Child Care Research Network, 1999b). Depressed mothers are less likely to interpret and respond to an infant's cries (Donovan, Leavitt, & Walsh, 1998).

Babies of depressed mothers may give up on sending emotional signals and learn that they have no power to draw responses from other people, that their mothers are unreliable, and that the world is untrustworthy. They also may become depressed themselves (Ashman & Dawson, 2002; Gelfand & Teti, 1995; Teti, Gelfand, Messinger, & Isabella, 1995), whether due to a failure of mutual regulation, an inherited predisposition to depression, or exposure to hormonal or other biochemical influences in the prenatal environment. It may be that a combination of genetic, prenatal, and environmental factors puts infants of depressed

mothers at risk. A bidirectional influence may be at work; an infant who does not respond normally may further depress the mother, and her unresponsiveness may in turn further depress the infant (T. Field, 1995, 1998a, 1998c; Lundy et al., 1999). Depressed mothers who are able to maintain good interactions with their infants tend to nurture better emotional regulation in their children than do other depressed mothers (Field, Diego, Hernandez-Reif, Schanberg, & Kuhn, 2003). Interactions with a nondepressed adult can help infants compensate for the effects of depressed mothering (T. Field, 1995, 1998a, 1998c).

Infants of depressed mothers tend to show unusual patterns of brain activity, similar to the mothers' patterns. Within 24 hours of birth, they show relatively less activity in the left frontal region of the brain, which seems to be specialized for approach emotions such as joy and anger, and more activity in the right frontal region, which controls *withdrawal* emotions, such as distress and disgust (G. Dawson et al., 1992, 1999; T. Field, 1998a, 1998c; T. Field, Fox, Pickens, Nawrocki, & Soutollo, 1995; N. A. Jones, Field, Fox, Lundy, & Davalos, 1997). Newborns of depressed mothers also tend to have higher levels of stress hormones (Lundy et al., 1999), lower scores on the Brazelton Neonatal Behavior Assessment Scale, and lower vagal tone, which is associated with attention and learning (T. Field, 1998a, 1998c; N. A. Jones et al., 1998). These findings suggest that a woman's depression during pregnancy may contribute to her newborn's neurological and behavioral functioning.

Children with depressed mothers tend to be insecurely attached (Gelfand & Teti, 1995; Teti et al., 1995). They are likely to grow poorly, to perform poorly on cognitive and linguistic measures, and to have behavior problems (T. Field, 1998a, 1998c; T. M. Field et al., 1985; Gelfand & Teti, 1995; NICHD Early Child Care Research Network, 1999b; Zuckerman & Beardslee, 1987). As toddlers these children tend to have trouble suppressing frustration and tension (Cole, Barrett, & Zahn-Waxler, 1992; Seiner & Gelfand, 1995), and in early adolescence they are at risk for violent behavior (Hay, 2003).

Antidepressant drugs such as Zoloft (a selective serotonin reuptake inhibitor) and nortriptyline (a tricyclic) appear to be safe and effective for treating postpartum depression (Wisner, Chambers, & Sit, 2006). Other techniques that may help improve a depressed mother's mood include listening to music, visual imagery, aerobics, yoga, relaxation, and massage therapy (T. Field, 1995, 1998a, 1998c). Massage also can help depressed

Continued

8.1

babies (T. Field, 1998a, 1998b; T. Field et al., 1996), possibly through effects on neurological activity (N. A. Jones et al., 1997). In one study, such mood-brightening measures—plus social, educational, and vocational rehabilitation for the mother and day care for the infant—improved their interaction behavior. The infants showed faster growth and had fewer pediatric problems, more normal biochemical values, and better developmental test scores than a control group (T. Field, 1998a, 1998b).

8.1

what's your view

Can you suggest ways to help depressed mothers and babies, other than those mentioned here?

checkpoint can you . . .

▷ Describe how mutual regulation works and explain its importance?

▷ Give examples of how infants seem to use social referencing?

floor or ceiling, both 12- and 18-month-olds moved closer to or farther from the toys depending on the experimenters' expressed emotional reactions ("Yecch!" or "Nice!"). In one pair of studies (Mumme & Fernald, 2003), 12-month-olds (but not 10-month-olds) adjusted their behavior toward certain unfamiliar objects according to nonvocal emotional signals given by an actress on a television screen. In another pair of studies (Hertenstein & Campos, 2004), whether 14-month-olds touched plastic creatures that dropped within their reach was related to the positive or negative emotions they had seen an adult express about the same objects an hour before; 11-month-olds responded to such emotional cues if the delay was very brief (3 minutes).

Social referencing—and the ability to retain information gained from it—may play a role in such key developments of toddlerhood as the rise of self-conscious emotions (embarrassment and pride), the development of a sense of self, and the processes of *socialization* and *internalization*, to which we turn later in this chapter.

guidepost

4 When and how does the sense of self arise, and how do toddlers exercise autonomy and develop standards for socially acceptable behavior?

Developmental Issues in Toddlerhood

About halfway between their first and second birthdays, babies become toddlers. This transformation can be seen, not only in such physical and cognitive skills as walking and talking but in the ways children express their personalities and interact with others. A toddler becomes a more active, intentional partner in interactions and sometimes initiates them. Caregivers can now more clearly read the child's signals. Such in-sync interactions help toddlers gain communicative skills and social competence and motivate compliance with a parent's wishes (Harrist & Waugh, 2002).

Let's look at three psychological issues that toddlers—and their caregivers—have to deal with: the emerging *sense of self*; the growth of *autonomy*, or self-determination; and *socialization*, or *internalization of behavioral standards*.

self-concept
Sense of self; descriptive and evaluative mental picture of one's abilities and traits.

THE EMERGING SENSE OF SELF

The **self-concept** is our image of ourselves—our total picture of our abilities and traits. It describes what we know and feel about ourselves and guides our actions (Harter, 1996, 1998). Children incorporate into their self-image the picture that others reflect back to them.

When and how does the self-concept develop? From a jumble of seemingly isolated experiences (say, from one breast-feeding session to another), infants begin to extract consistent patterns that form rudimentary concepts of self and other. Depending on what kind of care the infant receives and how she or he responds, pleasant or unpleasant

Self-awareness and an understanding that others can think things that you know are not true is also related to another developmental milestone: lying. While we do not generally think of it as such, lying is actually a profound developmental achievement.

emotions become connected with experiences that play an important part in the growing concept of the self (Harter, 1998).

Generally, 3-month-old infants pay attention to their mirror image (Courage & Howe, 2002). By 4–9 months, they show more interest in images of others than of themselves (Rochat & Striano, 2002). This early *perceptual* discrimination may be the foundation of the *conceptual* self-concept that develops in the middle of the 2nd year.

Between 4 and 10 months, when infants learn to reach, grasp, and make things happen, they experience a sense of personal *agency*, the realization that they can control external events. At about this time infants develop *self-coherence*, the sense of being a physical whole with boundaries separate from the rest of their world (Harter, 1998). These developments occur in interaction with caregivers in games such as peekaboo, in which the infant becomes increasingly aware of the difference between self and other ("I see you!").

The emergence of *self-representation* ("the idea of the me")—a conscious knowledge of the self as a distinct, identifiable being (Lewis, 2003)—builds on this dawning perceptual discrimination between self and others. Self-representation can be tested by studying whether infants recognize themselves in a mirror (Lewis & Carmody, 2008). In a classic line of research, investigators dabbed rouge on the noses of 6- to 24-month-olds and sat them in front of a mirror. Three-fourths of 18-month-olds and all 24-month-olds touched their red noses more often than before, whereas babies younger than 15 months never did. This behavior suggests that these toddlers had self-awareness. They knew they did not normally have red noses and recognized the image in the mirror as their own (Lewis, 1997; Lewis & Brooks, 1974). In a later study, 18- and 24-month-olds were about as likely to touch a sticker on their legs, which was visible only in a mirror, as on their faces (Nielsen, Suddendorf, & Slaughter, 2006). Once children can recognize themselves, they show a preference for looking at their own video image over an image of another child the same age (Nielsen, Dissanayake, & Kashima, 2003).

Pretend play, which typically begins during the last half of the 2nd year, is another measure or sign of self-representation—an early indication of the ability to understand others' mental states as well as the child's own (Lewis & Carmody, 2008). A third measure or sign of self-representation is the use of first-person pronouns, such as *me* and *mine*, usually at 20 to 24 months (Lewis, 1997; Lewis & Carmody, 2008). Between 19 and 30 months, children begin to apply descriptive terms ("big" or "little," "straight hair" or "curly hair") and evaluative ones ("good," "pretty," or "strong") to themselves. The rapid development of language enables children to think and talk about the self and to incorporate parents' verbal descriptions ("You're so smart!" "What a big boy!") into their emerging self-image (Stipek, Gralinski, & Kopp, 1990). Similarly, toddlers of this age demonstrate self-understanding through acknowledging objects that belong to them and those that belong to others (Fasig, 2000).

Brain maturation underlies the development of self-representation. MRI scans of 15- to 30-month-olds showed that signal intensities in a specific brain region (the left temporo-parietal junction) were strongest in children, regardless of age, who recognized their image in a mirror, engaged in pretend play with others, and used personal pronouns (Lewis & Carmody, 2008).

DEVELOPING AUTONOMY

As children mature—physically, cognitively, and emotionally—they are driven to seek independence from the very adults to whom they are attached. "Me do!" is the byword as toddlers use their developing muscles and minds to try to do everything on their own—not only to walk, but to feed and dress themselves and to explore their world.

Erikson (1950) identified the period from about 18 months to 3 years as the second stage in psychosocial development, **autonomy versus shame and doubt**, which is marked by a shift from external control to self-control. Having come through infancy with a sense of basic trust in the world and an awakening self-awareness, toddlers begin to substitute

Dabbing rouge on children's noses is known as the Rouge Task, and research has shown that dolphins, chimpanzees, and elephants also share our ability for self-recognition.

autonomy versus shame and doubt Erikson's second stage in psychosocial development, in which children achieve a balance between self-determination and control by others.

This toddler is showing autonomy—the drive to exert her own power over her environment.

their own judgment for their caregivers'. The virtue, or strength, that emerges during this stage is *will*. Toilet training is an important step toward autonomy and self-control. So is language. As children are better able to make their wishes understood, they become more powerful and independent. Since unlimited freedom is neither safe nor healthy, said Erikson, shame and doubt have a necessary place. Toddlers need adults to set appropriate limits, and shame and doubt help them recognize the need for those limits.

In the United States, the "terrible twos" are a normal sign of the drive for autonomy. Toddlers have to test the notions that they are individuals, that they have some control over their world, and that they have new, exciting powers. They are driven to try out their own ideas, exercise their own preferences, and make their own decisions. This drive typically shows itself in the form of *negativism*, the tendency to shout "No!" just for the sake of resisting authority. Almost all U.S. children show negativism to some degree; it usually begins before age 2, tends to peak at about 3½ to 4, and declines by age 6. Caregivers who view children's expressions of self-will as a normal, healthy striving for independence, not as stubbornness, can help them learn self-control, contribute to their sense of competence, and avoid excessive conflict. (Table 8.3 gives specific, research-based suggestions for dealing with the terrible twos.)

Many U.S. parents might be surprised to hear that the terrible twos are not universal. In some developing countries, the transition from infancy to early childhood is relatively smooth and harmonious, as we discuss in Box 8.2.

checkpoint
can you . . .

▷ Trace the early development of the sense of self?

▷ Describe the conflict of autonomy versus shame and doubt?

▷ Explain why the "terrible twos" is considered a normal phenomenon, and suggest reasons this transition may not exist in some cultures?

TABLE 8.3 Dealing with the Terrible Twos

The following research-based guidelines can help parents of toddlers discourage negativism and encourage socially acceptable behavior.

- *Be flexible.* Learn the child's natural rhythms and special likes and dislikes.

- *Think of yourself as a safe harbor,* with safe limits, from which a child can set out and discover the world and to which the child can keep coming back for support.

- *Make your home child-safe.* Make unbreakable objects that are safe to explore available.

- *Avoid physical punishment.* It is often ineffective and may even lead a toddler to do more damage.

- *Offer a choice*—even a limited one—to give the child some control. ("Would you like to have your bath now or after we read a book?")

- *Be consistent* in enforcing necessary requests.

- *Don't interrupt an activity unless absolutely necessary.* Try to wait until the child's attention has shifted.

- *If you must interrupt, give warning.* ("We have to leave the playground soon.")

- *Suggest alternative activities* when behavior becomes objectionable. (When Ashley is throwing sand in Keiko's face, say, "Oh, look! Nobody's on the swings now. Let's go over and I'll give you a good push!")

- *Suggest; don't command.* Accompany requests with smiles or hugs, not criticism, threats, or physical restraint.

- *Link requests with pleasurable activities.* ("It's time to stop playing so that you can go to the store with me.")

- *Remind the child of what you expect* ("When we go to this playground, we *never* go outside the gate.")

- *Wait a few moments before repeating a request* when a child doesn't comply immediately.

- *Use time-outs to end conflicts.* In a nonpunitive way, remove either yourself or the child from a situation.

- *Expect less self-control during times of stress* (illness, divorce, the birth of a sibling, or a move to a new home).

- *Expect it to be harder for toddlers to comply with "dos" than with "don'ts".* "Clean up your room" takes more effort than "Don't write on the furniture."

- *Keep the atmosphere as positive as possible.* Make your child want to cooperate.

Sources: Haswell, Hock, & Wenar, 1981: Kochanska & Aksan, 1995; Kopp, 1982; Kuczynski & Kochanska 1995; Power & Chapieski, 1986.

ARE STRUGGLES WITH TODDLERS NECESSARY?

Are the terrible twos a normal phase in child development? Many Western parents and psychologists think so. Actually, though, this transition does not appear to be universal.

In Zinacantan, Mexico, toddlers do not typically become demanding and resistant to parental control. Instead of asserting independence from their mothers, toddlerhood in Zinacantan is a time when children move from being mama's babies to being mother's helpers, responsible children who may tend a new baby and who help with household tasks (Edwards, 1994). A similar developmental pattern seems to occur in Mazahua families in Mexico and among Maya families in San Pedro, Guatemala. San Pedro parents "do not report a particular age when they expect children to become especially contrary or negative" (Mosier & Rogoff, 2003, p. 1058).

One arena in which issues of autonomy and control appear in Western cultures is in sibling conflicts over toys and the way children respond to parental handling of these conflicts. To explore these issues, a cross-cultural study compared 16 San Pedro families with 16 middle-class European American families in Salt Lake City. All of the families had toddlers 14 to 20 months old and older siblings 3 to 5 years old. The researchers interviewed each mother about her child-raising practices. They then handed the mother a series of attractive objects (such as nesting dolls and a jumping-jack puppet) and, in the presence of the older sibling, asked the mother to help the toddler operate them, with no instructions about the older child. Researchers who observed the ensuing interactions found striking differences in the way siblings interacted in the two cultures and in the way the mothers viewed and handled sibling conflict.

The older siblings in Salt Lake City often tried to take and play with the objects, but this generally did not happen in San Pedro. Instead, the older San Pedro children would offer to help their younger siblings work the objects, or the two children would play with them together. When there was a conflict over possession of the objects, mothers in both communities were more likely to endorse the toddler's right to have it first, but this tendency was far more characteristic of San Pedro mothers than of Salt Lake City mothers. San Pedro mothers favored the toddlers 94 percent of the time, even taking an object away from the older child if the younger child wanted it; and the older siblings tended to go along, willingly handing the objects to the toddlers or letting them have the

objects from the start. In contrast, in more than one-third of the interactions in Salt Lake City, the mothers tried to treat both children equally, negotiating with them or suggesting that they take turns or share. These observations were consistent with reports of mothers in both cultures of how they handled such issues at home. San Pedro children are given a privileged position until age 3; then they are expected to willingly cooperate with social expectations.

What explains these cultural contrasts? A clue emerged when the mothers were asked at what age children can be held responsible for their actions. Most of the Salt Lake City mothers maintained that their toddlers already understood the consequences of touching prohibited objects; several said this understanding arises as early as 7 months. Yet all but one of the San Pedro mothers placed the age of understanding social consequences of actions much later—between 2 and 3 years. The Salt Lake City mothers regarded their toddlers as capable of intentional misbehavior and punished their toddlers for it; most San Pedro mothers did not. All of the Salt Lake City preschoolers (toddlers and their siblings) were under direct caregiver supervision; 11 of the 16 San Pedro preschoolers were on their own much of the time and had more mature household responsibilities.

The researchers suggest that the terrible twos may be a phase specific to societies that place individual freedom before the needs of the group. Ethnographic research suggests that in societies that place higher value on group needs freedom of choice does exist, but it goes hand in hand with interdependence, responsibility, and expectations of cooperation. Salt Lake City parents seem to believe that responsible behavior develops gradually from engaging in fair competition and negotiations. San Pedro parents seem to believe that responsible behavior develops rapidly when children are old enough to understand the need to respect others' desires as well as their own.

what's your view

From your experience or observation of toddlers, which of the two ways of handling sibling conflict would you expect to be more effective?

THE ROOTS OF MORAL DEVELOPMENT: SOCIALIZATION AND INTERNALIZATION

Socialization is the process by which children develop habits, skills, values, and motives that make them responsible, productive members of society. Compliance with parental expectations can be seen as a first step toward compliance with societal standards. Socialization rests on **internalization** of these standards. Children who are successfully socialized no longer merely obey rules or commands to get rewards or avoid punishment; rather, they have internalized those standards and made them their own (Grusec & Goodnow, 1994; Kochanska, 2002; Kochanska & Aksan, 1995; Kochanska, Tjebkes, & Forman, 1998). They obey societal or parental dictates, not because they are afraid of getting in trouble, but because they themselves believe them to be right and true.

Developing Self-Regulation Laticia, age 2, is about to poke her finger into an electric outlet. In her child-proofed apartment, the sockets are covered, but not here in her grandmother's home. When Laticia hears her father shout "No!" the toddler pulls her arm back. The next time she goes near an outlet, she starts to point her finger, hesitates, and then says "No." She has stopped herself from doing something she remembers she is not supposed to do. She is beginning to show **self-regulation:** control of her behavior to conform to a caregiver's demands or expectations, even when the caregiver is not present.

Self-regulation is the foundation of socialization, and it links all domains of development—physical, cognitive, social, and emotional. Until Laticia was physically able to get around on her own, electric outlets posed no hazard. To stop herself from poking her finger into an outlet requires that she consciously understand and remember what her father told her. Cognitive awareness, however, is not enough; restraining herself also requires emotional control. By reading their parents' emotional responses to their behavior, children continually absorb information about what conduct their parents approve of. As children process, store, and act on this information, their strong desire to please their parents leads them to do as they know their parents want them to, whether or not the parents are there to see.

Before they can control their behavior, children need to be able to regulate, or control, their *attentional processes* and to modulate negative emotions (Eisenberg, 2000). Attentional regulation enables children to develop willpower and cope with frustration (Sethi, Mischel, Aber, Shoda, & Rodriguez, 2000). For example, control of attentional processes might allow a child to distract herself enough that she manages not to steal the cookies temptingly cooling on the counter.

The growth of self-regulation parallels the development of the self-conscious and evaluative emotions, such as empathy, shame, and guilt (Lewis, 1995, 1997, 1998). It requires the ability to wait for gratification. It is correlated with measures of conscience development, such as resisting temptation and making amends for wrongdoing (Eisenberg, 2000). In most children, the full development of self-regulation takes at least 3 years (Kopp, 1982).

Origins of Conscience: Committed Compliance Children, when young, cooperate with parental dictates because they know they are supposed to. While this self-regulation is important, the goal of parenting is often internalization of parental mores. Parents would like children to do the right thing and avoid doing the wrong thing because they truly believe it for themselves. In other words, the eventual goal is the development of a **conscience**, which involves both the ability to refrain from certain acts as well as to produce emotional discomfort as a result of a failure to do so.

Grazyna Kochanska (1993, 1995, 1997a, 1997b) and her colleagues have looked for the origins of conscience in a longitudinal study of a group of toddlers and mothers in Iowa. Researchers videotaped 103 children ages 26 to 41 months and their mothers playing together with toys for 2 to 3 hours, both at home and in a homelike laboratory setting (Kochanska & Aksan, 1995). After a free-play period, a mother would give her child 15 minutes to put away the toys. The laboratory had a special shelf with other, unusually attractive toys, such as a bubble gum machine, a walkie-talkie, and a music box. The child was told not to touch anything on the shelf. After about an hour, the experimenter asked the mother to go into an adjoining room, leaving the child alone with the toys. A few minutes later, a woman entered, played with several of the forbidden toys, and then left the child alone again for 8 minutes.

Some children could put the toys away as long as their parents were there to remind them. These children showed what is called **situational compliance**. They needed the extra assistance provided by their parents' reminder and prompts to complete the task, and, given a different situation which did not include those reminders, might fail to put the toys away. However, other children seemed to have internalized their parents' requests more fully. These children showed **committed compliance**—that is, they were committed to following requests and could do so without their parents' direct intervention (Kochanska, Coy, & Murray, 2001).

The roots of committed compliance go back to early infancy. Committed compliers, who are more likely to be girls than boys, tend to be those who, at 8 to 10 months, could refrain from touching when told "No!" Committed compliance tends to increase with age, whereas situational compliance decreases (Kochanska et al., 1998). Mothers of committed compliers, as contrasted with mothers of situational compliers, tend to rely on gentle guidance rather than force, threats, or other forms of negative control (Eisenberg, 2000; Kochanska & Aksan, 1995; Kochanska, Aksan, Knaack, & Rhines, 2004).

Receptive cooperation goes beyond committed compliance. It is a child's eager willingness to cooperate harmoniously with a parent, not only in disciplinary situations but in a variety of daily interactions, including routines, chores, hygiene, and play. Receptive cooperation enables a child to be an active partner in socialization. In a longitudinal study of 101 7-month-olds, those who were prone to anger, who received unresponsive parenting, or who were insecurely attached at 15 months tended to be low in receptive cooperation at 7 months. Children who were securely attached and whose mothers had been responsive to the child during infancy tended to be high in receptive cooperation (Kochanska, Aksan, & Carlson, 2005).

Factors in the Success of Socialization The way parents go about socializing a child, together with a child's temperament and the quality of the parent-child relationship, may help predict how hard or easy socialization will be. Factors in the success of socialization include security of attachment, observational learning from parents' behavior, and the mutual responsiveness of parent and child (Kochanska et al., 2004; Maccoby, 1992). All these as well as socioeconomic and cultural factors (Harwood, Schoelmerich, Ventura-Cook, Schulze, & Wilson, 1996) play a part in motivation to comply. However, not all children respond to socialization in the same way. For example, a temperamentally fearful toddler may respond better to gentle reminders than to strong admonitions whereas a more bold toddler may require more assertive parenting (Kochanska, Aksan, & Joy, 2007).

Secure attachment and a warm, mutually responsive parent-child relationship seem to foster committed compliance and conscience development. From the child's 2nd year until early school age, researchers observed more than 200 mothers and children in lengthy, naturalistic interactions: caregiving routines, preparing and eating meals, playing, relaxing, and doing household chores. Children who were judged to have mutually responsive relationships with

One new development in the parenting domain is the influence of instantly and always available technology. Research by Sherry Turkle of the Massachusetts Institute of Technology suggests that young children are increasingly experiencing hurt feelings as a result of competition with computers and smart phones.

Turkle, 2011

situational compliance
Kochanska's term for obedience of a parent's orders only in the presence of signs of ongoing parental control.

committed compliance
Kochanska's term for wholehearted obedience of a parent's orders without reminders or lapses.

receptive cooperation
Kochanska's term for eager willingness to cooperate harmoniously with a parent in daily interactions, including routines, chores, hygiene, and play.

what's your view

In view of Kochanska's research on the roots of conscience, what questions would you ask about the early socialization of antisocial adolescents and adults?

checkpoint can you . . .

▶ Tell when and how self-regulation develops and how it contributes to socialization?

▶ Distinguish among situational compliance, committed compliance, and receptive cooperation?

▶ Discuss how temperament and parenting practices affect socialization?

their mothers tended to show *moral emotions* such as guilt and empathy; *moral conduct* in the face of strong temptation to break rules or violate standards of behavior; and *moral cognition*, as judged by their response to hypothetical, age-appropriate moral dilemmas (Kochanska, 2002).

Constructive conflict over a child's misbehavior—conflict that involves negotiation, reasoning, and resolution—can help children develop moral understanding by enabling them to see another point of view. In one observational study, 2½-year-olds whose mothers gave clear explanations for their requests, compromised, or bargained with the child were better able to resist temptation at age 3 than children whose mothers had threatened, teased, insisted, or given in. Discussion of emotions in conflict situations ("How would you feel if . . .") also led to conscience development, probably by fostering the development of moral emotions (Laible & Thompson, 2002).

guidepost
5

When and how do gender differences appear?

Gender: How Different Are Baby Boys and Girls?

Being male or female affects how people look, how they move their bodies, and how they work, play, and dress. It influences what they think about themselves and what others think of them. All these characteristics—and more—are included in the word **gender:** what it means to be *male* or *female*.

GENDER DIFFERENCES IN INFANTS AND TODDLERS

gender
Significance of being male or female.

Measurable differences between baby boys and baby girls are few, at least in U.S. samples. Boys are a bit longer and heavier and may be slightly stronger but are physically more vulnerable from conception on. As mentioned in Chapter 4, beginning prenatally boys are more active than girls. Girls are less reactive to stress and more likely to survive infancy (Davis & Emory, 1995; Keenan & Shaw, 1997; Stevenson et al., 2000). Boys' brains at birth are about 10 percent larger than girls' brains, a difference that continues into adulthood (Gilmore et al., 2007). On the other hand, the two sexes are equally sensitive to touch and tend to teethe, sit up, and walk at about the same ages (Maccoby, 1980). They also achieve the other motor milestones of infancy at about the same times.

One of the earliest *behavioral* differences between boys and girls, appearing between ages 1 and 2, is in preferences for toys and play activities and for playmates of the same sex (Campbell, Shirley, Heywood, & Crook, 2000; Serbin, Poulin-Dubois, Colburne, Sen, & Eichstedt, 2001; Turner & Gervai, 1995). Boys as young as 17 months tend to play more aggressively than girls (Baillargeon et al., 2007). Between ages 2 and 3, boys and girls tend to say more words pertaining to their own gender (such as "necklace" versus "tractor") than to the other gender (Stennes, Burch, Sen, & Bauer, 2005).

By using age-appropriate tasks, cognitive psychologists have found evidence that infants begin to perceive differences between males and females long before their behavior is gender-differentiated and even before they can talk. Habituation studies have found that 6-month-olds respond differently to male and female voices. By 9 to 12 months, infants can tell the difference between male and female faces, apparently on the basis of hair and clothing. From about 24 to 36 months, infants begin to associate gender-typical toys, such as dolls, with a face of the correct gender. Boys are slower to develop this knowledge than girls (Martin, Ruble, & Szkrybalo, 2002). In elicited imitation studies (refer to Chapter 7), 25-month-old boys spend more time imitating "boy" tasks, such as shaving a teddy bear, whereas girls spend about the same amount of time imitating activities associated with each gender (Bauer, 1993).

Gender-typing is more strongly supported by fathers who tend to spend more time and play more roughly with sons than with daughters.

HOW PARENTS SHAPE GENDER DIFFERENCES

Parents in the United States tend to *think* baby boys and girls are more different than they actually are. In a study of 11-month-old infants who had recently begun crawling, mothers consistently had higher expectations for their sons' success in crawling down steep and narrow slopes than for their daughters. Yet, when tested on the slopes, the baby girls and boys showed identical levels of performance (Mondschein, Adolph, and Tamis-Lemonda, 2000).

U.S. parents also begin to influence boys' and girls' personalities very early. Fathers treat boys and girls more differently than mothers do, even during the 1st year (M. E. Snow, Jacklin, & Maccoby, 1983; Tenebaum & Leaper, 2003). During the 2nd year, fathers talk more and spend more time with sons than with daughters (Lamb, 1981). Mothers talk more, and more supportively, to daughters than to sons (Leaper, Anderson, & Sanders, 1998), and girls at this age tend to be more talkative than boys (Leaper & Smith, 2004). Fathers of toddlers play more roughly with sons and show more sensitivity to daughters (Kelley, Smith, Green, Berndt, & Rogers, 1998; Lindsey, Cremeens, & Caldera, 2010). Socialization processes such as these are known as **gender-typing** (Lytton & Romney, 1991). Through gender-typing, children learn the behavior that their culture considers appropriate for each sex.

Because cultures can have different conceptions of what it means to be male or female, gender-typing activities differ by culture. For example, a highly physical style of play, characteristic of many fathers in the United States, is not typical of fathers in all cultures. Swedish and German fathers usually do not play with their babies this way (Lamb, Frodi, Frodi, & Hwang, 1982; Parke, Grossman, & Tinsley, 1981). African Aka fathers (Hewlett, 1987) and those in New Delhi, India, also tend to play gently with small children (Roopnarine, Hooper, Ahmeduzzaman, & Pollack, 1993; Roopnarine, Talokder, Jain, Josh, & Srivastav, 1992). Such cross-cultural variations suggest that rough play may be a biologically based gender difference that is also culturally influenced.

We discuss gender-typing and gender differences in more depth in Chapter 11.

gender-typing
Socialization process by which children, at an early age, learn appropriate gender roles.

what's your view
Should parents try to treat male and female infants and toddlers alike?

checkpoint can you . . .

▷ Compare the roles of mothers and fathers in gender-typing?

Contact with Other Children

Although parents exert a major influence on children's lives, relationships with other children—both in the home and out of it—are important too, from infancy on.

How do infants and toddlers interact with siblings and other children?

guidepost 6

SIBLINGS

If you have brothers or sisters, your relationships with them are likely to be the longest lasting you will ever have. They share your roots: They knew you when you were young, they accepted or rejected the same parental values, and they probably deal with you more candidly than almost anyone else you know.

Sibling relationships begin with the birth of a new baby in a household and continue to develop, both positively and negatively, throughout childhood.

The Arrival of a New Baby Children react in various ways to the arrival of a sibling. To bid for the mother's attention, some suck their thumbs, wet their pants, or use baby talk. Others withdraw. Some suggest taking the baby back to the hospital or flushing it down the toilet. Some take pride in being the "big ones," who can dress themselves, use the potty, and help care for the baby.

Much of the variation in children's adjustment to a new baby may have to do with such factors as the older child's age, the quality of his or her relationship with the mother, and the family atmosphere. Not surprisingly, attachment to the mother often becomes temporarily less secure (Teti, Sakin, Kucera, Corns, & Eiden, 1996).

Affection and cooperation are common in sibling relationships as the younger sibling learns from the older.

The birth of a younger sibling may change the way a mother acts toward an older child, at least until the newcomer settles in. The mother is likely to play less with the older child, to be less sensitive to her or his interests, to give more orders, to have more confrontations, to use physical punishment, and to initiate fewer conversations and games that help develop skills. An older boy, especially, may show temporary behavior problems (Baydar, Greek, & Brooks-Gunn, 1997; Baydar, Hyle, & Brooks-Gunn, 1997; Dunn, 1985; Dunn & Kendrick, 1982). On the positive side, the arrival of a baby tends to enhance the older child's language development, perhaps because the child talks more than before with the father and other family members (Baydar, Greek, & Brooks-Gunn, 1997; Baydar, Hyle, & Brooks-Gunn, 1997).

How Siblings Interact Sibling relationships play a distinct role in socialization, different from the role of relationships with parents or peers (Vandell, 2000). Sibling conflicts can become a vehicle for understanding social relationships (Dunn & Munn, 1985; Ram & Ross, 2001). Lessons and skills learned from interactions with siblings carry over to relationships outside the home (Ji-Yeon, McHale, Couter, & Osgood, 2007; Brody, 1998).

Babies usually become attached to their older brothers and sisters. Although rivalry may be present, so is affection. The more securely attached siblings are to their parents, the better they get along with each other (Teti & Ablard, 1989).

Nevertheless, as babies begin to move around and become more assertive, they inevitably come into conflict with siblings—at least in U.S. culture (refer to Box 8.2). Sibling conflict increases dramatically after the younger child reaches age 18 months (Vandell & Bailey, 1992). During the next few months, younger siblings begin to participate more fully in family interactions and become more involved in family disputes. As they do, they become more aware of others' intentions and feelings. They begin to recognize what kind of behavior will upset or annoy an older brother or sister and what behavior is considered naughty or good (Dunn & Munn, 1985; Recchia & Howe, 2009).

As this cognitive and social understanding grows, sibling conflict tends to become more constructive, and the younger sibling participates in attempts to reconcile. Constructive conflict helps children recognize each other's needs, wishes, and point of view; and it helps them learn how to fight, disagree, and compromise within the context of a safe, stable relationship (Kramer, 2010; Vandell & Bailey, 1992).

SOCIABILITY WITH NONSIBLINGS

Infants and, even more so, toddlers show interest in people outside the home, particularly people their own size. During the first few months, they look, smile, and coo at other babies (T. M. Field, 1978). From about 6 to 12 months, they increasingly smile at, touch, and babble to them (Hay, Pedersen, & Nash, 1982). At about 1 year, when the biggest items on their agenda are learning to walk and to manipulate objects, babies pay less attention to other people (T. M. Field & Roopnarine, 1982). This stage does not last long, though. From about 1½ years to almost 3, children show growing interest in what other children do and an increasing understanding of how to deal with them (Eckerman, Davis, & Didow, 1989; Eckerman & Stein, 1982).

Toddlers learn by imitating one another. Games such as follow-the-leader help toddlers connect with other children and pave the way for more complex games during the preschool years (Eckerman et al., 1989). Imitation of each other's actions leads to more frequent verbal communication ("You go in playhouse," "Don't do it!" or

"Look at me"), which helps peers coordinate joint activity (Eckerman & Didow, 1996). Cooperative activity develops during the 2nd and 3rd years as social understanding grows (Brownell, Ramani, & Zerwas, 2006). As with siblings, conflict, too, can have a purpose, helping children learn how to negotiate and resolve disputes (Caplan, Vespo, Pedersen, & Hay, 1991; Kramer 2010). We learn as much from bullies as we do from friends.

Some children, of course, are more sociable than others, reflecting such temperament traits as their usual mood, readiness to accept new people, and ability to adapt to change. Sociability is also influenced by experience; babies who spend time with other babies, as in child care, become sociable earlier than those who spend all their time at home alone.

Children of Working Parents

Parents' work determines more than the family's financial resources. Much of adults' time, effort, and emotional involvement go into their occupations. How do their working and their child care arrangements affect young children? Most research on this subject pertains to mothers' work. (We discuss the impact of parents' work on older children in later chapters.)

EFFECTS OF MATERNAL EMPLOYMENT

More than half (55.8 percent) of mothers of infants in their 1st year of life and 54 percent of women with children under 3 were in the labor force in 2011, a dramatic increase since 1975 (U.S. Bureau of Labor Statistics, 2008a, 2012; Figure 8.2). However, labor force participation of *married* mothers of infants, which peaked in 1997 at 59.2 percent, fell to 54.6 percent in 2007, and the participation rate for married mothers of children under 3 dropped from about 64 percent in 1997–1998 to just over 60 percent in 2007 (Cohany & Sok, 2007; U.S. Bureau of Labor Statistics, 2008a, 2008b).

How does early maternal employment affect children? Longitudinal data on 900 European American children from the National Institute of Child Health and Human Development (NICHD) Study of Early Child Care, discussed in the next section, showed negative effects on cognitive development at 15 months to 3 years when mothers

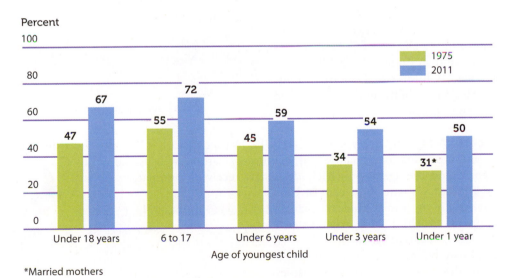

Percent

*Married mothers

Age of youngest child

Sources: Data from Hayghe, 1986; U.S. Bureau of Labor Statistics, 2012.

checkpoint
can you...

▷ Discuss factors affecting a child's adjustment to a new baby sister or brother?

▷ Describe changes in sibling interaction and sibling conflict during toddlerhood?

▷ Trace changes in sociability during the first 3 years and state two influences on it?

guidepost 7

How do parental employment and early child care affect infants' and toddlers' development?

FIGURE 8.2

Labor Force Participation Rates of Mothers with Children, 1975 and 2011

Labor force participation by mothers of children of all ages has increased dramatically in the past three decades. In 1975, fewer than half of all mothers were working or looking for work. In 2011, about 7 out of 10 mothers were labor force participants. Participation rates in 2011 ranged from 50 percent for mothers whose youngest child was under 1 year old to 72 percent for mothers whose youngest child was age 6 to 17.

worked 30 or more hours a week by a child's 9th month. Maternal sensitivity, a high-quality home environment, and high-quality child care lessened but did not eliminate these negative effects (Brooks-Gunn, Han, & Waldfogel, 2002).

Similarly, among 6,114 children from the National Longitudinal Survey of Youth (NLSY), those whose mothers worked full time in the 1st year after giving birth were more likely to show negative cognitive and behavioral outcomes at ages 3 to 8 than children whose mothers worked part time or not at all during their 1st year. Children in disadvantaged families showed fewer negative cognitive effects than children in more advantaged families (Hill, Waldfogel, Brooks-Gunn, & Han, 2005).

On the other hand, a longitudinal study of an ethnically, socioeconomically, and geographically diverse sample of 1,364 children during their first 3 years suggests that the economic and social benefits of maternal employment may outweigh any disadvantages resulting from reduced time with a child. Mothers who worked outside the home compensated for some of their work time by reducing time spent on non–child care activities. Differences in time spent with infants were modestly related to maternal sensitivity but did not seem to affect social or cognitive outcomes. Infants whose mothers spent more time with them did have more stimulating home environments, but so did infants whose mothers spent more time at work. It seems, then, that mothers who are temperamentally prone to be sensitive and to provide stimulating, warm home environments may find ways to do so whether or not they are employed (Huston & Aronson, 2005).

EARLY CHILD CARE

One factor in the impact of a mother's working outside the home is the type of substitute care a child receives. Recent data estimates that about 60 percent of U.S. children not yet in kindergarten are in some type of regular child care (Iruka & Carver, 2006). More than 50 percent of the 11.3 million children whose mothers were employed received care from relatives—30 percent from grandparents, 25 percent from their fathers, 3 percent from siblings, and 8 percent from other relatives. More than 30 percent were in organized day care or preschools. With nonrelative care averaging $129 a week (U.S. Census Bureau, 2008b) and center-based care in 33 states and the District of Columbia costing more than tuition at a public 4-year college (Children's Defense Fund, 2008b), affordability and quality of care are pressing issues.

> Although parents may feel guilty about how much time they spend with their children given the conflicting modern demands of work and family, research suggests that they actually spend more time with their kids than previous generations did. How do parents fit it in? Apparently, moms spend less time cooking and cleaning, and dads spend less time at the office.
>
> Ramey & Ramey, 2010

Factors Affecting Early Child Care The impact of early child care may depend on the type, amount, quality, and stability of care as well as the family's income and the age at which children start receiving nonmaternal care. By 9 months, about 50 percent of U.S. infants are in some kind of regular nonparental child care arrangement, and 86 percent of these infants enter child care before they reach 6 months. More than 50 percent of these babies are in child care more than 30 hours a week (NCES, 2005).

> In 2009, full-time child care costs for a year exceeded average yearly college tuition and fees in 40 states.
>
> National Association of Child Care Resource and Referral Agencies (NACCRRA), 2010

Caregivers' responsiveness to infants' needs is the most important factor in high-quality day care.

Temperament and gender may make a difference (Crockenberg, 2003). Shy children in child care experience greater stress, as shown by cortisol levels, than sociable children (Watamura, Donzella, Alwin, & Gunnar, 2003), and insecurely attached children undergo greater stress than securely attached children when introduced to full-time child care (Ahnert et al., 2004). Boys are more vulnerable to stress, in child care and elsewhere, than are girls (Crockenberg, 2003).

Quality of care contributes to cognitive and psychosocial competence (Marshall, 2004; de Schipper, Riksen-Walraven, & Geurts, 2006). Quality of care can be measured by *structural characteristics*, such as staff training and the ratio of children to caregivers; and by *process characteristics*, such as the warmth, sensitivity, and responsiveness of caregivers and the developmental appropriateness of activities. Structural quality and process quality may be related; in one study, well-trained caregivers and low child-staff ratios were associated with higher process quality, which, in turn, was associated with better cognitive and social outcomes (Marshall, 2004).

The most important element in quality of care is the caregiver; stimulating interactions with responsive adults are crucial to early cognitive, linguistic, and psychosocial development. Low staff turnover is important; infants need consistent caregiving to develop trust and secure attachments (Burchinal, Roberts, Nabors, & Bryant, 1996; Shonkoff & Phillips, 2000). Stability of care facilitates coordination between parents and child care providers, which may help protect against any negative effects of long hours of care (Ahnert & Lamb, 2003). The Checklist in Table 8.4 provides basic guidelines for selecting a high-quality child care facility.

The NICHD Study: Isolating Child Care Effects Because child care is an integral part of what Bronfenbrenner calls a child's bioecological system (refer to Chapter 2), it is difficult to measure its influence alone. The most comprehensive attempt to separate child care effects from such other factors as family characteristics, the child's characteristics, and the care the child receives at home is an ongoing study sponsored by the National Institute of Child Health and Human Development (NICHD).

This longitudinal study of 1,364 children and their families began in 1991 in 10 university centers across the United States, shortly after the children's birth. The sample was diverse socioeconomically, educationally, and ethnically; nearly 35 percent of the families were poor or near poor. Most infants entered nonmaternal care before

TABLE 8.4 Checklist for Choosing a Good Child Care Facility

- Is the facility licensed? Does it meet minimum state standards for health, fire, and safety? (Many centers and home care facilities are not licensed or regulated.)

- Is the facility clean and safe? Does it have adequate indoor and outdoor space?

- Does the facility have small groups, a high adult-to-child ratio, and a stable, competent, highly involved staff?

- Are caregivers trained in child development?

- Are caregivers warm, affectionate, accepting, responsive, and sensitive? Are they authoritative but not too restrictive and neither too controlling nor merely custodial?

- Does the program promote good health habits?

- Does it provide a balance between structured activities and free play? Are activities age appropriate?

- Do the children have access to educational toys and materials that stimulate mastery of cognitive and communicative skills at a child's own pace?

- Does the program nurture self-confidence, curiosity, creativity, and self-discipline?

- Does it encourage children to ask questions, solve problems, express feelings and opinions, and make decisions?

- Does it foster self-esteem, respect for others, and social skills?

- Does it help parents improve their child-rearing skills?

- Does it promote cooperation with public and private schools and the community?

Sources: American Academy of Pediatrics [AAP], 1986; Belsky, 1984; K. A. Clarke-Stewart, 1987; NICHD Early Child Care Research Network, 1996; S. W. Olds, 1989: Scarr, 1998.

4 months and received, on average, 33 hours of care each week. Child care arrangements varied widely in type and quality. Researchers measured the children's social, emotional, cognitive, and physical development at frequent intervals starting at the age of 1 month old.

The study showed that the amount and quality of care children received as well as the type and stability of care influenced specific aspects of development. Long days in child care have been associated with stress for 3- and 4-year-olds (Belsky et al., 2007; NICHD Early Child Care Research Network, 2003). And the 15 percent of 2- and 3-year-olds who experience more than one regular child care arrangement are at increased risk of behavior problems and are less likely to help and share (Morrissey, 2009).

On the other hand, children in child care centers with low child-staff ratios, small group sizes, and trained, sensitive, responsive caregivers who provide positive interactions and language stimulation tend to score higher on tests of language comprehension, cognition, and readiness for school than do children in lower-quality care. Their mothers also report fewer behavior problems (NICHD Early Child Care Research Network, 1999a, 2000, 2002). Children who received high-quality care before entering kindergarten are likely to have better vocabulary scores in fifth grade than children who received lower-quality care (Belsky et al., 2007).

However, factors related to child care are less influential than family characteristics, such as income, the home environment, the amount of mental stimulation the mother provides, and the mother's sensitivity to her child. These characteristics strongly predict developmental outcomes, regardless of how much time children spend in outside care

(Belsky et al., 2007; Marshall, 2004; NICHD Early Child Care Research Network, 1998a, 1998b, 2000, 2003).

Child care has no direct effect on attachment. However, when unstable, poor-quality, or more-than-minimal amounts of child care (10 or more hours a week) are combined with insensitive, unresponsive mothering, insecure attachment is more likely. On the other hand, high-quality care seems to help offset insensitive mothering (NICHD Early Child Care Research Network, 1997, 2001b).

It should not be surprising that what look like effects of child care often may be related to family characteristics. After all, stable families with favorable home environments are more able and therefore more likely to place their children in high-quality care. One area in which the NICHD study did find independent effects of child care was in interactions with peers. Between ages 2 and 3, children whose caregivers are sensitive and responsive tend to become more positive and competent in play with other children (NICHD Early Child Care Research Network, 2001a).

To sum up, the NICHD findings give high-quality child care good marks overall, especially for its impact on cognitive development and interaction with peers. Some observers say that the areas of concern the study pinpoints—stress levels in infants and toddlers and possible behavior problems related to amounts of care and multiple caregiving arrangements—might be counteracted by activities that enhance children's attachment to caregivers and peers, emphasize child-initiated learning and internalized motivation, and focus on group social development (Maccoby & Lewis, 2003).

The experiences of the first 3 years lay the foundation for future development. In Part IV, we'll see how young children build on that foundation.

what's your view

In the light of findings about effects of early child care, what advice would you give a new mother about the timing of her return to work and the selection of child care?

checkpoint
can you . . .

▷ Evaluate the impact of a mother's employment on her baby's well-being?

▷ List at least five criteria for good child care?

▷ Discuss the impact of child care and of family characteristics on emotional, social, and cognitive development?

summary and key terms

guidepost 1 — Foundations of Psychosocial Development

When and how do emotions develop, and how do babies show them?

- Crying, smiling, and laughing are early signs of emotion.
- Emotional development is orderly; complex emotions seem to develop from earlier, simpler ones.
- Self-conscious and evaluative emotions arise after the development of self-awareness.
- Emotional development is closely linked with brain development.
- Altruistic behavior and empathy typically emerge during the 2nd year of life and may result from the activity of mirror neurons. The roots of empathy can be seen in early infancy.
- Empathy is based on social cognition. Piaget suggested that egocentrism delays the development of this ability until middle childhood, but later research suggests that it begins much earlier.
- Between 9 and 12 months, infants begin to collaborate with caregivers on joint activities based on shared intentionality.

personality (*218*)

emotions (*218*)

self-conscious emotions (*221*)

self-awareness (*221*)

self-evaluative emotions (*222*)

altruistic behavior (*222*)

empathy (*222*)

mirror neurons (*223*)

social cognition (*223*)

egocentrism (*223*)

shared intentionality (*223*)

guidepost 2

How do infants show temperament differences, and how enduring are those differences?

- Many children seem to fall into one of three categories of temperament: easy, difficult, and slow-to-warm-up. Temperament patterns appear to be largely inborn and to have a biological basis. They are generally stable but can be modified by experience.
- Goodness of fit between a child's temperament and environmental demands aids adjustment.
- Cross-cultural differences in temperament may reflect child-raising practices.

temperament (*224*)

easy children (*224*)

difficult children (*224*)

slow-to-warm-up children (*224*)

goodness of fit (*226*)

guideposts for study

1. How do children's bodies change between ages 3 and 6?

2. What sleep patterns and problems tend to develop during early childhood?

3. How do children's brains develop between ages 3 and 6?

4. What are the main motor achievements of early childhood?

5. What are the nutritional needs of young children, and what risks are associated with undernutrition and obesity? What are the major health and safety risks for young children?

guidepost 1

How do children's bodies change between ages 3 and 6?

study smart

Patterns of Growth

Aspects of Physiological Development

In early childhood, children slim down and shoot up. They need less sleep and are more likely to develop sleep problems. They improve in running, hopping, skipping, jumping, and throwing balls. They also become better at tying shoelaces (in bows instead of knots), drawing with crayons (on paper rather than on walls), and pouring cereal (into the bowl, not onto the floor); and they begin to show a preference for using either the right or left hand.

BODILY GROWTH AND CHANGE

Children grow rapidly between ages 3 and 6 but less quickly than in infancy and toddlerhood. At about age 3, children begin to take on the slender, athletic appearance of childhood. As abdominal muscles develop, the toddler potbelly tightens. The trunk, arms, and legs grow longer. The head is still relatively large, but the other parts of the body continue to catch up as proportions steadily become more adultlike.

The pencil mark on the wall that shows Eve's height at 3 years is 38 inches from the floor, and she weighs about 30 pounds. Her twin brother Isaac, like most boys this age, is a little taller and heavier and has more muscle per pound of body weight, whereas Eve, like most girls, has more fatty tissue. Both boys and girls typically grow 2 to 3 inches a year during early childhood and gain about 4 to 6 pounds annually (Table 9.1). Boys' slight edge in height and weight continues until the growth spurt of puberty.

Muscular and skeletal growth progresses, making children stronger. Cartilage turns to bone at a faster rate than before, and bones become harder, giving the child a firmer shape and protecting the internal organs. These changes, coordinated by the still-maturing brain and nervous system, promote the development of a wide range of motor skills. The increased capacities of the respiratory and circulatory

At about age 6 and 50 inches in height, this girl is tall for her age.

TABLE 9.1	Physical Growth, Ages 3 to 6 (50th percentile*)			
	Height (inches)		Weight (pounds)	
Age	Boys	Girls	Boys	Girls
3	38.7	38.6	33.8	34.2
4	42.1	41.4	39.8	38.6
5	45.1	44	46.3	43.3
6	47.6	46.6	52.2	48.8

*Fifty percent of children in each category are above this height or weight level, and 50 percent are below it.

Source: McDowell, Fryar, Ogden, & Flegal, 2008; data from *Anthropometric Reference Data for Children and Adults: United States, 2003–2006,* National Health Statistics Report, No. 10, October 22, 2008.

systems build physical stamina and, along with the developing immune system, keep children healthier.

Sleep Patterns and Problems

Sleep patterns change throughout the growing-up years (Iglowstein, Jenni, Molinari, & Largo, 2003; Figure 9.1), and early childhood has its own distinct rhythms. Young children usually sleep more deeply at night than they will later in life. Most U.S. children average about 11 hours of sleep at night by age 5 and give up daytime naps

What sleep patterns and problems tend to develop during early childhood?

guidepost 2

FIGURE 9.1

Typical Sleep Requirements in Childhood

Unlike infants, who sleep about as long day and night, preschoolers get all or almost all their sleep in one long nighttime period. The number of hours of sleep steadily decreases throughout childhood, but individual children may need more or fewer hours than shown here.

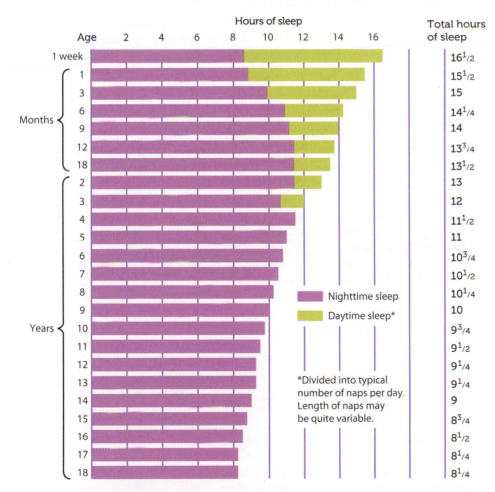

Source: Ferber, 1985; similar data in Iglowstein et al., 2003. Reprinted with the permission of Simon & Schuster, Inc., from *Solve Your Child's Sleep Problems,* by Richard Ferber. Copyright © 1985, 2006 by Richard Ferber, M.D. All rights reserved.

Regular, consistent sleep routines like reading before bedtime can minmize resistance to bedtime.

(Hoban, 2004). In some other cultures the timing of sleep may vary. Among the Gusii of Kenya, the Javanese in Indonesia, and the Zuni in New Mexico, young children have no regular bedtime and are allowed to stay up until they are sleepy. Among the Canadian Hare people, 3-year-olds take no naps but go to bed right after dinner and sleep as long as they wish in the morning (Broude, 1995).

Bedtime may bring on a form of separation anxiety, and the child may do all she or he can to avoid it. Young children may develop elaborate routines to put off retiring, and it may take them longer than before to fall asleep. More than half of U.S. parents or caregivers report that their preschool child stalls at bedtime and that it takes 15 minutes or more for the child to fall asleep. About one-third of preschoolers actively resist going to bed, and more than one-third awake at least once each night (National Sleep Foundation, 2004). Regular, consistent sleep routines can help minimize these problems. Children are likely to want a light left on and to sleep with a favorite toy or blanket. Such *transitional objects*, used repeatedly as bedtime companions, help a child shift from the dependence of infancy to the independence of later childhood. Young children who have become accustomed to going to sleep while feeding or rocking, however, may find it hard to fall asleep on their own (Hoban, 2004).

SLEEP DISTURBANCES AND DISORDERS

About 1 in 10 parents or caregivers of preschoolers say their child has a sleep problem (National Sleep Foundation, 2004). Sleep disturbances may be caused by accidental activation of the brain's motor control system (Hobson & Silvestri, 1999) or by incomplete arousal from a deep sleep (Hoban, 2004) or may be triggered by disordered breathing or restless leg movements (Guilleminault, Palombini, Pelayo, & Chervin, 2003). These disturbances tend to run in families (American Academy of Child & Adolescent Psychiatry [AACAP], 1997; Hobson & Silvestri, 1999; Hoban, 2004) and are often associated with separation anxiety (Petit, Touchette, Tremblay, Boivin, & Montplaisir, 2007). In most cases they are only occasional and usually are outgrown. Some sleep issues may be the result of ineffective parenting practices that exacerbate rather than ease the problem. Persistent sleep problems may indicate an emotional, physiological, or neurological condition that needs to be examined.

A child who experiences a *sleep* (or *night*) *terror* appears to awaken abruptly early in the night from a deep sleep in a state of agitation. The child may scream and sit up in bed, breathing rapidly and staring or thrashing about. Yet he is not really awake, quiets down quickly, and the next morning remembers nothing about the episode. Night terrors occur mostly between ages 3 and 13 (Laberge, Tremblay, Vitaro, & Montplaisir, 2000) and affect boys more often than girls (AACAP, 1997; Hobson & Silvestri, 1999).

Walking and talking during sleep are fairly common in early and middle childhood. Although sleepwalking itself is harmless, sleepwalkers may be in danger of hurting themselves (AACAP, 1997; Hoban, 2004; Vgontzas & Kales, 1999). However, it is best not to interrupt sleepwalking or night terrors, as interruptions may confuse and further frighten the child (Hoban, 2004; Vgontzas & Kales, 1999).

Nightmares are common during early childhood (Petit et al., 2007). They usually occur toward morning and are often brought on by staying up too late, eating a heavy meal close to bedtime, or overexcitement—for example, from watching an action-packed television program, seeing a terrifying movie, or hearing a frightening bedtime story (Vgontzas & Kales, 1999). An occasional bad dream is no cause for alarm, but frequent or persistent nightmares, especially those that make a child fearful or anxious during waking hours, may signal excessive stress (Hoban, 2004).

BED-WETTING

Most children stay dry, day and night, by age 3 to 5 years; but **enuresis**, repeated, involuntary urination at night by children old enough to be expected to have bladder control, is not unusual. About 10 to 15 percent of 5-year-olds, more commonly boys, wet the bed regularly, perhaps while sleeping deeply. More than half outgrow bed-wetting by age 8 without special help (Community Paediatrics Committee, 2005).

Children of preschool age normally recognize the sensation of a full bladder while asleep and awaken to empty it. Children who wet the bed do not yet have this awareness. Fewer than 1 percent of bed-wetters have a physical disorder, though they may have a small bladder capacity. Nor is persistent enuresis primarily an emotional, mental, or behavioral problem—though such problems can develop because of the way bed-wetters are treated by playmates and family (Community Paediatrics Committee, 2005; National Enuresis Society, 1995; Schmitt, 1997).

Enuresis runs in families. About 75 percent of bed-wetters have a close relative who also wets the bed, and identical twins are more concordant for the condition than fraternal twins (American Psychiatric Association, 1994; Fergusson, Horwood, & Shannon, 1986). The discovery of the approximate site of a gene linked to enuresis (von Gontard, Heron, & Joinson, 2011) points to heredity as a major factor, possibly in combination with slow motor maturation, allergies, or poor behavioral control (Goleman, 1995). The gene does not appear to account for occasional bed-wetting. Many children who wet the bed are lacking in an antidiuretic hormone, which concentrates urine during sleep. As a result, they produce more urine than their bladders can hold (National Enuresis Society, 1995).

Treatment is most effective if delayed until the child is able to understand and adhere to instructions. Enuresis alarms that wake the child when he or she begins to urinate can be helpful; however, the success rate is less than 50 percent even with older children who are highly motivated to overcome the problem. Drug therapy with desmopressin, a synthetic replacement for the hormone that reduces urine production during sleep, has become a standard treatment (Ramakrishnan, 2008). Recent studies on a treatment program that combines desmopressin with tolterodine, a bladder-control drug, showed a significant decrease in the risk of bed-wetting (Austin et al., 2008).

Children and their parents need to be reassured that enuresis is common and not serious. The child is not to blame and should not be punished. Generally parents need not do anything unless children themselves are distressed by bed-wetting. Enuresis that persists beyond age 8 to 10 may be related to poor self-concept or other psychological problems (Community Paediatrics Committee, 2005).

enuresis
Repeated urination in clothing or in bed.

Parents often view extended bed-wetting as deliberate, but generally it is not. It is a developmental issue, and no number of sticker charts or punishments will help a child outgrow enuresis until he or she is developmentally ready.

checkpoint
can you . . .

▷ Discuss age differences and cultural variations in sleep patterns?

▷ Identify four common sleep problems and give recommendations for handling them?

Brain Development

During the first few years of life, brain development is rapid and profound. This accelerated growth continues until about the age of 3 years. At this point, the brain is approximately 90 percent of adult weight (Gabbard, 1996). From ages 3 to 6, the most rapid brain growth occurs in the frontal areas that regulate planning and goal setting. Synapses connecting neighboring neurons continue to form during this time, and the density of synapses in the prefrontal cortex peaks at age 4 (Lenroot & Giedd, 2006). In addition, myelin (a fatty substance that coats the axons of nerve fibers and accelerates neural conduction) continues to form, and the myelination of pathways for hearing is completed (Benes, Turtle, Khan, & Farol, 1994). By age 6, the brain has attained about 95 percent of its peak volume. However, wide individual differences exist. Two normally functioning children of the same age could have as much as a 50 percent difference in brain volume (Lenroot & Giedd, 2006). From ages 6 to 11, rapid brain growth occurs in areas that support associative thinking, language, and spatial relations (P. M. Thompson et al., 2000).

The *corpus callosum* is a thick band of nerve fibers that connects both hemisphere of the brain and allows them to communicate with each other. The corpus callosum

How do children's brains develop between ages 3 and 6?

guidepost 3

Cuba, where child deaths have dropped more than 80 percent since 1970. In contrast, Haitian children still die at a rate of 133 per 1,000, almost double the rate in Bolivia, which has the next worst mortality record in the Americas (WHO, 2003).

In most countries, with the exception of China, India, Pakistan, and Nepal, boys are more likely to die than girls. In China, where families traditionally prefer boys, young girls have a 33 percent greater risk of dying—often, it has been reported, through abandonment, infanticide (Carmichael, 2004; Hudson & den Boer, 2004; Lee, 2004; Rosenthal, 2003), or benign neglect. Children in poor countries and children of the poor in rich countries are most likely to die young. Survival gains have been slower in rural than in urban areas and, in some countries, such as the United States, have disproportionately benefited those with higher incomes. But even poor U.S. children are less likely to die young than better-off children in Africa (WHO, 2003).

> **what's your view**
>
> What might be done to produce more rapid and more evenly distributed improvements in child mortality throughout the world?

earlier in this chapter) are quite different from those of infants or toddlers. Beginning at age 2, a healthy diet is the same as for adults: primarily fruits and vegetables, whole grains, low-fat and nonfat dairy products, beans, fish, and lean meats (American Heart Association et al., 2006).

Obesity is a serious problem among U.S. preschoolers. In 2003–2006, more than 12 percent of 2- to 5-year-olds had a body mass index (BMI) at or above the 95th percentile for their age, and about 12 percent more were at or above the 85th percentile (Ogden, Carroll, & Flegal, 2008). The greatest increase in prevalence of obesity is among children in low-income families (Ritchie et al., 2001), cutting across all ethnic groups (AAP Committee on Nutrition, 2003; Center for Weight and Health, 2001).

In 2008, Pixar films released *Wall-E,* an animated science fiction film in which humans were depicted as obese and sedentary, floating in a mechanized environment. Where do you think humans are headed if we do not change our ways? Could this view of humanity ever become a reality?

Worldwide, an estimated 22 million children under age 5 are obese (Belizzi, 2002). As junk food spreads through the developing world, as many as 20 to 25 percent of 4-year-olds in some countries, such as Egypt, Morocco, and Zambia, are overweight or obese—a larger proportion than are malnourished.

A tendency toward obesity can be hereditary, but the main factors driving the obesity epidemic are environmental (AAP, 2004). Excessive weight gain hinges on caloric intake and lack of exercise (AAP Committee on Nutrition, 2003). As growth slows, preschoolers need fewer calories in proportion to their weight than they did before. A key to preventing obesity may be to make sure older preschoolers are served appropriate portions—and not to force them to clean their plates (Rolls, Engell, & Birch, 2000; Table 9.3). Children 1 or 2 years old who are at risk of overweight or obesity may be given reduced fat (2 percent) milk; after age 2 they can drink skim (fat-free) milk (Daniels, Greer, & the Committee on Nutrition, 2008). Too little physical activity is an important factor in obesity as well. In a longitudinal study of 8,158 U.S. children, each additional hour of TV watching above 2 hours per day increased the likelihood of obesity at age 30 by 7 percent (Viner & Cole, 2005).

What children eat is as important as how much they eat. To avoid obesity and prevent cardiac problems, young children should get only about 30 percent of their total calories from fat, and no more than one-third of fat calories should come from saturated fat. Lean meat and dairy foods should remain in the diet to provide protein, iron, and calcium. Milk and other dairy products should be skim or low fat (AAP

> **what's your view**
>
> Much television advertising aimed at young children fosters poor nutrition by promoting fats and sugars rather than proteins and vitamins. How might parents counteract these pressures?

Committee on Nutrition, 2006). Studies have found no negative effects on height, weight, body mass, or neurological development from a moderately low-fat diet (Rask-Nissilä et al., 2000; Shea et al., 1993).

Prevention of obesity in the early years, when excessive weight gain usually begins, is critical; the long-term success of treatment, especially when it is delayed, is limited (AAP Committee on Nutrition, 2003; Quattrin, Liu, Shaw, Shine, & Chiang, 2005). Overweight children, especially those who have overweight parents, tend to become obese adults (AAP Committee on Nutrition, 2003; Whitaker, Wright, Pepe, Seidel, & Dietz, 1997), and excess body mass is a threat to health. Early childhood is a good time to treat obesity, when a child's diet is still subject to parental influence or control (Quattrin et al., 2005; Whitaker et al., 1997).

UNDERNUTRITION

Undernutrition is an underlying cause in more than half of all deaths before age 5 (Bryce, Boschi-Pinto, Shibuya, Black, & the WHO Child Health Epidemiology Reference Group, 2005). South Asia has the highest level of undernutrition; 42 percent of young children in South Asia are moderately or severely underweight as compared to 28 percent in sub-Saharan Africa, 7 percent in Latin America and the Caribbean, and 25 percent of young children worldwide (UNICEF, 2008a). Even in the United States, 17 percent of children under age 18 lived in food-insecure households in 2007 (Federal

While a healthy diet is important for the prevention of obesity, physical activity is also key.

TABLE 9.3 Encouraging Healthy Eating Habits
• Parents, not children, should choose mealtimes.
• If the child is not overweight, allow him or her to decide how much to eat. Don't pressure the child to clean the plate.
• Serve portions appropriate to the child's size and age.
• Serve simple, easily identifiable foods. Preschoolers often balk at mixed dishes such as casseroles.
• Serve finger foods as often as possible.
• Introduce only one new food at a time, along with familiar food the child likes. Offer small servings of new or disliked foods; give second helpings if wanted.
• After a reasonable time, remove the food and do not serve more until the next meal. A healthy child will not suffer from missing a meal, and children need to learn that certain times are appropriate for eating.
• Give the child a choice of foods containing similar nutrients: rye or whole wheat bread, a peach or an apple, yogurt or milk.
• Serve nonfat or lowfat dairy products as sources of calcium and protein.
• Encourage a child to help prepare food; a child can help make sandwiches or mix and spoon out cookie dough.
• Limit snacking while watching television or videos. Discourage nutrient-poor foods such as salty snacks, fried foods, ice cream, cookies, and sweetened beverages, and instead suggest nutritious snack foods, such as fruits and raw vegetables.
• Turn childish delights to advantage. Serve food in appealing dishes; dress it up with garnishes or little toys; make a party out of a meal.
• Don't fight rituals in which a child eats foods one at a time, in a certain order.
• Have regular family meals. Make mealtimes pleasant with conversation on interesting topics, keeping talk about eating itself to a minimum.

Sources: American Heart Association et al., 2006; Rolls, Engell, & Birch, 2000; Williams & Caliendo, 1984.

In 2010, ABC released a mini-series called *Jamie Oliver's Food Revolution.* Many people were shocked at his demonstration of how far removed the children featured in his program were from real food. In a striking segment, first graders were unable to identify fresh tomatoes, cauliflower, mushrooms, eggplant, or potatoes.

FOOD SECURITY

9.2

Most families in the United States are food secure—they have dependable access to enough food to support healthy living. Sadly, a growing number of families must deal with the challenges of insufficient food supplies for their households. Food insecurity is experienced when (1) the availability of future food is uncertain, (2) the amount and kind of food required for a healthy lifestyle is insufficient, or (3) individuals must resort to socially unacceptable ways to acquire food (NRC, 2006, p. 44).

In a recent study, the U.S. Department of Agriculture found that more than 36 million people suffered from "very low food security," a figure representing 12 percent of all Americans. The number in the worst-off category suffering the greatest hunger levels has risen 40 percent since 2000, and the prevalence of food insecurity for households with children is about twice that for households without children (Nord, Andrews, & Carlson, 2008).

Families with insufficient resources to provide food for the entire household usually try to protect children from disrupted eating and reduced food intake. Even so, 691,000 children went hungry in 2007, a 50 percent increase over 2006 statistics (Nord et al., 2008). With the challenging economic conditions currently facing the United States, it is highly likely this figure will continue to rise: "Increased demand at food stamp and WIC offices, social service agencies, and emergency food providers shows that growing economic dislocation is overwhelming the nation's first responders to hunger," notes Jim Weill, president of the Food Research and Action Center (FRAC).

Not surprisingly, food insecurity adversely affects children's health, cognitive abilities, and socioemotional well-being. The quality of food consumed is affected along with the quantity. As food budgets shrink, the first items to drop out of the diet are usually healthy foods such as whole grains, lean meats, dairy products, vegetables, and fruit. Energy-rich starches, sweets, and fats, which are often nutrient-poor, typically offer the cheapest way to fill hungry stomachs (Drewnowski & Eichelsdoerfer, 2009). Relatively moderate levels of food insecurity and lower quality diet have been linked to poor health, decreased learning capabilities, lowered motivation levels, and increased anxiety and depression.

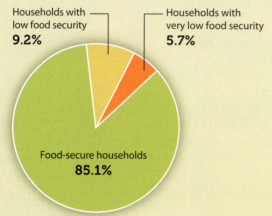

Food security status of U.S. households, 2011

Households with low food security
9.2%

Households with very low food security
5.7%

Food-secure households
85.1%

Food-insecure households include low and very low food security.

Source: Data from U.S. Department of Agriculture Economic Research Service, 2011.

what's your view

In some developing nations, famine is widespread and severe malnutrition prevalent. In the United States the effects of hunger are generally less severe, in part because federal nutrition programs provide assistance to low-income families. What programs are you aware of? What are the benefits (and drawbacks) of these types of programs?

Interagency Forum on Child and Family Statistics, 2007). See Box 9.2 for more about food insecurity.

Because undernourished children usually live in extremely deprived circumstances, the specific effects of malnutrition may be hard to determine. However, taken together, these deprivations may negatively affect not only growth and physical well-being but cognitive and psychosocial development as well. In an analysis of data on a nationally representative sample of 3,286 children 6 to 11 years old, those whose families had insufficient food were more likely to do poorly on arithmetic tests, to have repeated a grade, to have seen a psychologist, and to have had difficulty getting along with other children (Alaimo, Olson, & Frongillo, 2001). Moreover, cognitive effects of malnutrition may be long lasting. Among 1,559 children born on the island of Mauritius in a single year, those who were undernourished at age 3 had poorer verbal and spatial abilities, reading skills, scholastic ability, and neuropsychological performance than their peers at age 11 (Liu, Raine, Venables, Dalais, & Mednick, 2003).

> In view of childhood undernutrition's apparent long-term effects on physical, social, and cognitive development, what can and should be done to combat it?

Some studies suggest that some of the effects of malnutrition can be lessened with improved diet (Engle et al., 2007; Lewit & Kerrebrock, 1997), but the most effective treatments go beyond physical care. A longitudinal study (Grantham-McGregor, Powell, Walker, Chang, & Fletcher, 1994) followed two groups of Jamaican children with low developmental levels who had been hospitalized for severe undernourishment in infancy or toddlerhood and who came from extremely poor, often unstable homes. Health care paraprofessionals played with an experimental group in the hospital and, after discharge, visited them at home every week for 3 years, showing the mothers how to make toys and encouraging them to interact with their children. Three years after the program stopped, the experimental group's IQs were well above those of a control group who had received only standard medical care (though not as high as those of a third, well-nourished group). Furthermore, the IQs of the experimental group remained higher than those of the control group as much as 14 years after leaving the hospital.

Early education may help counter the effects of undernourishment. In the Jamaican study, the mothers in the experimental group enrolled their children in preschools at earlier ages than did the mothers in the control group. In another Mauritian study, 100 children 3 to 5 years old received nutritional supplements and medical examinations and were placed in special preschools with small classes. At age 17, these children had lower rates of antisocial behavior and mental health problems than a control group. The effects were greatest among those who had been undernourished to begin with (Raine, Mellingen, Liu, Venables, & Mednick, 2003).

FOOD ALLERGIES

A food allergy is an abnormal immune system response to a specific food. Reactions can range from tingling in the mouth and hives to more serious, life-threatening reactions like shortness of breath and even death. Ninety percent of food allergies can be attributed to seven foods: milk, eggs, peanuts, tree nuts, fish, soy, and wheat (Sampson, 2004; Sicherer, 2002). Food allergies are more prevalent in children than adults, and most children will outgrow their allergies (Branum & Lukas, 2008). In 2007, 4 out of every 100 children suffered from some type of food allergy.

Research on children under age 18 has demonstrated an increase in the prevalence of food allergies over the past 10 years (Branum & Lukacs, 2008). Hospitalizations related to food allergies have increased significantly as show in Figure 9.3. Changes in diet, how foods are processed, and decreased vitamin D based upon less exposure to the sun have all been suggested as contributors to the increase in allergy rates. Another theory—that society is too clean and that children's immune systems are less mature because they are not exposed to enough dirt and germs—has also been explored. Although possible explanations abound, not enough evidence exists to pinpoint a cause.

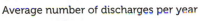

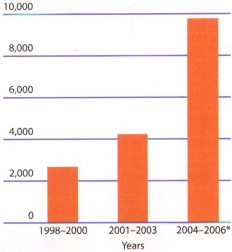

Average number of discharges per year

FIGURE 9.3

Average Number of Hospital Discharges per Year among Children Under Age 18 Years with Any Diagnosis Related to Food Allergy: United States, 1998–2006

Recent data show diagnoses related to food allergies have increased among children birth to 17 years old.

*Statistically significant trend.

From the CDC/NCHS, National Health Interview Survey.

Source: Branum & Lukacs, 2008.

ORAL HEALTH

By age 3, all the primary (baby) teeth are in place, and the permanent teeth, which will begin to appear at about age 6, are developing. Thus parents usually can safely ignore the common habit of thumbsucking in children under age 4. If children stop sucking thumbs or fingers by that age, their permanent teeth are not likely to be affected (American Dental Association, 2007).

Use of fluoride and improved dental care have dramatically reduced the incidence of tooth decay since the 1970s, but disadvantaged children still have more untreated cavities than other children (Bloom, Cohen, Vickerie, & Wondimu, 2003; Brown, Wall, & Lazar, 2000). Tooth decay in early childhood often stems from overconsumption of sweetened milk and juices in infancy together with a lack of regular dental care. Some of the worst effects have been found in children who take bottles to bed with them and bathe their teeth in sugar over the course of an afternoon or evening (American Academy of Pediatrics, 2000). In a longitudinal study of 642 Iowa children followed from age 1 through 5, consumption of regular (nondiet) soda pop, powdered beverages, and, to a lesser extent, 100-percent juice increased the risk of tooth decay (Marshall et al., 2003). Though decay in primary teeth has declined overall from the early 1970s, there has been a slight reverse in this trend since the mid-1990s (Centers for Disease Control and Prevention, 2007b).

ACCIDENTAL INJURIES AND DEATHS

Because young children are naturally venturesome and often are unaware of danger, it is hard for caregivers to protect them from harm without *over*protecting them. Although most cuts, bumps, and scrapes are "kissed away" and quickly forgotten, some accidental injuries result in lasting damage or death. Indeed, accidents are the leading cause of death after infancy throughout childhood and adolescence in the United States (Heron et al., 2009). More than 800,000 children die worldwide each year from burns, drowning, car crashes, falls, poisonings, and other accidents (WHO, 2008).

Many kindergartners and first graders walk alone to school, often crossing busy streets without traffic lights, although they may not know how to do this safely (Zeedyk, Wallace, & Spry, 2002). Some children are risk-prone. In one study, 5- and 6-year-olds who tended to take risks in a gambling game were more likely than their peers to say it was safe to cross a busy street between cars without a traffic light or crosswalk (Hoffrage, Weber, Hertwig, & Chase, 2003).

All 50 states and the District of Columbia require young children to ride in specially designed car seats or to wear seat belts. Four-year-olds who graduate from car seats to lap and shoulder belts may need booster seats until they grow bigger. Airbags are designed to protect adults, not children. They have been show to *increase* the risk of fatal injury to children under age 13 who are riding in the front seat. Campaigns to keep children in the back seats of cars have reduced the number of child deaths in motor vehicle crashes by 200 a year from 1996 to 2003 (Glassbrenner, Carra, & Nichols, 2005).

Most deaths from injuries, especially among preschoolers, occur in the home—from fires, drowning in bathtubs, suffocation, poisoning, or falls (Nagaraja et al., 2005). Everyday medications, such as aspirin, acetaminophen, cold and cough preparations, and even vitamins and minerals can be dangerous to inquisitive young children unless they are stored out of reach. During 2001–2003, more than 50,000 children age 4 and under were treated each year in U.S. hospital emergency departments for unintentional exposure to prescription and over-the-counter medicines (Burt, Annest, Ballesteros, & Budnitz, 2006).

U.S. laws requiring childproof caps on medicine bottles and other dangerous household products, regulation of product safety, car seats for young children, mandatory helmets for bicycle riders, and safe storage of firearms and of medicines have improved child safety. Making playgrounds safer would be another valuable measure. (Table 9.4 summarizes suggestions for reducing accident risks in various settings.)

checkpoint
can you . . .

▷ Summarize preschoolers' dietary needs and explain why obesity and tooth decay can become concerns at this age?

▷ Identify effects of malnutrition and factors that may influence its long-term outcome?

▷ Identify the most common foods that cause allergic reactions?

The typical symbol used for poison now is "Mr. Yuk"— a grimacing, green cartoon face sticking his tongue out. This graphic was put into use when researchers and public health agencies realized the traditional skull and crossbones, rather than indicating danger to young children, intrigued and interested them in the contents of containers.

checkpoint
can you . . .

▷ Compare the health status of young children in developed and developing countries?

▷ Tell where and how young children are most likely to be injured, and list ways in which injuries can be avoided?

TABLE 9.4 Reducing Accident Risks for Children

Activity	Precautions
Bicycling	Helmets reduce risk of head injury by 85 percent and brain injury by 88 percent.
Skateboarding and rollerblading	Children should wear helmets and protective padding on knees, elbows, and wrists.
Using fireworks	Families should not purchase fireworks for home use.
Lawn mowing	Children under 12 should not operate walk-behind mowers; those under 14 should not operate ride-on mowers; small children should not be close to a moving mower.
Swimming	Swimming pools should not be installed in backyards of homes with children under 5; pools already in place need a high fence all around, with gates having high, out-of-reach, self-closing latches. Adults need to watch children very closely near pools, lakes, and other bodies of water.
Playing on a playground	A safe surface under swings, slides, and other equipment can be 10-inch-deep sand, 12-inch-deep wood chips, or rubber outdoor mats; separate areas should be maintained for active play and quiet play, for older and younger children.
Using firearms	Guns should be kept unloaded and locked up, with bullets locked in a separate place; children should not have access to keys; adults should talk with children about the risks of gun injury.
Eating	To prevent choking, young children should not eat hard candies, nuts, grapes, and hot dogs (unless sliced lengthwise, then across); food should be cut into small pieces; children should not eat while talking, running, jumping, or lying down.
Ingesting toxic substances	Only drugs and toxic household products with safety caps should be used; toxic products should be stored out of children's reach. Suspected poisoning should be reported immediately to the nearest poison control center.
Riding in motor vehicles	Young children should sit in approved car seats, in the backseat. Adults should observe traffic laws and avoid aggressive drivers.

Source: Adapted in part from American Academy of Pediatrics (AAP) Committee on Injury and Poison Prevention, 1995, 2000; Rivara, 1999; Shannon, 2000.

HEALTH IN CONTEXT: ENVIRONMENTAL INFLUENCES

Why do some children have more illnesses or injuries than others? The genetic heritage contributes: Some children seem predisposed toward some medical conditions. In addition, environmental factors play major roles.

Socioeconomic Status and Race/Ethnicity The lower a family's socioeconomic status (SES), the greater a child's risks of illness, injury, and death (Chen, Matthews, & Boyce, 2002). Poor children—who represent 1 in 5 U.S. children under age 6 and are disproportionately minority children—are more likely than other children to have chronic conditions and activity limitations, to lack health insurance, and to have unmet medical and dental needs. However, the general health of poor children has been improving; between 1984 and 2003, the percentage of poor children in very good or excellent health rose from 62 percent to 71 percent, as compared with 86 to

89 percent for nonpoor children (Federal Interagency Forum on Child and Family Statistics, 2005, 2007).

Medicaid, a government program that provides medical assistance to eligible low-income persons and families, has been a safety net for many poor children since 1965. However, it has not reached millions of children whose families earn too much to qualify but too little to afford private insurance. In 1997 the federal government created the State Children's Health Insurance Program (SCHIP) to help states extend health care coverage to uninsured children in poor and near-poor families. Now known simply as CHIP, legislation passed in 2009 expanded the program and extended the coverage from 7 million to 11 million children (Centers for Medicare & Medicaid Services, 2009). Even with the expansion, health officials project there are about 7.3 million uninsured children in the United States in 2010 (Federal Interagency Forum on Child and Family Statistics, 2012). Children without insurance are more than 14 times as likely as children with insurance to lack a usual source of health care (Federal Interagency Forum on Child and Family Statistics, 2007).

Access to quality health care is a particular problem among black and Latino children, especially those who are poor or near poor (Flores, Olson, & Tomany-Korman, 2005). According to the Children's Defense Fund, 1 in 5 Latino children and 1 in 8 black children are uninsured compared with a rate of 1 in 13 for white children (Children's Defense Fund, 2008b). Language and cultural barriers and the need for more Latino care providers may help explain some of these disparities (Flores et al., 2002). Even Asian American children, who tend to be in better health than non-Hispanic white children, are less likely to access and use health care, perhaps because of similar barriers (NCHS, 2005; Yu, Huang, & Singh, 2004).

Homelessness Homelessness results from complex circumstances that force people to choose between food, shelter, and other basic needs (National Coalition for the Homeless, 2009). Since the 1980s, as affordable rental housing has become scarce and poverty has spread, homelessness has increased dramatically in the United States. An estimated 1.35 million children experience homelessness each year (National Coalition for the Homeless, 2009).

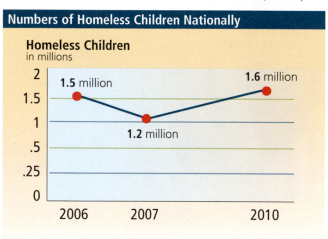

Numbers of Homeless Children Nationally

Homeless Children in millions

FIGURE 9.4

Families with Children as a Percentage of the Homeless Population in U.S. Cities

When people began to lose jobs in the economic downturn in the first decade in the 2000s, more children became homeless as this graph indicates.

Source: America's Youngest Outcasts, 2011.

Families now make up 33 percent of the homeless population, and the proportion is higher in rural areas (National Coalition for the Homeless, 2009). In fact, with the economic downturn in the late 2000s, the number of homeless children has increased to about one in every 45 children is homeless (America's Youngest Outcasts, 2011; Figure 9.4.) Many homeless families are headed by single mothers in their 20s (Buckner, Bassuk, Weinreb, & Brooks, 1999; Park, Metraux, & Culhane, 2010). Often these families are fleeing domestic violence (National Coalition for the Homeless, 2009).

Many homeless children spend their crucial early years in unstable, insecure, and often unsanitary environments. They and their parents may be cut off from a supportive community, family ties, and institutional resources and from ready access to medical care and schooling; and they often are unable to find stable housing again. These children suffer more health problems than poor children who have homes, and they are more likely to die in infancy. They are three times more likely than other children to lack immunizations and two to three times more likely to have iron deficiency anemia. They experience higher rates of several health problems including diarrhea, respiratory, skin, and eye and ear infections, asthma, and other chronic diseases. Homeless children also tend to suffer severe depression and anxiety and to have neurological

Families with children are the fastest-growing part of the homeless population. Homeless children tend to have more health problems than children with homes.

and visual deficits, developmental delays, behavior problems, and learning difficulties. As many as half do not go to school; if they do, they tend to have problems, partly because they miss a lot of it and have no place to do homework. They tend to do poorly on standardized reading and math tests, even when their cognitive functioning is normal, they are more likely to repeat a grade or be placed in special classes than are children with homes (AAP Committee on Community Health Services, 1996; Children's Defense Fund, 2004; Rubin et al., 1996; Weinreb et al., 2002). In large cities that have safe housing for poor and homeless families in stable, lower-poverty neighborhoods, the children's behavior and school performance improved greatly (CDF, 2004).

Exposure to Smoking, Air Pollution, Pesticides, and Lead Parental smoking is a preventable cause of childhood illness and death. The potential damage caused by exposure to tobacco smoke is greatest during the early years of life (DiFranza, Aligne, & Weitzman, 2004) when bodies are still developing. Children exposed to parental smoke are at increased risk of respiratory infections such as bronchitis and pneumonia, ear problems, worsened asthma, and slowed lung growth.

Air pollution is associated with increased risks of death and of chronic respiratory disease. Environmental contaminants also may play a role in certain childhood cancers, neurological disorders, attention-deficit/hyperactivity disorder, and mental retardation (Goldman et al., 2004; Woodruff et al., 2004). In 2006, 55 percent of U.S. children up to age 17 lived in counties that failed to meet one or more national air quality standard (Federal Interagency Forum on Child and Family Statistics, 2009).

Children are more vulnerable than adults to chronic pesticide damage (Goldman et al., 2004). There is some, though not definitive, evidence that low-dose pesticide exposure may affect the developing brain (Weiss, Amler, & Amler, 2004). Pesticide exposure is greater in children in agricultural and inner-city families (Dilworth-Bart & Moore, 2006). More than half of all reported pesticide poisonings—almost 50,000 per year—occur in children younger than age 6 (Weiss et al., 2004).

Children can get elevated concentrations of lead from lead-contaminated food or water, from airborne industrial wastes, from putting contaminated fingers in their mouths, or from inhaling dust or playing with paint chips in homes or schools where

Young children who live in old, dilapidated buildings with peeling lead paint are at risk for lead poisoning, which can adversely affect the developing brain.

TABLE 10.2 Immature Aspects of Preoperational Thought (according to Piaget)

Limitation	Description	Example
Centration: Inability to decenter	Children focus on one aspect of a situation and neglect others.	Jacob teases his younger sister that he has more juice than she does because his juice box has been poured into a tall, skinny glass, but hers has been poured into a short, wide glass.
Irreversibility	Children fail to understand that some operations or actions can be reversed, restoring the original situation.	Jacob does not realize that the juice in each glass can be poured back into the juice box from which it came, contradicting his claim that he has more than his sister.
Focus on states rather than on transformations	Children fail to understand the significance of the transformation between states.	In the conservation task, Jacob does not understand that transforming the shape of a liquid (pouring it from one container into another) does not change the amount.
Transductive reasoning	Children do not use deductive or inductive reasoning; instead they jump from one particular to another and see cause where none exists.	Luis was mean to his sister. Then she got sick. Luis concludes that he made his sister sick.
Egocentrism	Children assume everyone else thinks, perceives, and feels as they do.	Kara doesn't realize that she needs to turn a book around so that her father can see the picture she is asking him to explain to her. Instead, she holds the book directly in front of her, so only she can see it.
Animism	Children attribute life to inanimate objects.	Amanda says that spring is trying to come but winter is saying, "I won't go! I won't go!"
Inability to distinguish appearance from reality	Children confuse what is real with outward appearance.	Courtney is confused by a sponge made to look like a rock. She states that it looks like a rock and it really is a rock.

As this child pretends to listen to her father's heart, she is showing a major cognitive achievement, deferred imitation—the ability to repeat an action she observed some time before.

to use a simple map to find or place an object at the corresponding location in a similarly shaped but much larger space. Some 90 percent of 5-year-olds but only 60 percent of 4-year-olds were able to do so (Vasilyeva & Huttenlocher, 2004).

Understanding Causality Piaget maintained that preoperational children cannot yet reason logically about cause and effect. Instead, he said, they reason by **transduction**. They mentally link two events, especially events close in time, whether or not there is logically a causal relationship. For example, Luis may think that his "bad" thoughts or behavior caused his own or his sister's illness or his parents' divorce.

Piaget was incorrect in believing that young children could not understand causality. When tested in situations that are appropriate to their overall level of cognitive development, young children do grasp cause and effect. In naturalistic observations of 2½- to 5-year-olds' everyday conversations with their parents, children showed flexible causal reasoning, appropriate to the subject. Types of explanations ranged from physical ("The scissors have to be clean so I can cut better") to social–conventional ("I have to stop now because you said to") (Hickling & Wellman, 2001). However, preschoolers seem to view all causal relationships as equally and absolutely predictable. In one series of experiments, 3- to 5-year-olds, unlike adults, were just as sure that a person who does not wash his or her hands before eating will get sick as they were that a person who jumps up will come down (Kalish, 1998).

transduction
In Piaget's terminology, preoperational child's tendency to mentally link particular experiences, whether or not there is logically a causal relationship.

Understanding Identities and Categorization The world becomes more orderly and predictable as preschool children develop a better understanding of *identities:* the concept that people and many things are basically the same even if they change in form, size, or appearance. For example, putting on a wig does not make a person a different person; rather, it is just a surface change in appearance. This understanding underlies the emerging self-concept (see Chapter 11), and many of the processes involved in understanding the identity of others are mirrored in the understanding of one's own identity.

Categorization, or classification, requires a child to identify similarities and differences. By age 4, many children can classify by two criteria, such as color and shape. Children use this ability to order many aspects of their lives, categorizing people as "good" or "bad," "nice" or "mean," and so forth.

One type of categorization is the ability to distinguish living from nonliving things. When Piaget asked young children whether the wind and the clouds were alive, their answers led him to think they were confused about what is alive and what is not. The tendency to attribute life to objects that are not alive is called **animism**. However, when later researchers questioned 3- and 4-year-olds about something more familiar to them— differences between a rock, a person, and a doll—the children showed they understood that people are alive and rocks and dolls are not. They did not attribute thoughts or emotions to rocks, and they cited the fact that dolls cannot move on their own as evidence that dolls are not alive (Gelman, Spelke, & Meck, 1983; Jipson & Gelman, 2007). In general, it appears that children attribute animism to items that share characteristics with living things, for example, things that move, make sounds, or have lifelike features such as eyes.

animism
Tendency to attribute life to objects that are not alive.

Understanding Number As we discussed in Chapter 7, research by Karen Wynn suggests that infants as young as 4½ months have a rudimentary concept of number. They seem to know that if one doll is added to another doll, there should be two dolls, not just one. Other research has found that *ordinality*—the concept of comparing quantities (*more* or *less*, *bigger* or *smaller*)—seems to begin at around 9 to 11 months and at first is limited to comparisons of very few objects (Brannon, 2002; Siegler, 1998). By age 4, most children have words for comparing quantities. They can say that one tree is *bigger* than another or that one cup holds *more* juice than another. If they have one cookie and then get another cookie, they know they have more cookies than they had before and that if they give one cookie to another child, they have fewer cookies. They also can solve numerical ordinality problems ("Megan picked six apples, and Joshua picked four apples; which child picked more?") with up to nine objects (Byrnes & Fox, 1998).

Not until age 3½ or older do most children consistently apply the *cardinality* principle in counting (Sarnecka & Carey, 2007; Wynn, 1990). That is, when asked to count six items, children younger than 3½ tend to recite the number-names (one through six) but not to say how many items there are altogether (six). However, there is some evidence that children as young as 2½ use cardinality in practical situations, such as checking to make sure which plate has more cookies on it (Gelman, 2006). By age 5, most children can count to 20 or more and know the relative sizes of the numbers 1 through 10 (Siegler, 1998). Children intuitively devise strategies for adding by counting on their fingers or by using other objects (Naito & Miura, 2001).

By the time they enter elementary school, most children have developed basic "number sense" (Jordan, Kaplan, Oláh, & Locunia, 2006). This basic level of number skills (Table 10.3) includes *counting*, *number knowledge* (ordinality), *number transformations* (simple addition and subtraction), *estimation* ("Is this group of dots more or less than 5?"), and recognition of *number patterns* (2 plus 2 equals 4, and so does 3 plus 1).

Counting

TABLE 10.4 Tests of Various Kinds of Conservation

Conservation Task	What Child Is Shown*	Transformation	Question for Child	Preoperational Child's Usual Answers
Number	Two equal, parallel rows of candies	Space the candies in one row farther apart.	"Are there the same number of candies in each row or does one row have more?"	"The longer one has more."
Length	Two parallel sticks of the same length	Move one stick to the right.	"Are both sticks the same size or is one longer?"	"The one on the right (or left) is longer."
Liquid	Two identical glasses holding equal amounts of liquid	Pour liquid from one glass into a taller, narrower glass.	"Do both glasses have the same amount of liquid or does one have more?"	"The taller one has more."
Matter (mass)	Two balls of clay of the same size	Roll one ball into a sausage shape.	"Do both pieces have the same amount of clay or does one have more?"	"The sausage has more."
Weight	Two balls of clay of the same weight	Roll one ball into a sausage shape.	"Do both weigh the same or does one weigh more?"	"The sausage weighs more."
Area	Two toy rabbits, two pieces of cardboard (representing grassy fields), with blocks or toys (representing barns on the fields); same number of "barns" on each board	Rearrange the blocks on one piece of cardboard.	"Does each rabbit have the same amount of grass to eat or does one have more?"	"The one with the blocks close together has more to eat."
Volume	Two glasses of water with two equal-sized balls of clay in them	Roll one ball into a sausage shape.	"If we put the sausage back in the glass, will the water be the same height in each glass, or will one be higher?"	"The water in the glass with the sausage will be higher."

*Child then acknowledges that both items are equal.

checkpoint
can you...

▷ Tell how centration limits preoperational thought?

▷ Discuss research that challenges Piaget's views on egocentrism in early childhood?

▷ Give several reasons preoperational children have difficulty with conservation?

theory of mind
Awareness and understanding of mental processes.

failure to understand that an action can go in two or more directions. Because their thinking is concrete, preoperational children cannot mentally reverse the action and realize that the original state of the water can be restored by pouring it back into the other glass, and thus it must be the same. Preoperational children commonly think as if they were watching a slide show with a series of static frames: they *focus on successive states*, said Piaget, and do not recognize the transformation from one state to another.

DO YOUNG CHILDREN HAVE THEORIES OF MIND?

Theory of mind is the awareness of the broad range of human mental states—beliefs, intents, desires, dreams, and so forth—and the understanding that others have their own distinctive beliefs, desires and intentions. Having a theory of mind allows us to understand and predict the behavior of others and makes the social world understandable.

Piaget (1929) was the first scholar to investigate children's theory of mind. He sought to determine children's understanding of mind by asking them questions such as "Where do dreams come from?" and "What do you think with?" On the basis of their answers, he concluded that children younger than 6 cannot distinguish between thoughts or dreams and real physical entities and therefore have no theory of mind. However, more recent research indicates that between ages 2 and 5, and especially around age 4, children's knowledge about mental processes grows dramatically.

Again, methodology seems to have made the difference. Piaget's questions were abstract, and he expected children to be able to put their understanding into words. Contemporary researchers observe children in everyday activities or give them concrete examples. In this way, we have learned, for example, that 3-year-olds can tell the difference between a boy who has a cookie and a boy who is thinking about a cookie; they know which boy can touch, share, and eat it (Astington, 1993). Let's look at several aspects of theory of mind.

> We can see how important theory of mind is when we see what happens when it is broken, as in autism. Researchers believe that the failure to adequately develop theory of mind is one of the fundamental deficits found in this disorder.
>
> Baron-Cohen, Leslie, & Frith, 1985

Knowledge about Thinking and Mental States Between ages 3 and 5, children come to understand that thinking goes on inside the mind; that it can deal with either real or imaginary things; that someone can be thinking of one thing while doing or looking at something else; that a person whose eyes and ears are covered can think about objects; that someone who looks pensive is probably thinking; and that thinking is different from seeing, talking, touching, and knowing (Flavell, 2000; Flavell, Green, & Flavell, 1995).

However, preschoolers generally believe that mental activity starts and stops. Not until middle childhood do children know that the mind is continuously active (Flavell, 1993; Flavell, 2000; Flavell et al., 1995). Preschoolers also have little or no awareness that they or other people think in words, or "talk to themselves in their heads," or that they think while they are looking, listening, reading, or talking (Flavell, Green, Flavell, & Grossman, 1997).

Preschoolers tend to believe they can dream about anything they wish. Five-year-olds show a more adultlike understanding, recognizing that physical experiences, emotions, knowledge, and thoughts can affect the content of dreams. Not until age 11, however, do children fully realize that they cannot control their dreams (Woolley & Boerger, 2002).

Social cognition, the recognition that others have mental states, accompanies the decline of egocentrism and the development of empathy. By age 3, children realize that if someone gets what he wants he will be happy, and, if not, he will be sad (Wellman & Woolley, 1990). Four-year-olds begin to understand that people have differing beliefs about the world—true or mistaken—and that these beliefs affect their actions.

False Beliefs and Deception A researcher shows 3-year-old Madeline a candy box and asks what is in it. "Candy," she says. But when Madeline opens the box, she finds crayons, not candy. "What will a child who hasn't opened the box think is in it?" the researcher asks. "Crayons," says Madeline, not understanding that another child would be fooled by the box as she was. And then she says that she originally thought crayons would be in the box (Flavell, 1993; Flavell et al., 1995).

The understanding that people can hold false beliefs flows from the realization that people hold mental representations of reality, which can sometimes be wrong. Three-year-olds, like Madeline, appear to lack such an understanding (Flavell et al., 1995). An analysis of 178 studies in various countries, using a number of variations on false-belief tasks, found this consistent developmental pattern (Wellman & Cross, 2001; Wellman, Cross, & Watson, 2001).

However, when preschoolers were taught to respond to a false-belief task with gestures rather than with words, children near their fourth birthday—but not younger children—did better than on the traditional verbal-response tasks. Thus gestures may help children on the verge of grasping the idea of false beliefs to make that conceptual leap (Carlson, Wong, Lemke, & Cosser, 2005).

The young girl on the right is old enough to know that her cousin needs consoling. Empathy, the ability to understand another person's feelings, begins at an early age.

Three-year-olds' failure to recognize false beliefs may stem from egocentric thinking. At that age, children tend to believe that everyone else knows what they know and believes what they do, and, like Madeline, they have trouble understanding that their beliefs can be false (Lillard & Curenton, 1999). Four-year-olds understand that people who see or hear different versions of the same event may come away with different beliefs. Not until about age 6, however, do children realize that two people who see or hear the same thing may interpret it differently (Pillow & Henrichon, 1996).

Because deception is a deliberate effort to plant a false belief in someone else's mind, it requires a child to suppress the impulse to be truthful. Some studies have found that children become capable of deception as early as age 2 or 3, and others at 4 or 5. The difference may have to do with the means of deception children are expected to use. In a series of experiments, 3-year-olds were asked whether they would like to play a trick on an experimenter by giving a false clue about which of two boxes a ball was hidden in. The children were better able to carry out the deception when asked to put a picture of the ball on the wrong box or to point to that box with an arrow than when they pointed with their fingers, which children this age are accustomed to doing truthfully (Carlson, Moses, & Hix, 1998).

Piaget maintained that young children regard all falsehoods—intentional or not—as lies. However, when 3- to 6-year-olds were told a story about the danger of eating contaminated food and were given a choice between interpreting a character's action as a lie or a mistake, about three-fourths of the children in all age groups characterized it accurately (Siegal & Peterson, 1998). Apparently, then, even 3-year-olds have some understanding of the role of intent in deception.

Distinguishing between Appearance and Reality

According to Piaget, not until about age 5 or 6 do children understand the distinction between what *seems* to be and what *is*. Much research bears him out, though some studies have found this ability beginning to emerge before age 4 (Friend & Davis, 1993; Rice, Koinis, Sullivan, Tager-Flusberg, & Winner, 1997).

In one classic series of experiments (Flavell, Green, & Flavell, 1986), 3-year-olds apparently confused appearance and reality in a variety of tests. For example, when the children put on special sunglasses that made milk look green, they said the milk *was* green, even though they had just seen white milk. However, 3-year-olds' difficulty distinguishing appearance from reality may itself be more apparent than real. When children were asked questions about the uses of such objects as a candle wrapped like a crayon, only 3 out of 10 answered correctly. But when asked to respond with actions rather than words ("I want a candle to put on a birthday cake"), 9 out of 10 handed the experimenter the crayonlike candle (Sapp, Lee, & Muir, 2000).

Distinguishing between Fantasy and Reality

Sometime between 18 months and 3 years, children learn to distinguish between real and imagined events. Three-year-olds know the difference between a real dog and a dog in a dream, and between something invisible (such as air) and something imaginary. They can pretend and can tell when someone else is pretending (Flavell, 2000). By age 3, and, in some cases, by age 2, they know that pretense is intentional; they can tell the difference between trying to do something and pretending to do the same thing (Rakoczy, Tomasello, & Striano, 2004).

Still, the line between fantasy and reality may seem to blur at times. In one study (Harris, Brown, Marriott, Whittall, & Harmer, 1991), 4- to 6-year-olds, left alone in a room, preferred to touch a box holding an imaginary bunny rather than a box holding an imaginary monster, even though most of the children claimed they were just pretending. However, in a partial replication of the study, in which the experimenter stayed in the room and clearly ended the pretense, only about 10 percent of the children touched or looked in either of the boxes, and almost all showed a clear understanding that the creatures were imaginary (Golomb & Galasso, 1995). Thus it is difficult to know, when questioning children about pretend objects,

the everyday world

IMAGINARY COMPANIONS

At 3½, Anna had 23 "sisters" with such names as Och, Elmo, Zeni, Aggie, and Ankie. She often talked to them on the telephone because they lived about 100 miles away, in the town where her family used to live. During the next year, most of the sisters disappeared, but Och continued to visit, especially for birthday parties. Och had a cat and a dog (which Anna had begged for in vain), and whenever Anna was denied something she saw advertised on television, she announced that she already had one at her sister's house. But when a live friend came over and Anna's mother happened to mention one of her imaginary companions, Anna quickly changed the subject.

All 23 sisters—and some "boys" and "girls" who have followed them—lived only in Anna's imagination, as she well knew. Like an estimated 25 to 65 percent of children between ages 3 and 10 (Woolley, 1997), she created imaginary companions with whom she talked and played. This normal phenomenon of childhood is seen most often in firstborn and only children, who lack the close company of siblings. Like Anna, most children who create imaginary companions have many of them (Gleason, Sebanc, & Hartup, 2000). Girls are more likely than boys to have imaginary friends, or at least to acknowledge them; boys are more likely to impersonate imaginary characters (Carlson & Taylor, 2005).

Children who have imaginary companions can distinguish fantasy from reality, but in free-play sessions they are more likely to engage in pretend play than are children without imaginary companions (M. Taylor, Cartwright, & Carlson, 1993). They play more happily and more imaginatively than other children and are more cooperative with other children and adults (D. G. Singer & Singer, 1990; J. L. Singer & Singer, 1981); and they do not lack for friends at preschool (Gleason et al., 2000). They are more fluent with language, watch less television, and show more

curiosity, excitement, and persistence during play. In one study of 152 preschoolers, 4-year-olds who reported having imaginary companions did better on theory-of-mind tasks (such as differentiating appearance and reality and recognizing false beliefs) than children who did not create such companions (M. Taylor & Carlson, 1997), and these children showed greater emotional understanding 3 years later. Having imaginary companions remains common in the early school years; almost one-third of the children who reported having had imaginary companions (65 percent of the sample in all) were still playing with them at age 7 (Taylor, Carlson, Maring, Gerow, & Charley, 2004).

Children's relationships with imaginary companions are like peer relationships; they are usually sociable and friendly, in contrast with the way children "take care of" personified objects, such as stuffed animals and dolls (Gleason et al., 2000). Imaginary playmates are good company for an only child like Anna. They provide wish-fulfillment mechanisms ("There was a monster in my room, but Elmo scared it off with magic dust"), scapegoats ("I didn't eat those cookies—Och must have done it!"), a safe way to express the child's own fears ("Aggie is afraid she's going to be washed down the drain"), and support in difficult situations (When Anna went to a scary movie, she "took" her imaginary companion with her).

what's your view

How should parents respond to children's talk about imaginary companions?

whether children are giving serious answers or are keeping up the pretense (M. Taylor, 1997).

Magical thinking in children age 3 and older does not seem to stem from confusion between fantasy and reality. Often, magical thinking is a way to explain events that do not seem to have obvious realistic explanations (usually because children lack knowledge about them) or simply to indulge in the pleasures of pretending—as with the belief in imaginary companions, which we discuss in Box 10.1. Magical thinking tends to decline near the end of the preschool period (Woolley, Phelps, Davis, & Mandell, 1999).

All in all, then, the research on various theory-of-mind topics suggests that young children may have a clearer picture of reality than Piaget believed.

Typically, young infants are extremely interested in other people's eyes. What relationship might this have to theory of mind? What type of social information does eye gazing convey?

Influences on Individual Differences in Theory-of-Mind Development Some children develop theory-of-mind abilities earlier than others. In part this development reflects brain maturation and general improvements in cognition. What other influences explain individual differences?

Infant social attention has been closely linked to theory of mind development (Wellman & Liu, 2004). In a recent study, 45 children were evaluated as infants and then again as 4-year-olds. Measures of infant social attention significantly predicted later theory of mind. The fact that those infants who were better at paying attention later showed more facility with theory of mind tasks suggests that there is continuity in social cognition and that skills build on each other over time (Wellman, Lopez-Duran, LaBounty, & Hamilton, 2008).

Social competence and language development also contribute to an understanding of thoughts and emotions (Cassidy, Werner, Rourke, Zubernis, & Balaraman, 2003). Children whose teachers and peers rate them high on social skills are better able to recognize false beliefs, to distinguish between real and feigned emotion, and to take another person's point of view. These children also tend to have strong language skills (Cassidy et al., 2003; Watson, Nixon, Wilson, & Capage, 1999). The *kind* of talk a young child hears at home may affect the child's understanding of mental states. A mother's reference to others' thoughts and knowledge is a consistent predictor of a child's later mental state language. Children show the most benefit from "mother talk" when it fits the child's current level of understanding. Empathy usually arises earlier in children whose families talk a lot about feelings and causality (Dunn, 1991; Dunn 2006; Dunn, Brown, Slomkowski, Tesla, & Youngblade, 1991).

Families that encourage pretend play stimulate the development of theory-of-mind skills. As children play roles, they try to assume others' perspectives. Talking with children about how the characters in a story feel helps them develop social understanding (Lillard & Curenton, 1999).

Bilingual children, who speak and hear more than one language at home, do somewhat better than children with only one language on certain theory-of-mind tasks (Bialystok & Senman, 2004; Goetz, 2003). Bilingual children know that an object or idea can be represented linguistically in more than one way, and this knowledge may help them see that different people may have different perspectives. Bilingual children also recognize the need to match their language to that of their partner, and this may make them more aware of others' mental states. Finally, bilingual children tend to have better attentional control, and this may enable them to focus on what is true or real rather than on what only seems to be so (Bialystok & Senman, 2004; Goetz, 2003).

An incomplete or ineffective theory of mind may be a sign of a cognitive or developmental impairment. Individuals with this type of impairment have a hard time understanding things from any other perspective than their own. Thus they have difficulty determining the intentions of others, lack understanding of how their behavior affects others, and have a difficult time with social reciprocity. Research suggests that children with autism do not employ a theory of mind and that these children have particular difficulties with tasks requiring them to understand another person's mental state (Baron-Cohen, Leslie, & Frith, 1985).

checkpoint
can you . . .

▷ Give examples of research that challenges Piaget's views on young children's cognitive limitations?

▷ Describe changes between ages 3 and 6 in children's knowledge about the way their minds work?

guidepost

2

What memory abilities expand in early childhood?

Information-Processing Approach: Memory Development

During early childhood, children improve in attention and in the speed and efficiency with which they process information; and they begin to form long-lasting memories. Still, young children do not remember as well as older ones. For one thing, young children tend to focus on exact details of an event, which are easily forgotten, whereas older children and adults generally concentrate on the gist of what happened. Also, young children, because of their lesser knowledge of the world, may fail to notice important aspects of a situation, such as when and where it occurred, which could help jog their memory.

BASIC PROCESSES AND CAPACITIES

Information-processing theorists focus on the processes that affect cognition. According to this view, memory can be described as a filing system that has three steps, or processes: *encoding*, *storage*, and *retrieval*. **Encoding** is like putting information in a folder to be filed in memory; it attaches a "code" or "label" to the information so that it will be easier to find when needed. For example, if you were asked to list "things that are red," you might list apples, stop signs, and hearts. Presumably, all these items were tagged in memory with the concept "red" when they were originally encoded. This code, then, is what now allows you to access these seemingly disparate objects. **Storage** is putting the folder away in the filing cabinet. It is where the information is kept. When the information is needed, you access storage and through the process of **retrieval**, you search for the file and take it out.

The way the brain stores information is believed to be universal, though the efficiency of the system varies from one person to another (Siegler, 1998). Information processing models depict the brain as containing three types of storage: sensory memory, working memory, and long-term memory. **Sensory memory** is a temporary storehouse for incoming sensory information. For example, the light trail that is visible when a sparkler is moved quickly on a dark night illustrates visual sensory memory. Sensory memory shows little change from infancy on (Siegler, 1998). However, without processing (encoding), sensory memories fade quickly.

Information being encoded or retrieved is kept in **working memory**, a short-term storehouse for information a person is actively working on, trying to understand, remember, or think about. Brain imaging studies have found that working memory is located partly in the *prefrontal cortex*, the large portion of the frontal lobe directly behind the forehead (Nelson et al., 2000). Working memory has a limited capacity. Researchers can assess the capacity of working memory by asking children to recall a series of scrambled digits (for example, 2-8-3-7-5-1 if they heard 1-5-7-3-8-2). The capacity of working memory—the number of digits a child can recall—increases rapidly (Cowan, Nugent, Elliott, Ponomarev, & Saults, 1999). At age 4, children typically remember only two digits; at 12 they typically remember six (Zelazo, Müller, Frye, & Marcovitch, 2003). The growth of working memory may permit the development of **executive function**, the conscious control of thoughts, emotions, and actions to accomplish goals or to solve problems. Executive function enables children to plan and carry out goal-directed mental activity. It probably emerges around the end of an infant's 1st year and develops in spurts with age. Changes in executive function between ages 2 and 5 enable children to make up and use complex rules for solving problems (Zelazo et al., 2003; Zelazo & Müller, 2002).

> By the age of 3 or 4, children differentiate between fictional cartoon worlds. So, if Barney were to show up on Sesame Street, they would be extremely surprised.
>
> Skolnick Weisberg & Bloom, 2009

Long-term memory is a storehouse of virtually unlimited capacity that holds information for long periods of time. Presumably, this information is transferred from working memory if it is deemed important enough. But who decides its importance? According to a widely used model, a **central executive** controls processing operations in working memory (Baddeley, 1981, 1986, 1992, 1996, 1998, 2001). The central executive orders information encoded for transfer to long-term memory. The central executive also retrieves information from long-term memory for further processing. The central executive can temporarily expand the capacity of working memory by moving information into two separate subsidiary systems while the central executive is occupied with other tasks. One of these subsidiary systems holds verbal information (as in the digit task), and the other holds visual/spatial images.

encoding
Process by which information is prepared for long-term storage and later retrieval.

storage
Retention of information in memory for future use.

retrieval
Process by which information is accessed or recalled from memory storage.

sensory memory
Initial, brief, temporary storage of sensory information.

working memory
Short-term storage of information being actively processed.

executive function
Conscious control of thoughts, emotions, and actions to accomplish goals or solve problems.

long-term memory
Storage of virtually unlimited capacity that holds information for long periods.

central executive
In Baddeley's model, element of working memory that controls the processing of information.

checkpoint
can you . . .

▷ Identify the three basic processes and three storehouses of memory and discuss their development?

▷ Describe the purpose and development of the executive function?

▷ Compare preschoolers' recognition and recall ability?

RECOGNITION AND RECALL

Recognition and recall are types of retrieval. **Recognition** is the ability to identify something encountered before (for example, to pick out a missing mitten from a lost-and-found box). **Recall** is the ability to reproduce knowledge from memory (for example, to describe the mitten to someone). Preschool children, like all age groups, do better on recognition than on recall, but both abilities improve with age. The more familiar children are with an item, the better they can recall it.

Young children often fail to use strategies for remembering—even strategies they already know—unless reminded (Flavell, 1970). This tendency to not generate efficient strategies may reflect lack of awareness of how a strategy would be useful (Sophian, Wood, & Vong, 1995). Older children tend to become more efficient in the spontaneous use of memory strategies, as we discuss in Chapter 13.

FORMING AND RETAINING CHILDHOOD MEMORIES

Memory of experiences in early childhood is rarely deliberate: Young children simply remember events that made a strong impression, and most of these early conscious memories seem to be short-lived.

Early Memories: Three Types One investigator has distinguished three types of childhood memory that serve different functions: generic, episodic, and autobiographical (Nelson, 1993).

Generic memory, which begins at about age 2, produces a **script**, a general outline of a familiar, repeated event, such as riding the bus to preschool or having lunch at Grandma's house. It helps a child know what to expect and how to act.

Episodic memory refers to awareness of having experienced a particular event or episode that occurred at a specific time and place. Young children remember more clearly events that are new to them. Given a young child's limited memory capacity, episodic memories are temporary. Unless they recur several times (in which case they are transferred to generic memory), they last for a few weeks or months and then fade. For example, getting vaccinated at the pediatrician's office might originally be an episodic memory—a child might remember the particular event. Over time and repeated visits, a child might form a generic memory of the doctor's office as a place where shots are administered.

Autobiographical memory, a type of episodic memory, refers to memories of distinctive experiences that form a person's life history. Not everything in episodic memory becomes part of autobiographical memory—only those memories that have a special, personal meaning to the child (Fivush & Nelson, 2004). Autobiographical memory generally emerges between ages 3 and 4 (Howe, 2003; Fivush & Nelson, 2004; Nelson, 2005; Nelson & Fivush, 2004).

A suggested explanation for the relatively slow arrival of autobiographical memory is that children cannot store in memory events pertaining to their own lives until they develop a concept of self (Howe, 2003; Howe & Courage, 1993, 1997; Nelson & Fivush, 2004). Also critical is the emergence of language, which enables children to share memories and organize them into personal narratives (Fivush & Nelson, 2004; Nelson, 2005; Nelson & Fivush, 2004).

Influences on Memory Retention Why do some memories last longer and remain more clear than others? One important factor is the uniqueness of the event. When events are frequently repeated, children are likely to incorrectly recall specific details. For example, they might confuse a particular event, such as a trip to the supermarket, with other, similar events. When events are rare or unusual, children seem to remember them better (Powell & Thomson, 1996). In addition, events with emotional impact seem to be remembered better (Powell & Thomson, 1996), although there is some evidence suggesting that attention is focused in on central aspects of the situation rather than on peripheral details (Levine & Edelstein, 2009). So, for example, if you were frightened by a scary film you might show enhanced memory for events in the film but forget if you bought candy or what color sweater you were wearing when you watched it. Still another factor is children's active participation, either in the event itself or in its retelling or reenactment. Preschoolers tend to remember things they did better than things they merely saw (Murachver, Pipe, Gordon, Owens, & Fivush, 1996). Self-awareness matters as well. In one experiment, self-awareness at age 2 was predictive of the ability to retell stories more accurately at age 3 (Reese & Newcombe, 2007).

Finally, and most important, the way adults talk with a child about shared experiences strongly affects autobiographical memory as well as other cognitive and linguistic skills (Cleveland & Reese, 2005; Fivush & Haden, 2006; Nelson & Fivush, 2004; McGuigan & Salmon, 2004). Why might this be the case? The **social interaction model**, based on Vygotsky's sociocultural approach, provides a rationale for this process. Theorists argue that children collaboratively construct autobiographical memories with parents or other adults as they talk about shared events. Adults initiate and guide these conversations, and provide children with models of the narrative structure of memory, placing the past events in a coherent and meaningful framework (Fivush & Haden, 2006). For example, think of a mother and child sitting down and leafing through a photo album together. As they go through the book, the mother is likely to guide the child's recollection of events. "See—this is when we went to Grandma's house. Remember how we all played together in the living room, and you did that puzzle? That was fun wasn't it?"

Children will tend to remember those events that are frequently rehearsed with parents via conversations about past events. And, parents tend to have consistent styles of talking with children about shared experiences (Fivush & Haden, 2006). When a child gets stuck, adults with a *low elaborative style* repeat their own previous statements or questions. Such a parent might ask, "Do you remember how we traveled to Florida?" and then, receiving no answer, ask, "How did we get there? We went in the _____." A parent with a *high elaborative style* would ask a question that elicits more information: "Did we go by car or by plane?" In one study, children at ages 2 and 3 whose mothers had been trained to use highly elaborative techniques in talking with their children recalled richer memories than children of untrained mothers (Reese & Newcombe, 2007). Mothers tend to talk more elaboratively with girls than with boys. This finding may explain why women tend to have detailed, vivid recollections of childhood experiences from an earlier age than men do (Fivush & Haden, 2006; Nelson & Fivush, 2004).

How does elaborative talk promote autobiographical memory? It does so by providing verbal labels for aspects of an event and giving it an orderly, comprehensible structure (Nelson & Fivush, 2004). In reminiscing about past events, children learn to interpret those events and the thoughts and emotions connected with them. They build a sense of self as continuous in time, and they learn that their own perspective on an experience may differ from another person's perspective on the same experience (Fivush & Haden, 2006).

Influence of Culture The relationship between elaborative, parent-guided reminiscing and children's autobiographical memory has been replicated widely across cultures (Fivush & Haden, 2006). However, mothers in middle-class Western cultures tend to be more elaborative than mothers in non-Western cultures such as China (Fivush & Haden, 2006). In reminiscing with 3-year-olds, U.S. mothers might say, "Do you remember when you went swimming at Nana's? What did you do that was really neat?" Chinese mothers tend to ask leading questions, leaving little for the child to add ("What did you play at the skiing place? You sat on the ice ship, right?") (Nelson & Fivush, 2004).

social interaction model
Model, based on Vygotsky's sociocultural theory, that proposes that children construct autobiographical memories through conversation with adults about shared events.

checkpoint
can **you** . . .

▷ Identify three types of memories in early childhood?

▷ Identify several factors that affect how well a preschool child will remember an event?

▷ Discuss how conversations with adults influence memory construction and retention?

▷ Give an example of how culture influences memories?

guidepost

3 How is preschoolers' intelligence measured, and what factors influence it?

Intelligence: Psychometric and Vygotskian Approaches

One factor that may affect the strength of early cognitive skills is intelligence. Although the definition of intelligence is controversial, most psychologists agree that intelligence involves the ability to learn from situations, adapt to new experiences, and manipulate abstract concepts. Let's look at two ways intelligence is measured—through traditional psychometric tests and through newer tests of cognitive potential—and at influences on children's performance.

TRADITIONAL PSYCHOMETRIC MEASURES

Although preschool children are easier to test than infants and toddlers, they still need to be tested individually. Because 3- to 5-year-olds are more proficient with language than younger children, intelligence tests for this age group can include more verbal items; and these tests produce more reliable results than the largely nonverbal tests used in infancy. The two most commonly used individual tests for preschoolers are the Stanford-Binet Intelligence Scale and the Wechsler Preschool and Primary Scale of Intelligence.

The **Stanford-Binet Intelligence Scale** is used for children ages 2 and up and takes 45 to 60 minutes to complete. The child is asked to define words, string beads, build with blocks, identify the missing parts of a picture, trace mazes, and show an understanding of numbers. The child's score is supposed to measure fluid reasoning (the ability to solve abstract or novel problems), knowledge, quantitative reasoning, visual-spatial processing, and working memory. The fifth edition includes nonverbal methods of testing all five of these dimensions of cognition and permits comparisons of verbal and nonverbal performance. In addition to providing a full-scale IQ, the Stanford-Binet yields separate measures of verbal and nonverbal IQ plus composite scores spanning the five cognitive dimensions.

The **Wechsler Preschool and Primary Scale of Intelligence, Revised** (**WPPSI-III**) is an individual test taking 30 to 60 minutes. It has separate levels for ages 2½ to 4 and 4 to 7 and yields separate verbal and performance scores as well as a combined score. The most current version includes subtests designed to measure both verbal and nonverbal fluid reasoning, receptive versus expressive vocabulary, and processing speed. Both the Stanford-Binet and the WPPSI-III have been restandardized on samples of children representing the population of preschool-age children in the United States. The WPPSI-III also has been validated for special populations, such as children with intellectual disabilities, developmental delays, language disorders, and autistic disorders.

INFLUENCES ON MEASURED INTELLIGENCE

A common misconception is that IQ scores represent a fixed quantity of inborn intelligence. In reality, an IQ score is simply a measure of how well a child can do certain tasks at a certain time in comparison with others of the same age. Indeed, test scores of children in many industrialized countries have risen steadily since testing began, forcing test developers to raise standardized norms (Flynn, 1984, 1987). This trend was thought to reflect better nutrition, exposure to educational television, preschools, better-educated parents, smaller families in which each child receives more attention, and a wide variety of mentally demanding games, as well as changes in the tests themselves. However, in tests of Norwegian and Danish army recruits, the trend has slowed and even reversed since the 1970s and 1980s, perhaps because such influences have reached a saturation point (Sundet, Barlaug, & Torjussen, 2004; Teasdale & Owen, 2008).

The degree to which family environment influences a child's intelligence is uncertain. We do not know how much of parents' influence on intelligence comes from their genetic contribution and how much comes from their provision of a child's earliest environment for learning. Twin and adoption studies suggest that family life has its strongest influence

Stanford-Binet Intelligence Scale Individual intelligence test for ages 2 and up, used to measure knowledge, quantitative reasoning, visual-spatial processing, and working memory.

Wechsler Preschool and Primary Scale of Intelligence, Revised (WPPSI-III) Individual intelligence test for children ages 2½ to 7 that yields verbal and performance scores as well as a combined score.

Giving suggestions and strategies for solving a puzzle or problem—without showing approval or disapproval—can foster cognitive growth. Parental influence on cognitive development may be strongest in early childhood.

in early childhood, and this influence diminishes greatly by adolescence (Bouchard & McGue, 2003; McGue, 1997; Neisser et al., 1996) when children's exposure to different experiences is more self-driven. However, these studies have been done largely with white, middle-class samples; their results may not apply to low-income and nonwhite families (Neisser et al., 1996). In a longitudinal study of low-income African American children, the influence of the home environment remained substantial—at least as strong as the influence of the mother's IQ (Burchinal, Campbell, Bryant, Wassik, & Ramey, 1997).

The correlation between socioeconomic status and IQ is well documented (Neisser et al., 1996; Strenze, 2007). Family income is associated with cognitive development and achievement in the preschool years and beyond. Family economic circumstances can exert a powerful influence, not so much in themselves as in the way they affect other factors such as health, stress, parenting practices, and the atmosphere in the home (Brooks-Gunn, 2003; Evans, 2004; McLoyd, 1990, 1998; NICHD Early Child Care Research Network, 2005a; Rouse, Brooks-Gunn, & McLanahan, 2005).

Still, some economically deprived children do better on IQ tests than others. Both genetic and environmental factors are involved. In a study of 1,116 twin pairs born in England and Wales in 1994 and 1995 and assessed at age 5 (Kim-Cohen, Moffitt, Caspi, & Taylor, 2004), children in deprived families tended, as in other studies, to have lower IQs. However, children with outgoing temperament, warm mothering, and stimulating activities in the home (which, again, may be influenced by parental IQ) tended to do better than other economically deprived children.

TESTING AND TEACHING BASED ON VYGOTSKY'S THEORY

According to Vygotsky, children learn by internalizing the results of interactions with adults. This interactive learning is most effective in helping children cross the **zone of proximal development (ZPD)**, the imaginary psychological space between what they can do or know by themselves, and what they could do or know with help. (Refer to Chapter 2.) The ZPD can be assessed by *dynamic tests* (see Chapter 13) that, according to Vygotskyan theory, provide a better measure of children's intellectual potential than do traditional psychometric tests that measure what children have already mastered.

zone of proximal development (ZPD) Vygotsky's term for the difference between what a child can do alone and what the child can do with help.

scaffolding
Temporary support to help a child master a task.

what's your view

If you were a preschool or kindergarten teacher, would you find it more helpful to know a child's IQ or ZPD?

connect

study smart

Scaffolding

checkpoint

can you . . .

▷ Describe two commonly used individual intelligence tests for preschoolers?

▷ List and discuss several influences on measured intelligence?

▷ Describe Vygotsky's zone of proximal development (ZPD)?

guidepost

4

How does language improve, and what happens when its development is delayed?

Dynamic tests emphasize potential rather than present achievement. While traditional achievement tests measure a child's current abilities, dynamic tests strive to measure learning processes directly rather than through the products of past learning. Examiners help the child when necessary by asking questions, giving examples or demonstrations, and offering feedback, making the test itself a learning situation.

The ZPD, in combination with the related concept of **scaffolding**, can also help parents and teachers more efficiently guide children's cognitive progress. Scaffolding is the supportive assistance that a more sophisticated interaction partner provides, and ideally, it should be aimed at the ZPD. For example, consider what happens when you are trying to learn a new skill, such as playing pool. When you play with someone who is worse than you, you are not likely to improve. Likewise, when you play with someone who is a master, their skills are so above yours that they overwhelm you, and you are also not likely to learn a great deal. However, playing with someone who is just a bit better than you is likely to challenge you, illustrate strategies you might be successful at, and result in the greatest amount of learning. The reason for this is that the model they provided in their play scaffolded your emerging abilities. Ideally, scaffolding is lessened as children gain in skills. The less able a child is to do a task, the more scaffolding, or support, an adult must give. As the child can do more and more, the adult helps less and less. When the child can do the job alone, the adult takes away the scaffold that is no longer needed.

> Vygotsky believed play provided children with a great deal of scaffolding, enabling them to work at the higher end of their ZPD. If asked to pretend to be a statue, children are likely to be able to stand still longer than if asked to just remain motionless. The "rules" of being a statue provide support for the emerging regulatory abilities of the children.

By enabling children to become aware of and monitor their own cognitive processes and to recognize when they need help, parents can help children take responsibility for learning. Prekindergarten children who receive scaffolding are better able to regulate their own learning when they get to kindergarten (Neitzel & Stright, 2003). In a longitudinal study of 289 families with infants, the skills children developed during interactions with their mothers at 2 and 3½ enabled them, at 4½, to regulate goal-directed problem solving and to initiate social interactions. Also, 2-year-olds whose mothers helped maintain the child's interest in an activity—for example by asking questions, making suggestions or comments, or offering choices—tended, at 3½ and 4½, to show independence in cognitive and social skills, such as solving a problem and initiating social interaction (Landry, Smith, Swank, & Miller-Loncar, 2000).

Language Development

Preschoolers are full of questions: "How many sleeps until tomorrow?" "Who filled the river with water?" "Do babies have muscles?" "Do smells come from inside my nose?" Young children's growing facility with language helps them express their unique view of the world. Between ages 3 and 6, children make rapid advances in vocabulary, grammar, and syntax. The child who, at 3, describes how Daddy "hatches" wood (chops with a hatchet) or asks Mommy to "piece" her food (cut it into little pieces) may, by age 5, tell her mother, "Don't be ridiculous!" or proudly point to her toys and say, "See how I organized everything?"

VOCABULARY

At 3 the average child knows and can use 900 to 1,000 words. By age 6, a child typically has an *expressive* (speaking) vocabulary of 2,600 words and understands more than 20,000 (Owens, 1996). With the help of formal schooling, a child's *passive*, or *receptive*, vocabulary (words she or he can understand) will quadruple to 80,000 words by the time the child enters high school (Owens, 1996).

This rapid expansion of vocabulary may occur through **fast mapping**, which allows a child to pick up the approximate meaning of a new word after hearing it only once or twice in conversation. From the context, children seem to form a quick hypothesis about the meaning of the word, which then is refined with further exposure and usage. For example, suppose a child is at the zoo and encounters an emu for the first time. The mother might point to the emu and say, "Look at the emu over there." The child might use what she knows about the rules for forming words, about the context, and about the subject under discussion to form a hypothesis about the meaning of the word *emu*. Names of objects (nouns) seem to be easier to fast map than names of actions (verbs), which are less concrete. Yet one experiment showed that children just under age 3 can fast map a new verb and apply it to another situation in which the same action is being performed (Golinkoff, Jacquet, Hirsh-Pasek, & Nandakumar, 1996).

Many 3- and 4-year-olds seem able to tell when two words refer to the same object or action (Savage & Au, 1996). They also know that more than one adjective can apply to the same noun ("Fido is spotted and furry") and that an adjective can be combined with a proper name ("smart Fido!") (Hall & Graham, 1999).

GRAMMAR AND SYNTAX

The ways children combine syllables into words and words into sentences grow increasingly sophisticated during early childhood. This is because their understanding of grammar and syntax becomes more complex. When psychologists speak of grammar, they are not referring to the lessons learned in 7th grade English class; rather, they are referring to the deep underlying structure of a language that allows us both to produce and understand utterances. Syntax is a related concept and involves the rules for putting together sentences in a particular language.

At age 3, children typically begin to use plurals, possessives, and past tense and know the difference between I, you, and we. They can ask—and answer—*what* and *where* questions. (*Why* and *how* questions are harder to grasp at this age.) However, their sentences are generally short, simple, and declarative ("Kitty wants milk").

Between ages 4 and 5, sentences average four to five words and may be declarative ("I am big!"), negative ("I'm not hungry"), interrogative ("Why can't I go outside?"), or imperative ("Catch the ball!"). Four-year-olds use complex, multiclause sentences ("I'm eating because I'm hungry") more frequently if their parents often use such sentences (Huttenlocher, Vasilyeva, Cymerman, & Levine, 2002). Children this age tend to string sentences together in long run-on stories (". . . And then . . . And then . . ."). In some respects, comprehension may be immature. For example, 4-year-old Noah can carry out a command that includes more than one step ("Pick up your toys and put them in the cupboard"). However, if his mother tells him, "You may watch TV after you pick up your toys," he may process the words in the order in which he hears them and think he can first watch television and then pick up his toys.

By ages 5 to 7, children's speech has become quite adultlike. They speak in longer and more complicated sentences. They use more conjunctions, prepositions, and articles. They use compound and complex sentences and can handle all parts of speech.

Still, although children this age speak fluently, comprehensibly, and fairly grammatically, they have yet to master many fine points of language. They rarely use the passive voice ("I was dressed by Grandpa"), conditional sentences ("If I were big, I could drive the bus"), or the auxiliary verb *have* ("I have seen that lady before") (C. S. Chomsky, 1969). They often make errors because they have not yet learned exceptions to rules. Saying "holded" instead of "held" or "eated" instead of "ate" is a normal sign of linguistic progress. When young children discover a rule, such as adding *-ed* to a verb for past tense, they tend to overgeneralize—to use it even with words that do not conform to the rule. Eventually, they notice that *-ed* is not always used to form the past tense of a verb. Training can help children master such syntactical forms (Vasilyeva, Huttenlocher, & Waterfall, 2006).

fast mapping
Process by which a child absorbs the meaning of a new word after hearing it once or twice in conversation.

When exposed to rhymes, 5-year-olds from wealthier families show more localization of language in the left hemisphere (just like adults) than children from poorer families. This may result from children from wealthier homes being exposed to more complex vocabulary and syntax.

Raizada, Richards, Metlzoff, & Kuhl, 2008

This preschool girl can use her growing vocabulary and knowledge of grammar and syntax to communicate more effectively. She has learned how to ask her father for things, to carry on a conversation, and to tell a story, perhaps about what happened at preschool.

pragmatics
Practical knowledge needed to use language for communicative purposes.

social speech
Speech intended to be understood by a listener.

private speech
Talking aloud to oneself with no intent to communicate with others.

checkpoint
can **you** . . .

▷ **Trace normal progress in 3- to 6-year-olds' vocabulary, grammar, syntax, and conversational abilities?**

▷ **Give reasons why children of various ages use private speech?**

study smart

Language Challenges

Amalia, one of the children featured in the Milestones videos, was diagnosed with a speech delay at 18 months and received speech therapy for approximately a year and a half before she caught up with her peers. You may note that at younger ages, her speech is very difficult to understand.

PRAGMATICS AND SOCIAL SPEECH

Language is a social process. And, as children learn vocabulary, grammar and syntax, they also become more competent in **pragmatics**. Pragmatics involve the practical knowledge of how to use language to communicate. For example, a child is more likely to be successful with a request such as "May I please have a cookie?" than with "Give me a cookie now."

Pragmatics is related to theory of mind because to understand how to use language socially, you have to be able to put yourself in other people's shoes. This includes knowing how to ask for things, how to tell a story or joke, how to begin and continue a conversation, and how to adjust comments to the listener's perspective (M. L. Rice, 1982). These are all aspects of **social speech:** speech intended to be understood by a listener.

With improved pronunciation and grammar, it becomes easier for others to understand what children say. Most 3-year-olds are quite talkative, and they pay attention to the effect of their speech on others. If people cannot understand them, they try to explain themselves more clearly. Most 4-year-olds, especially girls, use parentese when speaking to 2-year-olds (Owens, 1996; Shatz & Gelman, 1973; refer to Chapter 7).

Most 5-year-olds can adapt what they say to what the listener knows. They can use words to resolve disputes, and they use more polite language and fewer direct commands in talking to adults than to other children. Almost half of 5-year-olds can stick to a conversational topic for about a dozen turns—if they are comfortable with their partner and if the topic is one they know and care about (Owens, 1996).

Private Speech **Private speech**, talking aloud to oneself with no intent to communicate with others, is normal and common in childhood. Piaget saw private speech as a sign of cognitive immaturity whereas Vygotsky saw it as a special form of communication. Research generally supports Vygotsky as to the functions of private speech (Berk, 1986a). Box 10.2 outlines the similarities and differences between Vygotsky and Piaget.

DELAYED LANGUAGE DEVELOPMENT

The fact that Albert Einstein did not start to speak until he was between 2 and 3 years old (Isaacson, 2007) may encourage parents of other children whose speech develops later than usual. About 5 to 8 percent of preschool children show speech and language delays (U.S. Preventive Services Task Force, 2006).

It is unclear why some children speak late. They do not necessarily lack linguistic input at home. Hearing problems and head and facial abnormalities can be associated with speech and language delays, as can premature birth, family history, socioeconomic factors, and some developmental delays (Dale et al., 1998; U.S. Preventive Services Task Force, 2006). Heredity seems to play a major role (Lyytinen, Poikkeus, Laakso, Eklund, & Lyytinen, 2001; Spinath, Price, Dale, & Plomin, 2004). Boys are more likely than girls to be late talkers (Dale et al., 1998; U.S. Preventive Services Task Force, 2006). Children with language delays may have problems in fast mapping; they may need to hear a new word more often than other children do before they can incorporate it into their vocabulary (Rice, Oetting, Marquis, Bode, & Pae, 1994).

Many children who speak late—especially those whose comprehension is normal—eventually catch up. One of the largest studies to date on language emergence determined that 80 percent of children with language delays at age 2 catch up with their peers by age 7 (Rice, Taylor, & Zubrick, 2008). However, some 40 to 60 percent of children with early language delays, if left untreated, may experience far-reaching cognitive, social, and emotional consequences (U.S. Preventive Services Task Force, 2006).

PREPARATION FOR LITERACY

To understand what is on the printed page, children first need to master certain prereading skills (Lonigan, Burgess, & Anthony, 2000; Muter, Hulme, Snowling, & Stevenson,

PRIVATE SPEECH: PIAGET VERSUS VYGOTSKY

10.2

Jacob, age 4, was alone in his room painting. When he finished, he was overheard saying aloud, "Now I have to put the pictures somewhere to dry. I'll put them by the window. They need to get dry now. I'll paint some more dinosaurs."

Private speech—speaking to oneself, as Jacob did—is normal and common in childhood, accounting for 20 to 50 percent of what 4- to 10-year-old children say (Berk, 1986a). Two- to three-year-olds engage in "crib talk," playing with sounds and words. Four- and five-year-olds use private speech as a way to express fantasies and emotions (Berk, 1992; Small, 1990). Older children "think out loud" or mutter in barely audible tones.

Piaget (1962/1923) saw private speech as a sign of cognitive immaturity and as merely a reflection on ongoing mental activity. Because young children are egocentric, he suggested, they are unable to recognize others' viewpoints and therefore are unable to communicate meaningfully. Instead, they simply vocalize whatever is on their minds. Another reason young children talk while they do things, said Piaget, is that they do not yet distinguish between words and the actions the words stand for, or symbolize. By the end of the preoperational stage, with cognitive maturation and social experience, children become less egocentric and more capable of symbolic thought and so discard private speech.

Like Piaget, Vygotsky (1962/1934) believed that private speech helps young children integrate language with thought. However, Vygotsky did not look on private speech as egocentric. He saw it as a special form of communication: conversation with the self. As such, he said, it serves an important function in the transition between early social speech (often experienced in the form of adult commands) and inner speech (thinking in words)—a transition toward the internalization of socially derived control of behavior ("Now I have to put the pictures somewhere to dry").

Research generally supports Vygotsky as to the functions of private speech. In an observational study of 3- to 5-year-olds, 86 percent of the children's remarks were *not* egocentric (Berk, 1986a). The most sociable children and those who engage in the most social speech tend to use the most private speech as well, apparently supporting Vygotsky's view that private speech is stimulated by social experience (Berk, 1986a, 1986b, 1992; Berk & Garvin, 1984; Kohlberg, Yaeger, & Hjertholm, 1968). There also is evidence for the role of private speech in self-regulation, as Jacob was doing (Berk & Garvin, 1984; Furrow, 1984). Private speech tends to increase when children are trying to perform difficult tasks, especially without adult supervision (Berk, 1992; Berk & Garvin, 1984).

Vygotsky proposed that private speech increases during the preschool years and then fades away during the early part of middle childhood as children become more able to guide and master their actions. However, the pattern now appears to be more complex than Vygotsky suggested. Some studies have reported no age changes in overall use of private speech; others have found variations in the timing of its decline. The brightest children tend to use it earliest. Whereas Vygotsky considered the need for private speech a universal stage of cognitive development, studies have found a wide range of individual differences, with some children using it very little or not at all (Berk, 1992).

Understanding the significance of private speech has practical implications, especially in school (Berk, 1986a). Talking to oneself or muttering should not be considered misbehavior; a child may be struggling with a problem, and thinking out loud may help in solving it.

what's your view

Have you ever seen a child talking to himself or herself? What purpose did the speech seem to serve?

2004). The development of fundamental skills that will eventually lead to being able to read is known as **emergent literacy**.

Prereading skills can be divided into two types: (1) oral language skills, such as vocabulary, syntax, narrative structure, and the understanding that language is used to communicate; and (2) specific phonological skills (linking letters with sounds) that help in decoding the printed word. Each of these types of skills seems to have its own independent effect (NICHD Early Child Care Research Network, 2005b; Lonigan et al., 2000; Whitehurst & Lonigan, 1998). In a 2-year longitudinal study of 90 British schoolchildren, the development of word recognition appeared critically dependent on phonological skills, whereas oral language skills such as vocabulary and

emergent literacy
Preschoolers' development of skills, knowledge, and attitudes that underlie reading and writing.

what's your view?

Suppose you wanted to set up a program to encourage preliteracy development in high-risk children. What elements would you include in your program, and how would you judge its success?

U.S. booksellers have noted a trend away from picture books and toward chapter books for young children, presumably as a result of parents' concerns about literacy. Do chapter books with fewer pictures and more text help develop children's imagination, or do they push them too quickly?

Bosman, 2010

checkpoint can you . . .

▷ Discuss possible causes, consequences, and treatment of delayed language development?

▷ Identify two types of prereading skills and explain how social interaction can promote preparation for literacy?

▷ Describe how exposure to media effects preschoolers' cognitive abilities?

grammatical skills were more important predictors of reading comprehension (Muter et al., 2004).

Social interaction can promote emergent literacy. Children are more likely to become good readers and writers if, during the preschool years, parents provide conversational challenges the children are ready for—if they use a rich vocabulary and center dinner-table talk on the day's activities, on mutually remembered past events, or on questions about why people do things and how things work (Reese, 1995; Snow, 1990, 1993).

As children learn the skills they will need to translate the written word into speech, they also learn that writing can express ideas, thoughts, and feelings. Preschool children in the United States pretend to write by scribbling, lining up their marks from left to right (Brenneman, Massey, Machado, & Gelman, 1996). Later they begin using letters, numbers, and letterlike shapes to represent words, syllables, or phonemes. Often their spelling is so inventive that they cannot read it themselves (Whitehurst & Lonigan, 1998, 2001).

Reading to children is one of the most effective paths to literacy. According to a U.S. government report, 86 percent of girls and 82 percent of boys are read to at home at least three times a week (Freeman, 2004). Children who are read to from an early age learn that reading and writing in English move from left to right and from top to bottom and that words are separated by spaces. They also are motivated to learn to read (Siegler, 1998; Whitehurst & Lonigan, 1998, 2001).

MEDIA AND COGNITION

Unlike infants and toddlers, preschool-age children comprehend the symbolic nature of television and can readily imitate behaviors they see (Bandura, Ross & Ross, 1963; Kirkorian, Wartella, & Anderson, 2008). By the age of 3 children are *active media users*, able to pay greater attention to dialogue and narrative (Huston & Wright, 1983). Exposure to television during the first few years of life may be associated with poorer cognitive development, but children over the age of 2 exposed to programs that follow an educational curriculum have demonstrated cognitive enhancement (Kirkorian et al., 2008). In one study, the more time 3- to 5-year-olds spent watching *Sesame Street*, the more their vocabulary improved (M. L. Rice, Huston, Truglio, & Wright, 1990). Program content is an important mediator. Parents who limit screen time, select well-designed, age-appropriate programs, and view the programs with their children can maximize the benefits of media (Table 10.5).

TABLE 10.5 Using Media Responsibly
• Limit screen time to the least amount possible.
• Set guidelines for appropriate viewing for all media, including TV, videos/DVDs, movies, and games.
• Protect children from inappropriate media.
• Require that children ask before turning on media.
• Remove TVs, video game systems, and computers from bedrooms.
• Watch programs and movies together and discuss what you are watching.
• Use media in a positive way to spark imagination and creativity.
• Limit the number of products you purchase for your child that are linked to TV programs.

Sources: Teachers Resisting Unhealthy Children's Entertainment [TRUCE]. (2008).

Early Childhood Education

What purpose does early childhood education serve, and how do children make the transition to kindergarten?

Going to preschool is an important step that widens a child's physical, cognitive, and social environment. The transition to kindergarten, the beginning of "real school," is another momentous step. Preschool enrollments have exploded over the past 20 years. Between 1985 and 2006, enrollment in prekindergarten increased 611 percent, while enrollment in other elementary grades increased 23 percent. The number of children enrolled in prekindergarten increased from 0.2 million in 1985 to 1.1 million in 2006 (U.S. Department of Education Institute of Education Statistics, 2008).

TYPES OF PRESCHOOLS

Preschools vary greatly in their goals and curriculums. Some programs emphasize academic achievement, and others focus on social and emotional development. In some countries, such as China, preschools provide academic preparation for schooling. In contrast, many preschools in the United States have followed progressive, child-centered philosophies stressing social and emotional growth in line with young children's developmental needs. Two of the most influential programs, Montessori and Reggio Emilia, were founded on similar philosophical premises.

The Montessori Method The nineteenth century saw major shifts in views on education and mental development. Philosophers such as Rousseau, Pestalozzi, and Seguin inspired educators to consider alternatives to traditional teaching methods. Maria Montessori was strongly influenced by the work of these philosphers. As Italy's first female physician, she dedicated herself to finding new and better methods for educating children with disabilities. Based on her success with these children, she was asked to start a school for underpriviledged children living in the slums of Italy. In 1907 Montessori opened Casa dei Bambini and began a movement that has since spread worldwide.

The Montessori method is based on the belief that children's natural intelligence involves rational, spiritual, and empirical aspects (Edwards, 2003). Montessori stresses the importance of children learning independently at their own pace, as they work with developmentally appropriate materials and self-chosen tasks. Children are grouped into multiage classrooms; infancy to age 3 is considered "the unconscious absorbent mind," and age 3 to 6 is considered the "conscious absorbent mind" (Montessori, 1995). Teachers serve as guides, and older children help younger ones. The curriculum is individualized but has a definite scope and prescribed sequencing. Teachers provide an environment of calm productivity, and the classrooms are organized to be orderly, pleasing environments (Standing, 1957).

Montessori's approach has proven effective. An evaluation of Montessori education in Milwaukee found that 5-year-old Montessori students were better prepared for elementary school in reading and math than children who attended other types of preschools (Lillard & Else-Quest, 2006).

The Reggio Emilia Approach In the late 1940s a group of Italian educators and parents devised a plan to revitalize a crumbling, post–World War II society through a new approach to education for young children. Their goal was to improve the lives of children and families by encouraging nonviolent dialogues and debates, developing problem-solving skills, and forging close, long-term relationships with teachers and classmates. Loris Malaguzzi, the school's founding director, was a social constructivist strongly influenced by Dewey, Piaget, Vygotsky, and Montessori. He envisioned an "education based on relationships" that supported the child's connections to people, society, and the environment (Malaguzzi, 1993).

Reggio Emilia is a less formal model than Montessori. Teachers follow children's interests and support them in exploring and investigating ideas and feelings through words, movement, dramatic play, and music. Learning is purposeful but less defined than with the Montessori curriculum. Teachers ask questions that draw out children's ideas and then create fleixble plans to explore these ideas with the children. Classrooms are carefully constructed to offer complexity, beauty, organization, and a sense of well-being (Ceppi & Zini, 1998; Edwards, 2002).

COMPENSATORY PRESCHOOL PROGRAMS

An estimated two-thirds of children in poor urban areas in the United States enter school unprepared to learn (Zigler, 1998). Since the 1960s, large-scale programs have been developed to help such children compensate for what they have missed and to prepare them for school.

The best-known compensatory preschool program for children of low-income families in the United States is Project Head Start, a federally funded program launched in 1965. Consistent with its whole child approach, its goals are not only to enhance cognitive skills but also to improve physical health and to foster self-confidence and social skills. The program provides medical, dental, and mental health care, social services, and at least one hot meal a day. Currently about one out of three Head Start children are from non-English-speaking homes (predominantly Hispanic), and a majority live in single-mother homes (Administration for Children and Families [ACF], 2006a).

Has Head Start lived up to its name? Data support its effectiveness in improving school readiness, and teacher and program quality continues to improve (ACF, 2006a, 2006b; USDHHS, 2003b). Similarly, children who attend the newer state-sponsored programs tend to show better cognitive and language skills and do better in school than children who do not attend (USDHHS, 2003a).

Head Start children make gains in vocabulary, letter recognition, early writing, early mathematics, and social skills; and the gap between their vocabulary and early reading scores and national norms has narrowed significantly since the late 1990s (ACF, 2006a). Furthermore, their skills continue to progress in kindergarten. Gains are closely related to parental involvement (ACF, 2006b).

An analysis of the long-term effects of Head Start suggests that the benefits outweigh the costs (Ludwig & Phillips, 2007). Children from Head Start and other compensatory programs are less likely to be placed in special education or to repeat a grade and are more likely to finish high school than low-income children who did not attend such programs (Deming, 2009; Neisser et al., 1996). "Graduates" of one such program, the Perry Preschool Project, were much less likely to become juvenile delinquents or to become pregnant in their teens (Berrueta-Clement, Schweinhart, Barnett, Epstein, & Weikart, 1985; Schweinhart, 2007; Schweinhart, Barnes, & Weikart, 1993; see Chapter 17). Outcomes are best with earlier and longer-lasting intervention through high-quality, center-based programs (Brooks-Gunn, 2003; Reynolds & Temple, 1998; Zigler & Styfco, 1993, 1994, 2001).

The Harlem Children's Zone is an extremely successful current program based in Brofenbrenner's bioecological model (see Chapter 2). One reason for its extraordinary success is the systems approach utilized to address children's deficiencies. The focus is as much on the community as it is on the children, with the goal of bringing about a "tipping point" of enriched events and environments that will, it is hoped, at some point become self-perpetuating.

These children in a Head Start program are getting a "head start" toward readiness for school. The most successful compensatory education programs start early and have well-trained staff, parental participation, and low staff-to-child ratios.

In 1995, an Early Head Start program began offering child and family development services to low-income families with infants and toddlers. By 2006, the program was operating in more than 700 communities and serving more than 85,000 children and more than 10,000 pregnant women (Center for Law and Social Policy, 2008). At ages 2 and 3, according to randomized studies, participants scored higher on standardized developmental and vocabulary tests and were at less risk of slow development than children not in the program. At age 3, they were less aggressive, more attentive to playthings, and more positively engaged with their parents. Early Head Start parents were more emotionally supportive, provided more learning and language stimulation, read to their children more, and spanked less. Programs that offered a mix of center-based services and home visits showed better results than those that concentrated on one setting or the other (Commissioner's Office of Research and Evaluation and Head Start Bureau, 2001; Love et al., 2002, 2005).

A growing consensus among early childhood educators is that the most effective way to ensure that gains achieved in early intervention and compensatory education programs are maintained is through a *PK–3* approach—a systematic program extending from prekindergarten through third grade. Such a program would (1) offer prekindergarten to all 3- and 4-year olds, (2) require full-day kindergarten, and (3) coordinate and align educational experiences and expectations from prekindergarten through Grade 3 through a sequenced curriculum based on children's developmental needs and abilities and taught by skilled professionals (Bogard & Takanishi, 2005).

State-funded preschool is becoming a national trend. Most of these programs are for disadvantaged children, but a growing number of states are offering universal preschool programs. In practice, "universal" usually means that the program is available to all on a voluntary basis.

THE SCHOOL OF THE TWENTY-FIRST CENTURY: UNIVERSAL PRESCHOOL

Montessori and Reggio Emilia schools and the Head Start program are structured to provide children with the cognitive and developmental foundation for successful academic performance. The correlation between good-quality early childhood education and future academic success has been closely investigated. Studies have indicated gaps in academic achievement between poor and middle-class students in the United States can be documented before children enter school (Sawhill, 2006). These findings have prompted interest in the development of **universal preschool**, a national system for early care and education using the public schools. The School of the 21st Century (21C), a model created by Edward Zigler, is an example of such a system.

21C is a comprisive school-based program that includes universally accessible preschool education and child care services. It provides all-day, year-round, developmentally appropriate care for 3- and 4-year-old children as well as before- and after-school and vacation care for school-age children. The goal of 21C is to improve school readiness and educational success by (1) providing access to high-quality child care and developmentally appropriate preschool, (2) building parent involvement, and (3) providing support services for parents that enhance family functioning. The program has been adopted by more than 1,300 schools in 20 states. Preliminary findings from the national 21C evaluation have indicated enhanced academic skills through second grade by children who have attended 21C preschools (Henrich, Ginicola, Finn-Stevenson, & Zigler, 2006).

THE CHILD IN KINDERGARTEN

For many years people thought of kindergarten as a transition time between home or preschool and the structure of grade school and academic instruction. Now, kindergarten in the United States has become more like first grade and emphasizes academics. Children spend more time on worksheets and preparing to read and less time on self-chosen activities. It is known that a successful transition from home or preschool to kindergarten lays the foundation for future academic achievement (Schulting, Malone, & Dodge, 2005).

Although some states do not require kindergarten, most 5-year-olds attend either a public or private kindergarten; and an increasing number (60 percent in 2001) spend

Should the primary purpose of preschool be to provide a strong academic foundation or to foster social and emotional development?

universal preschool
A national system for early care and education that makes access to preschool similar to kindergarten by using the public schools.

a full day in school instead of the traditional half day (National Center for Education Statistics, 2004a). Do children learn more in full-day kindergarten? Initially, they do. Full-day kindergarten has been associated with greater growth of reading and math skills from fall until spring, but overall these advantages tend to be small to moderate (Votruba-Drzal, Li-Grining, & Maldonado-Carreno, 2008). By the end of third grade, amount of time spent in kindergarten makes no substantial difference in reading, math, and science achievement (Rathbun, West, & Germino-Hausken, 2004).

Findings highlight the importance of the preparation a child receives *before* kindergarten. The resources with which children come to kindergarten—preliteracy skills and the richness of a home literacy environment—predict reading achievement in first grade, and these individual differences tend to persist or increase throughout the first 4 years of school (Denton, West, & Walston, 2003; Rathbun et al., 2004). Also, children with extensive preschool experience tend to adjust to kindergarten more easily than those who spent little or no time in preschool (Ladd, 1996).

Emotional and social adjustment affect readiness for kindergarten and strongly predict school success. More important than knowing the alphabet or being able to count to 20, kindergarten teachers say, are the abilities to sit still, follow directions, wait one's turn, and regulate one's own learning (Blair, 2002; Brooks-Gunn, 2003; Raver, 2002). Adjustment to kindergarten can be eased by enabling preschoolers and parents to visit before the start of kindergarten, shortening school days early in the school year, having teachers make home visits, holding parent orientation sessions, and keeping parents informed about what is going on in school (Schulting et al., 2005).

About 5 percent of children repeat kindergarten, according to a national longitudinal study of children who first entered kindergarten in 1998–1999. Low-SES children, those who did not attend preschool, and those with developmental delays were most likely to repeat kindergarten—typically, in the belief that a 2nd year of kindergarten would help them gain the skills they need to keep up. However, these children still tended to have lower reading and mathematics skills at the end of first grade than those who had spent only 1 year in kindergarten (Malone, West, Flanagan, & Park, 2006).

checkpoint
can **you** . . .

▷ Compare Montessori and Reggio Emilia preschool programs?

▷ Discuss compensatory preschool education and universal preschool?

▷ Describe factors that affect adjustment to kindergarten?

summary and key terms

guidepost ❶ Piagetian Approach: The Preoperational Child

What are typical cognitive advances and immature aspects of preschool children's thinking?

- Children in the preoperational stage show several important advances, as well as some immature aspects of thought.

- The symbolic function enables children to reflect on people, objects, and events that are not physically present. It is shown in deferred imitation, pretend play, and language.

- Early symbolic development helps preoperational children make more accurate judgments of spatial relationships. They can understand the concept of identity, link cause and effect, categorize living and nonliving things, and understand principles of counting.

- Centration keeps preoperational children from understanding principles of conservation, which develop gradually in middle childhood. Preoperational logic is limited also by irreversibility and a focus on states rather than transformations.

- Preoperational children appear to be less egocentric than Piaget thought; they (and even younger children) are capable of empathy.

- The theory of mind, which develops markedly between ages 3 and 5, includes awareness of one's own thought processes, social cognition, understanding that people can hold false beliefs, ability to deceive, ability to distinguish appearance from reality, and ability to distinguish fantasy from reality. Hereditary and environmental influences affect individual differences in theory-of-mind development.

preoperational stage (*274*)

symbolic function (*274*)

pretend play (*275*)

transduction (*277*)

animism (*277*)

centration (*278*)

decenter (*278*)

egocentrism (*278*)

conservation (*279*)

irreversibility (*279*)

theory of mind (*280*)

Information-Processing Approach: Memory Development

What memory abilities expand in early childhood?

- Information-processing models describe three steps in memory: encoding, storage, and retrieval.

- Although sensory memory shows little change with age, the capacity of working memory increases greatly. The central executive controls the flow of information to and from long-term memory.

- At all ages, recognition is better than recall, but both increase during early childhood.

- Early episodic memory is only temporary; it fades or is transferred to generic memory. Autobiographical memory begins at about age 3 or 4 and may be related to early self-recognition ability and language development. According to the social interaction model, children and adults co-construct autobiographical memories by talking about shared experiences.

- Children are more likely to remember unusual activities that they actively participate in. The way adults talk with children about events influences memory formation.

  encoding (*285*)

  storage (*285*)

  retrieval (*285*)

  sensory memory (*285*)

  working memory (*285*)

  executive function (*285*)

  long-term memory (*285*)

  central executive (*285*)

  recognition (*286*)

  recall (*286*)

  generic memory (*286*)

  script (*286*)

  episodic memory (*286*)

  autobiographical memory (*286*)

  social interaction model (*287*)

Intelligence: Psychometric and Vygotskian Approaches

How is preschoolers' intelligence measured, and what factors influence it?

- The two most commonly used psychometric intelligence tests for young children are the Stanford-Binet Intelligence Scale and the Wechsler Preschool and Primary Scale of Intelligence, Revised (WPPSI-III).

- Intelligence test scores may be influenced by social and emotional functioning as well as by parent-child interaction and socioeconomic factors.

- Newer tests based on Vygotsky's concept of the zone of proximal development (ZPD) indicate immediate potential for achievement. Such tests, when combined with scaffolding, can help parents and teachers guide children's progress.

  Stanford-Binet Intelligence Scale (*288*)

  Wechsler Preschool and Primary Scale of Intelligence, Revised (WPPSI-III) (*288*)

  zone of proximal development (ZPD) (*289*)

  scaffolding (*290*)

Language Development

How does language improve, and what happens when its development is delayed?

- During early childhood, vocabulary increases greatly, and grammar and syntax become fairly sophisticated. Children become more competent in pragmatics.

- Private speech is normal and common during early childhood.

- Causes of delayed language development are unclear. If untreated, language delays may have serious cognitive, social, and emotional consequences.

- Interaction with adults can promote emergent literacy.

  fast mapping (*291*)

  pragmatics (*292*)

  social speech (*292*)

  private speech (*292*)

  emergent literacy (*293*)

Early Childhood Education

What purpose does early childhood education serve, and how do children make the transition to kindergarten?

- Goals of preschool education vary across cultures. Montessori and Reggio Emilia are two popular child-centered approaches. Since the 1970s, the academic content of early childhood education programs in the United States has increased.

- Compensatory preschool programs have had positive outcomes, but participants generally have not equaled the performance of middle-class children. Compensatory programs that start early and extend into the primary grades have better long-term results.

- Interest in universal preschool has grown as results of pilot programs have shown positive outcomes in terms of children's school readiness and academic success.

- Many children today attend full-day kindergarten. Success in kindergarten depends in part on emotional and social adjustment and prekindergarten preparation.

  universal preschool (*297*)

1. How does the self-concept develop during early childhood, and how do children show self-esteem, emotional growth, and initiative?

2. How do boys and girls become aware of the meaning of gender, and what explains differences in behavior between the sexes?

3. How do preschoolers play, and how does play contribute to and reflect development?

4. How do parenting practices influence development?

5. Why do young children help or hurt others, and why do they develop fears?

6. How do young children get along with—or without—siblings, playmates, and friends?

guidepost 1

How does the self-concept develop during early childhood, and how do children show self-esteem, emotional growth, and initiative?

self-concept
Sense of self; descriptive and evaluative mental picture of one's abilities and traits.

self-definition
Cluster of characteristics used to describe oneself.

Although our self-descriptions do get more accurate with age, even adults wildly overestimate their positive qualities. The only people who are accurate? The clinically depressed.

The Developing Self

"Who in the world am I? Ah, *that's* the great puzzle," said Alice in Wonderland, after her size had abruptly changed—again. Solving Alice's "puzzle" is a lifelong process of getting to know one's self.

THE SELF-CONCEPT AND COGNITIVE DEVELOPMENT

The **self-concept** is our total picture of our abilities and traits. It is "a *cognitive construction*, . . . a system of descriptive and evaluative representations about the self," that determines how we feel about ourselves and guides our actions (Harter, 1996, p. 207). The sense of self also has a social aspect: Children incorporate into their self-image their growing understanding of how others see them.

The self-concept begins to come into focus in toddlerhood, as children develop self-awareness. It becomes clearer as a person gains in cognitive abilities and deals with the developmental tasks of childhood, of adolescence, and then of adulthood.

Changes in Self-Definition: The Five to Seven Shift Children's **self-definition**—the way they describe themselves—typically changes between about ages 5 and 7, reflecting self-concept development. At age 4, Jason says,

> My name is Jason and I live in a big house with my mother and father and sister, Lisa. I have a kitty that's orange and a television set in my own room. . . . I like pizza and I have a nice teacher. I can count up to 100, want to hear me? I love my dog, Skipper. I can climb to the top of the jungle gym, I'm not scared! Just happy. You can't be happy *and* scared, no way! I have brown hair, and I go to preschool. I'm really strong. I can lift this chair, watch me! (Harter, 1996, p. 208)

The way Jason describes himself is typical of U.S. children his age. Children of this age are very concrete in their thinking. Not surprisingly, Jason focuses on what he does, what he looks like, things he owns, and the people and animals in his life. He speaks in specifics, for example, mentioning a particular skill (climbing or counting) rather than general abilities (being athletic or good at math). He is somewhat inaccurate in his description, and like most children, is unrealistically positive about his abilities.

Moreover, his understanding of emotions is still forming, and he has difficulty understanding how conflicting emotions can exist simultaneously within one person.

Until Jason is about 7 years of age, his understanding of this aspect of the self will remain immature. At about 7, he will begin to be able to describe himself in terms of generalized traits such as popular, smart, or dumb; recognize that he can have conflicting emotions; and be self-critical while holding a positive overall self-concept.

What specific changes make up this so-called age 5 to 7 shift? A neo-Piagetian analysis (Case, 1985, 1992; Fischer, 1980) describes the 5 to 7 shift as occurring in three steps. At 4, Jason is at the first step, **single representations**. His statements about himself are one-dimensional ("I like pizza . . . I'm really strong"). His thinking jumps from particular to particular, without logical connections. This indicates his cognitive immaturity and lack of ability to decenter. At this stage he cannot imagine having two emotions at once ("You can't be happy *and* scared"). Because he cannot decenter, he cannot consider different aspects of himself at the same time. His thinking about himself is all-or-nothing. He cannot acknowledge that his **real self**, the person he actually is, is not the same as his **ideal self**, the person he would like to be. So he describes himself as a paragon of virtue and ability.

At about age 5 or 6, Jason moves up to the second step, **representational mappings**. He begins to make logical connections between one aspect of himself and another: "I can run fast, and I can climb high. I'm also strong. I can throw a ball real far, I'm going to be on a team some day!" (Harter, 1996, p. 215). However, his image of himself is still expressed in completely positive, all-or-nothing terms. He cannot see how he might be good at some things and not at others.

The third step, *representational systems*, takes place in middle childhood (see Chapter 14), when children begin to integrate specific features of the self into a general, multidimensional concept. As all-or-nothing thinking declines, Jason's self-descriptions will become more balanced and realistic ("I'm good at hockey but bad at arithmetic").

Cultural Differences in Self-Definition Parents transmit, often through everyday conversations, cultural ideas and beliefs about how to define the self. For example, Chinese parents tend to encourage *interdependent* aspects of the self: compliance with authority, appropriate conduct, humility, and a sense of belonging to the community. European American parents encourage *independent* aspects of the self: individuality, self-expression, and self-esteem.

A comparative study of 180 European American and Chinese preschoolers, kindergartners, and second graders (Wang, 2004) found that children absorb such differing cultural styles of self-definition as early as age 3 or 4, and these differences increase with age. European American children tend to describe themselves in terms of personal attributes and beliefs ("I am big"), whereas Chinese children talk more about social categories and relationships ("I have a sister"). European American children more often describe themselves in terms of personality traits and tendencies ("I'm good at sports"), whereas Chinese children describe specific, overt behaviors ("I play Snowmoon with my neighbor"). European American children tend to put themselves in an unqualified positive light ("I am smart"), whereas Chinese children and adults describe themselves more neutrally ("I sometimes forget my manners"). Thus differing cultural values influence the way children in each culture perceive and define themselves.

SELF-ESTEEM

Self-esteem is the evaluative part of the self-concept, the judgment children make about their overall self-worth. Self-esteem is based on children's growing cognitive ability to describe and define themselves.

Developmental Changes in Self-Esteem Although children do not generally talk about a concept of self-worth until about age 8, younger children often show by their behavior that they have one. In a study in Belgium (Verschueren, Buyck, & Marcoen,

This is related to why children fail conservation tasks. Just as it is difficult for young children to consider two different aspects of volume (height and width) at the same time, it is difficult for them to consider two different aspects of the self at the same time.

single representations
In neo-Piagetian terminology, first stage in development of self-definition, in which children describe themselves in terms of individual, unconnected characteristics and in all-or-nothing terms.

real self
Self one actually is.

ideal self
Self one would like to be.

representational mappings
In neo-Piagetian terminology, second stage in development of self-definition, in which a child makes logical connections between aspects of the self but still sees these characteristics in all-or-nothing terms.

self-esteem
Judgment a person makes about his or her self-worth.

2001), researchers measured various aspects of 5-year-olds' self-perceptions, such as physical appearance, scholastic and athletic competence, social acceptance, and behavioral conduct. Children's positive or negative self-perceptions at age 5 tended to predict their self-perceptions and socioemotional functioning at age 8.

While there are individual differences in self-esteem in young children, most children wildly overestimate their abilities. Their self-esteem is not necessarily based on reality. One reason for this is that self-esteem is, in part, the result of feedback received from other people, and adults tend to give positive and uncritical feedback (Harter, 2006). For example, a kindergartener's crude lettering is not generally critiqued as being messy; rather, parents and teachers are more likely to praise and encourage the child's efforts, even if the end result is not ideal.

In addition to being unrealistically high, children's self-esteem tends to be unidimensional. In other words, children either believe that they are all good or all bad (Harter, 1998). You may notice that this is similar to what is found in the self-concept, and presumably the same cognitive constraints underlie both processes. In middle childhood self-esteem will become more realistic, as personal evaluations of competence based on internalization of parental and societal standards begin to shape and maintain self-worth (Harter, 1998).

Contingent Self-Esteem: The "Helpless" Pattern When self-esteem is high, a child is motivated to achieve. However, if self-esteem is *contingent* on success, children may view failure or criticism as an indictment of their worth and may feel helpless to do better. About one-third to one-half of preschoolers, kindergartners, and first graders show elements of this "helpless" pattern, sometimes referred to as "learned helplessness" (Burhans & Dweck, 1995; Dweck, 2008; Ruble & Dweck, 1995). Instead of trying a different way to complete a puzzle, as a child with unconditional self-esteem might do, "helpless" children feel ashamed and give up. They assume they will fail and so do not bother to try. Whereas older children who fail may conclude that they are "dumb," preschoolers interpret poor performance as a sign of being "bad." Furthermore, this sense of being a bad person may persist into adulthood.

Children whose self-esteem is contingent on success tend to become demoralized when they fail. Often these children attribute poor performance or social rejection to their personality deficiencies, which they believe they are helpless to change. Rather than trying new strategies, they repeat unsuccessful ones or just give up. Children with noncontingent self-esteem, in contrast, tend to attribute failure or disappointment to factors outside themselves or to the need to try harder. For example, if such a child is unable to complete a puzzle, she might conclude there are missing pieces or that perhaps the puzzle is intended for older children. If initially unsuccessful or rejected, they persevere, trying new strategies until they find one that works (Erdley, Cain, Loomis, Dumas-Hines, & Dweck, 1997; Harter, 1998; Pomerantz & Saxon, 2001). Children with high self-esteem tend to have parents and teachers who give specific, focused feedback rather than criticize the child as a person ("Look, the tag on your shirt is showing in front," not, "Can't you see your shirt is on backwards?" or "When are you going to learn to dress yourself?").

The original research on learned helplessness involved restraining dogs as they were repeatedly shocked. Eventually they stopped struggling to get away and gave up. Research with human participants has to meet rigid ethical criteria, whereas research with animals is less constrained. What do you think of research such as this? Even if it gives us valuable information, is it ethical?

what's your view

Can you think of ways in which your parents or other adults helped you develop self-esteem?

That closet full of participation trophies may not be the best thing for your young child. Research on self-esteem suggests that when children are praised and rewarded for everything they do, regardless of performance, they believe that praise uncritically. When they inevitably fail at a task, they take that as a sign that they are deficient.

Dweck, 2008

UNDERSTANDING AND REGULATING EMOTIONS

"I hate you!" Maya, age 5, shouts to her mother. "You're a mean mommy!" Angry because her mother sent her to her room for pinching her baby brother, Maya cannot imagine ever loving her mother again. "Aren't you ashamed of yourself for making the baby cry?" her father asks Maya a little later. Maya nods, but only because she knows what response he wants. In truth, she feels a jumble of emotions—not the least of which is feeling sorry for herself.

The ability to understand and regulate, or control, one's feelings is one of the key advances of early childhood (Dennis, 2006). Children who can understand their emotions are better able to control the way they show them and to be sensitive to how others feel (Garner & Estep, 2001; Garner & Power, 1996). Emotional self-regulation helps children guide their behavior (Eisenberg, Fabes, & Spinrad, 2006; Laible & Thompson, 1998) and contributes to their ability to get along with others (Denham et al., 2003). It also helps children adjust their responses to meet societal expectations; being happy and showing appreciation for gifts they may not necesssarily like is an example of a type of emotional self-regulation.

Preschoolers can talk about their feelings and often can discern the feelings of others, and they understand that emotions are connected with experiences and desires (Saarni, Campos, Camras, & Witherington, 2006; Saarni, Mumme, & Campos, 1998). They understand that someone who gets what he wants will be happy, and someone who does not get what she wants will be sad (Lagattuta, 2005).

In addition to knowing how to regulate their emotions, children come to understand emotions in a more sophisticated manner over time. In preschool, children can talk about their feelings and can read the feelings of others. They know that experiences can elicit emotions and are often based on desires (Saarni et al., 1998). They understand that people are happy when they get something they want and sad when they do not (Lagattuta, 2005). So for example, a child might be able to theorize that a boy who did not get a present on his birthday would be sad, and that another boy who received the toy truck he had been coveting would be happy.

Emotional understanding becomes more complex with age, and there appears to be a fundamental shift in abilities between ages 5 to 7. For example, in one study, 32 children of different ages and adults were asked to speculate how a young boy would feel if his ball rolled into the street and he either retrieved it or refrained from going into the street to get it. The 4- and 5-year-olds believed the boy would be happy if he got the ball and unhappy if he did not. They seemingly ignored that the boy would have broken a rule about going into the street and did not consider the impact of that on emotions. The older children and the adults were more likely to believe that obedience to a rule would make the boy feel good and disobedience would make him feel bad (Lagattuta, 2005).

> Children as young as 2 or 3 years of age can experience true clinical depression, although they are generally unable to verbalize what is going on.

The impact of electronic media on children's emotional development has undergone much scientific scrutiny. Research has shown that media can have both positive and negative effects depending on the content (Wilson, 2008). One study found that regular viewing of *Sesame Street* helped preschoolers learn to recognize emotions and emotional situations, prompting the program to incorporate emotional and emotional coping into its curricular goals (Bogatz & Ball, 1971).

Understanding Conflicting Emotions One reason for younger children's confusion about their feelings is that they do not understand they can experience contrary emotional reactions at the same time. Individual differences in understanding conflicting emotions are evident by age 3. In one study, 3-year-olds who could identify whether a face looked happy or sad and who could tell how a puppet felt when enacting a situation involving happiness, sadness, anger, or fear were better able at the end of kindergarten to explain a story character's conflicting emotions. These children tended to come from families that often discussed why people behave as they do (Brown & Dunn, 1996). Most children acquire a more sophisticated understanding of conflicting emotions during middle childhood (Harter, 1996; see Chapter 14).

> Young children might be able to read your emotions better than you think. New research suggests that children as young as 6 can tell the difference between a real smile and a fake smile—but they're not great at it. They are only accurate about 60 percent of the time.
>
> Gosselin, Perron, & Maassarani, 2009

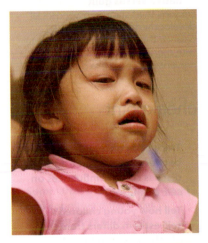

Being able to control and talk about their emotions is an important step in young children's psychological development.

> Temple Grandin, who has autism and speaks widely about her experiences, says people with autism also have difficulty feeling complex emotions. Feeling sad or happy is something she easily understands, but she has difficulty understanding how you can love someone and be angry at them at the same time.

TABLE 11.1 Five Perspectives on Gender Development

Theories	Major Theorists	Key Processes	Basic Beliefs
Biological Approach		Genetic, neurological, and hormonal activity	Many or most behavioral differences between the sexes can be traced to biological differences.
Evolutionary Developmental Approach	Charles Darwin	Natural sexual selection	Children develop gender roles in preparation for adult mating and reproductive behavior.
Psychoanalytic Approach Psychosexual theory	Sigmund Freud	Resolution of unconscious emotional conflict	Gender identity occurs when child identifies with same-sex parent.
Cognitive Approach Cognitive-developmental theory	Lawrence Kohlberg	Self-categorization	Once a child learns she is a girl or he is a boy, child sorts information about behavior by gender and acts accordingly.
Gender-schema theory	Sandra Bem, Carol Lynn Martin, & Charles F. Halverson	Self-categorization based on processing of cultural information	Child organizes information about what is considered appropriate for a boy or a girl on the basis of what a particular culture dictates and behaves accordingly. Child sorts by gender because the culture dictates that gender is an important schema.
Social Learning Approach Social cognitive theory	Albert Bandura	Observation of models, reinforcement	Child mentally combines observations of multiple models and creates own behavioral variations.

How do children acquire gender roles, and why do they adopt gender stereotypes? Are these purely social constructs, or do they reflect innate differences between males and females? The answers are not either-or. Let's look at five theoretical perspectives on gender development (summarized in Table 11.1): *biological, evolutionary developmental, psychoanalytic, cognitive,* and *social learning.* Each of these perspectives can contribute to our understanding, though none fully explains why boys and girls differ in some respects but not in others.

Biological Approach The existence of similar gender roles in many cultures suggests that some gender differences may be biologically based. In fact, if gender differences were purely cultural inventions, we would expect to see more variability in male and female roles and characteristics across cultures. Investigators are uncovering evidence of genetic, hormonal, and neurological explanations for gender differences.

Scientists have identified more than 50 genes that may explain differences in anatomy and function between the brains of male and female mice. If similar genetic differences exist in humans, then sexual identity may be hardwired into the brain even before sexual organs form and hormonal activity begins (Dewing, Shi, Horvath, & Vilain, 2003).

By age 5, when the brain reaches approximate adult size, boys' brains are about 10 percent larger than girls' brains, mostly because boys have more gray matter in the cerebral cortex, whereas girls have greater neuronal density (Reiss, Abrams, Singer, Ross, & Denckla, 1996).

However, what may be even more important is what occurs in the womb when the brain is forming. Hormones in the bloodstream before or about the time of birth affect the developing brain. The male hormone testosterone is related to aggressiveness in adult animals, but the relationship in humans is less clear (Simpson, 2001). For one thing, hormonal influences are hard to disentangle from genetic or later environmental influences (Iervolino et al., 2005). Although testosterone levels do not appear to be related to aggressiveness in children (Constantino et al., 1993), an analysis of fetal testosterone levels and the development of gender-typical play has shown a link between higher testosterone levels and male-typical play in boys (Auyeng et al., 2009).

Some research focuses on children with unusual prenatal hormonal histories. Girls with a disorder called *congenital adrenal hyperplasia* (CAH) have high prenatal levels of *androgens* (male sex hormones). Although raised as girls, they tend to develop into tomboys, showing preferences for "boys' toys," rough play, and male playmates, as well as strong spatial skills. *Estrogens* (female hormones) seem to have less influence on boys' gender-typed behavior. However, these studies are natural experiments and cannot establish cause and effect. Factors other than hormonal differences may play a role (Ruble & Martin, 1998).

Perhaps the most dramatic examples of biologically based research have to do with infants born with ambiguous sexual structures that appear to be part male and part female. John Money and his colleagues (Money, Hampson, & Hampson, 1955) developed guidelines for infants born with such disorders, recommending that the child be assigned as early as possible to the gender that holds the potential for the most nearly normal functioning. They based this recommendation on research conducted with identical twin boys, one of whom had his penis accidentally burned off during a circumcision. Money recommended to the family that the child be raised as a girl, arguing that social influences would shape gender development.

However, studies demonstrate the difficulty of predicting the outcome of sex assignment at birth. In one study, 14 genetically male children born without normal penises but with testes were legally and surgically assigned to female sex during the 1st month of life and were raised as girls. Between ages 5 and 16, eight declared themselves male (though two were living ambiguously). Five declared unwavering female identity but expressed difficulty fitting in with other girls; and one, after learning that she had been born male, refused to discuss the subject with anyone. Meanwhile, two boys whose parents had refused the initial sexual assignment remained male (Reiner & Gearhart, 2004). In another study, 25 of 27 genetically male children born without penises were raised as girls but considered themselves boys and, as children, engaged in rough play (Reiner, 2000). These cases suggest that gender identity may be rooted in chromosomal structure and cannot easily be changed (Diamond & Sigmundson, 1997).

Evolutionary Developmental Approach The evolutionary developmental approach sees gendered behavior as biologically based—with a purpose. From this controversial perspective, children's gender roles underlie the evolved mating and child-rearing strategies of adult males and females.

According to Darwin's (1871) **theory of sexual selection**, the selection of sexual partners is a response to the differing reproductive pressures that early men and women confronted in the struggle for survival of the species (Wood & Eagly, 2002). The more widely a man can "spread his seed," the greater his chances to pass on his genetic inheritance. Thus men in general tend to prefer more partners than women do. Men also value physical prowess because it enables them to compete for mates and for control of resources and social status, which women value. Because a woman invests more time and energy in pregnancy and can bear only a limited number of children, each child's survival is of greater importance to her. Thus she looks for a mate who will remain with her and support their offspring. The need to raise each child to reproductive maturity also explains why women tend to be more caring and nurturant than men (Bjorklund & Pellegrini, 2000; Wood & Eagly, 2002).

For years John Money promoted his twin study as a success and hid evidence to the contrary. It later came out that the boy had never successfully adjusted to life as a girl, had been unhappy throughout his childhood, and had made several suicide attempts in his youth, finally succeeding in adulthood. Because of Money's research, thousands of gender reassignment surgeries were conducted on infants under the presumption that gender is a malleable social construct. This series of events illustrates one of the primary reasons science needs to be transparent and honest—it can have profound repercussions in the real world.

theory of sexual selection
Darwinian theory, which holds that selection of sexual partners is influenced by the differing reproductive pressures that early men and women confronted in the struggle for survival of the species.

This approach does not imply that men and women are consciously striving to have lots of kids and pass on their genes. Instead, it is argued that men and women do things—like have sex—that make it more likely they will leave descendants.

According to evolutionary theory, male competitiveness and aggressiveness and female nurturance develop during childhood as preparation for these adult roles. Boys play at fighting; girls play at parenting. In caring for children, women often must put a child's needs and feelings ahead of their own. Thus young girls tend to be better able than young boys to control and inhibit their emotions and to refrain from impulsive behavior (Bjorklund & Pellegrini, 2000).

Some people misinterpret evolutionary approaches to be deterministic in nature. In other words, they assume that if evolution played a role in the development of gender roles, that means that gender roles are, in a way, preordained, and thus should be inflexible and highly resistant to change. It is indeed the case that in all cultures, women tend to be children's primary caregivers (Wood & Eagly, 2002). It is also the case, that in all cultures, men are overwhelmingly responsible for homicides (Daly & Wilson, 1998). But this does not mean that men never care for children, nor does it mean that women are never aggressive. Rather, it means that evolution has given us a slight "push" in one direction or another that can then be minimized or maximized by cultural and environmental influences. And, it is only when large numbers of individuals are examined that the gender differences thus emerge.

Critics of evolutionary theory suggest that society and culture are as important as biology in determining gender roles. But, evolutionary theorists have never argued that culture is insignificant. Rather, they have argued that men and women have cognitive adaptations designed to be sensitive to environmental input. Thus, while research suggests that men's primary ancestral role was to provide for subsistence while women's was to tend to the children, this does not mean that we are bound to these roles. Indeed, in some nonindustrial societies women are the main or equal providers, and men and women's mate preferences seem to be less pronounced in egalitarian societies where women have more reproductive freedom and educational opportunities (Wood & Eagly, 2002).

Gender roles, then, are best seen as a dynamic process. Evolutionary psychologists acknowledge that gender roles (such as men's involvement in child rearing) may change in an environment different from that in which these roles initially evolved (Crawford, 1998).

Psychoanalytic Approach "Dad, where will you live when I grow up and marry Mommy?" asks Juan, age 4. From the psychoanalytic perspective, Juan's question is part of his acquisition of gender identity. That process, according to Freud, is one of **identification**, the adoption of characteristics, beliefs, attitudes, values, and behaviors of the parent of the same sex. Freud considered identification an important personality development of early childhood; some social learning theorists also have used the term.

According to Freud, identification will occur for Juan when he represses or gives up the wish to possess the parent of the other sex (his mother) and identifies with the parent of the same sex (his father). But although this explanation for gender development has been influential, it has been difficult to test and has little research support (Maccoby, 1992, 2000). Despite some evidence that preschoolers tend to act more affectionately toward the other-sex parent and more aggressively toward the same-sex parent (Westen, 1998), the majority of developmental psychologists today favor other explanations.

Cognitive Approaches Sarah figures out she is a girl because people call her a girl. As she continues to observe and think about her world, she concludes that she will always be female. She comes to understand gender by actively thinking about and constructing her own gender-typing. This is the heart of Lawrence Kohlberg's (1966) cognitive-developmental theory.

Kohlberg's Cognitive-Developmental Theory In Kohlberg's theory, *gender knowledge precedes gendered behavior* ("I am a boy, so I like to do boy things"). Children *actively*

Worried about the boy down the street whose play is always too aggressive? In all likelihood, there's nothing to be concerned about. Research suggests no link between early aggressive play in boys and later criminality.

Parry, 2010

identification
In Freudian theory, process by which a young child adopts characteristics, beliefs, attitudes, values, and behaviors of the parent of the same sex.

search for cues about gender in their social world. As children come to realize which gender they belong to, they adopt behaviors they perceive as consistent with being male or female. Thus 3-year-old Sarah prefers dolls to trucks because she sees girls playing with dolls and therefore views playing with dolls as consistent with her being a girl. And she plays mostly with other girls, whom she assumes will share her interests (Martin & Ruble, 2004).

The acquisition of gender roles, said Kohlberg, hinges on **gender constancy**, more recently called *sex-category constancy*—a child's realization that his or her sex will always be the same. Once children achieve this realization, they are motivated to adopt behaviors appropriate to their sex. Gender constancy seems to develop in three stages: gender identity, gender stability, and gender consistency (Martin, Ruble, & Szkrybalo, 2002; Ruble & Martin, 1998; Szkrybalo & Ruble, 1999). *Gender identity* (awareness of one's own gender and that of others) typically occurs between ages 2 and 3. *Gender stability* comes when a girl realizes that she will grow up to be a woman, and a boy that he will grow up to be a man—in other words, that gender does not change. However, children at this stage may base judgments about gender on superficial appearances (clothing or hairstyle) and stereotyped behaviors. Sometime between ages 3 and 7, or even later—comes *gender consistency:* the realization that a girl remains a girl even if she has a short haircut and plays with trucks, and a boy remains a boy even if he has long hair and wears earrings. Once children realize that their behavior or dress will not affect their sex, they may become less rigid in their adherence to gender norms (Martin et al., 2002).

Much research challenges Kohlberg's view that gender-typing depends on gender constancy. Long before children attain the final stage of gender constancy, they show gender-typed preferences (Bussey & Bandura, 1992; Martin & Ruble, 2004; Ruble & Martin, 1998). For example, gender preferences in toys and playmates appear as early as 12 to 24 months. However, these findings do not challenge Kohlberg's basic insight: that gender concepts influence behavior (Martin et al., 2002).

Today, cognitive-developmental theorists no longer claim that gender constancy must precede gender-typing (Martin et al., 2002). Instead, they suggest that gender-typing may be heightened by the more sophisticated understanding that gender constancy brings (Martin & Ruble, 2004). Each stage of gender constancy increases children's receptivity to gender-relevant information. The achievement of gender identity may motivate children to learn more about gender; gender stability and gender consistency may motivate them to be sure they are acting "like a boy" or "like a girl." Studies have found significant links between levels of gender constancy and various aspects of gender development (Martin et al., 2002).

Gender-Schema Theory Another cognitive approach is **gender-schema theory**. Like cognitive-developmental theory, it views children as actively extracting knowledge about gender from their environment *before* engaging in gender-typed behavior. However, gender-schema theory places more emphasis on the influence of culture. Once children know what sex they are, they develop a concept of what it means to be male or female *in their culture*. Children then match their behavior to their culture's view of what boys and girls are "supposed" to be and do. Among the theory's leading proponents are Sandra Bem (1983, 1985, 1993), Carol Lynn Martin, and Charles F. Halverson (Martin & Halverson, 1981; Martin et al., 2002).

According to this theory, gender schemas promote gender stereotypes by influencing judgments about behavior. When a new boy his age moves in next door, 4-year-old Brandon knocks on his door, carrying a toy truck—apparently assuming that the new boy will like the same toys he likes. Bem suggests that children who show such stereotypical behavior may be experiencing pressure for gender conformity that inhibits healthy self-exploration. However, there is little evidence that gender schemas are at the root of stereotyped behavior or that children who are highly gender-typed necessarily feel pressure to conform (Yunger, Carver, & Perry, 2004). Indeed, as many

gender constancy
Awareness that one will always be male or female. Also called *sex-category constancy*.

study smart

Gender

gender-schema theory
Theory that children socialize themselves in their gender roles by developing a mentally organized network of information about what it means to be male or female in a particular culture.

According to Bem's gender-schema theory, parents can help their children avoid gender stereotypes by encouraging them to pursue their own interests, even when these interests are unconventional for their sex.

parents will attest, it can be difficult to encourage a child to behave in ways that are not stereotypically masculine or feminine.

Another problem with both gender-schema theory and Kohlberg's theory is that gender-stereotyping does not always become stronger with increased gender knowledge (Bandura & Bussey, 2004; Bussey & Bandura, 1999). In fact, gender-stereotyping rises and then falls in a developmental pattern (Ruble & Martin, 1998; Welch-Ross & Schmidt, 1996). Around ages 4 to 6, when, according to gender-schema theory, children are constructing and then consolidating their gender schemas, they notice and remember only information consistent with these schemas and even exaggerate it. In fact, they tend to *mis*remember information that challenges gender stereotypes, such as photos of a girl sawing wood or a boy cooking, and to insist that the genders in the photos were the other way around. Young children are quick to accept gender labels; when told that an unfamiliar toy is meant for the other sex, they will drop it quickly, and they expect others to do the same (C. L. Martin, Eisenbud, & Rose, 1995; Martin & Ruble, 2004; Ruble & Martin, 1998).

By ages 5 and 6, children develop a repertoire of rigid stereotypes about gender that they apply to themselves and others. A boy will pay more attention to what he considers boys' toys and a girl to girls' toys. A boy will expect to do better at boy things than at girl things, and if he does try, say, to dress a doll, he will be all thumbs. Then, around age 7 or 8, schemas become more complex as children begin to take in and integrate contradictory information, such as the fact that many girls have short hair. Children develop more complex beliefs about gender and become more flexible in their views about gender roles (Martin & Ruble, 2004; Trautner et al., 2005).

Cognitive approaches to gender development have made an important contribution by exploring how children think about gender and what they know about it at various ages. However, these approaches may not fully explain the link between knowledge and conduct. There is disagreement about precisely what mechanism prompts children to act out gender roles and why some children become more strongly gender-typed than others (Bussey & Bandura, 1992, 1999; Martin & Ruble, 2004; Ruble & Martin, 1998). Some investigators point to socialization.

> Coloring book and cereal box characters are not immune from gender stereotypes. Females are more likely to be portrayed as children or humans, males are more likely to be portrayed as animals, adults, and superheroes.

Social Learning Approach According to Walter Mischel (1966), a traditional social learning theorist, children acquire gender roles by imitating models and being rewarded for gender-appropriate behavior—in other words, by responding to environmental stimuli. Children generally choose models they see as powerful or nurturing. Typically, one model is a parent, often of the same sex, but children also pattern their behavior after other adults or after peers. Behavioral feedback, together with direct teaching by parents and other adults, reinforces gender-typing. A boy who models his behavior after his father is commended for acting "like a boy." A girl gets compliments on a pretty dress or hairstyle. In this model, *gendered behavior precedes gender knowledge* ("I am rewarded for doing boy things, so I must be a boy").

Since the 1970s, however, studies have cast doubt on the power of same-sex modeling alone to account for gender differences. As cognitive explanations have come to the fore, traditional social learning theory has lost favor (Martin et al., 2002). Albert Bandura's (1986; Bussey & Bandura, 1999) newer **social cognitive theory**, an expansion of social learning theory, incorporates some cognitive elements.

According to social cognitive theory, observation enables children to learn much about gender-typed behaviors before performing them. They can mentally combine observations of multiple models and generate their own behavioral variations. Instead of viewing the environment as a given, social cognitive theory recognizes that children

> Note that this explanation focuses on the learning approaches discussed in Chapter 1. Theories help us understand and make sense of the world, and in this case, we use the principles of reinforcement and punishment to explain gender. Note also that theories change in response to new data. Thus, when research began to indicate that cognition also mattered, the original approach was expanded to accommodate those findings.

social cognitive theory
Albert Bandura's expansion of social learning theory; holds that children learn gender roles through socialization.

select or even create their environments through their choice of playmates and activities. However, critics say that social cognitive theory does not explain how children differentiate between boys and girls before they have a concept of gender, or what initially motivates children to acquire gender knowledge, or how gender norms become internalized—questions that other cognitive theories attempt to answer (Martin et al., 2002).

For social cognitive theorists, socialization—the way a child interprets and internalizes experiences with parents, teachers, peers, and cultural institutions—plays a central part in gender development. Socialization begins in infancy, long before a conscious understanding of gender begins to form. Gradually, as children begin to regulate their activities, standards of behavior become internalized. A child no longer needs praise, rebukes, or a model's presence to act in socially appropriate ways. Children feel good about themselves when they live up to their internal standards and feel bad when they do not. A substantial part of the shift from socially guided control to self-regulation of gender-related behavior may take place between ages 3 and 4 (Bussey, 2011; Bussey & Bandura, 1992). In the following sections we address three primary sources of social influences on gender development: family, peer, and cultural.

Family Influences When former Louisiana governor Kathleen Blanco's 4-year-old grandson David was asked what he wanted to be when he grew up, he wasn't sure. He shrugged off all his mother's suggestions—firefighter, soldier, policeman, airplane pilot. Finally, she asked whether he'd like to be governor. "Mom," he replied, "I'm a boy!" (Associated Press, 2004a).

David's response illustrates how strong family influences may be, even fostering counterstereotypical preferences. Usually, though, experience in the family seems to reinforce gender-typical preferences and attitudes. We say "seems" because it is difficult to separate parents' genetic influence from the influence of the environment they create. Also, parents may be responding to rather than encouraging children's gender-typed behavior (Iervolino et al., 2005).

Boys tend to be more strongly gender-socialized concerning play preferences than girls. Parents, especially fathers, generally show more discomfort if a boy plays with a doll than if a girl plays with a truck (Lytton & Romney, 1991; Ruble & Martin, 1998; Ruble, Martin, & Berenbaum, 2006; Sandnabba & Ahlberg, 1999). Girls have more freedom than boys in their clothes, games, and choice of playmates (Fagot, Rogers, & Leinbach, 2000; Miedzian, 1991).

In egalitarian households, the father's role in gender socialization seems especially important (Deutsch, Servis, & Payne, 2001; Fagot & Leinbach, 1995). In an observational study of 4-year-olds in British and Hungarian cities, boys and girls whose fathers did more housework and child care were less aware of gender stereotypes and engaged in less gender-typed play than peers in more gender-typical families (Turner & Gervai, 1995). In an analysis of 43 studies, Tenenbaum and Leaper (2002) found that parents who adhered to traditional gender schemas were more likely to have children with gender-typed ideas about themselves and other individuals when compared to parents who had adhered to nontraditional gender schemas.

Siblings also influence gender development, according to a 3-year longitudinal study of 198 first- and secondborn siblings and their parents. Secondborns tend to become more like their older siblings in attitudes, personality, and leisure activities, whereas firstborns are more influenced by their parents and less by their younger siblings (McHale, Updegraff, Helms-Erikson, & Crouter, 2001). Young children with an older sibling of the same sex tend to be more gender-typed than those whose older sibling is of the other sex (Iervolino et al., 2005).

Peer Influences Anna, at age 5, insisted on dressing in a new way. She wanted to wear leggings with a skirt over them, and boots—indoors and out. When her mother asked her why, Anna replied, "Because Katie dresses like this—and Katie's the king of the girls!"

Did you know that pink used to be considered masculine and blue feminine? Blue was considered soothing, and so more appropriate for girls. Pink was a variation of red, a strong and active color, and was seen as more appropriate for boys.

letting children select from a wide range of activities. The Korean American preschool, in keeping with traditional Korean values, emphasized developing academic skills and completing tasks. The Anglo American preschools encouraged social interchange among children and collaborative activities with teachers. In the Korean American preschool, children were allowed to talk and play only during outdoor recess.

Not surprisingly, the Anglo American children engaged in more social play, whereas the Korean Americans engaged in more unoccupied or parallel play. At the same time, Korean American children played more cooperatively, often offering toys to other children—very likely a reflection of their culture's emphasis on group harmony. Anglo American children were more aggressive and often responded negatively to other children's suggestions, reflecting the competitiveness of American culture.

Parenting

As children increasingly become their own persons, their upbringing can be a complex challenge. Parents must deal with small people who have minds and wills of their own but who still have a lot to learn about what kinds of behavior work well in society.

FORMS OF DISCIPLINE

The word *discipline* means "instruction" or "training." In the field of child development, **discipline** refers to methods of molding character and of teaching self-control and acceptable behavior. In casual speech we tend to think of discipline as involving only punishment, but the psychological definition of the word also includes techniques such as rewarding desired behaviors and drawing attention to how actions affect others. Discipline can be a powerful tool for socialization with the goal of developing self-discipline. What forms of discipline work best? Researchers have looked at a wide range of techniques.

Reinforcement and Punishment "You're such a wonderful helper, Nick! Thank you so much for putting away your toys." Nick's mother smiles warmly at her son as he plops his dump truck into the toy box. Her words and actions provide gentle discipline for her son and teach him that putting away his toys is a positive behavior that should be repeated.

Parents sometimes punish children to stop undesirable behavior, but children usually learn more from being reinforced for good behavior. *External* reinforcements may be tangible (treats, more playtime) or intangible (a smile, a word of praise, a hug, extra attention, or a special privilege). Whatever the reinforcement, the child must see it as rewarding and must receive it fairly consistently and immediately after showing the desired behavior. Eventually, the behavior should provide an *internal* reinforcement: a sense of pleasure or accomplishment.

Still, at times punishment, such as isolation or denial of privileges, is necessary. Children cannot be permitted to run out into traffic or hit another child. Sometimes a child is willfully defiant. In such situations, punishment, if consistent, immediate, and clearly tied to the offense, may be effective. It should be administered calmly, in private, and aimed at eliciting compliance, not guilt. It is most effective when accompanied by a short, simple explanation (AAP Committee on Psychosocial Aspects of Child and Family Health, 1998; Baumrind, 1996a, 1996b). It is also important to remember that, in addition to punishment for undesired behaviors, the desired behaviors should be made clear. Children need to know what should be substituted for misbehavior.

Too harsh punishment, on the other hand, can be harmful. Children who are punished harshly and frequently may have trouble interpreting other people's actions and words; they may attribute hostile intentions where none exist (B. Weiss, Dodge, Bates, & Pettit, 1992). Young children who have been punished harshly may later act aggressively, even though the punishment is intended to stop what a parent sees as purposely

checkpoint
can you...

▷ Tell how gender and culture influence the way children play, and give examples?

guidepost
4 **How do parenting practices influence development?**

discipline
Methods of molding children's character and of teaching them to exercise self-control and engage in acceptable behavior.

A secure attachment with parents or a teacher in early childhood has been related to whether or not children view God as a "loving friend"—someone who is nice, loves you, and makes you happy. If you are religious, do you think your relationship with your parents affects your religious beliefs?

de Roos, 2006

aggressive behavior (Nix et al., 1999). Or such children may become passive because they feel helpless. Children may become frightened if parents lose control and may eventually try to avoid a punitive parent, undermining the parent's ability to influence behavior (Grusec & Goodnow, 1994).

Corporal punishment has been defined as "the use of physical force with the intention of causing a child to experience pain, but not injury, for the purpose of correction or control of the child's behavior" (Straus, 1994a, p. 4). It can include spanking, hitting, slapping, pinching, shaking, and other physical acts. Corporal punishment is popularly believed to be more effective than other remedies and to be harmless if done in moderation by loving parents (McLoyd & Smith, 2002), but a growing body of evidence points to serious negative consequences (Straus, 1999; Straus & Stewart, 1999; Box 11.2). An ongoing debate on the appropriateness of the use of corporal punishment in schools rages in the United States. Twenty states permit the use of corporal punishment in schools. In 2007 more than 200,000 students were hit as punishment. Some educators believe it is an effective deterant to harmful misbehaviors, like fighting, but others assert that corporal punishment degrades the educational environment (Human Rights Watch, 2008).

Unlike child abuse, which bears little or no relation to the child's personality or behavior, corporal punishment is more frequently used with children who are aggressive and hard to manage, characteristics that may be genetically based (Jaffee et al., 2004). The line between some forms of punishment and physical or emotional abuse is not always easy to draw, but discipline clearly becomes abusive when it results in injury to a child.

Psychological aggression refers to verbal attacks that may result in psychological harm, such as (1) yelling or screaming, (2) threatening to spank or hit the child, (3) swearing or cursing at the child, (4) threatening to send the child away or kick the child out of the house, and (5) calling the child dumb or lazy. Some psychologists equate the last three categories with emotional abuse. Psychological aggression, like physical aggression (spanking), is almost universal among U.S. parents. In a nationally representative sampling of 991 parents, 98 percent reported using some form of psychological aggression by the time a child was 5, and about 90 percent thereafter (Straus & Field, 2003).

Inductive Reasoning, Power Assertion, and Withdrawal of Love When Sara took candy from a store, her father did not lecture her on honesty, spank her, or tell her what a bad girl she had been. Instead, he explained how the owner of the store would be harmed by her failure to pay for the candy and how sad he would feel that it was gone. He asked Sara how she would feel in the same situation. Last, he took her back to the store to return the candy. Although he did not ask her to do so, Sara told the store owner she was sorry that she made him sad.

Inductive techniques, such as those Sara's father used, are designed to encourage desirable behavior or discourage undesirable behavior by reasoning with a child. They include setting limits, demonstrating logical consequences of an action, explaining, discussing, negotiating, and getting ideas from the child about what is fair. They also tend to include appeals to consider how one's actions affect how others feel. Inductive techniques are usually the most effective method of getting children to accept parental standards (M. L. Hoffman, 1970a, 1970b; Jagers, Bingham, & Hans, 1996; Kerr, Lopez, Olson, & Sameroff, 2004; McCord, 1996).

Inductive reasoning tends to arouse empathy for the victim of wrongdoing as well as guilt on the part of the wrongdoer (Kochanska, Gross, Lin, & Nichols, 2002; Krevans & Gibbs, 1996). Kindergartners whose mothers reported using reasoning were more likely to see the moral wrongness of behavior that hurts other people (as opposed to merely breaking rules) than children whose mothers took away privileges (Jagers et al., 1996).

Two other broad categories of discipline are power assertion and temporary withdrawal of love. **Power assertion** is intended to stop or discourage undesirable behavior through physical or verbal enforcement of parental control; it includes demands, threats,

corporal punishment
Use of physical force with the intention of causing pain but not injury so as to correct or control behavior.

Kids who come from homes in which there is domestic abuse, whether physical or emotional, are more likely to be spanked.

Taylor, Lee, Guterman, & Rice, 2010

Dante Cicchetti from the University of Minnesota has found that children from abusive homes are more likely to respond to a schoolmate's cries with aggression or withdrawal than are children from loving homes, who are more likely to try to comfort their schoolmate or go get a teacher. Why might abused children have developed this tendency? How might their parents' responses to their distress have shaped this?

psychological aggression
Verbal attack that may result in psychological harm.

inductive techniques
Disciplinary techniques designed to induce desirable behavior by appealing to a child's sense of reason and fairness.

power assertion
Disciplinary strategy designed to discourage undesirable behavior through physical or verbal enforcement of parental control.

THE CASE AGAINST CORPORAL PUNISHMENT

"Spare the rod and spoil the child" may sound old-fashioned, but corporal punishment has become a hot issue. Many people still believe that spanking instills respect for authority, motivates good behavior, and is a necessary part of responsible parenting (Kazdin & Benjet, 2003). Alternatively, some child development professionals view any corporal punishment as verging on child abuse (Straus, 1994b). Other professionals find no harm in corporal punishment in moderation when prudently administered by loving parents (Baumrind, 1996a, 1996b; Baumrind, Larzelere, & Cowan, 2002).

Corporal punishment is banned in many countries, including Austria, Bulgaria, Croatia, Cyprus, Denmark, Finland, Germany, Hungary, Iceland, Israel, Latvia, Norway, Romania, Sweden, and Ukraine. In the United States, all states except Minnesota allow parents to administer corporeal punishment, though some insist that it be reasonable, appropriate, moderate, or necessary, and some recognize that excessive corporal punishment can be abusive (Gershoff, 2002). Corporal punishment is allowed in schools in 20 states, though a bill introduced in 2010 aims to ban corporal punishment in all schools. The Supreme Court of Canada in January 2004 ruled out corporal punishment in schools and also forbade it for infants or teenagers in any setting (Center for Effective Discipline, 2005). The United Nations Convention on the Rights of Children opposes all forms of physical violence against children.

Nevertheless, some form of corporal punishment is widely used on U.S. infants and is near-universal among parents of toddlers. In interviews with a nationally representative sample of 991 parents in 1995, 35 percent reported using corporal punishment—usually hand slapping—on infants and fully 94 percent on 3- and 4-year-olds. About 50 percent of the parents used corporal punishment on 12-year-olds, 30 percent on 14-year-olds, and 13 percent on 17-year-olds (Straus & Stewart, 1999).

Why do parents hit children? No doubt, because hitting gets children to comply (Gershoff, 2002). However, a large body of research has found negative short- and long-term associations with its use. Apart from the risk of injury or abuse, these outcomes may include, in childhood, lack of moral internalization; poor parent-child relationships; increased physical aggressiveness, antisocial behavior, and delinquency; and diminished mental health. Outcomes in adulthood can include aggression, criminal or antisocial behavior, anxiety disorders, depression, alcohol problems, and partner or child abuse (Gershoff, 2002; MacMillan et al., 1999; Strassberg, Dodge, Pettit, & Bates, 1994).

A child who is spanked is likely to imitate that behavior. Studies show that children who are spanked tend to become aggressive.

Most of this research was cross-sectional or retrospective or did not consider that the spanked children may have been aggressive in the first place and that their aggressive behavior or some other factor might have led their parents to spank them (Gershoff, 2002). Since 1997, several large, nationally representative landmark studies of children from age 3 through adolescence (Brezina, 1999; Gunnoe & Mariner, 1997; Simons, Lin, & Gordon, 1998; Strauss & Paschall, 1999; Straus, Sugarman, & Giles-Sims, 1997) have controlled for the child's behavior at the time of first measurement. These studies found that the more physical punishment a child receives, the more aggressive the child becomes and the more likely the child is to be antisocial or aggressive as an adult (Straus & Stewart, 1999).

Why the link between corporal punishment and aggressive behavior? As social learning theory would predict, children may imitate the punisher and may come to consider infliction of pain an acceptable response to problems. Corporal punishment also may arouse anger and resentment, causing children to focus on their own

Continued

Continued

hurts instead of on the wrong they have done to others. Furthermore, as with any punishment, the effectiveness of spanking diminishes with repeated use; children may feel free to misbehave if they are willing to take the consequences. Also, reliance on physical punishment may weaken parents' authority when children become teenagers, too big and strong to spank even if spanking were appropriate (AAP Committee on Psychosocial Aspects of Child and Family Health, 1998; Gershoff, 2002; McCord, 1996). Frequent spanking may even inhibit cognitive development (Straus & Paschall, 1999).

Critics of this research point out that corporal punishment does not occur in isolation; we cannot be sure that the observed outcomes were attributable to it and not to other parental behaviors or family circumstances, such as stressful events, marital discord, lack of parental warmth, or substance abuse (Kazdin & Benjet, 2003). A 6-year study of 1,990 European American, African American, and Hispanic children found that spanking does not predict an increase in problem behavior if it is done in the context of a mother's strong emotional support (McLoyd & Smith, 2002). Also, physical discipline is less likely to cause aggression or anxiety in cultures where it is seen as normal, such as in Kenya (Lansford et al., 2005).

Still, the research strongly suggests that frequent or severe corporal punishment is potentially harmful to children.

Furthermore, there is no clear line between mild and harsh spanking, and one often leads to the other (Kazdin & Benjet, 2003). Thus, even though no harm from very mild spanking has been established (Larzalere, 2000), it seems prudent to choose other, less risky means of discipline that have no potentially adverse effects (Kazdin & Benjet, 2003).

The American Academy of Pediatrics Committee on Psychosocial Aspects of Child and Family Health (1998) urges parents to avoid spanking. Instead, the committee suggests teaching children to use words to express feelings, giving them choices and helping them evaluate the consequences, and modeling orderly behavior and cooperative conflict resolution. The committee recommends positive reinforcement to encourage desired behaviors and verbal reprimands, time-outs (brief isolation to give the child a chance to cool down), or removal of privileges to discourage undesired behaviors—all within a positive, supportive, loving parent-child relationship.

what's your view Did your parents ever spank you? If so, how often and in what kinds of situations? Would you spank, or have you ever spanked, your own child? Why or why not?

11.2

---

withdrawal of privileges, spanking, and other types of punishment. **Withdrawal of love** may include ignoring, isolating, or showing dislike for a child. Neither of these is as effective as inductive reasoning in most circumstances, and both may be harmful (Baumrind, Larzelere, & Owens, 2010; M. L. Hoffman, 1970a, 1970b; Jagers et al., 1996; McCord, 1996).

The effectiveness of parental discipline may hinge on how well the child understands and accepts the parent's message, both cognitively and emotionally (Grusec & Goodnow, 1994). For the child to accept the message, the child has to recognize it as appropriate, so parents need to be fair and accurate as well as clear and consistent about their expectations. They need to fit the discipline to the misdeed and to the child's temperament and cognitive and emotional level. A child may be more motivated to accept the message if the parents are normally warm and responsive and if they arouse the child's empathy for someone the child has harmed (Grusec & Goodnow, 1994; Kerr, Lopez, Olson & Sameroff, 2004). How well children accept a disciplinary method also may depend on whether the type of discipline used is accepted in the family's culture (Lansford et al., 2005).

One point on which many experts agree is that a child interprets and responds to discipline in the context of an ongoing relationship with a parent. Some researchers, therefore, look beyond specific parental practices to overall styles, or patterns, of parenting.

PARENTING STYLES

Why does Stacy hit and bite the nearest person when she cannot finish a jigsaw puzzle? What makes David sit and sulk when he cannot finish the puzzle, even though his teacher offers to help him? Why does Consuelo work on the puzzle for 20 minutes and

withdrawal of love Disciplinary strategy that involves ignoring, isolating, or showing dislike for a child.

what's your view As a parent, what form of discipline would you favor if your 3-year-old snuck a cookie from the cookie jar? Refused to take a nap? Hit his little sister? Tell why.

checkpoint can you . . .

▷ Compare various forms of discipline, and identify factors that influence their effectiveness?

TABLE 11.4 Parenting Styles

		WARMTH	
		High	Low
CONTROL	High	Authoritative	Authoritarian
	Low	Permissive	Neglectful

Diana Baumrind's research led her to classify parenting styles. Parenting styles can vary on warmth, or how responsive, loving, and supportive parents are; or on control, or how much behavioral compliance parents demand from their children.

then shrug and try another? Why are children so different in their responses to the same situation? Temperament is a major factor, of course, but some research suggests that styles of parenting affect children's competence in dealing with their world.

Diana Baumrind and the Effectiveness of Authoritative Parenting

In pioneering research, Diana Baumrind (1971, 1996b; Baumrind & Black, 1967) studied 103 preschool children from 95 families. Through interviews, testing, and home studies, she measured how children were functioning, identified three parenting styles, and described typical behavior patterns of children raised according to each. Baumrind's work and the large body of research it inspired have established strong associations between each parenting style and a particular set of child behaviors (Baumrind, 1989; Darling & Steinberg, 1993; Pettit, Bates, & Dodge, 1997; see Table 11.4).

Authoritarian parenting, according to Baumrind, emphasizes control and unquestioning obedience. Authoritarian parents try to make children conform rigidly to a set standard of conduct and punish them for violating it, often using power-assertive techniques. They are more detached and less warm than other parents. Their children tend to be more discontented, withdrawn, and distrustful.

Permissive parenting emphasizes self-expression and self-regulation. Permissive parents make few demands and allow children to monitor their own activities as much as possible. They consult with children about policy decisions and rarely punish. They are warm, noncontrolling, and undemanding or even indulgent. Their preschool children tend to be immature—the least self-controlled and the least exploratory.

> As a parent, what form of discipline would you favor if your 3-year-old took a cookie from the cookie jar? Refused to nap? Hit his little sister? Explain why.

Authoritative parenting emphasizes a child's individuality but also stress social constraints. Authoritative parents have confidence in their ability to guide children, but they also respect children's independent decisions, interests, opinions, and personalities. They are loving and accepting but also demand good behavior and are firm in maintaining standards. They impose limited, judicious punishment when necessary, within the context of a warm, supportive relationship. They favor inductive discipline, explaining the reasoning behind their stand and encouraging verbal negotiation and give-and-take. Their children apparently feel secure in knowing both that they are loved and what is expected of them. These preschoolers tend to be the most self-reliant, self-controlled, self-assertive, exploratory, and content.

Eleanor Maccoby and John Martin (1983) added a fourth parenting style—*neglectful,* or *uninvolved*—to describe parents who, sometimes because of stress or depression, focus on their own needs rather than on those of the child. Neglectful parenting has been linked with a variety of behavioral disorders in childhood and adolescence (Baumrind, 1991; Parke & Buriel, 1998; Steinberg, Eisengart, & Cauffman, 2006; R. A. Thompson, 1998).

---

authoritarian parenting
Parenting style emphasizing control and obedience.

permissive parenting
Parenting style emphasizing self-expression and self-regulation.

authoritative parenting
Parenting style blending warmth and respect for a child's individuality with an effort to instill social values.

Why does authoritative parenting tend to enhance children's social competence? It may be because authoritative parents set sensible expectations and realistic standards. By making clear, consistent rules, they let children know what is expected of them and give them a standard of behavior by which to judge themselves. In authoritarian homes, children are so strictly controlled that often they cannot make independent choices about their behavior; in permissive homes, children receive so little guidance that they may be uncertain and anxious about whether they are doing the right thing. In authoritative homes, children know when they are meeting expectations and can decide whether it is worth risking parental displeasure to pursue a goal. These children are expected to perform well, fulfill commitments, and participate actively in family duties as well as in family fun. They know the satisfaction of accepting responsibilities and achieving success. Parents who make reasonable demands show that they believe their children can meet them—and that they care enough to insist that their children do so.

When conflict arises, an authoritative parent can teach children positive ways to communicate their point of view and negotiate acceptable alternatives ("If you don't want to throw away those rocks you found, where do you think we should keep them?"). Internalization of this broader set of skills, not just of specific behavioral demands, may well be a key to the success of authoritative parenting (Grusec & Goodnow, 1994).

Support and Criticisms of Baumrind's Model In research based on Baumrind's work, the superiority of authoritative parenting (or similar conceptions of parenting style) has repeatedly been supported. Identifying and promoting positive parenting practices is crucial to preventing early-onset problem behavior (Dishion & Stormshak, 2007). In a longitudinal study of 585 ethnically and socioeconomically diverse families in Tennessee and Indiana with children from prekindergarten through Grade 6, four aspects of early supportive parenting—warmth, use of inductive discipline, interest and involvement in children's contacts with peers, and proactive teaching of social skills—predicted positive behavioral, social, and academic outcomes (Pettit et al., 1997). Families at high risk for problem behavior in children who participated in a "Family Check Up" program that provided critical parenting support services were able to improve childhood outcomes by an early focus on positive and proactive parenting practices (Dishion et al., 2008).

Still, Baumrind's model has provoked controversy because it seems to suggest that there is one "right" way to raise children. Also, because Baumrind's findings are correlational, they merely establish associations between each parenting style and a particular set of child behaviors. They do not show that different styles of child rearing *cause* children to be more or less competent. It is also impossible to know whether the children Baumrind studied were, in fact, raised in a particular style. It may be that some of the better-adjusted children were raised inconsistently, but by the time of the study their parents had adopted the authoritative pattern (Holden & Miller, 1999). In addition, Baumrind did not consider innate factors, such as temperament, that might have affected children's competence and exerted an influence on the parents. Children may elicit parenting styles based on their own behavior; an easy child might, for example, elicit authoritarian parenting.

Cultural Differences in Parenting Styles Another concern is that Baumrind's categories reflect the dominant North American view of child development and may not apply to some other cultures or socioeconomic groups. Among Asian Americans, obedience and strictness are not associated with harshness and domination but instead with caring, concern, involvement, and maintenance of family harmony. Traditional Chinese culture, with its emphasis on respect for elders, stresses adults' responsibility to maintain the social order by teaching children socially proper behavior. This obligation is carried out through firm and just control and governance of the child, and even by physical punishment if necessary (Zhao, 2002). Although Asian American

what's your view

To what extent would you like your children to adopt your values and behavioral standards? Give examples.

parenting is frequently described as authoritarian, the warmth and supportiveness that characterize Chinese American family relationships may more closely resemble Baumrind's authoritative parenting but without the emphasis on the American values of individuality, choice, and freedom (Chao, 1994) and with stricter parental control (Chao, 2001).

Indeed, a dichotomy between the individualistic values of Western parenting and the collectivist values of Asian parenting may be overly simplistic. In interviews with 64 Japanese mothers of 3- to 6-year-olds (Yamada, 2004), the mothers' descriptions of their parenting practices reflected the search for a balance between granting appropriate autonomy and exercising disciplinary control. The mothers let children make their own decisions within what they saw as the child's personal domain, such as play activities, playmates, and clothing, and this domain enlarged with the child's age. When health, safety, moral issues, or conventional social rules were involved, the mothers set limits or exercised control. When conflicts arose, the mothers used reason rather than power-assertive methods or sometimes gave in to the child, apparently on the theory that the issue wasn't worth struggling over—or that the child might be right after all.

Neighborhood Effects on Parenting Styles Increasing evidence has shown links between children's neighborhoods and their developmental outcomes (Brooks-Gunn, Duncan, Leventhal, & Aber, 1997; Goering & Feins, 2003). A recent longitudinal study of Canadian children found that residence in poor, disorganized neighborhoods led to more maternal depression and family dysfunction, which was linked to less consistent and more punitive parenting styles. The less supportive environment of these types of neighborhoods and the lack of cohesion among residents places higher demands on parents to oversee and protect their children. These neighborhoods have fewer positive role models and fewer institutional resources to support families (Kohen, Leventhal, Dahinten, & McIntosh, 2008).

Special Behavioral Concerns

Three specific issues of special concern to parents, caregivers, and teachers of preschool children are how to promote altruism, curb aggression, and deal with fears that often arise at this age.

PROSOCIAL BEHAVIOR

Alex, at 3½, responded to two preschool classmates' complaints that they did not have enough modeling clay, his favorite plaything, by giving them half of his. Alex was showing **altruism**: motivation to help another person with no expectation of reward. Altruistic acts like Alex's often entail cost, self-sacrifice, or risk. Altruism is at the heart of **prosocial behavior**, voluntary, positive actions to help others.

> Children think in concrete terms. When trying to encourage sharing between young children, it is better to encourage them to take turns (a concrete behavior) than to share (an abstract concept).

Even before the second birthday, children often help others, share belongings and food, and offer comfort. There are three different preferred styles for sharing resources. The first involves a preference for sharing with close relations. The second, known as reciprocity, involves a preference for sharing with those who have previously shared with you. Last there is indirect reciprocity; a preference to share with people who have shared with others. In a set of experiments on 3½-year-old children, researchers were able to demonstrate that these preferences are present and functional in young children (Olson & Spelke, 2008).

checkpoint
can **you**...

▷ Describe and evaluate Baumrind's model of parenting styles?

▷ Discuss how parents' ways of resolving conflicts with young children can contribute to the success of authoritative child rearing?

▷ Discuss criticisms of Baumrind's model and cultural variations in parenting styles?

guidepost
5
Why do young children help or hurt others, and why do they develop fears?

altruism
Motivation to help others without expectation of reward; may involve self-denial or self-sacrifice.

prosocial behavior
Any voluntary behavior intended to help others.

Is there a prosocial personality or disposition? A longitudinal study that followed 4- and 5-year-olds into early adulthood suggests that there is and that it emerges early and remains somewhat consistent throughout life. Preschoolers who were sympathetic and spontaneously shared with classmates tended to show prosocial understanding and empathic behavior as much as 17 years later. Preschoolers who are shy or withdrawn tend to be less prosocial, perhaps because they hesitate to reach out to others (Coplan et al., 2004).

> Remember "harmonizing" with your pals in preschool music circles? Research in Germany suggests that when kids make music together, they are more likely to cooperate with and help each other.
>
> Kirschner & Tomasello, 2010

Genes and environment each contribute to individual differences in prosocial behavior, an example of gene–environment correlation. This finding comes from a study of 9,319 twin pairs whose prosocial behavior was rated by parents and teachers at ages 3, 4, and 7. Parents who showed affection and followed positive (inductive) disciplinary strategies tended to encourage their children's natural tendency to prosocial behavior (Knafo & Plomin, 2006). Parents of prosocial children typically are prosocial themselves. They point out models of prosocial behavior and steer children toward stories, films, and television programs that depict cooperation, sharing, and empathy and encourage sympathy, generosity, and helpfulness (Singer & Singer, 1998). Media exposure to educational and youth-oriented programs has been shown to have prosocial effects by increasing children's altruism, cooperation, and even tolerance for others (Wilson, 2008). Relationships with siblings provide an important laboratory for trying out caring behavior and learning to see another person's point of view. Peers and teachers also can model and reinforce prosocial behavior (Eisenberg, 1992; Eisenberg & Fabes, 1998).

> Babies at about a year of age love give-and-take games, in which a toy is handed back and forth between two people. Researchers have suggested that playing these games might help encourage later sharing behaviors.
>
> Hay, 1994

Cultures vary in the degree to which they foster prosocial behavior. Traditional cultures in which people live in extended family groups and share work seem to foster prosocial values more than cultures that stress individual achievement (Eisenberg & Fabes, 1998).

what's your view?

In a society in which "good Samaritans" are sometimes blamed for "butting into other people's business" and are sometimes attacked by the very persons they try to help, is it wise to encourage children to offer help to strangers?

instrumental aggression
Aggressive behavior used as a means of achieving a goal.

AGGRESSION

Noah walks over to Jake, who is playing quietly with a toy car. Noah hits Jake and snatches the car away. He has used aggression as a tool with which to gain access to a wanted object. This is **instrumental aggression**, or aggression used as an instrument to reach a goal—the most common type in early childhood. Between ages 2½ and 5, children commonly struggle over toys and control of space. Instrumental aggression surfaces mostly during social play; children who fight the most also tend to be the most sociable and competent. In fact, the ability to show some instrumental aggression may be a necessary step in psychosocial development.

As children develop more self-control and become better able to express themselves verbally, they typically shift from showing aggression with blows to doing it with words (Coie & Dodge, 1998; Tremblay et al., 2004). However, individual differences remain. In a longitudinal

Children given responsibilities at home tend to develop prosocial qualities, such as cooperation and helpfulness. This 3-year-old boy, who is learning to cook, is likely to have caring relationships with people as well.

study of 383 preschoolers, 11 percent of the girls and 9 percent of the boys showed high levels of aggression between ages 2 and 5. Boys and girls who were inattentive at age 2, and girls who showed poor emotion regulation at that age, tended to have conduct problems at age 5 (Hill, Degan, Calkins, & Keane, 2006). Children who, as preschoolers, often engage in violent fantasy play may, at age 6, be prone to violent displays of anger (Dunn & Hughes, 2001).

connect

study smart

Relational Aggression

overt (direct) aggression
Aggression that is openly directed at its target.

relational (indirect or social) aggression
Aggression aimed at damaging or interfering with another person's relationships, reputation, or psychological well-being; can be overt or covert.

Gender Differences in Aggression Aggression is an exception to the generalization that boys and girls are more similar than different (Hyde, 2005). In all cultures studied, as among most mammals, boys are more physically and verbally aggressive than girls. This gender difference is apparent by age 2 (Archer, 2004; Baillargeon et al., 2007; Pellegrini & Archer, 2005). Research with genetically engineered mice suggests that the Sry gene on the Y chromosome may play a role (Gatewood et al., 2006).

However, when aggression is looked at more closely, it becomes apparent that boys and girls tend to use different kinds of aggression. Boys engage in more **overt (direct) aggression**, and tend to openly direct aggressive acts at a target. Girls, by contrast, tend to engage in a form of **indirect**, **social aggression**, also known as **relational aggression** (Putallaz & Bierman, 2004). This more subtle kind of aggression consists of damaging or interfering with relationships, reputation, or psychological well-being, often through teasing, manipulation, ostracism, or bids for control. It may include spreading rumors, name-calling, put-downs, or excluding someone from a group. It can be either overt or covert (indirect)—for example, making mean faces or ignoring someone. Among preschoolers, it tends to be direct and face-to-face ("You can't come to my party if you don't give me that toy") (Archer, 2004; Brendgen et al., 2005; Crick, Casas, & Nelson, 2002).

From an evolutionary perspective, boys' greater overt aggressiveness, like their greater size and strength, may prepare them to compete for a mate (Archer, 2004). Males produce many sperm; females generally produce only one ovum at a time. Males can increase their reproductive output by gaining access to females. Thus males are generally predicted to be more competitive and are more likely to take the risks of physical aggression. Females' reproductive output is limited by their own bodies; thus the need for physical aggression as a means by which to compete is diminished. Moreover, females are strongly motivated to protect and nurture the few offspring they have; thus they shy away from direct confrontations that could put them at physical risk (Pellegrini & Archer, 2005).

Influences on Aggression Why are some children more aggressive than others? Temperament may play a part. Children who are intensely emotional and low in self-control tend to express anger aggressively (Eisenberg, Fabes, Nyman, Bernzweig, & Pinuelas, 1994; Rubin, Burgess, Dwyer, & Hastings, 2003).

Both physical and social aggression have genetic and environmental sources, but their relative influence differs. Among 234 6-year-old twins, physical aggression was 50 to 60 percent heritable; the remainder of the variance was attributable to nonshared environmental influences (unique experiences). Social aggression was much more environmentally influenced; the variance was only 20 percent genetic, 20 percent explained by shared environmental influences, and 60 percent by unshared experiences (Brendgen et al., 2005).

Parental behaviors strongly influence aggressiveness. In one study, 5-year-old boys who had been exposed prenatally to cocaine and who lived in poor, unstable, or stressful environments with single mothers tended to be high in aggressive behavior, such as fighting and bullying (Bendersky, Bennett, & Lewis, 2006). In several longitudinal studies, insecure attachment and lack of maternal warmth and affection in infancy predicted aggressiveness in early childhood (Coie & Dodge, 1998; MacKinnon-Lewis, Starnes, Volling, & Johnson, 1997; Rubin, Burgess, & Hastings, 2002). Manipulative behaviors such as withdrawal of love and making a child feel guilty or ashamed may foster social aggression (Brendgen et al., 2005).

Aggressiveness may result from a combination of a stressful and unstimulating home atmosphere, harsh discipline, lack of maternal warmth and social support, family dysfunction, exposure to aggressive adults and neighborhood violence, poverty, and transient peer groups, which prevent stable friendships (Dodge, Pettit, & Bates, 1994; Grusec & Goodnow, 1994; Romano, Tremblay, Boulerice, & Swisher, 2005). In a study of 431 Head Start participants in an inner-city neighborhood, parents reported that more than half had witnessed gang activity, drug trafficking, police pursuits and arrests, or people carrying weapons, and some of the children and families had been victimized themselves. These children showed symptoms of distress at home and aggressive behavior at school (Farver, Xu, Eppe, Fernandez, & Schwartz, 2005).

Why does witnessing violence lead to aggression? In a classic social learning experiment (Bandura, Ross, & Ross, 1961), 3- to 6-year-olds individually watched films of adult models playing with toys. Children in one experimental group saw the adult model play quietly. The model for a second experimental group spent most of the 10-minute session punching, throwing, and kicking a life-size inflated doll. A control group did not see any model. After the sessions, the children, who were mildly frustrated by seeing toys they were not allowed to play with, went into another playroom. The children who had seen the aggressive model acted much more aggressively than those in the other groups, imitating many of the same things they had seen the model say and do. The children who had seen the quiet model were less aggressive than the control group. This finding suggests that parents may be able to moderate the effects of frustration by modeling nonaggressive behavior.

Electronic media including television, movies, and video games have enormous power for modeling either prosocial behavior or aggression. In Chapter 14 we discuss the influence of media violence on aggressive behavior.

In a classic experiment by Albert Bandura, children who had seen a film of an adult hitting and kicking an inflated clown were more likely to imitate the aggressive behavior if they had seen the adult being rewarded or experiencing no consequences than if they had seen the adult being punished.

Culture and Aggression How much influence does culture have on aggressive behavior? One research team asked closely matched samples of 30 Japanese and 30 U.S. middle- to upper-middle-class preschoolers to choose pictured solutions to hypothetical conflicts or stressful situations (such as having one's block tower knocked down, having to stop playing and go to bed, being hit, hearing parents argue, or fighting on a jungle gym). The children also were asked to act out such situations using dolls and props. The U.S. children showed more anger, more aggressive behavior and language, and less emotional control than the Japanese children (Zahn-Waxler, Friedman, Cole, Mizuta, & Hiruma, 1996).

These results are consistent with child-rearing values in the two cultures. In Japan, anger and aggression contradict the cultural emphasis on harmony. Japanese mothers are more likely than U.S. mothers to use inductive discipline, pointing out how aggressive behavior hurts others. Japanese mothers show strong disappointment when children fail to meet behavioral standards. However, the cross-cultural difference in children's anger and aggressiveness was significant even apart from mothers' behavior, suggesting that temperament differences also may have been at work (Zahn-Waxler et al., 1996).

FEARFULNESS

Passing fears are common in early childhood and are tied to cognitive development. Many 2- to 4-year-olds are afraid of the unfamiliar—strangers, animals, and loud noises. By age 6, children are more likely to be afraid of the dark and

When kids are little, their fears involve darkness, scary monsters, and imaginary threats. As they grow older, their fears become increasingly realistic. Why do you think this happens?

what's **your view**

Are there situations in which a child should be encouraged to be aggressive?

TABLE 11.5	Childhood Fears
Age	**Fears**
0–6 months	Loss of support; loud noises
7–12 months	Strangers; heights; sudden, unexpected, and looming objects
1 year	Separation from parent; toilet; injury; strangers
2 years	Many stimuli, including loud noises (vacuum cleaners, sirens and alarms, trucks, and thunder), animals, dark rooms, separation from parent, large objects or machines, changes in personal environment, unfamiliar peers
3 years	Masks; dark; animals; separation from parent
4 years	Separation from parent; animals; dark; noises (including noises at night)
5 years	Animals; "bad" people; dark; separation from parent; bodily harm
6 years	Supernatural beings (e.g., ghosts, witches); bodily injury; thunder and lightning; dark; sleeping or staying alone; separation from parent
7–8 years	Supernatural beings; dark; media events (e.g., news reports on the threat of nuclear war or child kidnapping); staying alone; bodily injury
9–12 years	Tests and examinations in school; school performances; bodily injury; physical appearance; thunder and lightning; death; dark

Source of Data: From Morris, R. J., & Kratochwill, T. R. *Treating Children's Fears and Phobias: A Behavioral Approach,* Allyn & Bacon, Boston, MA, 1983.

imaginary creatures (DuPont, 1983; Stevenson-Hinde & Shouldice, 1996). Eventually fears of imaginery things disappear as children grow older.

Young children's fears stem largely from their intense fantasy life and their tendency to confuse appearance with reality. Sometimes their imaginations get carried away, and they worry about being attacked by a lion or being abandoned. Also, they are more likely to be frightened by something that looks scary, such as a cartoon monster, than by something capable of doing great harm, such as a nuclear explosion (Cantor, 1994). For the most part, older children's fears are more realistic and self-evaluative (for example, fear of failing a test) (Stevenson-Hinde & Shouldice, 1996; Table 11.5).

Fears may stem from personal experience or from hearing about other people's experiences (Muris, Merckelbach, & Collaris, 1997). A preschooler whose mother is sick in bed may become upset by a story about a mother's death, even the death of an animal mother. Often fears result from appraisals of danger, such as the likelihood of being bitten by a dog, or are triggered by events, such as when a child who was hit by a car becomes afraid to cross the street. Children who have lived through an earthquake, a kidnapping, or some other frightening event may fear that it will happen again (Kolbert, 1994).

Parents can allay children's fears by instilling a sense of trust and normal caution without being too protective—and also by overcoming their own unrealistic fears. They can reassure a fearful child and encourage open expression of feelings. Ridicule ("Don't be such a baby!"), coercion ("Pat the nice doggie—it won't hurt you"), and logical persuasion ("The closest bear is 20 miles away, locked in a zoo!") are not helpful. Not until elementary school can children tell themselves that what they fear is not real (Cantor, 1994).

checkpoint
can **you** . . .

▷ Discuss influences that contribute to altruism, aggression, and fearfulness?

Relationships with Other Children

guidepost 6

How do young children get along with—or without—siblings, playmates, and friends?

Although the most important people in young children's world are the adults who take care of them, relationships with siblings and playmates become more important in early childhood. Virtually every characteristic activity and personality issue of this age, from gender development to prosocial or aggressive behavior, involves other children.

Let's look first at sibling relationships and then at children who grow up with no siblings. Then we will explore relationships with peers and friends.

SIBLING RELATIONSHIPS

"It's mine!"
"No, it's mine!"
"Well, I was playing with it first!"

The earliest, most frequent, and most intense disputes among siblings are over property rights—who owns a toy or who is entitled to play with it. Although exasperated adults may not always see it that way, sibling disputes and their settlement can be viewed as socialization opportunities, in which children learn to stand up for principles and negotiate disagreements (Ross, 1996). Joint dramatic play is another arena for socialization. Siblings who frequently play "let's pretend" develop a history of shared understandings that allow them to more easily resolve issues and build on each other's ideas (Howe, Petrakos, Pinaldi, & LeFebvre, 2005).

Despite the frequency of conflict, sibling rivalry is not the main pattern between brothers and sisters early in life. Although some rivalry exists, so do affection, interest, companionship, and influence. Observations spanning 3½ years that began when younger siblings were about age 1½ and older siblings ranged from 3 to 4½ found prosocial and play-oriented behaviors to be more common than rivalry, hostility, and competition (Abramovitch, Corter, & Lando, 1979; Abramovitch, Corter, Pepler, & Stanhope, 1986; Abramovitch, Pepler, & Corter, 1982). Older siblings initiated more behavior, both friendly and unfriendly; younger siblings tended to imitate the older siblings. As the younger children reached age 5, the siblings became less physical and more verbal, both in showing aggression and in showing care and affection.

At least one finding of this research has been replicated in many studies: Same-sex siblings, particularly girls, are closer and play together more peaceably than boy-girl siblings (Kier & Lewis, 1998). Because older siblings tend to dominate younger siblings, the quality of the relationship is more affected by the emotional and social adjustment of the older child (Pike, Coldwell, & Dunn, 2005).

The quality of sibling relationships tends to carry over to relationships with other children. A child who is aggressive with siblings is likely to be aggressive with friends as well (Abramovitch et al., 1986). Siblings who frequently play amicably together tend to develop prosocial behaviors (Pike et al., 2005).

Likewise, friendships can influence sibling relationships. Older siblings who have experienced a good relationship with a friend before the birth of a new sibling are likely to treat their younger siblings better and are less likely to develop antisocial behavior in adolescence (Kramer & Kowal, 2005). For a young child at risk for behavioral problems, a positive relationship with *either* a sibling or a friend can buffer the effect of a negative relationship with the other (McElwain & Volling, 2005).

THE ONLY CHILD

In the United States, approximately 21 percent of children under age 18 have no siblings in the home (Kreider & Fields, 2005). Are only children selfish, lonely, or spoiled?

> Younger siblings are more likely to take risks than older siblings. In one study on baseball statistics, 90 percent of younger brothers in major league baseball stole more bases than their older counterparts.
>
> Sulloway & Zweigenhaft, 2010

checkpoint
can you . . .

▷ Explain how the resolution of sibling disputes contributes to socialization?

▷ Tell how birth order and gender affect typical patterns of sibling interaction?

Generally, this stereotype of only children appears to be false. An analysis of 115 studies found that most "onlies" do well. With respect to academic outcomes and success in work, they perform slightly better than children with siblings. They tend to be more motivated to achieve and to have slightly higher self-esteem; and they do not differ in emotional adjustment, sociability, or popularity.

Why do onlies do better on some indices than children with siblings? Evolutionary theory suggests that these children do better because parents, who have limited time and resources to spend, focus more attention on only children, talk to them more, do more with them, and expect more of them than do parents with more than one child (Falbo, 2006; Falbo & Polit, 1986; Polit & Falbo, 1987). The more children are present in a family, the less individual time any one child receives. And, because most children today spend considerable time in play groups, child care, and preschool, only children do not lack opportunities for social interaction with peers (Falbo, 2006).

Research in China also has produced largely encouraging findings about only children. In 1979, to control an exploding population, the People's Republic of China established a controversial official policy of limiting families to one child. Although the policy has since been relaxed somewhat, most urban families now have only one child, and most rural families no more than two (Hesketh, Lu, & Xing, 2005). Thus, in many Chinese cities, schoolrooms are almost completely filled with children who have no brothers or sisters. This situation offered researchers a natural experiment: an opportunity to study the adjustment of large numbers of only children.

A review of the literature found no significant differences in behavioral problems (Tao, 1998). Indeed, only children seemed to be at a distinct psychological advantage in a society that favors and rewards such a child. Among 731 urban children and adolescents, those with siblings reported higher levels of fear, anxiety, and depression than only children, regardless of sex or age (Yang, Ollendick, Dong, Xia, & Lin, 1995).

Among 4,000 third and sixth graders, personality differences between only children and those with siblings—as rated by parents, teachers, peers, and the children themselves—were few. Only children's academic achievement and physical growth were about the same as, or better than, those with siblings (Falbo & Poston, 1993). In a randomized study in Beijing first-grade classrooms (Jiao, Ji, & Jing, 1996), only children outperformed classmates with siblings in memory, language, and mathematics skills. This finding may reflect the greater attention, stimulation, hopes, and expectations that parents shower on a child they know will be their first and last.

Most of the studies used urban samples. Further research may reveal whether the findings hold up in rural areas and small towns, where children with siblings are more numerous, and whether only children maintain their cognitive superiority as they move through school.

checkpoint
can you . . .

▷ Compare development of only children with that of children with siblings?

PLAYMATES AND FRIENDS

Friendships develop as people develop. Toddlers play alongside or near each other, but not until about age 3 do children begin to have what we could consider friends. The ability to relate to peers in groups, as opposed to one-on-one relationships, is a major transition that takes place in the preschool years (Hay, Payne, & Chadwick, 2004). Through friendships and interactions with casual playmates, young children learn how to get along with others. They learn that being a friend is the way to have a friend. They learn how to solve problems in relationships, they learn how to put themselves in another person's place, and they see models of various kinds of behavior. They learn moral values and gender-role norms, and they practice adult roles.

Preschoolers usually like to play with children of their own age and sex, and who are similar to them in observable characteristics. Children who have frequent positive experiences with each other are most likely to become friends (Rubin et al., 1998; Snyder, West, Stockemer, Gibbons, & Almquist-Parks, 1996). About three out of four preschoolers have such mutual friendships (Hartup & Stevens, 1999). Friendships are more satisfying—and more likely to last—when children see them as relatively harmonious and as validating their self-worth. Being able to confide in friends and get help from them is less important at this age than when children get older (Ladd, Kochenderfer, & Coleman, 1996).

The traits that young children look for in a playmate are similar to the traits they look for in a friend (Hart, DeWolf, Wozniak, & Burts, 1992). In one study, 4- to 7-year-olds rated the most important features of friendships as doing things together, liking and caring for each other, sharing and helping one another, and, to a lesser degree, living nearby or going to the same school. Younger children rated physical traits, such as appearance and size, higher than did older children, and they rated affection and support lower (Furman & Bierman, 1983).

Young children learn the importance of being a friend in order to have a friend.

Preschool children prefer prosocial playmates (Hart et al., 1992). They reject disruptive, demanding, intrusive, or aggressive children and tend to ignore those who are withdrawn, or tentative (Ramsey & Lasquade, 1996; Roopnarine & Honig, 1985).

Well-liked preschoolers and kindergartners and those who are rated by parents and teachers as socially competent generally cope well with anger. They respond directly in ways that minimize further conflict and keep relationships going. They avoid insults and threats. Unpopular children tend to hit, hit back, or tattle (Fabes & Eisenberg, 1992).

Peer relationships are affected by children's relationships with parents (Kerns & Barth, 1995), siblings (Herrera & Dunn, 1997), and teachers (Howes, Matheeson, & Hamilton, 1994). Parenting styles and practices can influence peer relationships. Popular children generally have warm, positive relationships with both mother and father. The parents are likely to be authoritative and the children to be both assertive and cooperative (Coplan et al., 2004; Isley, O'Neil, & Parke, 1996; Kochanska, 1992; Roopnarine & Honig, 1985).

summary *and* key terms

guidepost ❶ The Developing Self

How does the self-concept develop during early childhood, and how do children show self-esteem, emotional growth, and initiative?

- The self-concept undergoes major changes in early childhood. According to neo-Piagetians, self-definition shifts from single representations to representational mappings. Young children do not see the difference between the real self and the ideal self.

- Culture affects self-definition.

- Self-esteem in early childhood tends to be global and unrealistic, reflecting adult approval.

- Understanding of emotions directed toward the self and of simultaneous emotions develops gradually.

- According to Erikson, the developmental conflict of early childhood is initiative versus guilt. Successful resolution of this conflict results in the virtue of *purpose.*

self-concept (*302*)

self-definition (*302*)

single representations (*303*)

real self (*303*)

ideal self (*303*)

representational mappings (*303*)

self-esteem (*303*)

initiative versus guilt (*306*)

Gender

guidepost 2

How do boys and girls become aware of the meaning of gender, and what explains differences in behavior between the sexes?

- Gender identity is an aspect of the developing self-concept.
- The main gender difference in early childhood is boys' greater aggressiveness and activity level. Girls tend to be more empathic and prosocial and less prone to problem behavior. Some cognitive differences appear early and others not until preadolescence or later.
- Children learn gender roles at an early age through gender-typing. Gender stereotypes peak during the preschool years.
- Five major perspectives on gender development are biological, evolutionary, psychoanalytic, social learning, and cognitive approaches.
- Evidence suggests that some gender differences may be biologically based.
- Evolutionary theory sees children's gender roles as preparation for adult mating behavior.
- In Freudian theory, a child identifies with the same-sex parent after giving up the wish to possess the other parent.
- Cognitive-developmental theory maintains that gender identity develops from thinking about one's gender. Gender constancy enhances the acquisition of gender roles. Gender-schema theory holds that children categorize gender-related information by observing what males and females do in their culture.
- Children also learn gender roles through socialization. Parents, peers, the media, and culture influence gender-typing.

  gender identity (*306*)
  gender roles (*307*)
  gender-typing (*307*)
  gender stereotypes (*307*)
  theory of sexual selection (*309*)
  identification (*320*)
  gender constancy (*311*)
  gender-schema theory (*311*)
  social cognitive theory (*312*)

Play: The Business of Early Childhood

guidepost 3

How do preschoolers play, and how does play contribute to and reflect development?

- Play has physical, cognitive, and psychosocial benefits as well as evolutionary functions.
- Changes in the types of play children engage in reflect cognitive and social development.
- According to Smilansky, children progress cognitively from functional play to constructive play, dramatic play, and then formal games with rules. Dramatic play becomes

increasingly common during early childhood and helps children develop social and cognitive skills. Rough-and-tumble play also begins during early childhood.

- According to Parten, play becomes more social during early childhood. However, later research has found that nonsocial play is not necessarily immature.
- Children prefer to play with (and play more socially with) others of their sex.
- Cognitive and social aspects of play are influenced by the culturally approved environments adults create for children.

  functional play (*316*)
  constructive play (*316*)
  dramatic play (*317*)
  formal games with rules (*317*)
  gender segregation (*318*)

Parenting

guidepost 4

How do parenting practices influence development?

- Discipline can be a powerful tool for socialization.
- Both positive reinforcement and prudently administered punishment can be appropriate tools of discipline within the context of a positive parent-child relationship.
- Power assertion, inductive techniques, and withdrawal of love each can be effective in certain situations. Reasoning is generally the most effective and power assertion the least effective in promoting internalization of parental standards. Spanking and other forms of corporal punishment can have negative consequences.
- Baumrind identified three child-rearing styles: authoritarian, permissive, and authoritative. A fourth style, neglectful or uninvolved, was identified later by Maccoby and Martin. Authoritative parents tend to raise more competent children. However, Baumrind's findings may not apply to some cultures or socioeconomic groups.

  discipline (*320*)
  corporal punishment (*321*)
  psychological aggression (*321*)
  inductive techniques (*321*)
  power assertion (*321*)
  withdrawal of love (*323*)
  authoritarian parenting (*324*)
  permissive parenting (*324*)
  authoritative parenting (*324*)

Special Behavioral Concerns

guidepost 5

Why do young children help or hurt others, and why do they develop fears?

- The roots of altruism and prosocial behavior appear early. This may be an inborn disposition that can be cultivated by parental modeling and encouragement.
- Instrumental aggression—first physical, then verbal—is most common in early childhood.

- Most children become less aggressive after age 6 or 7, but the proportion of hostile aggression increases. Boys tend to practice overt aggression, whereas girls engage in relational or social aggression.
- Preschool children show temporary fears of real and imaginary objects and events; older children's fears tend to be more realistic.

  altruism (*326*)

  prosocial behavior (*326*)

  instrumental aggression (*327*)

  overt (direct) aggression (*328*)

  relational (indirect or social) aggression (*328*)

Relationships with Other Children

How do young children get along with—or without— siblings, playmates, and friends?

- Siblings learn to resolve disputes and negotiate differences.

- Most sibling interactions are positive. Older siblings tend to initiate activities, and younger ones to imitate. Same-sex siblings, especially girls, get along best.
- The kind of relationship children have with siblings often carries over into other peer relationships.
- Only children seem to develop at least as well as children with siblings in most respects.
- Preschoolers choose playmates and friends who are like them and with whom they have positive experiences. Aggressive children are less popular than prosocial children.
- Friends have more positive as well as more negative interactions with each other when compared to other playmates.
- Parenting can affect children's social competence with peers.

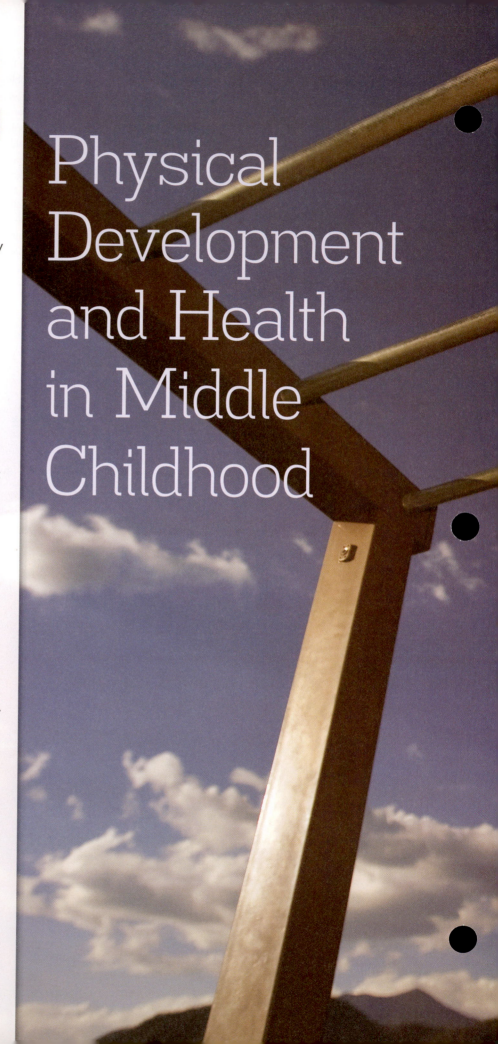

did you know?

▷ For optimal health, school-aged children need an average of 2,400 calories and 60 minutes of physical activity every day?

▷ Sleep disorders in school-aged children have been shown to affect behavior and cognitive abilities?

▷ More than half of children diagnosed with emotional, behavioral, and developmental problems struggle with issues related to aggression, defiance, or antisocial behavior?

Although motor abilities improve less dramatically in middle childhood than before, these years are important for development of the strength, stamina, endurance, and motor proficiency needed for sports and outdoor activities. In this chapter we look at these and other physical developments, beginning with normal growth and brain development, which depend on proper nutrition, adequate sleep, and good health. As children do more, their risk of accidents increases; we examine some ways to lower these risks. And finally we look at some mental health problems of childhood.

Physical Development and Health in Middle Childhood

It is easier to build strong children than to repair broken men.

—Frederick Douglass (1818–1895)

1. How do school-age children's bodies and brains grow and develop?

2. What are the nutritional and sleep needs of middle childhood?

3. What gains in motor skills typically occur at this age, and what kinds of physical play do boys and girls engage in?

4. What are the principal health and safety concerns in middle childhood?

5. What are some common mental health problems of childhood?

guidepost

1

How do school-age children's bodies and brains grow and develop?

Aspects of Physical Development

If we were to walk by a typical elementary school just as the the school day was ending, we would see a virtual explosion of children of all shapes and sizes. Tall ones, short ones, husky ones, and skinny ones would be bursting out of the school doors into the open air. We would see that school-age children look very different from children a few years younger.

HEIGHT AND WEIGHT

Growth during middle childhood slows considerably. Still, although day-by-day changes may not be obvious, they add up to a startling difference between 6-year-olds, who are still small children, and 11-year-olds, many of whom are now beginning to resemble adults.

Children grow about 2 to 3 inches each year between ages 6 and 11 and approximately double their weight during that period (McDowell, Fryar, Odgen, & Flegal, 2008; Table 12.1). Girls retain somewhat more fatty tissue than boys, a characteristic that will persist through adulthood. The average 10-year-old weighs about 11 pounds

TABLE 12.1	Physical Growth, Ages 6 to 11 (50th percentile*)			
	HEIGHT (INCHES)		**WEIGHT (POUNDS)**	
Age	**Girls**	**Boys**	**Girls**	**Boys**
6	46.6	47.6	48.8	52.2
7	49.5	49.3	56.6	56.4
8	51.4	51.3	62.1	64
9	54.5	54.0	75.0	71.2
10	56.6	55.7	89.2	82.2
11	59.6	58.8	104.3	97.4

*Fifty percent of children in each category are above this height or weight level, and 50 percent are below it.

Source: McDowell, Fryar, Odgen, & Flegal, 2008.

These girls proudly show off a childhood milestone—the normal loss of baby teeth, which will be replaced by permanent ones. U.S. children today have fewer dental cavities than in the early 1970s, probably owing to better nutrition, widespread use of fluoride, and better dental care.

more than 40 years ago—just under 85 pounds for a boy and 88 pounds for a girl (Ogden, Fryar, Carroll, & Flegal, 2004). African American boys and girls tend to grow faster than white children. By about age 6, African American girls have more muscle and bone mass than European American (white) or Mexican American girls, and Mexican American girls have a higher percentage of body fat than white girls the same size (Ellis, Abrams, & Wong, 1997).

Although most children grow normally, some do not. One type of growth disorder arises from the body's failure to produce enough growth hormone. Administration of synthetic growth hormone in such cases can produce rapid growth in height, especially during the first 2 years (Albanese & Stanhope, 1993; Vance & Mauras, 1999).

Growth hormone (GH) has been identified as an effective treatment for children with short stature. Although its use for this purpose has been controversial, it has been approved by the Food and Drug Administration for healthy children whose projected growth rate is too slow to reach a normal adult height (63 inches for men and 59 inches for women). Many variables affect short-statured children's responses to homone therapy, including whether they are GH deficient or not, what their early growth patterns were, and whether their parents are also short statured. In a recent study, children with short stature undergoing homone therapy treatment realized an average gain of 3 inches in their final height (Albertsson-Wikland et al., 2008). If unsuccessful, however, the therapy may do psychological harm by creating unfulfilled expectations or by giving short children the feeling that something is wrong with them (Lee, 2006).

TOOTH DEVELOPMENT AND DENTAL CARE

Most of the adult teeth arrive early in middle childhood. The primary teeth begin to fall out at about age 6 and are replaced by permanent teeth at a rate of about four teeth per year for the next 5 years.

In the past 20 years the number of U.S. children ages 6 to 18 with untreated cavities dropped nearly 80 percent. Improvements cut across ethnic and socioeconomic lines, although Hispanic children and those living in families with lower incomes have more decay (Centers for Disease Control [CDC], 2007b). Widespread use of fluoride has been a major factor in the decline in the prevalence and severity of dental caries in the United States and in other economically developed countries. Studies of community water fluoridation programs demonstrated a 30 to 50 percent reduction in childhood dental caries attributable to fluoridation (CDC, 2001).

Improvement in children's dental health is also attributed to use of adhesive sealants on the rough, chewing surfaces (Brown, Kaste, Selwitz, & Furman, 1996; Rethman, 2000). Dental sealants in children's teeth have increased from the early 1970s to the point where up to 30 percent of children age 6 to 11 have dental sealants (National Institute of Dental and Craniofacial Research, 2004). Access to proper dental care is important for young children. Untreated oral disease may lead to problems in eating, speaking, and sleeping (U.S. Department of Health and Human Services, 2001). The American Academy of Pediatric Dentistry recommends that all children visit the dentist within 6 months of the eruption of the first primary tooth and no later than after the first birthday (American Academy of Pediatric Dentistry, 2002).

BRAIN DEVELOPMENT

The Developing Brain

A number of cognitive advances occur in middle childhood that can be traced back to changes in the brain's structure and functioning. In general, these changes can be characterized as resulting in faster, more efficient information processing, as we as have an increased ability to filter out irrelevant or distracting information (Amso & Casey, 2006). For example, it becomes easier for children to concentrate on the teacher—even if it's a boring lesson—while filtering out the antics of the class clown sitting next to them.

The study of the brain's structure is complex and depends on the interaction between genetic, epigenetic, and environment factors. The use of new technologies has allowed us a window into this process. For example, one technology named *magnetic resonance imaging (MRI)* enables researchers to observe, with no health risk to the children under study, how the brain changes over time and how these changes vary from one child to another (Blakemore & Choudhury, 2006; Kuhn, 2006; Lenroot & Giedd, 2006).

MRI technology allows us to know, among other information, that the brain consists of both gray matter and white matter. Gray matter is composed of closely packed neurons in the cerebral cortex. White matter is made of glial cells, which provide support for neurons, and of myelinated axons, which transmit information across neurons. Both types of matter are necessary for effective cognition.

One important maturational change is a *loss in the density of gray matter* (Figure 12.1). While "less" gray matter may sound negative, the result is actually the opposite. This loss reflects pruning of unused dendrites. In other words, those connections that are used remain active; the unused connections eventually disappear. The result is that the brain becomes "tuned" to the experiences of the child.

Changes in the volume of gray matter peak at different times in the different lobes. Beneath the cortex, gray matter volume in the caudate—a part of the basal ganglia involved in control of movement and muscle tone and in mediating higher cognitive functions, attention, and emotional states—peaks at age 7 in girls and age 10 in boys. Gray matter volume in the parietal lobes, which deal with spatial understanding, and in the frontal lobes, which handle higher-order functions, peaks at age 11 in girls and age 12 for boys. At age 16 in both boys and girls, gray matter volume peaks in the temporal lobes, which deal with language (Lenroot & Giedd, 2006).

The amount of gray matter in the frontal cortex, which is largely genetic, is likely linked with differences in IQ (Thompson et al., 2001; Toga & Thompson, 2005). Some research suggests, however, that the key may not be how much gray matter a child has but rather the pattern of development of the prefrontal cortex. In children of average intelligence, the prefrontal cortex is relatively thick at age 7, peaks in thickness by age 8, and then gradually thins as unneeded connections are pruned (see Chapter 13).

The loss in density of gray matter with age is balanced by another change, which is a steady *increase in white matter*. The connections between neurons thicken and myelinate, beginning with the frontal lobes and moving toward the rear of the brain.

Structure and function

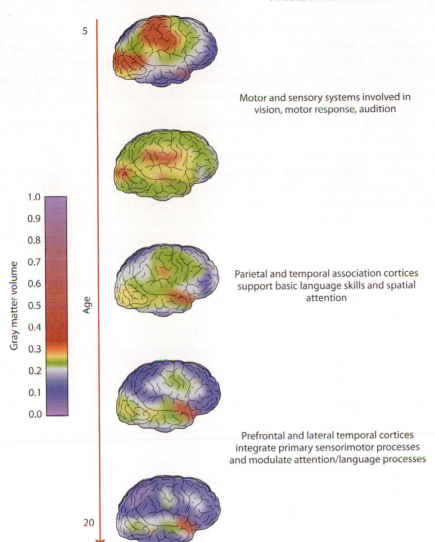

Motor and sensory systems involved in vision, motor response, audition

Parietal and temporal association cortices support basic language skills and spatial attention

Prefrontal and lateral temporal cortices integrate primary sensorimotor processes and modulate attention/language processes

FIGURE 12.1

Gray Matter Maturation in the Cerebral Cortex, Ages 5 to 20

Losses in gray matter density reflect maturation of various regions of the cortex, permitting more efficient functioning.

Source: Gogtay et al., 2004.

Between ages 6 and 13, striking growth occurs in connections between the temporal and parietal lobes. In fact, white matter growth may not begin to drop off until well into adulthood (Giedd et al., 1999; Kuhn, 2006; Lenroot & Giedd, 2006; NIMH, 2001b; Paus et al., 1999).

Last, children's brains also show *changes in the thickness of the cortex.* Researchers have observed cortical thickening between ages 5 and 11 in regions of the temporal and frontal lobes. At the same time, thinning occurs in the rear portion of the frontal and parietal cortex in the brain's left hemisphere. This change correlates with improved performance on the vocabulary portion of an intelligence test (Toga et al., 2006).

Nutrition and Sleep

To support their steady growth, brain development, and constant exertion, school-age children need to eat properly and get enough sleep. Unfortunately, too many children do neither.

NUTRITIONAL NEEDS

Schoolchildren need, on average, 2,400 calories every day—more for older children and less for younger ones. Nutritionists recommend a varied diet including plenty of grains,

checkpoint
can **you** . . .

▷ **Summarize typical growth patterns of boys and girls in middle childhood and give reasons for variations?**

▷ **Explain why health of permanent teeth has improved?**

▷ **Summarize changes in the brain during childhood and discuss their possible effects?**

What are the nutritional and sleep needs of middle childhood?

fruits, and vegetables and high levels of complex carbohydrates, found in potatoes, pasta, bread, and cereals.

Recommendations for children and adults state that about 30 percent of total calories should come from fat, and less than 10 percent of the total should come from saturated fat (AAP Committee on Nutrition, 1992; U.S. Department of Agriculture & USDHHS, 2000). Studies have found no negative effects on height, weight, body mass, or neurological development from a moderately low-fat diet at this age (Rask-Nissilä et al., 2000; Shea et al., 1993).

As children grow older, pressures and opportunities for unhealthy eating increase. Many children do not eat breakfast, or eat it hurriedly, and get at least one-third of their calories from snacks, including sweetened beverages (American Heart Association et al., 2006). School cafeterias and vending machines frequently offer unhealthy foods (National Center for Education Statistics, 2006). Children frequently eat out, often at fast-food restaurants. Many children prepare their own meals and snacks. The media strongly influence children's food choices, and not for the better. Socioeconomic status can be a factor as well because healthy, fresh food is often more expensive than highly processed, high-calorie food with low nutrient content.

Nutrition education in schools can be helpful when combined with parental education and changes in school lunch menus. Changes in food labeling, taxes on unhealthy foods, restrictions on foods provided by government-supported school lunch programs, regulation of food advertising directed toward children, and requiring restaurants to list nutrition information on their menus are among proposed legislative recommendations (American Heart Association et al., 2006).

SLEEP PATTERNS AND PROBLEMS

Sleep needs decline from about 11 hours a day at age 5 to little more than 10 hours at age 9 and about 9 hours at age 13. Even so, many U.S. children get less sleep than they need. First through fifth graders average 9½ hours a day, short of the recommended 10 to 11 hours. And, as children get older, about 1 in 4 get less sleep on weekends (National Sleep Foundation, 2004). Sleep problems, such as resistance to going to bed, insomnia, and daytime sleepiness are common during these years, in part because many children, as they grow older, are allowed to set their own bedtimes (Hoban, 2004). More than 40 percent of school-age children have a television set in their bedrooms, and these children get less sleep than other children (National Sleep Foundation, 2004).

Almost half of American children 6 to 17 years old have a television in their bedroom.

Sisson, Broyles, Newton, Baker, & Chernausek, 2011

A study of sleep patterns of 7- to 12-year-olds in Israel found significant age and gender differences. The older children went to sleep later and slept less (an hour less for 12-year-olds than for 7-year-olds). Older children also reported more morning drowsiness and were more likely to fall asleep during the day. At all ages, children woke up an average of almost twice each night. Girls slept longer and more soundly than boys. Family stress was associated with lower sleep quality (Sadeh, Raviv, & Gruber, 2000).

Although 1 in 5 children in this study experienced significant sleep difficulties, most of them went unnoticed by the children or their parents (Sadeh et al., 2000). Similar results were found in a National Sleep Foundation (2004) poll in the United States in which only 11 percent of parents or caregivers of school-age children reported sleeping problems. Yet 42 percent report that children regularly stall about going to bed, 29 percent have difficulty getting children up in the morning, and 14 percent need to attend to a child who has awakened at night. In one study, teachers noted that at least 10 percent of kindergarten through fourth-grade students struggled to stay awake in class (Owens, Spirito, McGuinn, & Nobile, 2000).

About one out of every five children under 18 snores. Persistent snoring, at least three times per week, may indicate a child has sleep-disordered breathing (SDB), a condition that has been linked to behavioral and learning difficulties (Halbower et al., 2006). Proper, early treatment of the condition is critical to helping a child afflicted with SDB realize his or her academic potential (Lamberg, 2007). Obstructive sleep apnea (OSA), a severe form of SDB, affects 1 in 20 children and is associated with significant deficits in IQ, memory, and verbal fluency (Halbower et al., 2006). Diagnosis can be difficult, however, and many children are misdiagnosed as having attention-deficit/hperactivity disorder (ADHD) (Chervin et al., 2006). Once diagnosed, many children with SDB may undergo the surgical removal of their adenoids and tonsils—a treatment that has been found to improve neurobehavioral deficits and improve quality of life (Chervin et al., 2006; Stewart, Glaze, Friedman, Smith, & Bautista, 2005). Children who are not candidates for surgery may benefit from continuous postive airway pressure (CPAP) therapy in which an electronic device keeps airways open via air pressure delivered through a nasal mask (Lamberg, 2007).

Motor Development and Physical Play

Motor skills continue to improve in middle childhood (Table 12.2). By this age, however, children in most nonliterate and transitional societies go to work, and this plus more household labor, especially for girls, leaves them with little time and freedom for

checkpoint can you . . .

▷ Identify nutritional and sleep needs of school-age children and tell why it is important to meet them?

▷ Give reasons why many children do not eat or sleep properly?

guidepost 3

What gains in motor skills typically occur at this age, and what kinds of physical play do boys and girls engage in?

TABLE 12.2	Motor Development in Middle Childhood
Age	**Selected Behaviors**
6	Girls are superior in movement accuracy; boys are superior in forceful, less complex acts. Skipping is possible. Children can throw with proper weight shift and step.
7	One-footed balancing without looking becomes possible. Children can walk 2-inch-wide balance beams. Children can hop and jump accurately into small squares. Children can execute accurate jumping-jack exercise.
8	Children have 12-pound pressure on grip strength. The number of games participated in by both sexes is greatest at this age. Children can engage in alternate rhythmic hopping in a 2-2, 2-3, or 3-3 pattern. Girls can throw a small ball 40 feet.
9	Boys can run 16½ feet per second. Boys can throw a small ball 70 feet.
10	Children can judge and intercept pathways of small balls thrown from a distance. Girls can run 17 feet per second.
11	A standing broad jump of 5 feet is possible for boys and of 4½ feet for girls.

Source of Data: Bryant J. Cratty, *Perceptual and Motor Development in Infants and Children,* 3rd ed., Pearson Education, Inc., Upper Saddle River, NJ, 1986.

study smart

Motor Skills

According to a nationally representative survey, nearly 40 percent of 9- to 13-year-olds participate in organized after-school sports, such as soccer. To help children improve motor skills, such programs should emphasize skill-building rather than competition and should include as many children as possible regardless of ability.

rough-and-tumble play
Vigorous play involving wrestling, hitting, and chasing, often accompanied by laughing and screaming.

physical play (Larson & Verma, 1999). In the United States, children's lives today are more sedentary. A nationally representative survey based on time-use diaries found that school-age children spend less time each week on sports and other outdoor activities than in the early 1980s and more hours on schooling and homework, in addition to time spent on television—an average of 12 to 14 hours a week—and on computer activities, which barely existed 20 years ago (Juster, Ono, & Stafford, 2004).

RECESS-TIME PLAY

The games schoolchildren play at recess tend to be informal and spontaneously organized. Boys play more physically active games, whereas girls favor games that include verbal expression or counting aloud, such as hopscotch and jumprope. Such recess-time activities promote growth in agility and social competence and foster adjustment to school (Pellegrini, Kato, Blatchford, & Baines, 2002).

About 10 percent of schoolchildren's free play in the early grades consists of **rough-and-tumble play**, vigorous play that involves wrestling, kicking, tumbling, grappling, and chasing, often accompanied by laughing and screaming (Bjorklund & Pellegrini, 2002). This kind of play may look like fighting but is done playfully among friends (Smith, 2005a).

Rough-and-tumble play peaks in middle childhood; the proportion typically drops to about 5 percent at age 11, about the same as in early childhood (Bjorklund & Pellegrini, 2002). Seemingly universal, rough-and-tumble play has been reported in such diverse places as India, Mexico, Okinawa, the Kalahari in Africa, the Philippines, Great Britain, and the United States as well as among most mammals (Bjorklund & Pellegrini, 2002; Humphreys & Smith, 1984). Boys around the world participate in rough-and-tumble play more than girls do, and this is the likely reason for sex segregation during play (Bjorklund & Pellegrini, 2002; Pellegrini et al., 2002; Smith, 2005a). From an evolutionary standpoint, rough-and-tumble play has important adaptive benefits. It hones skeletal and muscle development, offers safe practice for hunting and fighting skills, and channels aggression and competition. By age 11, it often becomes a way to establish dominance within the peer group (Bjorklund & Pellegrini, 2000, 2002; Smith, 2005b).

ORGANIZED SPORTS

When children outgrow rough-and-tumble play and begin playing games with rules, some join organized, adult-led sports. In a nationally representative survey of U.S. 9- to 13-year-olds and their parents, 38.5 percent reported participation in organized athletics outside of school hours—most of them in baseball, softball, soccer, or basketball. About twice as many children (77.4 percent) participated in unorganized physical activity, such as bicycling and shooting baskets (Duke, Huhman, & Heitzler, 2003). Girls tend to spend less time than boys on sports and more time on housework, studying, and personal care (Juster et al., 2004).

Besides improving motor skills, regular physical activity has immediate and long-term health benefits: weight control, lower blood pressure, improved cardiorespiratory functioning, and enhanced self-esteem and well-being. Active children tend to become active adults. Inactive children who spend many hours watching television tend to be overweight. They are likely to get too little exercise and eat too many fattening snacks. Thus organized athletic programs should include as many children as possible rather than concentrating on a few natural athletes and should focus on building skills rather than winning games. Programs should include a variety of sports that can be part of a lifetime fitness regimen, such as tennis, bowling, running, swimming, golf, and skating (Council on Sports Medicine and Fitness and Council on School Health, 2006). Six- to nine-year-olds need more flexible rules, shorter instruction time, and more free time for practice than older children. At this age girls and boys are about equal in weight, height, endurance, and motor skill development. Older children are better able to process instruction and learn team strategies.

Health and Safety

The development of vaccines for major childhood illnesses has made middle childhood a relatively safe time of life. The death rate in these years is the lowest in the life span. Still, too many children are overweight, and some suffer from chronic medical conditions or accidental injuries or from lack of access to health care.

OVERWEIGHT AND BODY IMAGE

Obesity in children has become a major health issue worldwide. The prevalence of childhood overweight and obesity has more than doubled in the past 25 years. Nearly 50 percent of the children in North and South America, 39 percent in Europe, and 20 percent in China are likely to be overweight (Wang & Lobstein, 2006).

In the United States, about 17 percent of children between the ages of 2 and 19 are obese and another 16.5 percent are overweight (Gundersen, Lohman, Garasky, Stewart, & Eisenmann, 2008). Boys are more likely to be overweight than girls (Ogden et al., 2006). Although overweight has increased in all ethnic groups (Center for Weight and Health, 2001), it is most prevalent among Mexican American boys (more than 25 percent) and non-Hispanic black girls (26.5 percent) (Ogden et al., 2006).

Unfortunately, children who try to lose weight are not always the ones who need to do so. Concern with **body image**—how one believes one looks—begins to be important early in middle childhood, especially for girls, and may develop into eating disorders that become more common in adolescence (see Chapter 15). In a recent study on the development of body image in 9- to 12-year-old girls, between 49 and 55 percent were dissatisfied with their weight, with heavier girls experiencing overall higher dissatisfaction (Clark & Tiggeman, 2008). Playing with Barbie dolls may be an influence in that direction, as we discuss in Box 12.1.

Causes of Overweight As we reported in Chapters 3 and 9, overweight (or obesity) often results from an inherited tendency aggravated by too little exercise and too much or the wrong kinds of food (AAP Committee on Nutrition, 2003; Chen et al., 2004). Children are more likely to be overweight if they have overweight parents or other relatives. From earlier in this chapter, we know that poor nutrition, encouraged by media advertising and wide availability of snack foods and beverages, also contributes (Council on Sports Medicine and Fitness and Council on School Health, 2006). Eating out is another culprit; children who eat outside the home consume an estimated 200 more calories a day than when the same foods are eaten at home (French, Story, & Jeffery, 2001). On a typical day, more than 30 percent of a nationally representative sample of children and adolescents reported eating fast foods high in fat, carbohydrates, and sugar additives (Bowman, Gortmaker, Ebbeling, Pereira, & Ludwig, 2004).

Inactivity is a major factor in the sharp rise in overweight. Even with the increase in organized sports, school-age children today spend less time than the children of 20 years ago in outdoor play and sports (Juster et al., 2004). Activity levels decrease signficantly as children get older, from an average level of approximately 180 minutes of activity per day for 9-year-olds to 40 minutes per day for 15-year-olds (Nader, Bradley, Houts, McRitchie, & O'Brien, 2008). According to one national survey, 22.6 percent of 9- to 13-year-olds engage in *no* free-time physical activity (Duke, Huhman, & Heitzler, 2003).

checkpoint
can you...

▶ Tell how boys' and girls' recess-time activities differ?

▶ Explain the evolutionary significance of rough-and-tumble play?

What are the principal health and safety concerns in middle childhood?

guidepost 4

body image
Descriptive and evaluative beliefs about one's appearance.

What's in children's lunchboxes? The typical composition is 1 sandwich, 1 piece of fruit, and 1.5 "extras." The number of extras, which are more likely to be processed and low in nutritional value, peaks on Wednesdays.
Miles, Matthews, Brennan, & Mitchell, 2010

the everyday world

DO BARBIE DOLLS AFFECT GIRLS' BODY IMAGE?

"I looked at a Barbie doll when I was 6 and said, 'This is what I want to look like,'" Cindy Jackson, a model, said on a CBS News broadcast. "I think a lot of little 6-year-old girls or younger even now are looking at that doll and thinking, 'I want to be her.'" It took 31 operations, 14 years, and $100,000, but Jackson's obsession with Barbie got her a new look and an entry in the *Guinness Book of World Records*.

Barbie is the best-selling fashion doll around the world. In the United States, 99 percent of 3- to 10-year-old girls own at least one Barbie doll, and the average girl owns eight. Though she is sold as "every girl," Barbie is far from average. Her body proportions are "unrealistic, unattainable, and unhealthy" (Dittmar, Halliwell, & Ive, 2006, p. 284). "If she were alive, Barbie would be a woman standing 7 feet tall with a waistline of 18 inches and a bust-line of 38 to 40 inches," writes the psychotherapist Abigail Natenshon (2006), a specialist in eating disorders. In fact, Barbie's waist, as compared to her bust size, is 39 percent *smaller* than that of a woman with the eating disorder anorexia (see Chapter 15). Fewer than 1 in 100,000 women actually have Barbie's body proportions.

According to Bandura's social-cognitive theory, Barbie dolls are role models for young girls, transmitting a cultural ideal of beauty. The media reinforce this ideal. Girls who do not measure up may experience *body dissatisfaction*—negative thoughts about their bodies, leading to low self-esteem. By age 6, studies show, many girls wish to be thinner than they are.

To test Barbie's effect on young girls' body image, researchers read picture books to 5½- to 8½-year-old girls. One group saw picture stories about Barbie; control groups saw stories about a full-figured fashion doll called Emme or about no doll (Dittmar et al., 2006). Afterward, the girls completed questionnaires in which they were asked to agree or disagree with such statements as "I'm pretty happy about the way I look" and "I really like what I weigh."

The findings were striking. Among the youngest girls (ages 5½ to 6½), a single exposure to the Barbie picture book significantly lowered body esteem and increased the discrepancy between actual and ideal body size.

This did not happen with the girls in the two control groups. The effect of Barbie on body image was even stronger in 6½- to 7½-year-olds. However, the findings for the oldest group, ages 7½ to 8½, were completely different: Pictures of Barbie had no direct effect on body image at this age.

What accounts for this difference? Girls up to age 7 may be in a sensitive period in which they acquire idealized images of beauty. As girls grow older, they may internalize the ideal of thinness as part of their emerging identity. Once the ideal is internalized, its power no longer depends on direct exposure to the original role model (Dittmar et al., 2006).

Or, it may be that girls simply outgrow Barbie. In another study (Kuther & McDonald, 2004), sixth- through eighth-grade girls were asked about their childhood experiences with Barbie. All the girls had owned at least two Barbie dolls but said they no longer played with them. Looking back, some of the girls saw Barbie as a positive influence: "She is like the perfect person . . . that everyone wants to be like." But most of the girls saw Barbie as an unrealistic role model: "Barbie dolls provide a false stereotype . . . as it is physically impossible to attain the same body size. . . . There wouldn't be enough room for organs and other necessary things. . . . Barbie has this perfect body and now every girl is trying to have her body because they are so unhappy with themselves."

Barbie now has a major competitor: Bratz, an ultrathin doll with a large round face, sassy mouth, and heavy makeup. Longitudinal research will help determine whether fashion dolls such as Barbie and Bratz have a lasting impact on body image.

what's your view

If you had (or have) a young daughter, would you encourage her to play with Barbie dolls? Why or why not?

Preadolescent girls in ethnic minorities, children with disabilities, children who live in public housing, and children in unsafe neighborhoods where facilities for outdoor exercise are lacking are most likely to be sedentary (Council on Sports Medicine and Fitness and Council on School Health, 2006).

Physical inactivity and sedentary behaviors vary among children in various ethnic groups. In a recent study more than 22 percent of immigrant Hispanic children were identified as physically inactive compared with 9.5 percent of white children. Overall, immigrant children were significantly more likely to be physically inactive and less likely to participate in sports than native children (Singh, Yu, Siahpush, & Kogan, 2008).

Television viewing appears to be an important indicator of a number of lifestyle behaviors likely to promote inactivity and obesity over time. Children who watch a lot of TV fill much of their free time with a sedentary activity. They are exposed to advertisements that encourage them to eat unhealthy foods, and they tend to snack on these types of foods while watching TV. As a result, children who watch TV 5 hours a day are 4.6 times as likely to be overweight as those who watch no more than 2 hours daily (Institute of Medicine of the National Academies, 2005).

Children who spend many hours watching television tend to get too little exercise and eat too many fattening foods.

Childhood Overweight Is a Serious Concern The adverse health affects of obesity for children are similar to those faced by adults. These children are at risk for behavior problems, depression, and low self-esteem (AAP Committee on Nutrition, 2003; Datar & Sturm, 2004a; Mustillo et al., 2003). They commonly have medical problems, including high blood pressure (discussed in the next section), high cholesterol, and high insulin levels (AAP Committee on Nutrition, 2003; NCHS, 2004). Childhood diabetes, discussed later in this chapter, is one of the prime results of rising obesity rates (Perrin, Finkle, & Benjamin, 2007). Overweight children often suffer emotionally and may compensate by indulging themselves with treats, making their physical and social problems even worse.

Overweight children tend to become obese adults, at risk for high blood pressure, heart disease, orthopedic problems, and diabetes. Indeed, childhood overweight may be a stronger predictor of some diseases than adult overweight (AAP Committee on Nutrition, 2003; AAP, 2004; Center for Weight and Health, 2001; Li et al., 2004; Must, Jacques, Dallal, Bajema, & Dietz, 1992). By midcentury, obesity that starts in childhood may shorten life expectancy by 2 to 5 years (Franks et al., 2010; Ludwig, 2007).

> Taking in calories through snacks rather than meals is increasingly common in children today. The average child snacks approximately three times a day and takes in 600 calories a day from snacks.
>
> Piernas & Popkin, 2010

In a longitudinal study of 1,456 primary students in Victoria, Australia, children classified as overweight or obese fell behind their classmates in physical and social functioning by age 10 (Williams, Wake, Hesketh, Maher, & Waters, 2005). When 106 severely obese children and adolescents were asked to rate their health-related quality of life (for example, their ability to walk more than one block, to sleep well, to get along with others, and to keep up in school), they reported significant impairment as compared with healthy peers (Schwimmer, Burwinkle, & Varni, 2003).

Prevention and Treatment of Overweight Healthy attitudes about food and appropriate activity levels are the best way to prevent and treat childhood obesity. Prevention of weight gain is easier, less costly, and more effective than treating overweight (Center for Weight and Health, 2001; Council on Sports Medicine and Fitness and Council on School Health, 2006). Effective education programs should include efforts of parents, schools, physicians, communities, and the larger culture (Krishnamoorthy, Hart, & Jelalian, 2006; Table 12.3). Less time in front of television and computers, changes in food labeling and advertising, healthier

> Cookie Monster's favorite cookie is chocolate chip, followed by oatmeal, and he is allergic to peanut butter cookies. However, since 2006, Cookie Monster admits that cookies are best used as "sometimes snacks."

TABLE 12.3 A Coordinated Strategy to Stop the "Overweight Epidemic"

WHERE SHOWN

What parents can do:

- Make sure children are offered healthy foods and get plenty of outdoor play time
- Limit food choices
- Limit television time and video games to 2 hours a day, and monitor what children watch
- Provide healthy role models

What schools can do:

- Develop school wellness policies in partnership with the local school board, parents, students, physical education teachers, and health care professionals
- Provide healthier foods in the cafeteria, vending machines, and school stores
- Make sure that all children spend at least 30 minutes a day in moderate to vigorous physical activity
- Eliminate advertising of low-nutrient foods on school buses and scoreboards and at school functions

What private industry can do:

- Offer employee medical benefits that include preventive coverage
- Develop healthy products that are attractive to children
- Offer incentives for healthy eating
- Use television advertising aimed at children to promote healthy products

What health care professionals can do:

- Identify and track children and adolescents at risk for obesity due to genetic and environmental factors
- Calculate body mass index annually for children and adolescents and refer to a weight control specialist those who are overweight or at risk of overweight
- Encourage parents and caregivers to promote healthy eating by offering nutritious snacks, letting children eat what they want within appropriate limits, and modeling healthy food choices
- Promote physical activity, including unstructured play time
- Recommend limiting screen time to a maximum of 2 hours a day
- Give parents information on appropriate nutrition and advise families on adopting healthier lifestyles

What communities can do:

- Offer after-school recreational programs emphasizing physical activity and classes in cooking, nutrition, health, and fitness
- Develop pedestrian friendly neighborhoods with shops and grocery stores within walking distance

What federal, state, or local governments can do:

- Give the Secretary of Agriculture authority over all foods available in schools—in vending machines and after-school programs as well as in the cafeteria
- Publish nutritional guidelines for all foods and beverages sold in schools
- Give the Federal Trade Commission authority to establish guidelines for advertising of junk foods aimed at children
- Sponsor media campaigns to promote healthy nutrition and physical activity
- Support community programs that foster an active environment, for example, road projects that accommodate bicycles and pedestrians
- Tax soft drinks and snack foods and partially subsidize the cost of fresh fruits and vegetables

Source: Krishnamoorthy, Hart, & Jelalian, 2006.

school meals, education to help children make better food choices, and more time spent in physical education would help. Schools that serve healthier foods and offer nutrition education have reduced the number of overweight children in their classrooms by 50 percent (Foster et al., 2008). The U.S. Department of Agriculture suggests that children need at least 60 minutes of moderate-to-vigorous physical activity (MPVA) per day (USDA & USDHHS, 2005). The average school, however, conducts only 85 to 98 minutes per week of physical education classes (National Center for Education Statistics, 2006). Adding just one hour of physical education per week in kindergarten and first grade could reduce by half the number of overweight girls that age (Datar & Sturm, 2004b).

Parents can encourage healthy habits by making exercise a family activity and by limiting television. Parents should watch children's eating and activity patterns and address excessive weight gain before a child becomes severely overweight (AAP Committee on Nutrition, 2003). A federal law (Public Law 108-265) requires that every school receiving federal funding for school lunches or breakfasts must set goals for healthy nutrition, physical activity, and wellness promotion with emphasis on prevention of childhood obesity.

Treatment of overweight should begin early, involve the family, and promote permanent changes in lifestyle, not weight loss alone (Barlow & Dietz, 1998; Miller-Kovach, 2003).

MEDICAL CONDITIONS

Illness in middle childhood tends to be brief. **Acute medical conditions**—occasional, short-term conditions, such as infections and warts—are common. Six or seven bouts a year with colds, flu, or viruses are typical as germs pass among children at school or at play (Behrman, 1992).

According to a nationally representative survey of more than 200,000 households, an estimated 12.8 percent of U.S. children have or are at risk for **chronic medical conditions**: long-lasting or recurrent physical, developmental, behavioral, or emotional conditions requiring special health services (Kogan, Newacheck, Honberg, & Strickland, 2005). Let's look at some chronic conditions that affect everyday living.

Although not an issue in the United States and most industrialized nations, children in tropical countries are at risk for diseases that cause lethargy and problems with attention. The cause? Tropical parasites such as hookworm or schistosomiasis.

Out of sight, out of mind: Hidden cost of neglected tropical diseases, 2010

Asthma **Asthma** is a chronic respiratory disease, apparently allergy-based and characterized by sudden attacks of coughing, wheezing, and difficulty in breathing. Its incidence is increasing worldwide (Asher et al., 2006), although it may have leveled off in some parts of the Western world (Eder, Ege, & von Mutius, 2006). Its prevalence in the United States more than doubled between 1980 and 1995 and has since remained at this historically high level (Akinbami, 2006). More than 13 percent of U.S. children and adolescents up to age 17 have been diagnosed with asthma at some time, and 9 percent currently have asthma (Federal Interagency Forum on Child and Family Statistics, 2007). It is 30 percent more likely to be diagnosed in boys than in girls and 20 percent more likely to be diagnosed in black children than in white children (McDaniel, Paxson, & Waldfogel, 2006).

The causes of the asthma explosion are uncertain, but a genetic predisposition is likely to be involved (Eder et al., 2006). Researchers have identified a gene mutation that increases the risk of developing asthma (Ober et al., 2008). Some researchers point to environmental factors: tightly insulated houses that intensify exposure to indoor air pollutants and allergens such as tobacco smoke, molds, and cockroach droppings. Allergies to household pets also have been suggested as risk factors (Bollinger, 2003; Etzel,

what's your view

In 2011, San Francisco banned including free toys with fast-food meals as a means by which to address the obesity epidemic. Is the legislation of such practices sound public health policy, or is it an intrusion into personal choice? What matters more?

checkpoint can you . . .

▷ Discuss why childhood overweight has increased, how it can affect health, and how it can be treated?

acute medical conditions
Occasional illnesses that last a short time.

chronic medical conditions
Long-lasting or recurrent physical, developmental, behavioral, and/or emotional conditions that require special health services.

asthma
A chronic respiratory disease characterized by sudden attacks of coughing, wheezing, and difficulty in breathing.

2003; Lanphear, Aligne, Auinger, Weitzman, & Byrd, 2001; Sly, 2000). However, findings regarding these proposed causes, except for smoke exposure, are inconclusive. Increasing evidence points to an association between obesity and asthma, perhaps because of an underlying lifestyle factor related to both conditions (Eder et al., 2006).

Diabetes **Diabetes** is one of the most common diseases in school-age children. More than 185,000 children in the United States have diabetes (National Diabetes Information Clearinghouse [NDIC], 2007). Diabetes is characterized by high levels of glucose in the blood as a result of defective insulin production, ineffectve insulin action, or both. Type 1 diabetes is the result of an insulin deficiency that occurs when insulin-producing cells in the pancreas are destroyed. Type 1 diabetes accounts for 5 to 10 percent of all diabetes cases and accounts for almost all diabetes in children under 10 years of age. Symptoms include thirst and urination, hunger, weight loss, blurred vision, and fatigue. Treatment includes insulin administration, nutrition management, and physical activity (National Diabetes Education Program, 2008).

Type 2 diabetes is characterised by insulin resistance and used to be found mainly in overweight and older adults. With the increase in childhood obesity, more and more children are being diagnosed with this form of diabetes. Each year about 3,700 children are diagnosed with type 2 diabetes, and statistics show increased incidence of the disease among African Americans, American Indians, and Latin Americans. Symptoms are similar to type 1 diabetes (Zylke & DeAngelis, 2007). Treatment with nutrition management and increased physical activity can be effective although glucose-lowering medication or insulin may be needed for resistant cases.

Childhood Hypertension **Hypertension** (high blood pressure) once was relatively rare in childhood, but it has been termed an "evolving epidemic" of cardiovascular risk, especially among ethnic minorities (Sorof, Lai, Turner, Poffenbarger, & Portman, 2004, p. 481). A series of screenings of 5,102 children ages 10 to 19 in eight Houston public schools found an estimated 4.5 percent prevalence of hypertension, with overweight the major contributing factor (Sorof et al., 2004).

Weight reduction through dietary modification and regular physical activity is the primary treatment for overweight-related hypertension. If blood pressure does not come down, drug treatment can be considered. However, care must be taken in prescribing such drugs, as their long-term effects on children are unknown—as are the long-term consequences of untreated hypertension in children (National High Blood Pressure Education Program Working Group on High Blood Pressure in Children and Adolescents, 2004).

Stuttering **Stuttering** is involuntary audible or silent repetition or prolongation of sounds or syllables. It usually begins between ages 2 and 5 (Büchel & Sommer, 2004). By fifth grade, it is 4 times more common in boys than in girls. Five percent of children stutter for a period of 6 months or more, but three-quarters of these recover by late childhood, leaving about 1 percent with a long-term problem (Stuttering Foundation, 2006).

Stuttering is now widely regarded as a neurological condition. It sometimes results from brain damage (for example, head trauma or a stroke). The more common type, *persistent developmental stuttering* (PDS), is especially noticeable at the beginning of a word or phrase or in long, complex sentences. The concordance rate is about 70 percent for monozygotic twins, 30 percent for dizygotic twins, and 18 percent for same-sex siblings, suggesting a genetic component (Kang et al., 2010). It seems likely that two factors are at work in PDS. The basic cause may be a structural or functional disorder of the central nervous system. This may then be reinforced by parental reactions to the stuttering, which may make the child nervous or anxious about speaking (Büchel & Sommer, 2004).

There is no known cure for stuttering, but speech therapy can help a child talk more easily and fluently (Stuttering Foundation, 2006). If stutterers become frustrated or anxious about their speech, they may learn to avoid speaking as much as possible. On the other hand, the actor Bruce Willis treated himself by joining a drama club, which forced him to speak before an audience (Büchel & Sommer, 2004). Many other famous people, including the actress Julia Roberts and the actor James Earl Jones, have succeeded despite having PDS.

FACTORS IN HEALTH AND ACCESS TO HEALTH CARE

Social disadvantage plays an important part in children's health. Poor children—who are disproportionately minority children—and those living with a single parent or parents with low educational status are more likely than other children to be in fair or poor health, to have chronic conditions or health-related limitations on activities, to miss school due to illness or injury, to be hospitalized, to have unmet medical and dental needs, and to experience delayed medical care (Bauman, Silver, & Stein, 2006; Bloom et al., 2003; Collins & LeClere, 1997; Flores et al., 2002; Newacheck et al., 1998), and the chances of health problems compound when more than one of these risk factors is present.

Why is this economic disadvantage important? Parents with higher socioeconomic and educational status tend to know more about good health habits and have better access to insurance and health care. Two-parent families tend to have higher incomes and more wholesome diets than single-parent families (Collins & LeClere, 1997), and their children are more likely to have health insurance (Fields, 2003). They can also more readily afford their children's participation in organized sports teams. Children in low-income and minority families are more likely than other children to be uninsured, to have no usual place of health care, or to go to clinics or hospital emergency rooms rather than doctors' offices (Bloom et al., 2003).

Access to health care is a particularly severe problem among Latino children, especially those who are poor or near poor and who have foreign-born parents with less than a high school education (Scott & Ni, 2004).

However, lack of access to insurance and health care accounts for only part of the disparity in disadvantaged children's health (Bauman et al., 2006). Asian American children, who tend to be in better health than non-Hispanic white children, are less likely to access and use health care, perhaps because of cultural and linguistic barriers (Yu, Huang, & Singh, 2004). Indeed, one factor in variations in health care is differing beliefs and attitudes about health and healing among cultural and ethnic groups, as we discuss in Box 12.2.

ACCIDENTAL INJURIES

As in early childhood, accidental injuries are the leading cause of death among school-age U.S. children (Heron et al., 2009). In 2004 nearly 950,000 children under the age of 18 worldwide died of an injury with the majority resulting from traffic accidents, drowning, or burns (WHO, 2008; Figure 12.2).

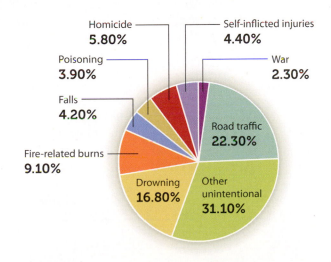

Homicide 5.80%
Self-inflicted injuries 4.40%
Poisoning 3.90%
War 2.30%
Falls 4.20%
Road traffic 22.30%
Fire-related burns 9.10%
Drowning 16.80%
Other unintentional 31.10%

FIGURE 12.2

Accidental Deaths for Children under Age 18

Traffic accidents, drowning, and burns are the most common causes of accidental deaths among children under 18 years of age.

Source: World Health Organization, 2008.

around the wrld

HOW CULTURAL ATTITUDES AFFECT HEALTH CARE

12.2

One morning Buddi Kumar Rai, a university-educated resident of Badel, a remote hill village in Nepal, carried his 2½-year-old daughter, Kusum, to the shaman, the local medicine man. Kusum's little face was sober, her usually golden complexion pale, and her almond-shaped eyes droopy from the upper-respiratory infection she had been suffering with the past week, complete with fever and a hacking cough.

Two days before, Kusum had been in her father's arms when he had slipped and fallen backward off a veranda to the ground about 3 feet below, still tightly holding his little daughter. Neither was hurt, but little Kusum had screamed in fright.

Now the shaman told Buddi that Kusum's illness was due to that fright. He prescribed incantations and put a mark, a charcoal smudge the size of a silver dollar, on the child's forehead to drive away the evil spirit that had entered her body when she had her scare.

Adherence to ancient beliefs about illness is common in parts of the industrialized world where people still cling to beliefs that are at odds with mainstream scientific and medical thinking. To provide better medical care to members of ethnic minorities, policymakers need to understand the cultural beliefs and attitudes that influence what people do and the decisions they make and how they interact with the broader society.

Many cultures see illness and disability as a form of punishment inflicted on someone who has transgressed in this or a previous life or is paying for an ancestor's sin. Another belief, common in Latin America and Southeast Asia, is that an imbalance of elements in the body causes illness, and the patient has to reestablish equilibrium. Arab Americans tend to attribute disease to such causes as the evil eye, grief and loss, exposure to drafts, and eating the wrong combinations of foods.

In many societies people believe that a severely disabled child will not survive. Since there is no hope, they do not expend time, effort, or money on the child—which often creates a self-fulfilling prophecy. In some religious households, parents hold out hope for a miracle and refuse surgery or other treatment.

Of course, standard medical practice in the United States is also governed by a cultural belief system. Often parents must make decisions about their child quickly, without consulting members of the extended family as would be done in many cultures. To foster independence and self-sufficiency, parents are discouraged from babying a disabled child. People from other cultures may not

This Peruvian healer treats a child with traditional methods, such as herbs and incantations. In many Latin American cultures, such practices are believed to cure illness by restoring the natural balance of elements in the body.

agree with these American values; parents may feel a need to consult their own parents about medical decisions and may not consider it important for a child with a disability to become self-sufficient.

Professionals need to explain clearly, in the family's language, what course of treatment they recommend, why they favor it, and what they expect to happen. Such concern can help prevent incidents like one that occurred when an Asian mother became hysterical as an American nurse took her baby to get a urine sample. Three children had been taken from this mother in Cambodia. None had returned.

Sources: Al-Oballi Kridli, 2002; Olds, 2002; Groce & Zola, 1993.

what's your view

▷ How would Piaget interpret the belief in some cultures that illness and disabilities are punishments for human actions?

▷ Does such a belief suggest that Piaget's theory is limited in its applicability to non-Western cultures?

Encouraging or requiring the use of safety devices has been shown to lower injury rates. Child seats, seat belts, and bicycle helmets have significantly lowered the number of injuries in the road environment, and smoke alarms and hot water temperature regulations have reduced the number of burns (WHO, 2008).

One reason for some accidents is children's immaturity, both cognitive (preventing them from being aware of some dangers) and emotional (leading them to take dangerous risks). We discuss cognitive development in middle childhood in Chapter 13 and emotional and social development in Chapter 14.

> About half of kids who drown do so within 25 yards of an adult. This happens partly because drowning doesn't look like it does in movies. A drowning child does not yell for help or splash. Signs to look for? Head low in the water, perhaps tilted back with hair covering the eyes, silence, glassy or closed eyes, mouth at or slightly below the water line, and ineffective attempts to roll over to the back or swim.
>
> Vittone, 2010

Safety approved helmets protect children from disabling or fatal head injuries.

Mental Health

COMMON EMOTIONAL DISTURBANCES

Children with emotional, behavioral, and developmental problems tend to be an underserved group. Compared with other children who have special health care needs, they are more likely to have conditions that affect their daily activities and cause them to miss school. They often have chronic physical conditions. Many of them lack adequate health insurance and have unmet health care needs (Bethell, Read, & Blumberg, 2005).

A reported 55.7 percent of children diagnosed with emotional, behavioral, and developmental problems have *disruptive conduct disorders:* aggression, defiance, or antisocial behavior. Almost all the rest, 43.5 percent, have *anxiety* or *mood disorders:* feeling sad, depressed, nervous, fearful, or lonely (Bethell et al., 2005).

Disruptive Conduct Disorders Temper tantrums and defiant, argumentative, hostile, or deliberately annoying behaviors—common among 4- and 5-year-olds—typically are outgrown by middle childhood. When such a pattern of behavior persists until age 8, children (usually boys) may be diagnosed with **oppositional defiant disorder (ODD)**, a pattern of defiance, disobedience, and hostility toward adult authority figures lasting at least 6 months and going beyond the bounds of normal childhood behavior. Children with ODD constantly fight, argue, lose their temper, snatch things, blame others, are angry and resentful, have few friends, are in constant trouble in school, and test the limits of adults' patience (American Psychiatric Association, 2000; National Library of Medicine, 2004).

Some children with ODD also develop **conduct disorder (CD)**, a persistent, repetitive pattern, beginning at an early age, of aggressive, antisocial acts, such as truancy, setting fires, habitual lying, fighting, bullying, theft, vandalism, assaults, and drug and alcohol use (American Psychiatric Association, 2000; National Library of Medicine, 2003). Between 6 and 16 percent of boys and between 2 and 9 percent of girls under age 18 in the United States have been diagnosed with clinical levels of externalizing behavior or conduct problems (Roosa et al., 2005). Some 11- to 13-year-olds progress from conduct disorder to criminal violence—mugging, rape, and break-ins—and by age 17 may be frequent, serious offenders (Boidy et al., 2003; Coie & Dodge, 1998). Between 25 and 50 percent of these highly antisocial children become antisocial adults (USDHHS, 1999b).

checkpoint
can **you** . . .

▷ Distinguish between acute and chronic medical conditions, and tell how specific chronic conditions can affect everyday life?

▷ Explain why socially disadvantaged children tend to have more health problems than their peers?

▷ Identify factors that increase the risks of accidental injury?

What are some common mental health problems of childhood?

oppositional defiant disorder (ODD) Pattern of behavior, persisting into middle childhood, marked by negativity, hostility, and defiance.

conduct disorder (CD) Repetitive, persistent pattern of aggressive, antisocial behavior violating societal norms or the rights of others.

What determines whether a particular child with antisocial tendencies will become severely and chronically antisocial? Neurobiological deficits, such as weak stress-regulating mechanisms, may fail to warn children to restrain themselves from dangerous or risky behavior. Such deficits may be genetically influenced or may be brought on by adverse environments such as hostile parenting or family conflict, or both (van Goozen, Fairchild, Snoek, & Harold, 2007). Also influential are stressful life events and association with deviant peers (Roosa et al., 2005).

School Phobia and Other Anxiety Disorders Children with **school phobia** have an unrealistic fear of going to school. Some children have realistic reasons to fear going to school: a sarcastic teacher, overly demanding work, or a bully in the school yard. In such cases, the environment may need changing, not the child. True school phobia may be a type of **separation anxiety disorder**, a condition involving excessive anxiety for at least 4 weeks concerning separation from home or from people to whom the child is attached.

Although separation anxiety is normal in infancy, when it persists in older children it is cause for concern. Separation anxiety disorder affects some 4 percent of children and young adolescents and may persist through the college years. These children often come from close-knit, caring families. They may develop the disorder spontaneously or after a stressful event, such as the death of a pet, an illness, or a move to a new school (American Psychiatric Association, 2000; Harvard Medical School, 2004). Many children with separation anxiety also show symptoms of depression (USDHHS, 1999b).

Sometimes school phobia may be a form of **social phobia**, or *social anxiety:* extreme fear and/or avoidance of social situations, such as speaking in class or meeting an acquaintance on the street. Social phobia affects about 5 percent of children. It runs in families, so there is likely a genetic component. Often these phobias are triggered by traumatic experiences, such as a child's mind going blank after being called on in class or having to write on the board in front of the class (Beidel & Turner, 1998; Rao, Beidel, Turner, Ammerman, Crosby, & Sallee, 2007). Social anxiety tends to increase with age, whereas separation anxiety decreases.

Some children have a **generalized anxiety disorder**, which is not focused on any specific aspect of their lives. These children worry about just about everything: school grades, storms, earthquakes, hurting themselves on the playground, or the amount of gas in the tank. They tend to be self-conscious, self-doubting, and excessively concerned with meeting the expectations of others. They seek approval and need constant reassurance, but their worry seems independent of performance or of how they are regarded by others (American Psychiatric Association, 1994; Harvard Medical School, 2004; USDHHS, 1999b).

Far less common is **obsessive-compulsive disorder (OCD)**. Those with this disorder may be obsessed by repetitive, intrusive thoughts, images, or impulses (often involving irrational fears) or may show compulsive behaviors, such as constant hand-washing, or both (American Psychiatric Association, 2000; Harvard Medical School, 2004; USD-HHS, 1999b).

Anxiety disorders tend to run in families (Harvard Medical School, 2004) and are twice as common among girls as among boys. The heightened female vulnerability to anxiety begins as early as age 6. Females also are more susceptible to depression, which is similar to anxiety and often goes hand in hand with it (Lewinsohn, Gotlib, Lewinsohn, Seeley, & Allen, 1998). Both anxiety and depression may be neurologically based or may stem from early experiences that make children feel a lack of control over what happens around them. Parents who reward an anxious child with attention to the anxiety may unwittingly perpetuate it through operant conditioning (Chorpita & Barlow, 1998; Harvard Medical School, 2004).

Childhood Depression **Childhood depression** is a disorder of mood that goes beyond normal, temporary sadness. Depression is estimated to occur in 2 percent of elementary school children (NCHS, 2004). Symptoms include inability to have fun or

---

school phobia
Unrealistic fear of going to school; may be a form of *separation anxiety disorder* or *social phobia*.

separation anxiety disorder
Condition involving excessive, prolonged anxiety concerning separation from home or from people to whom a person is attached.

social phobia
Extreme fear and/or avoidance of social situations.

generalized anxiety disorder
Anxiety not focused on any single target.

obsessive-compulsive disorder (OCD)
Anxiety aroused by repetitive, intrusive thoughts, images, or impulses, often leading to compulsive ritual behaviors.

childhood depression
Mood disorder characterized by such symptoms as a prolonged sense of friendlessness, inability to have fun or concentrate, fatigue, extreme activity or apathy, feelings of worthlessness, weight change, physical complaints, and thoughts of death or suicide.

concentrate, fatigue, extreme activity or apathy, crying, sleep problems, weight change, physical complaints, feelings of worthlessness, a prolonged sense of friendlessness, or frequent thoughts about death or suicide. Childhood depression may signal the beginning of a recurrent problem that is likely to persist into adulthood (Birmaher, 1998; Birmaher et al., 1996; Cicchetti & Toth, 1998; Kye & Ryan, 1995; USDHHS, 1999b; Weissman, Warner, Wickramaratne, & Kandel, 1999).

The exact causes of childhood depression are unknown, but depressed children tend to come from families with high levels of parental depression, anxiety, substance abuse, or antisocial behavior. The atmosphere in such families may increase children's risk of depression (Cicchetti & Toth, 1998; Franic, Middeldorp, Dolan, Ligthart, & Boomsma, 2010; USDHHS, 1999b).

Researchers have found a number of genes related to depression. One gene, 5-HTT, helps to control the brain chemical serotonin and affects mood. In a longitudinal study of 847 people born in the same year in Dunedin, New Zealand, those who had two short versions of this gene were more likely to become depressed than those who had two long versions (Caspi et al., 2003). A short form of another gene, SERT-s, which also controls serotonin, is associated with enlargement of the pulvinar, a brain region involved in negative emotions (Young et al., 2007).

Children as young as 5 or 6 can accurately report depressed moods and feelings that forecast later trouble, from academic problems to major depression and ideas of suicide (Ialongo, Edelsohn, & Kellam, 2001). Depression often emerges during the transition to middle school and may be related to stiffer academic pressures (Cicchetti & Toth, 1998), weak self-efficacy beliefs, and lack of personal investment in academic success (Rudolph, Lambert, Clark, & Kurlakowsky, 2001). Depression becomes more prevalent during adolescence (Costello et al., 2003), as discussed in Chapter 15.

TREATMENT TECHNIQUES

Psychological treatment for emotional disturbances can take several forms. In **individual psychotherapy**, a therapist sees a child one-on-one to help the child gain insights into his or her personality and relationships and to interpret feelings and behavior. Such treatment may be helpful at a time of stress, such as the death of a parent or parental divorce, even when a child has not shown signs of disturbance. Child psychotherapy is usually more effective when combined with counseling for the parents.

In **family therapy**, the therapist sees the family together, observes how members interact, and points out both growth-producing and growth-inhibiting, or destructive, patterns of family functioning. Therapy can help parents confront their own conflicts and begin to resolve them. This is often the first step toward resolving the child's problems as well.

Behavior therapy, or *behavior modification*, is a form of therapy that uses principles of learning theory to eliminate undesirable behaviors or to develop desirable ones. A statistical analysis of many studies found that psychotherapy is generally effective with children and adolescents, but behavior therapy is more effective than nonbehavioral methods. Results are best when treatment is targeted to specific problems and desired outcomes (Weisz, Weiss, Han, Granger, & Morton, 1995). *Cognitive behavioral therapy*, which seeks to change negative thoughts through gradual exposure, modeling, rewards, or positive self-talk, has proven the most effective treatment for anxiety disorders in children and adolescents (Harvard Medical School, 2004).

When children have limited verbal and conceptual skills or have suffered emotional trauma, **art therapy** can help them describe what is troubling them without the need to put their feelings into words. The child may express deep emotions through choice of colors and subjects (Hanney & Kozlowska, 2002; Kozlowska & Hanney, 1999). Observing how a family plans, carries out, and discusses an art project can reveal patterns of family interactions (Kozlowska & Hanney, 1999).

In **play therapy**, a child plays freely while a therapist occasionally comments, asks questions, or makes suggestions. Play therapy has proven effective with a variety of

individual psychotherapy
Psychological treatment in which a therapist sees a troubled person one-on-one.

family therapy
Psychological treatment in which a therapist sees the whole family together to analyze patterns of family functioning.

behavior therapy
Therapy that uses principles of learning theory to eliminate undesirable behaviors.

art therapy
Therapeutic approach that allows a person to express troubled feelings without words, using a variety of art materials and media.

play therapy
Therapeutic approach that uses play to help a child cope with emotional distress.

emotional, cognitive, and social problems, especially when consultation with parents or other close family members is part of the process (Athansiou, 2001; Bratton & Ray, 2002; Leblanc & Ritchie, 2001; Ryan & Needham, 2001; Wilson & Ryan, 2001).

The use of **drug therapy**—antidepressants, stimulants, tranquilizers, and antipsychotic medications—to treat childhood emotional disorders is controversial. In 2002, antipsychotic medications were prescribed for 1,438 in every 100,000 children and adolescents, as compared with only 275 per 100,000 during the mid-1990s (Olfson, Blanco, Liu, Moreno, & Laje, 2006). Sufficient research on the effectiveness and safety of many of these drugs, especially for children, is lacking (Murray, de Vries, & Wong, 2004; USDHHS, 1999b; Wong, Murray, Camilleri-Novak, & Stephens, 2004; Zito et al., 2003).

The use of *selective serotonin reuptake inhibitors* (SSRIs) to treat obsessive-compulsive, depressive, and anxiety disorders increased rapidly in the 1990s (Leslie, Newman, Chesney, & Perrin, 2005) but has since slipped by about 20 percent (Daly, 2005). Some studies show moderate risks of suicidal thought and behavior for children and adolescents taking antidepressants, whereas others show no significant added risk (Hammad, Laughren, & Racoosin, 2006; Simon, Savarino, Operskalski, & Wang, 2006) or lessened risk (Simon, 2006). An analysis of 27 randomized, placebo-controlled studies found that the benefits of antidepressant use for children and adolescents outweigh the risks (Bridge et al., 2007). (Use of antidepressant drugs for adolescent depression is discussed in Chapter 15.)

checkpoint can you . . .

▷ Identify causes and symptoms of disruptive behavior disorders, anxiety disorders, and childhood depression?

▷ Describe and evaluate six common types of therapy for emotional disorders?

summary and key terms

guidepost 1
Aspects of Physical Development

How do school-age children's bodies and brains grow and develop?

- Physical development is less rapid in middle childhood than in earlier years. Wide differences in height and weight exist.
- Children with retarded growth due to growth hormone deficiency may be given synthetic growth hormone. The hormone is sometimes prescribed for short children who do not have hormone deficiency; extreme caution is advised in such cases.
- The permanent teeth arrive in middle childhood. Dental health has improved, in part because of the use of sealants on chewing surfaces and the widespread use of flouride.
- Brain growth continues during childhood with a gradual increase in white matter and decrease in gray matter. The corpus callosum connecting the two hemispheres becomes progressively myelinated. These changes support the cognitive advances of middle childhood.

guidepost 2
Nutrition and Sleep

What are the nutritional and sleep needs of middle childhood?

- Proper nutrition and adequate sleep are essential for normal growth and health.

- Most children do not get enough sleep, and many have sleep problems.

guidepost 3
Motor Development and Physical Play

What gains in motor skills typically occur at this age, and what kinds of physical play do boys and girls engage in?

- Because of improved motor development, boys and girls in middle childhood can engage in a wide range of motor activities.
- About 10 percent of schoolchildren's free play, especially among boys, is rough-and-tumble play.
- Informal, spontaneous play helps develop physical and social skills. Boys' games are more physical and girls' games more verbal.
- Many children, mostly boys, engage in organized, competitive sports.
- A sound physical education program should aim at skill development for all children and should emphasize enjoyment and lifelong fitness rather than competition.

rough-and-tumble play (344)

 ❹ Health and Safety

What are the principal health and safety concerns in middle childhood?

- Middle childhood is a relatively healthy period; the death rate is the lowest in the life span. However, respiratory infections and other acute medical conditions are common.
- Concern with body image, especially among girls, may lead to eating disorders.
- Overweight, which is increasingly common among children, is influenced by genetic and environmental factors and can be prevented more easily than it can be treated.
- Obesity in children has increased at an alarming rate and is becoming a major health issue worldwide.
- Diabetes is becoming increasingly common and is linked to obesity.
- Stuttering is fairly common but usually not permanent.
- Chronic conditions such as asthma and hypertension are most prevalent among poor and minority children, who are least likely to be insured and to have regular health care.
- The prevalance of asthma has increased among children under the age of 17.
- Accidents are the leading cause of death in middle childhood. Use of helmets and other protective devices has been shown to lower injury rates.

body image (*345*)

acute medical conditions (*349*)

chronic medical conditions (*349*)

asthma (*349*)

diabetes (*350*)

hypertension (*350*)

stuttering (*350*)

❺ Mental Health

What are some common mental health problems of childhood?

- Common emotional and behavioral disorders among school-age children include disruptive behavioral disorders, anxiety disorders, and childhood depression.

oppositional defiant disorder (ODD) (*353*)

conduct disorder (CD) (*353*)

school phobia (*354*)

separation anxiety disorder (*354*)

social phobia (*354*)

generalized anxiety disorder (*354*)

obsessive-compulsive disorder (OCD) (*354*)

childhood depression (*354*)

- Treatment techniques include individual psychotherapy, family therapy, behavior therapy, art therapy, play therapy, and drug therapy. Often therapies are used in combination.

individual psychotherapy (*355*)

family therapy (*355*)

behavior therapy (*355*)

art therapy (*355*)

play therapy (*355*)

drug therapy (*356*)

Cognitive Development in Middle Childhood

did you know?

▷ IQ at age 11 may predict length of life, functional independence late in life, and the presence or absence of dementia?

▷ According to the neuropsychologist Howard Gardner, there are eight separate types of intelligence, and only three of them are measured by IQ tests?

▷ Children who believe they can master schoolwork are more likely to do so?

In this chapter we examine cognitive advances during the first 5 or 6 years of formal schooling, from about age 6 to 11. Entry into Piaget's stage of concrete operations enables children to think logically and to make more mature moral judgments. As children improve in memory and problem solving, intelligence tests become more accurate in predicting school performance. The abilities to read and write open the door to a wider world. We discuss all these changes, and we look at controversies over IQ testing, bilingual education, homework, and mathematics instruction. Finally, we examine influences on school achievement and how schools try to meet special educational needs.

What you learn today, for no reason at all, will help you discover all the wonderful secrets of tomorrow.

—Norton Juster, *The Phantom Tollbooth*

for **study**

guideposts

1. How do school-age children's thinking and moral reasoning differ from those of younger children?
2. What advances in information-processing skills occur during middle childhood?
3. How accurately can schoolchildren's intelligence be measured?
4. How do communicative abilities expand during middle childhood?
5. What factors influence school achievement?
6. How do schools meet special needs?

guidepost

1 How do school-age children's thinking and moral reasoning differ from those of younger children?

concrete operations
The third stage of Piagetian cognitive development (approximately from age 7 to 12) during which children develop logical but not abstract thinking.

Piagetian Approach: The Concrete Operational Child

At about age 7, according to Piaget, children enter the stage of **concrete operations** and begin to use mental operations to solve concrete (actual) problems. Children now can think logically because they can take multiple aspects of a situation into account. However, their thinking is still limited to real situations in the here and now. In the following section, we focus on the specific cognitive advances typical of this stage of development.

COGNITIVE ADVANCES

Children in the stage of concrete operations can perform many tasks at a much higher level than they could in the preoperational stage (Table 13.1). They have a better understanding of spatial concepts, causality, categorization, inductive and deductive reasoning, conservation, and number.

Spatial Relationships and Causality Eight year-old Ella stares intently at the map. "The star means we are here," she points, "so that must mean the store we want is there!" Ella turns to her mother with a smile and they both begin walking.

Ella is now in the stage of concrete operations. She is better able to understand spatial relationships. This allows her to interpret a map, find her way to and from school, more clearly estimate the time it would take to go from one place to another, and remember routes and landmarks. Experience plays a role in this development because children are more easily able to navigate a physical environment they have experience with. In addition, these spatial abilities improve as children age (Gauvain, 1993).

Another key development during middle childhood involves the ability to make judgments about cause and effect. These specific abilities also improve as children age. For example, when 5- to 12-year-old children are asked to predict how levers and balance scales work, the older children give more correct answers. In addition, when they are younger in middle childhood, they understand that the number of objects on each side of a scale impact performance. Some time later in this stage, they understand that the distance of objects from the center of a scale is also important (Amsel, Goodman, Savoie, & Clark, 1996).

TABLE 13.1 Advances in Selected Cognitive Abilities during Middle Childhood

Ability	Example
Spatial thinking	Danielle can use a map or model to help her search for a hidden object and can give someone else directions for finding the object. She can find her way to and from school, can estimate distances, and can judge how long it will take her to go from one place to another.
Cause and effect	Douglas knows which physical attributes of objects on each side of a balance scale will affect the result (i.e., number of objects matters but color does not). He does not yet know which spatial factors, such as position and placement of the objects, make a difference.
Categorization	Elena can sort objects into categories, such as shape, color, or both. She knows that a subclass (roses) has fewer members than the class of which it is a part (flowers).
Seriation and transitive inference	Catherine can arrange a group of sticks in order, from the shortest to the longest, and can insert an intermediate-size stick into the proper place. She knows that if one stick is longer than a second stick, and the second stick is longer than a third, then the first stick is longer than the third.
Inductive and deductive reasoning	Dominic can solve both inductive and deductive problems and knows that inductive conclusions (based on particular premises) are less certain than deductive ones (based on general premises).
Conservation	Felipe, at age 7, knows that if a clay ball is rolled into a sausage, it still contains the same amount of clay (conservation of substance). At age 9, he knows that the ball and the sausage weigh the same. Not until early adolescence will he understand that they displace the same amount of liquid if dropped in a glass of water.
Number and mathematics	Kevin can count in his head, can add by counting up from the smaller number, and can do simple story problems.

Categorization John sits at the kitchen table, working on his class project. He has been asked to make a timeline of six events in his life using photographs. His mother has given him six photographs of himself from infancy to the current time, and John carefully lays them in order from earliest to latest. "There!" he says, "I'm ready to start!"

Part of the reason that John is now able to complete tasks such as this class project is because he is becoming better able to categorize objects. This emerging ability helps him to think more logically, and involves a series of relatively sophisticated abilities. One such ability is **seriation**, arranging objects in a series according to one or more dimensions. Children become increasingly better at seriation for dimensions such as time (earliest to latest), length (shortest to longest), or color (lightest to darkest) (Piaget, 1952).

Another emerging ability is that of **transitive inferences** (if a < b and b < c, then a < c). This involves the ability to infer a relationship between two objects from the relationship between each of them and a third object. For example, Mateo is shown three sticks: a short yellow stick, a medium-length green stick, and a long blue stick. He is shown that the yellow stick is shorter than the green stick, and is then shown that the green stick is shorter than the blue stick. However, he is not shown all three sticks in order of their length. If John is able to understand transitive inferences, he should be able to quickly and easily infer that the yellow stick is shorter than the blue

seriation
Ability to order items along a dimension.

transitive inference
Understanding the relationship between two objects by knowing the relationship of each to a third object.

stick without physically comparing them (Chapman & Lindenberger, 1988; Piaget & Inhelder, 1967).

Last, class inclusion becomes easier. **Class inclusion** is the ability to see the relationship between a whole and its parts, and to understand the categories within a whole. For example, Piaget (1964) showed preoperational children 10 flowers—7 roses and 3 carnations—and asked them whether there were more roses or more flowers. Children in the preoperational stage of development tended to say there were more roses because they were comparing the roses with the carnations rather than the whole bunch of flowers. However, at about age 7 or 8, when children have reached the concrete operations stage, they are able to understand that roses are a subcategory of the flowers, and that there are therefore more flowers than there are roses (Flavell, 1963; Flavell, Miller, & Miller, 2002).

Inductive and Deductive Reasoning **Inductive reasoning** involves making observations about particular members of a class of people, animals, objects, or events, and then drawing conclusions about the class as a whole. For example, if one neighbor's dog barks and another neighbor's dog barks, then the conclusion might be, via inductive reasoning, that all dogs bark. Inductive reasoning must be tentative, however, because it is always possible to come across new information, for example, a dog that does not bark.

Deductive reasoning, by contrast, starts with a general statement—a premise—about a class and applies it to particular members of the class. If a premise is true of the whole class, and the reasoning is sound, then the conclusion must be true. So, for example, if the belief is that all dogs bark, and a new dog comes along, it might be reasonable to conclude that the new dog will also bark.

Piaget believed that children in the concrete operations stage of cognitive development only used inductive reasoning. Deductive reasoning, according to Piaget, did not develop until adolescence. But, is this really the case? Research suggests that Piaget underestimated the abilities of children. For example, in one study researchers gave inductive and deductive reasoning problems to kindergarteners, second graders, fourth graders, and sixth graders. Because they did not want children to use their knowledge of the real world, they used imaginary terms and words to create both inductive and deductive reasoning problems. For example, one of the inductive problems was "Tombor is a popgop. Tombor wears blue boots. Do all popgops wear blue boots?" The corresponding deductive reasoning problem was "All popgops wear blue boots. Tombor is a popgop. Does Tombor wear blue boots?" Contrary to Piagetian theory, second graders (but not kindergartners) were able to answer both kinds of problems correctly (Galotti, Komatsu, & Voelz, 1997; Pillow, 2002). Given age-appropriate testing methods, evidence of inductive and deductive reasoning is present considerably earlier than Piaget predicted.

what's **your VIEW**

How can parents and teachers help children improve their reasoning ability?

Conservation In the preoperational stage of development, children are focused on appearances and have difficulty with abstract concepts. For example, Camilla, who is at the preoperational stage of development, is likely to think that if one of two identical clay balls is rolled into a long thin snake, it will now contain more clay because it is longer. She is deceived by appearances and thus fails this conservation task. However, Felipe, who is in the stage of concrete operations, will say that the ball and the snake still contain the same amount of clay. What accounts for his ability to understand that they amount of clay remains unchanged regardless of the form it takes?

In solving various types of conservation problems, children in the stage of concrete operations can work out the answers in their heads; they do not have to measure or weigh the objects. Three primary achievements allow them to do this. First, they understand the principle of *identity*. For instance, Michael understands that the clay is still the same clay even though it has a different shape, because nothing was added or taken away from it. He is able to reason that it therefore must still be the same amount of clay for both shapes. Second, children in concrete operations understand the principle of *reversibility*. Michael can picture what would happen if he went backward in time and rolled the snake back into a ball. He can now reason that the snake must still be the same amount of clay, because if he rolled it back up into a ball, it would still be the same amount. Third, children at this stage can *decenter*. When Camilla looked at the snake, she focused only on its length, ignoring that it was thinner and flatter than the ball of clay. She centered on one dimension (length) while excluding the other (thickness). Michael, however, is able to decenter and to look at more than one aspect of the two objects at once. Thus, although the ball is shorter than the snake, it is also thicker.

Children do not gain the ability to pass the various types of conservations tasks at one point in time. Typically, children can solve problems involving conservation of matter, such as the clay task, at about age 7 or 8. However, it is not until age 8 or 9 that children can correctly solve conservation of weight tasks in which they are asked, for instance, whether or not the ball and the snake weigh the same. In tasks involving conservation of volume—In which children must judge whether the snake and ball displace the same amount of liquid when placed in a glass of water—children rarely answer correctly before age 12.

Piaget's term for the inconsistency in the development of different types of conservation is **horizontal décalage**. He argued that children's thinking at this stage is so concrete, so closely tied to a particular situation, that they cannot readily transfer what they have learned about one type of conservation to another type, even though the underlying principles are the same. Note that this is problematic for a stage theory, where it is assumed that once a stage is reached, all aspects of that stage come online together once the fundamental underlying skills are achieved. The fact that a child can reverse, decenter, or understand identity but cannot always pass conservation tasks, undermines the qualitative/stages aspect of Piaget's theory.

horizontal décalage
Piaget's term for an inability to transfer learning about one type of conservation to other types, which causes a child to master different types of conservation tasks at different ages.

Number and Mathematics By age 6 or 7, many children can count in their heads. They also learn to *count on:* to add 5 and 3, they start counting at 5 and then go on to 6, 7, and 8 to add the 3. It may take 2 or 3 more years for them to perform a comparable operation for subtraction, but by age 9 most children can either count up from the smaller number or down from the larger number to get the answer (Resnick, 1989).

Children also become more adept at solving simple story problems, such as "Pedro went to the store with $5 and spent $2 on candy. How much did he have left?" When the original amount is unknown ("Pedro went to the store, spent $2, and had $3 left. How much did he start out with?"), the problem is harder because the operation needed to solve it (addition) is not as clearly indicated. Few children can solve this kind of problem before age 8 or 9 (Resnick, 1989).

Research with minimally schooled people in developing countries suggests that children learn to add and subtract through concrete experience in a cultural context (Guberman, 1996; Resnick, 1989). These intuitive procedures are different from those taught in school. In a study of Brazilian street vendors ages 9 to 15, a researcher acting as a customer said, "I'll take two coconuts." Each one cost 40 cruzeiros; she paid with a 500-cruzeiros bill and asked, "What do I get back?" The child counted up from 80: "Eighty, 90, 100, . . ." and gave the customer 420 cruzeiros. However, when this same child was given a similar problem in the classroom ("What is 500 minus 80?"), he arrived at the wrong answer by incorrectly using a series of steps learned in school (Carraher, Schliemann, & Carraher, 1988). This observation suggests that there are different routes toward learning what needs to be learned in a culture. In fact, in cultural contexts where schooling is not as important, children do not standardly use abstract counting strategies.

Some intuitive understanding of fractions seems to exist by age 4, as children show when they distribute portions of pizza or separate a box of chocolates (Mix, Levine, & Huttenlocher, 1999; Singer-Freeman & Goswami, 2001; Sophian, Garyantes, & Chang, 1997). Young children tend not to think about the quantity a fraction represents; instead, they focus on the numerals that make it up. Thus, they may say that ½ plus ⅓ equals ⅖. Also difficult for many children to grasp at first is the fact that ½ is bigger than ¼—that the smaller fraction (¼) has the larger denominator (Geary, 2006; Siegler, 1998; Sophian & Wood, 1997).

The ability to estimate progresses with age. When asked to place 24 numbers along a line from 0 to 100, almost all kindergartners exaggerate the distances between low numbers and minimize the distances between high numbers. Most second graders produce number lines that are more evenly spaced (Siegler & Booth, 2004). Second, fourth, and sixth graders show a similar progression in producing number lines from 0 to 1,000 (Siegler & Opfer, 2003), most likely reflecting the experience older children gain in dealing with larger numbers. Besides improving in *number line estimation*, school-age children also improve in three other types of estimation: *computational estimation*, such as estimating the sum in an addition problem; *numerosity estimation*, such as estimating the number of candies in a jar; and *measurement estimation*, such as estimating the length of a line (Booth & Siegler, 2006).

INFLUENCES OF NEUROLOGICAL DEVELOPMENT AND SCHOOLING

Piaget maintained that the shift from the rigid, illogical thinking of younger children to the flexible, logical thinking of older children depends on both neurological development and experience in adapting to the environment. Support for a neurological influence comes from scalp measurements of brain activity during a conservation task. Children who had achieved conservation of volume had different brain wave patterns from those who had not yet achieved it, suggesting that they may have been using different brain regions for the task (Stauder, Molenaar, & Van der Molen, 1993).

While Piaget believed his theories described universal aspects of child development, it may be that abilities such as conservation may depend in part on familiarity with the materials being manipulated. Children can think more logically about things they know something about. Thus understanding of conservation may come, not only from new patterns of mental organization but also from culturally defined experience with the physical world.

Today's schoolchildren may not be advancing through Piaget's stages as rapidly as their parents did. When 10,000 British 11- and 12-year-olds were tested on conservation of volume and weight, their performance was 2 to 3 years behind that of their counterparts 30 years earlier (Shayer, Ginsburg, & Coe, 2007). These results suggest that today's schoolchildren may be getting too much instruction on the three Rs and less hands-on experience with the way materials behave.

MORAL REASONING

Piaget was also interested in how children's ways of thinking might impact their ability to reason about morality. To draw out children's moral thinking, Piaget (1932) would tell them a story about two little boys: "One day Augustus noticed that his father's inkpot was empty and decided to help his father by filling it. While he was opening the bottle, he spilled a lot of ink on the tablecloth. The other boy, Julian, played with his father's inkpot and spilled a little ink on the cloth." Then Piaget would ask, "Which boy was naughtier, and why?" Children younger than 7 usually considered Augustus naughtier because he made the bigger stain. Older children recognized that Augustus meant well and made the large stain by accident, whereas Julian made a small stain while doing something he should not have been doing. Immature moral judgments, Piaget concluded, center only on the *degree* of offense; more mature judgments consider *intent*.

Piaget (1932; Piaget & Inhelder, 1969) proposed that moral reasoning develops in three stages. Children move gradually from one stage to another, at varying ages. The first stage (around ages 2 to 7, corresponding with the preoperational stage) is based on *rigid obedience to authority*. Young children are egocentric, and tend to see things only from their point of view. Thus, they cannot imagine that there is more than one way of looking at a moral issue. Moreover, they are rigid in their views. They believe that rules cannot be bent or changed, that behavior is either right or wrong, and that any offense (like Augustus's) deserves punishment, regardless of intent.

According to Piaget, children develop concepts of fairness through interaction with peers, often in games with rules like musical chairs. As children grow older, they realize that rules need not be externally imposed but can be changed by mutual agreement.

The second stage (around ages 7 to 11, corresponding with the stage of concrete operations) is characterized by *increasing flexibility*. As children interact with more people and come into contact with a wider range of viewpoints, they begin to discard the idea that there is a single, absolute standard of right and wrong and to develop their own sense of justice based on fairness or equal treatment for all. Because they can consider more than one aspect of a situation, they can make more subtle moral judgments, such as taking into consideration the intent behind Augustus's and Julian's behavior. The decrease in egocentrism allows consideration of other perspectives.

Around age 11 or 12, when children may become capable of formal reasoning, the third stage of moral development arrives. The belief that everyone should be treated alike gives way to the ideal of *equity*, of taking specific circumstances into account. Thus a child of this age might say that a 2-year-old who spilled ink on the tablecloth should be held to a less demanding moral standard than a 10-year-old who did the same thing.

We discuss Lawrence Kohlberg's theory of moral reasoning, which builds on Piaget's, in Chapter 16.

Information-Processing Approach: Attention, Memory, and Planning

Clara walks by the kitchen, and smells the delicious cake she just helped bake cooling on the counter. A few short years ago, she might have darted into the kitchen and surreptitiously stuck her finger in the cake to steal a few bites. But now, older and wiser, she thinks to herself, "No, that cake is for later. If I take a bite, it will look ugly and I'll get in trouble like I did last time. I really, really want it. But, maybe if I go play

what's your view ?

▷ Do you agree that intent is an important factor in morality?

▷ How does the criminal justice system reflect this view?

► checkpoint can you . . .

▷ Describe Piaget's three stages of moral development and explain their links to cognitive maturation?

What advances in information-processing skills occur during middle childhood?

guidepost **2**

for a while, I won't want it so much." Clara's more sophisticated cognitive abilities have allowed her to control her behavior in ways that were previously unavailable to her.

As children move through the school years, they make steady progress in their abilities to regulate and sustain attention, process and retain information, and plan and monitor their own behavior. All of these interrelated developments are central to **executive function**, the conscious control of thoughts, emotions, and actions to accomplish goals or solve problems. As their knowledge expands, children become more aware of what kinds of information are important to pay attention to and remember. School-age children also understand more about how memory works, and this knowledge enables them to plan and use strategies, or deliberate techniques, to help them remember.

executive function
Conscious control of thoughts, emotions, and actions to accomplish goals or solve problems.

Attention Span

HOW DO EXECUTIVE SKILLS DEVELOP?

Executive functions allow children to be more thoughtful in their cognition and behavior, and these skills are vital to successful development. There are a number of influences that help children attain these skills, and as is typical within psychology, we can look at biological and environmental influences as working together to shape the developing child over time.

Executive functioning develops gradually from infancy to adolescence. As might be expected, it is accompanied by brain development, most notably in the prefrontal cortex (Lamm, Zelazo, & Lewis, 2006). As unneeded synapses are pruned away and pathways become myelinated, processing speed improves dramatically (Camarata & Woodcock, 2006; Luna, Garver, Urban, Lazar, & Sweeney, 2004). Faster, more efficient processing increases the amount of information children can keep in working memory. And, when children develop the ability to mentally juggle more concepts at the same time, they are also able to develop more complex thinking and goal-directed planning (Flavell et al., 2002; Luna et al., 2004).

In addition to the physical development of the brain, environmental influences also matter. For example, the home environment has been documented to contribute to the development of executive skills. In a longitudinal study of 700 children from infancy on, the quality of the family environment—including such factors as available resources, cognitive stimulation, and maternal sensitivity—predicted attentional and memory performance in first grade (NICHD Early Child Care Research Network, 2005c).

As children age, they become increasingly independent, and must make decisions for themselves rather than being told what to do by their parents. Executive functioning is involved in the capacity to make good decisions and monitor if goals are being met and the strategy being used is appropriate for those goals. These abilities develop gradually, and parenting practices and culture affect the pace at which children are given the opportunity to practice these skills. For example, school-age children develop planning skills by making decisions about their everyday activities. In a 3-year longitudinal study, the responsibility for planning children's informal activities gradually shifted between second and fourth grades from parent to child, and this change was reflected in children's improved ability to plan classroom work (Gauvain & Perez, 2005).

SELECTIVE ATTENTION

School-age children can concentrate longer than younger children and can focus on the information they need and want while screening out irrelevant information. For example, they can summon up from memory the appropriate meaning of a word and suppress other meanings that do not fit the context. Fifth graders are better able than first graders to keep unwanted information from reentering working memory and vying with other material for attention (Harnishfeger & Pope, 1996). This growth in *selective attention*—the ability to deliberately direct one's attention and shut out distractions—may hinge on the executive skill of *inhibitory control*, the voluntary suppression of unwanted responses (Luna et al., 2004). For example, in school, it may be necessary for a child to focus on a teacher's less-than-exciting lesson while simultaneously ignoring the antics of the class clown.

The increasing capacity for selective attention is believed to be due to neurological maturation and is one of the reasons memory improves during middle childhood (Bjorklund & Harnishfeger, 1990; Booth et al., 2003; Harnishfeger & Bjorklund, 1993). Older children may make fewer mistakes in recall than younger children because they are better able to select what they want to remember and what they can forget (Lorsbach & Reimer, 1997).

WORKING MEMORY

Working memory involves the short-term storage of information that is being actively processed, like a mental workspace. For example, if you are asked to compute what 42×60 is, you would use your working memory to keep part of the solved equation active while you solved the rest of it.

The efficiency of working memory increases greatly in middle childhood, laying the foundation for a wide range of cognitive skills. For example, between the ages of 6 to 10 there are improvements in processing speed (how quickly information is processed) and storage capacity (how many things can be simultaneously held in working memory) (Bayliss, Jarrod, Baddeley, Gunn, & Leigh, 2005). And, because working memory is necessary for storing information while other material is being mentally manipulated, the capacity of a child's working memory can directly affect academic success (Alloway, 2006). For example, children with low working memory struggle with structured learning activities. These difficulties are most apparent when there are lengthy instructions because children need to retain multiple items in working memory to be able to follow the instructions (Gathercole & Alloway, 2008). Individual differences in working memory capacity are also linked to a child's ability to acquire knowledge and new skills (Alloway, 2006).

Working memory issues are not just a theoretical concern; they are important in education. Research has indicated that as many as 10 percent of school-age children suffer from low working memory (Alloway, Gathercole, Kirkwood, & Elliot, 2009). The adoption of tools that assess working memory in the classroom could greatly influence achievement levels for children identified as possessing low working memory. Some strategies for overcoming memory-related failures are outlined in Table 13.2.

METAMEMORY: UNDERSTANDING MEMORY

Between ages 5 and 7, the brain's frontal lobes undergo significant development and reorganization. These changes may make possible improved **metamemory**, knowledge about the processes of memory (Chua, Schacter, Rand-Giovanetti, & Sperling, 2006; Janowsky & Carper, 1996). Metamemory can be thought of as thinking about memory. In other words, it involves the knowledge of and reflection about memory processes.

From kindergarten through fifth grade, children advance steadily in understanding memory (Flavell et al., 2002; Kreutzer, Leonard, & Flavell, 1975). Kindergartners and first graders know that people remember better if they study longer, that people forget things with time, and that relearning something is easier than learning it for the first time. By third grade, children know that some people remember better than others and that some things are easier to remember than others.

MNEMONICS: STRATEGIES FOR REMEMBERING

Were you ever taught the saying "please excuse my dear aunt Sally" as a technique to help you remember the order of operations in solving an equation? This is an example of a **mnemonic device**, a strategy to aid memory. The most common mnemonic strategy among both children and adults is use of *external memory aids*. Other common mnemonic strategies are *rehearsal*, *organization*, and *elaboration*.

Writing down a telephone number, making a list, setting a timer, and putting a library book by the front door are examples of **external memory aids**: prompts by something outside the person. Saying a telephone number over and over after looking it up, so as not to forget it before dialing, is a form of **rehearsal**, or conscious repetition.

study**smart**

Working Memory Capacity

metamemory
Understanding of processes of memory.

mnemonic device
Strategy to aid memory.

external memory aids
Mnemonic strategies using something outside the person.

rehearsal
Mnemonic strategy to keep an item in working memory through conscious repetition.

TABLE 13.2	Working Memory Challenges and Strategies
Challenge	**Strategy**
Following lengthy and detailed instructions	• Keep instructions as brief and simple as possible • Break down instructions into individual steps • Repeat instructions frequently • For tasks that take place over extended time periods, provide reminders of crucial information for each phase rather than repeating original instructions • Ask child to repeat instructions
Storing and processing information	• Decrease the processing demands by reducing complexity • Simplify vocabulary, syntax, and length of sentences
Staying focused in a complex activity	• Break down the activity into separate steps • Provide memory support such as external memory aids • Encourage practice using memory aids • Keep external aids close at hand
Working memory failures	• Encourage child to ask about forgotten information • Train child in the use of memory aids • Support and encourage child to complete complex tasks rather than abandon them

organization
Mnemonic strategy of categorizing material to be remembered.

elaboration
Mnemonic strategy of making mental associations involving items to be remembered.

Contestants in a spelling bee can make good use of mnemonic strategies—devices to aid memory—such as rehearsal (repetition), organization, and elaboration.

Organization is mentally placing information into categories (such as animals, furniture, vehicles, and clothing) to make it easier to recall. **Elaboration** involves cementing items in memory by thinking about the meaning of a term and relating it to material in long-term memory, or making mental associations with something else, such as an imagined scene or story. Essentially, it involves deeper processing of material. For example, to remember to buy lemons, ketchup, and napkins, a child might imagine a ketchup bottle balanced on a lemon, with a pile of napkins handy to wipe up spilled ketchup.

There are developmental changes in children's ability to use memory strategies. For example, when young children are taught to use a memory strategy, they tend to use it only in the particular context in which they were taught. Older children, however, are more likely to apply it to other situations (Flavell et al., 2002). This process occurs for spontaneous learning as well. As children grow older, they develop better strategies and use them more effectively (Bjorklund, 1997; Table 13.3). And older children often use more than one strategy for a task and choose different kinds of strategies for different problems (Coyle & Bjorklund, 1997).

While it is difficult to teach young children to use mnemonic devices, teaching older children about them if they are developmentally ready to learn such skills can result in memory gains. In other words, children have difficulty learning mnemonic devices when younger because they just aren't ready for them, but once they have the necessary capacities in place, they can benefit from instruction. Indeed, children's memory performance has been linked to aspects of the classroom context. Some teachers tend to request that their students remember more information than other teachers. Teachers with this orientation toward learning may teach their students to use more mnemonic strategies. The evidence of a link between the teacher's orientation toward

TABLE 13.3 Four Common Memory Strategies

Strategy	Definition	Development in Middle Childhood	Example
External memory aids	Prompting by something outside the person	5- and 6-year-olds can do this, but 8-year-olds are more likely to think of it.	Dana makes a list of the things she has to do today.
Rehearsal	Conscious repetition	6-year-olds can be taught to do this; 7-year-olds do it spontaneously.	Ian says the letters in his spelling words over and over until he knows them.
Organization	Grouping by categories	Most children do not do this until at least age 10, but younger children can be taught to do it.	Luis recalls the animals he saw in the zoo by thinking first of the mammals, then the reptiles, then the amphibians, then the fish, and then the birds.
Elaboration	Associating items to be remembered with something else, such as a phrase, scene, or story	Older children are more likely to do this spontaneously and remember better if they make up their own elaboration; younger children remember better if someone else makes it up.	Yolanda remembers the lines of the musical staff (E, G, B, D, F) by associating them with the phrase "*Every good boy does fine.*"

connect

study smart

Memory Strategies

learning and the children's memory performance reinforces the importance of the school context to children's memory development (Coffman, Ornstein, McCall, & Curran, 2008).

INFORMATION PROCESSING AND PIAGETIAN TASKS

Improvements in information processing may help explain the advances Piaget described. For example, 9-year-olds may be better able than 5-year-olds to find their way to and from school because they can scan a scene, take in its important features, and remember objects in context in the order in which they were encountered (Allen & Ondracek, 1995).

Improvements in memory may contribute to the mastery of conservation tasks. Young children's working memory is so limited that they may not be able to remember all the relevant information (Siegler & Richards, 1982). For example, they may have difficulty holding both the length and width of an item in working memory simultaneously, or have difficulty remembering that two differently shaped pieces of clay were originally identical. Gains in working memory may enable older children to solve such problems.

Robbie Case (1985, 1992), a neo-Piagetian theorist, suggested that as a child's application of a concept or scheme becomes more automatic, it frees space in working memory to deal with new information. This may help explain horizontal décalage: Children may need to be able to use one type of conservation without conscious thought before they can extend that scheme to other types of conservation.

checkpoint
can **you** . . .

▷ Identify at least three specific ways in which information processing improves during middle childhood?

▷ Name four common mnemonic aids?

▷ Tell how improved information processing helps explain advances Piaget described?

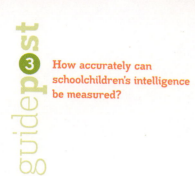

guidepost

③ How accurately can
schoolchildren's intelligence
be measured?

**Wechsler Intelligence Scale for
Children (WISC-III)**
Individual intelligence test for
schoolchildren that yields verbal
and performance scores as well as
a combined score.

**Otis-Lennon School Ability
Test (OLSAT8)**
Group intelligence test for kindergarten
through 12th grade.

Psychometric Approach: Assessment of Intelligence

Psychometrics is a branch of psychology involved in the quantitative measurement of psychological variables. One area of psychology in which psychometrics has had a major impact is intelligence, and psychometric techniques have been used extensively in the development of ways to measure intelligence. Schoolchildren's intelligence may be measured by either individual or group tests. The most widely used individual test is the **Wechsler Intelligence Scale for Children (WISC-III)**. This test for ages 6 through 16 measures verbal and performance abilities, yielding separate scores for each as well as a total score. The separate subtest scores pinpoint a child's strengths and help diagnose specific problems. For example, if a child does well on verbal tests (such as general information and basic arithmetic operations) but poorly on performance tests (such as doing a puzzle or drawing the missing part of a picture), the child may be slow in perceptual or motor development. A child who does well on performance tests but poorly on verbal tests may have a language problem. Another commonly used individual test is the Stanford-Binet Intelligence Scale, described in Chapter 10.

A popular group test, the **Otis-Lennon School Ability Test (OLSAT8)**, has levels for kindergarten through 12th grade. Children are asked to classify items, show an understanding of verbal and numerical concepts, display general information, and follow directions. Separate scores for verbal comprehension, verbal reasoning, pictorial reasoning, figural reasoning, and quantitative reasoning can identify strengths and weaknesses.

THE IQ CONTROVERSY

The use of psychometric intelligence tests such as those just described is controversial. On the positive side, because IQ tests have been standardized and widely used, there is extensive information about their norms, validity, and reliability (see Chapter 2). Scores on IQ tests taken during middle childhood are fairly good predictors of school achievement, especially for highly verbal children, and scores are more reliable than during the preschool years. IQ at age 11 even has been found to predict length of life, functional independence late in life, and the presence or absence of dementia (Starr, Deary, Lemmon, & Whalley, 2000; Whalley & Deary, 2001; Whalley et al., 2000).

On the other hand, critics claim that the tests underestimate the intelligence of children who are in ill health, tired, or, for one reason or another, do not do well on tests (Anastasi, 1988; Ceci, 1991; Sternberg, 2004). Because the tests are timed, they equate intelligence with speed and penalize a child who works slowly and deliberately. Their appropriateness for diagnosing learning disabilities has been questioned (Benson, 2003).

A more fundamental criticism is that IQ tests do not directly measure native ability; instead, they *infer* intelligence from what children already know. As we'll see, it is virtually impossible to design a test that requires no prior knowledge. Further, the tests are validated against measures of achievement, such as school performance, which are affected by such factors as schooling and culture (Sternberg, 2004, 2005). As we discuss in a subsequent section, there is also controversy over whether intelligence is a single, general ability or whether there are types of intelligence not captured by IQ tests. For these and other reasons, there is strong disagreement over how accurately these tests assess children's intelligence.

INFLUENCES ON INTELLIGENCE

Both heredity and environment influence intelligence. Keeping in mind the controversy over whether IQ tests actually measure intelligence, let's look more closely at these influences.

Genes and Brain Development Brain imaging research shows a moderate correlation between brain size or amount of gray matter and general intelligence, especially reasoning and problem-solving abilities (Gray & Thompson, 2004). One study found that the amount of gray matter in the frontal cortex is largely inherited, varies widely among individuals, and is linked with differences in IQ (Thompson et al., 2001). A later study suggests that the key is not the *amount* of gray matter a child has at a certain age, but rather the *pattern of development* of the prefrontal cortex, the seat of executive function and higher-level thinking. In children of average IQ, the prefrontal cortex is relatively thick at age 7, peaks in thickness by age 8, and then gradually thins as unneeded connections are pruned. In the most intelligent 7-year-olds, the cortex does not peak in thickness until age 11 or 12. The prolonged thickening of the prefrontal cortex may represent an extended critical period for developing high-level thinking circuits (Shaw et al., 2006; see Chapter 12).

Although reasoning, problem solving, and executive function are linked to the prefrontal cortex, other brain regions under strong genetic influence contribute to intelligent behavior. So does the speed and reliability of transmission of messages in the brain. Environmental factors, such as the family, schooling, and culture, also play a part; but heritability of intelligence (an estimate of the degree to which individual differences in intelligence are genetically caused) increases with age as children select or create environments that fit their genetic tendencies (Gray & Thompson, 2004).

Influence of Schooling on IQ Schooling seems to increase IQ scores (Ceci & Williams, 1997; Neisser et al., 1996). Children whose school entrance was significantly delayed—as happened, for example, in South Africa due to a teacher shortage and in the Netherlands during the Nazi occupation—lost as many as 5 IQ points each year, and some of these losses were never recovered (Ceci & Williams, 1997).

IQ scores also tend to drop during summer vacation (Ceci & Williams, 1997). Among a national sample of 1,500 children, language, spatial, and conceptual scores improved much more between October and April, the bulk of the school year, than between April and October, which includes summer vacation and the beginning and end of the school year (Huttenlocher, Levine, & Vevea, 1998).

Influences of Race/Ethnicity on IQ Average test scores vary among racial/ethnic groups, inspiring claims that the tests are unfair to minorities. Although some black people score higher than most whites, black children, on average, historically scored about 15 points lower than white children and showed a comparable lag on school achievement tests (Neisser et al., 1996). However, those gaps have narrowed in recent years—as much as 4 to 7 IQ points (Dickens & Flynn, 2006). Average IQ scores of Hispanic children fall between those of black and white children, and their scores, too, tend to predict school achievement (Ang, Rodgers, & Wanstrom, 2010; Neisser et al., 1996).

What accounts for these racial/ethnic differences in IQ? Some writers have argued for a substantial genetic factor (Herrnstein & Murray, 1994; Jensen, 1969; Rushton & Jensen, 2005). But although there is strong evidence of a genetic influence on *individual* differences in intelligence, there is no direct evidence that differences among ethnic, cultural, or racial groups are hereditary (Gray & Thompson, 2004; Neisser et al., 1996; Sternberg, Grigorenko, & Kidd, 2005). Instead, many studies attribute ethnic differences in IQ largely or entirely to inequalities in environment (Nisbett, 1998, 2005)—in income, nutrition, living conditions, health, parenting practices, early child care, intellectual stimulation, schooling, culture, or other circumstances such as the effects of oppression and discrimination that can affect self-esteem, motivation, and academic performance. Environmental differences also influence readiness for school (Rouse, Brooks-Gunn, & McLanahan, 2005), which, in turn, affects measured intelligence as well as achievement. In a longitudinal study of 500 healthy U.S. children, participants from low-income families had somewhat lower IQ and achievement test scores than those from higher-income families. However, these healthy low-income children did better than published norms for their income level, suggesting the importance of health as a factor in measured intelligence (Waber et al., 2007).

The recent narrowing of the gap between white and black children's test scores parallels an improvement in the life circumstances and educational opportunities of many black children (Nisbett, 2005). In addition, as we discussed in Chapter 7, some early intervention programs have had significant success in raising disadvantaged children's IQs (Nisbett, 2005).

The strength of genetic influence itself appears to vary with socioeconomic status. In a longitudinal study of 319 pairs of twins followed from birth, the genetic influence on IQ scores at age 7 among children from impoverished families was close to zero and the influence of environment was strong, whereas among children in affluent families the opposite was true. In other words, high SES strengthens genetic influence, whereas low SES tends to override it (Turkheimer, Haley, Waldron, D'Onofrio, & Gottesman, 2003). Still, although socioeconomic status and IQ are strongly related, SES does not seem to explain the entire intergroup variance in IQ (Neisser et al., 1996; Suzuki & Valencia, 1997).

What about Asian Americans, whose scholastic achievements consistently outstrip those of other ethnic groups? Although there is some controversy about their relative performance on intelligence tests, most researchers find that they do *not* seem to have a significant edge in IQ (Neisser et al., 1996). Instead, Asian American children's strong scholastic achievement seems to be best explained by their culture's emphasis on obedience and respect for elders, the supreme importance Asian American parents place on education as a route to upward mobility, and the devotion of Asian American students to homework and study (Chao, 1994, 1996; Fuligni & Stevenson, 1995; Huntsinger & Jose, 1995; Stevenson, 1995; Stevenson, Chen, & Lee, 1993; Stevenson, Lee, Chen, & Lummis, 1990; Stevenson et al., 1990; Sue & Okazaki, 1990).

Influence of Culture on IQ Various attempts have been made to explain why there are differences in IQ tests for people of different ethnicities. One possibility is that people of different ethnic groups have different cultures. Intelligence and culture are inextricably linked, and behavior seen as intelligent in one culture may be viewed as foolish in another (Sternberg, 2004). For example, when given a sorting task, North Americans would be likely to place a robin under the category of birds, whereas the Kpelle people in North Africa would consider it more intelligent to place the robin in the functional category of flying things (Cole, 1998). Thus a test of intelligence developed in one culture may not be equally valid in another. Furthermore, the schooling offered in a culture may prepare a child to do well in certain tasks and not in others, and the competencies taught and tested in school are not necessarily the same as the practical skills needed to succeed in everyday life (Sternberg, 2004, 2005). Intelligence might thus be better defined as the skills and knowledge needed for success within a particular social and cultural context. The mental processes that underlie intelligence may be the same across cultures, but their products may be different—and so should the means of assessing performance. (Sternberg, 2004). Thus, intelligence tests should be culturally relevant and include activities that are common and necessary in that culture.

These arguments have led to assertions that ethnic differences in IQ are not reflecting intelligence, but rather are an artifact of cultural bias. It may be that some questions use vocabulary or call for information or skills more familiar to some cultural groups than to others (Sternberg, 1985, 1987). Because these intelligence tests are built around the dominant thinking style and language of white people of European ancestry, this puts minority children at a disadvantage (Heath, 1989; Helms, 1992; Matsumoto & Juang, 2008).

Test developers have tried to design **culture-free tests**—tests with no culture-linked content—by posing tasks that do not require language, such as tracing mazes, putting the right shapes in the right holes, and completing pictures; but they have been unable to eliminate all cultural influences. Test designers also have found it virtually impossible to produce **culture-fair tests** consisting only of experiences common to people in various cultures. Thus, controlled studies have generally failed to show that cultural bias contributes substantially to overall group differences in IQ (Neisser et al., 1996).

culture-free test
An intelligence test that, if it were possible to design, would have no culturally linked content.

culture-fair test
An intelligence test that deals with experiences common to various cultures, in an attempt to avoid cultural bias.

▷ checkpoint
can *you* . . .

▶ Name and describe two traditional intelligence tests for schoolchildren?

▶ Discuss influences on measured intelligence and explanations that have been advanced for differences in the performance of children of various racial/ ethnic and cultural groups?

IS THERE MORE THAN ONE INTELLIGENCE?

A serious criticism of IQ tests is that they focus almost entirely on abilities used in school. While doing well in school is certainly important, doing well in life involves much more than just academics. Most IQ tests do not cover other important aspects of intelligent behavior, such as common sense, social skills, creative insight, and self-knowledge. Yet these abilities, in which some children with modest academic skills excel, may become equally or more important in later life and may even be considered separate forms of intelligence. Two of the chief advocates of this position are Howard Gardner and Robert Sternberg.

Gardner's Theory of Multiple Intelligences Is a child who is good at analyzing paragraphs and making analogies more intelligent than one who can play a challenging violin solo or organize a closet or pitch a curve ball at the right time? The answer is no, according to Gardner's (1993) **theory of multiple intelligences**.

Gardner, a neuropsychologist and educational researcher at Harvard University, identified eight independent types of intelligence. According to Gardner, conventional intelligence tests tap only three "intelligences": *linguistic, logical-mathematical*, and, to some extent, *spatial*. The other five, which are not reflected in IQ scores, are *musical, bodily-kinesthetic, interpersonal, intrapersonal*, and *naturalist*. (Table 13.4 provides definitions of each type of intelligence and examples of fields in which it is most useful.)

Gardner argued that these intelligences are distinct from each other, and that high intelligence in one area does not necessarily accompany high intelligence in any of the others. A person may be extremely gifted in art (spatial), precision of movement (bodily-kinesthetic), social relations (interpersonal), or self-understanding (intrapersonal). Thus the tennis champions Venus and Serena Williams, the painter Frida Kahlo, and the cellist Yo Yo Ma could be viewed as equally intelligent, each in a different area.

Gardner (1995) would assess each intelligence directly by observing its products—how well a child can tell a story, remember a melody, or get around in a strange area—and not with the typical standardized tests. This is because the type of intelligence being

theory of multiple intelligences
Gardner's theory that there are eight distinct forms of intelligence.

what's your view

▷ Which of Gardner's types of intelligence are you strongest in?

▷ Did your education include a focus on any of these aspects?

TABLE 13.4	Eight Intelligences, according to Gardner	
Intelligence	**Definition**	**Fields or Occupations Where Used**
Linguistic	Ability to use and understand words and nuances of meaning	Writing, editing, translating
Logical-mathematical	Ability to manipulate numbers and solve logical problems	Science, business, medicine
Spatial	Ability to find one's way around in an environment and judge relationships between objects in space	Architecture, carpentry, city planning
Musical	Ability to perceive and create patterns of pitch and rhythm	Musical composition, conducting
Bodily-kinesthetic	Ability to move with precision	Dancing, athletics, surgery
Interpersonal	Ability to understand and communicate with others	Teaching, acting, politics
Intrapersonal	Ability to understand the self	Counseling, psychiatry, spiritual leadership
Naturalist	Ability to distinguish species and their characteristics	Hunting, fishing, farming, gardening, cooking

Source: Based on Gardner, 1993, 1998.

assessed would impact the type of test that was required. To monitor spatial ability, for example, the examiner might hide an object from a 1-year-old, ask a 6-year-old to do a jigsaw puzzle, and give a Rubik's cube to a preadolescent. The purpose would be, not to compare individuals but to reveal strengths and weaknesses so as to help children realize their potential. Of course, such assessments would be far more time-consuming and more open to observer bias than paper-and-pencil tests.

But do Gardner's methods accurately describe and assess intelligence? Critics of Gardner argue that his multiple intelligences are actually more accurately labeled as talents or abilities and assert that *intelligence* is more closely associated with skills that lead to academic achievement. They further question his criteria for defining separate intelligences that largely overlap such as mathematical and spatial intelligence (Willingham, 2004).

Sternberg's Triarchic Theory of Intelligence While Gardner segmented intelligence on the basis of areas of ability, Sternberg's (1985, 2004) **triarchic theory of intelligence** focuses on the processes involved in intelligence behavior. In this approach, intelligence consists of three elements, or aspects, of intelligence: componential, experiential, and contextual.

- The **componential element** is the *analytic* aspect of intelligence; it determines how efficiently people process information. It tells people how to solve problems, how to monitor solutions, and how to evaluate the results. Some people are more effective information processors than others.

- The **experiential element** is *insightful* or *creative*; it determines how people approach novel or familiar tasks. It allows people to compare new information with what they already know and to come up with new ways of putting facts together—in other words, to think originally.

- The **contextual element** is *practical*; it determines how people deal with their environment. It is the ability to size up a situation and decide what to do. And, what actions are most appropriate for a given situation naturally depend on the particular context someone is in. A person might decide to adapt to a situation, change it, or get out of it.

According to Sternberg, everyone has these three kinds of abilities to a greater or lesser extent. A person may be strong in one, two, or all three. The *Sternberg Triarchic Abilities Test* (STAT) (Sternberg, 1993) seeks to measure each of the three aspects of intelligence—analytic, creative, and practical—through multiple-choice and essay questions. Because Sternberg focused on processes rather than content and those processes should predict intelligent behavior across domains of knowledge, there are three domains of intelligence that are assessed: *verbal*, *quantitative*, and *figural* (or spatial). For example, an item to test practical-quantitative intelligence might be to solve an everyday math problem having to do with buying tickets to a ball game or following a recipe for making cookies. A creative-verbal item might ask children to solve deductive reasoning problems that start with factually false premises (such as, "Money falls off trees"). An analytical-figural item might ask children to identify the missing piece of a figure. Validation studies have found positive correlations between the STAT and several other tests of critical thinking, creativity, and practical problem solving. As predicted, the three kinds of abilities are only weakly correlated with each other (Sternberg, 1997; Sternberg & Clinkenbeard, 1995).

How do Sternberg's tests compare to conventional IQ tests? Conventional tests, while relatively good at predicting school

Musical ability, which includes the ability to perceive and create patterns of pitch and rhythm, is one of eight separate kinds of intelligence, according to Howard Gardner.

performance, are less useful at predicting success in the outside world. According to Sternberg, this is to be expected. Conventional IQ tests measure mainly componential ability; because this ability is the kind most school tasks require in Western societies, it's not surprising that the tests predict academic success. Their failure to measure experiential (insightful or creative) and contextual (practical) intelligence may explain why they have less utility predicting outcomes in the outside world.

In the real world, book knowledge may not always be helpful. For example, children in many cultures have to learn practical skills, known as **tacit knowledge**, in order to succeed. These skills are not necessarily taught in schools. In studies in Usenge, Kenya, and among Yup'ik Eskimo children in southwestern Alaska, children's tacit knowledge of medicinal herbs, hunting, fishing, and preserving plants showed no correlation with conventional measures of intelligence (Grigorenko et al., 2004; Sternberg, 2004; Sternberg, Grigorenko, & Oh, 2001) but were necessary for survival.

OTHER DIRECTIONS IN INTELLIGENCE TESTING

Some other diagnostic and predictive tools are based on neurological research and information-processing theory. The second edition of the **Kaufman Assessment Battery for Children (K-ABC-II)** (Kaufman & Kaufman, 1983, 2003), an individual test for ages 3 to 18, is designed to evaluate cognitive abilities in children with diverse needs (such as autism, hearing impairments, and language disorders) and from varying cultural and linguistic backgrounds. It has subtests designed to minimize verbal instructions and responses as well as items with limited cultural content.

Dynamic tests based on Vygotsky's theories emphasize potential rather than present achievement. In contrast with traditional *static tests* that measure a child's current abilities, these tests seek to capture the dynamic nature of intelligence by measuring learning processes directly rather than through the products of past learning (Sternberg, 2004). Dynamic tests contain items up to 2 years above a child's current level of competence. Examiners help the child when necessary by asking leading questions, giving examples or demonstrations, and offering feedback; thus the test itself is a learning situation. Given that Vygotsky focused on interaction as the context in which development occurred, part of what it means to be intelligent thus includes the ability to learn via scaffolded interactions. The difference between the items a child can answer alone and the items the child can answer with help is the child's zone of proximal development (ZPD).

By pointing to what a child is ready to learn, dynamic testing may give teachers more useful information than does a psychometric test and can aid in designing interventions to help children progress. It can be particularly effective with disadvantaged children (Grigorenko & Sternberg, 1998; Rutland & Campbell, 1996). However, dynamic testing is quite labor-intensive, and the ZPD may be difficult to measure precisely.

Language and Literacy

Language abilities continue to grow during middle childhood. School-age children are better able to understand and interpret oral and written communication and to make themselves understood. These tasks are especially challenging for children who are not native-language speakers.

VOCABULARY, GRAMMAR, AND SYNTAX

As vocabulary grows during the school years, children use increasingly precise verbs. They learn that a word like *run* can have more than one meaning, and they can tell from the context which meaning is intended. *Simile* and *metaphor*, figures of speech in which a word or phrase that usually designates one thing is compared or applied to another,

tacit knowledge
Sternberg's term for information that is not formally taught or openly expressed but is necessary to get ahead.

Kaufman Assessment Battery for Children (K-ABC-II)
Nontraditional individual intelligence test designed to provide fair assessments of minority children and children with disabilities.

dynamic tests
Tests based on Vygotsky's theory that emphasize potential rather than past learning.

> checkpoint
can **you** . . .

▷ Compare Gardner's and Sternberg's theories, and name the specific abilities each proposed?

▷ Describe several other types of intelligence tests?

How do communicative abilities expand during middle childhood?

connect

study smart

Forms of Speech

School-age children's use of language is more sophisticated than that of younger children. They are better able to tell stories and secrets and make themselves understood.

become increasingly common (Owens, 1996; Vosniadou, 1987). Although grammar is quite complex by age 6, children during the early school years rarely use the passive voice (as in "The sidewalk is being shoveled").

Children's understanding of rules of *syntax* (the deep underlying structure of language that organizes words into understandable phrases and sentences) becomes more sophisticated with age (C. S. Chomsky, 1969). For example, most children under age 5 or 6 think the sentences "John promised Bill to go shopping" and "John told Bill to go shopping" both mean that Bill is the one to go to the store. Many 6-year-olds have not yet learned how to interpret constructions such as the one in the first sentence, even though they know what a promise is and can use and understand the word correctly in other sentences. By age 8, most children can interpret the first sentence correctly, and, by age 9, virtually all children can. They now look at the meaning of a sentence as a whole instead of focusing on word order alone.

Sentence structure continues to become more elaborate. Older children use more subordinate clauses ("The boy *who delivers the newspapers* rang the doorbell"). Still, some constructions, such as clauses beginning with *however* and *although*, do not become common until early adolescence (Owens, 1996).

In 1939, researchers at Iowa University conducted a study in which they attempted to deliberately induce stuttering in young children. In this "Monster study," a group of orphans were taunted and harassed over their speech in an attempt to demonstrate that stuttering was the result of psychological pressure. None of the children developed a stuttering problem, but many of them did develop psychological problems as a result of the experiment. Clearly, this study suffered from profound ethical issues, and in 2007 six of the children sued and were awarded settlements of approximately $1 million.

Huge payout in U.S. stuttering case, 2007

PRAGMATICS: KNOWLEDGE ABOUT COMMUNICATION

pragmatics
The social context of language.

The major area of linguistic growth during the school years is in **pragmatics**: the social context of language. Pragmatics includes both conversational and narrative skills.

Good conversationalists probe by asking questions before introducing a topic with which the other person may not be familiar. They quickly recognize a breakdown in communication and do something to repair it. There are wide individual differences in such skills; some 7-year-olds are better conversationalists than some adults (Anderson, Clark, & Mullin, 1994). There are also gender differences. In one study, 120 middle-class London fourth graders were paired up to solve a mathematical problem. When boys and girls worked together, boys tended to use more controlling statements and to utter more negative interruptions, whereas girls phrased their remarks in a more tentative, conciliatory way. Children's communication was more collaborative when working with a partner of the same sex (Leman, Ahmed, & Ozarow, 2005).

When first graders tell stories, they often relate a personal experience. Most 6-year-olds can retell the plot of a short book, movie, or television show. They are beginning to describe motives and causal links. By second grade, children's stories become longer and more complex. Fictional tales often have conventional beginnings and endings ("Once upon a time . . ." and "They lived happily ever after," or simply "The end"). Word use is more varied than before, but characters do not show growth or change, and plots are not fully developed.

Older children usually set the stage with introductory information about the setting and characters, and they clearly indicate changes of time and place during the story. They construct more complex episodes than younger children do, but with less unnecessary

If you want children to tell you the truth, ask them to promise to do so before asking your question. Researchers have found that children are less likely to lie after promising to tell the truth.

Evans & Lee, 2010

checkpoint can you . . .

▷ Summarize improvements in language skills during middle childhood?

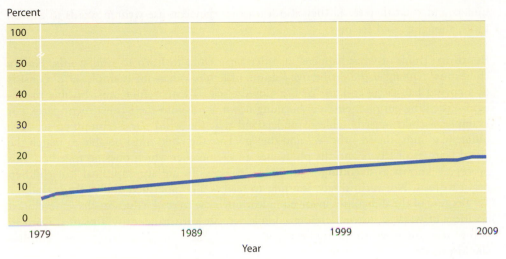

FIGURE 13.1

Percent of U.S. Children Whose Primary Language Is Not English, by Year

The number of U.S. children whose primary language is not English has risen steadily over 30 years from about 8 percent in 1979 to 21 percent in 2009.

Source: National Center for Education Statistics, 2009.

detail. They focus more on the characters' motives and thoughts, and they think through how to resolve problems in the plot.

SECOND-LANGUAGE LEARNING

In 2007, 21 percent of U.S. children ages 5 to 17 spoke a language other than English at home. The primary language most of these children spoke was Spanish, and more than 5 percent had difficulty speaking English (Federal Interagency Forum on Child and Family Statistics, 2009; Figure 13.1). About 11 percent of the public school population are defined as *English language learners* (ELLs) (National Center for Education Statistics [NCES], 2007).

Some schools use an **English-immersion approach** (sometimes called ESL, or English as a second language), in which language-minority children are immersed in English from the beginning, in special classes. Other schools have adopted programs of **bilingual education**, in which children are taught in two languages, first learning in their native language with others who speak it and then switching to regular classes in English when they become more proficient in it. These programs can encourage children to become **bilingual** (fluent in two languages) and to feel pride in their cultural identity.

Advocates of early *English immersion* claim that the sooner children are exposed to English and the more time they spend speaking it, the better they learn it. Proponents of *bilingual* programs claim that children progress faster academically in their native language and later make a smoother transition to all-English classrooms (Padilla et al., 1991). Some educators maintain that the English-only approach stunts children's cognitive growth; because foreign-speaking children can understand only simple English at first, the curriculum must be watered down, and children are less prepared to handle complex material later (Collier, 1995).

Statistical analyses of multiple studies conclude that children in bilingual programs typically outperform those in all-English programs on tests of English proficiency (Crawford, 2007; Krashen & McField, 2005). Even more successful, according to some research, is a another, less common, approach: **two-way (dual-language) learning**, in which English-speaking and foreign-speaking children learn together in their own and each other's languages. This approach avoids any need to place minority children in separate classes. By valuing both languages equally, it reinforces self-esteem and improves school performance. An added advantage is that English speakers learn a foreign language at an early age, when they can acquire it most easily (Collier, 1995; W. P. Thomas & Collier, 1997, 1998).

LITERACY

Learning to read and write frees children from the constraints of face-to-face communication. Now they have access to the ideas and imagination of people in faraway lands and long-ago times. Once children can translate the marks on a page into patterns of sound and meaning, they can develop increasingly sophisticated strategies to

English-immersion approach
Approach to teaching English as a second language in which instruction is presented only in English.

bilingual education
System of teaching non-English-speaking children in their native language while they learn English and later switching to all-English instruction.

bilingual
Fluent in two languages.

two-way (dual-language) learning
Approach to second-language education in which English speakers and non-English speakers learn together in their own and each other's languages.

checkpoint can you . . .

▷ Describe and evaluate three types of second-language education?

understand what they read. They also learn that they can use written words to express ideas, thoughts, and feelings.

Reading Think of what happens in order for a child to learn to read words. First, a child must remember the distinctive features of letters—that, for example, a "c" consists of a curved half-circle and an "o" is a closed circle. Then, a child must be able to recognize the different phonemes by breaking down words into their constituent parts. For example, a child must be able to understand that the word *dog* is composed of three different sounds, the "d," the "o," and the "g." Last the child must be able to match the visual features of letters and the phonemes and remember which ones go together. This process is known as **decoding**. Only when these skills are accomplished can children begin to read. Not surprisingly, learning to read is a complicated and difficult skill.

Because of the difficulties involved in learning how to read, educators have developed a variety of ways to instruct children. Children can learn to identify a printed word in two contrasting ways. In the traditional approach, called the **phonetic** (or **code emphasis**) **approach**, the child sounds out the word, translating it from print to speech before retrieving it from long-term memory. To do this, the child must master the phonetic code that matches the printed alphabet to spoken sounds (as described above). Instruction generally involves rigorous, teacher-directed tasks focused on memorizing sound-letter correspondences.

The **whole-language approach** emphasizes visual retrieval and the use of contextual cues. This approach is based on the belief that children can learn to read and write naturally, much as they learn to understand and use speech. By using **visually based retrieval**, the child simply looks at the word and then retrieves it. Whole-language proponents assert that children learn to read with better comprehension and more enjoyment if they experience written language from the outset as a way to gain information and express ideas and feelings, not as a system of isolated sounds and syllables to be learned by memorization and drill. Whole-language programs tend to feature real literature and open-ended, student-initiated activities.

Despite the popularity of the whole-language approach, research has found little support for its claims. A central claim of the approach, that we can learn to read as naturally and easily as we learn to speak, is fundamentally flawed, in that we are adapted for language, but not for reading. A long line of research supports the view that phonemic awareness and early phonics training are keys to reading proficiency for most children (Booth, Perfetti, & MacWhinney, 1999; Hatcher, Hulme, & Ellis, 1994; Jeynes & Littell, 2000; Liberman & Liberman, 1990; National Reading Panel, 2000; Stahl, McKenna, & Pagnucco, 1994).

Many experts recommend a blend of the best of both approaches (National Reading Panel, 2000). Children can learn phonetic skills along with strategies to help them understand what they read. For example, they might be drilled in sound—letter correspondences but also be asked to memorize certain common words such as "the" and "one" that are more difficult to decode. Because reading skills are the joint product of many functions in different parts of the brain, instruction solely in specific subskills—phonetics or comprehension—is less likely to succeed (Byrnes & Fox, 1998). Children who can summon both visually based and phonetic strategies, using visual retrieval for familiar words and phonetic decoding for unfamiliar words, become better, more versatile readers (Siegler, 1998, 2000).

Metacognitive abilities can help children develop literacy. **Metacognition** involves thinking about thinking. In other words, it involves awareness of one's own thinking processes and thus can help children monitor their understanding of what they read and develop strategies to address challenges. For example, children with good metacognitive skills might learn to use such strategies as reading more slowly, rereading difficult passages, trying to visualize information, or thinking of additional examples when trying to learn information in a challenging written passage. Metacognitive abilities can be encouraged by having students recall, summarize, and ask questions about what they read can enhance comprehension (National Reading Panel, 2000).

decoding
Process of phonetic analysis by which a printed word is converted to spoken form before retrieval from long-term memory.

phonetic (code emphasis) approach
Approach to teaching reading that emphasizes decoding unfamiliar words.

whole-language approach
Approach to teaching reading that emphasizes visual retrieval and use of contextual clues.

visually based retrieval
Process of retrieving the sound of a printed word on seeing the word as a whole.

study smart

Literacy

metacognition
Thinking about thinking, or awareness of one's own mental processes.

However, children who have early reading difficulties are not necessarily condemned to reading failure. One longitudinal study followed the progress of 146 low-income children whose first grade reading scores fell below the 30th percentile. Thirty percent of the children showed steady movement toward average reading skills from second through fourth grade. The children who improved the most were those who, as kindergartners, had shown relatively strong emergent literacy skills and better classroom behavior, which permitted them to pay attention and benefit from instruction (Spira, Bracken, & Fischel, 2005).

Writing The acquisition of writing skills goes hand in hand with the development of reading. Older preschoolers begin using letters, numbers, and letter-like shapes as symbols to represent words or parts of words—syllables or phonemes. Often their spelling is quite inventive—so much so that they may not be able to read it themselves (Ouellette & Sénéchal, 2008; Whitehurst & Lonigan, 1998).

Writing is difficult for young children. Unlike conversation, which offers constant feedback, writing requires the child to judge independently whether the communicative goal has been met. The child also must keep in mind a variety of other constraints: spelling, punctuation, grammar, and capitalization, as well as the basic physical task of forming letters (Siegler, 1998).

In many classrooms, children are discouraged from discussing their work with other children in the belief that they will distract one another. Research based on Vygotsky's social interaction model of language development suggests that such policies are misguided. In one study, fourth graders working in pairs wrote stories with more solutions to problems, more explanations and goals, and fewer errors in syntax and word use than did children working alone (Daiute, Hartup, Sholl, & Zajac, 1993).

Efforts to improve the teaching of reading and writing seem to be paying off. U.S. fourth graders scored higher than their counterparts in any of eight other industrialized countries except England on an international literacy test (Sen, Partelow, & Miller, 2005). The National Assessment of Educational Progress in 2007 found significant improvements in the proportion of fourth graders who read and write proficiently, particularly among lower- and middle-performing students (NCES, 2007). Still, in 2007, only 33 percent of fourth graders were at or above the proficient achievement level for reading (NCES, 2007).

The Child in School

The earliest school experiences are critical in setting the stage for future success or failure. Let's look at the first-grade experience and at how children learn to read and write. Then we'll examine influences on school achievement.

ENTERING FIRST GRADE

Even today, when most U.S. children go to kindergarten, children often approach the start of first grade with a mixture of eagerness and anxiety. The first day of "regular" school is a milestone—a sign of the developmental advances that make this new status possible.

To make the most academic progress, a child needs to be involved in what is going on in class. Interest, attention, and active participation are positively associated with achievement test scores and, even more so, with teachers' marks from first grade through at least fourth grade (Alexander, Entwisle, & Dauber, 1993).

Did you take psychology because you thought it would be easy? You're not alone. By the age of 7 children believe that psychology is easier than the natural sciences.

Keil, Lockhart, & Schlegel, 2010

what's your view

Why might social interaction improve children's writing?

checkpoint can you . . .

▷ Compare the phonetic and whole-language methods of teaching reading, and discuss how comprehension improves?

▷ Discuss factors that affect reading improvement in low-income beginning readers?

▷ Explain why writing is harder for younger children than for older children?

▷ Summarize trends in reading and writing achievement?

What factors influence school achievement?

guidepost 5

checkpoint
can you . . .

▶ Explain the impact of the first-
grade experience on a child's
school career, and identify
factors that affect success in
first grade?

In January 2011 a Roslyn,
New York, school bought
47 iPads to hand out to
students as part of a pilot
program. Administrators argue
that iPads will replace textbooks,
increase homework completion,
provide interactive material,
and make communication
with teachers more likely.
What do you think?

Hu, 2011

In a national longitudinal study, first graders at risk of school failure—either because of low SES or academic, attentional, or behavioral problems—progressed as much as their low-risk peers when teachers offered strong instructional and emotional support. Such support took the form of frequent literacy instruction, evaluative feedback, engaging students in discussions, responding to their emotional needs, encouraging responsibility, and creating a positive classroom atmosphere (Hamre & Pianta, 2005).

INFLUENCES ON SCHOOL ACHIEVEMENT

As Bronfenbrenner's bioecological theory would predict, in addition to children's own characteristics, each level of the context of their lives influences how well they do in school—from the immediate family to what goes on in the classroom to the messages children receive from peers and from the larger culture (such as "It's not cool to be smart"). Let's look at this web of influences. (We discuss the influence of culture on student motivation in Chapter 16.)

Self-Efficacy Beliefs Think of how you felt the last time you had a big exam to study for. Did you feel as if you could do well as long as you studied, and were you confident in your ability to master the material? Did you think you would be able to focus on studying well enough to learn? Or did you feel as if nothing you could do would matter, and that the material was just too hard? Your attitudes in this area can be described as involving a construct called *self-efficacy.* Those students high in self-efficacy believe they can master schoolwork and regulate their own learning. They are more likely to succeed than students who do not believe in their own abilities (Bandura, Barbaranelli, Caprara, & Pastorelli, 1996; Caprara et al., 2008; Zimmerman, Bandura, & Martinez-Pons, 1992). Self-regulated learners set challenging goals and use appropriate strategies to achieve them. They try hard, persist despite difficulties, and seek help when necessary. Students who do not believe in their ability to succeed tend to become frustrated and depressed—feelings that make success more elusive.

Gender Girls tend to do better in school than boys; they receive higher marks, on average, in every subject (Halpern et al., 2007), are less likely to repeat grades, have fewer school problems, and outperform boys in national reading and writing assessments (Freeman, 2004). In addition, in a study of more than 8,000 males and females ranging from 2 to 90 years old, girls and women tended to do better than boys and men on timed tests (Camarata & Woodcock, 2006). On the other hand, boys do significantly better than girls on science and math tests that are not closely related to material taught in school. However, differences in mathematical abilities in elementary school, when computational facility is stressed, are small and tend to favor girls. Girls' advantage in writing and boys' advantage in science are larger and more reliable (Halpern et al., 2007). Gender differences tend to become more prominent in high school, as we discuss in Chapter 16.

A combination of several factors—early experience, biological differences (including differences in brain size and structure), and cultural expectations—may help explain these differences (Halpern et al., 2007). Boys' advantage in spatial skills may be influenced by SES, according to a study of 547 urban second and third graders. Although middle- and high-SES boys did better than girls on spatial tasks, low-SES boys did not, perhaps because they were less likely to engage in spatially oriented activities such as building projects (Levine, Vasilyeva, Lourenco, Newcombe, & Huttenlocher, 2005).

Parenting Practices Parents of achieving children create an environment for learning. They provide a place to study and to keep books and supplies; they set times for meals, sleep, and homework; they monitor how much television their children watch and what their children do after school; and they show interest in their children's lives by talking with them about school and being involved in school activities. Children whose parents are involved in their schools do better in school (Hill & Taylor, 2004).

Parenting styles may affect children's motivation and their school success. In one study, the highest achieving fifth graders had *authoritative* parents. These children were curious and interested in learning; they liked challenging tasks and enjoyed solving problems. *Authoritarian* parents, who kept after children to do homework, supervised closely, and relied on extrinsic motivation, tended to have lower-achieving children. So did *permissive* parents, who did not seem to care how the children did in school (G. S. Ginsburg & Bronstein, 1993).

Socioeconomic Status Socioeconomic status can be a powerful factor in educational achievement—not in and of itself, but through its influence on such factors as family atmosphere, choice of neighborhood, and parenting practices (Evans, 2004; National Research Council [NRC], 1993a; Rouse et al., 2005). In a nationally representative study of children who entered kindergarten in 1998, achievement gaps between advantaged and disadvantaged students widened during the first 4 years of schooling (Rathbun, West, & Germino-Hausken, 2004). Summer vacation contributes to these gaps because of differences in the typical home environment and in the summer learning experiences the children have. Low-income children do not make up for this gap, which, according to a longitudinal study of Baltimore schoolchildren, substantially accounts for differences in high school achievement and completion and college attendance (Alexander, Entwisle, & Olson, 2007).

However, SES is not the only factor in school achievement. In a longitudinal study, children whose home environment was cognitively stimulating at age 8 showed higher intrinsic motivation for academic learning at ages 9, 10, and 13 than children who lived in less stimulating homes. This was true over and above effects of SES (Gottfried, Fleming, & Gottfried, 1998).

Why do some young people from disadvantaged homes and neighborhoods do well in school and improve their condition in life? One factor is **social capital**: the networks of community resources children and families can draw on (Coleman, 1988). In a 3-year experimental antipoverty intervention in which working poor parents received wage supplements and subsidies for child care and health insurance, their school-age children's academic achievement and behavior improved in comparison with a control group who did not participate (Huston et al., 2001). Two years after the families had left the program, the impact on school achievement and motivation held steady, especially for older boys, though the effect on social and problem behavior declined (Huston et al., 2005).

social capital
Family and community resources on which a person or family can draw.

Peer Acceptance Children who are liked and accepted by peers tend to do better in school. Among 248 fourth graders, those whose teachers reported that they were not liked by peers had poorer academic self-concepts and more symptoms of anxiety or depression in fifth grade and lower reading and math grades in sixth grade. Early teacher identification of children who exhibit social problems could lead to interventions that would improve such children's academic as well as emotional and social outcomes (Flook, Repetti, & Ullman, 2005).

The Educational System In the 1980s, a series of governmental and educational commissions proposed plans for improvement, ranging from more homework to a longer school day and school year to a total reorganization of schools and curricula. The debate over homework is analyzed in Box 13.1.

The federal No Child Left Behind (NCLB) Act of 2001 is a sweeping educational reform emphasizing accountability, parental options, and expanded local control and flexibility. The intent is to funnel federal funding to research-based programs and practices, with special emphasis on reading and mathematics. Students in grades 3 through 8 are tested annually to see if they are meeting statewide progress objectives. Children in schools that fail to meet state standards can transfer to another school.

More than 50 national education, civil rights, children's, and citizens groups have called for substantial changes in NCLB. Critics such as the National Education Association, a national teachers' organization, claim that NCLB emphasizes punishment rather than assistance for failing schools; rigid, largely unfunded mandates rather than

the research world

THE HOMEWORK DEBATE

13.1

The homework debate is far from new. In the United States, historical swings in homework use have reflected shifts in educational philosophy (Cooper, 1989b; Gill & Schlossman, 2000). During the nineteenth century, the mind was considered a muscle and homework a means of exercising it. Antihomework crusaders argued that assignments lasting far into the evening endangered children's physical and emotional health and interfered with family life. By the 1940s, "progressive," child-centered education had become popular and homework had lost favor. Many states and school districts banned it (Gill & Schlossman, 1996). In the 1950s, when the Soviet Union's *Sputnik* launch brought calls for more rigorous science and math education, and again in the early 1980s, amid worries about the United States' competitive position toward Japan, "More homework!" became a battle cry in campaigns to upgrade U.S. educational standards (Cooper, 1989b).

Homework advocates claim that it disciplines the mind, develops good work habits, improves retention, and enables students to cover more ground than they could in the classroom alone. Homework also is a bridge between home and school, increasing parental involvement. In the most comprehensive and rigorous analysis of data on research dating from the 1930s to 2003, researchers found a positive and statistically signficant relationship between the amount of homework students do and academic achievement (Cooper, 1989a; Cooper, Robinson, & Patall, 2006).

Opponents claim that too much homework leads to boredom, anxiety, or frustration; puts unnecessary pressure on children; discourages intrinsic motivation; and usurps time from other worthwhile activities. They say that parental help can be counterproductive if parents become overly intrusive or use teaching methods that conflict with those used at school (Cooper, 1989b). Once

again, some critics want to ban homework, at least for young children (Kralovec & Buell, 2000).

A comprehensive review of nearly 120 studies found that the value of homework depends on many factors, including the age, ability, and motivation of the child; the amount and purpose of homework; the home situation; and classroom follow-up. Although homework is highly beneficial for high school students, it has only moderate benefits for junior high school students, and has virtually no effect on elementary school students as compared with in-class study (Cooper, 1989b). Research-based recommendations range from one to three 15-minute assignments a week in the primary grades to four or five assignments a week, each lasting 75 to 120 minutes, in grades 10 to 12. Instead of grading homework, researchers suggest, teachers should use it to diagnose learning problems (Cooper, 1989b).

Homework, then, has value—but only in moderation and when geared to students' developmental levels. For grade school children, it can develop good study habits and an understanding that learning can take place at home as well as in school. In junior high, a mix of mandatory and voluntary homework can promote academic goals and motivate children to pursue studies that interest them. In high school, homework can provide opportunities for practice, review, and integration of what is being learned at school (Cooper, 1989b).

what's your view How much homework do you think is appropriate for children of various ages?

---

what's your view

Which approach to education do you favor for children in the primary grades: instruction in the basics, a more flexible, child-centered curriculum, or a combination of the two?

support for proven practices; and standardized testing rather than teacher-led, classroom-focused learning. Research on Sternberg's triarchic theory, for example, suggests that students learn better when taught in a variety of ways, emphasizing creative and practical skills as well as memorization and critical thinking (Sternberg, Torff, & Grigorenko, 1998). (Box 13.2 discusses the controversy over the best way to teach math.)

Recently proposed changes to NCLB would replace the law's pass-fail school grading system with one that measures individual students' academic growth. Schools would be judged not on test scores alone but also on attendance, graduation rates, and learning climate. The proposed changes also address the requirement that every American child attain proficiency in reading and math by replacing it with a new national target that all students graduate from high school prepared for college and a career.

THE MATH WARS

13.2

Should children learn math by rules and formulas or by manipulating colored blocks or pie-shaped segments to illustrate mathematical concepts? By memorizing and drilling with the multiplication tables or by using computer simulations and relating math problems to real life? Such questions have spurred heated argument between proponents of *traditional "skill-and-drill" math* teaching and advocates of *constructivist math* (or *whole math*), in which children actively build their own mathematical concepts.

Constructivist math de-emphasizes basic skills. Instead, it stresses understanding how mathematics works. Rather than passively absorbing rules from a teacher or textbook, children discover mathematical concepts for themselves, often on the basis of intuitive learning gleaned from telling time, playing board games, dealing with money, and other everyday experiences. Instead of arriving at precise answers by multiplying, say, $19 \times 3 \times 6$, children are encouraged to make estimates from more obvious relationships, such as $20 \times 3 \times 5$.

The math wars have split educators into opposing camps. Although constructivist methods were initially pronounced a failure, the first scientific studies on their effectiveness have been generally favorable. Among 2,369 big-city middle-school students, algebra performance actually improved after adoption of constructivist methods (Mayer, 1998). Contrary to claims that the constructivist approach was inappropriate for diverse populations, a randomized study of 104 low-achieving, mostly poor and minority third and fourth graders' performance on computation and word problems found otherwise. Students taught by problem solving and/or peer collaboration outperformed students taught by more traditional methods (Ginsburg-Block & Fantuzzo, 1998).

The Trends in International Mathematics and Science Study (TIMSS) reports the performance of U.S. students relative to their peers in other countries. In 2007, U.S. fourth graders scored higher than 23 of 35 competing nations on math literacy.

The TIMSS intensified the math wars. Some educators blamed constructivist teaching, while others insisted the real problem was the persistence of traditional methods in many schools (Murray, 1998). Some argued that the reforms did not go far enough in rooting out the worst features of old curricula (Jackson, 1997a, 1997b). Superficial teaching and textbooks were among the reformers' complaints.

As in the reading wars, the best approach may be a combination of old and new methods. That is what the National Center for Teachers of Mathematics (NCTM) now advocates. Its revised standards and principles, issued in 2000, strive for a balance between conceptual understanding and computational skills. In 2003, math scores on the National Assessment of Educational Progress rose sharply to their highest levels since the test began in 1990 (NCES, 2004b). In 2005 they inched higher. The percentage of fourth graders scoring at or above the basic level of achievement increased by 30 points since 1990, from 50 to 80 percent; and the percentage of eighth graders at that level increased 17 points, from 52 to 69 percent. However, only 36 percent of fourth graders and 30 percent of eighth graders were judged "proficient" in 2005 (Perie, Grigg, & Dion, 2005).

Meanwhile, in 2003, U.S. fourth and eighth graders scored well above average in the TIMSS but not as well as Asian students. The eighth graders scored higher than their counterparts in the 1990s, but fourth graders showed no improvement. Achievement gaps between white and black students at both grade levels narrowed (Gonzales et al., 2004).

A further step back to the basics is the National Center for Teachers of Mathematics (2006) issuance of "curriculum focal points." To help teachers and students wade through the dozens of topics set forth in state curriculum standards, the focal points specify the most important skills students need to learn in each grade.

what's your view Based on your own experience, which method of teaching math do you think would be more effective, or would you advocate a combination of both?

Class Size Most educators consider small class size a key factor in achievement, especially in the early grades, though findings on this point are mixed (Schneider, 2002). A longitudinal study found lasting academic benefits for students randomly assigned to classes of about 15 students in kindergarten through third grade and, especially for low-SES students, a greater likelihood of finishing high school (Finn, Gerber, & Boyd-Zaharias, 2005; Krueger, 2003; Krueger & Whitmore, 2000).

However, in most schools small classes are larger than that. In classroom observations of 890 first graders, classes with 25 students or less tended to be more social and interactive (with a bit more disruptive behavior) and to enable higher-quality instruction and emotional support. Students in these classes tended to score higher on standardized achievements tests and beginning reading skills (NICHD Early Childhood Research Network, 2004b).

Educational Innovations When the Chicago public schools ended **social promotion**, the practice of promoting children to keep them with their age-mates even when they do not meet academic standards, in 1996, many observers hailed the change. Others warned that, although grade retention in some cases can be a "wake-up call," more often it is the first step on a remedial track that leads to lowered expectations, poor performance, and dropping out of school (Fields & Smith, 1998; Lugaila, 2003; McCoy & Reynolds, 1999; McLeskey, Lancaster, & Grizzle, 1995; Temple, Reynolds, & Miedel, 2000). Indeed, studies by University of Chicago researchers found that Chicago's retention policy did not improve third graders' test scores, hurt sixth graders' scores, and greatly increased eighth-grade and high school dropout rates for retained students (Nagaoka & Roderick, 2004; Roderick, Engel, & Nagaoka, 2003).

Many educators say the only real solution to a high failure rate is to identify at-risk students early and intervene *before* they fail (Bronner, 1999). In 2000–2001, 39 percent of U.S. public school districts provided alternative schools or programs for at-risk students, offering smaller classes, remedial instruction, counseling, and crisis intervention (NCES, 2003). Summer school may be effective as an early intervention. In one study, first graders who attended summer instruction in reading and writing at least 75 percent of the time outscored 64 percent of their peers who did not participate (Borman, Boulay, Kaplan, Rachuba, & Hewes, 1999).

Some parents, unhappy with their public schools or seeking a particular style of education, are choosing charter schools or homeschooling. More than 1.3 million U.S. children now attend charter schools, some privately operated and others under charter from public school boards (Center for Education Reform, 2008). Charter schools tend to be smaller than regular public schools and tend to have a unique philosophy, curriculum, structure, or organizational style. Although parents are generally satisfied with their charter schools, studies of their effects on student outcomes have had mixed results (Braun, Jenkins, & Grigg, 2006; Bulkley & Fisler, 2002; Center for Education Reform, 2004; Detrich, Phillips, & Durett, 2002; Hoxby, 2004; National Assessment of Educational Progress, 2004; Schemo, 2004).

Homeschooling is legal in all 50 states. In 2007 some 1.5 million U.S. students representing 2.9 percent of the school-age population were homeschooled, 4 out of 5 of them full-time—a 36 percent increase from 2003 (NCES, 2008). In a nationally representative government survey, the main reasons parents gave for choosing to homeschool their children were the desire to provide religious or moral instruction and concern about a poor or unsafe learning environment (NCES, 2008).

Computer and Internet Use Access to the Internet in public schools has skyrocketed. In 1994 only 3 percent of classrooms had Internet access, compared with 94 percent in 2005 (Wells & Lewis, 2006). However, fewer black, Hispanic, and American Indian children than white and Asian children, and fewer poor children than nonpoor children, use these technologies. Girls and boys spend about the same amount of time on computer and Internet use (Day, Janus, & Davis, 2005; DeBell & Chapman, 2006).

Computer literacy and the ability to navigate the World Wide Web are opening new possibilities for individualized instruction, global communication, and early training in independent research skills. However, this tool poses dangers. Foremost is the risk of exposure to harmful or inappropriate material. Also, students need to learn to critically evaluate information they find in cyberspace and to separate facts from opinion and advertising. Finally, a focus on "visual literacy" could divert financial resources from other areas of the curriculum.

social promotion
Policy of automatically promoting children even if they do not meet academic standards.

checkpoint
can you . . .

▷ Tell how self-efficacy beliefs and parenting practices can influence school success?

▷ Discuss the impact of socioeconomic status and peer acceptance on school achievement?

▷ Describe changes and innovations in educational philosophy and practice, homework, and the teaching of math?

Educating Children with Special Needs

How do schools meet special needs?

Public schools have a tremendous job educating children of varying abilities from all sorts of families and cultural backgrounds. They must educate children who have special needs. Note that when most of us consider special needs, we are likely to focus on those children who have learning or behavioral disorders, as those concerns have earned center stage as a major condition affecting the development of school-age children (Pastor & Reuben, 2008). However, special needs also include a focus on children who are gifted, talented, or creative, as they have different educational needs than the typical child.

CHILDREN WITH LEARNING PROBLEMS

Just as educators have become more sensitive to teaching children from varied cultural backgrounds, they also have sought to meet the needs of children with special educational needs. These conditions vary in severity and can often be difficult to diagnose accurately.

Intellectual Disability **Intellectual disability** is significantly subnormal cognitive functioning. It is indicated by an IQ of about 70 or less, coupled with a deficiency in age-appropriate adaptive behavior (such as communication, social skills, and self-care), appearing before age 18 (Kanaya, Scullin, & Ceci, 2003). Intellectual disability is sometimes referred to as cognitive disability or mental retardation. Less than 1 percent of U.S. children are intellectually disabled (National Center for Health Statistics [NCHS], 2004; Woodruff et al., 2004).

> **intellectual disability**
> Significantly subnormal cognitive functioning. Also referred to as cognitive disability or mental retardation.

In 30 to 50 percent of cases the cause of intellectual disability is unknown. Known causes include genetic disorders, traumatic accidents, prenatal exposure to infection or alcohol, and environmental exposure to lead or high levels of mercury (Woodruff et al., 2004). Many cases may be preventable through genetic counseling, prenatal care, amniocentesis, routine screening and health care for newborns, and nutritional services for pregnant women and infants.

Most children with an intellectual disability can benefit from schooling. Intervention programs have helped many of those mildly or moderately disabled and those considered borderline (with IQs ranging from 70 up to about 85) to hold jobs, live in the community, and function in society. The profoundly disabled need constant care and supervision, usually in institutions. For some, day care centers, hostels for intellectually disabled adults, and homemaking services for caregivers can be less costly and more humane alternatives.

Learning Disorders The two most commonly diagnosed conditions causing behavioral and learning problems in school-age children are learning disability (LD) and attention-deficit/hyperactivity disorder (ADHD). A recent study of more than 23,000 children in the United States revealed that about 5 percent of children have learning disabilities, 5 percent of children have ADHD, and 4 percent of children have both conditions (Pastor & Reuben, 2008).

Learning Disabilities Nelson Rockefeller, former vice president of the United States, had so much trouble reading that he ad-libbed speeches instead of using a script. Rockefeller is just one of many people who struggle with **dyslexia**, a language-processing disorder in which reading is substantially below the level predicted by IQ or age. Other famous persons reportedly having dyslexia include actors Tom Cruise, Whoopi Goldberg, and Cher; baseball Hall-of-Famer Nolan Ryan; television host Jay Leno; and filmmaker Steven Spielberg.

> **dyslexia**
> Developmental disorder in which reading achievement is substantially lower than predicted by IQ or age.

learning disabilities (LDs)
Disorders that interfere with specific aspects of learning and school achievement.

Dyslexia is the most commonly diagnosed of a large number of **learning disabilities (LDs)**. These disorders interfere with specific aspects of school achievement, such as listening, speaking, reading, writing, or mathematics, resulting in performance substantially lower than would be expected given a child's age, intelligence, and amount of schooling (American Psychiatric Association, 1994). Mathematical disabilities, as an example, include difficulty in counting, comparing numbers, calculating, and remembering basic arithmetic facts. Each of these may involve distinct disabilities. A growing number of children—almost 4.6 million, or 5 percent of the U.S. school population—have been diagnosed with LD (Pastor & Reuben, 2008).

Children with LDs often have near-average to higher-than-average intelligence and normal vision and hearing, but they seem to have trouble processing sensory information. Although causes are uncertain, one factor is genetic. A review of quantitative genetic research concluded that the genes most responsible for the high heritability of the most common LDs—language impairment, reading disability, and mathematical disability—are also responsible for normal variations in learning abilities and that genes that affect one type of disability are also likely to affect other types. However, some genes are specific to particular learning disabilities (Plomin & Kovas, 2005). Environmental factors may include complications of pregnancy or birth, injuries after birth, nutritional deprivation, and exposure to lead (National Center for Learning Disabilities, 2004b).

Children with LDs tend to be less task oriented and more easily distracted than other children; they are less well organized as learners and less likely to use memory strategies. Of course, not all children who have trouble with reading, arithmetic, or other specific school subjects have LDs. Some haven't been taught properly, are anxious, have trouble reading or hearing directions, lack motivation or interest in the subject, or have a developmental delay, which may eventually disappear (Geary, 1993; Ginsburg, 1997; Roush, 1995).

> *People with dyslexia often fail to develop phonological awareness and have difficulty breaking speech sounds into their constituent parts. If you cannot "hear" that the word "dog" is made up of three distinct phonemes, then reading is definitely going to be a challenge.*
>
> Shaywitz et al., 2006

About 4 out of 5 children with LDs have been identified as dyslexic. Dyslexia is generally considered to be a chronic, persistent medical condition that tends to run in families (Shaywitz, 1998, 2003). It hinders the development of oral as well as written language skills and may cause problems with reading, writing, spelling, grammar, and understanding speech (National Center for Learning Disabilities, 2004a). Reading disability is more frequent in boys than in girls (Rutter et al., 2004).

Brain imaging studies have found that dyslexia is due to a neurological defect that disrupts recognition of speech sounds (Shaywitz, Mody, & Shaywitz, 2006). Several identified genes contribute to this disruption (Meng et al., 2005; Kere et al., 2005). Many children—and even adults—with dyslexia can be taught to read through systematic phonological training, but the process does not become automatic, as it does with most readers (Eden et al., 2004; Shaywitz, 1998, 2003).

attention-deficit/hyperactivity disorder (ADHD)
Syndrome characterized by persistent inattention and distractibility, impulsivity, low tolerance for frustration, and inappropriate overactivity.

Attention-Deficit/Hyperactivity Disorder **Attention-deficit/hyperactivity disorder (ADHD)** has been called the most common disorder in childhood (Wolraich et al., 2005). It is a chronic condition usually marked by persistent inattention, distractibility, impulsivity, low tolerance for frustration, and a great deal of activity at the wrong time and in the wrong place, such as the classroom (American Psychiatric Association, 1994; Woodruff et al., 2004). Among well-known people who reportedly have had ADHD are the singer and composer John Lennon, Senator Robert Kennedy, and the actors Robin Williams and Jim Carey.

ADHD may affect an estimated 2 to 11 percent of school-age children worldwide (Zametkin & Ernst, 1999). In 2006 about 2.5 million children in the United States were diagnosed with ADHD, a rate of about 4.7 percent. While the rate of diagnoses of LDs have remained relatively constant, the rate of ADHD has increased about 3 percent per year over the past 10 years (Pastor & Reuben, 2008; Figure 13.2).

ADHD is a somehat controversial diagnosis: Some research suggests that it may be underdiagnosed (Rowland et al., 2002), but physicians warn that it may be overdiagnosed, resulting in unnecessary overmedication of children whose parents or teachers do not know how to control them (Elliott, 2000). Similar to LD, ADHD diagnosis

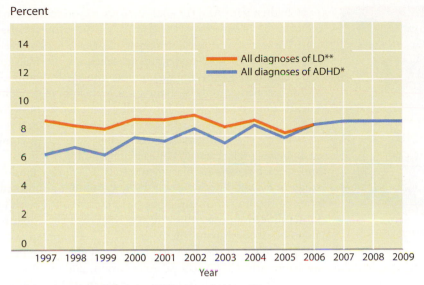

Percent

All diagnoses of LD**
All diagnoses of ADHD*

1997 1998 1999 2000 2001 2002 2003 2004 2005 2006 2007 2008 2009
Year

*"All diagnoses of ADHD" includes ADHD with and without LD.

**"All diagnoses of LD" includes LD with and without ADHD.

FIGURE 13.2

United States Diagnosis of Attention-Deficit/ Hyperactivity Disorder by Year

Diagnosis of learning disabilities has remained constant, but diagnosis of ADHD rose during the years from 1997 to 2009.

Source: CDC/NCHS, National Health Interview Surveys, 1997–2009.

rates vary greatly by gender, ethnicity, geographic area, and other contextual factors. Boys are more likely than girls to have each of the diagnoses and are twice as likely to have ADHD, and children living in a mother-only family were more likely to be diagnosed with LD or ADHD (Pastor & Reuben, 2008). ADHD rates may in part be related to pressures on children to succeed in school (Schneider & Eisenberg, 2006). Some of the diagnoses may be environmentally driven and related to the demands or characteristics of the school involved.

Some children with ADHD are inattentive but not hyperactive; others show the reverse pattern (USDHHS, 1999b). Because these characteristics appear to some degree in all children, some practitioners question whether ADHD is actually a distinct neurological or psychological disorder (Bjorklund & Pellegrini, 2002; Furman, 2005). Most experts agree, however, that there is cause for concern when symptoms are so severe that they interfere with the child's functioning in school and in daily life (AAP Committee on Children with Disabilities and Committee on Drugs, 1996; Barkley, 1998; USDHHS, 1999b).

Imaging studies reveal that brains of children with ADHD grow in a normal pattern, with different areas thickening and then thinning at different times; but the process is delayed by about 3 years in certain regions of the brain, particularly the frontal cortex. These frontal regions enable a person to control movement, suppress inappropriate thoughts and actions, focus attention, remember from moment to moment, and work for rewards— all functions that are often disturbed in children with ADHD. The motor cortex is the only area that matures faster than normal, and this mismatch may account for the restlessness and fidgeting characteristic of the disorder (Shaw, Krause, Liang, & Bennett, 2007).

ADHD seems to have a substantial genetic basis with heritability approaching 80 percent (Acosta, Arcos-Burgos, & Muenke, 2004; Barkley, 1998; Elia, Ambrosini, & Rapoport, 1999; USDHHS, 1999b; Zametkin & Ernst, 1999). In one of the largest genetic studies of ADHD, more than 600,000 genetic markers were examined. Results indicated that many genes are involved in ADHD, each contributing some small effect (Neale et al., 2008). Another group of researchers identified a variation of a gene for dopamine, a brain chemical essential for attention and cognition, low levels of which appear to be associated with ADHD (Shaw et al., 2007; Volkow et al., 2007). Birth complications also may play a part in ADHD. Prematurity, a prospective mother's alcohol or tobacco use, and oxygen deprivation (Barkley, 1998; Thapar et al., 2003; USDHHS, 1999b; Woodruff et al., 2004) have all been linked to ADHD. Children with ADHD are more likely to show early antisocial behavior if they were of low birth weight and have a variant of a gene called COMT (Thapar et al., 2005).

what's your view?

Long-term effects of drug treatment for ADHD are unknown, and leaving the condition untreated also carries risks. If you had a child with ADHD, what would you do?

Sign language can be used to integrate deaf children into classrooms with hearing classmates.

Children with ADHD tend to forget responsibilities, to speak aloud rather than give themselves silent directions, to be frustrated or angered easily, and to give up when they don't see how to solve a problem. Parents and teachers may be able to help these children by breaking down tasks into small "chunks," providing frequent prompts about rules and time, and giving frequent, immediate rewards for small accomplishments (Barkley, 1998).

ADHD is often managed with drugs, sometimes combined with behavioral therapy, counseling, training in social skills, and special classroom placement. In a 14-month randomized study of 579 children with ADHD, a carefully monitored program of Ritalin treatment, alone or in combination with behavior modification, was more effective than the behavioral therapy alone or standard community care (MTA Cooperative Group, 1999). However, the superior benefits of the program diminished during the following 10 months (MTA Cooperative Group, 2004a). A side effect of the combined treatment was slower growth in height and weight (MTA Cooperative Group, 2004b). Furthermore, long-term effects of Ritalin are unknown (Wolraich et al., 2005).

Educating Children with Disabilities In 2006, 14 percent of public school students in the United States were receiving special educational services under the Individuals with Disabilities Education Act, which ensures a free, appropriate public education for all children with disabilities. Most of these children had learning disabilities or speech or language impairments (NCES, 2007a). An individualized program must be designed for each child, with parental involvement. Children must be educated in the "least restrictive environment" appropriate to their needs—which means, whenever possible, the regular classroom.

Programs in which children with special needs are included in the regular classroom are known as *inclusion programs.* Here, children with disabilities are integrated with nondisabled children for all or part of the day, sometimes with assistance. In 2005, 52 percent of students with disabilities spent at least 80 percent of their time in regular classrooms (NCES, 2007a).

GIFTED CHILDREN

Sir Isaac Newton, who discovered gravity, did poorly in grade school. Thomas Edison, inventor of the lightbulb, was told as a boy that he was too stupid to learn. The British prime minister Winston Churchill failed sixth grade. The great operatic tenor Enrico Caruso was told as a child that he could not sing.

Giftedness is hard to define and identify. Educators disagree on who qualifies as gifted, on what basis, and on what kinds of educational programs these children need. Another source of confusion is that creativity and artistic talent are sometimes viewed as aspects or types of giftedness and sometimes as independent of it.

Identifying Gifted Children The traditional criterion of giftedness is high general intelligence as shown by an IQ score of 130 or higher. This definition tends to exclude highly creative children (whose unusual answers often lower their test scores), children from minority groups (whose abilities may not be well developed, though the potential is there), and children with specific aptitudes (who may be only average or even show learning problems in other areas). Most states and school districts have therefore adopted the broader definition in the U.S. Elementary and Secondary Education Act, which encompasses children who show high intellectual, creative, artistic, or leadership capacity or ability in specific academic fields, and who need special educational services and activities in order to fully develop those capabilities. Many school districts now use multiple criteria for admission to programs for the gifted, including achievement test scores, grades, classroom performance,

> checkpoint
can **you** . . .

▷ Describe the causes and prognoses for three common types of conditions that interfere with learning?

▷ Discuss the impact of federal requirements for the education of children with disabilities?

creative production, parent and teacher nominations, and student interviews; but IQ remains an important and sometimes the determining factor. An estimated 6 percent of the student population are considered gifted (National Association for Gifted Children, n.d.).

What Causes Giftedness? Psychologists who study the lives of extraordinary achievers find that high levels of performance require strong intrinsic motivation and years of rigorous training (Bloom, 1985; Czikszentmihalyi, 1996; Gardner, 1993; Gottfried, Cook, Gottfried, & Morris, 2005; Gruber, 1981; Keegan, 1996). However, motivation and training will not produce giftedness unless a child is endowed with unusual ability (Winner, 2000). Conversely, children with innate gifts are unlikely to show exceptional achievement without motivation and hard work (Achter & Lubinski, 2003).

Gifted children tend to grow up in enriched family environments with much intellectual or artistic stimulation. Their parents recognize and often devote themselves to nurturing the children's gifts but also give their children an unusual degree of independence. Parents of gifted children typically have high expectations and are hard workers and high achievers themselves. But although parenting can enhance the development of gifts, it cannot create them (Winner, 2000).

Brain research suggests that gifted children "are born with unusual brains that enable rapid learning in a particular domain" (Winner, 2000, p. 161). For example, children with mathematical, musical, and artistic gifts tend to have unusual activity in the right hemisphere while doing tasks normally done by the left. They are also more likely to be left-handed (Winner, 2000).

Defining and Measuring Creativity One definition of *creativity* is the ability to see things in a new light—to produce something never seen before or to discern problems others fail to recognize and find new and unusual solutions. High creativity and high academic intelligence (IQ) do not necessarily go hand in hand. Classic research found only modest correlations (Anastasi & Schaefer, 1971; Getzels, 1964, 1984; Getzels & Jackson, 1962, 1963).

The reason that creativity is not highly correlated with traditional IQ tests is that the traditional tests are measuring a different kind of thinking than is characteristic of creativity. J. P. Guilford (1956, 1959, 1960, 1967, 1986) distinguished two kinds of thinking: convergent and divergent. **Convergent thinking**—the kind IQ tests measure—seeks a single correct answer. For example, when solving an arithmetic problem, there is one correct answer upon which everyone is expected to converge. **Divergent thinking**, by contrast, involving comes up with a wide array of fresh possibilities, such as when children are asked to list how many different uses there might be for a paper clip, complete a figure, or write down what a sound brings to mind. There is no one right answer. Tests of creativity call for divergent thinking, and this ability can be assessed via the *Torrance Tests of Creative Thinking* (Torrance, 1966, 1974; Torrance & Ball, 1984), one of the most widely known tests of creativity.

A problem with these tests is that the score often depends partly on speed, which is not a hallmark of creativity. Moreover, although the tests yield fairly reliable results, there is dispute over whether they are valid—whether they identify children who are creative in everyday life (Simonton, 1990).

Educating Gifted Children Programs for gifted children generally stress either enrichment or acceleration. **Enrichment** programs may deepen students' knowledge and skills

17-year-old Sara Volz of Colorado Springs, Colorado—shown here in the makeshift lab she constructed under her loft bed—won the Intel Science Talent Search in 2013 for her experiments using artificial selection to improve oil yields from algae. This experiment has important applications for the use of biofuels. In addition to winning the Intel science contest, Sara is also involved in her high school's Science Olympiad, Science Bowl and debate teams, and has sung and acted in plays. The key to helping such children achieve lies in recognizing and nurturing their natural gifts.

> One possible reason creativity and academic achievement don't always relate is that the personality characteristics related to creativity are generally viewed negatively by teachers.
>
> Westby & Dawson, 1995

convergent thinking
Thinking aimed at finding the one right answer to a problem.

divergent thinking
Thinking that produces a variety of fresh, diverse possibilities.

what's your view

Would you favor strengthening, cutting back, or eliminating special educational programs for gifted students?

enrichment
Approach to educating the gifted that broadens and deepens knowledge and skills through extra activities, projects, field trips, or mentoring.

acceleration
Approach to educating the gifted that moves them through the curriculum at an unusually rapid pace.

checkpoint can you ...

▷ Describe how gifted children are identified, possible causes of giftedness, and ways giftedness is measured?

▷ Describe two approaches to the education of gifted children?

through extra classroom activities, research projects, field trips, or expert coaching. **Acceleration** programs speed up their education through early school entrance, grade skipping, placement in fast-paced classes, or advanced courses. Other options include ability grouping within the classroom (which has been found to help children academically and not harm them socially [Winner, 2000]), dual enrollment (for example, an eighth grader taking algebra at a nearby high school), magnet schools, and specialized schools for the gifted.

Moderate acceleration does not seem to harm social adjustment, at least in the long run (Winner, 1997). A 30-year study of 3,937 young people who took advanced placement (AP) courses in high school found that they were more satisfied with their school experience and ultimately achieved more than equally gifted young people who did not take AP courses (Bleske-Rechek, Lubinski, & Benbow, 2004).

summary and key terms

guidepost 1
Piagetian Approach: The Concrete Operational Child

How do school-age children's thinking and moral reasoning differ from those of younger children?

• A child from about age 7 to age 12 is in the stage of concrete operations. Children are less egocentric than before and are more proficient at tasks requiring logical reasoning, such as spatial thinking, understanding of causality, categorization, inductive and deductive reasoning, conservation, and working with numbers. However, their reasoning is largely limited to the here and now.

• Cultural experience, as well as neurological development, seems to contribute to the rate of development of conservation and other Piagetian skills.

• According to Piaget, moral development is linked with cognitive maturation and occurs in three stages in which children move from strict obedience to authority toward more autonomous judgments based first on fairness and later on equity.

concrete operations (360)
seriation (361)
transitive inference (361)
class inclusion (362)
inductive reasoning (362)
deductive reasoning (362)
horizontal décalage (363)

guidepost 2
Information-Processing Approach: Attention, Memory, and Planning

What advances in information-processing skills occur during middle childhood?

• Executive function—including attentional, memory, and planning skills—improves during middle childhood as a result of pruning of neurons in the prefrontal cortex.

• Processing speed, inhibitory control, selective attention, working memory capacity, metamemory, metacognition, and use of mnemonic strategies are specific skills that improve during the school years.

• Gains in information processing may help explain the advances Piaget described.

executive function (366)
metamemory (367)
mnemonic device (367)
external memory aids (367)
rehearsal (367)
organization (368)
elaboration (368)

guidepost 3
Psychometric Approach: Assessment of Intelligence

How accurately can schoolchildren's intelligence be measured?

• The intelligence of school-age children is assessed by group or individual tests. Although intended as aptitude tests, they are validated against measures of achievement.

• IQ tests are fairly good predictors of school success but may be unfair to some children.

• Differences in IQ among ethnic groups appear to result to a considerable degree from socioeconomic and other environmental differences. Schooling seems to increase measured intelligence.

• Attempts to devise culture-free or culture-fair tests have been unsuccessful.

• IQ tests tap only three of the intelligences in Howard Gardner's theory of multiple intelligences. According to Robert Sternberg's triarchic theory, IQ tests measure mainly the componential element of intelligence, not the experiential and contextual elements.

- Other directions in intelligence testing include the Sternberg Triarchic Abilities Test (STAT), the Kaufman Assessment Battery for Children (K-ABC-II), and dynamic tests based on Vygotskyan theory.

  Wechsler Intelligence Scale for Children (WISC-III) (370)

  Otis-Lennon School Ability Test (OLSAT8) (370)

  culture-free test (372)

  culture-fair test (372)

  theory of multiple intelligences (373)

  triarchic theory of intelligence (374)

  componential element (374)

  experiential element (374)

  contextual element (374)

  tacit knowledge (375)

  Kaufman Assessment Battery for Children (K-ABC-II) (375)

  dynamic tests (375)

guidepost 4 Language and Literacy

How do communicative abilities expand during middle childhood?

- Use of vocabulary, grammar, and syntax become increasingly sophisticated, but the major area of linguistic growth is in pragmatics.
- Methods of second-language education are controversial. Issues include speed and facility with English, long-term achievement in academic subjects, and pride in cultural identity.
- Metacognition contributes to progress in reading.
- Despite the popularity of whole-language programs, early phonics training is a key to reading proficiency.
- Interaction with peers fosters development of writing skills.

  pragmatics (376)

  English-immersion approach (377)

  bilingual education (377)

  bilingual (377)

  two-way (dual-language) learning (377)

  decoding (378)

  phonetic (code emphasis) approach (378)

  whole-language approach (378)

  visually based retrieval (378)

  metacognition (378)

guidepost 5 The Child in School

What factors influence school achievement?

- Because schooling is cumulative, the foundation laid in first grade is very important.

- Children's self-efficacy beliefs affect school achievement.
- Parents influence children's learning by becoming involved in their schooling, motivating them to achieve, and transmitting attitudes about learning.
- Socioeconomic status can influence parental beliefs and practices that, in turn, influence achievement. Poor families whose children do well in school tend to have more social capital than poor families whose children do not do well.
- The school environment and class size affect learning.
- Current educational issues and innovations include the amount of homework assigned, methods of teaching math, social promotion, charter schools, homeschooling, and computer literacy.

  social capital (381)

  social promotion (384)

guidepost 6 Educating Children with Special Needs

How do schools meet special needs?

- Three frequent sources of learning problems are intellectual disabilities, learning disabilities (LDs), and attention-deficit hyperactivity disorder (ADHD). Dyslexia is the most common learning disability.
- In the United States, all children with disabilities are entitled to a free, appropriate education. Children must be educated in the least restrictive environment possible, often in the regular classroom.
- An IQ of 130 or higher is a common standard for identifying gifted children. Broader definitions include creativity, artistic talent, and other attributes and rely on multiple criteria for identification. Minorities are underrepresented in programs for the gifted.
- In Terman's classic longitudinal study of gifted children, most turned out to be well adjusted and successful but not outstandingly so.
- Creativity and IQ are not closely linked. Tests of creativity seek to measure divergent thinking, but their validity has been questioned.
- Special educational programs for gifted, creative, and talented children usually stress enrichment or acceleration.

  intellectual disability (385)

  dyslexia (385)

  learning disabilities (LDs) (386)

  attention-deficit/hyperactivity disorder (ADHD) (386)

  convergent thinking (389)

  divergent thinking (389)

  enrichment (389)

  acceleration (390)

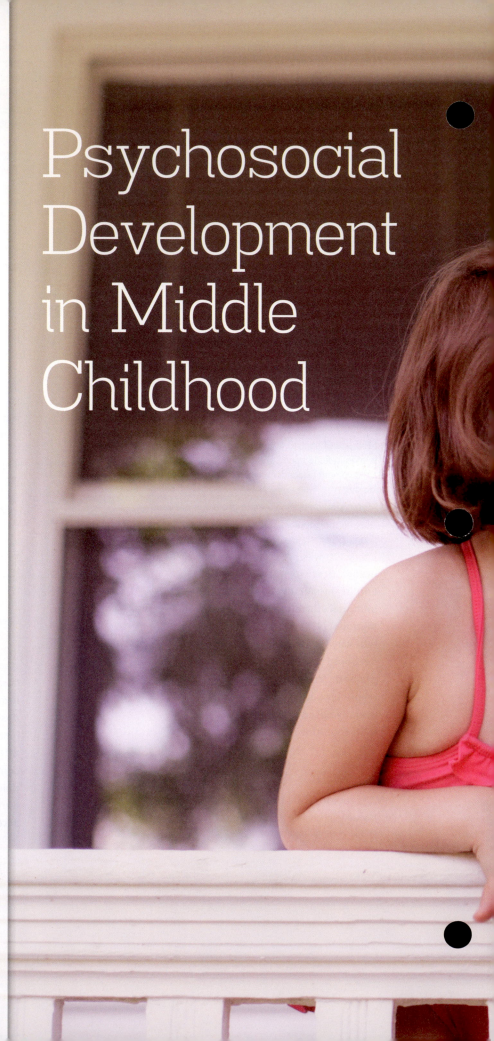

did you know outline

did you know?

▷ Children in single-parent households do better on achievement tests in countries with supportive family policies?

▷ Children reared by gay parents have been found to be as psychologically healthy as children reared by heterosexual parents?

▷ Research supports a cause-and-effect relationship between viewing media violence and aggressive behavior?

In this chapter, we trace the varied emotional and social lives of school-age children. We see how children develop a more realistic concept of themselves and achieve more competence, self-reliance, and emotional control. Through being with peers they make discoveries about their own attitudes, values, and skills. Still, the family remains a vital influence. Children's lives are affected, not only by the way parents approach child rearing, but also by whether and how they are employed, by the family's economic circumstances, and by its structure or composition—whether the child lives with one parent or two; whether the child has siblings and if so, how many; and whether the household includes other relatives, such as grandparents, aunt, and cousins. We also consider resilient children who emerge from the stresses of childhood healthier and stronger.

Psychosocial Development in Middle Childhood

Let us put our minds together and see what life we can make for our children.

Sitting Bull, Native American Chief of the Lakota Sioux (1831–1890)

1. How do the self-concept and self-esteem change in middle childhood, and how do school-age children show emotional growth?

2. What are the effects of family atmosphere and family structure, and what part do siblings play in children's development?

3. How do relationships with peers change in middle childhood, and what factors influence popularity and aggressive behavior?

4. How do children respond to the stresses of modern life?

guidepost 1

How do the self-concept and self-esteem change in middle childhood, and how do school-age children show emotional growth?

The Developing Self

The cognitive growth that takes place during middle childhood enables children to develop more complex concepts of themselves and to grow in emotional understanding and control.

SELF-CONCEPT DEVELOPMENT: REPRESENTATIONAL SYSTEMS

"At school I'm feeling pretty smart in certain subjects, Language Arts and Social Studies," says 8-year-old Lisa. "I got A's in these subjects on my last report card and was really proud of myself. But I'm feeling really dumb in Arithmetic and Science, particularly when I see how well the other kids are doing. . . . I still like myself as a person, because Arithmetic and Science just aren't that important to me. How I look and how popular I am are more important" (Harter, 1996, p. 208).

Earlier in development young children have difficulty with abstract concepts and with integrating various dimensions of the self. Their self-concepts focus on physical attributes, possessions, and global descriptions. However, at around age 7 or 8, children reach the third stage of self-concept development introduced in Chapter 11. At this time judgments about the self become more conscious, realistic, balanced, and comprehensive as children form **representational systems:** broad, inclusive self-concepts that integrate various aspects of the self (Harter, 1993, 1996, 1998).

We see these changes in Lisa's self-description. She can now focus on more than one dimension of herself. She has outgrown her earlier all-or-nothing, black-or-white self-definition. Now she recognizes that she can be "smart" in certain subjects and "dumb" in others. She can verbalize her self-concept better, and she can weigh different aspects of it. She can compare her *real self* (who she is) with her *ideal self* (who she wants to be) and can judge how well she measures up to social standards in comparison with others. All of these changes contribute to the development of self-esteem, her assessment of her *global self-worth* ("I still like myself as a person").

INDUSTRY VERSUS INFERIORITY

According to Erikson (1982), a major determinant of self-esteem is children's view of their capacity for productive work, which develops in his fourth stage of psychosocial development. As with all of Erikson's stages, there are two possible paths. There is an

representational systems
Broad, inclusive self-concepts that integrate various aspects of the self.

Middle childhood, according to Erikson, is a time for learning the skills one's culture considers important. In driving geese to market, this Vietnamese girl is developing a sense of competence and gaining self-esteem.

opportunity for growth represented by a sense of industry and a complementary risk represented by inferiority. This stage, therefore, is named **industry versus inferiority**.

In the event that children are unable to obtain the praise of adults or peers in their lives, or lack motivation and self-esteem, they may develop a feeling of low self-worth, and thus sink into inertia. In this case, children would have developed a sense of inferiority, which is problematic, because during middle childhood children must learn skills valued in their society. For example, if children feel inadequate compared with their peers, they may retreat to the protective embrace of the family and not venture further away from home.

Developing a sense of industry, by contrast, involves learning how to work hard to achieve goals. The details may vary across societies: Arapesh boys in New Guinea learn to make bows and arrows and to lay traps for rats; Arapesh girls learn to plant, weed, and harvest; Inuit children of Alaska learn to hunt and fish; and children in industrialized countries learn to read, write, do math, and use computers. What these different experiences share, however, is an emphasis on developing responsibility and motivation to succeed. If the stage is successfully resolved, children develop a view of the self as able to master skills and complete tasks. This can go too far—if children become too industrious, they may neglect social relationships and turn into workaholics.

Parents strongly influence a child's beliefs about competence. In a longitudinal study of 514 middle-class U.S. children, parents' beliefs about their children's competence in math and sports were strongly associated with the children's beliefs (Fredricks & Eccles, 2002).

EMOTIONAL GROWTH AND PROSOCIAL BEHAVIOR

As children grow older, they are more aware of their own and other people's feelings. They can better regulate or control their emotions and can respond to others' emotional distress (Saarni et al., 1998, 2006).

By age 7 or 8, children typically are aware of feeling shame and pride, and they have a clearer idea of the difference between guilt and shame (Harris, Olthof, Meerum Terwogt, & Hardman, 1987; Olthof, Schouten, Kuiper, Stegge, & Jennekens-Schinkel, 2000). These emotions affect their opinion of themselves (Harter, 1993, 1996). Children also understand their conflicting emotions. As Lisa says, "Most of the boys at school are pretty yucky. I don't feel that way about my little brother Jason, although he does get on my nerves. I love him but at the same time, he also does things that make me mad. But I control my temper; I'd be ashamed of myself if I didn't" (Harter, 1996, p. 208).

industry versus inferiority
Erikson's fourth crisis of psychosocial development, in which children must learn the productive skills their culture requires or else face feelings of inferiority.

checkpoint
can you . . .

▷ **Describe how the self-concept develops in middle childhood?**

▷ **Discuss the formation of representational systems?**

▷ **Describe Erikson's stage of industry versus inferiority?**

At about the age of 9, white American children start to self-censor their speech so as not to mention the race of others in an attempt to appear unprejudiced.

Apfelbaum, Pauker, Ambady, Sommers, & Norton, 2008

study smart

Emotional
Regulation

study smart

Understanding
Emotions

By middle childhood, children are aware of their culture's rules for acceptable emotional expression (Cole Bruschi, & Tamang, 2002). Children learn what makes them angry, fearful, or sad and how other people react to displays of these emotions, and they learn to behave accordingly. When parents respond to displays of negative emotions with disapproval or punishment, emotions such as anger and fear may become more intense and may impair children's social adjustment (Fabes, Leonard, Kupanoff, & Martin, 2001). Or the children may become secretive and anxious about their negative feelings. As children approach early adolescence, parental intolerance of negative emotion may heighten parent-child conflict (Eisenberg et al., 1999; Fabes et al., 2001).

Have you ever received a gift you didn't like or had to hold in your anger to avoid getting in trouble? The ability to fake liking a gift or to smile when you are mad involves emotion self-regulation. Emotional self-regulation involves effortful (voluntary) control of emotions, attention, and behavior (Eisenberg et al., 2004). There are individual differences in how effective different children are at doing this as well as developmental changes with age.

Children low in effortful control tend to become visibly angry or frustrated when interrupted or prevented from doing something they want to do. They cannot easily hide these signals. By contrast, children with high effortful control can stifle the impulse to show negative emotion at inappropriate times. Effortful control is to some extent a temperamentally based individual difference; however, it also generally improves with age. Still, those children with low effortful control when young are at higher risk for later behavior problems (Eisenberg et al., 2004).

> Self-regulation, specifically self-discipline, is more predictive of academic achievement than IQ.
>
> Duckworth & Seligman, 2005

Children tend to become more empathic and more inclined to prosocial behavior in middle childhood. Empathy appears to be "hard wired" into the brains of normal children. A recent study of brain activity in 7- to 12-year-olds found parts of their brains were activated when shown pictures of people in pain (Decety, Michalaska, Akitsuki, & Lahey, 2009). Children with high self-esteem tend to be more willing to volunteer to help those who are less fortunate than they are, and volunteering, in turn, helps build self-esteem (Karafantis & Levy, 2004). Prosocial children tend to act appropriately in social situations, to be relatively free from negative emotion, and to cope with problems constructively (Eisenberg, Fabes, & Murphy, 1996). Parents who acknowledge children's feelings of distress and help them focus on solving the root problem foster empathy, prosocial development, and social skills (Bryant, 1987; Eisenberg et al., 1996).

▷ **checkpoint** can **you** ...

▷ Identify some aspects of emotional growth in middle childhood, and tell how parental treatment may affect children's handling of negative emotions?

▷ Tell ways in which prosocial behavior increases in middle childhood?

The Child in the Family

School-age children spend more of their free time away from home than when they were younger, visiting and socializing with peers. They also spend more time at school and on their studies and less time at family meals than 20 or so years ago (Juster, Ono, & Stafford, 2004). Still, home and the people who live there remain an important part of most children's lives. Research suggests that family mealtimes are related both directly and to children's health and well-being, as discussed in Box 14.1.

guidepost

2

What are the effects of family atmosphere and family structure, and what part do siblings play in children's development?

> In general, adults are not very good at distinguishing when children lie. Adults are able to identify lies only slightly better than would be predicted by chance.
>
> Stromwall, Granhag, & Landstrom, 2007

> Recall the active genotype-environment interactions we discussed in Chapter 3. What does the growing independence of young children suggest about the importance of these correlations with age?

To understand the child in the family we need to look at the family environment—its atmosphere and structure. These in turn are affected by what goes on beyond the walls of the home. As Bronfenbrenner's theory predicts, wider layers of influence—including parents' work and socioeconomic status and societal trends such as urbanization, changes in family size, divorce, and remarriage—help shape the family environment and, thus, children's development.

the research w🌍rld

PASS THE MILK: FAMILY MEALTIMES AND CHILD WELL-BEING

14.1

There is no other activity that families share as a group more than daily meals. In one survey 56 percent of families with school-age children reported eating a meal together six to seven days per week (National Center on Addiction and Substance Abuse at Columbia University [CASA], 2006). And that's good news for children's health and well-being. These "densely packed events" that last an average of 20 minutes can have profound effects on a child's health and well-being (Fiese & Schwartz, 2008).

A few of the positive outcomes of family mealtimes include:

1. Promotion of language development: Frequency of family mealtimes has been linked to vocabulary growth (Beals & Snow, 1994), increased literary skills (Snow & Beals, 2006), and academic achievement (CASA, 2006).

2. Reduced risk for eating disorders and childhood obesity: Families who eat together regularly promote healthy eating habits and report fewer eating disorders (Neumark-Sztainer et al., 2007) and less obesity (Gable, Chung, & Krull, 2007). They eat more fruits and vegetables.

3. Reduced risk for substance abuse: Teens who eat regularly with their families are less likely to smoke cigarettes or marijuana and are at reduced risk for alcohol abuse (CASA, 2007).

4. Increased awareness of cultural traditions: Participating in family meals typically offers children opportunities to learn and identify with cultural traditions (Larson, 2008).

5. Fewer emotional problems: Mealtimes can offer a venue for positive communication between parents and children. This typically creates an environment where children engage in less risky behavior and have fewer emotional problems (Larson, 2008).

To optimize the likelihood of these positive outcomes, parents need to consider the climate of the mealtime experience. How the family interacts, where the meal is conducted, and the presence of television during the meal strongly influence the mealtime experience. The climate can support or discourage health and well-being. Meals that are well-organized and where parents are responsive to children have been linked to more positive outcomes (Fiese & Schwartz, 2008).

what's your view ? **What are some ways busy families can build family mealtimes into their schedules?**

Culture, too, defines the rhythms of family life and the roles of family members. Many African American families, for example, carry on extended-family traditions that include living near or with kin, a strong sense of family obligation, ethnic pride, and mutual aid (Parke & Buriel, 1998). Latino families tend to stress family commitment, respect for self and others, and moral education (Halgunseth, Ispa, & Rudy, 2006). As we look at the child in the family, then, we need to be aware of outside forces that affect it.

FAMILY ATMOSPHERE

The most important influences of the family environment on children's development come from the atmosphere in the home. One key factor is whether or not conflict is present in the home. Exposure to violence and conflict is harmful to children, both with respect to direct exposure via parental discord (Kaczynski, Lindahl, Malik, & Laurenceau, 2006), as well as via indirect influences on such variables as low family cohesion and anger regulation strategies (Houltberg, Henry, & Morris, 2012).

internalizing behaviors
Behaviors by which emotional problems
are turned inward; for example, anxiety
or depression.

externalizing behaviors
Behaviors by which a child acts out
emotional difficulties; for example,
aggression or hostility.

coregulation
Transitional stage in the control of
behavior in which parents exercise
general supervision and children
exercise moment-to-moment
self-regulation.

Children exposed to family conflict show a variety of different responses, which can be broadly characterized as including either externalizing or internalizing behaviors. **Internalizing behaviors** include anxiety, fearfulness, and depression—anger turned inward. **Externalizing behaviors** include aggression, fighting, disobedience, and hostility—anger turned outward. Both internalizing behaviors (Kaczynski et al., 2006; Fear et al., 2009) and externalizing behaviors (Kaczynski et al., 2006; Houltberg et al., 2012) are more likely in children that come from families with high levels of discord.

Another contributing factor to family atmosphere is how parents handle school-age children's growing need—and ability—to make their own decisions. Still another aspect is the family's economic situation. How does parents' work affect children's well-being?

Parenting Issues: From Control to Coregulation Babies don't have a lot of say in what happens to them; they are exposed to what their parents chose to expose them to and experience what their parents decide they should experience. Their parents run the show. However, as children grow and become more autonomous, there is a gradual shift in power. Over the course of childhood, control of behavior gradually shifts from parents to child. Children begin to request certain types of experiences, demand particular foods, negotiate for desired objects, and communicate their shifting needs to parents.

In middle childhood, social power becomes more equal between parent and child. Parent and child engage in **coregulation**, a stage that can include strategies where parents exercise oversight, but children enjoy moment-to-moment self-regulation (Maccoby, 1984; 1992). For example, with regard to problems among peers, parents might now rely less on direct intervention and more on discussion with their child (Parke & Buriel, 1998).

Coregulation is affected by the overall relationship between parent and child. Children are more apt to follow their parents' wishes when they believe the parents are fair and concerned about the child's welfare and that they may "know better" because of experience. This is particularly true when parents take pains to acknowledge children's maturing judgment and take strong stands only on important issues (Maccoby, 1984; 1992).

The shift to coregulation affects the way parents handle discipline (Kochanska, Aksan, Prisco, & Adams, 2008; Maccoby, 1984; Roberts, Block, & Block, 1984). Parents of school-age children are more likely to use inductive techniques. For example, 8-year-old Jared's father points out how his actions affect others: "Hitting Jermaine hurts him and makes him feel bad." In other situations, Jared's parents may appeal to his self-esteem ("What happened to the helpful boy who was here yesterday?") or moral values ("A big, strong boy like you shouldn't sit on the train and let an old person stand"). Above all, Jared's parents let him know that he must bear the consequences of his behavior ("No wonder you missed the school bus today—you stayed up too late last night! Now you'll have to walk to school").

The way parents and children resolve conflicts may be more important than the specific outcomes. If family conflict is constructive, it can help children see the need for rules and standards. They also learn what kinds of issues are worth arguing about and what strategies can be effective (Eisenberg, 1996). However, as children become preadolescents and their striving for autonomy becomes more insistent, the quality of family problem solving often deteriorates (Vuchinich, Angelelli, & Gatherum, 1996).

Effects of Parents' Work Most studies of the impact of parents' work on children's well-being have focused on employed mothers. From 1975 to 2000, the labor force participation rate of mothers with children under age 18 rose from 47 percent to a peak of 73 percent. By 2004, the rate for these mothers had receded to 71 percent, where it remained through 2007 (U.S. Bureau of Labor Statistics, 2008b). Thus many children have never known a time when their mothers were not working for pay.

In general, the more satisfied a mother is with her employment status, the more effective she is likely to be as a parent (Parke, 2004a; Parke & Buriel, 1998). However, the impact of a mother's work depends on many other factors, including the child's age, sex, temperament, and personality; whether the mother works full- or part-time; why she is working; whether she has a supportive or unsupportive partner, or none; the family's socioeconomic status; and the kind of care the child receives before and/ or after school (Parke & Buriel, 1998). Often a single mother must work to stave off economic disaster. How her working affects her children may hinge on how much time and energy she has left over to spend with them and what sort of role model she is (Barber & Eccles, 1992).

How well parents keep track of their children may be more important than whether the mother works for pay (Crouter, MacDermid, McHale, & Perry-Jenkins, 1990; Jacobson & Crockett, 2000). In 2005, 57 percent of students in kindergarten through eighth grade whose mothers worked full-time and 32 percent of those whose mothers worked part-time or were looking for work were in at least one regular nonparental after-school care arrangement, most often a school- or center-based program. Some children of employed mothers, especially younger children, are supervised by relatives. Many children receive several types of out-of-school care (Carver & Iruka, 2006). Like good child care for preschoolers, good after-school programs have relatively low enrollment, low child-staff ratios, and well-educated staff. Children, especially boys, in organized after-school programs with flexible programming and a positive emotional climate tend to adjust better and do better in school (Mahoney, Lord, & Carryl, 2005; Pierce, Hamm, & Vandell, 1999; Posner & Vandell, 1999).

About 9 percent of school-age children and 23 percent of early adolescents are reported to be in *self-care*, regularly caring for themselves at home without adult supervision (Hofferth & Jankuniene, 2000; NICHD Early Child Care Research Network, 2004a). This arrangement is advisable only for older children who are mature, responsible, and resourceful and know how to get help in an emergency—and, even then, only if a parent stays in touch by telephone.

Latch-key children, who care for themselves after school while parents work, need to be mature, responsible, and resourceful and should know how to get help in an emergency.

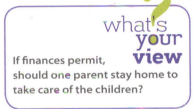

what's your view

If finances permit, should one parent stay home to take care of the children?

Poverty and Parenting Some 22 percent of U.S. children up to age 17—including 39 percent of black children and 35 percent of Hispanic children—lived in poverty in 2010. Children living with single mothers were nearly 5 times more likely to be poor than children living with married couples—43 percent as compared with 9 percent (Federal Interagency Forum on Child and Family Statistics, 2012a; Figure 14.1).

Poor children are more likely than other children to have emotional or behavioral problems (Wadsworth et al., 2008). In addition, their cognitive potential and school performance suffer even more (Brooks-Gunn, Britto, & Brady, 1998; Brooks-Gunn Duncan, Leventhal, & Aber, 1997; Duncan & Brooks-Gunn, 1997; McLoyd, 1998; Najman et al., 2009). Poverty can harm children's development through its impact on

FIGURE 14.1

Percentage of Children Ages 0 to 17 Living in Poverty

Children living with single mothers (female-householder families) are by far the most likely to be poor.

Source: Federal Interagency Forum on Child and Family Statistics, Fig. 4, 2012a.

NOTE: Estimates refer to children ages 0 to 17 who are related to the householder. In 2010, the average poverty threshold for a family of four was $22,113 in annual income.

parents' emotional state and parenting practices and on the home environment they create (Evans, 2004; NICHD Early Child Care Research Network, 2005a).

Vonnie McLoyd's (1990, 1998; Mistry, Vandewater, Huston, & McLoyd, 2002) analysis of the effects of poverty traces a route that leads to adult psychological distress, to effects on child rearing, and finally to emotional, behavioral, and academic problems in children. Parents who live in poverty are likely to become anxious, depressed, and irritable and thus may become less affectionate with and less responsive to their children. They may discipline inconsistently, harshly, and arbitrarily. The children also tend to become depressed, to have trouble getting along with peers, to lack self-confidence, to develop behavioral and academic problems, and to engage in antisocial acts (Brooks-Gunn et al., 1998; Evans, 2004; Evans & English, 2002; J. M. Fields & Smith, 1998; McLoyd, 1990, 1998; Mistry et al., 2002).

Fortunately, this pattern is not inevitable. Effective parenting can buffer children from the effects of low SES. Family interventions that reduce family conflict and anger and increase cohesion and warmth are especially beneficial (Repetti, Taylor, & Seeman, 2002). In a nationally representative study of 21,260 6-year-olds, it was not so much low income as material hardship—insufficient food, unstable housing, and inadequate medical care—that led to parental stress. This, in turn, affected how much time, money, and energy parents invested in their children's development and the way the parents treated their children; and these factors in turn predicted children's cognitive skills and social and emotional competence. Families that, despite poverty, managed to make ends meet did not show this pattern (Gershoff, Aber, Raver, & Lennon, 2007).

Parents who can turn to relatives or to community resources for emotional support, help with child care, and child-rearing information often can parent their children more effectively. A 4-year longitudinal study of 152 single mother–headed African American families in Georgia found a pattern opposite to the one McLoyd described. Mothers who, despite economic stress, were emotionally healthy and had relatively high self-esteem tended to have academically and socially competent children who reinforced the mothers' positive parenting; and this, in turn, supported the children's continued academic success and socially desirable behavior (Brody, Kim, Murry, & Brown, 2004).

FAMILY STRUCTURE

Family structure in the United States has changed dramatically. In earlier generations, the vast majority of children grew up in families with two married parents. Today, although about 2 out of 3 children under 18 live with two married biological, adoptive, or stepparents, that proportion represents a dramatic decline—from 77 percent in 1980 to 64 percent in 2012 (Child Trends Data Bank, 2013). Other increasingly common family types are gay and lesbian families and grandparent-headed families (discussed in Chapter 16). See Figure 14.2 for data on children's living arrangements.

FIGURE 14.2

Living Arrangements of Children Younger than 18, 1970 to 2012

Most children under 18 in the United States live with two parents, but the prevalence of that household type has been diminishing.

Source: Child Trends Data Bank, 2013.

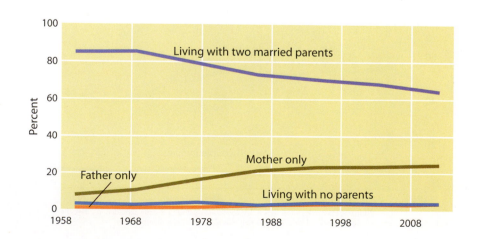

TABLE 14.1 Living Arrangements of Children, Age 0 to 14

Country	Two Parents in Same Household	Father and Mother Not in Same Household
Austria	86.6	0.5
Belgium	65	4.4
Bulgaria	85.2	1.6
Czech Republic	80.8	0.6
Denmark	81.3	1.4
Estonia	66.8	6.7
Finland	95.2	0.2
France	79.5	0.6
Germany	82	0
Greece	93.6	0.2
Hungary	82	1
Italy	92.1	0.1
Japan	87.7	0
Latvia	64.9	2.7
Lithuania	72.4	2
Luxembourg	91.5	0.7
Malta	90	0.5
Mexico	87.1	0
Netherlands	87.4	0.1
Poland	82	1.1
Portugal	86.6	1.8
Romania	88.9	1.9
Slovakia	86.4	0.5
Slovenia	87.7	0.9
Spain	91.5	0.7
Sweden	78	0
Switzerland	84.7	0.1
Turkey	91.5	0.7
United Kingdom	68.9	1.1
United States	70.7	3.5

Source: Organisation for Economic Co-operation and Development, 2012.

There is cross-national variation in living arrangements. In Finland 95 percent of children live with both parents, whereas only 65 percent of Belgian children live with both parents. Table 14.1 details international statistics on children's living arrangements.

Other things being equal, children tend to do better in families with two continuously married parents than in cohabiting, divorced, single-parent, or stepfamilies, or when the child is born outside of marriage (S. L. Brown, 2004). The distinction is even stronger for children growing up with two *happily* married parents. These children tend to experience a higher standard of living, more effective parenting, more cooperative co-parenting, closer relationships with both parents (especially fathers), and fewer stressful events (Amato, 2005). However, the parents' relationship, the quality of their parenting, and their ability to create a favorable family atmosphere may affect

Although paternal custody is still relatively rare, it is a growing trend. Whether or not a father has custody, as this man does, his son is likely to adjust better if his father remains involved in his life.

children's adjustment more than their marital status does (Amato, 2005; Bray & Hetherington, 1993; Bronstein, Clauson, Stoll, & Abrams, 1993; D. A. Dawson, 1991).

Family instability may be more harmful to children than the particular type of family they live in. In a study of a nationally representative sample of 5- to 14-year-olds, children who experienced several family transitions (for example, moving homes, changing schools, divorcing parents) were more likely to have behavior problems and to engage in delinquent behavior than children in stable families (Fomby & Cherlin, 2007).

A father's frequent and positive involvement with his child, from infancy on, is directly related to the child's well-being and physical, cognitive, and social development (Cabrera, Tamis-LeMonda, Bradley, Hofferth, & Lamb 2000; Kelley, Smith, Green, Berndt, & Rogers, 1998; Shannon, Tamis-LeMonda, London, & Cabrera, 2002). Unfortunately, in 2011, more than 30 percent of children live in homes without a biological father present (National Fatherhood Initiative, 2013). Furthermore, about 18 percent of European American children, 6 percent of black children, and 21 percent of Latino children had never met their father (NCES, 2004).

When Parents Divorce The United States has one of the highest divorce rates in the world. The annual number of divorces has tripled since 1960 (Harvey & Pauwels, 1999), but the divorce *rate* has remained stable at just around 3.5 percent per 1,000 people (Centers for Disease Control and Prevention, 2009; Munson & Sutton, 2004). More than 1.5 million children are involved in divorces each year (NIMH, 2002).

Adjusting to Divorce Divorce is stressful for children. First there is the stress of marital conflict and then of parental separation and the departure of one parent, usually the father. Children may not fully understand what is happening. Divorce is, of course, stressful for the parents as well and may negatively affect their parenting. The family's standard of living is likely to drop; and, if a parent moves away, a child's relationship with the noncustodial parent may suffer (Kelly & Emery, 2003). A divorced parent's remarriage can increase the stress on children, renewing feelings of loss (Ahrons & Tanner, 2003; Amato, 2003).

Children's emotional or behavioral problems may reflect the level of parental conflict *before* the divorce (Amato, 2005). In a longitudinal study of almost 11,000 Canadian children, those whose parents later divorced showed more anxiety, depression, or antisocial behavior than those whose parents stayed married (Strohschein, 2005). If predivorce parental discord is chronic, overt, or destructive, children may be as well or better off after a divorce (Amato, 2003, 2005; Amato & Booth, 1997).

A child's adjustment to divorce may depend in part on the child's age or maturity, gender, temperament, and psychosocial adjustment before the divorce. Younger children tend to be more anxious about divorce, have less realistic perceptions of what caused it, and are more likely to blame themselves. However, they may adapt more quickly than older children, who better understand what is going on. School-age children are sensitive to parental pressures and loyalty conflicts and, like younger children, may fear abandonment and rejection. Boys find it harder to adjust than girls do and are more susceptible to social and conduct problems (Amato, 2005; Hetherington, Bridges, & Insabella, 1998; Hines, 1997; Parke & Buriel, 1998).

Custody, Visitation, and Co-Parenting Different types of custody arrangements exist when parents divorce. In most divorce cases, the mother gets custody, sometimes referred to as *maternal custody*, though *paternal custody* is a growing trend, with the father being the custodial parent. *Joint custody*, shared by both parents, is another arrangement. When parents have *joint legal custody*, they share the right and responsibility to make decisions regarding the child's welfare. When they have *joint physical custody* (which is less common), the child lives part-time with each parent.

In the cases of one parent having custody, children do better after divorce if the custodial parent is warm, supportive, and authoritative; monitors the child's activities; and holds age-appropriate expectations. In addition, conflict between the divorced parents needs to be minimal, and the nonresident parent should maintain close contact and involvement (Ahrons & Tanner, 2003; Kelly & Emery, 2003). Children living with divorced mothers adjust better when the father pays child support, which may indicate the tie between father and child and may also indicate the level of cooperation between the ex-spouses (Amato & Gilbreth, 1999; Kelly & Emery, 2003). Many children of divorce say that losing contact with a father is one of the most painful results of divorce (Fabricius, 2003). However, frequency of contact with the father is not as important as the quality of the father-child relationship and the level of parental conflict. Children who are close to their nonresident fathers and whose fathers are authoritative parents tend to do better in school and are less likely to have behavior problems (Amato & Gilbreth, 1999; Kelly & Emery, 2003).

Joint custody can be advantageous for the child if the parents can cooperate, as both parents can continue to be closely involved with the child. An analysis of 33 studies found that children in either legal or physical joint custody were better adjusted and had higher self-esteem and better family relationships than children in sole custody arrangements. In fact, the joint custody children were as well-adjusted as children in nondivorced families (Bauserman, 2002). It is likely, though, that couples who choose joint custody are those that have less conflict.

In a national sample of 354 divorced families, *cooperative parenting*—active consultation between a mother and a nonresident father on parenting decisions—led to more frequent contact between father and child, and this, in turn, led to better father-child relationships and more responsive fathering (Sobolewski & King, 2005). Unfortunately, cooperative parenting is not the norm (Amato, 2005). Parent education programs that teach separated or divorced couples how to prevent or deal with conflict, keep lines of communication open, develop an effective co-parenting relationship, and help children adjust to divorce have been introduced in many courts with measurable success (Wolchik et al., 2002).

Long-Term Effects Most children of divorce adjust reasonably well. Children with divorced parents tend to have lower academic achievement and more problems with social relationships, but most do not suffer long-term negative outcomes (Lansford, 2009). However, the timing of the divorce often affects the outcome. In one study, children who experienced their parents' divorce during elementary school were more likely to develop internalizing or externalizing problems, whereas children whose parents divorced later were more likely to suffer a drop in grades (Lansford et al., 2006). In another study, children who experienced parental divorce before age 16 tended to have emotional and educational problems, to initiate sexual activity early, and to be at risk for depression and suicidal thoughts (D'Onofrio et al., 2006). In adolescence, parental divorce increases the risk of antisocial behavior, difficulties with authority figures (Amato, 2003, 2005; Kelly & Emery, 2003), and dropping out of school (McLanahan & Sandefur, 1994).

The anxiety connected with parental divorce may surface as children enter adulthood and try to form intimate relationships of their own (Amato, 2003; Wallerstein, Lewis, & Blakeslee, 2000). Having experienced their parents' divorce, some young adults are afraid of making commitments that might end in disappointment (Glenn & Marquardt, 2001; Wallerstein & Corbin, 1999). According to some research, 25 percent of children of divorce reach adulthood with serious social, emotional, or psychological problems, compared with 10 percent of children whose parents stay together (Hetherington & Kelly, 2002). As adults, the children of divorce tend to have lower SES, poorer psychological well-being, and a greater chance of having a birth outside marriage. Their marriages tend to be less satisfying and are more likely to end in divorce

(Amato, 2005). However, much depends on how young people resolve and interpret the experience of parental divorce. Some who saw a high degree of conflict between their parents are able to learn from that negative example and to form highly intimate relationships themselves (Shulman, Scharf, Lumer, & Maurer, 2001).

Living in a One-Parent Family One-parent families result from divorce or separation, unwed parenthood, or death. With rising rates of divorce and of parenthood outside of marriage, the percentage of single-parent families in the United States has more than doubled since 1970 (U.S. Census Bureau, 2008a). More than half of all black children live with a single parent, as compared with 19 percent of non-Hispanic white children and 26 percent of Hispanic children (Kreider & Fields, 2005).

Although children are far more likely to live with a single mother than with a single father, the number of father-only families has more than quadrupled since 1970, apparently due largely to the increase in paternal custody after divorce (Fields, 2004). Four percent of children do not live with either parent; a majority of these children live with their grandparents (see Figure 14.2).

Children in single-parent families do fairly well overall but tend to lag socially and educationally behind peers in two-parent families. This is true of both children born out of wedlock and those whose parents are divorced. What explains these findings? Children living with a single parent are exposed to many stressful experiences. For one thing, they tend to be economically disadvantaged. Because their parents are struggling to maintain the household, these children often receive poorer parenting. Losing contact with a parent or observing conflict and hostility between parents can produce emotional insecurity. Children living with married parents tend to have more daily interaction with their parents, are read to more often, progress more steadily in school, and participate more in extracurricular activities than children living with a single parent (Lugaila, 2003).

However, negative outcomes for children in one-parent families are far from inevitable. The child's age and level of development, the family's financial circumstances, whether there are frequent moves, and a nonresident father's involvement make a difference (Amato, 2005; Seltzer, 2000). In a longitudinal study of 1,500 white, black, and Hispanic families with 6- and 7-year-old children, the mother's educational and ability level and, to a lesser extent, family income and the quality of the home environment accounted for any negative effects of single parenting on academic performance and behavior (Ricciuti, 1999, 2004).

Because single parents often lack the resources needed for good parenting, potential risks to children in these families might be reduced or eliminated through increased access to economic, social, educational, and parenting support. In international math and science tests, the achievement gap between third and fourth graders living in single-parent households and those living with two biological parents was greater for U.S. children than for any other country except New Zealand. Children of single parents did better in countries with supportive family policies such as child and family allowances, tax benefits to single parents, maternity leave, and released time from work (Pong, Dronkers, & Hampden-Thompson, 2003).

Living in a Cohabiting Family Cohabiting families are similar in many ways to married families, but the parents tend to be more disadvantaged. They typically have less income and education, report poorer relationships, and have more mental health problems. Thus, it is not surprising that data from a national survey of almost 36,000 U.S. families showed worse emotional, behavioral, and academic outcomes for 6- to 11-year-old children living with cohabiting biological parents than for those living with married biological parents. The difference in outcomes was due largely to differences in economic resources, parental well-being, and parenting effectiveness (S. L. Brown, 2004).

Living in a Stepfamily Most divorced parents eventually remarry, and many single mothers marry men who were not the father of their children (Amato, 2005), thus forming step-, or blended, families. Some 15 percent of U.S. children live in blended families (Kreider & Fields, 2005).

Adjusting to a new stepparent may be stressful. A child's loyalties to an absent or dead parent may interfere with forming ties to a stepparent (Amato, 2005). Many stepchildren maintain ties with their noncustodial parents. Noncustodial mothers tend to keep in touch more than do noncustodial fathers and offer more social support (Gunnoe & Hetherington, 2004).

Some studies have found that boys—who often have more trouble than girls in adjusting to divorce and living with a single mother—benefit from a stepfather. A girl, though, may find the new man in the house a threat to her independence and to her close relationship with her mother (Bray & Hetherington, 1993; Hetherington, 1987; Hetherington, Stanley-Hagan, & Anderson, 1989; Hetherington et al., 1998; Hines, 1997). In a longitudinal study of a nationally representative sample of U.S. adults, mothers who remarried or formed new cohabiting relationships tended to use gentler discipline than mothers who remained single, and their children reported better relationships with them. However, supervision was greater in stable single-mother families (Thomson, Mosley, Hanson, & McLanahan, 2001).

Research has shown that children living with homosexual parents are no more likely than other children to have social or psychological problems or to turn out to be homosexual themselves.

Living with Gay or Lesbian Parents An estimated 9 million U.S. children and adolescents have at least one gay or lesbian parent. Some gays and lesbians are raising children born of previous heterosexual relationships. Others conceive by artificial means, use surrogate mothers, or adopt children (Pawelski et al., 2006; Perrin & AAP Committee on Psychosocial Aspects of Child and Family Health, 2002).

A considerable body of research has examined the development of children of gays and lesbians, including physical and emotional health, intelligence, adjustment, sense of self, moral judgment, and social and sexual functioning, and has indicated no special concerns (Paige, 2005). There is no consistent difference between homosexual and heterosexual parents in emotional health or parenting skills and attitudes; and where there are differences, they tend to favor gay and lesbian parents (Brewaeys, Ponjaert, Van Hall, & Golombok, 1997; Meezan & Rauch, 2005; Pawelski et al., 2006; Perrin & AAP Committee on Psychosocial Aspects of Child and Family Health,

Those who cite benefits for heterosexual parenting are generally drawing conclusions that the research does not warrant. Specifically, they often compare two-parent families with single-parent families. The appropriate comparisons are between homosexual and heterosexual two-parent families. And, when this comparison is made, no negative effects are found.

Biblarz & Stacey, 2010

2002; Wainright, Russell, & Patterson, 2004). The American Psychiatric Association's official policy statement concludes that gay or lesbian parents usually have positive relationships with their children, and the children are no more likely than children raised by heterosexual parents to have emotional, social, academic, or psychological problems (Paige, 2005; Chan, Raboy, & Patterson, 1998; Gartrell, Deck, Rodas, Peyser, & Banks, 2005; Golombok et al., 2003; Meezan & Rauch, 2005; Mooney-Somers & Golombok, 2000; Wainright et al., 2004). Furthermore, children of gays and lesbians are no more likely to be homosexual or to be confused about their gender than are children of heterosexuals (Anderssen, Amlie, & Ytteroy, 2002; Golombok et al., 2003; Meezan & Rauch, 2005; Pawelski et al., 2006; Wainright et al., 2004).

Such findings have social policy implications for legal decisions on custody and visitation disputes, foster care, and adoptions. In the face of controversy over gay and

The 2010 comedy-drama *The Kids Are Alright* encompasses this view within the very title. In this film, a lesbian couple meets the sperm donor they used for their children. Although this introduces challenges into their lives, they, and the kids, ultimately persevere.

These Inuit boys in a northern Canadian fishing camp enjoy caring for a baby brother. Children in nonindustrialized societies tend to have regular responsibility for siblings.

checkpoint
can you . . .

▷ Compare the roles and responsibilities of siblings in industrialized and nonindustrialized countries?

▷ Discuss how siblings affect each other's development?

guidepost

3 How do relationships with peers change in middle childhood, and what factors influence popularity and aggressive behavior?

prejudice
Unfavorable attitude toward members of certain groups outside one's own, especially racial or ethnic groups.

societies helps the family carry on its work and provide for aging members. In industrialized societies, siblings tend to be fewer and farther apart in age, enabling parents to focus more resources and attention on each child (Cicirelli, 1994).

Two longitudinal studies in England and in Pennsylvania found that changes in sibling relationships were most likely to occur when one sibling was between ages 7 and 9. Both mothers and children often attributed these changes to outside friendships, which led to jealousy and competitiveness or loss of interest in and intimacy with the sibling (Dunn, 1996).

Sibling relations can be a laboratory for conflict resolution. Siblings are motivated to make up after quarrels because they know they will see each other every day. They learn that expressing anger does not end a relationship. Children are more apt to squabble with same-sex siblings; two brothers quarrel more than any other combination (Cicirelli, 1976, 1995).

Siblings influence each other, not only *directly*, through their own interactions, but also *indirectly* through their impact on each other's relationship with the parents. Parents' experience with an older sibling influences their expectations and treatment of a younger one (Brody, 2004). Conversely, behavior patterns a child establishes with parents tend to "spill over" into the child's behavior with siblings. In a study of 101 English families, when the parent-child relationship was warm and affectionate, siblings tended to have positive relationships as well. When the parent-child relationship was conflictual, sibling conflict was more likely (Pike, Coldwell, & Dunn, 2005).

The Child in the Peer Group

In middle childhood the peer group comes into its own. Groups form naturally among children who live near one another or go to school together and often consist of children of the same racial or ethnic origin and similar socioeconomic status. Children who play together are usually close in age and of the same sex (Hartup, 1992; Pellegrini, Kato, Blatchford, & Baines, 2002).

How does the peer group influence children? What determines their acceptance by peers and their ability to make friends?

POSITIVE AND NEGATIVE EFFECTS OF PEER RELATIONS

Children benefit from doing things with peers. They develop skills needed for sociability and intimacy, and they gain a sense of belonging. They are motivated to achieve, and they attain a sense of identity. They learn leadership and communication skills, roles, and rules.

As children begin to move away from parental influence, the peer group opens new perspectives and frees them to make independent judgments. In comparing themselves with others their age, children can gauge their abilities more realistically and gain a clearer sense of self-efficacy. The peer group helps children learn how to get along in society—how to adjust their needs and desires to those of others, when to yield, and when to stand firm. The peer group offers emotional security. It is reassuring for children to find out that they are not alone in harboring thoughts that might offend an adult.

On the negative side, peer groups may reinforce **prejudice**, unfavorable attitudes toward "outsiders," especially members of certain racial or ethnic groups. Children tend to show biases toward children like themselves, but these biases, except for a preference for children of the same sex, diminish with age and cognitive development (Powlishta,

Serbin, Doyle, & White, 1994). Prejudice and discrimination can do real damage. In a 5-year longitudinal study of 714 African American 10- to 12-year-olds, those who saw themselves as targets of discrimination tended to show symptoms of depression or conduct problems during the next 5 years (Brody et al., 2006). In a study of 253 English children, prejudice against refugees was reduced by *extended contact:* reading them stories about close friendships between English children and refugee children, followed by group discussions (Cameron, Rutland, Brown, & Douch, 2006).

By the age of 10, children from both the United States and Korea think it's okay to dislike another child because he or she is aggressive or shy, but it's less acceptable to dislike another child because of his or her race or gender, characteristics that cannot change.

Park & Killen, 2010

The peer group also can foster antisocial tendencies. Preadolescent children are especially susceptible to pressure to conform. It is usually in the company of peers that some children shoplift and begin to use drugs (Dishion & Tipsord, 2011; Hartup, 1992). Of course, some degree of conformity to group standards is healthy. It is unhealthy when it becomes destructive or prompts young people to act against their better judgment.

what's your view?

How can parents and schools reduce racial, religious, and ethnic prejudice?

GENDER DIFFERENCES IN PEER-GROUP RELATIONSHIPS

Boys' and girls' peer groups engage in different types of activities. Groups of boys more consistently pursue gender-typed activities. They play in large groups with well-defined leadership hierarchies and engage in more competitive and rough-and-tumble play. Girls have more intimate conversations characterized by prosocial interactions and shared confidences (Rose & Rudolph, 2006). Also, girls are more likely than boys to engage in cross-gender activities, such as team sports (McHale, Kim, Whiteman, & Crouter, 2004).

Boys are apt to receive less emotional support from their friends than girls do. Girls tend to seek social connections and are more sensitive to others' distress. They are more likely than boys to worry about their relationships, to express emotions, and to seek emotional support (Rose & Rudolph, 2006).

Why do children segregate themselves by sex and engage in such different activities? One obvious reason is that males and females differ in body size, strength, and energy. Boys need more space and more physical exercise to build physical fitness (Pellegrini & Archer, 2005). Same-sex peer groups help children learn gender-appropriate behaviors and incorporate gender roles into their self-concept. In a 2-year study of 106 ethnically diverse third through seventh graders, a sense of being typical of one's gender and being content with that gender contributed to self-esteem and well-being, whereas feeling pressure—from parents, peers, or oneself—to conform to gender stereotypes lessened well-being (Yunger, Carver, & Perry, 2004).

checkpoint can you . . .

▷ Tell what characteristics members of a peer group tend to have in common?

▷ Identify positive and negative effects of peer groups?

▷ Discuss gender differences in peer-group activities and relationships?

POPULARITY

Humans are social creatures, and as such, our relationships have a profound effect on our outcomes. Early in life, this need is expressed primarily within the context of attachment relationships with parents. As children age, however, peer relationships become increasingly important. And, given that children most often interact with each other within the context of school and in groups, researchers have developed means by which to assess their standing in the social group.

Much of research in child development depends on asking children the right questions in the right way. If a researcher asked schoolchildren to tell her the social ranking of all the children in a classroom, she would most likely be met with a blank stare. However, children can easily say who they like to play with, who they like the most, or who they think other kids like the most. This is known as a *positive nomination.*

Children who squint are invited to fewer birthday parties.

Mojon-Azzi, Kunz, & Mojon, 2010

TABLE 14.2 Selman's Stages of Friendship

Stage	Description	Example
Stage 0: Momentary playmateship (ages 3 to 7)	On this *undifferentiated* level of friendship, children are egocentric and have trouble considering another person's point of view; they tend to think only about what they want from a relationship. Most very young children define their friends in terms of physical closeness and value them for material or physical attributes.	"She lives on my street" or "He has the Power Rangers."
Stage 1: One-way assistance (ages 4 to 9)	On this *unilateral* level, a "good friend" does what the child wants the friend to do.	"She's not my friend anymore because she wouldn't go with me when I wanted her to" or "He's my friend because he always says yes when I want to borrow his eraser."
Stage 2: Two-way fair-weather cooperation (ages 6 to 12)	This *reciprocal* level overlaps stage 1. It involves give-and-take but still serves many separate self-interests, rather than the common interests of the two friends.	"We are friends; we do things for each other" or "A friend is someone who plays with you when you don't have anybody else to play with."
Stage 3: Intimate, mutually shared relationships (ages 9 to 15)	On this *mutual* level, children view a friendship as having a life of its own. It is an ongoing, systematic, committed relationship that incorporates more than doing things for each other. Friends often become possessive and demand exclusivity.	"It takes a long time to make a close friend, so you really feel bad if you find out that your friend is trying to make other friends too."
Stage 4: Autonomous interdependence (beginning at age 12)	In this *interdependent* stage, children respect friends' needs for both dependency and autonomy.	"A good friendship is a real commitment, a risk you have to take; you have to support and trust and give, but you have to be able to let go too."

Source: Selman, 1980; Selman & Selman, 1979.

instrumental aggression
Aggressive behavior used as a means of achieving a goal.

hostile aggression
Aggressive behavior intended to hurt another person.

else's place, can understand another person's motives, and can find positive ways of asserting themselves. **Instrumental aggression** (aggression aimed at achieving an objective), the hallmark of the preschool period, becomes much less common (Coie & Dodge, 1998; Dodge et al., 2006). However, as aggression declines overall, **hostile aggression**—action intended to hurt another person—proportionately increases (Coie & Dodge, 1998; Dodge et al., 2006), often taking verbal rather than physical form (Pellegrini & Archer, 2005). Boys continue to engage in more *direct aggression*, and girls are increasingly more likely to engage in *social* or *indirect aggression*. A review of 148 studies of child and adolescent aggressive behavior, however, revealed neglible gender differences in levels of social or indirect aggression between boys and girls. These findings contradict the common portrayal of indirect agression as a predominantly female form of aggression (Card, Stucky, Sawalani, & Little, 2008).

A small minority of children do not learn to control physical aggression (Coie & Dodge, 1998). These children tend to have social and psychological problems, but it is not clear whether aggression causes these problems or is a response to them, or both (Crick & Grotpeter, 1995). Direct aggression has been linked to poor peer relations and low prosocial behavior (Card et al., 2008). Highly aggressive children often egg each other on to antisocial acts. Thus school-age boys who are physically aggressive may become juvenile delinquents in adolescence (Broidy et al., 2003).

Although aggressors tend to be personally disliked, physically aggressive boys and some relationally aggressive girls (those who, for example, talk behind another girl's back or exclude her socially) are perceived as among the most popular in the classroom (Cillessen & Mayeux, 2004; Rodkin, Farmer, Pearl, & Van Acker, 2000). In a study of peer-rejected fourth graders, aggressive boys tended to gain in social status by the end of fifth grade, suggesting that behavior shunned by younger children may be seen as cool or glamorous by preadolescents (Sandstrom & Coie, 1999). In a longitudinal study of a multiethnic group of 905 urban fifth through ninth graders, physical aggression became less disapproved as children moved into adolescence, and relational aggression was increasingly reinforced by high status among peers (Cillessen & Mayeux, 2004).

Types of Aggression and Social Information Processing What makes children act aggressively? One answer may lie in the way they process social information: what features of the social environment they pay attention to and how they interpret what they perceive (Crick & Dodge, 1994, 1996).

Instrumental, or *proactive*, aggressors view force and coercion as effective ways to get what they want. They act deliberately, not out of anger. In social learning terms, they are aggressive because they expect to be rewarded; and when they are rewarded, their belief in the effectiveness of aggression is reinforced (Crick & Dodge, 1996). For example, such a child might learn that in order to force another child to trade lunch items with him, he can threaten to hit the other child. If that strategy works, then the child has been reinforced for his aggressive acts, and his belief in aggression is confirmed. Compare this to a child who, while standing in line at lunch, is accidentally pushed by another child and pushes back angrily, assuming the bump was on purpose. This type of aggression is known as *hostile*, or *reactive*, aggression. All children might sometimes make this mistake, but some children habitually assume the worst of others in situations such as these. In other words, they have a **hostile attributional bias** that leads them to quickly conclude, in ambiguous situations, that others were acting with ill intent. They are likely to strike out in retaliation or self-defense. Generally, other children then respond to this hostility with aggression, thereby confirming the original hostile attributional bias and strengthening it (Crick & Dodge, 1996; de Castro, Veerman, Koops, Bosch, & Monshouwer, 2002; Waldman, 1996).

Children who seek dominance and control may react aggressively to threats to their status, which they may attribute to hostility (de Castro et al., 2002; Erdley Cain, Loomis, Dumas-Hines, & Dweck, 1997). Being a boy, having a reactive temperament, parental separation, early onset of motherhood, and controlling parenting have all been shown to contribute to physical aggression in 6- to 12-year-olds (Joussemet et al., 2008). Rejected children and those exposed to harsh parenting also tend to have a hostile attribution bias (Coie & Dodge, 1998; Masten & Coatsworth, 1998; Weiss, Dodge, Bates, & Pettit, 1992). Since people often do become hostile toward someone who acts aggressively toward them, a hostile bias may set in motion a cycle of aggression (de Castro et al., 2002). Hostile attribution bias becomes more common between ages 6 and 12 (Aber, Brown, & Jones, 2003).

Aggressors need to alter the way they process social information so that they do not interpret aggression as either useful or justified. Adults can help children curb aggression by teaching them how to recognize when they are getting angry and how to control their anger. In a New York City school study, children exposed to a conflict resolution curriculum that involved discussions and group role-playing showed less hostile attribution bias, less aggression, fewer behavior problems, and more effective responses to social situations than children who did not participate in the program (Aber et al., 2003).

Does Media Violence Stimulate Aggression? As television, movies, video games, cell phones, and computers take on larger roles in children's daily lives, it is critical to understand the impact mass media has on children's behavior. Children spend more time on entertainment media than on any other activity besides school and sleeping. On average, children spend about 4 hours a day in front of a television or computer screen—some much more than that (Anderson et al., 2003).

hostile attribution bias Tendency for individuals to perceive others as trying to hurt them and to strike out in retaliation or self-defense.

Violence is prevalent in U.S. media. About 6 out of 10 television programs portray violence, usually glamorized, glorified, or trivialized (Yokota & Thompson, 2000). In addition the 24-hour news stations provide constant, repetitive coverage of natural disasters and violent acts. Music videos disproportionately feature violence against women and blacks. The motion picture, music, and video game industries aggressively market violent, adult-rated products to children (AAP Committee on Public Education, 2001). In a recent study of U.S. children, 40 movies that were rated R for violence were seen by a median of 12.5 percent of an estimated 22 million children age 10 to 14. The most popular movie, *Scary Movie*, was seen by more than 10 million children (Worth et al., 2008).

Because of the significant amount of time that children spend interacting with media, the images they see can become primary role models and sources of information about how people behave. Evidence from research conducted over the past 50 years on exposure to violence on TV, movies, and video games supports a *causal* relationship between media violence and violent behavior on the viewer's part (Huesmann, 2007). Although the strongest single correlate of violent behavior is previous exposure to violence (AAP Committee on Public Education, 2001; Anderson, Berkowitz, et al., 2003; Anderson, Huston, Schmitt, Linebarger, & Wright, 2001; Huesmann, Moise-Titus, Podolski, & Eron, 2003), the effect of exposure to violence via mass media is significant (Figure 14.3).

How might media violence lead to long-term aggressiveness? Longitudinal studies have demonstrated that children's exposure to violent media seems to increase their risk for long-term effects based on observational learning, desensitization, and enactive learning that occur automatically in human children (Huesmann, 2007). Children's beliefs are influenced by their observation of behavior. Media provides visceral thrills without showing the human cost and may lead children to view aggression as acceptable. Children who see characters use violence to achieve their goals might conclude that force is an effective way to resolve conflicts. Moreover, repeated exposure can desensitize children.

What can and should be done to reduce children's exposure to violent television programs?

FIGURE 14.3

Effects of Threats to Public Health

The effect of media violence is the same as or greater than the effect of many other recognized threats to public health.

Source: Bushman & Huesmann, 2001.

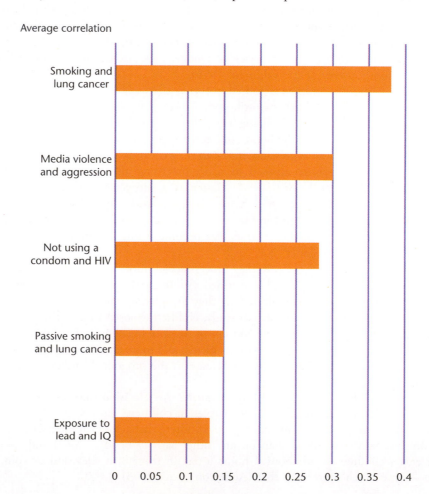

Average correlation

Negative reactions to violent scenes have been shown to decline in intensity with repeated exposure (Huesmann & Kirwil, 2007). And, the more realistically violence is portrayed, the more likely it is to be accepted (AAP Committee on Public Education, 2001; Anderson, Berkowitz, et al., 2003).

What processes might underlie these effects? Classic social learning research suggests that children imitate filmed models even more than live ones (Bandura et al., 1963). The influence is stronger if the child believes the violence on the screen is real, identifies with the violent character, finds that character attractive, and watches without parental supervision or intervention (Anderson, Berkowitz, et al., 2003; Coie & Dodge, 1998). Highly aggressive children are more strongly affected by media violence than are less aggressive children (Anderson, Berkowitz, et al., 2003). Most theorists believe that video games can result in similar processes (C. Anderson, 2000), especially as video game players are generally positively reinforced for onscreen violent action (Huesmann, 2007).

While the majority of researchers endorse the link between viewing violence and aggression, there are those that disagree. It may be that the certainty in claims are in part the result of adherence to the standard narrative on media influences and aggression in children (Ferguson, 2013). The link between media violence and aggression may have been overstated. For example, some researchers argue that methodological flaws such as a failure to consider confounding variables, difficulty generalizing from laboratory studies of aggression to real-world aggressive acts, and inappropriate statistical modeling call into question many of the earlier assertions made in this particular domain (Ferguson & Savage, 2012). In support of this assertion is data indicating that youth violence has declined dramatically, while exposure to violent media has remained stable (Ferguson, 2013).

Bullies and Victims Aggression becomes **bullying** when it is deliberately, persistently directed against a particular target: a victim. Bullying can be physical (hitting, punching, kicking, or damaging or taking of personal belongings), verbal (name-calling or threatening), or relational or emotional (isolating and gossiping, often behind the victim's back) (Berger, 2007; Veenstra et al., 2005). Bullying can be *proactive*—done to show dominance, bolster power, or win admiration—or *reactive*, responding to a real or imagined attack. *Cyberbullying*—posting negative comments or derogatory photos of the victim on a Web site—has become increasingly common (Berger, 2007). The increase in use of cell phones, text messaging, e-mail, and chat rooms has opened new venues for bullies that provide access to victims without the protection of family and community (Huesmann, 2007).

Some 24 percent of U.S. primary schools, 42 percent of middle schools, and 21 percent of high schools report student bullying at school at least once a week (Guerino, Hurwitz, Noonan, & Kaffenberger, 2006). Bullying is a problem in other industrialized countries as well (Hara, 2002; Kanetsuna & Smith, 2002; Ruiz & Tanaka, 2001). In a survey of 50,000 children in 34 European countries, almost one-third of the children said they were bullies, victims, or both (Currie et al., 2004). In Japan and Korea, school bullying has been associated with a growing wave of student suicide and suicidal thoughts and behavior (Kim, Koh, & Leventhal, 2005; Rios-Ellis, Bellamy, & Shoji, 2000).

Bullying may reflect a genetic tendency toward aggressiveness combined with environmental influences, such as coercive parents and antisocial friends (Berger, 2007). Most bullies are boys who tend to victimize other boys; female bullies tend to target other girls (Berger, 2007; Pellegrini & Long, 2002; Veenstra et al., 2005). Male bullies tend to use overt, physical aggression; female bullies may use relational aggression (Boulton, 1995; Nansel et al., 2001). Patterns of bullying and victimization may become established as early as kindergarten; as tentative peer groups form, aggressors soon get to know which children make the easiest targets. Physical bullying declines with age, but other forms of bullying increase, especially at ages 11 to 15. Whereas younger children reject an aggressive child, by early adolescence bullies are often dominant, respected, feared, and even liked (Berger, 2007).

Unlike the pattern for bullying, the likelihood of *being* bullied decreases steadily. As children get older, most of them may learn how to discourage bullying, leaving a smaller

bullying
Aggression deliberately and persistently directed against a particular target, or victim, typically one who is weak, vulnerable, and defenseless.

One innovative program that has shown some success in reducing negative aggression involves combating bullying with babies. In Canada's Roots of Empathy program, 2- to 4-month old babies are brought into classrooms, and children are encouraged to puzzle out what the baby is feeling, take the baby's point of view, and monitor the baby's achievements. Presumably, this practice in empathizing and perspective-taking has led to declines in negative behaviors.

Bornstein, 2010; Schonert-Reichl & Hymel, n.d.

Bullying tends to peak in middle grades. Boys are more likely to use overt aggression; girls, relational or social aggression.

pool of available victims (Pellegrini & Long, 2002; P. K. Smith & Levan, 1995). Most victims are small, passive, weak, and submissive and may blame themselves for being bullied. Other victims are provocative; they goad their attackers, and they may even attack other children themselves (Berger, 2007; Veenstra et al., 2005).

Risk factors for victimization seem to be similar across cultures (Schwartz, Chang, & Farver, 2001). Victims do not fit in. They tend to be anxious, depressed, cautious, quiet, and submissive and to cry easily, or to be argumentative and provocative (Hodges, Boivin, Vitaro, & Bukowski, 1999; Olweus, 1995; Veenstra et al., 2005). They have few friends and may live in harsh, punitive family environments (Nansel et al., 2001; Schwartz, Dodge, Pettit, Bates, & Conduct Problems Prevention Research Group, 2000). Victims are apt to have low self-esteem, though it is not clear whether low self-esteem leads to or follows from victimization (Boulton & Smith, 1994; Olweus, 1995). In a study of 5,749 Canadian children, those who were overweight were most likely to become either victims or bullies (Janssen, Craig, Boyce, & Pickett, 2004).

Bullying, especially emotional bullying, is harmful to both bullies and victims—and can even be fatal (Berger, 2007). Bullies are at increased risk of delinquency, crime, or alcohol abuse. In the wave of school shootings since 1994, the perpetrators often had been victims of bullying (Anderson, Kaufman, et al., 2001). Victims of chronic bullying tend to develop behavior problems. They may become more aggressive themselves or may become depressed (Schwartz, McFadyen-Ketchum, Dodge, Pettit, & Bates, 1998; Veenstra et al., 2005). Furthermore, frequent bullying affects the school atmosphere, leading to widespread underachievement, alienation from school, stomachaches and headaches, reluctance to go to school, and frequent absences (Berger, 2007).

The U.S. Department of Health and Human Services has promoted Steps to Respect, a program for grades 3 to 6 that aims to (1) increase staff awareness and responsiveness to bullying, (2) teach students social and emotional skills, and (3) foster socially responsible beliefs. A randomized controlled study of 1,023 third to sixth graders found a reduction in playground bullying and argumentative behavior and an increase in harmonious interactions among children who participated in the program, as well as less bystander incitement to bullying (Frey et al., 2005). However, analysis of research done on a broad variety of these types of intervention programs has indicated that while the programs may enhance students social competence and self-esteem, the impact on actual bullying behavior is minimal (Merrell, Gueldner, Ross, & Isava, 2008).

checkpoint
can you . . .

▷ Tell how aggression changes during middle childhood and how social information processing and televised violence can contribute to it?

▷ Discuss gender differences in aggression in school-age children?

▷ Tell how patterns of bullying and victimization become established and change?

▷ List risk factors for bullying and victimization?

guidepost
4

How do children respond to the stresses of modern life?

Stress and Resilience

Stressful events are part of childhood, and most children learn to cope with them. Stress that becomes overwhelming, however, can lead to psychological problems. Severe stressors, such as war or child abuse, may have long-term effects on physical and psychological well-being. Yet some children show remarkable resilience in surmounting such ordeals.

STRESSES OF MODERN LIFE

The child psychologist David Elkind (1981, 1986, 1997, 1998) has called today's child the "hurried child." He warns that the pressures of modern life are forcing children to grow up too soon and are making their childhood too stressful. Today's children are expected to succeed in school, to compete in sports, and to meet parents' emotional needs. Children are exposed to many adult problems on television and in real life before they have mastered the problems of childhood. They know about sex and violence, and they often must shoulder adult responsibilities. Many children move frequently and have to change schools and leave old friends. The tightly scheduled pace of life also can be stressful. Yet children are not small adults. They feel and think as children, and they need the years of childhood for healthy development.

Given how much stress children are exposed to, it should not be surprising that anxiety in childhood has increased greatly (Twenge, 2000). Fears of danger and death are the most consistent fears of children at all ages (Gullone, 2000; Silverman, La Greca, & Wasserstein, 1995). This intense anxiety about safety may reflect the high rates of crime and violence in the larger society—including the presence of street gangs and violence in schools (DeVoe et al., 2004).

Findings about children's fears have been corroborated in a wide range of developed and developing societies. Poor children—who may see their environment as threatening—tend to be more fearful than children of higher socioeconomic status (Gullone, 2000; Ollendick, Yang, King, Dong, & Akande, 1996). Children who grow up constantly surrounded by violence often have trouble concentrating and sleeping. Some become aggressive, and some come to take brutality for granted. Many do not allow themselves to become attached to other people for fear of more hurt and loss (Garbarino, Dubrow, Kostelny, & Pardo, 1992).

Children are more susceptible than adults to psychological harm from a traumatic event such as war or terrorism, and their reactions vary with age (Wexler, Branski, & Kerem, 2006; Table 14.3). Younger children, who do not understand why the event occurred, tend to focus on the consequences. Older children are more aware of, and worried about, the underlying forces that caused the event (Hagan et al., 2005).

TABLE 14.3 Children's Age-Related Reactions to Trauma	
Age	**Typical Reactions**
Age 5 or less	Fear of separation from parent Crying, whimpering, screaming, trembling Immobility or aimless motion Frightened facial expressions Excessive clinging Regressive behaviors (thumb sucking, bed-wetting, fear of dark)
Ages 6 to 11	Extreme withdrawal Disruptive behavior Inability to pay attention Stomachaches or other symptoms with no physical basis Declining school performance, refusal to go to school Depression, anxiety, guilt, irritability, or emotional numbing Regressive behavior (nightmares, sleep problems, irrational fears, outbursts of anger or fighting)
Ages 12 to 17	Flashbacks, nightmares Emotional numbing, confusion Avoidance of reminders of the traumatic event Revenge fantasies Withdrawal, isolation Substance abuse Problems with peers, antisocial behavior Physical complaints School avoidance, academic decline Sleep disturbances Depression, suicidal thoughts

Source: NIMH, 2001a.

Parents who are burned out at work are more likely to have kids who report they are burned out at school.

Salmela-Aro, Tynkkynen, & Vuori, 2010

Paraplush, a European toy company, has released a line of plush animals illustrating common psychological disorders. Their tagline is "Psychiatry for Abused Toys." The animals include a hallucinating snake, a depressed turtle, a paranoid crocodile, and others. Do you think this approach helps destigmatize mental disorders, or does it promote negative stereotypes and inaccurate perceptions?

the everyday world

TALKING TO CHILDREN ABOUT TERRORISM AND WAR

In today's world, caring adults are faced with the challenge of explaining violence, terrorism, and war to children. Although difficult, these conversations are extremely important. They give parents an opportunity to help their children feel more secure and better understand the world in which they live. Here are some pointers from the American Academy of Child & Adolescent Psychiatry:

1. *Listen to children.* Create a time and place for children to ask questions and help them express themselves. Sometimes children lack the cognitive ability to discuss their feelings and are more comfortable drawing pictures or playing with toys rather than talking.
2. *Answer their questions.* When you answer tough questions about violence, be honest. Use words the child can understand, and try not to overload him or her with too much information. You may have to repeat yourself. Be consistent and reassuring.
3. *Provide support.* Children are most comfortable with structure and familiarity. Try to establish a predictable routine. Avoid exposure to violent images on TV and video games. Watch for physical signs of stress, such as trouble sleeping or separation anxiety, and seek professional help if symptoms are persistent and/or pronounced.

Many young children feel confused and anxious when faced with the realities of war and terrorism. By creating an open environment where children are free to ask questions and receive honest, consistent, and supportive messages about how to cope with violence, caring adults can reduce the likelihood of emotional difficulties.

Source: Adapted from American Academy of Child & Adolescent Psychiatry, 2003.

what's your view How might you respond to a 6-year-old who asked you about what happened on September 11, 2001?

The impact of a traumatic event is also influenced by the type of event, how much exposure children have to it, and how much they and their families and friends are personally affected. Human-caused disasters, such as terrorism and war, are much harder on children psychologically than natural disasters, such as earthquakes and floods. Exposure to graphic news coverage can worsen the effects (Wexler et al., 2006). Most children who watched news coverage of the September 11, 2001, terrorist attacks on New York and Washington, D.C., experienced profound stress, even if they were not directly affected (Walma van der Molen, 2004).

Children's responses to a traumatic event typically occur in two stages: *first,* fright, disbelief, denial, grief, and relief if their loved ones are unharmed; *second,* several days or weeks later, developmental regression and signs of emotional distress—anxiety, fear, withdrawal, sleep disturbances, pessimism about the future, or play related to themes of the event. If symptoms last for more than 1 month, the child should receive counseling (Hagan et al., 2005).

For some children, the effects of a traumatic event may remain for years. Children who have been exposed to war or terrorism have high rates of depression, disruptive behaviors, and unexplained, recurring physical symptoms such as stomach distress and headaches. If they and their household have been personally affected, physical pain and loss of home and family may compound the psychological effects (Wexler et al., 2006). Parents' responses to a violent event or disaster and the way they talk with a child about it strongly influence the child's ability to recover (NIMH, 2001a). Providing parents with strategies for addressing terrorism-related news can reduce threat perceptions and lower anxiety related to potential terrorism attacks (Comer, Furr, Beidas, Weiner, & Kendall, 2008; Box 14.2).

COPING WITH STRESS: THE RESILIENT CHILD

Liz Murray grew up in abject poverty in a small apartment in the Bronx. Both her parents were drug addicts, and her childhood was marked by poverty, hunger, and

TABLE 14.4	Characteristics of Resilient Children and Adolescents
Source	**Characteristic**
Individual	Good Intellectual functioning
	Appealing, sociable, easygoing disposition
	Self-efficacy, self-confidence, high self-esteem
	Talents
	Faith
Family	Close relationship to caring parent figure
	Authoritative parenting: warmth, structure, high expectations
	Socioeconomic advantages
	Connections to extended supportive family networks
Extrafamilial context	Bonds to prosocial adults outside the family
	Connections to prosocial organizations
	Attending effective schools

Source: Masten & Coatsworth, 1998, p. 212.

chaos. She was teased in school for her dirty clothing, placed in a girls' home for cutting school, and at age 15, ran away from home and spent her nights sleeping on the subways and eating from trash bins. Most children, in this type of situation, would spiral down into a life of further misery. But Liz did not. She was able to realize that education was her ticket to freedom and finished high school while living on the streets. She won a *New York Times* scholarship and was eventually admitted to Harvard. In 2011, she became an author when she published a memoir of her brief but tumultuous life on the streets.

Much of the early history of psychology was marked by investigations into the various risks that can pull a child into a negative developmental trajectory. However, psychologists have increasingly come to realize that there is also value in examining resilience. **Resilient children**, like Liz Murray, are those who weather circumstances that might blight others, who maintain their composure and competence under challenge or threat, or who bounce back from traumatic events. These children do not necessarily possess extraordinary qualities. They simply manage, despite adverse circumstances, to hold on to the basic systems and resources that promote positive development in normal children (Masten, 2001; Table 14.4). The two most important **protective factors** that help children and adolescents overcome stress and contribute to resilience are *good family relationships* and *cognitive functioning* (Masten & Coatsworth, 1998).

Resilient children are likely to have good relationships and strong bonds with at least one supportive parent (Pettit Bates, & Dodge, 1997) or caregiver or other caring, competent adult (Masten & Coatsworth, 1998). Resilient children also tend to have high IQs and to be good problem solvers. Their superior information-processing skills may help them cope with adversity, protect themselves, regulate their behavior, and learn from experience. They may attract the interest of teachers, who can act as guides, confidants, or mentors (Masten & Coatsworth, 1998). They may even have protective genes, which may buffer the effects of an unfavorable environment (Caspi et al., 2002; Kim-Cohen, Moffitt, & Caspi, 2004).

Other frequently cited protective factors (Ackerman, Kogos, Youngstrom, Schoff, & Izard, 1999; Eisenberg et al., 2004; Eisenberg et al., 1997; Masten, Best, & Garmezy, 1990; Masten & Coatsworth, 1998; Werner, 1993) include the following:

- *The child's temperament or personality:* Resilient children are adaptable, friendly, well liked, independent, and sensitive to others. They are competent and have high self-esteem. They are creative, resourceful, independent, and pleasant to be with.

resilient children
Children who weather adverse circumstances, function well despite challenges or threats, or bounce back from traumatic events.

protective factors
Influences that reduce the impact of early stress and tend to predict positive outcomes.

what's **your view**

How can adults contribute to children's resilience? Give examples.

When under stress, they can regulate their emotions by shifting attention to something else.

- *Compensating experiences:* A supportive school environment or successful experiences in studies, sports, or music or with other children or adults can help make up for a destructive home life.

- *Reduced risk:* Children who have been exposed to only one of a number of risk factors for psychiatric disorder (such as parental discord, low social status, a disturbed mother, a criminal father, and experience in foster care or an institution) are often better able to overcome stress than children who have been exposed to more than one risk factor.

All this does not mean that bad things that happen in a child's life do not matter. In general, children with unfavorable backgrounds have more adjustment problems than children with more favorable backgrounds. Even some outwardly resilient children may suffer internal distress that may have long-term consequences (Masten & Coatsworth, 1998). Still, what is heartening about these findings is that negative childhood experiences do not necessarily determine the outcome of a person's life and that many children have the strength to rise above the most difficult circumstances.

checkpoint can you . . .

▷ Explain Elkind's concept of the "hurried chhiod"?

▷ Name the most common sources of stress, fear, and anxiety in children?

▷ Identify protective factors that contribute to resilience?

summary and key terms

guidepost ❶

The Developing Self

How do the self-concept and self-esteem change in middle childhood, and how do school-age children show emotional growth?

- The self-concept becomes more realistic during middle childhood, when children form representational systems.

- According to Erikson, the chief source of self-esteem is children's view of their productive competence. This virtue develops through resolution of the crisis of industry versus inferiority.

- Self-esteem is multidimensional.

- School-age children have internalized shame and pride and can better understand and control negative emotions.

- Empathy and prosocial behavior increase.

- Emotional growth is affected by parents' reactions to displays of negative emotions.

representational systems (394)

industry versus inferiority (395)

guidepost ❷

The Child in the Family

What are the effects of family atmosphere and family structure, and what part do siblings play in children's development?

- School-age children spend less time with parents and are less close to them than before, but relationships with parents continue to be important. Culture influences family relationships and roles.

- The family environment has two major components: family structure and family atmosphere. Family atmosphere includes both emotional tone and economic well-being.

- Development of coregulation may affect the way a family handles conflicts and discipline.

- The impact on the child of the mother's employment depends on many factors, including the mother's work and her feelings about it; whether she has a supportive partner; the family's socioeconomic status; and the kind of care the child receives.

- Parents living in persistent poverty may have trouble providing effective discipline and monitoring and emotional support.

- Many children today grow up in nontraditional family structures. Children tend to do better in traditional two-parent families than in divorced families, single-parent families, and stepfamilies. The structure of the family, however, is less important than its effects on family atmosphere.

- The amount of conflict in a marriage and the likelihood of conflict continuing after divorce may influence whether children are better off if the parents stay together.

- Children living with only one parent are at heightened risk of behavioral and academic problems, in part related to socioeconomic status.

- Boys tend to have more trouble than girls in adjusting to divorce and single-parent living but tend to adjust better to the mother's remarriage.

- Studies have found positive outcomes in children living with gay or lesbian parents.
- Adopted children are generally well adjusted, though they face special challenges.
- The roles and responsibilities of siblings in nonindustrialized societies are more structured than in industrialized societies.
- Siblings learn about conflict resolution from their relationships with each other. Relationships with parents affect sibling relationships.

internalizing behaviors (398)
externalizing behaviors (398)
coregulation (398)

The Child in the Peer Group

How do relationships with peers change in middle childhood, and what factors influence popularity and aggressive behavior?

- The peer group becomes more important in middle childhood. Peer groups generally consist of children who are similar in age, sex, ethnicity, and socioeconomic status and who live near one another or go to school together.
- The peer group helps children develop social skills, allows them to test and adopt values independent of parents, gives them a sense of belonging, and helps develop the self-concept. It also may encourage conformity and prejudice.
- Popularity influences self-esteem and future adjustment. Popular children tend to have good cognitive abilities and social skills. Behaviors that affect popularity may be derived from family relationships and cultural values.
- Intimacy and stability of friendships increase during middle childhood. Boys tend to have more friends, whereas girls tend to have closer friends.

- During middle childhood, aggression typically declines. Relational aggression becomes more common than overt aggression. Also, instrumental aggression generally gives way to hostile aggression, often with a hostile bias. Highly aggressive children tend to be unpopular, but this may change as children move into adolescence.
- Aggressiveness promoted by exposure to televised violence can extend into adult life.
- Middle childhood is a prime time for bullying; patterns may be established in kindergarten. Victims tend to be weak and submissive or argumentative and provocative and to have low self-esteem.

prejudice (408)
instrumental aggression (412)
hostile aggression (412)
hostile attribution bias (413)
bullying (415)

Stress and Resilience

How do children respond to the stresses of modern life?

- As a result of the pressures of modern life, many children experience stress. Children tend to worry about school, health, and personal safety.
- Resilient children are better able than others to withstand stress. Protective factors involve cognitive ability, family relationships, personality, degree of risk, and compensating experiences.

resilient children (419)
protective factors (419)

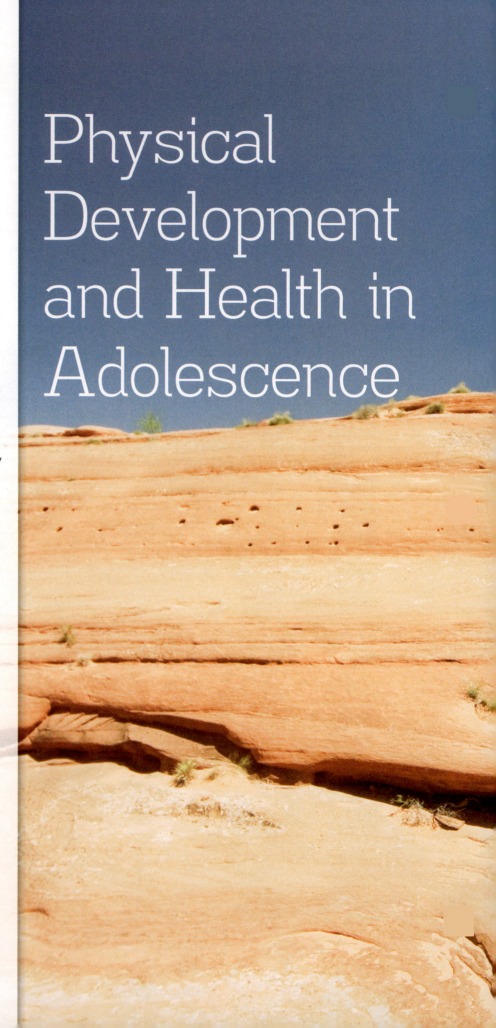

chapter

15

outline

outline

Adolescence: A Developmental Transition

Puberty: The End of Childhood

The Adolescent Brain

Physical and Mental Health

did you know?

did you know

▷ Adolescence was not recognized as a separate period of life in the Western world until the twentieth century?

▷ Boys and girls reach sexual maturity earlier in developed countries than in developing countries?

▷ More than 35 percent of U.S. adolescents have tried illicit drugs by the time they leave high school?

In this chapter we examine the physical transformations of adolescence and how they affect young people's feelings. We consider the impact of early or late maturation. We discuss health issues associated with this time of life, and we examine two serious problems: depression and teenage suicide.

Physical Development and Health in Adolescence

We know what we are but not what we may be.

Ophelia, *Hamlet*

1. What is adolescence, and what opportunities and risks does it entail?

2. What physical changes do adolescents experience, and how do these changes affect them psychologically?

3. What brain developments occur during adolescence, and how do they affect adolescent behavior?

4. What are some common health problems and health risks of adolescence, and how can they be prevented?

What is adolescence, and what opportunities and risks does it entail?

adolescence
Developmental transition between childhood and adulthood entailing major physical, cognitive, and psychosocial changes.

puberty
Process by which a person attains sexual maturity and the ability to reproduce.

connect

study smart

The Myth of Adolescence

Adolescence: A Developmental Transition

Rituals to mark a child's coming of age are common in many societies. For example, Apache tribes celebrate a girl's first menstruation with a 4-day ritual of sunrise-to-sunset chanting. In most modern societies, the passage from childhood to adulthood is marked, not by a single event, but by a long period known as **adolescence**—a developmental transition that involves physical, cognitive, emotional, and social changes and takes varying forms in different social, cultural, and economic settings (Larson & Wilson, 2004).

An important physical change is the onset of **puberty**, the process that leads to sexual maturity, or fertility—the ability to reproduce. Traditionally, adolescence and puberty were thought to begin at the same time, around age 13, but physicians in some Western societies now see pubertal changes before age 10. In this book, we define adolescence as encompassing the years between 11 and 19 or 20.

ADOLESCENCE AS A SOCIAL CONSTRUCTION

Adolescence is not a clearly defined physical or biological category—it is a social construction. In other words, the concept of adolescence is in a sense "made-up" by some cultures. In traditional and preindustrial cultures, children generally entered the adult world when they matured physically or when they began a vocational apprenticeship. In the Western world, adolescence was first recognized as a unique period in the life span in the twentieth century. Today, adolescence is recognized globally though it may take different forms in different cultures (Box 15.1).

In most parts of the world, adolescence lasts longer and is less clear-cut than in the past. There are a myriad of reasons for this social change. First, puberty generally begins earlier than it used to, which means that the period of adolescence begins at a younger age than in the past. In addition, as the world becomes more driven by technology and information, the amount of training that is required to be eligible for higher-paying occupations has increased. For example, in the United States, it used to be possible to graduate from high school and find a job that would allow a young person to live a middle-class life. Now, additional years of higher education are necessary to be eligible for higher-paying jobs. Because of this and other factors, the period of adolescence also has been extended upward as young adults tend to go to school for more years, delay

THE GLOBALIZATION OF ADOLESCENCE

Young people today live in a global neighborhood, a web of interconnections and interdependencies. Goods, information, electronic images, songs, entertainment, and fads sweep almost instantaneously around the planet. Western youth dance to Latin rhythms, and Arabic girls draw their images of romance from Indian cinema. Maori youth in New Zealand listen to African American rap music to symbolize their separation from adult society.

Adolescence is no longer solely a Western phenomenon. Globalization and modernization have set in motion societal changes the world over. Among these changes are urbanization, longer and healthier lives, reduced birthrates, and smaller families. Earlier puberty and later marriage are increasingly common. More women and fewer children work outside the home. The rapid spread of advanced technologies has made knowledge a prized resource. Young people need more schooling and skills to enter the labor force. Together these changes result in an extended transitional phase between childhood and adulthood.

Despite the forces of globalization and modernization, preadolescent children in some less-developed societies still follow traditional paths. These 9-year-old schoolgirls in Tehran celebrate the ceremony of Taqlif, which marks their readiness to begin the religious duties of Islam.

Puberty in less-developed countries traditionally was marked by initiation rites such as circumcision. Today adolescents in these countries are increasingly identified by their status as students removed from the working world of adults. In this changing world, new pathways are opening up for them. They are less apt to follow in their parents' footsteps and to be guided by their advice. If they work, they are more likely to work in factories than on the family farm.

This does *not* mean that adolescence is the same the world over. The strong hand of culture shapes its meaning differently in different societies. In the United States, adolescents are spending less time with their parents and confiding in them less. In India, adolescents may wear Western clothing and use computers, but they maintain strong family ties, and their life decisions often are influenced by traditional Hindu values. In Western countries, teenage girls strive to be as thin as possible. In Niger and other African countries, obesity can be considered beautiful.

In many non-Western countries, adolescent boys and girls seem to live in two separate worlds. In parts of the Middle East, Latin America, Africa, and Asia, puberty brings more restrictions on girls, whose virginity must be protected to uphold family status and ensure girls' marriageability. Boys, on the other hand, gain more freedom and mobility, and their sexual exploits are tolerated by parents and admired by peers.

Puberty heightens preparation for gender roles, which, for girls in most parts of the world, means preparation for domesticity. In Laos, a girl may spend 2½ hours a day husking, washing, and steaming rice. In Istanbul, a girl must learn the proper way to serve tea when a suitor comes to call. While boys are expected to prepare for adult work and to maintain family honor, adolescent girls in many less-developed countries, such as rural regions of China, do not go to school because the skills they would learn would be of no use after they married. Instead, they are expected to spend most of their time helping at home. As a result, girls rarely develop independent thinking and decision-making skills.

This traditional pattern is changing in some parts of the developing world as women's employment and self-reliance become financial necessities. During the past quarter-century, the advent of public education has enabled more girls to go to school, breaking down some of the taboos and restrictions on feminine activities. Better-educated girls tend to marry later and have fewer children,

Continued

enabling them to seek skilled employment in the new technological society.

Cultural change is complex; it can be both liberating and challenging. Today's adolescents are charting a new course, not always certain where it will lead.

Source: Larson & Wilson, 2004.

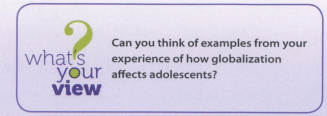

what's your view

Can you think of examples from your experience of how globalization affects adolescents?

marriage and childbirth longer, and settle into permanent careers later and less firmly than was previously the case.

ADOLESCENCE: A TIME OF OPPORTUNITIES AND RISKS

Any time of transition and change in the life span offers opportunities for both advances and risks. Adolescence is no different. It offers opportunities for growth, not only with respect to physical dimensions, but also in cognitive and social competence, autonomy, self-esteem, and intimacy. Young people who have supportive connections with parents, school, and community tend to develop in a positive, healthful way (Youngblade et al., 2007).

However, adolescence is also a time of potential risk, and adolescents in the United States today face hazards to their physical and mental well-being, including high death rates from accidents, homicide, and suicide (Eaton et al., 2008). Why is adolescence such a risky stage in the life span? Psychologists believe that the tendency to engage in risky behaviors may reflect the immaturity of the adolescent brain and is, to some extent, to be expected of young people. But, teens can and do respond to messages about safety and responsibility. Since the 1990s, adolescents have shown decreases across a wide range of risky behavior. For example, they are less likely to use alcohol, tobacco, or marijuana; to ride in a car without a seat belt or to ride with a driver who has been drinking; to carry weapons; to have sexual intercourse or to have it without condoms; or to attempt suicide (Centers for Disease Control and Prevention [CDC], 2012; Eaton et al., 2008). These positive trends increase the chance that young people will come through the adolescent years in good physical and mental health.

Why do you think these encouraging trends are occurring among high school students in recent years?

checkpoint can **you** . . .

▷ Explain why adolescence is a social construction?

▷ Point out similarities and differences among adolescents in various parts of the world?

▷ Identify risky behavior patterns common during adolescence?

guidepost 2

What physical changes do adolescents experience, and how do these changes affect them psychologically?

connect

study smart

Puberty in Boys

connect

study smart

Puberty in Girls

Puberty: The End of Childhood

Puberty involves dramatic biological changes. These changes are part of a long, complex process of maturation that begins even before birth, and their psychological ramifications may continue into adulthood.

HOW PUBERTY BEGINS: HORMONAL CHANGES

The advent of puberty is not caused by any one single factor. Rather, puberty results from a cascade of hormonal responses (see Figure 15.1). First, the hypothalamus releases elevated levels of gonadotropin releasing hormone (GnRH). The increased GnRH then triggers a rise in two key reproductive hormones: lutenizing hormone (LH) and follicle-stimulating hormone (FSH). These hormones exert their actions differentially on boys and girls. In girls, increased levels of FSH lead to the onset of menstruation. In boys, LH initiates the release of two additional hormones: testosterone and androstendione (Buck Louis et al., 2008).

Puberty takes many years to occur, and it can be broken down into two basic stages: (1) adrenarche, the activation of the adrenal glands, and (2) gonadarche, the maturing of the sex organs. The first stage occurs between ages 6 and 8. During this stage, the adrenal glands (located above the kidneys) secrete increasing levels of androgens,

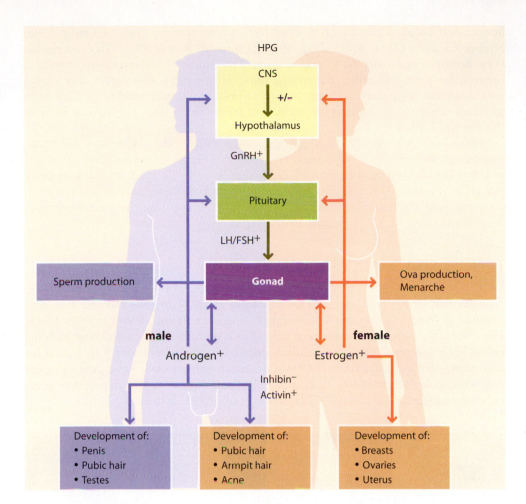

FIGURE 15.1

Regulation of Human Puberty Onset and Progression

HPG (hypothalamus-pituitary-gonadal) activation requires a signal from the central nervous system (CNS) to the hypothalamus, which stimulates the production of LH and FSH from the pituitary.

Source: Buck Louis et al., 2008.

most notably dehydroepiandrosterone (DHEA) (Susman & Rogol, 2004). Levels increase gradually but consistently, and by the time a child is 10 years of age, the levels of DHEA are 10 times what they were between ages 1 to 4. DHEA influences the growth of pubic, axillary (underarm), and facial hair. It also contributes to faster body growth, oilier skin, and the development of body odor.

The second stage is marked by the maturing of the sex organs, which triggers a second burst of DHEA production (McClintock & Herdt, 1996). During this time, a girl's ovaries increase their input of estrogen, which in turn stimulates the growth of female genitals, breasts, and the development of pubic and underarm hair. In boys, the testes increase the production of androgens, especially testosterone. This increase leads to the growth of male genitals, muscle mass, and body hair.

It is important to note that both boys and girls have both types of hormones, and that both types of hormones affect processes in children of both sexes. For example, girls have testosterone, which influences the growth of the clitoris and bones and the appearance of pubic and axillary hair. However, boys have more testosterone and, analogously, girls have higher levels of estrogens.

What determines the precise timing of when puberty begins? One important factor seems to be reaching a critical amount of body fat necessary for successful reproduction. When this level is hit at a younger age, puberty begins earlier. For example, girls who have a higher percentage of body fat in early childhood and those who experience unusual weight gain between ages 5 and 9 tend to show earlier pubertal development (Davison, Susman, & Birch, 2003; Lee et al., 2007).

What explains the link between body fat and puberty? It may be that leptin, a hormone associated with obesity, plays a role in this process (Kaplowitz, 2008). Increased levels of leptin may signal the pituitary and sex glands to increase their secretion of hormones (Chehab, Mounzih, Lu, & Lim, 1997; Clément et al., 1998; O'Rahilly, 1998; Strobel, Camoin, Ozata, & Strosberg, 1998; Susman & Rogol, 2004). This process has been demonstrated more frequently in girls. Few studies have shown a connection between body fat and earlier puberty in boys. This suggests that leptin may play a permissive role for puberty to start. In other words, leptin may need to be present in sufficient amounts for puberty to occur, but leptin alone does not initiate puberty (Kaplowitz, 2008).

Some research attributes the heightened emotionality and moodiness of early adolescence to these hormonal developments. Indeed, negative emotions such as distress and hostility, as well as symptoms of depression in girls, do tend to rise as puberty progresses (Susman & Rogol, 2004). However, other influences, such as sex, age, temperament, and the timing of puberty, may moderate or even override hormonal influences (Buchanan, Eccles, & Becker, 1992).

TIMING, SIGNS, AND SEQUENCE OF PUBERTY AND SEXUAL MATURITY

Changes that herald puberty now typically begin at age 8 in girls and age 9 in boys (Susman & Rogol, 2004), but a wide range of ages exists for various changes (Table 15.1). Recently, pediatricians have seen a significant number of girls with breast budding before age 8 (Slyper, 2006). The pubertal process typically takes about 3 to 4 years for both sexes. African American and Mexican American girls generally enter puberty earlier than white girls (Wu, Mendola, & Buck, 2002). Some African American girls experience pubertal changes as early as age 6 (Kaplowitz et al., 1999; Biro et al., 2010).

TABLE 15.1 Usual Sequence of Physiological Changes in Adolescence

Female Characteristics	Age of First Appearance
Growth of breasts	6–13
Growth of pubic hair	6–14
Body growth spurt	9.5–14.5
Menarche	10–16.5
Appearance of underarm hair	About 2 years after appearance of pubic hair
Increased output of oil- and sweat-producing glands (that may lead to acne)	About the same time as appearance of underarm hair
Male Characteristics	**Age of First Appearance**
Growth of testes, scrotal sac	9–13.5
Growth of pubic hair	12–16
Body growth spurt	10.5–16
Growth of penis, prostate gland, seminal vesicles	11–14.5
Change in voice	About the same time as growth of penis
Spermarche	About 1 year after beginning of growth of penis
Appearance of facial and underarm hair	About 2 years after appearance of pubic hair
Increased output of oil- and sweat-producing glands (that may lead to acne)	About the same time as appearance of underarm hair

TABLE 15.2	Secondary Sex Characteristics	
Girls	**Boys**
Breasts	Pubic hair
Pubic hair	Axillary (underarm) hair
Axillary (underarm) hair	Muscular development
Changes in voice	Facial hair
Changes in skin	Changes in voice
Increased width and depth of pelvis	Changes in skin
Muscular development	Broadening of shoulders

Primary and Secondary Sex Characteristics The **primary sex characteristics** are the organs necessary for reproduction. In the female, the sex organs include the ovaries, fallopian tubes, uterus, clitoris, and vagina. In the male, they include the testes, penis, scrotum, seminal vesicles, and prostate gland. During puberty, these organs enlarge and mature.

The **secondary sex characteristics** (Table 15.2) are physiological signs of sexual maturation that do not directly involve the sex organs, for example, the breasts of females and the broad shoulders of males. Other secondary sex characteristics are changes in the voice and skin texture; muscular development; and the growth of pubic, facial, axillary, and body hair.

These changes unfold in a sequence that is much more consistent than their timing, though even the sequence may vary somewhat. One girl may develop breasts and body hair at about the same rate; in another girl, body hair may reach adultlike growth a year or so before breasts develop. Similar variations in pubertal status (degree of pubertal development) and timing occur among boys. Let's look more closely at these changes.

Signs of Puberty The first external signs of puberty typically are breast tissue and pubic hair in girls and enlargement of the testes in boys (Susman & Rogol, 2004). A girl's nipples enlarge and protrude, the *areolae* (the pigmented areas surrounding the nipples) enlarge, and the breasts assume first a conical and then a rounded shape. Some adolescent boys, much to their distress, may experience temporary breast enlargement, however, this is normal and generally does not last longer than 18 months.

Pubic hair, at first straight and silky, eventually becomes coarse, dark, and curly. It appears in different patterns in males and females. Adolescent boys are usually happy to see hair on the face and chest, but girls are usually dismayed at the appearance of even a slight amount of hair on the face or around the nipples, though this is normal.

The voice deepens, especially in boys, partly in response to the growth of the larynx and partly in response to the production of male hormones. The skin becomes coarser and oilier. Increased activity of the sebaceous glands may give rise to pimples and blackheads. Acne is more common in boys and seems related to increased amounts of testosterone.

The Adolescent Growth Spurt The **adolescent growth spurt** generally begins in girls between ages 9½ and 14½ (usually at about 10) and in boys, between 10½ and 16 (usually at 12 or 13). It typically lasts about 2 years; soon after it ends, the young person reaches sexual maturity. Both growth hormone and the sex hormones (androgens and estrogen) contribute to this normal pubertal growth (Susman & Rogol, 2004).

Because girls' growth spurt usually occurs 2 years earlier than that of boys, girls between ages 11 and 13 tend to be taller, heavier, and stronger than boys the same age. After their growth spurt, boys are again larger, as before. Girls usually reach full height at age 15 and boys by age 17. The rate of muscular growth peaks at age 12½ for girls and 14½ for boys (Gans, 1990).

primary sex characteristics
Organs directly related to reproduction, which enlarge and mature during adolescence.

secondary sex characteristics
Physiological signs of sexual maturation (such as breast development and growth of body hair) that do not involve the sex organs.

adolescent growth spurt
Sharp increase in height and weight that precedes sexual maturity.

From ages 11 to 13, girls are, on average, taller, heavier, and stronger than boys, who reach their adolescent growth spurt later than girls do.

Boys and girls grow differently, not only in rate of growth but also in form and shape. A boy becomes larger overall: his shoulders wider, his legs longer relative to his trunk, and his forearms longer relative to his upper arms and his height. A girl's pelvis widens to make childbearing easier, and layers of fat accumulate under her skin, giving her a more rounded appearance. Fat accumulates twice as rapidly in girls as in boys (Susman & Rogol, 2004).

Because each of these changes follows its own timetable, parts of the body may be out of proportion for a while. The result is the familiar teenage gawkiness that accompanies unbalanced, accelerated growth.

These striking physical changes have psychological ramifications. Most young teenagers are more concerned about their appearance than about any other aspect of themselves, and some do not like what they see in the mirror. As we discuss in a subsequent section, these attitudes can lead to eating problems.

Signs of Sexual Maturity: Sperm Production and Menstruation The maturation of the reproductive organs brings the beginning of menstruation in girls and the production of sperm in boys. The principal sign of sexual maturity in boys is the production of sperm. The first ejaculation, or **spermarche**, occurs at an average age of 13. A boy may wake up to find a wet spot or a dried, hardened spot on the sheets—the result of a *nocturnal emission*, an involuntary ejaculation of semen (commonly referred to as a *wet dream*). Most adolescent boys have these emissions, sometimes in connection with an erotic dream.

The principal sign of sexual maturity in girls is *menstruation*, a monthly shedding of tissue from the lining of the womb. Girl's first menstruation, called **menarche**, occurs fairly late in the sequence of female development; its normal timing can vary from ages 10 to 16½ (refer to Table 15.1). The average age of menarche in U.S. girls has fallen from older than age 14 before 1900 to age 12½ in the 1990s. On average, a black girl first menstruates shortly after her 12th birthday and a white girl about 6 months later (S. E. Anderson, Dallal, & Must, 2003).

Influences on Timing of Puberty On the basis of historical sources, developmental scientists have found a **secular trend**—a trend that spans several generations—in the onset of puberty: a drop in the ages when puberty begins and when young people reach

spermarche
A boy's first ejaculation.

menarche
A girl's first menstruation.

secular trend
Trend that can be seen only by observing several generations, such as the trend toward earlier attainment of adult height and sexual maturity, which began a century ago.

adult height and sexual maturity. The trend, which also involves increases in adult height and weight, began about 100 years ago. It has occurred in such places as the United States, Western Europe, and Japan (S. E. Anderson et al., 2003).

One proposed explanation for this secular trend is a higher standard of living. Children who are healthier, better nourished, and better cared for might be expected to mature earlier and grow bigger (Slyper, 2006). Thus the average age of sexual maturity is earlier in developed countries than in developing countries. Because of the role of body fat in triggering puberty, a contributing factor in the United States during the last part of the twentieth century may be the increase in obesity among young girls (S. E. Anderson et al., 2003; Lee et al., 2007).

A combination of genetic, physical, emotional, and contextual influences may affect the timing of menarche (Graber, Brooks-Gunn, & Warren, 1995). Twin studies have documented the heritability of age of menarche (Mendle et al., 2006). Other research has found that the age of a girl's first menstruation tends to be similar to that of her mother *if* nutrition and standard of living remain stable from one generation to the next (Susman & Rogol, 2004). In several studies, family conflict was associated with early menarche, whereas parental warmth, harmonious family relationships, and paternal involvement in child rearing were related to later menarche (Belsky et al., 2007; Mendle et al., 2006). Girls who, as preschoolers, have had close, supportive relationships with their parents—especially with an affectionate, involved father—tend to enter puberty later than girls whose parental relationships were cold or distant or those who were raised by single mothers (Belsky et al., 2007; Ellis, McFadyen-Ketchum, Dodge, Pettit, & Bates, 1999). On the other hand, family disruption and residential separation from the father has been associated with earlier menarche (Tither & Ellis, 2008).

How might family relationships affect pubertal development? One possibility is that human males, like some animals, may give off *pheromones*, odorous chemicals that attract mates. As a natural incest-prevention mechanism, sexual development may be inhibited in girls who are heavily exposed to their fathers' pheromones, as would happen in a close father-daughter relationship. Contrarily, frequent exposure to the pheromones of unrelated adult males, such as a stepfather or a single mother's boyfriend, may speed up pubertal development (Ellis & Garber, 2000).

An alternative theory focuses on how experiences in infancy and childhood might provide the child with cues as to what type of future is likely. From an evolutionary point of view, different reproductive strategies may be used. For example, one species might evolve to have many offspring and invest very little in any of them; another species might evolve to have only a few offspring and invest a great deal in them. This analysis can be applied to different species as well as to individual differences in reproductive strategies within the same species. With respect to humans, some parents might have few children but spend a great deal of time and money on them, while other parents might have many children and invest less in each individual child.

How does this relate to the link between family relationships and puberty? One approach (Belsky, Steinberg, & Draper, 1991) argues that a childhood high in stress and conflict, or one lacking a consistent male figure, might signal to a developing child that the world is a stressful and dangerous place to live in, that male partners may be scarce or unwilling to help out, and that survival is not assured. Thus, it might be best, from an adaptive point of view, to have many children; investing less in each one but expecting that some, if not all, will live. So, puberty and sexual activity begin earlier. Alternatively, a childhood in which stress levels are low, the family environment is high quality, and adult males are consistently present may signal the opposite. In that situation, the strategy of having fewer offspring and making a higher investment in each one may make more sense. Subsequently, later puberty and maturation may follow from this situation. This evolutionary approach suggests that the social environment acts as a trigger to biological development, perhaps influenced by high stress levels. In support of this theory are findings that insecure attachment in infancy is related to early puberty (Belsky, Houts, & Fearon, 2010), and that girls with absent fathers (Bogaert, 2005,

2008) or from homes high in conflict (Mishra, Cooper, Tom, & Kuh, 2012) begin puberty earlier than those with fathers living in the home.

IMPLICATIONS OF EARLY AND LATE MATURATION

The onset of puberty can vary by as many as 5 years among normal boys and girls (Golub et al., 2008). Early maturation increases the likelihood of accelerated skeletal maturation and psychosocial difficulties and has been linked to adult health issues including reproductive tract cancers, obesity, type 2 diabetes, and cardiovascular disease (Golub et al., 2008). Other effects of early and late maturation vary in boys and girls, and the timing of maturation tends to influence adolescent mental health and health-related behaviors in adulthood (Susman & Rogol, 2004).

Research on early maturing boys has had mixed results. Some studies found that most boys like to mature early, and those who do so seem to gain in self-esteem (Alsaker, 1992; Weichold, Silbereisen, & Schmitt-Rodermund, 2003). Other studies have found early maturing boys to be more anxious or aggressive, more worried about being liked, more cautious, more reliant on others, and more bound by rules and routines (Ge, Conger, & Elder, 2001b; Graber, Lewinsohn, Seeley, & Brooks-Gunn, 1997; Gross & Duke, 1980). Early maturing boys demonstrate a higher incidence of conduct and behavioral disorders during adolescence (Golub et al., 2008). Late maturing boys, however, have been found to feel more inadequate, self-conscious, rejected, and dominated; to be more dependent, aggressive, insecure, or depressed; to have more conflict with parents and more trouble in school; and to have poorer social and coping skills (Graber et al., 1997; Mussen & Jones, 1957).

Girls are generally happier if their timing is about the same as that of their peers. Early maturing girls tend to be less sociable, less expressive, and less poised; more introverted and shy; and more negative about menarche than later maturing girls (Livson & Peskin, 1980; Ruble & Brooks-Gunn, 1982; Stubbs, Rierdan, & Koff, 1989). Perhaps because they feel rushed into confronting the pressures of adolescence before they are ready (Susman & Rogol, 2004), they are more vulnerable to psychological distress. They are more likely to associate with antisocial peers (Ge et al., 1996). They may have a poor body image and lower self-esteem than later maturing girls (Alsaker, 1992; Graber et al., 1997; Mendle, Turkheimer, & Emery, 2007; Simmons, Blyth, Van Cleave, & Bush, 1979). Early maturing girls are at increased risk of anxiety and depression; disruptive behavior; eating disorders; early smoking, drinking, and substance abuse; precocious sexual activity; early pregnancy; and attempted suicide (Deardorff, Gonzalez, Christopher, Roosa, & Millsap, 2005; Dick, Rose, Kaprio, & Viken, 2000; Graber et al., 1997; Susman & Rogol, 2004, Golub et al., 2008). They have difficulty coping with rejection and tend to use fewer problem-solving skills than their peers (Sontag, Graber, Brooks-Gunn, & Warren, 2008). However, this is less true of girls with no history of behavior problems (Susman & Rogol, 2004). Among both boys and girls, early maturers tend to be vulnerable to risky behavior and the influence of deviant peers (Orr & Ingersoll, 1995; Susman & Rogol, 2004).

It is hard to generalize about the psychological effects of pubertal timing because they depend on how the adolescent and other people in his or her world interpret the accompanying changes. Effects of early or late maturation are most likely to be negative when adolescents are much more or less developed than their peers; when they do not see the changes as advantageous; and when several stressful events, such as the advent of puberty and the transition to junior high school, occur at about the same time (Petersen, 1993; Simmons, Blyth, & McKinney, 1983). Contextual factors such as ethnicity, school, and neighborhood can make a difference. For example, African American and Hispanic late maturers report less satisfaction with their bodies, but timing of puberty for Asian American and European American youth does not seem to affect body image (Susman & Rogol, 2004). Also, early maturing girls are more likely to show problem behavior in mixed-gender schools than in all-girl schools and in disadvantaged urban communities than in rural or middle-class urban communities (Caspi, Lynam, Moffitt, & Silva, 1993; Dick et al., 2000; Ge, Brody, Conger, Simons, & Murry, 2002).

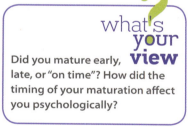

what's your view

Did you mature early, late, or "on time"? How did the timing of your maturation affect you psychologically?

checkpoint can you . . .

▷ Tell how puberty begins and how its timing and length vary?

▷ Identify typical pubertal changes in boys and girls and factors that affect psychological reactions to these changes?

The Adolescent Brain

Not long ago, most scientists believed that the brain was fully mature by puberty. Now imaging studies reveal that the adolescent brain is still a work in progress. Dramatic changes in brain structures involved in emotions, judgment, organization of behavior, and self-control take place between puberty and young adulthood. The immaturity of the adolescent brain has raised questions about the extent to which adolescents can reasonably be held legally responsible for their actions (Steinberg & Scott, 2003), prompting the U.S. Supreme Court in 2005 to rule the death penalty unconstitutional for a convicted murderer who was 17 or younger when the crime was committed (Mears, 2005).

Risk-taking appears to result from the interaction of two brain networks: (1) a *socioemotional network* that is sensitive to social and emotional stimuli, such as peer influence, and (2) a *cognitive-control network* that regulates responses to stimuli. The socioemotional network becomes more active at puberty, whereas the cognitive-control network matures more gradually into early adulthood. These findings may help explain teenagers' tendency toward emotional outbursts and risky behavior and why risk-taking often occurs in groups (Steinberg, 2007).

Brain development is rapid and profound at two points in the life span. One is in the early years of infancy, and the other is in adolescence. Recent advances in imaging technology have shown that both white and grey matter change in the adolescent brain.

There is a steady increase in white matter (nerve fibers that connect distant portions of the brain) during the teenage years. This allows nerve impulses to be transmitted more rapidly and helps neurons synchronize their firing rate (Fields & Stephens-Graham, 2002), thus improving adolescents' information-processing abilities. Though white matter increases across the brain as a whole, it is perhaps most marked in the corpus callosum. The corpus callosum is a band of axon fibers that connects the two hemispheres of the brain, allowing rapid and effective communication between them. During adolescence this band thickens, leading to better communication between the hemispheres (Geidd, 2008). This increase in white matter also occurs in the frontal, temporal, and parietal lobes (ACT for Youth, 2002; Blakemore & Choudhury, 2006; Kuhn, 2006; National Institute of Mental Health [NIMH], 2001b; Geidd, 2008).

There are also marked changes in gray matter composition. A major spurt in production of gray matter in the frontal lobes begins around puberty. After the growth spurt, the density of gray matter declines greatly, particularly in the prefrontal cortex, as unused synapses (connections between neurons) are pruned and those that remain are strengthened (ACT for Youth, 2002; Blakemore & Choudhury, 2006; Kuhn, 2006; NIMH, 2001b). This pruning process begins in the rear portions of the brain and moves forward generally reaching the frontal lobes during adolescence. Thus, by middle to late adolescence young people have fewer but stronger, smoother, and more effective neuronal connections, making cognitive processing more efficient (Kuhn, 2006).

Adolescents are capable of very strong emotions, and changes in white and gray matter in the amygdala and prefrontal cortex may help explain why teens sometimes make bad choices based on their emotions rather than more reasoned choices based on logic and foresight. The amygdala, broadly, is involved with strong emotional reactions. It matures before the prefrontal cortex. The prefrontal cortex is involved with planning, reasoning, judgment, emotional regulation, and impulse control. Thus, the areas of the brain involved with feeling strong emotions mature prior to the area of the brain responsible for making thoughtful decisions (Nelson, Thomas & deHann, 2006). This might explain some early adolescents' rash choices, such as substance abuse and sexual risk-taking. Immature brain development may permit feelings to override reason and may keep some adolescents from heeding warnings that seem logical and persuasive to adults (Baird et al., 1999; Yurgelun-Todd, 2002). Underdevelopment of frontal cortical systems associated with motivation, impulsivity, and addiction may help explain why adolescents tend to seek thrills and novelty and why many of them find it hard to focus on long-term goals (Bjork et al., 2004; Chambers, Taylor, & Potenza, 2003).

guidepost 3

What brain developments occur during adolescence, and how do they affect adolescent behavior?

study smart

Pubertal Brain Development

The immaturity of these brain centers, and the consequent propensity to act impulsively and without fully considering consequences, are one reason some people take issue with the death penalty being applied against teenagers. Do you think this is a valid argument? Why or why not?

Overweight teenagers tend to be in poorer health than their peers and are more likely to have difficulty attending school, performing household chores, or engaging in strenuous activity or personal care (Swallen, Reither, Haas, & Meier, 2005). They are at heightened risk of high cholesterol, hypertension, and diabetes (NCHS, 2005). They tend to become obese adults, subject to a variety of physical, social, and psychological risks (Gortmaker, Must, Perrin, Sobol, & Dietz, 1993). Given how many adolescents are overweight today, one research team projects that by 2035 more than 100,000 additional cases of cardiovascular disease will be attributable to an increased prevalence of overweight in young and middle-aged men and women (Bibbins-Domingo, Coxson, Pletcher, Lightwood, & Goldman, 2007).

Genetic and other factors, such as faulty regulation of metabolism and, at least in girls, depressive symptoms and having obese parents, can increase the likelihood of teenage obesity (Morrison et al., 2005; Stice, Presnell, Shaw, & Rohde, 2005). However a study of 878 California 11- to 15-year-olds revealed that lack of exercise was the *main* risk factor for overweight in boys and girls (Patrick et al., 2004).

Weight-loss programs that use behavioral modification techniques to help adolescents make changes in diet and exercise have had some success. For many preadolescents and adolescents, however, dieting may be counterproductive. In a prospective 3-year study of 8,203 girls and 6,769 boys ages 9 to 14, those who dieted gained more weight than those who did not diet (A. E. Field et al., 2003).

Body Image and Eating Disorders

Sometimes a determination not to become overweight can result in problems more serious than overweight itself. Concern with body image may lead to obsessive efforts at weight control (Davison & Birch, 2001; Vereecken & Maes, 2000). This pattern is more common among girls than among boys and is less likely to be related to actual weight problems.

Because of girls' normal increase in body fat during puberty, many girls, especially if they are advanced in pubertal development, become unhappy about their appearance, reflecting the cultural emphasis on women's physical attributes (Susman & Rogol, 2004). Girls' dissatisfaction with their bodies increases over the course of early to midadolescence, whereas boys, who are becoming more muscular, become more satisfied with their bodies (Feingold & Mazzella, 1998; Rosenblum & Lewis, 1999; Swarr & Richards, 1996). By age 15, more than half the girls sampled in 16 countries were dieting or thought they should be. The United States was at the top of the list, with 47 percent of 11-year-old girls and 62 percent of 15-year-olds concerned about overweight (Vereecken & Maes, 2000). Black girls are generally more satisfied with their bodies and less concerned about weight and dieting than white girls (Kelly, Wall, Eisenberg, Story, & Neumark-Sztainer, 2004; Wardle et al., 2004).

According to a large prospective cohort study, parental attitudes and media images play a greater part than peer influences in encouraging weight concerns. Girls who try to look like the unrealistically thin models they see in the media tend to develop excessive concern about weight and may develop eating disorders (Striegel-Moore & Bulik, 2007). In addition, both girls and boys who believe that thinness is important to their parents, especially to their fathers, tend to become constant dieters (Field et al., 2001).

Excessive concern with weight control and body image may be signs of *anorexia nervosa* or *bulimia nervosa*, both of which involve abnormal patterns of food intake. These chronic disorders

Concern with body image is more common among girls than among boys and is less likely to be related to actual weight problems. Normal increase in body fat during puberty causes many girls to become unhappy about their appearance, reflecting the cultural emphasis on being thin.

TABLE 15.3 Eating Disorders: Risk Factors and Symptoms

Risk Factors	• Accepting society's attitudes about thinness
	• Being a perfectionist
	• Being female
	• Experiencing childhood anxiety
	• Feeling increased concern or attention to weight and shape
	• Having eating and gastrointestinal problems during early childhood
	• Having a family history of addictions or eating disorders
	• Having parents who are concerned about weight and weight loss
	• Having a negative self-image

	Anorexia	Bulimia
Symptoms	• Using laxatives, enemas, or diuretics inappropriately in an effort to lose weight	• Abuse of laxatives, diuretics, or enemas to prevent weight gain
	• Binge eating	• Binge eating
	• Going to the bathroom right after meals	• Going to the bathroom right after meals
	• Exercising compulsively	• Frequent weighing
	• Restricting the amount of food eaten	• Self-induced vomiting
	• Cutting food into small pieces	• Overachieving behavior
	• Dental cavities due to self-induced vomiting	• Dental cavities due to self-induced vomiting
	• Confused or slow thinking	
	• Blotchy or yellow skin	
	• Depression	
	• Dry mouth	
	• Extreme sensitivity to cold	
	• Fine hair	
	• Low blood pressure	
	• No menstruation	
	• Poor memory or poor judgment	
	• Significant weight loss	
	• Wasting away of muscle and loss of body fat	

occur worldwide, mostly in adolescent girls and young women. Table 15.3 describes risk factors and common symptoms of these two disorders.

However, not enough study has been done of eating disorders among men and among nonwhite ethnic groups. Furthermore, the idea that eating disorders are the result of cultural pressure to be thin is too simplistic; biological factors, including genetic factors, play an equally important role (Striegel-Moore & Bulik, 2007). Twin studies have found associations between eating disorders and the brain chemical serotonin, a variant of the protein BDNF that influences food intake, and estrogen (Klump & Culbert, 2007).

Anorexia Nervosa **Anorexia nervosa**, or *self-starvation*, is potentially life-threatening. An estimated 0.3 to 0.5 percent of adolescent girls and young women and a smaller but growing percentage of boys and men in Western countries are known to be affected. People with anorexia have a distorted body image and, though typically severely underweight, think they are too fat. They often are good students but may be withdrawn or depressed and may engage in repetitive, perfectionist behavior. They are extremely afraid

anorexia nervosa
Eating disorder characterized by self-starvation and extreme weight loss.

of losing self-control and becoming overweight (AAP Committee on Adolescence, 2003; Martínez-González et al., 2003; Wilson, Grilo, & Vitousek, 2007). Early warning signs include determined, secret dieting; dissatisfaction after losing weight; setting new, lower weight goals after reaching an initial desired weight; excessive exercising; and interruption of regular menstruation.

Anorexia is, paradoxically, both deliberate and involuntary: An affected person deliberately refuses food needed for sustenance, yet cannot stop doing so even when rewarded or punished. These behavior patterns have been traced back to medieval times and seem to have existed in all parts of the world. Thus, anorexia may be in part a reaction to societal pressure to be slender, but this does not seem to be the only factor or even a necessary one (Keel & Klump, 2003; Striegel-Moore & Bulik, 2007).

Bulimia Nervosa **Bulimia nervosa** affects about 1 to 2 percent of international populations (Wilson et al., 2007). A person with bulimia regularly goes on huge, short-lived eating binges (2 hours or less) and then may try to purge the high caloric intake through self-induced vomiting, strict dieting or fasting, excessively vigorous exercise, or laxatives, enemas, or diuretics. These episodes occur at least twice a week for at least 3 months (American Psychiatric Association, 2000). People with bulimia are usually within normal weight ranges, but they are obsessed with their weight and shape. They tend to have low self-esteem and may become overwhelmed with shame, self-contempt, and depression (Wilson et al., 2007).

A related *binge eating disorder* involves frequent binging but without subsequent fasting, exercise, or vomiting. Not surprisingly, people who binge frequently tend to be overweight and to experience emotional distress and other medical and psychological disorders. An estimated 3 percent of the population are binge eaters (Wilson et al., 2007).

There is some overlap between anorexia and bulimia; some people with anorexia have bulimic episodes, and some people with bulimia lose large amounts of weight ("Eating Disorders—Part I," 1997). Unlike anorexia, there is little evidence of bulimia either historically or in cultures not subject to Western influence (Keel & Klump, 2003).

Treatment and Outcomes of Eating Disorders The immediate goal of treatment for anorexia is to get patients to eat and gain weight—goals that are often difficult to achieve given the strength of patients' beliefs about their bodies. One widely used treatment is a type of family therapy in which parents take control of their child's eating patterns. When the child begins to comply with parental directives, she (or he) may be given more age-appropriate autonomy (Wilson et al., 2007). Cognitive behavioral therapy, which seeks to change a distorted body image and rewards eating with such privileges as being allowed to get out of bed and leave the room, may be part of the treatment (Beumont, Russell, & Touyz, 1993; Wilson et al., 2007). Patients who show signs of severe malnutrition, are resistant to treatment, or do not make progress on an outpatient basis may be admitted to a hospital, where they can be given 24-hour nursing. Once their weight is stabilized, patients may enter less intensive daytime care (McCallum & Bruton, 2003).

Bulimia, too, is best treated with cognitive behavioral therapy (Wilson et al., 2007). Patients keep daily diaries of their eating patterns and are taught ways to avoid the temptation to binge. Individual, group, or family psychotherapy can help both anorexia and bulimia patients, usually after initial behavior therapy has brought symptoms under control. Because these patients are at risk for depression and suicide, antidepressant drugs are often combined with psychotherapy (McCallum & Bruton, 2003), but evidence of their long-term effectiveness on either anorexia or bulimia is lacking (Wilson et al., 2007).

Adolescents, with their need for autonomy, may reject family intervention and may need the structure of an institutional setting. Still, any treatment program for adolescents must involve the family. It also must provide for adolescents' developmental needs, which may be different from the needs of adult patients, and must offer the opportunity to keep up with schooling (McCallum & Bruton, 2003).

bulimia nervosa
Eating disorder in which a person regularly eats huge quantities of food and then purges the body by laxatives, induced vomiting, fasting, or excessive exercise.

what's your **view**

Can you suggest ways to reduce the prevalence of eating disorders?

checkpoint
can **you** . . .

▷ Summarize the normal nutritional needs and typical dietary deficiencies of adolescent boys and girls?

▷ Discuss risk factors for, effects of, treatment of, and prognoses for obesity, anorexia, and bulimia?

Mortality rates among those affected with anorexia nervosa have been estimated at about 10 percent of cases. Among the surviving anorexia patients, less than one-half make a full recovery and only one-third actually improve; 20 percent remain chronically ill (Steinhausen, 2002). It should also be noted that up to one-third of patients drop out of treatment before achieving an appropriate weight (McCallum & Bruton, 2003). Recovery rates from bulimia are a bit better and average 30 to 50 percent after cognitive behavioral therapy (Wilson et al., 2007).

USE AND ABUSE OF DRUGS

Although the great majority of adolescents do not abuse drugs, a significant minority do. **Substance abuse** is harmful use of alcohol or other drugs. It can lead to **substance dependence** (addiction), which may be physiological, psychological, or both and is likely to continue into adulthood. Addictive drugs are especially dangerous for adolescents because they stimulate parts of the brain that are changing in adolescence (Chambers et al., 2003). In 2003–2004, about 6 percent of young people ages 12 to 17 were identified as needing treatment for alcohol use and more than 5 percent as needing treatment for illicit drug use (National Survey on Drug Use and Health [NSDUH], 2006).

Trends in Drug Use More than 35 percent of U.S. adolescents have tried illicit drugs by the time they leave high school. An upsurge in drug use during the mid- to late 1990s accompanied a lessening of perceptions of its dangers and a softening of peer disapproval. However, that trend has begun to reverse. Student use of certain drugs, especially central nervous stimulants like methamphetamine and cocaine, has shown a gradual decline. LSD, ecstacy, and psychoactive drugs like vicodin have held steady, and use of marijuana and anabolic steroids have shown signs of increased usage.

These findings come from the latest in a series of annual government surveys of a nationally representative sample of 8th, 10th, and 12th graders from more than 400 schools across the United States (Johnston, O'Malley, Bachman, & Schulenberg, 2013; Figure 15.2). These surveys probably underestimate adolescent drug use because they are based on self-reports and do not reach high school dropouts, who are more likely to use drugs. Continued progress in eliminating drug abuse is slow because new drugs are continually introduced or rediscovered by a new generation, and young people do not necessarily generalize the adverse consequences of one drug to another (Johnston et al., 2013).

A recent trend is the abuse of nonprescription cough and cold medications; 3 percent of 8th graders, 4.7 percent of 10th graders, and 5.6 percent of 12th graders report taking medicines containing dextromethorphan (DXM), a cough suppressant, to get high within the past year (Johnston et al., 2013).

Risk Factors for Drug Abuse What is the likelihood that a particular young person will abuse drugs? Risk factors may include difficult temperament, poor impulse control, and a tendency to seek out sensation (Table 15.4). The more risk factors that are present, the greater the chance that an adolescent or young adult will abuse drugs.

Let's look more closely at alcohol, marijuana, and tobacco, the three drugs most popular with adolescents, and at influences on their use.

Alcohol, Marijuana, and Tobacco Alcohol, marijuana, and tobacco use among U.S. teenagers has followed a trend roughly parallel to that of harder drug use, with a dramatic rise during most of the 1990s followed by a smaller, gradual decline (Johnston et al., 2013).

Alcohol is a potent, mind-altering drug with major effects on physical, emotional, and social well-being. Its use is a serious problem in many

substance abuse
Repeated, harmful use of a substance, usually alcohol or other drugs.

substance dependence
Addiction (physical or psychological, or both) to a harmful substance.

study smart

Substance Abuse

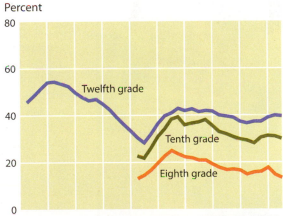

FIGURE 15.2

Trends in High School Students' Use of Illicit Drugs over the Previous 12 Months

Source: Johnston, O'Malley, Bachman, & Schulenberg, Fig. 1, 2013.

TABLE 15.4	Risk Factors for Teenage Drug Abuse

What is the likelihood that a particular young person will abuse drugs? Risk factors include the following:

- A "difficult" temperament

- Poor impulse control and a tendency to seek out sensation (which may have a biochemical basis)

- Family influences (such as a genetic predisposition to alcoholism, parental use or acceptance of drugs, poor or inconsistent parenting practices, family conflict, and troubled or distant family relationships)

- Early and persistent behavior problems, particularly aggression

- Academic failure and lack of commitment to education

- Peer rejection

- Associating with drug users

- Alienation and rebelliousness

- Favorable attitudes toward drug use

- Early initiation into drug use

The more risk factors that are present, the greater the chance that an adolescent will abuse drugs.

Sources: Hawkins, Catalano, & Miller, 1992; Johnson, Hoffmann, & Gerstein, 1996; Masse & Tremblay, 1997; Wong et al., 2006.

binge drinking
Consuming five or more drinks on one occasion.

connect

study smart

Attitudes about Drinking

Marijuana is the most widely used illicit drug in the United States. Aside from its own ill effects, marijuana use may lead to addiction to hard drugs.

countries (Gabhainn & François, 2000). In 2012, 11 percent of U.S. 8th graders, 27 percent of 10th graders, and 42 percent of 12th graders said they had consumed alcohol at least once during the past 30 days (Johnston et al., 2013). The majority of high school students who drink engage in **binge drinking**—consuming five or more drinks on one occasion. About 25 percent of high school seniors admitted to binge drinking (McQueeny et al., 2009). A recent MRI-based study has revealed that binge drinking in teenagers may affect thinking and memory by damaging sensitive "white matter" in the brain (McQueeny et al., 2009). In a representative national study, binge drinkers were more likely than other students to report poor school performance and to engage in other risky behaviors (Miller, Naimi, Brewer, & Jones, 2007).

Adolescents are more vulnerable than adults to both immediate and long-term negative effects of alcohol on learning and memory (White, 2001). In one study, 15- and 16-year-old alcohol abusers who stopped drinking showed cognitive impairments weeks later in comparison with nonabusing peers (Brown, Tapert, Granholm, & Delis, 2000).

Despite the decline in *marijuana* use since 1996–1997, it is still by far the most widely used illicit drug in the United States. In 2012, about 11 percent of 8th graders, 28 percent of 10th graders, and 36 percent of 12th graders admitted to having used it in the past year (Johnston et al., 2013).

Marijuana smoke typically contains more than 400 carcinogens, and its potency has doubled in the past 25 years (National Institute on Drug Abuse [NIDA], 2008). Heavy use can damage the brain, heart, lungs, and immune system and cause nutritional deficiencies, respiratory infections, and other physical problems. It may lessen motivation, worsen depression, interfere with daily activities, and cause family problems. Marijuana use also can impede memory, thinking speed, learning, and school performance. It can lessen perception, alertness, attention span, judgment, and the motor skills needed to drive a vehicle and thus can contribute to traffic accidents (Messinis, Krypianidou, Maletaki, & Papathanasopoulos, 2006; NIDA, 1996; Substance Abuse and Mental Health Services Administration [SAMHSA], 2006; Office of National Drug Control Policy, 2008; Solowij et al., 2002). In a recent survey conducted by the NIDA, more than 13 percent of high school seniors admitted to driving under the influence of marijuana (NIDA, 2008).

Contrary to common belief, marijuana use may be addictive (Tanda, Pontieri, & DeChiara, 1997). It has been associated with behaviors that meet the criteria for substance dependence established by the American Psychiatric Association (2000) in the *Diagnostic and Statistical Manual of Mental Disorders* (DSM-IV). These behaviors include (1) tolerance (needing more of the substance to achieve the same effects); (2) withdrawal symptoms; (3) using a drug even in the presence of adverse effects; and (4) giving up social, occupational, or recreational activities because of substance use.

In the United States, approximately 5 percent of eighth graders, 11 percent of tenth graders, and 17 percent of twelfth graders are current (past-month) smokers (Johnston et al., 2013). While this number is high and cause for concern, there is some good news. Smoking rates have declined between one-third to more than one-half among eighth to twelfth graders in the United States since the mid-1990s. And, adolescent tobacco use is a less widespread problem in the United States than in most other industrialized countries (Gabhainn & Françoise, 2000). Research has indicated that nicotine replacement therapy in concert with behavioral skills training can be effective in helping adolescents stop smoking (Killen et al., 2004).

Substance use often begins when children enter middle school, where they become more vulnerable to peer pressure. Fourth to sixth graders may start using cigarettes, beer, and inhalants and, as they get older, move on to marijuana or harder drugs (National Parents' Resource Institute for Drug Education, 1999). The earlier young people start using a drug, the more frequently they are likely to use it and the greater their tendency to abuse it (Wong et al., 2006).

> Although marijuana clearly has negative effects, there are also documented medical applications. For example, marijuana is an effective treatment for nausea in cancer patients, and it has been used to reduce ocular pressure in glaucoma patients.

The average age for starting to drink is 13 to 14, and some children start earlier. A recent study found nearly 28 percent of underage drinkers had a drink before age 13 (Faden, 2006). Young people who begin drinking early tend to have behavior problems or to have siblings who are alcohol dependent (Kuperman et al., 2005). Those who start drinking before age 15 are more than 5 times more likely to become alcohol dependent or alcohol abusers than those who do not start drinking until age 21 or later (SAMHSA, 2004).

Smoking often begins in the early teenage years as a sign of toughness, rebelliousness, and passage from childhood to adulthood. This desired image enables a young initate to tolerate initial distaste for the first few puffs, after which the effects of nicotine begin to take over to sustain the habit. Within a year or two after starting to smoke, these young people inhale the same amount of nicotine as adults and experience the same cravings and withdrawal effects if they try to quit. Young adolescents attracted to smoking often come from homes, schools, and neighborhoods where smoking is common. They also tend to be overweight, to have low self-esteem, and not to be succeeding at school (Jarvis, 2004).

Adolescents exposed to alcohol and drugs before the age of 15 demonstrate an increased risk for substance disorders (Hingson, Heeren, & Winte, 2006), risky sexual behavior (Stueve & O'Donnell, 2005), low educational attainment (King, Meehan, Trim & Chassin, 2006), and crime. Though many adolescents who have been exposed to substances have a history of conduct problems, a recent study has shown that even children with no conduct-problem history were still at an increased risk for negative outcomes based on early exposure to alcohol and drugs (Odgers et al., 2008).

Peer influence on both smoking and drinking has been documented extensively (Center on Addiction and Substance Abuse [CASA] at Columbia University, 1996; Cleveland & Wiebe, 2003). As with hard drugs, the influence of older siblings and their friends increases the likelihood of tobacco and alcohol use (Rende, Slomkowski, Lloyd-Richardson, & Niaura, 2005).

Adolescents who believe that their parents disapprove of smoking are less likely to smoke (Sargent & Dalton, 2001). Rational discussions with parents can counteract

what's your view

Should marijuana be legal, like alcohol? Why or why not? How can adolescents be helped to avoid or curtail substance use?

what's your view

A number of states have enacted medical marijuana laws, and some have even decriminalized recreational use of marijuana. Should marijuana be legal?

checkpoint
can you . . .

▷ Summarize recent trends in drug use among adolescents?

▷ Discuss risk factors and influences connected with use of drugs, specifically alcohol, marijuana, and tobacco?

▷ Tell why early initiation into substance use is dangerous?

Playing Tetris can help ameliorate the flashbacks associated with posttraumatic stress disorder.

Holmes, James, Kilford, & Deeprose, 2010

harmful influences and discourage or limit drinking (Austin, Pinkleton, & Fujioka, 2000; Turrisi, Wiersman, & Hughes, 2000). However, parents also can be a negative influence. In a longitudinal study that compared 514 children of alcoholics with a matched control group, having an alcoholic parent significantly increased the risk of early alcohol use and later alcohol problems (Wong et al., 2006). The omnipresence of substance use in the media is another important influence. Movies that depict smoking increase early initiation of smoking (Charlesworth & Glantz, 2005).

DEPRESSION

The prevalence of depression increases during adolescence. An annual average of just over 8 percent of young people ages 12 to 17 have experienced at least one episode of major depression, and only about 39 percent of them had been treated (NSDUH, 2012). Rates generally increase with increasing age as shown in Figure 15.3. Depression in young people does not necessarily appear as sadness but as irritability, boredom, or inability to experience pleasure. One reason it needs to be taken seriously is the danger of suicide (Brent & Birmaher, 2002).

Adolescent girls, especially early maturing girls, are more subject to depression than adolescent boys (Brent & Birmaher, 2002; Ge et al., 2001a; NSDUH, 2012; Stice, Presnell, & Bearman, 2001). This gender difference may be related to biological changes connected with puberty; studies show a correlation between advancing puberty status and depressive symptoms (Susman & Rogol, 2004). Other possible factors are the way girls are socialized (Birmaher et al., 1996) and their greater vulnerability to stress in social relationships (Ge et al., 2001a; U.S. Department of Health and Human Services [USDHHS], 1999b).

In addition to female gender, risk factors for depression include anxiety, fear of social contact, stressful life events, chronic illnesses such as diabetes or epilepsy, parent-child conflict, abuse or neglect, alcohol and drug use, sexual activity, and having a parent with a history of depression. Alcohol and drug use and sexual activity are more likely to lead to depression in girls than in boys (Brent & Birmaher, 2002; Hallfors, Waller, Bauer, Ford, & Halpern, 2005; NSDUH, 2012; Waller et al., 2006). Body-image problems and eating disturbances can aggravate depressive symptoms (Stice & Bearman, 2001).

Depressed adolescents who do not respond to outpatient treatment or who have substance dependence or psychosis or seem suicidal may need to be hospitalized. At

FIGURE 15.3

Depression Rates for 12- to 17-Year-Olds

Rates of depression typically go up with increasing age during adolesense.

Source: NSDUH, 2012.

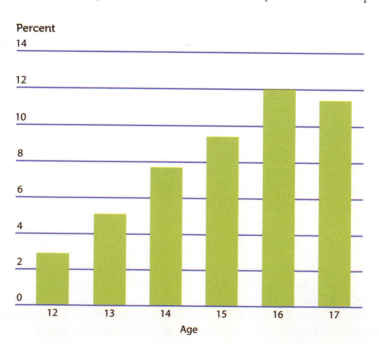

least 1 in 5 persons who experience bouts of depression in childhood or adolescence are at risk for bipolar disorder, in which depressive episodes (low periods) alternate with manic episodes (high periods) characterized by increased energy, euphoria, grandiosity, and risk-taking (Brent & Birmaher, 2002). Even adolescents with depressive symptoms not severe enough for a diagnosis of depression are at elevated risk of depression and suicidal behavior by age 25 (Fergusson, Horwood, Ridder, & Beautrais, 2005).

Selective serotonin reuptake inhibitors (SSRIs) are the only type of antidepressant medication currently approved for children and adolescents. However, as with the use of SSRIs for children, there is concern about the safety of these medications for adolescents. Not all SSRIs are effective, and a few have been associated with a slight increase in risk of suicidality (Williams, O'Connor, Eder, & Whitlock, 2009). Because of these safety issues, the U.S. Food and Drug Administration requires a warning to accompany their distribution and sale (Leslie, Newman, Chesney, & Perrin, 2005).

The only other treatment option is psychotherapy. An analysis of all available studies found modest short-term effectiveness of psychotherapy, cognitive or noncognitive, with effects lasting no more than 1 year (Weisz, McCarty, & Valeri, 2006). In view of the greater effectiveness of antidepressant medicine, especially fluoxetine, the Society for Adolescent Medicine supports its use for adolescents when clinically warranted and closely monitored, despite the risk (Lock, Walker, Rickert, & Katzman, 2005).

DEATH IN ADOLESCENCE

Death this early in life is always tragic and usually accidental but not entirely so. In the United States, 63 percent of all deaths among adolescents result from motor vehicle crashes, other unintentional injuries, homicide, and suicide (National Highway Traffic Safety Administration [NHTSA], 2009; Figure 15.4). The frequency of violent deaths in this age group reflects a violent culture as well as adolescents' inexperience and immaturity, which often lead to risk-taking and carelessness.

Deaths from Injuries Motor vehicle collisions are the leading cause of death among U.S. teenagers, accounting for 35 percent of all deaths in adolescence. The risk of collision is greater among 16- to 19-year-olds than for any other age group and especially so among 16- and 17-year-olds who have recently started to drive (McCartt, 2001; Miniño, Anderson, Fingerhut, Boudreault, & Warner, 2006; National Center for Injury Prevention and Control [NCIPC], 2004). Collisions are more likely to be fatal when teenage passengers are in the vehicle, probably because adolescents tend to drive more recklessly in the presence of peers (Chen, Baker, Braver, & Li, 2000). In the United States 64 percent of all drivers or motorcycle operators ages 15 to 20 who were involved in fatal traffic crashes and had a blood alcohol level of 0.08 or higher died as a result of the crash, suggesting that alcohol is a major factor in accident-related fatalities. Despite efforts aimed at increasing seat belt use among teens, observed use among teens and young adults was 76 percent in 2006—the lowest of any age group. In fact, in 2006, 58 percent of young people 16 to 20 years old involved in fatal motor vehicle crashes were unbuckled (NHTSA, 2009).

Firearm-Related Deaths Firearm-related deaths of 15- to 19-year-olds (including homicide, suicide, and accidental deaths) are far more common in the United States than in other industrialized countries. They comprise about one-third of all injury deaths and more than 85 percent of all homicides in that age group. The chief reason for these grim statistics seems to be the ease of obtaining a gun in the United States (AAP Committee on Injury and Poison Prevention, 2000). However, youth death rates from firearms have declined since 1993 (AAP Committee on Injury and Poison Prevention, 2000; NCHS, 2005), a period during which police have been confiscating guns on the street (Cole, 1999) and fewer young people have carried them (USDHHS, 1999b).

FIGURE 15.4

Leading Causes of Death in Adolescence

In the United States, motor vehicle crashes are responsible for the greatest percentage of deaths among adolescents, followed by other unintentional injuries, homicide, and suicide.

Source: NHTSA, 2009.

Access to guns is a major factor in the rise in teenage suicide.

Suicide Suicide is the fourth leading cause of death among U.S. 15- to 19-year-olds (CDC, 2010; NHTSA, 2009). The teenage suicide rate fell by 34 percent between 1990 and 2006 (CDC, 2008b). In 2004, however, the suicide rate did shoot back up by 8 percent—its highest level in 15 years, with the largest increases among teenage girls. Hanging surpassed handguns as the preferred method among girls, but boys remained more likely to use firearms (Lubell, Kegler, Crosby, & Karch, 2007).

Although suicide occurs in all ethnic groups, Native American boys have the highest rates and African American girls the lowest. Gay, lesbian, and bisexual youths, who have high rates of depression, also have unusually high rates of suicide and attempted suicide (AAP Committee on Adolescence, 2000; NCHS, 2009; Remafedi, French, Story, Resnick, & Blum, 1998).

Young people who consider or attempt suicide tend to have histories of emotional illness. They are likely to be either perpetrators or victims of violence and to have school problems, academic or behavioral. Many have suffered from maltreatment in childhood and have severe problems with relationships. They tend to think poorly of themselves, to feel hopeless, and to have poor impulse control and low tolerance for frustration and stress. These young people are often alienated from their parents and have no one outside the family to turn to. They also tend to have attempted suicide before or to have friends or family members who did so (Borowsky, Ireland, & Resnick, 2001; Brent & Mann, 2006; Garland & Zigler, 1993; Johnson et al., 2002; NIMH, 1999; "Suicide—Part I," 1996; Swedo et al., 1991). Alcohol plays a part in half of all teenage suicides (AAP Committee on Adolescence, 2000). Perhaps the key factor is a tendency toward impulsive aggression. Postmortem and imaging studies of the brains of persons who have completed or attempted suicide have identified alterations in regions of the prefrontal cortex involved in emotion, regulation, and behavioral inhibition (Brent & Mann, 2006). Protective factors that reduce the risk of suicide include a sense of connectedness to family and school, emotional well-being, and academic achievement (Borowsky et al., 2001).

PROTECTIVE FACTORS: HEALTH IN CONTEXT

Adolescents' development, like that of younger children, does not occur in a vacuum. As we have seen, family and school environments play an important part in physical and mental health.

A study of 12,118 seventh through twelfth graders in a random sample of 134 schools across the United States (Resnick et al., 1997) looked at risk factors and protective factors affecting four major aspects of adolescent health and well-being. These were emotional distress and suicidal behavior; involvement in fighting, threats of violence, or use of weapons; use of cigarettes, alcohol, and marijuana; and sexual experience, including age of sexual initiation and any history of pregnancy. The students completed questionnaires and had 90-minute home interviews. During the sensitive portions of the interview, the young people listened to the questions through earphones and entered their answers on laptop computers. School administrators also filled out questionnaires.

The findings underline the linkage of physical, cognitive, emotional, and social development. Perceptions of connectedness to others, both at home and at school, positively affected young people's health and well-being in all domains. One important factor was parents' spending time with and being available to their adolescent children. Even more important was the sense that parents and teachers were warm and caring and had high expectations for children's achievement. These findings are clear and consistent with other research: Adolescents who are getting emotional support at home and are well-adjusted at school have the best chance of avoiding the health hazards of adolescence.

checkpoint
can **you** . . .

▷ Discuss factors affecting gender differences in adolescent depression?

▷ Name the three leading causes of death among adolescents, and discuss the dangers of firearm injury?

▷ Discuss trends and risk factors for adolescent suicide?

▷ Identify factors that tend to protect adolescents from health risks?

summary and key terms

guidepost 1
Adolescence: A Developmental Transition

What is adolescence, and what opportunities and risks does it entail?

- Adolescence is the transition from childhood to adulthood. Neither its beginning nor its end is clearly marked in Western societies; it lasts about a decade, between ages 11 or 12 and 19 or 20.
- In some non-Western cultures, coming of age is signified by special rites.
- Adolescence is full of opportunities for physical, cognitive, and psychosocial growth but also of risks to healthy development. Risky behavior patterns, such as drinking alcohol, abusing drugs, engaging in sexual and gang activity, and using firearms tend to be established early in adolescence. About 4 out of 5 young people experience no major problems.

adolescence (424)

puberty (425)

guidepost 2
Puberty: The End of Childhood

What physical changes do adolescents experience, and how do these changes affect them psychologically?

- Puberty is triggered by hormonal changes, which may affect moods and behavior. Puberty takes about 4 years, typically begins earlier in girls than in boys, and ends when a person can reproduce.
- Primary sex characteristics (the reproductive organs) enlarge and mature during puberty. Secondary sex characteristics also appear.
- During puberty, both boys and girls undergo an adolescent growth spurt. A secular trend toward earlier attainment of adult height and sexual maturity began about 100 years ago, probably because of improvements in living standards.
- The principal signs of sexual maturity are production of sperm (for males) and menstruation (for females). Spermarche typically occurs at age 13. Menarche occurs, on average, between ages 12 and 13 in the United States.
- Teenagers, especially girls, tend to be sensitive about their physical appearance. Girls who mature early tend to adjust less easily than early maturing boys.

primary sex characteristics (429)

secondary sex characteristics (429)

adolescent growth spurt (429)

spermarche (430)

menarche (430)

secular trend (430)

guidepost 3
The Adolescent Brain

What brain developments occur during adolescence, and how do they affect adolescent behavior?

- The adolescent brain is not yet fully mature. Adolescents process information about emotions with the amygdala, whereas adults use the frontal lobe. Thus adolescents tend to make less accurate, less reasoned judgments.
- A wave of overproduction of gray matter, especially in the frontal lobes, is followed by pruning of excess dendrites. Continuing myelination of the frontal lobes facilitates maturation of cognitive processing.
- Underdevelopment of frontal cortical systems connected with motivation, impulsivity, and addiction may help explain adolescents' tendency toward risk-taking.
- Because of their developing brains, adolescents are particularly vulnerable to effects of alcohol and addictive drugs.

guidepost 4
Physical and Mental Health

What are some common health problems and health risks of adolescence, and how can they be prevented?

- For the most part, the adolescent years are relatively healthy. Health problems often are associated with poverty or a risk-taking lifestyle. Adolescents are less likely than younger children to get regular medical care.
- Many adolescents, especially girls, do not engage in regular vigorous physical activity.
- Many adolescents do not get enough sleep because the high school schedule is out of sync with their natural body rhythms.
- Three common eating disorders in adolescence are obesity, anorexia nervosa, and bulimia nervosa. All can have serious long-term effects. Anorexia and bulimia affect mostly girls. Outcomes for bulimia tend to be better than for anorexia.
- Adolescent substance abuse and dependence have lessened in recent years, but nonmedical use of prescription drugs has increased.
- Marijuana, alcohol, and tobacco are the most popular drugs with adolescents. All involve serious risks.
- Leading causes of death among adolescents include motor vehicle accidents, firearm use, and suicide.

anorexia nervosa (437)

bulimia nervosa (438)

substance abuse (439)

substance dependence (439)

binge drinking (440)

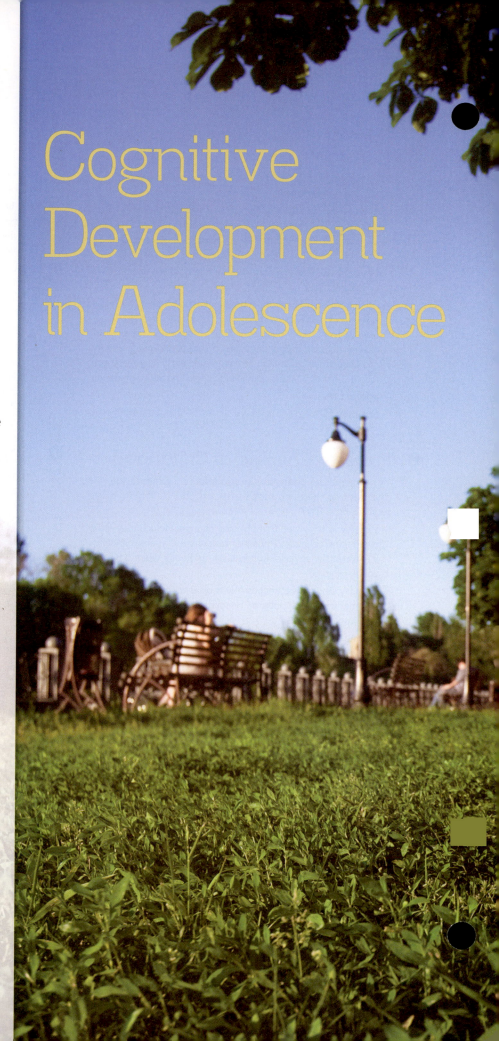

chapter 16

Cognitive
Development
in Adolescence

outline

Aspects of Cognitive Maturation

Moral Development

Educational and Vocational Issues

did you know?

▷ Adolescents with supportive, authoritative parents who stimulate them to question and expand on their moral reasoning tend to reason at higher levels?

▷ Girls tend to show more prosocial behavior than boys, and this difference becomes more pronounced in adolescence?

▷ Researchers disagree as to whether part-time work is beneficial or harmful to high school students?

In this chapter, we explore the Piagetian stage of formal operations. We look at adolescents' growth in information processing, including memory, knowledge, and reasoning, and in vocabulary and other linguistic skills. We note some immature aspects of adolescents' thought, and we examine adolescents' moral and spiritual development. Finally, we explore practical aspects of cognitive growth—issues of school and vocational choice.

outline

did you know

Life would be infinitely happier if we could only be born at the age of 80 and gradually approach 18.

Mark Twain, American Author and Humorist (1835–1910)

1. How do adolescents' thinking and use of language differ from younger children's?

2. On what basis do adolescents make moral judgments, and how does prosocial behavior vary?

3. What influences affect adolescents' school success and their educational and vocational planning and preparation?

guidepost 1

How do adolescents' thinking and use of language differ from younger children's?

Aspects of Cognitive Maturation

Adolescents not only look different from younger children, they also think and talk differently. Their speed of information processing continues to increase, though not as dramatically as in middle childhood. Although their thinking may remain immature in some ways, many adolescents are capable of abstract reasoning and sophisticated moral judgments, and they can plan more realistically for the future.

PIAGET'S STAGE OF FORMAL OPERATIONS

Adolescents enter what Piaget called the highest level of cognitive development—**formal operations**—when they move away from their reliance on concrete, real-world stimuli and develop the capacity for abstract thought. This development, usually around age 11, gives them a new, more flexible way to manipulate information. They can use symbols for symbols (for example, letting the letter X stand for an unknown numeral) and thus can learn algebra and calculus. They can better appreciate the hidden messages in metaphor and allegory and thus can find richer meanings in literature. They can think in terms of what *might be*, not just what *is*. They can imagine possibilities and can form and test hypotheses.

People in the stage of formal operations can integrate what they have learned in the past with the challenges of the present and make plans for the future. The ability to think abstractly has emotional implications too. Earlier, a child could love a parent or hate a classmate. Now an adolescent "can love freedom or hate exploitation. . . . The possible and the ideal captivate both mind and feeling" (H. Ginsburg & Opper, 1979, p. 201).

Hypothetical-Deductive Reasoning **Hypothetical-deductive reasoning** involves a methodical, scientific approach to problem solving and it characterizes formal operations thinking. It involves the ability to develop, consider, and test hypotheses, and the young person can be compared to a scientist exploring the various facets of life. To appreciate the difference formal reasoning makes, let's follow the progress of a typical child in dealing with a classic Piagetian problem, the pendulum problem.*

*This description of age-related differences in the approach to the pendulum problem is adapted from H. Ginsburg and Opper (1979).

formal operations
In Piaget's theory, final stage of cognitive development, characterized by the ability to think abstractly.

hypothetical-deductive reasoning
Ability, believed by Piaget to accompany the stage of formal operations, to develop, consider, and test hypotheses.

connect

study smart

Piaget's Formal Operations Substage

Like any other linguistic code,
outsiders (adults) out.

Vocabulary may differ by ge
and type of school (Labov, 19
and "jocks" engage in different
conversation. This talk, in turn
speech patterns in Naples, Italy
ture where teenagerhood consti

Teenage slang is part of the
from parents and the adult wo
newfound ability to play with v
tastes, and preferences" (Elkind

CHANGES IN INFORM

Changes in the way adolescents
frontal lobes and may help ex
neural connections wither and
rience. Thus progress in cogniti
(Kuhn, 2006).

Researchers have identified
tion processing: *structural chan*
at each.

Structural Change *Structural*
processing capacity and an inc
memory. The capacity of worki
may continue to increase durin
older adolescents to deal with
of information.

Information stored in long-t

- **Declarative knowledge** ("k
  a person has acquired (for
  Washington was the first U

- **Procedural knowledge** ("k
  has acquired, such as being

- **Conceptual knowledge** ("k
  an algebraic equation rema
  from both sides.

Functional Change Processe
functional aspects of cognition
all of which improve during a
Among the most importar
ing speed (Kuhn, 2006), and
ter 13), which includes such
control of impulsive responses,
to develop at varying rates (I
study, researchers tested proce
245 8- to 30-year-olds by m
tasks. For example, participar
appeared in their peripheral
center and then, after the ligh

*Unless otherwise referenced, the discus

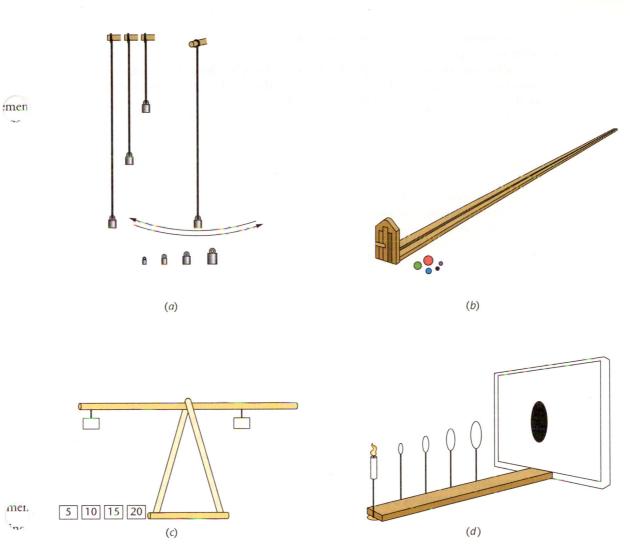

(a) (b)

(c) (d)

FIGURE 16.1
Piagetian Tasks for Measuring Attainment of Formal Operations

(a) *Pendulum. The pendulum's string can be shortened or lengthened, and weights of varying sizes can
be attached to it. The student must determine what variables affect the speed of the pendulum's swing.*
(b) *Motion in a horizontal plane. A spring device launches balls of varying sizes that roll in a horizontal
plane. The student must predict their stopping points. (c) Balance beam. A balance scale comes with weights
of varying sizes that can be hung at different points along the crossbar. The student must determine what
factors affect whether the scale will balance. (d) Shadows. A board containing a row of peg holes is attached
perpendicular to the base of a screen. A light source and rings of varying diameters can be placed in the
holes, at varying distances from the screen. The student must produce two shadows of the same size, using
different-sized rings.*

Source: Adapted from Small, Fig. 8-12, 1990.

The child, Adam, is shown the pendulum, an object hanging from a string. He is
then shown how he can change any of four factors: the length of the string, the weight
of the object, the height from which the object is released, and the amount of force he
uses to push the object. He is asked to figure out which factor or combination of factors determines how fast the pendulum swings. (Figure 16.1 depicts this and other
Piagetian tasks for assessing the achievement of formal operations.)

When Adam first sees the pendulum, he is not yet 7 years old and is in the preoperational stage. Unable to formulate a plan for attacking the problem, he tries one thing
after another in a hit-or-miss manner. First, he puts a light weight on a long string and
pushes it; then he tries swinging a heavy weight on a short string; then he removes the

imaginary audience Elkind's term for observer who exists only in an adolescent's mind and is as concerned with the adolescent's thoughts and actions as the adolescent is.

personal fable Elkind's term for conviction that one is special, unique, and not subject to the rules that govern the rest of the world.

▷ Describe Elkind's six proposed aspects of immature adolescent thought, and explain how they may grow out of the transition to formal operational thought?

▷ Identify several characteristics of adolescents' language development that reflect cognitive advances?

▷ Name two major kinds of changes in adolescents' cognitive processing and give examples of each?

On what basis do adolescents make moral judgments, and how does prosocial behavior vary?

preconventional morality First level of Kohlberg's theory of moral reasoning in which control is external and rules are obeyed in order to gain rewards or avoid punishment or out of self-interest.

Adolescents reached adult-level performance in response inhibition at age 14, processing speed at 15, and working memory at 19. Although each process appears to mature independently, each seems to aid in the development of the others (Luna, Garver, Urban, Lazar, & Sweeney, 2004).

However, improvements observed in laboratory situations do not necessarily carry over to real life, where behavior depends in part on motivation and emotion regulation. Many older adolescents make poorer real-world decisions than younger adolescents do. In the game Twenty Questions, the object is to ask as few yes-or-no questions as necessary to discover the identity of a person, place, or thing by systematically narrowing down the categories within which the answer might fall. In one study (Drumm & Jackson, 1996), high school students, especially boys, showed a greater tendency than either early adolescents or college students to jump to guessing the answer. As we discussed in Chapter 15, adolescents' rash judgments may be related to immature brain development, which may permit feelings to override reason.

Moral Development

As children grow older and attain higher cognitive levels, they become capable of more complex reasoning about moral issues. Adolescents are better able than younger children to take another person's perspective, to solve social problems, to deal with interpersonal relationships, and to see themselves as social beings. All of these tendencies foster moral development.

Let's look at Lawrence Kohlberg's seminal theory of moral reasoning, at Carol Gilligan's influential work on moral development in women and girls, and at research on prosocial behavior in adolescence.

KOHLBERG'S THEORY OF MORAL REASONING

A woman is near death from cancer. A druggist has discovered a drug that doctors believe might save her. The druggist is charging $2,000 for a small dose—10 times what the drug costs him to make. The sick woman's husband, Heinz, borrows from everyone he knows but can scrape together only $1,000. He begs the druggist to sell him the drug for $1,000 or let him pay the rest later. The druggist refuses, saying, "I discovered the drug and I'm going to make money from it." Heinz, desperate, breaks into the man's store and steals the drug. Should Heinz have done that? Why or why not? (Kohlberg, 1969).

Heinz's problem is the most famous example of Lawrence Kohlberg's approach to studying moral development. Starting in the 1950s, Kohlberg and his colleagues posed hypothetical dilemmas like this one to 75 boys ages 10, 13, and 16 and continued to question them periodically for more than 30 years. Kohlberg, borrowing Piaget's interview methodology, asked children about how they arrived at their answers. Kohlberg came to believe that moral development was a consequence of moral reasoning, which depended heavily on cognitive development. Moreover, he believed that at the heart of every dilemma was the concept of justice—a universal principle. In other words, Kohlberg believed moral reasoning was fundamentally concerned with sound reasoning about principles of justice.

Kohlberg's Levels and Stages Moral development in Kohlberg's theory bears some resemblance to Piaget's (refer to Chapter 13), but Kohlberg's model is more complex. On the basis of thought processes shown by responses to his dilemmas, Kohlberg (1969) described three levels of moral reasoning, each divided into two stages (Table 16.1):

- *Level I:* **Preconventional morality.** People act under external controls. They obey rules to avoid punishment or reap rewards, or act out of self-interest. This level is typical of children ages 4 to 10.

TABLE 16.1 Kohlberg's Six Stages of Moral Reasoning

Levels	Stages of Reasoning	Typical Answers to Heinz's Dilemma
Level I: Preconventional morality (ages 4 to 10)	*Stage 1: Orientation toward punishment and obedience.* "What will happen to me?" Children obey rules to avoid punishment. They ignore the motives of an act and focus on its physical form (such as the size of a lie) or its consequences (such as the amount of physical damage).	*Pro:* "He should steal the drug. It isn't really bad to take it. It isn't as if he hadn't asked to pay for it first. The drug he'd take is worth only $200; he's not really taking a $2,000 drug." *Con:* "He shouldn't steal the drug. It's a big crime. He didn't get permission; he used force and broke and entered. He did a lot of damage and stole a very expensive drug."
	Stage 2: Instrumental purpose and exchange. "You scratch my back, I'll scratch yours." Children conform to rules out of self-interest and consideration for what others can do for them. They look at an act in terms of the human needs it meets and differentiate this value from the act's physical form and consequences.	*Pro:* "It's all right to steal the drug, because his wife needs it and he wants her to live. It isn't that he wants to steal, but that's what he has to do to save her." *Con:* "He shouldn't steal it. The druggist isn't wrong or bad; he just wants to make a profit. That's what you're in business for—to make money."
Level II: Conventional morality (ages 10 to 13 or beyond)	*Stage 3: Maintaining mutual relations, approval of others, the golden rule.* "Am I a good boy or girl?" Children want to please and help others, can judge the intentions of others, and develop ideas of what a good person is. They evaluate an act according to the motive behind it or the person performing it, and they take circumstances into account.	*Pro:* "He should steal the drug. He is only doing something that is natural for a good husband to do. You can't blame him for doing something out of love for his wife. You'd blame him if he didn't love his wife enough to save her." *Con:* "He shouldn't steal. If his wife dies, he can't be blamed. It isn't because he's heartless or that he doesn't love her enough to do everything that he legally can. The druggist is the selfish or heartless one."
	Stage 4: Social concern and conscience. "What if everybody did it?" People are concerned with doing their duty, showing respect for higher authority, and maintaining the social order. They consider an act always wrong, regardless of motive or circumstances, if it violates a rule and harms others.	*Pro:* "You should steal it. If you did nothing, you'd be letting your wife die. It's your responsibility if she dies. You have to take it with the idea of paying the druggist." *Con:* "It is a natural thing for Heinz to want to save his wife, but it's still always wrong to steal. He knows he's taking a valuable drug from the man who made it."
Level III: Postconventional morality (early adolescence, or not until young adulthood, or never)	*Stage 5: Morality of contract, of individual rights, and of democratically accepted law.* People value the will of the majority and the welfare of society—they are focused on the greater good. They think this is achieved primarily by adherence to the law and that it is better for all when laws are followed. But, they understand there are times when human need and the law conflict.	*Pro:* "The law wasn't set up for these circumstances. Taking the drug in this situation isn't really right, but it's justified." *Con:* "You can't completely blame someone for stealing, but extreme circumstances don't really justify taking the law into your own hands. You can't have people stealing whenever they are desperate. The end may be good, but the ends don't justify the means."
	Stage 6: Morality of universal ethical principles. People act in accordance with what they consider to be universal moral principles, regardless of legal restrictions or the opinions of others. They act in accordance with what they believe to be true, knowing that they would condemn themselves if they did not.	*Pro:* "This is a situation that forces him to choose between stealing and letting his wife die. In a situation where the choice must be made, it is morally right to steal. He has to act in terms of the principle of preserving and respecting life." *Con:* "Heinz is faced with the decision of whether to consider the other people who need the drug just as badly as his wife. Heinz ought to act not according to his feelings for his wife, but considering the value of all the lives involved."

Source: Adapted from Kohlberg, 1969; Lickona, 1976.

- *Level II:* **Conventional morality** (or **morality of conventional role conformity**). People have internalized the standards of authority figures. They are concerned about being "good," pleasing others, and maintaining the social order. This level is typically reached after age 10; many people never move beyond it, even in adulthood.

- *Level III:* **Postconventional morality** (or **morality of autonomous moral principles**). People recognize conflicts between moral standards and make judgments on the basis of principles of right, fairness, and justice. People generally do not reach this level of moral reasoning until at least early adolescence, or more commonly in young adulthood, if ever.

In Kohlberg's theory, it is the reasoning underlying a person's response to a moral dilemma, not the answer itself, that indicates the stage of moral development. As shown in Table 16.1, two people who give opposite answers may be at the same stage if their reasoning is based on similar factors.

Some adolescents and even some adults remain at Kohlberg's level I. Like young children, they seek to avoid punishment or to satisfy their needs. Most adolescents and most adults seem to be at level II, usually in stage 3. They conform to social conventions, support the status quo, and do the "right" thing to please others or to obey the law. Stage 4 reasoning (upholding social norms) is less common but increases from early adolescence into adulthood. Often adolescents show periods of apparent disequilibrium when advancing from one level to another (Eisenberg & Morris, 2004) or fall back on other ethical systems, such as religious prescriptions, rather than Kohlberg's justice-based one (Thoma & Rest, 1999).

Kohlberg added a transitional level between levels II and III, when people no longer feel bound by society's moral standards but have not yet reasoned out their own principles of justice. Instead, they base their moral decisions on personal feelings. Before people can develop a fully principled (level III) morality, he said, they must recognize the relativity of moral standards. Many young people question their earlier moral views when they enter high school or college or the world of work and encounter people whose values, culture, and ethnic background are different from

Early adolescent girls have more intimate social relationships than early adolescent boys and are more concerned about caring for others. This may help explain why girls in this age group tend to score higher than boys on moral judgments.

their own. Still, few people reach a level where they can choose among differing moral standards. In fact, at one point Kohlberg questioned the validity of stage 6, morality based on universal ethical principles, because so few people seem to attain it. Later, he proposed a seventh, "cosmic" stage, in which people consider the effect of their actions not only on other people but on the universe as a whole (Kohlberg, 1981; Kohlberg & Ryncarz, 1990).

Evaluating Kohlberg's Theory Kohlberg, building on Piaget, inaugurated a profound shift in the way we look at moral development. Instead of viewing morality solely as the attainment of control over self-gratifying impulses, investigators now study how children and adults base moral judgments on their growing understanding of the social world. Kohlberg's work has influenced much additional research, including James Fowler's theory of spiritual development described in Box 16.1.

Initial research supported Kohlberg's theory. The American boys whom Kohlberg and his colleagues followed through adulthood progressed through Kohlberg's stages in sequence, and none skipped a stage. Their moral judgments correlated positively with age, education, IQ, and socioeconomic status (Colby, Kohlberg, Gibbs, & Lieberman, 1983). More recent research, however, has cast doubt on the delineation of some of Kohlberg's stages (Eisenberg & Morris, 2004). A study of children's judgments about laws and lawbreaking suggests that some children can reason flexibly about such issues as early as age 6 (Helwig & Jasiobedzka, 2001).

One reason the ages attached to Kohlberg's levels are so variable is that people who have achieved a high level of cognitive development do not always reach a comparably high level of moral development. A certain level of cognitive development is *necessary* but not *sufficient* for a comparable level of moral development. In other words, just because a person is capable of moral reasoning does not necessarily imply that the person actually engages in moral reasoning. Thus, other processes besides cognition must be at work. Some investigators suggest that moral activity is motivated, not only by abstract considerations of justice but also by such emotions as empathy, guilt, distress, and the internalization of prosocial norms (Eisenberg & Morris, 2004; Gibbs, 1991, 1995; Gibbs & Schnell, 1985). It also has been argued that Kohlberg's stages 5 and 6 cannot fairly be called the most mature stages of moral development because they restrict maturity to a select group of people given to philosophical reflection and to people who hold a particular view about the value of moral relativism.

Furthermore, there is not always a clear relationship between moral reasoning and moral behavior. For example, most people would characterize the actions of Pol Pot, the despotic Cambodian leader of the Khmer Rouge, as clearly amoral. From 1974–1979, the Khmer Rouge killed about 25 percent of the population of Cambodia—some 1 to 3 million people. Most people would describe this mass murder as profoundly evil. But, Pol Pot was driven by his idealistic belief in an idyllic Communist agrarian society. He believed that the actions he took were in the service of a higher ideal, and the justifications for the actions he took were cognitively complex and well formed. While this is an extreme example, it is clear that people at postconventional levels of reasoning do not necessarily act more morally than those at lower levels. Other factors, such as specific situations, conceptions of virtue, and concern for others contribute to moral behavior (Colby & Damon, 1992; Fischer & Pruyne, 2003). Generally speaking, however, adolescents who are more advanced in moral reasoning do tend to be more moral in their behavior as well as better adjusted and higher in social competence, whereas antisocial adolescents tend to use less mature moral reasoning (Eisenberg & Morris, 2004).

Influence of Parents, Peers and Culture Neither Piaget nor Kohlberg considered parents important to children's moral development, but more recent research emphasizes parents' contribution in both the cognitive and the emotional realms. Adolescents with supportive, authoritative parents who stimulate them to question and expand on their moral reasoning tend to reason at higher levels (Eisenberg & Morris, 2004).

what's **your** view

Can you think of a time when you or someone you know acted contrary to personal moral judgment? Why do you think this happened?

FOWLER'S STAGES OF FAITH

16.1

Can spiritual belief be studied from a developmental perspective? Yes, according to James Fowler (1981, 1989). Fowler defined faith as a way of seeing or knowing the world. To find out how people arrive at this way of seeing or knowing, Fowler and his students at Harvard Divinity School interviewed more than 400 people of all ages with various ethnic, educational, and socioeconomic backgrounds and various religious or secular identifications and affiliations.

Faith, according to Fowler, can be religious or nonreligious. People may have faith in a god, in science, in humanity, or in a cause to which they attach ultimate worth and that gives meaning to their lives. Faith develops, said Fowler, as do other aspects of cognition, through interaction between the maturing person and the environment. Fowler's stages correspond roughly to those described by Piaget, Kohlberg, and Erikson. New experiences—crises, problems, or revelations—that challenge or upset a person's equilibrium may prompt a leap from one stage to the next. The ages at which these transitions occur are variable, and some people never leave a particular stage; but the first three stages normally occur during childhood and adolescence.

- *Stage 1: Primal, or intuitive-projective, faith* (ages 18–24 months to 7 years). The beginnings of faith, says Fowler, arise after toddlers become self-aware, begin to use language and symbolic thought, and have developed *basic trust:* the sense that their needs will be met by powerful others. As young children struggle to understand the forces that control their world, they form powerful, imaginative, often terrifying images of God, heaven, and hell, drawn from the stories adults tell. These images are often irrational; preoperational children tend to be confused about cause and effect and about the difference between reality and fantasy. Still egocentric, they may identify God's point of view with their own or their parents'. They think of God mainly in terms of obedience and punishment.
- *Stage 2: Mythic-literal faith* (ages 7 to 12 years). Children capable of concrete operations begin to develop a more coherent view of the universe. As they adopt their family's and community's beliefs and observances, they tend to take religious stories and symbols literally. They can now see God as having a perspective, beyond their own, that takes into account people's effort and intent. They believe that God is fair and that people get what they deserve.

- *Stage 3: Synthetic-conventional faith* (adolescence or beyond). Adolescents capable of abstract thought form belief systems and commitments to ideals. As they search for identity, they seek a more personal relationship with God but look to others, usually peers, for moral authority. Their faith is unquestioning and conforms to community standards. This stage is typical of followers of organized religion; about 50 percent of adults may never move beyond it to Fowler's more advanced stages: critically examined faith and, finally, universalized faith.
- *Stage 4: Individuative-reflective faith* (early to middle 20s or beyond). Adults who reach this stage examine their faith critically and think out their own beliefs, independent of external authority and group norms.
- *Stage 5: Conjunctive faith* (midlife or beyond). Middle-aged people may become more aware of the limits of reason. They recognize life's paradoxes and contradictions, and they often struggle with conflicts between fulfilling their own needs and sacrificing for others. As they begin to anticipate death, they may achieve a deeper understanding and acceptance through faith.
- *Stage 6: Universalizing faith* (late life). In this rare category Fowler placed such moral and spiritual leaders as Mahatma Gandhi, Martin Luther King Jr., and Mother Teresa, whose vision or commitment profoundly inspires others. Because they threaten the established order, they may become martyrs; and though they love life, they do not cling to it. This stage parallels Kohlberg's proposed seventh stage of moral development.

As one of the first researchers to study faith systematically, Fowler has had great impact but has been criticized on several counts (Koenig, 1994). Critics say Fowler's concept of faith is at odds with conventional definitions. They challenge his emphasis on cognitive knowledge and claim that he underestimates the maturity of a simple, solid, unquestioning faith. Critics also question whether faith develops in universal stages or in those Fowler identified. Fowler's sample was not randomly selected; it consisted of paid participants who lived in or near North American cities with major colleges or universities. Thus the findings may be more representative of people with above-average intelligence and education, and they are not representative of non-Western cultures.

Continued

Continued

Some investigators have looked more narrowly at children's understanding of prayer, one aspect of religious activity, and have come up with stages somewhat different from Fowler's. One early study using Piaget-style questioning (Goldman, 1964) noted a progression from a magical stage before age 9, in which children believe that prayers come true as if by magic, toward rational and, finally, faith-based stages.

what's your view

▷ From your experience and observation, can faith be nonreligious?

▷ Can you recall having gone through any of Fowler's stages of faith? At which stage would you say you are now?

16.1

Peers also affect moral reasoning by talking with each other about moral conflicts. Having more close friends, spending quality time with them, and being perceived as a leader are associated with higher moral reasoning (Eisenberg & Morris, 2004).

Kohlberg's system does not seem to represent moral reasoning in non-Western cultures as accurately as in the Western culture in which it was originally developed (Eisenberg & Morris, 2004). Older people in countries other than the United States do tend to score at higher stages than younger people. However, people in non-Western cultures rarely score above stage 4 (Edwards, 1981; Nisan & Kohlberg, 1982; Snarey, 1985), suggesting that some aspects of Kohlberg's model may not fit the cultural values of these societies.

GILLIGAN'S THEORY: AN ETHIC OF CARE

Do men and women reason in the same fashion? This question was addressed by Carol Gilligan (1982), who asserted that Kohlberg's theory was sexist and oriented toward values more important to men than to women. Gilligan argued that men, Kohlberg included, viewed morality in terms of justice and fairness. Women held a different set of values, however, that placed caring and avoiding harm as higher goals than justice. Kohlberg's typology unfairly categorized women as less morally and cognitive complex because of the exclusive focus on justice (Eisenberg & Morris, 2004).

Research has not found much support for Gilligan's claim of a male bias in Kohlberg's stages (Brabeck & Shore, 2003; Jaffee & Hyde, 2000), and she has since modified her position. However, research has found small gender differences in care-related moral reasoning among adolescents in some cultures (Eisenberg & Morris, 2004). For example, early adolescent girls in the United States tend to emphasize care-related concerns more than boys do, especially when tested with open-ended questions ("How important is it to keep promises to a friend?") or self-chosen moral dilemmas related to their own experience (Garmon, Basinger, Gregg, & Gibbs, 1996). This may be because girls generally mature earlier and have more intimate social relationships (Garmon et al., 1996; Skoe & Diessner, 1994). In an analysis of 113 studies, girls and women were more likely to think in terms of care and boys and men in terms of justice, but these differences were small (Jaffee & Hyde, 2000).

PROSOCIAL BEHAVIOR AND VOLUNTEER ACTIVITY

Some researchers have studied prosocial (similar to care-oriented) moral reasoning as an alternative to Kohlberg's justice-based system. Prosocial moral reasoning is reasoning about moral dilemmas in which one person's needs or desires conflict with those of others in situations in which social rules or norms are unclear or nonexistent. For example, a child faced with the dilemma of deciding whether or not to intervene when a friend is being teased might run the risk of becoming a target of the bullies, too. So, such a child would engage in prosocial moral reasoning when deciding about a course of action. In a longitudinal study that followed children into early adulthood, prosocial reasoning based on personal reflection about consequences and on internalized values

checkpoint
can **you** . . .

▷ List Kohlberg's levels and stages, and discuss factors that influence how rapidly children and adolescents progress through them?

▷ Evaluate Kohlberg's theory with regard to the role of emotion and socialization, parent and peer influences, and cross-cultural validity?

▷ Explain the difference between Gilligan's and Kohlberg's standards of moral reasoning, and discuss gender effects?

▷ Discuss individual differences in prosocial behavior, such as volunteering?

guidepost
③ What influences affect adolescents' school success and their educational and vocational planning and preparation?

and norms increased with age, whereas reasoning based on such stereotypes as "it's nice to help" decreased from childhood into the late teens (Eisenberg & Morris, 2004).

Prosocial behavior, too, typically increases from childhood through adolescence (Eisenberg & Morris, 2004). Girls tend to show more prosocial behavior than boys (Eisenberg & Fabes, 1998), and this difference becomes more pronounced in adolescence (Fabes, Carlo, Kupanoff, & Laible, 1999). Girls tend to see themselves as more empathic and prosocial than boys do, and parents of girls emphasize social responsibility more than parents of boys (Eisenberg & Morris, 2004). In a large-scale study, this was true of 18-year-olds and their parents in seven countries—Australia, United States, Sweden, Hungary, Czech Republic, Bulgaria, and Russia (Flannagan, Bowes, Jonsson, Csapo, & Sheblanova, 1998). As with younger children, parents who use inductive discipline are more likely to have prosocial adolescents than parents who use power-assertive discipline. Inductive parenting techniques involve reasoning with children, explaining the consequences of their behaviors, and encouraging them to consider the effects of their actions on others.

About half of adolescents engage in some sort of community service or volunteer activity. These prosocial activities enable adolescents to become involved in adult society, to explore their potential roles as part of the community, and to link their developing sense of identity to civic involvement. Adolescent volunteers tend to have a high degree of self-understanding and commitment to others. Girls are more likely to volunteer than boys, and adolescents with high SES volunteer more than those with lower SES (Eisenberg & Morris, 2004). Students who do volunteer work outside of school tend, as adults, to be more engaged in their communities than those who do not (Eccles, 2004).

Educational and Vocational Issues

School is a central organizing experience in most adolescents' lives. It offers opportunities to learn information, master new skills, and sharpen old skills; to participate in sports, the arts, and other activities; to explore vocational choices; and to be with friends. It widens intellectual and social horizons. Some adolescents, however, experience school not as an opportunity but as one more hindrance on the road to adulthood.

In the United States, as in all other industrialized countries and in some developing countries as well, more students finish high school than ever before, and many enroll in higher education (Eccles et al., 2003; Organisation for Economic Co-operation and Development [OECD], 2004). In 2009, nearly 76 percent of U.S. 18- to 24-year-olds had received a high school diploma or equivalent credential. Rates vary by state; Wisconsin had the highest graduation rate at 90.7 percent and Nevada had the lowest rate at 56.3 percent (Aud, Hussar, Johnson, Kena, & Roth, 2012).

Among the 30 member countries of the Organisation for Economic Co-operation and Development, graduation rates vary from 15 percent in Turkey to 62 percent in Iceland (OECD, 2008a) The United States, with an average of 12.7 years of schooling, is on the high end of this international comparison. However, U.S. adolescents, on average, do less well on academic achievement tests than adolescents in many other countries. For example, U.S. students score lower on mathematics and scientific literacy than most other countries at a similar level of economic development. (Baldi, Jin, Skemer, Green, & Herget, 2007; Lemke et al., 2004; T. D. Snyder & Hoffman, 2001). Furthermore, although fourth- and eighth-grade student achievement, as measured by the National Assessment of Educational Progress (NAEP), has improved in some areas, twelfth-grade achievement generally has not (National Center for Education [NCES], 2009).

Let's look at influences on school achievement and then at young people who drop out of school. Then, we'll consider planning for higher education and vocations.

INFLUENCES ON SCHOOL ACHIEVEMENT

As in the elementary grades, such factors as parenting practices, socioeconomic status, and the quality of the home environment influence the course of school achievement in adolescence. Other factors include gender, ethnicity, peer influence, quality of schooling, and students' belief in themselves.

Student Motivation and Self-Efficacy In Western countries, particularly the United States, educational practices are based on the assumption that students are, or can be, motivated to learn. Educators emphasize the value of intrinsic motivation—the student's desire to learn for the sake of learning (Larson & Wilson, 2004). Unfortunately, many U.S. students are *not* self-motivated, and motivation often declines as they enter high school (Eccles, 2004; Larson & Wilson, 2004).

In these Western cultures, students high in *self-efficacy*—who believe that they can master tasks and regulate their learning—are likely to do well in school. So, for example, after failing a test, a student with high self-efficacy might assume that he didn't study enough, and that in order to do well in future tests he should study more. A student with low self-efficacy, by contrast, might conclude the material was too hard or the test was unfair. In a longitudinal study of 140 eighth graders, students' self-discipline was twice as important as IQ in accounting for their grades and achievement test scores and for selection into a competitive high school program at the end of the year (Duckworth & Seligman, 2005).

In the United States, where opportunities exist for most children, how much children learn is often based on their personal motivation. But, in many cultures, education is based not on personal motivation but on such factors as duty (India), submission to authority (Islamic countries), and participation in the family and community (sub-Saharan Africa). In the countries of East Asia, students are expected to learn in order to meet family and societal expectations. Learning is expected to require intense effort, and students who fail or fall behind feel obligated to try again. This may help explain why, in international comparisons in science and math, East Asian students substantially surpass U.S. students. In developing countries, issues of motivation pale in the light of social and economic barriers to education: inadequate or absent schools and educational resources, the need for child labor to support the family, barriers to schooling for girls or cultural subgroups, and early marriage (Larson & Wilson, 2004). Thus, as we discuss factors in educational success, which are drawn largely from studies in the United States and other Western countries, we need to remember that they do not apply to all cultures.

Gender On an international test of adolescents in 43 industrialized countries, girls in all countries were better readers than boys. Boys were ahead in mathematical literacy in about half of the countries, but these gender differences were less pronounced than in reading (OECD, 2004). Overall, beginning in adolescence, girls do better on verbal tasks that involve writing and language usage; boys do better in activities that involve visual and spatial functions helpful in math and science. Despite theories that boys possess some innate ability to do better at math, an evaluation of SAT results and math scores from 7 million students found no gender differences in math performance (Hyde, Lindberg, Linn, Ellis, & Williams, 2008).

What causes the observed gender differences? As with all aspects of development, research points to interacting biological and environmental contributions (Hyde & Mertz, 2009).

As we described in Chapter 9, male and female brains do show some differences in structure and organization. Moreover, these differences tend to become more pronounced with age. Girls have more gray matter, and their neurons also have more connections. In addition, their brains are more evenly balanced across the hemispheres. What are the consequences of these differences? The brain structure of girls appears to permit a wider range of cognitive abilities, and girls are better able to integrate verbal and analytic tasks (which occur in the left brain) with spatial and holistic tasks (which occur in the right

study**smart**

Mastery
Orientation

parents are sometimes described as authoritarian, get high grades and score better than European American students on math achievement tests, apparently because both parents and peers prize achievement (C. Chen & Stevenson, 1995). The strong school achievement of many young people from a variety of immigrant backgrounds reflects their families' and friends' strong emphasis on educational success (Fuligni, 1997; 2001).

Peer influence may help explain the downward trend in academic motivation and achievement that begins for many students in early adolescence. In a longitudinal study of students entering an urban middle school, motivation and grades declined, on average, during seventh grade. Students whose peer group were high achievers showed less decline in achievement and enjoyment of school, whereas those who associated with low achievers showed greater declines (Ryan, 2001).

Importance of SES and Related Family Characteristics Socioeconomic status is an important predictor of academic success. Parents' educational level and family income indirectly affect educational attainment based on how they influence parenting style, sibling relationships, and adolescent academic engagement (Melby, Conger, Fang, Wickrama, & Conger, 2008). According to a study of 15-year-olds' mathematical literacy in 20 relatively high-income countries, students with at least one postsecondary-educated parent performed better than students whose parents had lower educational levels (Hampden-Thompson & Johnston, 2006). A similar gap occurred between students whose parents had high occupational status and those whose parents were of middle or low occupational status. Having more than 200 books in the home was associated with higher scores, and living in a two-parent family was another key predictor of math competence in all 20 countries.

The School The quality of schooling strongly influences student achievement. A good middle or high school has an orderly, safe environment, adequate material resources, a stable teaching staff, and a positive sense of community. The school culture places a strong emphasis on academics and fosters the belief that all students can learn. It also offers opportunities for extracurricular activities, which keep students engaged and prevent them from getting into trouble after school. Teachers trust, respect, and care about students and have high expectations for them as well as confidence in their own ability to help students succeed (Eccles, 2004).

One of the issues with comparing historical research with current research is that the influence of particular variables can change over time. Electronic book readers such as the Kindle are becoming increasingly popular. What might this trend mean for the previous finding that number of books in the home is correlated with academic achievement?

Even though adolescents are more independent than younger children, the home atmosphere continues to influence school achievement. Parents help not only by monitoring homework, but also by taking an active interest in other aspects of teenagers' lives. Children of authoritative parents who discuss issues openly and offer praise and encouragement tend to do best in school.

Adolescents are more satisfied with school if they are allowed to participate in making rules and feel support from teachers and other students (Samdal & Dür, 2000) and if the curriculum and instruction are meaningful and appropriately challenging and fit their interests, skill level, and needs (Eccles, 2004). In a survey of students' perceptions of their teachers, high teacher expectations were the most consistent positive predictor of students' goals and interests, and negative feedback was the most consistent negative predictor of academic performance and classroom behavior (Wentzel, 2002).

A decline in academic motivation and achievement often begins with the transition from the intimacy and familiarity of elementary school to the larger, more pressured, and less supportive environment of middle school or junior high school (Eccles, 2004). For this reason, some cities have tried eliminating the middle school transition by extending elementary school to eighth grade or have consolidated some middle schools with small high schools (Gootman, 2007). Some big-city school systems, such as New York's, Philadelphia's, and Chicago's, are experimenting with small schools in which students, teachers, and parents form a learning community united by a common vision of good education and often a special curricular focus, such as music or ethnic studies (Meier, 1995; Rossi, 1996).

Another innovation is Early College High Schools—small, personalized, high-quality schools operated in cooperation with nearby colleges. By combining a nurturing atmosphere with clear, rigorous standards, these schools enable students to complete high school requirements plus the first 2 years of college ("The Early College High School Initiative," n.d.).

DROPPING OUT OF HIGH SCHOOL

More U.S. youths are completing high school than ever before. The percentage of those who drop out, known as the status dropout rate, includes all people in the 16- to 24-year-old age group who are not enrolled in school and who have not completed a high school program, regardless of when they left school. In 2009–2010, the status dropout rate for public school students in grades 9–12 was 3.4 percent, representing some 500,000 students. Average dropout rates are lower for white students (2.3 percent) than for both blacks (5.5 percent) and Hispanics (5.0 percent). Asian students are the least likely to dropout (1.9 percent) (Stillwell & Sable, 2013; Figure 16.2.).

Why are poor and minority adolescents more likely to drop out? One reason may be ineffective schooling: low teacher expectations or differential treatment of these students; less teacher support than at the elementary level; and the perceived irrelevance

checkpoint
can you . . .

▷ Explain how schools in various cultures motivate students to learn?

▷ Assess the influences of personal qualities, SES, gender, ethnicity, parents, and peers on academic achievement?

▷ Give examples of educational practices that can help high school students succeed?

The Gates Foundation has provided funding for a new program in which tenth graders who pass proficiency tests will be allowed to graduate early and immediately begin taking community college courses. Proponents argue that a system based on subject mastery rather than accumulated credits will lead to increased motivation for proficient students. Moreover, those students who do not pass the board exams will know which competencies they must work on to engage in college level work. What do you think?

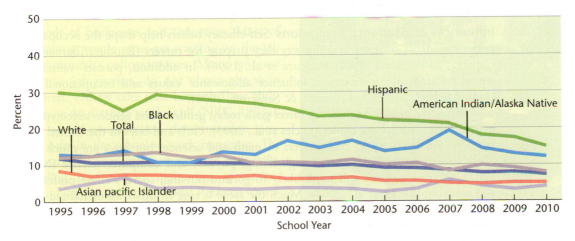

FIGURE 16.2

Status Dropout Rates of 16- through 24-Year-Olds between 1995 and 2010

Source: Stillwell & Sable, 2013.

likely to find jobs and earned higher wages than students who did not participate (Hughes, Bailey, & Mechur, 2001).

Adolescents in the Workplace In the United States, an estimated 80 to 90 percent of adolescents are employed at some time during high school, mostly in service and retail jobs (Staff, Mortimer, & Uggen, 2004). Researchers disagree over whether part-time work is beneficial to high school students (by helping them develop real-world skills and a work ethic) or detrimental (by distracting them from long-term educational and occupational goals).

Some research suggests that working students fall into two groups: those who are on an accelerated path to adulthood, and those who make a more leisurely transition, balancing schoolwork, paid jobs, and extracurricular activities. The "accelerators" work more than 20 hours a week during high school and spend little time on school-related leisure activities. Exposure to an adult world may lead them into alcohol and drug use, sexual activity, and delinquent behavior. Many of these adolescents have relatively low SES; they tend to look for full-time work right after high school and not to obtain college degrees. Intensive work experience in high school improves their prospects for work and income after high school, but not for long-term occupational attainment. The "balancers," in contrast, often come from more privileged backgrounds. For them, the effects of part-time work seem entirely benign. It helps them to gain a sense of responsibility, independence, and self-confidence and to appreciate the value of work but does not deter them from their educational paths (Staff et al., 2004).

For high school students who must or choose to work outside of school, then, the effects are more likely to be positive if they try to limit working hours and remain engaged in school activities. Cooperative educational programs that enable students to work part-time as part of their school program may be especially protective (Staff et al., 2004). These programs may also help students try out different vocations and begin the process of deciding on a career.

Career planning is an important aspect of the adolescent's overall search for identity. The question "What shall I do?" is very close to "Who shall I be?" People who feel they are doing something worthwhile, and doing it well, feel good about themselves. Those who feel that their work does not matter—or that they are not good at it—may wonder about the meaning of their lives. A prime personality issue in adolescence, which we discuss in Chapter 17, is the effort to define the self.

checkpoint can you . . .

▷ Discuss influences on educational and vocational aspirations and planning?

▷ Weigh factors in the value of part-time work for high school students?

summary and key terms

guidepost ①

Aspects of Cognitive Maturation

How do adolescents' thinking and use of language differ from younger children's?

- People in Piaget's stage of formal operations can engage in hypothetical-deductive reasoning. They can think in terms of possibilities, deal flexibly with problems, and test hypotheses.

- Since environmental stimulation plays an important part in attaining this stage, not all people become capable of formal operations; and those who are capable do not always use it.

- Piaget's proposed stage of formal operations does not take into account such developments as accumulation of knowledge and expertise, gains in information processing, and the growth of metacognition. Piaget also paid little

attention to individual differences, between-task variations, and the role of the situation.

- According to Elkind, immature thought patterns can result from adolescents' inexperience with formal thinking. These thought patterns include idealism and criticalness, argumentativeness, indecisiveness, apparent hypocrisy, self-consciousness, and an assumption of specialness and invulnerability. Research has cast doubt on the special prevalence of the latter two patterns during adolescence.

- Research has found both structural and functional changes in adolescent cognition, which reflect developments in the adolescent brain. Structural changes include increases in information-processing capacity, in the amount of knowledge in long-term memory, and in the capacity of working memory. Functional changes include progress in learning, remembering, and reasoning.

- Vocabulary and other aspects of language development, especially those related to abstract thought, such as social perspective-taking, improve in adolescence. Adolescents enjoy wordplay and create their own slang.

  formal operations (*448*)

  hypothetical-deductive reasoning (*448*)

  imaginary audience (*452*)

  personal fable (*452*)

  declarative knowledge (*453*)

  procedural knowledge (*453*)

  conceptual knowledge (*453*)

guidepost ❷ Moral Development

On what basis do adolescents make moral judgments, and how does prosocial behavior vary?

- According to Kohlberg, moral reasoning is based on a developing sense of justice and growing cognitive abilities. Kohlberg proposed that moral development progresses from external control to internalized societal standards to personal, principled moral codes.

- Kohlberg's theory has been criticized on several grounds, including failure to credit the roles of emotion, socialization, and parental guidance. The applicability of Kohlberg's system to people in non-Western cultures has been questioned. Research has found no significant gender differences in moral reasoning as measured by Kohlbergian methods.

- Gilligan proposed an alternative theory of moral development based on an ethic of caring, rather than on justice.

- Prosocial behavior continues to increase during adolescence, especially among girls. Many adolescents engage in volunteer community service.

- According to Fowler's theory of faith development, most adolescents are in the stage of conventional faith, in which they accept established community beliefs.

  preconventional morality (*454*)

  conventional morality (or morality of conventional role conformity) (*456*)

  postconventional morality (or morality of autonomous moral principles) (*456*)

guidepost ❸ Educational and Vocational Issues

What influences affect adolescents' school success and their educational and vocational planning and preparation?

- Motivation, self-efficacy beliefs, gender, parental practices, cultural and peer influences, and quality of schooling affect educational motivation and achievement.

- Although most Americans graduate from high school, the dropout rate is higher among poor, Hispanic, and black students. Active engagement in studies is an important factor in keeping adolescents in school.

- Educational and vocational aspirations are influenced by several factors, including self-efficacy beliefs, parental values, and gender.

- High school graduates who do not immediately go on to college can benefit from vocational training.

- Part-time work seems to have both positive and negative effects on educational, social, and occupational development. The long-term effects tend to be best when working hours are limited.

chapter 17

Psychosocial Development in Adolescence

did you know?

▷ Sex education programs that encourage *both* abstinence and safe sexual practices are more effective than abstinence-only programs in delaying sexual initiation?

▷ Most adolescents say they have good relationships with their parents?

▷ Studies have shown that online communication and social networking sites, such as Facebook, stimulate rather than reduce social connectedness?

In this chapter, we turn to psychosocial aspects of the quest for identity. We discuss how adolescents come to terms with their sexuality. We consider how teenagers' burgeoning individuality expresses itself in relationships with parents, siblings, and peers. We examine sources of antisocial behavior and ways of reducing the risks of adolescence in order to make it a time of positive growth and expanding possibilities. Finally, we take a cross-cultural view of late adolescence and the emerging adult.

Life is an experiment. The more experiments you make, the better.

—Ralph Waldo Emerson

1. How do adolescents form an identity, and what roles do gender and ethnicity play?

2. What determines sexual orientation, what sexual practices are common among adolescents, and what leads some to engage in risky sexual behavior?

3. How do adolescents relate to parents, siblings, and peers?

4. What causes antisocial behavior, and what can be done to reduce the risk of juvenile delinquency?

5. How do various cultures define what it means to become an adult, and what markers confer adult status?

guidepost

1 How do adolescents form an identity, and what roles do gender and ethnicity play?

identity
In Erikson's terminology, a coherent conception of the self made up of goals, values, and beliefs to which a person is solidly committed.

identity versus identity confusion
Erikson's fifth stage of psychosocial development, in which an adolescent seeks to develop a coherent sense of self, including the role she or he is to play in society. Also called *identity versus role confusion*.

The Search for Identity

The search for **identity**—according to Erikson, a coherent conception of the self made up of goals, values, and beliefs to which the person is solidly committed—comes into focus during the teenage years. Adolescents' cognitive development now enables them to construct a "theory of the self" (Elkind, 1998). In other words, adolescence is a time to figure out exactly who you are. As Erikson (1950) emphasized, the effort to make sense of the self is part of a healthy process that builds on the achievements of earlier stages—on trust, autonomy, initiative, and industry—and lays the groundwork for coping with the challenges of adult life. However, the identity crisis is seldom fully resolved in adolescence; issues concerning identity crop up again and again throughout life.

ERIKSON: IDENTITY VERSUS IDENTITY CONFUSION

The chief task of adolescence, said Erikson (1968), is to confront the crisis of **identity versus identity confusion** (or *identity versus role confusion*) so as to become a unique adult with a coherent sense of self and a valued role in society. His concept of the *identity crisis* was based in part on his own life experience. Growing up in Germany as the out-of-wedlock son of a Jewish woman from Denmark who had separated from her first husband, Erikson never knew his biological father. Though adopted at age 9 by his mother's second husband, a German Jewish pediatrician, he felt confusion about who he was. He floundered for some time before settling on his vocation. When he came to the United States, he needed to redefine his identity as an immigrant. All these issues found echoes in the identity crises he observed among disturbed adolescents, soldiers in combat, and members of minority groups (Erikson, 1968, 1973; Friedman, 1999).

Identity, according to Erikson, forms as young people resolve three major issues: the choice of an *occupation*, the adoption of *values* to live by, and the development of a satisfying *sexual identity*. During middle childhood, children acquire skills needed for success in their culture. As adolescents, they need to find constructive ways to use these skills. When young people have trouble settling on an occupational identity—or when their opportunities are limited—they may engage in behavior with serious negative consequences, such as criminal activity.

At least in Western countries such as the United States, some individuals enjoy a relatively long period of time during which they begin to take on adult responsibilities but are not fully independent. Erikson believed this time-out period, which he called *psychosocial moratorium*, was ideal for the development of identity and allowed young people the opportunity to search for commitments to which they could be faithful.

Adolescents who resolve the identity crisis satisfactorily, according to Erikson, develop the virtue of **fidelity**: sustained loyalty, faith, or a sense of belonging to a loved one or to friends and companions. Fidelity also can mean identification with a set of values, an ideology, a religion, a political movement, a creative pursuit, or an ethnic group (Erikson, 1982). By contrast, those individuals who do not develop a firm sense of their own identity and do not develop fidelity may have an unstable sense of self, be insecure, and fail to plan for themselves and the future.

Erikson saw this identity or role confusion as the prime danger of this stage. A failure to form a coherent sense of identity can greatly delay reaching psychological adulthood. (He did not resolve his own identity crisis until his mid-20s.) Some degree of identity confusion is normal, however. According to Erikson, it accounts for the seemingly chaotic nature of much adolescent behavior and for teenagers' painful self-consciousness. Cliquishness and intolerance of differences, both hallmarks of adolescence, are defenses against identity confusion.

Erikson's theory describes male identity development as the norm. According to Erikson, a man is not capable of real intimacy until after he has achieved a stable identity, whereas women define themselves through marriage and motherhood (something that may have been truer when Erikson developed his theory than it is today). Thus, said Erikson, women (unlike men) develop identity *through* intimacy, not before it. As we'll see, this male orientation of Erikson's theory has prompted criticism. Still, Erikson's concept of the identity crisis has inspired much valuable research.

Mastering the challenge of a ropes course may help this adolescent boy assess his abilities, interests, and desires. According to Erikson, the process of self-assessment helps adolescents resolve the crisis of identity versus identity confusion.

fidelity
A sustained loyalty, faith, or a sense of belonging that results from the successful resolution of Erikson's identiy versus identity confusion psychosocial stage of development.

MARCIA: IDENTITY STATUS—CRISIS AND COMMITMENT

Caterina, Andrea, Nick, and Mark are all about to graduate from high school. Caterina has considered her interests and her talents and plans to become an engineer. She has narrowed her college choices to three schools that offer good programs in this field.

Andrea knows exactly what she is going to do with her life. Her mother, a union leader at a plastics factory, has arranged for Andrea to enter an apprenticeship program there. Andrea has never considered doing anything else.

Nick is agonizing over his future. Should he attend a community college or join the army? He cannot decide what to do now or what he wants to do eventually.

> Identity formation includes attitudes about religion. Research indicates that 84 percent of U.S. teens age 13 to 17 believe in God, and about half of them say religion is very important to them. This number declines somewhat as teens age; however, by comparison to European countries, U.S. teens show higher religiosity.
>
> Lippman & McIntosh, 2010

Mark still has no idea what he wants to do, but he is not worried. He figures he can get some sort of a job and make up his mind about the future when he is ready.

These four young people are involved in identity formation. What accounts for the differences in the way they go about it, and how will these differences affect the outcome? According to research by the psychologist James E. Marcia (1966, 1980), these students are in four different **identity statuses**, states of ego (self) development.

identity statuses
Marcia's term for states of ego development that depend on the presence or absence of crisis and commitment.

TABLE 17.1 Identity-Status Interview

Sample Questions	Typical Answers for the Four Statuses
About occupational commitment: "How willing do you think you'd be to give up going into _____ if something better came along?"	*Identity achievement:* "Well, I might, but I doubt it. I can't see what 'something better' would be for me." *Foreclosure:* "Not very willing. It's what I've always wanted to do. The folks are happy with it and so am I." *Moratorium:* "I guess if I knew for sure, I could answer that better. It would have to be something in the general area—something related . . . " *Identity diffusion:* "Oh, sure. If something better came along, I'd change just like that."
About ideological commitment: "Have you ever had any doubts about your religious beliefs?"	*Identity achievement:* "Yes, I started wondering whether there is a God. I've pretty much resolved that now. The way it seems to me is . . . " *Foreclosure:* "No, not really; our family is pretty much in agreement on these things." *Moratorium:* "Yes, I guess I'm going through that now. I just don't see how there can be a God and still so much evil in the world." *Identity diffusion:* "Oh, I don't know. I guess so. Everyone goes through some sort of stage like that. But it really doesn't bother me much. I figure that one religion is about as good as another!"

Source: Adapted from Marcia, 1966.

Through 30-minute, semistructured *identity-status interviews* (Kroger, 2003; Table 17.1), Marcia distinguished these four types of identity status: *identity achievement, foreclosure, moratorium,* and *identity diffusion.* The four categories differ according to the presence or absence of **crisis** and **commitment**, the two elements Erikson saw as crucial to forming identity. Marcia defined *crisis* as a period of conscious decision making. Note that this is different from the everyday usage of the word. Crisis, within the context of Erikson's theories, does not refer to a stressful event such as losing your job or not being able to pay your bills. Rather, it refers to a period of active engagement with an aspect of identity—where a person is grappling with what to believe and who to be. *Commitment,* the other aspect of identity formation, involves a personal investment in an occupation or ideology (system of beliefs). Commitments can be held after they have been deeply considered, after crisis, or can be adopted without much thought put into them. He found relationships between identity status and such characteristics as anxiety, self-esteem, moral reasoning, and patterns of behavior. Building on Marcia's theory, other researchers have identified other personality and family variables related to identity status (Table 17.2). Here is a more detailed sketch of young people in each identity status:

- **Identity achievement** (*crisis leading to commitment*). Caterina has resolved her identity crisis. During the crisis period, she devoted much thought and some emotional struggle to major issues in her life. She has made choices and expresses strong commitment to them. Her parents have encouraged her to make her own decisions; they have listened to her ideas and given their opinions without

crisis
Marcia's term for a period of conscious decision making related to identity formation.

commitment
Marcia's term for personal investment in an occupation or system of beliefs.

identity achievement
Identity status, described by Marcia, that is characterized by commitment to choices made following a crisis, a period spent in exploring alternatives.

TABLE 17.2 Family and Personality Factors Associated with Adolescents in Four Identity Statuses*

Factor	Identity Achievement	Foreclosure	Moratorium	Identity Diffusion
Family	Parents encourage autonomy and connection with teachers; differences are explored within a context of mutuality.	Parents are overly involved with their children; families avoid expressing differences.	Adolescents are often involved in an ambivalent struggle with parental authority.	Parents are laissez-faire in child-rearing attitudes; are rejecting or not available to children.
Personality	High levels of ego development, moral reasoning, self-certainty, self-esteem, performance under stress, and intimacy.	Highest levels of authoritarianism and stereotypical thinking, obedience to authority, dependent relationships, low level of anxiety.	Most anxious and fearful of success; high levels of ego development, moral reasoning, and self-esteem.	Mixed results, with low levels of ego development, moral reasoning, cognitive complexity, and self-certainty; poor cooperative abilities.

*These associations have emerged from a number of separate studies. Because the studies have all been correlational rather than longitudinal, it is impossible to say that any factor caused placement in any identity status.

Source: Kroger, 1993.

pressuring her to adopt them. Research in a number of cultures has found people in this category to be more mature and more socially competent than people in the other three (Marcia, 1993).

- **Foreclosure** (*commitment without crisis*). Andrea has made commitments, not as a result of exploring possible choices, but by accepting someone else's plans for her life. She has not considered whether or not she believes in her commitments and has uncritically accepted others' opinions. She is happy and self-assured, perhaps even smug and self-satisfied, and she becomes dogmatic when her opinions are questioned. She has close family ties, is obedient, and tends to follow a powerful leader, like her mother, who accepts no disagreement.

- **Moratorium** (*crisis with no commitment yet*). Nick is actively grappling with his identity and trying to decide for himself who he wants to be and the path he wants his life to take. He is lively, talkative, self-confident, and scrupulous but also anxious and fearful. He is close to his mother but resists her authority. He wants to have a girlfriend but has not yet developed a close relationship. He will probably come out of his crisis eventually with the ability to make commitments and achieve identity.

- **Identity diffusion** (*no commitment, no crisis*). Mark has not seriously considered options and has avoided commitments. He is unsure of himself and tends to be uncooperative. His parents do not discuss his future with him; they say it's up to him. People in this category tend to be unhappy and often lonely.

These categories are not stages; they represent the status of identity development at a particular time, and they are likely to change in any direction as young people continue to develop (Marcia, 1979). Moreover, the same typology can be applied to any aspect of identity formation. Also, because our identity is multidimensional, our identity development is as well. For example, a young person may have decided upon a career path but not yet considered such aspects of identity as political or religious affiliation. When middle-aged people look back on their lives, they most commonly trace a path from foreclosure to moratorium to identity achievement (Kroger & Haslett, 1991). From late adolescence on, as Marcia proposed, more and more people are in moratorium or achievement: seeking or finding their identity. About half of late adolescents remain in foreclosure or diffusion, but when development does

foreclosure
Identity status, described by Marcia, in which a person who has not spent time considering alternatives (that is, has not been in crisis) is committed to other people's plans for his or her life.

moratorium
Identity status, described by Marcia, in which a person is considering alternatives (in crisis) and seems headed for commitment.

identity diffusion
Identity status, described by Marcia, that is characterized by absence of commitment and lack of serious consideration of alternatives.

what's your view

▷ Which of Marcia's identity statuses best described you as an adolescent?

▷ Has your identity status changed since then? If so, how?

occur, it is typically in the direction Marcia described (Kroger, 2003). Furthermore, although people in foreclosure seem to have made final decisions, that is often not so.

GENDER DIFFERENCES IN IDENTITY FORMATION

Does the identity development of men and women proceed in the same fashion? According to Carol Gilligan (1982, 1987a, 1987b; Brown & Gilligan, 1990), the female sense of self develops not so much through achieving a separate identity as through establishing relationships. Girls and women, says Gilligan, judge themselves on their handling of their responsibilities and on their ability to care for others as well as for themselves.

Most research supports Erikson's view that, for women, identity and intimacy develop together. Some researchers believe that this points to a weakness in Erikson's theory, which they claim is based on male-centered Western concepts of individuality, autonomy, and competitiveness. Moreover, given changes in social structure and the increased role of women in the workplace, it may be that these gender differences are less important than they were previously, and individual differences may play more of a role now (Archer, 1993; Marcia, 1993). In other research on Marcia's identity statuses, few gender differences have appeared (Kroger, 2003).

While identity formation in men and women may not necessarily conform to Erikson's original conception of it, it does appear that there are differences in the formation of self-esteem. Male self-esteem seems to be linked with striving for individual achievement, whereas female self-esteem depends more on connections with others (Thorne & Michaelieu, 1996). Some evidence suggests that adolescent girls have lower self-esteem, on average, than adolescent boys, though this finding has been controversial. Several large studies find that self-esteem drops during adolescence, more rapidly for girls than for boys, and then rises gradually into adulthood. These changes may be due in part to body image and other anxieties associated with puberty and with the transitions to junior high or middle school and high school (Robins & Trzesniewski, 2005).

ETHNIC FACTORS IN IDENTITY FORMATION

For a European American young person growing up in a predominantly white culture, the process of ethnic identify formation is not particularly troublesome, and an ethnic identity is generally entered into easily. However, for many young people in minority groups, race or ethnicity is central to identity formation. Following Marcia's model, some research has identified four ethnic identity statuses (Phinney, 1998):

- *Diffuse:* Juanita hasn't really thought about her identity. She has done little or no exploration of what her heritage means or what she thinks about it, and she does not clearly understand the issues involved.

- *Foreclosed:* Caleb has strong feelings about his identity, but those feelings are not really based on any serious exploration of his identity. Rather, he has absorbed the attitudes of other important people in his life. These feelings may be positive or negative.

- *Moratorium:* Cho-san has begun to think about what her ethnicity means to her but is still confused about it. She asks questions of others, talks about it with her parents, and thinks a great deal about it.

- *Achieved:* Diego has spent a good deal of time thinking about who he is and what his ethnicity means within that context. He now understands and accepts his ethnicity.

Table 17.3 includes representative statements by minority young people in each status.

Identity development can be especially complicated for young people from minority groups. Ethnicity may play a central part in their self-concept.

TABLE 17.3 Representative Quotations from Each Status of Ethnic Identity Development

Diffusion
"Why do I need to learn about who was the first black woman to do this or that? I'm just not that interested." (African American female)

Foreclosure
"I don't go looking for my culture. I just go by what my parents say and do, and what they tell me to do, the way they are." (Mexican American male)

Moratorium
"There are a lot of non-Japanese people around, and it gets pretty confusing to try and decide who I am." (Asian American male)

Achieved
"People put me down because I'm Mexican, but I don't care anymore. I can accept myself more." (Mexican American female)

Source: Phinney, 1998, Table 2, p. 277.

A study of 940 African American adolescents, college students, and adults found evidence of all four identity statuses in each age group. Only 27 percent of the adolescents were in the achieved group, as compared with 47 percent of the college students and 56 percent of the adults. Instead, adolescents were more likely to be in moratorium (42 percent), still exploring what it means to be African American. Some 25 percent of the adolescents were in foreclosure, with feelings about African American identity based on their family upbringing. All three of these groups (achieved, moratorium, and foreclosed) reported more positive regard for being African American than the 6 percent of adolescents who were diffused (neither committed nor exploring). Those of any age who were in the achieved status were most likely to view race as central to their identity (Yip, Seaton, & Sellers, 2006).

Another model focuses on three aspects of racial/ethnic identity: *connectedness* to one's own racial/ethnic group, *awareness of racism*, and *embedded achievement*, the belief that academic achievement is a part of group identity. A longitudinal study of low-income minority youth found that all three aspects of identity appear to stabilize and even to increase slightly by midadolescence. Thus, a positive racial/ethnic identity may buffer tendencies toward a drop in grades and connection to school during the transition from middle school to high school (Altschul, Oyserman, & Bybee, 2006). On the other hand, perceived discrimination during the transition to adolescence can interfere with positive identity formation and lead to conduct problems or depression. Protective factors include prosocial friends, strong academic performance, and nurturant, involved parents (Brody et al., 2006).

A 3-year longitudinal study of 420 African American, Latino American, and European American adolescents looked at two dimensions of ethnic identity: *group esteem* (feeling good about one's ethnicity) and *exploration of the meaning of ethnicity* in one's life. Group esteem rose during both early and middle adolescence, especially for African Americans and Latinos, whose group esteem was lower to begin with. Exploration of the meaning of ethnicity increased only in middle adolescence, perhaps reflecting the transition from relatively homogeneous neighborhood elementary or junior high schools into more ethnically diverse high schools. Interactions with members of other ethnic groups may stimulate young people to curiosity about their ethnic identity (French, Seidman, Allen, & Aber, 2006).

The term **cultural socialization** refers to parental practices that teach children about their racial or ethnic heritage, promote cultural customs and traditions, and promote racial/ethnic and cultural pride. For example, think about the holidays you celebrate. Those holidays generally include traditions and rituals important to your cultural group, and participating in them over time was part of your cultural socialization. Adolescents who have experienced cultural socialization tend to have stronger and more positive ethnic identity than those who have not (Hughes et al., 2006).

checkpoint
can you . . .

▷ List the three major issues involved in identity formation, according to Erikson?

▷ Describe four types of identity status found by Marcia?

▷ Discuss how gender and ethnicity affect identity formation?

cultural socialization
Parental practices that teach children about their racial/ethnic heritage and promote cultural practices and cultural pride.

FIGURE 17.1

Percentage of
Students in Grades
9 through 12 Who
Report They Are
Sexually Active

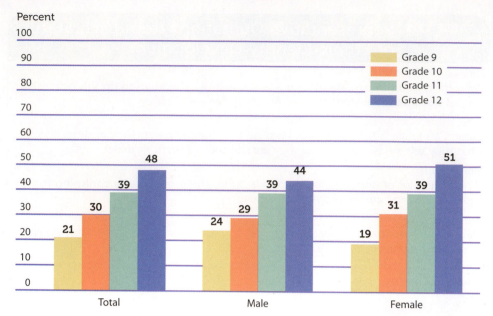

Source: Child Trends Databank, 2012.

guidepost

2

What determines sexual orientation, what sexual practices are common among adolescents, and what leads some to engage in risky sexual behavior?

sexual orientation
Focus of consistent sexual, romantic, and affectionate interest, either heterosexual, homosexual, or bisexual.

Most people experience their first crush at about 10 years of age, a process that appears to be related to the maturation of the adrenal glands. For those who will later identify as homosexual, this first crush is often on a member of the same sex.

Herdt & McClintock, 2000

Sexuality

Seeing oneself as a sexual being, recognizing one's sexual orientation, coming to terms with sexual stirrings, and forming romantic or sexual attachments all are parts of achieving *sexual identity*. Awareness of sexuality is an important aspect of identity formation, profoundly affecting self-image and relationships. Although this process is biologically driven, its expression is in part culturally defined.

During the twentieth century a major change in sexual attitudes and behavior in the United States and other industrialized countries brought more widespread acceptance of premarital sex, homosexuality, and other previously disapproved forms of sexual activity. Recent data indicate that 48 percent of twelfth graders report that they are sexually active (Figure 17.1). With widespread access to the Internet, casual sex with fleeting cyber-acquaintances who hook up through online chat rooms or singles' meeting sites has become common. Cell phones, e-mail, and instant messaging make it easy for adolescents to arrange hookups with disembodied strangers, insulated from adult scrutiny. These changes have brought increased concerns about sexual risk-taking. On the other hand, the AIDS epidemic has led many young people to abstain from sexual activity outside of committed relationships or to engage in safer sexual practices.

SEXUAL ORIENTATION AND IDENTITY

Although present in younger children, it is in adolescence that a person's **sexual orientation** generally becomes a pressing issue: whether that person will consistently be sexually attracted to persons of the other sex (*heterosexual*), of the same sex (*homosexual*), or of both sexes (*bisexual*). And, as with other important areas of development, teens may hold varying identity statuses as they form their sexual identity.

Heterosexuality predominates in nearly every known culture throughout the world. The prevalence of homosexual orientation varies widely, depending on how it is defined and measured. Depending on whether it is measured by sexual, or romantic, *attraction or arousal* as in the definition we just gave, or by sexual *behavior*, or by sexual *identity*, the rate of homosexuality in the U.S. population ranges from 1 to 21 percent (Savin-Williams, 2006).

Many young people have one or more homosexual experiences as they are growing up, but isolated experiences or even occasional homosexual attractions or fantasies do not determine sexual orientation. In a national survey, 4.5 percent of 15- to 19-year-old boys and 10.6 percent of 15- to 19-year-old girls reported ever having had same-sex sexual contact, but only 2.4 percent of the boys and 7.7 percent of the girls reported having done so in the past year (Mosher, Chandra, & Jones, 2005). Social stigma may bias such self-reports, underestimating the prevalence of homosexuality and bisexuality.

Attitudes towards homosexuality in the United States have changed far more rapidly than social scientists predicted, in part because of the increased visibility of advocacy groups.

Origins of Sexual Orientation Much research on sexual orientation has focused on efforts to explain homosexuality. Although it once was considered a mental illness, several decades of research have found no association between homosexual orientation and emotional or social problems—apart from those apparently caused by societal treatment of homosexuals, such as a tendency to depression (American Psychological Association (APA), n.d.; Meyer, 2003; Patterson, 1992, 1995a, 1995b). These findings led the psychiatric profession in 1973 to stop classifying homosexuality as a mental disorder.

Sexual orientation seems to be at least partly genetic (Diamond & Savin-Williams, 2003). The first full genome-wide scan for male sexual orientation has identified three stretches of DNA on chromosomes 7, 8, and 10 that appear to be involved (Mustanski et al., 2005). However, because identical twins are not perfectly concordant for sexual orientation, nongenetic factors also play a part (Diamond & Savin-Williams, 2003). Among more than 3,800 Swedish same-sex twin pairs, nonshared environmental factors accounted for about 64 percent of individual differences in sexual orientation. Genes explained about 34 percent of the variation in men and 18 percent in women. Shared family influences accounted for about 16 percent of the variation in women but had no effect in men (Långström, Rahman, Carlström, & Lichtenstein, 2008).

The more older biological brothers a man has, the more likely he is to be gay. In an analysis of 905 men and their biological, adoptive, half-, or stepsiblings, each older biological brother increased the chances of homosexuality in a younger brother by 33 percent. The significant factor in sexual orientation was the number of times a man's mother had borne boys. If rearing or social factors influenced the fraternal birth-order effect, then the number of nonbiological older brothers would predict sexual orientation, but they did not. Even when the number of nonbiological older brothers significantly exceeded the number of biological older brothers, and hence the opportunity for an effect via being reared with older male siblings was high, only the number of biological older brothers and not nonbiological older brothers predicted sexual orientation in men. This phenomenon may be a cumulative immunelike response to the presence of successive male fetuses in the womb (Bogaert, 2006).

Imaging studies have found similarities of brain structure and function between homosexuals and heterosexuals of the other sex. Brains of gay men and straight women are more symmetrical, whereas in lesbians and straight men the right hemisphere tends to be slightly larger. Also, in gays and lesbians, connections in the amygdala, which is involved in emotion, are typical of the other sex (Savic & Lindström, 2008). One researcher reported a difference in the size of the hypothalamus, a brain structure that governs sexual activity, in heterosexual and gay men (LeVay, 1991). In brain imaging studies on pheromones, odors that attract mates, the odor of male sweat activated the hypothalamus in gay men much as it did in heterosexual women. Similarly, lesbian women and straight men reacted more positively to female pheromones than to male ones (Savic, Berglund, & Lindström, 2005; Savic, Berglund, & Lindström, 2006). However, these differences may be an effect of homosexuality, not a cause.

Homosexual and Bisexual Identity Development Despite the increased acceptance of homosexuality in the United States, many adolescents who openly identify as

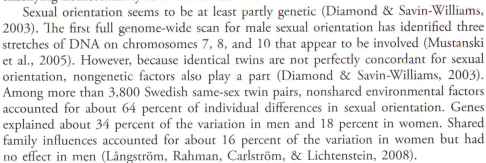

Homosexual teens are at risk for depression and suicide largely due to contextual variables such as bullying and a lack of acceptance. In 2010, columnist and author Dan Savage created a YouTube video that went viral and has now resulted in the "It Gets Better" campaign. In this video, teens are assured that happiness and hope are a distinct possibility for the future—that, indeed, it does get better.

gay, lesbian, or bisexual feel isolated in a hostile environment. They may be subject to discrimination and even violence. Others may be reluctant to disclose their sexual orientation, even to their parents, for fear of strong disapproval or a rupture in the family (Hillier, 2002; Patterson, 1995b). They may find it difficult to meet and identify potential same-sex partners. Thus homosexuals' recognition and expression of their sexual identity are more complex and follow a less defined timetable than heterosexuals' do (Diamond & Savin-Williams, 2003). Notice that, as in ethnic identity formation, not being from the majority group makes the process of identity formation more complex.

There is no single route to the development of gay, lesbian, or bisexual identity and behavior. Because of the lack of socially sanctioned ways to explore their sexuality, many gay and lesbian adolescents experience identity confusion (Sieving, Oliphant, & Blum, 2002). Gay, lesbian, and bisexual youth who are unable to establish peer groups that share their sexual orientation may struggle with the recognition of same-sex attractions (Bouchey & Furman, 2003; Furman & Wehner, 1997).

checkpoint
can you . . .

▷ Discuss theories and research regarding origins of sexual orientation?

▷ Discuss homosexual identity development?

SEXUAL BEHAVIOR

Internationally, there are wide variations in timing of heterosexual initiation. The percentage of women who report having first intercourse by age 17 is about 10 times greater in Mali (72 percent) than in Thailand (7 percent) or the Philippines (6 percent). Similar differences exist for men. Although earlier male initiation is the norm in most cultures, in Mali and Ghana more women than men become sexually active at an early age (Singh, Wulf, Samara, & Cuca, 2000).

In the United States, according to national surveys, 77 percent of young people have had sex by age 20. This proportion has been roughly the same since the mid-1960s and the advent of the pill (Finer, 2007). The average girl has her first sexual intercourse at 17, the average boy at 16, and approximately 25 percent of boys and girls report having had intercourse by age 15 (Klein & AAP Committee on Adolescence, 2005). Blacks and Latinos tend to begin sexual activity earlier than white youth (Kaiser Family Foundation, Hoff, Greene, & Davis, 2003). Whereas teenage boys in previous years were more likely to be sexually experienced than teenage girls, that is no longer true: In 2011, 44 percent of twelfth grade boys and 51 percent of girls in that age group reported being sexually active (U.S. Department of Health and Human Services [USDHHS], 2012).

Sexual Risk-Taking Two major concerns about adolescent sexual activity are the risks of contracting sexually transmitted infections (STIs) and, for heterosexual activity, of pregnancy. Most at risk are young people who start sexual activity early, have multiple partners, do not use contraceptives regularly, and have inadequate information—or misinformation—about sex (Abma, Chandra, Mosher, Peterson, & Piccinino, 1997). Other risk factors are living in a socioeconomically disadvantaged community, substance use, antisocial behavior, and association with deviant peers. Parental monitoring can help reduce these risks (Baumer & South, 2001; Capaldi, Stoolmiller, Clark, & Owen, 2002).

Why do some adolescents become sexually active at an early age? Various factors, including early entrance into puberty, poverty, poor school performance, lack of academic and career goals, a history of sexual abuse or parental neglect, and cultural or family patterns of early sexual experience, may play a part (Klein & AAP Committee on Adolescence, 2005). The absence of a father, especially early in life, is a strong factor (Ellis et al., 2003). Teenagers who have close, warm relationships with their mothers are more likely to delay sexual activity. So are those who perceive that their mothers disapprove of such activity (Jaccard & Dittus, 2000; Sieving, McNeely, & Blum, 2000). Other reasons teenagers give for not yet having had sex are that it is against their religion or morals and that they do not want to get (or get a girl) pregnant (Abma, Martinez, Mosher, & Dawson, 2004).

TABLE 17.4 Adolescents' Attitudes about Sexual Activity

PERCENT OF 15- TO 17-YEAR-OLDS WHO SAY THEY "STRONGLY" OR "SOMEWHAT" AGREE WITH EACH OF THE FOLLOWING

	Male	Female	Sexually Active	Not Sexually Active
Waiting to have sex is a nice idea but nobody really does.	66%	60%	69%	59%
There is pressure to have sex by a certain age.	59%	58%	58%	59%
Once you have had sex it is harder to say no the next time.	56%	47%	54%	50%
If you have been seeing someone for a while, it is expected that you will have sex.	50%	27%	52%	31%
Oral sex is not as big of a deal as sexual intercourse.	54%	38%	52%	42%

Source: Adapted from Kaiser Family Foundation et al., 2003, Table 8, p. 12, and Table 33, p. 39.

One of the most powerful influences is perception of peer group norms. Young people often feel under pressure to engage in activities they do not feel ready for. In a nationally representative survey, nearly one-third of 15- to 17-year-olds, especially boys, said they had experienced pressure to have sex (Kaiser Family Foundation et al., 2003; Table 17.4).

Among Asian American youths, males begin sexual activity later than white, African American, and Latino males. This pattern of delayed sexual activity may reflect strong cultural pressures to save sex for marriage or adulthood and then to have children who will carry on the family name (Dubé & Savin-Williams, 1999). New research supports the influence a family can have on sexual behavior. In a 10-year study of more than 3,000 adolescents and their families, researchers found that family activities like eating together and playing sports can be a tool in preventing risky sexual behavior (Coley, Votruba-Drzal, & Schindler, 2009).

As U.S. adolescents have become more aware of the risks of sexual activity, the percentage who have ever had intercourse has declined, especially among boys (Abma et al., 2004). However, noncoital forms of genital sexual activity, such as oral and anal sex and mutual masturbation, are common. Many heterosexual teens do not regard these activities as sex but as substitutes for, or precursors of, sex, or even as abstinence (Remez, 2000). In one national survey, just more than half of teenage boys and girls reported having given or received oral sex, more than had had vaginal intercourse (Mosher et al., 2005).

Use of Contraceptives The use of contraceptives among teenagers has increased since the 1990s (Abma et al., 2004). About 83 percent of girls and 91 percent of boys in one survey said they had used contraception the most recent time they had sex (Abma et al., 2004). Teens who, in their first relationship, delay intercourse, discuss contraception before having sex, or use more than one method of contraception are more likely to use contraceptives consistently throughout that relationship (Manlove, Ryan, & Franzetta, 2003).

The best safeguard for sexually active teens is regular use of condoms, which give some protection against STIs as well as against pregnancy. The use of many types of contraceptives has increased among sexually active teenage girls in recent years, including the pill and new hormonal and injectable methods or combinations of methods (Fig. 17.2; Centers for Disease Control and Prevention [CDC], 2012a). In 2011, 52 percent of sexually active high school girls and 75 percent of sexually active high school boys reported having used condoms the last time they had intercourse (Martinez,

what's your view

How can adolescents be helped to avoid or change risky sexual behavior?

Condoms have been in use for at least 400 years.

FIGURE 17.2

Current Contraceptive
Status among Females
Age 15–19 Who Had
Sex during the Past
Month, by Year,
Race/Ethnicity, and
Effectiveness of
Method Used

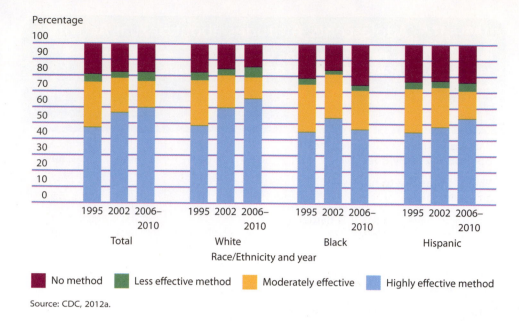

Source: CDC, 2012a.

Copen, & Abma, 2011). Adolescents who start using prescription contraceptives often stop using condoms, in some cases not realizing that they leave themselves unprotected against STIs (Klein & AAP Committee on Adolescence, 2005).

Where Do Teenagers Get Information about Sex? Adolescents get their information about sex primarily from friends, parents, sex education in school, and the media (Kaiser Family Foundation et al., 2003). Adolescents who can talk about sex with older siblings as well as with parents are more likely to have positive attitudes toward safer sexual practices (Kowal & Pike, 2004).

Since 1998, federal- and state-funded sex education programs stressing abstinence from sex until marriage as the best or only option have become common (Devaney, Johnson, Maynard, & Trenholm, 2002). Programs that encourage abstinence but also discuss STD prevention and safer sexual practices for the sexually active have been found to delay sexual initiation and increase contraceptive use (AAP Committee on Psychosocial Aspects of Child and Family Health and Committee on Adolescence, 2001).

However, some school programs promote abstinence as the only option, even though abstinence-only courses have *not* been shown to delay sexual activity (AAP Committee on Psychosocial Aspects of Child and Family Health and Committee on Adolescence, 2001; Satcher, 2001). Likewise, pledges to maintain virginity have shown little to no impact on sexual behavior other than a *decrease* in the likelihood to take precautions during sex (Rosenbaum, 2009). Although more than 4 out of 5 teenagers report receiving formal instruction in how to say no to sex, only 2 out of 3 have been taught about birth control. Only 1 out of 2 girls and 1 out of 3 boys ages 18 and 19 say they talked with a parent about birth control before age 18 (Abma et al., 2004).

Unfortunately, many teenagers get much of their "sex education" from the media, which present a distorted view of sexual activity, associating it with fun, excitement, competition, danger, or violence and rarely showing the risks of unprotected sex. Teens exposed to highly sexual television content were twice as likely to experience a pregnancy compared with lower level or no exposure (Chandra et al., 2008). Black teens, in contrast, appeared to be more influenced by parental expectations and their friends' behavior (J. D. Brown et al., 2006).

SEXUALLY TRANSMITTED INFECTIONS (STIs)

Sexually transmitted infections (STIs), sometimes called *sexually transmitted diseases* (STDs), are diseases spread by sexual contact. Table 17.5 summarizes some common STDs: their causes, most frequent symptoms, treatment, and consequences.

checkpoint
can **you** . . .

▷ Cite trends in sexual activity among adolescents?

▷ Identify factors that increase or decrease the risks of sexual activity?

sexually transmitted infections (STIs)
Diseases spread by sexual contact.

TABLE 17.5 Common Sexually Transmitted Infections

Disease	Cause	Symptoms: Male	Symptoms: Female	Treatment	Consequences If Untreated
Chlamydia	Bacterial infection	Pain during urination, discharge from penis	Vaginal discharge, abdominal discomfort[†]	Tetracycline or erythromycin	Can cause pelvic inflammatory disease or eventual sterility
Trichomoniasis	Parasitic infection, sometimes passed on in moist objects such as towels and bathing suits	Often absent	Absent or may include vaginal discharge, discomfort during intercourse, odor, painful urination	Oral antibiotic	May lead to abnormal growth of cervical cells
Gonorrhea	Bacterial infection	Discharge from penis, pain during urination*	Discomfort when urinating, vaginal discharge, abnormal menses[†]	Penicillin or other antibiotics	Can cause pelvic inflammatory disease or eventual sterility; can also cause arthritis, dermatitis, and meningitis
HPV (genital warts)	Human papilloma virus	Painless growths that usually appear on penis but may also appear on urethra or in rectal area*	Small, painless growths on genitals and anus; may also occur inside the vagina without external symptoms*	Removal of warts; but infection often reappears	May be associated with cervical cancer; in pregnancy, warts enlarge and may obstruct birth canal
Herpes	Herpes simplex virus	Painful blisters anywhere on the genitalia, usually on the penis*	Painful blisters on the genitalia, sometimes with fever and aching muscles; women with sores on cervix may be unaware of outbreaks*	No known cure but controlled with an antiviral drug, such as acyclovir	Possible increased risk of cervical cancer
Hepatitis B	Hepatitis B virus	Skin and eyes become yellow	Skin and eyes become yellow	No specific treatment; no alcohol	Can cause liver damage, chronic hepatitis
Syphilis	Bacterial infection	In first stage, reddish-brown sores on the mouth or genitalia or both, which may disappear, though the bacteria remain; in the second, more infectious stage, a widespread skin rash*	In first stage, reddish-brown sores on the mouth or genitalia or both, which may disappear, though the bacteria remain; in the second, more infectious stage, a widespread skin rash*	Penicillin or other antibiotics	Paralysis, convulsions, brain damage, and sometimes death

Continued

TABLE 17.5 Common Sexually Transmitted Infections *Continued*

Disease	Cause	Symptoms: Male	Symptoms: Female	Treatment	Consequences If Untreated
AIDS (acquired immune deficiency syndrome)	Human immunodeficiency virus (HIV)	Extreme fatigue, fever, swollen lymph nodes, weight loss, diarrhea, night sweats, susceptibility to other diseases*	Extreme fatigue, fever, swollen lymph nodes, weight loss, diarrhea, night sweats, susceptibility to other diseases*	No known cure; protease inhibitors and other drugs appear to extend life	Death, usually due to other diseases, such as cancer

*May be asymptomatic.

† Is often asymptomatic.

An estimated 19 million new STIs are diagnosed each year, and 65 million Americans have an incurable STI (Wildsmith, Schelar, Peterson, & Manlove, 2010.) An estimated 3.2 million adolescent girls in the United States—about 1 in 4 of those ages 14 to 19—has had at least one STI, according to a nationally representative study (Forhan et al., 2008). The chief reasons for the prevalence of STIs among teenagers include early sexual activity, which increases the likelihood of having multiple high-risk partners; failure to use condoms or to use them regularly and correctly; and, for women, a tendency to have sex with older partners (CDC, 2000b; Forhan et al., 2008). Despite the fact that teens are at higher risk for contracting STIs, they perceive their own personal risk as low (Wildsmith et al., 2010).

STIs in adolescent girls are most likely to develop undetected. In a *single* unprotected sexual encounter with an infected partner, a girl runs a 1 percent risk of acquiring HIV, a 30 percent risk of acquiring genital herpes, and a 50 percent risk of acquiring gonorrhea (Alan Guttmacher Institute [AGI], 1999). Although teenagers tend to view oral sex as less risky than intercourse, a number of STIs, especially pharyngeal gonorrhea, can be transmitted in that way (Remez, 2000).

The most common STI, affecting 18.3 percent of 14- to 19-year-olds, is human papilloma virus (HPV), or genital warts. Among girls with three or more partners, the risk of contracting HPV jumps to 50 percent (Forhan et al., 2008). There are approximately 40 types of HPV virus, a number of which have been identified as the leading cause of cervical cancer in women. A vaccine is available that prevents the types of HPV that cause most cases of cervical cancer and genital warts. The vaccine has been recommended for 11- and 12-year-old girls as well as for girls and women ages 13 through 26 who have not yet been vaccinated.

> According to Piaget, teens perceiving low personal risk is an example of adolescent egocentrism. Piaget called this the personal fable. Teens often seem to behave as if they believe that bad things won't happen to them because their "personal story" is different and unique.

The most common *curable* STIs are chlamydia and gonorrhea. These diseases, if undetected and untreated, can lead to severe health problems, including, in women, pelvic inflammatory disease (PID), a serious abdominal infection. In the United States, close to 1 in 10 teenage girls and 1 in 5 boys are affected by either chlamydia or gonorrhea, or both (Forhan et al., 2008).

Genital herpes simplex is a chronic, recurring, often painful, and highly contagious disease. It can be fatal to a person with a deficiency of the immune system or to the newborn infant of a mother who has an outbreak at the time of delivery. Its incidence has increased dramatically during the past three decades. Hepatitis B remains a prominent STI despite the availability, for more than 20 years, of a preventive vaccine. Also common among young people is trichomoniasis, a parasitic infection that may be passed along by moist towels and swimsuits (Weinstock, Berman, & Cates, 2004).

The human immunodeficiency virus (HIV), which causes AIDS, is transmitted through bodily fluids (mainly blood and semen), usually by sharing of intravenous drug needles or by sexual contact with an infected partner. The virus attacks the body's immune system, leaving a person vulnerable to a variety of fatal diseases. Symptoms of AIDS, which include extreme fatigue, fever, swollen lymph nodes, weight loss, diarrhea, and night sweats, may not appear until 6 months to 10 or more years after initial infection.

Worldwide, of the 4.1 million new HIV infections each year, about half are in young people ages 15 to 24 (UNAIDS, 2006). In the United States, more than 1 in 4 of the estimated 1,039,000 to 1,185,000 persons living with HIV or AIDS were infected in their teens (CDC, 2007a; Kaiser Family Foundation et al., 2003). As of now, AIDS is incurable, but increasingly the related infections that kill people are being stopped with antiviral therapy, including protease inhibitors (Palella et al., 1998; Weinstock et al., 2004). A Danish study found that young patients with HIV have an estimated median survival of more than 35 years (Lohse et al., 2007). Ironically, by reducing the scare factor, this advance may be responsible for giving sexually active teens less reason to take precautions when having sex. After holding steady for 3 years, the estimated number of new HIV infections in U.S. 15- to 19-year-olds took a 20 percent jump to 1,213 cases in 2005 (CDC, 2007a). Because symptoms may not appear until a disease has progressed to the point of causing serious long-term complications, early detection is important.

Comprehensive sex and STI/HIV education is critical to promoting responsible decision making and controlling the spread of STIs. Evidence for the positive impact of such programs is strong: More than 60 percent of programs that emphasized abstinence and condom use realized the positive outcomes of delayed and/or reduced sexually activity and increased use of condoms or contraceptives. Further, the programs did not increase sexual activity. In contrast, programs that emphasize abstinence only have shown little evidence of affecting sexual behavior (Kirby & Laris, 2009).

TEENAGE PREGNANCY AND CHILDBEARING

More than 4 in 10 adolescent girls in the United States have been pregnant at least once before age 20. More than half (51 percent) of pregnant teenagers in the United States have their babies, and 35 percent choose to abort. Fourteen percent of teen pregnancies end in miscarriage or stillbirth (Klein & AAP Committee on Adolescence, 2005).

A substantial decline in teenage pregnancy has accompanied steady decreases in early intercourse and in sex with multiple partners and an increase in contraceptive use. In 2011, births rates for teens dropped to their lowest rate yet—31.3 per 1,000 women age 15 to 19 (Martin, Hamilton, Ventura, Osterman, Wilson, & Mathews, 2012). Birthrates have fallen more sharply among younger teens (15 to 17 years old) than among 18- and 19-year-olds. Figure 17.3 shows the teen births by age. (For more on teenage pregnancy prevention, see Box 17.1.)

Although declines in teenage pregnancy and childbearing have occurred among all population groups, birthrates have fallen most sharply among black teenagers. Still, black and Hispanic girls are more likely to have babies than white, American Indian, or Asian American girls (Martin et al., 2012). And U.S. teens are more likely to become pregnant and give birth than teenagers in most other industrialized countries (Martin et al., 2005).

More than 90 percent of pregnant teenagers describe their pregnancies as unintended, and 50 percent of teen pregnancies occur within 6 months of sexual initiation

checkpoint can you . . .

▷ Identify and describe the most common sexually transmitted infections?

▷ List risk factors for developing an STI during adolescence, and describe effective prevention methods?

FIGURE 17.3

Teen Birth Rates
for Women in the
United States
by Age Group,
1960–2010

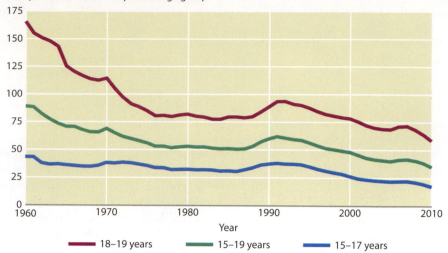

Rate per 1,000 women in specified age group

Year

■ 18–19 years   ■ 15–19 years   ■ 15–17 years

Source: CDC/NCHS. National Vital Statistics System

checkpoint
can you . . .

▷ Summarize trends in teenage pregnancy and birthrates?

▷ Describe ways to prevent teenage pregnancy?

▷ Discuss risk factors, problems, and outcomes connected with teenage pregnancy?

(Klein & the AAP Committee on Adolescence, 2005). Many of these girls grew up fatherless (Ellis et al., 2003). Among 9,159 women at a California primary care clinic, those who had become pregnant in adolescence were likely, as children, to have been physically, emotionally, or sexually abused and/or exposed to parental divorce or separation, domestic violence, substance abuse, or a household member who was mentally ill or engaged in criminal behavior (Hillis et al., 2004). Teenage fathers, too, tend to have limited financial resources, poor academic performance, and high dropout rates. At least one-third of teenage parents are themselves products of adolescent pregnancy (Klein & AAP Committee on Adolescence, 2005).

Outcomes of Teenage Pregnancy Teenage pregnancies often have poor outcomes. Many of the mothers are impoverished and poorly educated, and some are drug users. Many do not eat properly, do not gain enough weight, and get inadequate prenatal care or none at all. Their babies are likely to be premature or dangerously small and are at heightened risk of other birth complications; late fetal, neonatal, or infant death; health and academic problems; abuse and neglect; and developmental disabilities that may continue into adolescence (AAP Committee on Adolescence, 1999; AAP Committee on Adolescence and Committee on Early Childhood, Adoption, and Dependent Care, 2001; AGI, 1999; Children's Defense Fund, 1998, 2004; Klein & AAP Committee on Adolescence, 2005; Menacker, Martin, MacDorman, & Ventura, 2004).

Babies of more affluent teenage mothers also may be at risk. Among more than 134,000 white, largely middle-class girls and women, 13- to 19-year-olds were more likely than 20- to 24-year-olds to have low-birth-weight babies, even when the mothers were married and well educated and had adequate prenatal care. Prenatal care apparently cannot always overcome the biological disadvantage of being born to a still-growing girl whose own body may be competing for vital nutrients with the developing fetus (Fraser, Brockert, & Ward, 1995).

Teenage unwed mothers and their families are likely to suffer financially. Child support laws are spottily enforced, court-ordered payments are often inadequate, and many young fathers cannot afford them (AAP Committee on Adolescence, 1999). Unmarried parents under age 18 are eligible for public assistance only if they live with their parents and go to school.

Teenage mothers are likely to drop out of school and to have repeated pregnancies. They and their partners may lack the maturity, skills, and social support to be good parents. Their children, in turn, tend to have developmental and academic problems, to be depressed, to engage in substance abuse and early sexual activity,

PREVENTING TEENAGE PREGNANCY

Teenage pregnancy and birthrates in the United States are many times higher than in other industrialized countries, where adolescents begin sexual activity just as early or earlier (Darroch, Singh, Frost, & the Study Team, 2001). Teenage birthrates in recent years have been nearly 5 times as high in the United States as in Denmark, Finland, France, Germany, Italy, the Netherlands, Spain, Sweden, and Switzerland and 12 times as high as in Japan (Ventura, Mathews, & Hamilton, 2001).

Why are U.S. rates so high? Some observers point to such factors as the reduced stigma on unwed motherhood, media glorification of sex, the lack of a clear message that sex and parenthood are for adults, the influence of childhood sexual abuse, and failure of parents to communicate with children. Comparisons with the European experience suggest the importance of other factors: U.S. girls are more likely to have multiple sex partners and less likely to use contraceptives (Darroch et al., 2001).

Europe's industrialized countries have provided universal, comprehensive sex education for a much longer time than the United States. Comprehensive programs encourage young teenagers to delay intercourse but also aim to improve contraceptive use among sexually active adolescents. Such programs include education about sexuality and acquisition of skills for making responsible sexual decisions and communicating with partners. They provide information about risks and consequences of teenage pregnancy, about birth control methods, and about where to get medical and contraceptive help (AAP Committee on Psychosocial Aspects of Child and Family Health and Committee on Adolescence, 2001; AGI, 1994; Kirby, 1997; Stewart, 1994). Programs aimed at adolescent boys emphasize the wisdom of delaying fatherhood and the need to take responsibility when it occurs (Children's Defense Fund, 1998).

In the United States the provision and content of sex education programs are political issues. Some critics claim that community- and school-based sex education leads to more or earlier sexual activity, even though evidence shows otherwise (AAP Committee on Adolescence, 2001; Satcher, 2001).

An important component of pregnancy prevention in European countries is access to reproductive services. Contraceptives are provided free to adolescents in a number of European countries. Sweden showed a fivefold reduction in the teenage birthrate following introduction of birth control education, free access to contraceptives, and free abortion on demand (Bracher & Santow, 1999). Indeed, U.S. teens who use contraception in their first sexual experience are much less likely to bear a child by age 20 (Abma et al., 2004).

The problem of teenage pregnancy requires a multifaceted solution. It must include programs and policies to encourage postponing or refraining from sexual activity, but it also must recognize that many young people do become sexually active and need education and information to prevent pregnancy and infection. It requires attention to underlying factors that put teenagers and families at risk—reducing poverty, school failure, behavioral and family problems, and expanding employment, skills training, and family life education (AGI, 1994; Children's Defense Fund, 1998; Kirby, 1997)—and it should target those young people at highest risk (Klein & AAP Committee on Adolescence, 2005). Comprehensive early intervention programs for preschoolers and elementary school students have reduced teenage pregnancy (Lonczak, Abbott, Hawkins, Kosterman, & Catalano, 2002; Hawkins, Catalano, Kosterman, Abbott, & Hill, 1999; Schweinhart, Barnes, & Weikart, 1993). Because adolescents with high aspirations are less likely to become pregnant, programs that motivate young people to achieve and raise their self-esteem have had some success (Allen & Philliber, 2001).

what's your view

If you were designing a school-based or community-based sexuality education program, what would you include? Do you favor or oppose programs that provide contraceptives to teenagers?

to engage in gang activity, to be unemployed, and to become adolescent parents themselves (Klein & AAP Committee on Adolescence, 2005; Pogarsky, Thornberry, & Lizotte, 2006). The risks are especially great for sons of teenage mothers (Pogarsky et al., 2006). However, some of these outcomes, such as marijuana use, may be influenced by other factors, and not by early childbearing (Levine, Emery, & Pollack, 2007).

Indeed, poor outcomes of teenage parenting are far from inevitable. Several long-term studies find that, two decades after giving birth, most former adolescent mothers are not on welfare; many have finished high school and secured steady jobs, and do not have large families. Comprehensive adolescent pregnancy and home visitation programs seem to contribute to good outcomes (Klein & AAP Committee on Adolescence, 2005), as do contact with the father (Howard, Lefever, Borkowski, & Whitman, 2006) and involvement in a religious community (Carothers, Borkowski, Lefever, & Whitman, 2005).

Relationships with Family and Peers

Age becomes a powerful bonding agent in adolescence. Adolescents spend more time with peers and less with family. However, most teenagers' fundamental values remain closer to their parents' than is generally realized (Offer & Church, 1991). Even as adolescents increasingly turn toward peers to fulfill many of their social needs for role models, companionship, and intimacy, they still look to parents for a secure base from which they can try their wings. You may recall that toddlers use their parents as a secure base, and that those toddlers who feel as if their parents have their backs feel safer exploring the world—they know they have someone to count on if things go wrong. Similarly, those adolescents who have the most secure attachment relationships tend to have strong, supportive relationships with parents who permit and encourage their strivings for independence, while also providing a safe haven in times of emotional stress (Allen et al., 2003; Laursen, 1996).

IS ADOLESCENT REBELLION A MYTH?

The teenage years have been called a time of **adolescent rebellion**, involving emotional turmoil, conflict within the family, alienation from adult society, reckless behavior, and rejection of adult values. Yet school-based research on adolescents the world over suggests that only about 1 in 5 teenagers fits this pattern (Offer & Schonert-Reichl, 1992).

Most young people feel close to and positive about their parents, share similar opinions on major issues, and value their parents' approval (Blum & Rinehart, 2000; Hill, 1987; Offer, Ostrov, & Howard, 1989; Offer, Ostrov, Howard, & Atkinson, 1988). In a 34-year longitudinal study of 67 14-year-old suburban boys, the vast majority adapted well to their life experiences (Offer, Offer, & Ostrov, 2004). The relatively few deeply troubled adolescents tended to come from disrupted families and, as adults, continued to have unstable family lives and to reject cultural norms. Those raised in intact two-parent homes with a positive family atmosphere tended to sail through adolescence with no serious problems and, as adults, to have solid marriages and lead well-adjusted lives (Offer, Kaiz, Ostrov, & Albert, 2002).

Still, adolescence can be a tough time for young people and their parents. Family conflict, depression, and risky behavior are more common than during other parts of the life span (Arnett, 1999; Petersen et al., 1993). Negative emotionality and mood swings are most intense during early adolescence, perhaps due to the stress connected with puberty. Some research indicates that rebellion should be more common in technologically advanced cultures, where there is a disparity between feeling like an adult and the rights/responsibilities of being an adult. The case is also made that some level of antisocial behavior in the teenage years is developmentally normal (Moffitt, 1993). By late adolescence, emotionality tends to become more stable (Larson, Moneta, Richards, & Wilson, 2002).

Recognizing that adolescence may be a difficult time can help parents and teachers put trying behavior in perspective. But adults who assume that storm and stress are normal and necessary may fail to heed the signals of the relatively few young persons who need special help.

guidepost

3

How do adolescents relate to parents, siblings, and peers?

adolescent rebellion
Pattern of emotional turmoil, characteristic of a minority of adolescents, that may involve conflict with family, alienation from adult society, reckless behavior, and rejection of adult values.

what's
your
view

Can you think of values you hold that are different from those of your parents? How did you come to develop these values?

connect

study smart

Adolescence as a Social Construction

CHANGING TIME USE AND CHANGING RELATIONSHIPS

One way to assess changes in adolescents' relationships with the important people in their lives is to see how they spend their discretionary time. The amount of time U.S. adolescents spend with families declines during the teen years. However, the disengagement is not a rejection of the family but a response to developmental needs. Early adolescents often retreat to their rooms; they seem to need time alone to step back from the demands of social relationships, regain emotional stability, and reflect on identity issues (Larson, 1997).

Cultural variations in time use reflect varying cultural needs, values, and practices (Verma & Larson, 2003). Young people in tribal or peasant societies spend most of their time producing bare necessities of life and have much less time for socializing than adolescents in technologically advanced societies (Larson & Verma, 1999). In some postindustrial societies such as Korea and Japan, where the pressures of schoolwork and family obligations are strong, adolescents have relatively little free time. To relieve stress, they spend their time in passive pursuits, such as watching television and "doing nothing" (Verma & Larson, 2003). In India's family-centered culture, on the other hand, middle-class urban eighth graders spend 39 percent of their waking hours with family, compared with 23 percent for U.S. eighth graders, and report being happier when with their families than U.S. eighth graders do. For these young people, the task of adolescence is not to separate from the family but to become more integrated with it. Similar findings have been reported in Indonesia, Bangladesh, Morocco, and Argentina (Larson & Wilson, 2004). In comparison, U.S. adolescents have a good deal of discretionary time, most of which they spend with peers, increasingly of the other sex (Juster, Ono, & Stafford, 2004; Larson & Seepersad, 2003; Verma & Larson, 2003).

Ethnicity may affect family connectedness. In some research, African American teenagers, who may look on their families as havens in a hostile world, tended to maintain more intimate family relationships and less intense peer relations than white teenagers (Giordano, Cernkovich, & DeMaris, 1993). Among 489 ninth graders, however, those with European backgrounds reported as much or more family identification and closeness as did minority students. On the other hand, those from Mexican and Chinese families, particularly immigrant families, reported a stronger sense of family obligation and assistance and spent more time on activities that carried out those obligations (Hardway & Fuligni, 2006). Still, for Chinese American youth from immigrant families, the need to adapt to U.S. society often conflicts with the pull of traditional family obligations (Fuligni, Yip, & Tseng, 2002).

With such cultural variations in mind, let's look more closely at relationships with parents, and then with siblings and peers.

checkpoint
can you . . .

▷ Assess the extent of storm and stress during the teenage years?

▷ Identify age and cultural differences in how young people spend their time, and discuss their significance?

ADOLESCENTS AND PARENTS

As the English poet William Wordsworth wrote, "The child is the father of the man." This developmental pattern applies to adolescence as well. Relationships with parents during adolescence—the degree of conflict and openness of communication—are grounded largely in the emotional closeness developed in childhood; and adolescent relationships with parents, in turn, set the stage for the quality of the relationship with a partner in adulthood (Overbeek, Stattin, Vermulst, Ha, & Engels, 2007).

Most adolescents report good relations with their parents (Gutman & Eccles, 2007). Still, adolescence brings special challenges. Just as adolescents feel tension between dependency on their parents and the need to break away, parents want their children to be independent yet find it hard to let go. Parents have to walk a fine line between giving adolescents enough independence and protecting them from immature lapses in judgment. Tensions can lead to family conflict, and parenting styles can influence its shape and outcome. Effective monitoring depends on how much adolescents let parents know about their daily lives, and such disclosures may depend on the atmosphere parents have established. Also, as with younger children, adolescents' relationships with parents are affected by the parents' life situation—their work and marital and socioeconomic status.

individuation
Adolescent's struggle for autonomy
and differentiation, or personal identity.

connect

study smart

Conflict with Parents

Individuation and Family Conflict If you were like most teens, you probably listened to different music from your parents, dressed in a different style of clothing, and felt it was reasonable to keep certain things private from them. This process, called **individuation** by psychologists, begins in infancy and continues throughout adolescence. It involves the struggle for autonomy and differentiation, or personal identity. An important aspect of individuation is carving out boundaries of control between self and parents (Nucci, Hasebe, & Lins-Dyer, 2005), and this process may entail family conflict.

In a longitudinal study, 1,357 European American and African American youth were interviewed three times between the summer before high school entry and eleventh grade. What emerged was the importance of adolescents' perceptions of family relations. Young people who saw themselves as having a great deal of autonomy over their everyday activities tended to spend more time in unsupervised socializing with peers and were at risk for problem behavior by eleventh grade. On the other hand, those who saw their parents as highly intrusive in their personal lives tended to come under negative peer influence and to join their friends in risky behaviors. Thus parents of young adolescents must strike a delicate balance between too much freedom and too much intrusiveness (Goldstein, Davis-Kean, & Eccles, 2005).

Arguments most often concern control over everyday personal matters—chores, schoolwork, dress, money, curfews, dating, and friends—rather than issues of health and safety or right and wrong (Adams & Laursen, 2001; Steinberg, 2005). Teens generally feel they should have autonomy over personal matters. The emotional intensity of these conflicts—out of all proportion with the subject matter—may reflect the underlying individuation process. In a longitudinal study of 99 families, both individuation and family connectedness during adolescence predicted well-being in middle age (Bell & Bell, 2005).

The process of individuation can be rocky, and as teens work out the details of their new power dynamic, conflict can result. Both family conflict and positive identification with parents are highest at age 13 and then diminish until age 17, when they stabilize or increase somewhat. This shift reflects increased opportunities for independent adolescent decision making (Gutman & Eccles, 2007), enlarging the boundaries of what is considered the adolescent's own business (Steinberg, 2005).

Especially for girls, family relations can affect mental health. Adolescents given more decision-making opportunities report higher self-esteem than those given fewer such opportunities. In addition, negative family interactions are related to adolescent depression, whereas positive family identification is related to less depression (Gutman & Eccles, 2007).

The level of family discord may depend largely on family atmosphere. Among 335 two-parent rural midwestern families with teenagers, conflict declined during early to middle adolescence in warm, supportive families but worsened in hostile, coercive, or critical families (Rueter & Conger, 1995).

Parenting Styles and Parental Authority Authoritative parenting continues to foster healthy development (Baumrind, 1991, 2005). Parents who show disappointment in teenagers' misbehavior are more effective in motivating responsible behavior than parents who punish harshly (Krevans & Gibbs, 1996). Overly strict, authoritarian parenting may lead an adolescent to reject parental influence and to seek peer support and approval at all costs (Fuligni & Eccles, 1993).

Authoritative parents insist on important rules, norms, and values but are willing to listen, explain, and negotiate (Lamborn, Mounts, Steinberg, & Dornbusch, 1991). They exercise appropriate control over a child's conduct (*behavioral control*) but not over the child's feelings, beliefs, and sense of self (*psychological control*) (Steinberg & Darling, 1994). So, for example, they might ground their teenage son or daughter from using the car after breaking a family rule, but they would not insist that the teen agree with them about the wisdom of the broken rule. Generally, behavioral control is preferable. Psychological control, exerted through such emotionally manipulative techniques as

TABLE 17.6 Psychological Control Scale—Youth Self-Report

Ratings:

1 = Not like her (him); 2 = Somewhat like her (him); 3 = A lot like her (him)

My Mother (Father) is a person who . . .

1. changes the subject, whenever I have something to say.
2. finishes my sentences whenever I talk.
3. often interrupts me.
4. acts like she (he) knows what I'm thinking or feeling.
5. would like to be able to tell me how to feel or think about things all the time.
6. is always trying to change how I feel or think about things.
7. blames me for other family members' problems.
8. brings up my past mistakes when she (he) criticizes me.
9. tells me that I am not a loyal or good member of the family.
10. tells me of all the things she (he) had done for me.
11. says, if I really cared for her (him), I would not do things that cause her (him) to worry.
12. is less friendly with me, if I do not see things her (his) way.
13. will avoid looking at me when I have disappointed her (him).
14. if I have hurt her (his) feelings, stops talking to me until I please her (him) again.
15. often changes her (his) moods when with me.
16. goes back and forth between being warm and critical toward me.

Source: Adapted from Barber, 1996.

withdrawal of love, can harm adolescents' psychosocial development and mental health (Steinberg, 2005). (Table 17.6 is a checklist used for adolescents' self-reports on parents' use of psychological control.) Parents who are psychologically controlling tend to be unresponsive to their children's growing need for *psychological autonomy*, the right to their own thoughts and feelings (Steinberg, 2005).

Authoritative parenting seems to bolster an adolescent's self-image. A survey of 8,700 ninth to twelfth graders concluded that "the more involvement, autonomy granting, and structure that adolescents perceive from their parents, the more positively teens evaluate their own general conduct, psychosocial development, and mental health" (Gray & Steinberg, 1999, p. 584). When adolescents thought their parents were trying to dominate their psychological experience, their emotional health suffered more than when they thought their parents were trying to control their behavior. Teens whose parents were firm in enforcing behavioral rules had more self-discipline and fewer behavior problems than those with more permissive parents. Those whose parents granted them psychological autonomy tended to become self-confident and competent in both the academic and social realms.

Problems arise when parents overstep what adolescents perceive as appropriate bounds of legitimate parental authority. The existence of a mutually agreed personal domain in which authority belongs to the adolescent has been found in various cultures and social classes from Japan to Brazil. This domain expands as parents and adolescents continually renegotiate its boundaries (Nucci et al., 2005).

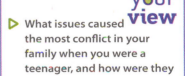

what's **your** **view**

▷ What issues caused the most conflict in your family when you were a teenager, and how were they resolved?

▷ If you lived with both parents, were your conflicts more with one parent than with the other? Did your mother and father handle such issues similarly or differently?

TABLE 17.7 Items Used to Assess Perceived Areas of Parental versus Adolescent Authority

Moral Items	Conventional Items	Prudential Items	Multifaceted Items	Multifaceted Friendship	Personal Items
Stealing money from parents	Not doing assigned chores	Smoking cigarettes	Not cleaning bedroom	When to start dating	Sleeping late on weekends
Hitting siblings	Talking back to parents	Drinking beer or wine	Getting ears pierced with multiple holes	Staying over at a friend's house	Choosing how to spend allowance money
Lying to parents	Using bad manners	Doing drugs	Staying out late	Seeing friends whom parents don't like	Choosing own clothes or hairstyles
Breaking a promise to parents	Cursing	Having sex	Watching cable TV	Seeing friends rather than going out with family	Choice of music

Source: Adapted from Smetana, Crean, & Campione-Barr, 2005.

Parental Monitoring and Adolescents' Self-Disclosure Young people's growing autonomy and the shrinking areas of perceived parental authority redefine the types of behavior adolescents are expected to disclose to parents (Smetana, Crean, & Campione-Barr, 2005; Table 17.7). In a study of 276 ethnically diverse suburban ninth and twelfth graders, both adolescents and parents saw *prudential* behavior related to health and safety (such as smoking, drinking, and drug use) as most subject to disclosure; followed by *moral* issues (such as lying); *conventional* issues (such as bad manners or swearing); and *multifaceted*, or borderline, issues (such as seeing an R-rated movie), which lie at the boundary between personal matters and one of the other categories. Both adolescents and parents saw *personal* issues (such as how teens spend their time and money) as least subject to disclosure. However, for each type of behavior parents were more inclined to expect disclosure than adolescents were to do it. This discrepancy diminished between ninth and twelfth grades as parents modified their expectations to fit adolescents' growing maturity (Smetana, Metzger, Gettman, & Campione-Barr, 2006).

In a study of 690 Belgian adolescents, young people were more willing to disclose information about themselves when parents maintained a warm, responsive family climate in which adolescents were encouraged to speak openly and when parents provided clear expectations without being overly controlling (Soenens, Vansteenkiste, Luyckx, & Goossens, 2006)—in other words, when parenting was authoritative. Adolescents, especially girls, tend to have closer, more supportive relationships with their mothers than with their fathers, and girls confide more in their mothers (Smetana et al., 2006). And, perhaps even more important, a large body of research shows that parental monitoring is one of the most consistently identified protective factors for teens (Racz & McMahon, 2011). Parental monitoring broadly involves keeping track of the young person's activities, for example, by signing the teen up for after-school activities, checking in with parents of their teen's friends, and keeping track of a teen's whereabouts.

Family Structure and Family Atmosphere Adolescents, like younger children, are sensitive to the atmosphere in the family home. And, conflict in the home can affect the process of individuation. In a longitudinal study of 451 adolescents and their parents, changes in marital distress or marital conflict—either for better or worse—predicted corresponding changes in adolescents' adjustment (Cui, Conger, & Lorenz, 2005). Divorce can impact this process as well. Adolescent boys and girls whose parents later divorced showed more academic, psychological, and behavioral problems before the breakup than peers whose parents did not later divorce (Sun, 2001). In addition, the distancing that can result for divorce tends to be more extreme for fathers. For example, research has shown that teens whose parents are still married report a close relationship with their father 48 percent of the time, while those whose parents are divorced report being close to their fathers only 25 percent of the time (Scott, Booth, King, & Johnson, 2007).

Adolescents living with their continuously married parents tend to have significantly fewer behavioral problems than those in any other family structure (single-parent, cohabiting, or stepfamilies), according to data from a major national longitudinal study. An important factor is father involvement. High-quality involvement of a nonresident father helps a great deal, but not as much as the involvement of a father living in the home (Carlson, 2006).

Adolescents in cohabiting families, like younger children, tend to have greater behavioral and emotional problems than adolescents in married families; and, when one of the cohabiting parents is not the biological parent, school engagement suffers as well. For adolescents, unlike younger children, these effects are independent of economic resources, parental well-being, or effectiveness of parenting, suggesting that parental cohabitation itself may be more troublesome for adolescents than for younger children (Brown, 2004).

On the other hand, a multiethnic study of 12- and 13-year-old children of single mothers—first assessed when the children were 6 and 7 years old—found no negative effects of single parenting on school performance and no greater risk of problem behavior. What mattered most were the mother's educational level and ability, family income, and the quality of the home environment (Ricciuti, 2004). This finding suggests that negative effects of living in a single-parent home can be offset by positive factors.

Mothers' Employment and Economic Stress The impact of a mother's work outside the home may depend on whether there are two parents or only one in the household. Often a single mother must work to stave off economic disaster; how her working affects her teenage children may hinge on how much time and energy she has left over to spend with them, how much parental monitoring she is able to provide. A longitudinal study of 819 10- to 14-year-olds from low-income urban families points up the importance of the type of care and supervision adolescents receive after school. Those who are on their own, away from home, tend to become involved in alcohol and drug use and in misconduct in school, especially if they have an early history of problem behavior. However, this is less likely to happen when parents monitor their children's activities and neighbors are actively involved (Coley, Morris, & Hernandez, 2004).

As we have discussed earlier, a major problem in many single-parent families is lack of money. In a national longitudinal study, adolescent children of low-income single mothers were negatively affected by their mother's unstable employment or being out of work for 2 years. The adolescents were more likely to drop out of school and to experience declines in self-esteem and mastery (Kalil & Ziol-Guest, 2005). Furthermore, family economic hardship during adolescence can affect adult well-being. The degree of risk depends on whether parents see their situation as stressful, whether that stress interferes with family relationships, and how much it affects children's educational and occupational attainments (Sobolewski & Amato, 2005).

On the other hand, many adolescents in economically distressed families may benefit from accumulated social capital—the support of kin and community. In 51 poor, urban African American families in which teenagers were living with their mothers, grandmothers, or aunts, women who had strong kinship networks exercised firmer control and closer monitoring while granting appropriate autonomy, and their teenage charges were more self-reliant and had fewer behavior problems (Taylor & Roberts, 1995).

checkpoint
can you . . .

▷ Identify factors that affect conflict with parents and adolescents' self-disclosure?

▷ Discuss the impact on adolescents of parenting styles and of marital status, mothers' employment, and economic stress?

Studies have found that the negative effects of living in a single-parent home can be offset by positive factors.

ADOLESCENTS AND SIBLINGS

There are several trends in sibling relationships across adolescence. In general, siblings spend less time together, their relationships become more equal, and they become more similar in their levels of competence.

Changes in sibling relationships in many ways precede and mirror the changes we see in the relationships of adolescents and their parents. As young people develop, they become more independent from their parents. They begin to exert their autonomy and spend less time with their parents and more time with their peers. This is similar to what occurs with adolescents and their siblings. As adolescents begin to spend more time with peers, they spend less time with siblings. Generally, and perhaps as a result of this, adolescents tend to be less close to siblings than to friends, and are less influenced by them. This distance grows across adolescence (Laursen, 1996). Moreover, as children approach high school, their relationships with their siblings become progressively more equal. Older siblings exercise less power over younger ones, and younger siblings no longer need as much supervision. As relative age differences shrink, so do differences in competence and independence (Buhrmester & Furman, 1990).

Older and younger siblings tend to have different feelings about their changing relationship. As the younger sibling grows up, the older sibling may look on a newly assertive younger brother or sister as a pesky annoyance. Younger siblings still tend to look up to older siblings and try to feel more grown up by identifying with and emulating them (Buhrmester & Furman, 1990).

A longitudinal study of 200 white families charted changes in sibling relations from middle childhood through adolescence (Kim, McHale, Osgood, & Crouter, 2006). As in previous research, sisters generally reported more intimacy than brothers or mixed pairs. Intimacy levels between same-sex siblings remained stable. Mixed-sex siblings, in contrast, became less intimate between middle childhood and early adolescence, but more so in middle adolescence, a time when most young people become more interested in the other sex. Sibling conflict declined across middle adolescence.

The study also found that sibling relations tend to reflect both parent-child relations and the parents' marital relationship. For example, siblings were more intimate if their mother was warm and accepting. Parent-child conflict was associated with sibling conflict. On the other hand, when fathers became less happy in their marriages, siblings became closer and quarreled less (Kim et al., 2006).

In a 5-year longitudinal study of 227 Latino and African American families, sibling relationships under certain circumstances had important effects on the younger sibling. In single-mother homes, a warm and nurturing relationship with an older sister tended to prevent a younger sister from engaging in substance use and risky sexual behavior. On the other hand, having a domineering older sister tended to increase a younger sibling's high-risk sexual behavior (East & Khoo, 2005). Older siblings may influence a younger one to smoke, drink, or use drugs (Pomery et al., 2005; Rende, Slomkowski, Lloyd-Richardson, & Niaura, 2005). In a longitudinal study of 206 boys and their younger siblings, younger siblings hanging out with an antisocial older brother were at serious risk for adolescent antisocial behavior, drug use, sexual behavior, and violence, regardless of parental discipline (Snyder, Bank, & Burraston, 2005). A meta-analysis supports the strong connection between warm relationships with little conflict and healthier psychological adjustment in siblings (Buist, Dekovic, & Prinzie, 2013).

PEERS AND FRIENDS

An important source of emotional support during the complex transition of adolescence—as well as a source of pressure for behavior that parents may deplore—is the peer group. The peer group is a source of affection, sympathy, understanding, and moral guidance; a place for experimentation; and a setting for achieving autonomy and independence from parents. It is a place to form intimate relationships that serve as rehearsals for adult intimacy.

what's your view

If you have one or more brothers or sisters, did your relationships with them change during adolescence?

Cliques and Crowds

In childhood, most peer interactions are *dyadic*, or one-to-one, though somewhat larger groupings begin to form in middle childhood. As children move into adolescence, *cliques*—structured groups of friends who do things together—become more important. A larger type of grouping, *crowds*, which does not normally exist before adolescence, is based not on personal interactions but on reputation, image, or identity. Crowd membership is a social construction, a set of labels by which young people divide the social map based on neighborhood, ethnicity, socioeconomic status, or other factors (such as the jocks, the nerds, the skaters, the stoners). All three levels of peer groupings may exist simultaneously, and some may overlap in membership, which may change over time. Both clique and crowd affiliations become looser as adolescence progresses (Brown & Klute, 2003).

> As an adolescent, were you part of a clique or crowd? If so, how did it affect your social relationships and attitudes?

The influence of peers normally peaks at ages 12 to 13 and declines during middle and late adolescence. At age 13 or 14, popular adolescents may engage in mildly antisocial behaviors, such as trying drugs or sneaking into a movie without paying, so as to demonstrate to their peers their independence from parental rules (Allen, Porter, McFarland, Marsh, & McElhaney, 2005). In a study about the influence of risk-taking, 306 adolescents, college-age youth, and young adults played a video game called "Chicken." For all ages groups, risk-taking was higher in the company of peers than alone, but this was especially true of younger participants (Gardner & Steinberg, 2005). However, attachment to peers in early adolescence is not likely to forecast real trouble unless the attachment is so strong that the young person is willing to give up obeying household rules, doing schoolwork, and developing his or her own talents in order to win peer approval and popularity (Fuligni, Eccles, Barber, & Clements, 2001).

Friendships The intensity and importance of friendships and the amount of time spent with friends are probably greater in adolescence than at any other time in the life span. Friendships tend to become more reciprocal, more equal, and more stable. Those that are less satisfying become less important or are abandoned.

Greater intimacy, loyalty, and sharing with friends mark a transition toward adultlike friendships. Adolescents begin to rely more on friends than on parents for intimacy and support, and they share confidences more than younger friends do (Berndt & Perry, 1990; Buhrmester, 1990, 1996; Hartup & Stevens, 1999; Laursen, 1996; Nickerson & Nagle, 2005). Girls' friendships tend to be more intimate than boys', with frequent sharing of confidences (Brown & Klute, 2003). Intimacy with same-sex friends increases during early to midadolescence, after which it typically declines as intimacy with the other sex grows (Laursen, 1996).

> It is true that those around you influence your propensity to take risks, but it is also true that some people, by virtue of their genetic makeup, are more likely to take risks. Researchers have recently found that mutations linked to the production of dopamine are involved in sensation-seeking.
> Derringer et al., 2011

The increased intimacy of adolescent friendship reflects cognitive as well as emotional development. Adolescents are now better able to express their private thoughts and feelings. They can more readily consider another person's point of view, and so it is easier for them to understand a friend's thoughts and feelings. Increased intimacy reflects early adolescents' concern with getting to know themselves. Confiding in a friend helps young people explore their own feelings, define their identity, and validate their self-worth (Buhrmester, 1996).

> There are indications that administering oxytocin, a hormone involved in social affiliation, results in better social cognitive abilities, but only for those people who are deficient in this hormone to start with.
> Bartz, 2010

Humans are social animals, and as such, the quality of our relationships matters greatly to outcomes. Friends are important. Thus, it is not surprising that the capacity for intimacy is related to psychological adjustment and social competence. Adolescents

The explosion of social networking sites like Facebook and Twitter has significantly affected how adolescents communicate with one another.

study smart

Social Networking

▷ **checkpoint**
can you . . .

▶ Describe typical changes in sibling relationships during adolescence?

▶ List several functions of the peer group in adolescence?

▶ Discuss how online communication affects social connectedness?

connect

study smart

Dating

who have close, stable, supportive friendships generally have a high opinion of themselves, do well in school, are sociable, and are unlikely to be hostile, anxious, or depressed (Berndt & Perry, 1990; Buhrmester, 1990; Hartup & Stevens, 1999). They also tend to have established strong bonds with parents (Brown & Klute, 2003). A bidirectional process seems to be at work: Good relationships foster adjustment, which in turn fosters good friendships.

Social Consequences of Online Communication The explosion of online communication technologies such as instant messaging, e-mail, and text messaging, as well as social networking sites like Instagram and Facebook, has changed the way many adolescents communicate. As a group, adolescents are the primary users of social interaction technologies. They spend more time online than adults, and spend a majority of their online time using the Internet to communicate. Early research suggested that online communication would reduce adolescents' social connectedness with friends and family members. Studies on the effects of Internet use in the 1990s and early 2000 showed that adolescents who spent a lot of time on the Internet spent less time with friends (Nie, 2001), had fewer friends (Mesch, 2001), and showed reduced social connectedness and well-being (Kraut et al., 1998).

There are social consequences to online communities . . . and there are academic ones as well. Students who are on Facebook while they study earn 20 percent lower grades than their peers who turn the computer off.

Kirschner & Karpinski, 2010

As access to the Internet has increased and as more sophisticated technologies like instant messaging (IM) and Facebook have replaced public chat rooms, the effect of increased Internet use has shifted from negative to positive. European and U.S. studies have shown that 88 percent of adolescents use IM to communicate with existing friends (Valkenburg & Peter, 2007). Recent studies have shown that online communication stimulates rather than reduces social connectedness (Kraut et al., 2002).

The ability of online communication to enhance online self-disclosure has been identified as a primary reason for improved social connectedness and well-being. Individuals often become unusually intimate in an online environment with reduced visual and auditory contextual cues. They are less concerned about how others perceive them and more free to express themselves (Tidewell & Walther, 2002; Valkenburg & Peter, 2009). Because adolescents connect self-disclosure with quality friendships, the elevated level of self-disclosure in online environments can also be linked to friendship quality and formation (McKenna & Bargh, 2000; Valkenburg & Peter, 2007), which in turn elevates social connectedness and well-being.

The aspects of online communication that enhance connectedness—the level of anonymity—has made it appealing for electronic bullies. As discussed previously, bullying is a form of aggression intended to harm. Verbal and physical bullying are the more prevalent types of bullying, but Internet bullying and victimization rates have been reported at about 25 percent of middle school students (Willard, 2006).

Romantic Relationships Romantic relationships are a central part of most adolescents' social worlds. They contribute to the development of both intimacy and identity. With the onset of puberty, most heterosexual boys and girls begin to think about and interact more with members of the other sex. Typically they move from mixed groups or group dates to one-on-one romantic relationships that involve passion and a sense of commitment (Bouchey & Furman, 2003; Furman & Wehner, 1997).

Romantic relationships tend to become more intense and more intimate across adolescence (Bouchey & Furman, 2003). Early adolescents think primarily about how a romantic relationship may affect their status in the peer group (Bouchey & Furman, 2003). They pay little or no attention to attachment or support needs, such as help, caring, and nurturance, and their attention to sexual needs is limited to how to engage in sexual activity and which activities to engage in (Bouchey & Furman, 2003; Furman & Wehner, 1997).

In midadolescence, most young people have had at least one exclusive partner lasting for several months to about a year, and the effect of the choice of partner on peer status tends to become less important (Furman & Wehner, 1997). In interviews with 1,316 junior high and high school students, boys revealed less confidence than girls about these early romantic relationships. Girls' greater ease in romantic relationships may be an extension of their greater intimacy in same-sex friendships (Giordano, Longmore, & Manning, 2006).

By age 16, adolescents interact with and think about romantic partners more than about parents, friends, or siblings (Bouchey & Furman, 2003). Not until late adolescence or early adulthood, though, do romantic relationships begin to meet the full gamut of emotional needs that such relationships can serve and then only in relatively long-term relationships (Furman & Wehner, 1997). Breakups with romantic partners are among the strongest predictors of depression and suicide (Bouchey & Furman, 2003).

Relationships with parents and peers may affect the quality of romantic relationships. The parents' marriage or romantic relationship may serve as a model for their adolescent child. The peer group forms the context for most romantic relationships and may affect an adolescent's choice of a partner and the way the relationship develops (Bouchey & Furman, 2003). Adverse relationships with parents and peers can lead to unhealthy and sometimes violent relationships.

Dating Violence Dating violence is a significant problem in the United States. The three common forms of dating violence are:

Physical—when a partner is hit, pinched, shoved, or kicked;

Emotional—when a partner is threatened or verbally abused; and

Sexual—when a partner is forced to engage in a nonconsensual sex act.

Statistics indicate that about 10 percent of students have been victims of physical dating violence, but the rate may actually be higher due to the fear students have about telling friends or family. The rates for emotional abuse are even higher: As many as 3 in 10 adolescents report being verbally or psychologically abused (Halpern, Young, Waller, Martin, & Kupper, 2003). Altogether, 1 in 4 adolescents reports verbal, physical, emotional, or sexual abuse from a dating partner each year (CDC, 2008d).

In addition to the physical harm caused by this type of abuse, teens who are victims of dating violence are more likely to do poorly in school and to engage in risky behaviors like drug and alcohol use. These students are also subject to eating disorders, depression, and suicide. Although the rates for overall victimization are similar for boys and girls, boys report slightly higher levels of victimization, but girls are disproportionately victims in cases of severe violence (Mulford & Giordano, 2008).

Risk factors that may predict violence include substance abuse, depression or anxiety, high sexual risk behaviors, or having been previously involved in an abusive relationship (Cutter-Wilson & Richmond, 2011). Unhealthy relationships can last a lifetime as victims carry patterns of violence into future relationships.

Antisocial Behavior and Juvenile Delinquency

What influences young people to engage in—or refrain from—violence (Box 17.2) or other antisocial acts? By what processes do antisocial tendencies develop? How do problem behaviors escalate into chronic delinquency? What determines whether a juvenile

checkpoint
can **you . . .**

▷ Describe developmental changes in romantic relationships?

▷ List the three forms of dating violence and the risk factors that may predict violence?

What causes antisocial behavior, and what can be done to reduce the risk of juvenile delinquency?

the everyday world

THE YOUTH VIOLENCE EPIDEMIC

On April 20, 1999, two Columbine High School students in Littleton, Colorado, killed 12 classmates and 1 teacher before fatally shooting themselves. On April 16, 2007, a 23-year-old Virginia Tech student killed 32 people before shooting himself, making the shooting rampage the most deadly in U.S. history. And, in 2012, a 20-year-old man first shot his mother, and then 20 children and 6 adults at Sandy Hook Elementary School in Newtown, Connecticut, before taking his own life.

While the publicity surrounding such acts of violence makes them highly salient to most people, in actuality they are rare, representing only 1 percent of homicides among school-age youth. Most such homicides involve only a single killer and a single victim. Indeed, despite the wave of school killings since 1999, rates of school-associated homicides declined overall between 1992 and 2006 (Modzeleski et al., 2008).

Sadly, though, victims of these highly publicized cases are only a small fraction of those affected by youth violence. In 2005, more than 721,000 young people ages 10 to 24 were treated in emergency departments for injuries sustained from violence (CDC, 2007c). Persons under age 25 comprised 44.5 percent of persons arrested for violent crime and 53.9 percent of persons arrested for property crime in the United States in that year (Federal Bureau of Investigation [FBI], 2007).

What causes such destructive behavior? Many influences may push young people to violent acts:

- The immature adolescent brain, particularly the prefrontal cortex, which is critical to judgment and impulse suppression.
- Ready access to guns in a culture that "romanticizes gunplay" (Weinberger, 2001, p. 2).
- The presence of gangs at school (National Center for Education Statistics [NCES], 2003; "Youth Violence," 2001).
- A rejecting, coercive, or chaotic childhood home environment, which tends to produce aggressive behavior in children. The hostility they evoke in others increases their own aggression. Their negative self-image prevents them from succeeding at

school or developing other constructive interests; and they generally associate with peers who reinforce their antisocial attitudes and behavior (Staub, 1996).

- Living in unstable, inner-city neighborhoods with low community involvement and support (Tolan, Gorman-Smith, & Henry, 2003), although middle-class students in suburban schools are not immune.
- Having witnessed or having been victims of neighborhood violence, or having been exposed to media violence (Brookmeyer, Henrich, & Schwab-Stone, 2005; Pearce, Jones, Schwab-Stone, & Ruchkin, 2003).

Psychologists point to potential warning signs. Adolescents likely to commit violence often refuse to listen to parents and teachers, ignore the feelings and rights of others, mistreat people, rely on violence or threats to solve problems, and believe that life has treated them unfairly. They tend to do poorly in school; to cut classes or play truant; to be held back or suspended or to drop out; to be victims of bullying; to use alcohol, inhalants, and/or other drugs; to engage in early sexual activity; to join gangs; and to fight, steal, or destroy property (American Psychological Association and American Academy of Pediatrics [AAP], 1996; Resnick et al., 1997; Smith-Khuri et al., 2004; "Youth Violence," 2001).

One of the worst myths about youth violence is that nothing can be done to prevent or treat violent behavior. This is not true. School-based programs for *all* children, not just those at risk, have reduced violence and aggressiveness at all grade levels. These programs are designed to prevent violent behavior by promoting social skills and emotional awareness and control (Hahn et al., 2007).

what's your view

What do you think is the most important factor in preventing youth violence?

delinquent will grow up to be a hardened criminal? Human behavior is complex and multiply determined. Thus, no one factor is responsible for antisocial behavior. Rather, the development of antisocial behavior involves a complex and reciprocal interaction between environment and biological risk factors (van Goozen, Fairchild, Snoek, and Harold, 2007).

BECOMING A DELINQUENT: GENETIC AND NEUROLOGICAL FACTORS

Antisocial behavior tends to run in families. Analyses of many studies have concluded that genes influence 40 to 50 percent of the variation in antisocial behavior within a population and 60 to 65 percent of the variation in aggressive antisociality (Rhee & Waldman, 2002; Tackett, Krueger, Iacono, & McGue, 2005). Genes alone, however, are not predictive of antisocial behavior. Recent research findings suggest that while genetics influence delinquency, environmental influences including family, friends, and school affect gene expression (Guo, Roettger, & Cai, 2008).

Neurobiological deficits, particularly in the portions of the brain that regulate reactions to stress, may help explain why some children become antisocial children and adolescents. As a result of these neurological deficits, which may result from the interaction of genetic factors or difficult temperament with adverse early environments, children may not receive or heed normal warning signals to restrain impulsive or reckless behavior (van Goozen et al., 2007). Children with attention-deficit/hyperactivity disorder (ADHD) are at higher risk for the development of comorbid conduct disorder (CD) and depression that contribute to antisocial behavior (Drabick, Gadow, & Sprafkin, 2006) Also, preliminary findings of an MRI investigation of empathetic response have indicated youth with aggressive conduct disorders have atypical responses to seeing others in pain (Decety, Michalaska, Akitsuki, & Lahey, 2009).

BECOMING A DELINQUENT: HOW FAMILY, PEER, AND COMMUNITY INFLUENCES INTERACT

Researchers have identified two types of antisocial behavior: an *early-onset* type, beginning by age 11, which tends to lead to chronic juvenile delinquency in adolescence, and a milder, *late-onset* type, beginning after puberty, which tends to arise temporarily in response to the changes of adolescence: the mismatch between biological and social maturity, increased desire for autonomy, and decreased adult supervision. Late-onset adolescents tend to commit relatively minor offenses (Schulenberg & Zarrett, 2006).

The early-onset type of antisocial behavior is influenced, as Bronfenbrenner's theory would suggest, by interacting factors ranging from microsystem influences, such as parent-child hostility, poor parenting practices, and peer deviance, to macrosystem influences, such as community structure and neighborhood social support (Buehler, 2006; Tolan et al., 2003). This network of interacting influences begins to be woven early in childhood.

Late-onset antisociality typically occurs in adolescents with normal family backgrounds. Parents of children who become chronically antisocial, by contrast, may have failed to reinforce good behavior in early childhood and may have been harsh or inconsistent—or both—in punishing misbehavior (Coie & Dodge, 1998; Snyder, Cramer, Frank, & Patterson, 2005). Through the years these parents may not have been closely and positively involved in their children's lives (Patterson, DeBaryshe, & Ramsey, 1989). The children may get payoffs for antisocial behavior: When they act up, they may gain attention or get their own way. These early negative patterns pave the way for negative peer influences that promote and reinforce antisocial behavior (Collins, Maccoby, Steinberg, Hetherington, & Bornstein, 2000; Brown, Mounts, Lamborn, & Steinberg, 1993).

By early adolescence, open hostility may exist between parent and child. When constant criticism, angry coercion, or rude, uncooperative behavior characterizes parent-child interactions, the child tends to show aggressive behavior problems, which then worsen the parent-child relationship (Buehler, 2006). Ineffective parenting can leave younger siblings to the powerful influence of a deviant older brother, especially if the siblings are close in age (Snyder et al., 2005).

The choice of antisocial peers is affected mainly by environmental factors (Iervolino et al., 2002). Young people gravitate to others brought up like themselves who are similar in school achievement, adjustment, and prosocial or antisocial tendencies (Collins et al., 2000; Brown et al., 1993). As in childhood, antisocial adolescents tend to have antisocial friends, and their antisocial behavior increases when they associate with

Teens who drop out of high school cost society approximately $240,000 in lost tax revenue, increased use of social services, and greater likelihood of being on welfare or incarcerated. In October 2008, approximately 30 million 16- to 24-year-olds were not in school and had not earned a high school diploma. This represents approximately 8 percent of eligible teens.

Chapman, Laird, & Kewal-Ramani, 2010

Some high schools, in an attempt to curb violent antisocial behavior, have installed metal detectors and security checkpoints for their students.

each other (Dishion, McCord, & Poulin, 1999; Hartup & Stevens, 1999; Vitaro, Tremblay, Kerr, Pagani, & Bukowski, 1997). The way antisocial teenagers talk, laugh, or smirk about rule breaking and nod knowingly among themselves seems to constitute a sort of "deviancy training" (Dishion et al., 1999). These problem children continue to elicit ineffective parenting, which predicts delinquent behavior and association with deviant peer groups or gangs (Simons, Chao, Conger, & Elder, 2001; Tolan et al., 2003).

Authoritative parenting, which involves high levels of warmth as well as control and rules, can help young people internalize standards that may insulate them against negative peer influences and open them to positive influences (Collins et al., 2000; Mounts & Steinberg, 1995). Improved parenting during adolescence can reduce delinquency by discouraging association with deviant peers (Simons et al., 2001). Adolescents whose parents know where they are and what they are doing are less likely to engage in delinquent acts (Laird, Pettit, Bates, & Dodge, 2003) or to associate with deviant peers (Lloyd & Anthony, 2003). In sum, parents who are warm, who monitor their teens, and who have clearly defined and well-enforced rules are the least likely to have delinquent adolescents.

Family economic circumstances may influence the development of antisocial behavior. Persistent economic deprivation can undermine sound parenting by depriving the family of social capital. Poor children are more likely than other children to commit antisocial acts, and those whose families are continuously poor tend to become more antisocial with time. Conversely, when families rise from poverty while a child is still young, the child is no more likely to develop behavior problems than a child whose family was never poor (Macmillan, McMorris, & Kruttschnitt, 2004).

Weak neighborhood social organization in a disadvantaged community can influence delinquency through its effects on parenting behavior and peer deviance (Chung & Steinberg, 2006). The strength of social connections within a neighborhood can be a protective factor for at-risk teens (Sampson, 1997). Psychologists define *collective efficacy* as a neighborhood-level influence, involving the willingness of individuals in a neighborhood to work together to achieve a common goal, intervene if a problem is apparent, and help each other out in times of need. A combination of nurturant, involved parenting and collective efficacy can discourage adolescents from association with deviant peers (Brody et al., 2001).

LONG-TERM PROSPECTS

The vast majority of these young people do not become adult criminals (Kosterman, Graham, Hawkins, Catalano, & Herrenkohl, 2001; Moffitt, 1993). Delinquency peaks at about age 15 and then declines as most adolescents and their families come to terms with young people's need to assert independence.

However, teenagers who do not see positive alternatives are more likely to adopt a permanently antisocial lifestyle (Elliott, 1993). Those most likely to persist in violence are boys who had early antisocial influences. Least likely to persist are boys and girls who were early school achievers and girls who showed early prosocial development (Kosterman et al., 2001). Because adolescents' character is still in flux, many developmental psychologists deplore the current trend toward transferring juvenile offenders from the juvenile court system, which is aimed at rehabilitation, to criminal courts where they are tried and sentenced as adults (Steinberg, 2000; Steinberg & Scott, 2003).

PREVENTING AND TREATING DELINQUENCY

Because juvenile delinquency has roots early in childhood, so should preventive efforts. Delinquency is multiply determined. Thus, to be most successful, interventions should attack the multiple factors that can lead to delinquency.

Adolescents who have taken part in certain early childhood intervention programs are less likely to get in trouble than their equally underprivileged peers who did not have these early experiences (Yoshikawa, 1994; Zigler, Taussig, & Black, 1992). Effective programs are those that target high-risk urban children and last at least 2 years during the child's first 5 years of life. They influence children directly, through high-quality day care or education, and at the same time indirectly, by offering families assistance and support geared to their needs (Berrueta-Clement, Schweinhart, Barnett, Epstein, & Weikart, 1985; Berrueta-Clement, Schweinhart, Barnett, & Weikart, 1987; Schweinhart et al., 1993; Seitz, 1990; Yoshikawa, 1994; Zigler et al., 1992).

These programs operate on Bronfenbrenner's mesosystem by affecting interactions between the home and the school and/or child care center. The programs also go one step further to the exosystem by creating supportive parent networks and linking parents with such community services as prenatal and postnatal care and educational and vocational counseling (Yoshikawa, 1994; Zigler et al., 1992). Through their multi-pronged approach, these interventions have an impact on several early risk factors for delinquency.

One such program is the Chicago Child-Parent Centers, a preschool program for disadvantaged children in the Chicago public schools. The program offers follow-up services through age 9. Participants studied at age 20 had better educational and social outcomes and fewer juvenile arrests than a comparison group who had received less extensive early interventions (Reynolds, Temple, Robertson, & Mann, 2001).

Once children reach adolescence, especially in poor, crime-ridden neighborhoods, interventions need to focus on spotting troubled adolescents and preventing gang recruitment (Tolan et al., 2003). Successful programs boost parenting skills through better monitoring, behavioral management, and neighborhood social support.

Programs such as teen hangouts and summer camps for behaviorally disturbed youth can be counterproductive because they bring together groups of deviant youth who tend to reinforce each other's deviancy. More effective programs—Scouts, sports, and church activities—integrate deviant youth into the nondeviant mainstream. Structured, adult-monitored, or school-based activities after school, on weekend evenings, and in summer, when adolescents are most likely to be idle and to get in trouble, can reduce their exposure to settings that encourage antisocial behavior (Dodge, Dishion, & Lansford, 2006).

Getting teenagers involved in constructive activities or job skills programs during their free time can pay long-range dividends. Participation in extracurricular school activities tends to cut down on dropout and criminal arrest rates among high-risk boys and girls (Mahoney, 2000).

Fortunately, the great majority of adolescents do not get into serious trouble. Those who show disturbed behavior can—and should—be helped. With love, guidance, and support, adolescents can avoid risks, build on their strengths, and explore their possibilities as they approach adult life.

Emerging Adulthood

In modern Western societies, entrance into adulthood takes longer and follows more varied routes than in the past. Before the mid-twentieth century, a young man just out of high school could, in short order, obtain a stable job, marry, and start a family. For a young woman, the chief route to adulthood was marriage, which occurred as soon as she could find a suitable mate. Now, the technological revolution has made higher education or specialized training increasingly essential. The gender revolution has brought more women into the workforce and broadened female roles (Furstenberg, Rumbaut, & Settersten, 2005; Fussell & Furstenberg, 2005). Today the road to adulthood may be marked by multiple milestones—entering college (full- or part-time), working (full- or part-time), moving away from home, getting married, and having children—and the order and timing of these transitions varies (Schulenberg, O'Malley,

what's your view

How should society deal with youthful offenders?

checkpoint
can you . . .

▷ Discuss how genetic/neurological factors influence delinquency and explain how family, peer, and community influences may interact to promote antisocial behavior and delinquency?

▷ Give examples of types of programs that have been successful in preventing or stopping delinquency and other antisocial behavior?

guidepost 5

How do various cultures define what it means to become an adult, and what markers confer adult status?

TABLE 17.8	Criteria for Adulthood	
Criteria		**% Who Felt Criteria Necessary***
Accept responsibility for consequences of actions		94
Decide on personal belief system independent of parents		78
Financially independent		73
Capable of running a household (man)		72
Establish adult relationship with parents		69
Avoid committing petty crimes (shoplifting and vandalism)		66
Capable of running a household (woman)		67
Use contraceptives and avoid pregnancy		65
Live independently from parents		60
Avoid drunk driving		55
Control emotions		50
Care for children		50
Avoid drugs		39

*Participants were asked to indicate whether they thought each item must be achieved before a person can be considered an adult.

Source: Arnett, Jeffrey Jensen. (1998). "Learning to Stand Alone: The Contemporary American Transition to Adulthood in Cultural and Historical Context," *Human Development* (Sept.–Dec.), 41.

emerging adulthood
Proposed transitional period between adolescence and adulthood, usually extending from the late teens through the mid-20s.

Bachman, & Johnston, 2005). Thus some developmental scientists suggest that the period from the late teens through the mid- to late 20s has become a distinct period of the life course: **emerging adulthood**—a time when young people are no longer adolescents but have not yet become fully adult (Arnett, 2007).

In the minds of many people today, the onset of adulthood is marked not so much by external criteria such as driving, voting, and work as by such internal indicators as a sense of autonomy, self-control, and personal responsibility. It is more a state of mind than a discrete event (Shanahan, Porfeli, & Mortimer, 2005). Individualistic criteria most likely to be considered important markers of the transition to adulthood include accepting responsibility for one's actions, deciding on one's beliefs and values, establishing an equal relationship with parents, and becoming financially independent (Arnett, 2001). Other criteria that are considered important in the onset of adulthood are included in Table 17.8.

Since the 1990s, surveys of emerging adult Americans (mostly white, urban, and middle class) have repeatedly come up with three top criteria for adulthood: "accepting responsibility for oneself, making independent decisions, and becoming financially independent"—criteria that reflect their society's values of individualism and self-sufficiency (Arnett & Galambos, 2003, p. 92). In similar studies of Israelis, Argentinians, U.S. minority groups, and Mormons, those same criteria were most widely expressed. However, emerging adults in those cultures also mentioned criteria reflecting collectivistic values. In Israel, universal military service is an important marker of adulthood (Mayseless & Scharf, 2003). Young Argentines, who have experienced severe economic crises and high unemployment in recent years, emphasize family responsibilities more than work (Facio & Micocci, 2003). Mormons cite religious rites of passage, such as being admitted to men's or women's organizations of their church (Nelson, 2003).

what's your view

▷ What criteria for adulthood do you consider most relevant?

▷ Do you think those criteria are influenced by the culture in which you live or grew up?

African Americans, Latinos, and Asian Americans are more likely than European Americans to mention criteria involving obligations to others (such as supporting one's family), recognized role transitions (such as marriage), and complying with social norms (such as avoiding illegal drug use). African Americans and Latinos who come from lower-SES families tend to believe they have reached adulthood at an earlier age than do European Americans and Asian Americans, probably because of greater and earlier family responsibilities (Arnett, 2003). As research on this topic continues, it will be interesting to see what adulthood means in rural, non-Westernized cultures, which tend to hold more strongly collectivist values.

The normal developmental changes in the early years of life are obvious and dramatic signs of growth. The infant lying in the crib becomes an active, exploring toddler. The young child enters and embraces the worlds of school and society. The adolescent, with a new body and new awareness, prepares to step into adulthood.

Growth and development do not screech to a stop even then. People change in important ways throughout adulthood. They continue to shape their development, as they have been doing since birth. What occurs in a child's world is significant, but it is not the whole story. We each continue to write the story of human development for ourselves and our society for as long as we live.

checkpoint can you . . .

▷ Explain the concept of emerging adulthood, and tell why it applies to modern Westernized societies?

▷ Discuss cultural conceptions of what it means to be an adult?

summary and key terms

guidepost 1 The Search for Identity

How do adolescents form an identity, and what roles do gender and ethnicity play?

- A central concern during adolescence is the search for identity, which has occupational, sexual, and values components. Erik Erikson described the psychosocial crisis of adolescence as the crisis of identity versus identity confusion. The virtue that should arise from this crisis is *fidelity*.

- James Marcia, in research based on Erikson's theory, described four identity statuses with differing combinations of crisis and commitment: identity achievement, foreclosure, moratorium, and identity diffusion.

- Some evidence suggests that self-esteem tends to fall during adolescence, especially for girls, and then gradually rises into adulthood.

- Ethnicity is an important part of identity. Minority adolescents seem to go through stages of ethnic identity development much like Marcia's identity statuses.

identity (472)
identity versus identity confusion (472)
fidelity (473)
identity statuses (473)
crisis (474)
commitment (474)
identity achievement (474)
foreclosure (475)
moratorium (475)
identity diffusion (475)
cultural socialization (477)

guidepost 2 Sexuality

What determines sexual orientation, what sexual practices are common among adolescents, and what leads some to engage in risky sexual behavior?

- Sexual orientation appears to be influenced by an interaction of biological and environmental factors and seems to be at least partly genetic.

- Teenage sexual activity is more prevalent and more accepted than in the past, but it involves risks of pregnancy and sexually transmitted infections (STIs). Adolescents at greatest risk are those who begin sexual activity early, have multiple partners, do not use contraceptives, and are ill informed about sex.

- The course of homosexual identity and relationship development may vary with cohort, gender, and ethnicity.

- Rates of STIs in the United States are the highest in the world, and especially high among adolescents. STIs are more likely to develop undetected in girls than in boys.

- Teenage pregnancy and birthrates in the United States have declined. Most of these births are to unmarried mothers.

- Teenage pregnancy and childbearing often have negative outcomes. Teenage mothers and their families tend to suffer ill health and financial hardship, and the children often suffer from ineffective parenting.

sexual orientation (478)
sexually transmitted infections (STIs) (482)

guidepost ③ Relationships with Family and Peers

How do adolescents relate to parents, siblings, and peers?

- Although relationships between adolescents and their parents are not always smooth, full-scale adolescent rebellion is unusual. For the majority of teens, adolescence is a fairly smooth transition. For the minority who seem more deeply troubled, it can predict a troubled adulthood.

- Adolescents spend an increasing amount of time with peers, but relationships with parents continue to be close and influential.

- Conflict with parents tends to be most frequent during early adolescence and most intense during middle adolescence. The intensity of minor conflicts may reflect the process of individuation.

- Authoritative parenting is associated with the most positive outcomes. These parents exercise appropriate behavioral control but not psychological control over their teenagers.

- Effective parental monitoring depends on adolescents' self-disclosure, which is influenced by the quality of the parent-child relationship.

- Effects of divorce, single parenting, and maternal employment on adolescents' development depend on such factors as how closely parents monitor adolescents' activity and the quality of the home environment.

- Economic stress affects relationships in both single-parent and two-parent families.

- Relationships with siblings tend to become more distant during adolescence, and the balance of power between older and younger siblings becomes more equal.

- The influence of the peer group is strongest in early adolescence. Adolescents who are rejected by peers tend to have the greatest adjustment problems.

- Peer relationships fall into three categories: friendships, cliques, and crowds. Friendships, especially among girls, become more intimate and supportive in adolescence.

- Cliques are highly status-based; crowds are based on common features, such as ethnicity or SES.

- Online communication appears to stimulate social connectedness.

- Romantic relationships involve several roles and develop with age and experience. One in four adolescents reports violence from a dating partner yearly.

adolescent rebellion (488)

individuation (490)

guidepost ④ Antisocial Behavior and Juvenile Delinquency

What causes antisocial behavior, and what can be done to reduce the risk of juvenile delinquency?

- Antisocial behavior is associated with multiple interacting risk factors, including genes, neurological deficits, ineffective parenting, school failure, peer influence, and low socioeconomic status.

- Programs that attack environmental risk factors from an early age have had success in preventing juvenile delinquency.

guidepost ⑤ Emerging Adulthood

How do various cultures define what it means to become an adult, and what markers confer adult status?

- A transitional period called emerging adulthood has developed in Westernized cultures in recent years.

- Emerging adults in various Westernized cultures hold similar views of what defines entrance into adulthood. The most widely accepted criteria are individualistic ones having to do with self-sufficiency and independence. However, some cultures also embrace collectivistic criteria, such as family responsibilities and conformity with social norms.

emerging adulthood (502)

glossary

acceleration Approach to educating the gifted that moves them through the curriculum at an unusually rapid pace. (390)

accommodation Piaget's term for changes in a cognitive structure to include new information. (34)

acquired immune deficiency syndrome (AIDS) Viral disease that undermines effective functioning of the immune system. (105)

acute medical conditions Occasional illnesses that last a short time. (349)

adaptation Piaget's term for adjustment to new information about the environment. (34)

adolescence Developmental transition between childhood and adulthood entailing major physical, cognitive, and psychosocial changes. (424)

adolescent growth spurt Sharp increase in height and weight that precedes sexual maturity. (429)

adolescent rebellion Pattern of emotional turmoil, characteristic of a minority of adolescents, that may involve conflict with family, alienation from adult society, reckless behavior, and rejection of adult values. (488)

alleles Two or more alternative forms of a gene that can occupy the same position on paired chromosomes and affect the same trait. (69)

altruism Motivation to help others without expectation of reward; may involve self-denial or self-sacrifice. (326)

altruistic behavior Activity intended to help another person with no expectation of reward. (222)

ambivalent (resistant) attachment Pattern in which an infant becomes anxious before the primary caregiver leaves, is extremely upset during his or her absence, and both seeks and resists contact on his or her return. (229)

animism Tendency to attribute life to objects that are not alive. (277)

anorexia nervosa Eating disorder characterized by self-starvation and extreme weight loss. (437)

A-not-B error Tendency for 8- to 12-month-old infants to search for a hidden object in a place where they previously found it rather than in the place where they most recently saw it being hidden. (189)

anoxia Lack of oxygen, which may cause brain damage. (125)

Apgar scale Standard measurement of a newborn's condition; it assesses appearance, pulse, grimace, activity, and respiration. (126)

art therapy Therapeutic approach that allows a person to express troubled feelings without words, using a variety of art materials and media. (355)

assimilation Piaget's term for incorporation of new information into an existing cognitive structure. (34)

assisted reproductive technology (ART) Methods used to achieve conception through artificial means. (65)

asthma A chronic respiratory disease characterized by sudden attacks of coughing, wheezing, and difficulty in breathing. (349)

attachment Reciprocal, enduring tie between two people—especially between infant and caregiver—each of whom contributes to the quality of the relationship. (228)

attention-deficit/hyperactivity disorder (ADHD) Syndrome characterized by persistent inattention and distractibility, impulsivity, low tolerance for frustration, and inappropriate overactivity. (386)

authoritarian parenting Parenting style emphasizing control and obedience. (324)

authoritative parenting Parenting style blending warmth and respect for a child's individuality with an effort to instill social values. (324)

autobiographical memory A type of episodic memory of distinctive experiences that form a person's life history. (286)

autonomy versus shame and doubt Erikson's second stage in psychosocial development, in which children achieve a balance between self-determination and control by others. (237)

autosomes In humans, the 22 pairs of chromosomes not related to sexual expression. (68)

avoidant attachment Pattern in which an infant rarely cries when separated from the primary caregiver and avoids contact on his or her return. (229)

basic sense of trust versus basic mistrust Erikson's first stage in psychosocial development, in which infants develop a sense of the reliability of people and objects. (227)

Bayley Scales of Infant and Toddler Development Standardized test of infants' and toddlers' mental and motor development. (181)

behavioral genetics Quantitative study of relative hereditary and environmental influences on behavior. (80)

behaviorism Learning theory that emphasizes the predictable role of environment in causing observable behavior. (31)

behaviorist approach Approach to the study of cognitive development that is concerned with the basic mechanics of learning. (178)

behavior therapy Therapy that uses principles of learning theory to eliminate undesirable behaviors. (355)

bilingual Fluent in two languages. (377)

bilingual education System of teaching non-English-speaking children in their native language while they learn English and later switching to all-English instruction. (377)

binge drinking Consuming five or more drinks on one occasion. (440)

bioecological theory Bronfenbrenner's approach to understanding processes and contexts of child development that identifies five levels of environmental influence. (36)

body image Descriptive and evaluative beliefs about one's appearance. (345)

Brazelton Neonatal Behavioral Assessment Scale (NBAS) Neurological and behavioral test to measure a neonate's responses to the environment. (127)

bulimia nervosa Eating disorder in which a person regularly eats huge quantities of food and then purges the body by laxatives, induced vomiting, fasting, or excessive exercise. (438)

bullying Aggression deliberately and persistently directed against a particular target, or victim, typically one who is weak, vulnerable, and defenseless. (415)

canalization Limitation on variance of expression of certain inherited characteristics. (83)

case study Study of a single subject, such as an individual or family. (46)

cell death In brain development, normal elimination of excess cells to achieve more efficient functioning. (153)

central executive   In Baddeley's model, element of working memory that controls the processing of information. (285)

central nervous system   Brain and spinal cord. (149)

centration   In Piaget's theory, tendency of preoperational children to focus on one aspect of a situation and neglect others. (278)

cephalocaudal principle   Principle that development proceeds in a head-to-tail direction; that is, that upper parts of the body develop before lower parts of the trunk. (92)

cesarean delivery   Delivery of a baby by surgical removal from the uterus. (120)

child development   Scientific study of processes of change and stability in children from conception through adolescence. (4)

child-directed speech (CDS)   Form of speech often used in talking to babies or toddlers; includes slow, simplified speech, a high-pitched tone, exaggerated vowel sounds, short words and sentences, and much repetition; also called *parentese*. (212)

childhood depression   Mood disorder characterized by such symptoms as a prolonged sense of friendlessness, inability to have fun or concentrate, fatigue, extreme activity or apathy, feelings of worthlessness, weight change, physical complaints, and thoughts of death or suicide. (354)

chromosomes   Coils of DNA that consist of genes. (67)

chronic medical conditions   Long-lasting or recurrent physical, developmental, behavioral, and/or emotional conditions that require special health services. (349)

chronosystem   Bronfenbrenner's term for effects of time on other developmental systems. (37)

circular reactions   Piaget's term for processes by which an infant learns to reproduce desired occurrences originally discovered by chance. (185)

classical conditioning   Learning based on association of a stimulus that does not ordinarily elicit a particular response with another stimulus that does elicit the response. (32, 179)

class inclusion   Understanding the relationship between a whole and its parts. (362)

code mixing   Use of elements of two languages, sometimes in the same utterance, by young children in households where both languages are spoken. (212)

code switching   Changing one's speech to match the situation, as in people who are bilingual. (212)

cognitive development   Pattern of change in mental abilities, such as learning, attention, memory, language, thinking, reasoning, and creativity. (6)

cognitive neuroscience   Study of links between neural processes and cognitive abilities. (45)

cognitive neuroscience approach   Approach to the study of cognitive development that links brain processes with cognitive ones. (179)

cognitive perspective   Perspective that looks at the development of mental processes such as thinking. (33)

cognitive-stage theory   Piaget's theory that children's cognitive development advances in a series of four stages involving qualitatively distinct types of mental operations. (33)

cohort   A group of people born at about the same time. (17)

commitment   Marcia's term for personal investment in an occupation or system of beliefs. (474)

committed compliance   Kochanska's term for wholehearted obedience of a parent's orders without reminders or lapses. (241)

componential element   Sternberg's term for the analytic aspect of intelligence. (374)

conceptual knowledge   Acquired interpretive understandings stored in long-term memory. (453)

concordant   Term describing the tendency of twins to share the same trait or disorder. (81)

concrete operations   The third stage of Piagetian cognitive development (approximately from age 7 to 12), during which children develop logical but not abstract thinking. (360)

conduct disorder (CD)   Repetitive, persistent pattern of aggressive, antisocial behavior violating societal norms or the rights of others. (353)

conscience   Internal standards of behavior, which usually control one's conduct and produce emotional discomfort when violated. (240)

conservation   Piaget's term for awareness that two objects that are equal according to a certain measure remain equal in the face of perceptual alteration so long as nothing has been added to or taken away from either object. (279)

constructive play   Second cognitive level of play, involving use of objects or materials to make something; also called *object play*. (316)

contextual element   Sternberg's term for the practical aspect of intelligence. (374)

contextual perspective   View of child development that sees the individual as inseparable from the social context. (36)

control group   In an experiment, a group of people, similar to those in the experimental group, who do not receive the treatment under study. (49)

conventional morality (or morality of conventional role conformity)   Second level in Kohlberg's theory of moral reasoning in which standards of authority figures are internalized. (456)

convergent thinking   Thinking aimed at finding the one right answer to a problem. (389)

coregulation   Transitional stage in the control of behavior in which parents exercise general supervision and children exercise moment-to-moment self-regulation. (398)

corporal punishment   Use of physical force with the intention of causing pain but not injury so as to correct or control behavior. (321)

correlational study   Research design intended to discover whether a statistical relationship between variables exists. (47)

crisis   Marcia's term for a period of conscious decision making related to identity formation. (474)

critical period   Specific time when a given event or its absence has a profound and specific impact on development. (18)

cross-modal transfer   Ability to use information gained by one sense to guide another. (193)

cross-sectional study   Study designed to assess age-related differences, in which people of different ages are assessed on one occasion. (51)

cultural socialization   Parental practices that teach children about their racial/ethnic heritage and promote cultural practices and cultural pride. (477)

culture   A society's or group's total way of life, including customs, traditions, beliefs, values, language, and physical products—all learned behavior passed on from adults to children. (11)

culture-fair test   An intelligence test that deals with experiences common to various cultures, in an attempt to avoid cultural bias. (372)

culture-free test   An intelligence test that, if it were possible to design, would have no culturally linked content. (372)

decenter   In Piaget's terminology, to think simultaneously about several aspects of a situation. (278)

declarative knowledge   Acquired factual knowledge stored in long-term memory. (453)

decoding   Process of phonetic analysis by which a printed word is converted to spoken form before retrieval from long-term memory. (378)

deductive reasoning   Type of logical reasoning that moves from a general premise about a class to a conclusion about a particular member or members of the class. (362)

deferred imitation   Piaget's term for reproduction of an observed behavior after the passage of time by calling up a stored symbol of it. (188)

Denver Developmental Screening Test   Screening test given to children age 1 month to 6 years to determine whether they are developing normally. (161)

deoxyribonucleic acid (DNA)   Chemical that carries inherited instructions for the development of all cellular forms of life. (67)

dependent variable   In an experiment, the condition that may or may not change as a result of changes in the independent variable. (49)

depth perception   Ability to perceive objects and surfaces in three dimensions. (163)

diabetes   One of the most common diseases of childhood. It is characterized by high levels of glucose in the blood as a result of defective insulin production, ineffectve insulin action, or both. (350)

differentiation   Process by which cells acquire specialized structure and function. (153)

difficult children   Children with irritable temperament, irregular biological rhythms, and intense emotional responses. (224)

discipline   Methods of molding children's character and of teaching them to exercise self-control and engage in acceptable behavior. (320)

dishabituation   Increase in responsiveness after presentation of a new stimulus. (192)

disorganized-disoriented attachment   Pattern in which an infant, after separation from the primary caregiver, shows contradictory behaviors on his or her return. (230)

divergent thinking   Thinking that produces a variety of fresh, diverse possibilities. (389)

dominant inheritance   Pattern of inheritance in which, when a child receives diffcrent alleles, only the dominant one is expressed. (69)

doula   An experienced mentor who furnishes emotional support and information for a women during labor. (122)

Down syndrome   Chromosomal disorder characterized by moderate-to-severe mental retardation and by such physical signs as a downward-sloping skin fold at the inner corners of the eyes. (76)

dramatic play   Play involving imaginary people or situations; also called *fantasy play*, *pretend play*, or *imaginative play*. (317)

drug therapy   Administration of drugs to treat emotional disorders. (356)

dual representation hypothesis   Proposal that children under age 3 have difficulty grasping spatial relationships because of the need to keep more than one mental representation in mind at the same time. (191)

dynamic systems theory (DST)   Thelen's theory that holds that motor development is a dynamic process of active coordination of multiple systems within the infant in relation to the environment. (164)

dynamic tests   Tests based on Vygotsky's theory that emphasize potential rather than past learning. (375)

dyslexia   Developmental disorder in which reading achievement is substantially lower than predicted by IQ or age. (385)

early intervention   Systematic process of providing services to help families meet young children's developmental needs. (184)

easy children   Children with a generally happy temperament, regular biological rhythms, and a readiness to accept new experiences. (224)

ecological theory of perception   Theory developed by Eleanor and James Gibson that describes developing motor and perceptual abilities as interdependent parts of a functional system that guides behavior in varying contexts. (163)

egocentrism   Piaget's term for an inability to consider another person's point of view; a characteristic of young children's thought. (223, 278)

elaboration   Mnemonic strategy of making mental associations involving items to be remembered. (368)

electronic fetal monitoring   Mechanical monitoring of fetal heartbeat during labor and delivery. (120)

elicited imitation   Research method in which infants or toddlers are induced to imitate a specific series of actions they have seen but not necessarily done before. (189)

embryonic stage   Second stage of prenatal development (2 to 8 weeks), characterized by rapid growth and development of major body systems and organs. (97)

emergent literacy   Preschoolers' development of skills, knowledge, and attitudes that underlie reading and writing. (293)

emerging adulthood   Proposed transitional period between adolescence and adulthood, usually extending from the late teens through the mid-20s. (502)

emotions   Subjective reactions to experience that are associated with physiological and behavioral changes. (218)

empathy   Ability to put oneself in another person's place and feel what the other person feels. (222)

encoding   Process by which information is prepared for long-term storage and later retrieval. (285)

English-immersion approach   Approach to teaching English as a second language in which instruction is presented only in English. (377)

enrichment   Approach to educating the gifted that broadens and deepens knowledge and skills through extra activities, projects, field trips, or mentoring. (389)

enuresis   Repeated urination in clothing or in bed. (257)

environment   Totality of nonhereditary, or experiential, influences on development. (9)

epigenesis   Mechanism that turns genes on or off and determines functions of body cells. (71)

episodic memory   Long-term memory of specific experiences or events, linked to time and place. (286)

equilibration   Piaget's term for the tendency to seek a stable balance among cognitive elements; achieved through a balance between assimilation and accommodation. (34)

ethnic gloss   Overgeneralization about an ethnic or cultural group that blurs or obscures variations within the group or overlaps with other such groups. (13)

ethnic group   A group united by ancestry, race, religion, language, or national origin that contributes to a sense of shared identity. (11)

ethnographic study   In-depth study of a culture, which uses a combination of methods including participant observation. (47)

ethology   Study of distinctive adaptive behaviors of species of animals that have evolved to increase survival of the species. (38)

evolutionary psychology   Application of Darwinian principles of natural selection to human psychology. (38)

evolutionary/sociobiological perspective   View of human development that focuses on evolutionary and biological bases of social behavior. (38)

executive function   Conscious control of thoughts, emotions, and actions to accomplish goals or solve problems. (285, 366)

exosystem   Bronfenbrenner's term for linkages between two or more settings, one of which does not contain the child. (37)

experiential element   Sternberg's term for the insightful aspect of intelligence. (374)

experiment   Rigorously controlled, replicable procedure in which the researcher manipulates variables to assess the effect of one on the other. (49)

experimental group   In an experiment, the group receiving the treatment under study. (49)

explicit memory Intentional and conscious memory, generally of facts, names, and events; sometimes called *declarative memory*. (200)

extended family Multigenerational kinship network of parents, children, and other relatives, sometimes living together in an extended-family household. (10)

externalizing behaviors Behaviors by which a child acts out emotional difficulties; for example, aggression or hostility. (398)

external memory aids Mnemonic strategies using something outside the person. (367)

family therapy Psychological treatment in which a therapist sees the whole family together to analyze patterns of family functioning. (355)

fast mapping Process by which a child absorbs the meaning of a new word after hearing it once or twice in conversation. (291)

fertilization Union of sperm and ovum to produce a zygote; also called *conception*. (61)

fetal alcohol syndrome (FAS) Combination of mental, motor, and developmental abnormalities affecting the offspring of some women who drink heavily during pregnancy. (103)

fetal stage Final stage of prenatal development (from 8 weeks to birth), characterized by increased differentiation of body parts and greatly enlarged body size. (99)

fidelity A sustained loyalty, faith, or a sense of belonging that results from the successful resolution of Erikson's identity versus identify confusion psychosocial stage of development. (473)

fine motor skills Physical skills that involve the small muscles and eye-hand coordination. (161, 258)

foreclosure Identity status, described by Marcia, in which a person who has not spent time considering alternatives (that is, has not been in crisis) is committed to other people's plans for his or her life. (475)

formal games with rules Organized games with known procedures and penalties. (317)

formal operations In Piaget's theory, final stage of cognitive development, characterized by the ability to think abstractly. (448)

functional play Lowest cognitive level of play, involving repetitive muscular movements; also called *locomotor play*. (316)

gender Significance of being male or female. (242)

gender constancy Awareness that one will always be male or female. Also called *sex-category constancy*. (311)

gender identity Awareness, developed in early childhood, that one is male or female. (306)

gender roles Behaviors, interests, attitudes, skills, and traits that a culture considers appropriate for each sex; differs for males and females. (307)

gender-schema theory Theory that children socialize themselves in their gender roles by developing a mentally organized network of information about what it means to be male or female in a particular culture. (311)

gender segregation Tendency to select playmates of one's own gender. (318)

gender stereotypes Preconceived generalizations about male or female role behavior. (307)

gender-typing Socialization process by which children, at an early age, learn appropriate gender roles. (243, 307)

generalized anxiety disorder Anxiety not focused on any single target. (354)

generic memory Memory that produces scripts of familiar routines to guide behavior. (286)

genes Small segments of DNA located in definite positions on particular chromosomes; functional units of heredity. (67)

genetic code Sequence of bases within the DNA molecule; a set of rules that govern the formation of proteins that determine the structure and functions of living cells. (67)

genetic counseling Clinical service that advises prospective parents of their probable risk of having children with hereditary defects. (77)

genotype Genetic makeup of a person, containing both expressed and unexpressed characteristics. (70)

genotype–environment correlation Tendency of certain genetic and environmental influences to reinforce each other; may be passive, reactive (evocative), or active. Also called *genotype–environment covariance*. (83)

genotype–environment interaction Effect of the interaction between genes and the environment on phenotypic variation. (83)

germinal stage First 2 weeks of prenatal development, characterized by rapid cell division, increasing complexity and differentiation, and implantation in the wall of the uterus. (93)

gestation Period of development between conception and birth. (92)

gestational age Age of an unborn baby, usually dated from the first day of an expectant mother's last menstrual cycle. (92)

goodness of fit Appropriateness of environmental demands and constraints to a child's temperament. (226)

gross motor skills Physical skills that involve the large muscles. (161, 258)

guided participation Participation of an adult in a child's activity in a manner that helps to structure the activity and to bring the child's understanding of it closer to that of the adult. (201)

habituation Type of learning in which familiarity with a stimulus reduces, slows, or stops a response. (192)

handedness Preference for using a particular hand. (259)

haptic perception Ability to acquire information about properties of objects, such as size, weight, and texture, by handling them. (163)

heredity Inborn characteristics inherited from the biological parents. (9)

heritability Statistical estimate of contribution of heredity to individual differences in a specific trait within a given population at a particular time. (80)

heterozygous Possessing differing alleles for a trait. (69)

historical generation A group of people strongly influenced by a major historical event during their formative period. (17)

holophrase Single word that conveys a complete thought. (205)

Home Observation for Measurement of the Environment (HOME) Instrument designed to measure the influence of the home environment on children's cognitive growth. (182)

homozygous Possessing two identical alleles for a trait. (69)

horizontal décalage Piaget's term for an inability to transfer learning about one type of conservation to other types, which causes a child to master different types of conservation tasks at different ages. (363)

hostile aggression Aggressive behavior intended to hurt another person. (412)

hostile attribution bias Tendency of individuals to respond to ambiguous situations as hostile and to then strike out in retaliation or self-defense. (413)

human genome The complete sequence of genes in the human body. (67)

hypertension High blood pressure. (350)

hypotheses Possible explanations for phenomena, used to predict the outcome of research. (24)

hypothetical-deductive reasoning Ability, believed by Piaget to accompany the stage of formal operations, to develop, consider, and test hypotheses. (448)

ideal self Self one would like to be. (303)

identification In Freudian theory, process by which a young child adopts characteristics, beliefs, attitudes, values, and behaviors of the parent of the same sex. (310)

identity In Erikson's terminology, a coherent conception of the self made up of goals, values, and beliefs to which a person is solidly committed. (472)

identity achievement Identity status, described by Marcia, that is characterized by commitment to choices made following a crisis, a period spent in exploring alternatives. (474)

identity diffusion Identity status, described by Marcia, that is characterized by absence of commitment and lack of serious consideration of alternatives. (475)

identity statuses Marcia's term for states of ego development that depend on the presence or absence of crisis and commitment. (473)

identity versus identity confusion Erikson's fifth stage of psychosocial development, in which an adolescent seeks to develop a coherent sense of self, including the role she or he is to play in society. Also called *identity versus role confusion*. (472)

imaginary audience Elkind's term for observer who exists only in an adolescent's mind and is as concerned with the adolescent's thoughts and actions as the adolescent is. (452)

implantation The attachment of the blastocyst to the uterine wall, occurring at about day 6. (93)

implicit memory Unconscious recall, generally of habits and skills; sometimes called *procedural memory*. (200)

imprinting Instinctive form of learning in which, during a critical period in early development, a young animal forms an attachment to the first moving object it sees, usually the mother. (17, 137)

incomplete dominance Pattern of inheritance in which a child receives two different alleles, resulting in partial expression of a trait. (75)

independent variable In an experiment, the condition over which the experimenter has direct control. (49)

individual differences Differences among children in characteristics, influences, or developmental outcomes. (9)

individual psychotherapy Psychological treatment in which a therapist sees a troubled person one-on-one. (355)

individuation Adolescent's struggle for autonomy and differentiation, or personal identity. (490)

inductive reasoning Type of logical reasoning that moves from particular observations about members of a class to a general conclusion about that class. (362)

inductive techniques Disciplinary techniques designed to induce desirable behavior by appealing to a child's sense of reason and fairness. (321)

industry versus inferiority Erikson's fourth crisis of psychosocial development, in which children must learn the productive skills their culture requires or else face feelings of inferiority. (395)

infant mortality rate Proportion of babies born alive who die within the 1st year. (166)

infertility Inability to conceive after 12 months of trying. (61)

information-processing approach Approach to the study of cognitive development by observing and analyzing the mental processes involved in perceiving and handling information. (35, 179)

initiative versus guilt Erikson's third stage in psychosocial development, in which children balance the urge to pursue goals with moral reservations that may prevent carrying them out. (306)

instrumental aggression Aggressive behavior used as a means of achieving a goal. (327, 412)

integration Process by which neurons coordinate the activities of muscle groups. (153)

intellectual disability Significantly subnormal cognitive functioning. Also referred to as cognitive disability or mental retardation. (385)

intelligent behavior Behavior that is goal oriented and adaptive to circumstances and conditions of life. (181)

internalization During socialization, process by which children accept societal standards of conduct as their own. (240)

internalizing behaviors Behaviors by which emotional problems are turned inward; for example, anxiety or depression. (398)

invisible imitation Imitation with parts of one's body that one cannot see. (187)

IQ (intelligence quotient) tests Psychometric tests that seek to measure intelligence by comparing a test-taker's performance with standardized norms. (181)

irreversibility Piaget's term for a preoperational child's failure to understand that an operation can go in two or more directions. (279)

kangaroo care Method of skin-to-skin contact in which a newborn is laid face down between the mother's breasts. (133)

Kaufman Assessment Battery for Children (K-ABC-II) Nontraditional individual intelligence test designed to provide fair assessments of minority children and children with disabilities. (375)

laboratory observation Research method in which all participants are observed under the same controlled conditions. (44)

language Communication system based on words and grammar. (202)

language acquisition device (LAD) In Chomsky's terminology, an inborn mechanism that enables children to infer linguistic rules from the language they hear. (208)

lateralization Tendency of each of the brain's hemispheres to have specialized functions. (150)

learning disabilities (LDs) Disorders that interfere with specific aspects of learning and school achievement. (386)

learning perspective View of human development that holds that changes in behavior result from experience. (31)

linguistic speech Verbal expression designed to convey meaning. (205)

literacy Ability to read and write. (213)

longitudinal study Study designed to assess changes in a sample over time. (51)

long-term memory Storage of virtually unlimited capacity that holds information for long periods. (285)

low-birth-weight babies Infants who weigh less than 5½ pounds (2,500 grams) at birth because of prematurity or being small-for-date. (129)

macrosystem Bronfenbrenner's term for a society's overall cultural patterns, including values, customs, and social systems. (37)

maturation Unfolding of a universal natural sequence of physical and behavioral changes. (9)

mechanistic model Model that views human development as a series of predictable responses to stimuli. (25)

menarche A girl's first menstruation. (430)

mesosystem Bronfenbrenner's term for linkages between two or more microsystems. (37)

metacognition Thinking about thinking, or awareness of one's own mental processes. (378)

metamemory Understanding of processes of memory. (367)

microsystem Bronfenbrenner's term for a setting in which a child interacts with others on an everyday, face-to-face basis. (36)

mirror neurons Neurons that fire when a person does something or observes someone else doing the same thing. (223)

mnemonic device Strategy to aid memory. (367)

moratorium Identity status, described by Marcia, in which a person is considering alternatives (in crisis) and seems headed for commitment. (475)

mother-infant bond Mother's feeling of close, caring connection with her newborn. (137)

multifactorial transmission Combination of genetic and environmental factors to produce certain complex traits. (71)

mutations Permanent alterations in genes or chromosomes that usually produce harmful characteristics but provide the raw material of evolution. (70)

mutual regulation Process by which infant and caregiver communicate emotional states to each other and respond appropriately. (234)

myelination Process of coating neurons with myelin, a fatty substance that enables faster communication between cells. (154)

nativism Theory that human beings have an inborn capacity for language acquisition. (208)

naturalistic observation Research method in which behavior is studied in natural settings without intervention or manipulation. (44)

natural, or prepared, childbirth Method of childbirth that seeks to reduce or eliminate the use of drugs, enable both parents to participate fully, and control perceptions of pain. (121)

neonatal jaundice Condition in many newborn babies caused by immaturity of the liver and evidenced by a yellowish appearance; can cause brain damage if not treated promptly. (126)

neonatal period First 4 weeks of life, a time of transition from intrauterine dependency to independent existence. (122)

neonate Newborn baby, up to 4 weeks old. (122)

neurons Nerve cells. (151)

nonnormative Characteristic of an unusual event that happens to a particular person or a typical event that happens at an unusual time of life. (17)

nonorganic failure to thrive In infancy, lack of appropriate growth for no known medical cause, accompanied by poor developmental and emotional functioning. (171)

nonshared environmental effects The unique environment in which each child grows up, consisting of distinctive influences or influences that affect one child differently from another. (84)

normative Characteristic of an event that occurs in a similar way for most people in a group. (15)

nuclear family Two-generational household unit consisting of one or two parents and their biological children, adopted children, or stepchildren. (10)

obesity Extreme overweight in relation to age, sex, height, and body type. (85)

object permanence Piaget's term for the understanding that a person or object still exists when out of sight. (189)

observational learning Learning through watching the behavior of. (33)

obsessive-compulsive disorder (OCD) Anxiety aroused by repetitive, intrusive thoughts, images, or impulses, often leading to compulsive ritual behaviors. (354)

operant conditioning Learning based on association of behavior with its consequences. (32, 179)

operational definition Definition stated solely in terms of the operations or procedures used to produce or measure a phenomenon. (45)

oppositional defiant disorder (ODD) Pattern of behavior, persisting into middle childhood, marked by negativity, hostility, and defiance. (353)

organismic model Model that views human development as internally initiated by an active organism, and as occurring in a sequence of qualitatively different stages. (26)

organization (1) Piaget's term for the creation of categories or systems of knowledge; (2) Mnemonic strategy of categorizing material to be remembered. (34, 368)

Otis-Lennon School Ability Test (OLSAT8) Group intelligence test for kindergarten through 12th grade. (370)

overt (direct) aggression Aggression that is openly directed at its target. (328)

participant observation Research method in which the observer lives with the people or participates in the activity being observed. (47)

parturition The act or process of giving birth. (118)

permissive parenting Parenting style emphasizing self-expression and self-regulation. (324)

personal fable Elkind's term for conviction that one is special, unique, and not subject to the rules that govern the rest of the world. (452)

personality The relatively consistent blend of emotions, temperament, thought, and behavior that makes each person unique. (218)

phenotype Observable characteristics of a person. (70)

phonetic (code emphasis) approach Approach to teaching reading that emphasizes decoding unfamiliar words. (378)

physical development Growth of body and brain, including biological and physiological patterns of change in sensory capacities, motor skills, and health. (6)

Piagetian approach Approach to the study of cognitive development that describes qualitative stages in cognitive functioning. (178)

plasticity Modifiability of the brain through experience. (18, 156)

play therapy Therapeutic approach that uses play to help a child cope with emotional distress. (355)

polygenic inheritance Pattern of inheritance in which multiple genes at different sites on chromosomes affect a complex trait. (70)

postconventional morality (or morality of autonomous moral principles) Third level in Kohlberg's theory of moral reasoning in which people follow internally held moral principles and can decide among conflicting moral standards. (456)

postmature A fetus not yet born as of 42 weeks' gestation. (134)

power assertion Disciplinary strategy designed to discourage undesirable behavior through physical or verbal enforcement of parental control. (321)

pragmatics The social context of language. (292, 376)

preconventional morality First level of Kohlberg's theory of moral reasoning in which control is external and rules are obeyed in order to gain rewards or avoid punishment or out of self-interest. (454)

prejudice Unfavorable attitude toward members of certain groups outside one's own, especially racial or ethnic groups. (408)

prelinguistic speech Forerunner of linguistic speech; utterance of sounds that are not words. Includes crying, cooing, babbling, and accidental and deliberate imitation of sounds without understanding their meaning. (202)

preoperational stage In Piaget's theory, the second major stage of cognitive development, in which children become more sophisticated in their use of symbolic thought but are not yet able to use logic. (274)

pretend play Play involving imaginary people or situations; also called *fantasy play*, *dramatic play*, or *imaginary play*. (275)

preterm (premature) infants Infants born before completing the 37th week of gestation. (129)

primary sex characteristics Organs directly related to reproduction, which enlarge and mature during adolescence. (429)

private speech Talking aloud to oneself with no intent to communicate with others. (292)

procedural knowledge Acquired skills stored in long-term memory. (453)

prosocial behavior Any voluntary behavior intended to help others. (326)

protective factors Factors that reduce the impact of potentially negative influences and tend to predict positive outcomes. (136, 419)

proximodistal principle Principle that development proceeds from within to without; that is, that parts of the body near the center develop before the extremities. (93)

psychoanalytic perspective View of human development as being shaped by unconscious forces. (27)

psychological aggression Verbal attack that may result in psychological harm to a child. (321)

psychometric approach Approach to the study of cognitive development that seeks to measure the quantity of intelligence a person possesses. (178)

psychosexual development In Freudian theory, an unvarying sequence of stages of personality development during infancy, childhood, and adolescence, in which gratification shifts from the mouth to the anus and then to the genitals. (29)

psychosocial development (1) Pattern of change in emotions, personality, and social relationships; (2) In Erikson's eight-stage theory, the socially and culturally influenced process of development of the ego, or self. (6, 31)

puberty Process by which a person attains sexual maturity and the ability to reproduce. (425)

punishment In operant conditioning, a process that decreases the likelihood that a behavior will be repeated. (32)

qualitative change Change in kind, structure, or organization, such as the change from nonverbal to verbal communication. (26)

qualitative research Research that involves the interpretation of nonnumerical data, such as subjective experiences, feelings, or beliefs. (41)

quantitative change Change in number or amount, such as in height, weight, or size of vocabulary. (26)

quantitative research Research that deals with objectively measurable data. (41)

random assignment Assignment of participants in an experiment to groups in such a way that each person has an equal chance of being placed in any group. (50)

random selection Selection of a sample in such a way that each person in a population has an equal and independent chance of being chosen. (43)

reaction range Potential variability, depending on environmental conditions, in the expression of a hereditary trait. (83)

real self Self one actually is. (303)

recall Ability to reproduce material from memory. (286)

receptive cooperation Kochanska's term for eager willingness to cooperate harmoniously with a parent in daily interactions, including routines, chores, hygiene, and play. (241)

recessive inheritance Pattern of inheritance in which a child receives identical recessive alleles, resulting in expression of a nondominant trait. (69)

reciprocal determinism Bandura's term for bidirectional forces that affect development. (33)

recognition Ability to identify a previously encountered stimulus. (286)

reflex behavior Automatic, involuntary, innate response to stimulation. (156)

rehearsal Mnemonic strategy to keep an item in working memory through conscious repetition. (367)

reinforcement In operant conditioning, a process that increases the likelihood that a behavior will be repeated. (32)

relational (indirect or social) aggression Aggression aimed at damaging or interfering with another person's relationships, reputation, or psychological well-being; can be overt or covert. (328)

representational ability Piaget's term for capacity to store mental images or symbols of objects and events. (187)

representational mappings In neo-Piagetian terminology, second stage in development of self-definition, in which a child makes logical connections between aspects of the self but still sees these characteristics in all-or-nothing terms. (303)

representational systems Broad, inclusive self-concepts that integrate various aspects of the self. (394)

resilient children Children who weather adverse circumstances, function well despite challenges or threats, or bounce back from traumatic events. (419)

retrieval Process by which information is accessed or recalled from memory storage. (285)

risk factors Conditions that increase the likelihood of a negative developmental outcome. (14)

rough-and-tumble play Vigorous play involving wrestling, hitting, and chasing, often accompanied by laughing and screaming. (344)

sample Group of participants chosen to represent the entire population under study. (42)

scaffolding Temporary support to help a child master a task. (35, 290)

schemes Piaget's term for organized patterns of thought and behavior used in particular situations. (34, 184)

schizophrenia Neurological disorder marked by loss of contact with reality; hallucinations and delusions; loss of coherent, logical thought; and inappropriate emotionality. (86)

school phobia Unrealistic fear of going to school; may be a form of *separation anxiety disorder* or *social phobia.* (354)

scientific method System of established principles and processes of scientific inquiry, which includes identifying a problem to be studied, formulating a hypothesis to be tested by research, collecting data, analyzing the data, forming tentative conclusions, and disseminating findings. (41)

script General remembered outline of a familiar, repeated event, used to guide behavior. (286)

secondary sex characteristics Physiological signs of sexual maturation (such as breast development and growth of body hair) that do not involve the sex organs. (429)

secular trend Trend that can be seen only by observing several generations, such as the trend toward earlier attainment of adult height and sexual maturity, which began a century ago. (430)

secure attachment Pattern in which an infant is quickly and effectively able to find comfort from a caregiver when faced with a stressful situation. (229)

self-awareness Realization that one's existence and functioning are separate from those of other people and things. (221)

self-concept Sense of self; descriptive and evaluative mental picture of one's abilities and traits. (236, 302)

self-conscious emotions Emotions, such as embarrassment, empathy, and envy, that depend on self-awareness. (221)

self-definition Cluster of characteristics used to describe oneself. (302)

self-efficacy Sense of one's capability to master challenges and achieve goals. (33)

self-esteem Judgment a person makes about his or her self-worth. (303)

self-evaluative emotions Emotions, such as pride, shame, and guilt, that depend on both self-awareness and knowledge of socially accepted standards of behavior. (222)

self-regulation A person's independent control of behavior to conform to understood social expectations. (240)

sensitive periods Times in development when a given event or its absence usually has a strong effect on development. (18)

sensorimotor stage In Piaget's theory, first stage in cognitive development, during which infants learn through senses and motor activity. (184)

sensory memory Initial, brief, temporary storage of sensory information. (285)

separation anxiety Distress shown by someone, typically an infant, when a familiar caregiver leaves. (232)

separation anxiety disorder Condition involving excessive, prolonged anxiety concerning separation from home or from people to whom a person is attached. (354)

sequential study Study design that combines cross-sectional and longitudinal techniques. (51)

seriation Ability to order items along a dimension. (361)

sex chromosomes Pair of chromosomes that determines sex: XX in the normal human female, XY in the normal human male. (68)

sex-linked inheritance Pattern of inheritance in which certain characteristics carried on the X chromosome inherited from the mother are transmitted differently to her male and female offspring. (75)

sexually transmitted infections (STIs) Diseases spread by sexual contact. (482)

sexual orientation Focus of consistent sexual, romantic, and affectionate interest, either heterosexual, homosexual, or bisexual. (478)

shaken baby syndrome Form of maltreatment in which shaking an infant or toddler can cause brain damage, paralysis, or death. (171)

shared intentionality Joint attention to a mutual goal. (223)

single representations In neo-Piagetian terminology, first stage in development of self-definition, in which children describe themselves in terms of individual, unconnected characteristics and in all-or-nothing terms. (303)

situational compliance Kochanska's term for obedience of a parent's orders only in the presence of signs of ongoing parental control. (241)

slow-to-warm-up children Children whose temperament is generally mild but who are hesitant about accepting new experiences. (224)

small-for-date (small-for-gestational-age) infants Infants whose birth weight is less than that of 90 percent of babies of the same gestational age as a result of slow fetal growth. (131)

social capital Family and community resources on which a person or family can draw. (381)

social cognition Ability to understand that other people have mental states and to gauge their feelings and intentions. (223)

social cognitive theory Albert Bandura's expansion of social learning theory; holds that children learn gender roles through socialization. (312)

social construction Concept about the nature of reality based on societally shared perceptions or assumptions. (7)

social-contextual approach Approach to the study of cognitive development that focuses on environmental influences, particularly parents and other caregivers. (179)

social interaction model Model, based on Vygotsky's sociocultural theory, that proposes that children construct autobiographical memories through conversation with adults about shared events. (287)

socialization Development of habits, skills, values, and motives shared by responsible, productive members of a society. (240)

social learning theory Theory that behaviors also are learned by observing and imitating models. Also called *social cognitive theory*. (33)

social phobia Extreme fear and/or avoidance of social situations. (354)

social promotion Policy of automatically promoting children even if they do not meet academic standards. (384)

social referencing Understanding an ambiguous situation by seeking out another person's perception of it. (234)

social speech Speech intended to be understood by a listener. (292)

sociocultural theory Vygotsky's theory of how contextual factors affect children's development. (35)

socioeconomic status (SES) Combination of economic and social factors, including income, education, and occupation, that describe an individual or family. (13)

spermarche A boy's first ejaculation. (430)

spontaneous abortion Natural expulsion from the uterus of a embryo that cannot survive outside the womb; also called *miscarriage*. (97)

Stanford-Binet Intelligence Scale Individual intelligence test for ages 2 and up, used to measure knowledge, quantitative reasoning, visual-spatial processing, and working memory. (288)

state of arousal Infant's physiological and behavioral status at a given moment in the periodic daily cycle of wakefulness, sleep, and activity. (128)

stillbirth Death of a fetus at or after the 20th week of gestation. (135)

still-face paradigm Research procedure used to measure mutual regulation in infants 2 to 9 months old. (234)

storage Retention of information in memory for future use. (285)

stranger anxiety Wariness of strange people and places, shown by some infants from age 6 to 12 months. (232)

Strange Situation Laboratory technique used to study infant attachment. (229)

stuttering Involuntary, frequent repetition or prolongation of sounds or syllables. (350)

substance abuse Repeated, harmful use of a substance, usually alcohol or other drugs. (439)

substance dependence Addiction (physical or psychological, or both) to a harmful substance. (439)

sudden infant death syndrome (SIDS) Sudden and unexplained death of an apparently healthy infant. (166)

symbolic function Piaget's term for ability to use mental representations (words, numbers, or images) to which a child has attached meaning. (274)

syntax Rules for forming sentences in a particular language. (206)

systems of action Increasingly complex combinations of motor skills that permit a wider or more precise range of movement and more control of the environment. (160, 258)

tacit knowledge Sternberg's term for information that is not formally taught or openly expressed but is necessary to get ahead. (375)

telegraphic speech Early form of sentence use consisting of only a few essential words. (206)

temperament Characteristic disposition or style of approaching and reacting to situations. (86, 224)

teratogen Environmental agent, such as a virus, a drug, or radiation, that can interfere with normal prenatal development and cause developmental abnormalities. (100)

theory Coherent set of logically related concepts that seeks to organize, explain, and predict data. (24)

theory of mind Awareness and understanding of mental processes in others. (280)

theory of multiple intelligences Gardner's theory that there are eight distinct forms of intelligence. (373)

theory of sexual selection Darwinian theory, which holds that selection of sexual partners is influenced by the differing reproductive pressures that early men and women confronted in the struggle for survival of the species. (309)

transduction In Piaget's terminology, preoperational child's tendency to mentally link particular experiences, whether or not there is logically a causal relationship. (277)

transitive inference Understanding the relationship between two objects by knowing the relationship of each to a third object. (361)

triarchic theory of intelligence Sternberg's theory describing three types of intelligence: componential (analytical ability), experiential (insight and originality), and contextual (practical thinking). (374)

two-way (dual-language) learning Approach to second-language education in which English speakers and non-English speakers learn together in their own and each other's languages. (377)

ultrasound Prenatal medical procedure using high-frequency sound waves to detect the outline of a fetus and its movements, used to determine whether a pregnancy is progressing normally. (99)

universal preschool   A national system for early care and education that makes access to preschool similar to kindergarten by using the public schools. (297)

violation-of-expectations   Research method in which dishabituation to a stimulus that conflicts with experience is taken as evidence that an infant recognizes the new stimulus as surprising. (197)

visible imitation   Imitation with parts of one's body that one can see. (187)

visual cliff   Apparatus designed to give an illusion of depth and used to assess depth perception in infants. (163)

visual guidance   Use of the eyes to guide movements of the hands or other parts of the body. (163)

visually based retrieval   Process of retrieving the sound of a printed word on seeing the word as a whole. (378)

visual preference   Tendency of infants to spend more time looking at one sight than another. (193)

visual recognition memory   Ability to distinguish a familiar visual stimulus from an unfamiliar stimulus when shown both at the same time. (193)

Wechsler Intelligence Scale for Children (WISC-III)   Individual intelligence test for schoolchildren that yields verbal and performance scores as well as a combined score. (370)

Wechsler Preschool and Primary Scale of Intelligence, Revised (WPPSI-III)   Individual intelligence test for children ages 2½ to 7 that yields verbal and performance scores as well as a combined score. (288)

whole-language approach   Approach to teaching reading that emphasizes visual retrieval and use of contextual clues. (378)

withdrawal of love   Disciplinary strategy that involves ignoring, isolating, or showing dislike for a child. (323)

working memory   Short-term storage of information being actively processed. (200, 285)

zone of proximal development (ZPD)   Vygotsky's term for the difference between what a child can do alone and what the child can do with help. (35, 289)

zygote   One-celled organism resulting from fertilization. (61)

Aaron, V., Parker, K. D., Ortega, S., & Calhoun, T. (1999). The extended family as a source of support among African Americans. *Challenge: A Journal of Research on African American Men, 10*(2), 23–36.

Abbey, A., Andrews, F. M., & Halman, J. (1992). Infertility and subjective wellbeing: The mediating roles of self-esteem, internal control, and interpersonal conflict. *Journal of Marriage and the Family, 54,* 408–417.

Aber, J. L., Brown, J. L., & Jones, S. M. (2003). Developmental trajectories toward violence in middle childhood: Course, demographic differences, and response to school-based intervention. *Developmental Psychology, 39,* 324–348.

Abma, J. C., Chandra, A., Mosher, W. D., Peterson, L., & Piccinino, L. (1997). Fertility, family planning, and women's health: New data from the 1995 National Survey of Family Growth. *Vital Health Statistics, 23*(19). Washington, DC: National Center for Health Statistics.

Abma, J. C., Martinez, G. M., Mosher, W. D., & Dawson, B. S. (2004). Teenagers in the United States: Sexual activity, contraceptive use, and childbearing, 2002. *Vital Health Statistics, 23*(24). Washington, DC: National Center for Health Statistics.

Abramovitch, R., Corter, C., & Lando, B. (1979). Sibling interaction in the home. *Child Development, 50,* 997–1003.

Abramovitch, R., Corter, C., Pepler, D., & Stanhope, L. (1986). Sibling and peer interactions: A final follow-up and comparison. *Child Development, 57,* 217–229.

Abramovitch, R., Pepler, D., & Corter, C. (1982). Patterns of sibling interaction among preschool-age children. In M. E. Lamb (Ed.), *Sibling relationships: Their nature and significance across the lifespan* (pp. 61–86). Hillsdale, NJ: Erlbaum.

Achter, J. A., & Lubinski, D. (2003). Fostering exceptional development in intellectually talented populations. In W. B. Walsh (Ed.), *Counseling psychology and optimal human functioning* (pp. 279–296). Mahwah, NJ: Erlbaum.

Ackerman, B. P., Kogos, J., Youngstrom, E., Schoff, K., & Izard, C. (1999). Family instability and the problem behaviors of children from economically disadvantaged families. *Developmental Psychology, 35*(1), 258–268.

Ackerman, M. J., Siu, B. L., Sturner, W. Q., Tester D. J., Valdivia, C. R., Makielski, J. C., & Towbin, J. A. (2001). Postmortem molecular analysis of SCN5A defects in sudden infant death syndrome. *Journal of the American Medical Association, 286,* 2264–2269.

Acosta, M. T., Arcos-Burgos, M., & Muenke, M. (2004). Attention deficit/hyperactivity disorder (ADHD): Complex phenotype, simple genotype? *Genetics in Medicine, 6,* 1–15.

ACT for Youth Upstate Center of Excellence. (2002). *Adolescent brain development. Research facts and findings.* [A collaboration of Cornell University, University of Rochester, and the NYS Center for School Safety.] Retrieved March 23, 2004, from www.human.cornell.edu/actforyouth

Adam, E. K., Gunnar, M. R., & Tanaka, A. (2004). Adult attachment, parent emotion, and observed parenting behavior: Mediator and moderator models. *Child Development, 75,* 110–122.

Adams, G. (2009, January 28). Octuplets born: It's a boy … a boy … four more boys … and two girls. *The Independent.* Retrieved January 30, 2009, from www.independent.co.uk/news/world/octuplets /americas-born-its-a-boy-a-boy-four-more-boys- and-two-girls-1517840.html

Adams, R., & Laursen, B. (2001). The organization and dynamics of adolescent conflict with parents and friends. *Journal of Marriage and the Family, 63,* 97–110.

Administration for Children and Families. (2006a). *FACES 2003 research brief and program quality in Head Start.* Washington, DC: Author.

Administration for Children and Families. (2006b). *FACES findings: New research on Head Start outcomes and program quality.* Washington, DC: Author.

Adolph, K. E. (2000). Specificity of learning: Why infants fall over a veritable cliff. *Psychological Science, 11,* 290–295.

Adolph, K. E. (2008). Learning to move. *Current Directions in Psychological Science, 17,* 213–218.

Adolph, K. E., & Eppler, M. A. (2002). Flexibility and specificity in infant motor skill acquisition. In J. Fagen & H. Hayne (Eds.), *Progress in infancy research* (Vol. 2, pp. 121–167). Mahwah, NJ: Erlbaum.

Adolph, K. E., Vereijken, B., & Shrout, P. E. (2003). What changes in infant walking and why. *Child Development, 74,* 475–497.

Ahnert, L., Gunnar, M. R., Lamb, M. E., & Barthel, M. (2004). Transition to child care: Associations with infant-mother attachment, infant negative emotion and corticol elevation. *Child Development, 75,* 639–650.

Ahnert, L., & Lamb, M. E. (2003). Shared care: Establishing a balance between home and child care settings. *Child Development, 74,* 1044–1049.

Ahrons, C. R., & Tanner, J. L. (2003). Adult children and their fathers: Relationship changes 20 years after parental divorce. *Family Relations, 52,* 340–351.

Ainsworth, M.D.S. (1967). *Infancy in Uganda: Infant care and the growth of love.* Baltimore: Johns Hopkins University Press.

Ainsworth, M.D.S., Blehar, M. C., Waters, E., & Wall, S. (1978). *Patterns of attachment: A psychological study of the strange situation.* Hillsdale, NJ: Erlbaum.

Akinbami, L. (2006). The state of childhood asthma, United States, 1980–2005. *Advance Data from Vital and Health Statistics, 381.* Hyattsville, MD: National Center for Health Statistics.

Alaimo, K., Olson, C. M., & Frongillo, E. A. (2001). Food insufficiency and American school-aged children's cognitive, academic, and psychosocial development. *Pediatrics, 108,* 44–53.

Alan Guttmacher Institute (AGI). (1994). *Sex & America's teenagers.* New York: Author.

Alan Guttmacher Institute (AGI). (1999). *Facts in brief: Teen sex and pregnancy.* Retrieved January 31, 2000, from www.agi_usa.org/pubs/fb_teen_sex .html#sfd

Alati, R., Al Mamun, A., Williams, G. M., O'Callaghan, M., Najman, J. M., & Bor, W. (2006). In utero alcohol exposure and prediction of alcohol disorders in early adulthood: A birth cohort study. *Archives of General Psychiatry, 63*(9), 1009–1016.

Albanese, A., & Stanhope, R. (1993). Growth and metabolic data following growth hormone treatment of children with intrauterine growth retardation. *Hormone Research, 39,* 8–12.

Albertsson-Wikland, K., Aronson, A. S., Gustafsson, J., Hagenäs, L., Ivarsson, S. A., Jonsson, B., et al. (2008). Dose-dependent effect of growth hormone on final height in children with short stature without growth hormone deficiency. *Journal of Clinical Endocrinology & Metabolism, 93*(11), 4342–4350.

Alexander, K. L., Entwisle, D. R., & Dauber, S. L. (1993). First-grade classroom behavior: Its short- and long-term consequences for school performance. *Child Development, 64,* 801–814.

Alexander, K. L., Entwisle, D. R., & Olson, L. S. (2007). Lasting consequences of the summer learning gap. *American Sociological Review, 72,* 167–180.

Alibeik, H., & Angaji, S. A. (2010). Developmental aspects of left handedness. *Australian Journal of Basic and Applied Sciences, 4*(5), 881–977.

Allen, G. L., & Ondracek, P. J. (1995). Age-sensitive cognitive abilities related to children's acquisition of spatial knowledge. *Developmental Psychology, 31,* 934–945.

Allen, J. P., McElhaney, K. B., Land, D. J., Kuperminc, G. P., Moore, C. W., O'Beirner-Kelly, H., & Kilmer, S. L. (2003). A secure base in adolescence: Markers of attachment security in the mother-adolescent relationship. *Child Development, 74,* 292–307.

Allen, J. P., & Philliber, S. (2001). Who benefits most from a broadly targeted prevention program? Differential efficacy across populations in the Teen Outreach Program. *Journal of Community Psychology, 29,* 637–655.

Allen, J. P., Porter, M. R., McFarland, F. C., Marsh, P., & McElhaney, K. B. (2005). The two faces of adolescents' success with peers: Adolescent popularity, social adaptation, and deviant behavior. *Child Development, 76*(3), 747–760.

Allen, K. R., Blieszner, R., & Roberto, K. A. (2000). Families in the middle and later years: A review and critique of research in the 1990s. *Journal of Marriage and the Family, 62,* 911–926.

Alloway, T. P. (2006). How does working memory work in the classroom? *Education Research and Reviews, 1,* 134–139.

Alloway, T. P., Gathercole, S. E., Kirkwood, H., & Elliot, J. (2009). The cognitive and behavioral characteristics of children with low working memory. *Child Development, 80*(2), 606–621.

Almeida, D. M., Wethington, E., & Chandler, A. L. (1999). Daily transmission of tensions between marital dyads and parent-child dyads. *Journal of Marriage and the Family, 61,* 49–61.

Al-Oballi Kridli, S. (2002). Health beliefs and practices among Arab Women. *MCN, The American Journal of Maternal/Child Nursing, 27,* 178–182.

Als, H., Duffy, F. H., McAnulty, G. B., Rivkin, M. J., Vajapeyam, S., Mulkern, R. V., et al. (2004). Early experience alters brain function and structure. *Pediatrics, 113,* 846–857.

Almli, C. R., Ball, R. H., & Wheeler, M. E. (2001). Human fetal and neonatal movement patterns: Gender differences and fetal-to-natal continuity. *Developmental Psychobiology, 38*(4), 252–273.

Alsaker, F. D. (1992). Pubertal timing, overweight, and psychological adjustment. *Journal of Early Adolescence, 12*(4), 396–419.

Altschul, I., Oyserman, D., & Bybee, D. (2006). Racial-ethnic identity in mid-adolescence: Content and change as predictors of academic achievement. *Child Development, 77,* 1155–1169.

Aluti, A., Cattaneo, F., Galimberti, S., Benninghoff, U., Cassani, B., Callegaro, L., et al. (2009). Gene therapy for immunodeficiency due to adenosine deaminase deficiency. *New England Journal of Medicine, 360,* 447–458.

Amato, P. R. (2003). Reconciling divergent perspectives: Judith Wallerstein, quantitative family research, and children of divorce. *Family Relations, 52,* 332–339.

Amato, P. R. (2005). The impact of family formation change on the cognitive, social, and emotional well-being of the next generation. *Future of Children, 15,* 75–96.

Amato, P. R., & Booth, A. (1997). *A generation at risk: Growing up in an era of family upheaval.* Cambridge, MA: Harvard University Press.

Amato, P. R., & Gilbreth, J. G. (1999). Nonresident fathers and children's wellbeing: A meta-analysis. *Journal of Marriage and the Family, 61,* 557–573.

American Academy of Child & Adolescent Psychiatry (AACAP). (1997). *Children's sleep problems.* [Fact sheet no. 34]. Washington, DC: Author.

American Academy of Child & Adolescent Psychiatry. (AACAP). (2003). Talking to children about terrorism and war. *Facts for Families #87.* Retrieved April 22, 2005, from www.aacap.org /publications/factsfam/87.htm

American Academy of Pediatric Dentistry, Council on Clinical Affairs. (2002). Clinical guideline on infant oral health. *Reference Manual,* 54.

American Academy of Pediatrics (AAP). (1986). *Positive approaches to day care dilemmas: How to make it work.* Elk Grove Village, IL: Author.

American Academy of Pediatrics (AAP). (2000). Shaken baby syndrome. Retrieved February 17, 2007, from http://aappolicy.aappublications.org /cgi/content/full/pediatrics;108/1/206

American Academy of Pediatrics (AAP). (2004, September 30). *American Academy of Pediatrics (AAP) supports Institute of Medicine's (IOM) childhood obesity recommendations.* [Press release]. Elk Grove Village, IL: Author.

American Academy of Pediatrics (AAP) and Canadian Paediatric Society. (2000). Prevention and management of pain and stress in the neonate. *Pediatrics, 105*(2), 454–461.

American Academy of Pediatrics (AAP) Committee on Adolescence. (1999). Adolescent pregnancy—current trends and issues: 1998. *Pediatrics, 103,* 516–520.

American Academy of Pediatrics (AAP) Committee on Adolescence. (2000). Suicide and suicide attempts in adolescents. *Pediatrics, 105*(4), 871–874.

American Academy of Pediatrics (AAP) Committee on Adolescence. (2001). Condom use by adolescents. *Pediatrics, 107*(6), 1463–1469.

American Academy of Pediatrics (AAP) Committee on Adolescence. (2003). Policy statement: Identifying and treating eating disorders. *Pediatrics, 111,* 204–211.

American Academy of Pediatrics (AAP) Committee on Adolescence and Committee on Early Childhood, Adoption, and Dependent Care. (2001). Care of adolescent parents and their children. *Pediatrics, 107,* 429–434.

American Academy of Pediatrics (AAP) Committee on Bioethics. (1992, July). Ethical issues in surrogate motherhood. *AAP News,* 14–15.

American Academy of Pediatrics (AAP) Committee on Children with Disabilities and Committee on Drugs. (1996). Medication for children with attentional disorders. *Pediatrics, 98,* 301–304.

American Academy of Pediatrics (AAP) Committee on Community Health Services. (1996). Health needs of homeless children and families. *Pediatrics, 88,* 789–791.

American Academy of Pediatrics Committee on Drugs. (1982). Psychotropicdrugs in pregnancy and lactation. *Pediatrics, 69,* 241–244.

American Academy of Pediatrics (AAP) Committee on Drugs (2001). The transfer of drugs and other chemicals into human milk. *Pediatrics, 108*(3), 776–789.

American Academy of Pediatrics (AAP) Committee on Environmental Health. (2005). Lead exposure in children: Prevention, detection, and management. *Pediatrics, 116,* 1036–1046.

American Academy of Pediatrics (AAP) Committee on Fetus and Newborn & American College of Obstetricians and Gynecologists (ACOG) Committee on Obstetric Practice. (1996). Use and abuse of the Apgar score. *Pediatrics, 98,* 141–142.

American Academy of Pediatrics (AAP) Committee on Fetus and Newborn & American College of Obstetricians and Gynecologists (ACOG) Committee on Obstetric Practice. (2006). The Apgar score. *Pediatrics, 117,* 1444–1447.

American Academy of Pediatrics (AAP) Committee on Genetics. (1996). Newborn screening fact sheet. *Pediatrics, 98,* 1–29.

American Academy of Pediatrics (AAP) Committee on Genetics. (1999). Folic acid for the prevention of neural tube defects. *Pediatrics, 104,* 325–327.

American Academy of Pediatrics (AAP) Committee on Injury and Poison Prevention (1995). Skateboard injuries. *Pediatrics, 95,* 611–612.

American Academy of Pediatrics (AAP) Committee on Injury and Poison Prevention. (2000). Firearm-related injuries affecting the pediatric population. *Pediatrics, 105*(4), 888–895.

American Academy of Pediatrics (AAP) Committee on Nutrition. (1992). Statement on cholesterol. *Pediatrics, 90,* 469–473.

American Academy of Pediatrics (AAP) Committee on Nutrition. (2003). Prevention of pediatric overweight and obesity. *Pediatrics, 112,* 424–430.

American Academy of Pediatrics (AAP) Committee on Nutrition. (2006). Dietary recommendations for children and adolescents: A guide for practitioners. *Pediatrics, 117*(2), 544–559.

American Academy of Pediatrics (AAP) Committee on Pediatric Research. (2000). Race/ethnicity, gender, socioeconomic status—research exploring their effects on child health: A subject review. *Pediatrics, 105,* 1349–1351.

American Academy of Pediatrics (AAP) Committee on Practice and Ambulatory Medicine and Section on Ophthalmology. (2002). Use of photoscreening for children's vision screening. *Pediatrics, 109,* 524–525.

American Academy of Pediatrics (AAP) Committee on Psychosocial Aspects of Child and Family Health. (1998). Guidance for effective discipline. *Pediatrics, 101,* 723–728.

American Academy of Pediatrics (AAP) Committee on Psychosocial Aspects of Child and Family Health. (2002). Coparent or second-parent adoption by same-sex parents. *Pediatrics, 109*(2), 339–340.

American Academy of Pediatrics (AAP) Committee on Psychosocial Aspects of Child and Family Health and Committee on Adolescence. (2001). Sexuality education for children and adolescence. *Pediatrics, 108*(2), 498–502.

American Academy of Pediatrics (AAP) Committee on Public Education. (2001). Policy statement: Children, adolescents, and television. *Pediatrics, 107,* 423–426.

American Academy of Pediatrics (AAP) Committee on Quality Improvement. (2002). *Making advances against jaundice in infant care (MAJIC).* Retrieved October 25, 2002, from www.aap.org /visit/majic.htm

American Academy of Pediatrics (AAP) Committee on Sports Medicine and Fitness and Committee on School Health. (2001). Organized sports for children and preadolescents. *Pediatrics, 107*(6) 1459–1462.

American Academy of Pediatrics (AAP) Committee on Substance Abuse. (2001). Tobacco's toll: Implications for the pediatrician. *Pediatrics, 107,* 794–798.

American Academy of Pediatrics (AAP) Section on Breastfeeding. (2005). Breastfeeding and the use of human milk. *Pediatrics, 115,* 496–506.

American Academy of Pediatrics (AAP), Stirling, J., Jr., and the Committee on Child Abuse and Neglect and Section on Adoption and Foster Care; American Academy of Child and Adolescent Psychiatry, Amaya-Jackson, L.; & National Center for Child Traumatic Stress, Amaya-Jackson, L. (2008). Understanding the behavioral and emotional consequences of child abuse. *Pediatrics, 122*(3), 667–673.

American Academy of Pediatrics (AAP) Task Force on Infant Sleep Position and Sudden Infant Death Syndrome. (2000). Changing concepts of sudden infant death syndrome: Implications for infant sleeping environment and sleep position. *Pediatrics, 105,* 650–656.

American Academy of Pediatrics Task Force on Sudden Infant Death Syndrome. (2005). The changing concept of sudden infant death syndrome: Diagnostic coding shifts, controversies regarding sleeping environment, and new variables to consider in reducing risk. *Pediatrics, 116,* 1245–1255.

American College of Nurse-Midwives. (2005). *Position statement: Home births.* Silver Spring, MD: Author.

American College of Obstetricians and Gynecologists (ACOG). (2002). *Early pregnancy loss: Miscarriage and molar pregnancy.* Washington, DC: Author.

American College of Obstetricians and Gynecologists (ACOG). (2008, February 6). *ACOG news release: ACOG statement on home births.* Retrieved November 13, 2008, from www. acog.org/from_publications/home/press_releases /nr02-06-08-2.cfm

American Congress of Obstetricians and Gynecologists (2002). Exercise during pregnancy and the postpartum period. ACOG Committee Opinion No. 267. *Obstetrics and Gynecology, 99,* 171–173.

American Dental Association (2007). Thumb sucking and pacifier use. *The Journal of the American Dental Association, 138*(8), 1176.

American Heart Association, Gidding, S. S., Dennison, B. A., Birch, L. L., Daniels, S. R., Gilman, M. W., et al. (2006). Dietary recommendations for children and adolescents: A guide for practitioners. *Pediatrics, 117,* 544–559.

American Medical Association House of Delegates. (2008, June). *Resolution 205: Home deliveries.* Proceedings of the American Medical Association House of Delegates, Fifteenth Annual Meeting, Chicago, IL. Retrieved from www.ama-assn.org /ama1/pub/mm/upload/471/205.doc

American Psychiatric Association. (1994). *Diagnostic and statistical manual of mental disorders* (4th ed.). Washington, DC: Author.

American Psychiatric Association. (2000). *Diagnostic and statistical manual of mental disorders* (4th ed., Text Revision). Washington, DC: Author.

American Psychological Association. (n.d.). *Answers to your questions about sexual orientation and homosexuality.* [Brochure]. Washington, DC: Author.

American Psychological Association (APA). (2002). Ethical principles of psychologists and code of conduct. *American Psychologist, 57,* 1060–1073.

American Psychological Association (APA) and American Academy of Pediatrics (AAP). (1996). *Raising children to resist violence: What you can do.* [Brochure]. Retrieved from www.apa.org /helpcenter/resist-violence.aspx

American Public Health Association. (2004). *Disparities in infant mortality. Fact sheet.* Retrieved April 18, 2004, from www.medscape.com /viewarticle/472721

America's Youngest Outcasts: 2010. (2011). The National Center on Family Homelessness, Needham, MA.

Ames, E. W. (1997). *The development of Romanian orphanage children adopted to Canada: Final report* (National Welfare Grants Program, Human Resources Development, Canada). Burnaby, BC, Canada: Fraser University, Psychology Department.

Amsel, E., Goodman, G., Savoie, D., & Clark, M. (1996). The development of reasoning about causal and noncausal influences on levers. *Child Development, 67,* 1624–1646.

Amso, D., & Casey, B. J. (2006). Beyond what develops when: Neuroimaging may inform how cognition changes with development. *Current Directions in Psychological Science, 15,* 24–29.

Anastasi, A. (1988). *Psychological testing* (6th ed.). New York: Macmillan.

Anastasi, A., & Schaefer, C. E. (1971). Note on concepts of creativity and intelligence. *Journal of Creative Behavior, 3,* 113–116.

Anderson, A. H., Clark, A., & Mullin, J. (1994). Interactive communication between children: Learning how to make language work in dialog. *Journal of Child Language, 21,* 439–463.

Anderson, C. (2000). *The impact of interactive violence on children.* Statement before the Senate Committee on Commerce, Science, and Transportation, 106th Congress, 1st session.

Anderson, D. A., & Hamilton, M. (2005). Gender role stereotyping of parents in children's picture books: The invisible father. *Sex Roles, 52,* 145–151.

Anderson, D. R., Huston, A. C., Schmitt, K. L., Linebarger, D. L., & Wright, J. C. (2001). Early childhood television viewing and adolescent behavior. *Monographs of the Society for Research in Child Development, 66*(1) [Serial No. 264].

Anderson, D. R., & Pempek, T. A. (2005). Television and very young children. *American Behavioral Scientist, 48*(5), 505–522.

Anderson, M., Kaufman, J., Simon, T. R., Barrios, L., Paulozzi, L., Ryan, G., et al. (2001). School-associated violent deaths in the United States, 1994–1999. *Journal of the American Medical Association, 286*(21), 2695–2702.

Anderson, P., Doyle, L. W., & the Victorian Infant Collaborative Study Group. (2003). *Journal of the American Medical Association, 289,* 3264–3272.

Anderson, P. O. (1995). Alcohol and breastfeeding. *Journal of Human Lactation, 11,* 321–323.

Anderson, R. N., & Smith, B. L. (2005). Deaths: Leading causes for 2002. *National Vital Statistics Reports, 53*(17). Hyattsville, MD: National Center for Health Statistics.

Anderson, S. E., Dallal, G. E., & Must, A. (2003). Relative weight and race influence average age at menarche: Results from two nationally representative surveys of U.S. girls studied 25 years apart. *Pediatrics 2003, 111,* 844–850.

Anderssen, N., Amlie, C., & Ytteroy, E. A. (2002). Outcomes for children with lesbian or gay parents: A review of studies from 1978 to 2000. *Scandinavian Journal of Psychology, 43*(4), 335–351.

Ang, S., Rodgers, J. L., & Wanstrom, L. (2010). The Flynn Effect within subgroups in the U.S.: Gender, race, income, education, and urbanization differences in the NLSY-Children data. *Intelligence, 38*(4), 367–384.

Antonarakis, S. E., & Down Syndrome Collaborative Group. (1991). Parental origin of the extra chromosome in trisomy 21 as indicated by analysis of DNA polymorphisms. *New England Journal of Medicine, 324,* 872–876.

Apfelbaum, E. P., Pauker, K., Ambady, N., Sommers, S. R., & Norton, M. I. (2008). Learning (not) to talk about race: When older children underperform in social categorization. *Developmental Psychology, 44*(5), 1513–1518. doi:10.1037/a0012835

Apgar, V. (1953). A proposal for a new method of evaluation of the newborn infant. *Current Research in Anesthesia and Analgesia, 32,* 260–267.

Archer, J. (2004). Sex differences in aggression in real-world settings: A meta-analytic review. *Review of General Psychology, 8,* 291–322.

Archer, S. L. (1993). Identity in relational contexts: A methodological proposal. In J. Kroger (Ed.), *Discussions on ego identity* (pp. 75–99). Hillsdale, NJ: Erlbaum.

Arcus, D., & Kagan, J. (1995). Temperament and craniofacial variation in the first two years. *Child Development, 66,* 1529–1540.

Arend, R., Gove, F., & Sroufe, L. A. (1979). Continuity of individual adaptation from infancy to kindergarten: A predictive study of ego-resiliency and curiosity in preschoolers. *Child Development, 50*(4), 950–959.

Arias, E., MacDorman, M. F., Strobino, D. M., & Guyer, B. (2003). Annual summary of vital statistics—2002. *Pediatrics, 112,* 1215–1230.

Arner, P. (2000). Obesity—a genetic disease of adipose tissue? *British Journal of Nutrition, 83*(1), 9–16.

Arnestad, M., Crotti, L., Rognum, T. O., Insolia, R., Pedrazzini, M., Ferrandi, C., et al. (2007). Prevalence of long-qt syndrome gene variants in sudden infant death syndrome. *Circulation, 115,* 361–367.

Arnett, J. J. (1998, September–December). Learning to stand alone: The contemporary American transition to adulthood in cultural and historical context. *Human Development, 41.*

Arnett, J. J. (1999). Adolescent storm and stress, reconsidered. *American Psychologist, 54,* 317–326.

Arnett, J. J. (2001). Conceptions of the transition to adulthood: Perspectives from adolescence through midlife. *Journal of Adult Development, 8*(2), 133–143.

Arnett, J. J. (2003). Conceptions of the transition to adulthood among emerging adults in American ethnic groups. In J. J. Arnett & N. L. Galambos (Eds.), Exploring cultural conceptions of the transition to adulthood. *New Directions for Child and Adolescent Development, 100,* 63–75.

Arnett, J. J. (2007). Emerging adulthood: What is it, and what is it good for? *Child Development Perspectives, 1,* 68–73.

Arnett, J. J., & Galambos, N. L. (2003). Culture and conceptions of adulthood. In J. J. Arnett & N. L. Galambos (Eds.), Exploring cultural conceptions of the transition to adulthood. *New Directions for Child and Adolescent Development, 100,* 91–98.

Asher, M. I., Montefort, S., Björkstén, B., Lai, C. K., Strachan, D. P., Weiland, S. K., et al. (2006). Worldwide time trends in the prevalence of symptoms of asthma, allergic rhinoconjunctivitis, and eczema in childhood: ISAAC phases one and three repeat multicountry cross-sectional surveys. *Lancet, 368*(9537), 733–743.

Ashman, S. B., & Dawson, G. (2002). Maternal depression, infant psychobiological development, and risk for depression. In S. H. Goodman, & I. H. Gotlib (Eds.), *Children of depressed parents: Mechanisms of risk and implications for treatment* (pp. 37–58). Washington, DC: American Psychological Association.

Associated Press. (2004a, November 22). *Boys have no place in politics: 4-year-old.* AP Newswire.

Associated Press. (2004b, April 29). *Mom in C-section case received probation: Woman originally charged with murder for delaying operation.* Retrieved June 8, 2004, from www.msnbc.msn .com/id/4863415/

Astington, J. W. (1993). *The child's discovery of the mind.* Cambridge, MA: Harvard University Press.

Athansiou, M. S. (2001). Using consultation with a grandmother as an adjunct to play therapy. *Family Journal—Consulting and Therapy for Couples and Families, 9,* 445–449.

Aud, S., Hussar, W., Johnson, F., Kena, G. & Roth, E. (2012). *The condition of education 2012.* (NCES 2012045). Hyattsville, MD: National Center on Education Statistics.

Austin, E. W., Pinkleton, B. E., & Fujioka, Y. (2000). The role of interpretation processes and parental discussion in the media's effects on adolescents' use of alcohol. *Pediatrics, 105*(2), 343–349.

Austin, P. F., Ferguson, G., Yan, Y., Campigotto, M., Royer, M., & Coplen, D. (2008). Combination therapy with desmopressin and an anticholinergic medication for nonresponders to desmopressin for monosymptomatic nocturnal enuresis: A randomized double-blind, placebo controlled trial. *Pediatrics, 122*(5), 1027–1032.

Auyeung, B., Baron-Cohen, S., Ashwin, E. Kinckmeyer, R., Taylor, K. Hackett, G., & Hines, M. (2009) Fetal testosterone predicts sexually differentiated childhood behavior in girls and in boys. *Psychological Science, 20,* 144–148.

Babu, A., & Hirschhorn, K. (1992). *A guide to human chromosome defects* (Birth Defects: Original Article Series, 28[2]). White Plains, NY: March of Dimes Birth Defects Foundation.

Bada, H. S., Das, A., Bauer, C. R., Shankaran, S., Lester, B., LaGasse, L., et al. (2007). Impact of prenatal cocaine exposure on child behavior problems through school age. *Pediatrics, 119,* 348–359.

Badcock, C., & Crespi, B. (2006). Imbalanced genomic imprinting in brain development: An evolutionary basis for the aetiology of autism. *Journal of Evolutionary Biology, 19,* 1007–1032.

Badcock, C., & Crespi, B. (2008). Battle of the sexes may set the brain. *Nature, 454,* 1054–1055.

Baddeley, A. (1996). Exploring the central executive. *Quarterly Journal of Experimental Psychology: Human Experimental Psychology* (Special Issue: Working Memory), *49A,* 5–28.

Baddeley, A. (1998). Recent developments in working memory. *Current Opinion in Neurobiology, 8,* 234–238.

Baddeley, A. D. (1981). The concept of working memory: A view of its current state and probable future development. *Cognition, 10,* 17–23.

Baddeley, A. D. (1986). *Working memory.* London, UK: Oxford University Press.

Baddeley, A. D. (1992). Working memory. *Science, 255,* 556–559.

Baddeley, A. D. (2001). Is working memory still working? *American Psychologist, 56,* 851–864.

Baddock, S. A., Galland, B. C., Bolton, D. P. G., Williams, S. M., & Taylor, B. J. (2006). Differences in infant and parent behaviors during routine bed sharing compared with cot sleeping in the home setting. *Pediatrics, 117,* 1599–1607.

Baer, J. S., Sampson, P. D., Barr, H. M., Connor, P. D., & Streissguth, A. P. (2003). A 21-year longitudinal analysis of the effects of prenatal alcohol exposure on young adult drinking. *Archives of General Psychiatry, 60,* 377–385.

Baillargeon, R. (1994). How do infants learn about the physical world? *Current Directions in Psychological Science, 3,* 133–140.

Baillargeon, R. (1999). Young infants' expectations about hidden objects. *Developmental Science, 2,* 115–132.

Baillargeon, R., & DeVos, J. (1991). Object permanence in young infants: Further evidence. *Child Development, 62,* 1227–1246.

Baillargeon, R. H., Zoccolillo, M., Keenan, K., Côté, S., Pérusse, D., Wu, H.-X., et al. (2007). Gender differences in physical aggression: A prospective population-based survey of children before and after 2 years of age. *Developmental Psychology, 43,* 13–26.

Bainbridge, J. W., Smith, A. J., Barker, S. S., Robbie, S., Henderson, R., Balaggan, K., et al. (2008). Effect of gene therapy on visual function in Leber's congenital amaurosis. *New England Journal of Medicine, 358,* 2282–2284.

Baird, A. A., Gruber, S. A., Fein, D. A., Maas, L. C., Steingard, R. J., Renshaw, P. F., et al. (1999). Functional magnetic resonance imaging of facial affect recognition in children and adolescents. *Journal of the American Academy of Child and Adolescent Psychiatry, 38,* 195–199.

Baird, G., Pickles, A., Simonoff, E., Charman, T., Sullivan, P., Chandler, S., et al. (2008, February 5). Measles vaccination and antibody response in autism spectrum disorders. *Archives of Disease in Childhood.* [ePub].

Baldi, S., Jin, Y., Skemer, J., Green, P., & Herget, D. (2007). *Highlights from PISA 2006: Performance of U.S. fifteen-year-olds in science and mathematics literacy in an international context* (NCES-016). Washington, DC: U.S. Department of Education, National Center for Education Statistics.

Balercia, G., Mosca, F., Mantero, F., Boscaro, M., Mancini, A., Ricciardo-Lamonica, G., & Littarru, G. (2004). Coenzyme q(10) supplementation in infertile men with idiopathic asthenozoospermia: An open, uncontrolled pilot study. *Fertility and Sterility, 81,* 93–98.

Baltes, P. B., & Smith, J. (2004). Lifespan psychology: From developmental contextualism to developmental biocultural co-constructivism. *Research in Human Development, 1,* 123–144.

Bandura, A. (1977). *Social learning theory.* Englewood Cliffs, NJ: Prentice Hall.

Bandura, A. (1986). *Social foundations of thought and action: A social cognitive theory.* Englewood Cliffs, NJ: Prentice Hall.

Bandura, A. (1989). Social cognitive theory. In R. Vasta (Ed.), *Annals of child development* (Vol. 6, pp. 1–60). Greenwich, CT: JAI.

Bandura, A., Barbaranelli, C., Caprara, G. V., & Pastorelli, C. (1996). Multifaceted impact of self-efficacy beliefs on academic functioning. *Child Development, 67,* 1206–1222.

Bandura, A., Barbaranelli, C., Caprara, G. V., & Pastorelli, C. (2001). Self-efficacy beliefs as shapers of children's aspirations and career trajectories. *Child Development 72*(1), 187–206.

Bandura, A., & Bussey, K. (2004). On broadening the cognitive, motivational, and sociostructural scope of theorizing about gender development and functioning: comment on Martin, Ruble, and Szkrybalo (2002). *Psychological Bulletin, 130*(5), 691–701.

Bandura, A., Ross, D., & Ross, S. A. (1961). Transmission of aggression through imitation of aggressive models. *Journal of Abnormal and Social Psychology, 63,* 575–582.

Bandura, A., Ross, D., & Ross, S. A. (1963). Imitation of film-mediated aggressive models. *Journal of Abnormal and Social Psychology, 66,* 3–11.

Bandura, A., & Walters, R. H. (1963). *Social learning and personality development.* New York: Holt, Rinehart, & Winston.

Banks, E. (1989). Temperament and individuality: A study of Malay children. *American Journal of Orthopsychiatry, 59,* 390–397.

Banta, D., & Thacker, S. B. (2001). Historical controversy in health technology assessment: The case of electronic fetal monitoring. *Obstetrical and Gynecological Survey, 56*(11), 707–719.

Barber, B. (1996). Parental psychological control: Revisiting a neglected construct. *Child Development, 67,* 3296–3319.

Barber, B. L., & Eccles, J. S. (1992). Longterm influence of divorce and single parenting on adolescent, family and work related values, behaviors, and aspirations. *Psychological Bulletin, 111*(1), 108–126.

Barkley, R. A. (1998, September). Attention-deficit hyperactivity disorder. *Scientific American,* pp. 66–71.

Barlow, S. E., & Dietz, W. H. (1998). Obesity evaluation and treatment: Expert committee recommendations. *Pediatrics, 102*(3), e29. Retrieved from http://pediatrics.aappublications.org/cgi/content/full/3/102/e29

Baron-Cohen, S. (2005). The essential difference: The male and female brain. *Phi Kappa Phi Forum, 85*(1), 23–26.

Baron-Cohen, S., Leslie, A. M., & Frith, U. (1985). Does the autistic child have a "theory of mind"? *Cognition, 21*(1), 37–46.

Bartick, M., & Reinhold, A. (2010). The burden of suboptimal breastfeeding in the United States: A pediatric cost analysis. *Pediatrics, 125,* 1048–1056.

Bartoshuk, L. M., & Beauchamp, G. K. (1994). Chemical senses. *Annual Review of Psychology, 45,* 419–449.

Bartz, J. A. (2010). Oxytocin electively improves empathic accuracy. *Psychological Science, 21*(10), 1426–1428. doi: 10.1177/0956797610383439

Bates, E., O'Connell, B., & Shore, C. (1987). Language and communication in infancy. In J. D. Osofsky (Ed.), *Handbook of infant development* (2nd ed., pp. 149–203). New York: Wiley.

Bauer, P. J. (1993). Memory for gender-consistent and gender-inconsistent event sequences by twenty-five-month-old children. *Child Development, 64,* 285–297.

Bauer, P. J. (1996). What do infants recall of their lives? Memory for specific events by 1- to 2-year-olds. *American Psychologist, 51,* 29–41.

Bauer, P. J. (2002). Long-term recall memory: Behavioral and neurodevelopmental changes in the first 2 years of life. *Current Directions in Psychological Science, 11,* 137–141.

Bauer, P. J., Wenner, J. A., Dropik, P. L., & Wewerka, S. S. (2000). Parameters of remembering and forgetting in the transition from infancy to early childhood. *Monographs of the Society for Research in Child Development, 65*(4). [Serial No. 263]. Malden, MA: Blackwell.

Bauer, P. J., Wiebe, S. A., Carver, L. J., Waters, J. M., & Nelson, C. A. (2003). Developments in long-term explicit memory late in the first year of life: Behavioral and electrophysiological indices. *Psychological Science, 14,* 629–635.

Bauman, L. J., Silver, E. J., & Stein, R.E.K. (2006). Cumulative social disadvantage and child health. *Pediatrics, 117,* 1321–1328.

Baumer, E. P., & South, S. J. (2001). Community effects on youth sexual activity. *Journal of Marriage and Family, 63,* 540–554.

Baumrind, D. (1971). Harmonious parents and their preschool children. *Developmental Psychology, 41,* 92–102.

Baumrind, D. (1989). Rearing competent children. In W. Damon (Ed.), *Child development today and tomorrow* (pp. 349–378). San Francisco, CA: Jossey-Bass.

Baumrind, D. (1991). Parenting styles and adolescent development. In J. Brooks-Gunn, R. Lerner, & A. C. Peterson (Eds.), *The encyclopedia of adolescence* (pp. 746–758). New York: Garland.

Baumrind, D. (1996a). A blanket injunction against disciplinary use of spanking is not warranted by the data. *Pediatrics, 88,* 828–831.

Baumrind, D. (1996b). The discipline controversy revisited. *Family Relations, 45,* 405–414.

Baumrind, D. (2005). Patterns of parental authority and adolescent autonomy. In J. Smetana (Ed.), *Changing boundaries of parental authority during adolescence: New directions for child and adolescent development* (No. 108, pp. 61–70). San Francisco, CA: Jossey-Bass.

Baumrind, D., & Black, A. E. (1967). Socialization practices associated with dimensions of competence in preschool boys and girls. *Child Development, 38,* 291–327.

Baumrind, D., Larzelere, R. E., & Cowan, P. A. (2002). Ordinary physical punishment: Is it harmful? Comment on Gershoff (2002). *Psychological Bulletin, 128,* 580–589.

Baumrind, D., Larzelere, R. E., & Owens, E. B. (2010). Effects of preschool parents' power assertive patterns and practices on adolescent development. *Parenting: Science and Practice, 10*(3), 157–201.

Bauserman, R. (2002). Child adjustment in joint-custody versus sole-custody arrangements: A meta-analytic review. *Journal of Family Psychology, 16,* 91–102.

Baydar, N., Greek, A., & Brooks-Gunn, J. (1997). A longitudinal study of the effects of the birth of a sibling during the first 6 years of life. *Journal of Marriage and the Family, 59,* 939–956.

Baydar, N., Hyle, P., & Brooks-Gunn, J. (1997). A longitudinal study of the effects of the birth of a sibling during preschool and early grade school years. *Journal of Marriage and the Family, 59,* 957–965.

Bayley, N. (1969). *Bayley Scales of Infant Development.* New York: Psychological Corporation.

Bayley, N. (1993). *Bayley Scales of Infant Development: II.* New York: Psychological Corporation.

Bayley, N. (2005). *Bayley Scales of Infant Development: III.* New York: Harcourt Brace.

Bayliss, D. M., Jarrold, C., Baddeley, A. D., Gunn, D. M., & Leigh, E. (2005). Mapping the developmental constraints on working memory span performance. *Developmental Psychology, 41*(4), 579–597.

Beals, D. E., & Snow, C. E. (1994). Thunder is when the angels are upstairs bowling: Narratives and explanations at the dinner table. *Journal of Narrative and Life History, 4,* 331–352.

Beauchamp, G. K., & Mennella, J. A. (2009). Early flavor learning and its impact on later feeding behavior. *Journal of Pediatric Gastroenterology and Nutrition, 48*(1), 25–30.

Beckett, C., Maughan, B., Rutter, M., Castle, J., Colvert, E., Groothues, C., et al. (2006). Do the effects of severe early deprivation on cognition persist into early adolescence? Findings from the English and Romanian adoptees study. *Child Development, 77,* 696–711.

Behne, R., Carpenter, M., Call, J., & Tomasello, M. (2005). Unwilling versus unable: Infants' understanding of intentional action. *Developmental Psychology, 41,* 328–337.

Behrman, R. E. (1992). *Nelson textbook of pediatrics* (13th ed.). Philadelphia, PA: Saunders.

Beidel, D. C., & Turner, S. M. (1998). *Shy children, phobic adults: Nature and treatment of social phobia.* Washington, DC: American Psychological Association.

Bekedam, D. J., Engelsbe1, S., Mol, B. W., Buitendijk, S. E., & van der Pal-de Bruin, K. M. (2002). Male predominance in fetal distress during labor. *American Journal of Obstetrics and Gynecology, 187,* 1605–1607.

Belizzi, M. (2002, May). *Obesity in children—what kind of future are we creating?* Presentation at the Fifty-Fifth World Health Assembly Technical Briefing, Geneva, Switzerland.

Bell, J. F., Zimmerman, F. J., & Diehr, P. K. (2008) Maternal work and birth outcome disparities. *Maternal & Child Health Journal, 12,* 415–426.

Bell, L. G., & Bell, D.C. (2005). Family dynamics in adolescence affect midlife well-being. *Journal of Family Psychology, 19,* 198–207.

Bell, M. A., & Fox, N. A. (1992). The relations between frontal brain electrical activity and cognitive development during infancy. *Child Development, 63,* 1142–1163.

Belsky, J. (1984). Two waves of day care research: Developmental effects and conditions of quality. In R. Ainslie (Ed.), *The child and the day care setting.* New York: Praeger.

Belsky, J. (1997). Variation in susceptibility to environmental influence: An evolutionary argument. *Psychological Inquiry, 8,* 230–235.

Belsky, J. (2005). Differential susceptibility to rearing influence: An evolutionary hypothesis and some evidence. In B. J. Ellis & D. F. Bjorklund (Eds.), *Origins of the social mind: Evolutionary psychology and child development* (pp.139–163). New York: Guilford Press.

Belsky, J., Fish, M., & Isabella, R. (1991). Continuity and discontinuity in infant negative and positive emotionality: Family antecedents and attachment consequences. *Developmental Psychology, 27,* 421–431.

Belsky J., Houts, R. M., & Fearon, R.M.P. (2010). Infant attachment and the timing of puberty: Testing an evolutionary hypothesis. *Psychological Science, 21,* 1195–1201, doi:10.1177 /0956797610379867

Belsky, J., Steinberg, L., & Draper, P. (1991). Childhood experience, interpersonal development and reproductive strategy: An evolutionary theory of socialization. *Child Development, 62,* 647–670.

Belsky, J., Steinberg, L. D., Houts, R. M., Friedman, S. L., DeHart, G., Cauffman, E., et al. (2007). Family rearing antecedents of pubertal timing. *Child Development, 78*(4), 1302–1321.

Bem, S. L. (1983). Gender schema theory and its implications for child development: Raising gender-aschematic children in a gender-schematic society. *Signs, 8,* 598–616.

Bem, S. L. (1985). Androgyny and gender schema theory: A conceptual and empirical integration. In T. B. Sondregger (Ed.), *Nebraska symposium on motivation, 1984: Psychology and gender.* Lincoln: University of Nebraska Press.

Bem, S. L. (1993). *The lenses of gender: Transforming the debate on sexual inequality.* New Haven, CT: Yale University Press.

Bendersky, M., Bennett, D., & Lewis, M. (2006). Aggression at age 5 as a function of prenatal exposure to cocaine, gender, and environmental risk. *Journal of Pediatric Psychology, 31,* 71–84.

Benenson, J. F. (1993). Greater preference among females than males for dyadic interaction in early childhood. *Child Development, 64,* 544–555.

Benes, F. M., Turtle, M., Khan, Y., & Farol, P. (1994). Myelination of a key relay zone in the hippocampal formation occurs in the human brain during childhood, adolescence, and adulthood. *Archives of General Psychiatry, 51,* 447–484.

Bennett, D.S., Bendersky, M., & Lewis, M. (2008). Children's cognitive ability from 4 to 9 years old as a function of prenatal cocaine exposure, environmental risk, and maternal verbal intelligence. *Developmental Psychology, 44,* 919–928.

Benson, E. (2003). Intelligent intelligence testing. *Monitor on Psychology, 43*(2), 48–51.

Berg, S. J, & Wynne-Edwards, K. E. (2001). Changes in testosterone, cortisol, and estradiol levels in men becoming fathers. *Mayo Clinic Proceedings, 76,* 582–592.

Bergeman, C. S., & Plomin, R. (1989). Genotype-environment interaction. In M. Bornstein & J. Bruner (Eds.), *Interaction in human development* (pp. 157–171). Hillsdale, NJ: Erlbaum.

Bergen, D. (2002). The role of pretend play in children's cognitive development. *Early Childhood Research & Practice, 4*(1). Retrieved from http://ecrp.uiuc.edu/v4n1/bergen.html

Berger, K. S. (2007). Update on bullying at school: Science forgotten? *Developmental Review, 27,* 91–92.

Berk, L. E. (1986a). Development of private speech among preschool children. *Early Child Development and Care, 24,* 113–136.

Berk, L. E. (1986b). Private speech: Learning out loud. *Psychology Today, 20*(5), 34–42.

Berk, L. E., & Garvin, R. A. (1984). Development of private speech among low income Appalachian children. *Developmental Psychology, 20,* 271–286.

Berk, L. E. (1992). Children's private speech: An overview of theory and the status of research. In R. M. Diaz & L. E. Berk (Eds.), *Private speech: From social interaction to self-regulation* (pp. 17–53). Hillsdale, NJ: Erlbaum.

Berkowitz, G. S., Skovron, M. L., Lapinski, R. H., & Berkowitz, R. L. (1990). Delayed childbearing and the outcome of pregnancy. *New England Journal of Medicine, 322,* 659–664.

Berkowitz, R. I., Stallings, V. A., Maislin, G., & Stunkard, A. J. (2005). Growth of children at high risk of obesity during the first 6 years of life: Implications for prevention. *American Journal of Clinical Nutrition, 81,* 140–146.

Berndt, T. J., & Perry, T. B. (1990). Distinctive features and effects of early adolescent friendships. In R. Montemayor, G. R. Adams, & T. P. Gullotta (Eds.), *From childhood to adolescence: A transitional period?* (Vol. 2, pp. 269–287). Newbury Park, CA: Sage.

Bernier, A., & Meins, E. (2008). A threshold approach to understanding the origins of attachment disorganization. *Developmental Psychology, 44,* 969–982.

Bernstein, P. S. (2003, December 12). Achieving equity in women's and perinatal health. *Medscape Ob/Gyn & Women's Health, 8.* [ePub].

Berrueta-Clement, J. R., Schweinhart, L. J., Barnett, W. S., Epstein, A. S., & Weikart, D. P. (1985). *Changed lives: The effects of the Perry Preschool Program on youths through age 19.* Ypsilanti, MI: High/Scope.

Berrueta-Clement, J. R., Schweinhart, L. J., Barnett, W. S., & Weikart, D. P. (1987). The effects of early educational intervention on crime and delinquency in adolescence and early adulthood. In J. D. Burchard & S. N. Burchard (Eds.), *Primary prevention of psychopathology: Vol. 10. Prevention of delinquent behavior* (pp. 220–240). Newbury Park, CA: Sage.

Berry, M., Dylla, D. J., Barth, R. P., & Needell, B. (1998). The role of open adoption in the adjustment of adopted children and their families. *Children and Youth Services Review, 20,* 151–171.

Berry, R. J., Li, Z., Erickson, J. D., Li, S., Moore, C. A., Wang, H., et al. (1999). Prevention of neural-tube defects with folic acid in China. *New England Journal of Medicine, 341,* 1485–1490.

Bertenthal, B. I., & Campos, J. J. (1987). New directions in the study of early experience. *Child Development, 58,* 560–567.

Bertenthal, B. I., Campos, J. J., & Barrett, K. C. (1984). Self-produced locomotion: An organizer of emotional, cognitive, and social development in infancy. In R. N. Emde & R. J. Harmon (Eds.), *Continuities and discontinuities in development* (pp. 175–209). New York: Plenum Press.

Bertenthal, B. I., Campos, J. J., & Kermoian, R. (1994). An epigenetic perspective on the development of self-produced locomotion and its consequences. *Current Directions in Psychological Science, 3*(5), 140–145.

Bertenthal, B. I., & Clifton, R. K. (1998). Perception and action. In W. Damon (Ed.-in-Chief), D. Kuhn & R. S. Siegler (Vol. Eds.), *Handbook of child psychology: Vol. 2. Cognition perception, and language* (pp. 51–102). New York: Wiley.

Bethell, C. D., Read, D., & Blumberg, S. J. (2005). Mental health in the United States: Health care and well being of children with chronic emotional, behavioral, or developmental problem—United States, 2001. *Morbidity and Mortality Weekly Report, 54,* 985–989.

Beumont, P J.V., Russell, J. D., & Touyz, S. W. (1993). Treatment of anorexia nervosa. *Lancet, 341,* 1635–1640.

Bialystok, E., & Senman, L. (2004). Executive processes in appearance-reality tasks: The role of inhibition of attention and symbolic representation. *Child Development, 75,* 562–579.

Biason-Lauber, A., Konrad, D., Navratil, F., & Schoenle, E. J. (2004). A WNT4 mutation associated with Mullerian-duct regression and virilization in a 46, XX woman. *New England Journal of Medicine, 351,* 792–798.

Bibbins-Domingo, K., Coxson, P., Pletcher, M. J., Lightwood, J., & Goldman, L. (2007). Adolescent overweight and future adult coronary heart disease. *New England Journal of Medicine, 357,* 2371–2379.

Biblarz, T. J., & Stacey, J. (2010). How does gender of the parent matter? *Journal of Marriage and Family, 72,* 3–22.

Bierman, K. L., Smoot, D. L., & Aumiller, K. (1993). Characteristics of aggressive rejected, aggressive (nonrejected), and rejected (non-aggressive) boys. *Child Development, 64,* 139–151.

Birmaher, B. (1998). Should we use antidepressant medications for children and adolescents with depressive disorders? *Psychopharmacology Bulletin, 34,* 35–39.

Birmaher, B., Ryan, N. D., Williamson, D. E., Brent, D. A., Kaufman, J., Dahl, R. E., et al. (1996). Childhood and adolescent depression: A review of the past 10 years. *Journal of the American Academy of Child, 35,* 1427–1440.

Biro, F. M., Galvez, M. P., Greenspan, L. C., Succop, P. A., Vengeepuram, N., Pinney, S. M., et al. (2010). Pubertal assessment method and baseline characteristics in a mixed longitudinal study of girls. *Pediatrics, 126*(3), 583–590.

Bittles, A. H., Bower, C., Hussain, R., & Glasson, E. J. (2006). The four ages of Down syndrome. *European Journal of Public Health, 17*(2), 221–225.

Bjork, J. M., Knutson, B., Fong, G. W., Caggiano, D. M., Bennett, S. M., & Hommer, D. W. (2004). Incentive-elicited brain activities in adolescents: Similarities and differences from young adults. *Journal of Neuroscience, 24,* 1793–1802.

Bjorklund, D. F. (1997). The role of immaturity in human development. *Psychological Bulletin, 122,* 153–169.

Bjorklund, D. F., & Harnishfeger, K. K. (1990). The resources construct in cognitive development: Diverse sources of evidence and a theory of inefficient inhibition. *Developmental Review, 10,* 48–71.

Bjorklund, D. F., & Pellegrini, A. D. (2000). Child development and evolutionary psychology. *Child Development, 71,* 1687–1708.

Bjorklund, D. F., & Pellegrini, A. D. (2002). *The origins of human nature: Evolutionary developmental psychology.* Washington, DC: American Psychological Association.

Black, J. E. (1998). How a child builds its brain: Some lessons from animal studies of neural plasticity. *Preventive Medicine, 27,* 168–171.

Black, M. M., & Krishnakumar, A. (1998). Children in low-income, urban settings: Interventions to promote mental health and well-being. *American Psychologist, 53,* 636–646.

Black, R. E., Morris, S. S., & Bryce, J. (2003). Where and why are 10 million children dying each year? *Lancet, 361,* 2226–2234.

Blair, C. (2002). School readiness: Integrating cognition and emotion in a neurobiological conceptualization of children's functioning at school entry. *American Psychologist, 57,* 111–127.

Blakemore, S., & Choudhury, S. (2006). Development of the adolescent brain: Implications for executive function and social cognition. *Journal of Child Psychology and Psychiatry, 47*(3), 296–312.

Blakeslee, S. (1997, April 17). Studies show talking with infants shapes basis of ability to think. *New York Times,* p. D21.

Bleske-Rechek, A, Lubinski, D., & Benbow, C. P. (2004). Meeting the educational needs of special populations. Advanced placement's role in developing exceptional human capital. *Psychological Sciences, 15,* 217–224.

Block, R. W., Krebs, N. F., the Committee on Child Abuse and Neglect, & the Committee on Nutrition. (2005). *Pediatrics, 116*(5), 1234–1237.

Bloom, B. (1985). *Developing talent in young people.* New York: Ballantine.

Bloom, B., Cohen, R. A., Vickerie, J. L., & Wondimu, E. A. (2003). Summary health statistics for U.S. children: National Health Interview Survey, 2001. *Vital and Health Statistics, 10*(216). Hyattsville, MD: National Center for Health Statistics.

Blum, R., & Reinhart, P. (2000). *Reducing the risk: Connections that make a difference in the lives of youth.* University of Minnesota, Division of General Pediatrics and Adolescent Health.

Boatman, D., Freeman, J., Vining, E., Pulsifer, M., Miglioretti, D., Minahan, R., et al. (1999). Language recovery after left hemispherectomy in children with late onset seizures. *Annals of Neurology, 46*(4), 579–586.

Bocskay, K. A., Tang, D., Orjuela, M. A., Liu, X., Warburton, D. P., & Perera, F. P. (2005). Chromosomal aberrations in cord blood are associated with prenatal exposure to carcinogenic polycyclic aromatic hydrocarbons. *Cancer Epidemiology Biomarkers and Prevention, 14,* 506–511.

Bodrova, E., & Leong, D. J. (2005). High quality preschool programs: What would Vygotsky say? *Early Education & Development, 16*(4), 437–446.

Bodrova, E., & Leong, D. J. (1998). Adult influences on play: The Vygotskian approach. In D. P. Fromberg & D. Bergen (Eds.), *Play from birth to twelve and beyond: Contexts, perspectives, and meanings* (pp. 277–282). New York: Garland.

Bogaert, A. F. (2005). Age at puberty and father absence in a national probability sample. *Journal of Adolescence, 28,* 541–546.

Bogaert, A. F. (2006). Biological versus nonbiological older brothers and men's sexual orientation. *Proceedings of the National Academy of Sciences, 103,* 10771–10774.

Bogaert A. F. (2008). Menarche and father absence in a national probability sample. *Journal of Biosocial Science, 40*(4), 623–636.

Bogard, K., & Takanishi, R. (2005). Pre-K through 3: An aligned and coordinated approach to education for children 3-8 years old. *Social Policy Report, 19*(3).

Bogatz, G. A., & Ball, S. (1971). *The second year of Sesame Street: A continuing education* (Vols. 1-2). Princetion, NJ: Educational Testing Service.

Bojczyk, K. E., & Corbetta, D. (2004). Object retrieval in the 1st year of life: Learning effects of task exposure and box transparency. *Developmental Psychology, 40,* 54–66.

Bollinger, M. B. (2003). Involuntary smoking and asthma severity in children: Data from the Third National Health and Nutrition Examination Survey (NHANES III). *Pediatrics, 112,* 471.

Bonham, V. L., Warshauer-Baker, E., & Collins, F. S. (2005). Race and ethnicity in the genome era. *American Psychologist, 60,* 9–15.

Booth, J. L., & Siegler, R. S. (2006). Developmental and individual differences in pure numerical estimation. *Developmental Psychology, 41,* 189–201.

Booth, J. R., Burman, D. D., Meyer, J. R., Lei, Z., Trommer, B. L., Davenport, D., et al. (2003). Neural development of selective attention and response inhibition. *Neuroimage, 20,* 737–751.

Booth, J. R., Perfetti, C.A., & MacWhinney, B. (1999). Quick, automatic, and general activation of orthographic and phonological representations in young readers. *Developmental Psychology, 35*(1), 3–19.

Borman, G., Boulay, M., Kaplan, J., Rachuba, L., & Hewes, G. (1999, December 13). *Evaluating the longterm impact of multiple summer interventions on the reading skills of low-income, early elementary students.* [Preliminary report, Year 1]. Baltimore, MD: Center for Social Organization of Schools, Johns Hopkins University.

Bornstein, D. (2010, November 8). Fighting bullying with babies. *The New York Times.* Retrieved from http://opinionator.blogs.nytimes.com /2010/11/08/fighting-bullying-with-babies /?emc=eta1

Bornstein, M. H. & Cote, L. R. (with Maital, S., Painter, K., Park, S. Y., Pascual, L., Pecheux, M. G., Ruel, J., et al.). (2004). Cross-linguistic analysis of vocabulary in young children: Spanish, Dutch, French, Hebrew, Italian, Korean, and American English. *Child Development, 75,* 1115–1139.

Bornstein, M. H., Hahn, C.-S., Bell, C., Haynes, O. M., Slater, A., Golding, J., et al. (2006). Stability in cognition across early childhood: A developmental cascade. *Psychological Science, 17,* 151–158.

Bornstein, M. H., Haynes, O. M., O'Reilly, A. W., & Painter, K. (1996). Solitary and collaborative pretense play in early childhood: Sources of individual variation in the development of representational competence. *Child Development, 67,* 2910–2929.

Bornstein, M. H., & Sigman, M. D. (1986). Continuity in mental development from infancy. *Child Development, 57,* 251–274.

Bornstein, M. H., & Tamis-LeMonda, C. S. (1994). Antecedents of information processing skills in infants: Habituation, novelty responsiveness, and cross-modal transfer. *Infant Behavior and Development, 17,* 371–380.

Borowsky, I. A., Ireland, M., & Resnick, M. D. (2001). Adolescent suicide attempts: Risks and protectors. *Pediatrics, 107*(3), 485–493.

Borse, N. N., Gilchrist, J., Dellinger, A. M., Rudd, R. A., Ballesteros, M. F., & Sleet, D. A. (2008). *CDC childhood injury reports: Patterns of unintentional injuries among 0-19 year olds in the United States, 2000–2006.* Atlanta, GA: Centers for Disease Control and Prevention, National Center for Injury Prevention and Control.

Bosch, J., Sullivan, S., Van Dyke, D. C., Su, H., Klockau, L., Nissen, K., et al. (2003). Promoting a healthy tomorrow here for children adopted from abroad. *Contemporary Pediatrics, 20*(2), 69–86.

Bosman, J. (2010, October). Picture books no longer a staple for children. *The New York Times.* Retrieved from http://www.nytimes.com /2010/10/08/us/08picture.html?emc=eta1

Boss, P. (2006). *Loss, trauma, and resilience: Therapeutic work with ambiguous loss*. New York: Norton.

Boss, P. (2007). Ambiguous loss theory: Challenges for scholars and practitioners. *Family Relations, 56*(2), 105–111.

Bouchard, T. J. (1994). Genes, environment, and personality. *Science, 264,* 1700–1701.

Bouchard, T. J. (2004). Genetic influence on human psychological traits: A survey. *Current Directions in Psychological Science, 13,* 148–154.

Bouchard, T. J., & McGue, M. (2003). Genetic and environmental influences on human psychological differences. *Developmental Neurobiology, 54*(1), 4–45.

Bouchey, H. A., & Furman, W. (2003). Dating and romantic experiences in adolescence. In G. R. Adams & M. D. Berzonsky (Eds.), *Blackwell handbook of adolescence* (pp. 313–329). Oxford, UK: Blackwell.

Boulton, M. J. (1995). Playground behaviour and peer interaction patterns of primary school boys classified as bullies, victims and not involved. *British Journal of Educational Psychology, 65,* 165–177.

Boulton, M. J., & Smith, P. K. (1994). Bully/victim problems in middle school children: Stability, self-perceived competence, peer perception, and peer acceptance. *British Journal of Developmental Psychology, 12,* 315–329.

Boutin, P., Dina, C., Vasseur, F., Dubois, S. S., Corset, L., Seron, K., et al. (2003). GAD2 on chromosome 10p12 is a candidate gene for human obesity. *Public Library of Science Biology, 1*(3), e68.

Bower, T.G.R. (1966). The visual world of infants. *Scientific American, 215,* 80–92.

Bowlby, J. (1951). Maternal care and mental health. *Bulletin of the World Health Organization, 3,* 355–534.

Bowlby, J. (1969). *Attachment and loss: Vol. I. Attachment.* London, UK: Hogarth Press & the Institute of Psychoanalysis.

Bowman, S. A., Gortmaker, S. L., Ebbeling, C. B., Pereira, M.A., & Ludwig, D. S. (2004). Effects of fast food consumption on energy intake and diet quality among children in a national household survey. *Pediatrics, 113,* 112–118.

Boyles, S. (2002, January 27). Toxic landfills may boost birth defects. *WebMD Medical News.* Retrieved February 5, 2007, from www.webmd.com /content/article/3606/25_1181.htm

Brabeck, M. M., & Shore, E. L. (2003). Gender differences in intellectual and moral development? The evidence refutes the claims. In J. Demick & C. Andreoletti (Eds.), *Handbook of adult development* (pp. 351–368). New York: Plenum Press.

Bracher, G., & Santow, M. (1999). Explaining trends in teenage childbearing in Sweden. *Studies in Family Planning, 30,* 169–182.

Bradley, R., & Caldwell, B. (1982). The consistency of the home environment and its relation to child development. *International Journal of Behavioral Development, 5,* 445–465.

Bradley, R., Caldwell, B., & Rock, S. (1988). Home environment and school performance: A ten-year follow-up and examination of three models of environmental action. *Child Development, 59,* 852–867.

Bradley, R. H. (1989). Home measurement of maternal responsiveness. In M. H. Bornstein (Ed.), *Maternal responsiveness: Characteristics and consequences* (pp. 63–74). [New Directions for Child Development No. 43]. San Francisco: Jossey-Bass.

Bradley, R. H., Corwyn, R. F., Burchinal, M., McAdoo, H. P., & Coll, C. G. (2001). The home environment of children in the United States: Part II: Relations with behavioral development through age thirteen. *Child Development, 72*(6), 1868–1886.

Bradley, R. H., Corwyn, R. F., McAdoo, H. P., & Coll, C. G. (2001). The home environment of children in the United States: Part I: Variation by age, ethnicity, and poverty status. *Child Development, 72*(6), 1844–1867.

Braine, M. (1976). Children's first word combinations. *Monographs of the Society for Research in Child Development, 41*(1). [Serial No. 164].

Brannon, E. M. (2002). The development of ordinal numerical knowledge in infancy. *Cognition, 83,* 223–240.

Branum, A., & Lukacs, S. L. (2008). *Food allergy among U.S. children: Trends in prevalence and hospitalizations.* [Data Brief No. 10]. Hyattsville, MD: National Center for Health Statistics.

Brass, L. M., Isaacsohn, J. L., Merikangas, K. R., & Robinette, C. D. (1992). A study of twins and stroke. *Stroke, 23*(2), 221–223.

Braswell, G. S. (2006). Sociocultural contexts for the early development of semiotic production. *Psychological Bulletin, 132,* 877–894.

Braswell, G. S., & Callanan, M. A. (2003). Learning to draw recognizable graphic representations during mother-child interactions. *Merrill-Palmer Quarterly, 49,* 471–494.

Bratton, S. C., & Ray, D. (2002). Humanistic play therapy. In D. J. Cain (Ed.), *Humanistic psychotherapies: Handbook of research and practice* (pp. 369–402). Washington, DC: American Psychological Association.

Braun, H., Jenkins, F., & Grigg, W. (2006). *A closer look at charter schools using hierarchical linear modeling* (NCES 2006-460). Washington, DC: U.S. Government Printing Office.

Braungart, J. M., Plomin, R., DeFries, J. C., & Fulker, D. W. (1992). Genetic influence on tester-rated infant temperament as assessed by Bayley's Infant Behavior Record: Nonadoptive and adoptive siblings and twins. *Developmental Psychology 28,* 40–47.

Braungart-Rieker, J. M., Garwood, M. M., Powers, B. P., & Wang, X. (2001). Parental sensitivity, infant affect, and affect regulation: Predictors of later attachment. *Child Development, 72,* 252–270.

Bray, J. H., & Hetherington, E. M. (1993). Families in transition: Introduction and overview. *Journal of Family Psychology, 7,* 3–8.

Brazelton, T. B. (1973). *Neonatal Behavioral Assessment Scale.* Philadelphia, PA: Lippincott.

Brazelton, T. B. (1984). *Neonatal Behavioral Assessment Scale.* Philadelphia, PA: Lippincott.

Brazelton, T. B., & Nugent, J. K. (1995). *Neonatal Behavioral Assessment Scale* (3rd ed.). Cambridge, England: Cambridge University Press.

Brazelton, T. B., & Nugent, J. K. (2001). *Neonatal Behavioral Assessment Scale* (4th ed.). Wiley.

Breastfeeding and HIV International Transmission Study Group. (2004). Late postnatal transmission of HIV-1 in breastfed children: An individual patient data meta-analysis. *Journal of Infectious Diseases, 189,* 2154–2166.

Brendgen, M., Dionne, G., Girard, A., Boivin, M., Vitaro, F., & Perusse, D. (2005). Examining genetic and environmental effects on social aggression: A study of 6-year-old twins. *Child Development, 76,* 930–946.

Brenneman, K., Massey, C., Machado, S. F., & Gelman, R. (1996). Young children's plans differ for writing and drawing. *Cognitive Development, 11,* 397–419.

Brenner, R. A., Sismons-Morton, B. G., Bhaskar, B., Revenis, M., Das, A., & Clemens, J. D. (2003). Infant-parent bed sharing in an inner-city population. *Archives of Pediatrics and Adolescent Medicine, 57,* 33–39.

Brent, D. A., & Birmaher, B. (2002). Adolescent depression. *New England Journal of Medicine, 347,* 667–671.

Brent, D. A., & Mann, J. J. (2006). Familial pathways to suicidal behavior—understanding and preventing suicide among adolescents. *New England Journal of Medicine, 355,* 2719–2721.

Brent, M. R., & Siskind, J. M. (2001). The role of exposure to isolated words in early vocabulary development. *Cognition, 81,* 33–34.

Bretherton, I. (1990). Communication patterns, internal working models, and the intergenerational transmission of attachment relationships. *Infant Mental Health Journal, 11*(3), 237–252.

Brewaeys, A., Ponjaert, I., Van Hall, V. E., & Golombok, S. (1997). Donor insemination: Child development and family functioning in lesbian mother families. *Human Reproduction, 12,* 1349–1359.

Brezina, T. (1999). Teenage violence toward parents as an adaptation to family strain: Evidence from a national survey of male adolescents. *Youth & Society, 30,* 416–444.

Bridge, J. A., Iyengar, S., Salary, C. B., Barbe, R. P., Birmaher, B., Pincus, H. A., et al. (2007). Clinical response and risk for reported suicidal ideation and suicide attempts in pediatric antidepressant treatment: A meta-analysis of randomized controlled trials. *Journal of the American Medical Association, 297,* 1683–1696.

Briggs, J. L. (1970). *Never in anger.* Cambridge, MA: Harvard University Press.

Brin, D. J. (2004). The use of rituals in grieving for a miscarriage or stillbirth. *Women & Therapy, 27,* 123–132.

Brodowski, M. L., Nolan, C. M., Gaudiosi, J. A., Yuan, Y. Y., Zikratova, L., Oritz, M. J., et al. (2008). Nonfatal maltreatment of infants—United States, October 2005–September 2006. *Morbidity & Mortality Weekly Report, 57*(13), 336–339.

Brody, G. H. (1998). Sibling relationship quality: Its causes and consequences. *Annual Review of Psychology, 49,* 1–24.

Brody, G. H. (2004). Siblings' direct and indirect contributions to child development. *Current Directions in Psychological Science, 13,* 124–126.

Brody, G. H., Chen, Y.-F., Murry, V. M., Ge, X., Simons, R. L., Gibbons, F. X., et al. (2006). Perceived discrimination and the adjustment of African American youths: A five-year longitudinal analysis with contextual moderation effects. *Child Development, 77*(5), 1170–1189.

Brody, G. H., Ge., X., Conger, R., Gibbons, F. X., Murry, V. M., Gerrard, M., & Simons, R. L. (2001). The influence of neighborhood disadvantage, collective socialization, and parenting on African American children's affiliation with deviant peers. *Child Development, 72*(4), 1231–1246.

Brody, G. H., Kim, S., Murry, V. M., & Brown, A. C. (2004). Protective longitudinal paths linking child competence to behavioral problems among African American siblings. *Child Development, 75,* 455–467.

Brody, J. E. (1995, June 28). Preventing birth defects even before pregnancy. *New York Times,* p. C10.

Brody, L. R., Zelazo, P. R., & Chaika, H. (1984). Habituation-dishabituation to speech in the neonate. *Developmental Psychology, 20,* 114–119.

Broekmans, F. J., Soules, M. R., & Fauser, B. C. (2009). Ovarian aging: Mechanisms and clinical consequences. *Endocrine Reviews, 30*(5), 465–493.

Broidy, L. M., Tremblay, R. E., Brame, B., Fergusson, D., Horwood, J. L., Laird, R., et al. (2003). Developmental trajectories of childhood disruptive behaviors and adolescent delinquency: A six-site cross-national study. *Developmental Psychology, 39*(2), 222–245.

Bronfenbrenner, U. (1979). *The ecology of human development.* Cambridge, MA: Harvard University Press.

Bronfenbrenner, U. (1986). Ecology of the family as a context for human development: Research perspectives. *Developmental Psychology, 22,* 723–742.

Bronfenbrenner, U. (1994). Ecological models of human development. In T. Husen & T. N. Postlethwaite (Eds.), *International encyclopedia of education* (Vol. 3, 2nd ed., pp. 1643–1647). Oxford, U.K.: Pergamon Press/Elsevier Science.

Bronfenbrenner, U., & Morris, P. A. (1998). The ecology of developmental processes. In W. Damon (Series Ed.) & R. Lerner (Vol. Ed.), *Handbook of child psychology: Vol. I. Theoretical models of human development* (5th ed., pp. 993–1028). New York: Wiley.

Bronner, E. (1999, January 22). Social promotion is bad; repeating a grade may be worse. *New York Times.* Retrieved from http://search.nytimes.com /search/daily/bin/fastweb?getdocPsitePsiteP13235 POPwAA APsocial%7Epromotion

Bronstein, P., Clauson, J., Stoll, M. F., & Abrams, C. L. (1993). Parenting behavior and children's social, psychological, and academic adjustment in diverse family structures. *Family Relations, 42,* 268–276.

Brookmeyer, K. A., Henrich, C. C., & Schwab-Stone, M. (2005). Adolescents who witness community violence: Can parent support and prosocial cognitions protect them from committing violence? *Child Development, 76,* 917–929.

Brooks, R., & Meltzoff, A. N. (2002). The importance of eyes: How infants interpret adult looking behavior. *Developmental Psychology, 38,* 958–966.

Brooks, R., & Meltzoff, A. N. (2005). The development of gaze following and its relation to language. *Developmental Science, 8,* 535–543.

Brooks, R., & Meltzoff, A. N. (2008). Infant gaze following and pointing predict accelerated vocabulary growth through two years of age: A longitudinal, growth curve modeling study. *Journal of Child Language, 35,* 207–220.

Brooks-Gunn, J. (2003). Do you believe in magic? What can we expect from early childhood intervention programs? *SRCD Social Policy Report, 17*(1).

Brooks-Gunn, J., Britto, P. R., & Brady, C. (1998). Struggling to make ends meet: Poverty and child development. In M. E. Lamb (Ed.), *Parenting and child development in "non-traditional" families* (pp. 279–304). Mahwah, NJ: Erlbaum.

Brooks-Gunn, J., Duncan, G. J., Leventhal, T., & Aber, J. L. (1997). Lessons learned and future directions for research on the neighborhoods in which children live. In J. Brooks-Gunn, G. J. Duncan, & J. L. Aber (Eds.), *Neighborhood poverty: Context and consequences for children* (Vol. 1, pp. 279–297). New York: Russell Sage Foundation.

Brooks-Gunn, J., Han, W.-J., & Waldfogel, J. (2002). Maternal employment and child cognitive outcomes in the first three years of life: The NICHD study of early child care. *Child Development, 73,* 1052–1072.

Broude, G. J. (1995). *Growing up: A crosscultural encyclopedia.* Santa Barbara, CA: ABC-CLIO.

Brousseau, E. (2006, May). *The effect of maternal body mass index on efficacy of dinoprosteone vaginal insert for cervical ripening.* Paper presented at the annual meeting of the American College of Obstetricians and Gynecologists, Washington, D.C.

Brown, A. L., Metz, K. E., & Campione, J. C. (1996). Social interaction and individual understanding in a community of learners: The influence of Piaget and Vygotsky. In A. Tryphon & J. Voneche (Eds.), *Piaget-Vygotsky: The social genesis of thought* (pp. 145–170). Hove, England: Psychology/Erlbaum (UK) Taylor & Francis.

Brown, A. S., Begg, M. D., Gravenstein, S., Schaefer, C. A., Wyatt, R. J., Bresnahan, M., Babulas, V. P., & Susser, E. S. (2004). Serologic evidence of prenatal influence in the etiology of schizophrenia. *Archives of General Psychiatry, 61,* 774–780.

Brown, A. S., Tapert, S. F., Granholm, E., & Delis, D. C. (2000) Neurocognitive functioning of adolescents: Effects of protracted alcohol use. *Alcoholism: Clinical and Experimental Research, 24,* 64–171.

Brown, B. B., & Klute, C. (2003). Friendships, cliques, and crowds. In G. R. Adams & M. D. Berzonsky. (Eds.). *Blackwell handbook of adolescence* (pp. 330–348). Malden, MA: Blackwell.

Brown, B. B., Mounts, N., Lamborn, S. D., & Steinberg, L. (1993). Parenting practices and peer group affiliation in adolescence. *Child Development, 64,* 467–482.

Brown, G. L., Schoppe-Sullivan, S. J., Mangelsdorf, S. C., & Neff, C. (2010). Observed and reported supportive coparenting as predictors of infant-mother and infant-father attachment security. *Early Child Development and Care, 180*(1–2), 121–137.

Brown, J. D., L'Engle, K. L., Pardun, C. J., Guo, G., Kenneavy, K., & Jackson, C. (2006). Sexy media matter: Exposure to sexual content in music, movies, television, and magazines predicts black and white adolescents' sexual behavior. *Pediatrics, 117,* 1018–1027.

Brown, J. L. (1987). Hunger in the U.S. *Scientific American, 256*(2), 37–41.

Brown, J. R., & Dunn, J. (1996). Continuities in emotion understanding from three to six years. *Child Development, 67,* 789–802.

Brown, L. J., Kaste, L. M., Selwitz, R. H., & Furman, L. J. (1996). Dental caries and sealant usage in U.S. children, 1988–1991. *Journal of the American Dental Association, 127,* 335–343.

Brown, L. J., Wall, T. P., & Lazar, V. (2000). Trends in untreated caries in primary teeth of children 2- to 10-years old. *Journal of the American Dental Association, 131,* 93–100.

Brown, L. M., & Gilligan, C. (1990, April). *The psychology of women and the development of girls.* Paper presented at the Laurel-Harvard Conference on the Psychology of Women and the Education of Girls, Cleveland, OH.

Brown, P. (1993, April 17). Motherhood past midnight. *New Scientist,* pp. 4–8.

Brown, S. L. (2004). Family structure and child well-being: The significance of parental cohabitation. *Journal of Marriage and Family, 66,* 351–367.

Brown, S. S. (1985). Can low birth weight be prevented? *Family Planning Perspectives, 17*(3), 112–118.

Browne, A., & Finkelhor, D. (1986). Impact of child sexual abuse: A review of research. *Psychological Bulletin, 99*(1), 66–77.

Brownell, C. A., Ramani, G. B., & Zerwas, S. (2006). Becoming a social partner with peers: Cooperation and social understanding in one- and two-year-olds. *Child Development, 77,* 803–821.

Bruer, J. T. (2001). A critical and sensitive period primer. In D. B. Bailey, J. T. Bruer, F. J. Symons, & J. W. Lichtman (Eds.), *Critical thinking about critical periods: A series from the National Center for Early Development and Learning* (pp. 289–292). Baltimore, MD: Paul Brooks.

Bruner, A. B., Joffe, A., Duggan, A. K., Casella, J. F., & Brandt, J. (1996). Randomised study of cognitive effects of iron supplementation in non-anaemic irondeficient adolescent girls. *Lancet, 348,* 992–996.

Brunson, K. L., Kramar, E., Lin, B., Chen, Y., Colgin, L. L., Yanagihara, T. K., Lynch, G., & Baram, T. Z. (2005). Mechanisms of late-onset cognitive decline after early-life stress. *Journal of Neuroscience, 25*(41), 9328–9338.

Bryant, B. K. (1987). Mental health, temperment, family, and friends: Perspectives on children's empathy and social perspective taking. In N. Eisenberg & J. Strayer (Eds.), Empathy and its development of competence in adolescence. *Child Development, 66,* 129–138.

Bryce, J., Boschi-Pinto, C., Shibuya, K., & the WHO Child Health Epidemiology Reference Group. (2005). WHO estimates of the causes of death in children. *Lancet, 365,* 1147–1152.

Buchanan, C. M., Eccles, J. S., & Becker, J. B. (1992). Are adolescents the victims of raging hormones? Evidence for activational effects of hormones on moods and behavior at adolescence. *Psychological Bulletin, 111*(1), 62–107.

Büchel, C., & Sommer, M. (2004). Unsolved mystery: What causes stuttering? *PLoS Biology, 2,* 0159–0163.

Buck Louis, G., Gray, L., Marcus, M., Ojeda, S., Pescovitz, O., Witchel, S., et al. (2008). Environmental factors and puberty timing: Expert panel research needs. *Pediatrics, 121,* S192–S207.

Buckner, J. C., Bassuk, E. L., Weinreb, L. F., & Brooks, M. G. (1999). Homelessness and its relation to the mental health and behavior of low-income school-age children. *Developmental Psychology, 35*(1), 246–257.

Buehler, C. (2006). Parents and peers in relation to early adolescent problem behavior. *Journal of Marriage and Family, 68,* 109–124.

Buhrmester, D. (1990). Intimacy of friendship, interpersonal competence, and adjustment during preadolescence and adolescence. *Child Development, 61,* 1101–1111.

Buhrmester, D. (1996). Need fulfillment, interpersonal competence, and the developmental contexts of early adolescent friendship. In W. M. Bukowski, A. F. Newcomb, & W. W. Hartup (Eds.), *The company they keep: Friendship in childhood and adolescence* (pp. 158–185). New York: Cambridge University Press.

Buhrmester, D., & Furman, W. (1990). Perceptions of sibling relationships during middle childhood and adolescence. *Child Development, 61,* 138–139.

Buist, K. L., Dekovic, M., & Prinzie, P. (2013). Sibling relationship quality and psychopathology of children and adolescents: A meta-analysis. *Clinical Psychology Review, 33*(1), 97–106.

Bulkley, K., & Fisler, J. (2002). *A decade of charter schools: From theory to practice.* Philadelphia, PA: Consortium for Policy Research in Education,

Graduate School of Education, University of Pennsylvania.

Bunikowski, R., Grimmer, I., Heiser, A., Metze, B., Schafer, A., & Obladen, M. (1998). Neurodevelopmental outcome after prenatal exposure to opiates. *European Journal of Pediatrics, 157,* 724–730.

Burchinal, M. R., Campbell, F. A., Bryant, D. M., Wasik, B. H., & Ramey, C. T. (1997). Early intervention and mediating processes in cognitive performance of children of low-income African American families. *Child Development, 68,* 935–954.

Burchinal, M. R., Roberts, J. E., Nabors, L. A., & Bryant, D. M. (1996). Quality of center child care and infant cognitive and language development. *Child Development, 67,* 606–620.

Burhans, K. K., & Dweck, C. S. (1995). Helplessness in early childhood: The role of contingent worth. *Child Development, 66,* 1719–1738.

Burns, B. J., Phillips, S. D., Wagner, H. R., Barth, R. P., Kolko, D. J., Campbell, Y., & Landsverk, J. (2004). Mental health need and access to mental health services by youths involved with child welfare: A national survey. *Journal of the American Academy of Child & Adolescent Psychiatry, 43,* 960–970.

Burt, A., Annest, J. L., Ballesteros, M. F., & Budnitz, D. S. (2006). Nonfatal, unintentional medication exposures among young children—United States, 2001–2003. *Morbidity and Mortality Weekly Report, 55,* 1–5.

Bushman, B. J., & Huesmann, L. R. (2001). Effects of televised violence on aggression. In J. Singer & D. Singer (Eds.), *Handbook of children and the media* (pp. 223–254). Thousand Oaks, CA: Sage.

Bushnell, E. W., & Boudreau, J. P. (1993). Motor development and the mind: The potential role of motor abilities as a determinant of aspects of perceptual development. *Child Development, 64,* 1005–1021.

Bussey, K. (2011). Gender identity development. In S. J. Schwarts, K. Luyckx, and V. L. Vignoles (Eds.). *Handbook of Identity Theory and Research: Vol. 1. structures and processes* (pp. 603–628). New York: NY: Springer.

Bussey, K., & Bandura, A. (1992). Self-regulatory mechanisms governing gender development. *Child Development, 63,* 1236–1250.

Bussey, K., & Bandura, A. (1999). Social cognitive theory of gender development and differentiation. *Psychological Review, 106,* 676–713.

Byrne, M., Agerbo, E., Ewald, H., Eaton, W. W., & Mortensen, P. B. (2003). Parental age and risk of schizophrenia. *Archives of General Psychiatry, 60,* 673–678.

Byrnes, J. P., & Fox, N. A. (1998). The educational relevance of research in cognitive neuroscience. *Educational Psychology Review, 10,* 297–342.

Bystron, I., Rakic, P., Molnar, Z., & Blakemore, C. (2006). The first neurons of the human cerebral cortex. *Nature Neuroscience, 9*(7), 880–886.

Caballero, B. (2006). Obesity as a consequence of undernutrition. *Journal of Pediatrics, 149*(5, Suppl. 1), 97–99.

Cabrera, N. J., Tamis-LeMonda, C. S., Bradley, R. H., Hofferth, S., & Lamb, M. E. (2000). Fatherhood in the twenty-first century. *Child Development, 71,* 127–136.

Cacciatore, J. (2007). Effects of support groups on post traumatic stress responses in women experiencing stillbirth. *Omega, 55,* 71–90.

Cacciatore, J., DeFrain, J., & Jones, K.L.C. (2008). When a baby dies: Ambiguity and stillbirth. *Marriage & Family Review, 44*(4), 439–454.

Caelli, K., Downie, J., & Letendre, A. (2002). Parents' experiences of midwife-managed care following the loss of a baby in a previous pregnancy. *Journal of Advanced Nursing, 39,* 127–136.

Caldji, C., Diorio, J., & Meaney, M. J. (2003). Variations in maternal care alter GABA(A) receptor subunit expression in brain regions associated with fear. *Neuropsychopharmacology, 28,* 1950–1959.

Caldwell, B. M., & Bradley, R. H. (1984). *Home observation for measurement of the environment.* Unpublished manuscript, University of Arkansas at Little Rock.

Calkins, S. D., & Fox, N. A. (1992). The relations among infant temperament, security of attachment, and behavioral inhibition at twenty-four months. *Child Development, 63,* 1456–1472.

Camarata, S., & Woodcock, R. (2006). Sex differences in processing speed: Developmental effects in males and females. *Intelligence, 34*(3), 231–252.

Cameron, L., Rutland, A., Brown, R., & Douch, R. (2006). Changing children's intergroup attitudes towards refugees: Testing different models of extended contact. *Child Development, 77,* 1208–1219.

Campbell, A., Shirley, L., & Candy, J. (2004). A longitudinal study of gender-related cognition and behaviour. *Developmental Science, 7,* 1–9.

Campbell, A., Shirley, L., Heywood, C., & Crook, C. (2000). Infants' visual preference for sex-congruent babies, children, toys, and activities: A longitudinal study. *British Journal of Developmental Psychology, 18,* 479–498.

Campbell, F. A., Ramey, C. T., Pungello, E., Sparling, J., & Miller-Johnson, S. (2002). Early childhood education: Young adult outcomes from the Abecedarian Project. *Applied Developmental Science, 6*(1), 42–57.

Campos, J., Bertenthal, B., & Benson, N. (1980, April). *Self-produced locomotion and the extraction of form invariance.* Paper presented at the meeting of the International Conference on Infant Studies, New Haven, CT.

Canfield, R. L., Henderson, C. R., Cory-Slechta, D. A., Cox, C., Jusko, T. A., & Lanphear, B. P. (2003). Intellectual impairment in children with blood lead concentrations below 10 adolescence to young adulthood: Prevalence, prediction, and association with STD contraction. *Developmental Psychology, 38,* 394–406.

Cantor, J. (1994). Confronting children's fright responses to mass media. In D. Zillman, J. Bryant, & A. C. Huston (Eds.), *Media, children, and the family: Social scientific, psychoanalytic, and clinical perspectives* (pp. 139–150). Hillsdale, NJ: Erlbaum.

Cao, A., Rosatelli, M. C., Monni, G., & Galanello, R. (2002). Screening for thalassemia: A model of success. *Obstetrics and Gynecology Clinics of North America, 29*(2), 305–328.

Capaldi, D. M., Stoolmiller, M., Clark, S., & Owen, L. D. (2002). Heterosexual risk behaviors in at-risk young men from early adolescence to young adulthood: Prevalence, prediction, and STD contraction. *Developmental Psychology, 38,* 394–406.

Caplan, M., Vespo, J., Pedersen, J., & Hay, D. F. (1991). Conflict and its resolution in small groups of one- and two-year olds. *Child Development, 62,* 1513–1524.

Caprara, G. V., Fida, R., Vecchione, M., Del Bove, G., Vecchio, G. M., Barbaranelli, et al. (2008). Longitudinal analysis of the role of perceived self-efficacy for self-regulated learning in academic continuance and achievement. *Journal of Educational Psychology, 100*(3), 525–534.

Capute, A. J., Shapiro, B. K., & Palmer, F. B. (1987). Marking the milestones of language development. *Contemporary Pediatrics, 4*(4), 24.

Card, N., Stucky, B., Sawalani, G., & Little, T., (2008) Direct and indirect aggression during childhood and adolescence: A meta-analytic review of gender differences, intercorrelations, and relations to maladjustment. *Child Development, 79*(5), 1185–1229.

Carlson, E. A. (1998). A prospective longitudinal study of attachment disorganization/disorientation. *Child Development, 69*(4), 1107–1128.

Carlson, E. A., Sroufe, L. A., & Egeland, B. (2004). The construction of experience: A longitudinal study of representation and behavior. *Child Development, 75,* 66–83.

Carlson, M. J. (2006). Family structure, father involvement, and adolescent behavioral outcomes. *Journal of Marriage and Family, 68,* 137–154.

Carlson, S. M., Moses, L. J., & Hix, H. R. (1998). The role of inhibitory processes in young children's difficulties with deception and false belief. *Child Development, 69*(3), 672–691.

Carlson, S. M., & Taylor, M. (2005). Imaginary companions and impersonated characters: Sex differences in children's fantasy play. *Merrill-Palmer Quarterly, 51*(1), 93–118.

Carlson, S. M., Wong, A., Lemke, M., & Cosser, C. (2005). Gesture as a window in children's beginning understanding of false belief. *Child Development, 76,* 73–86.

Carmichael, M. (2004, January 26). In parts of Asia, sexism is ingrained and gender selection often means murder. No girls please. *Newsweek,* p. 50.

Carnethon, M. R., Gulati, M., & Greenland, P. (2005). Prevalence and cardiovascular disease correlates of low cardiorespiratory fitness in adolescents and adults. *Journal of the American Medical Association, 294,* 2981–2988.

Carothers, S. S., Borkowski, J. G., Lefever, J. B., & Whitman, T. L. (2005). Religiosity and the socioemotional adjustment of adolescent mothers and their children. *Journal of Family Psychology, 19,* 263–275.

Carraher, T. N., Schliemann, A. D., & Carraher, D. W. (1988). Mathematical concepts in everyday life. In G. B. Saxe & M. Gearhart (Eds.), Children's mathematics. *New Directions in Child Development, 41,* 71–87.

Carrel, L., & Willard, B. F. (2005). X-inactivation profile reveals extensive variability in X-linked gene expression in females. *Nature, 434,* 400–404.

Carskadon, M.A., Acebo, C., Richardson, G. S., Tate, B. A., & Seifer, R. (1997). Long nights protocol: Access to circadian parameters in adolescents. *Journal of Biological Rhythms, 12,* 278–289.

Carter, R. C., Jacobson, S. W., Molteno, C. D., Chiodo, L. M., Viljoen, D., & Jacobson, J. L. (2005). Effects of prenatal alcohol exposure on infant visual acuity. *The Journal of Pediatrics, 147*(4), 473–479.

Carver, P. R., & Iruka, I. U. (2006). *After-school programs and activities: 2005* (NCES 2006-076). Washington, DC: National Center for Education Statistics.

Casaer, P. (1993). Old and new facts about perinatal brain development. *Journal of Child Psychology and Psychiatry, 34*(1), 101–109.

Case, R. (1985). *Intellectual development: Birth to adulthood.* Orlando, FL: Academic Press.

Case, R. (1992). Neo-Piagetian theories of child development. In R. Sternberg & C. Berg (Eds.), *Intellectual development* (pp. 161–196). New York: Cambridge University Press.

Case, R., & Okamoto, Y. (1996). The role of central conceptual structures in the development of children's thought. *Monographs of the Society for Research in Child Development, 61*(1–2). [Serial No. 246].

Casper, L. M. (1997). My daddy takes care of me: Fathers as care providers. *Current Population Reports* (P70–59). Washington, DC: U.S. Bureau of the Census.

Caspi, A. (2000). The child is father of the man: Personality continuity from childhood to adulthood. *Journal of Personality and Social Psychology, 78*, 158–172.

Caspi, A., Lynam, D., Moffitt, T. E., & Silva, P. (1993). Unraveling girls' delinquency: Biological, dispositional, and contextual contributions to adolescent misbehavior. *Developmental Psychology, 29*(1), 19–30.

Caspi, A., McClay, J., Moffitt, T. E., Mill, J., Martin, J., Craig, I. W., Taylor, A., & Poulton, R. (2002). Role of genotype in the cycle of violence in maltreated children. *Science, 297*, 851–854.

Caspi, A., & Silva, P. (1995). Temperamental qualities at age 3 predict personality traits in young adulthood: Longitudinal evidence from a birth cohort. *Child Development, 66*, 486–498.

Caspi, A., Sugden, K., Moffitt, T. E., Taylor, A., Craig, I. W., Harrington, H., et al. (2003). Influence of life stress on depression: Moderation by a polymorphism in the 5-HTT gene. *Science, 301*, 386–389.

Cassidy, K. W., Werner, R. S., Rourke, M., Zubernis, L. S., & Balaraman, G. (2003). The relationship between psychological understanding and positive social behaviors. *Social Development, 12*, 198–221.

Caughey, A. B., Hopkins, L. M., & Norton, M. E. (2006). Chorionic villus sampling compared with amniocentesis and the difference in the rate of pregnancy loss. *Obstetrics and Gynecology, 108*, 612–616.

Ceci, S. J. (1991). How much does schooling influence general intelligence and its cognitive components? A reassessment of the evidence. *Developmental Psychology, 27*, 703–722.

Ceci, S. J., & Gilstrap, L. L. (2000). Determinants of intelligence: Schooling and intelligence. In A. Kazdin (Ed.), *Encyclopedia of psychology*. Washington, DC, & New York: American Psychological Association and Oxford University Press.

Ceci, S. J., & Williams, W. M. (1997). Schooling, intelligence, and income. *American Psychologist, 52*(10), 1051–1058.

Celis, W. (1990, August 16). More states are laying school paddle to rest. *New York Times*, pp. A1, B12.

Center for Education Reform. (2004, August 17). *Comprehensive data discounts New York Time account; reveals charter schools performing at or above traditional schools.* [CER Press Release]. Retrieved from www.edreform.com/Press_Box/Press _Releases/?Charter_Schools_Produce_Strong _Student_Achievement&year=2004

Center for Education Reform. (2008). *Just the FAQs—charter schools.* Retrieved April 8, 2008, from www.edreform.com/index.cfm?fuseAction= document&documentID=60&sectionID=67& NEWSYEAR=2008

Center for Effective Discipline. (2005). *Facts about corporal punishment in Canada.* Retrieved April 20, 2005, from www.stophitting.com/news

Center for Law and Social Policy. (2008). *Head Start participants, programs, families, and staff in 2006.* [Fact sheet]. Washington, DC: Author.

Center for Weight and Health. (2001). *Pediatric overweight: A review of the literature: Executive summary.* Berkeley: University of California at Berkeley.

Center on Addiction and Substance Abuse at Columbia University (CASA). (1996, June). *Substance abuse and the American woman.* New York: Author.

Centers for Disease Control and Prevention (CDC). (2000a). *CDC's guidelines for school and community programs: Promoting lifelong physical activity.* Retrieved May 26, 2000, from www.cdc.gov /nccdphp/dash/phactaag.htm

Centers for Disease Control and Prevention (CDC). (2000b). *Tracking the hidden epidemic: Trends in STDs in the U.S., 2000.* Washington, DC: Author.

Centers for Disease Control and Prevention (CDC). (2001). Recommendations for using fluoride to prevent and control dental caries in the United States. *Morbidity and Mortality Weekly Report, 50*(RR14), 1–42.

Centers for Disease Control and Prevention (CDC). (2004). National, state, and urban area vaccination coverage among children aged 19–36 months— United States, 2003. *Morbidity and Mortality Weekly Report, 53*, 658–661.

Centers for Disease Control and Prevention (CDC). (2005a). *Assisted reproductive technology: Home.* Retrieved January 25, 2006, from www.cdc.gov /ART/

Centers for Disease Control and Prevention (CDC). (2006a). Achievements in public health: Reduction in perinatal transmission of HIV infection—United States, 1985–2005. *Morbidity and Mortality Weekly Report, 55*(21), 592–597.

Centers for Disease Control and Prevention (CDC). (2006b). Improved national prevalence estimates for 18 selected major birth defects—United States, 1999–2001. *Morbidity and Mortality Weekly Report, 54*(51 & 52), 1301–1305.

Centers for Disease Control and Prevention (CDC). (2006c). Recommendations to improve preconception health and health care—United States. *Morbidity and Mortality Weekly Report, 55*(RR06), 1–23.

Centers for Disease Control and Prevention (CDC). (2007a, June). Cases of HIV infection and AIDS in the United States and dependent areas, 2005. *HIV/AIDS Surveillance_Report, 17* (Rev. ed.).

Centers for Disease Control and Prevention (CDC). (2007b). Trends in oral health status: United States, 1988–1994 and 1999–2004. *Vital Health Statistics, 11*(248).

Centers for Disease Control and Prevention (CDC). (2007c). *Web-based Injury Statistics Query and Reporting System.* Retrieved June 2007 from www. cdc.gov/injury/wisqars/index.html

Centers for Disease Control and Prevention (CDC). (2008a). Prevalence of self-reported postpartum depressive symptoms—17 states, 2004–2005. *Morbidity and Mortality Weekly Report, 57*(14), 361–366.

Centers for Disease Control and Prevention (CDC). (2008b, Summer). *Suicide: Facts at a glance.* Atlanta, GA: Author.

Centers for Disease Control and Prevention (CDC). (2008c). *Understanding teen dating violence.* [Fact sheet]. Atlanta, GA: Author.

Centers for Disease Control and Prevention (CDC). (2009). Births, marriages, divorces, and deaths: Provisional data for 2008. *National Vital Statistics Reports, 57*(19).

Centers for Disease Control and Prevention (CDC). (2010). NCHS Data Brief: Mortality among teenagers aged 12–19 years: United States, 1999–2006. Retrieved January 4, 2013, from http://www.cdc.gov /nchs/data/databriefs/db37.htm

Centers for Disease Control and Prevention (CDC). (2012). Youth Risk Behavior Survveillance—2011. Accessed January 4, 2013: http://www.cdc.gov /mmwr/pdf/ss/ss6104.pdf

Centers for Disease Control and Prevention (CDC). (2012a). Sexual Experience and Contraceptive Use among Female Teens—United States, 1995, 2002, and 2006–2010. *Morbidity and Mortality Weekly Report, 61*(17), 297–301.

Centers for Medicare and Medicaid Services. (2009). *Low cost health insurance for families and children.* Retrieved from www.cms.hhs.gov /lowcosthealthinsfamchild/

Central Intelligence Agency. (2008, December 4.) *The world factbook: United States.* Retrieved December 14, 2008, from www.cia.gov/library /publications/the-world-factbook/geos/us.html

Ceppi, G., & Zini, M. (1998). *Children, spaces, relations: Metaproject for an environment for young children.* Eggio Emilia, Italy: Municipality of Reggio Emilia Inanzia ricerca.

Chambers, C. D., Hernandez-Diaz, S., Van Marter, L. J., Werler, M. M., Louik, C., Jones, K. L., & Mitchell, A. A. (2006). Selective serotonin-reuptake inhibitors and risk of persistent pulmonary hypertension of the newborn. *New England Journal of Medicine, 354*, 579–587.

Chambers, R. A., Taylor, J. R., & Potenza, M. N. (2003). Developmental neurocircuitry of motivation in adolescence: A critical period of addiction vulnerability. *American Journal of Psychiatry, 160*, 1041–1052.

Chan, R. W., Raboy, B., & Patterson, C. J. (1998). Psychosocial adjustment among children conceived via donor insemination by lesbian and heterosexual mothers. *Child Development, 69*, 443–457.

Chandra, A., Martin, S., Collins, R., Elliott, M., Berry, S., Kanouse, D., & Miu, A. (2008). Does watching sex on television predict teen pregnancy? Findings from a National Longitudinal Survey of Youth. *Pediatrics, 122*(5), 1047–1054.

Chao, R. K. (1994). Beyond parental control and authoritarian parenting style: Understanding Chinese parenting through the cultural notion of training. *Child Development, 65*, 1111–1119.

Chao, R. K. (1996). Chinese and European American mothers' beliefs about the role of parenting in children's school success. *Journal of Cross-Cultural Psychology, 27*, 403–423.

Chao, R. K. (2001). Extending research on the consequences of parenting style for Chinese Americans and European Americans. *Child Development, 72*, 1832–1843.

Chapman, C., Laird, J., & Kewal-Ramani, A. (2010). *Trends in high school dropout and completion rates in the United States: 1972–2008* (NCES 2011–012). Retrieved from National Center for Education Statistics website: http://nces.ed.gov/ pubsearch

Chapman, M., & Lindenberger, U. (1988). Functions, operations, and décalage in the development of transitivity. *Developmental Psychology, 24*, 542–551.

Charlesworth, A., & Glantz, S. A. (2005). Smoking in the movies increases adolescent smoking: A review. *Pediatrics, 116,* 1516–1528.

Chehab, F. F., Mounzih, K., Lu, R., & Lim, M. E. (1997). Early onset of reproductive function in normal female mice treated with leptin. *Science, 275,* 88–90.

Chen, A., & Rogan, W. J. (2004) Breastfeeding and the risk of postneonatal death in the United States. *Pediatrics, 113,* 435–439.

Chen, C., & Stevenson, H. W. (1995). Motivation and mathematics achievement: A comparative study of Asian-American, Caucasian-American, and East Asian high school students. *Child Development, 66,* 1215–1234.

Chen, E., Matthews, K. A., & Boyce, W. T. (2002). Socioeconomic differences in children's health: How and why do these relationships change with age? *Psychological Bulletin, 128,* 295–329.

Chen, L., Baker, S. B., Braver, E. R., & Li, G. (2000). Carrying passengers as a risk factor for crashes fatal to 16- and 17-year-old drivers. *Journal of the American Medical Association, 283*(12), 1578–1582.

Chen, P. C., & Wang, J. D. (2006). Parental exposure to lead and small for gestational age births. *American Journal of Industrial Medicine 49*(6), 417–422.

Chen, P-L., Avramopoulos, D., Lasseter, V. K., McGrath, J. A., Fallin, M. D., Liang, K-Y., et al. (2009). Fine mapping on chromosome 10q22-q23 implicates *Neuregulin 3* in schizophrenia. *American Journal of Human Genetics, 84,* 21–34.

Chen, W., Li, S., Cook, N. R., Rosner, B. A., Srinivasan, S. R., Boerwinkle, E., & Berenson, G. S. (2004). An autosomal genome scan for loci influencing longitudinal burden of body mass index from childhood to young adulthood in white sibships. The Bogalusa Heart Study. *International Journal of Obesity, 28,* 462–469.

Chen, X., Cen, G., Li, D., & He, Y. (2005). Social functioning and adjustment in Chinese children: The imprint of historical time. *Child Development, 76,* 182–195.

Cheruku, S. R., Montgomery-Downs, H. E., Farkas, S. L., Thoman, E. B., & Lammi-Keefe C. J. (2002). Higher maternal plasma docosahexaenoic acid during pregnancy is associated with more mature neonatal sleep-state patterning. *American Journal of Clinical Nutrition, 76,* 608–613.

Chervin, R. D., Ruzicka, D. L., Giordani, B. J., Weatherly, R. A., Dillon, J. E., Hodges, E. K., et al. (2006). Sleep-disordered breathing, behavior, and cognition in children before and after adeno-tonsillectomy. *Pediatrics, 117,* e-769–e788.

Chess, S., & Thomas, A. (1982). Infant bonding: Mystique and reality. *American Journal of Orthopsychiatry, 52*(2), 213–222.

Child Trends Databank. (2012). Sexually active teens: Indicators on children and youth. Retrieved April 4, 2013, from http://www.childtrendsdatabank.org /sites/default/files/23_Sexually_Active_Teens.pdf

Child Trends Data Bank. (2013). *Family structure: Indicators on children and youth.* Retrieved from http://www.childtrendsdatabank.org/sites/default /files/59_Family_Structure.pdf

Child Welfare Information Gateway. (2008a). *Child abuse and neglect fatalities: Statistics and interventions.* Retrieved November 4, 2008, from www.childwelfare.gov/factsheets/pubs/fatality.cfm

Child Welfare Information Gateway. (2008b). *Preventing child abuse and neglect.* Retrieved February 9, 2009, from www.childwelfare.gov /preventing/

Children in North America Project. (2008). *Growing up in North America: The economic well-being of children in Canada, the United States, and Mexico.* Baltimore, MD: Annie E. Casey Foundation.

Children's Defense Fund. (1998). *The state of America's children yearbook, 1998.* Washington, DC: Author.

Children's Defense Fund. (2004). *The state of America's children 2004.* Washington, DC: Author.

Children's Defense Fund. (2008). *The state of America's children 2008.* Washington, DC: Author.

Children's Defense Fund. (2012). *The state of America's children handbook 2012.* Retrieved January 7, 2013, from http://www.childrensdefense .org/child-research-data-publications/data /soac-2012-handbook.pdf

Chiriboga, C. A., Brust, J.C.M., Bateman, D., & Hauser, W. A. (1999). Dose-response effect of fetal cocaine exposure on newborn neurologic function. *Pediatrics, 103,* 79–85.

Chodirker, B. N., Cadrin, C., Davies, G., Summers, A. M., Wilson, R. D., Winsor, E.J.T., & Young, D. (2001, July). Canadian guidelines for prenatal diagnosis: Techniques of prenatal diagnosis. *JOGC Clinical Practice Guidelines, 105.*

Chomitz, V. R., Cheung, L.W.Y., & Lieberman, E. (1995). The role of lifestyle in preventing low birth weight. *The Future of Children, 5*(1), 121–138.

Chomsky, C. S. (1969). *The acquisition of syntax in children from five to ten.* Cambridge, MA: MIT Press.

Chomsky, N. (1957). *Syntactic structures.* The Hague, The Netherlands: Mouton.

Chomsky, N. (1972). *Language and mind* (2nd ed.). New York: Harcourt Brace Jovanovich.

Chomsky, N. (1995). *The minimalist program.* Cambridge, MA: MIT Press.

Chorpita, B. P., & Barlow, D. H. (1998). The development of anxiety: The role of control in the early environment. *Psychological Bulletin, 124,* 3–21.

Christakis, D. A., Zimmerman, F. J., DiGiuseppe, D. L., & McCarty, C. A. (2004). Early television exposure andsubsequent attentional problems in children. *Pediatrics, 113,* 708–713.

Christakis, N. A., & Fowler, J. H. (2007). The spread of obesity in a large social network over 32 years. *New England Journal of Medicine, 357,* 370–379.

Christian, M. S., & Brent, R. L. (2001). Teratogen update: Evaluation of the reproductive and developmental risks of caffeine. *Teratology, 64*(1), 51–78.

Christie, J. F. (1998). Play as a medium for literacy development. In D. P. Fromberg & D. Bergen (Eds.), *Play from birth to 12 and beyond: Contexts, perspectives, and meanings* (pp. 50–55). New York: Garland.

Chu, S. Y., Bachman, D. J., Callaghan, W. M., Whitlock, E. P., Dietz, P. M., Berg, C. J., et al. (2008). Association between obesity during pregnancy and increased use of health care. *New England Journal of Medicine, 358,* 1444–1453.

Chua, E. F., Schacter, D. L., Rand-Giovanetti, E., & Sperling, R. A. (2006). Understanding metamemory: Neural correlates of the cognitive process and subjective level of confidence in recognition memory. *Neuroimage, 29*(4), 1150–1160.

Chung, H. L., & Steinberg, L. (2006). Relations between neighborhood factors, parenting behaviors, peer deviance, and delinquency among serious juvenile offenders. *Developmental Psychology, 42,* 319–331.

Cicchetti, D., & Toth, S. L. (1998). The development of depression in children and adolescents. *American Psychologist, 53,* 221–241.

Cicchino, J. B., & Rakison, D. H. (2008). Producing and processing self-propelled motion in infancy. *Developmental Psychology, 44,* 1232–1241.

Cicero, S. Curcio, P., Papageorghiou, A., Sonek, J., & Nicolaides, K. (2001). Absence of nasal bone in fetuses with trisomy 21 at 11–14 weeks of gestation: An observational study. *Lancet, 358,* 1665–1667.

Cicirelli, V. G. (1976). Family structure and interaction: Sibling effects on socialization. In M. F. McMillan & S. Henao (Eds.), *Child psychiatry: Treatment and research* (pp. 190–203). New York: Brunner/Mazel.

Cicirelli, V. G. (1994). Sibling relationships in cross-cultural perspective. *Journal of Marriage and the Family, 56,* 7–20.

Cicirelli, V. G. (1995). *Sibling relationships across the life span.* New York: Plenum Press.

Cillessen, A.H.N., & Mayeux, L. (2004). From censure to reinforcement: Developmental changes in the association between aggression and social status. *Child Development, 75,* 147–163.

Clark, L., & Tiggeman, M. (2008) Sociocultural and individual psychology predictors of body image in young girls: A prospective study. *Developmental Psychology, 44,* 1124–1134.

Clark, S. L. (2012). Strategies for reducing maternal mortality. *Seminars in Perinatology, 36*(1), 42–47.

Clarke-Stewart, K. A. (1987). Predicting child development from day care forms and features: The Chicago study. In D. A. Phillips (Ed.), *Quality in child care: What does the research tell us?* Washington, DC: National Association for the Education of Young Children.

Clayton, E. W. (2003). Ethical, legal, and social implications of genomic medicine. *New England Journal of Medicine, 349,* 562–569.

Clearfield, M. W., & Mix, K. S. (1999). Number versus contour length in infants' discrimination of small visual sets. *Current Directions in Psychological Science, 10,* 408–411.

Clément, K., Vaisse, C., Lahlou, N., Cabrol, S., Pelloux, V., Cassuto, D., et al. (1998). A mutation in the human leptin receptor gene causes obesity and pituitary dysfunction. *Nature, 392,* 398–401.

Cleveland, E., & Resse, E. (2005). Maternal structure and autonomy support in conversations about the past: Contributions to children's autobiographical memory. *Development Psychology, 41,* 376–388.

Cleveland, H. H., & Wiebe, R. P. (2003). The moderation of adolescent-to-peer similarity in tobacco and alcohol use by school level of substance use. *Child Development, 74,* 279–291.

Clifton, R. K., Muir, D. W., Ashmead, D. H., & Clarkson, M. G. (1993). Is visually guided reaching in early infancy a myth? *Child Development, 64,* 1099–1110.

Coffman, J. L., Ornstein, P. A., McCall, L. W., & Curran, P. J. (2008) Linking teachers' memory-relevant language and the development of children's memory skills. *Developmental Psychology, 44,* 1640–1654.

Cohany, S. R., & Sok, E. (2007). Trends in labor force participation of married mothers of infants. *Monthly Labor Review,* 9–16.

Cohen, L. B., & Amsel, L. B. (1998). Precursors to infants' perception of the causality of a simple event. *Infant Behavior and Development, 21,* 713–732.

Cohen, L. B., Chaput, H. H., & Cashon, C. H. (2002). A constructivist model of infant cognition. *Cognitive Development, 17,* 1323–1343.

Cohen, L. B., & Marks, K. S. (2002). How infants process addition and subtraction events. *Developmental Science, 5,* 186–201.

Cohen, L. B., & Oakes, L. M. (1993). How infants perceive a simple causal event. *Developmental Psychology, 29,* 421–433.

Cohen, L. B., Rundell, L. J., Spellman, B. A., & Cashon, C. H. (1999). Infants' perception of causal chains. *Current Directions in Psychological Science, 10,* 412–418.

Cohn, J. F., & Tronick, E. Z. (1983). Three-month-old infants' reaction to simulated maternal depression. *Child Development, 54*(1), 185–193.

Coie, J. D., & Dodge, K. A. (1998). Aggression and antisocial behavior. In W. Damon (Series Ed.) & N. Eisenberg (Vol. ed.), *Handbook of child psychology: Vol. 3. Social, emotional, and personality development* (5th Ed., pp. 780–862). New York: Wiley.

Colby, A., & Damon, W. (1992). *Some do care: Contemporary lives of moral commitment.* New York: Free Press.

Colby, A., Kohlberg, L., Gibbs, J., & Lieberman, M. (1983). A longitudinal study of moral development. *Monographs of the Society for Research in Child Development, 48*(1–2). [Serial No. 200].

Cole, M. (1998). *Cultural psychology: A once and future discipline.* Cambridge, MA: Belknap.

Cole, P. M., Barrett, K. C., & Zahn-Waxler, C. (1992). Emotion displays in two-year-olds during mishaps. *Child Development, 63,* 314–324.

Cole, P. M., Bruschi, C. J., & Tamang, B. L. (2002). Cultural differences in children's emotional reactions to difficult situations. *Child Development, 73*(3), 983–996.

Cole, T. B. (1999). Ebbing epidemic: Youth homicide rate at a 14-year low. *Journal of the American Medical Association, 281,* 25–26.

Coleman, J. S. (1988). Social capital in the creation of human capital. *American Journal of Sociology, 94*(Suppl. 95), S95–S120.

Coleman-Phox, K., Odouli, R., & Li, D-K. (2008). Use of a fan during sleep and the risk of sudden infant death syndrome. *Archives of Pediatric & Adolescent Medicine, 162*(10), 963–968.

Coley, R. L., Morris, J. E., & Hernandez, D. (2004). Out-of-school care and problem behavior trajectories among low-income adolescents: Individual, family, and neighborhood characteristics as added risks. *Child Development, 75,* 948–965.

Coley, R. L., Votruba-Drzal, E., & Schindler, H. S. (2009). Fathers' and mothers' parenting predicting and responding to adolescent sexual risk behaviors. *Child Development, 80,* 808–827.

Collier, V. P. (1995). Acquiring a second language for school. *Directions in Language and Education, 1*(4), 1–11.

Collins, J. G., & LeClere, F. B. (1997). *Health and selected socioeconomic characteristics of the family: United States, 1988–90* (DHHS No. PHS 97–1523). Washington, DC: U.S. Government Printing Office.

Collins, W. A., Maccoby, E. E., Steinberg, L., Hetherington, E. M., & Bornstein, M. H. (2000). Contemporary research in parenting: The case for nature and nurture. *American Psychologist, 55,* 218–232.

Colombo, J. (1993). *Infant cognition: Predicting later intellectual functioning.* Thousand Oaks, CA: Sage.

Colombo, J. (2002). Infant attention grows up: The emergence of a developmental cognitive neuroscience perspective. *Current Directions in Psychological Science, 11,* 196–200.

Colombo, J., & Janowsky, J. S. (1998). A cognitive neuroscience approach to individual differences in infant cognition. In J. E. Richards (Ed.), *Cognitive neuroscience of attention* (pp. 363–391). Mahwah, NJ: Erlbaum.

Colombo, J., Kannass, K. N., Shaddy, J., Kundurthi, S., Maikranz, J. M., Anderson, C. J., et al. (2004). Maternal DHA and the development of attention in infancy and toddlerhood. *Child Development, 75,* 1254–1267.

Coltrane, S., & Adams, M. (1997). Work-family imagery and gender stereotypes: Television and the reproduction of difference. *Journal of Vocational Behavior, 50,* 323–347.

Comer, J., Furr, J., Beidas, R., Weiner, C., & Kendall, P. (2008) Children and terrorism-related news: Training parents in coping and media iteracy. *Journal of Consulting and Clinical Psychology, 76*(4), 568–578.

Commissioner's Office of Research and Evaluation and Head Start Bureau, Department of Health and Human Services. (2001). *Building their futures: How Early Head Start programs are enhancing the lives of infants and toddlers in low-income families. Summary report.* Washington, DC: Author.

Committee on Obstetric Practice. (2002). ACOG committee opinion: Exercise during pregnancy and the postpartum period. *International Journal of Gynaecology & Obstetrics, 77*(1), 79–81.

Community Paediatrics Committee, Canadian Paediatrics Society. (2005). Management of primary nocturnal enuresis. *Paediatrics and Child Health, 10,* 611–614.

Conde-Agudelo, A., Rosas-Bermúdez, A., & Kafury-Goeta, A. C. (2006). Birth spacing and risk of adverse perinatal outcomes: A meta-analysis. *Journal of the American Medical Association, 295,* 1809–1823.

Conel, J. L. (1939, 1941, 1947, 1951, 1955, 1959, 1963, 1967). *The Postnatal Development of the Human Cerebral Cortex, Vols. I-VIII. Cambridge, MA:* Harvard University Press.

Conger, R. D., & Conger, K. J. (2002). Resilience in midwestern families: Selected findings from the first decade of a prospective, longitudinal study. *Journal of Marriage and Family, 64*(2), 361–373.

Conger, R. D., Conger, K. J., Elder, G. H., Jr., Lorenz, F. O., Simons, R. L., & Whitbeck, L. B. (1993). Family economic stress and adjustment of early adolescent girls. *Developmental Psychology, 29,* 206–219.

Conger, R. D., & Elder, G. H., Jr. (1994). *Families in troubled times.* New York: DeGruyter.

Conger, R. D., Ge, X., Elder, G. H., Jr., Lorenz, F. O., & Simons, R. L. (1994). Economic stress, coercive family process, and developmental problems of adolescents. *Child Development, 65*(2), 541–561.

Constantino, J. N. (2003). Autistic traits in the general population: A twin study. *Archives of General Psychiatry, 60,* 524–530.

Constantino, J. N., Grosz, D., Saenger, P., Chandler, D. W., Nandi, R., & Earls, F. J. (1993). Testosterone and aggression in children. *Journal of the Academy of Child and Adolescent Psychiatry, 32,* 1217–1222.

Cooper, H. (1989a). *Homework.* White Plains, NY: Longman.

Cooper, H. (1989b, November). Synthesis of research on homework. *Educational Leadership,* 85–91.

Cooper, H., Robinson, J. C., & Pattall, E. A. (2006). Does homework improve academic achievement? A synthesis of research, 1987–2003. *Review of Educational Research, 76*(1), 1–62.

Cooper, R. P., & Aslin, R. N. (1990). Preference for infant-directed speech in the first month after birth. *Child Development, 61,* 1584–1595.

Cooper, W. O., Hernandez-Diaz, S., Arbogast, P. G., Dudley, J. A., Dyer, S., Gideon, P. S., Hall, K., & Ray, W. A. (2006). Major congenital formations after first-trimester exposure to ACE inhibitors. *New England Journal of Medicine, 354,* 2443–2451.

Coplan, R. J., Prakash, K., O'Neil, K., & Armer, M. (2004). Do you "want" to play? Distinguishing between conflicted-shyness and social disinterest in early childhood. *Developmental Psychology, 40,* 244–258.

Corbet, A., Long, W., Schumacher, R., Gerdes, J., Cotton, R., & the American Exosurf Neonatal Study Group 1. (1995). Double-blind developmental evaluation at 1-year corrected age of 597 premature infants with birth weight from 500 to 1,350 grams enrolled in three placebo-controlled trials of prophylactic synthetic surfactant. *Journal of Pediatrics, 126,* S5–S12.

Corbin, C. (1973). *A textbook of motor development.* Dubuque, IA: Wm. C. Brown.

Correa, A., Botto, L., Liu, V., Mulinare, J., & Erickson, J. D. (2003). Do multivitamin supplements attenuate the risk for diabetes-associated birth defects? *Pediatrics, 111,* 1146–1151.

Correa, A., Gilboa, S. M., Besser, L. M., Botto, L. D., Moore, C. A., Hobbs, C. A., et al. (2008). Diabetes mellitus and birth defects. *American Journal of Obstetrics & Gynecology, 199*(237), e1–e9.

Costello, E. J., Compton, S. N., Keeler, G., & Angold, A. (2003). Relationship between poverty and psychopathology: A natural experiment. *Journal of the American Medical Association, 290,* 2023–2029.

Council on Sports Medicine and Fitness and Council on School Health. (2006). Active healthy living: Prevention of childhood obesity through increased physical activity. *Pediatrics, 117,* 1834–1842.

Courage, M. L., & Howe, M. L. (2002). From infant to child: The dynamics of cognitive change in the second year of life. *Psychological Bulletin, 128,* 250–277.

Cowan, C. P., & Cowan, P. A. (2000). *When partners become parents: The big life change for couples.* Mahwah, NJ; Erlbaum.

Cowan, N., Nugent, L. D., Elliott, E. M., Ponomarev, I., & Saults, J. S. (1999). The role of attention in the development of short-term memory: Age differences in the verbal span of apprehension. *Child Development, 70,* 1082–1097.

Cowan, W. M. (1979, September). The development of the brain. *Scientific American, 241*(3), 113–133.

Coyle, T. R., & Bjorklund, D. F. (1997). Age differences in, and consequences of, multiple- and variable-strategy use on a multitrial sort-recall task. *Developmental Psychology, 33,* 372–380.

Crain-Thoreson, C., & Dale, P. S. (1992). Do early talkers become early readers? Linguistic precocity, preschool language, and emergent literacy. *Developmental Psychology, 28,* 421–429.

Crary, D. (2007, January 6). After years of growth, foreign adoptions by Americans decline sharply. *Associated Press.*

Cratty, B. J. (1986). *Perceptual and motor development in infants and children* (3rd ed.). Upper Saddle River, NJ: Pearson Education, Inc.

Crawford, C. (1998). Environments and adaptations: Then and now. In C. Crawford & D. L. Krebs (Eds.), *Handbook of evolutionary psychology: Ideas, issues, and applications* (pp. 275–302). Mahwah, NJ: Erlbaum.

Crawford, J. (2007). The decline of bilingual education: How to reverse a troubling trend? *International Multilingual Research Journal, 1*(1), 33–38.

Crespi, B., Summers, K., & Dorus, S. (2007). Adaptive evolution of genes underlying schizophrenia. *Proceedings of the Royal Society of London B, 274,* 2801–2810.

Crespi, B. J. (2008). Genomic imprinting in the development and evolution of psychotic spectrum conditions. *Biological Reviews, 83,* 441–493.

Crick, N. R., Casas, J. F., & Nelson, D. A. (2002). Toward a more comprehensive understanding of peer maltreatment: Studies of relational victimization. *Current Directions in Psychological Science, 11*(3), 98–101.

Crick, N. R., & Dodge, K. A. (1994). A review and reformulation of social information-processing mechanisms in children's social adjustment. *Psychological Bulletin, 115,* 74–101.

Crick, N. R., & Dodge, K. A. (1996). Social information-processing mechanisms in reactive and proactive aggression. *Child Development, 67,* 993–1002.

Crick, N. R., & Grotpeter, J. K. (1995). Relational aggression, gender, and social psychological adjustment. *Child Development, 66,* 710–722.

Crockenberg, S. C. (2003). Rescuing the baby from the bathwater: How gender and temperament influence how child care affects child development. *Child Development, 74,* 1034–1038.

Cronk, L. B., Ye, B., Tester, D. J., Vatta, M., Makielski, J. C., & Ackerman, M. J. (2006, May). *Identification of CAV3-encoded caveolin-3 mutations in sudden infant death syndrome.* Presentation at Heart Rhythm 2006, the 27th Annual Scientific Sessions of the Heart Rhythm Society, Boston.

Crouter, A., & Larson, R. (Eds.). (1998). *Temporal rhythms in adolescence: Clocks, calendars, and the coordination of daily life.* [New Directions in Child and Adolescent Development, No. 82]. San Francisco: Jossey-Bass.

Crouter, A. C., MacDermid, S. M., McHale, S. M., & Perry-Jenkins, M. (1990). Parental monitoring and perception of children's school performance and conduct in dual- and single-earner families. *Developmental Psychology, 26,* 649–657.

Crowley, S. L. (1993, October). Grandparents to the rescue. *AARP Bulletin,* pp. 1, 16–17.

Cui, M., Conger, R. D., & Lorenz, F. O. (2005). Predicting change in adolescent adjustment from change in marital problems. *Developmental Psychology, 41,* 812–823.

Cunniff, C., & Committee on Genetics. (2004). Prenatal screening and diagnosis for pediatricians. *Pediatrics, 114,* 889–894.

Cunningham, F. G., & Leveno, K. J. (1995). Childbearing among older women: The message is cautiously optimistic. *New England Journal of Medicine, 333,* 1002–1004.

Currie, C., Roberts, C., Morgan, A., Smith, R., Settertobulte, W., & Samdal, O. (Eds.). (2004). *Young people's health in context.* Geneva, Switzerland: World Health Organization.

Curtiss, S. (1977). *Genie.* New York: Academic Press.

Cutter-Wilson, E. & Richmond, T. (2011). Understanding teen dating violence: Practical screening and intervention strategies for pediatric and adolescent healthcare providers. *Current Opinions in Pediatrics, 23*(4), 379–383.

Czikszentmihalyi, M. (1996). *Creativity: Flow and the psychology of discovery and invention.* New York: HarperCollins.

Daiute, C., Hartup, W. W., Sholl, W., & Zajac, R. (1993, March). *Peer collaboration and written language development: A study of friends and acquaintances.* Paper presented at the meeting of the Society for Research in Child Development, New Orleans, LA.

Dale, P. S., Simonoff, E., Bishop, D.V.M., Eley, T. C., Oliver, B., Price, T. S., et al. (1998). Genetic influence on language delay in two-year-old children. *Nature Neuroscience, 1,* 324–328.

Daly, M., & Wilson, M. (1988). *Homicide.* Hawthorne, NY: Aldine de Gruyter.

Daly, R. (2005). Drop in youth antidepressant use prompts call for FDA monitoring. *Psychiatric News, 40*(19), 18.

Danesi, M. (1994). *Cool: The signs and meanings of adolescence.* Toronto, Canada: University of Toronto Press.

Daniel, I., Berg, C., Johnson, C. H., & Atrash, H. (2003). Magnitude of maternal morbidity during labor and delivery: United States, 1993–1997. *American Journal of Public Health, 93,* 633–634.

Daniels, S. R., Greer, F. R., & the Committee on Nurition. (2008). Lipid screening and cardiovascular health in childhood. *Pediatrics, 122,* 198–208.

Darling, N., Kolasa, M., & Wooten, K. G. (2008). National, state, and local area vaccination coverage among children aged 19–35 Months—United States, 2007. *Morbidity & Mortality Weekly Report, 57*(35), 961–966.

Darling, N., & Steinberg, L. (1993). Parenting style as context: An integrative model. *Psychological Bulletin, 113,* 487–496.

Darroch, J. E., Singh, S., Frost, J. J., & the Study Team. (2001). Differences in teenage pregnancy rates among five developed countries: The roles of sexual activity and contraceptive use. *Family Planning Perspectives, 33,* 244–250, 281.

Darwin, C. (1871). *The descent of man, and selection in relation to sex.* London: John Murray.

Darwin, C. (1872). *The expression of the emotions in man and animals.* Chicago, IL: University of Chicago Press.

Datar, A., & Sturm, R. (2004a). Childhood overweight and parent- and teacher-reported behavior problems. *Archives of Pediatric and Adolescent Medicine, 158,* 804–810.

Datar, A., & Sturm, R. (2004b). Duke physical education in elementary school and body mass index: Evidence from the Early Childhood Longitudinal Study. *American Journal of Public Health, 94,* 1501–1507.

David and Lucile Packard Foundation. (2004). Children, families, and foster care: Executive summary. *The Future of Children, 14*(1). Retrieved from www.futureofchildren.org

Davidson, J.I.F. (1998). Language and play: Natural partners. In D. P. Fromberg & D. Bergen (Eds.), *Play from birth to 12 and beyond: Contexts, perspectives, and meanings* (pp. 175–183). New York: Garland.

Davidson, R. J., & Fox, N. A. (1989). Frontal brain asymmetry predicts infants' response to maternal separation. *Journal of Abnormal Psychology, 948*(2), 58–64.

Davis, A. S. (2008). Children with Down syndrome: Implications for assessment and intervention in the school. *School Psychology Quarterly, 23,* 271–281.

Davis, B. E., Moon, R. Y., Sachs, H. C., & Ottolini, M. C. (1998). Effects of sleep position on infant motor development. *Pediatrics, 102*(5), 1135–1140.

Davis, M., & Emory, E. (1995). Sex differences in neonatal stress reactivity. *Child Development, 66,* 14–27.

Davison, K. K., & Birch, L. L. (2001). Weight status, parent reaction, and self concept in 5-year-old girls. *Pediatrics, 107,* 46–53.

Davison, K. K., Susman, E. J., & Birch, L. L. (2003). Percent body fat at age 5 predicts earlier pubertal development among girls at age 9. *Pediatrics, 111,* 815–821.

Dawson, D. A. (1991). Family structure and children's health and well-being. Data from the 1988 National Health Interview Survey on child health. *Journal of Marriage and the Family, 53,* 573–584.

Dawson, G. (2007). Despite major challenges, autism research continues to offer hope. *Archives of Pediatric and Adolescent Medicine, 161,* 411–412.

Dawson, G., Frey, K., Panagiotides, H., Yamada, E., Hessl, D., & Osterling, J. (1999). Infants of depressed mothers exhibit atypical frontal electrical brain activity during interactions with mother and with a familiar nondepressed adult. *Child Development, 70,* 1058–1066.

Dawson, G., Klinger, L. G., Panagiotides, H., Hill, D., & Spieker, S. (1992). Frontal lobe activity and affective behavior of infants of mothers with depressive symptoms. *Child Development, 63,* 725–737.

Day, J. C., Janus, A., & Davis, J. (2005). Computer and Internet use in the United States: 2003. *Current Population Reports* (P23-208). Washington, DC: U.S. Census Bureau.

Day, S. (1993, May). Why genes have a gender. *New Scientist, 138*(1874), 34–38.

de Castro, B. O., Veerman, J. W., Koops, W., Bosch, J. D., & Monshouwer, H. J. (2002). Hostile attribution of intent and aggressive behavior: A meta-analysis. *Child Development, 73,* 916–934.

de Roos, S. (2006). Young children's God concepts: Influences of attachment and religious socialization in a family and school context. *Religious Education, 101*(1), 84–103.

De Schipper, E., Riksen-Walraven, M., & Geurts, S. (2006). Effects of child-caregiver ratio on the interactions between caregivers and children in child-care centers: An experimental study. *Child Development, 77*(4), 861–874.

De Wolff, M. S., & van IJzendoorn, M. H. (1997). Sensitivity and attachment: A meta-analysis on parental antecedents of infant attachment. *Child Development, 68,* 571–591.

Deardorff, J., Gonzales, N. A., Christopher, S., Roosa, M. W., & Millsap, R. E. (2005). Early puberty and adolescent pregnancy: The influence of alcohol use. *Pediatrics, 116,* 1451–1456.

DeBell, M., & Chapman, C. (2006). *Computer and Internet use by students in 2003: Statistical analysis report* (NCES 2006-065). Washington, DC: National Center for Education Statistics.

DeCasper, A. J., & Fifer, W. P. (1980). Of human bonding: Newborns prefer their mothers' voices. *Science, 208,* 1174–1176.

DeCasper, A. J., Lecanuet, J. P., Busnel, M. C., Granier-Deferre, C., & Maugeais, R. (1994). Fetal reactions to recurrent maternal speech. *Infant Behavior and Development, 17,* 159–164.

DeCasper, A. J., & Spence, M. J. (1986). Prenatal maternal speech influences newborns' perceptions of speech sounds. *Infant Behavior and Development, 9,* 133–150.

Decety, J., Michalaska, K., Akitsuki, Y., & Lahey, B. (2009). Atypical empathetic responses in adolescents with aggressive conduct disorder: A functional MRI investigation. *Biological Psychology, 80,* 203–211.

Dee, D. L., Li, R., Lee, L., & Grummer-Strawn, L. M. (2007). Association between breastfeeding practices and young children's language and motor development. *Pediatrics, 119*(Suppl. 1), 592–598.

DeFranco, E. A., Stamilio, D. M., Boslaugh, S. E., Gross, G. A., & Muglia, L. J. (2007). A short interpregnancy interval is a risk factor for preterm birth and its recurrence. *American Journal of Obstetrics and Gynecology,* 197(264), e1–e6.

Dekovic, M., & Janssens, J. (1992). Parents' child-rearing style and child's sociometric status. *Developmental Psychology, 28,* 925–932.

Delaney, C. (2000). Making babies in a Turkish village. In J. DeLoache & A. Gottlieb (Eds.), *A world of babies: Imagined childcare guides for seven societies* (pp. 117–144). New York: Cambridge University Press.

DeLoache, J. S. (2006). Mindful of symbols. *Scientific American Mind, 17,* 70–75.

DeLoache, J., & Gottlieb, A. (2000). If Dr. Spock were born in Bali: Raising a world of babies. In J. DeLoache & A. Gottlieb (Eds.), *A world of babies: Imagined childcare guides for seven societies* (pp. 1–27). New York: Cambridge University Press.

DeLoache, J. S., Miller, K. F., & Pierroutsakos, S. L. (1998). Reasoning and problem solving. In D. Kuhn & R. S. Siegler (Eds.), *Handbook of child psychology: Vol. 2. Cognition, perception, and language* (5th ed., pp. 801–850). New York: Wiley.

DeLoache, J. S., Pierroutsakos, S. L., & Uttal, D. H. (2003). The origins of pictorial competence. *Current Directions in Psychological Science, 12,* 114–118.

DeLoache, J. S., Pierroutsakos, S. L., Uttal, D. H., Rosengren, K. S., & Gottlieb, A. (1998). Grasping the nature of pictures. *Psychological Science, 9,* 205–210.

DeLoache, J. S., Uttal, D. H., & Rosengren, K. S. (2004). Scale errors offer evidence for a perception-action dissociation early in life. *Science, 304,* 1027–1029.

Deming, D. (2009). Early childhood intervention and life-cycle skill development: Evidence from Head Start. *American Economic Journal: Applied Economics, 1*(3), 111–134.

DeNavas-Walt, C., Proctor, B. D., & Smith, J. C. (2012). U.S. Census Bureau, *Current Population Reports, P60-243, Income, Poverty, and Health Insurance* Washington, DC: U.S. Government Printing Office. *Coverage in the United States: 2011.* Washington, DC: U.S. Government Printing Office.

Denham, S. A., Blair, K. A., DeMulder, E., Levitas, J., Sawyer, K., Auerbach-Major, S., & Queenan, P. (2003). Preschool emotional competence: Pathway to social competence? *Child Development, 74,* 238–256.

Dennis, T. (2006). Emotional self-regulation in preschoolers: The interplay of child approach reactivity, parenting, and control capacities. *Developmental Psychology, 42,* 84–97.

Dennis, W. (1936). A bibliography of baby biographies. *Child Development, 7,* 71–73.

Denton, K., West, J., & Walston, J. (2003). *Reading—young children's achievement and classroom experiences: Findings from The Condition of Education 2003.* Washington, DC: National Center for Education Statistics.

Department of Immunization, Vaccines, and Biologicals, World Health Organization; United

Nations Children's Fund; Global Immunization Division, National Center for Immunization and Respiratory Diseases (proposed); & McMorrow, M. (2006). Vaccine preventable deaths and the global immunization vision and strategy, 2006–2015. *Morbidity and Mortality Weekly Report, 55,* 511–515.

Deptula, D. P., & Cohen, R. (2004). Aggressive, rejected, and delinquent children and adolescents: A comparison of their friendships. *Aggression and Violent Behavior, 9*(1), 75–104.

Derringer, J., Krueger, R. F., Dick, D. M., Saccone, S, Grucza, R. A., Agrawal, A., & Gene Environment Association Studies (GENEVA) Consortium. (2011). Predicting sensation seeking from dopamine genes: A candidate-system approach. *Psychological Science, 2,* 413–415. doi:10.1177/0956797610380699

Detrich, R., Phillips, R., & Durett, D. (2002). *Critical issue: Dynamic debate—determining the evolving impact of charter schools.* North Central Regional Educational Laboratory. Retrieved from www.ncrel.org/sdrs/areas/issues/envrnmnt/go/go800.htm

Deutsch, F. M., Servis, L. J. & Payne, J. D. (2001). Paternal participation in child care and its effects on children's self-esteem and attitudes toward gender roles. *Journal of Family Issues, 22*(8), 1000–1024.

Devaney, B., Johnson, A., Maynard, R., & Trenholm, C. (2002). *The evaluation of abstinence education programs funded under Title V, Section 510: Interim report.* Washington, DC: U.S. Department of Health and Human Services.

DeVoe, J. F., Peter, K., Kaufman, P., Miller, A., Noonan, M., Snyder, T. D., & Baum, K. (2004). *Indicators of school crime and safety: 2004* (NCES 2005-002/NCJ 205290). Washington, DC: U.S. Departments of Education and Justice.

Dewing, P., Shi, T., Horvath, S., & Vilain, E. (2003). Sexually dimorphic gene expression in mouse brain precedes gonadal differentiation. *Molecular Brain Research, 118,* 82–90.

Diamond, A. (1991). Neuropsychological insights into the meaning of object concept development. In S. Carey & R. Gelman (Eds.), *Epigensis of mind* (pp. 67–110). Hillsdale, NJ: Erlbaum.

Diamond, A. (2002). Normal development of prefrontal cortex from birth to young adulthood: Cognitive functions, anatomy, and biochemistry. In D.T. Strauss & R.T. Knight (Eds.), *Principles of frontal lobe function* (pp. 466–503). New York: Oxford University Press.

Diamond, A. (2007). Interrelated and interdependent. *Developmental Science, 10,* 152–158.

Diamond, L. M., & Savin-Williams, R. C. (2003). The intimate relationships of sexual-minority youths. In G. R. Adams & M. D. Berzonsky (Eds.), *Blackwell handbook of adolescence* (pp. 393–412). Malden, MA: Blackwell.

Diamond, M., & Sigmundson, H. K. (1997). Sex reassignment at birth: Longterm review and clinical implications. *Archives of Pediatric and Adolescent Medicine, 151,* 298–304.

Dick, D. M., Alieve, F., Kramer, J., Wang, J., Anthony, H., Bertelsen, S., et al. (2007). Association of CHRM2 with IQ: Converging evidence for a gene influencing intelligence. *Behavioral Genetics, 37*(2), 265–272.

Dick, D. M., Rose, R. J., Kaprio, J., & Viken, R. (2000). Pubertal timing and substance use: Associations between and within families across late adolescence. *Developmental Psychology, 36,* 180–189.

Dickens, W. T., & Flynn, J. R. (2006). Black Americans reduce the racial IQ gap: Evidence from standardization samples. *Psychological Science, 17*(10), 913–920.

Diemand-Yauman, C., Oppenheimer, D., & Vaughan, E. (2011). Fortune favors the bold (and the italicized): Effects of disfluency on educational outcomes. *Cognition, 118*(1), 111–115. doi: 10.1016/j.cognition.2010.09.012

Dietert, R. R. (2005). Developmental immunotoxicology (DIT): Is DIT testing necessary to ensure safety? *Proceedings of the 14th Immunotoxicology Summer School, Lyon, France, October 2005,* 246–257.

DiFranza, J. R., Aligne, C. A., & Weitzman, M. (2004). Prenatal and postnatal environmental tobacco smoke exposure and children's health. *Pediatrics, 113,* 1007–1015.

Dillon, R. M. (2009, February 1). Woman with octuplets obsessed with having kids: Mom. *Chicago Sun-Times,* p. 18A.

Dilworth-Bart, J. E., & Moore., C. F. (2006). Mercy mercy me: Social injustice and the prevention of environmental pollutant exposures among ethnic minority and poor children. (2006). *Child Development, 77*(2), 247–265.

DiMarco, M. A., Menke, E. M., & McNamara, T. (2001). Evaluating a support group for peri-natal loss. *MCN American Journal of Maternal and Child Nursing, 26,* 135–140.

Dingfelder, S. (2004). Programmed for psychopathology? Stress during pregnancy may increase children's risk for mental illness, researchers say. *Monitor on Psychology, 35*(2), 56–57.

DiPietro, J. A. (2004). The role of prenatal maternal stress in child development. *Current Directions in Psychological Science, 13*(2), 71–74.

DiPietro, J. A., Bornstein, M. H., Costigan, K. A., Pressman, E. K., Hahn, C. S., Painter, K., et al. (2002). What does fetal movement predict about behavior during the first two years of life? *Developmental Psychobiology, 40*(4), 358–371.

DiPietro, J. A., Hodgson, D. M., Costigan, K. A., Hilton, S. C., & Johnson, T.R.B. (1996). Development of fetal movement fetal heart rate coupling from 20 weeks through term. *Early Human Development, 44,* 139–151.

DiPietro, J. A., Novak, M.F.S.X., Costigan, K. A., Atella, L. D., & Reusing, S. P. (2006). Maternal psychological distress during pregnancy in relation to child development at age 2. *Child Development, 77*(3), 573–587.

Dishion, T. J., McCord, J., & Poulin, F. (1999). When intervention harms. *American Psychologist, 54,* 755–764.

Dishion, T. J., Shaw, D., Connell, A., Garnder, F., Weaver, C., & Wilson, M. (2008). The family check-up with high-risk indigent families: Preventing problem behavior by increasing parents' positive behavior support in early childhood. *Child Development, 79,* 1395–1414.

Dishion. T., J., & Stormshak, E. (2007) *Intervening in children's lives: An ecological, family-centered approach to mental health care.* Washington, DC: APA Books.

Dishion, T. J., & Tipsord, J.M. (2011). Peer contagion in child and adolescent social and emotional development. *Annual Review of Psychology, 62,* 189–214.

Dittmar, H., Halliwell, E., & Ive, S. (2006). Does Barbie make girls want to be thin? The effect of experimental exposure to images of dolls on the body image of 5- to 8-year-old girls. *Developmental Psychology, 42,* 283–292.

Dodge, K. A., Coie, J. D., & Lynam, D. (2006). Aggression and antisocial behavior in youth. In N. Eisenberg, W. Damon, and R. Lerner (Eds.) *Handbook of Child Psychology: Vol. 3, Social, emotional and personality development* (6th ed.), pp. 719–788. Hoboken, NJ: Wiley.

Dodge, K. A., Coie, J. D., Pettit, G. S., & Price, J. M. (1990). Peer status and aggression in boys' groups: Developmental and contextual analysis. *Child Development, 61,* 1289–1309.

Dodge, K. A., Dishion, T. J., & Lansford, J. E. (2006). Deviant peer influences in intervention and public policy for youth. *Social Policy Report, 20,* 3–19.

Dodge, K. A., Pettit, G. S., & Bates, J. E. (1994). Socialization mediators of the relation between socioeconomic status and child conduct problems. *Child Development, 65,* 649–665.

Dollinger, S. J. (2007). Creativity and conservatism. *Personality and Individual Differences, 43,* 1025–1035.

D'Onofrio, B. M., Turkheimer, E., Emery, R. E., Slutske, W. S., Heath, A. C., Madden, P. A., & Martin, N. G. (2006). A genetically informed study of the processes underlying the association between parental marital instability and offspring adjustment. *Developmental Psychology, 42,* 486–499.

Donovan, W. L., Leavitt, L. A., & Walsh, R. O. (1998). Conflict and depression predict maternal sensitivity to infant cries. *Infant Behavior and Development, 21,* 505–517.

Dougherty, T. M., & Haith, M. M. (1997). Infant expectations and reaction time as predictors of childhood speed of processing and IQ. *Developmental Psychology, 33,* 146–155.

Dowshen, S., Crowley, J., & Palusci, V. J. (2004). Shaken baby/shaken impact syndrome. Retrieved February 17, 2007, from www.kidshealth.org /parent/brain/medical/shaken.html

Dozier, M., Stovall, K. C., Albus, K. E., & Bates, B. (2001). Attachment for infants in foster care: The role of caregiver state of mind. *Child Development, 72,* 1467–1477.

Drabick, D.A.G., Gadow, K. D., & Sprafkin, J. (2006). Co-occurrence of conduct disorder and depression in a clinic-based sample of boys with ADHD. *Journal of Child Psychology and Pscyhiatry, 47*(8), 766–774.

Drewnowski, A., & Eichelsdoerfer, P. (2009). The Mediterranean diet: Does it have to cost more? *Public Health Nutrition, 12*(9A), 1621–1628.

Drug Policy Alliance. (2004, June 23). *South Carolina v. McKnight.* Retrieved April 6, 2005, from www.drugpolicy.org/womenpregnan/law /mcknight.cfm

Drumm, P., & Jackson, D. W. (1996). Developmental changes in questioning strategies during adolescence. *Journal of Adolescent Research, 11,* 285–305.

Dubé, E. M., & Savin-Williams, R. C. (1999). Sexual identity development among ethnic sexual-minority youths. *Developmental Psychology, 35*(6), 1389–1398.

Dube, S. R., Anda, R. F., Felitti, V. J., Chapman, D. P., Williamson, D. F., & Giles, W. H. (2001). Childhood abuse, household dysfunction, and the risk of attempted suicide throughout the life span: Findings from the Adverse Childhood Experiences Study. *Journal of the American Medical Association, 286*(24), 3089–3096.

Dube, S. R., Anda, R. F., Whitfield, C. L., Brown, D. W., Felitti, V. J., Dong, M., & Giles, W. H. (2005) Long-term consequences of childhood

sexual abuse by gender of victim. *American Journal of Preventative Medicine, 28*(5), 430–438.

Dube, S. R., Felitti, V. J., Dong, M., Chapman, D. P., Giles, W. H., & Anda, R. F. (2003, March). Childhood abuse, neglect, and household dysfunction and the risk of illicit drug use: The Adverse Childhood Experiences Study. *Pediatrics, 111*(3), 564–572.

Duckworth, A., & Seligman, M.E.P. (2005). Self-discipline outdoes IQ in predicting academic performance of adolescents. *Psychological Science, 26,* 939–944.

Duenwald, M. (2003, July 15). After 25 years, new ideas in the prenatal test tube. *New York Times.* Retrieved from www.nytimes.com/2003/07/15 /health/15IVF.html?ex

Duke, J., Huhman, M., & Heitzler, C. (2003). Physical activity levels among children aged 9–13 years—United States, 2002. *Morbidity and Mortality Weekly Report, 52,* 785–788.

Duncan, G. J., & Brooks-Gunn, J. (1997). Income effects across the life span: Integration and interpretation. In G. J. Duncan & J. Brooks-Gunn (Eds.), *Consequences of growing up poor* (pp. 596–610). New York: Russell Sage Foundation.

Dunn, J. (1985). *Sisters and brothers.* Cambridge, MA: Harvard University Press.

Dunn, J. (1991). Young children's understanding of other people: Evidence from observations within the family. In D. Frye & C. Moore (Eds.), *Children's theories of mind: Mental states and social understanding* (pp. 97–114). Hillsdale, NJ: Erlbaum.

Dunn, J. (1996). Sibling relationships and perceived self-competence: Patterns of stability between childhood and early adolescence. In A. J. Sameroff & M. M. Haith (Eds.), *The five to seven year shift: The age of reason and responsibility* (pp. 253–269). Chicago: University of Chicago Press.

Dunn, J. (2006). Moral development in early childhood and social interaction in the family. In M. Killen & J. Smetana (Eds), *Handbook of Moral Development,* (p. 331–350). Mahwah, NJ: Earlbaum.

Dunn, J., Brown, J., Slomkowski, C., Tesla, C., & Youngblade, L. (1991). Young children's understanding of other people's feelings and beliefs: Individual differences and antecedents. *Child Development, 62,* 1352–1366.

Dunn, J., & Hughes, C. (2001). "I got some swords and you're dead!": Violent fantasy, antisocial behavior, friendship, and moral sensibility in young children. *Child Development, 72,* 491–505.

Dunn, J., & Kendrick, C. (1982). *Siblings: Love, envy and understanding.* Cambridge, MA: Harvard University Press.

Dunn, J., & Munn, P. (1985). Becoming a family member: Family conflict and the development of social understanding in the second year. *Child Development, 56,* 480–492.

Dunham, P., Dunham, F., & O'Keefe, C. (2000). Two-year-olds' sensitivity to a parent's knowledge state: Mind reading or contextual cues? *British Journal of Developmental Psychology, 18*(4), 519 –532.

Dunson, D. (2002). *Late breaking research session. Increasing infertility with increasing age: Good news and bad news for older couples.* Paper presented at 18th Annual Meeting of the European Society of Human Reproduction and Embryology, Vienna.

Dunson, D. B., Colombo, B., & Baird, D. D. (2002). Changes with age in the level and duration of fertility in the menstrual cycle. *Human Reproduction, 17,* 1399–1403.

DuPont, R. L. (1983). Phobias in children. *Journal of Pediatrics, 102,* 999–1002.

Dux, P. E., Ivanoff, J. G., Asplund, C. L., & Marois, R. (2006). Isolation of a central bottleneck of information processing with time-resolved fMRI. *Neuron, 52*(6), 1109–1120.

Dweck, C. S. (2008). Mindsets: How praise is harming youth and what can be done about it. *School Library Medical Activities Monthly, 24*(5), 55–58.

Dweck, C. S., & Grant, H. (2008). Self theories, goals, and meaning. In J. Y. Shaw & W. L. Gardner (Eds.). *Handbook of motivation science* (pp. 405–416). New York: Guilford Press.

Dwyer, T., Ponsonby, A. L., Blizzard, L., Newman, N. M., & Cochrane, J. A. (1995). The contribution of changes in the prevalence of prone sleeping position to the decline in sudden infant death syndrome in Tasmania. *Journal of the American Medical Association, 273,* 783–789.

Dye, J. L. (2010). *Fertility of American women: 2008.* Retrieved November 20, 2012 from http:// www.census.gov/prod/2010pubs/p20-563.pdf

Dye, J. L., & Johnson, T. D. (2009). A child's day: 2006 (selected indicators of child well-being). *Current Population Reports* (P70-118). Washington, DC: U.S. Census Bureau.

East, P. L., & Khoo, S. T. (2005). Longitudinal pathways linking family factors and sibling relationship qualities to adolescent substance use and sexual risk behaviors. *Journal of Family Psychology, 19,* 571–580.

Eating disorders—Part I. (1997, October). *The Harvard Mental Health Letter,* pp. 1–5.

Eaton, D. K., Kann, L., Kinchen, S., Shanklin, S., Ross, J., Hawkins, J., et al. (2008). Youth risk behavior surveillance—United States, 2007. *Morbidity and Mortality Weekly Report, 57*(SS-4), 1–131.

Eccles, A. (1982). *Obstetrics and gynaecology in Tudor and Stuart England.* Kent, OH: Kent State University Press.

Eccles, J. S. (2004). Schools, academic motivation, and stage-environment fit. In R. M. Lerner & L. Steinberg (Eds), *Handbook of adolescent development* (2nd ed., pp. 125–153). Hoboken, NJ: Wiley.

Eccles, J. S., Wigfield, A., & Byrnes, J. (2003). Cognitive development in adolescence. In I. B. Weiner (Ed.), *Handbook of psychology: Vol. 6. Developmental psychology* (pp. 325–350). New York: Wiley.

Eccles, R. (1978). The central rhythm of the nasal cycle. *Acta Oto-laryngologica, 86* (5–6), 464–468.

Echeland, Y., Epstein, D. J., St-Jacques, B., Shen, L., Mohler, J., McMahon, J. A., & McMahon, A. P. (1993). Sonic hedgehog, a member of a family of putative signality molecules, is implicated in the regulation of CNS polarity. *Cell, 75,* 1417–1430.

Ecker, J. L., & Frigoletto, F. D., Jr. (2007). Cesarean delivery and the risk-benefit calculus. *New England Journal of Medicine, 356,* 885–888.

Eckerman, C. O., Davis, C. C., & Didow, S. M. (1989). Toddlers' emerging ways of achieving social coordination with a peer. *Child Development, 60,* 440–453.

Eckerman, C. O., & Didow, S. M. (1996). Nonverbal imitation and toddlers' mastery of verbal means of achieving coordinated action. *Developmental Psychology, 32,* 141–152.

Eckerman, C. O., & Stein, M. R. (1982). The toddler's emerging interactive skills. In K. H. Rubin & H. S. Ross (Eds.), *Peer relationships and social skills in childhood* (pp. 41–71). New York: Springer-Verlag.

Eddleman, K. A., Malone, F. D., Sullivan, L., Dukes, K., Berkowitz, R. L., & Kharbutli, Y., et al. (2006). Pregnancy loss rates after midtrimester amniocentesis. *Obstetrics and Gynecology, 108*(5), 1067–1072.

Eden, G. F., Jones, K. M., Cappell, K., Gareau, L., Wood, F. B., Zeffiro, T. A., et al. (2004). Neural changes following remediation in adult developmental dyslexia. *Neuron, 44,* 411–422.

Eder, W., Ege, M. J., & von Mutius, E. (2006). The asthma epidemic. *New England Journal of Medicine, 355,* 2226–2235.

Edwards, C. P. (1981). The comparative study of the development of moral judgment and reasoning. In R. Monroe, R. Monroe, & B. B. Whiting (Eds.), *Handbook of cross-cultural human development* (pp. 501–526). New York: Garland.

Edwards, C. P. (1994, April). *Cultural relativity meets best practice, or, anthropology and early education, a promising friendship.* Paper presented at the meeting of the American Educational Research Association, New Orleans.

Edwards, C. P. (2002). Three approaches from Europe: Waldorf, Montessori, and Reggio Emilia. *Early Childhood Research and Practice, 4*(1), 14–38.

Edwards, C. P. (2003). "Fine designs" from Italy: Montessori education and the Reggio Emilia approach. *Montesorri Life: Journal of the American Montessori Society, 15*(1), 33–38.

Ehrenreich, B., & English, D. (2005). *For her own good: Two centuries of the experts' advice to women.* New York: Anchor.

Eichler, E. E., & Zimmerman, A. W. (2008). A hot spot of genetic instability in autism. *New England Journal of Medicine, 358,* 737–739.

Eiger, M. S., & Olds, S. W. (1999). *The complete book of breastfeeding* (3rd ed.). New York: Workman.

Eimas, P. (1985). The perception of speech in early infancy. *Scientific American, 252*(1), 46–52.

Eimas, P., Siqueland, E., Jusczyk, P., & Vigorito, J. (1971). Speech perception in infants. *Science, 171,* 303–306.

Einarson, A., & Boskovic, R. (2009). Use and safety of antipsychotic drugs during pregnancy. *Journal of Psychiatric Practice, 15*(3), 183–192.

Eisenberg, A. R. (1996). The conflict talk of mothers and children: Patterns related to culture, SES, and gender of child. *Merrill-Palmer Quarterly, 42,* 438–452.

Eisenberg, N. (1992). *The caring child.* Cambridge, MA: Harvard University Press.

Eisenberg, N. (2000). Emotion, regulation, and moral development. *Annual Review of Psychology, 51,* 665–697.

Eisenberg, N., & Fabes, R. A. (1998). Prosocial development. In W. Damon (Series Ed.), & N. Eisenberg (Vol. Ed.), *Handbook of child psychology: Vol. 3. Social, emotional, and personality development* (5th ed., pp. 701–778). New York: Wiley.

Eisenberg, N., Fabes, R. A., & Murphy, B. C. (1996). Parents' reactions to children's negative emotions: Relations to children's social competence and comforting behavior. *Child Development, 67,* 2227–2247.

Eisenberg, N., Fabes, R. A., Nyman, M., Bernzweig, J., & Pinuelas, A. (1994). The relations of emotionality and regulation to children's anger-related reactions. *Child Development, 65,* 109–128.

Eisenberg, N., Fabes, R. A., Shepard, S. A., Guthrie, I. K., Murphy, B. C., & Reiser, M. (1999). Parental reactions to children's negative emotions: Longitudinal relations to quality of children's social functioning. *Child Development, 70*(2), 513–534.

Eisenberg, N., Fabes, R. A., & Spinrad, T. L. (2006). Prosocial development. In W. Damon & R. M. Lerner (Series Eds.) & N. Eisenberg (Vol. Ed.), *Handbook of child psychology: Vol 3. Social, emotional and personality development* (pp. 646–718). Hoboken: NJ: Wiley.

Eisenberg, N., Guthrie, I. K., Fabes, R. A., Reiser, M., Murphy, B. C., Holgren, R., Maszk, P., & Losoya, S. (1997). The relations of regulation and emotionality to resiliency and competent social functioning in elementary school children. *Child Development, 68,* 295–311.

Eisenberg, N., & Morris, A. D. (2004). Moral cognitions and prosocial responding in adolescence. In R. M. Lerner & L. Steinberg (Eds.), *Handbook of adolescent psychology* (2nd ed., pp. 155–188). Hoboken, NJ: Wiley.

Eisenberg, N., Spinrad, T. L., Fabes, R. A., Reiser, M., Cumberland, A., Shepard, S. A., et al. (2004). The relations of effortful control and impulsivity to children's resiliency and adjustment. *Child Development, 75,* 25–46.

Elder, G. H., Jr. (1974). *Children of the Great Depression: Social change in life experience.* Chicago: University of Chicago Press.

Elder, G. H., Jr. (1998). The life course as developmental theory. *Child Development, 69*(1), 1–12.

Elia, J., Ambrosini, P. J., & Rapoport, J. L. (1999). Treatment of attention-deficit hyperactivity disorder. *New England Journal of Medicine, 340,* 780–788.

Elicker, J., Englund, M., & Sroufe, L. A. (1992). Predicting peer competence and peer relationships in childhood from early parent-child relationships. In R. Parke & G. Ladd (Eds.), *Family peer relationships: Modes of linkage* (pp. 77–106). Hillsdale, NJ: Erlbaum.

Eliot, L. (1999). *What's going on in there? How the brain and mind develop in the first five years of life.* New York: Bantam Books.

Elkind, D. (1981). *The hurried child.* Reading, MA: Addison-Wesley.

Elkind, D. (1984). *All grown up and no place to go.* Reading, MA: Addison-Wesley.

Elkind, D. (1986). *The miseducation of children: Superkids at risk.* New York: Knopf.

Elkind, D. (1997). *Reinventing childhood: Raising and educating children in a changing world.* Rosemont, NJ: Modern Learning Press.

Elkind, D. (1998). Teenagers in crisis: *All grown up and no place to go.* Reading, MA: Perseus Books.

Elliott, D. S. (1993). Health enhancing and health compromising lifestyles. In S. G. Millstein, A. C. Petersen, & E. O. Nightingale (Eds.), *Promoting the health of adolescents: New directions for the twenty-first century* (pp. 119–145). New York: Oxford University Press.

Elliott, V. S. (2000, November 20). Doctors caught in middle of ADHD treatment controversy: Critics charge that medications are being both under- and overprescribed. *AMNews.* Retrieved April 21, 2005, from www.ama-assn.org/amednews /2000/11/20/hlsb1120.htm

Ellis, B. J., Bates, J. E., Dodge, K. A., Fergusson, D. M., Horwood, L. J., Pettit, G. S., & Woodward, L. (2003). Does father-absence place daughters at special risk for early sexual activity and teenage pregnancy? *Child Development, 74,* 801–821.

Ellis, B. J., & Garber, J. (2000). Psychosocial antecedents of variation in girls' pubertal timing: Maternal depression, stepfather presence, and marital family stress. *Child Development, 71*(2), 485–501.

Ellis, B. J., McFadyen-Ketchum, S., Dodge, K. A., Pettit, G. S., & Bates, J. E. (1999). Quality of early family relationships and individual differences in the timing of pubertal maturation in girls: A longitudinal test of an evolutionary model. *Journal of Personality and Social Psychology, 77,* 387–401.

Ellis, K. J., Abrams, S. A., & Wong, W. W. (1997). Body composition of a young, multiethnic female population. *American Journal of Clinical Nutrition, 65,* 724–731.

Ellison, M., Hotamisligil, S., Lee, H., Rich-Edwards, J., Pang, S., & Hall, J. (2005). Psychosocial risks associated with multiple births resulting from assisted reproduction. *Fertility and Sterility, 83,* 1422–1428.

Eltzschig, H. K., Lieberman, E. S., & Camann, W. R. (2003). Regional anesthesia and analgesia for labor and delivery. *New England Journal of Medicine, 348,* 319–332.

Emde, R. N., Plomin, R., Robinson, J., Corley, R., DeFries, J., Fulker, D. W., et al. (1992). Temperament, emotion, and cognition at 14 months: The MacArthur longitudinal twin study. *Child Development, 63,* 1437–1455.

Engle, P. L., Black, M. M., Behrman, J. R., de Mello, M. C., Gertler, P. J., Kapiriri, et al. (2007). Strategies to avoid the loss of developmental potential in more than 200 million children in the developing world. *The Lancet, 369*(9557), 20–26.

Engle, P. L., & Breaux, C. (1998). Fathers' involvement with children: Perspectives from developing countries. *Social Policy Report, 12*(1), 1–21.

Eogan, M. A., Geary, M. P., O'Connell, M. P., & Keane, D. P. (2003). Effect of fetal sex on labour and delivery: Retrospective review. *British Medical Journal, 326,* 137.

Erdley, C. A., Cain, K. M., Loomis, C. C., Dumas-Hines, F., & Dweck, C. S. (1997). Relations among children's social goals, implicit personality theories, and responses to social failure. *Developmental Psychology, 33,* 263–272.

Erikson, E. H. (1950). *The life cycle completed.* New York: Norton.

Erikson, E. H. (1968). *Identity: Youth and crisis.* New York: Norton.

Erikson, E. H. (1973). The wider identity. In K. Erikson (Ed.), *In search of common ground: Conversations with Erik H. Erikson and Huey P. Newton.* New York: Norton.

Erikson, E. H. (1982). *The life cycle completed.* New York: Norton.

Erikson, E. H., Erikson, J. M., & Kivnick, H. Q. (1986). *Vital involvement in old age: The experience of old age in our time.* New York: Norton.

Eriksson, P. S., Perfilieva, E., Björk- Eriksson, T., Alborn, A., Nordborg, C., Peterson, D. A., & Gage, F. H. (1998). Neurogenesis in the adult human hippocampus. *Nature Medicine, 4,* 1313–1317.

Etzel, R. A. (2003). How environmental exposures influence the development and exacerbation of asthma. *Pediatrics, 112*(1), 233–239.

Evans, A. D., & Lee, K. (2010). Promising to tell the truth makes 8- to 16-year-olds more honest. *Behavioral Sciences and the Law, 28*(6), 801–811.

Evans, G. W. (2004). The environment of childhood poverty. *American Psychologist, 59,* 77–92.

Evans, G. W., & English, K. (2002). The environment of poverty: Multiple stressor exposure, psycholophysiological stress and socioemotional adjustment. *Child Development, 73*(4), 1238–1248.

Fabes, R. A., Carlo, G., Kupanoff, K., & Laible, D. (1999). Early adolescence and prosocial/moral behavior: I. The role of individual processes. *Journal of Early Adolescence, 19,* 5–16.

Fabes, R. A., & Eisenberg, N. (1992). Young children's coping with interpersonal anger. *Child Development, 63*, 116–128.

Fabes, R. A., Leonard, S. A., Kupanoff, K., & Martin, C. L. (2001). Parental coping with children's negative emotions: Relations with children's emotional and social responding. *Child Development, 72*, 907–920.

Fabes, R. A., Martin, C. L., & Hanish, L. D. (2003, May). Young children's play qualities in same-, other-, and mixed-gender peer groups. *Child Development, 74*(3), 921–932.

Fabricius, W. V. (2003). Listening to children of divorce: New findings that diverge from Wallerstein, Lewis, and Blakeslee. *Family Relations, 52*, 385–394.

Facio, A., & Micocci, F. (2003). Emerging adulthood in Argentina. In J. J. Arnett & N. L. Galambos (Eds.), Exploring cultural conceptions of the transition to adulthood. *New Directions for Child and Adolescent Development, 100*, 21–32.

Faden, V. B. (2006). Trends in initiation of alcohol use in the United States: 1975–2003. *Alcoholism: Clinical and Experimental Research. 30*(6), 1011–1022.

Fagan, J. F., Holland, C. R., & Wheeler, K. (2007). The prediction, from infancy, of adult IQ. *Intelligence, 35*, 225–231.

Fagan, J., Palkovitz, R., Roy, K., & Farrie, D. (2009). Pathways to paternal engagement: Longitudinal effects of risk and resilience on nonresident fathers. *Developmental Psychology, 45*(5), 1389–1405.

Fagot, B. I. (1997). Attachment, parenting, and peer interactions of toddler children. *Developmental Psychology, 33*, 489–499.

Fagot, B. I., & Leinbach, M. D. (1995). Gender knowledge in egalitarian and traditional families. *Sex Roles, 32*, 513–526.

Fagot, B. I., Rogers, C. S., & Leinbach, M. D. (2000). Theories of gender socialization. In T. Eckes & H. M. Trautner (Eds.). *The developmental social psychology of gender.* Mahwah, NJ: Earlbaum.

Falbo, T. (2006). *Your one and only: Educational psychologist dispels myths surrounding only children.* Retrieved July 20, 2006, from www.utexas.edu/features/archive/2004/single.htm

Falbo, T., & Polit, D. F. (1986). Quantitative review of the only child literature: Research evidence and theory development. *Psychological Bulletin, 100*(2), 176–189.

Falbo, T., & Poston, D. L. (1993). The academic, personality, and physical outcomes of only children in China. *Child Development, 64*, 18–35.

Fantz, R. L. (1963). Pattern vision in newborn infants. *Science, 140*, 296–297.

Fantz, R. L. (1964). Visual experience in infants: Decreased attention to familiar patterns relative to novel ones. *Science, 146*, 668–670.

Fantz, R. L. (1965). Visual perception from birth as shown by pattern selectivity. In H. E. Whipple (Ed.), New issues in infant development. *Annals of the New York Academy of Science, 118*, 793–814.

Fantz, R. L., Fagen, J., & Miranda, S. B. (1975). Early visual selectivity. In L. Cohen & P. Salapatek (Eds.), *Infant perception: From sensation to cognition: Vol. 1. Basic visual processes* (pp. 249–341). New York: Academic Press.

Fantz, R. L., & Nevis, S. (1967). Pattern preferences and perceptual-cognitive development in early infancy. *Merrill-Palmer Quarterly, 13*, 77–108.

Farver, J.A.M., Kim, Y. K., & Lee, Y. (1995). Cultural differences in Korean and Anglo-American preschoolers' social interaction and play behavior. *Child Development, 66*, 1088–1099.

Farver, J.A.M., Xu, Y., Eppe, S., Fernandez, A., & Schwartz, D. (2005). Community violence, family conflict, and preschoolers' socioemotional functioning. *Developmental Psychology, 41*, 160–170.

Fasig, L. (2000). Toddlers' understanding of ownership: Implications for self-concept development. *Social Development, 9*, 370–382.

Fawzi, W. W., Msamanga, G. I., Urassa, W., Hertzmark, E., Petraro, P., Willett, W. C., & Spiegelman, D. (2007). Vitamins and perinatal outcomes among HIV-negative women in Tanzania. *New England Journal of Medicine, 356*, 1423–1431.

Fear, J. M., Champion, J. E., Reeslund, K. L., Forehand, R., Colletti, C., Roberts, L., & Compas, B. E. (2009). Parental depression and interparental conflict: Children and adolescents' self-blame and coping responses. *Journal of Family Psychology, 23*(5), 762–766. doi:10.1037/a0016381

Fearon, P., O'Connell, P., Frangou, S., Aquino, P., Nosarti, C., Allin, M., et al. (2004). Brain volume in adult survivors of very low birth weight: A sibling-controlled study. *Pediatrics, 114*, 367–371.

Fearon, R. P., Bakersmans-Kranenburg, M. K., VanIJzendoorn, M. H., Lapsley, A., & Roisman, G. I. (2010). The significance of insecure attachment and disorganization in the development of children's externalizing behavior: A meta-analytic study. *Child Development, 81*(2), 435–456.

Federal Bureau of Investigation (FBI). (2007). *Crime in the United States, 2005.* Retrieved June 2007 from www.fbi.gov/ucr/05cius

Federal Interagency Forum on Child and Family Statistics. (2005). *America's children: Key national indicators of well-being, 2005.* Washington, DC: U.S. Government Printing Office.

Federal Interagency Forum on Child and Family Statistics. (2007). *America's children: Key indicators of well-being, 2007.* Washington, DC: U.S. Government Printing Office.

Federal Interagency Forum on Child and Family Statistics. (2009). *America's children: Key national indicators of well-being, 2009.* Retrieved from www.childstats.gov/americaschildren/eco3.asp

Federal Interagency Forum on Child and Family Statistics. (2012). *America's children in brief: Key national indicators of well-being, (2012).* Retrieved from http://www.childstats.gov/americaschildren/care.asp

Federal Interagency Forum on Child and Family Statistics. (2012a). *America's children: Key indicators of well-being, 2012.* Retrieved from http://www.childstats.gov/americaschildren/eco.asp

Feingold, A., & Mazzella, R. (1998). Gender differences in body image are increasing. *Psychological Science, 9*(3), 190–195.

Ferber, R. (1985). *Solve your child's sleep problems.* New York: Simon & Schuster.

Ferber, S. G., & Makhoul, I. R. (2004). The effect of skin-to-skin contact (Kangaroo Care) shortly after birth on the neurobehavioral responses of the term newborn: A randomized, controlled trial. *Pediatrics, 113*, 858–865.

Ferguson, C. J. (2013). Violent video games and the Supreme Court: Lessons for the scientific community in the wake of Brown. vs Entertainment Merchants Association. *American Psychologist, 68*(2), 57–74.

Ferguson, C. J., & Savage, J. (2012). Have recent studies addressed methodological issues raised by five decades of television violence research? A critical review. *Aggression and Violent Behavior, 17*, 129–139.

Fergusson, D. M., Boden, J. M., & Horwood, L. J. (2008). Exposure to childhood sexual and physical abuse and adjustment in early adulthood. *Child Abuse & Neglect, 32*, 607–619.

Fergusson, D. M., Horwood, L. J., Ridder, E. M., & Beautrais, A. L. (2005). Subthreshold depression in adolescence and mental health outcomes in adulthood. *Archives of General Psychiatry, 62*(1), 66–72.

Fergusson, D. M., Horwood, L. J., & Shannon, F. T. (1986). Factors related to the age of attainment of nocturnal bladder control: An 8-year longitudinal study. *Pediatrics, 78*, 884–890.

Fernald, A., Perfors, A., & Marchman, V. A. (2006). Picking up speed in understanding: Speech processing efficiency and vocabulary growth across the second year. *Developmental Psychology, 42*, 98–116.

Fernald, A. (1985). Four-month-old infants prefer to listen to motherease. *Infant Behavior and Development, 8*, 181–195.

Fernald, A., Pinto, J. P., Swingley, D., Weinberg, A., & McRoberts, G. W. (1998). Rapid gains in speed of verbal processing by infants in the 2nd year. *Psychological Science, 9*(3), 228–231.

Fernald, A., Swingley, D., & Pinto, J. P. (2001). When half a word is enough: Infants can recognize spoken words using partial phonetic information. *Child Development, 72*, 1003–1015.

Field, A. E., Austin, S. B., Taylor, C. B., Malspeis, S., Rosner, B., Rockett, H. R., et al. (2003). Relation between dieting and weight change among preadolescents and adolescents. *Pediatrics, 112*(4), 900–906.

Field, A. E., Camargo, C. A., Taylor, B., Berkey, C. S., Roberts, S. B., & Colditz, G. A. (2001). Peer, parent, and media influence on the development of weight concerns and frequent dieting among preadolescent and adolescent girls and boys. *Pediatrics, 107*(1), 54–60.

Field, T. (1995). Infants of depressed mothers. *Infant Behavior and Development, 18*, 1–13.

Field, T. (1998a). Emotional care of the at-risk infant: Early interventions for infants of depressed mothers. *Pediatrics, 102*, 1305–1310.

Field, T. (1998b). Massage therapy effects. *American Psychologist, 53*, 1270–1281.

Field, T. (1998c). Maternal depression effects on infants and early intervention. *Preventive Medicine, 27*, 200–203.

Field, T. (2010). Touch for socioemotional and physical well-being: A review. *Developmental Review, 30*(4), 367–383.

Field, T., Diego, M., & Hernandez-Reif, M. (2007). Massage therapy research. *Developmental Review, 27*, 75–89.

Field, T., Diego, M., Hernandez-Reif, M., Schanberg, S., & Kuhn, C. (2003). Depressed mothers who are "good interaction" partners versus those who are withdrawn or intrusive. *Infant Behavior & Development, 26*, 238–252.

Field, T., Fox, N. A., Pickens, J., Nawrocki, T., & Soutollo, D. (1995). Right frontal EEG activation in 3- to 6-month-old infants of depressed mothers. *Developmental Psychology, 31*, 358–363.

Field, T., Grizzle, N., Scafidi, F., Abrams, S., Richardson, S., Kuhn, C., & Schanberg, S. (1996). Massage therapy for infants of depressed mothers. *Infant Behavior and Development, 19*, 107–112.

Field, T., Hernandez-Reif, M., & Freedman, J. (2004). Stimulation programs for preterm infants. *Social Policy Report, 18*(1), 1–19.

Field, T. M. (1978). Interaction behaviors of primary versus secondary caretaker fathers. *Developmental Psychology, 14*, 183–184.

Field, T. M., & Roopnarine, J. L. (1982). Infant-peer interaction. In T. M. Field, A. Huston, H. C. Quay, L. Troll, & G. Finley (Eds.), *Review of human development* (pp. 164–179). New York: Wiley.

Field, T. M., Sandberg, D., Garcia, R., Vega-Lahr, N., Goldstein, S., & Guy, L. (1985). Pregnancy problems, postpartum depression, and early infant-mother interactions. *Developmental Psychology, 21*, 1152–1156.

Fields, J. (2003). Children's living arrangements and characteristics: March 2002. *Current Population Reports* (p. 20–547). Washington, DC: U.S. Bureau of the Census.

Fields, J. (2004). America's families and living arrangements: 2003. *Current Population Reports* (P20–553). Washington, DC: U.S. Census Bureau.

Fields, J. M., & Smith, K. E. (1998, April). *Poverty, family structure, and child wellbeing: Indicators from the SIPP* (Population Division Working Paper No. 23, U.S. Bureau of the Census). Paper presented at the annual meeting of the Population Association of America, Chicago, IL.

Fields, R. D., & Stevens-Graham, B. (2002). New insights into neuron-glia communication. *Science, 298*, 556–62.

Fiese, B., & Schwartz, M. (2008). Reclaiming the family table: Mealtimes and child health and well-being. *Society for Research in Child Development Social Policy Report, 23*(4).

Fifer, W. P., & Moon, C. M. (1995). The effects of fetal experience with sound. In J. P. Lecanuet, W. P. Fifer, N. A. Krasnegor, & W. P. Smotherman (Eds.), *Fetal development: A psychobiological perspective* (pp. 351–366). Hillsdale, NJ: Erlbaum.

Finer, L. B. (2007). Trends in premarital sex in the United States, 1954–2003. *Public Health Reports, 122*, 73–78.

Finn, J. D. (2006). *The adult lives of at-risk students: The roles of attainment and engagement in high school* (NCES 2006–328). Washington, DC: U.S. Department of Education, National Center for Education Statistics.

Finn, J. D., Gerber, S. B., & Boyd-Zaharias, J. (2005). Small classes in the early grades, academic achievement, and graduating from high school. *Journal of Educational Psychology, 97*, 214–223.

Finn, J. D., & Rock, D. A. (1997). Academic success among students at risk for dropout. *Journal of Applied Psychology, 82*, 221–234.

Fiscella, K., Kitzman, H. J., Cole, R. E., Sidora, K. J., & Olds, D. (1998). Does child abuse predict adolescent pregnancy? *Pediatrics, 101*, 620–624.

Fischer, K. (1980). A theory of cognitive development: The control and construction of hierarchies of skills. *Psychological Review, 87*, 477–531.

Fischer, K. W. (2008). Dynamic cycles of cognitive and brain development: Measuring growth in mind, brain, and education. In A. M. Battro, K.W. Fischer, & P. Léna (Eds.), *The educated brain*. Cambridge, UK: Cambridge University Press, 127–150.

Fischer, K. W., & Pruyne, E. (2003). Reflective thinking in adulthood. In J. Demick & C. Andreoletti (Eds.), *Handbook of adult development* (pp. 169–198). New York: Plenum Press.

Fischer, K. W., & Rose, S. P. (1994). Dynamic development of coordination of components in brain and behavior: A framework for theory and research. In G. Dawson & K. W. Fischers (Eds.), *Human behavior and the developing brain* (pp. 3–66). New York: Guilford Press.

Fischer, K. W., & Rose, S. P. (1995, Fall). Concurrent cycles in the dynamic development of brain and behavior. *SRCD Newsletter*, pp. 3–4, 15–16.

Fischhoff, B., Bruine de Bruin, W., Parker, A. M., Millstein, S. G., & Halpern-Felsher, B. L. (2010). Adolescents' perceived risk of dying. *Journal of Adolescent Health, 46*, 265–269.

Fisher, C. B., Hoagwood, K., Boyce, C., Duster, T., Frank, D. A., Grisso, T., et al. (2002). Research ethics for mental health science involving ethnic minority children and youth. *American Psychologist, 57*, 1024–1040.

Fivush, R., & Haden, C. A. (2006). Elaborating on elaborations: Role of maternal reminiscing style in cognitive and socioemotional development. *Child Development, 77*, 1568–1588.

Fivush, R., & Nelson, K. (2004). Culture and language in the emergence of autobiographical memory. *Psychological Science, 15*, 573–577.

Flannagan, C. A., Bowes, J. M., Jonsson, B., Csapo, B., & Sheblanova, E. (1998). Ties that bind: Correlates of adolescents' civic commitment in seven countries. *Journal of Social Issues, 54*, 457–475.

Flavell, J. (1963). *The developmental psychology of Jean Piaget*. New York: Van Nostrand.

Flavell, J. H. (1970). Developmental studies of mediated memory. In H. W. Reese & L. P. Lipsitt (Eds.), *Advances in child development and behavior* (Vol. 5, pp. 181–211). New York: Academic.

Flavell, J. H. (1993). Young children's understanding of thinking and consciousness. *Current Directions in Psychological Science, 2*, 40–43.

Flavell, J. H. (2000). Development of children's knowledge about the mental world. *International Journal of Behavioral Development, 24*(1), 15–23.

Flavell, J. H., Green, F. L., & Flavell, E. R. (1986). Development of knowledge about the appearance-reality distinction. *Monographs of the Society for Research in Child Development, 51*(1). [Serial No. 212].

Flavell, J. H., Green, F. L., & Flavell, E. R. (1995). Young children's knowledge about thinking. *Monographs of the Society for Research in Child Development, 60*(1). [Serial No. 243].

Flavell, J. H., Green, F. L., Flavell, E. R., & Grossman, J. B. (1997). The development of children's knowledge about inner speech. *Child Development, 68*, 39–47.

Flavell, J. H., Miller, P. H., & Miller, S. A. (2002). *Cognitive development*. Englewood Cliffs, NJ: Prentice Hall.

Flook, L., & Fuligni, A. (2008). Family and school spillover in adolescents' daily lives. *Child Development, 79*(3), 776–787.

Flook, L., Repetti, R. L., & Ullman, J. B. (2005). Classroom social experiences as predictors of academic performance. *Developmental Psychology, 41*, 319–327.

Flores, G., Fuentes-Afflick, E., Barbot, O., Carter-Pokras, O., Claudio, L., Lara, M., et al. (2002). The health of Latino children: Urgent priorities, unanswered questions, and a research agenda. *Journal of the American Medical Association, 288*, 82–90.

Flores, G., Olson, L., & Tomany-Korman, S. C. (2005). Racial and ethnic disparities in early childhood health and health care. *Pediatrics, 115*, e183–e193.

Flynn, J. R. (1984). The mean IQ of Americans: Massive gains 1932 to 1978. *Psychological Bulletin, 95*, 29–51.

Flynn, J. R. (1987). Massive IQ gains in 14 nations: What IQ tests really measure. *Psychological Bulletin, 101*, 171–191.

Fomby, P., & Cherlin, A. J. (2007). Family instability and child well-being. *American Sociological Review, 72*(2), 181–204.

Fontanel, B., & d'Harcourt, C. (1997). *Babies, history, art and folklore*. New York: Abrams.

Ford, R. P., Schluter, P. J., Mitchell, E. A., Taylor, B. J., Scragg, R., & Stewart, A. W. (1998). Heavy caffeine intake in pregnancy and sudden infant death syndrome (New Zealand Cot Death Study Group). *Archives of Disease in Childhood, 78*(1), 9–13.

Forhan, S. E., Gottlieb, S. L., Sternberg, M. R., Xu, F., Datta, D., Berman, S., & Markowitz, L. E. (2008, March 13). *Prevalence of sexually transmitted infections and bacterial vaginosis among female adolescents in the United States: Data from the National Health and Nutritional Examination Survey (NHANES) 2003-2004*. Oral presentation at the meeting of the 2008 National STD Prevention Conference, Chicago.

Forste, R., & Hoffman, J. P. (2008). Are us mothers meeting the *Healthy People 2010* breastfeeding targets for initiation, duration, and exclusivity? The 2003 and 2004 national immunization surveys. *Journal of Human Lactation, 24*, 278–288.

Foster, E. M., & Watkins, S. (2010). The value of reanalysis: TV viewing and attention problems. *Child Development*.

Foster, G. D., Sherman, S., Borradaile, K. E., Grundy, K. M., Vander Veur, S. S., Nachmani, J., et al. (2008). A policy based school intervention to prevent obesity and overweight. *Pediatrics, 121*, e794–e802.

Fowler, J. (1981). *Stages of faith: The psychology of human development and the quest for meaning*. New York: Harper & Row.

Fowler, J. W. (1989). Strength for the journey: Early childhood development in selfhood and faith. In D. A. Blazer, J. W. Fowler, K. J. Swick, A. S. Honig, P. J. Boone, B. M. Caldwell, R. A. Boone, & L. W. Barber (Eds.), *Faith development in early childhood* (pp. 1–63). New York: Sheed & Ward.

Fox, M. K., Pac, S., Devaney, B., & Jankowski, L. (2004). Feeding Infants and Toddlers Study: What foods are infants and toddlers eating? *Journal of the American Dietetic Association, 104*, 22–30.

Fox, N. A., Hane, A. A., & Pine, D. S. (2007). Plasticity for affective neurocircuitry: How the environment affects gene expression. *Current Directions in Psychological Science, 16*(1), 1–5.

Fox, N. A., Kimmerly, N. L., & Schafer, W. D. (1991). Attachment to mother/attachment to father: A meta-analysis. *Child Development, 62*, 210–225.

Fraga, M., F., Ballestar, E., Paz, M. F., Ropero, S., Setien, F., Ballestar, M. L., et al. (2005). Epigenetic differences arise during the lifetime of monozygotic twins. *Proceedings of the National Academy of Sciences, USA, 102*, 10604–10609.

Franic, S., Middledorp, C. M., Dolan, C. V., Ligthart, L., & Boomsma, D. I. (2010). Childhood and adolescent anxiety and depression: Beyond heritability. *Journal of the American Academy of Child & Adolescent Psychiatry, 49*(8), 820–829.

Frank, D. A., Augustyn, M., Knight, W. G., Pell, T., & Zuckerman, B. (2001). Growth, development, and behavior in early childhood following prenatal cocaine exposure. *Journal of the American Medical Association, 285*, 1613–1625.

Frankenburg, W. K., Dodds, J., Archer, P., Bresnick, B., Maschka. P., Edelman, N., & Shapiro, H. (1992). *Denver II training manual*. Denver: Denver Developmental Materials.

Frankenburg, W. K., Dodds, J. B., Fandal, A. W., Kazuk, E., & Cohrs, M. (1975). *The Denver Developmental Screening Test: Reference manual.* Denver: University of Colorado Medical Center.

Franks, P. W., Hanson, R. L., Knowler, W. C., Sievers, M. L., Bennett, P. H., & Looker, H. C. (2010). Childhood obesity, other cardiovascular risk factors, and premature death. *New England Journal of Medicine, 362,* 485–493.

Frans, E. M., Sandin, S., Reichenberg, A., Lichtenstein, P., Långström, N., & Hultman, C. M. (2008). Advancing paternal age and bipolar disorder. *Archives of General Psychiatry, 65,* 1034–1040.

Fraser, A. M., Brockert, J. F., & Ward, R. H. (1995). Association of young maternal age with adverse reproductive outcomes. *New England Journal of Medicine, 332*(17), 1113–1117.

Fredricks, J. A., & Eccles, J. S. (2002). Children's competence and value beliefs from childhood through adolescence: Growth trajectories in two male-sex-typed domains. *Developmental Psychology, 38,* 519–533.

Freeark, K., Rosenberg, E. B., Bornstein, J., Jozefowicz-Simbeni, D., Linkevich, M., & Lohnes, K. (2005). Gender differences and dynamics shaping the adoption life cycle: Review of the literature and recommendations. *American Journal of Orthopsychiatry, 75,* 86–101.

Freeman, C. (2004). *Trends in educational equity of girls & women: 2004* (NCES 2005016). Washington, DC: National Center for Education Statistics.

Freking, K., & Neergaard, L. (2009, February 12). Health news court issues ruling in autism case. *Associated Press.* Retrieved February 12, 2009, from http://news.yahoo.com/s/ap/20090212/ap_on_go_ot/autism_ruling

French, R. M., Mareschal, D., Mermillod, M., & Quinn, P. C. (2004). The role of bottom-up processing in perceptual categorization by 3- to 4- month old infants: Simulations and data. *Journal of Experimental Psychology: General, 133*(3), 382–397.

French, S. A., Story, M., & Jeffery, R. W. (2001). Environmental influences on eating and physical activity. *Annual Review of Public Health, 22,* 309–335.

French, S. E., Seidman, E., Allen, L., & Aber, J. L. (2006). The development of ethnic identity during adolescence. *Developmental Psychology, 42,* 1–10.

Freud, S. (1953). *A general introduction to psycho-analysis* (J. Rivière, Trans.) New York: Perma-books. (Original work published 1935)

Freud, S. (1964a). New introductory lectures on psychoanalysis. In J. Strachey (Ed. & Trans.), *The standard edition of the complete psychological works of Sigmund Freud* (Vol. 22). London: Hogarth. (Original work published 1933)

Freud, S. (1964b). An outline of psychoanalysis. In J. Strachey (Ed. & Trans.), *The standard edition of the complete psychological works of Sigmund Freud* (Vol. 23). London: Hogarth. (Original work published 1940)

Frey, K. S., Hirschstein, M. K., Snell, J. L., Edstrom, L.V.S., MacKenzie, E. P., & Broderick, C. J. (2005). Reducing playground bullying and supporting beliefs: An experimental trial of the Steps to Respect program. *Developmental Psychology, 41,* 479–491.

Fried, P. A., & Smith, A. M. (2001). A literature review of the consequences of prenatal marijuana exposure: An emerging theme of a deficiency in aspects of executive function. *Neurotoxicology and Teratology, 23,* 1–11.

Friedman, L. J. (1999). *Identity's architect.* New York: Scribner.

Friend, M., & Davis, T. L. (1993). Appearance-reality distinction: Children's understanding of the physical and affective domains. *Developmental Psychology, 29,* 907–914.

Fromkin, V., Krashen, S., Curtiss, S., Rigler, D., & Rigler, M. (1974). The development of language in Genie: Acquisition beyond the "critical period." *Brain and Language, 15*(9), 28–34.

Fuligni, A. J. (1997). The academic achievement of adolescents from immigrant families: The roles of family background, attitudes, and behavior. *Child Development, 68,* 351–363.

Fuligni, A. J. (2001). Family obligation and the academic motivation of adolescents from Asian, Latin American, and European backgrounds. *New Directions for Child and Adolescent Development, 94,* 61–76.

Fuligni, A. J., & Eccles, J. S. (1993). Perceived parent-child relationships and early adolescents' orientation toward peers. *Developmental Psychology, 29,* 622–632.

Fuligni, A. J., Eccles, J. S., Barber, B. L., & Clements, P. (2001). Early adolescent peer orientation and adjustment during high school. *Developmental Psychology, 37*(1), 28–36.

Fuligni, A. J., & Stevenson, H. W. (1995). Time use and mathematics achievement among American, Chinese, and Japanese high school students. *Child Development, 66,* 830–842.

Fuligni, A. J., Yip, T., & Tseng, V. (2002). The impact of family obligation on the daily activities and psychological wellbeing of Chinese American adolescents. *Child Development, 73*(1), 302–314.

Furman, L. (2005). What is attention-deficit hyperactivity disorder (ADHD)? *Journal of Child Neurology, 20,* 994–1003.

Furman, L., Taylor, G., Minich, N., & Hack, M. (2003). The effect of maternal milk on neonatal morbidity of very low birth-weight infants. *Archives of Pediatrics and Adolescent Medicine, 157,* 66–71.

Furman, W. (1982). Children's friendships. In T. M. Field, A. Huston, H. C. Quay, L. Troll, & G. E. Finley (Eds.), *Review of human development* (pp. 327–342). New York: Wiley.

Furman, W., & Bierman, K. L. (1983). Developmental changes in young children's conception of friendship. *Child Development, 54,* 549–556.

Furman, W., & Buhrmester, D. (1985). Children's perceptions of the personal relationships in their social networks. *Developmental Psychology, 21,* 1016–1024.

Furman, W., & Wehner, E. A. (1997). Adolescent romantic relationships: A developmental perspective. In S. Shulman & A. Collins (Eds.), *Romantic relationships in adolescence: Developmental perspectives. New Directions for Child and Adolescent Development, 78,* 21–36.

Furrow, D. (1984). Social and private speech at two years. *Child Development, 55,* 355–362.

Furstenberg, Jr., F. F., Rumbaut, R. G., & Setterstein, Jr., R. A. (2005). On the frontier of adulthood: Emerging themes and new directions. In R. A. Settersten Jr., F. F. Furstenberg Jr., & R. G. Rumbaut (Eds.), *On the frontier of adulthood: Theory, research, and public policy* (pp. 3–25). Chicago: University of Chicago Press.

Fussell, E., & Furstenberg, F. (2005). The transition to adulthood during the twentieth century: Race, nativity, and gender. In R. A. Settersten Jr., F. F. Furstenberg Jr., & R. G. Rumbaut (Eds.), *On the frontier of adulthood: Theory, research, and public policy* (pp. 29–75). Chicago: University of Chicago Press.

Gabbard, C. P. (1996). *Lifelong motor development* (2nd ed.). Madison, WI: Brown and Benchmark.

Gabhainn, S., & François, Y. (2000). Substance use. In C. Currie, K. Hurrelmann, W. Settertobulte, R. Smith, & J. Todd (Eds.), *Health behaviour in schoolaged children: A WHO cross-national study (HBSC) international report* (pp. 97–114). [WHO Policy Series: Healthy Policy for Children and Adolescents, Series No. 1.] Copenhagen, Denmark: World Health Organization Regional Office for Europe.

Gable, S., Chang, Y., & Krull, J. L. (2007). Television watching and frequency of family meals are predictive of overweight onset and persistence in a national sample of school-age children. *Journal of the American Dietetic Association, 107,* 53–61.

Gabriel, T. (1996, January 7). High-tech pregnancies test hope's limit. *New York Times,* pp. 1, 18–19.

Gaffney, M., Gamble, M., Costa, P., Holstrum, J., & Boyle, C. (2003). Infants tested for hearing loss—United States, 1999–2001. *Morbidity and Mortality Weekly Report, 51,* 981–984.

Gagne, J. R., & Saudino, K. J. (2010). Wait for it! A twin study of inhibitory control in early childhood. *Behavioral Genetics, 40*(3), 327–337.

Galotti, K. M., Komatsu, L. K., & Voelz, S. (1997). Children's differential performance on deductive and inductive syllogisms. *Developmental Psychology, 33,* 70–78.

Ganger, J. & Brent, M. R. (2004). Reexamining the vocabulary spurt. *Developmental Psychology, 40,* 621–632.

Gannon, P. J., Holloway, R. L., Broadfield, D. C., & Braun, A. R. (1998). Asymmetry of chimpanzee planum temporale: Humanlike pattern of Wernicke's brain language homlog. *Science, 279,* 22–222.

Gans, J. E. (1990). *America's adolescents: How healthy are they?* Chicago: American Medical Association.

Garbarino, J., Dubrow, N., Kostelny, K., & Pardo, C. (1992). *Children in danger: Coping with the consequences of community violence.* San Francisco: Jossey-Bass.

Gardiner, H. W., & Kozmitzki, C. (2005). *Lives across cultures: Cross-cultural human development.* Boston: Allyn & Bacon.

Gardner, H. (1993). *Frames of mind: The theory of multiple intelligences.* New York: Basic. (Original work published 1983)

Gardner, H. (1995). Reflections on multiple intelligences: Myths and messages. *Phi Delta Kappan,* pp. 200–209.

Gardner, H. (1998). Are there additional intelligences? In J. Kane (Ed.), *Education, information, and transformation: Essays on learning and thinking.* Englewood Cliffs, NJ: Prentice Hall.

Gardner, M., & Steinberg, L. (2005). Peer influence on risk taking, risk preference, and risky decision making in adolescence and adulthood: An experimental study. *Developmental Psychology, 41,* 625–635.

Garland, A. F., & Zigler, E. (1993). Adolescent suicide prevention: Current research and social policy implications. *American Psychologist, 48*(2), 169–182.

Garlick, D. (2003). Integrating brain science research with intelligence research. *Current Directions in Psychological Science, 12,* 185–192.

Garmon, L. C., Basinger, K. S., Gregg, V. R., & Gibbs, J. C. (1996). Gender differences in stage and expression of moral judgment. *Merrill-Palmer Quarterly, 42,* 418–437.

Garner, P. W., & Estep, K. M. (2001). Emotional competence, emotional socialization, and young children's peer-related social competence. *Early Education & Development, 12*(1), 29–48.

Garner, P. W., & Power, T. G. (1996). Preschoolers' emotional control in the disappointment paradigm and its relation to temperament, emotional knowledge, and family expressiveness. *Child Development, 67,* 1406–1419.

Gartrell, N., Deck, A., Rodas, C., Peyser, H., & Banks, A. (2005). The National Lesbian Family Study: Interviews with the 10-year-old children. *American Journal of Orthopsychiatry, 75,* 518–524.

Gartstein, M. A., & Rothbart, M. K. (2003). Studying infant temperament via the Revised Infant Behavior Questionnaire. *Infant Behavior & Development, 26,* 64–86.

Gatewood, J. D., Wills, A., Shetty, S., Xu, J., Arnold, A. P., Burgoyne, P. S., & Rissman, E. F. (2006). Sex chromosome complement and gonadal sex influence aggressive and parental behaviors in mice. *Journal of Neuroscience, 26,* 2335–2342.

Gathercole, S. E., & Alloway, T. P. (2008). *Working memory and learning: A practical guide.* Thousand Oaks, CA: Sage.

Gauvain, M. (1993). The development of spatial thinking in everyday activity. *Developmental Review, 13,* 92–121.

Gauvain, M., & Perez, S. M. (2005). Parent-child participation in planning children's activities outside of school in European American and Latino families. *Child Development, 76,* 371–383.

Gazzaniga, M. S. (Ed.). (2000). *The new cognitive neurosciences* (2nd ed.). Cambridge, MA: MIT Press.

Ge, X., Brody, G. H., Conger, R. D., Simons, R. L., & Murry, V. (2002). Contextual amplification of pubertal transitional effect on African American children's problem behaviors. *Developmental Psychology, 38,* 42–54.

Ge, X., Conger, R. D., & Elder, G. H. (1996). Coming of age too early: Pubertal influences on girls' vulnerability to psychological distress. *Child Development, 67,* 3386–3400.

Ge, X., Conger, R. D., & Elder, G. H. (2001a). Pubertal transition, stressful life events, and the emergence of gender differences in adolescent depressive symptoms. *Developmental Psychology, 37*(3), 404–417.

Geary, D. C. (1993). Mathematical disabilities: Cognitive, neuropsychological, and genetic components. *Psychological Bulletin, 114,* 345–362.

Geary, D. C. (1999). Evolution and developmental sex differences. *Current Directions in Psychological Science, 8*(4), 115–120.

Geary, D. C. (2006). Development of mathematical understanding. In W. Damon (Ed.) & D. Kuhl & R. S. Siegler (Vol. Eds.), *Handbook of child psychology (6th ed.): Cognition, perception, and language,* Vol 2. (pp. 777–810). New York: John Wiley & Sons.

Gedo, J. (2001). *The enduring scientific contributions of Sigmund Freud.* Retrieved November 20, 2012, from http://www.pep-web.org/document .php?id=AOP.029.0105A.

Geidd, J. N. (2008). The teen brain: Insights from neuroimaging. *Journal of Adolescent Health, 42,* 321–323.

Geier, D. A., & Geier, M. R. (2006). Early downward trends in neurodevelopmental disorders following removal of thimerosal-containing vaccines. *Journal of American Physicians & Surgeons, 11*(1), 8–13.

Gelfand, D. M., & Teti, D. M. (1995, November). How does maternal depression affect children? *The Harvard Mental Health Letter,* p. 8.

Gélis, J. (1991). *History of childbirth: Fertility, pregnancy, and birth in early modern Europe.* Boston: Northeastern University Press.

Gelman, R. (2006). Young natural-number mathematicians. *Current Directions in Psychological Science, 15,* 193–197.

Gelman, R., Spelke, E. S., & Meck, E. (1983). What preschoolers know about animate and inanimate objects. In D. R. Rogers & J. S. Sloboda (Eds.), *The acquisition of symbolic skills* (pp. 297–326). New York: Plenum Press.

Genesee, F., Nicoladis, E., & Paradis, J. (1995). Language differentiation in early bilingual development. *Journal of Child Language, 22,* 611–631.

George, C., Kaplan, N., & Main, M. (1985). *The Berkeley Adult Attachment Interview.* [Unpublished protocol]. Department of Psychology, University of California, Berkeley, CA.

George, T. P., & Hartmann, D. P. (1996). Friendship networks of unpopular, average, and popular children. *Child Development, 67,* 2301–2316.

Gershoff, E. T. (2002). Corporal punishment by parents and associated child behaviors and experiences: A meta-analytic and theoretical review. *Psychological Bulletin, 128,* 539–579.

Gershoff, E. T., Aber, J. L., Raver, C. C., & Lennon, M. C. (2007). Income is not enough: Incorporating material hardship into models of income associations with parenting and child development. *Child Development, 78,* 70–95.

Gervai, J., Nemoda, Z., Lakatos, K., Ronai, Z., Toth, I., Ney, K., & Sasvari-Szekely, M. (2005). Transmission disequilibrium tests confirm the link between DRD4 gene polymorphism and infant attachment. *American Journal of Medical Genetics, Part B (Neuropsychiatric Genetics), 132B,* 126–130.

Gesell, A. (1929). Maturation and infant behavior patterns. *Psychological Review, 36,* 307–319.

Gettler, L. T., McDade, T. W., Feranil, A. B., & Kuzawa, C.W. (2011). Longitudinal evidence that fatherhood decreases testosterone in human males. *Proceedings of the National Academy of Science 108*(39), 1–6.

Getzels, J. W. (1964). Creative thinking, problem-solving, and instruction. In *Yearbook of the National Society for the Study of Education* (Part 1, pp. 240–267). Chicago: University of Chicago Press.

Getzels, J. W. (1984, March). *Problem finding in creativity in higher education.* The Fifth Rev. Charles F. Donovan, SJ, Lecture, Boston College, School of Education, Boston, MA.

Getzels, J. W., & Jackson, P. W. (1962). *Creativity and intelligence: Explorations with gifted students.* New York: Wiley.

Getzels, J. W., & Jackson, P. W. (1963). The highly intelligent and the highly creative adolescent: A summary of some research findings. In C. W. Taylor & F. Baron (Eds.), *Scientific creativity; Its recognition and development* (pp. 161–172). New York: Wiley.

Gibbons, L., Belizan, J. M., Lauer, J. A., Betran, A. P., Merialdi, M., & Althabe, F. (2010). The global numbers and costs of additionally needed and unnecessary caesarean sections performed per year: Overuse as a barrier to universal coverage. *World Health Report 30,* 2010.World Health Organization World Health Report Background Paper, 30. Retrieved from http://www.who.int /healthsystems/topics/financing/healthreport /30C-sectioncosts.pdf/

Gibbs, J. C. (1991). Toward an integration of Kohlberg's and Hoffman's theories of moral development. In W. M. Kurtines & J. L. Gewirtz (Eds.), *Handbook of moral behavior and development: Advances in theory, research, and application* (Vol. 1, pp. 183–222). Hillsdale, NJ: Erlbaum.

Gibbs, J. C. (1995). The cognitive developmental perspective. In W. M. Kurtines & J. L. Gewirtz (Eds.), *Moral development: An introduction.* Boston: Allyn & Bacon.

Gibbs, J. C., & Schnell, S. V. (1985). Moral development "versus" socialization. *American Psychologist, 40*(10), 1071–1080.

Gibson, E. J. (1969). *Principles of perceptual learning and development.* New York: Appleton-Century-Crofts.

Gibson, E. J., & Pick, A. D. (2000). *An ecological approach to perceptual learning and development.* New York: Oxford University Press.

Gibson, E. J., & Walker, A. S. (1984). Development of knowledge of visual tactual affordances of substance. *Child Development, 55,* 453–460.

Gibson, J. J. (1979). *The ecological approach to visual perception.* Boston: Houghton-Mifflin.

Giedd, J. N., Blumenthal, J., Jeffries, N. O., Castellanos, F. X., Zijdenbos, A., Paus, T., Evans, A. C., & Rapoport, J. L. (1999). Brain development during childhood and adolescence: A longitudinal MRI study. *Nature Neuroscience, 2,* 861–863.

Gilboa, S., Correa, A., Botto, L., Rasmussen, S., Waller, D., Hobbs, C., et al. (2009). Association between prepregnancy body mass index and congenital heart defects. *American Journal of Obstetrics and Gynecology, 202*(1), 51–61.

Gill, B., & Schlossman, S. (1996). "A sin against childhood": Progressive education and the crusade to abolish homework, 1897–1941. *American Journal of Education, 105,* 27–66.

Gill, B. P., & Schlossman, S. L. (2000). The lost cause of homework reform. *American Journal of Education, 109,* 27–62.

Gilligan, C. (1982). *In a different voice: Psychological theory and women's development.* Cambridge, MA: Harvard University Press.

Gilligan, C. (1987a). Adolescent development reconsidered. In E. E. Irwin (Ed.), *Adolescent social behavior and health* (pp. 63–92). San Francisco: Jossey-Bass.

Gilligan, C. (1987b). Moral orientation and moral development. In E. F. Kittay & D. T. Meyers (Eds.), *Women and moral theory* (pp. 19–33). Totowa, NJ: Rowman & Littlefield.

Gilmore, J., Lin, W., Prastawa, M. W., Looney, C. B., Vetsa, Y.S.K., Knickmeyer, R. C., et al. (2007). Regional gray matter growth, sexual dimorphism, and cerebral asymmetry in the neonatal brain. *Journal of Neuroscience, 27*(6), 1255–1260.

Ginsburg, G. S., & Bronstein, P. (1993). Family factors related to children's intrinsic/extrinsic motivational orientation and academic performance. *Child Development, 64,* 1461–1474.

Ginsburg, H., & Opper, S. (1979). *Piaget's theory of intellectual development* (2nd ed.). Englewood Cliffs, NJ: Prentice Hall.

Ginsburg, H. P. (1997). Mathematics learning disabilities: A view from developmental psychology. *Journal of Learning Disabilities, 30,* 20–33.

Ginsburg, K., & Committee on Communications & the Committee on Psychosocial Aspects of Child and Family Health, American Academy of

Pediatrics (AAP). (2007). The importance of play in promoting healthy child development. *Pediatrics, 119,* 182–191.

Ginsburg-Block, M. D., & Fantuzzo, J. W. (1998). An evaluation of the relative effectiveness of NCTM standards-based interventions for low-achieving urban elementary students. *Journal of Educational Psychology, 90,* 560–569.

Giordano, P. C., Cernkovich, S. A., & DeMaris, A. (1993). The family and peer relations of black adolescents. *Journal of Marriage and the Family, 55,* 277–287.

Giordano, P. C., Longmore, M. A., & Manning, W. D. (2006). Gender and the meanings of adolescent romantic relationships: A focus on boys. *American Sociological Review, 71*(2), 260–287.

Giscombé, C. L., & Lobel, M. (2005). Explaining disproportionately high rates of adverse birth outcomes among African Americans: The impact of stress, racism, and related factors in pregnancy. *Psychological Bulletin, 131,* 662–683.

Gjerdingen, D. (2003). The effectiveness of various postpartum depression treatments and the impact of antidepressant drugs on nursing infants. *Journal of American Board of Family Practice, 16,* 372–382.

Glaser, D. (2000). Child abuse and neglect and the brain: A review. *Journal of Child Psychiatry, 41,* 97–116.

Glassbrenner, D., Carra, J. S., & Nichols, J. (2005). Recent estimates of safety belt use. *Journal of Safety Research, 35*(2), 237–244.

Glasson, E. J., Bower, C., Petterson, B., de Klerk, N., Chaney, G., & Hallmayer, J. F. (2004). Perinatal factors and the development of autism: A population study. *Archives of General Psychiatry, 61,* 618–627.

Gleason, T. R., Sebanc, A. M., & Hartup, W. W. (2000). Imaginary companions of preschool children. *Developmental Psychology, 36,* 419–428.

Gleitman, L. R., Newport, E. L., & Gleitman, H. (1984). The current status of the motherese hypothesis. *Journal of Child Language, 11,* 43–79.

Glenn, N., & Marquardt, E. (2001). *Hooking up, hanging out, and hoping for Mr. Right: College women on dating and mating today.* New York: Institute for American Values.

Gluckman, P. D., Wyatt, J. S., Azzopardi, D., Ballard, R., Edwards, A. D., Ferriero, D. M., et al. (2005). Selective head cooling with mild systemic hypothermia after neonatal encephalopathy: Multicentre randomized trial. *Lancet, 365,* 663–670.

Goerning, J., & Feins, F. (Eds.). (2003). *Choosing a better life? Evaluating the moving to opportunity social experiment.* Washington, DC: Urban Institute Press.

Goetz, P. J. (2003). The effects of bilingualism on theory of mind development. *Bilingualism: Language and Cognition, 6,* 1–15.

Gogtay, N., Giedd, J. N., Lusk, L., Hayashi, K. M., Greenstein, D., Vaituzis, A. C., et al. (2004). Dynamic mapping of human cortical development during childhood through early adulthood. *Proceedings of the National Academy of Sciences, USA, 101,* 8174–8179.

Goldenberg, R. L., Kirby, R., & Culhane, J. F. (2004). Stillbirth: A review. *Journal of Maternal-Fetal & Neonatal Medicine, 16*(2), 79–94.

Goldenberg, R. L., & Rouse, D. J. (1998). Prevention of premature labor. *New England Journal of Medicine, 339,* 313–320.

Goldin-Meadow, S. (2007). Pointing sets the stage for learning language—and creating language. *Child Development, 78*(3), 741–745.

Goldman, L., Falk, H., Landrigan, P. J., Balk, S. J., Reigart, J. R., & Etzel, R. A. (2004). Environmental pediatrics and its impact on government health policy. *Pediatrics, 113,* 1146–1157.

Goldman, R. (1964). *Religious thinking from childhood to adolescence.* London: Routledge & Kegan Paul.

Goldstein, M., King, A., & West, M. (2003). Social interaction shapes babbling: Testing parallels between birdsong and speech. *Proceedings of the National Academy of Sciences, USA, 100,* 8030–8035.

Goldstein, S. E., Davis-Kean, P., E., & Eccles, J. E. (2005). Parents, peers, and problem behavior: A longitudinal investigation of the impact of relationship perceptions and characteristics on the development of adolescent problem behavior. *Developmental Psychology, 2,* 401–413.

Goleman, D. (1995, July 1). A genetic clue to bedwetting is located: Researchers say discovery shows the problem is not emotions! *New York Times,* p. 8.

Goler, N. C., Armstrong, M. A., Taillac, C. J., & Osejo, V, M. (2008). Substance abuse treatment linked with prenatal visits improves perinatal outcomes: A new standard. *Journal of Perinatology, 28,* 597–603.

Golinkoff, R. M., & Hirsch-Pasek, K. (2006). Baby wordsmith. *Current Directions in Psychological Science, 15,* 30–33.

Golinkoff, R. M., Jacquet, R. C., Hirsh-Pasek, K., & Nandakumar, R. (1996). Lexical principles may underlie the learning of verbs. *Child Development, 67,* 3101–3119.

Golomb, C., & Galasso, L. (1995). Make believe and reality: Explorations of the imaginary realm. *Developmental Psychology, 31,* 800–810.

Golombok, S., Perry B., Burston, A., Murray, C., Mooney-Summers, J., Stevens, M., & Golding, J. (2003). Children with lesbian parents: A community study. *Developmental Psychology, 39,* 20–33.

Golombok, S., Rust, J., Zervoulis, K., Croudace, T., Golding, J., & Hines, M. (2008). Developmental trajectories of sex-typed behaviors in boys and girls: A longitudinal general population study of children aged 2.5–8 years. *Child Development, 79,* 1583–1593.

Golub, M., Collman, G., Foster, P., Kimmel, C., Rajpert-De Meyts, E., Reiter, E., et al. (2008). Public health implications of altered puberty timing. *Pediatrics, 121,* S218–s230.

Göncü, A., Mistry, J., & Mosier, C. (2000). Cultural variations in the play toddlers. *International Journal of Behavioral Development, 24,* 321–329

Gonzales, N. A., Cauce, A. M., & Mason, C. A. (1996). Interobserver agreement in the assessment of parental behavior and parent-adolescent conflict: African American mothers, daughters, and independent observers. *Child Development, 67,* 1483–1498.

Gonzales, P., Guzman, J. C., Partelow, L., Pahlke, E., Jocelyn, L., Kastberg, D., & Williams, T. (2004). *Highlights from the Trends in International Mathematics and Science Study (TIMSS) 2003.* (NCES 2005-205). Washington, DC: National Center for Education Statistics, U.S. Department of Education, Institute of Education Sciences.

Gootman, E. (2007, January 22). Taking middle schoolers out of the middle. *New York Times,* p. A1.

Gopnik, A., Sobel, D. M., Schulz, L. E., & Glymour, C. (2001). Causal learning mechanisms in very young children: Two-, three-, and four-year-olds infer causal relations from patterns of variation and covariation. *Developmental Psychology, 37*(5), 620–629.

Gorman, M. (1993). Help and self-help for older adults in developing countries. *Generations, 17*(4), 73–76.

Gosselin, P., Perron, M., & Maassarani, R. (2009). Children's ability to distinguish between enjoyment and non-enjoyment smiles. *Infant and Child Development, 19*(3), 297–312. doi: 10.1002/icd.648

Gortmaker, S. L., Must, A., Perrin, J. M., Sobol, A. M., & Dietz, W. H. (1993). Social and economic consequences of overweight in adolescence and young adulthood. *New England Journal of Medicine, 329,* 1008–1012.

Gosden, R. G., & Feinberg, A. P. (2007). Genetics and epigenetics—nature's pen-and-pencil set. *New England Journal of Medicine, 356,* 731–733.

Gottfried, A., E., Fleming, J. S., & Gottfried, A. W. (1998). Role of cognitively stimulating home environment in children's academic intrinsic motivation: A longitudinal study. *Child Development, 69,* 1448–1460.

Gottfried, A. W., Cook, C. R., Gottfried, A. E., & Morris, P. E. (2005). Educational characteristics of adolescents with gifted academic intrinsic motivation: A longitudinal investigation from school entry through early adulthood. *Gifted Child Quarterly, 49*(2), 172–186.

Gottlieb, A. (2000). Luring your child into this life: A Beng path for infant care. In J. DeLoache & A. Gottlieb (Eds.), *A world of babies: Imagined child-care guides for seven societies* (pp. 55–89). New York: Cambridge University Press.

Gottlieb, G. (1991). Experiential canalization of behavioral development theory. *Developmental Psychology, 27*(1), 4–13.

Gottlieb, G. (2007). Probabilistic epigenesis. *Developmental Science, 10,* 1–11.

Gottman, J. M., & Notarius, C. I. (2000). Decade review: Observing marital interaction. *Journal of Marriage and the Family, 62,* 927–947.

Goubet, N. & Clifton, R. K. (1998). Object and event representation in 6 1/2-month-old infants. *Developmental Psychology, 34,* 63–76.

Gould, E., Reeves, A. J., Graziano, M.S.A., & Gross, C. G. (1999). Neurogenesis in the neocortex of adult primates. *Science, 286,* 548–552.

Graber, J. A., Brooks-Gunn, J., & Warren, M. P. (1995). The antecedents of menarcheal age: Heredity, family environment, and stressful life events. *Child Development, 66,* 346–359.

Graber, J. A., Lewinsohn, P. M., Seeley, J. R., & Brooks-Gunn, J. (1997). Is psychopathology associated with the timing of pubertal development? *Journal of the American Academy of Child and Adolescent Psychiatry, 36,* 1768–1776.

Grady, B. (2002, December). *Miscarriage: The need to grieve.* Retrieved April 9, 2006, from www.parenting-plus.newsletter/com0212.htm

Grantham-McGregor, S., Powell, C., Walker, S., Chang, S., & Fletcher, P. (1994). The long-term follow-up of severely malnourished children who participated in an intervention program. *Child Development, 65,* 428–439.

Gray, J. R., & Thompson, P. M. (2004). Neurobiology of intelligence: Science and ethics. *Neuroscience, 5,* 471–492.

Gray, M. R., & Steinberg, L. (1999). Unpacking authoritative parenting: Reassessing a multidimensional construct. *Journal of Marriage and the Family, 61,* 574–587.

Gray, P. B., Yang, C. J., & Pope Jr., H. G. (2006). Fathers have lower salivary testosterone levels than umarried men and married on-fathers in Beijing, China. *Proceedings of the Royal Society of Biological Sciences, 273*(1584), 333–339.

Green, R. E., Krause, J., Briggs, A. W., Maricic, T., Stenzel, U., Kircher, M., et al. (2010). A draft sequence of the Neandertal genome. *Science, 7*(328), 710–722. doi: 10.1126/science.1188021

Greene, M. F. (2002). Outcomes of very low birth weight in young adults. *New England Journal of Medicine, 346*(3), 146–148.

Greenfield, P. (2009). Technology and informal education: What is taught, what is learned. *Science, 323,* 69–71.

Greenfield, P. M., & Childs, C. P. (1978). Understanding sibling concepts: A developmental study of kin terms in Zinacanten. In P. R. Dasen (Ed.), *Piagetian psychology* (pp. 335–358). New York: Gardner.

Greenhouse, L. (2000a, February 29). Program of drug-testing pregnant women draws review by the Supreme Court. *New York Times,* p. A12.

Greenhouse, L. (2000b, September 9). Should a fetus's well-being override a mother's rights? *New York Times,* pp. B9, B11.

Greenstone, M., & Chay, K. (2003). The impact of air pollution on infant mortality: Evidence from geographic variation in pollution shocks induced by a recession. *Quarterly Journal of Economics, 118,* 1121–1167.

Gregg, V. R., Winer, G. A., Cottrell, J. E., Hedman, K. E., & Fournier, J. S. (2001). The persistence of a misconception about vision after educational interventions. *Psychonomic Bulletin and Review, 8,* 622–626.

Grigorenko, E. L., Meier, E., Lipka, J., Mohatt, G., Yanez, E., & Sternberg, R. J. (2004). Academic and practical intelligence: A case study of the Yup'ik in Alaska. *Learning and Individual Differences, 14*(4), 183–207.

Grigorenko, E. L., & Sternberg, R. J. (1998). Dynamic testing. *Psych Bulletin, 124,* 75–111.

Groce, N. E., & Zola, I. K. (1993). Multiculturalism, chronic illness, and disability. *Pediatrics, 91,* 1048–1055.

Gross, R. T., & Duke, P. (1980). The effect of early versus late physical maturation on adolescent behavior. [Special issue: I. Litt (Ed.), Symposium on adolescent medicine]. *Pediatric Clinics of North America, 27,* 71–78.

Grotevant, H. D., McRoy, R. G., Eide, C. L., & Fravel, D. L. (1994). Adoptive family system dynamics: Variations by level of openness in the adoption. *Family Process, 33*(2), 125–146.

Gruber, H. (1981). *Darwin on man: A psychological study of scientific creativity* (2nd ed.). Chicago: University of Chicago Press.

Grusec, J. E., & Goodnow, J. J. (1994). Impact of parental discipline methods on the child's internalization of values: A reconceptualization of current points of view. *Developmental Psychology, 30,* 4–19.

Guberman, S. R. (1996). The development of everyday mathematics in Brazilian children with limited formal education. *Child Development, 67,* 1609–1623.

Guendelman, S., Kosa, J. L., Pearl, M., Graham, S., Goodman, J., & Kharrazi, M. (2009). Juggling work and breastfeeding: Effects of maternity leave and occupational characteristics. *Pediatrics, 123,* e38–e46.

Guerino, P., Hurwitz, M. D., Noonan, M. E., & Kaffenberger, S. M. (2006). *Crime, violence, discipline, and safety in U.S. public schools: Findings from the School Survey on Crime and Safety: 2003–2004* (NCES 2007-303). Washington, DC: National Center for Education Statistics.

Guilford, J. P. (1956). Structure of intellect. *Psychological Bulletin, 53,* 267–293.

Guilford, J. P. (1959). Three faces of intellect. *American Psychologist, 14,* 469–479.

Guilford, J. P. (1960). Basic conceptual problems of the psychology of thinking. *Proceedings of the New York Academy of Sciences, 91,* 6–21.

Guilford, J. P. (1967). *The nature of human intelligence.* New York: McGraw-Hill.

Guilford, J. P. (1986). *Creative talents: Their nature, uses and development.* Buffalo, NY: Bearly.

Guilleminault, C., Palombini, L., Pelayo, R., & Chervin, R. D. (2003). Sleeping and sleep terrors in prepubertal children: What triggers them? *Pediatrics, 111,* e17–e25.

Gullone, E. (2000). The development of normal fear: A century of research. *Clinical Psychology Review, 20,* 429–451.

Gundersen, C., Lohman, B. J., Garasky, S., Stewart, S., & Eisenmann, J. (2008). Food security, maternal stressors, and overweight among low-income U.S. children: Results from the National Health and Nutrition Examination Survey (1999–2002). *Pediatrics, 122,* e529–e540.

Gunnar, M. R., Larson, M. C., Hertsgaard, L., Harris, M. L., & Brodersen, L. (1992). The stressfulness of separation among 9-month-old infants: Effects of social context variables and infant temperament. *Child Development, 63,* 290–303.

Gunnoe, M. L., & Hetherington, E. M. (2004). Stepchildren's perceptions of noncustodial mothers and noncustodial fathers: Differences in socioemotional involvement and associations with adolescent adjustment problems. *Journal of Family Psychology, 18,* 555–563.

Gunnoe, M. L., & Mariner, C. L. (1997). Toward a developmental-contextual model of the effects of parental spanking on children's aggression. *Archives of Pediatric and Adolescent Medicine, 151,* 768–775.

Gunturkun, O. (2003). Human behaviour: Adult persistence of head-turning asymmetry. *Nature, 421,* 711. doi:10.1038/421711a

Guo, G., Roettger, M., & Cai, T. (2008). The integration of genetic propensities into social-control models of delinquency and violence among male youths. *American Sociological Review, 73,* 543–568.

Gutman, L. M., & Eccles, J. S. (2007). Stage-environment fit during adolescence: Trajectories of family relations and adolescent outcomes. *Developmental Psychology, 43,* 522–537.

Guzick, D. S., Carson, S. A., Coutifaris, C., Overstreet, J. W., Factor-Litvak, P., Steinkampf, M. P., et al. (1999). Efficacy of superovulation and intrauterine insemination in the treatment of infertility. *New England Journal of Medicine, 340,* 177–183.

Hack, M., Flannery, D. J., Schluchter, M., Cartar, L., Borawski, E., & Klein, N. (2002). Outcomes in young adulthood for very-low-birth-weight infants. *New England Journal of Medicine, 346*(3), 149–157.

Hack, M., Youngstrom, E. A., Cartar, L., Schluchter, M., Taylor, H. G., Flannery, D., et al. (2004). Behavioral outcomes and evidence of psychopathology among very low birth weight infants at age 20 years. *Pediatrics, 114,* 932–940.

Hagan, J. F., Committee on Psychosocial Aspects of Child and Family Health, & Task Force on Terrorism. (2005). Psychosocial implications of disaster or terrorism on children: A guide for pediatricians. *Pediatrics, 116,* 787–796.

Hahn, R., Fuqua-Whitley, D., Wethington, H., Lowy, J., Liberman, A., Crosby, A., et al. (2007). The effectiveness of universal school-based programs for the prevention of violent and aggressive behavior: A report on recommendations of the Task Force on Community Preventive Services. *Morbidity and Mortality Weekly Report, 56*(RR07), 1–12.

Haig, D. (1993). Genetic conflicts in human pregnancy. *Quarterly Review of Biology, 68,* 495–532.

Haith, M. M. (1986). Sensory and perceptual processes in early infancy. *Journal of Pediatrics, 109*(1), 158–171.

Haith, M. M. (1998). Who put the cog in infant cognition? Is rich interpretation too costly? *Infant Behavior and Development, 21*(2), 167–179.

Haith, M. M., & Benson, J. B. (1998). Infant cognition. In D. Kuhn & R. S. Siegler (Eds.), *Handbook of child psychology: Vol. 2. Cognition, perception, and language* (5th ed., pp. 199–254). New York: Wiley.

Halbower, A. C., Degaonkar, M., Barker, P. B., Early, C. J., Marcus, C. L., Smith, P. L., et al. (2006) Childhood obstructive sleep apnea associates with neuropsychological deficits and neuronal brain injury. *PLoS Medicine, 3,* e301–e312.

Halgunseth, L. C., Ispa, J. M., & Rudy, D. (2006). Parental control in Latino families: An integrated review of the literature. *Child Development, 77,* 1282–1297.

Hall, D. G., & Graham, S. A. (1999). Lexical form class information guides word-to-object mapping in preschoolers. *Child Development, 70,* 78–91.

Hallfors, D. D. Waller, M. W., Bauer, D., Ford, C. A., & Halpern, C. T. (2005). Which comes first in adolescence—sex and drugs or depression? *American Journal of Preventive Medicine, 29,* 1163–1170.

Halpern, C., Young, M., Waller, M., Martin, S., & Kupper, L. (2003). Prevalence of partner violence in same-sex romantic and sexual relationships in a national sample of adolescents. *Journal of Adolescent Health, 35*(2), 124–131.

Halpern, D. F., Benbow, C. P., Geary, D. C., Gur, R. C., Hyde, J. S., & Gernsbacher, M. A. (2007). The science of sex differences in science and mathematics. *Psychological Science in the Public Interest, 8,* 1–51.

Hamilton, L., Cheng, S., & Powell, B. (2007). Adoptive parents, adaptive parents: Evaluating the importance of biological ties for parental involvement. *American Sociological Review, 72,* 95–116.

Hamilton, M. C., Anderson, D., Broaddus, M., & Young, K. (2006) Gender stereotyping and underrepresentation of female characters in 200 popular children's picture books: A 21st century update. *Sex Roles: A Journal of Research, 55,* 757–765.

Hamlin, J. K., Wynn, K., & Bloom, P. (2007). Social evaluation by preverbal infants. *Nature, 450,* 557–559.

Hammad, T. A., Laughren, T., & Racoosin, J. (2006). Suicidality in pediatric patients treated with antidepressant drugs. *Archives of General Psychiatry, 63,* 332–339.

Hampden-Thompson, G., & Johnston. J. S. (2006). *Variation in the relationship between nonschool factors and student achievement on international assessments* (NCES 2006-014). Washington, DC: U.S. Department of Education, National Center for Education Statistics.

Hamre, B. K., & Pianta, R. C. (2005). Can instructional and emotional support in the first-grade classroom make a difference for children at risk of school failure? *Child Development, 76,* 949–967.

Handmaker, N. S., Rayburn, W. F., Meng, C., Bell, J. B., Rayburn, B. B., & Rappaport, V. J. (2006). Impact of alcohol exposure after pregnancy recognition on ultrasonographic fetal growth measures. *Alcoholism: Clinical and Experimental Research, 30,* 892–898.

Hanney, L., & Kozlowska, K. (2002). Healing traumatized children: Creating illustrated storybooks in family therapy. *Family Process, 41*(1), 37–65.

Hannigan, J. H., & Armant, D. R. (2000). Alcohol in pregnancy and neonatal outcome. *Seminars in Neonatology, 5,* 243–254.

Hansen, D., Lou, H. C., & Olsen, J. (2000). Serious life events and congenital malformations: A national study with complete follow-up. *Lancet, 356,* 875–880.

Hansen, M., Janssen, I., Schiff, A., Zee, P. C., & Dubocovich, M. L. (2005). The impact of school daily schedule on adolescent sleep. *Pediatrics, 115,* 1555–1561.

Hara, H. (2002). Justifications for bullying among Japanese school children. *Asian Journal of Social Psychology, 5,* 197–204.

Hardway, C., & Fuligni, A. J. (2006). Dimensions of family connectedness among adolescents with Mexican, Chinese, and European backgrounds. *Developmental Psychology, 42,* 1246–1258.

Hardy, R., Kuh, D., Langenberg, C., & Wadsworth, M. E. (2003). Birth weight, childhood social class, and change in adult blood pressure in the 1946 British birth cohort. *Lancet, 362,* 1178–1183.

Hardy-Brown, K., & Plomin, R. (1985). Infant communicative development: Evidence from adoptive and biological families for genetic and environmental influences on rate differences. *Developmental Psychology, 21,* 378–385.

Hardy-Brown, K., Plomin, R., & DeFries, J. C. (1981). Genetic and environmental influences on rate of communicative development in the first year of life. *Developmental Psychology, 17,* 704–717.

Harlow, H. F., & Harlow, M. K. (1962). The effect of rearing conditions on behavior. *Bulletin of the Menninger Clinic, 26,* 213–224.

Harlow, H. F., & Zimmerman, R. R. (1959). Affectional responses in the infant monkey. *Science, 130,* 421–432.

Harnishfeger, K. K., & Bjorklund, D. F. (1993). The ontogeny of inhibition mechanisms: A renewed approach to cognitive development. In M. L. Howe & R. P. Pasnak (Eds.), *Emerging themes in cognitive development* (Vol. 1, pp. 28–49). New York: Springer-Verlag.

Harnishfeger, K. K., & Pope, R. S. (1996). Intending to forget: The development of cognitive inhibition in directed forgetting. *Journal of Experimental Psychology, 62,* 292–315.

Harris, G. (1997). Development of taste perception and appetite regulation. In G. Bremner, A. Slater, & G. Butterworth (Eds.), *Infant development: Recent advances* (pp. 9–30). East Sussex, UK: Psychology Press.

Harris, L. H., & Paltrow, L. (2003). The status of pregnant women and fetuses in U.S. criminal law. *Journal of the American Medical Association, 289,* 1697–1699.

Harris, P. L., Brown, E., Marriott, C., Whittall, S., & Harmer, S. (1991). Monsters, ghosts, and witches: Testing the limits of the fantasy-reality distinction in young children. In G. E. Butterworth, P. L. Harris, A. M. Leslie, & H. M. Wellman (Eds.), *Perspective on the child's theory of mind* (pp. 143–164). Oxford: Oxford University Press.

Harris, P. L., Olthof, T., Meerum Terwogt, M., & Hardman, C. (1987). Children's knowledge of situations that provoke emotion. *International Journal of Behavioral Development, 10,* 319–343.

Harrist, A. W., & Waugh, R. M. (2002). Dyadic synchrony: Its structure and function in children's development. *Developmental Review, 22,* 555–592.

Harrist, A. W., Zain, A. F., Bates, J. E., Dodge, K. A., & Pettit, G. S. (1997). Subtypes of social withdrawal in early childhood: Sociometric status and social-cognitive differences across four years. *Child Development, 68,* 278–294.

Hart, C. H., DeWolf, M., Wozniak, P., & Burts, D. C. (1992). Maternal and paternal disciplinary styles: Relations with preschoolers' playground behavioral orientation and peer status. *Child Development, 63,* 879–892.

Hart, C. H., Ladd, G. W., & Burleson, B. R. (1990). Children's expectations of the outcome of social strategies: Relations with sociometric status and maternal disciplinary style. *Child Development, 61,* 127–137.

Harter, S. (1990). Causes, correlates, and the functional role of global self-worth: A life-span perspective. In J. Kolligan & R. Sternberg (Eds.), *Competence considered: Perceptions of competence and incompetence across the life-span* (pp. 67–97). New Haven, CT: Yale University Press.

Harter, S. (1993). Developmental changes in self-understanding across the 5 to 7 shift. In A. Sameroff & M. Haith (Eds.), *Reason and responsibility: The passage through childhood* (pp. 207–236). Chicago: University of Chicago Press.

Harter, S. (1996). Developmental changes in self-understanding across the 5 to 7 shift. In J. Sameroff & M. M. Haith (Eds.), *The five to seven year shift: The age of reason and responsibility* (pp. 207–235). Chicago: University of Chicago Press.

Harter, S. (1998). The development of self-representations. In W. Damon (Series Ed.) & N. Eisenberg (Vol. Ed.), *Handbook of child psychology: Vol. 3. Social, emotional, and personality development* (5th ed., pp. 553–617). New York: Wiley.

Harter, S. (2006). The self. In W. Damon & R. M. Lerner (Series Eds.) & N. Eisenberg (Vol. Ed.), *Handbook of child psychology: Vol 3. Social, emotional and personality development* (pp. 505–570). Hoboken: NJ: Wiley.

Hartshorn, K., Rovee-Collier, C., Gerhardstein, P., Bhatt, R. S., Wondoloski, R. L., Klein, P., et al. (1998). The ontogeny of long-term memory over the first year-and-a-half of life. *Developmental Psychobiology, 32,* 69–89.

Hartup, W. W. (1992). Peer relations in early and middle childhood. In V. B. Van Hasselt & M. Hersen (Eds.), *Handbook of social development: A lifespan perspective* (pp. 257–281). New York: Plenum Press.

Hartup, W. W. (1996a). The company they keep: Friendships and their developmental significance. *Child Development, 67,* 1–13.

Hartup, W. W. (1996b). Cooperation, close relationships, and cognitive development. In W. M. Bukowski, A. F. Newcomb, & W. W. Hartup (Eds.), *The company they keep: Friendship in childhood and adolescence* (pp. 213–237). New York: Cambridge University Press.

Hartup, W. W., & Stevens, N. (1999). Friendships and adaptation across the life span. *Current Directions in Psychological Science, 8,* 76–79.

Harvard Medical School. (2004, December). Children's fears and anxieties. *Harvard Mental Health Letter, 21*(6), 1–3.

Harvey, J. H., & Pauwels, B. G. (1999). Recent developments in close relationships theory. *Current Directions in Psychological Science, 8*(3), 93–95.

Harwood, R. L., Schoelmerich, A., Ventura-Cook, E., Schulze, P. A., & Wilson, S. P. (1996). Culture and class influences on Anglo and Puerto Rican mothers' beliefs regarding long-term socialization goals and child behavior. *Child Development, 67,* 2446–2461.

Haswell, K., Hock, E., & Wenar, C. (1981). Oppositional behavior of preschool children: Theory and intervention. *Family Relations, 30,* 440–446.

Hatcher, P. J., Hulme, C., & Ellis, A. W. (1994). Ameliorating early reading failure by integrating the teaching of reading and phonological skills: The phonological linkage hypotheses. *Child Development, 65,* 41–57.

Hauck, F. R., Herman, S. M., Donovan, M., Iyasu, S., Moore, C. M., Donoghue, E., et al. (2003). Sleep environment and the risk of sudden infant death syndrome in an urban population: The Chicago Infant Mortality Study. *Pediatrics, 111,* 1207–1214.

Hauck, F. R., Omojokun, O. O., & Siadaty, M. S. (2005). Do pacifiers reduce the risk of sudden infant death syndrome? A meta-analysis. *Pediatrics, 116,* e716–e723.

Haugaard, J. J. (1998). Is adoption a risk factor for the development of adjustment problems? *Clinical Psychology Review, 18,* 47–69.

Hawes, A. (1996). Jungle gyms: The evolution of animal play. *ZooGoer, 25*(1). Retrieved July 18, 2006, from http://nationalzoo.si.edu/Publications /ZooGoer/1996/1/junglegyms.cfm

Hawkins, J. D., Catalano, R. F., Kosterman, R., Abbott, R., & Hill, K. G. (1999). Preventing adolescent health-risk behaviors by strengthening protection during childhood. *Archives of Pediatrics and Adolescent Medicine, 153,* 226–234.

Hawkins, J. D., Catalano, R. F., & Miller, J. Y. (1992). Risk and protective factors for alcohol and other drug problems in adolescence and early adulthood: Implications for substance abuse programs. *Psychological Bulletin, 112*(1), 64–105.

Hawks, J., Wang, E. T., Cochran, G. M., Harpending, H. C., & Moyzis, R. K. (2007). Recent acceleration of human adaptive evolution. *Proceedings of the National Academy of Sciences, USA, 104,* 20753–20758.

Hay, D (1994). Prosocial development. *Journal of Child Psychology and Psychiatry, 35,* 29–71.

Hay, D. (2003). Pathways to violence in the children of mothers who were depressed post partum. *Developmental Psychology, 39,* 1083–1094.

Hay, D. F., Payne, A., & Chadwick, A. (2004). Peer relations in childhood. *Journal of Child Psychology and Psychiatry, 45,* 84–108.

Hay, D. F., Pedersen, J., & Nash, A. (1982). Dyadic interaction in the first year of life. In K. H. Rubin & H. S. Ross (Eds.), *Peer relationships and social skills in children.* New York: Springer.

Hayashi, M., & Abe, A. (2008). Short daytime naps in a car seat to counteract daytime sleepiness: The effect of backrest angle. *Sleep and Biological Rhythms, 6,* 34–44.

Hayes, A., & Batshaw, M. L. (1993). Down syndrome. *Pediatric Clinics of North America, 40,* 523–535.

Hayghe, H. (1986, February). Rise in mothers' labor force activity includes those with infants. *Monthly Labor Review, 109,* 43–45.

Hayne, H., Barr, R., & Herbert, J. (2003). The effect of prior practice on memory reactivation and generalization. *Child Development, 74,* 1615–1627.

Healy, A. J., Malone, F. D., Sullivan, L. M., Porter, T. F., Luthy, D. A., Comstock, C. H., et al. (2006). Early access to prenatal care: Implications for racial disparity in perinatal mortality. *Obstetrics and Gynecology, 107,* 625–631.

Heath, S. B. (1989). Oral and literate tradition among black Americans living in poverty. *American Psychologist, 44,* 367–373.

Heffner, L. J. (2004). Advanced maternal age-how old is too old? *New England Journal of Medicine, 351,* 1927–1929.

Helms, J. E. (1992). Why is there no study of cultural equivalence in standardized cognitive ability testing? *American Psychologist, 47,* 1083–1101.

Helms, J. E., Jernigan, M., & Macher, J. (2005). The meaning of race in psychology and how to change it: A methodological perspective. *American Psychologist, 60,* 27–36.

Helwig, C. C., & Jasiobedzka, U. (2001). The relation between law and morality: Children's reasoning about socially beneficial and unjust laws. *Child Development, 72,* 1382–1393.

Henderson, H. A., Marshall, P. J., Fox, N. A., & Rubin, K. H. (2004). Psychophysiological and behavioral evidence for varying forms and functions of nonsocial behavior in preschoolers. *Child Development, 75,* 251–263.

Henrich, C., Ginicola, M., Finn-Stevenson, M., & Zigler, E. (2006). *The school of the 21st century is making a difference: Findings from two evaluations.* [Issue brief]. New Haven, CT: Zigler Center in Child Development and Social Policy, Yale University.

Herdt, G., & McClintock, M. (2000). The magical age of ten. *Archives of Sexual Behavior, 29*(6), 587–606. doi: 10.1023/A:1002006521067

Hernandez, D. J. (1997). Child development and the social demography of childhood. *Child Development, 68,* 149–169.

Hernandez, D. J. (2004, Summer). Demographic change and the life circumstances of immigrant families. In R. E. Behrman (Ed.), *Children of immigrant families* (pp. 17–48). *The Future of Children, 14*(2). Retrieved October 7, 2004, from www.futureofchildren.org

Hernandez, D. J., Denton, N. A., & Macartney, S. E. (2007). Child poverty in the U.S.: A new family budget approach with comparison to European countries. In H. Wintersberger, L. Alanen, T. Olk, & J. Qvortrup (Eds.), *Childhood, generational order and the welfare state: Exploring children's social and economic welfare. Volume 1 of COST A19 Children's Welfare* (pp. 109–140). Odense: University Press of Southern Denmark.

Hernandez, D. J., Denton, N. A., & Macartney, S. E. (2008). Children in immigrant families: Looking to America's future. *SRCD Social Policy Report, 22.* [No. 111].

Hernandez, D. J., & Macartney, S. E. (2008, January). *Racial-ethnic inequality in child well-being from 1985–2004: Gaps narrowing, but persist.* [No. 9]. New York: Foundation for Child Development.

Heron, M. P, Hoyert, D. L., Murphy, S. L., Xu, J. Q., Kochanek, K. D., & Tejada-Vera, B. (2009). Deaths: Final data for 2006. *National Vital Statistics Reports, 57*(14). Hyattsville, MD: National Center for Health Statistics.

Herrera, C., & Dunn, J. (1997). Early experinces with family conflict: Implications for arguments with a close friend. *Developmental Psychology, 33,* 869–881.

Herrnstein, R. J., & Murray, C. (1994). *The bell curve: Intelligence and class structure in American life.* New York: Free Press.

Hertenstein, M. J., & Campos, J. J. (2004). The retention effects of an adult's emotional displays on infant behavior. *Child Development, 75,* 595–613.

Hertz-Pannier, L., Chiron, C., Jambaque, I., Renaux-Kieffer, V., Van de Moortele, P.,

Delalande, O., et al. (2002). Late plasticity for language in a child's non-dominant hemisphere. A pre- and post-surgery fMRI study. *Brain, 125*(2), 361–372.

Hertz-Picciotto, I., & Delwiche, L. (2009). The rise in autism and the role of age at diagnosis. *Epidemiology, 20,* 84–90.

Hesketh, T., Lu, L., & Xing, Z. W. (2005). The effect of China's one-child policy after 25 years. *New England Journal of Medicine, 353,* 1171–1176.

Hespos, S. J., & Baillargeon, R. (2008). Young infants' actions reveal their developing knowledge of support variables: Converging evidence for violation-of-expectation findings. *Cognition, 107*(1), 304–316.

Hess, S. Y., & King, J. C. (2009). Effects of maternal zinc supplementation on pregnancy and lactation outcomes. *Food and Nutrition Bulletin, 30*(1), 60–78.

Hesso, N. A., & Fuentes, E. (2005). Ethnic differences in neonatal and postneonatal mortality. *Pediatrics, 115,* e44–e51.

Hetherington, E. M. (1987). Family relations six years after divorce. In K. Pasley & M. Ihinger-Tallman (Eds.), *Remarriage and stepparenting today: Research and theory* (pp. 185–205). New York: Guilford Press.

Hetherington, E. M., & Kelly, J. (2002). *For better or worse: Divorce reconsidered.* New York: Norton.

Hetherington, E. M., Stanley-Hagan, M., & Anderson, E. (1989). Marital transitions: Child's perspective. *American Psychologist, 44,* 303–312.

Hewlett, B. S. (1987). Intimate fathers: Patterns of paternal holding among Aka pygmies. In M. E. Lamb (Ed.), *The father's role: Cross-cultural perspectives* (pp. 295–330). Hillsdale, NJ: Erlbaum.

Hewlett, B. S. (1992). Husband-wife reciprocity and the father-infant relationship among Aka pygmies. In B. S. Hewlett (Ed.), *Father-child relations: Cultural and biosocial contexts* (pp. 153–176). New York: de Gruyter.

Hewlett, B. S., Lamb, M. E., Shannon, D., Leyendecker, B., & Schölmerich, A. (1998). Culture and early infancy among central African foragers and farmers. *Developmental Psychology, 34*(4), 653–661.

Hickling, A. K., & Wellman, H. M. (2001). The emergence of children's causal explanations and theories: Evidence from everyday conversations. *Developmental Psychology, 37*(5), 668–683.

Hickman, M., Roberts, C., & de Matos, M. G. (2000). Exercise and leisure time activities. In C. Currie, K. Hurrelmann, W. Settertobulte, R. Smith, & J. Todd (Eds.), *Health and health behaviour among young people: A WHO crossnational study (HBSC) international report* (pp. 73–82). [WHO Policy Series: Health Policy for Children and Adolescents, Series No. 1]. Copenhagen, Denmark: World Health Organization Regional Office for Europe.

Hill, A. L., Degan, K. A., Calkins, S. D., & Keane, S. P. (2006). Profiles of externalizing behavior problems for boys and girls across preschool: The roles of emotional regulation and inattention. *Developmental Psychology, 42,* 913–928.

Hill, D. A., Gridley, G., Cnattingius, S., Mellemkjaer, L., Linet, M., Adami, H.-O., et al. (2003). Mortality and cancer incidence among individuals with Down syndrome. *Archives of Internal Medicine, 163,* 705–711.

Hill, J. L., Waldfogel, J., Brooks-Gunn, J., & Han, W.-J. (2005). Maternal employment and child development: A fresh look using newer methods. *Developmental Psychology, 41,* 833–850.

Hill, J. P. (1987). Research on adolescents and their families: Past and prospect. In E. E. Irwin (Ed.), *New directions in child development: Adolescent social behavior and health* (pp. 13–32). San Francisco: Jossey-Bass.

Hill, N., & Tyson, D. (2009). Parental involvement in middle school: A meta-analytical assessment of the strategies that promote achievement. *Developmental Psychology, 45*(3), 740–763.

Hill, N. E., & Taylor, L. C. (2004). Parental school involvement and children's academic achievement: Pragmatics and issues. *Current Directions in Psychological Science, 13,* 161–168.

Hillier, L. (2002). "It's a catch-22": Same-sex-attracted young people on coming out to parents. In S. S. Feldman & D. A. Rosenthal (Eds.), Talking sexuality. *New Directions for Child and Adolescent Development, 97,* 75–91.

Hillier, T. A., Pedula, K. L., Vesco, K. K., Schmidt, M. M., Mullen, J. A., LeBlanc, E. S., & Pettitt, D. J. (2008). Excess gestational weight gain: Modifying fetal macrosomia risk associated with maternal glucose. *Obstetrics & Gynecology, 112,* 1007–1014.

Hillis, S. D., Anda, R. F., Dubé, S. R., Felitti, V. J., Marchbanks, P. A., & Marks, J. S. (2004). The association between adverse childhood experiences and adolescent pregnancy, long-term psychosocial consequences, and fetal death. *Pediatrics, 113,* 320–327.

Hinckley, A. F., Bachard, A. M., & Reif, J. S. (2005). Late pregnancy exposures to disinfection by-products and growth-related birth outcomes. *Environmental Health Perspectives, 113,* 1808–1813.

Hines, A. M. (1997). Divorce-related transitions, adolescent development, and the role of the parent-child relationship: A review of the literature. *Journal of Marriage and the Family, 59,* 375–388.

Hingson, R. W., Heeren., T., & Winter, M. R. (2006) Age at drinking onset and alcohol dependence: Age at onset, duration, and severity. *Archivers of Pediatrics & Adolescent Medicine, 160,* 739–746.

Hitchins, M. P., & Moore, G. E. (2002, May 9). Genomic imprinting in fetal growth and development. *Expert Reviews in Molecular Medicine, 4,* 1–9.

Hjelmborg, J., Iachine, I., Skythe, A., Vaupel, J., McGue, M., et. al., (2006). Genetic influence on human lifespan and longevity. *Human Genetics 199*(3), 312–321.

Hoban, T. F. (2004). Sleep and its disorders in children. *Seminars in Neurology, 24,* 327–340.

Hobson, J. A., & Silvestri, L. (1999, February). Parasomnias. *Harvard Mental Health Letter,* pp. 3–5.

Hodges, E.V.E., Boivin, M., Vitaro, F., & Bukowski, W. M. (1999). The power of friendship: Protection against an escalating cycle of peer victimization. *Developmental Psychology, 35,* 94–101.

Hodnett, E. D., Gates, S., Hofmeyr, G. J., & Sakala, C. (2005). Continuous support for women during childbirth (Cochrane Review). *The Cochrane Library,* Issue 1, Oxford.

Hoff, E. (2003). The specificity of environmental influence: Socioeconomic status affects early vocabulary development via maternal speech. *Child Development, 74,* 1368–1378.

Hoff, E. (2006). How social contexts support and shape language development. *Developmental Review, 26,* 55–88.

Hofferth, S. L., & Jankuniene, Z. (2000, April 2). *Children's after-school activities.* Paper presented at biennial meeting of the Society for Research on Adolescence, Chicago, IL.

Hoffman, M. L. (1970a). Conscience, personality, and socialization techniques. *Human Development, 13*, 90–126.

Hoffman, M. L. (1970b). Moral development. In P. H. Mussen (Ed.), *Carmichael's manual of child psychology* (Vol. 2, 3rd ed., pp. 261–360). New York: Wiley.

Hoffrage, U., Weber, A., Hertwig, R., & Chase, V. M. (2003). How to keep children safe in traffic: Find the daredevils early. *Journal of Experimental Psychology: Applied, 9*, 249–260.

Hofman, P. L., Regan, F., Jackson, W. E., Jefferies, C., Knight, D. B., Robinson, E. M., & Cutfield, W. S. (2004). Premature birth and later insulin resistance. *New England Journal of Medicine, 351*, 2179–2186.

Hogge, W. A. (2003). The clinical use of karyotyping spontaneous abortions. *American Journal of Obstetrics and Gynecology, 189*, 397–402.

Holden, G. W., & Miller, P. C. (1999). Enduring and different: A meta-analysis of the similarity in parents' child rearing. *Psychological Bulletin, 125*, 223–254.

Holditch-Davis, D., Scher, M., Schwartz, T., & Hudson-Barr, D. (2004). Sleeping and waking state development in preterm infants. *Early Human Development, 80*, 43–64.

Holmes E. A., James, E. L., Kilford, E. J., & Deeprose, C. (2010). Key steps in developing a cognitive vaccine against traumatic flashbacks: Visuospatial tetris versus verbal pub quiz. *PLoS ONE, 5*(11), e13706. doi:10.1371/journal.pone.0013706

Holowka, S., & Petitto, L. A. (2002). Left hemisphere cerebral specialization for babies while babbling. *Science, 297*, 1515.

Holtzman, N. A., Murphy, P. D., Watson, M. S., & Barr, P. A. (1997). Predictive genetic testing: From basic research to clinical practice. *Science, 278*, 602–605.

Honein, M. A., Paulozzi, L. J., Mathews, T. J., Erickson, J. D., & Wong, L.-Y. C. (2001). Impact of folic acid fortification of the U.S. food supply on the occurrence of neural tube defects. *Journal of the American Medical Association, 285*, 2981–2986.

Hong, Y., Morris, M. W., Chiu, C., & Benet-Martinez, V. (2000). Multicultural Minds: A dynamic constructivist approach to culture and cognition. Retrieved November 20, 2012, from http://test.scripts.psu.edu/users/n/x/nxy906/COMPS/indivdualismandcollectivism/culture%20lit/Hongminds.pdf

Hopkins, B., & Westra, T. (1988). Maternal handling and motor development: An intracultural study. *Genetic, Social and General Psychology Monographs, 14*, 377–420.

Hopkins, B., & Westra, T. (1990). Motor development, maternal expectations, and the role of handling. *Infant Behavior and Development, 13*, 177–122.

Horbar, J. D., Wright, E. C., Onstad, L., & the Members of the National Institute of Child Health and Human Development Neonatal Research Network. (1993). Decreasing mortality associated with the introduction of surfactant therapy: An observational study of neonates weighing 601 to 1300 grams at birth. *Pediatrics, 92*, 191–196.

Hornig, M., Briese, T., Buie, T., Bauman, M. L., Lauwer, G., Siemetzki, U., et al. (2008). Lack of association between measles virus vaccine and autism with enteropathy: A case-control study. *PloS One, 3*(9), e3140–1371.

Horwitz, B. N., Neiderhiser, J. M., Ganiban, J. M., Spotts, E. L., Lichtenstein, P., & Reiss, D. (2010). Genetic and environmental influences on global family conflict. *Journal of Family Psychology, 24*(2), 217–220.

Houltberg, B. J., Henry, C. S, & Morris, A. S. (2012), Family interactions, exposure to violence, and emotion regulation: Perceptions of children and early adolescents at risk. *Family Relations, 61*: 283–296. doi: 10.1111/j.1741-3729.2011.00699.x

Howard, K. S., Lefever, J. B., Borkowski, J. G., & Whitman, T. L. (2006). Fathers' influence in the lives of children with adolescent mothers. *Journal of Family Psychology, 20*, 468–476.

Howe, M. L. (2003). Memories from the cradle. *Current Directions in Psychological Science, 12*, 62–65.

Howe, M. L., & Courage, M. L. (1993). On resolving the enigma of infantile amnesia. *Psychological Bulletin, 113*, 305–326.

Howe, M. L., & Courage, M. L. (1997). The emergence and early development of autobiographical memory. *Psychological Review, 104*, 499–523.

Howe, N., Petrakos, H., Rinaldi, C. M., & LeFebvre, R. (2005). "This is a bad dog, you know …": Constructing shared meanings during sibling pretend play. *Child Development, 76*, 783–794.

Howell, R. R. (2006). We need expanded newborn screening. *Pediatrics, 117*, 1800–1805.

Howes, C., Matheeson, C. C., & Hamilton, C. E. (1994). Maternal, teaching, and child-care history correlates of children's relationships with peers. *Child Development, 65*, 264–273.

Howlett, N., Kirk, E., & Pine, K. J. (2010). Does "wanting the best" create more stress? The link between baby sign classes and maternal anxiety. *Infant and Child Development, 20*. Advance online publication. doi: 10.1002/icd.705

Hoyert, D. L., Heron, M. P., Murphy, S. L., & Kung, H. C. (2006). Deaths: Final data for 2003. *National Vital Statistics Reports, 54*(13). Hyattsville, MD: National Center for Health Statistics.

Hoyert, D. L., Mathews, T. J., Menacker, F., Strobino, D. M., & Guyer, B. (2006). Annual summary of vital statistics: 2004. *Pediatrics, 117*, 168–183.

Hoxby, C. M. (2004). *Achievement in charter schools and regular public schools in the United States: Understanding the differences.* Cambridge, MA: Department of Economics, Harvard University.

Hu, W. (2011, January 4). Math that moves: Schools embrace the iPad. *The New York Times.* Retrieved from http://www.nytimes.com/2011/01/05/education/05tablets.html?ref=education

Hudson, V. M., & den Boer, A. M. (2004). *Bare branches: Security implications of Asia's surplus male population.* Cambridge, MA: MIT Press.

Huesmann, L. R., & Kirwil, L. (2007). Why observing violence increases the risk of violent behavior in the observer. In D. Flannery, A. Vazinsyi, & I. Waldman (Eds.), *The Cambridge handbook of violent behavior and agression* (pp. 545–570). Cambridge, UK: University Press.

Huesmann, L. R., Moise-Titus, J., Podolski, C. L., & Eron, L. (2003). Longitudinal relations between children's exposure to TV violence and their aggressive and violent behavior in young adulthood: 1977–1992. *Developmental Psychology, 39*, 201–221.

Huesmann, R. (2007) The impact of electronic media violence: Scientific theory and research. *Journal of Adolescent Health, 41*, S6–S13.

Huge payout in U.S. stuttering case. (2007, August 17). *BBC News.* Retrieved from http://news.bbc.co.uk/2/hi/americas/6952446.stm

Hughes, D., Rodriguez, J., Smith, E. P., Johnson, D. J., Stevenson, H. C., & Spicer, P. (2006). Parents' ethnic-racial socialization practices: A review of research and directions for future study. *Developmental Psychology, 42*, 747–770.

Hughes, I. A. (2004). Female development—all by default? *New England Journal of Medicine, 351*, 748–750.

Hughes, K. L., Bailey, T. R., & Mechur, M. J. (2001). *School-to-work: Making a difference in education: A research report to America.* New York: Columbia University, Teachers College, Institute on Education and the Economy.

Huizink, A. C., Mulder, E.J.H., & Buitelaar, J. K. (2004). Prenatal stress and risk for psychopathology: Specific effects or induction of general susceptibility? *Psychological Bulletin 130*, 80–114.

Huizink, A., Robles de Medina, P., Mulder, E., Visser, G., & Buitelaar, J. (2002). Psychological measures of prenatal stress as predictors of infant temperament. *Journal of the American Academy of Child & Adolescent Psychiatry, 41*, 1078–1085.

Hujoel, P. P., Bollen, A.-M., Noonan, C. J., & del Aguila, M. A. (2004). Antepartum dental radiography and infant low birth weight. *Journal of the American Medical Association, 291*, 1987–1993.

Human Rights Watch. (2008). *A violent education: Corporeal punishment in U.S. public schools.* Retrieved April 15, 2010, from www.aclu.org/human-rights-racial-justice/violent-education-corporal-punishment-children-us-public-schools

Humphreys, A. P., & Smith, P. K. (1984). Rough-and-tumble in preschool and playground. In P. K. Smith (Ed.), *Play in animals and humans* (pp. 241–266). Oxford: Blackwell.

Humphreys, G. W. (2002). Cognitive neuroscience. In H. Pashler, & D. Medin (Eds.), *Steven's handbook of experimental psychology: Vol. 2. Memory and cognitive processes* (3rd ed., pp. 77–112). New York: Wiley.

Hunt, C. E. (1996). Prone sleeping in healthy infants and victims of sudden infant death syndrome. *Journal of Pediatrics, 128*, 594–596.

Huntsinger, C. S., & Jose, P. E. (1995). Chinese American and Caucasian American family interaction patterns in spatial rotation puzzle solutions. *Merrill-Palmer Quarterly, 41*, 471–496.

Huston, A. C., & Aronson, S. R. (2005). Mothers' time with infant and time in employment as predictors of mother-child relationships and children's early development. *Child Development, 76*, 467–482.

Huston, A. C., Duncan, G. J., McLoyd, V. C., Crosby, D. A., Ripke, M. N., Weisner, T. S., & Eldred, C. A. (2005). Impacts on children of a policy to promote employment and reduce poverty for low-income parents: New hope after 5 years. *Developmental Psychology, 41*, 902–918.

Huston, A. C., & Wright, J. C. (1983). Childrens' processing of television: The informative functions of formal features. In J. Bryant & D. R. Anderson (Eds.), *Children's understanding of television: Research on attention and comprehension* (pp. 35–68). New York: Academic Press.

Huston, H. C., Duncan, G. J., Granger, R., Bos, J., McLoyd, V., Mistry, R., et al. (2001). Work-based antipoverty programs for parents can enhance the performance and social behavior of children. *Child Development, 72*(1), 318–336.

Huttenlocher, J. (1998). Language input and language growth. *Preventive Medicine, 27*, 195–199.

Huttenlocher, J., Haight, W., Bryk, A., Seltzer, M., & Lyons, T. (1991). Early vocabulary growth: Relation to language input and gender. *Developmental Psychology, 27,* 236–248.

Huttenlocher, J., Levine, S., & Vevea, J. (1998). Environmental input and cognitive growth: A study using time period comparisons. *Child Development, 69,* 1012–1029.

Huttenlocher, J., Vasilyeva, M., Cymerman, E., & Levine, S. (2002). Language input and child syntax. *Cognitive Psychology, 45,* 337–374.

Hyde, J., Lindberg, S., Linn, M., Ellis, A., & Williams, C. (2008). Gender similarities characterize math performance. *Science, 321*(5888), 494–495.

Hyde, J., & Mertz, J. (2009). Gender, culture, and mathematics performance. *Proceedings of the National Academy of Sciences, 106*(8), 801–807.

Hyde, J. S. (2005). The gender similarity hypothesis. *American Psychologist, 60,* 581–592.

Iacoboni, M. (2008). *Mirroring people: The new science of how we connect with others.* New York: Farrar, Straus, & Giroux.

Iacoboni, M., & Mazziotta, J. C. (2007). Mirror neuron system: Basic findings and clinical applications. *Annals of Neurology, 62,* 213–218.

Ialongo, N. S., Edelsohn, G., & Kellam, S. G. (2001). A further look at the prognostic power of young children's reports of depressed mood and feelings. *Child Development, 72,* 736–747.

Iervolino, A. C., Hines, M., Golombok, S. E., Rust, J., & Plomin, R. (2005). Genetic and environmental influences on sex-types behavior during the preschool years. *Child Development, 76,* 826–840.

Iervolino, A. C., Pike, A., Manke, B., Reiss, D., Hetherington, E. M., & Plomin, R. (2002). Genetic and environmental influences in adolescent peer socialization: Evidence from two genetically sensitive designs. *Child Development, 73*(1), 162–174.

Iglowstein, I., Jenni, O. G., Molinari, L., & Largo, R. H. (2003). Sleep duration from infancy to adolescence: Reference values and generational trends. *Pediatrics, 111,* 302–307.

Imada, T., Zhang, Y., Cheour, M., Taulu, S., Ahonen, A., & Kuhl, P. (2006). Infant speech perception activates Broca's area: A developmental magnetoencephalography study. *NeuroReport, 17,* 957–962.

Ingersoll, E. W., & Thoman, E. B. (1999). Sleep/wake states of preterm infants: Stability, developmental change, diurnal variation, and relation with care giving activity. *Child Development, 70,* 1–10.

Ingram, J. L., Stodgell, C. S., Hyman, S. L., Figlewicz, D. A., Weitkamp, L. R., & Rodier, P. M. (2000). Discovery of allelic variants of HOXA1 and HOXB1: Genetic susceptibility to autism spectrum disorders. *Teratology, 62,* 393–406.

International Committee for Monitoring Assisted Reproductive Technologies (ICMART). (2006, June). *2002 World report on ART.* Report released at meeting of the European Society of Human Reproduction and Embryology, Prague.

Institute of Medicine of the National Academies. (2005). *Preventing childhood obesity: Health in the balance.* Washington, DC: Author.

Institute of Medicine National Academy of Sciences. (1993, November). *Assessing genetic risks: Implications for health and social policy.* Washington, DC: National Academy of Sciences.

Iruka, I. U., & Carver, P. R. (2006). *Initial results from the 2005 NHDS Early Childhood Program Participation Survey* (NCES 2006-075). Washington, DC: National Center for Education Statistics.

Isaacson, W. (2007). *Einstein: His life and universe.* New York: Simon & Schuster.

Isabella, R. A. (1993). Origins of attachment: Maternal interactive behavior across the first year. *Child Development, 64,* 605–621.

ISLAT Working Group. (1998). ART into science: Regulation of fertility techniques. *Science, 281,* 651–652.

Isley, S., O'Neil, R., & Parke, R. (1996). The relation of parental affect and control behaviors to children's classroom acceptance: A concurrent and predictive analysis. *Early Education and Development, 7,* 7–23.

Izard, C. E., Porges, S. W., Simons, R. F., Haynes, O. M., & Cohen, B. (1991). Infant cardiac activity: Developmental changes and relations with attachment. *Developmental Psychology, 27,* 432–439.

Jaccard, J., & Dittus, P. J. (2000). Adolescent perceptions of maternal approval of birth control and sexual risk behavior. *American Journal of Public Health, 90,* 1426–1430.

Jackson, A. (1997a). The math wars: California battles it out over mathematics, Education Reform (Part I). *Notices of the AMS.* Retrieved January 22, 1999, from www.ams.org/notices/199706/comm-calif.pdf

Jackson, A. (1997b). The math wars: California battles it out over mathematics, Education Reform (Part II). *Notices of the AMS.* Retrieved January 22, 1999, from www.ams.org/notices/199707/comm-calif2.pdf

Jacobsen, T., & Hofmann, V. (1997). Children's attachment representations: Longitudinal relations to school behavior and academic competency in middle childhood and adolescence. *Developmental Psychology, 33,* 703–710.

Jacobson, J. L., & Wille, D. E. (1986). The influence of attachment pattern on developmental changes in peer interaction from the toddler to the preschool period. *Child Development, 57,* 338–347.

Jacobson, K. C., & Crockett, L. J. (2000). Parental monitoring and adolescent adjustment: An ecological perspective. *Journal of Research on Adolescence, 10*(1), 65–97.

Jaffee, S., & Hyde, J. S. (2000). Gender differences in moral orientation: A meta-analysis. *Psychological Bulletin, 126,* 703–726.

Jaffee, S. R., Caspi, A., Moffitt, T. E., Dodge, K. A., Rutter, M., Taylor, A., & Tully, L. A. (2005). Nature x nature: Genetic vulnerabilities interact with physical maltreatment to promote conduct problems. *Developmental Psychopathology, 17,* 67–84.

Jaffee, S. R., Caspi, A., Moffitt, T. E., Polo-Tomas, M., Price, T., & Taylor, A. (2004). The limits of child effects: Evidence for genetically mediated child effects on corporal punishment but not on physical maltreatment. *Developmental Psychology, 40,* 1047–1058.

Jagers, R. J., Bingham, K., & Hans, S. L. (1996). Socialization and social judgments among inner-city African-American kindergartners. *Child Development, 67,* 140–150.

Jain, T., Missmer, S. A., & Hornstein, M. D. (2004). Trends in embryo-transfer practice and in outcomes of the use of assisted reproductive technology in the United States. *New England Journal of Medicine, 350,* 1639–1645.

Jankowiak, W. (1992). Father-child relations in urban China. In B. S. Hewlett (Ed.), *Father-child relations: Cultural and bisocial contexts* (pp. 345–363). New York: de Gruyter.

Jankowski, J. J., Rose, S. A., & Feldman, J. F. (2001). Modifying the distribution of attention in infants. *Child Development, 72,* 339–351.

Janowsky, J. S., & Carper, R. (1996). Is there a neural basis for cognitive transitions in school-age children? In A. J. Sameroff & M. M. Haith (Eds.), *The five to seven year shift: The age of reason and responsibility* (pp. 33–56). Chicago: University of Chicago Press.

Janssen, I., Craig, W. M., Boyce, W. F., & Pickett, W. (2004). Associations between overweight and obesity with bullying behaviors in school-aged children. *Pediatrics, 113,* 1187–1194.

Jarvis, M. J. (2004). Why people smoke. In J. Britton (Ed.), *ABC of smoking cessation* (pp. 4–6). Malden, MA: Blackwell.

Javaid, M. K., Crozier, S. R., Harvey, N. C., Gale, C. R., Dennison, E. M., Boucher, B. J., et al. (2006). Maternal vitamin D status during pregnancy and childhood bone mass at age 9 years: A longitudinal study. *Lancet, 367*(9504), 36–43.

Jensen, A. R. (1969). How much can we boost IQ and scholastic achievement? *Harvard Educational Review, 39,* 1–123.

Jeynes, W. H., & Littell, S. W. (2000). A meta-analysis of studies examining the effect of whole language instruction on the literacy of low-SES students. *Elementary School Journal, 101*(1), 21–33.

Ji, B. T., Shu, X. O., Linet, M. S., Zheng, W., Wacholder, S., Gao, Y. T., Ying, D. M., & Jin, F. (1997). Paternal cigarette smoking and the risk of childhood cancer among offspring of nonsmoking mothers. *Journal of the National Cancer Institute, 89,* 238–244.

Jiao, S., Ji, G., & Jing, Q. (1996). Cognitive development of Chinese urban only children and children with siblings. *Child Development, 67,* 387–395.

Jipson, J. L., & Gelman, S. A. (2007). Robots and rodents: Children's inferences about living and nonliving kinds. *Child Development, 78*(6), 1675–1688.

Ji-Yeon, K., McHale, S. M., Crouter, A. C., & Osgood, D. W. (2007). Longitudinal linkages between sibling relationships and adjustment from middle childhood through adolescence. *Developmental Psychology, 43*(4), 960–973.

Jodl, K. M., Michael, A., Malanchuk, O., Eccles, J. S., & Sameroff, A. (2001). Parents' roles in shaping early adolescents' occupational aspirations. *Child Development 72*(4), 1247–1265.

Johnson, C. P., Myers, S. M., & the Council on Children with Disabilities. (2007). Identification and evaluation of children with autism spectrum disorders. *Pediatrics, 120,* 1183–1215.

Johnson, D. J., Jaeger, E., Randolph, S. M., Cauce, A. M., Ward, J., & National Institute of Child Health and Human Development Early Child Care Research Network (2003). Studying the effects of early child care experiences on the development of children of color in the United States: Toward a more inclusive research agenda. *Child Development, 74,* 1227–1244.

Johnson, J. E. (1998). Play development from ages four to eight. In D. P. Fromberg & D. Bergen (Eds.), *Play from birth to twelve and beyond: Contexts, perspectives, and meanings* (pp. 145–153). New York: Garland.

Johnson, J. G., Cohen, P., Gould, M. S., Kasen, S., Brown, J., & Brook, J. S. (2002). Childhood adversities, interpersonal difficulties, and risk for suicide attempts during late adolescence and early adulthood. *Archives of General Psychiatry, 59,* 741–749.

Johnson, K. (2004, March 27). Harm to fetuses becomes issue in Utah and elsewhere. *New York*

Times. Retrieved March 29, 2004, from www .nytimes.com/2004/03027//national/27FETU.html? ex=1081399221&eu=1&en=ede725fc158cb2bd

Johnson, M. H. (1998). The neural basis of cognitive development. In D. Kuhn & R. S. Siegler (Eds.), *Handbook of child psychology: Vol. 2. Cognition, perception, and language* (5th ed., pp. 1–49). New York: Wiley.

Johnson, R. A., Hoffmann, J. P., & Gerstein, D. R. (1996). *The relationship between family structure and adolescent substance use* (No. SMA 96-3086). Washington, DC: U.S. Department of Health and Human Services.

Johnston, L. D., O'Malley, P. M., Bachman, J. G., & Schulenberg, J. E. (2013). *Monitoring the future national results on drug use: 2012 Overview, key findings on adolescent drug use*. Ann Arbor: Institute for Social Research, The University of Michigan.

Jones, H. W., & Toner, J. P. (1993). The infertile couple. *New England Journal of Medicine, 329*, 1710–1715.

Jones, N. A., Field, T., Fox, N. A., Davalos, M., Lundy, B., & Hart, S. (1998). Newborns of mothers with depressive symptoms are physiologically less developed. *Infant Behavior & Development, 21*(3), 537–541.

Jones, N. A., Field, T., Fox, N. A., Lundy, B., & Davalos, M. (1997). EEG activation in one-month-old infants of depressed mothers. *Development and Psychopathology, 9*, 491–505.

Jones, R., Homa, D., Meyer, P., Brody, D., Caldwell, K., Pirkle, J., & Brown., M. (2009). Trends in blood lead levels and blood lead testing among U.S. children aged 1 to 5 years, 1988–2004. *Pediatrics, 123*, e376–e385.

Jordan, B. (1993). *Birth in four cultures: A cross-cultural investigation of childbirth in Yucatan, Holland, Sweden, and the United States* (4th ed.). Prospect Heights, IL: Waveland Press. (Original work published 1978)

Jordan, N. C., Kaplan, D., Olah, L. N., & Locunia, M. N. (2006). Number sense growth in kindergarten: A longitudinal investigation of children at risk for mathematics difficulties. *Child Development, 77*, 153–175.

Joussemet, M., Vitaro, F., Barker, E., Cote, S., Nagin, D., Zoccolillo, M., & Tremblay, R. (2008). Controlling parenting and physical aggression during elementary school. *Child Development, 79*(2), 411–425.

Juffer, F., & van IJzendoorn, M. H. (2007). Adoptees do not lack self-esteem: A meta-analysis of studies on self-esteem of transracial, international, and domestic adoptees. *Psychological Bulletin APA, 133*(6), 1067–1083.

Juul-Dam, N., Townsend, J., & Courchesne, E. (2001). Prenatal, perinatal, and neonatal factors in autism, pervasive developmental disorder—not otherwise specified, and the general population. *Pediatrics, 107*(4), e63.

Jusczyk, P. W. (2003). The role of speech perception capacities in early language acquisition. In M. T. Banich & M. Mack (Eds.), *Mind, brain, and language: Multidisciplinary perspectives* (pp. 61–83). Mahwah, NJ: Erlbaum.

Jusczyk, P. W., & Hohne, E. A. (1997). Infants' memory for spoken words. *Science, 277*, 1984–1986.

Just, M. A., Cherkassky, V. L., Keller, T. A., Kana, R. K., & Minshew, N. J. (2007). Functional and anatomical cortical underconnectivity in autism: Evidence from an fMRI study of an executive function task and corpus callosum morphometry. *Cerebral Cortex, 17*(4), 951–961.

Juster, F. T., Ono. H., & Stafford, F. P. (2004). *Changing times of American youth: 1981–2003.* [Child Development Supplement]. Ann Arbor: University of Michigan Institute for Social Research.

Kaczynski, K. J., Lindahl, K. M., Malik, N. M., & Laurenceau, J. (2006). Marital conflict, maternal and paternal parenting, and child adjustment: A test of mediation and moderation. *Journal of Family Psychology, 20*, 199–208.

Kagan, J. (1997). Temperament and the reactions to unfamiliarity. *Child Development, 68*, 139–143.

Kagan, J. (2008). In defense of qualitative changes in development. *Child Development, 79*, 1606–1624.

Kagan, J., & Snidman, N. (2004). *The long shadow of temperament.* Cambridge, MA: Belknap.

Kaiser Family Foundation, Hoff, T., Greene, L., & Davis, J. (2003). *National survey of adolescents and young adults: Sexual health knowledge, attitudes and experiences.* Menlo Park, CA: Henry J. Kaiser Foundation.

Kalil, A., & Ziol-Guest, K. M. (2005). Single mothers' employment dynamics and adolescent well-being. *Child Development, 76*, 196–211.

Kalish, C. W. (1998). Young children's predictions of illness: Failure to recognize probabilistic cause. *Developmental Psychology, 34*(5), 1046–1058.

Kanaya, T., Scullin, M. H., & Ceci, S. J. (2003). The Flynn effect and U.S. policies: The impact of rising IQ scores on American society via mental retardation diagnoses. *American Psychologist, 58*, 778–790.

Kanetsuna, T., & Smith, P. K. (2002). Pupil insight into bullying and coping with bullying: A bi-national study in Japan and England. *Journal of School Violence, 1*, 5–29.

Kang, C., Riazuddin, S., Mundorff, J., Krasnewich, D., Friedman, P., Mullikin, J. C., & Drayna, D. (2010). Mutations in the lysosomal enzyme-targeting pathway and persistent stuttering. *New England Journal of Medicine, 362*, 677–685.

Kaplan, H., & Dove, H. (1987). Infant development among the Ache of East Paraguay. *Developmental Psychology, 23*, 190–198.

Kaplow, J. B., & Widom, C. S. (2007). Age of onset of child maltreatment predicts long-term mental health outcomes. *Journal of Abnormal Psychology, 116*, 176–187.

Kaplowitz, P. B. (2008). The link between body fat and the timing of puberty. *Pediatrics, 121*(2, Suppl. 3), S208–S217.

Kaplowitz, P. B., Oberfield, S. E., & the Drug and Therapeutics and Executive Committees of the Lawson Wilkins Pediatric Endocrine Society. (1999). Reexamination of the age limit for defining when puberty is precocious in girls in the United States: Implications for evaluation and treatment. *Pediatrics, 104*, 936–941.

Karafantis, D. M., & Levy, S. R. (2004). The role of children's lay theories about the malleability of human attributes in beliefs about and volunteering for disadvantaged groups. *Child Development, 75*, 236–250.

Karasick, L. B., Tamis-LeMonda, C. S., & Adolph, K.E. (2011). Transition from crawling to walking and infants' actions with objects and people. *Child Development, 82*(4), 1199–1209.

Katzman, R. (1993). Education and prevalence of Alzheimer's disease. *Neurology, 43*, 13–20.

Kaufman, A. S., & Kaufman, N. L. (1983). *Kaufman Assessment Battery for Children: Administration and scoring manual.* Circle Pines, MN: American Guidance Service.

Kaufman, A. S., & Kaufman, N. L. (2003). *Kaufman Assessment Battery for Children* (2nd ed.). Circle Pines, MN: American Guidance Service.

Kaufman, J., Yang, B-Z., Douglas-Palumberi, H., Houshyar, S., Lipschitz, D., Krystal, J. H., & Gelernter, J. (2004). Social supports and serotonin transporter gene moderate depression in maltreated children. *Proceedings of the National Academy of Sciences, USA, 101*, 17316–17321.

Kawabata, Y., & Crick, N. (2008). The roles of cross-racial/ethnic friendships in social adjustment. *Developmental Psychology, 44*(4), 1177–1183.

Kazdin, A. E., & Benjet, C. (2003). Spanking children: Evidence and issues. *Current Directions in Psychological Science, 12*, 99–103.

Keegan, R. T. (1996). Creativity from childhood to adulthood: A difference of degree and not of kind. *New Directions for Child Development, 72*, 57–66.

Keegan, R. T., & Gruber, H. E. (1985). Charles Darwin's unpublished "Diary of an Infant": An early phase in his psychological work. In G. Eckardt, W. G. Bringmann, & L. Sprung (Eds.), *Contributions to a history of developmental psychology: International William T. Preyer Symposium* (pp.127–145). Berlin, Germany: Walter de Gruyter.

Keel, P. K., & Klump, K. L. (2003). Are eating disorders culture-bound syndromes? Implications for conceptualizing their etiology. *Psychological Bulletin, 129*, 747–769.

Keenan, K., & Shaw, D. (1997). Developmental and social influences on young girls' early problem behavior. *Psychological Bulletin, 121*(1), 95–113.

Keil, F. C., Lockhart, K. L., & Schlegel, E. (2010). A bump on a bump? Emerging intuitions concerning the relative difficulty of the sciences. *Journal of Experimental Psychology. General, 139*(1), 1–15.

Keller, B. (1999, February 24). A time and place for teenagers. *Education Week on the WEB*. Retrieved March 11, 2004, from www.4uth.gov.ua/usa /english/educ/century/ew/vol-18/24studen.htm

Kelley, M. L., Smith, T. S., Green, A. P., Berndt, A. E., & Rogers, M. C. (1998). Importance of fathers' parenting to African-American toddler's social and cognitive development. *Infant Behavior & Development, 21*, 733–744.

Kellman, P. J., & Arterberry, M. E. (1998). *The cradle of knowledge: Development of perception in infancy.* Cambridge, MA: MIT Press.

Kellman, P. J., & Banks, M. S. (1998). Infant visual perception. In W. Damon (Series Ed.), D. Kuhn, & R. S. Siegler (Vol. Eds.), *Handbook of child psychology: Vol. 2, Cognition, perception, and language* (5th Ed., pp. 103–146). New York: Wiley.

Kellogg, N., & the Committee on Child Abuse and Neglect. (2005). The evaluation of sexual abuse in children. *Pediatrics, 116*(2), 506–512.

Kellogg, R. (1970). Understanding children's art. In P. Cramer (Ed.), *Readings in developmental psychology today.* Delmar, CA: CRM.

Kelly, A. M., Wall, M., Eisenberg, M., Story, M., & Neumark-Sztainer, D. (2004). High body satisfaction in adolescent girls: Association with demographic, socio-environmental, personal, and behavioral factors. *Journal of Adolescent Health, 34*, 129.

Kelly, J. B., & Emery, R. E. (2003). Children's adjustment following divorce: Risk and resiliency perspectives. *Family Relations, 52*, 352–362.

Kellymom Breast Feeding and Parenting. (2006). Average calorie and fat content of human milk. Retrieved from http://www.kellymom.com /nutrition/milk/change-milkfat.html

Kere, J., Hannula-Jouppi, K., Kaminen-Ahola, N., Taipale, M., Eklund, R., Nopola-Hemmi, J., & Kaariainen, H. (2005, October). *Identification of the dyslexia susceptibility gene for DYX5 on chromosome 3*. Paper presented at the American Society of Human Genetics meeting, Salt Lake City, UT.

Kerns, K. A., & Barth, J. M. (1995) Attachment and play-convergence across components of parent-child relationships and their relations to peer competence. *Journal of Social and Personal Relationships, 12,* 243–260.

Kerns, K. A., Don, A., Mateer, C. A., & Streissguth, A. P. (1997). Cognitive deficits in nonretarded adults with fetal alcohol syndrome. *Journal of Learning Disabilities, 30,* 685–693.

Kerr, D.C.R., Lopez, N. L., Olson, S. L., & Sameroff, A. J. (2004). Parental discipline and externalizing behavior problems in early childhood: The roles of moral regulation and child gender. *Journal of Abnormal Child Psychology, 32*(4), 369–383.

Kestenbaum, R., & Gelman, S. A. (1995). Preschool children's identification and understanding of mixed emotions. *Cognitive Development, 10,* 443–458.

Khashan, A. S., Abel, K. M., McNamee, R., Pedersen, M. G., Webb, R. T., Baker, P. N., Kenny, L. C., & Mortensen, P. B. (2008). Higher risk of offspring schizophrenia following antenatal maternal exposure to severe adverse life events. *Archives of General Psychiatry, 65,* 146–152.

Khoury, M. J., McCabe, L. L., & McCabe, E.R.B. (2003). Population screening in the age of genomic medicine. *New England Journal of Medicine, 348,* 50–58.

Kier, C., & Lewis, C. (1998). Preschool sibling interaction in separated and married families: Are same-sex pairs or older sisters more sociable? *Journal of Child Psychology and Psychiatry, 39,* 191–201.

Killen, J. D., Robinson, T. N., Ammerman, S., Hayward, C., Rogers, J., Stone, C., Samuels, D., Levin, S. K., Green, S., & Schatzberg, A. F. (2004). Randomized clinical trial of the efficacy of bupropion combined with nicotine patch in the treatment of adolescent smokers. *Journal of Consulting and Clinical Psychology, 72,* 729–735.

Kim, J., McHale, S. M., Osgood, D. W., & Crouter, A. C. (2006). Longitudinal course and family correlates of sibling relationships from childhood through adolescence. *Child Development, 77,* 1746–1761.

Kim, J., Peterson, K. E., Scanlon, K. S., Fitzmaurice, G. M., Must, A., Oken, E., et al. (2006). Trends in overweight from 1980 through 2001 among preschool-aged children enrolled in a health maintenance organization. *Obesity, 14*(7), 1107–1112.

Kim, K. J., Conger, R. D., Elder, G. H., Jr., & Lorenz, F. O. (2003). Reciprocal influences between stressful life events and adolescent internalizing and externalizing problems. *Child Development, 74*(1), 127–143.

Kim, Y, S., Koh, Y.-J., & Leventhal, B. (2005). School bullying and suicidal risk in Korean middle school students. *Pediatrics, 115,* 357–363.

Kim-Cohen, J., Moffitt, T. E., Caspi, A., & Taylor, A. (2004). Genetic and environmental processes in young children's resilience and vulnerability to socioeconomic deprivation. *Child Development, 75,* 651–668.

Kimball, M. M. (1986). Television and sexrole attitudes. In T. M. Williams (Ed.), *The impact of television: A natural experiment in three communities* (pp. 265–301). Orlando, FL: Academic Press.

King, K. M., Meehan, B. T., Trim, R. S., & Chassin, L. (2006). Market or mediator? The effects of adolescent substance use on young adult educational attainment. *Addiction, 101,* 1730–1740.

King, W. J., MacKay, M., Sirnick, A., & The Canadian Shaken Baby Study Group. (2003). Shaken baby syndrome in Canada: Clinical characteristics and outcomes of hospital cases. *Canadian Medical Association Journal, 168,* 155–159.

Kinney, H. C., Filiano, J. J., Sleeper, L. A., Mandell, F., Valdes-Dapena, M., & White, W. F. (1995). Decreased muscarinic receptor binding in the arcuate nucleus in sudden infant death syndrome. *Science, 269,* 1446–1450.

Kinsella, K., & Phillips, P. (2005). Global aging: The challenges of success. *Population Bulletin, No. 1.* Washington, DC: Population Reference Bureau.

Kinsella, K., & Velkoff, V. A. (200l). *An aging world: 2001.* U.S. [Census Bureau, Series P95/01–1]. Washington, DC: U.S. Government Printing Office.

Kinsley, C. H., & Meyer, E. A. (2010). The construction of the maternal brain: Theoretical comment on Kim et al. (2010). *Behavioral Neuroscience, 124*(5), 710–714.

Kirby, D. (1997). *No easy answers: Research findings on programs to reduce teen pregnancy.* Washington, DC: National Campaign to Prevent Teen Pregnancy.

Kirby, D., & Laris, B. (2009). Effective curriculum-based sex and STD/HIV education programs for adolescents. *Child Development Perspectives, 3,* 21–29.

Kirkorian, H. L., Wartella, E. A., & Anderson, D. R. (2008). Media and young children's learning. *Future of Children, 18,* 39–61.

Kirschner, P. A., & Karpinski, A. C. (2010). Facebook and academic performance. *Computers in Human Behavior, 26*(6), 1237–1245.

Kirschner, S., & Tomasello, M. (2010). Joint music making promotes prosocial behavior in 4-year-old children. *Evolution and Human Behavior, 31*(5), 354-364. doi: 10.1016/j.evolhumbehav .2010.04.004

Kisilevsky, B. S., & Hains, S.M.J. (2010). Exploring the relationship between fetal heart rate and cognition. *Infant and Child Development, 19,* 60–75.

Kisilevsky, B. S., Hains, S.M.J, Brown, C. A., Lee, C. T., Cowperthwaite, B., Stutzman, S. S., et al. (2009). Fetal sensitivity to properties of maternal speech and language. *Infant Behavior and Development, 32,* 59–71.

Kisilevsky, B. S., Hains, S. M., Lee, K., Xie, X., Huang, H., Ye, H. H., et al. (2003). Effects of experience on fetal voice recognition. *Psychological Science, 14*(3), 220–224.

Kisilevsky, B. S., Muir, D. W., & Low, J. A. (1992). Maturation of human fetal responses to vibro-acoustic stimulation. *Child Development, 63,* 1497–1508.

Klar, A.J.S. (1996). A single locus, RGHT, specifies preference for hand utilization in humans. *Cold Spring Harbor Symposia on Quantitative Biology 61,* 59–65. Cold Spring Harbor, NY: Cold Spring Harbor Laboratory Press.

Klaus, M. H., & Kennell, J. H. (1982). *Parent-infant bonding* (2nd ed.). St. Louis, MO: Mosby.

Klein, J. D., & the American Academy of Pediatrics Committee on Adolescence. (2005). Adolescent pregnancy: Current trends and issues. *Pediatrics, 116,* 281–286.

Kleinmann, R. E., Hall, S., Green, H., Korzec-Ramirez, D., Patton, K., Pagano, M. E., & Murphy, J. M. (2002). Diet, breakfast, and academic performance in children. *Annals of Nutrition and Metabolism, 46*(Suppl. 1), 24–30.

Klein-Velderman, M., Bakermans-Kranenburg, M. J., Juffer, F., & van IJzendoorn, M. H. (2006). Effects of attachment-based interventions on maternal sensitivity and infant attachment: Differential susceptibility of highly reactive infants. *Journal of Family Psychology, 20,* 266–274.

Klibanoff, R. S., Levine, S. C., Huttenlocher, J., Vasilyeva, M., & Hedges, L. V. (2006). Preschool children's mathematical knowledge: The effect of teacher "math talk." *Developmental Psychology, 42,* 59–69.

Klump, K. L., & Culbert, K. M. (2007). Molecular genetic studies of eating disorders: Current status and future directions. *Current Directions in Psychological Science, 16,* 37–41.

Knafo, A., & Plomin, R. (2006). Parental discipline and affection and children's prosocial behavior: Genetic and environmental links. *Journal of Personality and Social Psychology, 90,* 147–164.

Knecht, S., Drager, B., Deppe, M., Bobe, L., Lohmann, H., Floel, A., et al. (2000). Handedness and hemispheric language dominance in healthy humans. *Brain: A Journal of Neurology, 123*(12), 2512–2518.

Knickmeyer, R., Baron-Cohen, S., Raggatt, P., & Taylor, K. (2005). Foetal testosterone, social relationships, and restricted interests in children. *Journal of Child Psychology and Psychiatry, 46,* 198–210.

Knickmeyer, R. C., Gouttard, S., Kang, C, Evans, D., Wilber, K, Smith, J. K., et al. (2008). A structural MRI study of human brain development from birth to 2 years. *The Journal of Neuroscience, 28*(47), 12176–12182.

Knudsen, E. I. (1999). Early experience and critical periods. In M. J. Zigmond (Ed.), *Fundamental neuroscience* (pp. 637–654). San Diego, CA: Academic.

Kochanska, G. (1992). Children's interpersonal influence with mothers and peers. *Developmental Psychology, 28,* 491–499.

Kochanska, G. (1993). Toward a synthesis of parental socialization and child temperament in early development of conscience. *Child Development, 64,* 325–437.

Kochanska, G. (1995). Children's temperament, mothers' discipline, and security of attachment: Multiple pathways to emerging internalization. *Child Development, 66,* 597–615.

Kochanska, G. (1997a). Multiple pathways to conscience for children with different temperaments: From toddlerhood to age 5. *Developmental Psychology, 33,* 228–240.

Kochanska, G. (1997b). Mutually responsive orientation between mothers and their young children: Implications for early socialization. *Child Development, 68,* 94–112.

Kochanska, G. (2001). Emotional development in children with different attachment histories: The first three years. *Child Development, 72,* 474–490.

Kochanska, G. (2002). Mutually responsive orientation between mothers and their young children: A context for the early development of conscience. *Current Directions in Psychological Science, 11,* 191–195.

Kochanska, G., & Aksan, N. (1995). Mother-child positive affect, the quality of child compliance to requests and prohibitions, and maternal control as correlates of early internalization. *Child Development, 66,* 236–254.

Kochanska, G., Aksan, N., & Carlson, J. J. (2005). Temperament, relationships, and young children's receptive cooperation with their parents. *Developmental Psychology, 41,* 648–660.

Kochanska, G., Aksan, N., & Joy, M. E. (2007). Children's fearfulness as a moderator of parenting in early socialization: Two longitudinal studies. *Developmental Psychology, 43,* 222–237.

Kochanska, G., Aksan, N., Knaack, A., & Rhines, H. M. (2004). Maternal parenting and children's conscience: Early security as moderator. *Child Development, 75,* 1229–1242.

Kochanska, G., Askan, N., Prisco, T. R., & Adams, E. E. (2008). Mother-child and father-child mutually responsive orientation in the first two years and children's outcomes at preschool age: Mechanisms of influence. *Child Development, 79,* 30–44.

Kochanska, G., Coy, K. C., & Murray, K. T. (2001). The development of self-regulation in the first four years of life. *Child Development, 72*(4), 1091–1111.

Kochanska, G., Gross, J. N., Lin, M. H., & Nichols, K. E. (2002). Guilt in young children: Development, determinants, and relations with a broader system of standards. *Child Development, 73*(2), 461–482.

Kochanska, G., Tjebkes, T. L., & Forman, D. R. (1998). Children's emerging regulation of conduct: Restraint, compliance, and internalization from infancy to the second year. *Child Development, 69*(5), 1378–1389.

Koenig, H. G. (1994). *Aging and God.* New York: Haworth.

Kogan, M. D., Blumberg, S. J., Schieve, L. A., Boyle, C. A., Perrin, J. M., Chandour, R. M., et al. (2009). Prevalence of parent-reported diagnosis of autism spectrum disorder among children in the U.S., 2007. *Pediatrics, 124*(5), 1395–1403.

Kogan, M. D., Newacheck, P. W., Honberg, L., & Strickland, B. (2005). Association between under-insurance and access to care among children with special health care needs in the United States. *Pediatrics, 116,* 1162–1169.

Kohen, D. E., Leventhal, T., Dahinten, V. S., & McIntosh, C. N. (2008). Neighborhood disadvantage: Pathways of effects for young children. *Child Development, 79,* 156–169.

Kohlberg, L. (1966). A cognitive developmental analysis of children's sex role concepts and attitudes. In E. E. Maccoby (Ed.), *The development of sex differences.* Stanford CA: Stanford University Press.

Kohlberg, L. (1969). Stage and sequence: The cognitive-developmental approach to socialization. In D. A. Goslin (Ed.), *Handbook of socialization theory and research* (pp 347–480). Chicago: Rand McNally.

Kohlberg, L. (1981). *Essays on moral development.* San Francisco: Harper & Row.

Kohlberg, L., & Gilligan, C. (1971, Fall). The adolescent as a philosopher: The discovery of the self in a postconventional world. *Daedalus, 100,* 1051–1086.

Kohlberg, L., & Ryncarz, R. A. (1990). Beyond justice reasoning: Moral development and consideration of a seventh stage. In C. N. Alexander & E. J. Langer (Eds.), *Higher stages of human development* (pp. 191–207). New York: Oxford University Press.

Kohlberg, L., Yaeger, J., & Hjertholm, E. (1968). Private speech: Four studies and a review of theories. *Child Development, 39,* 691–736.

Kolata, G. (2003, February 18). Using genetic tests, Ashkenazi Jews vanquish a disease. *New York Times,* pp. D1, D6.

Kolbert, E. (1994, January 11). Canadians curbing TV violence. *New York Times,* pp. C15, C19.

Kopp, C. B. (1982). Antecedents of self-regulation. *Developmental Psychology, 18,* 199–214.

Koren, G., Pastuszak, A., & Ito, S. (1998). Drugs in pregnancy. *New England Journal of Medicine, 338,* 1128–1137.

Korner, A. (1996). Reliable individual differences in preterm infants' excitation management. *Child Development, 67,* 1793–1805.

Korner, A. F., Zeanah, C. H., Linden, J., Berkowitz, R. I., Kraemer, H. C., & Agras, W. S. (1985). The relationship between neonatal and later activity and temperament. *Child Development, 56,* 38–42.

Kosterman, R., Graham, J. W., Hawkins, J. D., Catalano, R. F., & Herrenkohl, T. I. (2001). Childhood risk factors for persistence of violence in the transition to adulthood: A social development perspective. *Violence & Victims. Special Issue: Developmental Perspectives on Violence and Victimization, 16*(4), 355–369.

Kowal, A. K., & Pike, L. B. (2004). Sibling influences on adolescents' attitudes toward safe sex practices. *Family Relations, 53,* 377–384.

Kozhimannil, K. B., Pereira, M., & Harlow, B. (2009). Association between diabetes and perinatal depression among low-income mothers. *Journal of the American Medical Association, 301,* 842–847.

Kozlowska, K., & Hanney, L. (1999). Family assessment and intervention using an interactive art exercise. *Australia and New Zealand Journal of Family Therapy, 20*(2), 61–69.

Kralovec, E., & Buell, J. (2000). *The end of homework.* Boston: Beacon.

Kramer, L. (2010). The essential ingredients of successful sibling relationships: An emerging framework for advancing theory and practice. *Child Development Perspectives, 4*(2), 80–86.

Kramer, L., & Kowal, A. K. (2005). Sibling relationship quality from birth to adolescence: The enduring contributions of friends. *Journal of Family Psychology, 19,* 503–511.

Kramer, M. S., Aboud, F., Mironova, E., Vanilovich, I., Platt, R. W., Matush, L., et al. for the Promotion of Breastfeeding Intervention Trial (PROBIT) Study Group. (2008). Breastfeeding and child cognitive development: New evidence from a large randomized trial. *Archives of General Psychiatry, 65*(5), 578–584.

Kramer, M. S., Chalmers, B., Hodnett, E. D., Sevkovskaya, Z., Dzikovich, I., Shapiro, S., et al. (2001). Promotion of Breastfeeding Intervention Trial (PROBIT): A randomized trial in the Republic of Belarus. *Journal of the American Medical Association, 285,* 413–420.

Krashen, S., & McField, G. (2005). What works? Reviewing the latest evidence on bilingual education. *Language Learner, 1*(2), 7–10, 34.

Krause, K. W. (2009, January–February). Change we can believe in: "Race" and continuing selection in the human genome. *The Humanist,* pp. 20–22.

Krauss, S., Concordet, J. P., & Ingham, P. W. (1993). A functionally conserved homolog of the Drosophila segment polarity gene hh is expressed in tissues with polarizing activity in zebrafish embryos. *Cell, 75,* 1431–1444.

Krausz, C. (2010). Genetic Testing of Male Infertility. In D. T. Carrell & C. M. Peterson (Eds.), *Reproductive endocrinology and infertility* (pp. 431–444). New York: Springer.

Kraut, R., Kiesler S., Boneva, B., Cummings, J. Helgeson, V., & Crawford, A. (2002). Internet paradox revisited. *Journal of Social Issues, 58,* 49–74.

Kraut, R., Patterson, M., Lunmark, V., Kiesler, S., Mukopadhyay, T., & Scherlis, W. (1998). Internet paradox: A social technology that reduces social involvement and psychological well being? *American Psychologist, 53,* 1017–1031.

Kreider, R. M. (2003). Adopted children and stepchildren: 2000. *Census 2000 Special Reports.* Washington, DC: U.S. Bureau of the Census.

Kreider, R. M. (2008). Living arrangements of children: 2004. *Current Population Reports.* [No. 70-114]. Washington, DC: U.S. Census Bureau.

Kreider, R. M., & Fields, J. (2005). *Living arrangements of children: 2001.* Current Population Reports. [No. P70-104]. Washington, DC: U.S. Census Bureau.

Kreutzer, M., Leonard, C., & Flavell, J. (1975). An interview study of children's knowledge about memory. *Monographs of the Society for Research in Child Development, 40*(1). [Serial No. 159].

Krevans, J., & Gibbs, J. C. (1996). Parents' use of inductive discipline: Relations to children's empathy and prosocial behavior. *Child Development, 67,* 3263–3277.

Kringelbach, M. L., Lehtonen, A., Squire, S., Harvey, A. G., Craske, M. G., Holliday, I. E., et al. (2008). A specific and rapid neural signature for parental instinct. *PLoS ONE, 3*(2), e1664–1673.

Krishnamoorthy, J. S., Hart, C., & Jelalian, E. (2006). The epidemic of childhood obesity: Review of research and implications for public policy. *Society for Research in Child Development (SRCD) Social Policy Report, 20*(2).

Kroger, J. (1993). Ego identity: An overview. In J. Kroger (Ed.), *Discussions on ego identity* (pp. 1–20). Hillsdale, NJ: Erlbaum.

Kroger, J. (2003). Identity development during adolescence. In G. R. Adams & M. D. Berzonsky (Eds.), *Blackwell handbook of adolescence* (pp. 205–226). Malden, MA: Blackwell.

Kroger, J., & Haslett, S. J. (1991). A comparison of ego identity status transition pathways and change rates across five identity domains. *International Journal of Aging and Human Development, 32,* 303–330.

Krueger, A. B. (2003, February). Economic considerations and class size. *The Economic Journal, 113,* F34–F63.

Krueger, A. B., & Whitmore, D. M. (2000, April). *The effect of attending a small class in the early grades on college-test taking and middle school test results: Evidence from Project STAR.* [NBER Working Paper No. W7656]. Cambridge, MA: National Bureau of Economic Research.

Kuczmarski, R. J., Ogden, C. L., Grummer-Strawn, L. M., Flegal, K. M., Guo, S. S., Wei, R., et al. (2000). *CDC growth charts: United States.* [Advance data, No. 314]. Washington, DC: Centers for Disease Control and Prevention.

Kuczynski, L., & Kochanska, G. (1995). Function and content of maternal demands: Developmental significance of early demands for competent action. *Child Development, 66,* 616–628.

Kuhl, P., & Rivera-Gaxiola, M. (2008). Neural substrates of language acquisition. *Annual Review of Neuroscience, 31,* 511–534.

Kuhl, P. K. (2004). Early language acquisition: Cracking the speech code. *Nature Reviews Neuroscience, 5,* 831–843.

Kuhl, P. K., Andruski, J. E., Chistovich, I. A., Chistovich, L. A., Kozhevnikova, E. V., Ryskina, V. L., et al. (1997). Cross-language analysis of phonetic units in language addressed to infants. *Science, 277,* 684–686.

Kuhl, P. K., Conboy, B. T., Padden, D., Nelson, T., & Pruitt, J. (2005). Early speech perception and later language development: Implications for the "critical period." *Language Learning and Development, 1,* 237–264.

Kuhl, P. K., Williams, K. A., Lacerda, F., Stevens, K. N., & Lindblom, B. (1992). Linguistic experience alters phonetic perception in infants by 6 months of age. *Science, 255,* 606–608.

Kuhn, D. (2006). Do cognitive changes accompany developments in the adolescent brain? *Perspectives on Psychological Science, 1,* 59–67.

Kuhn. D., & Dean, D. (2005). Is developing scientific thinking all about learning to control variables? *Psychological Science, 16,* 866–870.

Kumwenda, N. I., Hoover, D. R., Mofenson, L. M., Thigpen, M. C., Kafulafula, G., Li, Q., et al. (2008). Extended antiretroviral prophylaxis to reduce breast-milk HIV-1 transmission. *New England Journal of Medicine, 359,* 119–129.

Kung, H-C., Hoyert, D. L., Xu, J., & Murphy, S. L. (2008). Deaths: Final data for 2005. *National Vital Statistics Reports, 56*(10). Hyattsville, MD: National Center for Health Statistics.

Kuperman, S., Chan, G., Kramer, J. R., Bierut, L., Buckholz, K. K., Fox, L., et al. (2005). Relationship of age of first drink to child behavioral problems and family psychopathology. *Alcoholism: Clinical and Experimental Research, 29*(10), 1869–1876.

Kupersmidt, J. B., & Coie, J. D. (1990). Preadolescent peer status, aggression, and school adjustment as predictors of externalizing problems in adolescence. *Child Development, 61,* 1350–1362.

Kurjak, A., Kupesic, S., Matijevic, R., Kos, M., & Marton, M. (1999). First trimester malformation screening. *European Journal of Obstetrics & Gynecology and Reproductive Biology, 85*(1), 93–96.

Kushnir, T., Xu, F., & Wellman, H. M. (2010). Young children use statistical sampling to infer the preferences of other people. *Psychological Science, 21,* 1134–1140.

Kuther, T., & McDonald, E. (2004). Early adolescents' experiences with, and views of, Barbie. *Adolescence, 39,* 39–51.

Kye, C., & Ryan, N. (1995). Pharmacologic treatment of child and adolescent depression. *Child and Adolescent Psychiatric Clinics of North America, 4,* 261–281.

Labarere, J., Gelbert-Baudino, N., Ayral, A. S., Duc, C., Berchotteau, M., Bouchon, N., et al. (2005). Efficacy of breast-feeding support provided by trained clinicians during an early, routine, preventive visit: A prospective, randomized, open trial of 226 mother-infant pairs. *Pediatrics, 115,* e139–e146.

Laberge, L., Tremblay, R. E., Vitaro, F., & Montplaisir, J. (2000). Development of parasomnias from childhood to early adolescence. *Pediatrics, 106,* 67–74.

Labov. T. (1992). Social and language boundaries among adolescents. *American Speech, 67,* 339–366.

Ladd, G., Herald-Brown, S., & Reiser, M. (2008). Does chronic classroom peer rejection predict the development of children's classroom participation during the grade school years? *Child Development, 79*(4), 1001–1015.

Ladd, G. W. (1996). Shifting ecologies during the 5- to 7-year period: Predicting children's adjustment during the transition to grade school. In A. J. Sameroff & M. M. Haith (Eds.), *The five to seven year shift: The age of reason and responsibility* (pp. 363–386). Chicago: University of Chicago Press.

Ladd, G. W., Kochenderfer, B. J., & Coleman, C. C. (1996). Friendship quality as a predictor of young children's early school adjustment. *Child Development, 67,* 1103–1118.

LaFontana, K. M., & Cillessen, A.H.N. (2002). Children's perceptions of popular and unpopular peers: A multi-method assessment. *Developmental Psychology, 38,* 635–647.

Lagattuta, K. H. (2005). When you shouldn't do what you want to do: Young children's understanding of desires, rules, and emotions. *Child Development, 76,* 713–733.

Lagercrantz, H., & Slotkin, T. A. (1986). The "stress" of being born. *Scientific American, 254*(4), 100–107.

Laible, D. J., & Thompson, R. A. (1998). Attachment and emotional understanding in preschool children. *Developmental Psychology, 34*(5), 1038–1045.

Laible, D. J., & Thompson, R. A. (2002). Mother-child conflict in the toddler years: Lessons in emotion, morality, and relationships. *Child Development, 73,* 1187–1203.

Laird, J., Lew, S., DeBell, M., & Chapman, C. (2006). *Dropout rates in the United States: 2002 and 2003* (NCES 2006-062). Washington, DC: U.S. Department of Education, National Center for Education Statistics.

Laird, R. D., Pettit, G. S., Bates, J. E., & Dodge, K. A. (2003). Parents' monitoring relevant knowledge and adolescents' delinquent behavior: Evidence of correlated developmental changes and reciprocal influences. *Child Development, 74,* 752–768.

Lakatos, K., Nemoda, Z., Toth, I., Ronai, Z., Ney, K., Sasvari-Szekely, M., & Gervai, J. (2002). Further evidence for the role of the dopamine D4 receptor gene (DRD4) in attachment disorganization: Interaction of the III exon 48 bp repeat and the _521 C/T promoter polymorphisms. *Molecular Psychiatry, 7,* 27–31.

Lakatos, K., Toth, I., Nemoda, Z., Ney, K., Sasvari-Szekely, M., & Gervai, J. (2000). Dopamine D4 receptor (DRD4) gene polymorphism is associated with attachment disorganization. *Molecular Psychiatry, 5,* 633–637.

Lalonde, C. E., & Werker, J. F. (1995). Cognitive influences on cross-language speech perception in infancy. *Infant Behavior and Development, 18,* 459–475.

Lamason, R. L., Mohideen, M.A.P.K., Mest, R., Wong, A. C., Norton, H. L., Arcs, M. C., et al. (2005). SLC24A5, a putative cation exchanger affects pigmentation in zebrafish and humans. *Science, 310,* 1782–1786.

Lamb, M. E. (1981). The development of father-infant relationships. In M. E. Lamb (Ed.), *The role of the father in child* development (2nd ed., pp. 459–488). New York: Wiley.

Lamb, M. E. (1983). Early mother-neonate contact and the mother-child relationship. *Journal of Child Psychology & Psychiatry & Allied Disciplines, 24,* 487–494.

Lamb, M. E., Frodi, A. M., Frodi, M., & Hwang, C. P. (1982). Characteristics of maternal and paternal behavior in traditional and non-traditional Swedish families. *International Journal of Behavior Development, 5,* 131–151.

Lamberg, A. (2007) Sleep-disordered breathing may spur behavioral learning problems in children. *Journal of the American Medical Association, 297,* 2681–2683.

Lamborn, S. D., Mounts, N. S., Steinberg, L., & Dornbusch, S. M. (1991). Patterns of competence and adjustment among adolescents from authoritative, authoritarian, indulgent, and neglectful families. *Child Development, 62,* 1049–1065.

Lamm, C., Zelazo, P. D., & Lewis, M. D. (2006) Neural correlates of cognitive control in childhood and adolescence: Disentangling the contributions of age and executive function. *Neuropsychologia, 44,* 2139–2148.

Landon, M. B., Hauth, J. C. Leveno, K. J., Spong, C. Y., Leindecker, S., Varner, M. W., et al. (2004). Maternal and perinatal outcomes associated with trial of labor after prior cesarean delivery. *New England Journal of Medicine, 351,* 2581–2589.

Landry, S. H., Smith, K. E., Swank, P. R., & Miller-Loncar, C. L. (2000). Early maternal and child influences on children's later independent cognitive and social functioning. *Child Development, 71,* 358–375.

Långström, N., Rahman, Q., Carlström, E., & Lichtenstein, P. (2008). Genetic and environmental effects on same-sex sexual behavior: A population study of twins in Sweden. *Archives of Sexual Behavior* (ePub).

Lanphear, B. P. Aligne, C. A., Auinger, P., Weitzman, M., & Byrd, R. S. (2001). Residential exposure associated with asthma in U.S. children. *Pediatrics, 107,* 505–511.

Lansford, J. (2009). Parental divorce and children's adjustment. *Perspectives on Psychological Science, 4*(2), 14–152.

Lansford, J. E., Chang, L., Dodge, K. A., Malone, P. S., Oburu, P., Palmérus, K., et al. (2005). Physical discipline and children's adjustment: Cultural normativeness as a moderator. *Child Development, 76,* 1234–1246.

Lansford, J. E., & Dodge, K. A. (2008) Cultural norms for adult corporal punishment of children and societal rates of endorsement and use of violence. *Parenting: Science & Practice, 8*(3), 257–270.

Lansford, J. E., Dodge, K. A., Pettit, G. S., Bates, J. E., Crozier, J., & Kaplow, J. (2002). A 12-year prospective study of the long-term effects of early child physical maltreatment on psychological, behavioral, and academic problems in adolescence. *Archives of Pediatric and Adolescent Medicine, 156*(8), 824–830.

Lansford, J. E., Malone, P. S., Castellino, D. R., Dodge, K. A., Pettit, G. S., & Bates, J. E. (2006). Trajectories of internalizing, externalizing, and grades for children who have and have not experienced their parents' divorce or separation. *Journal of Family Psychology, 20,* 292–301.

Lanting, C. I., Fidler, V., Huisman, M., Touwen, B.C.L., & Boersma, E. R. (1994). Neurological differences between 9-year-old children fed breast-milk or formula-milk as babies. *Lancet, 334,* 1319–1322.

Larsen, D. (1990, December–1991, January). Unplanned parenthood. *Modern Maturity,* pp. 32–36.

Larson, R. (2008). Family mealtimes as a developmental context. *Social Policy Report, 22*(4), 21.

Larson, R., & Seepersad, S. (2003). Adolescents' leisure time in the United States: Partying, sports, and the American experiment. In S. Verma & R. Larson (Eds.), Examining adolescent leisure time across cultures: Developmental opportunities and risks. *New Directions for Child and Adolescent Development, 99,* 53–64.

Larson, R., & Wilson, S. (2004). Adolescents across place and time: Globalization and the changing pathways to adulthood. In R. M. Lerner & L. Steinberg (Eds.), *Handbook of adolescent psychology* (2nd ed., pp. 299–331). Hoboken, NJ: Wiley.

Larson, R. W. (1997). The emergence of solitude as a constructive domain of experience in early adolescence. *Child Development, 68,* 80–93.

Larson, R. W., Moneta, G., Richards, M. H., & Wilson, S. (2002). Continuity, stability, and change in daily emotional experience across adolescence. *Child Development, 73,* 1151–1165.

Larson, R. W., & Verma, S. (1999). How children and adolescents spend time across the world: Work, play, and developmental opportunities. *Psychological Bulletin, 125,* 701–736.

Larzalere, R. E. (2000). Child outcomes of nonabusive and customary physical punishment by parents: An updated literature review. *Clinical Child and Family Psychology Review, 3,* 199–221.

Laucht, M., Esser, G., & Schmidt, M. H. (1994). Contrasting infant predictors of later cognitive functioning. *Journal of Child Psychology and Psychiatry, 35,* 649–652.

Laursen, B. (1996). Closeness and conflict in adolescent peer relationships: Interdependence with friends and romantic partners. In W. M. Bukowski, A. F. Newcomb, & W. W. Hartup (Eds.), *The company they keep: Friendship in childhood and adolescence* (pp. 186–210). New York: Cambridge University Press.

Lavelli, M. & Fogel, A. (2005). Developmental changes in the relationship between the infant's attention and emotion during early face-to-face communication: The 2-month transition. *Developmental Psychology, 41,* 265–280.

Lawn, J. E., Cousens, S., & Zupan, J., for the Lancet Neonatal Survival Steering Team. (2005). 4 million neonatal deaths: When? Where? Why? *The Lancet, 365,* 891–900.

Lawn, J. E., Gravett, M. G., Nunes, T. M., Rubens, C. E., Stanton, C., & the GAPPS Review Group. (2010). Global report on preterm birth and stillbirth (1 of 7): Definitions, description of the burden and opportunities to improve data. *BMC Pregnancy and Childbirth, 10*(Suppl. 1), S1.

Le, H. N. (2000). Never leave your little one alone: Raising an Ifaluk child. In J. S. DeLoache & A. Gottlieb (Eds.), *A world of babies: Imagined child-care guides for seven societies* (pp. 199–201). Cambridge, UK: Cambridge University Press.

Leaper, C., Anderson, K. J., & Sanders, P. (1998). Moderators of gender effects on parents' talk to their children: A meta-analysis. *Developmental Psychology, 34*(1), 3–27.

Leaper, C., & Smith, T. E. (2004). A meta-analytic review of gender variations in children's language use: Talkativeness, affiliative speech, and assertive speech. *Developmental Psychology, 40,* 993–1027.

Leblanc, M., & Ritchie, M. (2001). A meta-analysis of play therapy outcomes. *Counseling Psychology Quarterly, 14,* 149–163.

Lecanuet, J. P., Granier-Deferre, C., & Busnel, M-C. (1995). Human fetal auditory perception. In J. P. Lecanuet, W. P. Fifer, N. A. Krasnegor, & W. P. Smotherman (Eds.), *Fetal development: A psychobiological perspective* (pp. 239–262). Hillsdale, NJ: Erlbaum.

Lee, F. R. (2004, July 3). Engineering more sons than daughters: Will it tip the scales toward war? *New York Times,* pp. A17, A19.

Lee, J. M., Appugliese, D., Kaciroti, N., Corwyn, R. F., Bradley, R., & Lumeng, J. C. (2007). Weight status in young girls and the onset of puberty. *Pediatrics, 119,* E624–E630.

Lee, M. M. (2006). Idiopathic short stature. *New England Journal of Medicine, 354,* 2576–2582.

Lee, S. J., Ralston, H.J.P., Drey, E. A., Partridge, J. C., & Rosen, M. A. (2005). Fetal pain: A systematic multidisciplinary review of the evidence. *Journal of the American Medical Association, 294,* 947–954.

Lee, S. M., & Edmonston, B. (2005). New marriages, new families: U.S. racial and Hispanic intermarriage. *Population Bulletin, 60*(2). Washington, DC: Population Reference Bureau.

Legerstee, M., & Varghese, J. (2001). The role of maternal affect mirroring on social expectancies in three-month-old infants. *Child Development, 72,* 1301–1313.

Leman, P. J., Ahmed, S., & Ozarow, L. (2005). Gender, gender relations, and the social dynamics of children's conversations. *Developmental Psychology, 41,* 64–74.

Lemke, M., Sen, A., Pahlke, E., Partelow, L., Miller, D., Williams, T., Kastberg, D., & Jocelyn, L. (2004). *International outcomes of learning in mathematics literacy and problem solving: PISA 2003. Results from the U.S. Perspective* (NCES 2005–003). Washington, DC: National Center for Education.

Lenneberg, E. H. (1967). *Biological functions of language.* New York: Wiley.

Lenneberg, E. H. (1969). On explaining language. *Science, 164*(3880), 635–643.

Lenroot, R. K., & Giedd, J. N. (2006). Brain development in children and adolescents: Insights from anatomical magnetic resonance imaging. *Neuroscience and Biobehavioral Reviews, 30*(6), 718–729.

Lesch, K. P., Bengel, D., Heils, A., Sabol, S. Z., Greenberg, B. D., Petri, S., et al. (1996). Association of anxiety-related traits with a polymorphism in the serotonin transporter gene regulatory region. *Science, 274,* 1527–1531.

Leslie, A. M. (1982). The perception of causality in infants. *Perception, 11,* 173–186.

Leslie, A. M. (1984). Spatiotemporal continuity and the perception of causality in infants. *Perception, 13,* 287–305.

Leslie, A. M. (1995). A theory of agency. In D. Sperber, D. Premack, and A. J. Premack, (Eds.), *Causal Cognition.* Oxford: Clarendon Press, 121–149.

Leslie, L. K., Newman, T. B., Chesney, J., & Perrin, J. M. (2005). The Food and Drug Administration's deliberations on antidepressant use in pediatric patients. *Pediatrics, 116,* 195–204.

Lester, B. M., & Boukydis, C.F.Z. (1985). *Infant crying: Theoretical and research perspectives.* New York: Plenum Press.

LeVay, S. (1991). A difference in hypothalamic structure between heterosexual and homosexual men. *Science, 253,* 1034–1037.

Levine, J. A., Emery, C. R., & Pollack, H. (2007). The well-being of children born to teen mothers. *Journal of Marriage and Family, 69,* 105–122.

Levine, L. J., & Edelstein, R. S. (2009). Emotion and memory narrowing: A review and goal-relevance approach. *Cognition and Emotion, 23*(5), 833–875.

LeVine, R. A. (1974). Parental goals: A cross-cultural view. *Teacher College Record, 76,* 226–239.

LeVine, R. A. (1989). Human parental care: Universal goals, cultural strategies, individual behavior. In R. A. LeVine, P. M. Miller, & M. M. West (Eds.), *Parental behavior in diverse societies* (pp. 3–12). San Francisco: Jossey-Bass.

LeVine, R. A. (1994). *Child care and culture: Lessons from Africa.* Cambridge, UK: Cambridge University Press.

Levine, S. C., Vasilyeva, M., Lourenco, S. E., Newcombe, N. S., & Huttenlocher, J. (2005). Socioeconimic status modifies the sex differences in spatial skills. *Psychological Science, 16,* 841–845.

Levron, J., Aviram, A., Madgar, I., Livshits, A., Raviv, G., Bider, D., et al. (1998, October). *High rate of chromosomal aneupoloidies in testicular spermatozoa retrieved from azoospermic patients undergoing testicular sperm extraction for in vitro fertilization.* Paper presented at the 16th World Congress on Fertility and Sterility and the 54th annual meeting of the American Society for Reproductive Medicine, San Francisco, CA.

Levy-Shiff, R., Zoran, N., & Shulman, S. (1997). International and domestic adoption: Child, parents, and family adjustment. *International Journal of Behavioral Development, 20,* 109–129.

Lewinsohn, P. M., Gotlib, I. H., Lewinsohn, M., Seeley, J. R., &Allen, N. B. (1998). Gender differences in anxiety disorders and anxiety symptoms in adolescence. *Journal of Abnormal Psychology, 107,* 109–117.

Lewis, M. (1995). Self-conscious emotions. *American Scientist, 83,* 68–78.

Lewis, M. (1997). The self in self-conscious emotions. In S. G. Snodgrass & R. L. Thompson (Eds.), *The self across psychology: Self-recognition, self-awareness, and the self-concept* (Vol. 818, pp. 119–142). New York: Annals of the New York Academy of Sciences.

Lewis, M. (1998). Emotional competence and development. In D. Pushkar, W. Bukowski, A. E. Schwartzman, D. M. Stack, & D. R. White (Eds.), *Improving competence across the lifespan* (pp. 27–36). New York: Plenum Press.

Lewis, M. (2003). The emergence of consciousness and its role in human development. *Annals of the New York Academy of Sciences, 1001,* 104–133.

Lewis, M. (2007). Early emotional development. In A. Slater and M. Lewis (Eds.), *Introduction to infant development.* Malden, MA: Blackwell.

Lewis, M., & Brooks, J. (1974). Self, other, and fear: Infants' reaction to people. In H. Lewis & L. Rosenblum (Eds.), *The origins of fear: The origins of behavior* (Vol. 2, pp. 195–228). New York: Wiley.

Lewis, M., & Carmody, D. P. (2008). Self-representation and brain development. *Developmental Psychology, 44,* 1329–1334.

Lewit, E., & Kerrebrock, N. (1997). Population-based growth stunting. *The Future of Children, 7*(2), 149–156.

Li, R., Chase, M., Jung, S., Smith, P.J.S., Loeken, M. R. (2005). Hypoxic stress in diabetic pregnancy contributes to impaired embryo gene expression and defective development by inducing oxidative stress. *American Journal of Physiology: Endocrinology and Metabolism, 289,* 591–599.

Li, X., Li, S., Ulusoy, E., Chen, W., Srinivasan, S. R., & Berenson, G. S. (2004). Childhood adiposity as a predictor of cardiac mass in adulthood. *Circulation, 110,* 3488–3492.

Liberman, I. Y., & Liberman, A. M. (1990). Whole language vs. code emphasis: Underlying assumptions and their implications for reading instruction. *Annals of Dyslexia, 40,* 51–76.

Lickliter, R., & Honeycutt, H. (2003). Developmental dynamics: Toward a biologically plausible evolutionary psychology. *Psychological Bulletin, 129,* 819–835.

Lickona, T. (Ed.). (1976). *Moral development and behavior.* New York: Holt.

Lillard, A., & Curenton, S. (1999). Do young children understand what others feel, want, and know? *Young Children, 54*(5), 52–57.

Lillard, A., & Else-Quest, N. (2006). The early years: Evaluating Montessori education. *Science, 313*, 1893–1894.

Lin, S., Hwang, S. A., Marshall, E. G., & Marion, D. (1998). Does paternal occupational lead exposure increase the risks of low birth weight or prematurity? *American Journal of Epidemiology, 148*, 173–181.

Lin, S. S., & Kelsey, J. L. (2000). Use of race and ethnicity in epidemiological research: Concepts, methodological issues, and suggestions for research. *Epidemiologic Reviews, 22*(2), 187–202.

Lindsey, E. W., Cremeens, P. R., & Caldera, Y. M. (2010). Gender differences in mother-toddler and father-toddler verbal initiations and responses during a caregiver and play context. *Sex Roles, 63*, 399–411.

Linnet, K. M., Wisborg, K., Obel, C., Secher, N. J., Thomsen, P. H., Agerbo, E., & Henriksen, T. B. (2005). Smoking during pregnancy and the risk of hyperkinetic disorder in offspring. *Pediatrics, 116*, 462–467.

Lippman, L. H., & McIntosh, H. (2010). *The demographics of spirituality and religiosity among youth: International and U. S. patterns (2010–21).* Retrieved from http://www.childtrends.org/Files//Child_Trends-2010_09_27_RB_Spirituality.pdf

Lissau, I., Overpeck, M. D., Ruan, J., Due, P., Holstein, B. E., Hediger, M. L., & Health Behaviours in School-Aged Children Obesity Working Group. (2004). Body mass index and overweight in adolescents in 13 European countries, Israel, and the Untied States. *Archives of Pediatric and Adolescent Medicine, 158*, 27–33.

Liszkowski, U., Carpenter, M., Striano, T., & Tomasello, M. (2006). 12- and 18-month-olds point to provide information for others. *Journal of Cognition and Development, 7*, 173–187.

Liszkowski, U., Carpenter, M., & Tomasello, M. (2008). Twelve-month-olds communicate helpfully and appropriately for knowledgeable and ignorant partners. *Cognition, 108*, 732–739.

Littleton, H., Breitkopf, C., & Berenson, A. (2006, August 13). *Correlates of anxiety symptoms during pregnancy and association with perinatal outcomes: A meta-analysis.* Presentation at the 114th annual convention of the American Psychological Association, New Orleans, LA.

Liu, J., Raine, A., Venables, P. H., Dalais, C., & Mednick, S. A. (2003). Malnutrition at age 3 years and lower cognitive ability at age 11 years. *Archives of Pediatric and Adolescent Medicine, 157*, 593–600.

Liu, S. V. (2006). Evolution: An integrated theory—criticisms on Darwinism—fifteen years ago. *Pioneer 1*, 10–28.

Livson, N., & Peskin, H. (1980). Perspectives on adolescence from longitudinal research. In J. Adelson (Ed.), *Handbook of adolescent psychology* (pp. 47–80). New York: Wiley.

Lloyd, J. J., & Anthony, J. C. (2003). Hanging out with the wrong crowd: How much difference can parents make in an urban environment? *Journal of Urban Health, 80*, 383–399.

Lloyd, T., Andon, M. B., Rollings, N., Martel, J. K., Landis, J. R., Demers, L. M., et al. (1993). Calcium supplementation and bone mineral density in adolescent girls. *Journal of the American Medical Association, 270*, 841–844.

LoBue, V., & DeLoache, J. (2011). Pretty in pink: The early development of gender-stereotyped colour preferences. *British Journal of Developmental Psychology, 29*(3), 656–667. doi: 10.1111/j.2044-835X.2011.02027.x

Lock, A., Young, A., Service, V., & Chandler, P. (1990). Some observations on the origin of the pointing gesture. In V. Volterra & C. J. Erting (Eds.), *From gesture to language in hearing and deaf children* (pp. 42–55). New York: Springer.

Lock, J., Walker, L. R., Rickert, V. I., & Katzman, D. K. (2005). Suicidality in adolescents being treated with antidepressant medications and the black box label: Position paper of the Society for Adolescent Medicine. *Journal of Adolescent Health, 36*, 92–93.

Lockwood, C. J. (2002). Predicting premature delivery—no easy task. *New England Journal of Medicine, 346*, 282–284.

Lohse, N., Hansen, A. E., Pedersen, G., Kronborg, G., Gerstoft, J., Sørensen, H. T., et al. (2007). Survival of persons with and without HIV infection in Denmark, 1995–2005. *Annals of Internal Medicine, 146*, 87–95.

Lonczak, H. S., Abbott, R. D., Hawkins, J. D., Kosterman, R., & Catalano, R. F. (2002). Effects of the Seattle Social Development Project on sexual behavior, pregnancy, birth, and sexually transmitted disease. *Archives of Pediatric and Adolescent Medicine, 156*, 438–447.

Longnecker, M. P., Klebanoff, M. A., Zhou, H., & Brock, J. W. (2001). Association between maternal serum concentration of the DDT metabolite DDE and preterm and small-for-gestational-age babies at birth. *Lancet, 358*, 110–114.

Longworth, H. L., & Kingdon, C. K. (2010) Fathers in the birth room: What are they expecting and experiencing? A phenomenological study. *Midwifery, 27*(5), 588–594.

Lonigan, C. J., Burgess, S. R., & Anthony, J. L. (2000). Development of emergent literacy and early reading skills in preschool children: Evidence from a latent-variable longitudinal study. *Developmental Psychology, 36*, 593–613.

Lorenz, K. (1957). Comparative study of behavior. In C. H. Schiller (Ed.), *Instinctive behavior.* New York: International Universities Press.

Lorsbach, T. C., & Reimer, J. F. (1997). Developmental changes in the inhibition of previously relevant information. *Journal of Experimental Child Psychology, 64*, 317–342.

Louise Brown: The world's first "test-tube baby" ushered in a revolution in fertility. (1984, March). *People Weekly*, p. 82.

Love, J. M., Kisker, E. E., Ross, C., Raikes, H., Constantine, J., Boller, K., et al. (2005). The effectiveness of Early Head Start for 3-year-old children and their parents: Lessons for policy and programs. *Developmental Psychology, 41*, 885–901.

Love, J. M., Kisker, E. E., Ross, C. M., Schochet, P. Z., Brooks-Gunn, J., Paulsell, D., et al. (2002). *Making a difference in the lives of infants and toddlers and their families: The impacts of Early Head Start.* Washington, DC: Administration on Children, Youth, and Families, U.S. Department of Health and Human Services.

Lubell, K. M., Kegler, S. R., Crosby, A. E., & Karch, M. D. (2007). Suicide trends among youths and young adults aged 10–24 years—United States, 1990–2004. *Morbidity and Mortality Weekly Report, 56*(35), 905–908.

Lucile Packard Children's Hospital at Stanford. (2009). *Failure to thrive.* Retrieved February 9, 2009, from www.lpch.org/DiseaseHealthInfo/Health/growth/Library/thrive.html

Ludwig, D. S. (2007). Childhood obesity—the shape of things to come. *New England Journal of Medicine, 357*, 2325–2327.

Ludwig, J., & Phillips, D. (2007). The benefits and costs of head start. *Social Policy Report, 21*, 3–20.

Lugaila, T. A. (2003). A child's day: 2000 (Selected indicators of child well-being). *Current Population Reports* (P70-89). Washington, DC: U.S. Census Bureau.

Luke, B., Mamelle, N., Keith, L., Munoz, F., Minogue, J., Papiernik, E., et al. (1995). The association between occupational factors and preterm birth: A United States nurses' study. *American Journal of Obstetrics and Gynecology, 173*, 849–862.

Luna, B., Garver, K. E., Urban, T. A., Lazar, N. A., & Sweeney, J. A. (2004). Maturation of cognitive processes from late childhood to adulthood. *Child Development, 75*, 1357–1372.

Lundy, B. L. (2003). Father- and mother-infant face-to-face interactions: Differences in mind-related comments and infant attachment? *Infant Behavior & Development, 26*, 200–212.

Lundy, B. L., Jones, N. A., Field, T., Nearing, G., Davalos, M., Pietro, P. A., et al. (1999). Prenatal depression effects on neonates. *Infant Behavior and Development, 22*, 119–129.

Luthar, S. S., & Latendresse, S. J. (2005). Children of the affluence: Challenges to well-being. *Current Directions in Psychological Science, 14*, 49–53.

Lyons-Ruth, K., Alpern, L., & Repacholi, B. (1993). Disorganized infant attachment classification and maternal psychosocial problems as predictors of hostile-aggressive behavior in the preschool classroom. *Child Development, 64*, 572–585.

Lytton, H., & Romney, D. M. (1991). Parents' differential socialization of boys and girls: A meta-analysis. *Psychological Bulletin, 109*(2), 267–296.

Lyytinen, P., Poikkeus, A., Laakso, M., Eklund, K., & Lyytinen, H. (2001). Language development and symbolic play in children with and without familial risk for dyslexia. *Journal of Speech, Language, and Hearing Research, 44*, 873–885.

Maccoby, E. (1980). *Social development.* New York: Harcourt Brace Jovanovich.

Maccoby, E. E. (1984). Middle childhood in the context of the family. In W. A. Collins (Ed.), *Development during middle childhood* (pp. 184–239). Washington, DC: National Academy.

Maccoby, E. E. (1992). The role of parents in the socialization of children: An historical overview. *Developmental Psychology, 28*, 1006–1017.

Maccoby, E. E. (2000). Perspectives on gender development. *International Journal of Behavioral Development, 24*(4), 398–406.

Maccoby, E. E. (2002). Gender and group process: A developmental perspective. *Current Directions in Psychological Science, 11*, 54–58.

Maccoby, E. E., & Jacklin, C. N. (1987). Gender segregation in childhood. *Advances in Child Development and Behavior, 20*, 239–287.

Maccoby, E. E., & Lewis, C. C. (2003). Less day care or different day care? *Child Development, 74*, 1069–1075.

Maccoby, E. E., & Martin, J. A. (1983). Socialization in the context of the family: Parent-child interaction. In P. H. Mussen (Series Ed.) & E. M. Hetherington (Vol. Ed.), *Handbook of child psychology: Vol. 4. Socialization, personality, and social development* (pp. 1–101). New York: Wiley.

MacDonald, K. (1998). Evolution and development. In A. Campbell & S. Muncer (Eds.), *Social development* (pp. 21–49). London: UCL Press.

Macdonald, K., & Hershberger, S. (2005). Theoretical issues in the study of evolution and development. In R. Burgess & K. MacDonald (Eds.), *Evolutionary Perspectives on Human Development* (2nd ed., pp. 21–72). Thousand Oaks, CA: Sage.

MacDorman, M. F., & Kirmeyer, S. (2009). Fetal and perinatal mortality, United States, 2005. *National Vital Statistics Reports, 57*(8). Hyattsville, MD: National Center for Health Statistics.

MacDorman, M. F., & Mathews, T. J. (2008). Recent trends in infant mortality in the United States. *NCHS Data Brief, 9.* Hyattsville, MD: National Center for Health Statistics.

MacKinnon-Lewis, C., Starnes, R., Volling, B., & Johnson, S. (1997). Perceptions of parenting as predictors of boys' sibling and peer relations. *Developmental Psychology, 33,* 1024–1031.

MacLean, K. (2003). The impact of institutionalization in child development. *Development and Psychopathology, 15*(4), 853–884.

Macmillan, C., Magder, L. S., Brouwers, P., Chase, C., Hittelman, J., Lasky, T., et al. (2001). Head growth and neurodevelopment of infants born to HIV-infected drug-using women. *Neurology, 57,* 1402–1411.

MacMillan, H. M., Boyle, M. H., Wong, M.Y.-Y., Duku, E. K., Fleming, J. E., & Walsh, C. A. (1999). Slapping and spanking in childhood and its association with lifetime prevalence of psychiatric disorders in a general population sample. *Canadian Medical Association Journal, 161,* 805–809.

Macmillan, R., McMorris, B. J., & Kruttschnitt, C. (2004). Linked lives: Stability and change in maternal circumstances and trajectories of antisocial behavior in children. *Child Development, 75,* 205–220.

Maestripieri, D., Higley, J., Lindell, S., Newman, T., McCormack, K., & Sanchez, M. (2006). Early maternal rejection affects the development of monoaminergic systems and adult abusive parenting in Rhesus Macaques (Macaca mulatta). *Behavioral Neuroscience, 120,* 1017–1024.

Mahoney, J. L. (2000). School extracurricular activity participation as a moderator in the development of antisocial patterns. *Child Development, 71*(2), 502–516.

Mahoney, J. L., Lord, H., & Carryl, E. (2005). An ecological analysis of after-school program participation and the development of academic performance and motivational attributes for disadvantaged children. *Child Development, 76*(4), 811–825.

Main, M. (1995). Recent studies in attachment: Overview, with selected implications for clinical work. In S. Goldberg, R. Muir, & J. Kerr (Eds.), *Attachment theory: Social, developmental, and clinical perspectives* (pp. 407–470). Hillsdale, NJ: Analytic Press.

Main, M., Kaplan, N., & Cassidy, J. (1985). Security in infancy, childhood and adulthood: A move to the level of representation. In I. Bretherton & E. Waters (Eds.), Growing points in attachment. *Monographs of the Society for Research in Child Development, 50*(1–20), 66–104.

Main, M., & Solomon, J. (1986). Discovery of an insecure, disorganized/disoriented attachment pattern: Procedures, findings, and implications for the classification of behavior. In M.Yogman & T. B. Brazelton (Eds.), *Affective development in infancy* (pp. 95–124). Norwood, NJ: Ablex.

Makino, M., Tsuboi, K., & Dennerstein, L. (2004). Prevalence of eating disorders: A comparison of Western and non-Western countries. *Medscape General Medicine, 6*(3). Retrieved September 27, 2004, from www.medscape.com/viewarticle/487413

Makrides, M., Gibson, R. A., McPhee, A. J., Collins, C. T., Davis, P. G., Doyle, L. W., et al. (2009). Neurodevelopmental outcomes of preterm infants fed high-dose docosahexaenoic acid. *Journal of the American Medical Association, 301,* 175–182.

Malaguzzi, L. (1993). For an education based on relationships. *Young Children, 49*(1), 9–12.

Malaspina, D., Harlap, S., Fennig, S., Heiman, D., Nahon, D., Feldman, D., & Susser, E. S. (2001). Advancing paternal age and the risk of schizophrenia. *Archives of General Psychiatry, 58,* 361–371.

Malloy, M. H. (2008). Impact of Cesarean section on neonatal mortality rates among very preterm infants in the United States, 2000–2003. *Pediatrics, 122,* 285–292.

Malone, F. D., Canick, J. A., Ball, R. H., Nyberg, D. A., Comstock, C. H., Bukowski, R., et al. (2005). First-trimester or second-trimester screening, or both, for Down's syndrome. *New England Journal of Medicine, 353,* 2001–2011.

Malone, L. M., West, J., Flanagan, K. D., & Park, J. (2006). *Statistics in brief: The early reading and mathematics achievement of children who repeated kindergarten or who began school a year late* (NCES 2006-064). Washington, DC: National Center for Education Statistics.

Mandler, J. M. (1998). Representation. In D. Kuhn & R. S. Siegler (Eds.), *Handbook of child psychology: Vol. 2. Cognition, perception, and language* (5th ed., pp. 255–308). New York: Wiley.

Mandler, J. M. (2007). On the origins of the conceptual system. *American Psychologist, 62,* 741–751.

Mandler, J. M., & McDonough, L. (1993). Concept formation in infancy. *Cognitive Development, 8,* 291–318.

Mandler, J. M., & McDonough, L. (1996). Drinking and driving don't mix: Inductive generalization in infancy. *Cognition, 59,* 307–335.

Mandler, J. M., & McDonough, L. (1998). Cognition across the life span: On developing a knowledge base in infancy. *Developmental Psychology, 34,* 1274–1288.

Manlove, J., Ryan, S., & Franzetta, K. (2003). Patterns of contraceptive use within teenagers' first sexual relationships. *Perspectives on Sexual and Reproductive Health, 35,* 246–255.

March of Dimes Birth Defects Foundation. (1987). *Genetic counseling: A public health information booklet* (Rev. ed.). White Plains, NY: Author.

March of Dimes Birth Defects Foundation.(2004a). *Cocaine use during pregnancy.* [Fact sheet]. Retrieved October 29, 2004, from www.marchofdimes.com/professionals/681_1169.asp

March of Dimes Birth Defects Foundation. (2004b). *Marijuana: What you need to know.* Retrieved October 29, 2004, from www.marchofdimes.com/pnhec/159_4427.asp

March of Dimes Foundation. (2002). *Toxoplasmosis.* [Fact sheet]. Wilkes-Barre, PA: Author.

Marchman, V. A., & Fernald, A. (2008). Speed of word recognition and vocabulary knowledge in infancy predict cognitive and language outcomes in later childhood. *Developmental Science, 11,* F9–16.

Marcia, J. E. (1966). Development and validation of ego identity status. *Journal of Personality and Social Psychology, 3*(5), 551–558.

Marcia, J. E. (1979, June). *Identity status in late adolescence: Description and some clinical implications.* Address given at Symposium on Identity Development, Rijksuniversitat Groningen, The Netherlands.

Marcia, J. E. (1980). Identity in adolescence. In J. Adelson (Ed.), *Handbook of adolescent psychology* (pp. 159–187). New York: Wiley.

Marcia, J. E. (1993). The relational roots of identity. In J. Kroger (Ed.), *Discussions on ego identity* (pp. 101–120). Hillsdale, NJ: Erlbaum.

Markoff, J. (1992, October 12). Miscarriages tied to chip factories. *New York Times,* pp. A1, D2.

Marks, H. (2000). Student engagement in instructional activity: Patterns in the elementary, middle, and high school years. *American Education Research Journal, 37,* 153–184.

Marlow, N., Wolke, D., Bracewell, M. A., & Samara, M., for the EPICure Study Group. (2005). Neurologic and developmental disability at six years of age after extremely preterm birth. *New England Journal of Medicine, 352,* 9–19.

Marshall, N. L. (2004). The quality of early child care and children's development. *Current Directions in Psychological Science, 13,* 165–168.

Marshall, T. A., Levy, S. M., Broffitt, B., Warren, J. J., Eichenberger-Gilmore, J. M., Burns, T. L., & Stumbo, P. J. (2003) Dental caries and beverage consumption in young children. *Pediatrics, 112,* e184–e191.

Martin, C. L., Eisenbud, L., & Rose, H. (1995). Children's gender-based reasoning about toys. *Child Development, 66,* 1453–1471.

Martin, C. L., & Fabes, R. A. (2001). The stability and consequences of young children's same-sex peer interactions. *Developmental Psychology, 37,* 431–446.

Martin, C. L., & Halverson, C. F. (1981). A schematic processing model of sex typing and stereotyping in children. *Child Development, 52,* 1119–1134.

Martin, C. L., & Ruble, D. (2004). Children's search for gender cues: Cognitive perspectives on gender development. *Current Directions in Psychological Science, 13,* 67–70.

Martin, C. L., Ruble, D. N., & Szkrybalo, J. (2002). Cognitive theories of early gender development. *Psychological Bulletin, 128,* 903–933.

Martin, J. A., Hamilton, B. E., Sutton, P. D., Ventura, S. J., Menacker, F., & Kirmeyer, S. (2006). Births: Final data for 2004. *National Vital Statistics Reports, 55*(1). Hyattsville, MD: National Center for Health Statistics.

Martin, J. A., Hamilton, B. E., Sutton, P. D., Ventura, S. J., Menacker, F., Kirmeyer, S., & Mathews, T. J. (2009). Births: Final data for 2006. *National Vital Statistics Reports, 57*(7). Hyattsville, MD: National Center for Health Statistics.

Martin, J. A., Hamilton, B. E., Sutton, P. D., Ventura, S. J., Menacker, F., Kirmeyer, S., & Munson, M. (2007). Births: Final data for 2005. *National Vital Statistics Reports, 56*(6). Hyattsville, MD: National Center for Health Statistics.

Martin, J. A., Hamilton, B. E., Sutton, P. D., Ventura, S. J., Menacker, F., & Munson, M. L. (2005). Births: Final data for 2003. *National Vital Statistics Reports, 54*(2). Hyattsville, MD: National Center for Health Statistics.

Martin, J. A., Hamilton, B. E., Ventura, S. J., Osterman, M.J.K., Wilson, E. C., & Mathews, T. J. (2012). Births: Final data for 2010. *National Vital Statistics Report, 61*(1). Hyattsville, MD: National Center for Health Statistics.

Martin, N., & Montgomery, G. (2002, March 18). *Is having twins, either identical or fraternal, in someone's genes? Is there a way to increase your chances of twins or is having twins just luck?* Retrieved March 7, 2006, from http://genepi.qimr.edu.au/Scientific American Twins.html

Martin, R., Noyes, J., Wisenbaker, J., & Huttunen, M. (2000). Prediction of early childhood negative emotionality and inhibition from maternal distress during pregnancy. *Merrill-Palmer Quarterly, 45,* 370–391.

Martinez, G., Copen, C. E., & Abma, J. C. (2011). Teenagers in the United States: Sexual activity, contraceptive use, and childbearing, 2006–2010 National Survey of Family Growth. National Center for Health Statistics. *Vital Health Stat 23*(31).

Martínez-González, M. A., Gual, P., Lahortiga, F., Alonso, Y., de Irala-Estévez, J., & Cervera, S. (2003). Parental factors, mass media influences, and the onset of eating disorders in a prospective population-based cohort. *Pediatrics, 111,* 315–320.

Marwick, C. (1997). Health care leaders from drug policy group. *Journal of the American Medical Association, 278,* 378.

Marwick, C. (1998). Physician leadership on national drug policy finds addiction treatment works. *Journal of the American Medical Association, 279,* 1149–1150.

Masse, L. C., & Tremblay, R. E. (1997). Behavior of boys in kindergarten and the onset of substance use during adolescence. *Archives of General Psychiatry, 54,* 62–68.

Masten, A., Best, K., & Garmezy, N. (1990). Resilience and development: Contributions from the study of children who overcome adversity. *Development and Psychopathology, 2,* 425–444.

Masten, A. S. (2001). Ordinary magic: Resilience processes in development. *American Psychologist, 56,* 227–238.

Masten, A. S., & Coatsworth, J. D. (1998). The development of competence in favorable and unfavorable environments: Lessons from research on successful children. *American Psychologist, 53,* 205–220.

Mathews, T. J., & MacDorman, M. F. (2008). Infant mortality statistics from the 2005 period linked birth/infant death data set. *National Vital Statistics Report, 57*(2), 1–32.

Mathie, A., & Carnozzi, A. (2005). *Qualitative research for tobacco control: A how-to introductory manual for researchers and development practitioners.* Ottawa, Ontario, Canada: International Development Research Centre.

Matsumoto, D., & Juang, L. (2008). *Culture and psychology* (4th ed.). Belmont, CA: Wadsworth.

May, K. A., & Perrin, S. P. (1985). Prelude: Pregnancy and birth. In S.M.H. Hanson & F. W. Bozett (Eds.), *Dimensions of fatherhood* (pp. 64–91). Beverly Hills, CA: Sage.

Mayer, D. P. (1998). Do new teaching standards undermine performance on old tests? *Educational Evaluation and Policy Analysis, 20,* 53–73.

Mayo Clinic (2013). Retrieved March 15, 2013, from www.mayoclinic.com/health/infertility /DS00310/DSECTION=causes

Mayo Foundation for Medical Education and Research. (2009, January). Beyond the human genome: Meet the epigenome. *Mayo Clinic Health Letter, 27*(1), pp. 4–5.

Mayseless, O., & Scharf, M. (2003). What does it mean to be an adult? The Israeli experience. In J. J. Arnett & N. L. Galambos (Eds.), Exploring cultural conceptions of the transition to adulthood. *New Directions for Child and Adolescent Development, 100,* 5–20.

McCall, D. D., & Clifton, R. K. (1999). Infants' means-end search for hidden objects in the absence of visual feedback. *Infant Behavior and Development, 22*(2), 179–195.

McCall, R. B., & Carriger, M. S. (1993). A meta-analysis of infant habituation and recognition memory performance as predictors of later IQ. *Child Development, 64,* 57–79.

McCallum, K. E., & Bruton, J. R. (2003). The continuum of care in the treatment of eating disorders. *Primary Psychiatry, 10*(6), 48–54.

McCartt, A. T. (2001). Graduated driver licensing systems: Reducing crashes among teenage drivers. *Journal of the American Medical Association, 286,* 1631–1632.

McCarty, M. E., Clifton, R. K., Ashmead, D. H., Lee, P., & Goubet, N. (2001). How infants use vision for grasping objects. *Child Development, 72,* 973–987.

McClearn, G. E., Johansson, B., Berg, S., Pedersen, N. L., Ahern, F., Petrill, S. A., & Plomin, R. (1997). Substantial genetic influence on cognitive abilities in twins 80 or more years old. *Science, 276,* 1560–1563.

McClintock, M. K., & Herdt, G. (1996). Rethinking puberty: The development of sexual attraction. *Current Directions in Psychological Science, 5*(6), 178–183.

McCord, J. (1996). Unintended consequences of punishment. *Pediatrics, 88,* 832–834.

McCoy, A. R., & Reynolds, A. J. (1999). Grade retention and school performance: An extended investigation. *Journal of School Psychology, 37,* 273–298.

McCrink, K., & Wynn, K. (2004). Large-number addition and subtraction by 9-month-old infants. *Psychological Science, 15,* 776–781.

McDaniel, M., Paxson, C., & Waldfogel, J. (2006). Racial disparities in childhood asthma in the United States: Evidence from the National Health Interview Survey, 1997 to 2003. *Pediatrics, 117,* 868–877.

McDowell, M., Fryar, C., Odgen, C., & Flegal, K. (2008). Anthropometric reference data for children and adults: United States, 2003–2006. *National health statistics report* (No. 10). Hyattsville, MD: National Center for Health Statistics.

McDowell, M. M., Wang, C.-Y., & Kennedy-Stephenson, J. (2008). *Breastfeeding in the United States: Findings from the National Health and Nutrition Examination Surveys, 1999–2006.* [NCHS Data Briefs, No. 5]. Hyattsville, MD: National Center for Health Statistics.

McElwain, N. L., & Volling, B. L. (2005). Preschool children's interactions with friends and older siblings: Relationship specificity and joint contributions to problem behavior. *Journal of Family Psychology, 19,* 486–496.

McGue, M. (1997). The democracy of the genes. *Nature, 388,* 417–418.

McGuffin, P., Owen, M. J., & Farmer, A. E. (1995). Genetic basis of schizophrenia. *Lancet, 346,* 678–682.

McGuffin, P., Riley, B., & Plomin, R. (2001). Toward behavioral genomics. *Science, 291,* 1232–1249.

McGuigan, F. & Salmon, K. (2004). The time to talk: The influence of the timing of adult-child talk on children's event memory. *Child Development, 75,* 669–686.

McHale, S. M., Kim, J., Whiteman, S., & Crouter, A. C. (2004). Links between sex-typed time use in middle childhood and gender development in early adolescence. *Developmental Psychology, 40,* 868–881.

McHale, S. M., Updegraff, K. A., Helms- Erikson, H., & Crouter, A. C. (2001). Sibling influences on gender development in middle childhood and early adolescence: A longitudinal study. *Developmental Psychology, 37,* 115–125.

McKenna, J. J., & Mosko, S. (1993). Evolution and infant sleep: An experimental study of infant-parent cosleeping and its implications for SIDS. *Acta Paediatrica, 389*(Suppl.), 31–36.

McKenna, J. J., Mosko, S. S., & Richard, C. A. (1997). Bedsharing promotes breastfeeding. *Pediatrics, 100,* 214–219.

McKenna, K.Y.A., & Bargh, J. A. (2000). Plan 9 from cyberspace: The implication of the Internet for personality and social psychology. *Personality and Social Psychology Review, 4,* 57–75.

McKusick, V. A. (2001). The anatomy of the human genome. *Journal of the American Medical Association, 286*(18), 2289–2295.

McLanahan, S., & Sandefur, G. (1994). *Growing up with a single parent.* Cambridge, MA: Harvard University Press.

McLeod, R., Boyer, K., Karrison, T., Kasza, K., Swisher, C., Roizen, N., et al. (2006). Outcome of treatment for congenital toxoplasmosis, 1981–2004: The national collaborative Chicago-based, congenital toxoplasmosis study. *Clinical Infectious Diseases: An Official Publication of the Infectious Diseases Society of America, 42*(10), 1383–1394.

McLeskey, J., Lancaster, M., & Grizzle, K. L. (1995). Learning disabilities and grade retention: A review of issues with recommendations for practice. *Learning Disabilities Research & Practice, 10,* 120–128.

McLoyd, V. C. (1990). The impact of economic hardship on black families and children: Psychological distress, parenting, and socioemotional development. *Child Development, 61,* 311–346.

McLoyd, V. C. (1998). Socioeconomic disadvantage and child development. *American Psychologist, 53,* 185–204.

McLoyd, V. C., & Smith, J. (2002). Physical discipline and behavior problems in African American, European American, and Hispanic children: Emotional support as a moderator. *Journal of Marriage and Family, 64,* 40–53.

McQueeny, T., Schweinsburg, B. C., Schweinsburg, A. D., Jacobus, J., Bava, S., Frank, L. R, & Tapert, S. F. (2009). Altered white matter integrity in adolescent binge drinkers. *Alcoholism: Clinical and Experimental Research, 33*(7), 1278–1285.

McQuillan, J., Greil, A. L., White, L., & Jacob, M. C. (2003). Frustrated fertility: Infertility and psychological distress among women. *Journal of Marriage and Family, 65,* 1007–1018.

Mears, B. (2005, March 1). *High court: Juvenile death penalty unconstitutional: Slim majority cites 'evolving standards' in American society.* Retrieved March 30, 2005, from http://cnn.com./2005 /LAW/03/01/scotus.death.penalty

Medland, S. E., Duffy, D. L., Wright, M. J., Geffen, G. M., Hay, D. A., Levy, F., et al. (2009). Genetic influences on handedness: Data from 25, 732 Australian and Dutch twin families. *Neuropsychologica,47*(2), 33–337.

Meeks, J. J., Weiss, J., & Jameson, J. L. (2003, May). Dax1 is required for testis formation. *Nature Genetics, 34,* 32–33.

Meezan, W., & Rauch, J. (2005). Gay marriage, same-sex parenting, and America's children. *Future of Children, 15,* 97–115.

Meier, D. (1995). *The power of their ideas.* Boston: Beacon.

Meier, R. (1991, January–February). Language acquisition by deaf children. *American Scientist, 79,* 60–70.

Meijer, A. M., & van den Wittenboer, G.L.H. (2007). Contributions of infants' sleep and crying to marital relationship of first-time parent couples in the 1st year after childbirth. *Journal of Family Psychology, 21,* 49–57.

Meins, E. (1998). The effects of security of attachment and maternal attribution of meaning on children's linguistic acquisitional style. *Infant Behavior and Development, 21,* 237–252.

Meis, P. J., Klebanoff, M., Thom, E., Dombrowski, M. P., Sibai, B., Moawad, A. H., et al. (2003). Prevention of recurrent preterm delivery by 17 alpha-hydroxyprogesterone caproate. *New England Journal of Medicine, 348,* 2379–2385.

Melby, J., Conger, R, Fang, S., Wickrama, K., & Conger, K. (2008). Adolescent family experiences and educational attainment during early adulthood. *Developmental Psychology, 44*(6), 1519–1536.

Meltzoff, A. N. (2007). "Like me": A foundation for social cognition. *Developmental Science, 10,* 126–134.

Meltzoff, A. N., & Moore, M. K. (1989). Imitation in newborn infants: Exploring the range of gestures imitated and the underlying mechanisms. *Developmental Psychology, 25,* 954–962.

Meltzoff, A. N., & Moore, M. K. (1994). Imitation, memory, and the representation of persons. *Infant Behavior and Development, 17,* 83–99.

Meltzoff, A. N., & Moore, M. K. (1998). Object representation, identity, and the paradox of early permanence: Steps toward a new framework. *Infant Behavior & Development, 21,* 201–235.

Menacker, F., & Hamilton, B. E. (2010, March). *Recent trends in cesarean delivery in the United States.* NCHS Data Brief No. 35. Hyattsville, MD: National Center for Health Statistics.

Menacker, F., Martin, J. A., MacDorman, M. F., & Ventura, S. J. (2004). Births to 10–14 year-old mothers, 1990–2002: Trends and health outcomes. *National Vital Statistics Reports, 53*(7). Hyattsville, MD: National Center for Health Statistics.

Mendle, J., Turkheimer, E., D'Onofrio, B. M., Lynch, S. K., Emery, R. E., Slutske, W. S., & Martin, N. G. (2006). Family structure and age at menarche: A children-of-twins approach. *Developmental Psychology, 42,* 533–542.

Mendle, J., Turkheimer, E., & Emery, R. E. (2007). Detrimental psychological outcomes associated with early pubertal timing in adolescent girls. *Developmental Review, 27,* 249–266.

Menegaux, F., Baruchel, A., Bertrand, Y., Lescoeur, B., Leverger, G., Nelken, B., et al. (2006). Household exposure to pesticides and risk of childhood acute leukaemia. *Occupational and Environmental Medicine, 63*(2), 131–134.

Meng, H., Smith, S. D., Hager, K., Held, M., Liu, J., Olson, R. K., et al. (2005, October). *A deletion in DCDC2 on 6p22 is associated with reading disability.* Paper presented at the American Society of Human Genetics meeting, Salt Lake City, UT.

Mennella, J. A., & Beauchamp, G. K. (1996). The early development of human flavor preferences. In E. D. Capaldi (Ed.), *Why we eat what we eat: The psychology of eating* (pp. 83–112). Washington DC: American Psychological Association.

Mennella, J. A., & Beauchamp, G. K. (2002). Flavor experiences during formula feeding are related to preferences during childhood. *Early Human Development, 68,* 71–82.

Mennella, J. A., Jagnow, C. P., & Beauchamp, G. K. (2001). Prenatal and postnatal flavor learning by human infants. *Pediatrics, 107,* E88.

Ment, L. R., Vohr, B., Allan, W., Katz, K. H., Schneider, K. C., Westerveld, M., et al. (2003). Changes in cognitive function over time in very low-birth-weight infants. *Journal of the American Medical Association, 289,* 705–711.

Merewood, A., Mehta, S. D., Chamberlain, L. B., Philipp, B. L., & Bauchner, H. (2005). Breastfeeding rates in US baby-friendly hospitals: Results of a national survey. *Pediatrics, 116,* 628–634.

Merrell, K., Gueldner, B., Ross, S., & Isava, D. (2008). How effective are school bullying intervention programs? A meta-analysis of intervention research. *School Psychology Quarterly, 23*(1), 26–42.

Mesch, G. (2001). Social relationships and Internet use among adolescents in Israel. *Social Science Quarterly, 82,* 329–340.

Messinger, D. S., Bauer, C. R., Das, A., Seifer, R., Lester, B. M., Lagasse, L. L., et al. (2004). The maternal lifestyle study: Cognitive, motor, and behavioral outcomes of cocaine-exposed and opiate-exposed infants through three years of age. *Pediatrics, 113,* 1677–1685.

Messinis, L., Krypianidou, A., Maletaki, S., & Papathanasopoulos, P. (2006). Neuropsychological deficits in long-term cannabis users. *Neurology, 66,* 737–739.

Meyer, I. H. (2003). Prejudice, social stress, and mental health in lesbian, gay, and bisexual populations: Conceptual issues and research evidence. *Psychological Bulletin, 129,* 674–697.

Miech, R. A., Kumanyika, S. K., Stettler, N., Link, B., Phelan, J. C., & Chang, V. W. (2006). Trends in the association of poverty with overweight among US adolescents, 1971–2004. *Journal of the American Medical Association, 295,* 2385–2393.

Miedzian, M. (1991). *Boys will be boys: Breaking the link between masculinity and violence.* New York: Doubleday.

Migeon, B. R. (2006). The role of X inactivation and cellular mosaicism in women's health and sex-specific disorders. *Journal of the American Medical Association, 295,* 1428–1433.

Mikkola, K., Ritari, N., Tommiska, V., Salokorpi, T., Lehtonen, L., Tammela, O., et al. (2005). Neurodevelopmental outcome at 5 years of age of a national cohort of extremely low birth weight infants who were born in 1996-1997. *Pediatrics, 116,* 1391–1400.

Miles C. L., Matthews, J., Brennan, L., & Mitchell, S. (2010). Changes in the content of children's school lunches across the school week. *Health Promotion Journal of Australia, 21*(3), 196–201.

Miller, J. W., Naimi, T. S., Brewer, R. D., & Jones, S. E. (2007). Binge drinking and associated health risk behaviors among high school students. *Pediatrics, 119,* 76–85.

Miller-Kovach, K. (2003). *Childhood and adolescent obesity: A review of the scientific literature.* Unpublished manuscript. Weight Watchers International.

Millman, R. P., Working Group on Sleepiness in Adolescents/Young Adults, & AAP Committee on Adolescents. (2005). Excessive sleepiness in adolescents and young adults: Causes, consequences, and treatment strategies. *Pediatrics, 115,* 1774–1786.

Mills, J. L., & England, L. (2001). Food fortification to prevent neural tube defects: Is it working? *Journal of the American Medical Association, 285,* 3022–3033.

Mindell, J. A., Sadeh, A., Wiegand, B., How, T. H., & Goh, D.Y.T. (2010). Cross-cultural differences in infant and toddler sleep. *Sleep Medicine, 11,* 274–289.

Miniño, A. M., Anderson, R. N., Fingerhut, L. A., Boudreault, M. A., & Warner, M. (2006). Deaths: Injuries, 2002. *National Vital Statistics Reports, 54*(10). Hyattsville, MD: National Center for Health Statistics.

Mischel, W. (1966). A social learning view of sex differences in behavior. In E. Maccoby (Ed.), *The development of sex differences* (pp. 57–81). Stanford, CA: Stanford University Press.

Mishra G. D., Cooper R., Tom, S. E., & Kuh, D. (2009). Early life circumstances and their impact on menarche and menopause. *Women's Health* (Lond Engl) 5, 175–190.

Mistry, R. S., Vandewater, E. A., Huston, A. C., & McLoyd, V. (2002). Economic well-being and children's social adjustment: The role of family process in an ethnically diverse low income sample. *Child Development, 73,* 935–951.

Mirchell, E. A., Blair, P. S., & L'Hoir, M. P. (2006). Should pacifiers be recommended to prevent sudden infant death syndrome? *Pediatrics, 117,* 1755–1758.

Miyake, K., Chen, S., & Campos, J. (1985). Infants' temperament, mothers' mode of interaction and attachment in Japan: An interim report. In I. Bretherton & E. Waters (Eds.), Growing points of attachment theory and research. *Monographs of the Society for Research in Child Development, 50*(1–2, Serial No. 109), 276–297.

Mix, K. S., Huttenlocher, J., & Levine, S. C. (2002). Multiple cues for quantification in infancy: Is number one of them? *Psychological Bulletin, 128,* 278–294.

Mix, K. S., Levine, S. C., & Huttenlocher, J. (1999). Early fraction calculation ability. *Developmental Psychology, 35,* 164–174.

Mlot, C. (1998). Probing the biology of emotion. *Science, 280,* 1005–1007.

Modzeleski, W., Feucht, T., Rand, M., Hall, J. E., Simon, T. R., Butler, L., et al. (2008). School-associated student homicides—United States, 1992–2006. *Morbidity and Mortality Weekly Report, 57*(2), 33–36.

Moffitt, T. E. (1993). Adolescent-limited and life-course persistent antisocial behavior: A developmental taxonomy. *Psychological Review, 100,* 674–701.

Mohajer, S. T. (2009a, February 10). Octuplets' mom had controversial doctor. *Associated Press.* Retrieved February 10, 2009, from http://news.aol.com/article/octuplets-nadya-suleman/328104

Mohajer, S. T. (2009b, February 6). Octuplet mom's doctor is investigated. *Associated Press.* Retrieved February 6, 2009, from http://news.aol.com/article/octuplets-mom-speaks/331827?icid=200100397x1217799767x1201239528

Mohajer, S. T. (2009c, February 12). Octuplet mom seeks donations online: Plus, taxpayers may have to help cover her costs. *Associated Press.* Retrieved February 12, 2009, from http://news.aol.com/octuplets/article-mom-web-site/334503

Mojon-Azzi, S., Kunz, A., & Mojon D. S. (2010). Strabismus and discrimination in children: Are children with strabismus invited to fewer birthday parties? *British Journal of Opthalmology, 95*(4), 473–476. doi: 10.1136/bjo.2010.185793

Mondschein, E. R., Adolph, K. E., & Tamis-Lemonda, C. S. (2000). Gender bias in mothers' expectations about infant crawling. *Journal of Experimental Child Psychology. Special Issue on Gender, 77,* 304–316.

Money, J., Hampson, J. G., & Hampson, J. L. (1955). Hermaphroditism: Recommendations concerning assignment of sex, change of sex and psychologic management. *Buletin of the Johns Hopkins Hospital, 97*(4), 284–300.

Montague, D.P.F., & Walker-Andrews, A. S. (2001). Peekaboo: A new look at infants' perception of emotion expressions. *Developmental Psychology, 37,* 826–838.

Montessori, M. (with Chattin-McNichogls, J.). (1995). *The absorbent mind.* New York: Holt.

Moon, C., Cooper, R. P., & Fifer, W. P. (1993). Two-day-olds prefer their native language. *Infant Behavior and Development, 16,* 495–500.

Moon, R. Y., Sprague, B. M., & Patel, K. M. (2005). Stable prevalence but changing risk factors for sudden infant death syndrome in child care settings in 2001. *Pediatrics, 116,* 972–977.

Mooney-Somers, J., & Golombok, S. (2000). Children of lesbian mothers: From the 1970s to the new millennium. *Sexual & Relationship Therapy 15*(2), 121–126.

Moore, S. E., Cole, T. J., Poskitt, E.M.E., Sonko, B. J., Whitehead, R. G., McGregor, I. A., & Prentice, A. M. (1997). Season of birth predicts mortality in rural Gambia. *Nature, 388,* 434.

Morelli, G. A., Rogoff, B., Oppenheim, D., & Goldsmith, D. (1992). Cultural variation in infants' sleeping arrangements: Questions of independence. *Developmental Psychology, 28,* 604–613.

Morgan, R. A., Dudley, M. E., Wunderlich, J. R., Hughes, M. S., Yang, J. C., Sherry, R. M., et al. (2006, August 31). *Cancer regression in patients mediated by transfer of genetically engineered lymphocytes.* Retrieved from www.sciencemag.org /cgi/content/abstract/1129003v1. doi: 10.1126 /science.1129003

Morison, P., & Masten, A. S. (1991). Peer reputation in middle childhood as a predictor of adaptation in adolescence: A seven-year follow-up. *Child Development, 62,* 991–1007.

Morris, R. J., & Kratochwill, T. R. (1983). *Treating children's fears and phobias: A behavioral approach.* Boston: Allyn & Bacon.

Morrison, J. A., Friedman, L. A., Harlan, W. R., Harlan, L. C., Barton, B. A., Schreiber, G. B., & Klein, D. J. (2005). Development of the metabolic syndrome in black and white adolescent girls. *Pediatrics, 116,* 1178–1182.

Morrissey, T. W. (2009). Multiple child-care arrangements and young children's behavioral outcomes. *Child Development, 80,* 59–76.

Mortensen, E. L., Michaelson, K. F., Sanders, S. A., & Reinisch, J. M. (2002). The association between duration of breastfeeding and adult intelligence. *Journal of the American Medical Association, 287,* 2365–2371.

Morton, H. (1996). *Becoming Tongan: An ethnography of childhood.* Honolulu: University of Hawaii Press.

Moses, L. J., Baldwin, D. A., Rosicky, J. G., & Tidball, G. (2001). Evidence for referential understanding in the emotions domain at twelve and eighteen months. *Child Development, 72,* 718–735.

Mosher, W. D., Chandra, A., & Jones, J. (2005). *Sexual behavior and selected health measures: Men and women 15–44 years of age, United States, 2002.*

[Advance data from vital and health statistics; No. 362]. Hyattsville, MD: Centers for Disease Control and Prevention, National Center for Health Statistics.

Mosier, C. E., & Rogoff, B. (2003). Privileged treatment of toddlers: Cultural aspects of individual choice and responsibility. *Developmental Psychology, 39,* 1047–1060.

Moster, D., Lie, R.T., & Markestad, T. (2008). Long-term medical and social consequences of preterm birth. *New England Journal of Medicine, 359,* 262–273.

Moulson, M. C., Fox, N. A., Zeanah, C. H., & Nelson, C. A. (2009). Early adverse experiences and the neurobiology of facial emotion processing. *Developmental Psychology, 45,* 17–30.

Mounts, N. S., & Steinberg, L. (1995). An ecological analysis of peer influence on adolescent grade point average and drug use. *Developmental Psychology, 31,* 915–922.

Msall, M.S.E. (2004). Developmental vulnerability and resilience in extremely preterm infants. *Journal of the American Medical Association, 292,* 2399–2401.

MTA Cooperative Group. (1999). A 14-month randomized clinical trial of treatment strategies for attention deficit/hyperactivity disorder. *Archives of General Psychiatry, 56,* 1073–1986.

MTA Cooperative Group. (2004a). National Institute of Mental Health multimodal treatment study of ADHD follow-up: Changes in effectiveness and growth after the end of treatment. *Pediatrics, 113,* 762–769.

MTA Cooperative Group. (2004b). National Institute of Mental Health multimodal treatment study of ADHD follow-up: 24-month outcomes of treatment strategies for attention-deficit/ hyperactivity disorder. *Pediatrics, 113,* 754–769.

Mulford, C., & Giordano, P. (2008). Teen dating violence: A closer look at adolescent romantic relationships. *National Institute of Justice Journal, 261.*

Mullan, D., & Currie, C. (2000). Socioeconomic equalities in adolescent health. In C. Currie, K. Hurrelmann, W. Settertobulte, R. Smith, & J. Todd (Eds.), *Health and health behaviour among young people: A WHO crossnational study (HBSC) international report* (pp. 65–72). [WHO Policy Series: Healthy Policy for Children and Adolescents, Series No. 1]. Copenhagen, Denmark: World Health Organization Regional Office for Europe.

Mumme, D. L., & Fernald, A. (2003). The infant as onlooker: Learning from emotional reactions observed in a television scenario. *Child Development, 74,* 221–237.

Munakata, Y. (2001). Task-dependency in infant behavior: Toward an understanding of the processes underlying cognitive development. In F. Lacerda, C. von Hofsten, & M. Heimann (Eds.), *Emerging cognitive abilities in early infancy* (pp. 29–52). Hillsdale, NJ: Erlbaum.

Munakata, Y., McClelland, J. L., Johnson, M. J., & Siegler, R. S. (1997). Rethinking infant knowledge: Toward an adaptive process account of successes and failures in object permanence tasks. *Psychological Review, 104,* 686–714.

Munk-Olsen, T., Laursen, T. M., Pedersen, C. B., Mors, O., & Mortensen, P. B. (2006). New parents and mental disorders: A population-based register study. *Journal of the American Medical Association, 296,* 2582–2589.

Munson, M. L., & Sutton, P. D. (2004). Births, marriages, divorces, and deaths: Provisional data

for November 2003. *National Vital Statistics Reports, 52*(20). Hyattsville, MD: National Center for Health Statistics.

Murachver, T., Pipe, M., Gordon, R., Owens, J. L., & Fivush, R. (1996). Do, show, and tell: Children's event memories acquired through direct experience, observation, and stories. *Child Development, 67,* 3029–3044.

Murchison, C., & Langer, S. (1927). Tiedemann's observations on the development of the mental facilities of children. *Journal of Genetic Psychology, 34,* 204–230.

Muris, P., Merckelbach, H., & Collaris, R. (1997). Common childhood fears and their origins. *Behaviour Research and Therapy, 35,* 929–937.

Murray, B. (1998, June). Dipping math scores heat up debate over math teaching: Psychologists differ over the merits of teaching children "whole math." *APA Monitor, 29*(6), 34–35.

Murray, M. L., deVries, C. S., & Wong, I.C.K. (2004). A drug utilisation study of anti-depressants in children and adolescents using the General Practice Research data base. *Archives of the Diseases of Children, 89,* 1098–1102.

Mussen, P. H., & Jones, M. C. (1957). Self-conceptions, motivations, and interpersonal attitudes of late- and early-maturing boys. *Child Development, 28,* 243–256.

Must, A., Jacques, P. F., Dallal, G. E., Bajema, C. J., & Dietz, W. H. (1992). Long-term morbidity and mortality of overweight adolescents: A follow-up of the Harvard Growth Study of 1922 to 1935. *New England Journal of Medicine, 327*(19), 1350–1355.

Mustanski, B. S., DuPree, M. G., Nievergelt, C. M., Bocklandt, S., Schork, N. J., & Hamer, D. H. (2005). A genomewide scan of male sexual orientation. *Human Genetics, 116,* 272–278.

Mustillo, S., Worthman, C., Erkanli, A., Keeler, G., Angold, A., & Costello, E. J. (2003). Obesity and psychiatric disorder: Developmental trajectories. *Pediatrics, 111,* 851–859.

Muter, V., Hulme, C., Snowling, M. J., & Stevenson, J. (2004). Phonemes, rimes, vocabulary, and grammatical skill as foundations of early reading development: Evidence from a longitudinal study. *Developmental Psychology, 40,* 665–681.

Myers, S. M., Johnson, C. P., & Council on Children With Disabilities. (2007). Management of children with autism spectrum disorders. *Pediatrics, 120*(5), 1162–1182.

Nader, P. R., Bradley, R. H., Houts, R. M., McRitchie, S. L., & O'Brien, M. (2008). Moderate-to-vigorous physical activity from ages 9 to 15 years. *Journal of the American Medical Association, 300,* 295–305.

Nadig, A. S., Ozonoff, S., Young, G. S., Rozga, A., Sigman, M., & Rogers, S. J. (2007). A prospective study of response to name in infants at risk for autism. (Name response at 12 months as screening tool for ASDs). *Archives of Pediatric and Adolescent Medicine, 161,* 378–383.

Nagaoka, J., & Roderick, M. (April 2004). *Ending social promotion: The effects of retention.* Chicago: Consortium on Chicago School Research.

Nagaraja, J., Menkedick, J., Phelan, K. J., Ashley, P., Zhang, X., & Lanphear, B. P. (2005). Deaths from residential injuries in US children and adolescents, 1985–1997. *Pediatrics, 116,* 454–461.

Nagy, E. (2008). Innate intersubjectivity: Newborns' sensitivity to communication disturbance. *Developmental Psychology, 44*(6), 1779–1784.

Naito, M., & Miura, H. (2001). Japanese childrens' numerical competencies: Age- and school-related influences on the development of number concepts and addition skills. *Developmental Psychology, 37,* 217–230.

Najman, J. M., Hayatbakhsh, M. R., Heron, M. A., Bor, W., O'Callaghan, M. J., & Williams, G.M. (2009). The impact of episodic and chronic poverty on child cognitive development. *The Journal of Pediatrics, 154*(2), 284–289.

Nansel, T. R., Overpeck, M., Pilla, R. S., Ruan, W. J., Simons-Morton, B., & Scheidt, P. (2001). Bullying behaviors among U.S. youth: Prevalence and association with psychosocial adjustment. *Journal of the American Medical Association, 285,* 2094–2100.

Napier, J. L., & Jost, J. T. (2008). Why are conservatives happier than liberals? *Psychological Science, 19*(6), 565–572. doi:10.1111/j.1467-9280.2008 .02124.x

Nash, J. M. (1997, February 3). Fertile minds. *Time,* pp. 49–56.

Natenshon, A. (2006). *Parental influence takes precedence over Barbie and the media.* Retrieved December 15, 2007, from www.empoweredparents .com/prevention/1prevention_09.htm

Nathanielsz, P. W. (1995). The role of basic science in preventing low birth weight. *The Future of Our Children, 5*(1), 57–70.

National Assessment of Educational Progress: The Nation's Report Card. (2004). *America's charter schools: Results from the NAEP 2003 Pilot Study* (NCES 2005-456). Jessup, MD: U.S. Department of Education.

National Association of Child Care Resource and Referral Agencies (NACCRRA). (2010). *Parents and the high cost of child care: 2010 update.* Retrieved from http://www.naccrra.org/docs/High_Cost _Report_2010_One_Pager_072910a-final.pdf

National Association for Gifted Children. (n.d.). *Frequently asked questions.* Retrieved April 29, 2010, from www.nagc.org/index2.aspx?id=548

National Center for Education Statistics (NCES). (2001). *The condition of education 2001* (Publication No. 2001–072). Washington, DC: U.S. Government Printing Office.

National Center for Education Statistics (NCES). (2003). *The condition of education, 2003* (Publication No. 2003–067). Washington, DC: Author.

National Center for Education Statistics (NCES). (2004a). *National assessment of educational progress: The nation's report card, Mathematics highlights 2003* (NCES 2004–451). Washington, DC: U.S. Department of Education.

National Center for Education Statistics (NCES). (2004b). *National Assessment of Educational Progress: The nation's report card. Reading highlights 2003* (NCES 2004–452). Washington, DC: U.S. Department of Education.

National Center for Education Statistics. (2005). *Children born in 2001—first results from the base year of Early Childhood Longitudinal Study, Birth Cohort (ECLS-B).* Retrieved November 19, 2004, from http://nces.ed.gov/pubs2005 /children/index.asp

National Center for Education Statistics. (2006). *Calories in, calories out: Food and exercise in public elementary schools, 2005* (NCES 2006-057). Washington, DC: Author.

National Center for Education Statistics (NCES). (2007). *The condition of education 2007* (NCES2007-064). Washington, DC: U.S. Government Printing Office.

National Center for Education Statistics (NCES). (2007a, July). *Demographic and school characteristics of students receiving special education in the elementary grades.* Retrieved April 29, 2010, from http://nces.ed.gov/pubsearch/pubsinfo .asp?pubid=2007005

National Center for Education Statistics (NCES). (2008). *1.5 million homeschooled students in the United States in 2007.* [Issue Brief]. Washington, DC: Author.

National Center for Education Statistics (NCES). (2009). *The condition of education 2009* (NCES 2009-081). Washington, DC: Author.

National Center for Health Statistics (NCHS). (1999). Abstract adapted from *Births: Final data for 1999* by mid-Atlantic parents of multiples. Retrieved March 7, 2006, from www.orgsites.com /va/mapom/_pgg1.php3

National Center for Health Statistics (NCHS). (2004). *Health, United States, 2004 with chartbook on trends in the health of Americans* (DHHS Publication No. 2004–1232). Hyattsville, MD: Author.

National Center for Health Statistics (NCHS). (2005). *Health, United States, 2005* (DHHS Publication No. 2005-1232). Hyattsville, MD: Author.

National Center for Health Statistics (NCHS). (2006). *Health, United States, 2006.* Hyattsville, MD: Author.

National Center for Health Statistics (NCHS). (2007). Trends in oral health status: United States, 1988–1994 and 1999–2004. *Vital Health Statistics, 11*(248). Hyattsville, MD: Author.

National Center for Health Statistics (NCHS). (2009). Distribution of teen births by age, 2007. *Vital Statistics Reports.* Hyattsville, MD: Author.

National Center for Injury Prevention and Control (NCIPC). (2004). *Fact sheet: Teen drivers.* Retrieved May 7, 2004, from www.cdc.gov/ncipc

National Center for Learning Disabilities. (2004a). *Dyslexia: Learning disabilities in reading.* [Fact sheet]. Retrieved May 30, 2004, from www.ld.org /LDInfoZone/InfoZone_FactSheet_Dyslexia.cfm

National Center for Learning Disabilities. (2004b). *LD at a glance.* [Fact sheet]. Retrieved May 30, 2004, from www.ld.org/LDInfoZone/InfoZone _FactSheet_LD.cfm

National Center on Addiction and Substance Abuse (CASA). (2006, September). *The importance of family dinners III.* New York: Columbia University.

National Center on Addiction and Substance Abuse (CASA). (2007, September). *The importance of family dinners IV.* Retrieved from www.casacolumbia.org/

National Center on Shaken Baby Syndrome. (2000). *SBS questions.* Retrieved from www.dontshake .com/sbsquestions.html

National Clearinghouse on Child Abuse and Neglect Information (NCCANI). (2004). Long-term consequences of child abuse and neglect. Retrieved October, 5, 2004, from http://nccanch.acf.hhs .gov/pubs/factsheets/long term consequences.cfm

National Coalition for the Homeless. (2009). *Why are people homeless?* [NCH fact sheet #1]. Retrieved from www.nationalhomeless.org /factsheets/why.html

National Commission for the Protection of Human Subjects of Biomedical and Behavioral Research. (1978). *Report.* Washington, DC: Author.

National Conference of State Legislatures. (2008). *Fetal homicide.* Retrieved November 2, 2008, from www.ncsl.org/programs/health /fethom.htm

National Council of Teachers of Mathematics (NCTM). (2006). *Curriculum focal points for prekindergarten through grade 8 mathematics.* Reston, VA: Author.

National Diabetes Education Program. (2008). *Overview of diabetes in children and adolescents. A fact sheet from the National Diabetes Education Program.* Retrieved from http://ndep.nih.gov /media/diabetes/youth/youth_FS.htm

National Diabetes Information Clearinghouse (NDIC). (2007). *National diabetes statistics.* Retrieved from http://diabetes.niddk.nih.gov /DM/PUBS/statistics/#allages

National Enuresis Society. (1995). *Enuresis.* [Fact sheet]. New York: Author.

National Fatherhood Initiative. (2013). *The father factor: Data on the consequences of father absence.* Retrieved from http://www.fatherhood.org/media /consequences-of-father-absence-statistics

National High Blood Pressure Education Program Working Group on High Blood Pressure in Children and Adolescents. (2004). The fourth report on the diagnosis, evaluation, and treatment of high blood pressure in children and adolescents. *Pediatrics, 114*(2-Suppl.), 555–576.

National Highway Traffic Safety Administration. (2009, November). *Traffic safety facts research note.* Washington, DC: Author.

National Institute of Child Health and Development (NICHD). (2008). *Facts about Down Syndrome.* Retrieved from www.nichd.nih .gov/publications/pubs/downsyndrome.cfm

National Institute of Child Health and Health Development (NICHD). (2010). Phenylketonuria (PKU). Retrieved February 5, 2012, from www .nichd.nih.gov/health/topics/phenylketonuria.cfm

National Institute of Dental and Craniofacial Research. (2004). *Dental sealants in children (Age 6 to 11).* Retrieved from www.nidcr.nih.gov /DataStatistics/FindDataByTopic/DentalSealants /Children

National Institute of Mental Health (NIMH). (1999, April). *Suicide facts.* Retrieved from www.nimh.nih.gov/research/suifact.htm

National Institute of Mental Health (NIMH). (2001a). *Helping children and adolescents cope with violence and disasters: Fact sheet* (NIH Publication No. 01-3518). Bethesda, MD: Author.

National Institute of Mental Health (NIMH). (2001b). *Teenage brain: A work in progress.* Retrieved March 11, 2004, from www.nimh.gov /publicat/teenbrain.cfm

National Institute of Mental Health (NIMH). (2002). Preventive sessions after divorce protect children into teens. Retrieved April 5, 2012, from www.nimh.nih.gov

National Institute of Mental Health (NIMH). (2009). *Autism spectrum disorders.* Retrieved from www.nimh.nih.gov/health/publications/autism /complete-index.shtml

National Institute of Neurological Disorders and Stroke (NINDS). (2006, January 25). NINDS *Shaken baby syndrome information page.* Retrieved June 20, 2006, from www.ninds.nih.gov/disorders /shakenbaby/shakenbaby.htm

National Institute of Neurological Disorders and Stroke (NINDS). (2007). NINDS *Asperger syndrome information page.* Retrieved from www .ninds.nih.gov/disorders/asperger/asperger.htm

National Institutes of Health. (2010). Consensus Development Conference on Vaginal Birth after Cesarean: New Insights. Bethesda, MD, March 8–10.

National Institutes of Health Consensus Development Panel. (2001). National Institutes of Health Consensus Development conference statement: Phenylketonuria screening and management. October 16–18, 2000. *Pediatrics, 108*(4), 972–982.

National Library of Medicine. (2003). *Medical encyclopedia: Conduct disorder.* Retrieved April 23, 2005, from www.nlm.nih.gov/medlineplus/ency/article/000919.htm

National Library of Medicine. (2004). *Medical encyclopedia: Oppositional defiant disorder.* Retrieved April 23, 2005, from www.nlm.nih.gov/medlineplus/ency/article/001537.htm

National Institute on Drug Abuse (NIDA). (1996). *Monitoring the future.* Washington, DC: National Institutes of Health.

National Institute on Drug Abuse (NIDA). (2008). *Quarterly report: Potency Monitoring Project (Report 100). December 16, 2007 thru March 15, 2008.* Conducted by National Center for Natural Products Research, University of Mississippi.

National Parents' Resource Institute for Drug Education. (1999, September 8). *PRIDE surveys, 1998–99 national summary: Grades 6–12.* Bowling Green, KY: Author.

National Reading Panel. (2000). *Report of the National Reading Panel: Teaching children to read: An evidence-based assessment of the scientific research literature on reading and its implications for reading instruction: Reports of the subgroups.* Washington, DC: U.S. Government Printing Office.

National Research Council (NRC). (1993a). *Losing generations: Adolescents in high risk settings.* Washington, DC: National Academy Press.

National Research Council (NRC). (1993b). *Understanding child abuse and neglect.* Washington, DC: National Academy Press.

National Research Council (NRC). (2006). *Food insecurity and hunger in the United States: An assessment of the measure.* Washington, DC: National Academies Press.

National Sleep Foundation. (2004). *Sleep in America.* Washington, DC: Author.

National Survey on Drug Use and Health (NSDUH). (2006). Substance use treatment need among adolescents: 2003-2004. *The NSDUH Report* (Issue 24). Rockville, MD: Office of Applied Statistics, Substance Abuse and Mental Health Services Administration (SAMHSA), U.S. Department of Health and Human Services (USDHHS).

National Survey on Drug Use and Health (NSDUH). (2012). Substance Abuse and Mental Health Services Administration, *Results from the 2011 national survey on drug use and health: Mental health findings,* NSDUH Series H-45, HHS Publication No. (SMA) 12-4725. Rockville, MD: Substance Abuse and Mental Health Services Administration, 2012. Retrieved April 1, 2013, from www.samhsa.gov/data/NSDUH/2k11MH_FindingsandDetTables/2K11MHFR/NSDUHmhfr2011.htm

Neale, B. M., Lasky-Su., J., Anney, R., Franke, B., Zhou, K., Maller, J. B., et al. (2008). Genome-wide association scan of attention deficit hyperactivity disorder. *American Journal of Medical Genetics Part B: Neuropsychiatric Genetics, 147B*(8), 1337–1344.

Nef, S., Verma-Kurvari, S., Merenmies, J., Vassallt, J.-D., Efstratiadis, A., Accili, D., & Parada, L. F. (2003). Testis determination requires insulin receptor family function in mice. *Nature, 426,* 291–295.

Neisser, U., Boodoo, G., Bouchard, T. J., Jr., Boykin, A. W., Brody, N., Ceci, S. J., et al. (1996). Intelligence: Knowns and unknowns. *American Psychologist, 51*(2), 77–101.

Neitzel, C., & Stright, A. D. (2003). Relations between parents' scaffolding and children's academic self-regulation: Establishing a foundation of self-regulatory competence. *Journal of Family Psychology, 17,* 147–159.

Nelson, C. A. (1995). The ontogeny of human memory: A cognitive neuroscience perspective. *Developmental Psychology, 31,* 723–738.

Nelson, C. A. (2008). A neurobiological perspective on early human deprivation. *Child Development Perspectives, 1,* 13–18.

Nelson, C. A., Monk, C. S., Lin, J., Carver, L. J., Thomas, K. M., & Truwit, C. L. (2000). Functional neuroanatomy of spatial working memory in children. *Developmental Psychology, 36,* 109–116.

Nelson, C. A., Thomas, K. M., & deHaan, M. (2006). Neural bases of cognitive development In W. Damon & R. Lerner (Eds.), *Handbook of Child Psychology* (6th ed.). New York: Wiley.

Nelson, K. (1993). The psychological and social origins of autobiographical memory. *Psychological Science, 47,* 7–14.

Nelson, K. (2005). Evolution and development of human memory systems. In B. J. Ellis & D. F. Bjorklund (Eds.), *Origins of the social mind: Evolutionary psychology and child development* (pp. 319–345). New York: Guilford Press.

Nelson, K., & Fivush, R. (2004). The emergence of autobiographical memory: A social cultural developmental theory. *Psychological Bulletin, 111,* 486–511.

Nelson, K. B., Dambrosia, J. M., Ting, T. Y., & Grether, J. K. (1996). Uncertain value of electronic fetal monitoring in predicting cerebral palsy. *New England Journal of Medicine, 334,* 613–618.

Nelson, L. J. (2003). Rites of passage in emerging adulthood: Perspectives of young Mormons. In J. J. Arnett & N. L. Galambos (Eds.), Exploring cultural conceptions of the transition to adulthood. *New Directions for Child and Adolescent Development, 100,* 33–49.

Nelson, L. J., & Marshall, M. F. (1998). *Ethical and legal analyses of three coercive policies aimed at substance abuse by pregnant women.* Princeton, NJ: Robert Wood Johnson Substance Abuse Policy Research Foundation.

Nelson, M. C., & Gordon-Larsen, P. (2006). Physical activity and sedentary behavior patterns are associated with selected adolescent risk behaviors. *Pediatrics, 117,* 1281–1290.

Neumark-Sztainer, D., Wall, M., Haines, J., Story, M., Sherwood, N. E., & van den Berg, P. A. (2007). Shared risk and protective factors for overweight and disordered eating in adolescents. *American Journal of Preventive Medicine, 33,* 359–369.

Neville, A. (n.d.). *The emotional and psychological effects of miscarriage.* Retrieved April 9, 2006, from www.opendoors.com.au/EffectsMiscarriage/EffectsMiscarriage.htm

Neville, H. J., & Bavelier, D. (1998). Neural organization and plasticity of language. *Current Opinion in Neurobiology, 8*(2), 254–258.

Newacheck, P. W., Strickland, B., Shonkoff, J. P., Perrin, J. M., McPherson, M., McManus, M., et al. (1998). An epidemiologic profile of children with special health care needs. *Pediatrics, 102,* 117–123.

Newcomb, A. F., & Bagwell, C. L. (1995). Children's friendship relations: A meta-analytic review. *Psychological Bulletin, 117*(2), 306–347.

Newcomb, A. F., Bukowski, W. M., & Pattee, L. (1993). Children's peer relations: A meta-analytic review of popular, rejected, neglected, controversial, and average sociometric status. *Psychological Bulletin, 113,* 99–128.

Newman, D. L., Caspi, A., Moffitt, T. E., & Silva, P. A. (1997). Antecedents of adult interpersonal functioning: Effects of individual differences in age 3 temperament. *Developmental Psychology, 33,* 206–217.

Newman, R. S. (2005). The cocktail party effect in infants revisited: Listening to one's name in noise. *Developmental Psychology, 41,* 352–362.

Newport, E., & Meier, R. (1985). The acquisition of American Sign Language. In D. Slobin (Ed.), *The crosslinguistic study of language acquisition* (Vol. 1, pp. 881–938). Hillsdale, NJ: Erlbaum.

Newport, E. L. (1991). Contrasting concepts of the critical period for language. In S. Carey & R. Gelman (Eds.), *The epigenesis of mind: Essays on biology and cognition* (pp. 111–130). Hillsdale, NJ: Erlbaum.

Newport, E. L., Bavelier, D., & Neville, H. J. (2001). Critical thinking about critical periods: Perspectives on a critical period for language acquisition. In E. Dupoux (Ed.), *Language, brain, and cognitive development: Essays in honor of Jacques Mehler* (pp. 481–502). Cambridge, MA: MIT Press.

NICHD Early Child Care Research Network. (1996). Characteristics of infant child care: Factors contributing to positive caregiving. *Early Childhood Research Quarterly, 11,* 269–306.

NICHD Early Child Care Research Network. (1997). The effects of infant child care on infant-mother attachment security: Results of the NICHD study of early child care. *Child Development, 68,* 860–879.

NICHD Early Child Care Research Network. (1998a). Early child care and self-control, compliance and problem behavior at 24 and 36 months. *Child Development, 69,* 1145–1170.

NICHD Early Child Care Research Network. (1998b). Relations between family predictors and child outcomes: Are they weaker for children in child care? *Developmental Psychology, 34,* 1119–1127.

NICHD Early Child Care Research Network. (1999a). Child outcomes when child care center classes meet recommended standards for quality. *American Journal of Public Health, 89,* 1072–1077.

NICHD Early Child Care Research Network. (2000). The relation of child care to cognitive and language development. *Child Development, 71,* 960–980.

NICHD Early Child Care Research Network. (2001a). Child care and children's peer interaction at 24 and 36 months: The NICHD Study of Early Child Care. *Child Development, 72,* 1478–1500.

NICHD Early Child Care Research Network. (2001b). Child-care and family predictors of preschool attachment and stability from infancy. *Developmental Psychology, 37,* 847–862.

NICHD Early Child Care Research Network. (2002). Child-care structure "process" outcome: Direct and indirect effects of child-care quality on young children's development. *Psychological Science, 13,* 199–206.

NICHD Early Child Care Research Network. (2003). Does amount of time spent in child care predict socioemotional adjustment during the transition to kindergarten? *Child Development, 74,* 976–1005.

NICHD Early Child Care Research Network. (2004a). Are child developmental outcomes related to before- and after-school care arrangement? Results from the NICHD Study of Early Child Care. *Child Development 75,* 280–295.

NICHD Early Child Care Research Network. (2004b). Does class size in first grade relate to children's academic and social performance or observed classroom processes? *Developmental Psychology, 40,* 651–664.

NICHD Early Child Care Research Network. (2005a). Duration and developmental timing of poverty and children's cognitive and social development from birth through third grade. *Child Development, 76,* 795–810.

NICHD Early Child Care Research Network. (2005b). Early child care and children's development in the primary grades: Follow-up results from the NICHD study of early child care. *American Educational Research Journal, 42*(3), 537–570.

NICHD Early Child Care Research Network. (2005c). Predicting individual differences in attention, memory, and planning in first graders from experiences at home, child care, and school. *Developmental Psychology, 41,* 99–114.

NICHD Early Child Care Research Network. (2006). Infant-mother attachment classification: Risk and protection in relation to changing maternal caregiving quality. *Developmental Psychology, 42,* 38–58.

Nickerson, A. B., & Nagel, R. J. (2005). Parent and peer attachment in late childhood and early adolescence. *Journal of Early Adolescence, 25,* 223–249.

Nie, N. H. (2001). Sociability, interpersonal relations and the Internet: Reconciling conflicting findings: *American Behavioral Scientist, 45,* 420–435.

Nielsen, M., Dissanayake, C., & Kashima, Y. (2003). A longitudinal investigation of self-other discrimination and the emergence of mirror self-recognition. *Infant Behavior & Development, 26,* 213–226.

Nielsen, M., Suddendorf, T., & Slaughter, V. (2006). Mirror self-recognition beyond the face. *Child Development, 77,* 176–185.

Nielsen, M., & Tomaselli, K. (2010). Overimitation in Kalahari Bushman children and the origins of human cultural cognition. *Psychological Science, 21* (5), 729–736.

Nilsen, E. S., & Graham, S.A. (2009). The relations between children's communicative perspective-taking and executive functioning. *Cognitive Psychology, 58,* 220–249.

Nirmala, A., Reddy, B. M., & Reddy, P. P. (2008). Genetics of human obesity: An overview. *International Journal of Human Genetics, 8,* 217–226.

Nisan, M., & Kohlberg, L. (1982). Universality and variation in moral judgment: A longitudinal and cross sectional study in Turkey. *Child Development, 53,* 865–876.

Nisbett, R. E. (1998). Race, genetics, and IQ. In C. Jencks & M. Phillips (Eds.), *The black-white test score gap* (pp. 86–102). Washington, DC: Brookings Institution.

Nisbett, R. E. (2005). Heredity, environment, and race differences in IQ: A commentary on Rushton and Jensen (2005). *Psychology, Public Policy, and Law, 11,* 302–310.

Nix, R. L., Pinderhughes, E. E., Dodge, K. A., Bates, J. E., Pettit, G. S., & McFadyen-Ketchum, S. A. (1999). The relation between mothers' hostile attribution tendencies and children's externalizing behavior problems: The mediating role of mothers' harsh discipline practices. *Child Development, 70*(4), 896–909.

Nobre, A. C., & Plunkett, K. (1997). The neural system of language: Structure and development. *Current Opinion in Neurobiology, 7,* 262–268.

Noirot, E., & Algeria, J. (1983). Neonate orientation towards human voice differs with type of feeding. *Behavioral Processes, 8,* 65–71.

Noll, J. G., Trickett, P. K., & Putnam, F. M. (2003). A prospective investigation of the impact of childhood sexual abuse on the development of sexuality. *Journal of Consulting and Clinical Psychology, 71*(3), 575–586.

Nord, M., Andrews, A., & Carlson, S. (2008). *Household food security in the United States, 2007* (ERR-66). Retrieved from www.ers.usda.gov /publications/err66

Noriuchi, M., Kikuchi, Y., & Senoo, A. (2008). The functional neuroanatomy of maternal love: Mother's response to infant's attachment behaviors. *Biological Psychiatry, 63,* 415–423.

Nourot, P. M. (1998). Sociodramatic play: Pretending together. In D. P. Fromberg & D. Bergen (Eds.), *Play from birth to twelve and beyond: Contexts, perspectives, and meanings* (pp. 378–391). New York: Garland.

Nucci, L., Hasebe, Y., & Lins-Dyer, M. T. (2005). Adolescent psychological well-being and parental control. In J. Smetana (Ed.), *Changing boundaries of parental authority during adolescence: New directions for child and adolescent development* (pp. 17–30). San Francisco: Jossey-Bass.

Nugent, J. K., Lester, B. M., Greene, S. M., Wieczorek-Deering, D., & O'Mahony, P. (1996). The effects of maternal alcohol consumption and cigarette smoking during pregnancy on acoustic cry analysis. *Child Development, 67,* 1806–1815.

Oakes, L. M. (1994). Development of infants' use of continuity cues in their perception of causality. *Developmental Psychology, 30,* 869–879.

Oakes, L. M., Coppage, D. J., & Dingel, A. (1997). By land or by sea: The role of perceptual similarity in infants' categorization of animals. *Developmental Psychology, 33,* 396–407.

Ober, C., Tan, Z., Sun, Y., Possick, J. D., Pan, L., Nicolae, R., et al. (2008). *New England Journal of Medicine, 358,* 1682–1691.

Oberman, L. M., & Ramachandran, V. S. (2007). The simulating social mind: The role of the mirror neuron system and simulation in the social and communicative deficits of autism spectrum disorders. *Psychological Bulletin, 133,* 310–327.

O'Brien, C. M., & Jeffery, H. E. (2002). Sleep deprivation, disorganization and fragmentation during opiate withdrawal in newborns. *Pediatric Child Health, 38,* 66–71.

O'Brien, M., & Huston, A. C. (1985). Development of sex-typed play behavior in toddlers. *Developmental Psychology, 21*(5), 866–871.

O'Connor, T., Heron, J., Golding, J., Beveridge, M., & Glover, V. (2002). Maternal antenatal anxiety and children's behavioural/emotional problems at 4 years. *British Journal of Psychiatry, 180,* 502–508.

Odgers, C., Caspi, A., Nagin, D., Piquero, A., Slutske, W., Milne, B., et al. (2008). Is it important to prevent early exposure to drugs and alcohol among adolescents? *Psychological Science, 19*(10), 1037–1044.

Offer, D., & Church, R. B. (1991). Generation gap. In R. M. Lerner, A. C. Petersen, & J. Brooks-Gunn (Eds.), *Encyclopedia of adolescence* (pp. 397–399). New York: Garland.

Offer, D., Kaiz, M., Ostrov, E., & Albert, D. B. (2002). Continuity in the family constellation. *Adolescent and Family Health, 3,* 3–8.

Offer, D., Offer, M. K., & Ostrov, E. (2004). *Regular guys: 34 years beyond adolescence.* Dordrecht, The Netherlands: Kluwer Academic.

Offer, D., Ostrov, E., & Howard, K. I. (1989). Adolescence: What is normal? *American Journal of Diseases of Children, 143,* 731–736.

Offer, D., Ostrov, E., Howard, K. I., & Atkinson, R. (1988). *The teenage world: Adolescents' self-image in ten countries.* New York: Plenum Press.

Offer, D., & Schonert-Reichl, K. A. (1992). Debunking the myths of adolescence: Findings from recent research. *Journal of the American Academy of Child and Adolescent Psychiatry, 31,* 1003–1014.

Office of National Drug Control Policy. (2008). *Teen marijuana use worsens depression: An analysis of recent data shows "self-medicating" could actually make things worse.* Washington, DC: Executive Office of the President.

Offit, P. A., Quarles, J., Gerber, M. A., Hackett, C. J., Marcuse, E. K., Kollman, T. R., et al. (2002). Addressing parents' concerns: Do multiple vaccines overwhelm or weaken the infant's immune system? *Pediatrics, 109,* 124–129.

Ofori, B., Oraichi, D., Blais, L., Rey, E., & Berard, A. (2006). Risk of congenital anomalies in pregnant users of non-steroidal anti-inflammatory drugs: A nested case-control study. *Birth Defects Research. Part B, Developmental and Reproductive Toxicology, 77*(4), 268–279.

Ogbuanu, I. U., Karmaus, W., Arshad, S. H., Kurukulaaratchy, R. J., & Ewart, S. (2009). Effect of breastfeeding duration on lung function at age 10 years: a prospective birth cohort study. *Thorax, 64,* 62–66.

Ogden, C. L., Carroll, M. D., Curtin, L. R., McDowell, M. A., Tabak, C. J., & Flegal, K. M. (2006). Prevalence of overweight and obesity in the United States, 1999–2004. *Journal of the American Medical Association, 295,* 1549–1555.

Ogden, C. L., Carroll, M. D., & Flegal, K. M. (2008). High body mass index for age among U.S. children and adolescents, 2003–2006. *Journal of the American Medical Association, 299,* 2401–2405.

Ogden, C. L., Fryar, C. D., Carroll, M. D., & Flegal, K. M. (2004). Mean body weight, height, and body mass index, United States 1960–2002. *Advance Data from Vital and Health Statistics, No 347.* Hyattsville, MD: National Center for Health Statistics.

Olds, S. W. (1989). *The working parents' survival guide.* Rocklin, CA: Prima.

Olds, S. W. (2002). *A balcony in Nepal: Glimpses of a Himalayan village.* Lincoln, NE: ASJA Books, an imprint of iUniverse.

O'Leary, C., Nassar, N., Kurinczuk, J., & Bower, C. (2009). Impact of maternal alcohol consumption on fetal growth and preterm birth. *BJOG, 116,* 390–400.

Olfson, M., Blanco, C., Liu, L., Moreno, C., & Laje, G. (2006). National trends in the outpatient treatment of children and adolescents with antipsychotic drugs. *Archives of General Psychiatry, 63,* 679–685.

Ollendick, T. H., Yang, B., King, N. J., Dong, Q., & Akande, A. (1996). Fears in American, Australian, Chinese, and Nigerian children and adolescents: A crosscultural study. *Journal of Child Psychology and Psychiatry, 37,* 213–220.

Olson, K. R., & Spelke, E. S. (2008). Foundations of cooperation in young children. *Cognition, 108,* 222–231.

Olthof, T., Schouten, A., Kuiper, H., Stegge, H., & Jennekens-Schinkel, A. (2000). Shame and guilt in children: Differential situational antecedents and experiential correlates. *British Journal of Developmental Psychology, 18,* 51–64.

Olweus, D. (1995). Bullying or peer abuse at school: Facts and intervention. *Current Directions in Psychological Science, 4,* 196–200.

Opdal, S. H., & Rognum, T. O. (2004). The sudden infant death syndrome gene: Does it exist? *Pediatrics, 114,* e506–e512.

O'Rahilly, S. (1998). Life without leptin. *Nature, 392,* 330–331.

Orenstein, P. (2002, April 21). Mourning my miscarriage. Retrieved from www.NYTimes.com

Organization for Economic Co-operation and Development (OECD). (2004). Education at a glance: OECD indicators—2004. *Education & Skills, 2004*(14), 1–456.

Organisation for Economic Co-operation and Development. (OECD). (2008a). *Education at a glance.* Paris, France: Author.

Organisation for Economic Co-operation and Development (2012). *Living arrangements of children.* Retrieved from http://www.oecd.org/els/soc/41919559.pdf

Orr, D. P., & Ingersoll, G. M. (1995). The contribution of level of cognitive complexity and pubertal timing behavioral risk in young adolescents. *Pediatrics, 95*(4), 528–533.

Oshima-Takane, Y., Goodz, E., & Derevensky, J. L. (1996). Birth order effects on early language development: Do secondborn children learn from overheard speech? *Child Development, 67,* 621–634.

Ossorio, P., & Duster, T. (2005). Race and genetics: Controversies in biomedical, behavioral, and forensic sciences. *American Psychologist, 60,* 115–128.

Ott, M. G., Schmidt, M., Schwarzwaelder, K., Stein, S., Siler, U., Koehl, U., et al. (2006). Correction of X-linked chronic granulomatous disease by gene therapy, augmented by insertional activation of MDS1-EVI1, PRDM16 or SETBP1. *Nature Medicine, 12,* 401–409.

Ouellette, G. P., & Sénéchal, M. (2008). A window into early literacy: Exploring the cognitive and linguistic underpinnings of invented spelling. *Scientific Studies of Reading, 12*(2), 195–219.

Out of sight, out of mind: Hidden cost of neglected tropical diseases (2010, November 25). *The Guardian.* Retrieved from http://www.guardian.co.uk/science/blog/2010/nov/25/neglectedtropical-diseases

Overbeek, G., Stattin, H., Vermulst, A., Ha, T., & Engels, R.C.M.E. (2007). Parent-child relationships, partner relationships, and emotional adjustment: A birth-to-maturity prospective study. *Developmental Psychology, 43,* 429–437.

Owen, C. G., Whincup, P. H., Odoki, K., Gilg, J. A., & Cook, D. G. (2002). Infant feeding and blood cholesterol: A study in adolescents and a systematic review. *Pediatrics, 110,* 597–608.

Owens, J., Spirito, A., McGuinn, N., & Nobile, C. (2000). Sleep habits and sleep disturbance in elementary school children. *Developmental and Behavioral Pediatrics, 21,* 27–30.

Owens, R. E. (1996). *Language development* (4th ed.). Boston: Allyn & Bacon.

Padden, C. A. (1996). Early bilingual lives of deaf children. In I. Parasnis (Ed.), *Cultural and language diversity and the deaf experience* (pp. 99–116). New York: Cambridge University Press.

Padilla, A. M., Lindholm, K. J., Chen, A., Duran, R., Hakuta, K., Lambert, W., & Tucker, G. R. (1991). The English-only movement: Myths, reality, and implications for psychology. *American Psychologist, 46*(2), 120–130.

Paige, R. U. (2005). Proceedings of the American Psychological Association, Incorporated, for the legislative year 2004. Minutes of the meeting of the Council of Representatives July 28 & 30, 2004, Honolulu, HI. Retrieved November 18, 2004, from http://www.apa.org/governance/

Palella, F. J., Delaney, K. M., Moorman, A. C., Loveless, M. O., Fuhrer, J., Satten, G. A., et al. (1998). Declining morbidity and mortality among patients with advanced human immunodeficiency virus infection. *New England Journal of Medicine, 358,* 853–860.

Paley, B., & O'Connor, M. J. (2011). Behavioral interventions for children and adolescents with fetal alcohol spectrum disorders. *Alcohol Research & Health, 34*(1), 64–75

Palkovitz, R. (1985). Fathers' birth attendance, early contact, and extended contact with their newborns: A critical review. *Child Development, 56,* 392–406.

Pan, B. A., Rowe, M. L., Singer, J. D., & Snow, C. E. (2005). Maternal correlates of growth in toddler vocabulary production in low-income families. *Child Development, 76,* 763–782.

Panigrahy, A., Filiano, J., Sleeper, L. A., Mandell, F., Valdes-Dapena, M., Krous, H. F., et al. (2000). Decreased serotonergic receptor binding in rhombic lip-derived regions of the medulla oblongata in the sudden infant death syndrome. *Journal of Neuropathology and Experimental Neurology, 59,* 377–384.

Papadatou-Pastou, M. Martin, M., Munafo, M., & Jones, G. (2008). Sex differences in left-handedness: A meta-analysis of 144 studies. *American Psychological Association Bulletin, 134*(5), 677–699.

Papalia, D. (1972). The status of several conservation abilities across the lifespan. *Human Development, 15,* 229–243.

Park, J. M., Metraux, S., & Culhane, D. P. (2010). Behavioral health services use among heads of homeless and housed poor families. *Journal of Health Care for the Poor and Underserved, 21*(2), 582–590.

Park, S., Belsky, J., Putnam, S., & Crnic, K. (1997). Infant emotionality, parenting, and 3-year inhibition: Exploring stability and lawful discontinuity in a male sample. *Developmental Psychology, 33,* 218–227.

Park, Y., & Killen, M. (2010). When is peer rejection justifiable? Children's understanding across two cultures. *Cognitive Development, 25*(3), 290–301. doi: 10.1016/j.cogdev.2009.10.004

Parke, R. D. (2004a). Development in the family. *Annual Review of Psychology, 55,* 365–399.

Parke, R. D. (2004b). The Society for Research in Child Development at 70: Progress and promise. *Child Development, 75,* 1–24.

Parke, R. D., & Buriel, R. (1998). Socialization in the family: Ethnic and ecological perspectives. In W. Damon (Series Ed.) & N. Eisenberg (Vol. Ed.), *Handbook of child psychology: Vol. 3. Social, emotional, and personality development* (5th ed., pp. 463–552). New York: Wiley.

Parke, R. D., Grossman, K., & Tinsley, R. (1981). Father-mother-infant interaction in the newborn period: A German-American comparison. In T. M. Field, A. M. Sostek, P. Viete, & P. H. Leideman (Eds.), *Culture and early interaction* (pp. 95–114). Hillsdale, NJ: Erlbaum.

Parker, J. D., Woodruff, T. J., Basu, R., & Schoendorf, K. C. (2005). Air pollution and birth weight among term infants in California. *Pediatrics, 115,* 121–128.

Parker, L., Pearce, M. S., Dickinson, H. O., Aitkin, M., & Craft, A. W. (1999). Stillbirths among offspring of male radiation workers at Sellafield Nuclear Reprocessing Plant. *Lancet, 354,* 1407–1414.

Parry, W. (2010, August 29). Bring it: Boys make benefit from aggressive play. *Today Health.* Retrieved from http://today.msnbc.msn.com/id/38882665/ns/health kids_and_parenting/

Parten, M. B. (1932). Social play among preschool children. *Journal of Abnormal and Social Psychology, 27,* 243–269.

Pascual-Leone, A., Amedi, A., Fregni, F., & Merabet, L. B. (2005). The plastic human brain cortex. *Annual Review of Neuroscience, 28,* 377–401.

Pastor, P. N., & Reuben, C. A. (2008). Diagnosed attention deficit hyperactivity disorder and learning disability, United States, 2004–2006. National Center for Health Statistics. *Vital Health Statistics, 10*(237).

Patenaude, A. F., Guttmacher, A. E., & Collins, F. S. (2002). Genetic testing and psychology: New roles, new responsibilities. *American Psychologist, 57,* 271–282.

Paterson, D. S., Trachtenberg, F. L., Thompson, E. G., Belliveau, R. A., Beggs, A. H., Darnell, R., et al. (2006). Multiple serotogenic brainstem abnormalities in sudden infant death syndrome. *Journal of the American Medical Association, 296,* 2124–2132.

Patrick, K., Norman, G. J., Calfas, K. J., Sallis, J. F., Zabinski, M. F., Rupp, J., & Cella, J. (2004). Diet, physical activity, and sedentary behaviors as risk factors for overweight in adolescence. *Archives of Pediatric Adolescent Medicine, 158,* 385–390.

Patterson, C. J. (1992). Children of lesbian and gay parents. *Child Development, 63,* 1025–1042.

Patterson, C. J. (1995a). Lesbian mothers, gay fathers, and their children. In A. R. D'Augelli & C. J. Patterson (Eds.), *Lesbian, gay, and bisexual identities over the lifespan: Psychological perspectives* (pp. 293–320). New York: Oxford University Press.

Patterson, C. J. (1995b). Sexual orientation and human development: An overview. *Developmental Psychology, 31,* 3–11.

Patterson, G. R., DeBaryshe, B. D., & Ramsey, E. (1989). A developmental perspective on antisocial behavior. *American Psychologist, 44*(2), 329–335.

Pauen, S. (2002). Evidence for knowledge-based category discrimination in infancy. *Child Development, 73,* 1016–1033.

Pauli-Pott, U., Mertesacker, B., Bade, U., Haverkock, A., & Beckman, D. (2003). Parental perceptions and infant temperament development. *Infant Behavior and Development, 26,* 27–48.

Paus, T., Zijdenbos, A., Worsley, K., Collins, D. L., Blumenthal, J., Giedd, J. N., et al. (1999). Structural maturation of neural pathways in children and adolescents: In vivo study. *Science, 283,* 1908–1911.

Pawelski, J. G., Perrin, E. C., Foy, J. M., Allen, C. E., Crawford, J. E., Del Monte, M., et al. (2006). The effects of marriage, civil union, and domestic partnership laws on the health and well-being of children. *Pediatrics, 118,* 349–364.

Pearce, M. J., Jones, S. M., Schwab-Stone, M. E., & Ruchkin, V. (2003). The protective effects of religiousness and parent involvement on the development of conduct problems among youth exposed to violence. *Child Development, 74,* 1682–1696.

Pellegrini, A. D., & Archer, J. (2005). Sex differences in competitive and aggressive behavior: A view from sexual selection theory. In B. J. Ellis & D. F. Bjorklund (Eds.), *Origins of the social mind: Evolutionary psychology and child development* (pp. 219–244). New York: Guilford Press.

Pellegrini, A. D., Kato, K., Blatchford, P., & Baines, E. (2002). A short-term longitudinal study of children's playground games across the first year of school: Implications for social competence and adjustment to school. *American Educational Research Journal, 39,* 991–1015.

Pellegrini, A. D., & Long, J. D. (2002). A longitudinal study of bullying, dominance, and victimization during the transition from primary school through secondary school. *British Journal of Developmental Psychology, 20,* 259–280.

Pendlebury, J. D., Wilson, R.J.A., Bano, S., Lumb, K. J., Schneider, J. M., & Hasan, S. U. (2008). Respiratory control in neonatal rats exposed to prenatal cigarette smoke. *American Journal of Respiratory and Critical Care Medicine, 177,* 1255–1261.

Pennington, B. F., Moon, J., Edgin, J., Stedron, J., & Nadel, L. (2003). The neuropsychology of Down syndrome: Evidence for hippocampal dysfunction. *Child Development, 74,* 75–93.

Pepper, S. C. (1942). *World hypotheses.* Berkeley: University of California Press.

Pepper, S. C. (1961). *World hypotheses.* Berkeley: University of California Press.

Perera, F., Tang, W-y., Herbstman, J., Tang, D., Levin, L., Miller, R., & Ho, S.-m. (2009). Relation of DNA methylation of 5'-CpG island of *ACSL3* to transplacental exposure to airborne polycyclic aromatic hydrocarbons and childhood asthma. *PLoS ONE 4,* e44–e48.

Perera, F. P., Rauh, V., Whyatt, R. M., Tsai, W.-Y., Bernert, J. T., Tu, Y.-H., et al. (2004). Molecular evidence of an interaction between prenatal environmental exposures and birth outcomes in a multiethnic population. *Environmental Health Perspectives, 112,* 626–630.

Perie, M., Grigg, W. S., & Dion, G. S. (2005). *The nation's report card: Mathematics 2005* (NCES 2006 453). U.S. Department of Education, Institute of Education Sciences, National Center for Education Statistics. Washington, DC: U.S. Government Printing Office.

Perrin, E. C., & the AAP Committee on Psychosocial Aspects of Child and Family Health. (2002). Technical report: Coparent or second-parent adoption by same-sex parents. *Pediatrics, 109*(2), 341–344.

Perrin, E. M., Finkle, J. P., & Benjamin, J. T. (2007). Obesity prevention and the primary care pediatrician's office. *Current Opinion in Pediatrics, 19*(3), 354–361.

Pesonen, A., Raïkkönen, K., Keltikangas-Järvinen, L., Strandberg, T., & Järvenpää, A. (2003). Parental perception of infant temperament: Does parents' joint attachment matter? *Infant Behavior & Development, 26,* 167–182.

Petersen, A. C. (1993). Presidential address: Creating adolescents: The role of context and process in developmental transitions. *Journal of Research on Adolescents, 3*(1), 1–18.

Petersen, A. C., Compas, B. E., Brooks-Gunn, J., Stemmler, M., Ey, S., & Grant, K. E. (1993). Depression in adolescence. *American Psychologist, 48*(2), 155–168.

Petit, D., Touchette, E., Tremblay, R. E., Boivin, M., & Montplaisir, J. (2007). Dyssomnias and parasomnias in early childhood. *Pediatrics, 119*(5), e1016–e1025.

Petitto, L. A., Holowka, S., Sergio, L., & Ostry, D. (2001). Language rhythms in babies' hand movements. *Nature, 413,* 35–36.

Petitto, L. A., Katerelos, M., Levy, B., Gauna, K., Tetrault, K., & Ferraro, V. (2001). Bilingual signed and spoken language acquisition from birth: Implications for mechanisms underlying bilingual language acquisition. *Journal of Child Language, 28,* 1–44.

Petitto, L. A., & Kovelman, I. (2003). The bilingual paradox: How signing-speaking bilingual children help us to resolve it and teach us about the brain's mechanisms underlying all language acquisition. *Learning Languages, 8,* 5–18.

Petitto, L. A., & Marentette, P. F. (1991). Babbling in the manual mode: Evidence for the ontogeny of language. *Science, 251,* 1493–1495.

Petrill, S. A., Lipton, P. A., Hewitt, J. K., Plomin, R., Cherny, S. S., Corley, R., & DeFries, J. C. (2004). Genetic and environmental contributions to general cognitive ability through the first 16 years of life. *Developmental Psychology, 40,* 805–812.

Pettit, G. S., Bates, J. E., & Dodge, K. A. (1997). Supportive parenting, ecological context, and children's adjustment: A seven-year longitudinal study. *Child Development, 68,* 908–923.

Phillips, D. F. (1998). Reproductive medicine experts till an increasingly fertile field. *Journal of the American Medical Association, 280,* 1893–1895.

Phinney, J. S. (1998). Stages of ethnic identity development in minority group adolescents. In R. E. Muuss & H. D. Porton (Eds.), *Adolescent behavior and society: A book of readings* (pp. 271–280). Boston: McGraw-Hill.

Piaget, J. (1929). *The child's conception of the world.* New York: Harcourt Brace.

Piaget, J. (1932). *The moral judgment of the child.* New York: Harcourt Brace.

Piaget, J. (1952). *The origins of intelligence in children.* New York: International Universities Press. (Original work published 1936)

Piaget, J. (1962). *The language and thought of the child* (M. Gabain, Trans.). Cleveland, OH: Meridian. (Original work published 1923)

Piaget, J. (1964). *Six psychological studies.* New York: Vintage.

Piaget, J. (1969). *The child's conception of time* (A. J. Pomerans, Trans.). London: Routledge & Kegan Paul.

Piaget, J. (1972). Intellectual evolution from adolescence to adulthood. *Human Development, 15,* 1–12.

Piaget, J., & Inhelder, B. (1967). *The child's conception of space.* New York: Norton.

Piaget, J., & Inhelder, B. (1969). *The psychology of the child.* New York: Basic Books.

Picker, J. (2005). The role of genetic and environmental factors in the development of schizophrenia. *Psychiatric Times, 22,* 1–9.

Pickett, W., Streight, S., Simpson, K., & Brison, R. J. (2003). Injuries experienced by infant children: A population-based epidemiological analysis. *Pediatrics, 111,* e365–e370.

Pierce, K. M., Hamm, J. V., & Vandell, D. L. (1999). Experiences in after-school programs and children's adjustment in first-grade classrooms. *Child Development, 70*(3), 756–767.

Piernas, C., & Popkin, B. M. (2010). Trends in snacking among U.S. children. *Health Affairs, 29*(3), 398–404.

Pierroutsakos, S. L., & DeLoache, J. S. (2003). Infants' manual exploration of pictorial objects varying in realism. *Infancy, 4,* 141–156.

Pike, A., Coldwell, J., & Dunn, J. F. (2005). Sibling relationships in early/middle childhood: Links with individual adjustment. *Journal of Family Psychology, 19,* 523–532.

Pillow, B. H. (2002). Children's and adult's evaluation of the certainty of deductive inferences, inductive inferences and guesses. *Child Development, 73*(3), 779–792.

Pillow, B. H., & Henrichon, A. J. (1996). There's more to the picture than meets the eye: Young children's difficulty understanding biased interpretation. *Child Development, 67,* 803–819.

Pines, M. (1981). The civilizing of Genie. *Psychology Today, 15*(9), 28–34.

Plant, L. D., Bowers, P. N., Liu, Q., Morgan, T., Zhang, T., State, M. W., et al. (2006). A common cardiac sodium channel variant associated with sudden infant death in African Americans, SCN5A S1103Y. *Journal of Clinical Investigation, 116*(2), 430–435.

Pleck, J. H. (1997). Paternal involvement: Levels, sources, and consequences. In M. E. Lamb (Ed.), *The role of the father in child development* (3rd ed., pp. 66–103). New York: Wiley.

Plomin, R. (1990). The role of inheritance in behavior. *Science, 248,* 183–188.

Plomin, R. (1996). Nature and nurture. In M. R. Merrens & G. G. Brannigan (Eds.), *The developmental psychologist: Research adventures across the life span* (pp. 3–19). New York: McGraw-Hill.

Plomin, R. (2004). Genetics and developmental psychology. *Merrill-Palmer Quarterly, 50,* 341–352.

Plomin, R., & Daniels, D. (1987). Why are children in the same family so different from one another? *Behavioral and Brain Sciences, 10,* 1–16.

Plomin, R., & Daniels, D. (2011). Why are children in the same family so different from one another? *International Journal of Epidemiology, 40*(3), 563–582.

Plomin, R., & DeFries, J. C. (1999). The genetics of cognitive abilities and disabilities. In S. J. Ceci & W. M. Williams (Eds.), *The nature nurture debate: The essential readings* (pp. 178–195). Malden, MA: Blackwell.

Plomin, R., & Kovas, Y. (2005). Generalist genes and learning disabilities. *Psychological Bulletin, 131,* 592–617.

Plomin, R., Owen, M. J., & McGuffin, P. (1994). The genetic bases of behavior. *Science, 264,* 1733–1739.

Plomin, R., & Rutter, M. (1998). Child development, molecular genetics, and what to do with genes once they are found. *Child Development, 69*(4), 1223–1242.

Plomin, R., & Spinath, F. M. (2004). Intelligence: Genetics, genes, and genomics. *Journal of Personality and Social Psychology, 86,* 112–129.

Pogarsky, G., Thornberry, T. P., & Lizotte, A. J. (2006). Developmental outcomes for children of young mothers. *Journal of Marriage and Family, 68,* 332–344.

Polit, D. F., & Falbo, T. (1987). Only children and personality development: A quantitative review. *Journal of Marriage and the Family, 49,* 309–325.

Pollack, S. D. (2008). Mechanisms linking early experience and the emergence of emotions: Illustration from the study of maltreated children. *Current Directions in Psychological Science, 17,* 370–375.

Pollak, S. D., & Kistler, D. J. (2002). Early experience is associated with the development of categorical representations for facial expressions of emotion. *Proceedings of the National Academy of Sciences, USA, 99,* 9072–9076.

Pomerantz, E. M., & Saxon, J. L. (2001). Conceptions of ability as stable and self-evaluative processes: A longitudinal examination. *Child Development, 72,* 152–173.

Pomery, E. A., Gibbons, F. X., Gerrard, M., Cleveland, M. J., Brody, G. H., & Wills, T. A. (2005). Families and risk: Prospective analyses of familial and social influences on adolescent substance use. *Journal of Family Psychology, 19,* 560–570.

Pong, S., Dronkers, J., & Hampden-Thompson, G. (2003). Family policies and children's school achievement in single-versus two-parent families. *Journal of Marriage and the Family, 65,* 681–699.

Pope, A. W., Bierman, K. L., & Mumma, G. H. (1991). Aggression, hyperactivity, and inattention-immaturity: Behavior dimensions associated with peer rejection in elementary school boys. *Developmental Psychology, 27,* 663–671.

Population Reference Bureau. (2006). *2006 world population data sheet.* Washington, DC: Author.

Posada, G., Gao, Y., Wu, F., Posada, R., Tascon, M., Schoelmerich, A., et al. (1995). The secure-base phenomenon across cultures: Children's behavior, mothers' preferences, and experts' concepts. In E. Waters, B. E. Vaughn, G. Posada, & K. Kondo-Ikemura (Eds.), Care-giving, cultural, and cognitive perspectives on secure-base behavior and working models: New growing points of attachment theory and research (pp. 27–48). *Monographs of the Society for Research in Child Development, 60*(2–30). [Serial No. 244].

Posner, J. K., & Vandell, D. L. (1999). After-school activities and the development of low-income urban children: A longitudinal study. *Developmental Psychology, 35*(3), 868–879.

Posner, M. L., & DiGirolamo, G. J. (2000). Cognitive neuroscience: Origins and promise. *Psychological Bulletin, 126*(6), 873–889.

Posthuma, D., & de Gues, E.J.C. (2006). Progress in the molecular-genetic study of intelligence. *Current Directions in Psychological Science, 36*(1), 1–3.

Powell, M. B., & Thomson, D. M. (1996). Children's memory of an occurrence of a repeated event: Effects of age, repetition, and retention interval across three question types. *Child Development, 67,* 1988–2004.

Power, T. G., & Chapieski, M. L. (1986). Childrearing and impulse control in toddlers: A naturalistic investigation. *Developmental Psychology, 22,* 271–275.

Powlishta, K. K., Serbin, L. A., Doyle, A. B., & White, D. R. (1994). Gender, ethnic, and body type biases: The generality of prejudice in childhood. *Developmental Psychology, 30,* 526–536.

Practice Committee of the American Society for Reproductive Technology, American Society for Reproductive Medicine. (2006). Guidelines on number of embryos transferred. *Fertility & Sterility, 86*(Suppl. 5), S52.

Prechtl, H.F.R., & Beintema, D. J. (1964). The neurological examination of the full-term newborn infant. *Clinics in developmental medicine* (No.12). London: Heinemann.

Preissler, M., & Bloom, P. (2007). Two-year-olds appreciate the dual nature of pictures. *Psychological Science, 18*(1), 1–2.

Pruden, S. M., Hirsch-Pasek, K., Golinkoff, R. M., & Hennon, E. A. (2006). The birth of words: Ten-month-olds learn words through perceptual salience. *Child Development, 77,* 266–280.

Putallaz, M., & Bierman, K. L. (Eds.). (2004). *Aggression, antisocial behavior, and violence among girls: A developmental perspective.* New York: Guilford Press.

Putnam, F. (2002). Ten-year research update review: Child sexual abuse. *Journal of the American Academy of Child & Adolescent Psychiatry, 42*(3), 269–278.

Quadrel, M. J., Fischoff, B., & Davis, W. (1993). Adolescent (in) vulnerability. *American Psychologist, 48,* 102–116.

Quattrin, T., Liu, E., Shaw, N., Shine, B., & Chiang, E. (2005). Obese children who are referred to the pediatric oncologist: Characteristics and outcome. *Pediatrics, 115,* 348–351.

Quinn, P. C., Eimas, P. D., & Rosenkrantz, S. L. (1993). Evidence for representations of perceptually similar natural categories by 3-month-old and 4-month-old infants. *Perception, 22,* 463–475.

Quinn, P. C., Westerlund, A., & Nelson, C. A. (2006). Neural markers of categorization in 6-month-old infants. *Psychological Science, 17,* 59–66.

Rabiner, D., & Coie, J. (1989). Effect of expectancy induction on rejected peers' acceptance by unfamiliar peers. *Developmental Psychology, 25,* 450–457.

Racz, S. J., & McMahon, R. J. (2011). The relationship between parental knowledge and monitoring and child and adolescent conduct: A 10-year update. *Clinical Child and Family Psychology Review, 14*(4), 377–398.

Raikes, H., Pan, B. A., Luze, G., Tamis-LeMonda, C. S., Brooks-Gunn, J., Constantine, J., et al. (2006). Mother-child book-reading in low-income families: Correlates and outcomes during three years of life. *Child Development, 77,* 924–953.

Raine, A., Mellingen, K., Liu, J., Venables, P., & Mednick, S. (2003). Effects of environmental enrichment at ages 3–5 years in schizotypal personality and antisocial behavior at ages 17 and 23 years. *American Journal of Psychiatry, 160,* 1627–1635.

Raizada, R., Richards, T., Meltzoff, A., & Kuhl, P. (2008). Socioeconomic status predicts hemispheric specialisation of the left inferior frontal gyrus in young children. *NeuroImage, 40*(3), 1392–1401. doi: 10.1016/j.neuroimage.2008.01.021

Rakison, D. H. (2005). Infant perception and cognition. In B. J. Ellis & D. F. Bjorklund (Eds.), *Origins of the social mind* (pp. 317–353). New York: Guilford Press.

Rakoczy, H., Tomasello, M., & Striano. T. (2004). Young children know that trying is not pretending: A test of the "behaving-as-if" construal of children's early concept of pretense. *Developmental Psychology, 40,* 388–399.

Rakyan, V., & Beck., S. (2006). Epigenetic inheritance and variation in mammals. *Current Opinion in Genetics and Development, 16*(6), 573–577.

Ram, A., & Ross, H. S. (2001). Problem solving, contention, and struggle: How siblings resolve a conflict of interests. *Child Development, 72,* 1710–1722.

Ramagopalan, S. V., Maugeri, N. J., Handunnetthi, L., Lincoln, M. R., Orton, S-M., Dyment, D. A., et al. (2009). Expression of the multiple sclerosis–associated MHC class II allele *HLA-DRB1*1501* is regulated by vitamin D. *PLoS Genetics, 5*(2), (ePub).

Ramakrishnan K. (2008). Evaluation and treatment of enuresis. *American Family Physician, 78*(4), 489–496.

Ramani, G. B., & Siegler, R. S. (2008). Promoting broad and stable improvements in low-income children's numerical knowledge through playing number board games. *Child Development, 79,* 375–394.

Ramey, C. T., & Ramey, S. L. (1996). Early intervention: Optimizing development for children with disabilities and risk conditions. In M. Wolraich (Ed.), *Disorders of development and learning: A practical guide to assessment and management* (2nd ed., pp. 141–158). Philadelphia: Mosby.

Ramey, C. T., & Ramey, S. L. (1998a). Early intervention and early experience. *American Psychologist, 53,* 109–120.

Ramey, C. T., & Ramey, S. L. (1998b). Prevention of intellectual disabilities: Early interventions to improve cognitive development. *Preventive Medicine, 21,* 224–232.

Ramey, C. T., & Ramey, S. L. (2003, May). *Preparing America's children for success in school.* Paper prepared for an invited address at the White House Early Childhood Summit on Ready to Read, Ready to Learn, Denver, CO.

Ramey, G., & Ramey, V. (2010). The rug rat race. In D. H. Romer & J. Wolfers (Eds.), *Brookings papers on economic activity* (pp. 129–200). Washington, DC: Brookings Institution.

Ramey, S. L., & Ramey, C. T. (1992). Early educational intervention with disadvantaged children—to what effect? *Applied and Preventive Psychology, 1,* 131–140.

Ramoz, N., Reichert, J. G., Smith, C. J., Silverman, J. M., Bespalova, I. N., Davis, K. L., & Buxbaum, J. D. (2004). Linkage and association of the mitochondrial aspartate/glutamate carrier SLC25A12 gene with autism. *American Journal of Psychiatry, 161,* 662–669.

Ramsey, P. G., & Lasquade, C. (1996). Preschool children's entry attempts. *Journal of Applied Developmental Psychology, 17,* 135–150.

Rao, P. A., Beidel, D. C., Turner, S. M., Ammerman, R. T., Crosby, L. E., & Sallee, F. R. (2007). Social anxiety disorder in children and adolescence: Descriptive psychopathology. *Behaviour Research and Therapy, 45*(6), 1181–1191.

Rapoport, J. L., Addington, A. M., Frangou, S., & Psych, M. (2005). The neurodevelopmental model of schizophrenia: Update 2005. *Molecular Psychiatry, 10,* 434–449.

Rask-Nissilä, L., Jokinen, E., Terho, P., Tammi, A., Lapinleimu, H., Ronnemaa, T., et al. (2000). Neurological development of 5-year-old children receiving a low-saturated fat, low cholesterol diet since infancy. *Journal of the American Medical Association, 284*(8), 993–1000.

Rathbun, A., West, J., & Germino-Hausken, E. (2004). *From kindergarten through third grade: Children's beginning school experiences* (NCES 2004–007). Washington, DC: National Center for Education Statistics.

Rauh, V. A., Whyatt, R. M., Garfinkel, R., Andrews, H., Hoepner, L., Reyes, A., et al. (2004). Developmental effects of exposure to environmental tobacco smoke and material hardship among inner-city children. *Neurotoxicology and Teratology, 26,* 373–385.

Raver, C. C. (2002). Emotions matter: Making the case for the role of young children's emotional development for early school readiness. *Social Policy Report, 16*(3).

Reaney, P. (2006, June 21). Three million babies born after fertility treatment. *Medscape.* Retrieved January 29, 2007, from www.medscape.com/viewarticle/537128

Recchia, H. E. & Howe, N. (2009). Associations between social understanding, sibling relationship quality, and siblings' conflict strategies and outcomes. *Child Development, 80*(5), 1564–1578.

Reef, S. E., Strebel, P., Dabbagh, A., Gacic-Dobo, M., & Cochi, S. (2011). Progress toward control of rubella and prevention of congential rubella syndrome—worldwide, 2009. *Journal of Infectious Diseases, 204*,(1), 24–27.

Reefhuis, J., Honein, M. A., Schieve, L. A., Correa, A., Hobbs, C. A., Rasmussen, S. A., and the National Birth Defects Prevention Study. (2008). Assisted reproductive technology and major structural birth defects in the United States. *Human Reproduction, 387*, 1–7.

Reese, D. (2000). A parenting manual, with words of advice for Puritan mothers. In J. DeLoache & A. Gottlieb (Eds.), *A world of babies: Imagined child-care guides for seven societies* (pp. 29–54). New York: Cambridge University Press.

Reese, E. (1995). Predicting children's literacy from mother-child conversations. *Cognitive Development, 10*, 381–405.

Reese, E., & Cox, A. (1999). Quality of adult book reading affects children's emergent literacy. *Developmental Psychology, 35*, 20–28.

Reese, E., & Newcombe, R. (2007). Training mothers in elaborative reminiscing enhances children's autobiographical memory and narrative. *Child Development, 78*(4), 1153–1170.

Reichenberg, A., Gross, R., Weiser, M., Bresnahan, M., Silverman, J., Harlap, S., et al. (2006). Advancing paternal age and autism. *Archives of General Psychiatry, 63*(9), 1026–1032.

Reiner, W. (2000, May 12). *Cloacal exstrophy: A happenstance model for androgen imprinting.* Presentation at the meeting of the Pediatric Endocrine Society, Boston.

Reiner, W. G., & Gearhart, J. P. (2004). Discordant sexual identity in some genetic males with cloacal exstrophy assigned to female sex at birth. *New England Journal of Medicine, 350*(4), 333–341.

Reiss, A. L., Abrams, M. T., Singer, H. S., Ross, J. L., & Denckla, M. B. (1996). Brain development, gender and IQ in children: A volumetric imaging study. *Brain, 119*, 1763–1774.

Remafedi, G., French, S., Story, M., Resnick, M. D., & Blum, R. (1998). The relationship between suicide risk and sexual orientation: Results of a population-based study. *American Journal of Public Health, 88*, 57–60.

Remez, L. (2000). Oral sex among adolescents: Is it sex or is it abstinence? *Family Planning Perspectives, 32*, 298–304.

Rende, R., Slomkowski, C., Lloyd-Richardson, E., & Niaura, R. (2005). Sibling effects on substance use in adolescence: Social contagion and genetic relatedness. *Journal of Family Psychology, 19*, 611–618.

Repetti, R. L., Taylor, S. E., & Seeman, T. S. (2002). Risky families: Family social environments and the mental and physical health of the offspring. *Psychological Bulletin, 128*(2), 330–366.

Resnick, L. B. (1989). Developing mathematical knowledge. *American Psychologist, 44*, 162–169.

Resnick, M. D., Bearman, P. S., Blum, R. W., Bauman, K. E., Harris, K. M., Jones, J., et al. (1997). Protecting adolescents from harm: Findings from the National Longitudinal Study on Adolescent Health. *Journal of the American Medical Association, 278*, 823–832.

Rethman, J. (2000). Trends in preventative care: Caries risk assessment and indications for sealants. *The Journal of the American Dental Association, 131*(1), 85–125.

Reuters. (2004b). *Senate passes unborn victims bill.* Retrieved March 29, 2004, from www.nytimes.com/reuters/politics/politics-congress-unborn.html?ex=1081399302&ei=1&en=636394338d275008

Reutter, M. (2005, November 8). *Fetal rights: Pregnant alcohol and drug users.* Retrieved November 2, 2008, from www.worldlawdirect.com/article/2024/Fetal_rights:_Pregnant_alcohol_and_drug_users.html

Reynolds, A. J., & Temple, J. A. (1998). Extended early childhood intervention and school achievement: Age thirteen findings from the Chicago Longitudinal Study. *Child Development, 69*, 231–246.

Reynolds, A. J., Temple, J. A., Robertson, D. L., & Mann, E. A. (2001). Long-term effects of an early childhood intervention on educational achievement and juvenile arrest. A 15-year follow-up of low-income children in public schools. *Journal of American Medical Association, 285*(18), 2339–2346.

Rhee, S. H. & Waldman, I. D. (2002). Genetic and environmental influences on antisocial behavior: A meta-analysis of twin and adoption studies. *Psychological Bulletin, 128*, 490–529.

Rhoton-Vlasak, A. (2000). Infections and infertility. *Primary Care Update for OB/GYNS, 7*(5), 200–206.

Ricciuti, H. N. (1999). Single parenthood and school readiness in white, black, and Hispanic 6- and 7-year-olds. *Journal of Family Psychology, 13*, 450–465.

Ricciuti, H. N. (2004). Single parenthood, achievement, and problem behavior in white, black, and Hispanic children. *Journal of Educational Research, 97*, 196–206.

Rice, C., Koinis, D., Sullivan, K., Tager-Flusberg, H., & Winner, E. (1997). When 3-year-olds pass the appearance-reality test. *Developmental Psychology, 33*, 54–61.

Rice, M., Oetting, J. B., Marquis, J., Bode, J., & Pae, S. (1994). Frequency of input effects on SLI children's word comprehension. *Journal of Speech and Hearing Research, 37*, 106–122.

Rice, M. L. (1982). Child language: What children know and how. In T. M. Field, A. Huston, H. C. Quay, L. Troll, & G. E. Finley (Eds.), *Review of human development research.* New York: Wiley.

Rice, M. L. (1989). Children's language acquisition. *American Psychologist, 44*(2), 149–156.

Rice, M. L., Huston, A. C., Truglio, R., & Wright, J. (1990). Words from "Sesame Street": Learning vocabulary while viewing. *Developmental Psychology, 26*, 421–428.

Rice, M. L., Taylor, C. L., & Zubrick, S. R. (2008). Language outcomes of 7-year-old children with or without a history of late language emergence at 24 months. *Journal of Speech, Language, and Hearing Research, 51*, 394–407.

Richardson, J. (1995). *Achieving gender equality in families: The role of males.* Innocenti Global Seminar, Summary Report. Florence, Italy: UNICEF International Child Development Centre, Spedale degli Innocenti.

Riddle, R. D., Johnson, R. L., Laufer, E., & Tabin, C. (1993). Sonic hedgehog mediates the polarizing activity of the ZPA. *Cell, 75*, 1401–1416.

Rideout, V. J., Vandewater, E. A., & Wartella, E. A. (2003). *Zero to six: Electronic media in the lives of infants, toddlers and preschoolers.* Menlo Park, CA: Kaiser Family Foundation.

Riemann, M. K., & Kanstrup Hansen, I. L. (2000). Effects on the fetus of exercise in pregnancy. *Scandinavian Journal of Medicine & Science in Sports. 10*(1), 12–19.

Rifkin, J. (1998, May 5). Creating the "perfect" human. *Chicago Sun-Times,* p. 29.

Rios-Ellis, B., Bellamy, L., & Shoji, J. (2000). An examination of specific types of *ijime* within Japanese schools. *School Psychology International, 21*, 227–241.

Ritchie, L., Crawford, P., Woodward-Lopez, G., Ivey, S., Masch, M., & Ikeda, J. (2001). *Prevention of childhood overweight: What should be done?* Berkeley, CA: Center for Weight and Health, U.C. Berkeley.

Ritter, J. (1999, November 23). Scientists close in on DNA code. *Chicago Sun-Times,* p. 7.

Rivara, F. (1999). Pediatric injury control in 1999: Where do we go from here? *Pediatrics, 103*(4), 883–888.

Rivera, J. A., Sotres-Alvarez, D., Habicht, J.-P., Shamah, T., & Villalpando, S. (2004). Impact of the Mexican Program for Education, Health and Nutrition (Progresa) on rates of growth and anemia in infants and young children. *Journal of the American Medical Association, 291*, 2563–2570.

Rivera, S. M., Wakeley, A., & Langer, J. (1999). The drawbridge phenomenon: Representational reasoning or perceptual preference? *Developmental Psychology, 35*(2), 427–435.

Roberts, G. C., Block, J. H., & Block, J. (1984). Continuity and change in parents' child-rearing practices. *Child Development, 55*, 586–597.

Robin, D. J., Berthier, N. E., & Clifton, R. K. (1996). Infants' predictive reaching for moving objects in the dark. *Developmental Psychology, 32*, 824–835.

Robins, R. W., & Trzesniewski, K. H. (2005). Self-esteem development across the lifespan. *Current Directions in Psychological Science, 14*(3), 158–162.

Rochat, P., Querido, J. G., & Striano, T. (1999). Emerging sensitivity to the timing and structure of proto conversations in early infancy. *Developmental Psychology, 35*, 950–957.

Rochat, P., & Striano, T. (2002). Who's in the mirror? Self-other discrimination in specular images by 4- and 9-month-old infants. *Child Development, 73*, 35–46.

Roderick, M., Engel, M., & Nagaoka, J. (2003). *Ending social promotion: Results from Summer Bridge.* Chicago: Consortium on Chicago School Research.

Rodier, P. M. (2000, February). The early origins of autism. *Scientific American,* pp. 56–63.

Rodkin, P. C., Farmer, T. W., Pearl, R., & Van Acker, R. (2000). Heterogeneity of popular boys: Antisocial and prosocial configurations. *Developmental Psychology, 36*(1), 14–24.

Rogan, W. J, Dietrich, K. N., Ware, J. H., Dockery, D. W., Salganik, M., Radcliffe, J., et al. (2001). The effect of chelation therapy with succimer on neuropsychological development in children exposed to lead. *New England Journal of Medicine, 344*, 1421–1426.

Rogler, L. H. (2002). Historical generations and psychology: The case of the Great Depression and World War II. *American Psychologist, 57*(12), 1013–1023.

Rogoff, B., Mistry, J., Göncü, A., & Mosier, C. (1993). Guided participation in cultural activity by toddlers and caregivers. *Monographs of the Society for Research in Child Development, 58*(8). [Serial No. 236].

Rogoff, B., & Morelli, G. (1989). Perspectives on children's development from cultural psychology. *American Psychologist, 44,* 343–348.

Rolls, B. J., Engell, D., & Birch, L. L. (2000). Serving portion size influences 5-year-old but not 3-year-old children's food intake. *Journal of the American Dietetic Association, 100,* 232–234.

Romano, E., Tremblay, R. E., Boulerice, B., & Swisher, R. (2005). Multi-level correlates of childhood physical aggression and prosocial behavior. *Journal of Abnormal Child Psychology, 33*(5), 565–578.

Ronca, A. E., & Alberts, J. R. (1995). Maternal contributions to fetal experience and the transition from prenatal to postnatal life. In J. P. Lecanuet, W. P. Fifer, N. A. Krasnegor, & W. P. Smotherman (Eds.), *Fetal development: A psychobiological perspective* (pp. 331–350). Hillsdale, NJ: Erlbaum.

Roopnarine, J., & Honig, A. S. (1985, September). The unpopular child. *Young Children,* 59–64.

Roopnarine, J. L., Hooper, F. H., Ahmeduzzaman, M., & Pollack, B. (1993). Gentle play partners: Mother-child and father-child play in New Delhi, India. In K. MacDonald (Ed.), *Parent-child play* (pp. 287–304). Albany: State University of New York Press.

Roopnarine, J. L., Talokder, E., Jain, D., Josh, P., & Srivastav, P. (1992). Personal well-being, kinship ties, and mother-infant and father-infant interactions in single-wage and dual-wage families in New Delhi, India. *Journal of Marriage and the Family, 54,* 293–301.

Roosa, M. W., Deng, S., Ryu, E., Burrell, G. L., Tein, J., Jones, S., Lopez, V., & Crowder, S. (2005). Family and child characteristics linking neighborhood context and child externalizing behavior. *Journal of Marriage and Family, 667,* 515–529.

Rose, A. J., & Rudolph, K. D. (2006). A review of sex differences in peer relationship processes: Potential trade-offs for the emotional and behavioral development of girls and boys. *Psychological Bulletin, 132,* 98–131.

Rose, S. A., & Feldman, J. F. (1995). Prediction of IQ and specific cognitive abilities at 11 years from infancy measures. *Developmental Psychology, 31,* 685–696.

Rose, S. A., & Feldman, J. F. (1997). Memory and speed: Their role in the relation of infant information processing to later IQ. *Child Development, 68,* 630–641.

Rose, S. A., & Feldman, J. F. (2000). The relation of very low birth weight to basic cognitive skills in infancy and childhood. In C. A. Nelson (Ed.), *The effects of early adversity on neurobehavioral development. The Minnesota Symposia on Child Psychology* (Vol. 31, pp. 31–59). Mahwah, NJ: Erlbaum.

Rose, S. A., Feldman, J. F., & Jankowski, J. J. (2001). Attention and recognition memory in the 1st year of life: A longitudinal study of preterm and full-term infants. *Developmental Psychology, 37,* 135–151.

Rose, S. A., Feldman, J. F., & Jankowski, J. J. (2002). Processing speed in the 1st year of life: A longitudinal study of preterm and full-term infants. *Developmental Psychology, 38,* 895–902.

Rose, S., Jankowski, J., & Feldman, J. (2002). Speed of processing and face recognition at 7 and 12 months. *Infancy, 3*(4), 435–455.

Rosenbaum, J. (2009). Patient teenagers? A comparison of the sexual behavior of virginity pledgers and matched nonpledgers. *Pediatrics, 123,* e110–e120.

Rosenblum, G. D., & Lewis, M. (1999). The relations among body image, physical attractiveness, and body mass in adolescence. *Child Development, 70,* 50–64.

Rosenthal, E. (2003, July 20). Bias for boys leads to sale of baby girls in China. *New York Times,* sec. 1, p. 6.

Ross, H. S. (1996). Negotiating principles of entitlement in sibling property disputes. *Developmental Psychology, 32,* 90–101.

Rossi, R. (1996, August 30). Small schools under microscope. *Chicago Sun-Times,* p. 24.

Rossoni, E., Feng, J., Tirozzi, B., Brown, D., Leng, G., & Moos, F. (2008). Emergent synchronous bursting of oxytocin neuronal network. *PloS Computational Biology, 4*(7). (ePub).

Rothbart, M. K., Ahadi, S. A., & Evans, D. E. (2000). Temperament and personality: Origins and outcomes. *Journal of Personality and Social Psychology, 78,* 122–135.

Rothbart, M. K., Ahadi, S. A., Hershey, K. L., & Fisher, P. (2001). Investigations of temperament at three to seven years: The Children's Behavior Questionnaire. *Child Development, 72,* 1394–1408.

Rothbart, M. K., & Hwang, J. (2002). Measuring infant temperament. *Infant Behavior & Development, 25*(1), 113–116.

Rouse, C., Brooks-Gunn, J., & McLanahan, S. (2005). Introducing the issue. *The Future of Children, 15*(1), 5–14.

Roush, W. (1995). Arguing over why Johnny can't read. *Science, 267,* 1896–1898.

Rovee-Collier, C. (1996). Shifting the focus from what to why. *Infant Behavior and Development, 19,* 385–400.

Rovee-Collier, C. (1999). The development of infant memory. *Current Directions in Psychological Science, 8,* 80–85.

Rowe, M. L., Ozcaliskan, S., & Goldin-Meadow, S. (2008). Learning words by hand: Gesture's role in predicting vocabulary development. *First Language, 28,* 182–199.

Rowland, A. S., Umbach, D. M., Stallone, L., Naftel, J., Bohlig, E. M., & Sandler, D. P. (2002). Prevalence of medication treatment for attention-deficit hyperactivity disorder among elementary school children in Johnston County, North Carolina. *American Journal of Public Health, 92,* 231–234.

Rubin, D. H., Erickson, C. J., San Agustin, M., Cleary, S. D., Allen, J. K., & Cohen, P. (1996). Cognitive and academic functioning of homeless children compared with housed children. *Pediatrics, 97,* 289–294.

Rubin, D. H., Krasilnikoff, P. A., Leventhal, J. M., Weile, B., & Berget, A. (1986, August 23). Effect of passive smoking on birth weight. *Lancet,* 415–417.

Rubin, K. (1982). Nonsocial play in preschoolers: Necessary evil? *Child Development, 53,* 651–657.

Rubin, K. H., Bukowski, W., & Parker, J. G. (1998). Peer interactions, relationships, and groups. In W. Damon (Series Ed.) & N. Eisenberg (Vol. Ed.), *Handbook of child psychology: Vol. 3. Social, emotional, and personality development* (5th ed., pp. 619–700). New York: Wiley.

Rubin, K. H., Burgess, K. B., Dwyer K. M. & Hastings, P. D. (2003). Predicting preschoolers' externalizing behavior from toddler temperament, conflict, and maternal negativity. *Developmental Psychology, 39*(1), 164–176.

Rubin, K. H., Burgess, K. B., & Hastings, P. D. (2002). Stability and social-behavioral consequences of toddlers' inhibited temperament and parenting behaviors. *Child Development, 73*(2), 483–495.

Ruble, D. M., & Brooks-Gunn, J. (1982). The experience of menarche. *Child Development, 53,* 1557–1566.

Ruble, D. N., & Dweck, C. S. (1995). Self-conceptions, person conceptions, and their development. In N. Eisenberg, (Ed.), *Social development: Review of personality and social psychology* (pp. 109–139). Thousand Oaks, CA: Sage.

Ruble, D. N., & Martin, C. L. (1998). Gender development. In W. Damon (Series Ed.) & N. Eisenberg (Vol. Ed.), *Handbook of child psychology: Vol. 3. Social, emotional, and personality development* (5th ed., pp. 933–1016). New York: Wiley.

Ruble, D. N., Martin, C. L., & Berenbaum, S. A. (2006). Gender development. In W. Damon & R. M. Lerner (Series Eds.) & D. Kuhn & R. S. Seigler (Vol. Eds.), *Handbook of child psychology: Vol 2. Cognition, perception, and language* (pp. 858–932). Hoboken, NJ: Wiley.

Rudolph, K. D., Lambert, S. F., Clark, A. G., & Kurlakowsky, K. D. (2001). Negotiating the transition to middle school: The role of self-regulatory processes. *Child Development, 72*(3), 929–946.

Rueda, M. R., & Rothbart, M. K. (2009). The influence of temperament on the development of coping: The role of maturation and experience. *New Directions for Child and Adolescent Development, 124,* 19–31.

Rueter, M. A., & Conger, R. D. (1995). Antecedents of parent-adolescent disagreements. *Journal of Marriage and the Family, 57,* 435–448.

Rueter, M. A., & Koerner, A. F. (2009). The effect of family communication patterns on adopted adolescent adjustment. *Journal of Marriage and Family, 70*(3), 715–727.

Ruiz, F., & Tanaka, K. (2001). The *ijime* phenomenon and Japan: Overarching consideration for cross-cultural studies. *Psychologia: An International Journal of Psychology in the Orient, 44,* 128–138.

Rushton, J. P., & Jensen, A. R. (2005). Thirty years of research on race differences in cognitive ability. *Psychology, Public Policy, and Law, 11,* 235–294.

Rutland, A. F., & Campbell, R. N. (1996). The relevance of Vygotsky's theory of the "zone of proximal development" to the assessment of children with intellectual disabilities. *Journal of Intellectual Disability Research, 40,* 151–158.

Rutter, M. (2002). Nature, nurture, and development: From evangelism through science toward policy and practice. *Child Development, 73,* 1–21.

Rutter, M. (2007). Gene-environment interdependence. *Developmental Science, 10,* 12–18.

Rutter, M., O'Connor, T. G., & the English and Romanian Adoptees (ERA) Study Team. (2004). Are there biological programming effects for psychological development? Findings from a study of Romanian adoptees. *Developmental Psychology, 40,* 81–94.

Ryan, A. (2001). The peer group as a context for the development of young adolescent motivation and achievement. *Child Development, 72*(4), 1135–1150.

Ryan, A. S. (1997). The resurgence of breast-feeding in the United States. *Pediatrics, 99.* Retrieved from www.pediatrics.org/cgi/content/full/99/4/e12

Ryan, A. S., Wenjun, Z., & Acosta, A. (2002). Breastfeeding continues to increase into the new millennium. *Pediatrics, 110,* 1103–1109.

Ryan, V., & Needham, C. (2001). Nondirective play therapy with children experiencing psychic trauma. *Clinical Child Psychology and Psychiatry, 6,* 437–453. [Special Issue].

Rymer, R. (1993). *An abused child: Flight from silence.* New York: HarperCollins.

Saarni, C., Campos, J. J., Camras, A., & Witherington, D. (2006). Emotional development: Action, communication, and understanding. In N. Eisenberg, W. Damon, and R. Lerner (Eds.) *Handbook of Child Psychology: Vol. 3, Social, emotional and personality development* (6th ed.), pp. 226–299. Hoboken, NJ: Wiley.

Saarni, C., Mumme, D. L., & Campos, J. J. (1998). Emotional development: Action, communication, and understanding. In W. Damon (Series Ed.) & N. Eisenberg (Vol. Ed.), *Handbook of child psychology: Vol. 3. Social, emotional, and personality development* (5th ed., pp. 237–309). New York: Wiley.

Sadeh, A., Raviv, A., & Gruber, R. (2000). Sleep patterns and sleep disruptions in school age children. *Developmental Psychology, 36*(3), 291–301.

Saffran, J. R., Pollak, S. D., Seibel, R. L., & Shkolnik, A. (2007). Dog is a dog is a dog: Infant rule learning is not specific to language. *Cognition, 105*(3), 669–680.

Saigal, S., Hoult, L. A., Streiner, D. L., Stoskopf, B. L., & Rosenbaum, P. L. (2000). School difficulties at adolescence in a regional cohort of children who were extremely low birth weight. *Pediatrics, 105,* 325–331.

Saigal, S., Stoskopf. B., Streiner, D., Boyle, M., Pinelli, J., Paneth, N., & Goddeeris, J. (2006). Transition of extremely-low-birth-weight infants from adolescence to young adulthood: Comparison with normal birth-weight controls. *Journal of the American Medical Association, 295,* 667–675.

Saigal, S., Stoskopf, B. L., Streiner, D. L., & Burrows, E. (2001). Physical growth and current health status of infants who were of extremely low birth weight and controls at adolescence. *Pediatrics, 108*(2), 407–415.

Salkind, N. J. (Ed.). (2005). Smiling. *The encyclopedia of human development.* Thousand Oaks, CA: Sage.

Salmela-Aro, K., Tynkkynen, L., & Vuori, J. (2010). Parents' work burnout and adolescents' school burnout: Are they shared? *European Journal of Developmental Psychology, 8*(2), 215–227. doi: 10.1080/17405620903578060

Samara, M., Marlow, N., Wolke, D. for the EPICure Study Group. (2008). Pervasive behavior problems at 6 years of age in a total-population sample of children born at 25 weeks of gestation. *Pediatrics, 122,* 562–573.

Samdal, O., & Dür, W. (2000). The school environment and the health of adolescents. In C. Currie, K. Hurrelmann, W. Settertobulte, R. Smith, & J. Todd (Eds.), *Health and health behaviour among young people: A WHO cross-national study (HBSC) international report* (pp. 49–64). WHO Policy Series: Health Policy for Children and Adolescents, Series No. 1. Copenhagen, Denmark: World Health Organization Regional Office for Europe.

Sampson, R. J. (1997). The embeddedness of child and adolescent development: A community-level perspective on urban violence. In J. McCord (Ed.), *Violence and childhood in the inner city* (pp. 31–77). Cambridge, England: Cambridge University Press.

Samuelsson, M., Radestad, I., & Segesten, K. (2001). A waste of life: Fathers' experience of losing a child before birth. *Birth, 28,* 124–130.

Sandler, D. P., Everson, R. B., Wilcox, A. J., & Browder, J. P. (1985). Cancer risk in adulthood from early life exposure to parents' smoking. *American Journal of Public Health, 75,* 487–492.

Sandler, W., Meir, I., Padden, C., & Aronoff, M. (2005). The emergence of grammar: Systematic structure in a new language. *Proceedings of the National Academy of Sciences, 102,* 2661–2665.

Sandnabba, H. K., & Ahlberg, C. (1999). Parents' attitudes and expectations about children's cross-gender behavior. *Sex Roles, 40,* 249–263.

Sandstrom, M. J., & Coie, J. D. (1999). A developmental perspective on peer rejection: Mechanisms of stability and change. *Child Development 70*(4), 955–966.

Santos, I. S., Victora, C. G., Huttly, S., & Carvalhal, J. B. (1998). Caffeine intake and low birth weight: A population-based case-control study. *American Journal of Epidemiology, 147,* 620–627.

Sapienza, C. (1990, October). Parental imprinting of genes. *Scientific American,* pp. 52–60.

Sapp, F., Lee, K., & Muir, D. (2000). Three-year-olds' difficulty with the appearance-reality distinction: Is it real or apparent? *Developmental Psychology, 36,* 547–560.

Sargent, J. D., & Dalton, M. (2001). Does parental disapproval of smoking prevent adolescents from becoming established smokers? *Pediatrics, 108*(6), 1256–1262.

Sarnecka, B. W. & Carey, S. (2007). How counting represents number: What children must learn and when they learn it. *Cognition, 108*(3), 662–674.

Saswati, S., Chang, J., Flowers, L., Kulkarni, A., Sentelle, G., Jeng, G., et al. (2009). *Assisted reproductive technology surveillance—United States, 2006* (Centers for Disease Control: June, 2009).

Satcher, D. (2001). *Women and smoking: A report of the Surgeon General.* Washington, DC: Department of Health and Human Services.

Saudino, K. J. (2003a). Parent ratings of infant temperament: Lessons from twin studies. *Infant Behavior & Development, 26,* 100–107.

Saudino, K. J. (2003b). The need to consider contrast effects in parent-rated temperament. *Infant Behavior & Development, 26,* 118–120.

Saudino, K. J., Wertz, A. E., Gagne, J. R., & Chawla, S. (2004). Night and day: Are siblings as different in temperament as parents say they are? *Journal of Personality and Social Psychology, 87,* 698–706.

Saunders, N. (1997, March). Pregnancy in the 21st century: Back to nature with a little assistance. *Lancet, 349,* s17–s19.

Savage, J. S., Fisher, J. O., & Birch, L. L. (2007). Parental influence on eating behavior: Conception to Adolescence. *Journal of Law, Medicine, and Ethics, 35*(1), 22–34.

Savage, S. L., & Au, T. K. (1996). What word learners do when input contradicts the mutual exclusivity assumption. *Child Development, 67,* 3120–3134.

Savic, I., Berglund, H., & Lindström, P. (2005). Brain response to putative pheromones in homosexual men. *Proceedings of the National Academy of Sciences, 102,* 7356–7361.

Savic, I., Berglund, H., & Lindström, P. (2006). Brain response to putative pheromones. *Proceedings of the National Academy of Sciences, 102*(20), 7356–7361.

Savic, I., & Lindström, P. (2008). PET and MRI show differences in cerebral assymetry and functional connectivity between homo- and heterosexual subjects. *Proceedings of the National Academy of Sciences USA, 105*(27), 9403–9408.

Savin-Williams, R. C. (2006). Who's gay? Does it matter? *Current Directions in Psychological Science, 15,* 40–44.

Sawhill, I. (2006). *Opportunity in America: The role of education: Policy brief Fall 2006.* Princeton-Brookings: The Future of Education. Retrieved from www.brookings.edu/es/research/projects /foc/20060913foc.pdf

Saxe, R., & Carey, S. (2006). The perception of causality in infancy. *Acta Psychologica, 123,* 144–165.

Saxe, R., Tenenbaum, J. B., & Carey, S. (2005). Secret agents: Inferences about hidden causes by 10- and 12-month old infants. *Psychological Science, 16,* 995–1001.

Saxe, R., Tzelnic, T., & Carey, S. (2007). Knowing who dunnit: Infants identify the causal agent in an unseen causal interaction. *Developmental Psychology, 43,* 149–158.

Scarr, S. (1992). Developmental theories for the 1990s: Development and individual differences. *Child Development, 63,* 1–19.

Scarr, S. (1998). American child care today. *American Psychologist, 53,* 95–108.

Scarr, S., & McCartney, K. (1983). How people make their own environments: A theory of genotype-environment effects. *Child Development, 54,* 424–435.

Schacter, D. L. (1999). The seven sins of memory: Insights from psychology and cognitive neuroscience. *American Psychologist, 54,* 182–203.

Scheers, N. J., Rutherford, G. W., & Kemp, J. S. (2003). Where should infants sleep? A comparison of risk for suffocation of infants sleeping in cribs, adult beds, and other sleeping locations. *Pediatrics, 112,* 883–889.

Scheidt, P., Overpeck, M. D., Whatt, W., & Aszmann, A. (2000). In C. Currie, K. Hurrelmann, W. Settertobulte, R. Smith, & J. Todd (Eds.), *Health and health behaviour among young people: A WHO cross-national study (HBSC) international report* (pp. 24–38). [WHO Policy Series: Healthy Policy for Children and Adolescents, Series No. 1]. Copenhagen, Denmark: World Health Organization Regional Office for Europe.

Schemo, D. J. (2004, August 19). Charter schools lagging behind, test scores show. *New York Times,* pp. A1, A16.

Scher, A., Epstein, R., & Tirosh, E. (2004). Stability and changes in sleep regulation: A longitudinal study from 3 months to 3 years. *International Journal of Behavioral Development, 28*(3), 268–274.

Scher, M. S., Richardson, G. A., & Day, N. L. (2000). Effects of prenatal crack/cocaine and other drug exposure on electroencephalographic sleep studies at birth and one year. *Pediatrics, 105,* 39–48.

Schieve, L. A., Meikle, S. F., Ferre, C., Peterson, H. B., Jeng, G., & Wilcox, L. S. (2002). Low and very low birth weight in infants conceived with use of assisted reproductive technology. *New England Journal of Medicine, 346,* 731–737.

Schmidt, M. E., Rich, M., Rifas-Shiman, S., Oken, E., & Taveras, E. (2009). Television viewing in infancy and child cognition at 3 years of age in a US cohort. *Pediatrics, 123*(3), 370–375.

Schmitt, B. D. (1997). Nocturnal enuresis. *Pediatrics in Review, 18,* 183–190.

Schmitt, S. A., Simpson, A. M., & Friend, M. (2011). A longitudinal assessment of the home literacy environment and early language. *Infant and Child Development, 20*(6), 409–431.

Schmitz, S., Saudino, K. J., Plomin, R., Fulker, D. W., & DeFries, J. C. (1996). Genetic and environmental influences on temperament in middle childhood: Analyses of teacher and tester ratings. *Child Development, 67,* 409–422.

Schnaas, L., Rothenberg, S. J., Flores, M., Martinez, S., Hernandez, C., Osorio, E., et al. (2006). Reduced intellectual development in children with prenatal lead exposure. *Environmental Health Perspectives, 114*(5), 791–797.

Schneider, B. H., Atkinson, L., & Tardif, C. (2001). Child-parent attachment and children's peer relations: A quantitative review. *Developmental Psychology, 37,* 86–100.

Schneider, H., & Eisenberg, D. (2006). Who receives a diagnosis of attention-deficit hyperactivity disorder in the United States elementary school population? *Pediatrics, 117,* 601–609.

Schneider, M. (2002). *Do school facilities affect academic outcomes?* Washington, DC: National Clearinghouse for Educational Facilities.

Scholten, C. M. (1985). *Childbearing in American society: 1650–1850.* New York: New York University Press.

Schöner, G., & Thelen, E. (2006). Using dynamic field theory to rethink infant habituation. *Psychological Review, 113,* 273–299.

Schonert-Reichl, K. A., & Hymel, S. (n.d.). *Educating the heart as well as the mind.* Canadian Education Association. Retrieved from http://www.greenbankms.ocdsb.ca/educating%20the%20heart.pdf

Schore, A. N. (1994). *Affect regulation and the origin of the self: The neurobiology of emotional development.* Hillsdale, NJ: Erlbaum.

Schug, J., Yuki, M., & Maddux, W. (2010). Relational mobility explains between and within culture differences in self-disclosure to close friends. *Psychological Science, 2*(10), 1471–1478. doi: 10.1177/0956797610382786

Schulenberg, J., O'Malley, P., Backman, J., & Johnston, L. (2005). Early adult transitions and their relation to well-being and substance use. In R. A. Settersten Jr., F. F. Furstenberg Jr., & R. G. Rumbaut (Eds.), *On the frontier of adulthood: Theory, research, and public policy* (pp. 417–453). Chicago: University of Chicago Press.

Schulenberg, J. E., & Zarrett, N. R. (2006). Mental health during emerging adulthood: Continuity and discontinuity in courses, causes, and functions. In J. J. Arnett & J. L. Tanner (Eds.), *Emerging adults in America: Coming of age in the 21st century* (pp. 135–172). Washington DC: American Psychological Association.

Schulting, A. B., Malone, P. S., & Dodge, K. A. (2005). The effect of school-based kindergarten transition policies and practices on child academic outcomes. *Developmental Psychology, 41,* 860–871.

Schulz, M. S., Cowan, C. P., & Cowan, P. A. (2006). Promoting healthy beginnings: A randomized controlled trial of a preventive intervention to preserve marital quality during the transition to parenthood. *Journal of Consulting and Clinical Psychology, 74,* 20–31.

Schumann, C. M., & Amaral, D. G. (2006). Stereological analysis of amygdala neuron number in autism. *The Journal of Neuroscience, 26*(29), 7674–7679.

Schumann, J. (1997). The view from elsewhere: Why there can be no best method for teaching a second language. *The Clarion: Magazine of the European Second Language Acquisition, 3*(1), 23–24.

Schwartz, D., Chang, L., & Farver, J. M. (2001). Correlates of victimization in Chinese children's peer groups. *Developmental Psychology, 37*(4), 520–532.

Schwartz, D., Dodge, K. A., Pettit, G. S., Bates, J. E., & the Conduct Problems Prevention Research Group. (2000). Friendship as a moderating factor in the pathway between early harsh home environment and later victimization in the peer group. *Developmental Psychology, 36,* 646–662.

Schwartz, D., McFadyen-Ketchum, S. A., Dodge, K. A., Pettit, G. S., & Bates, J. E. (1998). Peer group victimization as a predictor of children's behavior problems at home and in school. *Developmental and Psychopathology, 10,* 87–99.

Schwartz, L. L. (2003). A nightmare for King Solomon: The new reproductive technologies. *Journal of Family Psychology, 17,* 292–237.

Schweinhart, L. J. (2007). Crime prevention by the High/Scope Perry preschool program. *Victims & Offenders, 2*(2), 141–160.

Schweinhart, L. J., Barnes, H. V., & Weikart, D. P. (1993). *Significant benefits: The High/Scope Perry Preschool Study through age 27* (Monographs of the High/Scope Educational Research Foundation No. 10). Ypsilanti, MI: High/Scope.

Schwimmer, J. B., Burwinkle, T. M., & Varni, J. W. (2003, April). Health-related quality of life of severely obese children and adolescents. *Journal of the American Medical Association, 289*(14), 1813–1819.

Scott, G., & Ni, H. (2004). Access to health care among Hispanic/Latino children: United States, 1998–2001. *Advance Data from Vital and Health Statistics* [No. 344]. Hyattsville, MD: National Center for Health Statistics.

Scott, M., Booth, A., King. V., & Johnson, D. (2007). Post-divorce father-adolescent closeness. *Journal of Marriage and Family, 69,* 1194–1208.

Seifer, R. (2003). Twin studies, biases of parents, and biases of researchers. *Infant Behavior & Development, 26,* 115–117.

Seifer, R., Schiller, M., Sameroff, A. J., Resnick, S., & Riordan, K. (1996). Attachment, maternal sensitivity, and infant temperament during the first year of life. *Developmental Psychology, 32,* 12–25.

Seiner, S. H., & Gelfand, D. M. (1995). Effects of mother's simulated withdrawal and depressed affect on mother-toddler interactions. *Child Development, 60,* 1519–1528.

Seitz, V. (1990). Intervention programs for impoverished children: A comparison of educational and family support models. *Annals of Child Development, 7,* 73–103.

Selman, R. L. (1980). *The growth of interpersonal understanding: Developmental and clinical analyses.* New York: Academic.

Selman, R. L., & Selman, A. P. (1979, April). Children's ideas about friendship: A new theory. *Psychology Today,* pp. 71–80.

Seltzer, J. A. (2000). Families formed outside of marriage. *Journal of Marriage and the Family, 62,* 1247–1268.

Sen, A., Partelow, L., & Miller, D. C. (2005). *Comparative indicators of education in the United States and other G8 countries: 2004* (NCES 2005-021). Washington, DC: National Center for Education Statistics.

Sénéchal, M., & LeFevre, J. (2002). Parental involvement in the development of children's reading skill: A five-year longitudinal study. *Child Development, 73*(2), 445–460.

Senghas, A., & Coppola, M. (2001). Children creating language: How Nicaraguan sign language acquired a spatial grammar. *Psychological Science, 12,* 323–328.

Senghas, A., Kita, S., & Ozyürek, A. (2004). Children creating core properties of language: Evidence from an emerging sign language in Nicaragua. *Science, 305,* 1779–1782.

Serbin, L., Poulin-Dubois, D., Colburne, K. A., Sen, M., & Eichstedt, J. A. (2001). Gender stereotyping in infancy: Visual preferences for knowledge of gender-stereotyped toys in the second year. *International Journal of Behavioral Development, 25,* 7–15.

Serbin, L. A., Moller, L. C., Gulko, J., Powlishta, K. K., & Colburne, K. A. (1994). The emergence of gender segregation in toddler playgroups. In C. Leaper (Ed.), *Childhood gender segregation: Causes and consequences* (New Directions for Child Development No. 65, pp. 7–17). San Francisco: Jossey-Bass.

Servin, A., Bohlin, G., & Berlin, L. (1999). Sex differences in a 1-, 3-, and 5-year-olds' choice in a structured play session. *Scandinavian Journal of Pschology, 40,* 43–48.

Sethi, A., Mischel, W., Aber, J. L., Shoda, Y., & Rodriguez, M. L. (2000). The role of strategic attention deployment in development of self-regulation: Predicting preschoolers' delay of gratification from mother-toddler interactions. *Developmental Psychology, 36,* 767–777.

Shachar-Dadon, A., Schulkin, J., & Leshem, M. (2009). Adversity before conception will affect adult progeny in rats. *Developmental Psychology, 45*(1), 9–16.

Shackman, J. E., Shackman, A. J., & Pollak, S. D. (2007). Physical abuse amplifies attention to threat and increases anxiety in children. *Emotion, 7,* 838–852.

Shah, T., Sullivan, K., & Carter, J. (2006). Sudden infant death syndrome and reported maternal smoking during pregnancy. *American Journal of Public Health, 96*(10), 1757–1759.

Shanahan, M., Porfeli, E., & Mortimer, J. (2005). Subjective age identity and the transition to adulthood: When do adolescents become adults? In R. A. Settersten Jr., F. F. Furstenberg Jr., & R. G. Rumbaut (Eds.), *On the frontier of adulthood: Theory, research, and public policy* (pp. 225–255). Chicago: University of Chicago Press.

Shankaran, S., Bada, H. S., Smeriglio, V. L., Langer, J. C., Beeghly, M., & Poole, W. K. (2004). The maternal lifestyle study: Cognitive, motor, and behavioral outcomes of cocaine-exposed and opiate-exposed infants through three years of age. *Pediatrics, 113,* 1677–1685.

Shannon, J. D., Tamis-LeMonda, C. S., London, K., & Cabrera, N. (2002). Beyond rough and tumble: Low income fathers' interactions and children's cognitive development at 24 months. *Parenting: Science & Practice, 2*(2), 77–104.

Shannon, M. (2000) Ingestion of toxic substances by children. *New England Journal of Medicine, 342,* 186–191.

Shapiro, A. F., & Gottman, J. M. (2003, September). Bringing baby home: Effects on marriage of a psycho-education intervention with couples undergoing the transition to parenthood, evaluation at 1-year post intervention. In A. J. Hawkins (Chair), *Early family interventions.* Symposium conducted at the meeting of the National Council on Family Relations, Vancouver, British Columbia.

Shapiro-Mendoza, C. K., Kimball, M., Tomashek, K. M., Anderson, R. N., & Blanding, S. (2009). U.S. infant mortality trends attributable to accidental suffocation and strangulation in bed from 1984 through 2004: Are rates increasing? *Pediatrics, 123,* 533–539.

Sharma, A. R., McGue, M. K., & Benson, P. L. (1996a). The emotional and behavioral adjustment of United States adopted adolescents, Part I: An overview. *Children and Youth Services Review, 18,* 83–100.

Sharma, A. R., McGue, M. K., & Benson, P. L. (1996b). The emotional and behavioral adjustment of United States adopted adolescents, Part II: Age at adoption. *Children and Youth Services Review, 18,* 101–114.

Sharon, T., & DeLoache, J. S. (2003). The role of perseveration in children's symbolic understanding and skill. *Developmental Science, 6*(3), 289–296.

Shatz, M., & Gelman, R. (1973). The development of communication skills: Modifications in the speech of young children as a function of listener. *Monographs of the Society for Research in Child Development, 38*(5). [Serial No. 152].

Shaw, B. A., Krause, N., Liang, J., & Bennett, J. (2007). Tracking changes in social relations throughout late life. *Journal of Gerontology: Social Sciences, 62B,* S90–S99.

Shaw, P., Greenstein, D., Lerch, J., Clasen, L., Lenroot, R., Gogtay, N., et al. (2006). Intellectual ability and cortical development in children and adolescents. *Nature, 440,* 676–679.

Shayer, M., Ginsburg, D., & Coe, R. (2007). Thirty years on—a large anti-Flynn effect? The Piagetian Test Volume & Heaviness norms 1975–2003. *British Journal of Educational Psychology, 77*(1), 25–41.

Shaywitz, S. (2003). *Overcoming dyslexia: A new and complete science-based program for overcoming reading problems at any level.* New York: Knopf.

Shaywitz, S. E. (1998). Current concepts: Dyslexia. *New England Journal of Medicine, 338,* 307–312.

Shaywitz, S. E., Mody, M., & Shaywitz, B. A. (2006). Neural mechanisms in dyslexia. *Current Directions in Psychological Science, 15,* 278–281.

Shea, K. M., Little, R. E., & the ALSPAC Study Team. (1997). Is there an association between preconceptual paternal X-ray exposure and birth outcome? *American Journal of Epidemiology, 145,* 546–551.

Shea, S., Basch, C. E., Stein, A. D., Contento, I. R., Irigoyen, M., & Zybert, P. (1993). Is there a relationship between dietary fat and stature or growth in children 3 to 5 years of age? *Pediatrics, 92,* 579–586.

Shiono, P. H., & Behrman, R. E. (1995). Low birth weight: Analysis and recommendations. *The Future of Children, 5*(1), 4–18.

Shonkoff, J., & Phillips, D. (2000). Growing up in child care. In I. Shonkoff & D. Phillips (Eds.), *From neurons to neighborhoods* (pp. 297–327). Washington, DC: National Research Council/Institute of Medicine.

Shulman, S., Scharf, M., Lumer, D., & Maurer, O. (2001). Parental divorce and young adult children's romantic relationships: Resolution of the divorce experience. *American Journal of Orthopsychiatry, 71,* 473–478.

Shwe, H. I., & Markman, E. M. (1997). Young children's appreciation of the mental impact of their communicative signals. *Developmental Psychology, 33*(4), 630–636.

Sicherer, S. H. (2002). Food allergy. *Lancet, 360*(9334), 701–710.

Siegal, M., & Peterson, C. C. (1998). Preschoolers' understanding of lies and innocent and negligent mistakes. *Developmental Psychology, 34*(2), 332–341.

Siegler, R. S. (1998). *Children's thinking* (3rd ed.). Upper Saddle River, NJ: Prentice Hall.

Siegler, R. S. (2000). The rebirth of children's learning. *Child Development, 71*(1), 26–35.

Siegler, R. S., & Booth, J. L. (2004). Development of numerical estimation in young children. *Child Development, 75,* 428–444.

Siegler, R. S., & Opfer, J. E. (2003). The development of numerical estimation: Evidence for multiple representations of numerical quantity. *Psychological Science, 14,* 237–243.

Siegler, R. S., & Richards, D. (1982). The development of intelligence. In R. Sternberg (Ed.), *Handbook of human intelligence* (pp. 897–971). London: Cambridge University Press.

Sieving, R. E., McNeely, C. S., & Blum, R. W. (2000). Maternal expectations, mother-child connectedness, and adolescent sexual debut. *Archives of Pediatric & Adolescent Medicine, 154,* 809–816.

Sieving, R. E., Oliphant, J. A., & Blum, R. W. (2002). Adolescent sexual behavior and sexual health. *Pediatrics in Review, 23,* 407–416.

Sigman, M., Cohen, S. E., & Beckwith, L. (1997). Why does infant attention predict adolescent intelligence? *Infant Behavior and Development, 20,* 133–140.

Silverman, W. K., La Greca, A. M., & Wasserstein, S. (1995). What do children worry about? Worries and their relation to anxiety. *Child Development, 66,* 671–686.

Simmons, R. G., Blyth, D. A., & McKinney, K. L. (1983). The social and psychological effect of puberty on white females. In J. Brooks-Gunn & A. C. Petersen (Eds.), *Girls at puberty: Biological and psychological perspectives* (229–272). New York: Plenum Press.

Simmons, R. G., Blyth, D. A., Van Cleave, E. F., & Bush, D. M. (1979). Entry into early adolescence: The impact of school structure, puberty, and early dating on self-esteem. *American Sociological Review, 44*(6), 948–967.

Simon, G. E. (2006). The antidepressant quandary—considering suicide risk when treating adolescent depression. *New England Journal of Medicine, 355,* 2722–2723.

Simon, G. E., Savarino, J., Operskalski, B., & Wang, P. S. (2006). Suicide risk during antidepressant treatment. *American Journal of Psychiatry, 163,* 41–47.

Simons, R. L., Chao, W., Conger, R. D., & Elder, G. H. (2001). Quality of parenting as mediator of the effect of childhood defiance on adolescent friendship choices and delinquency: A growth curve analysis. *Journal of Marriage and the Family, 63,* 63–79.

Simons, R. L., Lin, K.-H., & Gordon, L. C. (1998). Socialization in the family of origin and male dating violence: A prospective study. *Journal of Marriage and the Family, 60,* 467–478.

Simonton, D. K. (1990). Creativity and wisdom in aging. In J. E. Birren & K. W. Schaie (Eds.), *Handbook of the psychology of aging* (pp. 320–329). New York: Academic Press.

Simpson, J. E. (2005). Choosing the best prenatal screening protocol. *New England Journal of Medicine, 353,* 2068–2070.

Simpson, K. (2001). The role of testosterone in aggression. *McGill Journal of Medicine, 6,* 32–40.

Sines, E., Syed, U., Wall, S., & Worley, H. (2007). Postnatal care: A critical opportunity to save mothers and newborns. *Policy Perspectives on Newborn Health.* Washington, DC: Save the Children and Population Reference Bureau.

Singer, D. G., & Singer, J. L. (1990). *The house of make-believe: Play and the developing imagination.* Cambridge, MA: Harvard University Press.

Singer, J. L., & Singer, D. G. (1981). *Television, imagination, and aggression: A study of preschoolers.* Hillsdale, NJ: Erlbaum.

Singer, J. L., & Singer, D. G. (1998). *Barney & Friends* as entertainment and education: Evaluating the quality and effectiveness of a television series for preschool children. In J. K. Asamen & G. L. Berry (Eds.), *Research paradigms, television, and social behavior* (pp. 305–367). Thousand Oaks, CA: Sage.

Singer, L. T., Minnes, S., Short, E., Arendt, K., Farkas, K., Lewis, B., et al. (2004). Cognitive outcomes of preschool children with prenatal cocaine exposure. *Journal of the American Medical Association, 291,* 2448–2456.

Singer-Freeman, K. E., & Goswami, U. (2001). Does half a pizza equal half a box of chocolates? Proportional matching in an analogy task. *Cognitive Development, 16*(3), 811–829.

Singh, G. K., Kogan, M. D., & Dee, D. L. (2007). Nativity/immigrant status, race/ethnicity, and socioeconomic determinants of breastfeeding initiation and duration in the United States, 2003. *Pediatrics, 119*(Suppl. 1), 538–547.

Singh, G. K., Yu, S. M., Siahpush, M., & Kogan, M. D. (2008). High levels of physical inactivity and sedentary behaviors among U.S. immigrant children and adolescents. *Archives of Pediatrics and Adolescent Medicine, 162*(8), 756–763.

Singh, S., Wulf, D., Samara, R., & Cuca, Y. P. (2000). Gender differences in the timing of first intercourse: Data from 14 countries. *International Family Planning Perspectives, Part 1, 26,* 21–28.

Singhal, A., Cole, T. J., Fewtrell, M., & Lucas, A. (2004). Breastmilk feeding and lipoprotein profile in adolescents born preterm: Follow-up of a prospective randomised study. *Lancet, 363,* 1571–1578.

Sipos, A., Rasmussen, F., Harrison, G., Tynelius, P., Lewis, G., Leon, D. A., et al. (2004). Paternal age and schizophrenia: A population based cohort study. *British Medical Journal, 329,* 1070–1073.

Sisson, S. B., Broyles, S. T., Newton, R. L., Baker, B. L., & Chernausek, S. D. (2011). TVs in the bedrooms of children: Does it impact health and behavior? *Preventive Medicine, 52*(2), 104–108.

Skadberg, B. T., Morild, I., & Markestad, T. (1998). Abandoning prone sleeping: Effects on the risk of sudden infant death syndrome. *Journal of Pediatrics, 132,* 234–239.

Skinner, B. F. (1938). *The behavior of organisms: An experimental approach.* New York: Appleton-Century.

Skinner, B. F. (1957). *Verbal behavior.* New York: Appleton-Century-Crofts.

Skinner, D. (1989). The socialization of gender identity: Observations from Nepal. In J. Valsiner (Ed.), *Child development in cultural context* (pp. 181–192). Toronto: Hogrefe & Huber.

Skoe, E. E., & Diessner, R. E. (1994). Ethic of care, justice, identity, and gender: An extension and replication. *Merrill-Palmer Quarterly, 40,* 272–289.

Skolnick Weisberg, D., & Bloom, P. (2009). Young children separate multiple pretend worlds. *Developmental Science, 12*(5), 699–705. doi: 10.1111/j.1467-7687.2009.00819.x

Slade, A., Belsky, J., Aber, J. L., & Phelps, J. L. (1999). Mothers' representation of their relationships with their toddlers: Links to adult attachment and observed mothering. *Developmental Psychology, 35,* 611–619.

Slobin, D. (1970). Universals of grammatical development in children. In W. Levitt & G. Flores d'Arcais (Eds.), *Advances in psycholinguistic research* (pp. 174–186). Amsterdam, The Netherlands: North Holland.

Slobin, D. (1973). Cognitive prerequisites for the acquisition of language. In C. Ferguson & D. Slobin (Eds.), *Studies of child language development* (pp. 175–208). New York: Holt, Rinehart, & Winston.

Slobin, D. (1983). Universal and particular in the acquisition of grammar. In E. Wanner & L. Gleitman (Eds.), *Language acquisition: The state of the art* (pp. 128–170). Cambridge, UK: Cambridge University Press.

Slobin, D. (1990). The development from child speaker to native speaker. In J. W. Stigler, R. A. Schweder, G. H. Herdt (Eds.) *Cultural Psychology: Essays on comparative human development.* New York: Cambridge University Press, 233–258.

Sly, R. M. (2000). Decreases in asthma mortality in the United States. *Annal of Allergy, Asthma, and Immunology, 85,* 121–127.

Slyper, A. H. (2006). The pubertal timing controversy in the USA, and a review of possible causative factors for the advance in timing of onset of puberty. *Clinical Endocrinology, 65,* 1–8.

Small, M. Y. (1990). *Cognitive development.* New York: Harcourt Brace.

Smedley, A., & Smedley, B. D. (2005). Race as biology is fiction, racism as a social problem is real: Anthropological and historical perspectives on the social construction of race. *American Psychologist, 60,* 16–26.

Smetana, J., Crean, H., & Campione-Barr, N. (2005). Adolescents' and parents' changing conceptions of parental authority. In J. Smetana (Ed.), *Changing boundaries of parental authority during adolescence: New directions for child and adolescent development, no. 108* (pp. 31–46). San Francisco: Jossey-Bass.

Smetana, J. G., Metzger, A., Gettman, D. C., & Campione-Barr, N. (2006). Disclosure and secrecy in adolescent-parent relationships. *Child Development, 77,* 201–217.

Smilansky, S. (1968). *The effects of sociodramatic play on disadvantaged preschool children.* New York: Wiley.

Smith, G.C.S., Pell, J. P., Cameron, A. D., & Dobbie, R. (2002). Risk of perinatal death associated with labor after previous cesarean delivery in uncomplicated term pregnancies. *Journal of the American Medical Association, 287,* 2684–2690.

Smith, L. B., & Thelen, E. (2003). Development as a dynamic system. *Trends in Cognitive Sciences, 7,* 343–348.

Smith, L. M., LaGasse, L. L., Derauf, C., Grant, P., Shah, R., Arria, A., et al. (2006). The infant development, environment, and lifestyle study: Effects of prenatal methamphetamine exposure, polydrug exposure, and poverty on intrauterine growth. *Pediatrics, 118,* 1149–1156.

Smith, P. K. (2005a). Play: Types and functions in human development. In A. D. Pellegrini & P. K. Smith (Eds.), *The nature of play* (pp. 271–291). New York: Guilford Press.

Smith, P. K. (2005b). Social and pretend play in children. In A. D. Pellegrini & P. K. Smith (Eds.), *The nature of play* (pp. 173–209). New York: Guilford Press.

Smith, P. K., & Levan, S. (1995). Perceptions and experiences of bullying in younger pupils. *British Journal of Educational Psychology, 65,* 489–500.

Smith, R. (1999, March). The timing of birth. *Scientific American,* pp. 68–75.

Smith, R. (2007). Parturition. *New England Journal of Medicine, 356,* 271–283.

Smith-Khuri, E., Iachan, R., Scheidt, P. C., Overpeck, M. D., Gabhainn, S. N., Pickett, W., & Harel, Y. (2004). A cross-national study of violence-related behaviors in adolescents. *Archives of Pediatrics and Adolescent Medicine, 158,* 539–544.

Smolak, L., & Murnen, S.K. (2002). A meta-analytic examination of the relationship between child sexual abuse and eating disorders. *International Journal of Eating Disorders, 31,* 136–150.

Smotherman, W. P., & Robinson, S. R. (1995). Tracing developmental trajectories into the prenatal period. In J. P. Lecanuet, W. P. Fifer, N. A. Krasnegor, & W. P. Smotherman (Eds.), *Fetal development. A psychobiological perspective* (pp. 15–32). Hillsdale, NJ: Erlbaum.

Smotherman, W. P., & Robinson, S. R. (1996). The development of behavior before birth. *Developmental Psychology, 32,* 425–434.

Snarey, J. R. (1985). Cross-cultural universality of social-moral development: A critical review of Kohlbergian research. *Psychological Bulletin, 97,* 202–232.

Snow, C. E. (1990). The development of definitional skill. *Journal of Child Language, 17,* 697–710.

Snow, C. E. (1993). Families as social contexts for literacy development. In C. Daiute (Ed.), *The development of literacy through social interaction* (New Directions for Child Development No. 61, pp. 11–24). San Francisco: Jossey-Bass.

Snow, C. E., & Beals, D. E. (2006). Mealtime talk that supports literacy development. In R. W. Larson, A. R. Wiley, & K. R. Branscomb (Eds.), *Family mealtime as a context of development and socialization,* No. 111 (pp. 51–66). San Francisco: Jossey-Bass.

Snow, M. E., Jacklin, C. N., & Maccoby, E. E. (1983). Sex-of-child differences in father-child interaction at one year of age. *Child Development, 54,* 227–232.

Snyder, E. E., Walts, B., Perusse, L., Chagnon, Y. C., Weisnagel, S. J., Raniken, T., & Bouchard, C. (2004). The human obesity gene map. *Obesity Research, 12,* 369–439.

Snyder, J., Bank, L., & Burraston, B. (2005). The consequences of antisocial behavior in older male siblings for younger brothers and sisters. *Journal of Family Psychology, 19,* 643–653.

Snyder, J., Cramer, A., Frank, J., & Patterson, G. R. (2005). The contributions of ineffective discipline and parental hostile attributions of child misbehavior to the development of conduct problems at home and school. *Developmental Psychology, 41,* 30–41.

Snyder, J., West, L., Stockemer, V., Gibbons, S., & Almquist-Parks, L. (1996). A social learning model of peer choice in the natural environment. *Journal of Applied Developmental Psychology, 17,* 215–237.

Snyder, T. D., & Hoffman, C. M. (2001). *Digest of education statistics, 2000.* Washington, DC: National Center for Education Statistics.

Sobel, D. M., Tenenbaum, J. B., & Gopnik, A. (2004). Children's causal inferences from indirect evidence: Backwards blocking and Bayesian reasoning in preschoolers. *Cognitive Science, 28,* 303–333.

Sobolewski, J. M., & Amato, P. J. (2005). Economic hardship in the family of origin and children's psychological well-being in adulthood. *Journal of Marriage and Family, 67,* 141–156.

Sobolewski, J. M., & King, V. (2005). The importance of the coparental relationship for nonresident fathers' ties to children. *Journal of Marriage and Family, 67,* 1196–1212.

Society for Assisted Reproductive Technology & the American Fertility Society. (1993). Assisted reproductive technology in the United States and Canada: 1991 results from the Society for Assisted Reproductive Technology generated from the American Fertility Society Registry. *Fertility and Sterility, 59,* 956–962.

Society for Assisted Reproductive Technology & the American Society for Reproductive Medicine. (2002). Assisted reproductive technology in the United States: 1998 results generated from the American Society for Reproductive Medicine/Society for Assisted Reproductive Technology Registry. *Fertility & Sterility, 77*(1), 18–31.

Society for Neuroscience. (2008). Neural disorders: Advances and challenges. *In Brain facts: A primer on the brain and nervous system* (pp. 36–54). Washington, DC: Author.

Society for Research in Child Development (SRCD). (2007). *Ethical standards for research with children.* Retrieved May 20, 2008, from www.srcd.org/ethicalstandards.html

Soenens, B., Vansteenkiste, M., Luyckx, K., & Goossens, L. (2006). Parenting and adolescent problem behavior: An integrated model with adolescent self-disclosure and perceived parental knowledge as intervening variables. *Developmental Psychology, 42,* 305–318.

Sokol, R. J., Delaney-Black, V., & Nordstrom, B. (2003). Fetal alcohol spectrum disorder. *Journal of the American Medical Association, 209,* 2996–2999.

Sokol, R. Z., Kraft, P., Fowler, I. M., Mamet, R., Kim, E., & Berhane, K. T. (2006). Exposure to environmental ozone alters semen quality. *Environmental Health Perspectives, 114*(3), 360–365.

Soliday, E. (2007). Infant feeding and cognition: Integrating a developmental perspective. *Child Development Perspectives, 1*(1), 19–25.

Solowij, N., Stephens, R. S., Roffman, R. A., Babor, T., Kadden, R., Miller, M., et al. (2002). Cognitive functioning of long-term heavy cannabis users seeking treatment. *Journal of the American Medical Association, 287,* 1123–1131.

Sondergaard, C., Henriksen, T. B., Obel, C., & Wisborg, K. (2001). Smoking during pregnancy and infantile colic. *Pediatrics, 108*(2), 342–346.

Sontag, L. M., Graber, J. A., Brooks-Gunn, J., & Warren, M. (2008). Coping with social stress: Implications for psychopathology in young adolescent girls. *Journal of Abnormal Child Psychology, 36*(8), 1159–1174.

Sood, B., Delaney-Black, V., Covington, C., Nordstrom-Klee, B., Ager, J., Templin, T., et al. (2001). Prenatal alcohol exposure and childhood behavior at age 6 to 7 years: I. Dose-response effect. *Pediatrics, 108*(8), e461–e462.

Sophian, C., Garyantes, D., & Chang, C. (1997). When three is less than two: Early developments in children's understanding of fractional quantities. *Developmental Psychology, 33,* 731–744.

Sophian, C., & Wood, A. (1997). Proportional reasoning in young children: The parts and the whole of it. *Journal of Educational Psychology, 89,* 309–317.

Sophian, C., Wood, A., & Vong, K. I. (1995). Making numbers count: The early development of numerical inferences. *Developmental Psychology, 31,* 263–273.

Sorof, J. M., Lai, D., Turner, J., Poffenbarger, T., & Portman, R. J. (2004). Overweight, ethnicity, and the prevalence of hypertension in school-aged children. *Pediatrics, 113,* 475–482.

Souter, V. L., Parisi, M. A., Nyholt, D. R., Kapur, R. P., Henders, A. K., Opheim, K. E., et al. (2007). A case of true hermaphroditism reveals an unusual mechanism of twinning. *Human Genetics Journal, 121*(2), 179–185.

Spelke, E. (1994). Initial knowledge: Six suggestions. *Cognition, 50,* 431–445.

Spelke, E. S. (1998). Nativism, empiricism, and the origins of knowledge. *Infant Behavior and Development, 21*(2), 181–200.

Spelke, E. S. (2005). Sex differences in intrinsic aptitude for mathematics and science? A critical review. *American Psychologist, 60,* 950–958.

Spencer, J. P., Clearfield, M., Corbetta. D., Ulrich, B., Buchanan, P., & Schöner, G. (2006). Moving toward a grand theory of development: In memory of Esther Thelen. *Child Development, 77,* 1521–1538.

Spencer, J. P., Smith, L. B., & Thelen, E. (2001). Tests of a dynamic systems account of the A-not-B error: The influence of prior experience on the spatial memory abilities of two-year-olds. *Child Development, 72,* 1327–1346.

Sperling, M. A. (2004). Prematurity—a window of opportunity? *New England Journal of Medicine, 351,* 2229–2231.

Spiegel, D. (1985). The use of hypnosis in controlling cancer pain. *CA: A Cancer Journal for Clinicians, 35*(4), 221–231.

Spinath, F. M., Price, T. S., Dale, P. S., & Plomin, R. (2004). The genetic and environmental origins of language disability and ability. *Child Development, 75,* 445–454.

Spinrad, T. L., Eisenberg, N., Harris, E., Hanish, L., Fabes, R. A., Kupanoff, K., et al. (2004). The relation of children's everyday nonsocial peer play behavior to their emotionality, regulation, and social functioning. *Developmental Psychology, 40,* 67–80.

Spira, E. G., Brachen, S. S., & Fischel, J. E. (2005). Predicting improvement after first-grade reading difficulties: The effects of oral language, emergent literacy, and behavior skills. *Developmental Psychology, 41,* 225–234.

Spitz, R. A. (1945). Hospitalism: An inquiry into the genesis of psychiatric conditioning in early childhood. In D. Fenschel et al. (Eds.), *Psychoanalytic studies of the child* (Vol. 1, pp. 53–74). New York: International Universities Press.

Spitz, R. A. (1946). Hospitalism: A followup report. In D. Fenschel et al. (Eds.), *Psychoanalytic studies of the child* (Vol. 1, pp. 113–117). New York: International Universities Press.

Spohr, H. L., Willms, J., & Steinhausen, H.-C. (1993). Prenatal alcohol exposure and long-term developmental consequences. *Lancet, 341,* 907–910.

Sroufe, L. A. (1979). Socioemotional development. In J. Osofsky (Ed.), *Handbook of infant development* (pp. 462–515) New York: John Wiley.

Sroufe, L. A. (1997). *Emotional development.* Cambridge, UK: Cambridge University Press.

Sroufe, L. A., Carlson, E., & Shulman, S. (1993). Individuals in relationships: Development from infancy through adolescence. In D. C. Funder, R. D. Parke, C. Tomlinson-Keasey, & K. Widaman (Eds.), *Studying lives through time: Personality and development* (pp. 315–342). Washington, DC: American Psychological Association.

Sroufe, L. A., Coffino, B., & Carlson, E. A. (2010). Conceptualizing the role of early experience: Lessons from the Minnesota Longitudinal Study. *Developmental Review, 30*(1), 36–51.

Sroufe, L. A., Egeland, B., Carlson, E. A., & Collins, W. A. (2005). *The development of the person: The Minnesota study of risk and adaptation from birth to adulthood.* New York: Guilford Publications.

St. Clair, D., Xu, M., Wang, P., Yu, Y., Fang, Y., Zhang, F., et al. (2005). Rates of adult schizophrenia following prenatal exposure to the Chinese famine of 1959–1961. *Journal of the American Medical Association, 294,* 557–562.

Staff, J., Mortimer, J. T., & Uggen, C. (2004). Work and leisure in adolescence. In R. M. Lerner & L. Steinberg (Eds.), *Handbook of adolescent development* (2nd ed., pp. 429–450). Hoboken, NJ: Wiley.

Stahl, S. A., McKenna, M. C., & Pagnucco, J. R. (1994). The effects of whole-language instruction: An update and a reappraisal. *Educational Psychologist, 29,* 175–185.

Standing, E. M. (1957). *Maria Montessori: Her life and work.* New York: Plume.

Standley, J. M. (1998). Strategies to improve outcomes in critical care—the effect of music and multimodal stimulation on responses of premature infants in neonatal intensive care. *Pediatric Nursing, 24,* 532–538.

Starr, J. M., Deary, I. J., Lemmon, H., & Whalley, L. J. (2000). Mental ability age 11 years and health status age 77 years. *Age and Ageing, 29,* 523–528.

Staub, E. (1996). Cultural-societal roots of violence: The examples of genocidal violence and of contemporary youth violence in the United States. *American Psychologist, 51,* 117–132.

Stauder, J.E.A., Molenaar, P.C.M., & Van der Molen, M. W. (1993). Scalp topography of event-related brain potentials and cognitive transition during childhood. *Child Development, 64,* 769–788.

Steinberg, L. (2000, January 19). *Should juvenile offenders be tried as adults? A developmental perspective on changing legal policies.* Paper presented as part of a Congressional Research Briefing entitled "Juvenile Crime: Causes and Consequences." Washington, DC: Government Printing Office.

Steinberg, L. (2005). Psychological control: Style or substance? In J. Smetana (Ed.), *Changing boundaries of parental authority during adolescence: New directions for child and adolescent development, no. 108* (pp. 71–78). San Francisco: Jossey-Bass.

Steinberg, L. (2007). Risk taking in adolescence: New perspectives from brain and behavioral science. *Current Directions in Psychological Science, 16,* 55–59.

Steinberg, L., & Darling, N. (1994). The broader context of social influence in adolescence. In R. Silberstein & E. Todt (Eds.), *Adolescence in context* (pp. 25–45). New York: Springer.

Steinberg, L., Dornbusch, S. M., & Brown, B. B. (1992). Ethnic differences in adolescent achievement: An ecological perspective. *American Psychologist, 47,* 723–729.

Steinberg, L., Eisengard, B., & Cauffman, E. (2006). Patterns of competence and adjustment among adolescents from authoritative, authoritarian, indulgent, and neglectful homes: A replication in a sample of serious juvenile offenders. *Journal of Research on Adolescence, 16*(1), 47–58.

Steinberg, L., & Scott, E. S. (2003). Less guilty by reason of adolescence: Developmental immaturity, diminished responsibility, and the juvenile death penalty. *American Psychologist, 58,* 1009–1018.

Steinhausen, H. C. (2002). The outcome of anorexia nervosa in the 20th century. *American Journal of Psychiatry, 159,* 1284–1293.

Stennes, L. M., Burch, M. M., Sen, M. G., & Bauer, P. J. (2005). A longitudinal study of gendered vocabulary and communicative action in young children. *Developmental Psychology, 41,* 75–88.

Sternberg, R. J. (1985). *Beyond IQ: A triarchic theory of human intelligence.* New York: Cambridge University Press.

Sternberg, R. J. (1987, September 23). The use and misuse of intelligence testing: Misunderstanding meaning, users over-rely on scores. *Education Week,* pp. 22, 28.

Sternberg, R. J. (1993). *Sternberg Triarchic Abilities Test.* Unpublished manuscript.

Sternberg, R. J. (1997). The concept of intelligence and its role in lifelong learning and success. *American Psychologist, 52,* 1030–1037.

Sternberg, R. J. (2004). Culture and intelligence. *American Psychologist, 59,* 325–338.

Sternberg, R. J. (2005). There are no public policy implications: A reply to Rushton and Jensen (2005). *Psychology, Public Policy, and Law, 11,* 295–301.

Sternberg, R. J., & Clinkenbeard, P. (1995). A triarchic view of identifying, teaching, and assessing gifted children. *Roeper Review, 17,* 255–260.

Sternberg, R. J., Grigorenko, E. L., & Kidd, K. K. (2005). Intelligence, race, and genetics. *American Psychologist, 60,* 46–59.

Sternberg, R. J., Grigorenko, E. L., & Oh, S. (2001). The development of intelligence at midlife. In M. E. Lachman (Ed.), *Handbook of midlife development* (pp. 217–247). New York: Wiley.

Sternberg, R. J., Torff, B., & Grigorenko, E. L. (1998). Teaching triarchically improves school achievement. *Journal of Educational Psychology, 90*(3), 374–384.

Stevens, J. H., & Bakeman, R. (1985). A factor analytic study of the HOME scale for infants. *Developmental Psychology, 21,* 1106–1203.

Stevenson, D., Verter, J., Fanaroff, A., Oh, W., Ehrenkranz, R., Shankaran, S., et al. (2000). Sex differences of very low birthweight infants: The newborn male disadvantage. *Archives of Disease in Childhood: Fetal and Neonatal, 83*(3), 182–185.

Stevenson, H. W. (1995). Mathematics achievement of American students: First in the world by the year 2000? In C. A. Nelson (Ed.), *The Minnesota Symposia on Child Psychology: Vol. 28. Basic and applied perspectives on learning, cognition, and development* (pp. 131–149). Mahwah, NJ: Erlbaum.

Stevenson, H. W., Chen, C., & Lee, S. Y. (1993). Mathematics achievement of Chinese, Japanese, and American children: Ten years later. *Science, 258*(5081), 53–58.

Stevenson, H. W., Lee, S., Chen, C., & Lummis, M. (1990). Mathematics achievement of children in

China and the United States. *Child Development, 61*, 1053–1066.

Stevenson, H. W., Lee, S. Y., Chen, C., Stigler, J. W., Hsu, C. C., & Kitamura, S. (1990). Contexts of achievement: A study of American, Chinese, and Japanese children. *Monographs of the Society for Research in Child Development, 55*(1–2). [Serial No. 221].

Stevenson-Hinde, J., & Shouldice, A. (1996). Fearfulness: Developmental consistency. In A. J. Sameroff & M. M. Haith (Eds.), *The five- to seven-year shift: The age of reason and responsibility* (pp. 237–252). Chicago: University of Chicago Press.

Stewart, I. C. (1994, January 29). Two part message [Letter to the editor]. *New York Times,* p. A18.

Stewart, M. G., Glaze, D. G., Friedman, E. M., Smith, E. O., & Bautista, M. (2005). Quality of life and sleep study findings after adenotonsillectomy in children with obstructive sleep apnea. *Archives of Otolaryngology-Head and Neck Surgery, 131*, 308–314.

Stice, E., & Bearman, K. (2001). Body image and eating disturbances prospectively predict increases in depressive symptoms in adolescent girls: A growth curve analysis. *Developmental Psychology, 37*(5), 597–607.

Stice, E., Presnell, K., & Bearman, S. K. (2001). Relation of early menarche to depression, eating disorders, substance abuse, and comorbid psychopathology among adolescent girls. *Developmental Psychology, 37*, 608–619.

Stice, E., Presnell, K., Shaw, H., & Rohde, P. (2005). Psychological and behavioral risk factors for obesity onset in adolescent girls: A prospective study. *Journal of Consulting and Clinical Psychology, 73*, 195–202.

Stice, E., Spoor, S., Bohon, C., & Small, D. M. (2008). Relation between obesity and blunted striatal response to food is moderated by TaqIA A1 allele. *Science, 322*, 449–452.

Stillwell, R., & Sable, J. (2013). Public school graduates and dropouts from the common core of data: School year 2009–10: First look (Provisional Data) (NCES 2013-309). U.S. Department of Education. Washington, DC: National Center for Education Statistics. Retrieved April 4, 2013, from http://nces.ed.gov/pubsearch

Stipek, D. J., Gralinski, H., & Kopp, C. B. (1990). Self-concept development in the toddler years. *Developmental Psychology, 26*, 972–977.

Stoecker, J. J., Colombo, J., Frick, J. E., & Allen, J. R. (1998). Long- and short-looking infants' recognition of symmetrical and asymmetrical forms. *Journal of Experimental Child Psychology, 71*, 63–78.

Stoelhorst, M.S.J., Rijken, M., Martens, S. E., Brand, R., den Ouden, A. L., Wit, J.-M., et al. (2005). Changes in neonatology: Comparison of two cohorts of very preterm infants (gestational age <32 weeks): The Project on Preterm and Small for Gestational Age Infants 1983 and the Leiden Follow-up Project on Prematurity 1996–1997. *Pediatrics, 115*, 396–405.

Stoll, B. J., Hansen, N. I., Adams-Chapman, I., Fanaroff, A. A., Hintz, S. R., Vohr, B., et al. (2004). Neurodevelopmental and growth impairment among extremely low-birth-weight infants with neonatal infection. *Journal of the American Medical Association, 292*, 2357–2365.

Stone, W. L., McMahon, C. R., Yoder, P. J., & Walden, T. A. (2007). Early social-communicative and cognitive development of younger siblings of children with autism spectrum disorders.

Archives of Pediatric and Adolescent Medicine, 161, 384–390.

Stothard, K. J., Tennant, P.W.G., Bell, R., & Rankin, J. (2009). Maternal overweight and obesity and the risk of congenital anomalies: A systematic review and meta-analysis. *Journal of the American Medical Association, 301,* 636–650.

Stout, H. (2010, October 15). Toddlers' favorite toy: The iPhone. *The New York Times.* Retrieved from http://www.nytimes.com/2010/10/17/fashion/17TODDLERS.html?pagewanted=2&_r=1&emc=eta1

Strassberg, Z., Dodge, K. A., Pettit, G. S., & Bates, J. E. (1994). Spanking in the home and children's subsequent aggression toward kindergarten peers. *Development and Psychopathology, 6,* 445–461.

Strathearn, L., Li, J., Fonagy, P., & Montague, P. R. (2008). What's in a smile? Maternal brain responses to infant facial cues. *Pediatrics, 122,* 40–51.

Straus, M. A. (1994a). *Beating the devil out of them: Corporal punishment in American families.* San Francisco, CA: Jossey-Bass.

Straus, M. A. (1994b). Should the use of corporal punishment by parents be considered child abuse? In M. A. Mason & E. Gambrill (Eds.), *Debating children's lives: Current controversies on children and adolescents* (pp. 196–222). Newbury Park, CA: Sage.

Straus, M. A. (1999). Is it time to ban corporal punishment of children? *Canadian Medical Association Journal, 161,* 821–822.

Straus, M. A. (2010). Prevalence, societal causes, and trends in corporal punishment by parents in world perspective. *Law and Contemporary Problems, 73*(1), 1–30.

Straus, M. A., & Field, C. J. (2003). Psychological aggression by American parents: National data on prevalence, chronicity, and severity. *Journal of Marriage and Family, 65,* 795–808.

Straus, M. A., & Paschall, M. J. (1999, July). *Corporal punishment by mothers and children's cognitive development: A longitudinal study of two age cohorts.* Paper presented at the Sixth International Family Violence Research Conference, University of New Hampshire, Durham, NH.

Straus, M. A., & Stewart, J. H. (1999). Corporal punishment by American parents: National data on prevalence, chronicity, severity, and duration, in relation to child and family characteristics. *Clinical Child and Family Psychology Review, 2*(21), 55–70.

Straus, M. A., Sugarman, D. B., & Giles-Sims, J. (1997). Spanking by parents and subsequent antisocial behavior of children. *Archives of Pediatric and Adolescent Medicine, 151,* 761–767.

Strayer, D., & Drews, F. (2004). Profiles in driver distraction: Effects of cell phone conversations on younger and older drivers. *Human Factors, 4*(4), 640–649.

Strayer, D., & Drews, F. (2007). Cell-phone-induced driver distratction. *Current Directions in Psychological Science, 16*(3), 128–131.

Strayer, D. L., Drews, F. A., & Crouch, D. J. (2006). A comparison of the cell phone driver and the drunk driver. *Human Factors, 48*(2), 381–391.

Streissguth, A. P., Aase, J. M., Clarren, S. K., Randels, S. P., LaDue, R. A., & Smith, D. F. (1991). Fetal alcohol syndrome in adolescents and adults. *Journal of the American Medical Association, 265,* 1961–1967.

Streissguth, A. P., Bookstein, F. L., Barr, H. M., Sampson, P. D., O'Malley, K., & Young, J. K. (2004). Risk factors for adverse life outcomes in fetal alcohol syndrome and fetal alcohol effects.

Journal of Developmental & Behavioral Pediatrics, 25, 228–238.

Strenze, T. (2007). Intelligence and socioeconomic success: A meta-analytic review of longitudinal research. *Intelligence, 35*(5), 401–426.

Striano, T. (2004). Direction of regard and the still-face effect in the first year: Does intention matter? *Child Development, 75,* 468–479.

Striegel-Moore, R. H., & Bulik, C. (2007). Risk factors for eating disorders. *American Psychologist, 62,* 181–198.

Stright, A. D., Gallagher, K. C., & Kelley, K. (2008). Infant temperament moderates relations between maternal parenting in early childhood and children's adjustment in first grade. *Child Development, 79,* 186–200.

Strobel, A., Camoin, T.I.L., Ozata, M., & Strosberg, A. D. (1998). A leptin missense mutation associated with hypogonadism and morbid obesity. *Nature Genetics, 18,* 213–215.

Strohschein, L. (2005). Parental divorce and child mental health trajectories. *Journal of Marriage and Family, 67,* 1286–1300.

Strömland, K., & Hellström, A. (1996). Fetal alcohol syndrome—an ophthalmological and socioeducational prospective study. *Pediatrics, 97,* 845–850.

Stromwall, L. A., Granhag, P. A., & Landstrom, S. (2007). Children's prepared and unprepared lies: Can adults see through their strategies? *Applied Cognitive Psychology, 21,* 457–471.

Stubbs, M. L., Rierdan, J., & Koff, E. (1989). Developmental differences in menstrual attitudes. *Journal of Early Adolescence, 9*(4), 480–498.

Stueve, A., & O'Donnell, L. N. (2005). Early alcohol initiation and subsequent sexual and alcohol risk behaviors among urban youths. *American Journal of Public Health, 95,* 887–893.

Stuttering Foundation. (2006). *Stuttering: Straight talk for teachers* (Pub. No. 0125). Memphis, TN: Author.

Substance Abuse and Mental Health Services Administration (SAMHSA). (2004, October 22). Alcohol dependence or abuse and age at first use. *The NSDUH Report.* Retrieved December 18, 2004, from http://oas.samhsa.gov/2k4/ageDependence/ageDependence.htm

Substance Abuse and Mental Health Services Administration (SAMHSA), Office of Applied Studies. (2006). Academic performance and substance use among students aged 12 to 17: 2002, 2003, and 2004. *The NSDUH Report* (Issue 18). Rockville, MD: Author.

Sue, S., & Okazaki, S. (1990). Asian-American educational achievements: A phenomenon in search of an explanation. *American Psychologist 45*(8), 913–920.

Suicide—Part I. (1996, November). *The Harvard Mental Health Letter,* pp. 1–5.

Sun, Y. (2001). Family environment and adolescents' well-being before and after parents' marital disruption. *Journal of Marriage and the Family, 63,* 697–713.

Sundet, J., Barlaug, D., & Torjussen, T. (2004). The end of the Flynn Effect? A study of secular trends in mean intelligence test scores of Norwegian conscripts during half a century. *Intelligence, 32,* 349–362.

Suomi, S., & Harlow, H. (1972). Social rehabilitation of isolate-reared monkeys. *Developmental Psychology, 6,* 487–496.

Surkan, P. J., Stephansson, O., Dickman, P. W., & Cnattingius, S. (2004). Previous preterm and small-for-gestational-age births and the subsequent risk of stillbirth. *New England Journal of Medicine, 350,* 777–785.

Susman, E. J., & Rogol, A. (2004). Puberty and psychological development. In R. M. Lerner & L. Steinberg (Eds.), *Handbook of adolescent psychology* (2nd ed., pp. 15–44). Hoboken, NJ: Wiley.

Susman-Stillman, A., Kalkoske, M., Egeland, B., & Waldman, I. (1996). Infant temperament and maternal sensitivity as predictors of attachment security. *Infant Behavior and Development, 19,* 33–47.

Susser, E. S., & Lin, S. P. (1992). Schizophrenia after prenatal exposure to the Dutch hunger winter of 1944–1945. *Archives of General Psychiatry, 49,* 983–988.

Suzuki, L. A., & Valencia, R. R. (1997). Race-ethnicity and measured intelligence: Educational implications. *American Psychologist, 52,* 1103–1114.

Swain, I., Zelano, P., & Clifton, R. (1993). Newborn infants' memory for speech sounds retained over 24 hours. *Developmental Psychology, 29,* 312–323.

Swain, I. U., Zelazo, P. R., & Clifton, R. K. (1993). Newborn infants' memory for speech sounds retained over 24 hours. *Developmental Psychology, 29,* 312–323.

Swain, J. E., Tasgin, E., Mayes, L. C., Feldman, R., Constable, R. T., & Leckman, J. F. (2008). Maternal brain response to own baby-cry is affected by cesarean section delivery. *Journal of Child Psychology and Psychiatry, 49,* 1042–1052.

Swallen, K. C., Reither, E. N., Haas, S. A., & Meier, A. M. (2005). Overweight, obesity, and health-related quality of life among adolescents: The National Longitudinal Study of Adolescent Health. *Pediatrics, 115,* 340–347.

Swamy, G. K., Ostbye, T., & Skjaerven, R. (2008). Association of preterm birth with long-term survival, reproduction, and next-generation preterm birth. *Journal of the American Medical Association, 299,* 1429–1436.

Swan, S. H., Kruse, R. L., Liu, F., Barr, D. B., Drobnis, E. Z., Redmon, J. B., et al. (2003). Semen quality in relation to biomarkers of pesticide exposure. *Environmental Health Perspectives, 111,* 1478–1484.

Swanston, H. Y., Tebbutt, J. S., O'Toole, B. I., & Oates, R. K. (1997). Sexually abused children 5 years after presentation: A case-control study. *Pediatrics, 100,* 600–608.

Swarr, A. E., & Richards, M. H. (1996). Longitudinal effects of adolescent girls' pubertal development, perceptions of pubertal timing, and parental relations on eating problems. *Developmental Psychology, 32,* 636–646.

Swedo, S., Rettew, D. C., Kuppenheimer, M., Lum, D., Dolan, S., & Goldberger, E. (1991). Can adolescent suicide attemptors be distinguished from at-risk adolescents? *Pediatrics, 88*(3), 620–629.

Swingley, D. (2008). The roots of the early vocabulary in infants' learning from speech. *Current Directions in Psychological Science, 17,* 308–312.

Swingley, D., & Fernald, A. (2002). Recognition of words referring to present and absent objects by 24-month olds. *Journal of Memory and Language, 46,* 39–56.

Szaflarski, J. P., Holland, S. K., Schmithorst, V. J., & Weber-Byars, A. (2004). *An fMRI study of cerebral language lateralization in 121 children and adults.* Paper presented at the 56th Annual Meeting of the American Academy of Neurology, San Francisco, CA.

Szatmari, P., Paterson, A. D., Zwaigenbaum, L., Roberts, W., Brian, J., Liu, X.-Q., et al. (2007).

Mapping autism risk loci using genetic linkage and chromosomal rearrangements. *Nature Genetics, 39,* 319–328.

Szkrybalo, J., & Ruble, D. N. (1999). God made me a girl: Sex category constancy judgments and explanations revisited. *Developmental Psychology, 35,* 392–403.

Tackett, J. L., Krueger, R. F., Iacono, W. G., & McGue, M. (2005). Symptom-based subfactors of DSM-defined conduct disorder: Evidence for etiologic distinctions. *Journal of Abnormal Psychology, 114,* 483–487.

Tamis-LeMonda, C. S., Bornstein, M. H., & Baumwell, L. (2001). Maternal responsiveness and children's achievement of language milestones. *Child Development, 72*(3), 748–767.

Tamis-LeMonda, C. S., Shannon, J. D., Cabrera, N. J., & Lamb, M. E. (2004). Fathers and mothers at play with their 2- and 3-year-olds: Contributions to language and cognitive development. *Child Development, 75,* 1806–1820.

Tanda, G., Pontieri, F. E., & DiChiara, G. (1997). Cannabinoid and heroin activation of mesolimbic dopamine transmission by a common N1 opioid receptor mechanism. *Science, 276,* 2048–2050.

Tao, K.-T. (1998). An overview of only child family mental health in China. *Psychiatry and Clinical Neurosciences, 52*(Suppl.), S206–S211.

Tarkan, L. (2005, November 22). Screening for abnormal embryos can offer hope after heartbreak. *New York Times.*

Taveras, E. M., Capra, A. M., Braveman, P. A., Jensvold, N. G., Escobar, G. J., & Lieu, T. A. (2003). Clinician support and psychosocial risk factors associated with breastfeeding discontinuation. *Pediatrics, 112,* 108–115.

Taylor, C. A., Lee, S. J., Guterman, N. B., & Rice, J. C. (2010). Use of spanking for 3-year-old children and associated intimate partner aggression or violence. *Pediatrics, 126*(3), 415–424. doi: 10.1542/peds.2010-0314

Taylor, M. (1997). The role of creative control and culture in children's fantasy/reality judgments. *Child Development, 68,* 1015–1017.

Taylor, M., & Carlson, S. M. (1997). The relation between individual differences in fantasy and theory of mind. *Child Development, 68,* 436–455.

Taylor, M., Carlson, S. M., Maring, B. L., Gerow, L., & Charley, C. M. (2004). The characteristics and correlates of fantasy in school-age children: Imaginary companions, impersonation, and social understanding. *Developmental Psychology, 40,* 1173–1187.

Taylor, M., Cartwright, B. S., & Carlson, S. M. (1993). A developmental investigation of children's imaginary companions. *Developmental Psychology, 28,* 276–285.

Taylor, R. D., & Roberts, D. (1995). Kinship support in maternal and adolescent well-being in economically disadvantaged African-American families. *Child Development, 66,* 1585–1597.

Teachers Resisting Unhealthy Children's Entertainment (TRUCE). (2008). *Media action guide.* Retrieved April 15, 2010, from www.truceteachers.org/mediaviolence.html

Teachman, J. D., Tedrow, L. M., & Crowder, K. D. (2000). The changing demography of America's families. *Journal of Marriage and Family, 62,* 1234–1246.

Teasdale, T. W., & Owen, D. R. (2008). Secular declines in cognitive test scores: A reversal of the Flynn effect. *Intelligence, 36,* 121–126.

Temple, J. A., Reynolds, A. J., & Miedel, W. T. (2000). Can early intervention prevent high

school dropout? Evidence from the Chicago Child-Parent Centers. *Urban Education, 35*(1), 31–57.

Tenenbaum, H., & Leaper, C. (2002). Are parents' gender schemas related to their children's gender-related cognitions? A meta-analysis. *Developmental psychology, 38*(4), 615–630.

Tenenbaum, H. R., & Leaper, C. (2003). Parent-child conversations about science: The socialization of gender inequities. *Developmental Psychology, 39*(1), 34–47.

Termine, N. T., & Izard, C. E. (1988). Infants' responses to their mothers' expressions of joy and sadness. *Developmental Psychology, 24,* 223–229.

Tester, D. J., Carturan, E., Dura, M., Reiken, S., Wronska, A., Marks, A. R., & Ackerman, M. J. (2006, May). *Molecular and functional characterization of novel RyR2-encoded cardiac ryanodine receptor/calcium release channel mutations in sudden infant death syndrome.* Presentation at Heart Rhythm 2006, the 27th annual scientific sessions of the Heart Rhythm Society, Boston.

Test-tube baby: It's a girl. (1978, August 7). *Time,* p. 68.

Teti, D. M., & Ablard, K. E. (1989). Security of attachment and infant-sibling relationships: A laboratory study. *Child Development, 60,* 1519–1528.

Teti, D. M., Bo-Ram, K., Mayer, G., & Countermine, M. (2010). Maternal emotional availability at bedtime predicts infant sleep quality. *Journal of Family Psychology, 24*(3), 307–315.

Teti, D. M., Gelfand, D. M., Messinger, D. S., & Isabella, R. (1995). Maternal depression and the quality of early attachment: An examination of infants, preschoolers, and their mothers. *Developmental Psychology, 31,* 364–376.

Teti, D. M., Sakin, J. W., Kucera, E., Corns, K. M., & Eiden, R. D. (1996). And baby makes four: Predictors of attachment security among preschool-age firstborns during the transition to siblinghood. *Child Development, 67,* 579–596.

Thapar, A., Fowler, T., Rice, F., Scourfield, J., van den Bree, M., Thomas, H., Harold, G., & Hay, D. (2003). Maternal smoking during pregnancy and attention deficit hyperactivity disorder symptoms in offspring. *American Journal of Psychiatry, 160,* 1985–1989.

Thapar, A., Langley, K., Fowler, T., Rice, F., Turic, D., Whittinger, N., et al. (2005). Catechol O-methyltransferase gene variant and birth weight predict early-onset antisocial behavior in children with attention-deficit/hyperactivity disorder. *Archives of General Psychiatry, 62,* 1275–1278.

The Early College High School Initiative. (n.d.). Retrieved March 31, 2004, from www.earlycolleges.org

The First Test-tube baby. (1978, July 31). *Time,* pp. 58–70.

Thelen, E. (1995). Motor development: A new synthesis. *American Psychologist, 50*(2), 79–95.

Thelen, E., & Fisher, D. M. (1982). Newborn stepping: An explanation for a "disappearing" reflex. *Developmental Psychology, 18,* 760–775.

Thelen, E., & Fisher, D. M. (1983). The organization of spontaneous leg movements in newborn infants. *Journal of Motor Behavior, 15,* 353–377.

Thoma, S. J., & Rest., J. R. (1999). The relationship between moral decision making and patterns of consolidation and transition in moral judgment development. *Developmental Psychology, 35,* 323–334.

Thomas, A., & Chess, S. (1977). *Temperament and development.* New York: Brunner/Mazel.

Thomas, A., & Chess, S. (1984). Genesis and evolution of behavioral disorders: From infancy to early adult life. *American Journal of Orthopsychiatry, 141*(1), 1–9.

Thomas, A., Chess, S., & Birch, H. G. (1968). *Temperament and behavior disorders in children.* New York: New York University Press.

Thomas, W. P., & Collier, V. P. (1997). *School effectiveness for language minority students.* Washington, DC: National Clearinghouse for Bilingual Education.

Thomas, W. P., & Collier, V. P. (1998). Two languages are better than one. *Educational Leadership, 55*(4), 23–28.

Thompson, L. A., Goodman, D. C., Chang, C-H., & Stukel, T. A. (2005). Regional variation in rates of low birth weight. *Pediatrics, 116,* 1114–1121.

Thompson, P. M., Cannon, T. D., Narr, K. L., van Erp, T., Poutanen, V., Huttunen, M., et al. (2001). Genetic influences on brain structure. *Nature Neuroscience, 4,* 1253–1258.

Thompson, P. M., Giedd, J. N., Woods, R. P., MacDonald, D., Evans, A. C., & Toga, A. W. (2000). Growth patterns in the developing brain detected by using continuum mechanical tensor maps. *Nature, 404,* 190–193.

Thompson, R. A. (1990). Vulnerability in research: A developmental perspective on research risk. *Child Development, 61,* 1–16.

Thompson, R. A. (1991). Emotional regulation and emotional development. *Educational Psychology Review, 3,* 269–307.

Thompson, R. A. (1998). Early sociopersonality development. In W. Damon (Series Ed.) & N. Eisenberg (Vol. Ed.), *Handbook of child psychology: Vol. 3. Social, emotional, and personality development* (4th ed., pp. 25–104). New York: Wiley.

Thompson, R. A. (2011). Emotion and emotion regulation: Two sides of the developing coin. *Emotion Review, 3*(1), 53–61.

Thompson, W. W., Price, C., Goodson, B., Shay, D. K., Benson, P., Hinrichsen, V. L., et al. (2007). Early thimerosal exposure and neuropsychological outcomes at 7 to 10 years. *New England Journal of Medicine, 357,* 1281–1292.

Thomson, E., Mosley, J., Hanson, T. L., & McLanahan, S. S. (2001). Remarriage, cohabitation, and changes in mothering behavior. *Journal of Marriage and Family, 63,* 370–380.

Thorne, A., & Michaelieu, Q. (1996). Situating adolescent gender and self-esteem with personal memories. *Child Development, 67,* 1374–1390.

Tidwell, L. C., & Walther, J. B. (2002). Computer-mediated communication effects on disclosure, impressions, and interpersonal evaluations: Getting to know one another a bit at a time. *Human Communication Research, 28*(3), 317–348.

Tincoff, R., & Jusczyk, P. W. (1999). Some beginnings of word comprehension in 6-month-olds. *Psychological Science, 10,* 172–177.

Tisdale, S. (1988). The mother. *Hippocrates, 2*(3), 64–72.

Tita, A.T.N., Landon, M. B., Spong, C. Y., Lai, Y., Leveno, K. J., Varner, M. W., et al. (2009). Timing of elective repeat cesarean delivery at term and neonatal outcomes. *New England Journal of Medicine, 360,* 111–120.

Tither, J., & Ellis, B. (2008) Impact of fathers on daughter's age at menarche: A genetically and environmentally controlled sibling study. *Developmental Psychology, 44*(5), 1409–1420.

Toga, A., & Thompson, P. M. (2005). Genetics of brain structure and intelligence. *Annual Review of Neurology, 28,* 1–23.

Toga, A. W., Thompson, P. M., & Sowell, E. R. (2006). Mapping brain maturation. *Trends in Neurosciences, 29*(3), 148–159.

Tolan, P. H., Gorman-Smith, D., & Henry, D. B. (2003). The developmental ecology of urban males' youth violence. *Developmental Psychology, 39,* 274–291.

Tomasello, M. (2007). Cooperation and communication in the 2nd year of life. *Child Development Perspectives, 1,* 8–12.

Tomasello, M., Carpenter, M., & Liszkowski, U. (2007). A new look at infant pointing. *Child Development, 78,* 705–722.

Tomashek, K. M., Hsia, J., & Iyasu, S. (2003). Trends in postneonatal mortality attributable to injury, United States, 1988–1998. *Pediatrics, 111,* 1215–1218.

Torrance, E. P. (1966). *The Torrance Tests of Creative Thinking: Technical norms manual* (Research ed.). Princeton, NJ: Personnel Press.

Torrance, E. P. (1974). *The Torrance Tests of Creative Thinking: Technical norms manual.* Bensonville, IL: Scholastic Testing Service.

Torrance, E. P., & Ball, O. E. (1984). *Torrance Tests of Creative Thinking: Streamlined (revised) manual, Figural A and B.* Bensonville, IL: Scholastic Testing Service.

Totsika, V., & Sylva, K. (2004). The Home Observation for Measurement of the Environment revisited. *Child and Adolescent Mental Health, 9,* 25–35.

Townsend, N. W. (1997). Men, migration, and households in Botswana: An exploration of connections over time and space. *Journal of Southern African Studies, 23,* 405–420.

Trautner, H. M., Ruble, D. N., Cyphers, L., Kirsten, B., Behrendt, R., & Hartmann, P. (2005). Rigidity and flexibility of gender stereotypes in childhood: Developmental or differential? *Infant and Child Development, 14*(4), 365–381.

Tremblay, R. E., Nagin, D. S., Séguin, J. R., Zoccolillo, M., Zelazo, P. D., Boivin, M., et al. (2004). Physical aggression during early childhood: Trajectories and predictors. *Pediatrics, 114,* e43–e50.

Trimble, J. E., & Dickson, R. (2005). Ethnic gloss. In C. B. Fisher & R. M. Lerner (Eds.), *Encyclopedia of applied developmental science* (Vol. 1, pp. 412–415). Thousand Oaks, CA: Sage.

Trionfi, G., & Reese, E. (2009). A good story: Children with imaginary companions create richer narratives. *Child Development, 80*(4), 1301–1313.

Troiano, R. P. (2002). Physical inactivity among young people. *New England Journal of Medicine, 347,* 706–707.

Tronick, E. (1972). Stimulus control and the growth of the infant's visual field. *Perception and Psychophysics, 11,* 373–375.

Tronick, E., Als, H., Adamson, L., Wise, S., & Brazelton, T. B. (1978). The infant's response to entrapment between contradictory messages in face-to-face interaction. *Journal of the American Academy of Child Psychiatry, 17*(1), 1–13.

Tronick, E. Z. (1989). Emotions and emotional communication in infants. *American Psychologist, 44*(2), 112–119.

Tronick, E. Z., Morelli, G. A, & Ivey, P. (1992). The Efe forager infant and toddler's pattern of social relationships: Multiple and simultaneous. *Developmental Psychology, 28,* 568–577.

Troseth, G. L., & DeLoache, J. S. (1998). The medium can obscure the message: Young children's understanding of video. *Child Development, 69,* 950–965.

Troseth, G. L., Saylor, M. M., & Archer, A. H. (2006). Young children's use of video as a source of socially relevant information. *Child Development, 77,* 786–799.

Tryba, A. K., Peña, F., & Ramirez, J. M. (2006). Gasping activity in vitro: A rhythm dependent on 5-HT2A receptors. *Journal of Neuroscience, 26*(10), 2623–2634.

Tsao, F. M., Liu, H. M., & Kuhl, P. K. (2004). Speech perception in infancy predicts language development in the second year of life: A longitudinal study. *Child Development, 75,* 1067–1084.

Tsuchiya, K., Matsumoto, K., Miyachi, T., Tsujii, M., Nakamura, K., Takagai, S., et al. (2008). Paternal age at birth and high-functioning autistic-spectrum disorder in offspring. *British Journal of Psychiatry, 193,* 316–321.

Tupler, L. A., & De Bellis, M. D. (2006). Segmented hippocampal volute in children and adolescents with posttraumatic stress disorder. *Biological Psychiatry, 59,* 523–529.

Turati, C., Simion, F., Milani, I., & Umilta, C. (2002). Newborns' preference for faces: What is crucial? *Developmental Psychology, 38,* 875–882.

Turkheimer, E., Haley, A., Waldron, J., D'Onofrio, B., & Gottesman, I. I. (2003). Socioeconomic status modifies heritability of IQ in young children. *Psychological Science, 14,* 623–628.

Turkle, S. (2011). *Alone together: Why we expect more from technology and less from each other.* New York: Basic Books.

Turner, P. J., & Gervai, J. (1995). A multidimensional study of gender typing in preschool children and their parents: Personality, attitudes, preferences, behavior, and cultural differences. *Developmental Psychology, 31,* 759–772.

Turrisi, R., Wiersman, K. A., & Hughes, K. K. (2000). Binge-drinking-related consequences in college students: Role of drinking beliefs and mother-teen communication. *Psychology of Addictive Behaviors, 14*(4), 342–345.

Twenge, J. M. (2000). The age of anxiety? Birth cohort change in anxiety and neuroticism, 1952–1993. *Journal of Personality and Social Psychology, 79,* 1007–1021.

Twenge, J. M., Campbell, W. K., & Foster, C. A. (2003). Parenthood and marital satsifaction: A meta-analytic review. *Journal of Marriage and Family, 65,* 574–583.

UNAIDS. (2006). *Report on the global AIDS epidemic.* Geneva: Author.

United Nations Children's Fund (UNICEF). (2007). *The state of the world's children 2008: Child survival.* New York: Author.

United Nations Children's Fund. (UNICEF). (2008a). *State of the world's children: Child survival.* Retrieved from www.unicef.org/sowc08/

United Nations Children's Fund (UNICEF). (2008b). *State of the world's children 2009: Maternal and newborn health.* New York: Author.

United Nations Children's Fund (UNICEF). (2009). *Worldwide deaths of children under five decline, continuing positive trend.* Retrieved from www.unicef.org/childsurvival/index_51095.html

United Nations Children's Fund (UNICEF). (2012). *State of the World's Children 2012: Children in an Urban World.* New York: Author.

United Nations Children's Fund (UNICEF) and World Health Organization (WHO). (2004). *Low birthweight: Country, regional and global estimates.* New York: UNICEF.

United Nations High Commissioner for Human Rights. (1989, November 20). *Convention on* the *Rights of the Child*. General Assembly Resolution 44/25.

United States Breastfeeding Committee. (2002). *Benefits of breastfeeding*. Raleigh, NC: Author.

University of Virginia Health System. (2004). *How chromosome abnormalities happen: Meiosis, mitosis, maternal age, environment*. Retrieved September 16, 2004, from www.healthsystem.virginia.edu /UVAHealth/peds_genetics/happen.cfm

U.S. Bureau of Labor Statistics. (2008a, May 30). *Employment characteristics of families in 2007*. [News release]. Washington, DC: U.S. Department of Labor.

U.S. Bureau of Labor Statistics. (2008b). *Women in the labor force: A databook* (Report 1011). Washington, DC: U.S. Department of Labor.

U.S. Bureau of Labor Statistics. (2012, April 26). Employment characteristics of families in 2011. [News release]. Washington, DC: U.S. Department of Labor. (http://www.bls.gov /news.release/famee.nr0.htm).

U.S. Census Bureau. (2001, September 7; revised November 17, 2008). *Multigenerational households number 4 million according to Census 2000*. [Press release]. Retrieved January 23, 2009, from www .census.gov/Press-Release/www/releases/archives /aging_population/000374.html

U.S. Census Bureau. (2008a, August 14). *An older and more diverse nation by midcentury*. [Press release]. Retrieved November 8, 2008, from hwww/census.gov/PressRelease/www/releases /archives/population/012496.html

U.S. Census Bureau. (2008b). *Who's minding the kids? Child care arrangements: Spring 2005*. Washington, DC: U.S. Census Bureau, Housing and Household Economic Statistics Division, Fertility & Family Statistics Branch.

U.S. Census Bureau. (2009a). *Births, deaths, and life expectancy by country or area, Table 3*. Washington, DC: U.S. Census Bureau, International Data Base. Retrieved from www.census.gov/compendia /statab/2010/tables/10s1303.xls

U.S. Census Bureau. (2009b). School enrollment in the United States, 2007, Table 1: Enrollment status of the population 3 years old and over, by sex, age, race, Hispanic origin, foreign born, and foreign-born parentage: October 2007, Hispanic. *School enrollment—social and economic characteristics of students: October 2007*. Washington, DC: Author.

U.S. Census Bureau. (2009c). School enrollment in the United States, 2007, Table 3. Nursery and primary school enrollment of people 3 to 6 years old, by control of school, attendance status, age, race, Hispanic origin, mother's labor force status and education, and family income. *School enrollment—social and economic chrcateristics of students: October 2007*. Washington, DC: Author.

U.S. Census Bureau. (2009d). *Census bureau estimates nearly half of children under age 5 are minorities*. Retrieved November 20, 2012, from www.census.gov/newsroom/releases /archives/population/cb09-75.html

U.S. Department of Agriculture & U.S. Department of Health and Human Services (USDHHS). (2000). *Dietary guidelines for Americans* (5th ed.). [USDA Home and Garden Bulletin No. 232]. Washington, DC: U.S. Department of Agriculture.

U.S. Department of Agriculture & U.S. Department of Health and Human Services (USDHHS). (2005). *Dietary guidelines for Americans, 2005*. Washington, DC: U.S. Government Printing Office.

U.S. Department of Agriculture Economic Research Service. (2011). *Food security stats of U. S. households in 2011*. Retrieved April 1, 2013, from http:// www.ers.usda.gov/topics/food-nutrition-assistance /food-security-in-the-us/key-statistics-graphics .aspx#foodsecure

U.S. Department of Education Institute of Education Sciences. (2008). *K–12 practitioners' circle*. Retrieved April 15, 2010, from http://nces .ed.gov/practitioners/parents.asp

U.S. Department of Education, National Center for Education Statistics. (2004). *Early Childhood Longitudinal Study, Birth Cohort, Restricted-Use File (NCES 2004–093)*.

U.S. Department of Education, National Center for Education Statistics, Integrated Postsecondary Education Data System (IPEDS). (2010, Fall). *Graduate fields of study*. Retrieved from http://nces .ed.gov/programs/coe/indicator_gfs.asp

U.S. Department of Energy Office of Science, Office of Biological and Environmental Research, Human Genome Program. (2008a). *Human genome project information: Gene testing*. Retrieved December 22, 2008, from www.ornl.gov/sci /techresources/Human_Genome/medicine /genetest.shtml

U.S. Department of Energy Office of Science, Office of Biological and Environmental Research, Human Genome Program. (2008b). *Human genome project information: Gene therapy*. Retrieved August 16, 2008, from www.ornl.gov/sci /techresources/Human_Genome/medicine /genetherapy.shtml

U.S. Department of Health and Human Services (USDHHS). (1996a). *Health, United States, 1995* (DHHS Publication No. PHS 96–1232). Washington, DC: U.S. Government Printing Office.

U.S. Department of Health and Human Services (USDHHS). (1996b). *HHS releases study of relationship between family structure and adolescent substance abuse*. [Press release]. Retrieved from www.hhs.gov

U.S. Department of Health and Human Services (USDHHS). (1999a). *Blending perspectives and building common ground: A report to Congress on substance abuse and child protection*. Washington, DC: U.S. Government Printing Office.

U.S. Department of Health and Human Services (USDHHS). (1999b). *Mental health: A report of the Surgeon General*. Rockville, MD: U.S. Department of Health and Human Services, Substance Abuse and Mental Health Services Administration, National Institutes of Health, National Institute of Mental Health.

U.S. Department of Health and Human Services (USDHSS). (2001). *Oral health in America: A report of the Surgeon General* (NIH Publication No. 00-4713). Rockville, MD: U.S. Department of Health and Human Services, Insitute of Dental and Craniofacial Research.

U.S. Department of Health and Human Services (USDHHS). (2003a). *State funded prekindergarten: What the evidence shows*. Retrieved from http://aspe.hhs.gov/hsp/state-funded-pre -k/index.htm

U.S. Department of Health and Human Services (USDHHS). (2003b). *Strengthening Head Start: What the evidence shows*. Retrieved from http:// aspe.hhs.gov/hsp/StrengthenHeadStart03 /index.htm

U.S. Department of Health and Human Services (USDHHS), Administration on Children, Youth, and Families. (2006). *Child maltreatment 2004*. Washington, DC: U.S. Government Printing Office.

U.S. Department of Health and Human Services (USDHHS), Administration on Children, Youth and Families. (2008). *Child maltreatment 2006*. Washington, DC: U.S. Government Printing Office.

U.S. Department of Health and Human Services (USDHHS), Office on Child Abuse and Neglect. (2009). *Protecting children in families affected by substance abuse disorders*. Retrieved February 15, 2012, from www.childwelfare.gov/pubs /usermanuals/substanceuse/substanceuse.pdf

US Department of Health and Human Services (USDHHS). (2012). *Youth risk behavior surveillance: United States 2011*. MMWR Surveillance Summaries, 61(4): Table 65. Retrieved April 12, 2013, from http://www.cdc.gov/mmwr/pdf/ss /ss6104.pdf

U.S. National Library of Medicine. National Institutes of Health. Topiramate monograph. Retrieved February 5, 2012, from http://www .nlm.nih.gov/medlineplus/druginfo/meds /a697012.html.

U. S. Preventive Services Task Force. (2006). Screening for speech and language delay in preschool children: Recommendation statement. *Pediatrics, 117,* 497–501.

Vainio, S., Heikkiia, M., Kispert, A., Chin, N., & McMahon, A. P. (1999). Female development in mammals is regulated by Wnt-4 signaling. *Nature, 397,* 405–409.

Valadez-Meltzer, A., Silber, T. J., Meltzer, A. A., & D'Angelo, L. J. (2005). Will I be alive in 2005? Adolescent level of involvement in risk behaviors and belief in near-future death. *Pediatrics, 116,* 24–31.

Valkenburg, P., & Peter, J. (2009). Social consequences of the Internet for adolescents: A decade of research. *Current Directions in Psychological Science, 18*(11), 1–5.

Valkenburg, P. M., & Peter, J. (2007). Preadolescents and adolescents' online communication and their closeness to friends. *Developmental Psychology, 43,* 267–277.

Van, P. (2001). Breaking the silence of African American women: Healing after pregnancy loss. *Health Care Women International, 22,* 229–243.

Van den Boom, D. C. (1989). Neonatal irritability and the development of attachment. In G. A. Kohnstamm, J. E. Bates, & M. K. Rothbart (Eds.), *Temperament in childhood* (pp. 299–318). Chichester, UK: Wiley.

Van den Boom, D. (1994). The influence of temperament and mothering on attachment and exploration: An experimental manipulation of sensitive responsiveness among lower-class mothers with irritable infants. *Child Development, 65,* 1457–1477.

van Goozen, S., Fairchild, G., Snoek, H., & Harold, G. (2007). The evidence for a neurobiological model of childhood antisocial behavior. *Psychological Bulletin, 133,* 149–182.

van IJzendoorn, M. H., & Bakermans-Kranenburg, M. J. (2006). DRD47-repeat polymorphism moderates the association between maternal unresolved loss or trauma and infant disorganization. *Attachment & Human Development, 8*(4), 291–307.

van IJzendoorn, M. H., & Juffer, F. (2005). Adoption is a successful natural intervention enhancing adopted children's IQ and school performance. *Current Directions in Psychological Science, 14,* 326–330.

van IJzendoorn, M. H., Juffer, F., & Poelhuis, C.W.K. (2005). Adoption and cognitive development: A meta-analytic comparison of adopted and nonadopted children's IQ and school performance. *Psychological Bulletin, 131,* 301–316.

van IJzendoorn, M. H., & Kroonenberg, P. M. (1988). Cross-cultural patterns of attachment: A meta-analysis of the Strange Situation. *Child Development, 59,* 147–156.

van IJzendoorn, M. H., & Sagi, A. (1997). Cross-cultural patterns of attachment: Universal and contextual dimensions. In J. Cassidy & P. R. Shaver (Eds.), *Handbook on attachment theory and research* (pp. 713–734). New York: Guilford Press.

van IJzendoorn, M. H., & Sagi, A. (1999). Cross-cultural patterns of attachment: Universal and contextual dimensions. In J. Cassidy & P. R. Shaver (Eds.), *Handbook of attachment: Theory, research, and clinical applications* (pp. 713–734). New York: Guilford Press.

van IJzendoorn, M. H., Schuengel, C., & Bakermans-Kranenburg, M. J. (1999). Disorganized attachment in early childhood: Meta-analysis of precursors, concomitants, and sequelae. *Development and Psychopathology, 11,* 225–250.

van IJzendoorn, M. H., Vereijken, C.M.J.L., Bakermans-Kranenburg, M. J., & Riksen-Walraven, J. M. (2004). Assessing attachment security with the Attachment Q Sort: Meta-analytic evidence for the validity of the observer AQS. *Child Development, 75,* 1188.

Van Voorhis, B. J. (2007). In vitro fertilization. *New England Journal of Medicine, 356,* 379–386.

Vance, M. L., & Mauras, N. (1999). Growth hormone therapy in adults and children. *New England Journal of Medicine, 341*(16), 1206–1216.

Vandell, D. L. (2000). Parents, peer groups, and other socializing influences. *Developmental Psychology, 36,* 699–710.

Vandell, D. L., & Bailey, M. D. (1992). Conflicts between siblings. In C. U. Shantz & W. W. Hartup (Eds.), *Conflict in child and adolescent development* (pp. 242–269). New York: Cambridge University Press.

Vandewater, E. A., Rideout, V. J., Wartella, E. A., Huang, X., Lee, J. H., & Shim, M.-s. (2007). Digital childhood: Electronic media and technology use among infants, toddlers, and preschoolers. *Pediatrics, 119,* e1006–e1015.

Varendi, H., Porter, R. H., & Winberg J. (1997). Natural odour preferences of newborn infants change over time. *Acta Paediatrica,* 86, 985–990.

Vargha-Khadem, F., Gadian, D. G., Watkins, K. E., Connelly, A., Van Paesschen, W., & Mishkin, M. (1997). Differential effects of early hippocampal pathology on episodic and semantic memory. *Science, 277,* 376–380.

Vasilyeva, M., & Huttenlocher, J. (2004). Early development of scaling ability. *Developmental Psychology, 40,* 682–690.

Vasilyeva, M., Huttenlocher, J., & Waterfall, H. (2006). Effects of language intervention on syntactic skill levels in preschoolers. *Developmental Psychology, 42,* 164–174.

Vaughn, B. E., Stevenson-Hinde, J., Waters, E., Kotsaftis, A., Lefever, G. B., Shouldice, A., et al. (1992). Attachment security and temperament in infancy and early childhood: Some conceptual clarifications. *Developmental Psychology, 28,* 463–473.

Veenstra, R., Lindenberg, S., Oldehinkel, A. J., De Winter, A. F., Verhulst, F. C., & Ormel, J. (2005). Bullying and victimization in elementary schools: A comparison of bullies, victims, bully/victims, and uninvolved preadolescents. *Developmental Psychology, 41,* 672–682.

Ventura, A. K., & Mennella, J. A. (2011). Innate and learned preferences for sweet taste during childhood. *Current Opinion in Clinical Nutrition and Metabolic Care, 14*(4), 379–384.

Ventura, S. J., Mathews, T. J., & Hamilton, B. E. (2001). Births to teenagers in the United States, 1940–2000. *National Vital Statistics Reports, 49*(10). Hyattsville, MD: National Center for Health Statistics.

Vereecken, C., & Maes, L. (2000). Eating habits, dental care and dieting. In C. Currie, K. Hurrelmann, W. Settertobulte, R. Smith, & J. Todd (Eds.), *Health and health behaviour among young people: A WHO cross-national study (HBSC) international report* (pp. 83–96). [WHO Policy Series: Healthy Policy for Children and Adolescents, Series No. 1]. Copenhagen, Denmark: World Health Organization Regional Office for Europe.

Verlinsky, Y., Rechitisky, S., Verlinsky, O., Masciangelo, C., Lederer, K., & Kuliev, A. (2002). Preimplantation diagnosis for early onset Alzheimer disease caused by V717L mutation. *Journal of the American Medical Association, 287,* 1018–1021.

Verma, S., & Larson, R. (2003). Editors' notes. In S. Verma & R. Larson (Eds.), *Chromosomal congenital anomalies and residence near hazardous waste landfill sites. Lancet, 359,* 320–322.

Verschueren, K., Buyck, P., & Marcoen, A. (2001). Self-representations and socioemotional competence in young children: A 3-year longitudinal study. *Developmental Psychology, 37,* 126–134.

Verschueren, K., Marcoen, A., & Schoefs, V. (1996). The internal working model of the self, attachment, and competence in five-year-olds. *Child Development, 67,* 2493–2511.

Vgontzas, A. N., & Kales, A. (1999). Sleep and its disorders. *Annual Review of Medicine, 50,* 387–400.

Viner, R. M., & Cole, T. J. (2005). Television viewing in early childhood predicts adult body mass index. *Journal of Pediatrics, 147,* 429–435.

Vitaro, F., Tremblay, R. E., Kerr, M., Pagani, L., & Bukowski, W. M. (1997). Disruptiveness, friends' characteristics, and delinquency in early adolescence: A test of two competing models of development. *Child Development, 68,* 676–689.

Vittone, M. (2010, June 16). *Drowning doesn't look like drowning.* Retrieved from http://gcaptain.com/maritime/blog/drowning/?10981

Vohr, B. R., Wright, L. L., Poole, K., & McDonald, S. A. for the NICHD Neonatal Research Network Follow-up Study. (2005). Neurodevelopmental outcomes of extremely low birth weight infants <30 weeks' gestation between 1993 and 1998. *Pediatrics, 116,* 635–643.

Volkow, N., Wang, G-J., Newcorn, J., Telang, F., Solanto, M. V., Fowler, J. S., et al. (2007). Depressed dopamine activity in caudate and preliminary evidence of limbic involvement in adults with attention-deficit/hyperactivity disorder. *Archives of General Psychiatry, 64,* 932–940.

Vondra, J. I., & Barnett, D. (1999). A typical attachment in infancy and early childhood among children at developmental risk. *Monographs of the Society for Research in Child Development, 64*(3). [Serial No. 258].

von Gontard, A., Heron, J., & Joinson, C. (2011). Family history of nocturnal enuresis and urinary incontinence: Results from a large epidemiological study. *The Journal of Urology, 185*(6), 2303–2307.

von Hofsten, C. (2004). An action perspective on motor development. *Cognitive Sciences, 8*(1), 266–272.

Vosniadou, S. (1987). Children and metaphors. *Child Development, 58,* 870–885.

Votruba-Drzal, E., Li-Grining, C. R., & Maldonado-Carreno, C. (2008). A developmental perspective on full- versus part-day kindergarten and children's academic trajectories through fifth grade. *Child Development, 79,* 957–978.

Vrijenhoek, T., Buizer-Voskamp, J. E., van der Stelt, I., Strengman, E., Sabatti, C., van Kessel, A. G., et al. (2008). Recurrent CNVs disrupt three candidate genes in schizophrenia patients. *American Journal of Human Genetics, 83,* 504–510.

Vrijheld, M., Dolk, H., Armstrong, B., Abramsky, L., Bianchi, F., Fazarinc, I., et al. (2002). Chromosomal congenital anomalies and residence near hazardous waste landfill sites. *The Lancet, 359*(9303), 320–322.

Vuchinich, S., Angelelli, J., & Gatherum, A. (1996). Context and development in family problem solving with preadolescent children. *Child Development, 67,* 1276–1288.

Vuoksimaa, E., Koskenvuo, M., Rose, R. J., & Kaprio, J. (2009). Origins of handedness: A nationwide study of 30,161 adults. *Neuropsychologia, 7*(5), 1294–1301.

Vuori, L., Christiansen, N., Clement, J., Mora, J., Wagner, M., & Herrera, M. (1979). Nutritional supplementation and the outcome of pregnancy: 2. Visual habitation at 15 days. *Journal of Clinical Nutrition, 32,* 463–469.

Vygotsky, L. S. (1962). *Thought and language.* Cambridge, MA: MIT Press. (Original work published 1934)

Vygotsky, L. S. (1978). *Mind in society: The development of higher psychological processes.* Cambridge, MA: Harvard University Press.

Waber, D. P., De Moor, C., Forbes, P. W., Almli, C. R., Botteron, K. N., Leonard, G., et al. (2007). The NIH MRI study of normal brain development: Performance of a population based sample of healthy children aged 6 to 18 years on a neuropsychological battery. *Journal of the International Neuropsychological Society, 13*(5), 729–746.

Wadsworth, M. E., Raviv, T., Reinhard, C., Wolff, B., Santiago, C. D., & Einhorn, L. (2008). An indirect effects model of the association between poverty and child functioning: The role of children's poverty related stress. *The Journal of Loss and Trauma: International Perspectives on Stress and Coping, 13*(2–3), 156–185.

Wadsworth, M. E., & Santiago, C. D. (2008). Risk and resiliency processes in ethnically diverse families in poverty. *Journal of Family Psychology, 22,* 299–410.

Wahlbeck, K., Forsen, T., Osmond, C., Barker, D.J.P., & Erikkson, J. G. (2001). Association of schizophrenia with low maternal body mass index, small size at birth, and thinness during childhood. *Archives of General Psychiatry, 58,* 48–55.

Wainright, J. L., Russell, S. T., & Patterson, C. J. (2004). Psychosocial adjustment, school outcomes, and romantic relationships of adolescents with same-sex parents. *Child Development, 75,* 1886–1898.

Waisbren, S. E., Albers, S., Amato, S., Ampola, M., Brewster, T. G., Demmer, L., et al. (2003). Effect of expanded newborn screening for biochemical disorders on child outcomes and parental stress. *Journal of the American Medical Association, 290,* 2564–2572.

Wakefield, M., Reid, Y., Roberts, L., Mullins, R., & Gillies, P. (1998). Smoking and smoking cessation among men whose partners are pregnant: A qualitative study. *Social Science and Medicine, 47,* 657–664.

Waknine, Y. (2006). Highlights from MMWR: Prevalence of U.S. birth defects and more. *Medscape.* Retrieved January 9, 2006, from www.medscape.com/viewarticle/521056

Wald, N. J. (2004). Folic acid and the prevention of neural-tube defects. *New England Journal of Medicine, 350,* 101–103.

Waldman, I. D. (1996). Aggressive boys' hostile perceptual and response biases: The role of attention and impulsivity. *Child Development, 67,* 1015–1033.

Walk, R. D., & Gibson, E. J. (1961). A comparative and analytical study of visual depth perception. *Psychology Monographs, 75*(15).

Waller, M. W., Hallfors, D. D., Halpern, C. T., Iritani, B., Ford, C. A., & Guo, G. (2006). Gender differences in associations between depressive symptoms and patterns of substance use and risky sexual behavior among a nationally representative sample of U.S. adolescents. *Archives of Women's Mental Health, 9,* 139–150.

Waller, N. G., Kojetin, B. A., Bouchard, T. J. Jr., Lykken, D. T., & Tellegen, A. (1990). Genetic and environmental influences on religious interests, attitudes, and values: A study of twins reared apart and together. *Psychological Science, 1*(2), 138–142.

Wallerstein, J., & Corbin, S. B. (1999). The child and the vicissitudes of divorce. In R. M. Galatzer-Levy & L. Kraus (Eds.), *The scientific basis of child custody decisions* (pp. 73–95). New York: Wiley.

Wallerstein, J. S., Lewis, J. M., & Blakeslee, S. (2000). *The unexpected legacy of divorce: A 25-year landmark study.* New York: Hyperion.

Walma van der Molen, J. (2004). Violence and suffering in television news: Toward a broader conception of harmful television content for children. *Pediatrics, 113,* 1771–1775.

Walsh, T., McClellan, J. M., McCarthy, S. E., Addington, A. M., Pierce, S. B., Cooper, G. M., et al. (2008). Rare structural variants disrupt multiple genes in neurodevelopmental pathways in schizophrenia. *Science, 320,* 539–43.

Wang, D. W., Desai, R. R., Crotti, L., Arnestad, M., Insolia, R., Pedrazzini, M., et al. (2007). Cardiac sodium channel dysfunction in sudden infant death syndrome. *Circulation, 115,* 368–376.

Wang, H., Parry, S., Macones, G., Sammel, M. D., Kuivaniemi, H., Tromp, G., et al. (2006). A functional SNP in the promoter of the SERPINH1 gene increases risk of preterm premature rupture of membranes in African Americans. *Proceedings of the National Academy of Sciences, USA, 103,* 13463–13467.

Wang, Q. (2004). The emergence of cultural self-constructs: Autobiographical memory and self-description in European American and Chinese children. *Developmental Psychology, 40,* 3–15.

Wang, Y., & Lobstein, T. (2006). Worldwide trends in childhood overweight and obesity. *International Journal of Obesity, 1*(1), 11–25.

Wardle, J., Robb, K. A., Johnson, F., Griffith, J., Brunner, E., Power, C., & Tovèe, M. (2004). Socioeconomic variation in attitudes to eating and weight in female adolescents. *Health Psychology, 23,* 275–282.

Warneken, F., & Tomasello, M. (2006). Altruistic helping in human infants and young chimpanzees. *Science, 311,* 1301–1303.

Warneken, F., & Tomasello, M. (2008). Extrinsic rewards undermine altruistic tendencies in 20-month-olds. *Developmental Psychology, 44,* 1785–1788.

Warner, J. (2008, January 4). Domestic disturbances. *New York Times.* Retrieved February 11, 2008, from http://warner.blogs.nytimes.com/2008/01/03/outsourced-wombs/

Wasik, B. H., Ramey, C. T., Bryant, D. M., & Sparling, J. J. (1990). A longitudinal study of two early intervention strategies: Project CARE. *Child Development, 61,* 1682–1696.

Watamura, S. E., Donzella, B., Alwin, J., & Gunnar, M. R. (2003). Morning-to-afternoon increases in cortisol concentrations for infants and toddlers at child care: Age differences and behavioral correlates. *Child Development, 74,* 1006–1020.

Waters, E., & Deane, K. E. (1985). Defining and assessing individual differences in attachment relationships: Methodology and the organization of behavior in infancy and early childhood. *Monographs of the Society for Research in Child Development, 50,* 41–65.

Waters, E., Wippman, J., & Sroufe, L. A. (1979). Attachment, positive affect, and competence in the peer group: Two studies in construct validation. *Child Development, 50,* 821–829.

Waters, K. A., Gonzalez, A., Jean, C., Morielli, A., & Brouillette, R. T. (1996). Face-straight-down and face-near-straightdown positions in healthy prone-sleeping infants. *Journal of Pediatrics, 128,* 616–625.

Watkins, M., Rasmussen, S. A., Honein, M. A., Botto, L. D., & Moore, C. A. (2003). Maternal obesity and risk for birth defects. *Pediatrics, 111,* 1152–1158.

Watson, A. C., Nixon, C. L., Wilson, A., & Capage, L. (1999). Social interaction skills and theory of mind in young children. *Developmental Psychology, 35*(2), 386–391.

Watson, J. B., & Rayner, R. (1920). Conditioned emotional reactions. *Journal of Experimental Psychology, 3,* 1–14.

Weese-Mayer, D. E., Berry-Kravis, E. M., Maher, B. S., Silvestri, J. M., Curran, M. E., & Marazita, M. L. (2004). Sudden infant death syndrome: Association with a promoter polymorphism of the serotonin transporter gene. *American Journal of Medical Genetics, 117A,* 268–274.

Wegienka, G., Johnson, C. C., Havstad, S., Ownby, D. R., Nicholas, C., & Zoratti, E. M. (2011). Lifetime dog and cat exposure and dog- and cat-specific sensitization at age 18 years. *Clinical & Experimental Allergy, 41*(7), 979–986.

Wegman, M. E. (1992). Annual summary of vital statistics—1991. *Pediatrics, 90,* 835–845.

Weichold, K., Silbereisen, R. K., & Schmitt-Rodermund, E. (2003). Short-term and long-term consequences of early vs. late physical maturation in adolescents. In C. Haywood (Ed.), *Puberty and Psychopathology.* New York: Cambridge University Press.

Weinberg, M. K., & Tronick, E. Z. (1996). Infant affective reactions to the resumption of maternal interaction after the still-face. *Child Development, 67*(3), 905–914.

Weinberger, B., Anwar, M., Hegyi, T., Hiatt, M., Koons, A., & Paneth, N. (2000). Antecedents and neonatal consequences of low Apgar scores in preterm newborns. *Archives of Pediatric and Adolescent Medicine, 154,* 294–300.

Weinberger, D. R. (2001, March 10). A brain too young for good judgment. *New York Times.* Retrieved from www.nytimes.com/2001/03/10/opinion/10WEIN.html?ex_985250309&ei_1&en_995bc03f7a8c7207

Weinraub, M. (1978). The effects of height on infants' social responses to unfamiliar persons. *Child Development, 49*(3), 598–603.

Weinreb, L., Wehler, C., Perloff, J., Scott, R., Hosmer, D., Sagor, L., & Gundersen, C. (2002). Hunger: Its impact on children's health and mental health. *Pediatrics, 110,* 816.

Weinstock, H., Berman, S., & Cates, W., Jr. (2004). Sexually transmitted diseases among American youth: Incidence and prevalence estimates, 2000. *Perspectives on Sexual and Reproductive Health, 36,* 6–10.

Weisner, T. S. (1993). Ethnographic and ecocultural perspectives on sibling relationships. In Z. Stoneman & P. W. Berman (Eds.), *The effects of mental retardation, visibility, and illness on sibling relationships* (pp. 51–83). Baltimore, MD: Brooks.

Weiss, B., Amler, S., & Amler, R. W. (2004). Pesticides. *Pediatrics, 113,* 1030–1036.

Weiss, B., Dodge, K. A., Bates, J. E., & Pettit, G. S. (1992). Some consequences of early harsh discipline: Child aggression and a maladaptive social information processing style. *Child Development, 63,* 1321–1335.

Weiss, L. A., Shen, Y., Korn, J. M., Arking, D. E., Miller, D. T., Fossdal, R., et al. (2008). Association between microdeletion and microduplication at 16p11.2 and autism. *New England Journal of Medicine, 358,* 667–675.

Weissman, M. M., Warner, V., Wickramaratne, P. J., & Kandel, D. B. (1999). Maternal smoking during pregnancy and psychopathology in offspring followed to adulthood. *Journal of the American Academy of Child and Adolescent Psychiatry, 38,* 892–899.

Weisz, J. R., McCarty, C. A., & Valeri, S. M. (2006). Effects of psychotherapy for depression in children and adolescents: A meta-analysis. *Psychological Bulletin, 132,* 132–149.

Weisz, J. R., Weiss, B., Han, S. S., Granger, D. A., & Morton, T. (1995). Effects of psychotherapy with children and adolescents revisited: A meta-analysis of treatment outcome studies. *Psychological Bulletin, 117*(3), 450–468.

Welch-Ross, M. K., & Schmidt, C. R. (1996). Gender-schema development and children's story memory: Evidence for a developmental model. *Child Development, 67,* 820–835.

Wellman, H. M., & Cross, D. (2001). Theory of mind and conceptual change. *Child Development, 72,* 702–707.

Wellman, H. M., Cross, D., & Watson, J. (2001). Meta-analysis of theory-of-mind development: The truth about false belief. *Child Development, 72,* 655–684.

Wellman, H. M., & Liu, D. (2004). Scaling theory-of-mind tasks. *Child Development, 75,* 523–541.

Wellman, H. M., Lopez-Duran, S., LaBounty, J., & Hamilton, B. (2008). Infant attention to intentional action predicts preschool theory of mind. *Developmental Psychology, 44,* 618–623.

Wellman, H. M., & Woolley, J. D. (1990). From simple desires to ordinary beliefs: The early development of everyday psychology. *Cognition, 35,* 245–275.

Wells, G. (1985). Preschool literacy-related activities and success in school. In D. R. Olson, N. Torrence, & A. Hilyard (Eds.), *Literacy, language, and learning* (pp. 229–255). New York: Cambridge University Press.

Wells, J., & Lewis, L. (2006). *Internet access in the U.S. public schools and classrooms: 1990–2005*

(NCES 2007-020). Washington, DC: National Center for Education Statistics.

Weng, X., Odouli, R., & Li, D.-K. (2008). Maternal caffeine consumption during pregnancy and the risk of miscarriage: A prospective cohort study. *American Journal of Obstetrics and Gynecology, 198*(3), e279–e287.

Wentworth, N., Benson, J. B., & Haith, M. M. (2000). The development of infants' reaches for stationary and moving targets. *Child Development, 71,* 576–601.

Wentzel, K. R. (2002). Are effective teachers like good parents? Teaching styles and student adjustment in early adolescence. *Child Development, 73,* 287–301.

Werker, J. F. (1989). Becoming a native listener. *American Scientist, 77,* 54–59.

Werker, J. F., Pegg, J. E., & McLeod, P. J. (1994). A cross-language investigation of infant preference for infant-directed communication. *Infant Behavior and Development, 17,* 323–333.

Werner, E., Bierman, L., French, F. E., Simonian, K., Conner, A., Smith, R., & Campbell, M. (1968). Reproductive and environmental casualties: A report on the 10-year follow-up of the children of the Kauai pregnancy study. *Pediatrics, 42,* 112–127.

Werner, E., & Smith, R. S. (2001). *Journeys from childhood to midlife.* Ithaca, NY: Cornell University Press.

Werner, E. E. (1985). Stress and protective factors in children's lives. In A. R. Nichol (Ed.), *Longitudinal studies in child psychology and psychiatry* (pp. 335–355). New York: Wiley.

Werner, E. E. (1987, July 15). *Vulnerability and resiliency: A longitudinal study of Asian Americans from birth to age 30.* Invited address at the ninth biennial meeting of the International Society for the Study of Behavioral Development, Tokyo, Japan.

Werner, E. E. (1989). Children of the garden island. *Scientific American, 260*(4), 106–111.

Werner, E. E. (1993). Risk and resilience in individuals with learning disabilities: Lessons learned from the Kauai longitudinal study. *Learning Disabilities Research and Practice, 8,* 28–34.

Werner, E. E. (1995). Resilience in development. *Current Directions in Psychological Science, 4*(3), 81–85.

Westby, E. L., & Dawson, V. L. (1995). Creativity: Asset or burden in the classroom. *Creativity Research Journal, 8*(1), 1–10.

Westen, D. (1998). The scientific legacy of Sigmund Freud: Toward a psychodynamically informed psychological science. *Psychological Bulletin, 124,* 333–371.

Wexler, A. (2008, August 12). Groundbreaking genetic non-discrimination bill signed into law. *HemOnc Today: Clinical News in Oncology and Hematology.* Retrieved December 14, 2008, from www.hemonctoday.com/article.aspx?rid=30268

Wexler, I. D., Branski, D., & Kerem, E. (2006). War and children. *Journal of the American Medical Association, 296,* 579–581.

Whalley, L. J., & Deary, I. J. (2001). Longitudinal cohort study of childhood IQ and survival up to age 76. *British Medical Journal, 322,* 819.

Whalley, L. J., Starr, J. M., Athawes, R., Hunter, D., Pattie, A., & Deary, I. J. (2000). Childhood mental ability and dementia. *Neurology, 55,* 1455–1459.

Whitaker, R. C., Wright, J. A., Pepe, M. S., Seidel, K. D., & Dietz, W. H. (1997). Predicting obesity in young adulthood from childhood and parental obesity. *New England Journal of Medicine, 337,* 869–873.

White, A. (2001). *Alcohol and adolescent brain development.* Retrieved from www.duke.edu/~amwhite/alc_adik_pf.html

White, B. L. (1971, October). *Fundamental early environmental influences on the development of competence.* Paper presented at the third Western Symposium on Learning: Cognitive Learning, Western Washington State College, Bellingham, WA.

White, B. L., Kaban, B., & Attanucci, J. (1979). *The origins of human competence.* Lexington, MA: Heath.

Whitehurst, G. J., Falco, F. L., Lonigan, C. J., Fischel, J. E., DeBaryshe, B. D., Valdez-Menchaca, M. D., & Caulfield, M. (1988). Accelerating language development through picture book reading. *Developmental Psychology, 24,* 552–559.

Whitehurst, G. J., & Lonigan, C. J. (1998). Child development and emergent literacy. *Child Development, 69,* 848–872.

Whitehurst, G. J., & Lonigan, C. J. (2001). Emergent literacy: Development from prereaders to readers. In S. B. Neuman & D. K. Dickinson (Eds.) *Handbook of Early Literacy Research* (pp. 11–29). New York: Guilford Press.

Whyatt, R. M., Rauh, V., Barr, D. B., Camann, D. E., Andrews, H. F., Garfinkel, R., et al. (2004). Prenatal insecticide exposures and birth weight and length among an urban minority cohort. *Environmental Health Perspectives, 112*(110), 1125–1132.

Widaman, K. F. (2009). Phenylketonuria in children and mothers: Genes, environment, behavior. *Current Directions in Psychological Science, 18*(1), 48–52.

Wilcox, A. J., Dunson, D., & Baird, D. D. (2000). The timing of the "fertile window" in the menstrual cycle: Day specific estimates from a prospective study. *British Medical Journal, 321,* 1259–1262.

Wildsmith, E., Schelar, E., Peterson, K., & Manlove, J. (2010) *Sexually transmitted diseases among young adults: Prevalence, perceived risk and risk-taking behaviors* (Publication 2010-10). Retrieved from http://www.childtrends.org/Files/Child_Trends-2010_05_01_RB_STD.pdf.

Willard, N. E. (2006). *Cyberbullying and cyberthreats.* Eugene, OR: Center for Safe and Responsible Internet Use.

Williams, D. L., Goldstein, G., & Minshew, N. J. (2006). Neuropsychologic functioning in children with autism: Further evidence for disordered complex information-processing. *Child Neuropsychology: A Journal on Normal and Abnormal Development in Childhood and Adolescence, 12*(4–5), 279–298.

Williams, E. R., & Caliendo, M. A. (1984). *Nutrition: Principles, issues, and applications.* New York: McGraw-Hill.

Williams, J., Wake, M., Hesketh, K., Maher, E., & Waters, E. (2005). Health-related quality of life of overweight and obese children. *Journal of the American Medical Association, 293,* 70–76.

Williams, S., O'Connor, E., Eder, M., & Witlock, E. (2009). Screening for child and adolescent depression in primary care settings: A systematic evidence review for the U.S. Preventive Services Task Force. *Pediatrics, 123*(4), 716–735.

Willinger, M., Hoffman, H. T., & Hartford, R. B. (1994). Infant sleep position and risk for sudden infant death syndrome: Report of meeting held January 13 and 14, 1994. *Pediatrics, 93,* 814–819.

Willinger, M., Ko, C.-W., Hoffman, H. J., Kessler, R. C., & Corman, M. J. (2003). Trends in infant bed sharing in the United States, 1993–2000: The National Infant Sleep Position Study.

Archives of Pediatrics & Adolescent Medicine, 157, 43–49.

Wilson, B. J. (2008). Media and children's aggression, fear, and altruism. *Future of Children, 18,* 87–118.

Wilson, E. O. (1975). *Sociobiology: The new synthesis.* Cambridge, MA: Harvard University Press.

Wilson, G. T., Grilo, C. M., & Vitousek, K. M. (2007). Psychological treatment of eating disorders. *American Psychologist, 62,* 199–216.

Wilson, K., & Ryan, V. (2001). Helping parents by working with their children in individual child therapy. *Child and Family Social Work, 6,* 209–217. [Special issue].

Wilson-Costello, D., Friedman, H., Minich, N., Siner, B., Taylor, G., Schluchter, M., & Hack, M. (2007). Improved neurodevelopmental outcomes for extremely low birth weight infants in 2000–2002. *Pediatrics, 119,* 37–45.

Winner, E. (1997). Exceptionally high intelligence and schooling. *American Psychologist, 52*(10), 1070–1081.

Winner, E. (2000). The origins and ends of giftedness. *American Psychologist, 55,* 159–169.

Wismer Fries, A. B., Ziegler, T., Kurian, J., Jacoris, S., & Pollak, S. (2005, November 22). Early experience in humans is associated with changes in neuropeptides critical for regulating social behavior. *Proceedings of the National Academy of Sciences of the United States of America, 102*(47), 17237–17240.

Wisner, K. L., Chambers, C., & Sit, D.K.Y. (2006). Postpartum depression: A major public health problem. *Journal of the American Medical Association, 296,* 2616–2618.

Woese, C. (1998). Evolution: The universal ancestor. *Proceedings of the National Academy of Sciences, 95,* 6854–6859.

Wolchik, S. A., Sandler, I. N., Millsap, R. E., Plummer, B. A., Greene, S. M., Anderson, E. R., et al. (2002). Six year follow-up of a randomized, controlled trial of preventive interventions for children of divorce. *Journal of the American Medical Association, 288,* 1874–1881.

Wolff, P. H. (1963). Observations on the early development of smiling. In B. M. Foss (Ed.), *Determinants of infant behavior* (Vol. 2). London: Methuen.

Wolff, P. H. (1969). The natural history of crying and other vocalizations in early infancy. In B. M. Foss (Ed.), *Determinants of infant behavior* (Vol. 4, pp. 81–109). London: Methuen.

Wolfson, A. R., Carskadon, M. A., Mindell, J. A., & Drake, C. *The National Sleep Foundation: Sleep in America poll. 2006.* Retrieved March 28, 2013, from www.sleepfoundation.org/sites/default/files/2006_summary_of_findings.pdf

Wolraich, M. L., Wibbelsman, C. J., Brown, T. E., Evans, S. W., Gotlieb, E. M., Knight, J. R., et al. (2005). Attention-deficit/hyperactivity disorder among adolescents: A review of the diagnosis, treatment, and clinical implications. *Pediatrics, 115,* 1734–1746.

Wong, C. A., Scavone, B. M., Peaceman, A. M., McCarthy, R. J., Sullivan, J. T., Diaz, N. T., et al. (2005). The risk of cesarean delivery with neuraxial analgesia given early versus late in labor. *New England Journal of Medicine, 352,* 655–665.

Wong, C. K., Murray, M. L., Camilleri-Novak, D., & Stephens, P. (2004). Increased prescribing trends of paediatric psychotropic medications. *Archives of the Diseases of Children, 89,* 1131–1132.

Wong, H., Gottesman, I., & Petronis, A. (2005). Phenotypic differences in genetically identical organisms: The epigenetic perspective. *Human Molecular Genetics, 14*(Review Issue 1), R11–R18.

Wong, M. M., Nigg, J. T., Zucker, R. A., Puttler, L. I., Fitzgerald, H. E., Jester, J. M., Glass, J. M., & Adams, K. (2006). Behavioral control and resiliency in the onset of alcohol and illicit drug use: A prospective study from preschool to adolescence. *Child Development, 77,* 1016–1033.

Wood, D. (1980). Teaching the young child: Some relationships between social interaction, language, and thought. In D. Olson (Ed.), *The social foundations of language and thought* (pp. 280–296). New York: Norton.

Wood, D., Bruner, J., & Ross, G. (1976). The role of tutoring in problem solving. *Journal of Child Psychiatry and Psychology, 17,* 89–100.

Wood, J. J., & Repetti, R. L. (2004). What gets dad involved? A longitudinal study of change in parental child caregiving involvement. *Journal of Family Psychology, 18*(1) 237–249.

Wood, R. M., & Gustafson, G. E. (2001). Infant crying and adults' anticipated caregiving responses: Acoustic and contextual influences. *Child Development, 72,* 1287–1300.

Wood, W., & Eagly, A. (2002). A cross-cultural analysis of the behavior of women and men: Implications for the origins of sex differences. *Psychological Bulletin, 128,* 699–727.

Woodruff, T. J., Axelrad, D. A., Kyle, A. D., Nweke, O., Miller, G. G., & Hurley, B. J. (2004). Trends in environmentally related childhood illnesses. *Pediatrics, 113,* 1133–1140.

Woodward, A. L., Markman, E. M., & Fitzsimmons, C. M. (1994). Rapid word learning in 13- and 18-month olds. *Development Psychology, 30,* 553–566.

Woolley, J. D. (1997). Thinking about fantasy: Are children fundamentally different thinkers and believers from adults? *Child Development, 68*(6), 991–1011.

Woolley, J. D., & Boerger, E. A. (2002). Development of beliefs about the origins and controllability of dreams. *Developmental Psychology, 38*(1), 24–41.

Wooley, J. D., Phelps, K. E., Davis, D. L., & Mandell, D. J. (1999). Where theories of mind meet magic: The development of children's beliefs about wishing. *Child Development, 70,* 571–587.

World Bank. (2006). *Repositioning nutrition as central to development.* Washington, DC: Author.

World Bank (2012). *World development indicators database.* Retrieved from http://data.worldbank.org/indicator

World Health Organization (WHO). (2008). *Global burden of disease report: 2004 update.* Retrieved from www.who.int/healthinfo/global_burden_disease/2004_report_update/en/index.html

World Health Organization (WHO). (2010). *Causes of child mortality for the year 2010.* Retrieved from http://www.who.int/gho/child_health/mortality/causes/en/index.html

Worth, K., Gibson, J., Chambers, M. S., Nassau, D., Balvinder, K., Rakhra, A. B., & Sargent, J. (2008). Exposure of U.S. adolescents to extremely violent movies, *Pediatrics, 122*(2), 306–312.

Wright, V. C., Chang, J., Jeng, G., & Macaluso, M. (2006). Assisted reproduction technology surveillance—United States, 2003. *Morbidity and Mortality Weekly Report, 55*(SS04), 1–22.

Wright, V. C., Chang, J., Jeng, G., & Macaluso, M. (2008). Assisted reproduction technology surveillance—United States, 2005. *Morbidity and Mortality Weekly Report, 57*(SS05), 1–23.

Wright, V. C., Schieve, L. A., Reynolds, M. A., & Jeng, G. (2003). Assisted reproductive technology surveillance—United States, 2000. *Morbidity and Mortality Weekly Report, 55*(SS04), 1–22.

Wu, T., Mendola, P., & Buck, G. M. (2002). Ethnic differences in the presence of secondary sex characteristics and menarche among U.S. girls: The Third National Health and Nutrition Survey, 1988–1994. *Pediatrics, 11,* 752–757.

Wulczyn, F. (2004). Family reunification. *The Future of Children, 14*(1). Retrieved from www.princeton.edu/futureofchildren/publications/docs/14_01_05.pdf

Wynn, K. (1990). Children's understanding of counting. *Cognition, 36,* 155–193.

Wynn, K. (1992). Evidence against empiricist accounts of the origins of numerical knowledge. *Mind and Language, 7,* 315–332.

Wyrobek, A. J., Eskenazi, B., Young, S., Arnheim, N., Tiemann-Boege, I., Jabs, E. W., et al. (2006). Advancing age has differential effects on DNA damage, chromatin integrity, gene mutations, and aneuploidies in sperm. *Proceedings of the National Academy of Sciences of the United States of America, 103*(25), 9601–9606.

Yamada, H. (2004). Japanese mothers' views of young children's areas of personal discretion. *Child Development, 75,* 164–179.

Yamazaki, J. N., & Schull, W. J. (1990). Perinatal loss and neurological abnormalities among children of the atomic bomb. *Journal of the American Medical Association, 264,* 605–609.

Yang, B., Ollendick, T. H., Dong, Q., Xia, Y., & Lin, L. (1995). Only children and children with siblings in the People's Republic of China: Levels of fear, anxiety, and depression. *Child Development, 66,* 1301–1311.

Yim, I. S., Glynn, L. M., Schetter, C. D., Hobel, C. J., Chicz-DeMet, A., & Sandman, C. A. (2009). Risk of postpartum depressive symptoms with elevated corticotrophin-releasing hormone in human pregnancy. *Archives of General Psychiatry, 66,* 162–169.

Yingling, C. D. (2001). Neural mechanisms of unconscious cognitive processing. *Clinical Neurophysiology, 112*(1), 157–158.

Yip, T., Seaton, E. K., & Sellers, R. M. (2006). African American racial identity across the lifespan: Identity status, identity content, and depressive symptoms. *Child Development, 77,* 1504–1517.

Yokota, F., & Thompson, K. M. (2000). Violence in G-rated animated films. *Journal of the American Medical Association, 283,* 2716–2720.

Yoshikawa, H. (1994). Prevention as cumulative protection: Effects of early family support and education on chronic delinquency and its risks. *Psychological Bulletin, 115*(1), 28–54.

Yoshikawa, H., Weisner, T. S., Kalil, A., & Way, N. (2008). Mixing qualitative and quantitative research in developmental science: Uses and methodological choices. *Developmental Psychology, 44,* 344–354.

Young, K., Holcomb, L., Bonkale, W., Hicks, P., Yazdaini U., & German, D. (2007). 5HTTLPR polymorphism and enlargement of the pulvinar: Unlocking the backdoor to the limbic system. *Biological Psychiatry, 61*(6), 813–818.

Youngblade, L. M., & Belsky, J. (1992). Parent-child antecedents of 5-year-olds' close friendships: A longitudinal analysis. *Developmental Psychology, 28,* 700–713.

Youngblade, L. M., Theokas, C., Schulenberg, J., Curry, L., Huang, I-C., & Novak, M. (2007). Risk and promotive factors in families, schools, and communities: A contextual model of positive youth development in adolescence. *Pediatrics, 119*(Suppl.), S47–S53.

Youth violence: A report of the Surgeon General. (2001, January). Retrieved from www.surgeongeneral.gov/library/youthviolence/default.htm

Yu, S. M., Huang, Z. J., & Singh, G. K. (2004). Health status and health services utilization among U.S. Chinese, Asian Indian, Filipino, and Other Asian/Pacific Islander children. *Pediatrics, 113*(1), 101–107.

Yunger, J. L., Carver, P. R., & Perry, D. G. (2004). Does gender identity influence children's psychological well-being? *Developmental Psychology, 40,* 572–582.

Yurgelon-Todd, D. (2002). Inside the teen brain. Retrieved from www.pbs.org/wgbh/pages/frontline/shows/teenbrain/interviews/todd.html

Zahn-Waxler, C., Friedman, R. J., Cole, P. M., Mizuta, I., & Hiruma, N. (1996). Japanese and U.S. preschool children's responses to conflict and distress. *Child Development, 67,* 2462–2477.

Zahn-Waxler, C., Radke-Yarrow, M., Wagner, E., & Chapman, M. (1992). Development of concern for others. *Developmental Psychology, 28,* 126–136.

Zametkin, A. J., & Ernst, M. (1999). Problems in the management of attention deficit-hyperactivity disorder. *New England Journal of Medicine, 340,* 40–46.

Zanardo, V., Svegliado, G., Cavallin, F., Giustardi, A., Cosmi, E., Litta, P., & Trevisanuto, D. (2010). Elective cesarean delivery: Does it have a negative effect on breastfeeding? *Birth, 37*(4), 275–279.

Zeedyk, M. S., Wallace, L., & Spry, L. (2002). Stop, look, listen, and think? What young children really do when crossing the road. *Accident Analysis and Prevention, 34*(1), 43–50.

Zeiger, J. S., Beaty, T. H., & Liang, K. (2005). Oral clefts, maternal smoking, and TGFA: A meta-analysis of gene-environment interaction. *The Cleft palate-Craniofacial Journal, 42*(1), 58–63.

Zelazo, P. D., & Müller, U. (2002). Executive function in typical and atypical development. In U. Goswami (Ed.), *Handbook of childhood cognitive development* (pp. 445–469). Oxford: Blackwell.

Zelazo, P. D., Müller, U., Frye, D., & Marcovitch, S. (2003). The development of executive function in early childhood. *Monographs of the Society for Research in Child Development, 68*(3). [Serial No. 274].

Zelazo, P. R., Kearsley, R. B., & Stack, D. M. (1995). Mental representations for visual sequences: Increased speed of central processing from 22 to 32 months. *Intelligence, 20,* 41–63.

Zeskind, P. S., & Stephens, L. E. (2004). Maternal selective serotonin reuptake inhibitor use during pregnancy and newborn neurobehavior. *Pediatrics, 11,* 368–375.

Zhang, X., Huang, C. T., Chen, J., Pankratz, M. T., Xi, J., Li, J., et al. (2010). Pax6 is a human neuroectoderm cell fate determinant. *Cell Stem Cell, 7*(1), 90–100.

Zhao, Y. (2002, May 29). Cultural divide over parental discipline. *New York Times.* Retrieved from www.nytimes.com/2002/05/29/nyregion/cultural-divide-over-parental-discipline.html

Zhao, D., Zhang, Q., Fu, M., Tang, Y., & Zhao, Y. (2010). Effects of physical positions on sleep architectures and post-nap functions among habitual nappers. *Biological Psychology, 83*(3), 207–213. doi: 10.1016/j.biopsycho.2009.12.008

Zhu, B.-P., Rolfs, R. T., Nangle, B. E., & Horan, J. M. (1999). Effect of the interval between pregnancies on perinatal outcomes. *New England Journal of Medicine, 340,* 589–594.

Zigler, E. (1998). School should begin at age 3 years for American children. *Journal of Developmental and Behavioral Pediatrics, 19,* 37–38.

Zigler, E., & Styfco, S. J. (1993). Using research and theory to justify and inform Head Start expansion. *Social Policy Report of the Society for Research in Child Development, 7*(2).

Zigler, E., & Styfco, S. J. (1994). Head Start: Criticisms in a constructive context. *American Psychologist, 49*(2), 127–132.

Zigler, E., & Styfco, S. J. (2001). Extended childhood intervention prepares children for school and beyond. *Journal of the American Medical Association, 285,* 2378–2380.

Zigler, E., Taussig, C., & Black, K. (1992). Early childhood intervention: A promising preventative for juvenile delinquency. *American Psychologist, 47,* 997–1006.

Zimmerman, B. J., Bandura, A., & Martinez-Pons, M. (1992). Self-motivation for academic attainment: The role of self-efficacy beliefs and personal goal setting. *American Educational Research Journal, 29,* 663–676.

Zimmerman, F. J., Christakis, D. A., & Meltzoff., A. N. (2007). Associations between media viewing and language development in children under age 2 years. *Journal of Pediatrics, 151*(4), 364–368.

Zito, J. M., Safer, D. J., dosReis, S., Gardner, J. F., Magder, L., Soeken, K., et al. (2003). Psychotropic practice patterns for youth: A 10-year perspective. *Archives of Pediatrics and Adolescent Medicine 57*(1), 17–25.

Zuckerman, B. S., & Beardslee, W. R. (1987). Maternal depression: A concern for pediatricians. *Pediatrics, 79,* 110–117.

Zylke, J., & DeAngelis, C. (2007). Pediatric chronic diseases—stealing childhood. *Journal of the American Medical Association, 297*(24), 2765–2766.

Image Researcher: Toni Michaels/PhotoFind, L.L.C.
Interior design: Maureen McCutcheon
Cover design: Maureen McCutcheon

TEXT AND ILLUSTRATIONS

Chapter 1

Figure 1-1: From Papalia, *Experience Human Development*, 12th ed. Copyright © 2011. Reprinted by permission of The McGraw-Hill Companies, Inc.

Figure 1-2: World Development Indicators Database. http://data.worldbank.org/indicator/NY.GNP.MKTP.CN

Chapter 2

Figure 2-2: From Papalia, *Experience Human Development*, 12th ed. Copyright © 2011. Reprinted by permission of The McGraw-Hill Companies, Inc.

Figure 2-4: From Papalia, *Experience Human Development*, 12th ed. Copyright © 2011. Reprinted by permission of The McGraw-Hill Companies, Inc.

Figure 2-5: From Papalia, *Experience Human Development*, 12th ed. Copyright © 2011. Reprinted by permission of The McGraw-Hill Companies, Inc.

Chapter 3

Figure 3-2: From Papalia, *Human Development*, 10th ed. Copyright © 2007. Reprinted by permission of The McGraw-Hill Companies, Inc.

Figure 3-3: From Papalia, *Experience Human Development*, 12th ed. Copyright © 2011. Reprinted by permission of The McGraw-Hill Companies, Inc.

Figure 3-4: From Martorell, *Child: From Birth to Adolescence.* Copyright © 2012. Reprinted by permission of The McGraw-Hill Companies, Inc.

Figure 3-5: From Papalia, *Experience Human Development*, 12th ed. Copyright © 2011. Reprinted by permission of The McGraw-Hill Companies, Inc.

Figure 3-7: From Papalia, *Experience Human Development*, 12th ed. Copyright © 2011. Reprinted by permission of The McGraw-Hill Companies, Inc.

Figure 3-8: Reprinted by permission of Nature Publishing Group

Chapter 4

Figure 4-2: From Papalia, *Human Development*, 10th ed. Copyright © 2007. Reprinted by permission of The McGraw-Hill Companies, Inc.

Figure 4-4: From Papalia, *Experience Human Development*, 12th ed. Copyright © 2011. Reprinted by permission of The McGraw-Hill Companies, Inc.

Chapter 5

Figure 5-1: From Papalia, *Experience Human Development*, 12th ed. Copyright © 2011. Reprinted by permission of The McGraw-Hill Companies, Inc.

Figure 5-2: From Papalia, *Experience Human Development*, 12th ed. Copyright © 2011. Reprinted by permission of The McGraw-Hill Companies, Inc.

Figure 5-3: From Martorell, *Child: From Birth to Adolescence.* Copyright © 2012. Reprinted by permission of The McGraw-Hill Companies, Inc.

Figure 5-4: From Papalia, *Experience Human Development*, 12th ed. Copyright © 2011. Reprinted by permission of The McGraw-Hill Companies, Inc.

Chapter 6

Figure 6-1: From Papalia, *Experience Human Development*, 12th ed. Copyright © 2011. Reprinted by permission of The McGraw-Hill Companies, Inc.

Figure 6-2: From Papalia, *Experience Human Development*, 12th ed. Copyright © 2011. Reprinted by permission of The McGraw-Hill Companies, Inc.

Figure 6-4: From Martorell, *Child: From Birth to Adolescence.* Copyright © 2012. Reprinted by permission of The McGraw-Hill Companies, Inc.

Figure 6-5: From Martorell, *Child: From Birth to Adolescence.* Copyright © 2012. Reprinted by permission of The McGraw-Hill Companies, Inc.

Figure 6-6: From *The Postnatal Development of the Human Cerebral Cortex* by Jesse Leroy Conel. Copyright © 1939 by the President and Fellows of Harvard College. Reprinted by permission.

Figure 6-8: UNICEF, The State of the World's Children 2011, UNICEF, New York, 2011, p. 91. Reprinted by permission.

Figure 6-8: UNICEF, The State of the World's Children 2011, UNICEF, New York, 2011, p. 91. Reprinted by permission.

Chapter 7

Table 7-1: Reproduced by permission of Wiley, Inc.

Table 7-4: From Papalia, *Human Development*, 10th ed. Copyright © 2007. Reprinted by permission of The McGraw-Hill Companies, Inc.

Figure 7-1: "Zero to Six: Electronic Media in the Lives of Infants, Toddlers and Preschoolers" (#3378), The Henry J. Kaiser Family Foundation, October 2003. This information was reprinted with permission from the Henry J. Kaiser Family Foundation. The Kaiser Family Foundation, a leader in health policy analysis, health journalism and communication, is

dedicated to filling the need for trusted, independent information on the major health issues facing our nation and its people. The Foundation is a non-profit private operating foundation, based in Menlo Park, California.

Chapter 8

Figure 8-1: From "The Self in self-conscious emotions," by M. Lewis in S. G. Snodgrass and R. L. Thompson (eds.), "The Self across psychology: Self-recognition, self-awareness, and the self-concept," 1997. *Annals of the New York Academy of Sciences,* Vol. 818, Figure 1, p. 120. Reprinted by permission obtained via RightsLink.

Figure 8-2: From Papalia, *Experience Human Development*, 12th ed. Copyright © 2011. Reprinted by permission of The McGraw-Hill Companies, Inc.

Chapter 9

Figure 9-1: From *Papalia, Experience Human Development*, 12th ed. Copyright © 2011. Reprinted by permission of The McGraw-Hill Companies, Inc.

Figure 9-2: From Papalia, *Experience Human Development*, 12th ed. Copyright © 2011. Reprinted by permission of The McGraw-Hill Companies, Inc.

Figure 1, Box 9-1: Reproduced, with the permission of the publisher, from "Global Health: Today's Challenges," in The World Health Report: Shaping the Future. Geneva, World Health Organization, 2003.

Figure 1, Box 9-1: Reproduced, with the permission of the publisher, from *The Global Burden of Disease.* Geneva, World Health Organization, 2004 (update 2008).

Figure 9-4: America's Yongest Outcasts: 2010. (2011). The National Center on Family Homelessness, Needham, MA.

Chapter 10

Table 10-3: Key Elements of Number Sense in Young Children by Nancy C. Jordan, David Kaplan, Leslie Nabors Olah & Maria N. Locuniak. *Child Development*, 77, 1. 2006. Reproduced with permission of Wiley, Inc.

Figure 10-1: From Martorell, *Child: From Birth to Adolescence.* Copyright © 2012. Reprinted by permission of The McGraw-Hill Companies, Inc.

Chapter 11

Table 11-2: M.B. Parten, "Social Play Among Preschool Children." *Journal of Abnormal Psychology* 27, 243–269, 1932. Reprinted by permission of the American Psychological Association.

Chapter 12

Figure 12-1: From "Dynamic mapping of human cortical development during childhood through early adulthood," by N. Gogtay, et al. *Proceedings of the National Academy of Sciences* Vol. 101, No. 21, pp. 8174–8179. May 2004. © 2004 National Academy of Sciences, U.S.A.

Figure 12-2: Reproduced, with the permission of the publisher, from *World Report on Child Injury Prevention*. Geneva, World Health Organization, 2008.

Chapter 14

Figure 14-3: "Effects of televised violence on aggression," in Singer, J., ed., *Handbook of Children and the Media*. Reproduced by permission of SAGE Publications, Inc.

Chapter 15

Figure 15-1: Reprinted by permission of the American Academy of Pediatrics.

Chapter 16

Figure 16-1: From Small. *Cognitive Development*, 1E. © 1990 Wadsworth, a part of Cengage Learning, Inc. Reproduced by permission. www.cengage.com/permissions

Chapter 17

Table 17-1: Adapted from "Developmetal and validation of ego identity status," by J.E. Marcia in *Journal of Personality and Social Psychology* 3 (5), pp. 551–558. Copyright © 1966 by the American Psychological Association

Table 17-1: Adapted from "Developmetal and validation of ego identity status," by J.E. Marcia in *Journal of Personality and Social Psychology* 3 (5), pp. 551–558. Copyright © 1966 by the American Psychological Association

Table 17-2: From "Ego Identity: An Overview" in *Discussion of Ego Identity,* edited by J. Kroger, 1993. Reprinted by permission of the author.

Table 17-3: Reprinted by permission of SAGE Publications.

Table 17-4: "National Survey of Adolescents and Young Adults: Sexual Health Knowledge, Attitudes and Experiences", (#3218), The Henry J. Kaiser Family Foundation, April 2003 http://www.kff.org/hivaids/report/national-survey-of-adolescents-and-young-adults/

Table 17-6: "Parental psychological control: Revisiting a neglected construct," in *Child Development,* Vol. 67, No. 6, pp. 3296–3319. 1996. Reproduced with permission of Wiley, Inc.

Table 17-7: "Adolescents' and parents' changing conceptions of parental authority," by J. Smetana et al, in *Changing boundaries of parental authority during adolescence: New directions for child and adolescent development.* No. 108, pp. 31–46. Reproduced with permission of Wiley, Inc.

DESIGN ELEMENTS

Around the World, © iStock Photos/Jani Bryson
The Everyday World, © iStock Photos/Jani Bryson
The Research World, © iStock Photos/Jan Rysavy

PHOTOS

Chapter 1

Opener: © Peter Cade/Getty Images; p. 4: © BananaStock/Punchstock RF; p. 7: © Angela Hampton Picture Library/Alamy; p. 13: © Barcroft Media/Landov; p. 16: © Library of Congress [LC-USF34-T01-009095-C].

Chapter 2

Opener: © Ariel Skelley/Blend Images/Blend Images RF; p. 29: © National Library of Medicine; p. 31: © Bettmann/Corbis Images; p. 33(top): © Bachrach/Getty Images; p. 33(bottom): © Vladimir Godnik/Getty Images RF; p. 34: © Bill Anderson/Science Source/Photo Researchers; p. 35: © A.R. Luria/Dr. Michael Cole, Laboratory of Human Cognition, University of California, San Diego; p. 45: © WDCN/University College London/Science Source.

Chapter 3

Opener: © Debbie Boccabella/Oredia Eurl/SuperStock; p. 70(bottom): © Rubberball/Getty Images RF; 3.4(top left): © Plush Studios/Blend Images RF; 3.4(top right): © Ariel Skelley/Blend Images RF; 3.4(center far left): © Glow Images RF; 3.4(center far right): © Pixtal/AGE Fotostock RF; 3.4(center left): © Sean Justice/Corbis RF; 3.4(center right): © Glow Images RF; p. 72: © AP Photo/Pat Sullivan; p. 77: © Stockbyte/Veer RF; p. 81: © T.K. Wanstal/The Image Works; p. 82: © AP Photo/Peter DeJong.

Chapter 4

Opener: © Jose Luis Pelaez Inc./Blend Images RF; p. 94(1 mo.): © Petit Format/Nestle/Science Source/Photo Researchers; p. 94(3 mo.): © Lennart Nilsson/Albert Bonniers Forlag AB, *A Child Is Born,* Dell Publishing Company; p. 94(4 mo.): © Ralph Hutchings/Visuals Unlimited; p. 94(5 mo.): © James Stevenson/Photo Researchers; p. 94(7 wks.): © Petit Format/Nestle/Science Source/Photo Researchers; p. 95(6 mo.): © Lennart Nilsson/Albert Bonniers Forlag AB, *A Child Is Born,* Dell Publishing Company; p. 95(7-8 mo.): © Petit Format/Nestle/Science Source/Photo Researchers; p. 95(9 mo.): © Tom Galliher/Galliher Photography; p. 99: © Keith Brofsky/Getty Images RF; p. 102: © Blend Images/Corbis RF; p. 104: © Pixtal/age fotostock RF.

Chapter 5

Opener: © Creatas/PictureQuest RF; p. 124: © Comstock Images RF; p. 130: © Angela Hampton/Alamy; p. 133: © Corbis RF; p. 136: Emmy E. Werner and Ruth S. Smith. *Overcoming the Odds.* Cornell University Press, 1992; p. 138: Harlow Primate Laboratory, University of Wisconsin; p. 139: © Brand X Pictures/Jupiterimages RF.

Chapter 6

Opener: © 2004 image100 Ltd. RF; p. 148: © Diane McDonald/Getty Images RF; p. 157 (top left): © Mimi Forsyth; p. 157(top center): © Lew Merrim/Photo Researchers; p. 157(top right): © Laura Dwight; p. 157(bottom left): © Elizabeth Crews; p. 157(bottom center): © Astier/Photo Researchers; p. 157(bottom right): © BSIP/UIG/Getty Images; p. 158(both): Courtesy, Children's Hospital of Michigan; p. 159: © Blend Images/Getty Images RF; p. 161: © Kwame Zikomo/Purestock/SuperStock RF; p. 164: © Mark Richards/PhotoEdit; p. 170: © Science Photo Library RF/Getty Images RF.

Chapter 7

Opener: © ImageSource/age fotostock RF; p. 180: © Bananastock/PictureQuest RF; p. 186: © Laura Dwight; p. 187: © Enrico Ferorelli; p. 190: DeLoache, J. S., Uttal, D. H., & Rosengren, K. S. (2004). Scale errors offer evidence for a perception-action dissociation early in life. *Science,* 304, 1047–1029 @2004 American Association for the Advancement of Science. Photo by Jackson Smith.; p. 192: © James Kilkelly; p. 194: © Mint Photography/Alamy; p. 202: Courtesy Department Library Services/American Museum of Natural History. Neg. No. 326799; p. 205: © Rubberball/PictureQuest RF; p. 211: © Brand X Pictures/Punchstock RF; p. 212: © Ariel Skelley/Getty Images RF.

Chapter 8

Opener: © Laoshi/Getty Images RF; p. 220(top): © PhotoAlto/PictureQuest RF; p. 220(bottom): © Jose Luis Pelaez Inc./Blend Images RF; 8.1(top): © Frare/Davis Photography/Brand X/Corbis RF; 8.1(center): © Amos Morgan/Getty Images RF; 8.1(bottom): © Comstock Images RF; p. 224: © JGI/Jamie Grill/Blend Images RF; p. 228: © Jonathan Finlay; p. 230: © Brand X Pictures/Punchstock RF; p. 237: © Robert Brenner/PhotoEdit; p. 242: © The McGraw-Hill Companies, Inc./Andrew Resek, photographer; p. 244: © Eyewire/Photodisc/Getty Images RF; p. 247: © Digital Vision/Getty Images RF.

Chapter 9

Opener: © Ariel Skelley/Blend Images RF; p. 254: © Janis Christie/Getty Images RF; p. 256: © KidStock/Getty Images RF; p. 263: Courtesy, Gabriela Martorell; p. 269(both): © Tony Freeman/PhotoEdit.

Chapter 10

Opener: © Kidstock/Getty Images RF; p. 276: © Floresco Productions/Corbis RF; p. 281: © Sheila Sheridan; p. 289: © Brand X Pictures/Punchstock RF; p. 292: © Design Pics/Don Hammond RF; p. 296: © Paul Conklin/PhotoEdit.

Chapter 11

Opener: © Ariel Skelley/Getty Images RF; p. 305: © Keith Eng 2007 RF; p. 311: © Erika Stone/Photo Researchers; p. 319(left): © Corbis RF; p. 319(right): © LWA/Dann Tardif/Getty Images RF; p. 322: © Myrleen Ferguson Cate/PhotoEdit; p. 327: © White Rock/Getty Images RF; p. 329(both): © Albert Bandura; p. 333: Courtesy, Gabriela Martorell.

name index

Bratton, S. C., 356
Braun, A. R., 208
Braun, H., 384
Braungart, J. M., 226
Braungart-Rieker, J. M., 231
Braver, E. R., 443
Bray, J. H., 402, 405
Brazelton, T. B., 127, 234
Breastfeeding and HIV International Transmission Study Group, 148
Breaux, C., 139
Breitkopf, C., 107
Brendgen, M., 328, 329
Brenner, R. A., 169
Brent, D. A., 442, 443, 444
Brent, M. R., 206, 211
Brent, R. L., 104
Brewaeys, A., 405
Brewer, R. D., 440
Brezina, T., 322
Bridge, J. A., 356
Bridges, M., 402
Briggs, J. L., 7
Brin, D. J., 98
Brison, R. J., 169
Britto, P. R., 399
Broadfield, D. C., 208
Brock, J. W., 109
Brockert, J. E., 109, 486
Brodersen, L., 232
Brodowski, M. L., 171
Brody, G. H., 244, 400, 408, 409, 432, 477, 500
Brody, L. R., 160
Broekmans, F.J., 62
Broidy, L. M., 353, 412
Bronfenbrenner, U., 36
Bronner, E., 384
Bronstein, P., 381, 402
Brookmeyer, K. A., 498
Brooks, J., 237
Brooks, M. G., 268
Brooks, R., 194
Brooks-Gunn, J., 184, 244, 246, 289, 296, 326, 371, 399, 400, 432
Broude, G. J., 7, 116, 129, 146, 169, 256
Brouillette, R. T., 168
Brousseau, E., 101
Browder, J. P., 110
Brown, A. C., 400
Brown, A. L., 451
Brown, A. S., 87, 440
Brown, B. B., 463, 495, 496, 499
Brown, E., 282
Brown, G. L., 230
Brown, J., 62, 284
Brown, J. D., 482
Brown, J. L., 102, 413
Brown, J. R., 305
Brown, L., 62
Brown, L. J., 266, 340
Brown, L. M., 10, 476

Brown, P., 109
Brown, R., 409
Brown, S. L., 401, 404, 493
Brown, S. S., 132
Browne, A., 174
Brownell, C. A., 245
Bruer, J. T., 18
Bruine de Bruin, W., 452
Bruner, A. B., 435
Bruner, J., 35
Brunson, K. L., 173
Bruschi, C. J., 219, 396
Brust, J. C. M., 105
Bruton, J. R., 438, 439
Bryant, D. M., 184, 247, 289
Bryce, J., 147, 261, 263
Bryk, A., 211
Büchel, C., 350, 351
Buck, G. M., 428
Buck Louis, G., 426
Buckner, J. C., 268
Budnitz, D. S., 266
Buehler, C., 499
Buell, J., 382
Buhrmester, D., 411, 494, 495, 496
Buist, K. L., 494
Buitelaar, J., 107
Buitelaar, J. K., 107
Buitendijk, S. E., 129
Bukowski, W., 317
Bukowski, W. M., 410, 416
Bulik, C., 436, 437, 438
Bulkley, K., 384
Bunikowski, R., 105
Burch, M. M., 242
Burchinal, M., 183
Burchinal, M. R., 247, 289
Burgess, K. B., 328
Burhans, K. K., 304
Buriel, R., 324, 397, 398, 399, 402
Burleson, B. R., 410
Burns, B. J., 172
Burraston, B., 494
Burrows, E., 134
Burt, A., 266
Burts, D. C., 333
Burwinkle, T. M., 347
Bush, D. M., 432
Bushnell, E. W., 18, 160, 163
Busnel, M. C., 100
Busnel, M. C., 203
Bussey, K., 311, 312, 313, 314
Buyck, P., 303
Bybee, D., 477
Byrd, R. S., 350
Byrne, M., 87, 110
Byrnes, J., 450
Byrnes, J. P., 277, 378
Bystron, I., 151

Caballero, B., 101
Cabrera, N., 139
Cabrera, N. J., 139, 402

Cacciatore, J., 98, 135
Caelli, K., 98
Cai, T., 499
Cain, K. M., 304, 413
Caldera, Y. M., 243
Caldji, C., 138
Caldwell, B., 183
Caldwell, B. M., 182
Calhoun, T., 10
Caliendo, M. A., 263
Calkins, S. D., 233, 328
Call, J., 223
Callanan, M. A., 260
Camann, W. R., 122
Camarata, S., 366, 380
Cameron, A. D., 121
Cameron, L., 409
Camilleri-Novak, D., 356
Camoin, T. I. L., 428
Campbell, A., 242, 307
Campbell, F. A., 184, 289
Campbell, R. N., 375
Campbell, W. K., 139
Campione, J. C., 451
Campione-Barr, N., 492
Campos, J., 231
Campos, J. J., 162, 234, 236, 305
Camras, A., 305
Canadian Paediatric Society, 159
Canadian Shaken Baby Study Group, 172
Candy, J., 307
Canfield, R. L., 270
Cantor, J., 330
Cao, A., 78
Capage, L., 284
Capaldi, D. M., 480
Caplan, M., 245
Caprara, G. V., 380, 466
Capute, A. J., 203
Card, N., 412
Carey, S., 196, 197, 277
Carlo, G., 460
Carlson, E., 233
Carlson, E. A., 230, 232, 233
Carlson, J. J., 241
Carlson, M. J., 493
Carlson, S. M., 233, 281, 282, 283
Carlström, E., 479
Carmichael, M., 262
Carmody, D. P., 237
Carnethon, M. R., 434
Carnozzi, A., 45
Carothers, S. S., 488
Carpenter, M., 204, 223
Carper, R., 367
Carra, J. S., 266
Carraher, D. W., 363
Carraher, T. N., 363
Carrel, L., 68
Carriger, M. S., 193, 194
Carroll, M. D., 262, 339
Carryl, E., 399
Carskadon, M. A., 435

Carter, J., 104
Carter, R. C., 104
Cartwright, B. S., 283
Carvalhal, J. B., 104
Carver, L. J., 189
Carver, P. R., 246, 311, 399, 409
Casaer, P., 150
Casas, J. F., 328
Case, R., 35, 303, 369, 451
Casella, J. F., 435
Casey, B. J., 340
Cashon, C. H., 197
Casper, L. M., 139
Caspi, A., 15, 174, 226, 289, 355, 419, 432
Cassidy, J., 233
Cassidy, K. W., 284
Catalano, R. F., 440, 487, 500
Cates, W., Jr., 485
Cauce, A. M., 48
Cauffman, E., 324
Caughey, A. B., 110
Ceci, S. J., 86, 370, 371, 385
Celis, W., 172
Cen, G., 410
Center for Education Reform, 384
Center for Effective Discipline, 322
Center for Law and Social Policy, 297
Center for Weight and Health, 262, 345, 347
Center on Addiction and Substance Abuse at Columbia University (CASA), 441
Centers for Disease Control and Prevention (CDC), 61, 72, 105, 235, 266, 339, 340, 402, 426, 434, 444, 480, 484, 485
Centers for Medicare and Medicaid Services, 268
Central Intelligence Agency, 13
Ceppi, G., 296
Cernkovich, S. A., 489
Chadwick, A., 332
Chaika, H., 160
Chambers, C., 235
Chambers, C. D., 103
Chambers, R. A., 433, 439
Chan, R. W., 405
Chandler, A. L., 462
Chandler, P., 205
Chandra, A., 479, 480, 482
Chang, C., 363
Chang, C. H., 132
Chang, J., 61, 65
Chang, L., 416
Chang, S., 265
Chang, Y., 397
Chao, R. K., 326, 372
Chao, W., 500
Chapieski, M. L., 238
Chapman, C., 384, 466
Chapman, M., 222, 362

Jones, H. W., 62
Jones, J., 479
Jones, K. L. C., 135
Jones, M. C., 432
Jones, N. A., 235
Jones, R., 270
Jones, S. E., 440
Jones, S. M., 413, 498
Jonsson, B., 460
Jordan, B., 116
Jordan, N. C., 277
Jose, P. E., 372
Josh, P., 243
Joussemet, M., 413
Joy, M. E., 241
Juang, L., 372
Juffer, F., 233, 406
Jung, S., 107
Jusczyk, P., 160
Jusczyk, P. W., 202, 205, 206
Just, M. A., 152
Juster, F. T., 344, 345, 396, 489
Juul-Dam, N., 152

Kaban, B., 183
Kaczynski, K. J., 397, 398
Kaffenberger, S. M., 415
Kafury-Goeta, A. C., 132
Kagan, J., 188, 199, 200, 226, 227
Kaiser Family Foundation, 463, 480, 482, 485
Kaiz, M., 488
Kales, A., 256
Kalil, A., 45, 493
Kalish, C. W., 277
Kalkoske, M., 231
Kamrava, M., 66
Kana, R. K., 152
Kanaya, T., 385
Kandel, D. B., 355
Kanetsuna, T., 415
Kang, C., 350
Kanstrup Hansen, I. L., 102
Kaplan, D., 277
Kaplan, H., 165
Kaplan, J., 384
Kaplan, N., 233
Kaplow, J. B., 173
Kaplowitz, P. B., 427, 428
Kaprio, J., 259, 432
Karafantis, D. M., 396
Karasik, L. B., 162
Karch, M. D., 444
Karmaus, W., 147
Kashima, Y., 237
Kaste, L. M., 340
Katerelos, M., 209, 211, 212
Kato, K., 344, 408
Katzman, D. K., 443
Katzman, R., 47
Kaufman, A. S., 375
Kaufman, J., 174, 416
Kaufman, N. L., 375

Kawabata, Y., 411
Kazdin, A. E., 322, 323
Kazuk, E., 161
Keane, D. P., 129
Keane, S. P., 328
Kearsley, R. B., 193
Keegan, R. T., 5, 389
Keel, P. K., 438
Keeler, G., 50–51
Keenan, K., 242, 307
Kegler, S. R., 444
Kellam, S. G., 355
Keller, B., 7
Keller, T. A., 152
Kelley, K., 226
Kelley, M. L., 139, 243, 402
Kellman, P. J., 160
Kellogg, R., 259
Kelly, A. M., 436
Kelly, J., 403
Kelly, J. B., 402, 403
Kelsey, J. L., 13
Keltikangas-Järvinen, L., 233
Kemp, J. S., 168
Kena, G., 460
Kendall, P., 418
Kendrick, C., 244
Kennedy-Stephenson, J., 146
Kennell, J. H., 137
Kere, J., 386
Kerem, E., 417
Kermoian, R., 162
Kerns, K. A., 104, 333
Kerr, D. C. R., 321, 323
Kerrebrock, N., 265
Kessler, R. C., 169
Kestenbaum, R., 306
Khan, Y., 257
Khoo, S. T., 494
Khoury, M. J., 79
Kidd, K. K., 13, 371
Kier, C., 331
Kikuchi, Y., 228
Killen, J. D., 441
Kim, J., 148, 409, 494
Kim, K. J., 17
Kim, S., 400
Kim, Y. S., 415
Kim, Y. K., 319
Kimball, M., 168
Kim-Cohen, J., 15, 289, 419
Kimmerly, N. L., 230
King, A., 211
King, J. C., 102
King, K. M., 441
King, N. J., 417
King, V., 403
King, W. J., 172
Kingdon, C. K., 137
King, V., 493
Kinney, H. C., 168
Kinsella, K., 10, 407
Kirby, D., 485, 487
Kirby, R., 135

Kirkorian, H. L., 294
Kirkwood, H., 367
Kirmeyer, S., 135
Kirwil, L., 415
Kisilevsky, B. S., 100
Kispert, A., 68
Kistler, D. J., 173
Kita, S., 209
Kitzman, H. J., 174
Kivnick, H. Q., 31
Klar, A. J. S., 259
Klaus, M. H., 137
Klebanoff, M. A., 109
Klein, J. D., 480, 482, 485, 486, 487, 488
Kleinmann, R. E., 4
Klein-Velderman, M., 233
Klibanoff, R. S., 278
Klump, K. L., 437, 438
Klute, C., 495, 496
Knaack, A., 241
Knafo, A., 327
Knecht, S., 210
Knickmeyer, R. C., 150
Knight, W. G., 105
Knudsen, E. I., 18
Ko, C.-W., 169
Kochanska, G., 232, 233, 238, 240, 241, 321, 333, 398
Kochenderfer, B. J., 333
Koenig, H. G., 458
Koerner, A. F., 406
Koff, E., 432
Kogan, M. D., 146, 347, 349
Kogos, J., 419
Koh, Y.-J., 415
Kohen, D. E., 326
Kohlberg, L., 310, 454, 455, 457, 459
Koinis, D., 282
Kolasa, M., 170
Kolata, G., 77
Kolbert, E., 330
Komatsu, L. K., 362
Konrad, D., 68
Koops, W., 413
Kopp, C. B., 237, 238
Koren, G., 103
Korner, A., 225–226
Koskenvuo, M., 259
Kostelny, K., 417
Kosterman, R., 487, 500
Kovas, Y., 386
Kovelman, I., 209, 211
Kowal, A. K., 482
Kozhimannil, K. B., 235
Kozlowska, K., 355
Kozmitzki, C., 116, 165, 450
Kralovec, E., 382
Kramer, L., 244, 245
Kramer, M. S., 147
Krashen, S., 19, 377
Krasilnikoff, P. A., 110
Kratochwill, T. R., 330

Krause, K. W., 68
Krause, N., 387
Krauss, S., 92
Krausz, C., 62
Kraut, R., 496
Krebs, N. F., 171
Kreider, R. M., 331, 404, 405, 406, 407
Kreutzer, M., 367
Krevans, J., 321, 490
Krishnakumar, A., 15
Krishnamoorthy, J. S., 347, 348
Kroger, J., 474, 475, 476
Kroonenberg, P. M., 229
Krueger, A. B., 383
Krueger, R. F., 499
Krull, J. L., 397
Kruttschnitt, C., 500
Krypianidou, A., 440
Kucera, E., 243
Kuczmarski, R. J., 145
Kuczynski, L., 238
Kuh, D., 134, 341, 432
Kuhl, P., 203, 206, 211, 212, 213
Kuhl, P. K., 18, 203, 204, 210
Kuhn, C., 235
Kuhn, D., 340, 433, 434, 450, 451, 453
Kuiper, H., 395
Kung, H.-C., 72, 131
Kung, H. C., 131, 135
Kupanoff, K., 396, 460
Kuperman, S., 441
Kupersmidt, J. B., 410
Kupper, L., 497
Kurian, J., 173
Kurinczuk, J., 132
Kurlakowsky, K. D., 355
Kurukulaaratchy, R. J., 147
Kuther, T., 346
Kuzawa, C. W., 137
Kye, C., 355

Laakso, M., 292
Labarere, J., 147
Laberge, L., 256
LaBounty, J., 284
Labov, T., 453
Lacerda, F., 204
Ladd, G., 410
Ladd, G. W., 298, 333
LaFontana, K. M., 410
Lagattuta, K. H., 305
Lagercrantz, H., 121
La Greca, A. M., 417
Lahey, B., 396, 499
Lai, D., 350
Laible, D., 460
Laible, D. J., 242, 305
Laird, J., 466
Laird, R. D., 500
Laje, G., 356
Lakatos, K., 230

Mann, J. J., 444
Manning, W. D., 497
Marchman, V. A., 202, 206
March of Dimes Birth Defects
  Foundation, 104, 105, 107
Marcia, J. E., 473, 474, 475, 476
Marcoen, A., 233, 303
Marcovitch, S., 285
Marentette, P. F., 209
Mareschal, D., 196
Mariner, C. L., 322
Maring, B. L., 283
Marion, D., 109
Markestad, T., 133, 168
Markman, E. M., 205, 206
Markoff, J., 109
Marks, H., 466
Marks, K. S., 198
Marlow, N., 134
Marois, R., 463
Marquardt, E., 403
Marquis, J., 292
Marriott, C., 282
Marsh, P., 495
Marshall, E. G., 109
Marshall, M. F., 106
Marshall, N. L., 247, 249
Marshall, P. J., 317
Martin, C. L., 242, 307, 309, 311,
  312, 313, 314, 318, 319, 396
Martin, J. A., 92, 99, 101, 104,
  108, 109, 110, 112, 117, 120,
  121, 126, 127, 131, 132, 133,
  134, 324, 485, 486
Martin, M., 259
Martin, N., 64
Martin, R., 107
Martin, S., 497
Martinez, G., 480–481
Martinez, G. M., 480
Martínez-González, M. A., 438
Martinez-Pons, M., 380
Marwick, C., 106
Mason, C. A., 48
Masse, L. C., 440
Masten, A., 419
Masten, A. S., 410, 413, 419
Mateer, C. A., 104
Matheeson, C. C., 333
Mathews, T. J., 64, 104, 131, 132,
  166, 167, 485, 487
Mathews, T. J., 102
Mathie, A., 45
Matsumoto, D., 372
Matthews, K. A., 267
Maugeais, R., 203
Mauras, N., 339
Maurer, O., 404
May, K. A., 137
Mayeux, L., 410, 413
Maynard, R., 482
Mayo Foundation for Medical
  Education and Research,
  71, 72

Mayseless, O., 502
Mazzella, R., 436
Mazziotta, J. C., 223
McAdoo, H. P., 183
McCabe, E.R.B., 79
McCabe, L. L., 79
McCall, D. D., 163
McCall, L. W., 369
McCall, R. B., 193, 194
McCallum, K. E., 438, 439
McCartney, K., 83, 85
McCartt, A. T., 443
McCarty, C. A., 194, 443
McCarty, M. E., 163
McClearn, G. E., 84, 86
McClelland, J. L., 199
McClintock, M. K., 427
McCord, J., 321, 323, 500
McCoy, A. R., 384
McDade, T. W., 137
McDaniel, M., 349
McDonald, E., 346
McDonald, S. A., 133
McDonough, L., 196
McDowell, M., 146, 338
McElhaney, K. B., 495
McElwain, N. L., 331
McFadyen-Ketchum, S., 431
McFadyen-Ketchum, S. A., 416
McFarland, F. C., 495
McField, G., 377
McGue, M., 289, 499
McGue, M. K., 406, 407
McGuffin, P., 81, 84, 87
McGuigan, F., 287
McGuinn, N., 342
McHale, S. M., 244, 313, 399,
  409, 494
McIntosh, C. N., 326
McKenna, J. J., 169
McKenna, K.Y.A., 496
McKenna, M. C., 378
McKinney, K. L., 432
McKusick, V. A., 79
McLanahan, S., 289, 371, 403
McLanahan, S. S., 405
McLeod, P. J., 213
McLeod, R., 107
McLeskey, J., 384
McLoyd, V., 400
McLoyd, V. C., 289, 321, 323, 399
McMahon, A. P., 68
McMahon, C. R., 153
McMahon, R. J., 492
McMorris, B. J., 500
McMorrow, M., 170
McNamara, T., 98
McNeely, C. S., 480
McQueeny, T., 440
McQuillan, J., 62
McRitchie, S. L., 345, 434
McRoberts, G. W., 206
McRoy, R. G., 406
Meaney, M. J., 138

Mechur, M. J., 468
Meck, E., 277
Medland, S. E., 259
Mednick, S., 265
Mednick, S. A., 265
Meehan, B. T., 441
Meeks, J. J., 68
Meerum Terwogt, M., 395
Meezan, W., 405
Meier, A. M., 436
Meier, D., 465
Meier, R., 209
Meijer, A. M., 139
Meins, E., 230, 232
Meir, I., 209
Meis, P. J., 132
Melby, J., 464
Mellingen, K., 265
Meltzer, A. A., 452
Meltzoff, A. N., 187, 189, 194
Meltzoff., A. N., 195
Menacker, F., 64, 104, 120, 486
Mendel, G., 24, 69
Mendle, J., 431, 432
Mendola, P., 428
Meng, H., 386
Menke, E. M., 98
Mennella, J. A., 100, 159
Ment, L. R., 134
Merabet, L. B., 156
Merckelbach, H., 330
Merikangas, K. R., 85
Mermillod, M., 196
Merrell, K., 416
Mertz, J., 461, 462
Mesch, G., 496
Messinger, D. S., 105, 235
Messinis, L., 440
Metraux, S., 268
Metz, K. E., 451
Metzger, A., 492
Meyer, I. H., 479
Michael, A., 466
Michaelieu, Q., 476
Michaelson, K. F., 147
Michalaska, K., 396, 499
Micocci, F., 502
Middledorp, C. M., 355
Miech, R. A., 435
Miedel, W. T., 384
Miedzian, M., 313
Migeon, B. R., 69
Mikkola, K., 134
Milani, I., 193
Miller, D. C., 379
Miller, J. W., 440
Miller, J. Y., 440
Miller, K. F., 275
Miller, P. C., 325
Miller, P. H., 362, 451
Miller, S. A., 362, 451
Miller-Johnson, S., 184
Miller-Kovach, K., 349
Millman, R. P., 435

Mills, J. L., 102
Millsap, R. E., 432
Millstein, S. G., 452
Mindell, J.A., 129
Mindell, J. A., 435
Minich, N., 133
Miniño, A. M., 443
Minshew, N. J., 152
Miranda, S. B., 193
Mischel, W., 240, 312
Mishra, G. D., 432
Missmer, S. A., 64
Mistry, J., 201
Mistry, R. S., 400
Mitchell, E. A., 168
Miura, H., 277
Mix, K. S., 198, 363
Miyake, K., 231
Mizuta, I., 329
Mlot, C., 222
Mody, M., 386
Moffitt, T. E., 15, 226, 289, 419,
  432, 488, 500
Mohajer, S. T., 64, 66
Moise-Titus, J., 414
Mol, B. W., 129
Molenaar, P. C. M., 364
Molinari, L., 435
Moller, L. C., 319
Molnar, Z., 151
Mondschein, E. R., 161, 243
Moneta, G., 488
Money, J., 309
Monni, G., 78
Monshouwer, H. J., 413
Montague, D. P. F., 234
Montague, P. R., 229
Montessori, M., 295
Montgomery, G., 64
Montgomery-Downs, H. E., 101
Montplaisir, J., 256
Moon, C., 100
Moon, J., 76
Moon, R. Y., 168
Mooney-Somers, J., 405
Moore, C. A., 101, 189
Moore, G. E., 72
Moore, M. K., 187
Moore, S. E., 102
Moore., C. F., 269
Morelli, G., 48
Morelli, G. A., 137, 169
Moreno, C., 356
Morgan, R. A., 79
Morielli, A., 168
Morild, I., 168
Morison, P., 410
Morris, A. D., 456, 457, 459, 460
Morris, A. S., 397
Morris, J. E., 493
Morris, M. W., 35
Morris, P. A., 36
Morris, P. E., 389
Morris, R. J., 330

Morris, S. S., 147
Morrison, J. A., 436
Morrissey, T. W., 248
Mors, O., 235
Mortensen, E. L., 147
Mortensen, P. B., 87, 110, 235
Mortimer, J., 502
Mortimer, J. T., 468
Morton, H., 7
Morton, T., 355
Moses, L. J., 234, 282
Mosher, W. D., 479, 480
Mosier, C., 201
Mosier, C. E., 239
Mosko, S. S., 169
Mosley, J., 405
Moster, D., 133
Moulson, M. C., 159
Mounts, N., 499
Mounts, N. S., 490, 500
Mounzih, K., 428
Moyzis, R. K., 68
Msall, M. S. E., 133
MTA Cooperative Group., 388
Muenke, M., 387
Muglia, L. J., 132
Muir, D., 282
Muir, D. W., 100, 163
Mulder, E., 107
Mulder, E.J.H., 107
Mulford, C., 497
Mulinare, J., 107
Mullan, D., 434
Müller, U., 152, 285
Mullin, J., 376
Mullins, R., 110
Mumma, G. H., 410
Mumme, D. L., 236, 305
Munafo, M., 259
Munakata, Y., 199
Munk-Olsen, T., 235
Munn, P., 244
Murachver, T., 287
Murchison, C., 5
Muris, P., 330
Murnen, S. K., 174
Murphy, B. C., 396
Murphy, P. D., 79
Murphy, S. L., 72, 131
Murray, C., 371
Murray, K. T., 241
Murray, M. L., 356
Murry, V., 432
Murry, V. M., 400
Mussen, P. H., 432
Must, A., 347, 430, 436
Mustillo, S., 347
Muter, V., 294
Myers, S. M., 153

Nabors, L. A., 247
Nadel, L., 76
Nader, P. R., 345, 434

Nadig, A. S., 153
Nagaoka, J., 384
Nagel, R. J., 495
Nagy, E., 234
Naimi, T. S., 440
Naito, M., 277
Najman, J. M., 399
Nandakumar, R., 291
Nangle, B. E., 132
Nansel, T. R., 415, 416
Nash, A., 244
Nassar, N., 132
Natenshon, A., 346
Nathanielsz, P. W., 132
National Assessment of Educational
    Progress, 384, 460
National Center for Child
    Traumatic Stress, 156, 173
National Center for Education
    Statistics (NCES), 246, 298,
    342, 377, 379, 384, 402,
    460, 466
National Center for Health
    Statistics (NCHS), 64,
    112, 167, 347, 354, 385,
    434, 435, 436, 444
National Center for Injury
    Prevention and Control, 443
National Center for Learning
    Disabilities, 386
National Center for Teachers of
    Mathematics, 383
National Center on Addiction and
    Substance Abuse at Columbia
    University, 397
National Center on Shaken Baby
    Syndrome, 172
National Clearinghouse on
    Child Abuse and Neglect
    Information (NCCANI),
    173, 174
National Coalition for the
    Homeless, 268
National Commission for the
    Protection of Human Subjects
    of Biomedical and Behavioral
    Research, 54
National Conference of State
    Legislatures, 106
National Diabetes Education
    Program, 350
National Diabetes Information
    Clearinghouse, 350
National Enuresis Society, 257
National Fatherhood Initiative, 402
National High Blood Pressure
    Education Program Working
    Group on High Blood
    Pressure in Children and
    Adolescents, 350
National Highway Traffic Safety
    Administration, 443
National Insitute of Drug Abuse
    (NIDA), 440

National Institute of Child Health
    and Human Development
    (NICHD), 77, 127, 247
    Early Child Care Research
        Network., 233, 235, 289, 293,
        384, 399, 400
    Study of Early Child Care, 53,
        231, 245
National Institute of Dental and
    Craniofacial Research, 340
National Institute of Mental Health
    (NIMH), 152, 341, 402, 418,
    433, 444
National Institute of Neurological
    Disorders and Stroke
    (NINDS), 171, 172
National Institutes of Health, 121
National Library of Medicine, 353
National Parents' Resource Institute
    for Drug Education, 441
National Reading Center, 378
National Research Council (NRC),
    173, 174, 264, 381, 467
National Sleep Foundation, 256, 342
National Survey on Drug Use and
    Health (NSDUH), 439, 442
Navratil, F., 68
Nawrocki, T., 235
Needell, B., 406
Needham, C., 356
Neergaard, L., 152
Neff, C., 230
Neisser, U., 289, 296, 371, 372
Nelson, C. A., 156, 158, 159, 189,
    196, 285, 433
Nelson, D. A., 328
Nelson, K., 179, 187, 200, 286, 287
Nelson, K. B., 120
Nelson, L. J., 106, 502
Nelson, M. C., 434
Nelson, T., 18, 204
Neumark-Sztainer, D., 397, 436
Neville, A., 97
Neville, H. J., 19
Nevis, S., 193
Newacheck, P. W., 349, 351
Newcomb, A. F., 410
Newcombe, R., 287
Newman, D. L., 226
Newman, N. M., 168
Newman, R. S., 205
Newman, T. B., 356, 443
Newport, E. L., 19, 213
Niaura, R., 494
Nichols, J., 266
Nichols, K. E., 321
Nickerson, A. B., 495
Nicoladis, E., 212
Nie, N. H., 496
Nielsen, M., 237
Nilsen, E. S., 279
Nirmala, A., 85
Nisan, M., 459
Nisbett, R. E., 371, 372

Nix, R. L., 321
Nixon, C. L., 284
Nobile, C., 342
Nobre, A. C., 210
Noirot, E., 100
Noll, J. G., 174
Noonan, C. J., 109
Noonan, M. E., 415
Nord, M., 264
Nordstrom, B., 103
Noriuchi, M., 228
Norton, M. E., 110
Notarius, C. I., 44
Nourot, P. M., 318
Novak, M. F. S. X., 107
Noyes, J., 107
Nucci, L., 490, 491
Nugent, J. K., 103, 127
Nugent, L. D., 285
Nyman, M., 328

Oakes, L. M., 196, 197
Oates, R. K., 174
Obel, C., 104
Ober, C., 349
Oberman, L. M., 223
O'Brien, C. M., 105
O'Brien, M., 318, 345, 434
O'Connell, B., 203, 204
O'Connell, M. P., 129
O'Connor, E., 443
O'Connor, M. J., 104
O'Connor, T., 107
O'Connor, T. G., 158
Odent, M., 121
Odgen, C., 146, 338
Odoki, K., 147
O'Donnell, L. N., 441
Odouli, R., 104, 168
Oetting, J. B., 292
Offer, D., 488
Offer, M. K., 488
Office of National Drug Control
    Policy, 440
Offit, P. A., 170
Ofori, B., 103
Ogbuanu, I. U., 147
Ogden, C. L., 262, 339, 345, 435
Okamoto, Y., 35, 451
Okazaki, S., 372
O'Keefe, C., 206
Oken, E., 195
Olah, L. N., 277
Olds, D., 174
Olds, S. W., 123, 130, 352
O'Leary, C., 132
Olfson, M., 356
Oliphant, J. A., 480
Ollendick, T. H., 332, 417
Olsen, J., 108
Olson, C. M., 265
Olson, K. R., 326
Olson, L., 167, 268

Olson, L. S., 381
Olson, S. L., 321, 323
Olthof, T., 395
Olweus, D., 416
O'Mahony, P., 103
O'Malley, P. M., 439
O'Malley, P., 501–502
Omojokun, O. O., 168
Ondracek, P. J., 369
O'Neil, K., 317
O'Neil, R., 333
Ono, H., 344, 396, 489
Opdal, S. H., 168
Operskalski, B., 356
Opfer, J. E., 364
Oppenheim, D., 169
Opper, S., 448
O'Rahilly, S., 428
Oraichi, D., 103
O'Reilly, A. W., 187
Orenstein, P., 98
Organization for Economic
    Co-operation and Development
    (OECD), 460, 466
Ornstein, P. A., 369
Orr, D. P., 432
Ortega, S., 10
Osejo, V. M., 105
Osgood, D. W., 244, 494
Oshima-Takane, Y., 213
Osmond, C., 87
Ossorio, P., 13
Ostbye, T., 133
Osterman, M. J. K., 485
Ostrov, E., 488
Ostry, D., 209
O'Toole, B. I., 174
Ott, M. G., 79
Ouellette, G.P., 379
Overbeek, G., 489
Overpeck, M. D., 434
Owen, C. G., 147
Owen, D. R., 288
Owen, L. D., 480
Owen, M. J., 84, 87
Owens, E. B., 323
Owens, J., 342
Owens, J. L., 287
Owens, R. E., 210, 290, 291, 292,
    376, 452
Oyserman, D., 477
Ozarow, L., 376
Ozata, M., 428
Ozcaliskan, S., 205
Ozyürek, A., 209

Pac, S., 148
Padden, C., 209
Padden, C. A., 209
Padden, D., 18, 204
Padilla, A. M., 377
Pae, S., 292
Pagnucco, J. R., 378

Paige, R. U., 405
Painter, K., 187
Paley, B., 104
Palkovitz, R., 137
Palmer, F. B., 203
Palombini, L., 256
Paltrow, L., 106
Palusci, V. J., 172
Pan, B. A., 211
Panigrahy, A., 168
Panwar, O., 108
Papadatou-Pastou, M., 259
Papathanasopoulos, P., 440
Paradis, J., 212
Pardo, C., 417
Park, J., 298
Park, J. M., 268
Park, S., 227
Parke, R., 333, 398, 399
Parke, R. D., 6, 13, 18, 48, 79, 243,
    324, 397, 398, 402
Parker, A. M., 452
Parker, J. G., 317
Parker, K. D., 10
Parker, L., 109
Partelow, L., 379
Parten, M. B., 317, 318
Partridge, J. C., 99, 159
Paschall, M. J., 322, 323
Pascual-Leone, A., 156
Pastor, P. N., 385, 386, 387
Pastorelli, C., 380, 466
Pastuszak, A., 103
Patel, K. M., 168
Patenaude, A. F., 79
Patrick, K., 436
Pattall, E. A., 382
Pattee, L., 410
Patterson, C. J., 405, 479, 480
Patterson, G. R., 499
Pauen, S., 196
Paulozzi, L. J., 102
Paus, T., 341
Pauwels, B. G., 402
Pavlov. I., 32
Pawelski, J. G., 405, 406
Paxson, C., 349
Payne, A., 332
Payne, J. D., 313
Pearce, M. J., 498
Pearce, M. S., 109
Pearl, R., 413
Pedersen, C. B., 235
Pedersen, J., 244, 245
Pegg, J. E., 213
Pelayo, R., 256
Pell, J. P., 121
Pell, T., 105
Pellegrini, A. D., 38, 118, 137, 187,
    307, 309, 310, 315, 316, 317,
    318, 319, 328, 344, 387, 408,
    409, 415, 416
Pempek, T. A., 195
Peña, F., 168

Pendlebury, J. D., 104
Pennington, B. F., 76, 77
Pepe, M. S., 263
Pepler, D., 331
Pepper, S. C., 25, 26
Pereira, M., 235
Pereira, M. A., 345
Perera, F., 109
Perera, F. P., 110
Perez, S. M., 366
Perfetti, C. A., 378
Perfors, A., 202
Perrin, E. C., 405
Perrin, E. M., 347
Perrin, J. M., 356, 436, 443
Perrin, S. P., 137
Perry, D. G., 311, 409
Perry, T. B., 495, 496
Perry-Jenkins, M., 399
Peskin, H., 432
Pesonen, A., 233
Peter, J., 496
Petersen, A. C., 432, 488
Peterson, C. C., 282
Peterson, K., 484
Peterson, K. E., 148
Peterson, L., 480
Petit, D., 256
Petitto, L. A., 209, 210, 211, 212
Petrakos, H., 331
Petrill, S. A., 86
Petronis, A., 72
Pettit, G. S., 317, 320, 322, 324,
    325, 329, 410, 413, 416, 419,
    431, 500
Peyser, H., 405
Phelps, J. L., 233
Phelps, K. E., 283
Philliber, S., 487
Phillips, D., 247, 296
Phillips, D. F., 62
Phillips, P., 10
Phillips, R., 384
Phinney, J. S., 476, 477
Piaget, J., 33–35, 179, 187, 191,
    274, 279, 281, 317, 361, 362,
    364, 450
Pianta, R. C., 380
Piccinino, L., 480
Pick, A. D., 163
Pickens, J., 235
Picker, J., 87
Pickett, W., 169, 416
Pierce, K. M., 399
Pierroutsakos, S. L., 190, 275
Pike, A., 331, 408
Pike, L. B., 482
Pillow, B. H., 282, 362
Pine, D. S., 227
Pines, M., 19
Pinkleton, B. E., 442
Pinto, J. P., 206
Pinuelas, A., 328
Pipe, M., 287

Plant, L. D., 168
Pleck, J. H., 139
Pletcher, M. J., 436
Plomin, R., 79, 81, 83, 84, 85,
    86, 211, 226, 292, 307,
    327, 386
Plunkett, K., 210
Podolski, C. L., 414
Poelhuis, C. W. K., 406
Poffenbarger, T., 350
Pogarsky, G., 487
Poikkeus, A., 292
Polit, D. F., 332
Pollack, B., 243
Pollack, H., 487
Pollack, S. D., 173, 174
Pollak, S., 173
Pollak, S. D., 173, 204
Pomerantz, E. M., 304
Pomery, E. A., 494
Pong, S., 404
Ponjaert, I., 405
Ponomarev, I., 285
Ponsonby, A. L., 168
Pontieri, F. E., 441
Poole, K., 133
Pope, A. W., 410
Pope, H. G., Jr., 137
Pope, R. S., 366
Population Reference Bureau, 14
Porfeli, E., 502
Porges, S. W., 231
Porter, M. R., 495
Porter, R. H., 100
Portman, R. J., 350
Posner, J. K., 399
Posner, M. I., 45
Posthuma, D., 86
Potenza, M. N., 433
Poulin, F., 500
Poulin-Dubois, D., 242
Powell, B., 406
Powell, C., 265
Powell, M. B., 286
Power, T. G., 238, 305
Powers, B. P., 231
Powlishta, K. K., 319, 408–409
Practice Committee, 65
Prakash, K., 317
Preissler, M., 190
Presnell, K., 436, 442
Price, J. M., 410
Price, T. S., 292
Prinzie, P., 494
Prisco, T. R., 398
Proctor, B. D., 14
Pruden, S. M., 205
Pruitt, J., 18, 204
Pruyne, E., 457
Psych, M., 87
Public Law 108-265, 349
Pungello, E., 184
Putallaz, M., 328
Putnam, F., 174

Soenens, B., 492
Sok, E., 245
Sokol, R. J., 103, 104, 109
Soliday, E., 147
Solomon, J., 230
Solowij, N., 440
Sommer, M., 350, 351
Sondergaard, C., 104
Sontag, L. M., 432
Sood, B., 104
Sophian, C., 286, 363
Sorof, J. M., 350
Sotres-Alvarez, D., 102
Soules, M.R., 62
Souter, V. L., 64
South, S. J., 480
Soutollo, D., 235
Sowell, E. R., 150, 258
Sparling, J., 184
Sparling, J. J., 184
Spelke, E., 199
Spelke, E. S., 277, 307, 326
Spellman, B. A., 197
Spence, M. J., 100
Spencer, J. P., 164, 190
Sperling, M. A., 133
Sperling, R. A., 367
Spinath, F. M., 86, 292
Spinrad, T. L., 305, 317, 318
Spira, E. G., 379
Spirito, A., 342
Spitz, R., 232
Spohr, H. L., 104
Spoor, S., 85
Sprafkin, J., 499
Sprague, B. M., 168
Spry, L., 266
Srivastav, P., 243
Sroufe, L. A., 220, 222, 232, 233
Stack, D. M., 193
Staff, J., 468
Stafford, F. P., 344, 396, 489
Stahl, S. A., 378
Stallings, V. A., 149
Stamilio, D. M., 132
Standing, E. M., 295
Standley, J. M., 133
Stanhope, L., 331
Stanhope, R., 339
Stanley-Hagan, M., 405
Starnes, R., 328
Starr, J. M., 370
State Children's Health Insurance
    Program (SCHIP), 268
Stattin, H., 489
Staub, E., 498
Stauder, J. E. A., 364
St. Clair, D., 87
Stedron, J., 76
Stegge, H., 395
Stein, M. R., 244
Stein, R. E. K., 351
Steinberg, L., 81, 324, 431, 433,
    463, 490, 491, 499, 500

Steinhausen, H. C., 104, 439
Stennes, L. M., 242
Stephansson, O., 135
Stephens, L. E., 103
Stephens, P., 356
Steptoe, P., 62
Sternberg, R. J., 13, 370, 371, 372,
    374, 375, 382, 467
Stevens, J. H., 183
Stevens, K. N., 204
Stevens, N., 333, 495, 496, 500
Stevens-Graham, B., 433
Stevenson, H. W., 372, 463
Stevenson-Hinde, J., 330
Stewart, I. C., 487
Stewart, J. H., 172, 321, 322
Stewart, M. G., 343
Stewart, S., 345
Stice, E., 85, 436, 442
Stillwell, R., 465
Stipek, D. J., 237
Stirling, J., Jr., 156, 173
Stockemer, V., 332
Stoecker, J. J., 193
Stoelhorst, M. S. J., 133
Stoll, B. J., 132
Stoll, M. F., 402
Stone, W. L., 153
Stoolmiller, M., 480
Stormshak, E., 325
Story, M., 345, 436, 444
Stoskopf, B. L., 134
Stothard, K. J., 101
Stovall, K. C., 233
Strandberg, T., 233
Strassberg, Z., 322
Strathearn, L., 229
Straus, M. A., 172, 321, 322, 323
Strayer, D., 463
Strebel, P., 105
Streight, S., 169
Streiner, D. L., 134
Streissguth, A. P., 103, 104
Striano, T., 204, 211, 234, 237
Strickland, B., 349
Striegel-Moore, R. H., 436, 437, 438
Stright, A. D., 226
Strobel, A., 428
Strobino, D. M., 64, 104, 132, 167
Strohschein, L., 402
Strömland, K., 104
Strosberg, A. D., 428
Stubbs, M. L., 432
Stucky, B., 412
Stueve, A., 441
Stukel, T. A., 132
Stunkard, A. J., 149
Sturm, R., 347, 349
Stuttering Foundation, 350
Styfco, S. J., 296
Substance Abuse and Mental Health
    Services Administration
    (SAMHSA), 440, 441
Suddendorf, T., 237

Sue, S., 372
Sugarman, D. B., 322
Suleman, N., 64, 66
Sullivan, K., 104, 282
Summers, K., 87
Sun, Y., 493
Sundet, J., 288
Surkan, P. J., 135
Susman, E. J., 427, 428, 429, 430,
    431, 432, 442
Susman-Stillman, A., 231
Susser, E. S., 87
Suzuki, L. A., 372
Swain, I. U., 160, 193
Swain, J. E., 121
Swallen, K. C., 436
Swamy, G. K., 133
Swan, S. H., 109
Swanston, H. Y., 174
Swedo, S., 444
Sweeney, J. A., 366, 454
Swingley, D., 206
Swisher, R., 329
Syed, U., 117, 166
Sylva, K., 182
Szaflarski, J. P., 210
Szatmari, P., 152
Szkrybalo, J., 242, 311

Tabin, C., 92
Tackett, J. L., 499
Tager-Flusberg, H., 282
Taillac, C. J., 105
Takanishi, R., 297
Talokder, E., 243
Tamang, B. L., 219, 396
Tamis-Lemonda, C. S., 161, 243
Tamis-LeMonda, C. S., 139, 162,
    194, 211, 402
Tanaka, A., 233
Tanaka, K., 415
Tanda, G., 441
Tanner, J. L., 402, 403
Tao, K.-T., 332
Tapert, S. F., 440
Tardif, C., 233
Tate, B. A., 435
Taussig, C., 501
Taveras, E., 195
Taveras, E. M., 148
Taylor, A., 15, 289
Taylor, B. J., 169
Taylor, C. L., 292
Taylor, G., 133
Taylor, J. R., 433
Taylor, L. C., 380
Taylor, M., 283
Taylor, R. D., 493
Taylor, S. E., 400
Teachman, J. D., 10
Teasdale, T. W., 288
Tebbutt, J. S., 174

Tedrow, L. M., 10
Temple, J. A., 296, 384, 501
Tenenbaum, H. R., 243, 313
Tenenbaum, J. B., 197
Tennant, P. W. G., 101
Termine, N. T., 234
Tesla, C., 284
Tester, D. J., 168
Teti, D. M., 235, 243, 244
Thacker, S. B., 120
Thapar, A., 387
Thelen, E., 164, 165, 189, 190, 199
Thoma, S. J., 456
Thoman, E. B., 101, 128, 133
Thomas, A., 86, 137, 224, 225, 226
Thomas, K. M., 433
Thomas, W. P., 377
Thompson, K. M., 414
Thompson, L. A., 132
Thompson, P. M., 86, 150, 257,
    258, 340, 371
Thompson, R. A., 55, 220, 242,
    305, 324
Thomson, D. M., 286
Thomson, E., 405
Thornberry, T. P., 487
Thorne, A., 476
Tidball, G., 234
Tidwell, L. C., 496
Tiedemann, D., 5
Tiggeman, M., 345
Tincoff, R., 205
Ting, T. Y., 120
Tinsley, R., 243
Tipsord, J.M., 409
Tipsord, J. M., 410
Tirosh, E., 128
Tita, A. T. N., 121
Tither, J., 431
Tjebkes, T. L., 240
Toga, A., 86, 156, 340, 341
Toga, A. W., 150, 258
Tolan, P. H., 498, 499, 500, 501
Tom, S. E., 432
Tomany-Korman, S. C., 167, 268
Tomasello, M., 204, 222, 223, 224
Tomashek, K. M., 168, 169
Toner, J. P., 62
Torff, B., 382
Torjussen, T., 288
Torrance, E. P., 389
Toth, S. L., 355
Totsika, V., 182
Touchette, E., 256
Touwen, B. C. L., 147
Touyz, S. W., 438
Townsend, J., 152–153
Townsend, N. W., 139
Trautner, H. M., 312
Tremblay, R. E., 256, 327, 329, 440
Trends in International
    Mathematics and Science
    Study (TIMSS), 383
Trenholm, C., 482

Trickett, P. K., 174
Trim, R. S., 441
Trimble, J. E., 13
Troiano, R. P., 434
Tronick, E., 160
Tronick, E. Z., 137, 234
Troseth, G. L., 190
Truglio, R., 294
Tryba, A. K., 168
Trzesniewski, K. H., 476
Tsao, F. M., 204
Tseng, V., 489
Tsuboi, K., 435
Tsuchiya, K., 110
Tupler, L. A., 173
Turati, C., 193
Turkheimer, E., 372, 432
Turner, J., 350
Turner, P. J., 242, 313, 314
Turner, S. M., 354
Turrisi, R., 442
Turtle, M., 257
Twenge, J. M., 139, 417
Tyson, D., 463

Uggen, C., 468
Ullman, J. B., 381
Umilta, C., 193
United Nations Children's Fund
    (UNICEF), 14, 110, 131, 132,
    146, 166, 170, 261, 263
United States Breastfeeding
    Committee, 147
Updegraff, K. A., 313
Urban, T. A., 366, 454
U.S. Bureau of Labor Statistics,
    245, 398
U.S. Census Bureau, 11, 167,
    246, 404
U.S. Department of Agriculture,
    342, 349
U.S. Department of Education,
    National Center for Education
    Statistics, 295
U.S. Department of Energy, Office
    of Science, 79
U.S. Department of Health and
    Human Services (USDHHS),
    99, 112, 171, 172, 174, 342,
    353, 355, 356, 387, 480
U. S. Preventive Services Task
    Force, 292
Uttal, D. H., 190, 191

Vainio, S., 68
Valadez-Meltzer, A., 452
Valencia, R. R., 372
Valeri, S. M., 443
Valkenburg, P., 496
Van, P., 98
Van Acker, R., 413
Vance, M. L., 339

Van Cleave, E. F., 432
Vandell, D. L., 244, 399
Van den Boom, D. C., 231
van den Wittenboer, G. L. H., 139
Van der Molen, M. W., 364
van der Pal-de Bruin, K. M., 129
Vandewater, E. A., 195, 400
van Goozen, S., 354, 498, 499
Van Hall, V. E., 405
van IJzendoorn, M. H., 229, 230,
    231, 232, 233, 406
Vansteenkiste, M., 492
Van Voorhis, B. J., 65, 66
Varendi, H., 100
Vargha-Khadem, F., 200
Varghese, J., 234
Varni, J. W., 347
Vasilyeva, M., 276, 278, 291
Vaughn, B. E., 231
Veenstra, R., 415, 416
Veerman, J. W., 413
Velkoff, V. A., 407
Venables, P., 265
Venables, P. H., 265
Ventura, A. K., 159
Ventura, S. J., 485, 486, 487
Ventura-Cook, E., 241
Vereecken, C., 435, 436
Vereijken, B., 162
Vereijken, C. M. J. L., 231
Verma, S., 344, 489
Vermulst, A., 489
Verschueren, K., 233, 303
Vespo, J., 245
Vevea, J., 371
Vgontzas, A. N., 256
Vickerie, J. L., 266
Victora, C. G., 104
Victorian Infant Collaborative
    Study Group, 134
Vigorito, J., 160
Viken, R., 432
Vilain, E., 308
Villalpando, S., 102
Viner, R. M., 262
Visser, G., 107
Vitaro, F., 256, 416
Vitousek, K. M., 438
Voelz, S., 362
Vohr, B. R., 133
Volkow, N., 387
Volling, B., 328
Volling, B. L., 331
Vondra, J. I., 229, 230
Vong, K. I., 286
von Gontard, A., 257
von Hofsten, C., 163
von Mutius, E., 349
Vosniadou, S., 376
Votruba-Drzal, E., 298, 480
Vrijenhoek, T., 87
Vrijheld, M., 109
Vuchinich, S., 398
Vuoksimaa, E., 259

Vuori, L., 102
Vygotsky, L. S., 35, 293

Waber, D. P., 371
Wadsworth, M. E., 14, 134, 399
Wagner, E., 222
Wahlbeck, K., 87
Wainright, J. L., 405
Waisbren, S. E., 127
Wake, M., 347
Wakefield, M., 110
Wakeley, A., 199
Waknine, Y., 72
Wald, N. J., 102
Walden, T. A., 153
Waldfogel, J., 246, 349
Waldman, I., 231
Waldman, I. D., 413, 499
Waldron, J., 372
Walk, R. D., 163
Walker, A. S., 193
Walker, L. R., 443
Walker, S., 265
Walker-Andrews, A. S., 234
Wall, M., 436
Wall, S., 117, 166, 229
Wall, T. P., 266
Wallace, L., 266
Waller, M., 497
Waller, M. W., 442
Wallerstein, J., 403
Wallerstein, J. S., 403
Walma van der Molen, J., 418
Walsh, R. O., 235
Walsh, T., 87
Walston, J., 298
Walters, R. H., 33
Walther, J. B., 496
Wang, C.-Y., 146
Wang, D. W., 168
Wang, E. T., 68
Wang, J. D., 109
Wang, P. S., 356
Wang, Q., 303
Wang, X., 231
Wang, Y., 132, 345
Wanstrom, L., 371
Ward, R. H., 109, 486
Wardle, J., 436
Warneken, F., 222
Warner, J., 66
Warner, M., 443
Warner, V., 355
Warren, M., 432
Warshauer-Baker, E., 13
Wartella, E. A., 195, 294
Wasik, B. H., 184, 289
Wasserstein, S., 417
Watamura, S. E., 247
Waterfall, H., 291
Waters, E., 229, 231, 233, 347
Waters, J. M., 189
Waters, K. A., 168

Watkins, M., 101
Watkins, S., 194
Watson, A. C., 284
Watson, J., 281
Watson, J. B., 32
Watson, M. S., 79
Waugh, R. M., 236
Way, N., 45
Weber, A., 266
Weber-Byars, A., 210
Weese-Mayer, D. E., 168
Wegman, M. E., 132
Wehner, E. A., 480, 496, 497
Weichold, K., 432
Weikart, D., 501
Weikart, D. P., 296, 487
Weile, B., 110
Weill, J., 264
Weinberg, A., 206
Weinberg, M. K., 234
Weinberger, B., 133
Weinberger, D. R., 498
Weiner, C., 418
Weinreb, L., 269
Weinreb, L. F., 268
Weinstock, H., 485
Weisner, T. S., 45, 407
Weiss, B., 269, 320, 355, 413
Weiss, J., 68
Weiss, L. A., 152
Weissman, M. M., 355
Weisz, J. R., 355, 443
Weitzman, M., 104, 269, 350
Welch-Ross, M. K., 312
Wellman, H. M., 276, 281, 284
Wells, J., 384
Wenar, C., 238
Weng, X., 104
Wenjun, Z., 148
Wenner, J. A., 189
Wentworth, N., 163
Wentzel, K. R., 465
Werker, J. F., 203, 204, 213
Werner, E. E., 135, 136, 419
Werner, R. S., 284
Wertz, A. E., 86
West, J., 298, 381
West, L., 332
West, M., 211
Westen, D., 29
Westerlund, A., 196
Westra, T., 165
Wethington, E., 462
Wexler, A., 79, 418
Wexler, I. D., 417
Whalley, L. J., 370
Whatt, W., 434
Wheeler, K., 193
Wheeler, M.E., 100
Whincup, P. H., 147
Whitaker, R. C., 263
White, A., 440
White, B. L., 183
White, D. R., 408–409

subject index

amniotic cavity, 95, 96f
amniotic sac, 95, 96f
amygdala, 433, 479
anal stage, 29, 30t
androgens, 103, 309
anencephaly, 73t
anger, externalizing behaviors, 398
angiotensin-converting enzyme
    (ACE) inhibitors, 103
angry cry, 219
animism, **277**
anorexia nervosa, **437**, 437–439
A-not-B error, **189**
anoxia, **125**
antidepressants, 103
antisocial behavior, in adolescence,
    497–501
antitrypsin deficiency, 73t
anxiety
    divorce and, 403
    internalizing behaviors, 398
    during pregnancy, 107–108
    school phobia, 354
    separation, 232
    separation anxiety disorder, 354
    social phobia, 354
    stranger, 232
Apache, coming of age ritual, 424
Apgar scale, **126**, 126–127, 126t
appearance, distinguishing from
    reality and, 282
apprenticeships, 467
Arab Americans, health care in, 353
Arapesh, sense of industry, 395
Argentina, adulthood criteria, 502
argumentativeness, adolescent
    thought and, 451
Around the World boxes
    childbirth in Himalayas, 123
    children of immigrant families, 12
    cross-cultural research purposes, 48
    cultural attitudes affect on health
        care, 352
    globalization of adolescence,
        425–426
    preventing teenage pregnancy, 487
    sign language invention, 209
    sleep customs, 169
    surviving first five years of life,
        261–262
    toddler struggles, 239
artificial insemination, 65
artificial insemination by a donor
    (AID), 65
artistic development, in early
    childhood, 259–260
art therapy, **355**
Asia
    adolescence in, 425
    child mortality in, 261
    emotions and, 218–219
    grandparents as caregivers, 407
    low-birth-weight babies,
        131, 131t

motor development, 165
school achievement, 461
sibling relationships, 407–408
Asian Americans
    adulthood criteria, 503
    health care access, 351
    high school dropout rates,
        465–466, 465f
    IQ, 372
    parenting style, 325–326
    peer influence on school
        achievement, 463–464
    puberty timing and, 432
    sexual activity, 481
Asperger syndrome, 152
assimilation, **34**
assisted reproductive technology
    (ART), 62, **65**, 65–66
asthma, **349**
    in middle childhood, 349–350
attachment, **228**
    ambivalent (resistant), 229
    Attachment Q-set (AQS), 231
    avoidant, 229
    developing in infancy, 228–233
    disorganized-disoriented, 230
    establishing, 230–231
    as factors in successful
        socialization, 241–242
    intergenerational transmission of
        patterns, 233
    long-term effects of, 232–233
    postpartum depression and, 235
    secure, 229
    as secure base, 231
    separation anxiety and stranger
        anxiety, 232
    Stranger Situation, 229, 230, 231
    studying patterns of,
        229–230, 231
    temperament role in, 231–232
    trust and, 231
Attachment Q-set (AQS), 231
attention
    control of attentional processes
        and self-regulation, 240
    joint, 194
    selective, 366–367
    television watching and
        attentional development, 194
attention-deficit/hyperactivity
    disorder (ADHD), **386**,
    386–388
    juvenile delinquency risk, 499
Australia
    overweight children in, 347
    prosocial behavior study, 460
authoritarian parenting, **324**,
    324–325, 333
    adolescent relationships and,
        490–491
    child popularity and, 410
    school achievement and, 381,
        462–463

authoritative parenting, **324**,
    324–325, 333
    adolescent relationships and,
        490–491
    child popularity and, 410
    juvenile delinquency influenced
        by, 500
    school achievement and, 381,
        462–463
autism, 72, 152–153
Autism Spectrum Disorders
    (ASD), 152
autobiographical memory, **286**
autonomic nervous system,
    emotional development, 222
autonomy
    autonomy versus shame and
        doubt, 237–238
    developing, 237–238
    terrible twos and, 238, 238t
    in toddlerhood, 237–239
autonomy versus shame and doubt,
    237, 237–238
autonomy vs. shame and doubt, 30t
autosomes, **68**
avoidant attachment, **229**
axons, 153

babbling, 202, 211
Babinski reflex, 157f, 157t
baby acne, 124t
baby biographies, 5
Baby-Friendly hospitals, 147
baby talk, 212
basic sense of trust versus basic
    mistrust, **227**
basic trust vs. mistrust, 30t, 31
Bayley Scales of Infant and Toddler
    Development, **181**, 181–182
bed sharing, 179
bed-wetting, 257
behavior, intelligent, 202–213
behavioral genetics, **80**
behavioral inhibition, 226–227
behavioral measures, 43t
behaviorism, **31**, 31–33
    behavior modification, 33
    classical conditioning, 32
    operant conditioning, 32–33
behaviorist approach, **178**
    infancy and toddlerhood,
        179–180
    language acquisition, 207–208
behavior modification, 33
    in middle childhood, 355
behavior therapy, **355**
Belgium
    self-disclosure of adolescents, 492
    self-esteem, 303–304
Beng of West Africa, 136
Berkeley Growth and Guidance
    Studies, 5
beta thalassemia, 73t, 78

bilingual, **377**
bilingual children
    theory-of-mind tasks and, 284
    vocabularies of, 211–212
bilingual education, **377**
binge drinking, **440**
binge eating disorder, 438
binocular vision, 160
bioecological theory, **36**, 36–38, 37f
biological approach to gender
    development, 308–309, 308t
biosocial theory, gender
    development, 314
birth. *See* childbirth
birth defects, 72–78, 73t–74t, 76t
    as cause of infant deaths, 166
    chromosomal abnormalities,
        76–77, 76t
    dominant or recessive inheritance
        of, 74–75
    folic acid and, 101–102
    genetic testing for, 77–78
    inheritance of, 74–75
    period when embryo most
        vulnerable to, 97, 97f
    sex-linked inheritance of,
        75–76, 76t
birth trauma, 125
bisexual, 478, 479–480
blastocyst, 93
blended families, 405
bodily-kinesthetic intelligence,
    373, 373t
body dissatisfaction, 346
body fat, onset of puberty and,
    427–428, 431
body image, **345**
    Barbie dolls and, 346
    eating disorders and adolescents,
        436–439
    in middle childhood, 345
boldness, 226–227
bonding, childbirth and, 137–138
Botswana, father's role, 138
bottlefeeding, 146–148, 147t
Bradley Method of childbirth, 121
brain
    cells of, 151, 153–154
    growth spurts, 150, 151
    lateralization, 150
    major parts of, 150–151, 151f
    myelination, 154–155, 155f
    neurological deficits and juvenile
        delinquency, 499
    plasticity, 156
    reflex behavior, 156, 157t
    sexual orientation and, 479
    stuttering, 350
brain development
    in adolescence, 433–434
    in early childhood, 257–258
    early reflexes, 156, 157t
    emotional development and, 222
    during gestation, 150, 150f

gray matter maturation,
340–341, 341*t*
in infancy and toddlerhood,
149–159
integration and differentiation,
153–154
intelligence and, 371
language development and, 210
in middle childhood, 340–341,
341*f*, 364
molding brain with experience,
156–159
brain stem, 150, 151*f*, 210
SIDS and, 168
Braxton-Hicks contractions, 119
Brazelton Neonatal Behavioral
Assessment Scale (NBAS), **127**
Brazil, cultural context of learning
math, 363
breastfeeding, 146–148, 147*t*
colostrum, 123
breasts, puberty and, 429
Bucharest Early Intervention Project
(BEIP), 158–159
Bulgaria, prosocial behavior
study, 460
bulimia nervosa, 438, **438**
bullying, **415**
Internet and, 496
in middle childhood, 415–416
risk factors for victimization
of, 416

caffeine, during pregnancy, 104
Canada
corporal punishment, 322–323
low-birth-weight babies, 134
Canadian Hare people, sleep
customs for children, 256
canalization, 82–83, **83**
cardinality principle of counting,
277–278
caregivers
emotional communication with,
234–236
language development and, 210
mutual regulation, 234–236
temperament and goodness
of fit, 226
case study, **46**, 46–47
categorization, 196, 361*t*
in middle childhood, 361–362
preoperational thought
and, 277
causality, 196–197, 276–277
spatial relationships and, 360
cause and effect, 360, 361*t*
cell death, **153**, 153–154
Central America, sibling
relationships, 407–408
central executive, **285**
central nervous system, **149**, 149*f*
centration, 278, **278**, 279

cephalocaudal principle, **92**, 144,
145*f*, 161
cerebellum, 150, 151*f*
cerebral cortex, 151
emotional development, 222
cerebrum, 150, 151*f*
cervix, dilation of, in childbirth, 119
cesarean delivery, **120**, 120–121
charter schools, 384
Chicago Child-Parent Centers, 501
childbirth
bonding and, 137–138
complications of, 129–136
contemporary settings for, 118
culture and, 116–118
electronic fetal monitoring, 120
medicated vs. nonmedicated
delivery, 121–122
mortality rates, 117–118, 117*f*
multiple, 64–65
natural or prepared, 121–122
process of, 118–122
risk reduction in, 117–118
stages of, 119–120, 119*f*
vaginal birth after cesarean
(VBAC), 121
vaginal vs. cesarean delivery,
120–121
childbirth complications
low-birth-weight babies, 129–134
postmature, 134
stillbirth, 135
supportive environment for,
135–136
child care
after-school programs, 399
checklist for good, 248*t*
early, 246–249
in middle childhood, 399
NICHD study, 247–249
child development, **4**. *See also
specific stages*
active or reactive, 25–26
adolescence, 8*t*
basic concepts of, 6–9
context of, 10–15
continuous or discontinuous, 26
culture and race/ethnicity
influences, 11–13
domains of, 6–7
early approaches, 5
early childhood, 8*t*
emerging consensus, 18–20
environment influence on, 9–10
family influences, 10–11
heredity influence on, 9–10
immigrant families, 11–12
individual differences, 9
infancy, 8*t*
influences on, 9–18
language acquisition, 19
maturation influence on, 9–10
mechanistic model, 25–26
middle childhood, 8*t*

new frontiers, 6
normative and nonnormative
influences, 15–17
organismic model, 26
periods of, 7–9, 8*t*
poverty and, 14
prenatal period, 8*t*
risk factors, 14
socioeconomic status influence
on, 13–15
study of, 4–9
timing of influences, 17–18
toddlerhood, 8*t*
child-directed speech (CDS), **212**,
212–213
childhood depression, **354**, 354–355
Child Protective Services, 172
Children in North America
Project, 12
China
attachment research in, 231
child abuse rate, 172
folic acid and birth defects,
101–102
only children, 332
overweight, 345
parenting, 139
popularity, 410
reasoning of adolescents, 450
self-definition, 306
Chinese Americans
infant mortality rates and, 167
teenagers time use, 489
chlamydia, 483*t*, 484
chorion, 95, 96*f*
chorionic villus sampling (CVS),
111*t*
chromosomes, **67**
abnormalities of, 76–77, 76*t*
sex, 68–69, 69*f*
chronic medical conditions, **349**
chronosystem, **37**
circular reactions, **185**,
185–187, 186*f*
classical conditioning, 32, **32**, **179**
class inclusion, **362**
cleft palate, 101
cliques, 495
cocaine, during pregnancy, 104–105
code mixing, **212**
code switching, **212**
cognition
convergent thinking, 389
divergent thinking, 389
media and, 294
cognitive behavioral therapy, 355
eating disorder treatment, 438
cognitive construction, 302
cognitive-control network, 433
cognitive development, **6**
cognitive development, adolescence
dropping out of high school,
465–466
ethic of care, 459

formal operations, 448–451
hypothetical-deductive reasoning,
448–450
imaginary audience, 452
immature characteristics of
thought, 451–452
information processing, 453–454
language development, 452–453
moral development, 454–469
personal fable, 452
preparing for higher education or
vocations, 466–468
prosocial behavior and volunteer
activity, 459–460
school achievement influences,
460–465
cognitive development, early
childhood
causality, 276–277
false beliefs and deception,
281–282
forming and maintaining
childhood memories, 286–287
imaginary companions, 283
information-processing approach,
284–287
intelligence measurements,
288–290
language development, 290–294
magical thinking, 283
media use and, 294
memory, 285–287
numbers, 277–278
preoperational child, Piagetian
approach, 274–284
preschools and kindergarten,
295–298
pretend play, 275
private speech, 293
psychometric approach, 288–290
theory of mind, 280–284
cognitive development, infancy and
toddlerhood
behaviorist approach, 179–180
cognitive neuroscience approach,
200–201
dual representation
hypothesis, 191
early intervention, 184
guided participation, 201
home environment impact,
182–183
imitation, 187–189
infant memory, 179–180
information-processing approach,
184–191
intelligence testing, 181–184
joint attention, 194
language development, 202–213
memory and, 200–201
object permanence, 189–190
psychometric approach, 181–184
sensorimotor stage, Piagetian
approach, 184–191

episiotomy, 120
episodic memory, **286**
equilibration, **34**
Erickson's industry versus inferiority, 394–395
erythema toxicum, 124*t*
estimation, in middle childhood, 364
estrogen
  gender development and, 309
  puberty and, 427
ethics, of research
  deception avoidance, 55
  developmental consideration for children an, 54, 55*t*
  informed consent, 54–55
  privacy and confidentiality, 55–56
  self-esteem right, 55
ethnic gloss, **13**
ethnic group, 11. *See also specific group*
ethnicity. *See* race/ethnicity
ethnographic study, 47, **47**
ethology, **38**
Europe
  overweight, 345
  reasoning of adolescents, 450
European Americans
  adulthood criteria, 503
  identity formation, 476–477, 477*t*
  peer influence on school achievement, 463
  puberty timing and, 432
  teenagers time use, 489
Everyday World boxes
  Barbie dolls and body image, 346
  comforting crying baby, 130
  corporal punishment, 322–323
  fetal welfare vs. mother's rights, 106
  food security, 264
  growing up in hard times, 16–17
  imaginary companions, 283
  math wars, 383
  multitasking and Gen M, 463
  postpartum depression and early development, 235–236
  television watching of infants/toddlers, 195
  terrorism and war discussions, 418
  youth violence epidemic, 498
evocative correlations, 84
evolutionary development, 39
evolutionary psychology, **38**, 38–39
evolutionary/sociobiological perspective, 28*t*, **38**, 38–39
  gender development, 308*t*, 309–310
  immaturity, adaptive value of, 40
  only children, 332
  play, 316
  puberty onset timing, 431
  rough-and-tumble play, 344
evolved mechanisms, 38
executive function, **285**, **366**, 453

exercise
  in adolescence, 434
  during pregnancy, 102
exosystem, **37**, 37*f*
experience, molding brain through, 156–159
experiential element, **374**
experiment, **49**, 49–51
  degree of control, 50
  groups and variables, 49
  laboratory, field and natural experiments, 50–51
  random assignment, 49–50
experimental group, **49**
explicit memory, **200**
expressive vocabulary, 206
extended family, **10**
externalizing behaviors, **398**
external memory aids, **367**, 367–369, 369*t*

Facebook, 496
failure factor, 55
faith, stages of, 458–459
false beliefs, 281–282
family, 399
  adolescent relationships, 489–494
  adoptive, 406–407
  atmosphere of, 492–493
  blended, 405
  characteristics of abusive/neglectful, 172
  child development influenced by, 10–11
  cohabiting, 404
  conflict, 397–398
  divorce of parents, 402–404
  extended, 10
  of gay or lesbian parents, 405–406
  gender development influenced by, 313
  grandparents, 407
  instability of, 402
  juvenile delinquency influenced by, 499–500
  mealtime, 397
  nuclear, 10
  one-parent, 399–400, 404
  parental monitoring, 492
  puberty onset influenced by, 431
  self-disclosure of adolescents, 492
  sexual activity influenced by, 481
  sibling relationships, 407–408
  single parent, 399–400, 404
  skip-generation families, 407
  stepfamilies, 404–405
  structure of, and changes in, 400–402, 401*t*
  two-parent, 401–402
Family and Medical Leave Act, 407
family studies, 80
family therapy, **355**

Family Transitions Project, 16–17
fantasy, distinguishing from reality and, 282
fantasy play, 275
fast mapping, **291**
fathers/fathering
  bonding with newborns, 137–138
  divorce and child relationship, 403
  early sexual activity influenced by, 480
  environmental factors in prenatal development, 109–110
  gay parents, 405–406
  gender development influenced by, 313
  importance of involvement, 402
  marital satisfaction related to parenthood, 139–140
  newborns and role of, 138–139
  puberty onset influenced by, 431
  relationship with adolescents, 493
  as single parent, 404
  stepfather, 405
fear
  anxiety disorders, 354
  internalizing behaviors, 398
  school phobia, 354
  social phobia, 354
fearfulness, 329–330
fears
  anxiety and fears of children, 417
  socioeconomic status (SES) and, 417
Fels Research Institute Study, 5
females
  ADHD, 387
  adolescent growth spurt, 429–430
  aggression, 328, 412
  anxiety disorders, 354
  asthma, 349
  body image, 345, 436–437
  body image and Barbie dolls, 346
  bullying, 415
  child mortality, 262
  communication, 376
  conduct disorders, 353
  depression, 354
  depression and, 442
  divorce adjustment, 402
  early and late maturers, 432
  fetus activity level, 99–100
  gender identity development, 306–314
  genetic determinants of, 68–69, 69*f*
  growth patterns, 145, 145*f*
  handedness, 259
  identity formation, 476
  imaginary friends, 283
  infants and toddlers, 242–243
  infertility causes, 62, 63*t*
  mathematical abilities, 307, 380
  miscarriage grief, 98

moral development, 459
overweight, 345
peer-group relationships, 409
play, 318–319
prosocial behavior, 460
puberty and, 426–432, 427*f*, 428*t*
recess-time play, 344
rough-and-tumble play, 344
school achievement, 380, 461–462
sexual activity and age, 478*f*, 480
sleep patterns in middle childhood, 342
stepfather adjustment, 405
stuttering, 350
verbal abilities, 307
vocational choices and, 466–467, 467*f*
volunteerism associated with, 460
fertilization, **61**
fetal alcohol syndrome (FAS), **103**, 103–104
fetal stage, **99**, 99–100
fetus, 92
  fetal welfare vs. mother's rights, 106
  sense of smell and hearing, 100
fidelity, **473**
field experiment, 50
fine motor skills, **161**, **258**, 258–259
Finland
  low-birth-weight babies, 134
  teenage pregnancy in, 487
firearm, deaths related to, 443, 443*f*
first grade, 379–380
first sentences, 206–207
first words, 205–206
fixation, 29
folic acid, pregnancy and, 101–102
follicle stimulating hormone (FSH), puberty and, 426–427, 427*f*
fontanels, 124
food allergies, in early childhood, 265
foreclosure, 474–476, 474*t*, **475**, 476*t*
formal games with rules, **317**
formal operations, 448–451, **488**
formal operations stage, 30*t*
formula feeding, 146–148, 147*t*
Foster care, 172–173
France
  family living arrangements, 401*t*
  teenage pregnancy in, 487
Freudian psychosexual development, 27–29, 30*t*
friends/friendship. *See also* peers
  in adolescence, 494–497
  in early childhood, 332–333
  in middle childhood, 411, 412*t*
  stages of, 412*t*
  unpopular children, 411

frontal lobe, 150–151, 151*f*, 433
  emotional development, 222
frustration cry, 220
functional changes, in information
    processing, 453–454
functional magnetic resonance
    imaging (fMRI), 45
functional play, **316**

galactosemia, 127
gamete intrafallopian transfer
    (GIFT), 66
gays
  families with gay parents,
    405–406
  suicide rate for adolescents, 444
gender, **242**. *See also* females; males
  vocational choices and,
    466–467, 467*f*
gender consistency, 311
gender constancy, **311**
gender development
  biological approach, 308–309
  cognitive approach, 310–314
  evolutionary approach,
    309–310
  five perspectives on,
    307–308, 308*t*
  gender-schema theory, 311–312
  Kohlberg's cognitive-
    developmental theory,
    310–311
  psychoanalytic approach, 310
  social learning approach,
    312–314
gender differences
  ADHD, 387
  aggression, 328, 412
  anxiety disorders, 354
  asthma, 349
  bullying, 415
  communication, 376
  conduct disorders, 353
  in early childhood, 306–307
  fetus activity level, 99–100
  identity formation, 476
  in infancy and toddlerhood,
    242–243
  mathematical abilities, 380
  moral development, 459
  overweight, 345
  parents influence on, 243
  peer-group relationships, 409
  play and, 318–319
  prosocial behavior, 460
  recess-time play, 344
  rough-and-tumble play, 344
  school achievement, 380,
    461–462
  sleep patterns, 342
  stuttering, 350
gender identity, **306**, 311
gender roles, **307**

gender-schema theory, **311**,
    311–312
gender segregation, **318**
gender similarities hypothesis, 307
gender stability, 311
gender stereotypes, **307**
gender-typing, **243**, **307**
gene-environment interaction
  disorganized attachment
    and, 230
  prosocial behavior, 327
general anesthesia, 122
generalized anxiety disorder, **354**
generativity vs. stagnation, 30*t*
generic memory, **286**
genes, **67**
gene therapy, 79
genetic code, **67**, 67–68, 67*f*
  human genome, 67
genetic counseling and testing, **77**,
    77–78, 79
genetic determinism, 79
genetics. *See also* heredity
  ADHD, 387
  aggression, 328
  anxiety disorders, 354
  autism and, 152
  behavioral genetics, 80
  depression, 355
  epigenesis, 71–72
  genetic transmission
    patterns, 69–72
  handedness, 259
  intelligence and, 289
  IQ associated with, 371
  juvenile delinquency and, 499
  learning disabilities, 386
  medical genetics, 79
  prosocial behavior, 327
  sex determinants, 68–69, 69*f*
  sexual orientation, 478
  SIDS and, 168
  stuttering, 350
genital stage, **29**, 30*t*
Gen M, 463
genome imprinting, 72
genomics, 79
genotype, **70**, 70–71
genotype-environment
    correlation, **83**
genotype-environment interaction,
    83, 83–84, 83*f*
German measles, 105
Germany
  apprentice system ion, 467
  attachment research in, 231
  family living arrangements, 401*t*
  teenage pregnancy in, 487
germinal stage, **93**,
    93–96, 96*f*
gestation, **92**
gestational age, **92**
gestures, 204–205
Ghana, sexuality in, 480

gifted children
  causes of, 389
  defining and measuring
    creativity, 389
  educating, 389–390
  identifying, 388–389
glaucoma, 74
glia cells, 151
globalization, of adolescence,
    425–426
global self-worth, 394
gonadarche, 426–427
gonadotropin releasing hormone
    (GnRH), puberty and,
    426–427, 427*f*
gonorrhea, 483*t*, 484
goodness of fit, **226**
grammar, 291, 375–376
grandparents, as caregivers, 407
grasping reflex, 156, 157*t*, 162
gray matter, 340–341, 341*t*, 433
  intelligence and, 371
Great Britain
  gender development
    influences, 313
  rough-and-tumble play in, 344
Great Depression, 16–17, 52
gross motor skills, **161**, **258**,
    258–259
group esteem, 477
growth
  adolescent growth spurt, 429–430
  in early childhood, 254, 255*t*
  in infancy and toddlerhood,
    144–146, 145*f*, 145*t*
  in middle childhood, 338–339
growth hormone, 339
Guatemala
  guided participation, 201
  sleep customs for infants, 179
guided participation, **201**
Gusii people, 137
  attachment behavior, 230
  sleep customs for children, 256

habituation, **192**, 192–193
hand control, 162
handedness, **259**
handling routines, 165
haptic perception, **163**
Hare, of Canada, 129, 256
head control, 161–162
Head Start, 296–297
health and safety
  in early childhood, 260–270
  in infancy and toddlerhood,
    166–170
  in middle childhood, 345–353
health care
  access to, 351
  cultural attitudes affect on, 352
hearing, in infancy and
    toddlerhood, 160

height, in middle childhood,
    338–339
helpless pattern, 304
hemophilia, 73*t*, 76
Hepatitis B, 483*t*, 484–485
heredity, **9**, 66–87
  bed-wetting and, 257
  birth defects, 72–78,
    73*t*–74*t*, 76*t*
  child development influenced by,
    9–10
  chromosomal abnormalities,
    76–77, 76*t*
  delayed language development
    and, 292
  dominant inheritance, 69–70,
    70*f*, 74–75
  epigenesis, 71–72
  genetic code, 67–68, 67*f*
  genetic transmission patterns,
    69–72
  genotype and phenotype, 70–71
  genotype-environment
    interaction, 83–84, 83*f*
  intelligence and, 86, 371–372
  measuring, 80–81
  mechanism of, 66–72
  multifactorial transmission, 71
  obesity and, 85
  personality and, 86
  reaction range and canalization,
    82–83
  recessive inheritance, 69–70, 70*f*,
    74–75
  schizophrenia and, 86–87
  sex determinants, 68–69, 68*f*
  sex-linked inheritance, 75–76, 75*f*
heritability, **80**, 80–81
herpes, 483*t*, 484
heterosexuality, 478–480
heterozygous, **69**
high blood pressure
  in middle childhood, 350
  overweight children and, 347
high elaborative style, 287
high school dropouts,
    465–466, 465*f*
hippocampus
  emotional development, 222
  memory and, 200
Hispanics. *See also* Latinos
  high school dropout rates,
    465–466, 465*f*
  inactivity and sedentary behavior,
    346–347
  infant mortality rates and, 167
  IQ, 371–372
  population projections for,
    11, 11*f*
  poverty and, 399
  prenatal care, 113
  puberty timing and, 432
  teenage pregnancy, 485
  tooth decay, 339

historical generation, **17**
HIV/AIDS, **105**
  breastfeeding and, 148
  cause and symptoms, 484*t*
  early childhood deaths
    caused by, 261
  incidence of, 485
  perinatal transmission, 105
  transmission of, 485
holophrase, **205**
home environment
  gender differences in school
    achievement, 462
  infant and toddler intelligence
    and, 182–183
  intelligence and, 288–289
  school achievement
    and, 381
homelessness, in early childhood,
  268–269
Home Observation for
  Measurement of the
  Environment (HOME),
  182, 182–183
homeschooling, 384
homework, 382
homosexuals/homosexuality
  families with gay or lesbians
    parents, 405–406
  identity development and,
    478–480
  origins of, 479
  rate of, 478
homozygous, **69**
horizontal décalage, **363**
hormones
  gender development and,
    309–310
  growth hormone, 339
  puberty and changes in,
    426–428, 427*f*
hostile aggression, **412**, 413
hostile attribution bias, **413**
HPV (genital warts), 483*t*, 484
Huhot of Inner Mongolia, 139
human genome, **67**
Hungary
  gender development
    influences, 313
  prosocial behavior study, 460
hunger cry, 219
hungry season, 102
Huntington's disease, 72, 74
hyaline membrane disease, 133
hydroxyprogesteronecaproate
  (17P), 132
hypertension, **350**
  in middle childhood, 350
hypocrisy, adolescent thought
  and, 451
hypothalamus, 479
  emotional development, 222
  puberty and, 426–427, 427*f*
hypotheses, 24

hypothetical-deductive reasoning,
  448–450, **488**
hypothyroidism, congenital, 127
hypoxia, 125

id, 27–28
idealism, adolescent thought
  and, 451
ideal self, **303**, 394
identification, **310**
identity, **472**
  ethnic factors in formation of,
    476–477, 477*t*
  fidelity and, 473
  gender differences in
    formation, 476
  identity statuses, 472–476,
    474*t*, 475*t*
  identity versus identity confusion,
    472–473
  occupational identity, 472
  role confusion and, 472–473
  search for, in adolescence,
    472–477, 474*t*, 475*t*, 477*t*
  sexual identity, 472, 478
  sexual orientation and formation
    of, 478–480
identity achievement, **474**,
  474–476, 474*t*, 476*t*
identity crisis, 31, 472
  preoperational thought
    and, 277
identity diffusion, 474–476, 474*t*,
  475, 476*t*
identity principle, 362
identity statuses, 472–476, **473**,
  474*t*, 475*t*
identity-status interviews, 474
identity versus identity confusion,
  472, 472–473
identity vs. identity confusion, 30*t*
Ifaluk people, 136
imaginary audience, **452**
imaginary companions, 283
imaginary play, 275
imitation
  deferred, 188–189, 275
  early language development, 202
  elicited, 189
  invisible, 187
  visible, 187
immaturity, adaptive value of, 40
immigrants, children of, 11–12
immunization, in infancy and
  toddlerhood, 170
implantation, **93**
implicit memory, **200**
imprinting, **17**, **137**
inclusion programs, 388
incomplete dominance, **75**
indecisiveness, adolescent thought
  and, 451
independent variable, **49**

India
  adolescence in, 425
  rough-and-tumble play in, 344
  school achievement, 461
  teenagers time use, 489
indirect aggression, 328
individual differences, **9**
individual psychotherapy, **355**
Individuals with Disabilities
  Education Act, 388
individuation, **490**
individuative-reflective faith, 458
inductive reasoning, 361*t*, **362**
inductive techniques, **321**
industry vs. inferiority, 30*t*,
  394–395, **395**
infancy and toddlerhood, cognitive
  development
  behaviorist approach, 179–180
  cognitive neuroscience approach,
    200–201
  dual representation
    hypothesis, 191
  early intervention, 184
  guided participation, 201
  home environment impact,
    182–183
  imitation, 187–189
  infant memory, 179–180
  information-processing approach,
    184–191
  intelligence testing, 181–184
  joint attention, 194
  language development, 202–213
  memory and, 200–201
  object permanence, 189–190
  psychometric approach,
    181–184
  sensorimotor stage, Piagetian
    approach, 184–191
  social-contextual approach in, 201
  television watching and, 195
  visual and auditory processing
    abilities, 193–194
infancy and toddlerhood, physical
  development and health
  abuse, 171–174
  brain and reflex behavior,
    149–159
  breastfeeding or bottlefeeding,
    146–148, 147*t*
  health, 166–170
  immunizations, 170
  injuries, 168–169
  maltreatment, 171–174
  motor development, 160–166
  neglect, 171–174
  nutrition and feeding methods,
    146–149
  overweight problem, 148–149
  principles of early growth,
    144–146, 145*f*, 145*t*
  reducing infant mortality, 166–169
  reflex behavior, 156, 157*t*

  sensory capacity, 159–160
  solid foods, 148
  sudden infant death syndrome
    (SIDS), 166, 167–168
infancy and toddlerhood,
  psychosocial development
  attachment development,
    228–233
  autonomy, 237–239
  child care, 246–249
  development issues in, 227–242
  emotional communication with
    caregivers, 234–236
  emotions, 218–224
  foundations of, 218–227
  gender differences, 242–243
  highlights of, 218, 219*t*
  moral development, 240–242
  mutual regulation, 234–236
  nonsibling sociability, 244–245
  other children influences,
    243–245
  postpartum depression
    influencing, 235–236
  self-concept, 236–237
  self-regulation, 240
  sibling influences, 243–244
  socialization and internalization,
    240–242
  social referencing, 234–235
  temperament, 224–227
  trust, 227–228
  working parents and, 245–249
infant mortality rate, **166**
  reducing, 166–169
infants, 8*t. See also* infancy and
  toddlerhood, cognitive
  development; infancy and
  toddlerhood, physical
  development and health;
  infancy and toddlerhood,
  psychosocial development
  cross-cultural view of infant care,
    136–137
  low-birth-weight babies,
    129–134
  mortality rates, 117–118, 117*f*
  mother-infant bond, 137–138
  postmature, 134
inferiority, industry versus,
  394–395
infertility, **61**
  assisted reproductive technology
    (ART), 62, 65–66
  causes and treatments for,
    62, 63*t*
  incidence of, 61
information-processing approach,
  35, **179**
  in adolescence, 453–454
  basic processes and capacities of
    memory, 285
  categorization, 196
  causality, 196–197

Project CARE, 184
Project Head Start, 296–297
prosocial behavior, **326**
  in early childhood, 326–327
  volunteer activity and
    adolescents, 459–460
protective factors, **136**, **419**
  in adolescence, 444
proximity-seeking, 38
proximodistal principle, **93**, 144, 161
Prozac, 103
psychic reflexes, 32
psychoanalytic perspective, **27**,
  27–29, 28t, 30t
  gender development, 308t, 310
psychological aggression, **321**
psychological autonomy, 491
psychometric approach, **178**
  early childhood, 288–290
  in infancy and toddlerhood,
    181–184
  in middle childhood, 370–375
psychopathology, heredity and
  environmental influences,
  86–87
psychosexual development, of
  Freud, 27–29, **29**, 30t
psychosocial development, **6**, **31**
psychosocial development,
  adolescence
  adolescent rebellion, 488
  adulthood emerging,
    501–503, 502t
  antisocial behavior, 497–501
  identity search, 472–477
  juvenile delinquency, 497–501
  parent influences, 489–493
  peers and friend relationships,
    494–497
  sexuality, 478–488, 478f, 481t,
    482t–484t, 486t
  sibling relationships, 494
  teenage pregnancy, 485–488
psychosocial development, early
  childhood
  aggression, 327–329
  discipline, 320–323
  emotions, 304–306
  fearfulness, 329–330
  gender development,
    307–314
  gender differences, 306–307
  only child, 331–332
  parenting styles, 323–326
  play, 315–320
  playmates and friends, 332–333
  prosocial behavior, 326–327
  self-concept, 302–303
  self-esteem, 303–304
  sibling relationships, 331
psychosocial development, infancy
  and toddlerhood
  attachment development,
    228–233

autonomy, 237–239
child care, 246–249
development issues in,
  227–242
emotional communication with
  caregivers, 234–236
emotions, 218–224
  foundations of, 218–227
  gender differences, 242–243
  highlights of, 218, 219t
  moral development, 240–242
  mutual regulation, 234–236
  nonsibling sociability, 244–245
  other children influences,
    243–245
  postpartum depression
    influencing, 235–236
  self-concept, 236–237
  self-regulation, 240
  sibling influences, 243–244
  socialization and internalization,
    240–242
  social referencing, 234–235
  temperament, 224–227
  trust, 227–228
  working parents and, 245–249
psychosocial development, middle
  childhood
  aggression and bullying,
    411–416
  emotional growth, 395–396
  emotional growth and prosocial
    behavior, 395–396
  family structure, 400–408
  friendship, 411
  industry versus inferiority,
    394–395
  parenting issues, 397–400
  peer group issues, 408–416
  popularity, 409–411
  prosocial behavior, 395–396
  self-concept development, 394
  self-esteem, 394–395
  sibling relationships, 407–408
  stress and resilience, 416–420
psychosocial moratorium, 473
psychotherapy, 355
puberty, **424**, 426–432
  body fat and onset of, 427–428
  early and late maturers, 432
  growth spurt, 429–430
  hormonal changes,
    426–428, 427f
  influences on timing of,
    430–431
  in less developed countries, 425
  sexual maturity, 430
  signs of, 429
  timing, signs and sequence of,
    428–432, 428t
pubic hair, 429
pubilect, 452–453
Puerto Ricans, infant mortality rates
  and, 167

punishment, **32**
  corporal, 321, 322–323
  physical punishment and
    abuse, 172
  reinforcement and, 320–321

qualitative change, **26**
qualitative methods, 41–42
qualitative research, **41**
  compared to quantitative, 42t
  evaluating, 45–46
quantitative change, **26**
quantitative research, **41**, 41–42, 42t
  compared to qualitative, 42t
  evaluating, 45–46
questionnaires, 43t, 44

race/ethnicity
  child development influenced
    by, 11–13
  cultural socialization, 477
  early childhood health
    and, 267–268
  embedded achievement, 477
  group esteem, 477
  identity formation, 476–477, 477t
  infant mortality rates and, 167
  IQ influenced by, 371–372
  population projections for,
    11, 11f
  poverty rate by, 15f
  as social construct, 13
random assignment, **50**
random selection, **43**
reaction range, 82–83, 82f, **83**
reactive aggression, 413
reactive correlations, 84
reactive development, 25–26
reading
  in middle childhood, 378–379
  phonetic approach, 378
  whole-language approach, 378
reading aloud, 213
reality
  distinguishing from appearances
    and, 282
  distinguishing from fantasy and,
    282–283
real self, **303**, 394
reasoning
  deductive, 362
  inductive, 362
recall, **286**
receptive cooperation, **241**
receptive vocabulary, 206,
  290–291
recessive inheritance, **69**, 69–70,
  70f, 74–75
recess-time play, 344
reciprocal determinism, **33**
recognition, **286**
reflex behavior, 156, **156**, 157t

reflexes
  early, 156, 157t
  primitive, 156
Reggio Emilia preschool approach,
  295–296
regional (epidural or spinal)
  anesthesia, 122
rehearsal, as memory device,
  367, 369t
reinforcement, **32**
  punishment and, 320–321
relational (indirect or social)
  aggression, **328**
representational gestures, 205
representational mappings, **303**
representational systems, **394**
research methods, 41–56
  basic designs of, 46–51
  case studies, 46–47
  collaborative, 53–54
  correlational studies, 47–49
  cross-cultural, 48
  cross-sectional, longitudinal and
    sequential studies, 51–53, 52t
  data collection forms, 43–45
  developmental designs, 51–52
  ethics of, 54–56
  ethnographic studies, 47
  meta-analysis, 53
  qualitative methods, 41–42,
    42t, 45–46
  quantitative research, 41–42,
    42t, 45–46
  random selection, 43
  sampling, 42–43
  scientific method, 41
Research World boxes
  adaptive value of immaturity, 40
  autism epidemic, 152–153
  evolutionary basis of play, 316
  family mealtime and child
    well-being, 397
  genetic testing, 79
  homework debate, 382
  language acquisition, 19
  private speech, 293
  stages of faith, 458–459
resilient child, 418–420, 419t
resilient children, 174, **419**
  birth complications and, 136
respiratory distress syndrome, 133
reticent play, 317–318
retrieval, **285**
reversibility principle, 362–363
rights in research studies, 54–56
risk factors, **14**
risk-taking, in adolescence,
  426, 433
role confusion, 472–473
Romanian brain development
  study, 158
romantic relationships,
  496–497
rooting reflex, 157f, 157t

socioeconomic status (SES), **13**
  child development influenced by, 13–15
  cohabiting families, 404
  development indicators by country, 14f
  early childhood health and, 267–268
  fearfulness and, 417
  health in middle childhood, 351
  intelligence and, 289
  juvenile delinquency influenced by, 500
  low-birth-weight babies, 132
  one-parent families, 404
  poverty rate in United Sates, 14, 15f
  preschool study of, 296–297
  school achievement and, 381, 464
  volunteerism associated with, 460
socioemotional network, 433
sociometric popularity, 410
South Africa, schooling and IQ, 371
South America
  overweight, 345
  sibling relationships, 407–408
Southeast Asia, health care in, 353
Spain, teenage pregnancy in, 487
spanking, 322–323
spatial intelligence, 373, 373t
spatial relationships, 360, 361t
speech. *See also* language development
  characteristics of early, 207
  prelinguistic speech, 202
  private speech, 292, 293
  social speech, 292
  stuttering, 350–351
  telegraphic, 206
sperm, 61
  infertility and, 62
  puberty and, 430
spermarche, **430**
spillover, 462
spina bifida, 73t
spinal cord, 149, 149f
spontaneous abortion, **97**
sports, organized sports in middle childhood, 344–345
stage theories, 26, 27f
standardized tests, 45
standing, motor development an, 162
Stanford-Binet Intelligence Scale, **288**
State Children's Health Insurance Program (SCHIP), 268
state of arousal, 127–129, **128**, 128t
Steps to Respect, 416
Sternberg Triarchic Abilities Test (STAT), 374–375
stillbirth, 99, **135**
  mourning, 98
still-face paradigm, **234**

stimulus-response theories, 32
storage, **285**
stork bites, 124t
stranger anxiety, **232**
Strange Situation, **229**, 230, 231
strawberry hemangioma, 124t
stress
  coping with, 418–420
  in middle childhood, 416–420
  of modern life, 416–418
  one-parent families, 403
  during pregnancy, 107–108
  protective factors, 419
  resilient child, 418–420
  traumatic event, 417–418
structural changes, in information processing, 453
structured interview, 44
stuttering, **350**, 350–351
substance abuse, **439**
  in adolescence, 439–442
substance dependence, **439**
sudden infant death syndrome (SIDS), 166, **166**, 167–168, 170t
suicide, adolescents, 443f, 444
superego, 27, 29
surrogate mother, 66
survival of the fittest, 38
Sweden
  family living arrangements, 401t
  prosocial behavior study, 460
  teenage pregnancy in, 487
swimming reflex, 157t
Switzerland, teenage pregnancy in, 487
symbolic development, 190
symbolic function, **274**, 274–275
symbolic gestures, 205
sympathetic nervous system, emotional development, 222
synapses, 153
syntax, **206**, 291, 375–376
synthetic-conventional faith, 458
syphilis, 483t
systems of action, **160**, 160–161, **258**, 258–259

tabula rasa (blank slate), 25
tacit knowledge, **375**
Tahiti, child abuse rate, 172
taste, sense of, in infancy and toddlerhood, 159
Tay-Sachs disease, 74, 74t
teenage pregnancy, 109, 485–488
teeth and dental care
  in middle childhood, 339–340
  oral health in early childhood, 266
teething, 146
telegraphic speech, **206**

television watching
  attentional development, 194
  gender development influenced by, 314
  inactivity and obesity, 347
  infants and toddlers, 195
  media violence and aggression, 413–415
temperament, **86**, **224**
  adjustment and, 226
  attachment and, 231–232
  biological and cultural influences, 226
  difficult children, 224–225, 225t
  easy children, 224–225, 225t
  in infancy and toddlerhood, 224–227
  measuring, 225
  shyness and boldness, 226–227
  slow-to-warm-up children, 224–225, 225t
  stability of, 225–226
  studying patterns of, 224–225, 225t
temporal lobe, 150–151, 151f
teratogen, **100**, 100–101
terrible twos and, 238, 238t, 239
terrorism, children's reaction to, 417–418
tertiary circular reaction, 186f, 187
testes, puberty and, 427, 429
testosterone
  gender development and, 309–310
  puberty and, 427
tests, standardized, 45
test-tube baby, 62, 65
thalidomide, 103
theoretical perspectives
  active or reactive development, 25–26
  cognitive, 28t, 33–36
  contextual, 28t, 36–38, 37f
  continuous or discontinuous development, 26
  evolutionary/sociobiological, 28t, 38–39
  learning, 28t, 31–33
  mechanistic model, 25–26
  organismic model, 26
  psychoanalytic, 27–29, 28t, 30t
  shifting of balance, 39–40
  stage theories, 26
  summary of, 28t
theory, **24**
theory of mind, **280**, 280–284
  appearance and reality, 282
  false beliefs and deception, 281–282
  fantasy and reality, 282–283
  individual differences influencing, 283
  thinking and mental states, 281

theory of multiple intelligences, **373**, 373–374, 373t
theory of self, 472
theory of sexual selection, **309**, 309–310
therapy, for mental health issues, 355–356
thimerosal, 152
three-mountain task, 278–279, 279f
toddlerhood. *See* infancy and toddlerhood, cognitive development; infancy and toddlerhood, physical development and health; infancy and toddlerhood, psychosocial development
toilet training, 238
tonic neck, 157f, 157t
Torrance Tests of Creative Thinking, 389
touch, sense of, in infancy and toddlerhood, 159
toxoplasmosis, 107
transduction, 276–277, **277**
transforming growth factor alpha, 101
transitional object, 256
transitive inference, **361**, 361t
traumatic event, children's reaction to, 417–418
triarchic theory of intelligence, **374**, 374–375
trichomoniasis, 483t
trisomy-21, 76–77
trust
  attachment and, 231
  basic sense of trust versus basic mistrust, 227–228
  developing in infancy, 227–228
Turkey
  guided participation, 201
  high school graduation rate, 460
Turner syndrome, 76, 76t
21C, 297
twins, fraternal and identical, 64
twin studies, 80, 81
two-parent families, 401–402
two-way (dual-language) learning, **377**

Uganda, motor development, 165
ultrasound, **99**, 99f, 111t
umbilical cord, 95, 96f, 125
  sampling, 111t
Unborn Victims of Violence Act, 106
undernutrition, in early childhood, 263–265
uninvolved parenting, 324
United Kingdom
  family living arrangements, 401t
  low-birth-weight babies, 134